Praise for previous editions of
Children with Disabilities

"A complete and thorough compendium of useful information regarding young children with disabilities and their families. . . . *Children with Disabilities* is a resource that will be (and should be) heavily used by professionals, laypersons, and families alike."

—Disability Studies Quarterly

"Up-to-date information about the medical and biological aspects of development and disability . . . an excellent resource for any professional or student interested in developmental disabilities."

—American Journal on Mental Retardation

"Covers a very wide breadth of knowledge in a well-illustrated, articulate manner which can be understood by those without a special educational background, but in enough depth to make it a valuable text for professionals working with children and families."

—Physical and Occupational Therapy in Pediatrics

"A useful reference for physical therapists . . . recommended for inclusion in clinical libraries."

—Pediatric Physical Therapy

"A good family resource for information on medical aspects of a child's disabilities . . . an excellent introduction to the medical and personal effects of disability on children and their families."

—Quest, a journal of the Muscular Dystrophy Association

"An excellent resource. . . . The text's clarity and up-to-date references make it valuable as an aid in explanations of complex issues to families and the public. The appendices make it a valuable reference for all."

—Developmental Medicine & Child Neurology

"A very useful source of reference for child health and as such deserves a place on the shelves of the pediatric department, where it could be accessed by all members of the multi-disciplinary team."

—NAPOT Journal

"[Provides] detailed descriptions of all of the major types of disabilities from mild to severe and [examines] their known and suspected causes . . . suitable for parents and students [and] an extremely useful background resource for workers in a wide range of fields."

—Journal of the Institute of Health Education

"A universal resource that addresses the needs of children with disabilities."

—ADVANCE for Physical Therapists

"An excellent book. The clear explanations of disabilities in children . . . cannot be too highly commended. The contents are truly a resource essential for everyone concerned with helping children with disabilities."

—Disability News

Children
with
Disabilities

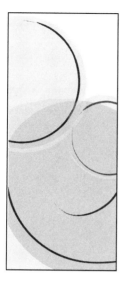

Children with Disabilities

FIFTH EDITION

edited by

Mark L. Batshaw, M.D.

"Fight for Children" Chair of Academic Medicine and Chief Academic Officer
Children's National Medical Center
Director, Children's Research Institute

Professor and Chairman of Pediatrics
Associate Dean for Academic Affairs
The George Washington University School of Medicine and Health Sciences

Washington, D.C.

·P A U L·H·
BROOKES
PUBLISHING C° ®

Baltimore • London • Sydney

Paul H. Brookes Publishing Co.
Post Office Box 10624
Baltimore, Maryland 21285-0624

www.brookespublishing.com

Typeset by Integrated Publishing Solutions, Grand Rapids, Michigan.
Manufactured in the United States of America by
The Maple Press Co., York, Pennsylvania.

Appendix C, Commonly Used Medications, which appears on pages 775–793, provides information
about numerous drugs frequently used to treat children with disabilities. This appendix is in no way
meant to substitute for a physician's advice or expert opinion; readers should consult a medical
practitioner if they are interested in more information.

The vignettes in the book are composites based on the authors' experiences. In all instances, names and
identifying details have been changed to protect confidentiality.

Library of Congress Cataloging-in-Publication Data

Children with disabilities / edited by Mark L. Batshaw.—5th ed.
    p.   cm.
Includes bibliographical reference and index.
ISBN 1-55766-581-8
    1. Child development deviations.   2. Child development deviations—Etiology.
3. Developmentally disabled children—Care.   4. Children with disabilities—Care.
I. Batshaw, Mark L., 1945–
   [DNLM: 1. Disabled Children. WS 368 C537 2002]
RJ135 .B38   2002
618.92—dc21   2002018496

British Library Cataloguing in Publication data are available from the British Library.

Contents

I As Life Begins

   Genetic Disorders
   Chromosomes
   Cell Division and Its Disorders
   Genes and Their Disorders
   Revising Mendelian Genetics
   Multifactorial Inheritance

   Genetic Assessment
   Screening Evaluations During Pregnancy
   Invasive Diagnostic Testing
   Prevention, Fetal Therapy, and Alternative Reproductive Choices
   Psychosocial Implications

   Fertilization
   Embryonic and Fetal Development
   Maternal Nutrition
   Malformations

   Dating a Pregnancy
   Deciding When to Deliver the Baby
   Perinatal Mortality
   Labor
   Monitoring Labor
   Delivery
   Cesarean Section
   Abnormal Labor or Dystocia
   Pregnancy Complications
   Birth Injuries and Defects

IV   Interventions, Families, and Outcomes

List of Tables and Figures

About the Editor

Mark L. Batshaw, M.D., is currently the "Fight for Children" Chair of Academic Medicine and Chief Academic Officer at the Children's National Medical Center (CNMC) in Washington, D.C., and serves as Professor and Chairman of Pediatrics and Associate Dean for Academic Affairs at The George Washington University School of Medicine and Health Sciences in Washington, D.C. Dr. Batshaw is also Director of the Children's Research Institute at CNMC.

Dr. Batshaw is a board-certified neurodevelopmental pediatrician who has treated children with developmental disabilities for more than 25 years. Before moving to Washington in 1998, he was Physician-in-Chief of Children's Seashore House, the child development and rehabilitation institute of The Children's Hospital of Philadelphia, and held the W.T. Grant Chair in Child Development at the University of Pennsylvania School of Medicine. Dr. Batshaw is a graduate of the University of Pennsylvania and of the University of Chicago Pritzker School of Medicine. Following pediatric residency in his native Canada at the Hospital for Sick Children in Toronto, he completed a fellowship in developmental pediatrics at the Kennedy Institute (now called the Kennedy Krieger Institute) and The Johns Hopkins Medical Institutions in Baltimore. He remained a professor at Johns Hopkins for 13 years and won the prestigious Alexander Schaffer teaching award while there.

A Joseph P. Kennedy, Jr., Scholar and recipient of major grants from the March of Dimes Birth Defects Foundation and the National Institutes of Health (NIH), Dr. Batshaw is director of the NIH-funded Mental Retardation and Developmental Disabilities Research Center at CNMC and continues to pursue his research on innovative treatments for inborn errors of metabolism, including gene therapy.

Dr. Batshaw has published more than 130 articles, chapters, and reviews on his research interests and on the medical aspects of the care of children with disabilities. Dr. Batshaw was the founding editor in chief (1995–2001) of the journal *Mental Retardation and Developmental Disabilities Research Reviews*. He is also the editor of *When Your Child Has a Disability: The Complete Sourcebook of Daily and Medical Care, Revised Edition* (Paul H. Brookes Publishing Co., 2001), and *Handbook of Developmental Disabilities* (co-edited with Kurtz, Dowrick, & Levy; Aspen Publishers, 1996). Dr. Batshaw is a Fellow of the American Academy of Pediatrics and is a member of the American Pediatric Society, the Society for Inherited Metabolic Disorders, the Society for Pediatric Research, and the Society for Developmental Pediatrics.

Dr. Batshaw's investment in the well-being of children was first sparked by his parents, both of whom were social workers; his father was involved in modernizing the juvenile justice system in Québec. Dr. Batshaw's wife, Karen, is a social worker in the field of international adoptions. His children also continue this legacy of making a difference: His daughter, Elissa, is a special education teacher and co-authored the chapter on special education in this edition of *Children with Disabilities*; his son Michael is a social worker; and his younger son, Drew, has overcome the challenges of attention-deficit/hyperactivity disorder to graduate from Vassar College and enter business school.

Contributors

George Acs, D.M.D., M.P.H.
Associate Professor of Pediatrics
The George Washington University School of
  Medicine and Health Sciences
Children's National Medical Center
111 Michigan Avenue NW
Washington, D.C. 20010

Terry Adirim, M.D., M.P.H.
Assistant Professor of Pediatrics, Emergency
  Medicine, and Prevention & Community Health
The George Washington University School
  of Medicine and Health Sciences
Children's National Medical Center
111 Michigan Avenue NW
Washington, D.C. 2001

Lowell Arye, M.S.S.A.
Executive Director
Alliance for the Betterment of Citizens with
  Disabilities (ABCD)
127 Route 206, Suite 18
Hamilton, NJ 08610

Paula J. Beckman, Ph.D., M.A.
Professor, Department of Special Education
University of Maryland at College Park
1308 Benjamin Building
College Park, MD 20910

Leila T. Beker, Ph.D., RD
Director
Bionutrition Research Core
Clinical Research Center
Children's National Medical Center
Assistant Clinical Professor of Pediatrics and
  Prevention & Community Health
The George Washington University School of
  Medicine and Health Sciences
111 Michigan Avenue NW
Washington, D.C. 20010

Andrew M. Bonwit, M.D.
Director
Infectious Disease and Special Immunology
  Clinics
Children's National Medical Center
Assistant Professor of Pediatrics
The George Washington University School of
  Medicine and Health Sciences
111 Michigan Avenue NW
Washington, D.C. 20010

Robin P. Church, Ed.D.
Assistant Vice President for Education
Kennedy Krieger Institute
Associate Professor of Education
The Johns Hopkins University
3835 Greenspring Avenue
Baltimore, MD 21211

Elissa Batshaw Clair, M.Ed.
Special Education Teacher
Special School District of St. Louis County
1150 Ross Avenue
St. Louis, MO 60146

Charles J. Conlon, M.D.
Chief
Division of Developmental Pediatrics
Children's National Medical Center
Assistant Professor of Pediatrics
The George Washington University School of
  Medicine and Health Sciences
111 Michigan Avenue NW
Washington, D.C. 20010

Shad H. Deering, M.D.
Captain
United States Army
Fellow
Division of Maternal-Fetal Medicine
Georgetown University Hospital
3800 Reservoir Road NW
Washington, D.C. 20007

John P. Dormans, M.D.
Chief of Orthopaedic Surgery
The Children's Hospital of Philadelphia
Professor of Orthopaedic Surgery
University of Pennsylvania School of Medicine
Wood Building
Second Floor
34th Street and Civic Center Boulevard
Philadelphia, PA 19104

Ann-Christine Duhaime, M.D.
Director
Pediatric Neurosurgery and Pediatric Neuroscience
  Programs
Dartmouth Hitchcock Medical Center
Dartmouth Medical School
Lebanon, NH 03756

Andrea Edelman, M.Ed., CRC
Clinical Supervisor
Adolescent Employment Readiness Center
Children's National Medical Center
111 Michigan Avenue NW
Washington, D.C. 20010

Lisa E. Efron, Ph.D.
Clinical Psychologist
Children's National Medical Center
Assistant Professor of Psychiatry & Behavioral
    Sciences and Pediatrics
The George Washington University School
    of Medicine and Health Sciences
111 Michigan Avenue NW
Washington, D.C. 20010

Peggy S. Eicher, M.D.
Medical Director
Center for Pediatric Feeding and Swallowing
    Disorders
St. Joseph's Hospital and Medical Center
703 Main Street
Paterson, NJ 07503

Abigail F. Farber, M.D.
Clinical Associate Professor
The Children's Hospital of Philadelphia
34th Street and Civic Center Boulevard
Philadelphia, PA 19104

Kenneth M. Fine, M.D.
Assistant Professor of Orthopaedic Surgery
The George Washington University Medical
    Faculty Associates
2150 Pennsylvania Avenue NW
Washington, D.C. 20037

Angelo P. Giardino, M.D., Ph.D.
Associate Chair, Operations
Assistant Professor of Pediatrics
University of Pennsylvania School of Medicine
34th Street and Civic Center Boulevard
Philadelphia, PA 19104

Marianne Glanzman, M.D.
Clinical Associate Professor of Pediatrics
University of Pennsylvania School of Medicine
Attending Physician
Division of Child Development and Rehabilitation
    Medicine
Children's Seashore House
The Children's Hospital of Philadelphia
3405 Civic Center Boulevard
Philadelphia, PA 19104

Karl F. Gumpper, B.S. Pharm, BCNSP
Clinical Pharmacy Coordinator
Children's National Medical Center
111 Michigan Avenue NW
Washington, D.C. 20010

William H.J. Haffner, M.D.
Chair and Professor
Department of Obstetrics and Gynecology
Uniformed Services University of the Health
    Sciences
4301 Jones Bridge Road
Bethesda, MD 20814

Adadot Hayes, M.D.
Developmental Disabilities Physician Consultant
State of Tennessee, Division of Mental
    Retardation
Post Office Box 910
Greeneville, TN 37744

Mark L. Helpin, D.M.D.
Chief
Division of Dentistry
The Children's Hospital of Philadelphia
34th Street and Civic Center Boulevard
Chairman and Associate Professor of Pediatric
    Dentistry
University of Pennsylvania School of Dental
    Medicine
4001 Spruce Street
Philadelphia, PA 19104

Gilbert R. Herer, Ph.D.
Director Emeritus
Children's Hearing and Speech Center
Children's National Medical Center
Professor of Pediatrics
The George Washington University School
    of Medicine and Health Sciences
111 Michigan Avenue NW
Washington, D.C. 20010

James B. Hill, M.D.
Chief Resident
Walter Reed Army Medical Center
6900 Georgia Avenue NW
Washington, D.C. 20307

Robert F. Keating, M.D.
Department of Neurosurgery
Children's National Medical Center
Associate Professor of Neurological Surgery and
    Pediatrics
The George Washington University School
    of Medicine and Health Sciences
111 Michigan Avenue NW
Washington, D.C. 20010

Carol A. Knightly, M.A., CCC-A
Director of Audiology
Center for Childhood Communication
The Children's Hospital of Philadelphia
34th Street and Civic Center Boulevard
Philadelphia, PA 19104

Alan E. Kohrt, M.D.
Medical Director
Children's Health Net
The Children's Hospital of Philadelphia
Clinical Associate Professor
University of Pennsylvania School of Medicine
34th Street and Civic Center Boulevard
Philadelphia, PA 19104

Lisa A. Kurtz, M.Ed., OTR/L, BCP
Assistant Clinical Professor of Occupational
   Therapy
University of New England
11 Hills Beach Road
Biddeford, ME 04005

Mary F. Lazar, Psy.D.
Pediatric Neuropsychologist
Adjunct Assistant Professor
Institute for Graduate Clinical Psychology
Widener University
Chester, PA 19013

Arabella I. Leet, M.D.
Assistant Professor
Department of Orthopedics
The Johns Hopkins University School
   of Medicine
601 North Caroline Street
Baltimore, MD 21287

Susan E. Levy, M.D.
Clinical Associate Professor
University of Pennsylvania School of Medicine
Children's Seashore House
The Children's Hospital of Philadelphia
3405 Civic Center Boulevard
Philadelphia, PA 19104

M.E.B. Lewis, Ed.D.
Principal
Lower School
Kennedy Krieger Institute
1750 East Fairmount Avenue
Baltimore, MD 21231

Gregory S. Liptak, M.D., M.P.H.
Associate Professor of Pediatrics
University of Rochester Medical Center
Post Office Box 671
601 Elmwood Avenue
Rochester, NY 14642

David Lynch, M.D., Ph.D.
Attending Physician
Division of Neurology
The Children's Hospital of Philadelphia
Assistant Professor of Neurology and Pediatrics
University of Pennsylvania School of Medicine
34th Street and Civic Center Boulevard
Philadelphia, PA 19104

Joyce E. Mauk, M.D.
President and CEO
Child Study Center
1300 West Lancaster
Fort Worth, TX 76102

Susan K. McCune, M.D.
Attending Neonatologist
Children's National Medical Center
Associate Professor of Pediatrics
The George Washington University School
   of Medicine and Health Sciences
111 Michigan Avenue NW
Washington, D.C. 20010

Sheryl J. Menacker, M.D.
Clinical Associate
Division of Ophthalmology
University of Pennsylvania School of Medicine
34th Street and Civic Center Boulevard
Philadelphia, PA 19104

Gretchen A. Meyer, M.D.
Commander, United States Navy
Neurodevelopmental Pediatrician

Linda J. Michaud, M.D., M.Ed.
Aaron W. Perlman Professor of Pediatric Physical
   Medicine & Rehabilitation
Associate Professor of Clinical Physical Medicine
   & Rehabilitation and Clinical Pediatrics
Director of Pediatric Rehabilitation
Cincinnati Children's Hospital Medical Center
University of Cincinnati College of Medicine
3333 Burnet Avenue
Cincinnati, OH 45229

Marijean M. Miller, M.D.
Attending Physician
Department of Ophthalmology
Children's National Medical Center
Assistant Professor of Ophthalmology
   and Pediatrics
The George Washington University School
   of Medicine and Health Sciences
111 Michigan Avenue NW
Washington, D.C. 20010

Man Wai Ng, D.D.S., M.P.H.
Chief
Division of Pediatric Dentistry
Children's National Medical Center
Assistant Professor of Pediatrics
The George Washington University School of
   Medicine and Health Sciences
111 Michigan Avenue NW
Washington, D.C. 20010

Maureen O'Rourke, M.D.
Assistant Professor of Anesthesia and Pediatrics
The Children's Hospital of Philadelphia
34th Street and Civic Center Boulevard
Philadelphia, PA 19104

John M. Parrish, Ph.D.
Executive Director
The Erickson Foundation
701 Maiden Choice Lane
Catonsville, MD 21228

Louis Pellegrino, M.D.
Director
Division of Developmental Pediatrics
St. Peter's University Hospital and Health
    Systems
254 Easton Avenue
New Brunswick, NJ 08903

K. Rais-Bahrami, M.D.
Attending Neonatologist
Children's National Medical Center
Professor of Pediatrics
The George Washington University School
    of Medicine and Health Sciences
111 Michigan Avenue NW
Washington, D.C. 20010

Mark Reber, M.D.
Consulting Psychiatrist
Woods Services
Langhorne, PA 19047

Nancy J. Roizen, M.D.
Professor of Pediatrics
SUNY Upstate Medical University
750 East Adams Street
Syracuse, NY 13210

Margaret Rose
Administrator
Mental Retardation and Developmental Disabilities
    Research Center
Children's National Medical Center
111 Michigan Avenue NW
Washington, D.C. 20010

Howard M. Rosenberg, D.D.S., M.Ed.
Associate Professor of Pediatric Dentistry
Department of Pediatric Dentistry
University of Pennsylvania School of Dental
    Medicine
4001 Spruce Street
Philadelphia, PA 19104

Andrew J. Satin, M.D.
Professor and Vice Chair
Department of Obstetrics and Gynecology
Uniformed Services University of the Health
    Sciences
4301 Jones Bridge Road
Bethesda, MD 20814

Cheryl Scacheri, M.S.
Senior Genetic Counselor
GeneDx, Inc.
9700 Great Seneca Highway
Suite 211
Rockville, MD 20850

Peter C. Scheidt, M.D., M.P.H.
Director, Program Office
Longitudinal Cohort Study of Environmental
    Influences on Child Health and Development
National Institute of Child Health and Human
    Development
National Institutes of Health
6100 Executive Boulevard
Bethesda, MD 20892

Wendy B. Schiff, Ph.D.
Assistant Professor
Argosy University
Washington, D.C., Campus
1550 Wilson Boulevard
Suite 600
Arlington, VA 22209

Rhonda L. Schonberg, M.S.
Coordinator
Center for Prenatal Evaluation
Children's National Medical Center
111 Michigan Avenue NW
Washington, D.C. 20010

Vincent Schuyler, B.S.W., A.B.D.A.
Program Director
Adolescent Employment Readiness Center
Children's National Medical Center
111 Michigan Avenue NW
Washington, D.C. 20010

Jennifer Semel-Concepción, M.D.
Director
Physical Medicine and Rehabilitation
Children's National Medical Center
Assistant Professor of Pediatrics
The George Washington University School of
    Medicine and Health Sciences
111 Michigan Avenue NW
Washington, D.C. 20010

Bruce Shapiro, M.D.
Associate Professor of Pediatrics
The Johns Hopkins University School of Medicine
Vice President, Training
Kennedy Krieger Institute
707 North Broadway
Baltimore, MD 21205

Billie Lou Short, M.D.
Chief
Division of Neonatology
Children's National Medical Center
Professor of Pediatrics
The George Washington University School of
    Medicine and Health Sciences
111 Michigan Avenue NW
Washington, D.C. 20010

Tomas Jose Silber, M.D., M.A.S.S.
Director
Office of Ethics
Children's National Medical Center
Professor of Pediatrics, International Public
    Health, and Prevention & Community Health
Adjunct Professor of Health Care Sciences
The George Washington University School of
    Medicine and Health Sciences
111 Michigan Avenue NW
Washington, D.C. 20010

Caple A. Spence, M.D.
Chief Resident
Neurosurgery
The George Washington University Medical
    Center
2150 Pennsylvania Avenue NW
Washington, D.C. 20037

Hans M.L. Spiegel, M.D., Ph.D.
Attending Physician
Special Immunology Service
Children's National Medical Center
Assistant Professor of Pediatrics and Microbiology
    & Tropical Medicine
The George Washington University School
    of Medicine and Health Sciences
111 Michigan Avenue NW
Washington, D.C. 20010

Mark A. Stein, Ph.D.
Chief
Division of Psychology
Children's National Medical Center
Professor of Psychiatry & Behavioral Sciences and
    Pediatrics
The George Washington University School
    of Medicine and Health Sciences
111 Michigan Avenue NW
Washington, D.C. 20010

Annie G. Steinberg, M.D.
Director
Deafness and Family Communication Center
Department of Child and Adolescent
    Psychiatry
The Children's Hospital of Philadelphia
3535 Market Street
Ninth Floor
Philadelphia, PA 19104

Sheela Stuart, Ph.D., CCC-SLP
Director
Speech-Language Pathology
Children's National Medical Center
Washington, D.C. 20010

Cynthia J. Tifft, M.D., Ph.D.
Chief
Division of Medical Genetics
Children's National Medical Center
Associate Professor of Pediatrics
The George Washington University School of
    Medicine and Health Sciences
111 Michigan Avenue NW
Washington, D.C. 20010

Laura L. Tosi, M.D.
Chief
Division of Orthopaedic Surgery
Children's National Medical Center
Associate Professor of Orthopaedic Surgery and
    Pediatrics
The George Washington University School of
    Medicine and Health Sciences
111 Michigan Avenue NW
Washington, D.C. 20010

Kenneth E. Towbin, M.D.
Professor of Psychiatry & Behavioral Sciences
    and Pediatrics
The George Washington University School
    of Medicine and Health Sciences
National Institute of Mental Health
Building 10, Room 3S228A
9000 Rockville Pike
Bethesda, MD 20892

Mendel Tuchman, M.D.
Mary Elizabeth McGehee Joyce Chair for Genetic
    Research
Children's National Medical Center
Professor of Pediatrics and Biochemistry
    & Molecular Biology
The George Washington University School
    of Medicine and Health Sciences
111 Michigan Avenue NW
Washington, D.C. 20010

Laura Placke Ward, M.D.
Department of Neonatology
Children's National Medical Center
111 Michigan Avenue NW
Washington, D.C. 20010

Steven Weinstein, M.D.
Associate Chief
Division of Pediatric Neurology
Children's National Medical Center
Professor of Neurology and Pediatrics
The George Washington University School
  of Medicine and Health Sciences
111 Michigan Avenue NW
Washington, D.C. 20010

Nora Wells, Ed.D.
Director of Research Activities
Family Voices @ the Federation for Children
  with Special Needs
1135 Tremont Street
Suite 420
Boston, MA 02120

Patience H. White, M.D.
Chief
Division of Rheumatology
Children's National Medical Center
Professor of Medicine and Pediatrics
The George Washington University School
  of Medicine and Health Sciences
111 Michigan Avenue NW
Washington, D.C. 20010

Martha J. Wunsch, M.D.
Assistant Professor
Division of Addiction Psychiatry
Virginia Commonwealth University
1200 East Broad Street
Richmond, VA 23298

Colleen Comonitski Yanni, M.S., R.D.
Clinical Dietitian
The Children's Hospital of Philadelphia
34th Street and Civic Center Boulevard
Philadelphia, PA 19104

A Personal Note to the Reader

As it enters its fifth edition, *Children with Disabilities* has changed in ways that mirror changes in my own life. The first edition evolved from lectures I developed for a special education course I taught at The Johns Hopkins University in Baltimore. The book contained 464 pages in 23 chapters, and I authored or co-authored all of them. When I started writing the first edition, I was 33 years old and 3 years out of my developmental pediatrics fellowship training program, and I thought I knew everything there was to know about developmental disabilities! I was also an expert in my own children's development, having just welcomed into our family our third child, Andrew.

As I prepared this fifth edition, I turned 55. The book is 912 pages long, with 38 chapters and four appendices. I have authored or co-authored fewer than one third of the chapters, an acknowledgment of the fact that I do not have the expertise I once thought I had. Our son Andrew, who was diagnosed as having attention-deficit/hyperactivity disorder in elementary school, became a software engineer and is now enrolled in business school.

It has been both personally and professionally rewarding to develop this book over almost a quarter century. Many of those rewards have come from the students, colleagues, and parents who have shared with me their thoughts and advice about the book. It is my hope that *Children with Disabilities* will continue to fill the needs of its diverse users for many years and many editions to come.

Mark L. Batshaw

Preface

One of the first questions asked about a subsequent edition of a textbook is "What's new?" The challenge of determining what to revise, what to add, and, in some cases, what to delete is always significant in preparing a new edition in a field changing as rapidly as developmental disabilities. Since the publication of the fourth edition in 1997, the fields of neuroscience and genetics have been revolutionized, greatly enhancing our understanding of the brain and inheritance and bringing forth the possibilities of treatments previously not thought possible for children with developmental disabilities. The human genome has been mapped, the brain probed by functional imaging techniques, the potential of gene therapy explored. The need to examine and explain these enormous advances and their significance for children with disabilities has necessitated an increase in the depth and breadth of the subjects covered in the book. Yet, while the book is now more expansive and has several new chapters, I have worked hard to ensure that it retains its clarity and cohesion. Its mission continues to be to provide the individual working with and caring for children with disabilities the necessary background to understand different disabilities and their treatments, thereby enabling affected children to reach their full potential.

THE AUDIENCE

Since it was originally published, *Children with Disabilities* has been used by students in a wide range of disciplines as a medical textbook addressing the impact of disabilities on child development and function. It has also served as a professional reference for special educators, general educators, physical therapists, occupational therapists, speech-language pathologists, psychologists, child life specialists, social workers, nurses, physicians, advocates, and others providing care for children with disabilities. Finally, as a family resource, parents, grandparents, siblings, and other family members and friends have found useful information on the medical and (re)habilitative aspects of care for the child with developmental disabilities.

FEATURES FOR THE READER

I have been told that the strengths of previous editions of this book have been the accessible writing style, the clear illustrations, and the up-to-date information and references. We have dedicated our efforts to retaining these strengths. Some of the features you will find include the following:

- *Teaching goals*—Each chapter begins with learning objectives to orient you to the content of that particular chapter.
- *Situational examples*—Most chapters include one or more stories, or case studies, to help bring alive the conditions and issues discussed in the chapter. In response to feedback from readers, many of these case studies have been expanded in this edition.
- *Key terms*—As medical terms are introduced in the text, they appear in boldface type at their first use; definitions for these terms appear in the Glossary (Appendix A).
- *Illustrations and tables*—More than 220 drawings, photographs, X rays, brain scans, and tables reinforce the points of the text and provide ways for you to more easily understand and remember the material you are reading.
- *Summary*—Each chapter closes with a final section that reviews its key elements and provides you with an abstract of the covered material.

- *References*—The reference list accompanying each chapter can be thought of as more than just a list of the literature cited in the chapter. These citations include review articles, reports of study findings and research discoveries, and other key references that can help you find additional information.
- *Appendices*—In addition to the Glossary, there are three other helpful appendices: Syndromes and Inborn Errors of Metabolism, a mini-reference of pertinent information on more than 110 inherited disorders causing disabilities; Commonly Used Medications, to describe indications and side effects of medications often prescribed for children with disabilities; and Resources for Children with Disabilities, a directory of a wide range of national organizations, federal agencies, information sources, self-advocacy and accessibility programs, and support groups that can provide assistance to families and professionals.

CONTENT

In developing this fifth edition, I have aimed for a balance between consistency with the text that many of you have come to know so well in its previous editions and innovation in exploring the new topics that demand our attention in the 21st century. All of the chapters from the fourth edition have been rewritten to include an expanded focus on psychosocial, (re)habilitative, and educational interventions as well as to provide information discovered through medical and scientific advances since 1997. In addition, three new chapters have been added to address early intervention, special education, and sports and recreation. These new chapters were added in response to readers who suggested that the text be further expanded beyond its medical focus to acknowledge the integral relationship between medical care and education and extracurricular activities in promoting a child's development.

The chapters are grouped in sections and have been reorganized to help guide readers through the breadth of content. The book starts with a section titled As Life Begins, which addresses what happens before, during, or shortly after birth to cause a child at risk to have a developmental disability. The concepts and consequences of genetics, embryology and fetal development, the birth process, and prematurity are explained. The next section of the book, The Developing Child, covers environmental causes of developmental disabilities and examines the various organ systems—how they develop and work and what can go wrong. Substance abuse, HIV infection, nutrition, vision, hearing, language, and the brain and musculoskeletal systems are discussed in individual chapters. As its title implies, the third section, Developmental Disabilities, provides comprehensive descriptions of various developmental disabilities and genetic syndromes causing disabilities and includes chapters on mental retardation, Down syndrome, fragile X syndrome, inborn errors of metabolism, psychiatric disorders in developmental disabilities, pervasive developmental disorders, attention-deficit/hyperactivity disorder, specific learning disabilities, cerebral palsy, neural tube defects, epilepsy, and traumatic brain injury. The final section, Interventions, Families, and Outcomes, contains chapters that focus on various interventions including early intervention and special education services, feeding, dental care, behavior management, technology assistance, and physical and occupational therapy. This section also concentrates on the ethical, legal, emotional, and transition-to-adulthood issues that are common to most families of children with disabilities and to professionals who work with them. The book closes with a discussion of the prospects for providing health care in the 21st century.

THE AUTHORS AND EDITORS

I have chosen physicians and other health care professionals who are experts in the areas they write about as authors of *Children with Disabilities*. Most are my colleagues from Children's

National Medical Center or former colleagues from Children's Seashore House of The Children's Hospital of Philadelphia. Each chapter in the book has undergone extensive editing at Paul H. Brookes Publishing Co. by Acquisitions Editor Heather Shrestha; Editorial Supervisor Mika Wendy Sam; and myself to ensure consistency in style and accessibility of content. Once the initial drafts were completed, each chapter was sent for peer review by two or three major clinical and academic leaders in the field and was revised according to their input.

A FEW NOTES ABOUT TERMINOLOGY AND STYLE

As is the case with any book of this scope, the editor or author faces decisions about the use of particular words or the presentation style of information. I'd like to share with you some of the decisions we have made for this book.

- *Reference style*—In general, the citation style of the American Psychological Association has been followed, with one particular exception. To conserve space, given the number of co-authors so often listed on primary source material, we have elected to use the "et al." format for all references with more than three names.
- *Categories of mental retardation*—This book uses the American Psychiatric Association's categories of mental retardation (i.e., mild, moderate, severe, profound) when discussing medical diagnosis and treatment and uses the categories that the American Association on Mental Retardation established in 1992 (i.e., requiring limited, intermittent, extensive, or pervasive support) when discussing educational and other interventions, thus emphasizing the capabilities rather than the impairments of individuals with mental retardation.
- *"Typical" and "normal"*—Recognizing diversity and the fact that no one type of person or lifestyle is inherently "normal," we have chosen to refer to the general population of children as "typical" or "typically developing," meaning that they follow the natural continuum of development.
- *Person-first language*—We have tried to preserve the dignity and personhood of all individuals with disabilities by consistently using person-first language, speaking, for example, of "a child with autism," instead of "an autistic child." In this way, we are able to emphasize the person, not define him or her by the condition.

As you read this fifth edition of *Children with Disabilities*, I hope you will find that the text continues to address the frequently asked question "Why this child?" and to provide the medical background you need to care for children with developmental disabilities.

FOR THE COURSE COMPANION WEB SITE USER

Children with Disabilities, Fifth Edition, has a Course Companion Web Site designed to enhance the learning experience of instructors and students using this book in a college course. Readers will find key terms, objectives, and outlines for each chapter; hundreds of annotated links to useful material on related web sites; student study questions and exercises; and relevant readings and case studies on education and intervention. In addition, visitors can quickly link to PubMed abstracts of journal articles from the chapter reference lists and search a complete glossary of terms and other material from the book's appendices.

The course companion web site is free for all readers. Readers can access the web site at http://textbooks.brookespublishing.com/batshaw.

Acknowledgments

A book such as *Children with Disabilities* is best understood with illustrations that help to explain medical concepts. A medical illustrator is indispensable in this effort, and two of the best, Lynn Reynolds and Elaine Kasmer, have contributed to this endeavor. They were given the ideas that needed illustration and produced the more than 100 beautiful images that fill this book. I gratefully acknowledge their important contribution. Lynn Reynolds contributed the following figures: 1.3–1.5, 1.8, 1.9, 1.11, 1.12, 1.14, 1.15, 1.17–1.21, 2.3–2.6, 3.1, 4.1, 4.2, 5.1–5.3, 6.6, 7.1, 8.1, 10.7, 11.4, 11.7, 11.8, 11.11–11.13, 14.2–14.5, 14.6a, 16.1, 16.2, 18.1–18.4, 22.1, 23.1, 23.3, 23.7, 23.8, 23.10, 23.13, 24.1–24.7, 27.1–27.4, 27.7–27.9, 28.1, 28.3, 31.1, 32.1–32.4, and 33.1. Elaine Kasmer contributed the following figures: 1.1, 1.2, 1.7, 1.10, 1.16, 5.4, 6.3, 6.4, 10.1–10.5, 10.8, 10.9, 11.1, 11.3, 11.5, 11.6, 13.1–13.6, 13.7 (drawings only), 13.8–13.11, 14.1, 14.6b, 14.7, 14.8, 14.10 (drawings only), 23.2 (drawings only), 23.4, 23.6, 23.9, 23.11 (drawings only), 25.1, 25.2, and 28.2.

I also acknowledge my assistant, Margaret Rose, who helped to copyedit the manuscript, obtained letters of consent, compiled and revised the resource section, and kept me and my colleagues on schedule throughout the production of this fifth edition. I also thank my colleagues at Paul H. Brookes Publishing Co., Editorial Supervisor Mika Wendy Sam and Acquisitions Editor Heather Shrestha, who both enhanced the book with careful and expert editing.

Finally, many colleagues at Children's National Medical Center and elsewhere reviewed and edited the manuscript for content and accuracy. I would like to acknowledge their efforts: Michael Batshaw, Allan Bloom, Robert Cooke, Felicitas Lacbawan, Ruth Nussbaum, and Daniel J. Silber. In addition, although the following individuals did not participate in this fifth edition, their contributions to past editions of the book have been the foundation for this edition: Yvonne M. Perret, Lisa J. Bain, Marleen Ann Baron, Judy C. Bernbaum, Nathan J. Blum, Breck G. Borcherding, Lawrence W. Brown, Jacquelyn R. Evans, Iraj Forouzan, Ernest M. Graham, the late Mark A. Morgan, Nancy C. Rose, Richard M. Rutstein, Symme Wilson Trachtenberg, and Paul P. Wang.

Preceding book production, Paul H. Brookes Publishing Co. shared early versions of the manuscript with professionals who specialize in various associated fields. I extend my thanks to all of the peer reviewers, both those who chose to remain anonymous and those who are listed here: Pasquale J. Accardo, Michael G. Aman, Alison Anthony, Bruce L. Baker, Glenis Benson, W. Carl Cooley, Elizabeth Crais, Larry W. Desch, Brenda M. Finucane, Robert Fletcher, Sam Goldstein, Michael J. Guralnick, Randi Hagerman, Lewis Jackson, Timothy R.B. Johnson, Mark Korson, Libby Kumin, Paul Lipkin, Stephanie Porter, Lisa Steege, and Edwin Trevathan.

Mark L. Batshaw

Why me?
Why me?
Why do I have to do so much more than others?
Why am I so forgetful?
Why am I so hyperactive?
And why can't I spell?
Why me? O'why me?

I remember when I almost failed first grade because I couldn't read. I would cry hour after hour because my mother would try to make me read. Now I love to read. I couldn't write in cursive but my mother helped me and now I can. I don't have as bad a learning disability as others. At lest I can go to a normal school. I am trying as hard as I can (I just hope it is enough). My worst nightmare is to go to a special school because I don't want to be treated differently.

I am getting to like working. I guess since my dad is so successful and has a learning disability, it helps make me not want to give up. Many people say that I am smart, but sometimes I doubt it. I am very good at math, but sometimes I read a number like 169 as 196, so that messes things up. I also hear things incorrectly, for instants entrepreneur as horse manure (that really happened). I guess the reason why a lot of people don't like me is because I say the wrong answer a lot of times.

I had to take medication, but then I got off the medication and did well. Then in 7th grade I wasn't doing well but I didn't tell my parents because I thought they would just scream at me. My dad talked to the guidance counselor and found out. It wasn't till a week ago that I started on the medication again; I have been doing fine since than. As I have been getting more organized, I have had more free time. I guess I feel good when I succeed in things that take hard work.

This is my true story. . .

Andrew Batshaw

Andrew Batshaw
1989

In applying to colleges during my senior year of high school, I found that most had as an essay topic, "Tell us something about yourself." I decided to write about my ADHD and learning disability as it is a big part of who I am. I wrote "I have found that while a disability inherently leaves you with a weakness, adapting to that disability can provide rewards. I feel that from coping with my disability, I have gained pride, determination, and a strength that will be with me all of my life." I guess Vassar College agreed; they admitted me.

When it came time for high school graduation, we had a problem. My sister was graduating from the University of Chicago on the same day that I graduated from high school in Philadelphia. The only solution was for one parent to attend my graduation while the other one was with my sister in Chicago. The decision as to who would go to which graduation was easy. My mother insisted that she attend my graduation because it was a product of her hard work as well as my own. I remember she said to me that day, "When I think of the boy who cried himself to sleep because he could not remember how to spell the word 'who,' it makes me so happy to see you now."

My parents expressed themselves in different ways about my leaving for college. My mother and I found ourselves getting into many arguments over simple things (the old severing of the umbilical cord; I am the baby of the family). My father, however, made sure to remind me to start my stimulant medication 2 weeks before classes began!

The first semester I took four courses: Poetry, Linear Algebra, Computer Science, and Music Theory. As the semester continued, I developed an increasing interest in computer science, until finally I decided to become a computer science major. I was very flattered, however, when during a meeting with my English professor, she asked if I planned to be an English major. To think that someone who could not read until the end of second grade would become a member of the Vassar English department seemed almost unbelievable. Well, I might have been proud but not that proud. I stuck with computer science.

On the whole, I would say that my freshman year was a good one. I learned a great deal, both inside and outside of classes, about myself and others. What will I do after college? What will I end up doing with my life? These are questions that continually run through my mind. I have no clear answers, but there is one thing of which I am sure: My disability will not keep me from doing anything. I will not let it.

Andrew Batshaw

Andrew Batshaw
June 1996

As a college graduate, I find that my ADHD and learning disabilities are much less of an issue; however, that was not the case during my early college years. In my second year of college, I took a year-long introductory German class that fulfilled my language requirement. Forgetting that languages don't come easily to me, I chose the intensive German class that met an extra day a week and moved faster than the regular class. I watched my exam grades slowly slide into the C range during the first semester and decided to switch to the regular class for the rest of the year. While this was happening, some medical warnings were issued concerning the stimulant medication I was taking, so I decided to discontinue its use.

In the new German class, we had exams every other week, so I received regular feedback on how I was doing. Unfortunately, it was not positive feedback. After receiving an F on the first quiz, I decided that I needed to work harder in the class. I started studying more and was less than relieved when on my next exam my grade rose to a D! Again, I studied even more and still received a D on the test that followed. At this point, I began to doubt myself. I felt like I was doing everything I could, and still I wasn't improving. I said to myself, "I know you have always told yourself that you could do anything you really gave your all to, but maybe there are just some things you can't do." I was disheartened, but felt that I had no choice but to just keep working. I received a C and then a C+ on my next two exams, but my overall class grade was still very low. My professor spoke to me and said that as long as I received at least a C+ on the final exam, he would pass me. I did all I could to prepare for the test and took the exam without reservation, simply willing to accept the results, whatever they might be. I ran into my professor a week after the final exam and was told that not only had I passed the final exam, but that I had received an A, one of the highest grades in the class. As you might expect, I was ecstatic. I looked back on the day when I had thought, "Maybe there really are things that I just can't do," and smiled, because I proved myself wrong. On top of that, I had accomplished it without the help of medication. That was when I truly felt that I had overcome my ADHD and learning disabilities.

In fact, some of the most important activities in my life are things that at first glance you wouldn't think someone with ADHD would find attractive. I meditate every day, which involves sitting in one place and not moving for long periods of time. When I meditate, I am actually watching how my mind works. I see how easily I am distracted from simply sitting by thinking about all kinds of things, like what I did yesterday or what I am going to do later. Nevertheless, I keep bringing myself back, over and over again, and sometimes my mind becomes very quiet and clear. I find that this has had a positive impact on all aspects of my life. I was talking with my older brother, Michael, after attending my first 3-day meditation retreat, and he told me how proud he was of me. He said that after seeing me bounce off the walls and have such difficulty concentrating while growing up, he was amazed that I could sit still and meditate for 3 days.

After 4 years, including 6 months at the University of York in England, I graduated from Vassar College with a B.A. in Computer Science in May 1999. After graduation, I worked for a year as a software engineer and then started my own company with my brother and a friend. Unfortunately, after developing the company for a year, we became one of the many casualties of the dot-com collapse. Naturally, I was very disappointed, but it was an incredible experience that I will always value. It sparked in me a passion for entrepreneurship that led to my decision to attend business school.

Throughout the process of applying to business school, it became clear to me how my learning disability had been transformed from a hindrance to an asset. The work habits I had developed to overcome my disability allowed me to stick to a rigorous preparation program for my business school entrance exams. As a result, I scored in the 98th percentile. In addition, when preparing my applications, I chose to include an essay about how overcoming a disability had taught me to treat failure as a natural and necessary part of important accomplishments. Furthermore, it instilled in me a drive to achieve and to take calculated risks that are essential to being successful in business. I will be attending the University of Southern California Business School with a full scholarship.

Drew Batshaw
April 2002

To Margaret Rose,
who has been an invaluable assistant and friend for 15 years

I As Life Begins

1 Chromosomes and Heredity

A Toss of the Dice

Mark L. Batshaw

Upon completion of this chapter, the reader will:

- be able to explain errors in mitosis and meiosis, including nondisjunction, deletion, and translocation, and understand chromosomal structural abnormalities

- know the differences and similarities among autosomal recessive, autosomal dominant, and X-linked genetic disorders

- understand the concepts of genomic imprinting, anticipation, and mitochondrial inheritance

- understand the ways in which environment and heredity contribute to the development of multifactorial disorders

Whether we have brown or blue eyes is determined by genes passed on to us from our parents. Other traits, such as height and weight, are affected by genes and by our environments both before and after birth. In a similar manner, genes alone or in combination with environmental factors can lead to many disorders, including birth defects. The spectrum ranges from purely genetic disorders, such as muscular dystrophy, which results from a single-gene defect, and Down syndrome, which results from an extra chromosome, to purely environmental conditions, including infectious diseases such as **meningitis**. Between these two extremes are multifactorial disorders such as meningomyelocele, the occurrence of which is influenced by genetics and environment.

As an introduction to the discussion in the chapters that follow, this chapter describes the human cell and explains what chromosomes are. It also reviews and provides some illustrations of the errors that can occur in the processes of **mitosis** and **meiosis** and discusses inheritance patterns of single-gene disorders. As you progress through this book, bear in mind that the purpose of this discussion is to focus on the abnormalities that can occur in human development; however, few infants are affected by these disorders.

GENETIC DISORDERS

Our bodies are composed of approximately 100 trillion cells. There are many cell types, including nerve cells, muscle cells, white blood cells, and skin cells, to name a few. Each cell is divided into two compartments: 1) a central, enclosed core—the nucleus; and 2) an outer area—the **cytoplasm** (Figure 1.1), except for the red blood cell, which does not have a nucleus. The nucleus houses chromosomes (Greek for "colored bodies"). These structures contain the genetic code **(deoxyribonucleic acid [DNA]),** organized into hundreds of units of heredity, termed **genes.** These genes are responsible for our physical properties and biological functions. Under the direction of the nucleus, the products that are needed for the growth and functioning of the

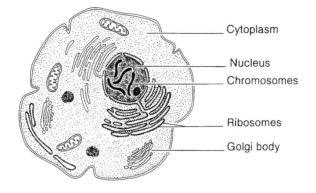

Cytoplasm

Nucleus
Chromosomes

Ribosomes

Golgi body

Figure 1.1.   An idealized cell. The genes within chromosomes direct the creation of a product on the ribosomes. The product is then packaged in the Golgi apparatus and released from the cell.

organism, including waste disposal and the release of energy, are made in the cytoplasm. The nucleus, then, contains the blueprint for an individual's development, and the cytoplasm manufactures the products needed to complete the task.

When there is a defect within this system, the result may be a genetic disorder. There is a continuum of genetic disorders ranging from the addition (e.g., Down syndrome) or loss (e.g., Turner syndrome) of an entire chromosome in each cell, to the loss of a part of a chromosome (e.g., cri-du-chat syndrome), to a **microdeletion** of a number of contiguous genes within a chromosome (e.g., velocardiofacial syndrome [VCFS]), to a defect within a single gene (e.g., phenylketonuria). In general, the larger the defect, the more severe the disorder. Therefore, extra chromosomes tend to lead to multiple malformations and more severe cognitive defects than do microdeletions. This chapter discusses each of these types of genetic defects, beginning with chromosomes and problems in their division.

CHROMOSOMES

Each organism has a fixed number of chromosomes that direct cellular activities. In humans, in each cell there are 46 chromosomes. Each chromosome contains somewhere between 250 and 2,000 genes. The 46 chromosomes, termed the **diploid** number, are organized into 23 pairs, termed the **haploid** number, of complementary chromosomes. One chromosome from each pair comes from the mother and one from the father. Egg and sperm cells, however, each contain only 23 chromosomes. During conception, these **germ cells** fuse to produce a fertilized egg with the full complement of 46 chromosomes.

Twenty-two of the twenty-three pairs of chromosomes are termed **autosomes.** The twenty-third pair consists of the X and Y chromosomes, or the **sex chromosomes.** The Y chromosome, which determines "maleness," is one third to one half as long as the X chromosome and has a different shape. Two X chromosomes determine the child to be female. An X and a Y chromosome determine the child to be male.

CELL DIVISION AND ITS DISORDERS

Cells have the ability to divide into daughter cells that contain identical genetic information. The prenatal development of a human being is accomplished through cell division, differentiation (into different cell types), and movement (to different locations in the body). There are two kinds of cell division: mitosis and meiosis. In mitosis, or nonreductive division, two daughter cells, each containing 46 chromosomes, are formed from one parent cell. In meiosis, or reductive division, four daughter cells, each containing only 23 chromosomes, are formed from one parent cell. Although mitosis occurs in all cells, meiosis takes place only in the germ cells and creates sperm and eggs (Jorde et al., 2001).

The ability of cells to continue to undergo mitosis throughout the life span is essential for proper functioning. Cells divide at different rates, however, ranging from once every 10 hours for skin cells to once a year for liver cells. This is why a skin abrasion heals in a few days but the liver may take a year to recover from hepatitis. By adulthood, some cells, including muscle and nerve cells, appear to have a significantly decreased ability to divide. This limits the body's capacity to recover after a stroke or other acquired brain injury.

Mitosis occurs in four steps: **prophase, metaphase, anaphase,** and **telophase** (Figure 1.2). This cycle, once begun, takes only 1–2 hours to complete. Therefore, all cells, even rapidly dividing skin cells, spend most of their lives in **interphase,** which is the rest period between cycles of mitosis.

Unlike mitosis, meiosis involves two cell divisions instead of one: The first division is reductive, the second replicative (Figure 1.3). Each division has analogous stages of prophase, metaphase, anaphase, and telophase. It takes a sperm cell but a few hours to undergo meiosis, whereas the process can take decades in an egg cell. Because meiosis is a much more complicated process than mitosis, it is more often associated with abnormalities (Gelehrter et al., 1998).

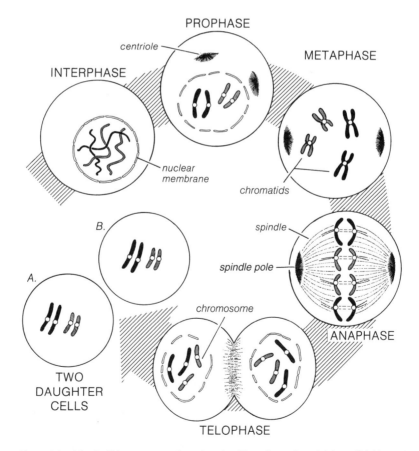

Figure 1.2.   Mitosis. This process produces two daughter cells, each containing a diploid number (46) of chromosomes. (*Source:* Jorde et al., 2001.)

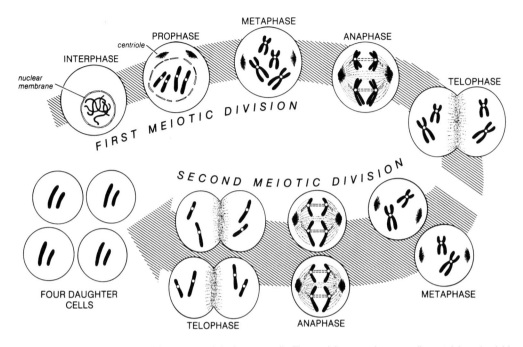

Figure 1.3.   Meiosis. This reductive division occurs only in the germ cells. The result is egg and sperm cells containing a haploid number (23) of chromosomes. (*Source:* Jorde et al., 2001.)

One of the primary differences between mitosis and meiosis can be seen during the first meiotic division (termed *meiosis I*). During prophase I, the corresponding chromosomes line up beside each other in pairs (e.g., the two chromosome 1s line up together). Unlike in mitosis, however, the chromosomes intertwine and may "cross over," exchanging genetic material (Figure 1.4). Although this **crossover** (or recombination) of chromosomes may result in disorders, it also allows for the mutual transfer of genetic information, reducing the chance that individuals end up as exact copies of their brothers and sisters. Some of the variability among siblings can also be attributed to the random assortment of maternal and paternal chromosomes in meiosis I.

Throughout the life span of the male, meiosis of the immature sperm continually produces spermatocytes with 23 chromosomes each. These cells will lose most of their cytoplasm, sprout tails, and become mature sperm. In the female, meiosis forms oocytes that will ultimately become mature eggs. By the time a girl is born, her body has produced all of the 2 million eggs she will ever have.

A number of events that adversely affect a child's development can occur during cell division (McFadden & Friedman, 1997). Often, when chromosomes divide unequally, in a process known as **nondisjunction,** the cells die. On occasion, however, they survive and can lead to a child's being born with too many or too few chromosomes. For example, sometimes during mitosis, a pair of **chromatids** does not split during anaphase, resulting in one daughter cell that contains 47 chromosomes **(trisomy)** and another daughter cell that contains 45 chromosomes **(monosomy)**.

Most abnormalities, however, occur during meiosis (Nicolaidis & Petersen, 1998). The loss or addition of part of a chromosome or an entire chromosome can result in the **deletion** or addition of hundreds of genes, which can have severe consequences. Among children who survive these genetic missteps, mental retardation, unusual facial appearances, and various **congenital** malformations are common. In the general population, chromosomal errors occur in 0.6%–0.9% of all live births. In children who have mental retardation, however, this incidence increases 10- to 40-fold (Flint et al., 1995).

Nondisjunction of Autosomes

The most frequent chromosomal abnormality is nondisjunction of autosomes, and the most common clinical consequence is trisomy 21, or Down syndrome (see Chapter 16). Nondisjunction can occur during either mitosis or meiosis but is more common in meiosis (Figure 1.5). When nondisjunction occurs during the first meiotic division, both copies of chromosome 21 end up in one cell. Instead of an equal distribution of chromosomes (23 each) among cells, one daughter cell receives 24 chromosomes, whereas the other receives only 22. The cell containing 22 chromosomes is unable to survive. The egg (or sperm) with 24 chromosomes, however, occasionally can survive. After fertilization with a sperm (or egg) containing 23 chromosomes, the resulting embryo contains three copies of chromosome 21, or trisomy 21. The child will be born with Down syndrome (Figure 1.6).

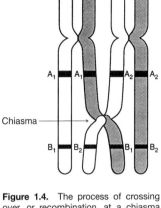

Figure 1.4. The process of crossing over, or recombination, at a chiasma permits exchange of genetic material among chromosomes and accounts for much of the genetic variability of human traits. In this illustration, there is an exchange on the banding area labeled B between two chromosomes. (*Source:* Jorde et al., 2001.)

A majority of individuals with Down syndrome (approximately 90%) acquire it as a result of a nondisjunction during meiosis of the egg; only 5% acquire Down syndrome from nondisjunction of the sperm (Ballesta et al., 1999; Savage et al., 1998). Another 5% of individuals acquire Down syndrome as a result of nondisjunction or **translocation** (discussed later) during mitosis of the embryo, resulting in **mosaicism** (some cells being affected and others not; discussed later).

Other nonsex chromosomes that seem particularly susceptible to nondisjunction are chromosomes 13 and 18. The resulting trisomy 13 and trisomy 18 are associated with even more severe cognitive impairments than Down syndrome and often with early death (Baty, Blackburn, & Carey, 1994; Baty, Jorde, & Blackburn, 1994; Root & Carey, 1994).

Nondisjunction of Sex Chromosomes—Klinefelter Syndrome

Klinefelter syndrome (47,XXY), occurring in one in every 500 male births, is the most common disorder arising from nondisjunction of the sex chromosomes (Smyth & Bremner, 1998). Males with Klinefelter syndrome are born with an extra X chromosome, derived from the mother 60% of the time. This gives them a total of 47 chromosomes, instead of the usual 46. As a consequence, these males produce inadequate **testosterone** and do not develop many of the typical secondary male sexual characteristics. They grow to be tall, slender men with disproportionately long arms and legs, underdeveloped testes, infertility, and small genitalia. They generally have IQ scores in the range of 75–90. Testosterone replacement therapy is given to promote the male physique, but this does not reverse the infertility.

Other sex chromosome abnormalities resulting from nondisjunction do exist, although they are extremely rare: 47,XXX (the only one of these disorders in females); 47,XYY; 48,XXXY; 48,XXYY; and 49,XXXYY syndromes (Linden, Bender, & Robinson, 1995; Peet, Weaver, & Vance, 1998). Abnormal physical, sexual, and cognitive development characterize these syndromes, and the severity increases with the number of extra sex chromosomes (Jones, 1997).

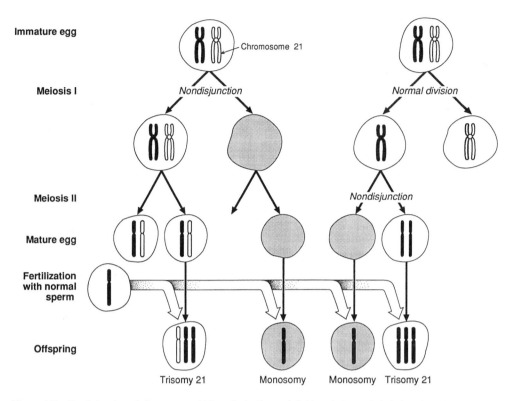

Immature egg

Meiosis I

Meiosis II

Mature egg

Fertilization with normal sperm

Offspring

Chromosome 21

Nondisjunction

Normal division

Nondisjunction

Trisomy 21   Monosomy   Monosomy   Trisomy 21

Figure 1.5.   Nondisjunction of chromosome 21 in meiosis. Unequal division during meiosis I or meiosis II can result in trisomy or monosomy.

Chromosomal Loss—Turner Syndrome

Turner syndrome (45,X), which affects girls, is the only disorder in which a fetus can survive despite the loss of an entire chromosome. Even so, more than 99% of the 45,X conceptions appear to be miscarried (Hall, 1992). Females with Turner syndrome (1 in every 5,000 live births) have only a single X chromosome and no second X or Y chromosome, for a total of 45 rather than 46 chromosomes. In contrast to Down syndrome, 80% of individuals with **monosomy X** conditions are affected by meiotic errors in sperm production; these children usually receive an X chromosome from their mothers but no sex chromosome from their fathers.

Girls with Turner syndrome have short stature and a webbed neck, a broad "shield-like" chest with widely spaced nipples, and nonfunctional ovaries. Twenty percent have obstruction of the left side of the heart, most commonly caused by a **coarctation** of the **aorta**. Unlike children with Down syndrome, most girls with Turner syndrome have IQ scores in the average range (IQ 85–115). They do, however, have visual-perceptual impairments that predispose them to develop nonverbal learning disabilities (Money, 1993; Ross et al., 1995). Human growth hormone injections have been effective in increasing height in girls with Turner syndrome, and **estrogen** supplementation can lead to the emergence of secondary sexual characteristics; however, these girls remain sterile (Haeusler, 1998; Saenger, 1999).

About half of all individuals with Turner syndrome have a 45,X karyotype in all of their cells; 30%–40% have mosaicism (discussed next). The remainder have structural X chromosome abnormalities involving a deletion of some part or all of the short arm of the X chromosome or involving an **isochromosome** (having two copies of one arm of the X chromosome but no copy of the short arm).

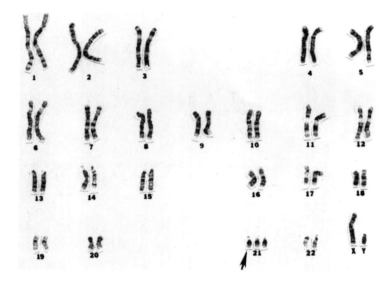

Figure 1.6. Karyotype of a boy with Down syndrome (47,XY). Note that the child has 47 chromosomes; the extra one is a chromosome 21.

Mosaicism

In mosaicism, different cells have a different genetic makeup (Colman et al., 1996; Johnson & Wapner, 1997). For example, a child with the mosaic form of Down syndrome may have trisomy 21 in blood cells but not in skin cells or in some, but not all, brain cells. Children with mosaicism often appear as if they have the condition (in this case, Down syndrome), although the physical features and cognitive impairments may be less severe. Usually mosaicism occurs when some cells in a trisomy conception lose the extra chromosome via nondisjunction during mitosis. Mosaicism also can occur if some cells lose a chromosome after a normal conception (e.g., some cells lose an X chromosome in mosaic Turner syndrome). Mosaicism is rare and accounts for only 5%–10% of all children with chromosomal abnormalities (Delatycki & Gardner, 1997).

Translocations

A relatively common dysfunction in cell division, translocation, can occur during mitosis and meiosis when the chromosomes exchange parts with other chromosomes. Translocation involves the transfer of a portion of one chromosome to a completely different chromosome. For example, a portion of chromosome 21 might attach itself to chromosome 14 (Figure 1.7). If this occurs during meiosis, one daughter cell will then have 23 chromosomes but will have both a chromosome 21 and a chromosome 14/21 translocation. Fertilization of this egg or sperm with a cell containing the normal complement of 23 chromosomes will result in a child with 46 chromosomes, including two copies of chromosome 21, one chromosome 14/21, and one chromosome 14. This child will have Down syndrome because of the partial trisomy 21 caused by the translocation.

Deletions

Another somewhat common dysfunction in cell division is deletion. Chromosomal deletions occur in two forms, visible deletions and microdeletions. Those that are large enough to be seen through the microscope are called *visible deletions*. Those that are so small that they can be detected only by technicians using special chromosomal banding techniques are called *microdeletions*.

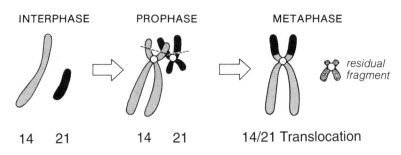

INTERPHASE   PROPHASE   METAPHASE

residual
fragment

14   21   14   21   14/21 Translocation

Figure 1.7. Translocation. During prophase of meiosis in a parent, there may be a transfer of a portion of one chromosome to another. In this figure, the long arm of chromosome 21 is translocated to chromosome 14, and the residual fragments are lost.

The cri-du-chat ("cat cry") syndrome is an example of a visible chromosomal deletion in which a portion of the short arm of chromosome 5 is lost. Cri-du-chat syndrome affects 1 in 50,000 children, causing **microcephaly** and an unusual facial appearance with a round face, widely spaced eyes, **epicanthal folds**, and low-set ears. Individuals with the syndrome have a high-pitched cry and mental retardation.

Examples of microdeletion syndromes are Williams syndrome and VCFS. The former is due to a deletion in the long arm of chromosome 7 and the latter to a deletion in the long arm of chromosome 22 (McDonald-McGinn et al., 1997). Children with VCFS have cleft palates, congenital heart defects, a characteristic facial appearance, and nonverbal learning disabilities (Gerdes et al., 1999). Children with Williams syndrome have a distinctive facial appearance, cardiac defects, and a unique cognitive profile with better expressive language skills (with excessive loquaciousness) than would be expected by their degree of mental retardation (Lashkari, Smith, & Graham, 1999).

Microdeletion syndromes are also called **contiguous gene syndromes** because they involve the deletion of multiple adjacent genes. As a general rule, microdeletion disorders result in less severe developmental disabilities than do visible deletion syndromes. A few microdeletion syndromes, including Williams syndrome and VCFS, can now be diagnosed using a new technique designated by the whimsical acronym FISH (fluorescent *in situ* hybridization; Elcioglu et al., 1998; Meyer et al., 2000). This technique employs a chemically labeled probe that binds with and identifies a specific gene sequence on the chromosome.

Other Structural Abnormalities

Chromosome breakage during meiosis or mitosis can yield rare structural abnormalities, including **ring chromosomes, inversions,** and isochromosomes (Eggermann et al., 1999; MacLean et al., 2000; Pettenati et al., 1995). A ring chromosome forms when deletions occur at both tips of a chromosome, with subsequent fusion of the two "sticky" ends (Figure 1.8). The deletion of chromosomal material usually causes clinical abnormalities; in ring chromosome 6, for example, affected children have short stature, mental retardation, microcephaly, and eye abnormalities (Teyssier et al., 1992).

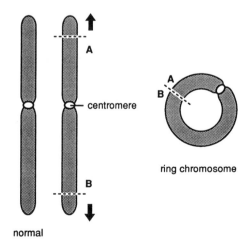

centromere

ring chromosome

normal

Figure 1.8. The formation of a ring chromosome requires deletion at both tips of the chromosome with subsequent fusing of the ends. (From Jorde, L.B., Carey, J.C., & Bamshad, M.J., et al. [2001]. *Medical genetics* [Rev. 2nd ed., p. 130]. St. Louis: Mosby; adapted by permission.)

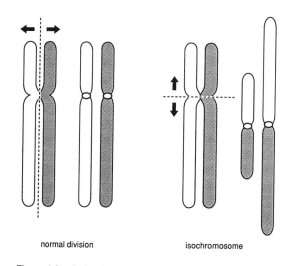

normal division   isochromosome

Figure 1.9. An isochromosome has two copies of one arm of a chromosome and no copies of the other. (From Jorde, L.B., Carey, J.C., & Bamshad, M.J., et al. [2001]. *Medical genetics* [Rev. 2nd ed., p. 132]. St. Louis: Mosby; adapted by permission.)

Inversions result when a chromosome breaks in two places and is then reconnected in reverse order. Because the affected individual still maintains the normal complement of genes, he or she is not affected by the inversion. As a parent, however, this individual can pass on the inversion to offspring, leading to chromosomal deletions or duplications (Pettenati et al., 1995).

An isochromosome has two copies of one arm of a chromosome and no copies of the other (Figure 1.9). As noted previously, some incidences of Turner syndrome result from an isochromosome X.

In total, about 25% of eggs and 3%–4% of sperm have an extra or missing chromosome, and an additional 1% and 5%, respectively, have a structural chromosomal abnormality (Nicolaidis & Petersen, 1998). As a result, 10%–15% of all conceptions have a chromosomal abnormality. Somewhat more than half of these abnormalities are trisomies, 20% are monosomies, and 15% are **triploids** (69 chromosomes). The remainder are composed of structural abnormalities and **tetraploids** (92 chromosomes). It may therefore seem surprising that more children are not born with chromosomal abnormalities (Jacobs et al., 1992). The explanation is that more than 95% of fetuses with chromosomal abnormalities do not survive to term. In fact, fetuses with certain abnormalities never survive; for example, trisomy 16 is the most common trisomy at conception but has never been reported in a live birth (Benn, 1998).

GENES AND THEIR DISORDERS

The underlying problem with the previously mentioned chromosomal disorders is the presence of too many or too few genes, resulting from extra or deleted chromosomal material. Genetic disorders can also result from an abnormality in a single gene. The Human Genome Project, a public–private partnership developed to unravel the genetic makeup of mankind, published a sequence of the human **genome** (the set of all genes) in 2001 that is thought to be more than 95% complete (Venter et al., 2001). The project appears to have confirmed that the human genome contains about 100,000 genes.

Genes are responsible for producing specific protein products (e.g., hormones, enzymes, blood-type proteins) as well as regulating the development and function of the body. Single-gene defects have already been shown to play a primary role in about 7,000 disorders (Mc-

Kusick, 1998). Now that the genetic sequence of the human genome is known, the next step is understanding how genes express protein products, a field called proteomics. This new knowledge is likely to help in developing new diagnostic and therapeutic tools in treating conditions causing developmental disabilities.

The particular genes that a person possesses determine that person's **genotype,** whereas the manner in which those genes are expressed is called the **phenotype.** For some clinical disorders, the same genotype can produce quite different phenotypes, depending on environmental influences. For example, a child with the **inborn error of metabolism** called phenylketonuria (PKU) will develop mental retardation if the PKU is not treated early but will have typical development if it is treated from infancy (see Chapter 18). Conversely, very different genotypes can produce the same phenotype. For example, two separate enzyme deficiencies, caused by gene defects on different chromosomes, can lead to the elevated levels of the chemical phenylalanine that cause brain damage in PKU. Thus, a person's genetic makeup may not always predict what will be observed biochemically or physically, and the converse is also true.

Genes provide the cells with a blueprint for producing the specific proteins needed for body functions, such as insulin for the metabolism of glucose. These instructions are encoded by DNA. DNA is formed as a **double helix,** a structure that resembles a twisted ladder. The sides of the ladder are composed of sugar and phosphate, whereas the rungs are made up of four chemicals called **nucleotide bases:** cytosine (C), guanine (G), adenine (A), and thymine (T) (Figure 1.10). Pairs of nucleotides interlock to form each rung: Cytosine bonds with guanine, and adenine with thymine. The sequence of nucleotide bases on a segment of DNA (spelled out by the 4-letter alphabet C, G, A, T) make up one's genetic code. Genes range in size, containing from 1,500 to more than 2 million nucleotide base pairs.

The production of a specific protein begins when the DNA for that gene unwinds and the two strands, or sides of the ladder, unzip to expose the code (Jorde et al., 2001). The exposed DNA sequence then serves as a template for the formation, or **transcription,** of a similar nucleotide sequence called **messenger ribonucleic acid** (mRNA; Figure 1.11). In **RNA,** the nucleotides are the same as in DNA except that uracil (U) substitutes for thymine (T). As might be expected, errors or **mutations** may occur during transcription; however, a proofreading enzyme generally catches and corrects these errors. If not corrected, the transcription error can lead to the production of a disordered protein and a disease state.

Once transcribed, the single-stranded mRNA detaches, and the double-stranded DNA zips back together. The mRNA then moves out of the nucleus into the cytoplasm, where it provides instructions for the production of a protein, a process termed **translation** (Figure 1.12). Once in the cytoplasm, the mRNA attaches itself to a **ribosome.** The ribosome moves along the mRNA strand, reading the message like a videocassette recorder in three-letter "words," or **codons,** such as GCU, CUA, and UAG. Most of these triplets code for specific **amino acids,**

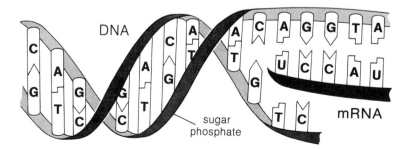

Figure 1.10.   DNA. Four nucleotides (C, cytosine; G, guanine; A, adenosine; T, thymine) form the genetic code. On the mRNA molecule, uracil (U) substitutes for thymine. The DNA unzips to transcribe its message as mRNA.

the building blocks of proteins. As these triplets are read, another type of RNA, **transfer RNA (tRNA),** carries the requisite amino acids to the ribosome, where they are linked to form a protein. Certain triplets, termed stop codons, instruct the ribosome to terminate the sequence. The stop codon indicates that all of the correct amino acids are in place to form the complete protein.

Once the protein is complete, the mRNA, ribosome, and protein separate, and the protein is released into the cytoplasm. The protein is either used by the cytoplasm or prepared for release into the bloodstream. If the protein is to be secreted, it is transferred to the Golgi body (Figure 1.1), which packages it in a form that can be released through the cell membrane and carried throughout the body.

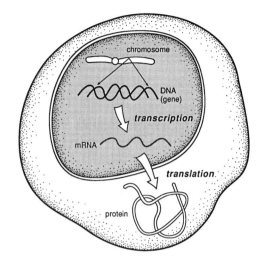

Figure 1.11. A summary of the steps leading from gene to protein formation. Transcription of the DNA (gene) onto mRNA occurs in the cell nucleus. The mRNA is then transported to the cytoplasm, where translation into protein occurs.

Mutations

An abnormality at any step in this translation process can cause the body to produce a structurally abnormal protein, reduced amounts of a protein, or no protein at all. When the error occurs in the gene itself, thus disrupting the subsequent steps, that mistake is called a *mutation*. The likelihood of mutations occurring increases with the size of the gene. In egg and sperm cells, the mutation rate also increases with parental age, especially in males (Figure 1.13; Green et al., 1999). Although most mutations occur spontaneously, they can be induced by ionizing and nonionizing radiation, chemicals, and viruses. Once they occur, mutations become part of a person's genetic code (and are present in the person's egg or sperm cells) and can be passed down from one generation to the next.

Point Mutations

The most common type of mutation is a single base pair substitution (Gelehrter et al., 1998), also called a point mutation. Because there is redundancy in our DNA, many of these mutations have no adverse consequences. Depending on where in the gene they occur, however, point mutations are capable of causing a **missense mutation** or a **nonsense mutation** (Figure 1.14). A missense mutation results in a change in the triplet code that substitutes a different amino acid in the protein chain. For example, in PKU, a single base substitution causes an error in the production of phenylalanine hydroxylase, the enzyme necessary to metabolize the amino acid phenylalanine. The result is an accumulation of phenylalanine in blood and brain that can cause brain damage. In a nonsense mutation, the single base pair substitution produces a stop codon that prematurely terminates the protein formation. In this case, no useful protein is formed. Neurofibromatosis is an example of a disorder commonly caused by a nonsense mutation. Here, neurofibromin, a tumor suppressor, is not formed. As a result, multiple neurofibroma tumors form on the body and in the brain. Children with the disorder have a high incidence of attention-deficit/hyperactivity disorder.

Insertions and Deletions

Mutations may also involve the insertion or deletion of one or more bases. The most common mutation in individuals with spinal muscular atrophy involves an insertion in the survival

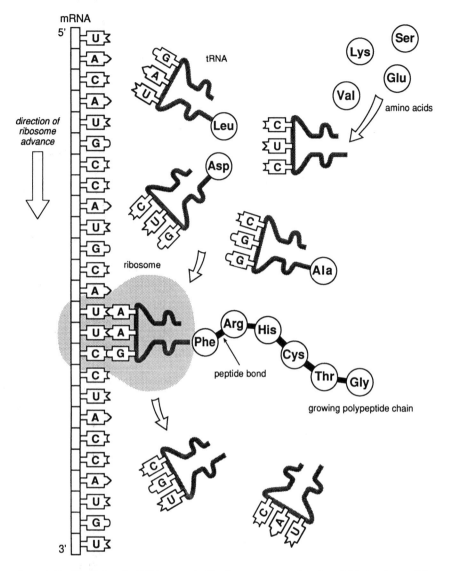

Figure 1.12. Translation of mRNA into protein. The ribosome moves along the mRNA strand assembling a growing polypeptide (protein) chain using tRNA–amino acid complexes. In this example, it has already assembled six amino acids (phenylalanine [Phe], arginine [Arg], histidine [His], cystine [Cys], threonine [Thr], and glycine [Gly]) into a polypeptide chain.

motor neuron gene, rendering it defective and resulting in a polio-like disorder. In contrast, a common mutation in Duchenne muscular dystrophy involves a deletion. Base additions or subtractions may also lead to a **frame shift** in which the three base pair reading frame is shifted, as occurs when one places the left index finger on the *G* rather than the *F* typewriter key. All subsequent triplets are misread, leading to the production of a nonfunctional protein (Figure 1.14). Certain children with Tay-Sachs disease (discussed later) have this type of mutation.

Other mutations can affect regions of the gene that regulate transcription but that do not actually code for an amino acid. These areas are called *promoter and enhancer areas.* Mutations here may result in a normal protein being formed but at a much slower rate than usual, leading to an enzyme or other protein deficiency.

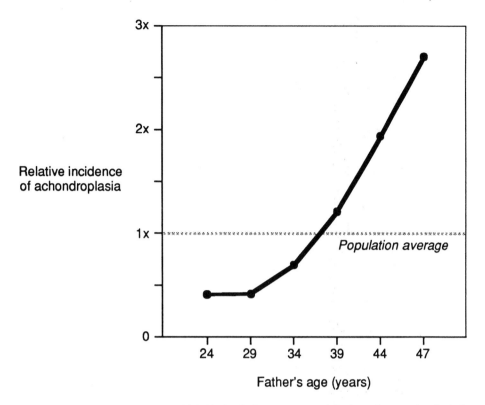

Figure 1.13. The risk of producing a child with the single-gene autosomal dominant disease achondroplasia (y-axis) increases with the father's age (x-axis). (From Vogel, F., & Rathenberg, R. [1975]. Spontaneous mutation in man. *Advances in Human Genetics, 5,* 267; reprinted by permission.)

Triplet Repeat Expansion

Another type of mutation involves a **triplet repeat expansion.** For reasons not fully understood, some triplet codes are repeated multiple times in certain regions of normal genes. However, if the number of triplet copies is expanded markedly, usually during defective meiosis, a gene can be turned off, leading to conditions such as Huntington disease or fragile X syndrome (Chakrabarti & Davies, 1997; Margolis et al., 1999). Triplet repeats are further described in the discussion of fragile X syndrome in Chapter 17.

Selective Advantage

The incidence of a genetic disease in a population depends on the difference between the rate of mutation production and that of mutation removal. Typically, genetic diseases enter populations through mutation errors. Natural selection, the process by which individuals with a selective advantage survive and pass on their genes, works to remove these errors. For instance, because individuals with sickle cell anemia, an autosomal recessive inherited blood disorder, often have a decreased life span, the gene that causes the disorder would be expected to be gradually removed from the gene pool. Sometimes natural selection, however, favors the individual who carries one copy of a mutated recessive gene. In the case of sickle cell anemia, unaffected carriers who appear clinically healthy actually have minor differences in their hemoglobin structure that make it more resistant to a malarial parasite. In Africa, where malaria is endemic, this resistance gives the carriers a selective advantage. This selection has maintained the sickle cell trait among Africans. Northern Europeans, for whom malaria is not an issue, do not carry the sickle cell gene at all; this mutation has presumably died out via natural selection.

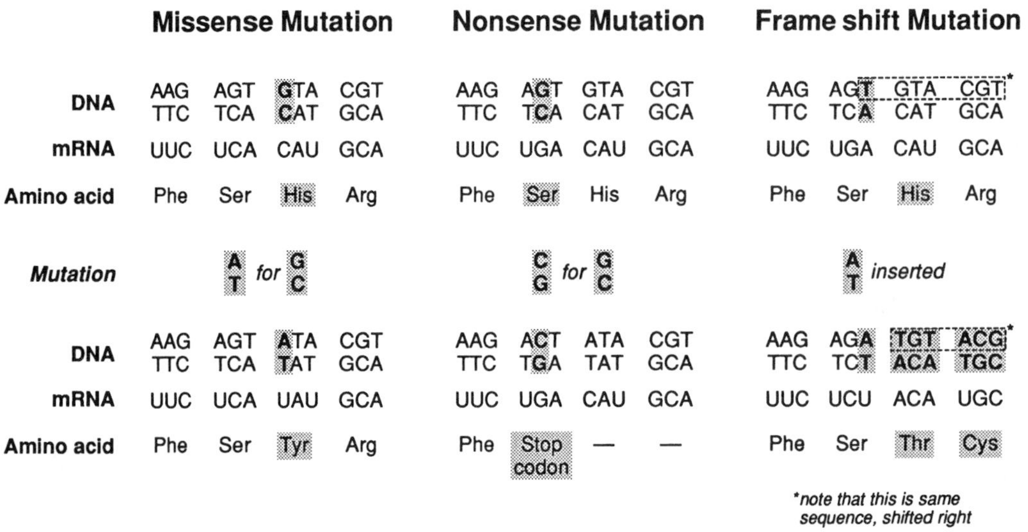

Missense Mutation   **Nonsense Mutation**   **Frame shift Mutation**

	Missense Mutation	Nonsense Mutation	Frame shift Mutation
DNA	AAG AGT GTA CGT / TTC TCA CAT GCA	AAG AGT GTA CGT / TTC TCA CAT GCA	AAG AGT GTA CGT* / TTC TCA CAT GCA
mRNA	UUC UCA CAU GCA	UUC UGA CAU GCA	UUC UGA CAU GCA
Amino acid	Phe Ser His Arg	Phe Ser His Arg	Phe Ser His Arg
Mutation	A/T for G/C	C/G for G/C	A/T inserted
DNA	AAG AGT ATA CGT / TTC TCA TAT GCA	AAG ACT ATA CGT / TTC TGA TAT GCA	AAG AGA TGT ACG* / TTC TCT ACA TGC
mRNA	UUC UCA UAU GCA	UUC UGA CAU GCA	UUC UCU ACA UGC
Amino acid	Phe Ser Tyr Arg	Phe Stop codon — —	Phe Ser Thr Cys

*note that this is same sequence, shifted right

Figure 1.14.   Examples of single-gene mutations: Missense mutation, nonsense mutation, and frame shift mutation. The shaded areas mark the point of mutation.

Likewise, the absence of malaria in the United States eliminates the selective advantage that has allowed sickle cell anemia to survive in Africa (Jorde et al., 2001). The result is that African Americans have a lower incidence of sickle cell anemia than do Africans.

Geneticists note that everyone carries a number of mutations that they can pass on to their children. Some of these mutations are part of the process of natural evolution. For example, a mutation leading to increased height might confer a selective advantage. Other mutations are harmful and predispose one to various diseases, including diabetes and cancer. Most have no observable effect and do not pose a serious threat to our well-being.

Mendelian Disorders

Gregor Mendel (1822–1884), an Austrian monk, pioneered our understanding of single-gene defects. While cultivating pea plants, he noted that when he bred two differently colored plants—yellow and green—the **hybrid** offspring all were green rather than mixed in color. Mendel concluded that the green trait was **dominant,** whereas the yellow trait was **recessive** (from the Latin for "hidden"). Yet, this yellow trait sometimes appeared in subsequent generations. Later, scientists determined that many human traits, including some birth defects, are also inherited in this fashion. They are referred to as **Mendelian traits** (Connor, Connor, & Ferguson-Smith, 1997).

Table 1.1 indicates the prevalence of the more common genetic disorders. Approximately 1% of the population has a Mendelian, or single-gene, disorder. These disorders can be transmitted to offspring on the autosomes or on the X chromosome. Mendelian traits may be either dominant or recessive. Thus, Mendelian disorders are characterized as being **autosomal recessive, autosomal dominant,** or X-linked.

Autosomal Recessive Disorders

For a child to inherit a disorder that is autosomal recessive, he or she must receive an abnormal gene from both mother and father. Tay-Sachs disease is an example of an autosomal recessive, progressive neurological disorder. It is caused by the absence of an enzyme, hexosaminidase A, that normally metabolizes a potentially toxic product of nerve cell metabolism (Kaplan, 1998).

In individuals with Tay-Sachs disease, this product cannot be broken down and is stored in the brain, leading to damage and early death. A child with Tay-Sachs disease initially develops typically. At about 6 months of age, however, the child's health begins to deteriorate, and he or she can no longer sit or babble. The disease progresses rapidly, causing blindness, mental retardation, and early death.

Alternate forms of the gene for hexosaminidase A are known to exist. The different forms of a gene, called **alleles,** include the normal gene, which can be symbolized by a capital *A* as it is dominant, and the mutated allele (in this example, carrying Tay-Sachs disease), which can be symbolized by the lowercase *a* as it is recessive (Figure 1.15). Upon fertilization, the embryo receives two genes for hexosaminidase A, one from the father and one from the mother. The following combinations of alleles could theoretically occur: **homozygous** (carrying the same allele) combinations, AA and aa; and **heterozygous** (carrying alternate allele) combinations, aA and Aa. Because Tay-Sachs disease is a recessive disorder, two abnormal recessive genes (aa) are needed to produce a child who has the disease. Therefore, a child with aa would be homozygous for the Tay-Sachs gene (i.e., have 2 copies and manifest the disease), a child with aA or Aa would be heterozygous and a healthy carrier of the Tay-Sachs gene, and a child with AA would be a healthy noncarrier.

If two heterozygotes (carrying alternate alleles) were to have children (e.g., aA x Aa), the following combinations could occur: AA, aA or Aa, or aa (Figure 1.15). According to the law of probability, each pregnancy would carry a 1 in 4 chance of the child's being a noncarrier (AA), a 1 in 2 chance of the child's being a carrier (aA or Aa), and a 1 in 4 risk of the child's having Tay-Sachs disease (aa). If a carrier has children with a noncarrier (aA x AA), each pregnancy carries a 1 in 2 chance of the child's being a carrier (aA, Aa), and a 1 in 2 chance of the child's being a noncarrier (AA); no child would be at risk for having Tay-Sachs disease (Figure 1.15). The significance is that siblings of affected children, even if they are carriers, are unlikely to produce children with the disease. This can only occur if they have children with another carrier, an unlikely occurrence in these rare diseases.

The 1 in 4 risk when two carriers have children is a probability risk. This does not mean that if a family has one affected child, the next three will be unaffected. Each new pregnancy carries the same 1 in 4 risk; the parents could by chance have three affected children in a row or five unaffected ones. In the case of Tay-Sachs disease, carrier screening and prenatal diagnosis are available to help alter these odds (see Chapter 2).

Because it is unlikely for a carrier of an unusual disease to have children with another carrier of the same disease, these types of disorders are quite rare in the general population, ranging from 1 in 2,000 to 1 in 200,000 births (McKusick, 1998). When intermarriage within an extended family or among ethnically, religiously, or geographically isolated populations occurs, however, the incidence of these disorders increases markedly, which probably underlies

Table 1.1. Prevalence of genetic disorders

Disease	Approximate prevalence
Chromosomal disorders	
Down syndrome	1/700–1/1,000
Klinefelter syndrome	1/1,000 males
Trisomy 13	1/10,000
Trisomy 18	1/6,000
Turner syndrome	1/2,500–1/10,000
Single-gene disorders	
Duchenne muscular dystrophy	1/3,500 males
Fragile X syndrome	1/1,500 males; 1/2,500 females
Neurofibromatosis	1/3,000–1/3,500
Phenylketonuria	1/14,000
Tay-Sachs disease	1/3,000 in Ashkenazi Jews
Multifactorial inheritance	
Cleft lip/palate	1/500–1/1,000
Club foot	1/1,000
Neural tube defects	1/1,000
Pyloric stenosis	3/1,000
Mitochondrial inheritance	
Leber hereditary optic neuropathy	Rare
MELAS and MERRF	Rare
Mitochondrial encephalopathy	Rare

Source: Jorde et al., 2001.

Key: MELAS, **m**itochondrial **e**ncephalomyelopathy, **l**actic **a**cidosis, and **s**troke-like episodes; MERRF, **my**oclonic **e**pilepsy and **r**agged **r**ed **f**ibers.

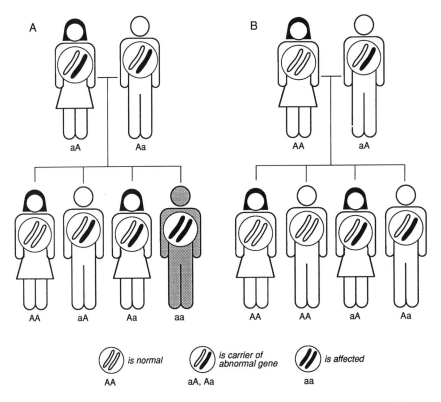

Figure 1.15. Inheritance of autosomal recessive disorders. Two copies of the abnormal gene (aa) must be present to produce the disease state. A) Two carriers mating, will result, on average, in 25% of the children being affected, 50% being carriers, and 25% not being affected. B) A carrier and a noncarrier mating, will result in 50% normal children and 50% carriers. No children will be affected.

the biblical proscription and taboo in many cultures against marrying one's immediate relatives (Figure 1.16). For example, Tay-Sachs disease tends to occur among Jewish children, and another inborn error of metabolism, glutaric acidemia, tends to occur among the Amish.

Like Tay-Sachs disease, many autosomal recessive disorders are caused by mutations that lead to an enzyme deficiency of some kind. In most cases, a number of different mutations within the gene can produce the same disease. Because these enzyme deficiencies generally lead to biochemical abnormalities involving either the insufficient production of a needed product or the buildup of toxic materials, developmental disabilities or early death may result (see Chapter 18). These disorders affect males and females equally, and there tends to be clustering in families (i.e., more than one affected child per family). Yet, a history of the disease in past generations rarely exists unless blood relatives have had children together (**consanguinity**).

Autosomal Dominant Disorders

Autosomal dominant disorders (Table 1.2) are quite different from autosomal recessive disorders in mechanism, incidence, and clinical characteristics. Because autosomal dominant disorders are caused by a single abnormal allele, individuals with the genotypes AA, Aa, or aA are all affected.

To better understand this, consider neurofibromatosis, the neurological disorder discussed previously. Suppose *a* represents the normal recessive gene and *A* indicates the mutated dominant gene for neurofibromatosis. If a person with neurofibromatosis (aA or Aa) has a child with an unaffected individual (aa), there is a 1 in 2 risk, statistically speaking, that the child will have the disorder (aA or Aa), and a 1 in 2 chance he or she will be unaffected (aa; Figure 1.17).

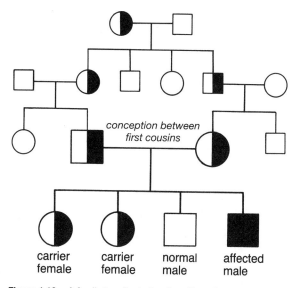

Figure 1.16. A family tree illustrating the effect of consanguinity (in this case, a conception between first cousins) on the risk of inheriting an autosomal recessive disorder. The chance of both parents being carriers is usually less than 1 in 300. When first cousins conceive a child, however, the chance of both parents being carriers rises to 1 in 8. The risk, then, of having an affected child increases almost 40-fold.

An unaffected child will not carry the abnormal allele and, therefore, cannot pass it to his or her children.

Autosomal dominant disorders affect men and women with equal frequency. They tend to involve structural (physical) abnormalities rather than enzymatic defects. In affected individuals, there is often a family history of the disease, but about half of affected individuals represent a new mutation. Although individuals with a new mutation will risk passing the mutated gene to their offspring, their parents are unaffected and at no greater risk than the general population of having a second affected child.

X-Linked Disorders

Unlike autosomal recessive and autosomal dominant disorders, which involve genes located on the 22 nonsex chromosomes, X-linked (previously called sex-linked) recessive disorders involve mutant genes located on the X chromosome. X-linked disorders primarily affect males. Because males have only one X chromosome, a single dose of the abnormal recessive gene causes disease. As females have two X chromosomes, a single recessive allele should not cause disease, provided there is a normal allele on the second X chromosome. Approximately 400 X-

Table 1.2. Comparison of autosomal recessive, autosomal dominant, and X-linked inheritance patterns

	Autosomal recessive	Autosomal dominant	X-linked
Type of disorder	Enzyme deficiency	Structural abnormalities	Mixed
Examples of disorder	Tay-Sachs disease Phenlyketonuria (PKU)	Achondroplasia Neurofibromatosis	Fragile X syndrome Muscular dystrophy
Carrier expresses disorder	No	Yes	Sometimes
Increased risk in other family members from consanguinity	Yes	No	No

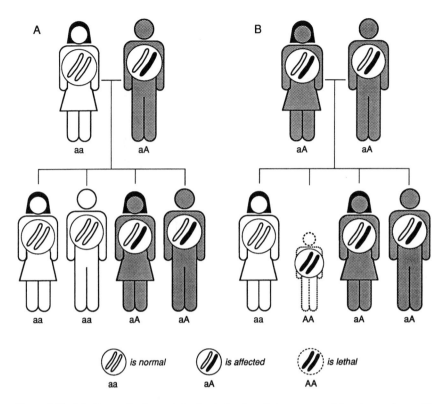

Figure 1.17. Inheritance of autosomal dominant disorders. Only one copy of the abnormal gene (A) must be present to produce the disease state. A) If an affected person conceives a child with an un- affected person, statistically speaking, 50% of the children will be affected and 50% will be unaffected. B) If two affected people have children, 25% of the children will be unaffected, 50% will be affected, and 25% will have an often fatal double dose of the abnormal gene.

linked disorders have been described (McKusick, 1998), including Duchenne muscular dystro- phy and hemophilia (Figure 1.18). These disorders are passed on from one generation to the next by carrier mothers.

As an example, children with Duchenne muscular dystrophy develop a progressive muscle weakness, typically requiring the use of a wheelchair by adolescence (Anderson & Rando, 1999; Tawil, 1999; Tsao & Mendell, 1999). The disease results from a mutation in the dystrophin gene, located on the X chromosome, the function of which is to ensure stability of the muscle cell membrane. Because the disease affects all muscles, eventually the heart muscle and the di- aphragmatic muscles needed for circulation and breathing are impaired, leading to early death.

Dystrophin is also required for typical brain development and function, so affected boys often have cognitive impairments. In fact, approximately 25% of males with mental retarda- tion and 10% of females with learning disabilities are affected by X-linked conditions (Chelly, 1999; Gecz & Mulley, 2000; Neri & Chiurazzi, 1999; Teague et al., 1998). The most common of these is fragile X syndrome (Warren, 1997; see Chapter 17). The finding that males are more likely to have mental retardation than females is probably attributable to X-linked disorders af- fecting males disproportionately more than females.

The mechanism for passing an **X-linked recessive trait** to the next generation is as fol- lows: Women who have a recessive mutation (Xa) on one of their X chromosomes are desig- nated carriers of the gene. Although usually clinically unaffected, they can pass on the abnor- mal gene to their children. Assuming the father is unaffected, each female child born to a carrier mother has a 1 in 2 chance of being a carrier (i.e., inheriting the mutant Xa allele from her mother and the normal X allele from her father; Figure 1.18). The male child (who has only

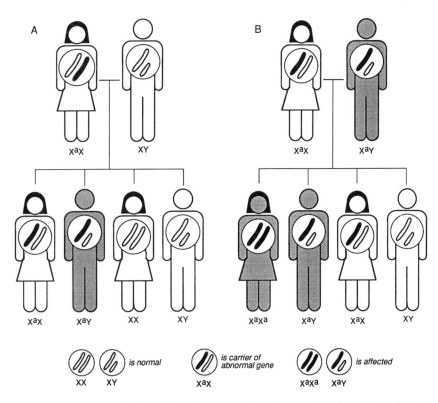

Figure 1.18. Inheritance of X-linked disorders. A) A carrier woman mates with an unaffected man. Among the female children, statistically speaking, 50% will be carriers and 50% will be unaffected; among the male children, 50% will be affected and 50% will be unaffected. B) A carrier woman mates with an affected man. Of the female children, 50% will be carriers and 50% will be affected. Of the male children, statistically speaking, 50% will be unaffected and 50% will be affected.

one X chromosome), however, has a 1 in 2 risk of having the disorder. This occurs if he inherits the X chromosome containing the mutated gene (XaY) instead of the normal one (XY). A family tree frequently reveals that some maternal uncles and male siblings have the disease.

Occasionally, females are affected by X-linked diseases. This can occur if the woman has adverse **lyonization** (unequal inactivation of X chromosomes) or if the disorder is X-linked dominant. Regarding the former mechanism, geneticist Mary Lyon questioned why women have the same amount of X-chromosome–directed gene product as men instead of twice as much as would be expected from their genetic makeup. Dr. Lyon postulated that early in embryogenesis, one of the two X chromosomes in each cell was inactivated, making every female fetus a mosaic. This implied that some cells would contain an active X chromosome derived from the father, whereas others would contain an active X chromosome derived from the mother. This lyonization hypothesis was later proved to be correct. In most instances, the cells in a woman's body have a fairly equal division between maternally and paternally derived active X chromosomes. In a minority of women, however, the distribution is very unequal. If the normal X chromosome is inactivated preferentially in cells of a carrier of an X-linked disorder, the woman will manifest the disease, although usually in a less severe form than a male would.

The second mechanism for a female to manifest an X-linked disorder is if the disorder is transmitted as X-linked dominant. Although most X-linked disorders are recessive, a few appear to be dominant. One example is Rett syndrome (Amir et al., 1999). It appears that in this disorder, the presence of the abnormal gene on the X chromosome of a male embryo leads to lethality. When it occurs in one of the X chromosomes of the female, however, it is compatible with survival but results in a syndrome marked by microcephaly, mental retardation, and autism-like behaviors.

REVISING MENDELIAN GENETICS

Genomic Imprinting

According to Mendelian genetics, the phenotype, or appearance, of an individual should be the same whether the given gene is inherited from the mother or the father. This is not always the case, however, because of a phenomenon called **genomic imprinting** (Mannens & Alders, 1999; Nicholls, 2000). Researchers have found that certain genes passed on from the mother, although containing the identical DNA sequence as in the father, differ in their effect on the fetus. For instance, if a particular deletion occurs on the long arm of the chromosome 15 derived from the father, the child will have Prader-Willi syndrome (Couper, 1999). If the same deletion occurs on the chromosome 15 derived from the mother, however, the child will develop Angelman syndrome (Jiang et al., 1999; Lalande et al., 1999). Prader-Willi syndrome is associated with short stature, obesity, and mental retardation; children with Angelman syndrome also have mental retardation but are not obese and have epilepsy and a gait abnormality (Khan & Wood, 1999). The exact mechanism for genomic imprinting remains unclear.

Anticipation

Mendel also predicted that an inherited trait should look the same from one generation to the next in a given family. In a few disorders associated with expanded triplet repeats, however, the manifestations actually increase in severity in each subsequent generation—a phenomenon called **anticipation** (McInnis, 1996; see Chapter 17). For example, the expanded triplet repeat (CAG) that causes Huntington disease—an autosomal dominant, progressive neurological disease associated with a movement disorder (chorea), cognitive impairment, and behavior disturbances (Reddy, Williams, & Tagle, 1999)—increases in each generation (Figure 1.19). The greater the expansion of triplet repeats, the more severe the manifestations of the disorder.

Mitochondrial Inheritance

Each cell contains several hundred mitochondria in its cytoplasm (Figure 1.1). Mitochondria produce the energy needed for cellular function through a complex process termed **oxidative phosphorylation.** It has been proposed that mitochondria were originally independent microorganisms that invaded our bodies during the process of human evolution and then developed a symbiotic relationship with the cells in the human body. They are unique among cellular organelles (the specialized parts of a cell) in that they possess their own DNA, which is circular rather than helical and contains genes different from those contained in nuclear DNA (Figure 1.20). A mutation in a mitochondrial gene can result in defective energy production and a disease state (Simon & Johns, 1999). Examples include MELAS (*m*itochondrial *e*ncephalomyelopathy, *l*actic *a*cidosis, and *s*troke-like episodes), a progressive neurological disorder marked by episodes of stroke and **dementia**, and MERRF (*m*yoclonic *e*pilepsy and *r*agged *r*ed *f*ibers), a disorder associated with seizures; muscle weakness; and cardiac, kidney, and endocrine abnormalities (Nissenkorn et al., 2000; Uusimaa et al., 2000).

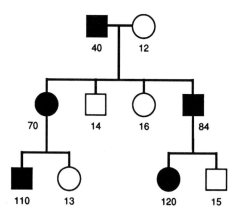

Figure 1.19.   Triplet repeat expansion (anticipation) in an extended family in which multiple members have Huntington disease. This disorder is inherited as an autosomal dominant trait. Numbers indicate the number of CAG triplet repeats. Normal range is 11–34; affected, 37–121. In subsequent generations, the number of triplet repeats increases in affected individuals. Shading indicates affected individuals. Squares represent males, circles females.

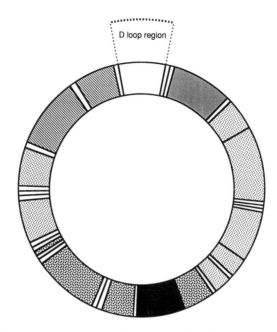

Figure 1.20. Mitochondrial DNA genome. The genes code for various enzyme complexes involved in energy production in the cell. The displacement loop (D loop) is not involved in energy production. (*Key:* ▨ Complex I genes [NADH dehydrogenase], ▨ Complex III genes [ubiquinol: cytochrome *c* oxidoreductase], ☐ tRNA genes, ▨ Complex IV genes [cytochrome *c* oxidase], ■ Complex V genes [ATP synthase], ▨ ribosomal RNA genes.) (From Jorde, L.B., Carey, J.C., & Bamshad, M.J., et al. [2001]. Medical genetics [Rev. 2nd ed., p. 105]. St. Louis: Mosby; adapted by permission.)

Other mitochondrial disorders can lead to blindness or deafness (DeVries et al., 1996; Leonard & Schapira, 2000a, 2000b).

Because eggs, but not sperm, contain cytoplasm, all mitochondria are inherited from one's mother. As a result, mitochondrial disorders are passed on from generally unaffected mothers to their children, both male and female. As expected, men affected by mitochondrial disorders cannot pass the trait to their children (Figure 1.21).

MULTIFACTORIAL INHERITANCE

Many traits and some disorders are inherited in a multifactorial manner—involving both genetics and the environment. In terms of traits, although bright parents tend to have bright children and tall parents tend to have tall children, the interaction of genetics with the pre- and postnatal environments allows for many possible outcomes. For example, it has been found that as a result of an increased protein intake during childhood, second-generation Asian Americans who grow up in the United States are significantly taller than their parents who grew up in Asia. Diabetes, meningomyelocele, cleft palate, and pyloric stenosis are examples of disorders that have both genetic and environmental influences (Cordell & Todd, 1995; Guo & Lange, 2000). Meningomyelocele, for example, is more likely to occur in children born to parents of Irish descent. This genetic predisposition, however, needs to be triggered by inadequate folate ingestion by the mother during the first trimester of pregnancy in order to produce a child with meninogmyelocele (see Chapter 24). Thus, this environmental factor influences gene expression. The prophylactic treatment of pregnant women during the first trimester with folate has markedly reduced the incidence of **neural tube** defects (see Chapter 24).

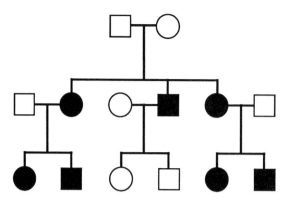

Figure 1.21. Mitochondrial inheritance. As mitochondria are inherited exclusively from the mother, defects in mitochondrial disease will be passed on from the mother to her children, as illustrated in this pedigree. Shading indicates affected individuals. Squares are males, circles females.

SUMMARY

Each human cell contains a full complement of genetic information encoded in genes contained in 46 chromosomes. Not only does this genetic code determine our physical appearance and biochemical makeup, but it is also the legacy we pass on to our children. The unequal division of the reproductive cells, the deletion of a part of a chromosome, or the mutation in a single gene can each have significant consequences. Yet, despite these and other potential problems that can occur during the development of the embryo and fetus, about 95% of infants are born without birth defects.

REFERENCES

Amir, R.E., Van den Veyver, I.B., Wan, M., et al. (1999). Rett syndrome is caused by mutations in X-linked MECP2, encoding methyl-CpG-binding protein 2. *Nature Genetics, 23,* 185–158.

Anderson, P.B., & Rando, T.A. (1999). Neuromuscular disorders of childhood. *Current Opinion in Pediatrics, 11,* 497–503.

Ballesta, F., Queralt, R., Gomez, D., et al. (1999). Parental origin and meiotic stage of non-disjunction in 139 cases of trisomy 21. *Annales de Génétique, 42,* 11–5.

Baty, B.J., Blackburn, B.L., & Carey, J.C. (1994). Natural history of trisomy 18 and trisomy 13, I: Growth, physical assessment, medical histories, survival and recurrence risk. *American Journal of Medical Genetics, 49,* 175–188.

Baty, B.J., Jorde, L.B., & Blackburn, B.L. (1994). Natural history of trisomy 18 and trisomy 13, II: Psychomotor development. *American Journal of Medical Genetics, 49,* 189–194.

Benn, P. (1998). Trisomy 16 and trisomy 16 mosaicism: A review. *American Journal of Medical Genetics, 79,* 121–133.

Chakrabarti, L., & Davies, K.E. (1997). Fragile X syndrome. *Current Opinion in Neurology, 10,* 142–147.

Chelly, J. (1999). Breakthroughs in molecular and cellular mechanisms underlying X-linked mental retardation. *Human Molecular Genetics, 8,* 1833–1838.

Colman, S.D., Rasmussen, S.A., Ho, V.T., et al. (1996). Somatic mosaicism in a patient with neurofibromatosis type I. *American Journal of Human Genetics, 58,* 484–490.

Connor, J., Connor, J.M., & Ferguson-Smith, M.A. (1997). *Essential medical genetics* (5th ed.). St. Louis: Blackwell Science.

Cordell, H.J., & Todd, J.A. (1995). Multifactorial inheritance in type 1 diabetes. *Trends in Genetics, 11,* 499–504.

Couper, R. (1999). Prader-Willi syndrome. *Journal of Paediatrics and Child Health, 35,* 331–334.

Delatycki, M., & Gardner, R.J. (1997). Three cases of trisomy 13 mosaicism and a review of the literature. *Clinical Genetics, 51,* 403–407.

DeVries, D.D., Went, L.N., Bruyn, G.W., et al. (1996). Genetic and biochemical impairment of mitochondrial complex I activity in a family with Leber hereditary optic neuropathy and hereditary spastic dystonia. *American Journal of Human Genetics, 58,* 703–711.

Eggermann, T., Schubert, R., Engels, H., et al. (1999). Formation of supernumerary euchromatic short arm isochromosomes: Parent and cell stage of origin in new cases and review of the literature. *Annales de Génétique, 42,* 75–80.

Elcioglu, N., Mackie-Ogilvie, C., Daker, M., et al. (1998). FISH analysis in patients with clinical diagnosis of Williams syndrome. *Acta Paediatrica, 87,* 48–53.

Flint, J., Wilkie, A.O., Buckle, V.J., et al. (1995). The detection of subtelomeric chromosomal rearrangements in idiopathic mental retardation. *Nature Genetics, 9,* 132–140.

Gecz, J., & Mulley, J. (2000). Genes for cognitive function: Developments on the X. *Genome Research, 10,* 157–163.

Gelehrter, T.D., Collins, F.S., Gelehrter, T.F., et al. (1998). *Principles of medical genetics* (2nd ed.). Philadelphia: Lippincott Williams & Wilkins.

Gerdes, M., Solot, C., Wang, P.P., et al. (1999). Cognitive and behavior profile of preschool children with chromosome 22q11.2 deletion. *American Journal of Medical Genetics, 85*, 127–133.

Green, P.M., Saad, S., Lewis, C.M., et al. (1999). Mutation rates in humans, I: Overall and sex-specific rates obtained from a population study of hemophilia B. *American Journal of Human Genetics, 65*, 1572–1579.

Guo, S.W., & Lange, K. (2000). Genetic mapping of complex traits: Promises, problems, and prospects. *Theoretical Population Biology, 57*, 1–11.

Haeusler, G. (1998). Growth hormone therapy in patients with Turner syndrome. *Hormone Research, 49*(Suppl. 2), 62–66.

Hall, J.C. (1992). Turner syndrome. In R.A. King, J.I. Rotter, & A.G. Motulsky (Eds.), *The genetic basis of common disease* (pp. 895–914). Oxford, England: Oxford University Press.

Jacobs, P.A., Browne, C., Gregson, N., et al. (1992). Estimates of the frequency of chromosome abnormalities detectable in unselected newborns using moderate levels of banding. *Journal of Medical Genetics, 29*, 103–108.

Jiang, Y., Lev-Lehman, E., Bressler, J., et al. (1999). Genetics of Angelman syndrome. *American Journal of Human Genetics, 65*, 1–6.

Johnson, A., & Wapner, R.J. (1997). Mosaicism: Implications for postnatal outcome. *Current Opinion in Obstetrics and Gynecology, 9*, 126–135.

Jones, K.L. (Ed.). (1997). *Smith's recognizable patterns of human malformation* (5th ed.). Philadelphia: W.B. Saunders.

Jorde, L.B., Carey, J.C., & Bamshad, M.J., et al. (2001). *Medical genetics* (Rev. 2nd ed.). St. Louis: Mosby.

Kaplan, F. (1998). Tay-Sachs disease carrier screening: A model for prevention of genetic disease. *Genetic Testing, 2*, 271–292.

Khan, N.L., & Wood, N.W. (1999). Prader-Willi and Angelman syndromes: Update on genetic mechanisms and diagnostic complexities. *Current Opinion in Neurology, 12*, 149–154.

Lalande, M., Minassian, B.A., DeLorey, T.M., et al. (1999). Parental imprinting and Angelman syndrome. *Advances in Neurology, 79*, 421–429.

Lashkari, A., Smith, A.K., & Graham, J.M., Jr. (1999). Williams-Beuren syndrome: An update and review for the primary physician. *Clinical Pediatrics, 38*, 189–208.

Leonard, J.V., & Schapira, A.H. (2000a). Mitochondrial respiratory chain disorders, I: Mitochondrial DNA defects. *Lancet, 355*, 299–304.

Leonard, J.V., & Schapira, A.H. (2000b). Mitochondrial respiratory chain disorders, II: Neurodegenerative disorders and nuclear gene defects. *Lancet, 355*, 389–394.

Linden, M.G., Bender, B.G., & Robinson, A. (1995). Sex chromosome tetrasomy and pentasomy. *Pediatrics, 96*, 672–682.

MacLean, J.E., Teshima, I.E., Szatmari, P., et al. (2000). Ring chromosome 22 and autism: Report and review. *American Journal of Medical Genetics, 90*, 382–385.

Mannens, M., & Alders, M. (1999). Genomic imprinting: Concept and clinical consequences. *Annals of Medicine. 31*, 4–11.

Margolis, R.L., McInnis, M.G., Rosenblatt, A., et al. (1999). Trinucleotide repeat expansion and neuropsychiatric disease. *Archives of General Psychiatry, 56*, 1019–1031.

McDonald-McGinn, D.M., LaRossa, D., Goldmuntz, E.,

et al. (1997). The 22q11.2 deletion: Screening, diagnostic workup, and outcome of results; report on 181 patients. *Genetic Testing, 1*, 99–108.

McFadden, D.E., & Friedman, J.M. (1997). Chromosome abnormalities in human beings. *Mutation Research, 396*, 129–140.

McInnis, M.G. (1996). Anticipation: An old idea in new genes. *American Journal of Human Genetics, 59*, 973–979.

McKusick, V.A. (1998). *Mendelian inheritance in man: A catalog of human genes and genetic disorders* (12th ed.). Baltimore: The Johns Hopkins University Press.

Meyer, L.M., Ramin, K.D., Ramsey, P.S., et al. (2000). Fluorescent in situ hybridization technique for the rapid detection of chromosomal abnormalities. *Obstetrics and Gynecology. 95*(4, Suppl. 1), S64.

Money, J. (1993). Specific neuro-cognitive impairments associated with Turner (45,X) and Klinefelter (47,XXY) syndromes: A review. *Social Biology, 40*, 147–151.

Neri, G., & Chiurazzi, P. (1999). X-linked mental retardation. *Advances in Genetics, 41*, 55–94.

Nicholls, R.D. (2000). The impact of genomic imprinting for neurobehavioral and developmental disorders. *Journal of Clinical Investigation, 105*, 413–418.

Nicolaidis, P., & Petersen, M.B. (1998). Origin and mechanisms of non-disjunction in human autosomal trisomies. *Human Reproduction, 13*, 313–319.

Nissenkorn, A., Zeharia, A., Lev, D., et al. (2000). Neurologic presentations of mitochondrial disorders. *Journal of Child Neurology, 15*, 44–48.

Peet, J., Weaver, D.D., & Vance, G.H. (1998). 49,XXXXY: A distinct phenotype. Three new cases and a review. *Journal of Medical Genetics, 35*, 420–424.

Pettenati, M.J., Rao, P.N., Phelan, M.D., et al. (1995). Paracentric inversions in humans: A review of 446 paracentric inversions with presentation of 120 new cases. *American Journal of Medical Genetics, 55*, 171–187.

Reddy, P.H., Williams, M., & Tagle, D.A. (1999). Recent advances in understanding the pathogenesis of Huntington's disease. *Trends in Neuroscience, 22*, 248–255.

Root, S., & Carey, J.C. (1994). Survival in trisomy 18. *American Journal of Medical Genetics, 49*, 170–174.

Ross, J.L., Stefanatos, G., Roeltgen, D., et al. (1995). Ullrich-Turner syndrome: Neurodevelopmental changes from childhood through adolescence. *American Journal of Medical Genetics, 58*, 74–82.

Saenger, P. (1999). Growth-promoting strategies in Turner's syndrome. *Journal of Clinical Endocrinology and Metabolism, 84*, 4345–4348.

Savage, A.R., Petersen, M.B., Pettay, D., et al. (1998). Elucidating the mechanisms of paternal non-disjunction of chromosome 21 in humans. *Human Molecular Genetics, 7*, 1221–1227.

Simon, D.K., & Johns, D.R. (1999). Mitochondrial disorders: Clinical and genetic features. *Annual Review of Medicine, 50*, 111–127.

Smyth, C.M., & Bremner, W.J. (1998). Klinefelter syndrome. *Archives of Internal Medicine, 158*, 1309–1314.

Tawil, R. (1999). Outlook for therapy in the muscular dystrophies. *Seminars in Neurology, 19*, 81–86.

Teague, J.W., Morton, N.E., Dennis, N.R., et al. (1998). FRAXA and FRAXE: Evidence against segregation distortion and for an effect of intermediate alleles on learning disability. *Proceedings of the National Academy of Sciences of the United States of America, 95*, 719–724.

Teyssier, M., Charrin, C., Corgiolu Theuil, G., et al. (1992). Ring chromosome 17: Case report and review of the literature. *Annales de Génétique, 35*, 75–78.

Tsao, C.Y., & Mendell, J.R. (1999). The childhood muscular dystrophies: Making order out of chaos. *Seminars in Neurology, 19,* 9–23.

Uusimaa, J., Remes, A.M., Rantala, H., et al. (2000). Childhood encephalopathies and myopathies: A prospective study in a defined population to assess the frequency of mitochondrial disorders. *Pediatrics, 105,* 598–603.

Venter, J.C., Adams, M.D., Meyers, E.W., et al. (2001). The sequence of the human genome. *Science, 291,* 1304–1351.

Vogel, F., & Rathenberg, R. (1975). Spontaneous mutation in man. *Advances in Human Genetics, 5,* 223–318.

Warren, S.T. (1997). Trinucleotide repetition and fragile X syndrome. *Hospital Practice (Office Edition), 32*(4), 73–76, 81–85, 90–92.

2

Birth Defects, Prenatal Diagnosis, and Fetal Therapy

Rhonda L. Schonberg and Cynthia J. Tifft

Upon completion of this chapter, the reader will:

- be knowledgeable about the indications, risks, and limitations of maternal serum screening for birth defects, ultrasonography, fetal magnetic resonance imaging, and echocardiography

- understand the techniques of amniocentesis and chorionic villus sampling and be able to determine when invasive diagnostic testing is indicated

- be familiar with alternative reproductive techniques and realize in what circumstances couples might benefit from such technologies

- become familiar with current approaches to fetal therapy

- be sensitive to the psychosocial needs of families who are at increased risk for bearing children with genetic disorders or birth defects

The birth of a child with disabilities can have a devastating impact on parents and extended family members. As couples grieve the loss of their expected "normal" child and work to accept the child they have, they look to the future to understand what happened to them and why. Although most infants are born without complications, 3%–5% of births result in a child who has a birth defect or a genetic disorder. These can affect any couple regardless of age or ethnicity. Although we know of circumstances that increase the risk, some of which are discussed in this chapter, most newborns with a birth defect/genetic disorder will be born to couples who are unaware they are at risk and have no family history of similarly affected children. When this occurs, genetic evaluation can help determine a diagnosis and/or mode of inheritance (discussed in Chapter 1). Advances in prenatal diagnosis have given couples the opportunity to gain information about their pregnancy, including birth defects or genetic disorders that may affect their child, and to examine a range of family planning alternatives.

This chapter discusses the genetic screening available prior to and during pregnancy, diagnostic testing available for pregnancies determined to be at an increased risk for specific genetic disorders, alternative reproductive choices, and recent advances in fetal therapy.

CHELSEA

Susan, a 31-year-old who had previously miscarried, was enjoying her second pregnancy. She started prenatal care early and was eating well and exercising regularly. Her fears were raised in the second trimester when a maternal serum screening test revealed an elevated **alpha-fetoprotein (AFP)** level. Her obstetrician recommended a detailed fetal ultrasound, which showed a fetal abdominal wall defect **(gastroschisis).** Susan and her husband Rick met with the genetics staff who explained that gastroschisis was usually an isolated malformation not associated with a chromosome abnormality, additional medical problems, or learning disabilities. After considering the information provided and weighing the risks, the couple decided not to undergo amniocentesis. They met with a pediatric surgeon to discuss the management of an infant with gastroschisis and visited the high-risk nursery where their baby would be treated after birth. On the basis of the information they received, Susan and Rick decided to continue the pregnancy and prepared for the birth of their child. Susan had ultrasounds every 3–4 weeks throughout the remainder of the pregnancy to monitor fetal growth and **amniotic fluid** volume. When delivery came, the family and the surgical team were prepared. Surgery was performed on baby Chelsea's first day of life with an uneventful recovery. At 1 year of age, Chelsea is a growing, thriving, healthy child.

GENETIC ASSESSMENT

Many individuals wonder what their risk of having a child with a birth defect or genetic disorder might be. A genetic counselor may assist families in obtaining this information. Genetic counselors are individuals specially trained to gather and interpret information provided by families in an effort to assess their "genetic risk." They can identify the need for specialized testing, discuss possible diagnostic alternatives, and educate families about their reproductive options. Throughout the United States, many centers offer the skills of a genetic counselor combined with the medical expertise of physicians trained in genetics. (A listing of these centers can be found at http://www.GeneClinics.org.) Assessing reproductive risk generally involves reviewing the individual's medical history and obtaining an extended family history, including birth defects, genetic disorders, unexplained infant deaths, and recurrent pregnancy loss. Information on medication use and occupational exposure can also provide clues to possible reproductive risks. In addition, many perinatologists and obstetricians have received specialized genetic training and can offer information about outcome and management of pregnancies known to be complicated by a fetal birth defect or a genetic disorder.

Knowing an individual's ethnic background is one of the steps in assessing the risk of having a child with a specific genetic disorder. Individuals from some defined ethnic backgrounds have a higher risk of being carriers for particular genetic disorders (Table 2.1). Molecular and/or biochemical analyses can identify carriers of these genetic variations before an affected

Table 2.1. Disorders with increased carrier frequencies in particular ethnic groups (carrier testing and prenatal diagnosis is available for each of these disorders)

Ethnic group	Disorder at risk	Estimated carrier frequency
African American or West African	Sickle cell anemia	1 in 12
Ashkenazi Jewish (Eastern European Jewish)	Tay-Sachs disease	1 in 27
	Canavan disease	1 in 40
	Cystic fibrosis	1 in 25
	Gaucher disease (type I)	1 in 15
	Bloom syndrome	1 in 100
	Niemann-Pick disease (type A)	1 in 90
	Fanconi anemia	1 in 90
Asian	Alpha thalassemia	1 in 8 to 1 in 20
European and North American (Caucasian)	Cystic fibrosis	1 in 25
French Canadian	Tay-Sachs disease	1 in 27
Mediterranean	Beta thalassemia	1 in 15 to 1 in 20

From Seashore, M.R. (1999). Clinical genetics. In B.N. Burrow & T.P. Duffy (Eds.), *Medical complications during pregnancy* (p. 216). Philadelphia: W.B. Saunders; adapted by permission.

child is conceived. Most of the disorders amenable to carrier screening are autosomal recessive (see Chapter 1) and have high morbidity and mortality. If both members of a couple are identified as carriers, there is a 1 in 4 chance with each pregnancy that the resulting child will be affected. Advanced knowledge of this risk provides couples the opportunity to consider alternative reproductive options or utilize prenatal diagnostic testing that is available for many of these disorders. Couples of mixed ethnicity may also want to meet with a genetic counselor to discuss their individual situation.

A couple may also be identified as being at risk for having a child with a specific genetic disorder through the prior birth of a child with the disorder or by the occurrence of the disorder in a member(s) of the extended family. A genetic counselor and/or clinical geneticist may meet with the couple to elicit a family history, to review medical records, or to examine the affected individual to verify the diagnosis and discuss reproductive risks and testing options.

As of 2002, genetic testing is available for almost 900 genetic disorders, and the number continues to grow. Medical centers providing genetic services have the most up-to-date information on the limitations and availability of genetic testing. Clinical genetic staff can also help locate appropriate resources and support groups for families. (One such resource is http://www.geneticalliance.org.)

SCREENING EVALUATIONS DURING PREGNANCY

It is now considered standard of care for prenatal service providers in developed countries to offer screening evaluations during pregnancy. These evaluations monitor the growth and development of the fetus and help identify pregnancies that are potentially at risk for birth defects/ genetic disorders. Two primary approaches, maternal serum screening and ultrasonography, are employed. Magnetic resonance imaging (MRI) and fetal echocardiography are also used sometimes.

Maternal Serum Screening

The levels of certain biochemical compounds in maternal serum can indicate an increased risk for specific disorders including neural tube defects (e.g., **spina bifida, anencephaly;** see Chapter 24) and some chromosome disorders (e.g., Down syndrome, see Chapter 16; trisomy 18 syndrome, see Appendix B). It is important to remember, however, that maternal serum screening is not diagnostic; if results are abnormal, additional studies are needed.

Maternal serum screening is offered to all pregnant women who will be younger than 35 at the expected delivery date. (Women older than 35 are offered diagnostic testing for chromosome disorders as described later.) A blood specimen is drawn at approximately 16 weeks of gestation and analyzed for alpha-fetoprotein (AFP), human chorionic gonadotropin (hCG) and unconjugated serum estriol (uE3). The level of these three analytes, in combination with maternal age, weight, race, diabetes status, and number of fetuses is entered into a complex formula to predict the likelihood that a fetus has one of the specific birth defects being screened (Haddow et al., 1992). Screening tests are designed to maximize the number of affected fetuses correctly identified while limiting the number of false positive results. A false positive rate of 5%, used by most screening programs, means that 5% of all women screened will have abnormal test results when there is an unaffected pregnancy. Further testing is *always* necessary to confirm a suspected diagnosis. For example, increased levels of AFP suggest a fetus with a neural tube defect, an abdominal wall defect (**omphalocele** or gastroschisis), or a rare kidney disorder. It can also be associated with a multiple gestation; gestational age greater than originally thought (Milunsky, 1998); or a pregnancy at a higher risk for preterm delivery, stillbirth, or intrauterine loss (Waller et al., 1991; Waller et al., 1996). A detailed ultrasound can resolve some of these concerns.

Low levels of AFP and uE3, when associated with an elevated hCG, are more frequently observed when a fetus has Down syndrome. If the maternal serum screen suggests an increased risk for Down syndrome or trisomy 18 (low levels of AFP, hCG, and estriol), diagnostic testing by amniocentesis and a detailed ultrasound evaluation are recommended. (Low levels of AFP can also occur if fetal gestation is less than expected.) Currently, second trimester maternal serum screening for Down syndrome in women younger than 35 detects approximately 60% of affected pregnancies (Haddow et al., 1992). Some physicians choose to offer maternal serum screening to women 35 and older to modify their age-related risks. Limitations of screening versus diagnostic testing must be carefully presented because these women may decline amniocentesis based on their serum screen result and pregnancies with Down syndrome or other chromosome anomalies may thus go undetected.

Second trimester screening, with appropriate follow-up, leads to a diagnosis at 18–20 weeks' gestation. First trimester screening accommodates earlier confirmatory testing and genetic counseling. A combination of ultrasound findings, maternal serum free beta-hCG, and pregnancy-associated plasma protein A (PAPP-A) can be evaluated at 10–14 weeks' gestation (Krantz et al., 1996). Elevations in PAPP-A and free beta-hCG combined with an ultrasound finding of increased nuchal translucency (increased thickness of the soft tissues of the neck) has been found to correctly identify 87% of fetuses with Down syndrome (Orlandi et al., 1997). Studies are in progress to identify additional biochemical markers that will improve the sensitivity and specificity of screening tests with a goal of reducing the number of invasive procedures.

Ultrasonography

Approximately two thirds of pregnant women undergo **real-time ultrasonography** during their pregnancy. Ultrasound can identify structures of varying density such as the heart, liver, bone, or fluid-filled spaces. This variation in reflected sound waves is collected and displayed on a monitor to create a real-time image of the fetus. In the first trimester, ultrasound can establish fetal viability, determine the number of fetuses (useful when a patient has had in vitro fertilization), locate placental position, and measure the nuchal translucency (transparency or cyst at the nape of the neck). An ultrasound finding of increased nuchal translucency in the first trimester has been strongly correlated with the presence of a chromosomal abnormality in the fetus (Taipale et al., 1997). In second trimester studies, advances in ultrasound technology and practitioners' clinical experience has improved, resulting in the ability to identify subtle findings that can be associated with chromosomal abnormalities or other genetic disorders (Benacerraf, Nadel, & Bromley, 1994; Smith-Bindman et al., 2001). In addition to neural tube defects and abdominal wall defects (omphalocele or gastroschisis), facial clefts, renal anomalies, skeletal anomalies, hydrocephalus, and certain brain malformations can be diagnosed.

Three-dimensional ultrasound, which is currently being piloted at specialized centers, may enhance the ability of physicians to detect variations such as facial clefts (Johnson et al., 2000). Although the identification of birth defects by ultrasound is improving, it cannot replace definitive diagnostic testing for chromosomal abnormalities, genetic mutations, and biochemical analyses that are possible using **amniocentesis** or **chorionic villus sampling (CVS).**

Magnetic Resonance Imaging

High-resolution ultrasound has revolutionized our ability to identify fetal anatomic abnormalities; however, the technology has some limitations. In selected circumstances, MRI can add to the clinical understanding of an ultrasound variation at 20 weeks' gestation or later (Levine et al., 1997). Because MRI uses ultra-fast imaging sequences, neither mother nor fetus requires sedation for a detailed study. Although there is no known risk associated with the use of MRI, as a new technology, the long-term effects are unknown (Quinn, Hubbard, & Adzick,

1998). MRI of the **central nervous system** can demonstrate the presence or absence of the corpus callosum (the band of tissue connecting the two cerebral hemispheres), Chiari malformations of the brain (seen in spina bifida), and the cause of enlarged ventricles (hydrocephalus; Levine et al., 1998). Another ultrasound finding that may be clarified by MRI is the amount of normal lung tissue present in a fetus with a diaphragmatic hernia (an incompletely formed diaphragm, which allows the stomach and intestines to herniate into the fetal chest, compromising lung development; Figure 2.1). The additional information gleaned from MRI can assist obstetricians, surgeons, and neonatologists in preparing for delivery of a baby in need of immediate assistance, such as a fetus with a large neck mass who may present with an occluded airway (Hubbard, Crombleholme, & Adzick, 1998; Kathary et al., 2001). MRI can also confirm normal anatomy when an abnormality has been suspected on ultrasound.

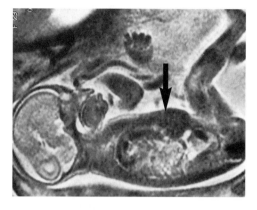

Figure 2.1.   MRI image of fetus with a diaphragmatic hernia demonstrating bowel loops (intestine) in the chest area. (Courtesy of Dorothy I. Bulas, M.D., Department of Diagnostic Imaging, Children's National Medical Center, Washington, D.C.)

Fetal Echocardiography

Echocardiography has become a valuable tool in the assessment of a fetus with congenital heart disease (CHD). This targeted ultrasound, performed at 18–20 weeks' gestation, when the fetal heart is approximately the size of an adult's thumbnail, monitors fetal blood flow and evaluates the structure and function of the fetal heart. A family history of CHD or maternal diabetes or a fetal diagnosis of Down syndrome, velocardiofacial syndrome (VCFS; see Appendix B), or another genetic disorder increases the likelihood that a congenital heart defect will be identified. Because fetal circulation differs from that of the newborn, coarctation (severe narrowing) of the aorta, interrupted aortic arch, and small atrial or ventricular septal defects (ASD or VSD) may not be accurately diagnosed using fetal echocardiography. A careful cardiac evaluation should be performed in infants known to be at increased risk for CHD.

Conversely, when a heart defect is identified **in utero,** a detailed ultrasound study is indicated to screen for other malformations. Approximately 10%–15% of infants with CHD have an underlying chromosome abnormality and will often have additional anomalies, developmental delay, or mental retardation (Table 2.2; Brown, 2000). When a fetus is identified with CHD, diagnostic testing via amniocentesis and genetic counseling are warranted because the long-term outcome for a child with an isolated CHD can be much different from the expected outcome for a child with a chromosome disorder. A multidisciplinary team including a geneticist, cardiologist, neonatologist, and surgeon gives parents the opportunity to discuss etiology, prognosis, testing, and treatment options.

Table 2.2.   Ultrasound findings in certain chromosomal abnormalities

Syndrome	Findings
Trisomy 13	Cleft lip and palate
	Congenital heart defect
	Cystic kidneys
	Extra finger or toe
	Midline facial defect
Trisomy 18	Clenched hands with overlapping fingers
	Congenital heart defect
	Excessive amniotic fluid
	Growth retardation
	Rocker-bottom feet
Trisomy 21	Abnormal gastrointestinal tract
	Congenital heart defect
	Excess neck skin

Source: D'Alton & DeCherney, 1993.

INVASIVE DIAGNOSTIC TESTING

Although the screening techniques just described can be diagnostic for a number of abnormalities, they are *not* diagnostic for chromosomal abnormalities. Maternal serum screening tests and ultrasound may strongly suggest the presence of a chromosomal abnormality, but diagnostic studies are needed to confirm the suspicion.

The leading indication for invasive diagnostic testing is advanced maternal age. When a woman is 35 years old, the chance of having a baby born with Down syndrome or another chromosomal abnormality is 1 in 230. By age 45, this risk increases to 1 in 20 live births (Figure 2.2; Hook, 1981). In the United States, the standard of care is to offer prenatal diagnosis by amniocentesis or CVS to any women who will be 35 years or older at the birth of her child. Additional indications for prenatal diagnosis are noted in Table 2.3. Not all individuals who are eligible will choose to undergo invasive testing, but the options should be presented. The fetal cells obtained by amniocentesis or CVS can also be used for molecular analysis of fetal DNA and biochemical analysis by enzyme determination (Thompson, McInnes, & Willard, 1991). Amniocentesis and CVS each have advantages and limitations.

Amniocentesis

Amniocentesis is traditionally performed between 15 and 18 weeks after the last menstrual period. Under ultrasound guidance in a sterile field, a needle is inserted just below the umbilicus through the abdominal and uterine wall. It enters the amniotic sac and 1–2 ounces of amniotic fluid are aspirated (Figure 2.3). Through natural processes (mostly fetal urination), the fluid is replaced within 24 hours. Often, the amniocentesis is performed at the time of a detailed ultrasound. The risk of pregnancy loss following a genetic amniocentesis at 15+ weeks ranges from 0.5% to 1.1% (Wilson, 2000). Early amniocentesis, performed before 14 weeks' gesta-

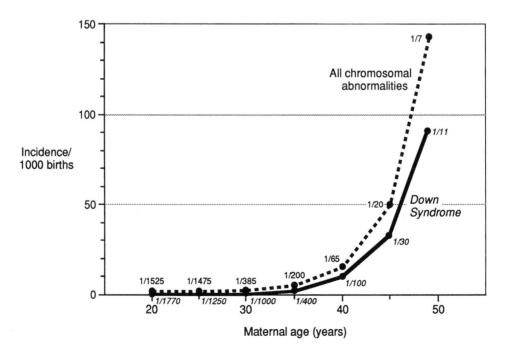

Figure 2.2. Risk of trisomy 21 and all chromosomal abnormalities in pregnant women of various ages. Risk increases markedly after 35 years of age. (*Source:* Hook, 1981.)

Table 2.3. Common indications for amniocentesis or chorionic villus sampling (CVS)

Indication	CVS	Amniocentesis
Maternal age 35 or older	X	X
Previous offspring with a chromosomal abnormality	X	X
Increased risk of having a child with a genetic disorder (e.g., previous affected child, positive carrier testing, carrier of X-linked disorder)	X	X
Previous offspring with a neural tube defect (e.g., spina bifida, anencephaly)		X
Increased risk of having a child with a chromosomal abnormality or neural tube defect based on a maternal serum screening test		X
Anatomic abnormality identified via ultrasound		X

tion, has been implemented in some centers as an alternative to CVS in the first trimester. A multi-center, randomized trial, however, found an increased risk of pregnancy loss, a higher incidence of musculoskeletal (most often clubfoot) deformities, and a greater chance of amniotic fluid leakage (Delisle & Wilson, 1999; Wilson et al., 1998). For this reason, CVS continues to be the preferred procedure for first trimester diagnosis (Jenkins & Wapner, 1999).

One advantage of amniocentesis is the ability to assay the amniotic fluid directly for abnormal levels of biochemical compounds such as AFP. Although ultrasound evaluations have improved in specificity and accuracy, an elevated amniotic fluid AFP of greater than 2.0 multiples of the median with a positive acetylcholinesterase test is diagnostic for a neural tube defect in greater than 98% of cases. Abdominal wall defects and some kidney disorders can also be diagnosed based on elevations in the amniotic fluid AFP (Milunsky, 1998; Nyberg, Mahoney, & Pretorius, 1990).

Chorionic Villus Sampling

CVS is a minute biopsy of the **chorion**, the outermost membrane surrounding the embryo. Chorionic **villi**, consisting of rapidly dividing cells of fetal origin, can be analyzed directly or after first being grown in culture (Blakemore, 1988). CVS is performed at 10–12 weeks' gestation, before a woman may appear pregnant and prior to "quickening" (the detection of fetal movement by the mother). Using ultrasound guidance, a chorionic villus biopsy is performed either by suction through a small catheter passed through the cervix or by aspiration via a needle inserted through the abdominal wall and uterus (Figure 2.4). The method used depends on the position of the **placenta** and the experience of the practitioner. CVS increases the risk of first trimester pregnancy loss by 1% (Goldberg, Porter, & Golbus, 1990). Limb reduction defects (foreshortened fingers, arms, or legs) have been reported in slightly fewer than 1 in 1,000 procedures. This may be the result of placental bleeding or hypoxia caused by the procedure. Limb reduction abnormalities have been reported more often when the CVS was performed prior to 10 weeks' gestation or by an operator not fully experienced with the technique (Burton, Schultz, & Burd, 1992). For that reason, CVS is now routinely offered after 10 weeks' gestation.

Diagnostic Testing of Fetal Cells

Both CVS and amniocentesis are well-established techniques for obtaining fetal cells. The most common test requested is chromosomal analysis; however, biochemical analysis for inborn errors of metabolism such as Tay-Sachs disease or DNA analysis for disorders such as fragile X syndrome can be performed on the cells. Indeed, any genetic disorder for which a fa-

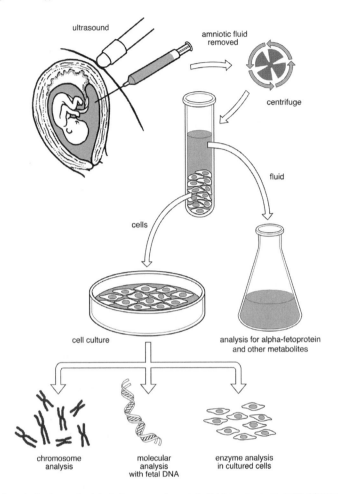

Figure 2.3.   Amniocentesis. Approximately 1–2 ounces of amniotic fluid are removed at 16–18 weeks' gestation. The fluid is spun in a centrifuge to separate the fluid from the fetal cells. The alpha-fetoprotein (AFP) in the fluid is used to test for a neural tube defect. The fluid can also be used to check for metabolites associated with inborn errors of metabolism when indicated. The cells are grown for a week, and then karyotype, enzyme, or DNA analyses can be performed. Most results are available in 10–14 days. (*Source:* Rose & Mennuti, 1993.)

milial DNA mutation has been identified can be analyzed using DNA isolated from the fetal cells (Figure 2.5).

Fluorescent *in situ* hybridization (FISH) is a technique that utilizes short pieces of DNA of known sequence (called a *DNA probe*) that can hybridize, or attach, to a unique region on a chromosome. The probe contains a fluorescent tag, making it visible under a fluorescent microscope. FISH is used to identify chromosomes or to indicate small deletions of a defined region of a specific chromosome. When a rapid result is required for prenatal diagnosis, this technique can be used to test for trisomies 13, 18, and 21 and variations in the number of X or Y chromosomes (Ward et al., 1993). In addition, FISH can be used to diagnose some genetic syndromes caused by chromosome deletions too small to be detected by conventional analysis. For example, the discovery of certain CHDs by fetal ultrasound or echocardiography should prompt consideration of using FISH analysis to detect the 22q11.2 deletion that occurs in 1 in 4,000 live births and is associated with VCFS (see Appendix B). Additional disorders that can be diagnosed by FISH analysis when clinically indicated include Angelman, Prader-Willi, and Williams syndromes (see Appendix B).

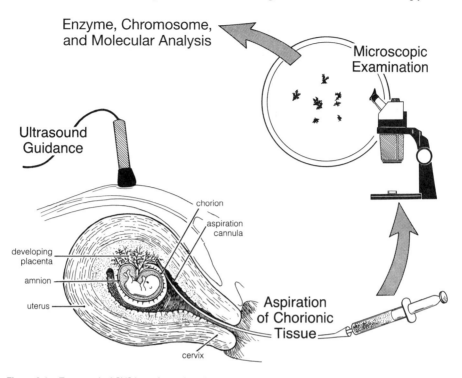

Enzyme, Chromosome, and Molecular Analysis

Microscopic Examination

Ultrasound Guidance

chorion

aspiration cannula

developing placenta

amnion

uterus

Aspiration of Chorionic Tissue

cervix

Figure 2.4. Transcervical CVS is performed at 10–12 weeks' gestation. A hollow instrument is inserted through the vagina and passed into the uterus, guided by ultrasound. A small amount of chorionic tissue is removed by suction. The tissue is then examined under a microscope to make sure it is sufficient. Karyotype, enzyme, and/or DNA analyses can be performed without first growing the cells, although cell culture is needed for most analyses. Results are available in a few days in select situations; more often they are ready in 10–14 days.

Emerging technologies, such as spectral **karyotyping** (the labeling of each chromosome in the cell in which each projects a unique color) offer additional cytogenetic information in select cases (Schrock et al., 1997). As of 2002, however, this technology is not widely available.

Percutaneous Umbilical Blood Sampling

Percutaneous umbilical blood sampling (PUBS), also referred to as cordocentesis, is performed after 20 weeks' gestation. Under ultrasound guidance, a needle is inserted through the abdominal and uterine walls and directed to the umbilical vein to obtain a small sample of fetal blood. PUBS has been used to detect intrauterine infection, fetal **anemia**, blood type in Rh-sensitized women, and clotting factors for fetuses at risk for bleeding disorders such as hemophilia A (Hickock & Mills, 1992). It can provide additional information when amniocentesis is uninformative or access to fetal blood is critical for clinical diagnostic studies, such as for certain inborn errors of metabolism (Seashore, 1999). With a risk of pregnancy loss approaching 2%, and the increase in availability of molecular diagnosis by amniocentesis or CVS, the use of PUBS has diminished.

As technology improves and laboratory tests using molecular and biochemical techniques become more precise, the indications for prenatal diagnosis will increase. Unfortunately, even the most sophisticated technology cannot guarantee the birth of a typical child. Most of the disorders that cause developmental disabilities in the absence of structural malformations are not amenable to prenatal diagnosis at this time. Prenatal testing, however, has offered some parents at high risk for having a child with a severe genetic disorder the opportunity of having healthy children who otherwise would not have been conceived.

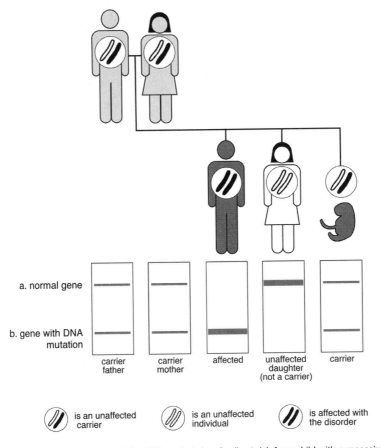

Figure 2.5. Prenatal diagnosis by DNA analysis in a family at risk for a child with a recessive disorder. The top of the figure illustrates the members of the family. This couple's first son was diagnosed with an autosomal recessive disorder. Blood samples from the child and his parents were obtained, and DNA was extracted. The DNA was digested with enzymes that broke it into different lengths depending on whether a genetic change (mutation) was present or not. The samples were then applied to a special gel and separated by size using an electric current. The upper band (a) is associated with the functional (normal) gene, whereas the lower band (b) is associated with the gene that contains a mutation that renders it nonfunctional. Genes are present in pairs, and as expected, each carrier parent was found to carry one gene containing the DNA mutation associated with this disease and one functional gene (represented by two bands on the gel). Their son with the autosomal recessive disorder had a single (b) band of greater intensity, which represents two copies of the nonfunctional gene. On the basis of this information, the next pregnancy was monitored with prenatal diagnosis, and the couple learned that their daughter would not be affected—after DNA analysis on amniotic fluid cells, only an (a) band was found. The couple are again pregnant and have decided to have prenatal testing. This time the fetus was found to be a carrier with two bands identified (a and b). The family can feel reassured that the new baby will not have the disorder.

PREVENTION, FETAL THERAPY, AND ALTERNATIVE REPRODUCTIVE CHOICES

Prevention

Although birth defects cannot be prevented, attention to a number of factors can contribute to a favorable outcome. Recommendations such as receiving early prenatal care, avoiding alcoholic beverages and smoking, and minimizing unnecessary medication are familiar to most women. In addition, ingestion of 0.4 mg of folic acid (found in most multivitamins) by all women of childbearing age starting 3 months before attempted conception is now recommended to reduce the risk of neural tube defects. Recent evidence indicates that folic acid may also reduce the incidence of other birth defects, including cardiac malformations and facial clefts (Desposito et al., 1999).

A number of maternal conditions can predispose an infant to birth defects or developmental delay. For example, a woman with phenylketonuria (PKU) is at risk of having a child with microcephaly and mental retardation if she does not maintain a phenylalanine-restricted diet during pregnancy (see Chapter 18). Other maternal disorders such as diabetes or certain medications taken to control illness such as anticonvulsants for a seizure disorder also increase the risk of birth defects (see Chapter 3).

Fetal Therapy

When a fetal abnormality is identified, questions about prognosis and treatment immediately arise. Some birth defects can be repaired soon after birth and have a very good outcome: isolated cleft lip/palate, gastroschisis, and some forms of CHD, for example. With other birth defects, fetal condition can worsen as the pregnancy continues, compromising the ability of the child to survive after birth. In these extreme circumstances, fetal surgery has been explored. Surgeries have been performed for obstructive uropathy (Crombleholme, 1994); diaphragmatic hernia (Kitano et al., 1999); and, most recently, spina bifida (Olutoye & Adzick, 1999; Tulipan et al., 1999). Families considering this option should be provided accurate information about the procedures, limitations, risks, and prognosis following birth. Multidisciplinary teams composed of surgeons, obstetricians, and neonatologists are available at some major medical centers to address these concerns and advise couples regarding their particular situation. Fetal surgery remains controversial due to maternal and fetal complications.

In utero transplantation of human stem cells also shows promise for disorders such as severe combined immune deficiency and beta thalassemia major (a blood disorder causing life-threatening anemia; Raudrant, Touraine, & Rebaud, 1992; Touraine et al., 1992). Eligibility criteria for fetal surgery and in utero stem cell transplantation need further study to assess the risk and outcome for both mother and child.

Alternative Reproductive Choices

In Vitro Fertilization

Some families known to be at increased risk of having a child with a serious genetic disorder and who prefer not to face the decision of interrupting an affected pregnancy may seek other reproductive options. Mendelian genetic disorders may be inherited as autosomal recessive (with two carrier parents), X-linked recessive (with a carrier mother), or autosomal dominant (with one parent being affected) as described in Chapter 1. Techniques such as artificial insemination using donor sperm or in vitro fertilization (IVF) with a donor egg may be appropriate considerations under these circumstances. Couples considering these options should assess how donors are chosen: what carrier testing is done to make sure the donor is not a carrier for an identifiable genetic disease, the ethnic/racial background of the donor, and the donor's family history. Families should also inquire about the rate of successful pregnancies resulting from IVF in the center they are considering and the risk for multiple gestation (e.g., twins, triplets).

Intracytoplasmic sperm injection (ICSI) is a technology available to some infertile males, including those with low sperm counts or poor sperm motility (Palermo et al., 1998). Sperm from the prospective father are harvested, and the cytoplasmic portions of the sperm are removed. A sperm nucleus is then introduced into a harvested egg by microinjection, and the developing blastocyst is subsequently transferred into the uterus. Genetic causes of male infertility, including microdeletion within fertility-associated regions of the Y chromosome, carriers for certain **cystic fibrosis** mutations, and Klinefelter syndrome, may be indications for ICSI.

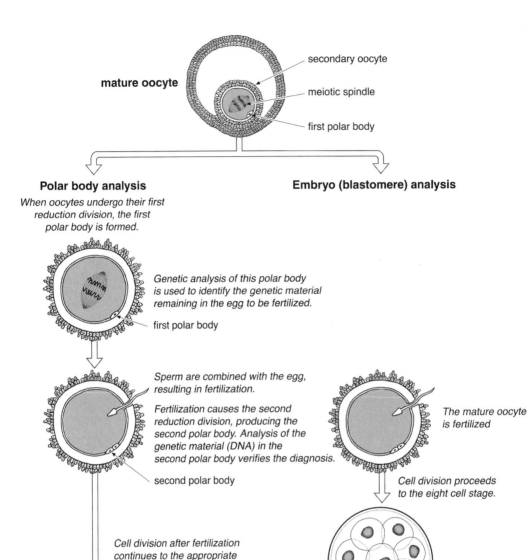

mature oocyte

secondary oocyte

meiotic spindle

first polar body

Polar body analysis

When oocytes undergo their first reduction division, the first polar body is formed.

Genetic analysis of this polar body is used to identify the genetic material remaining in the egg to be fertilized.

first polar body

Sperm are combined with the egg, resulting in fertilization.

Fertilization causes the second reduction division, producing the second polar body. Analysis of the genetic material (DNA) in the second polar body verifies the diagnosis.

second polar body

Cell division after fertilization continues to the appropriate stage of development.

Embryo (blastomere) analysis

The mature oocyte is fertilized

Cell division proceeds to the eight cell stage.

At this stage, one cell is removed for genetic testing.

Unaffected embryos are implanted in the uterus.

Figure 2.6. Preimplantation genetic diagnosis (PGD). Individuals who undergo PGD begin the process as they would for in vitro fertilization. The ovary is stimulated to produce mature oocytes, which are then harvested for fertilization outside of the woman's body. These mature oocytes can be used for polar body analysis, or they can be fertilized and processed for embryo (blastomere) analysis. This figure describes the path toward the preimplantation diagnosis using both methods. Polar body analysis is limited to detecting disorders or variations that would be present in the maternal genetic material, whereas an embryo biopsy can analyze both maternal and paternal genetic contributions. As with in vitro fertilization, not all pregnancies will progress to term. Prenatal diagnosis at a later stage of gestation by chorionic villus sampling (CVS) or by amniocentesis is recommended to confirm the preimplantation diagnosis.

It should be noted that there are reports of sex chromosome aneuploidy (e.g., an extra X or Y chromosome) in approximately 1% of conceptions accomplished through ICSI. Therefore, genetic counseling is suggested prior to initiating ICSI (Pauer et al., 1997).

Preimplantation Genetic Diagnosis

A few centers offer preimplantation genetic diagnosis (PGD) for couples who are at high risk to have a child with a defined genetic disorder and who wish to conceive an unaffected child that is biologically their own. PGD requires that the specific genetic mutations the couple is carrying be known and amenable to molecular analysis. There are two approaches to PGD as described in Figure 2.6. The first involves polar body testing of the woman's eggs to establish the presence or absence of the mutation in question. Only embryos from fertilized eggs determined to contain the normal gene are transferred to the mother's uterus to establish a pregnancy.

The second approach is to perform in vitro fertilization on harvested eggs and allow them to develop in culture to the eight-cell, or blastomere, stage. A single cell is then microdissected from each blastomere and analyzed for the presence of the mutation. Only unaffected embryos are subsequently transferred to the uterus. Pregnancies utilizing these methods have been successful for couples at high risk for bearing a child with cystic fibrosis, sickle cell disease, long-chain acyl-CoA dehydrogenase deficiency (an inborn error of metabolism), or thalassemia (Munne et al., 2000; Strom et al., 2000).

Assisted reproductive technologies are costly in terms of physical, emotional, and financial resources, and these services are rarely covered by health insurance plans. An individual is charged for each attempt, whether or not a successful pregnancy is achieved. The risk of multiple gestations is also a consideration, particularly if fetal reduction (i.e., abortion of one or more fetuses) is not a consideration. Couples should request from the center they are considering detailed information regarding the techniques that are used, the cost per attempt, the rate of successful pregnancies, and the risk of multiple gestation.

PSYCHOSOCIAL IMPLICATIONS

When a woman gives birth to a child with special needs or a child who does not survive, the experience can be devastating for the family. The woman may feel very vulnerable and fearful of attempting another pregnancy. It is imperative that health care professionals focus on the family's psychosocial needs as well as the clinical information the couple is requesting. Often, support groups or individual counseling can be beneficial.

A preliminary discussion that is difficult and often avoided is an exploration of how the couple would respond to a recurrence of the same problem in their next child (e.g., would they consider pregnancy interruption or are they primarily interested in obtaining diagnostic information to maximize the outcome of the next pregnancy). Many of these issues are best addressed prior to attempting another pregnancy so that prenatal diagnostic techniques, genetic screening, and other specialized tests can be investigated. Each family is unique, and assumptions by health care providers as to what a family should or should not do in a given situation must be avoided. Genetic counselors and medical geneticists who are trained in nondirective counseling can often help families understand their options and choose a course of action that is consistent with their own values and resources.

SUMMARY

A wealth of information exists for couples considering a pregnancy. This is particularly true for couples who have an increased risk for conceiving a child with a specific genetic disorder or who have previously conceived a child with a birth defect or genetic disorder. The vast array of screening and diagnostic tests can be both overwhelming and reassuring. Health care providers working together with genetics professionals are in a unique position to help families carefully consider and understand their reproductive options and the effects that prenatal diagnosis or genetic screening will have on them physically, emotionally, and financially.

REFERENCES

Benacerraf, B.R., Nadel, A., & Bromley, B. (1994). Identification of second-trimester fetuses with autosomal trisomy by use of a sonographic scoring index. *Radiology, 193,* 135–140.

Blakemore, K.J. (1988). Prenatal diagnosis by chorionic villus sampling. *Obstetrics and Gynecology Clinics of North America, 15,* 179–213.

Brown, D.L. (2000). Family history of congenital heart disease. In C.B. Benson, P.H. Arger, & E.I. Bluth (Eds.), *Ultrasonography in obstetrics and gynecology: A practical approach* (pp. 155–166). New York: Thieme Medical Publishers.

Burton, B.K., Schultz, C.J., & Burd, L.I. (1992). Limb abnormalities associated with chorionic villus sampling. *Obstetrics and Gynecology, 79,* 726–730.

Crombleholme, T.M. (1994). Invasive fetal therapy: Current status and future directions. *Seminars in Perinatology, 18,* 385–397.

D'Alton, M.E., & DeCherney, A.H. (1993). Prenatal diagnosis. *New England Journal of Medicine, 328,* 114–119.

Delisle, M., & Wilson, R.D. (1999). First trimester prenatal diagnosis. *Seminars in Perinatology, 23,* 414–423.

Desposito, F., Cuniff, C., Frias, J.L., et al. (1999). Folic acid for the prevention of neural tube defects. *Pediatrics, 104,* 325–327.

Goldberg, J.D., Porter, A.E., & Golbus, M.S. (1990). Current assessment of fetal losses as a direct consequence of chorionic villus sampling. *American Journal of Medical Genetics, 35,* 174–177.

Haddow, J.E., Palomaki, G.E., Knight, G.J., et al. (1992). Prenatal screening for Down's syndrome with use of maternal serum markers. *New England Journal of Medicine, 327,* 588–593.

Hickock, D.E., & Mills, M. (1992). Percutaneous umbilical blood sampling: Results from a multicenter collaborative registry. *American Journal of Obstetrics and Gynecology, 166,* 1614–1617.

Hook, E.B. (1981). Rates of chromosomal abnormalities at different maternal ages. *Obstetrics and Gynecology, 58,* 282–285.

Hubbard, A.M., Crombleholme, T.M., & Adzick, N.S. (1998). Prenatal evaluation of giant neck masses in preparation for the fetal EXIT procedure. *American Journal of Perinatology, 15,* 253–257.

Jenkins, T.J., & Wapner, R.J. (1999). First trimester prenatal diagnosis: Chorionic villus sampling. *Seminars in Perinatology, 223,* 403–413.

Johnson, D.D., Pretorius, D.H., Budorick, N.E., et al. (2000). Fetal lip and primary palate: Three-dimensional versus two-dimensional US. *Radiology, 217,* 236–239.

Kathary, N., Bulas, D.I., Newman, K.D., et al. (2001). MRI imaging and fetal neck masses with airway compromise: Utility in delivery planning. *Pediatric Radiology, 31,* 727–731.

Kitano, Y., Flake, A.W., Crombleholme, T.M., et al. (1999). Open fetal surgery for life threatening fetal malformations. *Seminars in Perinatology, 223,* 448–461.

Krantz, D.A., Larsen, J.W., Buchanan, P.D., et al. (1996).

First-trimester Down syndrome screening: Free-human chorionic gonadotropin and pregnancy-associated plasma protein A. *American Journal of Obstetrics and Gynecology, 174,* 612–616.

Levine, D., Barnes, P.D., Madsen, J.R., et al. (1997). Fetal central nervous system anomalies: MR imaging augments sonographic diagnosis. *Radiology, 204,* 635–642.

Levine, D., Barnes, P.D., Sher, S., et al. (1998). Fetal fast MR imaging: Reproducibility, technical quality, and conspicuity of anatomy. *Radiology, 206,* 549–554.

Milunsky, A. (1998). Maternal serum screening for neural tube defects. In A. Milunsky (Ed.), *Genetic disorders and the fetus: Diagnosis, prevention, and treatment* (4th ed., pp. 507–511). Baltimore: The Johns Hopkins University Press.

Munne, S., Sepulveda, S., Balmaceda, J., et al. (2000). Selection of the most common chromosomal abnormalities in oocytes prior to ICSI. *Prenatal Diagnosis, 20,* 582–586.

Nyberg, D.A., Mahoney, B.S., & Pretorius, D.H. (Eds.). (1990). *Diagnostic ultrasound of fetal anomalies: Text and atlas.* St. Louis: Mosby.

Olutoye, O.O., & Adzick, N.S. (1999). Fetal surgery for myelomeningocele. *Seminars in Perinatology, 23,* 462–473.

Orlandi, F., Damaini, G., Hallahan, T.W., et al. (1997). First-trimester screening for fetal aneuploidy: Biochemistry and nuchal translucency. *Ultrasound in Obstetrics and Gynecology, 10,* 381–386.

Palermo, G.D., Schlegel, P.N., Sills, E.S., et al. (1998). Births after intracytoplasmic injection of sperm obtained by testicular extraction from men with nonmosaic Klinefelter's syndrome. *New England Journal of Medicine, 338,* 588–590.

Pauer, H.U., Hinney, B., Michelmann, H.W., et al. (1997). Relevance of genetic counseling in couples prior to intracytoplasmic sperm injection. *Human Reproduction, 12,* 1909–1912.

Quinn, T.M., Hubbard, A.M., & Adzick, N.S. (1998). Prenatal magnetic resonance imaging enhances fetal diagnosis. *Journal of Pediatric Surgery, 33,* 553–558.

Raudrant, D., Touraine, J.L., & Rebaud, A. (1992). In utero transplantation of stem cells in humans: Technical aspects and clinical experience during pregnancy. *Bone Marrow Transplantation, 9*(Suppl. 1), 98–100.

Rose, N.C., & Mennuti, M.T. (1993). Alpha-fetoprotein and neural tube defects. In J.J. Sciarra & P.V. Dilts, Jr. (Eds.), *Gynecology and obstetrics* (Rev. ed., pp. 1–14). New York: HarperCollins.

Schrock, E., Veldman, T., Padilla-Nash, H., et al. (1997). Spectral karyotyping refines cytogenetic diagnostics of constitutional chromosomal abnormalities. *Human Genetics, 101,* 255–262.

Seashore, M.R. (1999). Clinical genetics. In B.N. Burrow & T.P. Duffy (Eds.), *Medical complications during pregnancy* (5th ed., pp. 197–223). Philadelphia: W.B. Saunders.

Smith-Bindman, R., Hosmer, W., Feldstein, V.A., et al. (2001). Second-trimester ultrasound to detect fetuses with Down syndrome. *Journal of the American Medical Association, 285,* 1044–1055.

Strom, C.M., Levin, R., Strom, S., et al. (2000). Neonatal outcome of preimplantation genetic diagnosis by polar body removal: The first 109 infants. *Pediatrics, 106,* 650–653.

Taipale, P., Hiilesmaa, V., Salonen, R., et al. (1997). Increased nuchal translucency as a marker for fetal chromosome defects. *New England Journal of Medicine, 337,* 1654–1658.

Thompson, M.W., McInnes, R.R., & Willard, H.F. (Eds.). (1991). *Thompson & Thompson genetics in medicine* (5th ed.). Philadelphia: W.B. Saunders.

Touraine, J.L., Raudrant, D., Rebaud, A., et al. (1992). In utero transplantation of stem cells in humans: Immunological aspects and clinical follow-up of patients. *Bone Marrow Transplantation, 9*(Suppl. 1), 121–126.

Tulipan, N., Bruner, J.P., Hernanz-Schulman, M., et al. (1999). Effect of intrauterine myelomeningocele repair on central nervous system structure and function. *Pediatric Neurosurgery, 31,* 183–188.

Waller, D.K., Lustig, L.S., Cunningham, G.C., et al. (1991). Second-trimester maternal serum alpha-fetoprotein levels and the risk of subsequent fetal death. *New England Journal of Medicine, 325,* 6–10.

Waller, D.K., Lustig, L.S., Cunningham, G.C., et al. (1996). The association between maternal serum alpha-fetoprotein and preterm birth, small for gestational age infants, preeclampsia and placental complications. *Obstetrics and Gynecology, 88,* 816–822.

Ward, B.E., Gersen, S.L., Carelli, M.P., et al. (1993). Rapid prenatal diagnosis of chromosomal aneuploidies by fluorescence in situ hybridization: Clinical experience with 4,500 specimens. *American Journal of Medical Genetics, 52,* 854–865.

Wilson, R.D. (2000). Amniocentesis and chorionic villus sampling. *Current Opinion in Obstetrics and Gynecology, 12,* 81–86.

Wilson, R.D., Johnson, J.M., Dansereau, J., et al. (1998). Randomized trial to assess safety and fetal outcome of early and midtrimester amniocentesis. *Lancet, 351,* 242–247.

3 Growth Before Birth

James B. Hill and William H.J. Haffner

Upon completion of this chapter, the reader will:

- understand the fertilization and implantation process
- be aware of the various stages of prenatal development
- be able to discuss the effects of maternal nutrition on fetal development
- know the various causes of malformations, including the major teratogens
- be able to identify some of the causes of deformities

The greatest risk for severe developmental disabilities occurs in the period between conception/ **implantation** and birth (Decoufle et al., 2001). Both genetic and environmental influences can adversely affect the developing organism, and there can be interactions between the two. Environmental agents that can affect fetal development are called **teratogens.** These range from heavy metals and radiation to medications and drugs of abuse, from infectious agents to chronic maternal illnesses. The susceptibility of the fetus depends on his or her genetic sensitivity in combination with the timing, magnitude, and duration of exposure to the teratogen and its ability to cross the placenta. This chapter discusses some of the factors that can lead to abnormalities in fetal growth and development.

FERTILIZATION

If sexual intercourse occurs near the time of ovulation, when the mature ovum (egg) is released, conception can occur. During ejaculation, 300 million sperm or more are released and deposited in the vagina; however, only about 200 reach the fallopian tubes. The sperm travel through the cervix and uterus into the fallopian tubes and can remain viable in the tubes for 2–3 days (Figure 3.1). In contrast, the egg can be fertilized only for 12–24 hours after ovulation. Once it is released from the ovary, the egg is actively moved by the finger-like fimbria from the opening of the fallopian tube inward to the junction of the outer two thirds of the tube. There, if a sperm successfully penetrates the ovum, fertilization occurs. The fertilized egg becomes a zygote, a diploid cell containing 46 chromosomes, 23 each contributed by the egg and sperm. While still in the fallopian tube, the zygote undergoes a series of divisions resulting in the formation of a blastomere (an eight-cell stage of division). Cleavage continues for 4 days after fertilization until a solid mulberry-like ball of compacted blastomeres is formed, called a **morula,** which then arrives in the uterine cavity (Figure 3.1). Fluid accumulates within the morula over the next few days, forming the **blastocyst.** The blastocyst lies free in the uterine cavity for about 2 days before attaching, or implanting, to an inside wall of the uterus (endometrium). This marks the formal beginning of pregnancy, nearly 5–7 days after ovulation and fertilization.

On one end of the blastocyst are cells comprising the inner cell mass, which is destined to produce the embryo. At the other end is a mass of cells that becomes the trophoblasts (Figure 3.1), forming part of the placenta. The trophoblasts invade the endometrium so that the blastocyst soon becomes covered. The endometrium becomes the site for subsequent development of the

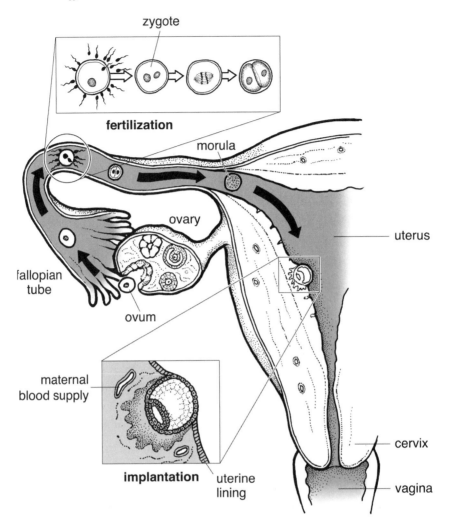

Figure 3.1. Fertilization and implantation. The ovum, or egg, is dropped from the ovary into the fallopian tube, where it is fertilized by a sperm. The fertilized egg thus gains its diploid number of chromosomes and starts dividing as it travels toward the uterus. It reaches the uterus after 5–7 days, and implantation of the embryo (trophoblast) then takes place.

embryo/fetus and placenta. The embryonic stem cells differentiate into three types of cells that ultimately form the various body organs: the ectoderm (skin, spinal cord, teeth), mesoderm (blood vessels, muscle, bone), and endoderm (lungs and digestive and urinary systems). By week 3 after ovulation and fertilization, the placenta has formed and is becoming the principal site of nutrient transfer between the embryo and the mother.

The blastocyst sometimes can become implanted in an abnormal location such as a fallopian tube, an ovary, the cervix, or even in the abdominal cavity. This is referred to as an ectopic pregnancy. Such a condition is very important to recognize because it can be associated with significant bleeding and possibly maternal mortality.

EMBRYONIC AND FETAL DEVELOPMENT

In utero development can be divided into two periods: embryonic and fetal. The embryonic period lasts from week 3 to week 8 after ovulation and fertilization, or week 5 to week 10 after

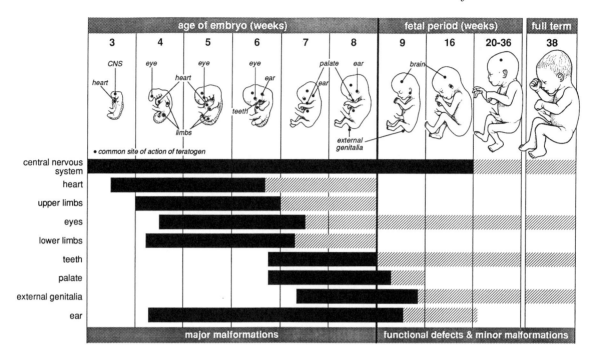

Figure 3.2. Embryogenesis and fetal development. The changes that take place during embryogenesis, between 3 and 8 weeks after fertilization, are enormous. All body systems are formed, and the embryo takes on a human form. Length increases 20-fold during this time. The fetal period lasts from 9 weeks to birth. Teratogens cause malformations if acting during the time a specific organ or group of organs are being formed. Damage to an organ during the time represented by a solid bar will lead to a major malformation, and damage during the time represented by the hatched bar will lead to functional defects or minor morphological abnormalities. (From Moore, K.L., & Persaud, T.V.N. [1993]. *Before we are born: Essentials of embryology and birth defects* [4th ed., inside back cover]. Philadelphia: W.B. Saunders; adapted by permission.)

the first day of the last menstrual period (Figure 3.2). During this time, organs form. Exposure to teratogens during this period may lead to structural abnormalities or fetal death. In contrast, exposure to a teratogen prior to this time will usually lead to either a spontaneous abortion (miscarriage) or to an unaffected fetus. This is true because so few cells exist at this stage of development that irreparable damage to some cells tends to be lethal to all. If the embryo survives, however, there is generally no organ damage because repair or replacement occurs.

As the embryo grows, it becomes surrounded by a cavity of amniotic fluid, a majority of which is thought to be formed in the fetal compartment. Later in pregnancy, much of the fluid is derived from fetal urine. Obstruction of the fetal urinary tract can lead to a diminished amount of amniotic fluid, a condition called **oligohydramnios.** Conversely, an inability of the fetus to swallow or absorb the amniotic fluid will result in excessive amniotic fluid in the uterine cavity, a condition called **polyhydramnios.** Thus, too little or too much amniotic fluid can serve as a marker for certain congenital malformations.

The head and tail folds of the embryo are distinctly developed by days 24–27 after ovulation and fertilization. At this time, the optic vesicles and lens form the embryonic eye; the limb buds are present; and the heart, liver, lungs, and thyroid gland appear. The cardiovascular system is the first fetal system to reach a functional state, beginning to contract by day 22 (Figure 3.2). An ebb and flow circulation occurs. Placental transfer of substances is usually established by the fifth week after ovulation and fertilization. Blood from the placenta carries oxygen and other nutrients from the mother, traveling to the fetus through the umbilical vein.

The central nervous system (CNS) starts to form by the third week after ovulation and fertilization. It begins as the neural folds form, rise, and fuse to form a neural tube starting in the midbrain region. Fusion proceeds both above and below, leaving both ends open. Exposure to a drug or teratogen when the heart or CNS is forming can result in congenital heart disease or a neural tube defect (NTD; see Chapter 24), respectively. Once the neural tube closes, it continues to develop and ultimately produces the distinct regions of the brain and spinal cord. As a result, the CNS is sensitive to teratogens throughout the embryonic and fetal development periods.

In terms of palate formation, two processes begin projecting vertically downward on either side of the tongue, subsequently meeting in the midline and fusing. If midline fusion fails, the nasal cavity and mouth are not separated normally and a cleft lip or palate results. The timing of this event is precise; cleft lip and cleft palate are known to occur between 7 and 8 weeks after ovulation and fertilization.

The four **branchial arches** (destined to form structures of the **pharynx** and throat) are present by day 27–29. The first branchial arch is known as the mandibular arch and is divided into two processes. The first forms the mandible and the second forms the maxilla, the lower and upper jawbones, respectively. Problems at this stage lead to abnormal development of the jaw.

The fetal development period begins 8 weeks after ovulation and fertilization. Most pregnancy tests are positive by this time. Development during this period consists of growth and maturation of structures that were formed during the embryonic period. Teratogen exposure at this time is more likely to lead to placental functional deficits or fetal growth restriction rather than to the types of birth defects that occur during the embryonic period.

The placenta continues to grow and supply nutrients to the fetus. By the end of the 12th week after ovulation and fertilization the fetus is 6–7 centimeters (2½ inches) in length and weighs approximately 100 grams (3 ounces). Individual fingers and toes become evident, and the external genitalia show signs of male or female differentiation. In the absence of TDF (testis-determining factor), which is coded on the short arm of the Y chromosome, ovaries develop during weeks 11–12.

MATERNAL NUTRITION

The growth and development of the fetus requires a continuous supply of nutrients, which are transported across the placental membrane and absorbed by the fetus. A typical pregnancy requires a woman to consume approximately 300 additional calories per day. Most healthy women who eat a well-balanced diet with a caloric balance of approximately 50%–60% from complex carbohydrates, 10%–20% from proteins, and 20%–30% from fats satisfactorily meet the daily nutritional requirements during pregnancy. There is no evidence that a high-protein diet is beneficial (Hay et al., 1997).

Women with poor weight gain during pregnancy, however, are at increased risk for having newborns with low birth weight (Abrams & Selvin, 1995; Smith et al., 1998). To prevent this and other fetal complications, it is recommended that most women gain at least 15 pounds during pregnancy. If the mother is below ideal body weight prior to pregnancy, she should gain even more weight. Women who are classified as obese are encouraged to gain no more than 15 pounds. Greater weight gain in obese women is associated with an increased risk for stillbirth, among other problems in pregnancy (Institute of Medicine, 1990).

There has been considerable interest about the potential impact of vitamin supplementation during pregnancy on the health of the newborn. Most healthy women who consume a well-balanced diet and gain an appropriate amount of weight during pregnancy will only need to take typical prenatal vitamins. In order to prevent NTDs, however, the American College of Obstetricians and Gynecologists (ACOG; 1995a) recommends that all women take 0.4 mg of folic acid daily prior to conception and that this supplement be continued through the first 12 weeks of gestation. Women who have had a prior child with an NTD should take a higher dosage: 4 mg per day. This higher level of folic acid supplementation is also recommended for women who have multiple gestation, who have hemoglobinopathies such as sickle cell anemia, or who are taking antiepileptic medication (Hernandez-Diaz et al., 2000).

The recommended daily allowance of vitamin A is 2,700 IU per day. This amount is contained in most diets, so supplementation is not recommended. In fact, studies have shown that intake of more than 10,000 IU per day of vitamin A is associated with an increased incidence of NTDs (Azais-Braesco & Pascal, 2000; Rothman et al., 1995). Therefore, the acne medication Accutane (isotretinoin), which contains vitamin A, should not be used by a woman who is pregnant or who is considering a pregnancy.

MALFORMATIONS

Knowledge is steadily increasing as to the causes of congenital malformations. Even so, among children born in the United States with congenital malformations, approximately two thirds of the malformations are caused by unknown sources (Beckman & Brent, 1986). Identifiable causes include single-gene defects (20%); chromosomal disorders (3%–5%); environmental exposure to teratogens, such as to radiation and certain medications or drugs (2%–3%); maternal infection, including bacterial, protozoal, or viral agents (2%–3%); and maternal chronic illness, such as hypertension or diabetes (1%). Development issues related to single-gene defects are discussed in Chapter 1. This chapter addresses the other known causes of congenital malformations.

Chromosomal Disorders

Chromosomal disorders include absence of a single chromosome, presence of an extra chromosome, or even presence of one or two entire extra sets of 23 chromosomes (triploidy or tetraploidy, respectively). These can lead to early or late pregnancy loss for the more severe chromosomal abnormalities and to structural or functional disorders in affected live-born infants. Approximately 15%–20% of all clinically diagnosed pregnancies end in spontaneous abortion. At least half of early spontaneous abortions are related to chromosomal abnormalities, with the monosomy Turner syndrome (45,X) being the most common. Turner syndrome is characterized by a large cystic swelling in the affected individual's neck region that is generally identifiable by ultrasound. Trisomies as a group constitute almost a quarter of all spontaneous abortions. These include trisomy 18, trisomy 13, and trisomy 21 (Down syndrome). Multiple clinical effects are typically present in such pregnancies, including fetal growth restriction and small placentas. Overall, the prevalence of live-born infants with one of these three chromosomal disorders is about 1 in 1,000. The fetal occurrence of these disorders, however, is many times this number, but most of these fetuses die in utero.

Environmental Exposure to Teratogens

Radiation

Imaging studies such as X-rays, **magnetic resonance imaging (MRI), computed tomography (CT),** and ultrasonography are frequently performed for diagnostic purposes during pregnancy in both routine and emergency situations. These can have a range of effects on the developing embryo and fetus from none at all to causing pregnancy loss.

With regard to X-rays, the risk of exposure from radiation is greatest during weeks 8 to 15 after ovulation and fertilization (Hall, 1991). Exposure to less than 5 **rad,** however, has not been associated with an increased risk of congenital malformations, miscarriage, or growth restriction (Brent, 1999). For example, the amount of fetal exposure from a standard chest X-ray is approximately 0.07 rad (Table 3.1). The standard intravenous pyelogram (IVP), which is often used to diagnose kidney stones, usually requires more than one film. These additional films can expose the fetus to more than 1 rad. A single-shot IVP, however, could reduce this dose to less than 1 rad. Thus, most diagnostic X-rays pose little or no significant risk to the fetus (ACOG, 1995b).

Exposure to higher doses of radiation, however, can cause gene mutations, chromosomal abnormalities, enzyme inhibition, and interference with cell division. These doses would only occur during radiation therapy for cancer. If such radiation therapy is required during the first trimester of pregnancy, pregnancy termination may be considered.

Table 3.1.   Dose to the uterus for common radiological procedures of concern in obstetrics

Study	Dose/study (rads)
Skull	Less than .0001
Chest	Less than .0001
Mammogram	Less than .02
Spine	Less than .4
Abdomen	Less than .3
Intravenous pyelogram	0.5–1.4

Source: Cunningham et al., 2001.

Computed tomography (CT) pelvimetry is often used to determine appropriate pelvic measurements in a patient who is being evaluated for a possible vaginal breech delivery (e.g., rather than for elective cesarean section). Fetal radiation exposure in CT scanning is usually less than 1.5 rad and can be further reduced depending on the technique used.

Diagnostic ultrasound, in contrast to X-rays, uses sound waves, not irradiation, to produce energy at a very low intensity range. Diagnostic ultrasound examinations have not been causally associated with adverse fetal effects. Similarly, magnetic resonance imaging (MRI) scans use the natural magnetic forces in the body rather than external radiation and thus pose no known risk to the fetus.

Medications and Drugs

Medications and drugs taken in pregnancy, whether prescription or nonprescription, often have no adverse effect on fetal development. Some, however, are known to cause significant problems and should be avoided if at all possible.

For example, thalidomide was commonly used in Europe (but was never approved for sale in the United States) in the late 1950s as an agent to control nausea and vomiting during the first trimester of pregnancy. It was discovered, however, that at least 20% of the children whose mothers had used thalidomide between 35 and 50 days after ovulation and fertilization demonstrated teratogenic effects. These included **duodenal atresia** (absence of part of the small intestine), limb reduction abnormalities, **microtia** (tiny ears), and spinal malformations (Newman, 1985; Taussig, 1962). Thalidomide was removed from the market in Europe. In 1998, however, it was approved in the United States for the treatment of leprosy, under extremely restrictive circumstances and only by specially registered physicians and pharmacists. According to the Food and Drug Administration, even a single dose taken by a pregnant woman can cause severe birth defects.

Seizure disorders in pregnant women are associated with an increase in congenital malformations (Holmes et al., 2001). It is not clear whether the disease process leading to the seizures or the antiepileptic drugs used to treat them causes the observed increase in birth defects. It is clear, however, that during pregnancy a single antiepileptic drug should be used whenever possible and at the lowest dosage needed for seizure control. Certain antiepileptics interfere with folic acid metabolism, and their use in pregnancy can lead to fetal NTDs (Centers for Disease Control, 1992). Overall, there is an approximately 8% chance that a fetus will develop birth defects if exposed to one of the commonly used antiepileptics (phenytoin [Dilantin], phenobarbital [Luminal], carbamazepine [Carbatrol, Tegretol], and valproic acid [Depakene, Depakote]; Kaneko et al., 1988; Nakane et al., 1980). Carbamazepine, when used alone in the first trimester, carries a 1%–2% risk of NTD, mostly in the lumbosacral region (Rosa, 1991). It is also associated with microcephaly, growth restriction, and developmental delay.

The phenytoin syndrome, characterized by limb defects, growth restriction, mental retardation, microcephaly, heart defects, and unusual **craniofacial** features, is seen in fewer than 10% of fetuses exposed to phenytoin in utero. The effects depend on whether the fetus inherits a mutant gene that decreases the production of an enzyme that is needed to break down phenytoin. Valproic acid is associated with NTDs, especially spina bifida. Phenobarbital has been associated with microcephaly in animal studies.

Like radiation therapy, chemotherapy used to treat cancer during pregnancy places the fetus at risk. This risk of exposure must be balanced against the risk of the malignant disease process that is being treated. The first 12 weeks of gestation are the most critical, and the use of these agents during this period can potentially cause congenital malformations, fetal death, or growth restriction (Gililland & Weinstein, 1983). If chemotherapy is needed during pregnancy, it should be delayed whenever possible until after the first 12 weeks of gestation. If such a delay is not possible, then termination of the pregnancy is often considered. Of the drugs used to treat cancer, those most commonly associated with teratogenic effects are folic acid **antagonists** such as methotrexate. Methotrexate has been shown to cause delayed skull formation, limb deformities, and cerebral anomalies.

Patients who have chronic hypertension or develop hypertension as part of preeclampsia (a medical condition of pregnancy that includes **hypertension**, protein in the urine, and **edema**) may require antihypertensive medication during pregnancy. Most of the drugs are safe for the fetus but a few require caution. The use of angiotensin-converting enzyme (ACE) inhibitor medication, such as captopril, during pregnancy has been associated with fetal kidney abnormalities. Pregnant women taking ACE inhibitors should be advised to discontinue them, especially because safer alternatives are available. Alpha-methyldopa (Aldomet) is considered the first-line antihypertensive agent for use during pregnancy because it is the only drug for which safety has been demonstrated in long-term follow-up studies. In addition, labetolol (Normodyne) and atenolol (Tenormin) are acceptable alternatives. In terms of the use of **diuretics** such as furosemide (Lasix) or chlorothiazide (Diuril) for blood pressure control, there are no data demonstrating an increased perinatal mortality rate or decreased birth weight when maternal diuretic therapy is begun before 24 weeks of gestation. Although there is a theoretical risk of dehydration when diuretics are used later in pregnancy, they may be continued as long as there is no clinical evidence of growth restriction or reduced uterine or placental blood flow.

Alcohol freely crosses the placenta, and its fetal toxicity is known to be dose related. The greatest risk of exposure is during the first twelve weeks of gestation. It is difficult to calculate an exact risk because of the frequent presence of confounders such as multiple drug use (both legal and illicit) and cigarette smoking. In the United States, however, 1 in every 500–1,000 deliveries is affected by maternal alcohol use. Alcohol use during pregnancy is the most commonly identified preventable cause of mental retardation in the United States.

Heroin use during pregnancy can cause growth restriction, preterm labor and delivery, stillbirth, and neonatal mortality. Furthermore, affected newborns are at risk for narcotic withdrawal syndrome in the first days of life that can be potentially fatal. A high-pitched cry, tremors, irritability, and occasional seizures characterize this withdrawal syndrome. Treatment of the mother with methadone improves pregnancy outcome, but neonatal narcotic withdrawal syndrome for methadone can be more severe and prolonged than for heroin due to the longer half-life of methadone.

Exposure to cocaine in the first trimester is associated with an increased risk of spontaneous abortion, fetal death, growth restriction, and separation of the placenta (placental abruption, or abruptio placenta). It is also associated with congenital malformations of the heart, limbs, face, and genitourinary tract. The exact risk of exposure is difficult to establish because of the frequent concurrent abuse of other substances. (See Chapter 7 for further discussion of the effects of prenatal exposure to alcohol, cocaine, heroin, and other drugs.)

Maternal Infection

Maternal infections, too, can cause a range of effects on the developing fetus from none at all to highly significant. For example, **syphilis** is a chronic disease process caused by the organism *Treponema pallidum;* in its severe form, the disease is associated with poor pregnancy outcomes. All pregnant women should be screened for this disease. Syphilis is acquired through sexual contact and has an incubation period of 10–90 days. As recommended by the Centers for Disease Control and Prevention (CDC, 1998), penicillin is the most effective treatment available. Untreated syphilis in a pregnant woman is associated with congenital syphilis, stillbirth, preterm labor and delivery, and neonatal death. It had been believed that *Treponema pallidum* was incapable of traversing the placenta prior to 26 weeks of gestation, but it is now known to be capable of causing intrauterine infection at any stage of pregnancy. In the third trimester of pregnancy, the transmission rate approaches 100% and fetal death occurs in almost 40% of cases. In surviving infants, the clinical manifestations of congenital syphilis include rash, oral **lesions,** enlarged liver, **jaundice,** and inflammation of the eye (chorioretinitis and iritis). Congenital syphilis that is untreated or incompletely treated after birth can lead to late manifestations resulting from chronic inflammation of bone, teeth, and the CNS. These findings include Hutchinson's teeth (barrel-shaped upper central incisors), sensorineural deafness, saddle nose (depression of the nasal root), and saber shins (bowing of the tibia).

Toxoplasmosis is a protozoan infection caused by *Toxoplasma gondii.* The incidence of acute maternal infection is 0.1%–0.5% in the United States. Acute congenital toxoplasmosis occurs in the fetuses of about 10%–20% of affected women. Pregnant women can acquire this infection by eating inadequately cooked meat that contains the parasite's tissue cysts or by ingesting food contaminated with minute amounts of cat feces containing the *Toxoplasmosis* oocysts (fertile cysts). Although the risk of fetal infection is lower in the first 12 weeks of gestation, the severity of congenital infection is greater during that time. The diagnosis of toxoplasmosis can be suggested by ultrasound findings of enlarged cerebral **ventricles**, placental thickness, intracranial calcifications in the fetus, excessive fluid in the abdominal cavity, and liver enlargement. Amniocentesis or fetal blood sampling can confirm the diagnosis prenatally and may lead to the consideration of pregnancy termination.

Varicella (chickenpox) is caused by a DNA herpesvirus. Prior varicella infection confers lifelong immunity. Herpesvirus varicella is responsible for both varicella and its recurrent manifestation, herpes zoster (shingles). Herpes zoster is usually self-limiting and does not cause fetal problems. Varicella infection during the first 12 weeks after ovulation and fertilization, however, is associated with the development of a congenital syndrome characterized by limb defects, scars, microcephaly, chorioretinitis, and cataracts. Furthermore, if the mother develops chickenpox within 5 days of delivery, the virus may cross the placenta and result in neonatal varicella. Because of inadequate **antibody** transfer, the neonate who has been exposed to the varicella virus should receive varicella **immunoglobulin** to protect against a severe case of chickenpox.

A vaccination program implemented in 1977 has greatly reduced the incidence of congenital **rubella** (German measles). In women who contract rubella during the first 12 weeks of gestation, there is a 90% risk of their fetus developing congenital rubella syndrome. Microcephaly, mental retardation, cataracts, deafness, and congenital heart defects characterize this syndrome. Women are now offered testing for immunity to rubella prior to becoming pregnant and are vaccinated if they are found to lack immunity. Administration of rubella vaccine, a live virus vaccine, however, is contraindicated during pregnancy. Although there is no evidence to suggest that the vaccine causes birth defects or illness, there is about a 2% theoretical risk that the virus could cross the placenta and infect the fetus.

Cytomegalovirus (CMV) infection is prevalent at child care centers and is caused by a double-stranded DNA herpesvirus. It is the most common cause of congenital viral infection in the United States, ranging in incidence from 0.2% to 2.2% of all live-born infants. CMV can be transmitted by blood transfusion, by sexual contact, and during breast feeding. The diagnosis of congenital CMV infection is based on ultrasound findings of symmetrical growth restriction, **microphthalmia**, cerebral calcifications, hydrocephalus, and microcephaly. The long-term effects include deafness, microcephaly, and mental retardation (Noyola et al., 2001). Amniocentesis or fetal blood sampling can confirm CMV infection.

Maternal Chronic Illness

Studies have suggested that several maternal chronic illnesses, including hypertension, thyroid disease, diabetes mellitus, and autoimmune disorders, can result in impaired intrauterine fetal growth and development.

Hypertensive disorders occur in approximately 1%–5% of all pregnancies in the United States and in a higher percentage among older pregnant women (Sibai, 1996). These disorders are a significant cause of perinatal morbidity (complications) and mortality. The direct fetal effects seen with hypertensive disorders include growth restriction and decreased volume of amniotic fluid. These are thought to result from decreased maternal blood flow to the uterus, placenta, and kidneys. Other maternal and fetal risks include preeclampsia, abruptio placenta, and preterm delivery. If antihypertensive medication is initiated during pregnancy, it is important to observe the fetus for further growth restriction (Butler, Kennedy, & Rubin, 1990).

Most medications commonly used to treat thyroid disease (thyrotoxicosis) in nonpregnant women can be safely used during pregnancy (Mulder, 1998). Propylthiouracil (PTU), the drug of choice for treatment of thyrotoxicosis, however, crosses the placenta and can potentially cause **hypothyroidism** in the fetus as well as a fetal **goiter**. Another drug used for **hyperthyroidism**, methimazole (Tapazole), also crosses the placenta, leading to an increased risk for development of an unusual scalp defect. There is no consistent evidence, however, that suggests that PTU or methimazole is teratogenic. Fetuses of mothers who are exposed to increased amounts of iodide for long periods of time are at increased risk of developing hypothyroidism and a fetal goiter because iodide easily crosses the placenta and is absorbed by the fetal thyroid. Therefore, radioiodine studies are not generally recommended during pregnancy unless the mother has severe thyrotoxicosis; thyroidectomy, however, can be safely carried out. Women who continue to have hyperthyroidism despite medical therapy and those whose disease remains untreated are at increased risk for developing pregnancy-induced hypertension and congestive heart failure, leading to an increased incidence of fetal death and preterm labor and delivery.

Because thyroid deficiency is commonly associated with infertility, most pregnancies are not complicated by overt hypothyroidism. For the most part, infants of mothers with hypothyroidism are healthy and show no evidence of thyroid dysfunction. Nevertheless, there is an increased incidence of pregnancy-induced hypertension and placental abruption in women with thyroid deficiency. Depending upon the degree of thyroid deficiency, children of mothers with hypothyroidism may have lower IQ scores (Haddow et al., 1999).

Diabetes is one of the most common medical complications of pregnancy. Gestational diabetes accounts for approximately 90% of all patients with diabetes during pregnancy. This diagnosis is made in a pregnant woman who has abnormally elevated blood **glucose** levels after consuming a specific amount of an oral glucose solution. In these patients, the disorder is usually well controlled with the American Diabetes Association diet for gestational diabetes (Casey et al., 1997).

Poorly treated maternal diabetes, both gestational and pregestational, however, is associated with an increased incidence of fetal anomalies, delayed lung maturity, large fetal body size (**macrosomia**), and fetal death. Preconceptional counseling (Willhoite et al., 1993) and maintenance of tight metabolic control of the mother's glucose levels throughout the pregnancy can decrease the risk of these complications.

Women with autoimmune conditions such as antiphospholipid antibody syndrome or systemic lupus erythematosus (SLE, or lupus) are at increased risk for recurrent pregnancy losses. Antiphospholipid antibody syndrome is associated with pregnancy loss, thrombosis (stroke), and decreased platelet count. In maternal SLE, a severe multisystem chronic illness associated with skin rash, hypertension, kidney disease, and potentially **encephalopathy**, infants can also be born with lupus and have blood, heart, and skin abnormalities (Peaceman & Ramsey-Goldman, 2001).

SUMMARY

Although this chapter has focused on the many complications that can occur during pregnancy, it is important to emphasize that the vast majority of all children are born well. There are certain things that a woman can do to decrease the risk of fetal development complications in pregnancy. These include eating a nutritious and well-balanced diet, seeking early prenatal care, taking only medically recommended dosages of vitamin supplements, and avoiding environmental agents that can potentially harm the developing fetus. If there is exposure to a potential teratogenic agent, the risk to the fetus depends on the specific teratogen; the extent, duration, and timing of exposure; the ability of the teratogen to cross the placenta; and genetic predisposition. Teratogenic agents include radiation, certain medications, drugs of abuse, bacteria, protozoa, and viruses. In addition, certain chronic maternal illnesses such as diabetes, thyroid disease, and lupus can place the fetus at risk. Adverse effects of teratogens can range from growth restriction, to malformations, to fetal death. The best protection from most of the known factors leading to problems in pregnancy is prevention or early detection and, when possible, intervention.

REFERENCES

Abrams, B., & Selvin, S. (1995). Maternal weight gain pattern and birth weight. *Obstetrics and Gynecology, 86*, 163.

American College of Obstetricians and Gynecologists. (1995a). *Folic acid for the prevention of recurrent neural tube defects* (ACOG Committee Opinion 120). Washington, DC: Author.

American College of Obstetricians and Gynecologists. (1995b). *Guidelines for diagnostic imaging during pregnancy* (ACOG Committee Opinion 158). Washington, DC: Author.

Azais-Braesco, V., & Pascal, G. (2000). Vitamin A in pregnancy: Requirements and safety limits. *American Journal of Clinical Nutrition, 71*(5, Suppl.), 1325S–1333S.

Beckman, A.A., & Brent, R.L. (1986). Mechanism of known environmental teratogens: Drugs and chemicals. *Clinics in Perinatology, 13*, 649–687.

Brent, R.L. (1999). The effect of embryonic and fetal exposure to x-ray, microwaves, and ultrasound: Reproductive risks from pre- and post-conception environmental radiation exposures. *Teratology, 59*, 182.

Butler, L., Kennedy, S., & Rubin, P.C. (1990). Atenolol in essential hypertension during pregnancy. *British Medical Journal, 301*, 587–590.

Casey, B.M., Lucas, M.J., McIntire, D.D., et al. (1997). Pregnancy outcomes in women with gestational diabetes compared with the general obstetric population. *Obstetrics and Gynecology, 90*, 869–873.

Centers for Disease Control. (1992). Recommendations for the use of folic acid to reduce the number of cases of spina bifida and other neural tube defects. *MMWR, 41*(RR-14), 1–7.

Centers for Disease Control and Prevention. (1998). Guidelines for the treatment of sexually transmitted diseases. *MMWR, 47*(RR-1), 28–48.

Cunningham, F.G., MacDonald, P.C., Leveno, K.J., et al. (2001). *Williams obstetrics* (21st ed.). New York: McGraw-Hill.

Decoufle, P., Boyle, C.A., Paulozzi, L.J., et al. (2001). Increased risk for developmental disabilities in children who have major birth defects: A population-based study. *Pediatrics, 108*, 728–734.

Gililland, J., & Weinstein, L. (1983). The effects of cancer chemotherapeutic agents on the developing fetus. *Obstetrical and Gynecological Survey, 38*, 6–13.

Haddow, J.E., Palomaki, G.E., Allan, W.C., et al. (1999). Maternal thyroid deficiency during pregnancy and subsequent neuropsychological development of the child. *New England Journal of Medicine, 341*, 549–555.

Hall, E.J. (1991). Scientific view of low-level radiation risks. *Radiographics, 11*, 509.

Hay, W.W., Catz, C.S., Grave, G.D., et al. (1997). Workshop summary: Fetal growth. Its regulation and disorders. *Journal of Pediatrics, 99*, 585–592.

Hernandez-Diaz, S., Werler, M.M., Walker, A.M., et al. (2000). Folic acid antagonists during pregnancy and the risk of birth defects. *New England Journal of Medicine, 343*, 1608–1614.

Holmes, L.B., Harvey, E.A., & Coull, B.A. (2001). The teratogenicity of anticonvulsant drugs. *New England Journal of Medicine, 344*, 1132–1138.

Institute of Medicine. (1990). *Nutrition during pregnancy*. Washington, DC: National Academy Press.

Kaneko, S., Otani, K., Fukushima, Y., et al. (1988). Teratogenicity of anti-epileptic drugs: Analysis of possible risk factors. *Epilepsia, 29*, 459–467.

Moore, K.L., & Persaud, T.V.N. (1993). *Before we are born: Essentials of embryology and birth defects.* Philadelphia: W.B. Saunders.

Mulder, J.E. (1998). Thyroid disease in women. *Medical Clinics of North America, 82*, 104–125.

Nakane, Y., Okuma, T., Takahashi, R., et al. (1980). Multi-institutional study on the teratogenicity and fetal toxicity of anti-epileptic drugs: A report of collaborative study group in Japan. *Epilepsia, 21*, 663–380.

Newman, C.G. (1985). Teratogen update: Clinical aspects of thalidomide embryopathy. A continuing preoccupation. *Teratology, 32*, 133–144.

Noyola, D.E., Demmler, G.J., Nelson, C.T., et al. (2001). Early predictors of neurodevelopmental outcome in symptomatic congenital cytomegalovirus infection. *Journal of Pediatrics, 138*, 324–331.

Peaceman, A.M., & Ramsey-Goldman, R. (2001). Autoimmune connective tissue disease in pregnancy. *Sciarra's Obstetrics and Gynecology, 3*(20), 1–5.

Rosa, F.W. (1991). Spina bifida in infants of women treated with carbamazepine during pregnancy. *New England Journal of Medicine, 324*, 674–677.

Rothman, K.J., Moore, L.L., Singer, M.R., et al. (1995). Teratogenicity of high vitamin A intake. *New England Journal of Medicine, 333*, 1369.

Sibai, B. (1996). Treatment of hypertension in pregnant women. *New England Journal of Medicine, 335*, 257–265.

Smith, G., Smith, M., McNay, M.B., et al. (1998). First trimester growth and the risk of low birth weight. *New England Journal of Medicine, 339*, 1817–1822.

Taussig, H.B. (1962). Thalidomide: A lesson in remote effects of drugs. *American Journal of Diseases of Children, 104*, 111–113.

Willhoite, M.B., Benvert, H.W., Palomaki, G.E., et al. (1993). The impact of preconception counseling on pregnancy outcomes: The experience of the Maine Diabetes in Pregnancy Program. *Diabetes Care, 16*, 450–455.

4 Having A Baby
The Birth Process

Shad H. Deering and Andrew J. Satin

Upon completion of this chapter, the reader will:

- be able to describe the stages of labor and techniques for monitoring labor
- be able to identify causes of abnormal labor, or dystocia
- be aware of pregnancy complications that influence the condition of the newborn
- be aware of special pregnancy conditions that are associated with increased risk to mother and fetus

In the past, it was thought that many developmental disabilities resulted from complications that occurred during the period of labor and delivery. Now it is known that in fact, complications during this period account for fewer than 10% of all cases of severe disabilities in childhood. The reason for this change in our perception is twofold. First, it is now understood that the most important causes of severe disability are genetic errors that occur very early in gestation. These errors currently cannot be treated or prevented, and these fetuses are at greater risk for perinatal complications. They are more likely to have a breech presentation, to not breathe spontaneously, and so forth. Thus, their problems during labor and delivery are secondary to their underlying condition rather than a primary cause of their disability. Second, changes in fetal monitoring and delivery practices have led to fewer perinatal complications and resultant disability in fetuses from otherwise uncomplicated pregnancies. This chapter focuses on the processes of labor and delivery and the technology that is being employed to prevent perinatal brain injury.

DATING A PREGNANCY

One of the most crucial steps in antepartum (prenatal) care is to date the pregnancy. Several different terms are used to define the duration of pregnancy. Estimated gestational age (EGA) or menstrual age is the time from the first day of the last menstrual period (LMP). It should be noted that gestational age is 14 days longer than conceptional age because of the time between the LMP and ovulation and implantation of the embryo. The average duration of a pregnancy is 280 days, or 40 weeks EGA. Obstetricians typically refer to the EGA during prenatal care. The estimated due date (EDD) and **estimated date of confinement (EDC)** are terms used interchangeably. A quick estimate of the EDD can be made by adding 7 days to the first day of the LMP and subtracting 3 months. For example, if the first day of a woman's LMP is October 15, her due date will be July 22. A pregnancy is considered full term between 38 and 42 weeks EGA. **Preterm birth** is delivery prior to 37 complete weeks. **Postterm birth** is delivery with an EGA greater than 42 weeks.

DECIDING WHEN TO DELIVER THE BABY

The most important decision an obstetrician makes is if and when to influence labor. **Tocolysis** is the prescribing of medications in an effort to prevent preterm labor. Labor augmentation, or induction, comprises efforts to stimulate the uterus to contract. Obstetric decision analysis balances the risk of delivery versus pregnancy continuation for both mother and fetus. These decisions can be particularly difficult when the decision to deliver may be medically beneficial to the mother but clearly disadvantageous to the fetus. Knowledge of gestational age is central to these treatment decisions.

PERINATAL MORTALITY

Over the past 50 years, both perinatal and maternal mortality rates have declined dramatically. Improvements in the quality of care during pregnancy and labor have contributed to the decline in the stillbirth rate, and improved intensive care of newborns has resulted in a decline in neonatal deaths. Fetal and neonatal deaths may arise from difficulties originating antepartum, during labor, or at birth. Perinatal mortality, which is defined as stillbirths (intrauterine death occurring after 20 weeks' gestation but prior to delivery) plus neonatal deaths (deaths that occur in the first 28 days of life), has been falling steadily since the 1970s. In 2000, the infant mortality rate in the United States was 6.9 per 1,000 births (Table 4.1), the lowest ever recorded (Hoyert et al., 2001). The prevalence of neonatal deaths has also declined. Perinatal mortality in high-risk pregnancies has been reduced fourfold since 1984 (Creasy & Resnik, 1999). The most common cause of neonatal death is low birth weight, usually as a result of preterm delivery. Preterm delivery is the major source of long-term complications due to issues of prematurity and accounts for 85% of all perinatal complications (Norwitz, Robinson, & Challis, 1999).

LABOR

Labor is defined by the presence of regular uterine contractions leading to progressive effacement (thinning) and dilation of the cervix and expulsion of the fetus. Labor is divided into three stages. The first stage begins when uterine contractions bring about effacement and progressive dilation of the cervix. This stage ends when the cervix is fully effaced, or paper-thin, and completely dilated, typically 10 centimeters. The first stage of labor is divided into a latent and an active phase. The latent phase is characterized by infrequent and irregular contractions, which typically result in only modest discomfort. The active phase is characterized by regular,

Table 4.1.   Infant mortality rates in 2000 in the United States for leading causes per 100,000 live births

Cause	Death rate
Congenital anomalies	142
Preterm birth and low birth weight	106
Sudden infant death syndrome	53
Respiratory distress syndrome	25
Maternal complications of pregnancy	33
Delivery complications of pregnancy	25
Infections	18
Accidents and adverse effects	20
Intrauterine hypoxia or birth asphyxia	16

Source: Hoyert et al., 2001.

intense, and typically painful contractions. This phase typically begins when the cervix is 3–4 centimeters dilated and concludes when the cervix is 10 centimeters dilated. The second stage of labor begins when dilation of the cervix is complete and ends with expulsion of the fetus. The third stage of labor begins immediately after delivery of the fetus and ends with the delivery of the placenta.

MONITORING LABOR

Once labor begins, the fetal heart rate (FHR) and uterine contractions are monitored. Continuous electronic fetal monitoring (EFM) has been used routinely in obstetrics in the United States since the 1960s. EFM may be done with either external or internal monitors. External monitors employ Doppler ultrasound technology to monitor the FHR and a tocodynamometer to measure contraction activity. Internal monitors include a fetal scalp electrode and an intrauterine pressure catheter, which have the advantage of providing exact measurements of FHR and contraction strength, respectively.

When EFM was first introduced, there was great hope that fetal deaths and neonatal morbidity (complications) and mortality could be decreased by closely monitoring the fetus. Although multiple **retrospective** studies of FHR monitoring have demonstrated a reduction in fetal deaths, all but one randomized, controlled trial found no difference between intermittent auscultation (checking the fetal heart manually with a stethoscope) and continuous EFM (American College of Obstetricians and Gynecologists [ACOG], 1995b; Vintzileos, Antsaklis, & Varvarigos, 1993).

Evaluation of a fetal heart tracing should include analysis of rate, variability, and periodic changes. A normal baseline FHR is between 120 and 160 beats per minute (bpm). Fetal **bradycardia** (slowed heart rate) is present if the baseline heart rate remains less than 120 bpm for more than 15 minutes (Freeman, Garite, & Nageotte, 1991). Severe bradycardia is a FHR less than 80 bpm for 3 minutes or longer. Causes of fetal bradycardia may include uterine hypertonus (excessive tone), epidural-induced hypotension, **placental abruption** (discussed later in this chapter), and any other problems that decrease blood flow to the fetus. Treatment of fetal bradycardia involves determining the cause and correcting it to restore adequate blood flow to the fetus. If bradycardia does not resolve in a timely manner, then delivery is accomplished either by cesarean delivery or by forceps or vacuum extraction, depending on which can be accomplished more quickly.

Fetal **tachycardia** (rapid heart rate) is diagnosed when there is a sustained FHR of greater than 160 bpm. Intra-amniotic infection may cause a maternal fever, which in turn causes fetal tachycardia. Other causes include fetal arrhythmia and administration of certain medications to the mother. Although mild tachycardia (160–180 bpm) in the absence of other concerning findings may be monitored, severe tachycardia (greater than 200 bpm) often requires delivery. Accelerations, or increases in the FHR of as much as 15 bpm for 15 seconds, should not be confused with sustained tachycardia. The presence of accelerations is similar to FHR variability in that when present, fetal compromise is rare.

It is normal for FHR to be variable. Short-term variability consists of the beat-to-beat changes of the FHR and long-term variability comprises changes that occur over 1-minute intervals. Decreased short- and long-term variability may be observed during normal fetal sleep cycles or after administration of narcotics during labor. Nevertheless, severely diminished or absent variability in the presence of decelerations can be an ominous sign of a compromised fetus. Decelerations, or periodic decreases in the FHR, should be evaluated in relation to contractions, as the cause and treatment of different types of decelerations may vary.

Alterations in FHR related to contractions are referred to as *periodic changes*. With each uterine contraction, the fetus experiences significant physiological changes. Contractions decrease placental blood flow, which in turn decreases oxygen delivery to the fetus for short periods of time. Although a healthy fetus does well and can compensate for this stress, fetuses affected by **preeclampsia** (discussed later in this chapter), intrauterine growth restriction (IUGR), or genetic syndromes or those who are extremely premature may become **hypoxic** (deprived of oxygen) during labor and develop abnormal FHR patterns. Contractions may also compress the umbilical cord and/or the head of the fetus, which can cause characteristic changes in the fetal heart tracing.

When the head of the fetus is compressed by contractions, which usually occurs during the second stage of labor, the FHR may drop in a manner that mirrors the contraction. This form of deceleration is termed an *early deceleration* and is not a sign of distress. In contrast, when the umbilical cord is compressed during a uterine contraction, the fetal heart decelerations are not uniform in nature and do not occur exactly with contractions (Figure 4.1a). Variable decelerations may be treated with maternal position changes, amnioinfusion (infusion of 250–500 cubic centimeters of fluid into the uterine cavity after the amniotic sac has broken), or with one of a group of drugs referred to as *tocolytics*, which are designed to stop contractions for a short period of time. When variable decelerations are persistently below 70 bpm for more than 60 seconds and demonstrate slow return to baseline or decreased variability or when tachycardia is present between decelerations, there is a correlation with fetal distress.

Late decelerations are symmetric in appearance, much like early decelerations, but they do not begin until after the peak of a contraction and do not return to baseline until after the contraction has ended. Late decelerations are not usually as obvious as variable decelerations and only decrease the FHR by 30–40 bpm below baseline. Late decelerations are of great concern as they are indicative of uteroplacental insufficiency and fetal jeopardy (Figure 4.1b). Late decelerations may be seen with maternal hypotension from **epidural anesthesia** or uterine hy-

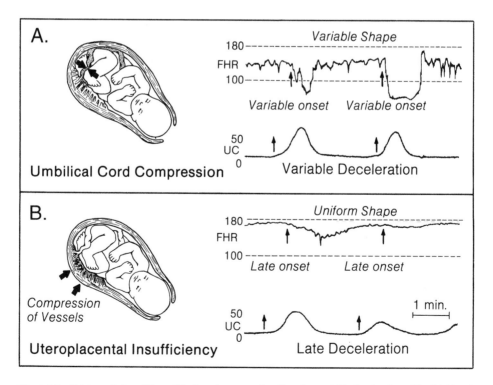

Figure 4.1. Fetal monitoring. A) In umbilical cord compression, there is a variable deceleration of the fetal heart rate (FHR). This abnormal finding of early, mid-, and late deceleration suggests compression and obstruction of the umbilical cord circulation during labor. B) In uteroplacental insufficiency, late deceleration of FHR occurs if the placental blood vessels are abnormally pressed together during the end of the uterine contraction (UC; see arrows). (From Hon, E. [1968]. *An atlas of fetal heart rate patterns.* New Haven, CT: Harty; adapted by permission.)

peractivity but may also be present with preeclampsia, diabetes, or placental abruption. If late decelerations are repetitive and associated with decreased variability, then immediate delivery is indicated.

A newer method of fetal monitoring that has recently been approved by the U.S. Food and Drug Administration is fetal pulse oximetry. Fetal pulse oximetry measures the oxygen saturation of arterial **hemoglobin** (Yam, Chua, & Arulkumaran, 2000a). If the fetal oxygen saturation falls below 30%, intervention is warranted (Yam, Chua, & Arulkumaran, 2000b). This technology is not yet in widespread use and is still being investigated but may be commonplace in the near future. Whether it will improve perinatal outcomes is yet to be determined.

DELIVERY

Most deliveries occur spontaneously and are referred to as spontaneous vaginal deliveries (SVD). The infant's head is delivered, and the nose and mouth are bulb-suctioned to clear the airway. When the umbilical cord is wrapped around the neck, as it is in approximately one quarter of births, it is called a *nuchal cord* and is either manually released or clamped and cut. Following delivery of the shoulders, the cord is clamped and cut, and the infant is placed on the mother's abdomen or under a warmer to be cleaned and resuscitated if needed.

An episiotomy is an incision in the perineum (pelvic outlet), which may be made in an attempt to prevent tearing at delivery. Although there are reasons for cutting an episiotomy when a larger passage is required, such as in breech deliveries and operative deliveries, it is not recommended on a routine basis.

Operative deliveries include the use of forceps and vacuum devices to assist or expedite delivery. These devices are used only when the cervix is fully dilated, fetal head position is known, and the fetus is sufficiently far enough down in the pelvis to be reached without difficulty. Indications for operative delivery include fetal distress, maternal exhaustion, and the need to avoid "pushing" for maternal factors (e.g., maternal cardiac conditions that might be exacerbated by cardiovascular stress). When forceps or vacuum devices are used in an appropriate manner, there do not appear to be any long-term differences in developmental outcome in infants delivered using these devices compared with those born spontaneously (Wesley, Van den Berg, & Reece, 1992).

CESAREAN SECTION

Cesarean deliveries, which involve delivering the baby through an incision in the abdomen and uterus, may be performed in cases of fetal jeopardy; if necessary, the infant can be delivered within minutes. Cesareans are also done when the fetus is too large or the pelvis is too small for vaginal delivery. Cesareans may also be used in cases of malpresentation (e.g., footling breech presentation) or for high-order multiple pregnancies (e.g., triplets or more). Cesarean delivery is usually performed under either epidural or spinal anesthesia with the patient awake, with general anesthesia being used only in emergency cases or when contraindications to epidural/spinal anesthesia are present.

Cesareans have become much more common in the United States since the mid-1960s, increasing from 5% of deliveries in 1965 to 24.7% by 1988 (Eskew et al., 1994). The reasons for this are many but include the use of continuous fetal monitoring with increased diagnosis of fetal distress, a decrease in the number of vaginal breech deliveries, and an increase in elective repeat cesareans. Data suggest that the rate of cesareans currently being performed, although lower than before, remains too high at 21% (DiMarco et al., 2000). It was initially felt that all patients who had a cesarean needed a repeat cesarean with subsequent pregnancies, but now most women are encouraged to attempt a vaginal birth after cesarean (VBAC). VBAC success rates range from 60% to 80% (Flamm, 1995; Rosen, Dickinson, & Westhoff, 1991). Contraindications to VBAC include a previous classical cesarean (in which the uterine incision is vertical rather than horizontal and enters into the upper, contractile portion of the uterus); previous uterine surgery in which the endometrial cavity was entered; or a previous uterine rupture. It is important to remember that regardless of the route of delivery, the majority of deliveries result in a healthy newborn.

ABNORMAL LABOR OR DYSTOCIA

Dystocia is defined as difficult labor or childbirth. Typically, labor abnormalities are characterized as slower than normal (protraction disorders) or complete cessation of progress (arrest disorders). Shown in Table 4.2 are the criteria for diagnosing labor abnormalities (ACOG, 1995a). Identification of the potential cause of dystocia involves assessment of the three Ps: *p*ower (uterine contraction intensity), *p*assenger (fetus), and *p*assage (maternal anatomy). Uterine hypocontractility (decreased power of contraction) is a common cause of dystocia. It may be treated with a carefully administered intravenous infusion of oxytocin. Oxytocin stimulates the uterus to contract. The size, presentation, and position of the fetus may contribute to dystocia. Fetal anomalies such as hydrocephalus and spina bifida may obstruct labor. Infrequently, the maternal bony pelvis may contribute to dystocia. This may be seen after trauma or with severe **malnutrition**.

PREGNANCY COMPLICATIONS

Pregnancy and labor complications undoubtedly influence the condition of the newborn. Although a definitive discussion of all complications of pregnancy is beyond the scope of this chapter, several problems merit review. Diabetes, hypertension, and trauma are maternal conditions that can influence newborn status. Preterm labor, preterm rupture of membranes, and placental abruption are obstetric conditions that may result in preterm birth. Perinatal viral, parasitic, and bacterial infections may affect both mother and child.

Maternal Conditions

Diabetes

Diabetes mellitus is classified as type I or type II, depending on whether insulin is required. Approximately 2%–3% of pregnancies are affected by diabetes, with 90% of these being gestational diabetics, or diabetes diagnosed in pregnancy (ACOG, 1994). Type I diabetics (requir-

Table 4.2.   Diagnostic criteria for abnormal labor patterns

Labor pattern	Nulligravida	Mulitpara (has previously delivered children)
Protraction disorders		
Dilation	< 1.2 cm/hour	< 1.5 cm/hour
Descent	< 1.2 cm/hour	< 1.5 cm/hour
Arrest disorders		
Dilation	> 2 hours	> 2 hours
Descent	> 1 hour	> 1 hour

From American College of Obstetricians and Gynecologists. (1995a). *Dystocia and the augmentation of labor* (ACOG Technical Bulletin 218). Washington, DC: Author; reprinted by permission.

ing insulin) are at a 3% risk for developing diabetic ketoacidosis (DKA; an acute elevation of blood sugar associated with acid buildup in the blood) during pregnancy. Ten percent of women with DKA suffer an intrauterine fetal death (Chauhan et al., 1996). It is also important to recognize that type I diabetic women who have poor glucose control during the period of organogenesis have a fourfold increase in the likelihood of having a baby with major congenital malformations (ACOG, 1994).

Uncontrolled diabetes in pregnancy also places the fetus at increased risk for preterm delivery, polyhydramnios (increased amniotic fluid), IUGR, preeclampsia, fetal macrosomia (large body size), and stillbirth (Dunne, 1999). For these reasons, tight control of glucose levels in pregnancy is extremely important to maximize chances for a good outcome for the infant. If good glucose control is not maintained during labor and delivery, the excessive insulin secreted by the fetus in response to maternal **hyperglycemia** can cause severe **hypoglycemia** in the infant soon after birth as the maternal glucose source is removed and the excess insulin remains. Because of this, insulin-dependent diabetics are monitored very closely in labor with frequent blood sugar checks and are treated with insulin to prevent this complication. Fetuses of diabetics are also at risk for developing macrosomia, which increases the need for a cesarean delivery because the fetus is too large to fit through the pelvis.

Although women with gestational diabetes (see Chapter 3) do not have the same increased risk for bearing a child with congenital anomalies as do those who are diabetic prior to pregnancy, their offspring are at risk for developing fetal macrosomia and as many as 50% of the mothers will develop overt diabetes within 20 years (O'Sullivan, 1982). Most pregnant women are screened for diabetes between 24 and 28 weeks of gestation, with a 50-gram glucose load and a serum glucose test 1 hour later. A blood glucose value greater than 140 milligrams per deciliter is thought to be abnormal, and a follow-up 3-hour 100-gram glucose tolerance test is administered. If this is abnormal, the patient is diagnosed with gestational diabetes and a diabetic diet and close monitoring are prescribed. If dietary management does not maintain glucose levels in the appropriate range, then insulin therapy is started and the patient is managed in the same manner as a pregestational diabetic.

Hypertensive Disorders of Pregnancy

The National Institutes of Health (NIH) working group on hypertension classifies hypertension disorders during pregnancy as chronic hypertension (CHTN), preeclampsia–eclampsia, preeclampsia superimposed on chronic hypertension, and transient hypertension. CHTN occurs in 1%–5% of pregnancies (Sibai, 1996). It is defined as elevated blood pressure (greater than 140/90 mm Hg) that occurs either before pregnancy or prior to 20 weeks' gestation. Ninety percent of women with CHTN have essential (i.e., unknown cause) hypertension, with the other 10% having underlying medical problems, such as kidney, collagen vascular (e.g., lupus), endocrine, or vascular diseases. Risk factors for CHTN include obesity, heredity, race, and diabetes (Mroz, 1999). Pregnant women with CHTN must be monitored closely for development of IUGR (fetal weight less than 10th percentile for gestational age) and superimposed preeclampsia–eclampsia during their pregnancy. They are also at increased risk for placental abruption.

Preeclampsia is hypertension occurring after the 20th week of gestation accompanied by proteinuria (protein in the urine) or edema (the accumulation of fluid in tissue). Preeclampsia complicates 7% of pregnancies (Creasy & Resnik, 1999). It is a disease that most commonly affects women having their first baby. Other risk factors include extremes of childbearing age, multiple gestation, and certain medical disorders (e.g., CHTN, renal disease, diabetes). The cause of preeclampsia is not known; however, several physiological changes are evident that result in decreased placental perfusion (i.e., blood flow; Napolitano et al., 1997). Because of these changes, the fetus often has IUGR.

In a small number of preeclamptic patients, eclampsia, or seizures, may develop. Thus, whenever patients with mild preeclampsia worsen or develop signs of severe preeclampsia, delivery is usually indicated, even in the case of prematurity. In addition to induction of labor, magnesium sulfate is administered to prevent seizures during both labor and postpartum. Interestingly, it has been suggested that very low birth weight infants whose mothers received magnesium sulfate have a significantly decreased risk of developing **cerebral palsy** or mental retardation (Schendel et al., 1996). In patients with eclampsia, the perinatal mortality rate has been reported to be between 130 and 300 per 1,000 cases, and eclampsia recurs in approximately 5% of subsequent pregnancies (Cunningham et al., 1997).

Trauma and Abuse

It has been reported that 1 in 12 women will suffer some form of trauma during pregnancy (Cunningham et al., 2001). Trauma in pregnancy can be divided into blunt and penetrating abdominal trauma. Motor vehicle accidents are the most common type of blunt abdominal trauma seen, with falls and assaults being seen with approximately equal lesser frequency (Connolly et al., 1997). The most common complication seen with blunt abdominal trauma in pregnancy is preterm labor, which occurs in up to 28% of cases. There is some evidence that frontal automobile collisions are associated with fewer maternal and fetal complications than side-impact collisions are as evidenced by fewer contractions and more term deliveries (Aitokallio-Tallberg & Halmesmaki, 1997). A more serious complication of blunt abdominal trauma is placental abruption, which can progress rapidly and can result in both maternal and fetal morbidity and/or mortality. Penetrating abdominal trauma is less common than blunt trauma in pregnancy. The pregnant uterus is actually protective of the mother's internal organs. The incidence of organ injury in pregnant patients who suffer penetrating abdominal trauma, usually from gunshot or stab wounds, is between 16% and 38%, which is considerably lower than the 80%–90% injury rate in the general population (Stone, 1999).

Obstetric Conditions

Preterm Labor

Preterm labor puts the fetus at significant risk, with 75% of all neonatal deaths not associated with congenital anomalies attributable to preterm delivery. One third of preterm deliveries are associated with placental hemorrhage or maternal hypertension. Importantly, two thirds are due to spontaneous preterm labor with or without rupture of membranes (Meis et al., 1995). Many factors increase the risk of preterm delivery. Prior preterm delivery is most predictive of recurrent preterm birth, with a rate of 20%–30%. Other contributing causes include an overdistended uterus (e.g., from multiple gestations), uterine or **cervical** abnormalities, low socioeconomic status, sexually transmitted diseases, intrauterine infections, and substance abuse. In the United States, women presenting with spontaneous preterm labor between 24 and 34 weeks' gestation and contractions are often treated with a tocolytic drug. The efficacy of tocolytics is questionable, but there are data to suggest they may delay delivery 24–48 hours. This may provide the opportunity to transport the mother to a tertiary care center and to administer corticosteroids to promote fetal lung maturity.

Preterm Membrane Rupture

Preterm membrane rupture between 24 and 34 weeks EGA occurs in less than 2% of pregnancies but contributes to 20% of all prenatal deaths during that period (Cox, Williams, & Leveno, 1988; Parry & Strauss, 1998). Preterm membrane rupture is associated with other obstetric complications, including multifetal gestation, **chorioamnionitis** (infection of the amniotic membranes), and FHR abnormalities. Tocolytics have not been effective in delaying delivery in the presence of rupture of membranes. Although a NIH Consensus Conference concluded that the use of corticosteroids to promote fetal lung maturation in the presence of rupture of membranes is controversial, these medications are often given. Antibiotics are prescribed to these women as they prolong the interval between rupture of membranes and delivery (Mercer & Arheart, 1995).

Abruption

Placental abruption, or abruptio placenta, is premature separation of the placenta from the uterus (Figure 4.2). It is a significant cause of maternal and fetal mortality and occurs in approximately 1% of pregnancies in the United States (Saftlas et al., 1991). The usual presentation of an abruption includes bleeding, uterine contractions, and FHR abnormalities. The uterine contractions are painful and often very close together, resulting in rapid delivery. The fetus may develop distress rapidly and then may deteriorate quickly secondary to the significant and ongoing blood loss. A cesarean delivery is often necessary because of fetal distress. Perinatal mortality rates associated with placental abruption range from 20% to 40%. Risk factors for abruption include ruptured membranes, chorioamnionitis, preeclampsia, maternal age greater than 35 years, and cocaine abuse (Kramer et al., 1997). The risk of recurrence is reported to be between 4% and 12%. Cigarette smoking is associated with placental abruptions, with each pack per day smoked increasing the risk by 40%, and the perinatal mortality rate when placental abruption occurs is also significantly increased (Raymond & Mills, 1993). Trauma is also a significant cause of placental abruption. Interestingly, abruption occurs more frequently with a male fetus.

Perinatal Infections

Cytomegalovirus (CMV), **parvovirus** B19, varicella zoster virus (chickenpox), and toxoplasmosis may be acquired by the mother and lead to adverse perinatal consequences. Typically, perinatal infections have more severe fetal consequences when acquired early in pregnancy.

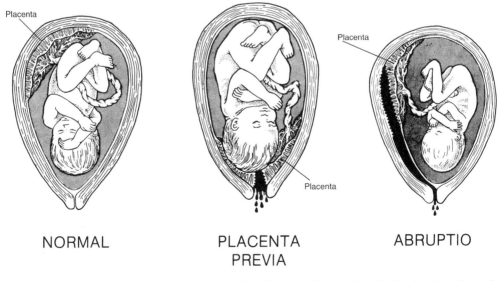

NORMAL   PLACENTA   ABRUPTIO
                   PREVIA

Figure 4.2. A normal placenta is located in the upper third of the uterus. In placenta previa, the placenta is abnormally placed so that it lies over the cervical opening. During labor, as the cervix dilates, the placenta may tear and bleeding may occur. In abruptio placenta, a normally placed placenta becomes partially separated from the uterine wall in the second or third trimester, and bleeding results.

(See Chapter 3 for discussion of the effects of CMV, varicella zoster, and toxoplasmosis infections on prenatal development.)

Although viral infections are usually contracted prior to or during delivery, most bacterial infections develop after birth, with the exception of Group B streptococcal (GBS) infection. GBS is the most common cause of neonatal meningitis and **sepsis** (McKenna & Iams, 1998). Approximately 8,000 cases of neonatal GBS infections occur yearly, with an incidence of 1.8 cases per 1,000 live births. Although maternal GBS infections are fairly benign, neonatal GBS infections carry a high risk of morbidity and mortality. Therefore, penicillin G (Bicillin) is recommended in labor for women colonized with GBS or those at high risk.

Risk factors indicating antibiotic **prophylaxis** during labor include prematurity, preterm rupture of membranes, membrane rupture more than 18 hours before delivery, previous birth of a child with GBS infection, or maternal fever during labor greater than or equal to 38.0° C. Maternal GBS colonization is diagnosed by lower vaginal or rectal culture or presence in maternal urine. ACOG concurs with recommendations of the Centers for Disease Control and Prevention to culture all pregnant women at 35–37 weeks' gestation or to adopt a strategy for selective screening based on clinical risk factors.

Special Conditions

Some other conditions seen in pregnancy that are associated with increased risk to the mother and fetus include cases of abnormal placentation (placement of the placenta), multiple gestations, and presentation of the fetus during labor in a position other than head-down, or **vertex**.

Abnormal Placentation

Usually, the placenta is attached to the upper third of the uterus. Approximately 1 in every 200 pregnancies, however, is complicated by **placenta previa,** in which the placenta is implanted low in the uterus and lies over the cervical opening (Love & Wallace, 1996; Figure 4.2). The more extensive the overlay, the greater the risk of bleeding when the cervix dilates during labor. Even before labor begins, the effacement of the cervix or uterine contractions can cause bleeding. Significant hemorrhaging may endanger both the fetus and the mother.

With improvements in obstetric care, including cesarean sections and blood transfusions, maternal mortality is rare. Perinatal infant mortality remains a concern, however, primarily as a result of preterm birth in women with placenta previa. Placenta previa is more common in women who are older than 35 years of age or who have had multiple abortions. In addition, maternal smoking and a past cesarean place women at increased risk for a placenta previa. Women with placenta previa are often placed on both bed rest and pelvic rest (i.e., no intercourse), to prolong pregnancy and avoid bleeding. A cesarean is frequently performed in an attempt to avoid life-threatening hemorrhage, once it is has been determined that the fetus is mature enough to survive outside the uterus. At the time of cesarean delivery, women with placenta previa have a 5%–10% likelihood of requiring a hysterectomy. The recurrence rate for placenta previa is about 2.5% (Rasmussen, Albrechtsen, & Dalaker, 1996).

Another type of abnormal implantation is called *placenta accreta*, which is a result of the placenta abnormally attaching itself directly to the muscular wall of the uterus. Placenta accreta is usually associated with significant hemorrhage when the placenta is removed after delivery. Risk factors for developing placenta accreta include placenta previa, prior cesarean delivery, prior uterine curettage, and advanced maternal age (greater than 35 years old at delivery). Patients with placenta previa and one previous cesarean delivery have a 25% risk of having placenta accreta. The risk of placenta accreta rises to 50%–60% when there is a history of multiple cesarean births. These cases often result in such significant hemorrhage that transfusion and hysterectomy are required.

Multiple Gestations

With the advent and now commonplace use of assisted reproductive technology, the incidence of multiple gestation pregnancies has increased dramatically. Between 1974 and 1994, the rate of twins increased from 1 per 54 to 1 per 40 births and triplets from 1 per 3,144 to 1 per 838 births (Luke, 1998), which are 35% and 275% increases, respectively. Multiple gestations now account for more than 2% of all pregnancies (Figure 4.3). This is important because multiple gestations are at significantly increased risk for low birth weight and preterm labor and birth. Given that the two strongest factors related to perinatal survival are gestational age at delivery and relative birth weight, it is easy to see that multiple gestations are at special risk for short- and long-term complications.

Abnormal Presentations

A breech presentation is one in which the fetal buttocks or lower extremities are the presenting part or parts. A frank breech presentation means the infant's legs are flexed at the hip and extended at the knees. This kind of breech may be a candidate for vaginal delivery. An incomplete breech presentation is one in which a foot or knee is the presenting part; the risk of umbilical cord prolapse is increased in this case. The incidence of breech presentation at term is approximately 3%. Some factors that increase the likelihood of a breech presentation include multiple gestation, uterine anomalies, polyhydramnios, and pelvic tumors. If a breech infant is delivered vaginally, the umbilical cord is compressed by the infant's body until the head is delivered. For this reason, it is extremely important for the breech infant to be delivered in a timely manner. Although a vaginal breech delivery may be performed safely, strict criteria must be met in order to accomplish this. Most breech infants are delivered by cesarean.

An alternative to breech vaginal delivery or cesarean is external cephalic version (ECV). In an ECV, an attempt is made to turn the fetus to the vertex (head down) position by manipulating the maternal abdomen. It is usually attempted at 37 weeks' gestation and has a success rate of approximately 60%. The rate of conversion back to a breech position is very low. Thus, most

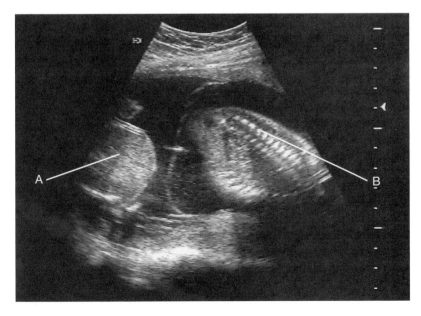

Figure 4.3. Ultrasound of a pregnant woman carrying twins. This is a cross-section view through the maternal abdomen. The head of one fetus (A) and the spinal column of the second fetus (B) can be seen.

fetuses that are successfully turned will be delivered vaginally, allowing the mother to avoid a cesarean.

A transverse presentation of the fetus at term occurs in approximately 1 in 360 deliveries. It is often initially suspected by inspection of the maternal abdomen that appears unusually wide. Common causes and associated anomalies in transverse lies include previous multiple gestations, excessive amniotic fluid, prematurity, and placenta previa. If the fetus remains in a transverse position, vaginal delivery is impossible. If the amniotic sac breaks, the fetus is at risk for prolapsing the umbilical cord, necessitating emergency cesarean delivery.

Face presentation, in which the neck of the fetus is hyperextended and the chin is the presenting part, occurs in only 2 per 1,000 pregnancies. It is diagnosed by vaginal exam. Risk factors include previous multiple gestations, an anencephalic fetus (see Chapter 24), and a large fetus. With normal labor, face presentations will often convert to the normal vertex position and can be delivered vaginally.

BIRTH INJURIES AND DEFECTS

Birth injuries occur in 2–7 per 1,000 deliveries (Creasy & Resnik, 1999). Some of the most common injuries include facial nerve palsy, fracture of the clavicle, and brachial plexus injuries.

The facial nerve can be injured during delivery by compression. Although often attributed to forceps delivery, the majority of cases are encountered after either cesarean or spontaneous vaginal deliveries. Nearly all of these injuries resolve quickly within the first few days of life.

Fractured clavicles occur in approximately 4 per 1,000 vaginal births (Roberts et al., 1995). Although these may occur during deliveries complicated by shoulder dystocia (in which the shoulder becomes lodged in the mother's pelvic opening after delivery of the baby's head), they often occur during uncomplicated births. A large study of more than 65,000 deliveries looked at the occurrence of clavicular fractures in an attempt to determine what factors may be associated and therefore avoided. The researchers concluded that this injury appears to be unpredictable, but fortunately it does not cause long-term problems (Roberts et al., 1995).

Brachial plexus injuries are reported to occur in approximately 1–2 per 1,000 deliveries (Gilbert, Thomas, & Beate, 1999). There are multiple factors associated with brachial plexus injuries, but none of them have been found to be predictive enough to permit prevention. It is known, however, that women with gestational diabetes who undergo a forceps delivery or vacuum extraction or who experience shoulder dystocia are at increased risk for delivering a baby with a brachial plexus injury. The most common types of brachial plexus injuries are Erb's palsy and Klumpke's palsy. In Erb's palsy, the affected arm of the infant lies limp at the side; the grasp reflex remains intact. In Klumpke's palsy, the hand is paralyzed, and the grasp reflex is absent. Fortunately, more than 90% of all brachial plexus injuries resolve within 6 months with no sequelae (Nocon et al., 1993).

Certain malformations of the fetus may make labor and delivery difficult or may necessitate a cesarean delivery. For example, fetuses with hydrocephalus may have such an enlarged head that vaginal delivery is impossible. Fetuses with enlarged bladders or renal/hepatic tumors also may not be candidates for vaginal delivery because of the enlarged fetal abdomen.

SUMMARY

The period of late pregnancy, labor, and delivery is a critical one for the live birth and normal development of the infant. Complications can result from such different sources as chronic maternal diseases, preeclampsia, preterm labor and delivery, premature rupture of membranes, perinatal maternal illness, abnormal placentation, breech presentation, multiple gestation, and birth injuries. The impact of such complications can be severe and long lasting. Fortunately, the vast majority of babies are born well, and improved prenatal care and surveillance have improved outcomes in high-risk pregnancies. Yet, additional public health measures, including improved prenatal care for teenagers and women who are homeless, are needed to ensure the health of pregnant women and their infants.

REFERENCES

Aitokallio-Tallberg, A., & Halmesmaki, E. (1997). Motor vehicle accident during the second or third trimester of pregnancy. *Acta Obstetricia et Gynecologica Scandinavica, 76,* 313–317.

American College of Obstetricians and Gynecologists (ACOG). (1994). *Diabetes and pregnancy* (ACOG Technical Bulletin 200). Washington, DC: Author.

American College of Obstetricians and Gynecologists (ACOG). (1995a). *Dystocia and the augmentation of labor* (ACOG Technical Bulletin 218). Washington, DC: Author.

American College of Obstetricians and Gynecologists. (1995b). *Fetal heart rate patterns: Monitoring, interpretation, and management* (ACOG Technical Bulletin 207). Washington, DC: Author.

Chauhan, S.P., Perry, K.G., Jr., McLaughlin, B.N., et al. (1996). Diabetic ketoacidosis complicating pregnancy. *Journal of Perinatology, 16,* 173–175.

Connolly, A., Katz, V.L., Bash, K.L., et al. (1997). Trauma and pregnancy. *American Journal of Perinatology, 14,* 331–336.

Cox, S., Williams, M.L., & Leveno, K.J. (1988). The natural history of preterm ruptured membranes: What to expect from expectant management. *Obstetrics and Gynecology, 71,* 558.

Creasy, R.K., & Resnik, R. (1999). *Maternal–fetal medicine* (4th ed.). Philadelphia: W.B. Saunders.

Cunningham, F.G., MacDonald, P.C., Gant, N.F., et al. (1997). *Williams obstetrics* (20th ed.). Norwalk, CT: Appleton & Lange.

Cunningham, F.G., MacDonald, P.C., Leveno, K.J., et al. (2001). *Williams obstetrics* (21st ed.). New York: McGraw-Hill.

DiMarco, C.S., Ramsey, P.S., Williams, L.H., et al. (2000). Temporal trends in operative obstetric delivery: 1992–1999. *Obstetrics and Gynecology, 95*(4, Suppl. 1), S39.

Dunne, F.P. (1999). Pregestational diabetes mellitus and pregnancy. *Trends in Endocrinology and Metabolism, 10,* 179–182.

Eskew, P.N., Jr., Saywell, R.M., Jr., Zollinger, T.W., et al. (1994). Trends in the frequency of cesarean delivery: A 21-year experience, 1970–1990. *Journal of Reproductive Medicine, 39,* 809–817.

Flamm, B.L. (1995). Vaginal birth after cesarean section. In B.L. Flamm & E.J. Quilligan (Eds.), *Cesarean section: Guidelines for appropriate utilization* (pp. 51–64). New York: Springer-Verlag.

Freeman, R.K., Garite, T.H., & Nageotte, M.P. (1991). *Fetal heart rate monitoring* (2nd ed.). Philadelphia: Lippincott Williams & Wilkins.

Gilbert, W.M., Thomas, N.S., & Beate, D. (1999). Associated factors in 1611 cases of brachial plexus injuries. *Obstetrics and Gynecology, 93,* 536–540.

Hoyert, D.L, Freedman, M.A., Strobino, D.M., et al. (2001). Annual summary of vital statistics: 2000. *Pediatrics, 108,* 1241–1255.

Kramer, M.S., Usher, R.H., Pollack, R., et al. (1997). Etiologic determinants of abruptio placentae. *Obstetrics and Gynecology, 89,* 221–226.

Love, C.D., & Wallace, E.M. (1996). Pregnancies complicated by placenta previa: What is appropriate management? *British Journal of Obstetrics and Gynaecology, 103,* 864.

Luke, B. (1998). What is the influence of maternal weight gain on the fetal growth of twins? *Clinical Obstetrics and Gynecology, 41,* 57–64.

Meis, P.T., Michielutte, R., Peters, T.J., et al. (1995). Factors associated with preterm birth in Cardiff, Wales. *American Journal of Obstetrics and Gynecology, 173,* 590.

Mercer, B.M., & Arheart, K.L. (1995). Antimicrobial therapy in expectant management of preterm premature rupture of membranes. *Lancet, 346,* 1271.

McKenna, D.S., & Iams, J.D. (1998). Group B streptococcal infections. *Seminars in Perinatology, 22,* 267–276.

Mroz, L.A. (1999). Hypertensive disorders of pregnancy. *Anesthesiology Clinics of North America, 17,* 679–691.

Napolitano, P.G., Hoeldtke, N., Moore, K., et al. (1997). The fetoplacental pressor effects of low-dose acetylsalicylic acid and angiotensin II in the ex vivo cotyledon model. *American Journal of Obstetrics and Gynecology, 177,* 1093–1096.

Nocon, J.J., McKenzie, D.K., Thomas, L.J., et al. (1993). Shoulder dystocia: An analysis of risks and obstetric maneuvers. *American Journal of Obstetrics and Gynecology, 168*(6, Pt. 1), 1732–1737; discussion 1737–1739.

Norwitz, E., Robinson, J., & Challis, J. (1999). The control of labor. *New England Journal of Medicine, 341,* 660–666.

O'Sullivan, J.B. (1982). Body weight and subsequent diabetes mellitus. *Journal of the American Medical Association, 248,* 949–952.

Parry, S., & Strauss, J.F., III. (1998). Premature rupture of the fetal membranes. *New England Journal of Medicine, 338,* 663–670.

Rasmussen, S., Albrechtsen, S., & Dalaker, D. (1996). Obstetric history and the risk of placenta previa. *Acta Obstetricia et Gynecologica Scandinavica, 79,* 502–507.

Raymond, E.G., & Mills, J.L. (1993). Placental abruption: Maternal risk factors and associated fetal conditions. *Acta Obstetricia et Gynecologica Scandinavica, 72,* 633–639.

Roberts, S.W., Hernandez, C., Maberry, M.C., et al. (1995). Obstetric clavicular fracture: The enigma of normal birth. *Obstetrics and Gynecology, 86,* 978.

Rosen, M.G., Dickinson, J.C., & Westhoff, C.L. (1991). Vaginal birth after cesarean: A meta-analysis of morbidity and mortality. *Obstetrics and Gynecology, 77,* 465–470.

Saftlas, A.F., Olson, D.R., Atrash, H.K., et al. (1991). National trends in the incidence of abruptio placentae, 1979–1987. *Obstetrics and Gynecology, 78,* 1081–1086.

Schendel, D.E., Berg, C.J., Yeargin-Allsopp, M., et al. (1996). Prenatal magnesium sulfate exposure and the risk for cerebral palsy or mental retardation among very low-birth-weight children aged 3 to 5 years. *Journal of the American Medical Association, 276,* 1805–1843.

Sibai, B. (1996). Treatment of hypertension in pregnant women. *New England Journal of Medicine, 335,* 257–265.

Stone, I.K. (1999). Trauma in the obstetric patient. *Obstetrics and Gynecology Clinics of North America, 26,* 459–467.

Vintzileos, A.M., Antsaklis, A., Varvarigos, I., et al. (1993). A randomized trial of intrapartum electronic fetal heart rate monitoring versus intermittent auscultation. *Obstetrics and Gynecology, 81,* 899–907.

Wesley, B., Van den Berg, B., & Reece, E.A. (1992). The effect of operative vaginal delivery on cognitive development. *American Journal of Obstetrics and Gynecology, 166,* 288.

Yam, J., Chua, S., & Arulkumaran, S. (2000a). Intrapartum fetal pulse oximetry, Part 1: Principles and technical issues. *Obstetrical and Gynecological Survey, 55,* 163–172.

Yam, J., Chua, S., & Arulkumaran, S. (2000b). Intrapartum fetal pulse oximetry, Part 2: Clinical application. *Obstetrical and Gynecological Survey, 55,* 173–183.

5 The First Weeks of Life

Laura Placke Ward and Susan K. McCune

Upon completion of this chapter, the reader will:

- understand changes in the function of the heart and lungs at birth
- understand the meaning of the Apgar score and its uses and limitations
- know clinical signs of common congenital malformations
- understand causes and potential treatments for hypoxic-ischemic encephalopathy and intracranial hemorrhages
- grasp the basic components of the immune system and the most common neonatal infections
- be able to discuss causes and consequences of hypoglycemia and other metabolic disturbances, including inborn errors of metabolism
- know causes and the significance of neonatal seizures

The transition of the infant from the protected intrauterine environment to physiological independence from the mother is difficult. The circulatory system must change so that blood reaches the lungs to be oxygenated, the lungs must expand so the infant can breathe, and body temperature and biochemistry must be regulated, to name but a few transitions needed after birth. It is therefore reassuring that most infants make this transition successfully. Those who do not, however, are at risk for life-threatening medical problems and for developmental disabilities. This chapter details the changes that must occur in the first days after birth and the complications that may result if these are not successfully accomplished.

MARY

Jane's pregnancy had been unremarkable except for gestational diabetes that had been controlled with diet. Her daughter, Mary, was born without difficulty and had a heart rate of 130 beats per minute and a good cry. Her extremities, however, only had slight flexion, and her arms and legs were blue at 1 minute of age. By 5 minutes, she was active with a lusty cry and good heart rate, but her hands and feet continued to be blue. On the basis of the **Apgar scoring system** (Table 5.1), Mary received Apgar scores of 8 at 1 minute and 9 at 5 minutes. She was taken from the delivery room to the nursery after being briefly held by Jane. There, she was noted to have a low glucose of 30 milligrams per deciliter. Mary was fed frequently, and her blood sugar stabilized over 24 hours. She was able to be discharged with her mother the next day.

MICHAEL

Nancy became very concerned when she could no longer feel her baby moving in her 38th week. She was rushed to the hospital, where her doctors had difficulty detecting a fetal heart rate. An emergency cesarean section was performed. Michael was ashen and limp

Table 5.1.   The Apgar scoring system and sample scores

	Points			1-minute score		5-minute score	
	0	1	2	Mary	Michael	Mary	Michael
Heart rate	Absent	Less than 100	More than 100	2	0	2	2
Respiratory effort	Absent	Slow, irregular	Normal respiration; crying	2	0	2	0
Muscle tone	Limp	Some flexion	Active motion	1	0	2	0
Gag reflex	No response	Grimace	Sneeze; cough	2	0	2	1
Color	Blue all over; pale	Blue extremities	Pink all over	1	0	1	1
			Totals	8	0	9	4

with no breathing efforts, reflexes, or heartbeat. A tube was inserted into his **trachea** to inflate his lungs. Catheters were placed in his umbilical blood vessels, and he was given **adrenaline**. By 5 minutes, his heart rate responded to the ventilation and medication and was 120 beats per minute, but he continued to be limp with no respiratory effort of his own. His body had become pink, but his extremities remained pale. After continued resuscitation, by 10 minutes he had a stable heart rate and made some weak respirations on his own. There was some flexion of the extremities and a facial grimace. His extremities remained pale. Based on these physical findings, his Apgar scores were estimated to be 0 at 1 minute, 4 at 5 minutes, and 6 at 10 minutes (Table 5.1). He was taken to the intensive care nursery (ICN), where his **acidosis** was corrected and his blood pressure supported with fluid and medication. Over the next few days, he continued to have difficulty maintaining adequate oxygen levels in his blood, and he developed seizures that required treatment with phenobarbital (Luminal). Gradually, Michael's lungs improved and he could be taken off the **ventilator.** A computed tomography (CT) scan of his head initially showed diffuse cerebral edema (brain swelling) that resolved within a week. An **electroencephalogram (EEG)** was abnormal but also improved within a week. He gradually became more alert and awake and did not have further seizures. He was able to be discharged after spending 2 weeks in the ICN. Even though he appeared "normal" at the time of discharge, Michael's low Apgar scores and his early clinically abnormal neurological exam suggest that he may be at significant risk for having developmental disabilities.

CHANGES IN CARDIOPULMONARY FUNCTION AT BIRTH

Significant changes in the **pulmonary** (lung) and cardiovascular (heart and blood vessel) systems must occur at the time of birth. The infant must change from being totally dependent on the mother and the placenta to becoming self-sufficient in a brief period of time. The first breath is both the most critical in this process and the most difficult. The fluid that filled the lungs during fetal life must be replaced with air. This change is aided by the passage through the birth canal, which expels fluid, and the first cry usually supplies sufficient force to inflate the lungs. Once the **alveoli** (air sacs) in the lungs are open, they normally maintain their shape because of the presence of a chemical called surfactant (see Chapter 6).

During fetal life, less than 10% of the blood flow from the heart goes through the lungs. Instead, oxygen reaches the fetus through the placenta (Figure 5.1). At birth, air entry into the lungs leads to a decrease in pulmonary blood pressure, encouraging blood flow to the lungs. During the first few hours to days after birth, these changes are tenuous, and any perturbation

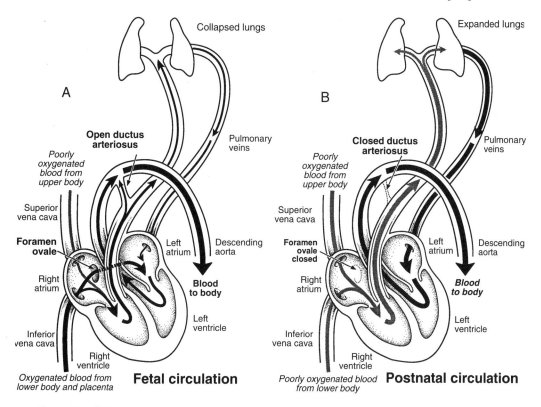

Figure 5.1. A) Fetal circulation. The foramen ovale and patent (open) ductus arteriosus allow the blood flow to bypass the unexpanded lungs. B) Postnatal circulation. The fetal bypasses close off with expansion of the lungs.

will cause the infant to revert to the fetal circulation (with little blood flow passing through the lungs). When the fetal form of circulation continues after birth, it is called *persistent pulmonary hypertension of the newborn* (PPHN). This can be life threatening and may require treatment with mechanical ventilation, high-frequency ventilation, or certain medications (e.g., nitric oxide). In the most severe cases, a heart–lung bypass procedure called *extracorporeal membrane oxygenation* (ECMO) may be needed to allow the heart and lungs time to rest and go through the typical transition.

In addition to undergoing the changes seen in the heart and lungs, the infant must take over the function of removing toxins from the blood. When the cord is clamped, the umbilical vein and ductus venosus close, allowing blood to pass through the liver, where it is **detoxified** prior to entering the heart (Figure 5.2).

The newborn must also quickly be able to regulate body temperature and take in nutrition. In the delivery room, thermoregulation is difficult because the infant is wet and has a large surface area and little body fat. This is the reason that newborns are quickly dried and placed under a warmer prior to being swaddled in blankets. Nutrition starts early, with the infant being put to the mother's breast in the delivery room if possible. If the infant is too sick or if the suck and swallow mechanism is inefficient, nutrition may be given as intravenous fluids or nasogastric feeds.

Prematurity may also disrupt the normal transition process. Infants born at less than 32 weeks' gestation often produce insufficient surfactant to keep the alveoli in the lungs open, placing these infants at significant risk for developing respiratory distress syndrome (Avery, Fletcher, & MacDonald, 1999; see Chapter 6).

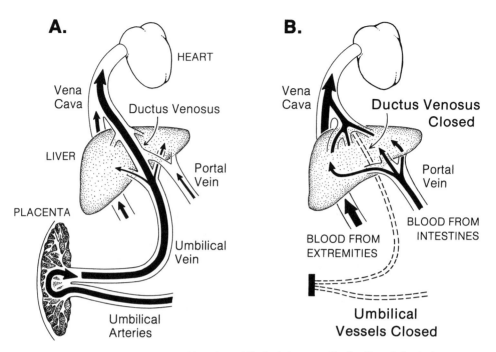

Figure 5.2. A) Fetal circulation. The blood from the umbilical vein bypasses the liver through the ductus venosus. B) Postnatal circulation. The umbilical vein ceases to function and the ductus venosus closes. Now blood from the body passes through the liver, where it is cleansed.

THE APGAR SCORE

In the past, physicians found that they needed a way to communicate with each other concerning the severity of illness in the immediate neonatal period. Dr. Virginia Apgar provided such a means through a scoring system she developed in the early 1950s. There are five components to the score: heart rate, respiratory effort, muscle tone, reflex irritability, and color. Each is scored between 0 and 2, with a maximum total score of 10. A perfect score of 10, however, is rare due to the normal cyanosis (blueness) of the infant's hands and feet in the first minutes after birth. A low Apgar score (less than 5) provides evidence that the infants was in distress in the delivery room. The initial hypothesis was that a low Apgar score would correlate with developmental disabilities. It was subsequently shown, however, that although a typical Apgar score, such as Mary's, generally predicts a good outcome, an abnormal score such as Michael's is not necessarily predictive of developmental disability. One study found that of children with an Apgar score of less than 4 at 5 minutes who survived, 64% were developmentally typical (Jain et al., 1991). Conversely, in a study of children with cerebral palsy, only 27% of them had received an Apgar score of less than 6 five minutes after birth (Nelson, 1989). More recent studies have demonstrated that an elevated nucleated (fetal) red blood cell count at birth (Buonocore et al., 1999), moderate to severe encephalopathy (Aggarwal et al., 1998), and/or an abnormal neurobehavioral assessment at the time of hospital discharge (Wolf et al., 1998) are more highly correlated with subsequent developmental disability than is the 5-minute Apgar score. In addition, certain findings of EEG and brain imaging studies have enhanced the predictability of developmental disabilities (Rose & Lombroso, 1970). Hence, although Michael's Apgar scores are worrisome, the fact that he had only a mild encephalopathy and that his neurodevelopmental exam was unremarkable prior to discharge are reassuring, but he will need to have close neurodevelopmental follow-up.

NEONATAL MORBIDITY AND MORTALITY

In 2000 in the United States, there were approximately 4 million births. During the first year of life, 6.9 per 1,000 of these infants died, more than half in the first month of life (Hoyert et al., 2001). The most common causes of mortality in the first month include congenital malformations, prematurity and/or low birth weight, respiratory distress syndrome, infections, perinatal complications, and intrauterine hypoxia or **asphyxia** (Guyer et al., 1999). In addition to mortality, there is a significant risk of **morbidity** (complications; Table 5.2), including intracranial hemorrhage, infection, hypoglycemia and **hypocalcemia,** inborn errors of metabolism, consequences of maternal substance abuse, jaundice, and seizures. Many of these neonatal disorders can be seen in both full-term and premature infants but may be manifest in a different manner in premature infants. This chapter focuses on the full-term infant; issues concerning the premature infant are covered in Chapter 6.

Congenital Malformations

Congenital malformations can occur in any organ in the body and can be associated with genetic defects, exposure to teratogens (substances capable of producing physical defects in the developing fetus), or a combination of genetic and environmental factors. The malformations that lead to developmental disabilities (e.g., neural tube defects; holoprosencephaly or lissencephaly, see Appendix B; **agenesis of the corpus callosum;** abnormalities of neuronal migration, see Chapter 13) predominantly occur during the development of the central nervous system. Many of these defects are incompatible with survival outside the womb. Infants who do survive have an increased susceptibility to various complications in the newborn period, including intracranial hemorrhage, apnea, hypoglycemia, and infection. After the neonatal period, these children are likely to develop seizures, cerebral palsy, mental retardation, or other developmental disabilities as a result of the underlying congenital abnormality and newborn complications. For many of these infants, treatment of the abnormality is not available or will have little effect on outcome. It is important, however, that these children be identified so that they can receive early intervention services to prevent secondary impairments and so that their families can receive assistance in obtaining appropriate care and psychosocial support.

Hypoxic-Ischemic Encephalopathy

Hypoxic-ischemic injury results from alterations in oxygen delivery and blood flow to the brain of the fetus or newborn. This is the most important cause of morbidity in term infants, but fortunately it occurs in only 2%–3% of these infants (Simon, 1999). It is also a major problem in preterm infants (see Chapter 6).

Similar to the Apgar score, there is a scoring system for hypoxic-ischemic encephalopathy (Sarnat & Sarnat, 1976). Stage I infants have mild encephalopathy and typical long-term neurodevelopment. Stage II (moderate) and stage III (severe) infants generally have early signs of neurological dysfunction, and almost all of these infants eventually have developmental disabilities. Premature infants who suffer a hypoxic-ischemic **insult** appear to have a better outcome than their full-term counterparts. The reason for this difference in outcome is not well understood.

The initial step in treating this disorder is accurate diagnosis. This involves using the Sarnat scoring system followed by a neuroimaging procedure (CT or MRI [magnetic resonance imaging] scan; Blankenberg et al., 2000). There is a specific neuroimaging pattern of white

Table 5.2. Medical disorders in newborns

Hypoxic-ischemic encephalopathy
Intracranial hemorrhage
Sepsis
Hypoglycemia
Hypocalcemia
Inborn errors of metabolism
Effects of maternal substance abuse
Hyperbilirubinemia
Seizures

matter injury following hypoxic-ischemic insult in full-term infants (Campistol et al., 1999). The parasagittal area of the brain (around the central plane of the head) is most vulnerable because it is at the far reaches of blood supplies and therefore at the highest risk of receiving inadequate oxygen and nutrients (Figure 5.3a). In addition, there may be **focal infarcts** (strokes) due to the blockage of a single major artery (Figure 5.3b). Finally, prolonged hypoxic-ischemic injury can result in cerebral edema that can progress to generalized **atrophy** in the brain (loss of tissue; Figure 5.3c).

The more localized the lesion, the more specific the neurological dysfunction. One example is hemiplegic cerebral palsy, in which the injury occurs on one side of the brain and leads to weakness and spasticity in the limbs on the other side. Another example is damage to the basal ganglia in the center of the brain, which results in **dyskinetic cerebral palsy** (Hill & Volpe, 1989; see Chapter 23). More global insults result in generalized motor and cognitive dysfunction.

Long-term consequences of hypoxic-ischemic injury are a result of the length and severity of the insult. They range in severity from **spastic quadriplegia** and mental retardation to learning disabilities (Robertson & Finer, 1988; Volpe, 2001). Infants subjected to asphyxia are at particular risk for visual and hearing impairments (Simon, 1999).

It would be useful to have early prognostic indicators of outcome following a hypoxic-ischemic insult. The classic approach has been to use the neurological examination (Wolf et al., 1998), MRI, and EEGs (Torres & Blaw, 1968; Whyte, 1993). Newer modalities such as **magnetic resonance spectroscopy (MRS), single photon emission computed tomography (SPECT),** and **positron emission tomography (PET)** scanning are being tested to assess the severity of the initial insult on metabolic function and blood flow to the brain. These studies have not yet demonstrated the value of these tests in predicting long-term neurological outcome (Shankaran, Kottamasu, & Kuhns, 1993). Finally, some biochemical markers such as elevated cerebrospinal fluid levels of lactate (a marker for acidosis) and interleukin-6 (an immune compound) may also correlate with the severity of the hypoxic-ischemic insult, but long-term studies have not been done to correlate these markers with neurodevelopmental outcome (Fernandez et al., 1986; Martin-Ancel et al., 1997).

Effective therapy to protect the brain from hypoxic-ischemic encephalopathy has been elusive. Antioxidants, such as vitamins E and C (ascorbic acid), have been beneficial in animal models but have been less promising in human trials. Magnesium and calcium channel blocking agents (antihypertensive agents) have also been studied to prevent neuronal cell death under hypoxic-ischemic conditions, but the results have been equivocal. In one study, infants who suffered hypoxic-ischemic insults and were treated with a high dose of phenobarbital (to induce a protective coma) had improved neurodevelopmental outcome when studied at 3 years

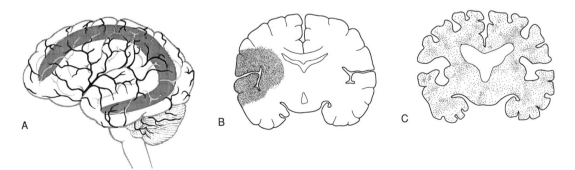

Figure 5.3.   Types of hypoxic-ischemic brain injury. A) A watershed infarct (shaded) occurs in the border zone between two major arterial circulation supplies. B) A focal infarct (stippled) occurs due to complete disruption of flow of a major artery. C) Diffuse hypodense areas (stippled) and generalized brain atrophy usually occur because of prolonged lack of oxygen.

of age (Hall, Hall, & Daily, 1998). Other promising therapies include brain hypothermia (lowering brain temperature), and new classes of medications such as monosialogangliosides, nitric oxide synthase inhibitors, excitatory amino acid antagonists, and nerve growth factors (Tan & Parks, 1999). Future success in ameliorating the long-term neurodevelopmental consequences of hypoxic-ischemic injury depends on accurate diagnosis and early implementation of one or more of the therapeutic modalities that are currently under investigation.

Intracranial Hemorrhage

Birth is a traumatic event, so bleeding into the head (Figure 5.4) is not uncommon or unexpected. The most common hemorrhage is **cephalohematoma** (superficial bleeding in the parietal region of the skull), which occurs in 1%–3% of newborns (Taeusch, Ballard, & Avery, 1991). In general, no treatment is necessary and the swelling resolves within the first few weeks of life. This bleeding is outside the skull; however, less commonly infants can suffer bleeding within the skull called *intracranial hemorrhage*. The major types of intracranial hemorrhage are **subdural hemorrhage, subarachnoid hemorrhage,** intracerebellar hemorrhage, intraventricular hemorrhage, and intraparenchymal hemorrhage.

Subdural hemorrhage is the least common, and it is clinically serious but can often be evacuated surgically. It involves bleeding below the outer protective layer of the brain, the dura. It occurs most frequently in the full-term infant and is most commonly caused by a traumatic birth. Precipitating factors include a large infant in a small birth canal, rigid pelvic structures, very brief or very long labor, or a delivery that requires forceps or vacuum extraction (Volpe, 2001).

Subarachnoid hemorrhage involves bleeding of the blood vessels below the middle covering of the brain. This is more likely to occur in the premature infant and is relatively benign. Occasionally, an infant has seizures associated with a subarachnoid hemorrhage, but 90% of children with seizures and subarachnoid hemorrhage develop typically.

Intracerebellar hemorrhage, bleeding into the cerebellum, can be serious and is more common in the premature infant. It most often results from trauma or hypoxia.

Intraventricular hemorrhage (bleeding into the ventricles, the spaces in the brain that are filled with cerebrospinal fluid) is more common in premature infants but can also occur in full-

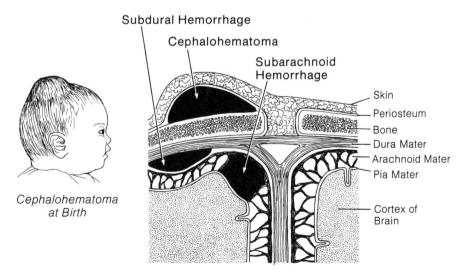

Figure 5.4. Types of hemorrhages in the newborn. Cephalohematoma is frequent; the child with this disorder has a good outcome. Subdural and subarachnoid hemorrhages carry more guarded prognoses.

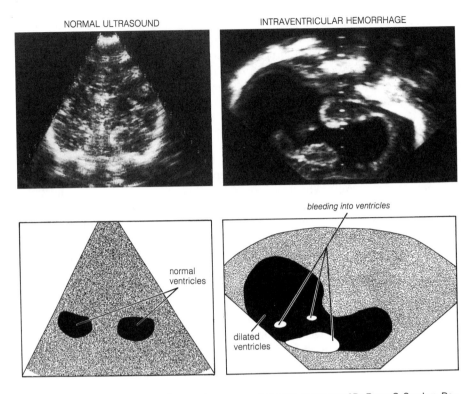

NORMAL ULTRASOUND

INTRAVENTRICULAR HEMORRHAGE

bleeding into ventricles

normal
ventricles

dilated
ventricles

Figure 5.5. Intraventricular hemorrhage as shown on an ultrasound. (Courtesy of Dr. Roger C. Sanders, Department of Radiology, Los Alamos Hospital, Los Alamos, NM.)

term infants (Figure 5.5). Trauma and hypoxic-ischemic injury are the major factors, but in a quarter of infants with intraventricular hemorrhage, no known factor can be identified. Intraventricular hemorrhage presents clinically as irritability, stupor, and seizures. Approximately half of affected infants develop **hydrocephalus** (increased fluid in the ventricles of the brain) and about one-third develop cerebral palsy (Roland, Flodmark, & Hill, 1990). (See Chapter 6 for further discussion of intraventricular hemorrhage.)

Intraparenchymal hemorrhage (bleeding into the brain substance) is uncommon and occurs predominantly in the full-term infant. The most common factors are trauma, stroke, and clotting defect (Volpe, 2001). The outcome generally relates to the location and the extent of the hemorrhage. Death may occur if the hemorrhage is quite severe.

Infection and the Immune System

The immune system functions as the newborn's defense against infection. It is composed of several well-integrated components. Neutrophils (white blood cells) migrate to the site of infection and engulf foreign material including bacteria. Another type of white blood cell, the B **lymphocyte,** generates antibodies that bind to bacteria so they can be recognized and degraded by the neutrophils. A third group of white blood cells, T lymphocytes, are able to kill virus-infected cells. Finally, the complement system includes a cascade of proteins that mediate a range of anti-inflammatory reactions.

Newborns are more susceptible to bacterial, fungal, viral, and parasitic infections because of the immaturity of the various components of the immune system (Wilson, 1986). For instance, an infant's reserve of neutrophils is less than that of an adult. As a result, the infant's supply is rapidly depleted in the face of a serious infection, and his or her ability to replenish this reserve is diminished (Schelonka & Infante, 1998). These cells are also less efficient at binding and ingesting foreign material. Levels of the various complement components are also reduced compared with levels in adults. In addition, newborns are generally able to generate only one class of antibody, IgM, to provide a primary response to infection. Infants must therefore rely on their mother's antibodies, passed on by placental transport or breast milk, to provide additional protection against infection. Finally, the cell-mediated killing capability of T cells is diminished in this age group (Schelonka & Infante, 1998).

Generalized infections (sepsis, or blood poisoning) in the newborn period are most commonly caused by bacterial organisms. Group B *Streptococcus* (GBS) has been the most prevalent causative agent since the 1970s. Approximately 30% of pregnant women are colonized with GBS in their genital tracts, placing 1%–2% of their infants at risk for developing sepsis (Baker, 1997). Several factors increase the risk of this "vertical" transmission of GBS from mother to child: severe colonization or illness in the mother, premature rupture of membranes, prematurity, multiple gestation, and a sibling with a history of GBS sepsis.

GBS infection has two patterns of clinical presentation in the newborn period. The majority of cases are early-onset disease. This type occurs in 1–2 per 1,000 live births, usually presents in the first 24 hours of life, and has a mortality rate of 5%–20% (Baker, 1997). Respiratory distress is the most prominent initial finding, and pneumonia, meningitis, or a generalized life-threatening illness follows. In contrast, late-onset disease occurs less commonly (0.4 per 1,000 live births), and the presentation is later—generally 7 days to 3 months of age (Baker, 1997). Meningitis occurs more frequently in late-onset GBS and mortality is lower.

The second most significant bacterial infection in the neonatal period is caused by ***Escherichia coli***, or ***E. coli***. Together, GBS and *E. coli* account for about 70% of neonatal sepsis (Kaftan & Kinney, 1998). Other microorganisms responsible for bacterial infections in the neonate include *Listeria monocytogenes*, *Haemophilus influenzae*, *Enterococcus*, and *Staphylococcus aureus*. A ramification of the widespread use of broad-spectrum antibiotics is the development of resistant organisms (Toltzis & Blumer, 1995). The judicious use of antibiotics, meticulous attention to hand washing, and isolation of infants at risk are warranted to prevent the emergence of untreatable strains of bacteria.

With the higher survival rates of very low birth weight infants necessitating longer hospital stays, hospital-acquired (nosocomial) infections are becoming more frequent, occurring at a rate of 15%–20% in neonatal intensive care units (Baltimore, 1998). Different pathogens are responsible for this type of infection. The bacteria *Staphylococcus epidermidis* becomes part of the normal skin **flora** within days after birth. It may, however, cause infection in premature infants due to its propensity to adhere to foreign bodies, such as the plastic intravenous catheters that are often necessary to maintain adequate nutrition in these infants. In addition, these infants are more likely to have received intravenous medication to treat suspected sepsis. This treatment may result in suppression of normal bowel flora and allow for the growth of fungus. *Candida albicans*, or **thrush,** is the most common nosocomial fungal infection. *Malassezia furfur* is also an important disease-causing fungus in the ICN, as it flourishes in the lipid-rich environment of the intravenous nutrition given to many premature infants.

In addition to these bacterial and fungal causes of infection in the newborn period, several viruses and other microbes can lead to chronic intrauterine infections and transmission to the neonate during delivery. The most common of these viruses is **herpes simplex virus (HSV) type 2**, which is transmitted via intimate person-to-person contact. Symptoms in adults include painful ulcerations in the genital area, regional lymph node enlargement, fever, and malaise. Studies have shown that one in five pregnant women has a specific antibody to HSV type 2, but a majority of these women have no clinical history of symptomatic disease (Kohl, 1997). Transmission to the infant appears to be a consequence of active viral "shedding" around the time of delivery. The rate of transmission to the infant is much higher (50%) during an initial infection than in recurrent disease (2%–5%; Kohl, 1997). There are three clinical patterns to congenital HSV in the infant. The first pattern, the disseminated form, usually presents between 9 and 11 days of age as sepsis with a clotting disorder, liver dysfunction, pneumonia, and shock; mortality approaches 90%, and survivors often have marked impairments (Kohl, 1997). The encephalitic form presents later, at approximately 3–4 weeks of life, with a brain infection and accompanying seizures. Although the mortality rate is lower than with the disseminated form, long-term neurodevelopmental outcome is often poor. The third type, localized congenital HSV, holds the best outcome. Infants with this type present with skin or eye lesions that respond well to treatment with the antiviral drug acyclovir (Zovirax); however, if treatment is delayed, the infection can progress to become the disseminated or encephalitic form. Because skin lesions are present in only 30% of infants with HSV infection (Kohl, 1997) and because most infants who develop the disease are born to asymptomatic women, congenital HSV must remain a high candidate in the differential diagnosis of causes for fever and sepsis in infants less than 1 month of age.

Infants born to mothers infected with the human immunodeficiency virus (HIV) are at risk for contracting the virus, most commonly during labor and delivery. Great advances have been made in preventing transmission from mother to infant. This infection is discussed in Chapter 8.

Hypoglycemia and Hypocalcemia

After the umbilical cord is clamped, the placenta ceases its role as the infant's primary energy source, and the infant must begin to mobilize its own fuel stores. These stores, however, may be inadequate, and infants often have developmentally immature regulatory enzyme systems, resulting in inefficient use of glucose. Thus, newborns are particularly vulnerable to hypoglycemia, and because glucose is the main energy source for the neonatal brain, its prolonged insufficiency can lead to brain injury.

Unfortunately, the diagnosis of hypoglycemia may be difficult to make because its symptoms are often subtle and nonspecific. These may include lethargy, irritability, jitteriness, vomiting, poor feeding, **hypothermia,** apnea, cyanosis, a high-pitched cry, and seizures. It is not uncommon for affected infants to be asymptomatic; therefore, one must have a high index of suspicion, particularly in high-risk infants.

Certain newborns are particularly prone to hypoglycemia. Because the majority of energy storage (as the polysaccharide **glycogen**) occurs in the fetal liver during the third trimester, premature infants may be born with fewer stores. Likewise, chronically stressed fetuses (e.g., those whose mothers have **toxemia**) may utilize the stored energy before birth. Therefore, both premature and growth-restricted infants are likely to become hypoglycemic shortly after birth. In addition, any acute stress in the newborn period may result in higher energy needs for the infant. Newborns with asphyxia, hypoxia, or sepsis are particularly prone to developing hypoglycemia.

Another category of infants at high risk for hypoglycemia are those with excessive levels of circulating insulin. There are several causes for this, the most common being diabetes in the mother. In infants born to diabetic mothers, the high maternal glucose levels cross the placenta, resulting in fetal hyperglycemia. This, in turn, causes chronic overstimulation of the fetal pancreas in an effort to produce enough insulin to counteract the high sugar levels. Once the umbilical cord is cut following delivery, the elevated glucose levels disappear. The newborn pancreas, however, remains overactive, and the glucose levels can drop precipitously. Other causes of hyperinsulinism are certain maternal medications that can stimulate the fetal pancreatic cells to produce insulin. One example is beta-sympathomimetic agents, which are used to treat preterm labor. Finally, malformations, inborn errors of metabolism, and genetic syndromes may be associated with neonatal hypoglycemia. In these cases, the hypoglycemia is usually a result of the liver's inability to release glucose from its glycogen stores.

Controversy exists over the parameters that define hypoglycemia (Halamek, Benaron, & Stevenson, 1997). Yet, because the risks of treatment are minimal whereas the neurodevelopmental consequences of hypoglycemia may be devastating, most physicians advocate a conservative approach by maintaining the serum glucose above 40 milligrams per deciliter.

For clinically stable infants, treatment of hypoglycemia involves early feedings either by mouth or by nasogastric tube. For infants in whom feedings are not possible, intravenous dextrose should be administered. In more severe cases of hypoglycemia, pharmacologic management with glucagon or steroids may be warranted.

Hypocalcemia is another metabolic perturbation to which the neonate is prone. Preterm newborns, infants of diabetic mothers, and infants with asphyxia are at particular risk. Signs of hypocalcemia are often nonspecific or are similar to hypoglycemia and include jitteriness, apnea, seizures, and cardiac rhythm abnormalities. It is therefore prudent to monitor serum calcium levels in high-risk infants to avoid these consequences.

Inborn Errors of Metabolism

A number of rare congenital enzyme deficiencies can be detected in the first few weeks of life. Some infants present with acute metabolic crises because toxic byproducts are no longer cleared by the placenta. Infants in metabolic crises have episodes of vomiting and lethargy that progress rapidly to coma and death if there is no swift intervention. Clinical management is directed toward preventing further accumulation of the toxic substances and removal of the existing toxins. Initially, it can be difficult to differentiate these infants from those with sepsis. With current diagnosis and treatment, however, many of these infants with life-threatening metabolic abnormalities are surviving. In most cases, the long-term neurological outcome depends on the degree of the initial neurological injury. Newborn screening programs have helped to identify many of these children (further discussed in Chapter 18).

Maternal Substance Abuse

It has been estimated that approximately 5% of all pregnancies are complicated by maternal drug use. The most common drugs of abuse include alcohol, cocaine, heroin, and marijuana. In addition, there is the risk of overuse or inappropriate use of therapeutic drugs. All of these drugs can lead to problems in the newborn period. Seizures can be a complication of withdrawal from heroin, methadone, barbiturates, propoxyphene (Darvon), tricyclic **antidepressants,** and alcohol or of the lingering effects of maternal cocaine use (see Chapter 7). The best described of these types of withdrawal is heroin withdrawal syndrome, which consists of jitteriness, poor feeding, sneezing, rapid respiration, diarrhea, a high-pitched cry, hyperactivity, and occasionally seizures. The onset of heroin withdrawal is generally within the first 24 hours of life. Methadone withdrawal generally presents later and can last for 2–4 weeks or more because methadone is metabolized differently than heroin. Treatment for withdrawal symptoms involves placing the infant in a quiet, dark environment in which stimulation is limited. Severe symptoms can be treated with paregoric or with phenobarbital. The long-term effects of drug exposure are difficult to assess because of polydrug use or confounding socioeconomic or environmental factors (see Chapter 7).

Jaundice

Jaundice refers to the yellowish discoloration of the skin that results from the accumulation in the tissues of a pigment called *bilirubin*, a breakdown product of hemoglobin. Bilirubin is released into the bloodstream, predominantly in the unconjugated, or indirect form. It then enters the liver, where it is conjugated so that it can be subsequently excreted into the biliary system and then into the gastrointestinal tract and out of the body.

A transient elevation in the indirect fraction of bilirubin is universally present to a certain degree in all newborns and is clinically evident as jaundice in 60% of full-term infants (Melton & Akinbi, 1999). This phenomenon is referred to as physiologic jaundice, and its cause is two-fold. First, infants undergo a large breakdown of hemoglobin, due to the relatively increased red blood cell volume in utero and the shorter life span of their red blood cells. Second, the newborn's ability to take up, conjugate, and then excrete bilirubin is not yet fully developed. This resulting physiologic jaundice generally resolves spontaneously within the first week of life.

Not all jaundice in the newborn period, however, is physiologic. One must differentiate physiologic jaundice from jaundice that has a pathologic cause, which is characterized by an earlier onset (for instance, within the first 24 hours of life), an accelerated rise of bilirubin, an excessive level of bilirubin (generally higher than 12 milligrams per deciliter), jaundice that persists for 2 weeks or more, or an elevated direct (conjugated) fraction of bilirubin.

Some infants may have a risk factor that renders them more susceptible to pathologic jaundice, including hemolysis (breakdown of red blood cells), which can be secondary to several conditions. For instance, fetal–maternal blood group incompatibility, such as ABO or **Rh incompatibility,** can result in rapid destruction of neonatal red blood cells. Mothers who are Rh negative should receive RhoGAM, and it is important to note this in the history. Furthermore, newborns of Asian or Native American descent have a genetic predisposition for jaundice. Breast-fed infants are also more likely to develop pathologic jaundice than their formula-fed counterparts for two reasons. One cause is a disorder known as *breast-feeding jaundice*, which is seen in the first week of life. It is generally secondary to mild dehydration and inadequate caloric intake due to the mother's initially low milk production. A second cause is *breast-milk jaundice*, which resolves once feedings with breast milk are interrupted. It is postulated that this condition is due to certain fatty acids in the breast milk that interfere with bilirubin uptake and conjugation. Jaundice also occurs more frequently in newborns who have sepsis or who have cephalohematoma, infants of diabetic mothers, newborns whose mothers underwent induction of labor, and infants with intestinal obstruction.

Pathologic jaundice is more dangerous to the newborn than physiological jaundice is because high levels of indirect bilirubin can injure the brain cells, leading to kernicterus, the yellow staining of certain central brain regions (the basal ganglia). The exact bilirubin level at which neurotoxicity occurs is not known, particularly in the premature infant. Early clinical signs include lethargy, poor feeding, and a high-pitched cry. Many infants with kernicterus do not survive; those that do often have severe neurological complications including seizures, hearing loss, mental retardation, and dyskinetic cerebral palsy.

The goal of treatment of jaundice is to prevent the indirect bilirubin from rising to a level that can be injurious to the brain (kernicterus). Historically, severe jaundice was treated with exchange transfusion, which decreased the concentration of bilirubin in the blood but carried some risk. More recently, phototherapy has been found to be effective in lowering indirect **hyperbilirubinemia** by forming chemical compounds that are more readily excreted in the urine. This safe treatment has obviated the need for exchange transfusions in many cases and has contributed to the marked decline in the incidence of kernicterus since the 1970s.

Despite these therapies, pediatricians continue to see cases of severe jaundice, and new treatments for jaundice are being investigated. These include tin protoporphyrin, a substance that inhibits the conversion of the heme portion of hemoglobin into bilirubin, and intravenous gammaglobulin, which has been effective in the prevention of red blood cell destruction (Hammerman & Kaplan, 2000). It is hoped that these strategies will help decrease the need for exchange transfusion, but given early hospital discharge, neonates continue to be readmitted with significant pathologic jaundice.

Seizures

Seizures in the neonatal period are complications of many of the common neonatal problems that have been described in this chapter. The most common causes of neonatal seizures are developmental defects, hypoxic-ischemic encephalopathy, intracranial hemorrhage, sepsis, hypoglycemia, hypocalcemia, inborn errors of metabolism, and maternal drug use. Manifestations of seizures in the neonatal period differ from those in the older child or adult. Neonatal seizures tend to be subtler (not clonic, tonic, or myoclonic) and localized (focal) rather than generalized because the network of neurons is less complex in the neonate (Volpe, 2001; see Figure 5.6 and Chapter 25). Based on data from EEGs combined with either videotape or direct observation, it has been noted that subtle seizures are more common in the premature infant. The most common manifestations are sustained eye opening in the premature infant and lateral gaze deviation in the full-term infant. There can also be blinking, lip smacking, pedaling leg movements, or rotary arm movements. Apnea also can be a manifestation of seizures, particularly in the full-term infant (Watanabe, Hara, & Miyazaki, 1982).

The most common cause of seizures in the neonatal period is hypoxic-ischemic injury, with the majority of seizures occurring within the first 24 hours of life. Slow, rhythmic clonic seizures are the most common manifestation of hypoxic-ischemic injury.

In terms of outcome, full-term infants with seizures are more likely to have subsequent typical development than are premature infants with seizures because most premature infants with seizures have an accompanying intraventricular hemorrhage (Volpe, 2001). The cause of the seizures also has a bearing on outcome. The best outcome occurs in infants with seizures secondary to drug withdrawal or late-onset hypocalcemia, almost all of whom, if treated effectively, develop typically. Also faring well are infants with subarachnoid hemorrhage, 90% of whom subsequently have typical development. About half of infants with hypoxic-ischemic en-

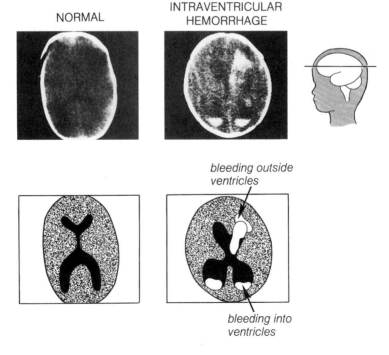

Figure 5.6. Intraventricular hemorrhage as shown on a CT scan. (Courtesy of Dr. Roger C. Sanders, Department of Radiology, Los Alamos Hospital, Los Alamos, NM.)

cephalopathy, early-onset hypocalcemia, hypoglycemia, or bacterial meningitis had a good out-come (Volpe, 2001). Infants with intraventricular hemorrhage and seizures have only a 10% chance of developing typically. None of the infants with malformation in the central nervous system such as holoprosencephaly or lissencephaly (see Appendix B) or abnormalities in neuronal migration have typical development (Volpe, 2001; see Chapter 13).

Seizures need to be quickly diagnosed and treated because of their impact on circulation, ventilatory function, and cerebral metabolism (Volpe, 2001). The first treatment is to correct any metabolic abnormality. Antiepileptic medication consists of phenobarbital as the first-line drug, followed by phenytoin (Dilantin) and lorazepam (Ativan). For most infants, therapy can be discontinued in the first month of life. In approximately 10%–30% of those infants, however, seizures persist beyond infancy. If the neurological exam is normal, there is little risk of ongoing seizure activity. For infants who have sustained hypoxic-ischemic injury, there is a 30% chance of seizure recurrence, whereas there is an almost 100% chance of further seizures for infants with an underlying structural brain abnormality (Volpe, 2001; see Chapter 25).

SUMMARY

Birth is a critical and often hazardous process. Once the baby is born, many cardiorespiratory alterations must occur. A number of underlying problems can affect this transition process and can lead to problems in the neonatal period. Many congenital anomalies can be surgically repaired in the first few years of life, but some other anomalies, particularly in the central nervous system, can be devastating and irreparable. Disorders such as hypoxic-ischemic injury, intracranial hemorrhage, sepsis, metabolic abnormalities, drug withdrawal, hyperbilirubinemia, and seizures require prompt diagnosis and intervention. With advances in medical care for neonates, the long-term neurological outcome for these sick infants has improved. It is important to emphasize that the vast majority of infants undergo the trauma of birth without sequelae. Health care professionals need to continue to improve care for those 7 in every 1,000 newborns that die and need to continue to push the frontiers of medical science to diagnose and treat infants at risk for long-term neurodevelopmental disability.

REFERENCES

Aggarwal, P., Chaudhari, S., Bhave, S., et al. (1998). Clinical predictors of outcome in hypoxic ischemic encephalopathy in term neonates. *Annals of Tropical Paediatrics, 18,* 117–121.

Avery, G.B., Fletcher, M.A., & MacDonald, M.G. (Eds.). (1999). *Neonatology: Pathophysiology and management of the newborn* (5th ed.). Philadelphia: Lippincott Williams & Wilkins.

Baker, C.J. (1997). Group B streptococcal infections. *Clinics in Perinatology, 24,* 59–70.

Baltimore, R.S. (1998). Neonatal nosocomial infections. *Seminars in Perinatology, 22,* 25–32.

Blankenberg, F.G., Loh, N.N., Bracci, P., et al. (2000). Sonography, CT, and MR imaging: A prospective comparison of neonates with suspected intracranial ischemia and hemorrhage. *American Journal of Neuroradiology, 21,* 213–218.

Buonocore, G., Perrone, S., Gioia, D., et al. (1999). Nucleated red blood cell count at birth as an index of perinatal brain damage. *American Journal of Obstetrics and Gynecology, 181,* 1500–1505.

Campistol, J., Poo, P., Fernandez Alvarez, E., et al. (1999). Parasagittal cerebral injury: magnetic resonance findings. *Journal of Child Neurology, 14,* 683–685.

Fernandez, F., Verdu, A., Quero, J., et al. (1986). Cerebrospinal fluid lactate levels in term infants with perinatal hypoxia. *Pediatric Neurology, 2,* 39–42.

Guyer, B., Hoyert, D.L., Martin, J.A., et al. (1999). Annual summary of vital statistics: 1998. *Pediatrics, 104,* 1229–1246.

Halamek, L.P., Benaron, D.A., & Stevenson, D.K. (1997). Neonatal hypoglycemia, Part I: Background and definition. *Clinics in Pediatrics, 36,* 675–680.

Hall, R.T., Hall, F.K., & Daily, D.K. (1998). High-dose phenobarbital therapy in term newborn infants with severe perinatal asphyxia: A randomized, prospective study with three-year followup. *Journal of Pediatrics, 132,* 345–348.

Hammerman, C., & Kaplan, M. (2000, February). Recent developments in the management of neonatal hyperbilirubinemia. *NeoReviews, 1,* e19–e24.

Hill, A., & Volpe, J.J. (1989). Perinatal asphyxia: Clinical aspects. *Clinics in Perinatology, 16,* 435–457.

Hoyert, D.L., Freedman, M.A., Strobino, D.M., et al. (2001). Annual summary of vital statistics: 2000. *Pediatrics, 108,* 1241–1255.

Jain, L., Ferre, C., Vidyasagar, D., et al. (1991). Cardiopulmonary resuscitation of apparently stillborn infants: Survival and long-term outcome. *Journal of Pediatrics, 118,* 778–782.

Kaftan, H., & Kinney, J.S. (1998). Early onset neonatal bacterial infections. *Seminars in Perinatology, 22,* 15–24.

Kohl, S. (1997). Neonatal herpes simplex infection. *Clinics in Perinatology, 24,* 129–150.

Martin-Ancel, A., Garcia-Alix, A., Pascual-Salcedo, D., et al. (1997). Interleukin-6 in the cerebrospinal fluid after perinatal asphyxia is related to early and late neurologic manifestations. *Pediatrics, 100,* 789–794.

Melton, K., & Akinbi, H. (1999). Neonatal jaundice: Strategies to reduce bilirubin-induced complications. *Postgraduate Medicine, 106,* 167–171.

Nelson, K.B. (1989). Relationship of intrapartum and delivery room events to long-term neurologic outcome. *Clinics in Perinatology, 16,* 995–1007.

Robertson, C.M.T., & Finer, N.N. (1988). Educational readiness of survivors of neonatal encephalopathy associated with birth asphyxia at term. *Journal of Developmental and Behavioral Pediatrics, 9,* 298–306.

Roland, E.H., Flodmark, D., & Hill, A. (1990). Thalamic hemorrhage with intraventricular hemorrhage in the full-term newborn. *Pediatrics, 85,* 737–741.

Rose, A.L., & Lombroso, C.T. (1970). A study of clinical, pathological and electroencephalographic features in 137 full-term babies with a long-term followup. *Pediatrics, 45,* 404–425.

Sarnat, H.B., & Sarnat, M.S. (1976). Neonatal encephalopathy following fetal distress: A clinical and electroencephalographic study. *Archives of Neurology, 33,* 696–705.

Schelonka, R.L., & Infante, A.J. (1998). Neonatal immunology. *Seminars in Perinatology, 22,* 2–14.

Shankaran, S., Kottamasu, S.R., & Kuhns, L. (1993). Brain sonography, computed tomography, and single-photon emission computed tomography in term neonates with perinatal asphyxia. *Clinics in Perinatology, 20,* 379–394.

Simon, N.P. (1999). Long-term neurodevelopmental outcome of asphyxiated newborns. *Clinics in Perinatology, 26,* 767–778.

Taeusch, H.W., Ballard, R.A., & Avery, M.E. (1991). *Schaffer and Avery's diseases of the newborn* (6th ed.). Philadelphia: W.B. Saunders.

Tan, S., & Parks, D.A. (1999). Preserving brain function during neonatal asphyxia. *Clinics in Perinatology, 26,* 733–747.

Toltzis, P., & Blumer, J. (1995). Antibiotic-resistant gram-negative bacteria in the critical care setting. *Pediatric Clinics of North America, 42,* 687–702.

Torres, F., & Blaw, M.E. (1968). Longitudinal EEG: Clinical correlations in children from birth to 4 years of age. *Pediatrics, 41,* 945–954.

Volpe, J.J. (2001). *Neurology of the newborn* (4th ed.). Philadelphia: W.B. Saunders.

Watanabe, K., Hara, K., Miyazaki, S., et al. (1982). Apneic seizures in the newborn. *American Journal of Diseases in Childhood, 136,* 980–984.

Whyte, H.E. (1993). Visual-evoked potentials in neonates following asphyxia. *Clinics in Perinatology, 20,* 451–461.

Wilson, C.B. (1986). Immunologic basis for increased susceptibility of the neonate to infection. *Journal of Pediatrics, 108,* 1–12.

Wolf, M.J., Beunen, G., Casaer, P., et al. (1998). Neonatal neurological examination as a predictor of neuromotor outcome at 4 months in term low-Apgar-score babies in Zimbabwe. *Early Human Development, 51,* 179–186.

6

Premature and Small-for-Dates Infants

K. Rais-Bahrami, Billie Lou Short, and Mark L. Batshaw

Upon completion of this chapter, the reader will:

- recognize some of the causes of prematurity and being small for gestational age
- be able to identify physical characteristics of the premature infant
- understand the complications and illnesses associated with preterm birth
- be aware of the methods used to care for low birth weight infants
- know the results of outcome studies

The preterm infant is at an immediate disadvantage compared with the full-term infant. In addition to facing all of the usual challenges of making the transition from intrauterine to extrauterine life (see Chapter 5), the preterm infant must make these changes using organs that are not ready to perform the task. Almost every organ is immature. Decreased production of a substance called **surfactant** in the lungs can lead to respiratory distress syndrome (RDS); immaturity of the central nervous system places the preterm infant at increased risk for an intraventricular hemorrhage (IVH), **periventricular leukomalacia (PVL),** and hydrocephalus; and inadequate kidney function makes fluid and metabolic management difficult. An immature gastrointestinal tract impairs the infant's ability to digest and absorb certain nutrients and places the gut at risk for developing a life-threatening disorder called **necrotizing enterocolitis (NEC)** that results from inadequate blood supply. Finally, the preterm infant's eyes are more susceptible to the damaging effects of the oxygen that is used to treat respiratory distress. This may result in retinopathy of prematurity (ROP) and subsequent vision loss. Given these risks, it is remarkable that most preterm infants overcome these acute problems with little residual effects. A minority, however, do sustain long-term medical and neurodevelopmental complications. A discussion of these complications and their prevention is the focus of this chapter.

DIAMOND

Diamond was born 2½ months prematurely, at 26 weeks' gestation, and weighed less than 900 grams (2 pounds). During Diamond's first day of life, she needed artificial ventilation and surfactant therapy to keep open the air passages in her lungs. By 1 month of age, she was doing well enough to receive a pressurized oxygen–air mixture through nasal prongs (continuous positive airway pressure, or CPAP), but she had brief breathing arrests (apnea) associated with a slowed heart rate (bradycardia). This was treated successfully with **caffeine** and frequent physical stimulation. Meeting her nutritional requirements was also a problem. Initially, Diamond needed intravenous nutrition. Gradually, she was able to accept increasing amounts of breast milk by a **nasogastric tube,** and by 2 months she was strong enough to receive her feedings by bottle. At her 69th day of life (postconceptional age of 36 weeks) weighing 2,000 grams (4½ pounds), Diamond went home on oxygen and caffeine and was hooked up to an apnea monitor. Her parents had been instructed how to administer oxygen therapy; how to use the monitor; and how to administer cardio-pulmonary resuscitation (CPR), if needed. Although her prognosis is good, Diamond will need continued medical and neurodevelopmental monitoring until school age.

DEFINITIONS OF PREMATURITY AND LOW BIRTH WEIGHT

A preterm or premature infant is one born before the 37th week of gestation. Although there is no universal system for birth weight classification, it is commonly accepted that an infant with a birth weight less than 2,500 grams (5½ pounds) is **low birth weight (LBW);** an infant born weighing less than 1,500 grams (3⅓ pounds) is **very low birth weight (VLBW);** and an infant with a birth weight lower than 1,000 grams (2¼ pounds) is **extremely low birth weight (ELBW).** An infant weighing less than 800 grams (1¾ pounds) is sometimes called a **micro-preemie.** Assessment of gestational age is also important, as infants of low birth weight may represent prematurely born infants or those who are small for gestational age (SGA).

Small-for-Gestational-Age Infants

SGA infants can be either full term or premature. In either case they have a birth weight below the 10th percentile for a population-specific birth weight verses gestational age plot (Figure 6.1). SGA infants are also referred to as dysmature, light for dates, or small for dates. They not only are small but also appear malnourished, usually because of intrauterine growth restriction. About one half of SGA births are attributable to maternal illness, smoking, or malnutrition.

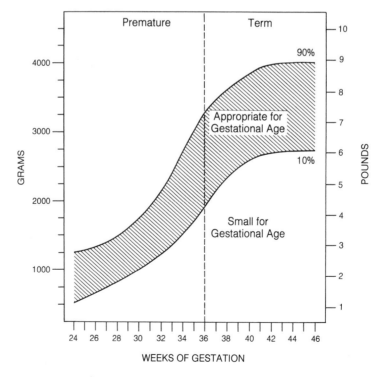

Figure 6.1.   Newborn weight by gestational age. The shaded area between the 10th and 90th percentiles represents infants who are appropriate for gestational age. Weight below the 10th percentile makes an infant small for gestational age (SGA). Prematurity is defined as being born before 36 weeks' gestation. (From Lubchenco, L.O. [1976]. *The high risk infant.* Philadelphia: W.B. Saunders; reprinted by permission.)

These infants tend to be underweight but have normal length and head circumference; they are said to have asymmetric SGA because of this discrepancy in growth pattern. The other half of SGA births are said to have *symmetric SGA* (equally deviant in length, weight, and head circumference). These infants may have been exposed in utero to alcohol or to infections such as cytomegalovirus (see Chapter 3). Infants with certain chromosomal and other genetic disorders also present as symmetrical SGA infants (Leger & Czernichow, 1994; Rasmussen et al., 2001; Suresh et al., 2001). SGA infants, whether full term or preterm, are recognized as having an increased risk for many complications in the newborn period (e.g., hypoxia, hypothermia, hypoglycemia), long-term growth impairments, developmental disabilities, and perinatal and neonatal mortality (Hediger et al., 1998; Hokken-Koelega et al., 1995; Leger et al., 1998; O'Shea & Dammann, 2000; Paz et al., 1995).

Assessment of Gestational Age

Assessment of gestational age helps distinguish an appropriate-for-gestational-age infant from a SGA infant. In addition, it will influence treatment approaches, neurodevelopmental assessment, and outcome. The gestational age is calculated from the projected birth date, or estimated date of confinement (EDC). This can be obtained using the Nägele rule: Add 7 days and subtract 3 months from the date of the last menstrual period. The accuracy of menstrual dating, however, is quite variable, especially in anticipated preterm deliveries. In most cases, uterine size is an accurate predictor of gestational age and can be measured by clinical and ultrasound examination (Persson & Weldner, 1986). Another way of estimating gestational age is by noting when fetal activity first develops. **Quickening** is first felt by the mother at approximately 16–18 weeks' gestation, and fetal heart sounds can be first detected at approximately 10–12 weeks by ultrasound and at 20 weeks by fetoscope (similar to a stethoscope). Following birth, the gestational age can be assessed using a clinical scoring system called the *modified Dubowitz examination* (discussed next). Another technique allows for estimating the degree of prematurity by examining the maturity of the lens of the eye in the first 24–48 hours of life (Hittner, Hirsch, & Rudolph, 1977). Using a combination of these methods increases the accuracy of gestational age assessment.

Physical and Behavioral Characteristics of the Premature Infant

Several physical and developmental characteristics distinguish the premature from the full-term infant. A scoring system developed by Dubowitz, Dubowitz, and Goldberg (1970) and updated by Ballard et al. (1991; Figure 6.2) takes these characteristics into account and enables the physician to estimate the infant's gestational age with some accuracy. The limitation of this scoring system is the postnatal age of the infant. If the scoring is not performed within the first 24 hours of birth, neurological and some physical features (such as skin texture) can change and make the infant appear more mature than is the case. Also, any severely ill infant can be difficult to evaluate due to altered neurological status.

The main physical characteristics that distinguish a premature from a full-term infant are the presence in the premature infant of fine body hair (**lanugo**); smooth, reddish skin; and the absence of skin creases, ear cartilage, and breast buds (Figure 6.3). In addition to the physical appearance, premature infants display distinctive neurological and behavioral characteristics, including reduced muscle tone and activity and increased joint mobility (Amiel-Tison, 1968; Constantine et al., 1987). Low muscle tone is particularly evident in the infant born before 28 weeks' gestation; it gradually improves with advancing gestational age, starting with the legs and moving up to the arms by 32 weeks. Thus, although the premature infant lies in a floppy, extended position, the full-term infant rests in a semi-flexed position. As flexion tone improves over the weeks after birth, increased joint mobility disappears. Finally, as compared with the full-term infant, the premature infant appears behaviorally passive and disorganized in the first weeks of life (Mandrich et al., 1994).

Neuromuscular Maturity

	−1	0	1	2	3	4	5
Posture							
Square Window (wrist)	>90°	90°	60°	45°	30°	0°	
Arm Recoil		180°	140°–180°	110°–140°	90°–110°	<90°	
Popliteal Angle	180°	160°	140°	120°	100°	90°	<90°
Scarf Sign							
Heel to Ear							

Physical Maturity

Skin	sticky friable transparent	gelatinous red, translucent	smooth pink, visible veins	superficial peeling &/or rash, few veins	cracking pale areas rare veins	parchment deep cracking no vessels	leathery cracked wrinkled
Lanugo	none	sparse	abundant	thinning	bald areas	mostly bald	
Plantar Surface	heel-toe 40-50mm:-1 <40mm:-2	>50mm no crease	faint red marks	anterior transverse crease only	creases ant. 2/3	creases over entire sole	
Breast	imperceptible	barely perceptible	flat areola no bud	stippled areola 1-2mm bud	raised areola 3-4mm bud	full areola 5-10mm bud	
Eye/Ear	lids fused loosely:-1 tightly:-2	lids open pinna flat stays folded	sl. curved pinna; soft; slow recoil	well-curved pinna; soft but ready recoil	formed &firm instant recoil	thick cartilage ear stiff	
Genitals male	scrotum flat, smooth	scrotum empty faint rugae	testes in upper canal rare rugae	testes descending few rugae	testes down good rugae	testes pendulous deep rugae	
Genitals female	clitoris prominent labia flat	prominent clitoris small labia minora	prominent clitoris enlarging minora	majora & minora equally prominent	majora large minora small	majora cover clitoris & minora	

Maturity Rating

score	weeks
−10	20
−5	22
0	24
5	26
10	28
15	30
20	32
25	34
30	36
35	38
40	40
45	42
50	44

Figure 6.2.   Scoring system to assess newborn infants. The score for each of the neuromuscular and physical signs is added together to obtain a score called the *total maturity score*. Gestational age is determined from this score. (From Ballard, J.L., Khoury, J.C., Wedig, K., et al. [1991]. New Ballard score, expanded to include extremely premature infants. *Journal of Pediatrics, 119*, 418; reprinted by permission.)

INCIDENCE OF PRETERM BIRTHS

Preterm birth occurs in only 11% of all pregnancies. Yet, it is responsible for the majority of neonatal deaths and nearly one half of all cases of neonatal-onset neurodevelopmental disabilities, including cerebral palsy (Hoyert et al., 2001). This risk is highest in those infants born before 32 weeks' gestation, representing 2% of all births (Robertson et al., 1992). The incidence of preterm births has risen over the past 15 years, and preterm births occur twice as frequently in African Americans as in Caucasians (Goldenberg & Rouse, 1998). Of LBW infants weighing less than 2,500 grams, 70% are preterm and 30% are full-term infants who are SGA (National Center for Chronic Disease Prevention and Health Promotion, Division of Nutrition;

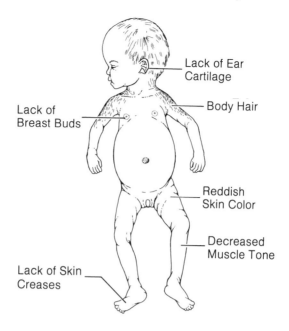

Figure 6.3. Typical physical features of a premature infant.

National Center for Health Statistics, Division of Vital Statistics; & Centers for Disease Control and Prevention, 1994).

CAUSES OF PREMATURE BIRTH

The two most common causes of preterm delivery are maternal infections and adolescence, and these often occur together (Table 6.1). Although less than 5% of all pregnancies occur in adolescents, these pregnancies account for 20% of all preterm births (Cooper, Leland, & Alexander, 1995). In addition, up to 80% of early preterm births (births before 30 weeks' gestation) are associated with an intrauterine infection that precedes the rupture of membranes (Andrews, Goldenberg, & Hauth, 1995; Gibbs et al., 1992). Other risk factors include inadequate prenatal care, poverty, acute and chronic maternal illness, multiple-gestation births, a history of previous premature pregnancies, smoking, and substance abuse (Adams et al., 2000). Congenital anomalies or injuries to the fetus may also lead to premature birth, and certain fetal conditions such as Rh incompatibility and poor fetal growth may require early delivery.

COMPLICATIONS OF PREMATURITY

The premature infant must undergo the same physiologic transitions to extrauterine life as the full-term infant (see Chapter 5). The preterm infant, however, must accomplish this difficult task using immature body organs. The result is a significant risk of complications in virtually every organ system in the body. This risk increases with the degree of prematurity.

Table 6.1. Known causes of prematurity

Amniotic fluid/membrane infection (chorioamnionitis)
Drug/alcohol abuse
Fetal distress
Maternal age (adolescent or older mother)
Maternal chronic illnesses
Maternal bacterial vaginosis
Maternal pyelonephritis (kidney infection)
Multiple gestation
Placental bleeding (abruptio, previa)
Polyhydramnios (excessive amniotic fluid)
Poor prenatal care
Premature rupture of the membranes
Preeclampsia
Uterine abnormalities/incompetent cervix

Respiratory Problems

Hyaline Membrane Diseases

Hyaline membrane diseases (HMDs) are a group of disorders characterized by respiratory distress in the newborn period (Verma, 1995). They affect approximately 20% of all premature infants, and the most common is RDS. The underlying abnormality is decreased production of surfactant that normally keeps the alveoli (the terminal airway passages) stable, permitting the exchange of oxygen and carbon dioxide (Figure 6.4). A chest X ray can clinically confirm HMD, showing a "ground glass" appearance of the lungs. This results from the collapsed alveoli appearing dense and hazy in comparison with the translucent, air-filled lung of a typical full-term newborn, which appears black (Figure 6.5). The clinical course of HMD involves peak severity between 24 and 48 hours after birth, followed by improvement over the next 24–48 hours. In uncomplicated cases, HMD will resolve by 72–96 hours after birth. This classical course of HMD has fortunately been modified by the administration of surfactant replacement therapy as soon as the diagnosis is made, in the first day of life. Improvement in pulmonary function usually begins within minutes after the first dose of surfactant, and effective gas exchange can be achieved with a significantly lower level of oxygen and ventilatory support after one or two doses. Except in severe cases of HMD, it is unusual for an infant to require more than two doses of surfactant.

Infants with mild HMD generally do well with supplemental oxygen alone or in combination with CPAP. CPAP involves providing a mixture of oxygen and air under continuous pressure; this prevents the alveoli from collapsing between breaths. More severely affected infants may require the placement of an endotracheal tube for mechanical ventilatory support as well as for administration of surfactant. Although surfactant therapy has significantly reduced mortality in ELBW premature infants, there has been no appreciable change in long-term pulmonary and neurodevelopmental complications in these infants (Bergman, 1998; Wagner et al., 1995). Therefore, close follow-up to school entry is important.

A related approach to treating surfactant deficiency is to stimulate its production. There is evidence that administration of **steroids** to mothers 24–36 hours before delivery stimulates surfactant production and pulmonary maturation in the fetus. This lessens the likelihood

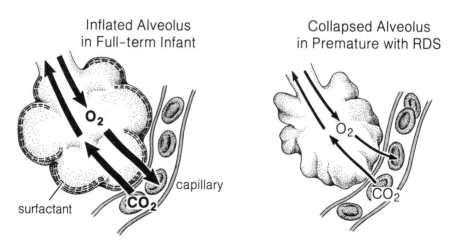

Figure 6.4.   Schematic drawing of alveoli in a normal newborn and in a premature infant with respiratory distress syndrome (RDS). Note that the inflated alveolus is kept open by surfactant. Oxygen (O_2) moves from the alveolus to the red blood cells in the pulmonary capillary. Carbon dioxide (CO_2) moves in the opposite direction. This exchange is much less efficient when the alveolus is collapsed. The result is hypoxia.

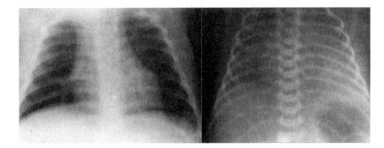

Figure 6.5.   Chest X rays of a normal newborn (left) and of a premature infant with respiratory distress syndrome (RDS; right), which shows a "white out" of the lungs due to surfactant deficiency.

and/or severity of HMD (Kari et al., 1994). The effect of antenatal steroids is additive to surfactant replacement therapy in reducing respiratory distress and mortality. It is therefore recommended that steroids be given prior to birth for potential preterm delivery of fetuses between 24 and 34 weeks' gestational age (NIH Consensus Development Panel on the Effect of Corticosteroids for Fetal Maturation on Perinatal Outcomes, 1995).

Bronchopulmonary Dysplasia

The improved survival of ELBW newborns has increased the number of infants at risk for various forms of respiratory morbidity associated with mechanical ventilation, including **bronchopulmonary dysplasia (BPD).** This term is generally used to describe infants who require supplemental oxygen and/or mechanical ventilation beyond 28 days postnatal age and who have persistently abnormal chest X rays and respiratory examinations (e.g., rapid breathing, wheezing; Bancalari et al., 1995; Farrell & Fiascone, 1997). BPD primarily occurs in infants who are born at less than 32 weeks' gestation and require mechanical ventilation during the first week of life for treatment of HMD (Farrell & Fiascone, 1997).

The development of BPD has been attributed to lung injury from a combination of **barotrauma** (pressure damage from prolonged mechanical ventilation), oxygen toxicity, infection, and inflammation; the exact mechanism of BPD remains poorly understood. Since the 1970s, newer methods of respiratory support, including high-frequency ventilation and surfactant therapy, have increased the survival rate of smaller and less mature infants, but the total number of infants who develop BPD has not decreased. BPD remains the most common chronic lung disease of infancy in the United States, with some 7,000 new cases being diagnosed each year. Long-term studies of pulmonary function in this population indicate that as these infants grow, there is clinical improvement. Abnormalities in airway resistance and pulmonary compliance, however, persist into adulthood, resulting in a high risk of asthma (Kennedy et al., 2000; Mallory et al., 1991).

Approaches to postnatal prevention and treatment of BPD have included corticosteroid therapy, supplemental vitamin A, high-frequency ventilation, use of bronchodilators (asthma medication), and administration of diuretics (to increase urinary excretion; Abman & Groothius, 1994). The use of postnatal corticosteroid medication such as dexamethasone (Decadron) for prevention and treatment of BPD has been a matter of controversy. There is evidence that early treatment with dexamethasone reduces pulmonary inflammation and decreases the need for supplemental oxygen and mechanical ventilation (Durand, Sardesai, & McEvoy, 1995; Rastogi et al., 1996; Tapia et al., 1998). Its potential for adverse long-term effects on physical growth and neurodevelopment, however, has been of concern (Papile et al., 1998). It is not unusual for infants with BPD to require prolonged support with supplemental oxygen, diuretics, and bronchodilators after discharge from the hospital. Even with supportive care and treatment, infants with BPD continue to have long-term problems, including limited tolerance of physical exercise, poor physical growth, excessive nutritional caloric requirement, and an increased risk of developmental disabilities (Laudry et al., 1993; Pederson et al., 2000; Valleur-Masson et al., 1993).

Neurologic Problems

Intraventricular Hemorrhage

IVH is an important neurological complication of extremely premature infants. The risk of IVH correlates directly with the degree of prematurity (Shankaran, Bauer, et al., 1996). Fortunately, its incidence appears to be declining (Tortorolo et al., 1999). About 50% of IVH occurs during the first day of life and 90% by the third day of life (Dolfin et al., 1983). Ultrasound of the head is the most reliable and safest technique for diagnosis of IVH. IVH is commonly graded by severity into four levels (Volpe, 2001). Grade I is defined by a bleed into the germinal matrix, a network of blood vessels in the roof of the lateral ventricles. If the hemorrhage expands beyond the germinal matrix into the ventricular system, it is Grade II. Grade I and II account for the majority of IVH, and significant neurological impairment is rare with these types of IVH. About 20% of hemorrhages, however, are severe enough to dilate the ventricle (Grade III) or invade the brain substance (Grade IV). Grade IV is often called *periventricular hemorrhagic infarction*. These hemorrhages can lead to damage of the white matter surrounding the ventricles, a condition termed *periventricular leukomalacia* (PVL; Volpe, 2001). The long-term neurological outcome is related to the severity of the hemorrhage, with cerebral palsy and/or mental retardation seen in 30% of the patients with Grade III hemorrhages and in 75% of those with Grade IV hemorrhages (Vohr & Ment, 1996).

Avoidance of hypoxic-ischemic events that lead to fluctuations in cerebral blood pressure, expert delivery room stabilization, effective resuscitation and ventilation, gentle handling, and use of muscle relaxants during mechanical ventilation have all been associated with a reduction in the incidence and severity of IVH (Volpe, 2001; Wells & Ment, 1995). A number of medications have been studied for preventing or treating IVH, with varied results. These include antenatal use of steroids and postnatal use of phenobarbital (Luminal), vitamin K, vitamin E, and indomethacin (Greer, 1995; Leviton et al., 1993; Shankaran, Cepeda, et al., 1996; Shankaran et al., 1997; Thorpe et al., 1995). Indomethacin given soon after birth appears to significantly reduce the incidence and severity of IVH, but the other medications do not appear to benefit the infant (Ment et al., 2000).

Periventricular Leukomalacia

The periventricular white matter is the region of the brain closest to the ventricles. It is especially vulnerable to injury in the premature infant. The blood supply is not fully developed until full term and is therefore vulnerable to disturbances in cerebral blood flow and in the delivery of oxygen and glucose (Kumazaki et al., 2002; Volpe, 2001). In addition, the glial cells, a major constituent of white matter, undergo rapid growth by the end of the second trimester and are more susceptible to injury caused by fluctuations in cerebral blood pressure during this period. Finally, there is evidence that maternal infection involving the membranes surrounding the fetus (chorioamnionitis) increases the risk of PVL (Grether et al., 1999).

PVL has been reported to occur in 4%–15% of premature infants (Perlman, Risser, & Broyles, 1996). It may occur in association with IVH or independently (Figure 6.6). The diagnosis of PVL is best made by serial head ultrasounds that may show the development of cystic lesions in the white matter. These have been shown to be an important predictor of the subsequent development of **spastic diplegia** (a form of cerebral palsy that impairs lower extremity function) and **hemiplegia** (a form of cerebral palsy that affects one side of the body; Kuban &

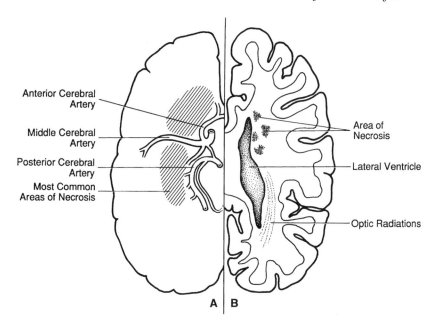

Figure 6.6. Periventricular leukomalacia (PVL). A) The blood vessel supply to the brain, and B) the brain structures. The area of the white matter surrounding the lateral ventricle (particularly the top part) is especially susceptible to hypoxic-ischemic damage because it is not well supplied by blood vessels. It lies in a watershed area between the anterior, middle, and posterior cerebral arteries. In premature infants, poor oxygenation and decreased blood flow associated with respiratory distress syndrome (RDS) may lead to necrosis of this brain tissue, a condition termed *periventricular leukomalacia*. When the posterior portion is affected, the optic radiations may be damaged, resulting in cortical blindness.

Leviton, 1994; see Chapter 23). Large cysts (greater than 3 millimeters in diameter) place the child at increased risk of developing spastic quadriplegia (a form of cerebral palsy that affects all four limbs), visual impairment, mental retardation, and seizures in early childhood (Dammann, Allred, & Veelken, 1998).

Hearing Impairment

ELBW infants are at increased risk for hearing loss because of multisystem illness and the frequent use of medications such as aminoglycoside antibiotics and diuretics, which can be toxic to the auditory system. The overall prevalence of sensorineural hearing impairment is about 4 per 10,000 in full-term infants. This increases to 13 per 10,000 in LBW infants and to 51 per 10,000 among VLBW infants (Van Naarden & Decoufle, 1999). In 1994, the Joint Committee on Infant Hearing recommended that all VLBW infants undergo auditory screening. The committee further expanded this statement in 2000 to advocate testing for all newborns. The most commonly performed tests are **auditory brainstem response** and evoked otoacoustic emission (Meyer et al., 1999; see Chapter 11).

Apnea and Bradycardia

Apnea is clinically defined as a respiratory pause lasting 15–20 seconds associated with a decrease in heart rate to below 80–100 beats per minute. It is the most common disorder of respiratory control found in the neonatal intensive care unit (NICU) and is related to immaturity of the central nervous system in the premature infant. About 10% of all LBW infants and more than 40% of VLBW infants experience clinically significant apnea (Bhatia, 2000; Scanlon, 1994).

Apnea that occurs with sustained bradycardia (very low heart rate) may be symptomatic of an underlying medical condition. If all serious underlying causes have been ruled out, the infant is said to have *apnea of prematurity.* Medications such as caffeine and theophylline can stimulate respiration and are commonly used to treat apnea of prematurity (Larsen et al., 1995). Caffeine and theophylline appear to have comparable therapeutic efficacy, but the frequency of reported side effects is greater with theophylline. Therefore, caffeine is usually used in centers that can measure caffeine levels in blood to ensure that therapeutic levels are maintained. Theophylline is used, however, in the infant who has both apnea and reactive airway disease (asthma) because it is a known bronchodilator, whereas caffeine is not.

The risk of apnea of prematurity declines with advancing postnatal maturation. Developmental immaturity of respiratory control underlies the pathogenesis of neonatal apnea. Even after apparent resolution, however, apnea can recur in certain clinical situations, particularly with respiratory syncytial virus infection and severe anemia (Baker & Ryan, 1999).

Sudden Infant Death Syndrome

Sudden infant death syndrome (SIDS) occurs more than twice as frequently in premature infants as in full-term infants, usually between 2 and 5 months of life. Contrary to earlier beliefs, apnea of prematurity is not a major predisposing factor for SIDS (Hodgman, 1998). Because of the increased incidence of SIDS, however, the extremely premature infant who is having significant **apneic** spells in the 2 weeks before discharge may be sent home on an apnea monitor (Tauman & Sivan, 2000). Although these monitors emit an alarm if the infant stops breathing, studies on their use have not shown effectiveness in reducing the incidence of SIDS. The monitors do, however, provide reassurance to parents and physicians about the status of the infant (Abendroth et al., 1999). Parents of such high-risk infants should be trained in neonatal CPR prior to taking their infant home on an apnea monitor. The monitor is generally not required for more than a few months.

In order to prevent SIDS, in 1992 the American Academy of Pediatrics began recommending that infants be placed on their back for sleep. In addition, fluffy blankets and toys should not be placed in the crib during sleep times and the home environment should be smoke free. These changes have resulted in a 40% reduction in the incidence of SIDS (Gibson et al., 2000).

Cardiovascular Problems

The most common cardiovascular problem in LBW infants is a **patent ductus arteriosus (PDA).** The **ductus arteriosis** is the fetal vessel that diverts blood flow around the lungs. It normally closes at birth, allowing blood to flow to the lungs and be oxygenated. About 30% of all premature infants, and more than 50% of those born weighing less than 1,000 grams, will have a patent (open) ductus arteriosis diagnosed during the first few days of life (Gonzalez & Centura-Junca, 1991). This is especially true in premature infants who have RDS (Scanlon, 1994). In these children, a PDA will divert blood from the lung and further decrease **oxygenation** to the body and brain, increasing the work of the heart. This can lead to both hypoxia-ischemia and heart failure. The presence of a PDA can be detected by echocardiography, a form of ultrasound of the heart. Its management involves medical and supportive measures, including fluid restriction, diuresis (stimulation of urination), and the use of CPAP. If this fails, closure is possible using the medications indomethacin or ibuprofen (Couser et al., 1996; Fowlie, 1996; Van Overmeire et al., 2000). In a small percentage of infants, surgical closure is required (Mavroudis, Backer, & Gevitz, 1994).

Gastrointestinal Problems

Although premature infants may be born with a suck-and-swallow response, it is immature and poorly coordinated until approximately 32 to 34 weeks' gestation. Thus, most premature infants require nasogastric or nasojejunal tube feedings until they can make the transition to oral feeds (see Chapter 27; Canadian Paediatrics Society, Nutrition Committee, 1995; Chan, Borschel, & Jacobs, 1994; Karlberg & Albertsson-Wikland, 1995). The nutritional needs of the premature infant are also different from those of the full-term infant and require the use of specialty formulas (see Chapter 9). In addition to physiological problems, premature infants are at increased risk for two disorders, necrotizing enterocolitis (NEC) and **gastroesophageal reflux (GER),** that can inhibit growth and be life threatening.

Necrotizing Enterocolitis

NEC is the most commonly acquired life-threatening intestinal disease in premature infants (Caplan & Jilling, 2001). It involves severe injury to a portion of the bowel wall. The exact cause of NEC is unknown, but prematurity appears to be the most common predisposing factor. Approximately 80% of infants with NEC were born at less than 38 weeks' gestation and weighed less than 2,500 grams at birth. Other precipitating factors include fetal distress, premature rupture of membranes, low Apgar scores, and exchange transfusion. The incidence of NEC is 1–2 per 1,000 live births, and the overall mortality rate for infants with NEC is 20%. The mortality rate of ELBW infants with NEC is greater than 40% (Snyder et al., 1997).

Medical management of NEC involves withholding feedings combined with providing nasogastric **suction** to decrease pressure on the bowel wall, antibiotics to fight the suspected underlying infection, and intravenous fluids and nutrition to prevent dehydration and weight loss. Although medical treatment can be successful in many infants with NEC, approximately half require surgery to remove the diseased section of the bowel (Chandler & Hebra, 2000). Survivors of NEC may experience a variety of postoperative complications related to the disease, the operation, or treatment measures (Horwitz et al., 1995). For example, surgery for NEC is the leading cause of short bowel syndrome in infancy (Grosfeld et al., 1991). The removal of a large portion of the bowel leads to decreased absorption of nutrients. This occurs in up to 11% of postsurgical NEC survivors and results in chronic diarrhea, malabsorption, nutritional deficiencies, impaired growth, and the long-term need for intravenous nutrition (an intravenous infusion of nutrients, fats, carbohydrates, and amino acids).

Gastroesophageal Reflux

The immaturity of gastric sphincter muscular control and delayed stomach emptying in premature infants may result in GER, a syndrome in which the contents of the stomach are regurgitated back into the **esophagus** (Marino et al., 1995; Novak, 1996). Infants with severe GER are at increased risk for vomiting and **aspiration pneumonia** (an infection precipitated by the **aspiration** of food into the lung). This may be worsened by nasogastric tube feedings. Signs of GER include refusal of oral feeding, apnea, and back arching. Treatment is targeted toward special positioning techniques and medications (see Chapter 27).

Ophthalmologic Problems

Abnormalities in the retinal vascular development after preterm birth lead to *retinopathy of prematurity,* formerly called *retrolental fibroplasia.* ELBW infants are at the greatest risk for developing ROP (Msall et al., 2000; O'Connor et al., 2002). An examination by a pediatric **ophthalmologist** should be performed at 4–6 weeks after birth or at 32–33 weeks' gestation (whichever comes first) for early detection of ROP. Follow-up examinations should be done until retinal vascularization is complete, around term (see Chapter 10). Preventive therapy with vitamin E may decrease the severity of ROP in susceptible infants (Johnson et al., 1995; Raju et al., 1997). Severe ROP is treated by laser to prevent permanent retinal detachment.

Immunologic Problems

The premature infant is born with an immature immune system. As a result, the infant is at increased risk for infection in the first months of life. Generalized bacterial and fungal infections, occurring in around 30% of extremely premature infants, are major life-threatening illnesses and can lead to a poor neurodevelopmental outcome (Wheater & Renie, 2000). Premature infants who remain in the hospital for prolonged periods should receive normal immunizations based on their chronological age.

Other Physiologic Abnormalities

Premature infants are at increased risk for many of the same transient physiological abnormalities that occur in full-term infants (see Chapter 5). These include hyperbilirubinemia, anemia, hypo- and hyperglycemia, hypocalcemia, and hypothermia. In addition, some develop transient hypothyroidism that is not seen in full-term infants (Fisher, 1999). These problems place the premature infant at increased risk for brain damage.

Acidosis and hypoxia can increase the permeability of the blood–brain barrier to bilirubin, making preterm infants more susceptible to kernicterus (see Chapter 5). Thus, the bilirubin level that is used to determine whether phototherapy or an exchange transfusion should be performed is lower for the preterm infant than for the full-term infant (Watchko & Claassen, 1994). Glucose and **electrolyte** instability are also common in premature infants, especially the micropreemie.

Anemia is also more of a problem for the premature infant as it decreases the oxygen-carrying capacity of the red blood cells and can lead to hypoxic-ischemic brain damage. In severe cases, correction of anemia with blood transfusion and/or treatment with erythropoietin, to stimulate the bone marrow to produce red blood cells, may be necessary (Obladen & Maier, 1995; Yu & Bascain, 1994).

Since the late 1990s, studies have shown that changes in transfusion practices have significantly reduced the need for transfusion in the LBW premature infant and reduced the need for erythropoietin, which is very costly (e.g., Cohen & Manno, 1998; Ohis, 2000). Most studies have found that by using more liberal transfusion practices (i.e., allowing **hematocrits** to drop into the mid-30s for the sick premature infant and mid-20s for the recovering premature infant) prior to transfusion has reduced the need for transfusion among these infants. Thus, the use of erythropoietin has come to be reserved for specific cases in which family or religious views restrict the use of blood transfusions.

Finally, premature infants often have a transient deficiency of thyroid hormone production. In severe cases, thyroid replacement therapy is indicated to prevent long-term neurodevelopmental impairments (Leviton et al., 1999; Reuss et al., 1996); in most cases, however, the hypothyroidism resolves without the need for therapy.

MEDICAL AND DEVELOPMENTAL CARE OF LOW BIRTH WEIGHT INFANTS

The best treatment for LBW infants is prevention of preterm births. This starts with identifying women at risk and providing them with education and prenatal health care; detecting preterm labor early; and using labor-arresting agents and antenatal steroids (Joffe et al., 1995). Prenatal care has improved appreciably since the 1970s, but the incidence of preterm delivery remains high and might even be rising (Dammann & Leviton, 1999; Goldenberg & Rouse, 1998). Preterm and SGA infants are best managed and cared for in high-risk obstetrical centers with NICUs.

As survival rates of preterm infants have improved, the focus of care is now including a consideration of the optimal environment within the NICU for the premature infant to develop. Traditional NICU care has focused on medical protocols and procedures. A newer approach uses a more relationship-based, individualized, developmentally supportive model (Als & Gilkerson, 1997). This approach recognizes that the usual NICU setting is not optimal for the premature infant's developmental progress. Typical NICU care has involved the infant experiencing prolonged diffuse sleep states, unattended crying, a high ambient noise level, a lack of opportunity for sucking, poorly timed social and caregiving interactions, and so forth. The newer approach seeks to observe the infant's behavior and respond to it appropriately and actively involve the parents in their infant's care (Als & Gilkerson, 1997). It involves documenting infant behavior, including breathing pattern, color fluctuations, startles, posture, sleep state, and so forth. This then leads to caregiving suggestions and environmental modifications. One of the techniques involving the parent in caregiving is termed continuous skin-to-skin or "kangaroo" care. Once the premature infant has reached physiologic stability and does not require major respiratory support, he or she is placed on the parent's chest. Using these developmental approaches has been associated with improved functioning in the NICU, including reduced number of apnea events, improved oxygenation, faster weight gain, and improved motor maturity and state organization (Feldman & Eidelman, 1998; Walburn, Heermann, & Balsillie, 1997). Research is ongoing to determine whether this approach carries long-term benefits (Kleberg, Westrup, & Stjernqvist, 2000).

In addition to environmental modifications to stimulate development, early intervention services can be provided even before the child is discharged from the NICU. Once the infant is medically stable, a team consisting of a physical and an occupational therapist, a developmental psychologist, and/or a developmental pediatrician should evaluate the child (Westrup et al., 2000). Care plans should be developed for the ongoing developmental needs of the child leading to referral to an early intervention program prior to discharge (see Chapter 29).

SURVIVAL OF LOW BIRTH WEIGHT INFANTS

Advances in the technology of newborn intensive care and their application to the premature infant have been very successful in reducing mortality. Since 1960, survival of LBW infants has improved from 50% to more than 90% (Table 6.2). This improvement is even more remarkable in ELBW infants. Furthermore, in one study comparing the 1980s with the 1990s, the survival to discharge from the NICU among infants born at 23–25 weeks' gestation increased from 27% to 42% (Emsley et al., 1998; O'Shea et al., 1997; O'Shea et al., 1998).

CARE AFTER DISCHARGE FROM THE HOSPITAL

The medical cost of the hospitalization and care of the preterm infant who requires NICU care is extraordinarily high, often measured in hundreds of thousands of dollars. Length of stay is a major factor in this cost. Because of this, many centers are developing care pathways, which allow the medical team to consider earlier discharge of the stable premature infant than previously practiced. This new approach needs to be monitored closely to ensure that earlier discharge does not compromise the health of the child and result in an increased risk of readmission to the hospital for treatment of medical complications.

Clinical criteria for discharging preterm LBW infants are based on the achievement of sufficient weight and maturity of body organ function to en-

Table 6.2. Improvement in survival rate of premature infants

	Survival (%)	
Birth weight	1960	1990
0.5–0.75 kilograms (kg)	10	30
0.75–1.0 kg	20	70
1.0–1.5 kg	30	90
1.5–2.0 kg	50	90

Sources: Emsley et al., 1998; O'Shea et al., 1997; O'Shea et al., 1998.

sure medical stability and continued growth in a home environment (Casiro et al., 1993; Rawlings, Smith, & Garcia, 1993). This generally involves the infant being able to feed well by mouth, continue to gain weight, maintain a stable body temperature outside of an isolette, and no longer experience episodes of apnea and bradycardia. Most preterm LBW infants meet these eligibility criteria at a postconceptional age of 35–37 weeks. For ELBW infants, discharge at a postconceptional age of 37–42 weeks is a more realistic goal (Rawlings & Scott, 1996). At the time of discharge, most infants weight between 1,800 and 2,000 grams (4–4½ pounds).

When the child comes home, the parents may be faced with the stress and difficulty of caring for an infant with many special needs. In addition, the infant may be more irritable, cry more often, and have a poorer sleep–wake cycle compared with a full-term infant. Because of an immature sucking pattern, the infant also requires more frequent feedings and may need a specialized formula or breast milk supplemented with a human milk fortifier to meet caloric needs. The prolonged duration of hospitalization and separation from parents also may have interfered with the usual mother–infant bonding.

As a result of these stresses, it is important to provide adequate support for the family after discharge, including close medical supervision and home care visits by nursing and/or social work staff to ensure technical, emotional, and financial support (Hadden, 1999; Robinson & Jackson, 1993). Parental education and understanding of the needs of a growing preterm infant are also extremely important. Ideally the infant should be discharged to a home environment that is free of smoke and any other potential respiratory irritants such as kerosene heaters, fresh paint, and people with respiratory-related viral illness. Each of these factors plays a crucial role in causing subsequent respiratory illnesses or in exacerbating the underlying lung disease.

To prepare for discharge, most centers provide rooming-in services for the parents. This allows the parents to take over the care of their infant under the supervision of the NICU staff to determine whether there are unforeseen problems. The parents also learn about the care of their infant, thereby reducing the stress and anxiety of taking a preterm infant home.

EARLY INTERVENTION PROGRAMS

Early intervention programs have been shown to have a beneficial effect on the neurodevelopment of most premature infants through 3 years of age, although longer-term effects are still debated (Bennett & Scott, 1997; Blair, Ramey, & Hardin, 1995; Brooks-Gunn et al., 1994; Guralnick, 1997; Ramey, Ramey, & Friedlander, 1999). In many premature infants, these programs should start at discharge from the hospital and continue until 36 months corrected age. (Corrected age is calculated by subtracting the number of weeks earlier than 40 weeks' gestation that the infant was born from the infant's current chronological age; e.g., corrected age of an 8-month-old born at 28 weeks' gestation is 5 months.) The intervention strategy incorporates parent group meetings; home visits; and, after 24 months chronological age, attendance at a multidisciplinary child development center with a low teacher–infant ratio (1:3–1:4; see Chapter 29). It is important to recognize that even after completion of the early intervention program, many of these children continue to need special education services, including speech-language therapy, special education, behavior therapy, and treatment of emotional problems (Ross, Lipper, & Ald, 1990). If these children do not receive these services, the benefits of early intervention may be lost over time.

NEURODEVELOPMENTAL OUTCOME

Most infants born prematurely can be viewed during infancy as developing at a typical rate when their corrected or adjusted age is determined from their expected date of birth rather than from their actual birth date. There are, however, differences between full-term and preterm infants, even when gestational age is taken into account. In terms of motor skills, although few premature infants develop cerebral palsy, they often lack the smooth, rhythmic movement patterns of full-term infants. Devices such as walkers and jumpers should be avoided because they encourage the infant to stand on tiptoe and walk in an abnormal pattern. In later infancy, visual-motor tasks that require the planned use of arms and hand are also more difficult. Coordinating reach and grasp, scooping with a spoon, managing a standard cup, copying block constructions, and completing crayon/paper tasks can be more difficult (Glass, 2001).

By school age the developmental status of children who had birth weights above 1,500 grams is not very different from full-term infants (Huddy, Johnson, & Hope, 2001). Below this birth weight, however, there is an increased risk for developmental disabilities. About half of children who were VLBW at birth will demonstrate behavior (especially attention-deficit/hyperactivity disorder [ADHD]) or learning problems by school age (Emsley et al., 1998; Lou, 1996; McCarton et al., 1996; O'Shea et al., 1998). In terms of behavior issues, children born prematurely are at risk for lower levels of social competence, are less adaptable, less regular in their habits, less persistent, and more withdrawn (Chapieski & Evankovich, 1997). ADHD is also more common in this group. Signs of ADHD may appear as early as 2 years of age as hyperactivity and difficulty following verbal directions and listening to a story in a small group. In addition, there may be behavior differences such as sleep disturbances, feeding difficulties, tantrums, or resistance to limit setting. Learning problems may be anticipated in children whose language is delayed and who demonstrate poor visual-motor coordination. Family factors have also been found to be strong predictors of future school performance (Gross et al., 2001). Optimal school outcome has been significantly associated with increased parental education, child rearing by two parents, and stability in family composition and geographic residence.

In studies of children with birth weight less than 1,000 grams (ELBW and micropreemies), major developmental disabilities have been found in about one quarter of children. This includes cerebral palsy (15%), hearing impairment (9%–11%), and visual impairment (1%–9%; Hack et al., 2000; Vohr et al., 2000). At 18–22 months corrected age, the mean Bayley Mental Developmental Index (Bayley, 1993) was 75, and 29% of the children had a score less than 70. Although cerebral palsy, especially spastic diplegia, is not uncommon in children who were VLBW, many "outgrow" this diagnosis by school age and simply appear to lack coordination. Predictors of neurological abnormality included abnormal findings (IVH/PVL) on cerebral ultrasound and chronic lung disease (Baud et al., 1998; Olsen et al., 1998; Pederson et al., 2000; Pinto-Martin et al., 1995; Skranes et al., 1998). Sensorineural impairments were correlated with neonatal sepsis and jaundice. Neurological, developmental, neurosensory, and functional morbidities increased with decreasing birth weight, and overall, males were more at risk for disabilities than were females.

SUMMARY

LBW infants are at greater risk when compared with full-term infants for many problems in the newborn period that may lead to long-term complications. Physiologic immaturity of organ systems leads to RDS, hyperbilirubinemia, hypoglycemia, and hypocalcemia. Fortunately, the infants usually recover from these complications without major long-term sequelae. Other problems, however, such as IVH, PVL, sepsis, and persistent apnea and bradycardia are associated with poor neurodevelopmental outcome. With increased public awareness, improved prenatal care, and advanced neonatal intensive care, the outcome of premature and SGA infants is likely to continue to improve.

REFERENCES

Abendroth, D., Moser, D.K., Dracup, K., et al. (1999). Do apnea monitors decrease emotional distress in parents of infants at high risk for cardiopulmonary arrest? *Journal of Pediatric Health Care, 13,* 50–57.

Abman, S.H., & Groothius, J.R. (1994). Pathophysiology and treatment of bronchopulmonary dysplasia: Current issues. *Pediatric Clinics of North America, 41,* 277–315.

Adams, M.M., Elam-Evans, L.D., Wilson, H.G., et al. (2000). Rates of and factors associated with recurrence of preterm delivery. *Journal of the American Medical Association, 283,* 1591–1596.

Als, H., & Gilkerson, L. (1997). The role of relationship-based developmentally supportive newborn intensive care in strengthening outcome of preterm infants. *Seminars in Perinatology, 21,* 178–189.

American Academy of Pediatrics Task Force on Infant Position and SIDS. (1992). Position and SIDS. *Pediatrics, 89,* 1120–1126.

Amiel-Tison, C. (1968). Neurological evaluation of the maturity of newborn infants. *Archives of Disease in Childhood, 43,* 89–93.

Andrews, W.W., Goldenberg, R.L., & Hauth, J.C. (1995). Preterm labor: Emerging role of genital tract infections. *Infectious Agents and Disease, 4,* 196–211.

Baker, K.A., & Ryan, M.E. (1999). RSV infection in infants and young children: What's new in diagnosis, treatment, and prevention? *Postgraduate Medicine, 106,* 97–99, 103–104, 107–108.

Ballard, J.L., Khoury, J.C., Wedig, K., et al. (1991). New Ballard score, expanded to include extremely premature infants. *Journal of Pediatrics, 119,* 417–423.

Bancalari, E., Abdenour, G.E., Feller, R., et al. (1995). Bronchopulmonary dysplasia: Clinical presentation. *Journal of Pediatrics, 95,* 819–823.

Baud, O., d'Allest, A., Lacaze-Masmonteil, T., et al. (1998). The early diagnosis of periventricular leukomalacia in premature infants with positive rolandic sharp waves on serial electroencephalography. *Journal of Pediatrics, 132,* 813–817.

Bayley, N. (1993). *Bayley Scales of Infant Development—Second Edition.* San Antonio, TX: The Psychological Corporation.

Bennett, F.C., & Scott, D.T. (1997). Long-term perspective on premature infant outcome and contemporary intervention issues. *Seminars in Perinatology, 21,* 190–201.

Bergman, J. (1998). Developmental outcomes in very low birth weight infants. Current status and future trends. *Pediatric Clinics of North America, 45,* 673–690.

Bhatia, J. (2000). Current options in the management of apnea of prematurity. *Clinical Pediatrics, 39,* 327–336.

Blair, C., Ramey, C.T., & Hardin, J.M. (1995). Early intervention for low birthweight, premature infants: Participation and intellectual development. *American Journal of Mental Retardation, 99,* 542–554.

Brooks-Gunn, J., McCarton, C.M., Casey, P.H., et al. (1994). Early intervention in low-birth-weight premature infants: Results through age 5 years from the Infant Health and Development Program. *Journal of the American Medical Association, 272,* 1257–1262.

Canadian Paediatrics Society, Nutrition Committee. (1995). Nutrient needs and feeding of premature infants. *Canadian Medical Association Journal, 152,* 1765–1785.

Caplan, M.S., & Jilling, T. (2001). New concepts in necrotizing enterocolitis. *Current Opinion in Pediatrics, 13,* 111–115.

Casiro, O.G., McKenzie, M.E., McFadyen, L., et al. (1993). Early discharge with community-based intervention for low birth weight infants: A randomized trial. *Pediatrics, 92,* 128–134.

Chan, G.M., Borschel, M.W., & Jacobs, J.R. (1994). Effects of human milk or formula feeding on the growth, behavior, and protein status of preterm infants discharged from the newborn intensive care unit. *American Journal of Clinical Nutrition, 60,* 710–716.

Chandler, J.C., & Hebra, A. (2000). Necrotizing enterocolitis in infants with very low birth weight. *Seminars in Pediatric Surgery, 9,* 63–72.

Chapieski, M.L., & Evankovich, K.D. (1997). Behavioral effects of prematurity. *Seminars in Perinatology, 21,* 221–239.

Cohen, A., & Manno, C. (1998). Transfusion practices in infants receiving assisted ventilation. *Clinics in Perinatology, 25,* 97–111.

Constantine, N.A., Kraemer, H.C., Kendall-Tackett, K.A., et al. (1987). Use of physical and neurologic observations in assessment of gestational age in low-birth-weight infants. *Journal of Pediatrics, 110,* 921–928.

Cooper, L.G., Leland, N.L., & Alexander, G. (1995). Effect of maternal age on birth outcomes among young adolescents. *Social Biology, 42,* 22–35.

Couser, R.J., Ferrara, T.B., Wright, G.B., et al. (1996). Prophylactic indomethacin therapy in the first twenty-four hours of life for the prevention of patent ductus arteriosus in preterm infants treated prophylactically with surfactant in the delivery room. *Journal of Pediatrics, 128,* 631–637.

Dammann, O., Allred, E.N., & Veelken, N. (1998). Increased risk of spastic diplegia among very low birth weight children after preterm labor or prelabor rupture of membranes. *Journal of Pediatrics, 132,* 531–535.

Dammann, O., & Leviton, A. (1999). Brain damage in preterm newborns: Might enhancement of developmentally regulated endogenous protection open a door for prevention? *Pediatrics, 104,* 541–550.

Dolfin, T., Skidmore, M.B., Fong, K.W., et al. (1983). Incidence, severity and timing of subependymal and intraventricular hemorrhages in preterm infants born in a perinatal unit as detected by serial real-time ultrasound. *Pediatrics, 71,* 541–546.

Dubowitz, L.M., Dubowitz, V., & Goldberg, C. (1970). Clinical assessment of gestational age in the newborn infant. *Journal of Pediatrics, 77,* 1–10.

Durand, M., Sardesai, S., & McEvoy, C. (1995). Effects of early dexamethasone therapy on pulmonary mechanics and chronic lung disease in very low birth weight infants: A randomized, controlled trial. *Pediatrics, 95,* 584–590.

Emsley, H.C.A., Wardle, S.P., Sims, D.G., et al. (1998). Increased survival and deteriorating developmental outcome in 23 to 25 week old gestation infants, 1990–4 compared with 1984–9. *Archives of Disease in Childhood, Fetal and Neonatal Edition, 78,* F99–F104.

Farrell, P.A., & Fiascone, J.M. (1997). Bronchopulmonary dysplasia in the 1990s: A review for the pediatrician. *Current Problems in Pediatrics, 27,* 129–163.

Feldman, R., & Eidelman, A.I. (1998). Intervention programs for premature infants. *Clinics in Perinatology, 25,* 613–626.

Fisher, D.A. (1999). Hypothyroxinemia in premature infants: Is thyroxine treatment necessary? *Thyroid, 9,* 715–720.

Fowlie, P.W. (1996). Prophylactic indomethacin: Systemic review and meta-analysis. *Archives of Disease in Childhood, 74,* F81–F87.

Gibbs, R.S., Romero, R., Hillier, S.L., et al. (1992). A review of premature birth and subclinical infection. *American Journal of Obstetrics and Gynecology, 166*, 1515–1528.

Gibson, E., Dembofsky, C.A., Rubin, S., et al. (2000). Infant sleep position practices 2 years into the "back to sleep" campaign. *Clinical Pediatrics, 39*, 285–289.

Glass, P. (2001). Your baby was born prematurely. In M.L. Batshaw (Ed.), *When your child has a disability: The complete sourcebook of daily and medical care* (Rev. ed., pp. 59–71). Baltimore: Paul H. Brookes Publishing Co.

Goldenberg, R.L., & Rouse, D.J. (1998). Prevention of premature birth. *New England Journal of Medicine, 339*, 313–320.

Gonzalez, A., & Centura-Junca, P. (1991). Incidence of patent ductus arteriosus in premature infants less than 2000 grams. *Revista chilena de pediatría, 62*, 354–358.

Greer, F.R. (1995). Vitamin K deficiency and hemorrhage in infancy. *Clinics in Perinatology, 22*, 759–777.

Grether, J.K., Nelson, K.B., Dambrosia, J.M., et al. (1999). Interferons and cerebral palsy. *Journal of Pediatrics, 134*, 324–332.

Grosfeld, J.L., Cheu, H., Schlatter, M., et al. (1991). Changing trends in necrotizing enterocolitis: Experience with 302 cases in two decades. *Annals of Surgery, 214*, 300–307.

Gross, S.J., Mettelman, B.B., Dye, T.D., et al. (2001). Impact of family structure and stability on academic outcome in preterm children at 10 years of age. *Journal of Pediatrics, 138*, 16–75.

Guralnick, M.J. (Ed.). (1997). *The effectiveness of early intervention.* Baltimore: Paul H. Brookes Publishing Co.

Hack, M., Wilson-Costello, D., Friedman, H., et al. (2000). Neurodevelopment and predictors of outcome of children with birth weights of less than 1000g: 1992–1995. *Archives of Pediatric and Adolescent Medicine, 154*, 725–731.

Hadden, D.S. (1999). The long anticipated day: Strategies for success when a premature infant comes home from the neonatal intensive care unit. *Young Exceptional Children, 3*, 21–26.

Hediger, M.L., Overpeck, M.D., Maurer, K.R., et al. (1998). Growth of infants and young children born small or large for gestational age: Findings from the Third National Health and Nutrition Examination Survey. *Archives of Pediatrics and Adolescent Medicine, 152*, 1225–1231.

Hittner, H.M., Hirsch, N.J., & Rudolph, A.J. (1977). Assessment of gestational age by examination of the anterior vascular capsule of the lens. *Journal of Pediatrics, 91*, 455–458.

Hodgman, J.E. (1998). Apnea of prematurity and the risk for SIDS. *Pediatrics, 102*, 969–971.

Hokken-Koelega, A.C., De Ridder, M.A., Lemmen, R.J., et al. (1995). Children born small for gestational age: Do they catch up? *Pediatric Research, 38*, 267–271.

Horwitz, J.R., Lally, K.P., Cheu, H.W., et al. (1995). Complications after surgical intervention for necrotizing enterocolitis: A multicenter review. *Journal of Pediatric Surgery, 30*, 994–998.

Hoyert, D.L., Freedman, M.A., Strobino, D.M., et al. (2001). Annual summary of vital statistics: 2000. *Pediatrics, 108*, 1241–1255.

Huddy, C.L., Johnson, A., & Hope, P.L. (2001). Educational and behavioural problems in babies of 32–35 weeks gestation. *Archives of Disease in Childhood, Fetal and Neonatal Edition, 85*, F23–F28.

Joffe, G.M., Symonds, R., Alverson, D., et al. (1995). The effect of a comprehensive prematurity prevention program on the number of admissions to the neonatal intensive care unit. *Journal of Perinatology, 15*, 305–309.

Johnson, L., Quinn, G.E., Abbasi, S., et al. (1995). Severe retinopathy of prematurity in infants with birth weights less than 1250 grams: Incidence and outcome of treatment with pharmacologic serum levels of vitamin E in addition to cryotherapy from 1985–1991. *Journal of Pediatrics, 127*, 632–639.

Joint Committee on Infant Hearing. (2000). Year 2000 position statement: Principles and guidelines for early hearing detection and intervention programs. *Pediatrics, 106*, 798–817.

Kari, M.A., Hallman, M., Eronen, M., et al. (1994). Prenatal dexamethasone treatment in conjunction with rescue therapy of human surfactant: A randomized placebo-controlled multicenter study. *Pediatrics, 93*, 730–736.

Karlberg, J., & Albertsson-Wikland, K. (1995). Growth in full-term small-for-gestational-age infants: From birth to final height. *Pediatric Research, 38*, 733–739.

Kennedy, J.D., Edward, L.J., Bates, D.J., et al. (2000). Effects of birthweight and oxygen supplementation on lung function in late childhood in children of very low birth weight. *Pediatric Pulmonology, 30*, 32–40.

Kleberg, A., Westrup, B., & Stjernqvist, K. (2000). Developmental outcome, child behavior and mother-child interaction at 3 years of age following newborn individualized developmental care and intervention program (NIDCAP). *Early Human Development, 60*, 123–135.

Kuban, K.C., & Leviton, A. (1994). Medical progress: Cerebral palsy. *New England Journal of Medicine, 330*, 188–195.

Kumazaki, K., Nakayama, M., Sumida, Y., et al. (2002). Placental features in preterm infants with periventricular leukomalacia. *Pediatrics, 109*, 650–655.

Larsen, P.B., Brendstrup, L., & Skov, L., et al. (1995). Aminophylline versus caffeine citrate for apnea and bradycardia prophylaxis in premature neonates. *Acta Paediatrica, 84*, 360–364.

Laudry, S.H., Fletcher, J.M., Denson, S.E., et al. (1993). Longitudinal outcome for low birth weight infants: Effects of intraventricular hemorrhage and bronchopulmonary dysplasia. *Journal of Clinical Experimental Neuropsychology, 15*, 205–218.

Leger, J., & Czernichow, P. (1994). Retardation of intrauterine growth: Prognosis and therapeutic perspectives [Editorial]. *Presse Médicale, 23*, 969–971.

Leger, J., Limoni, C., Collin, D., et al. (1998). Prediction factors in the determination of final height in subjects born small for gestational age. *Pediatric Research, 43*, 808–812.

Leviton, A., Kuban, K., Bagano, M., et al. (1993). Antenatal corticosteroids appear to reduce the risk of postnatal germinal matrix hemorrhage in intubated low birth weight newborns. *Pediatrics, 81*, 1083–1088.

Leviton, A., Paneth, N., Reuss, L., et al. (1999). Hypothyroxinemia of prematurity and the risk of cerebral white matter damage. *Journal of Pediatrics, 134*, 706–711.

Lou, H.C. (1996). Etiology and pathogenesis of attention-deficit hyperactivity disorder (ADHD): Significance of prematurity and perinatal hypoxic-haemodynamic encephalopathy. *Acta Paediatrica, 85*, 1266–1271.

Mallory, G.B., Chaney, H., Mutich, R.L., et al. (1991). Longitudinal changes in lung function during the first three years of premature infants with moderate to severe bronchopulmonary dysplasia. *Pediatric Pulmonology, 11*, 8–14.

Mandrich, M., Simons, C.J., Ritchie, S., et al. (1994). Motor development, infantile reactions and postural responses of preterm, at-risk infants. *Developmental Medicine and Child Neurology, 36*, 397–405.

Marino, A.J., Assing, E., Carbone, M.T., et al. (1995). The incidence of gastroesophageal reflux in preterm infants. *Journal of Perinatology, 15*, 369–371.

Mavroudis, C., Backer, C.L., Gevitz, M. (1994). Forty-six years of patent ductus arteriosus division at Children's Memorial Hospital of Chicago: Standards for comparisons. *Annals of Surgery, 220,* 402–409.

McCarton, C.M., Wallace, I.F., Divon, M., et al. (1996). Cognitive and neurologic development of the premature, small for gestational age infant through age 6: Comparison by birth weight and gestational age. *Pediatrics, 98,* 1167–1169.

Ment, L.R., Vohr, B., Allan, W., et al. (2000). Outcome of children in the indomethacin intraventricular hemorrhage trial. *Pediatrics, 105,* 485–491.

Meyer, C., Witte, J., Hildmann, A., et al. (1999). Neonatal screening for hearing disorders in infants at risk: Incidence, risk factors, and follow-up. *Pediatrics, 104,* 900–904.

Msall, M.E., Phelps, D.L., DiGaudio, K.M., et al. (2000). Severity of neonatal retinopathy of prematurity is predictive of neurodevelopmental functional outcome at age 5.5 years. *Pediatrics, 106,* 998–1005.

National Center for Chronic Disease Prevention and Health Promotion, Division of Nutrition; National Center for Health Statistics, Division of Vital Statistics; and Centers for Disease Control and Prevention. (1994). Increasing incidence of LBW: United States, 1981–1991. *MMWR, 43,* 335.

NIH Consensus Development Panel on the Effect of Corticosteroids for Fetal Maturation on Perinatal Outcomes. (1995). Effect of corticosteroids for fetal maturation on perinatal outcomes. *Journal of the American Medical Association, 273,* 413–418.

Novak, D.A. (1996). Gastroesophageal reflux in the premature infant. *Clinical Perinatology, 23,* 305–320.

Obladen, M., & Maier, R.F. (1995). Recombinant erythropoietin for "prevention" of anemia in preterm infants. *Journal of Perinatal Medicine, 23,* 119–126.

O'Connor, A.R., Stephenson, T., Johnson, A., et al. (2002). Long-term ophthalmic outcome of low birth weight children with and without retinopathy of prematurity. *Pediatrics, 109,* 12–18.

Ohis, R.H. (2000). The use of erythropoietin in neonates. *Clinics in Perinatology, 27,* 681–696.

Olsen, P., Vainionpaa, L., Paakko, E., et al. (1998). Psychological findings in preterm children related to neurologic status and magnetic resonance imaging. *Pediatrics, 102,* 329–336.

O'Shea, T.M., & Dammann, O. (2000). Antecedents of cerebral palsy in very low-birth weight infants. *Clinics in Perinatology, 27,* 285–302.

O'Shea, T.M., Klinepeter, K.L., Goldstein, D.J., et al. (1997). Survival and developmental disability in infants with birth weights of 501 to 800 grams, born between 1979 and 1994. *Pediatrics, 100,* 982–986.

O'Shea, T.M., Preisser, J.S., Klinepeter, K.L., et al. (1998). Trends in mortality and cerebral palsy in a geographically based cohort of very low birth weight neonates born between 1982 to 1994. *Pediatrics, 101,* 642–647.

Papile, L., Tyson, J.E., Stoll, B.J., et al. (1998). A multicenter trial of two dexamethasone regimens in ventilator-dependent premature infants. *New England Journal of Medicine, 338,* 1112–1118.

Paz, I., Gale, R., Laor, A., et al. (1995). The cognitive outcome of full-term small for gestational age infants at late adolescence. *Obstetrics and Gynecology, 85,* 452–456.

Pederson, B.S., Vohr, B., Staib, L.H., et al. (2000). Regional brain volume abnormalities and long-term cognitive outcome in preterm infants. *Journal of the American Medical Association, 284,* 1939–1947.

Perlman, J.M., Risser, R., & Broyles, R.S. (1996). Bilateral cystic periventricular leukomalacia in premature infants: Associated risk factors. *Pediatrics, 97,* 822–827.

Persson, P.H., & Weldner, B.M. (1986). Reliability of ultrasound fetometry in estimating gestational age in the second trimester. *Acta Obstetricia et Gynecologica Scandinavica, 65,* 481–483.

Pinto-Martin, J.A., Riolo, S., Cnaan, A., et al. (1995). Cranial ultrasound prediction of disabling and nondisabling cerebral palsy at age two in a low birth weight population. *Pediatrics, 95,* 249–254.

Raju, T.N.K., Langenberg, P., Bhutani, V., et al. (1997). Vitamin E prophylaxis to reduce retinopathy of prematurity: A reappraisal of published trials. *Journal of Pediatrics, 131,* 844–850.

Ramey, S.L., Ramey, C.T., & Friedlander, M.J. (1999). Early experience and early intervention. *Mental Retardation and Developmental Disabilities Research Reviews, 5,* 1–99.

Rasmussen, S.A., Moore, C.A., Paulozzi, L.J., et al. (2001). Risk for birth defects among premature infants: A population-based study. *Journal of Pediatrics, 138,* 668–673.

Rastogi, A., Akintorin, S.M., Bez, M.L., et al. (1996). A controlled trial of dexamethasone to prevent bronchopulmonary dysplasia in surfactant-treated infants. *Pediatrics, 98,* 204–210.

Rawlings, J.S., & Scott, J.S. (1996). Postconceptional age of surviving preterm low-birth-weight infants at hospital discharge. *Archives of Pediatrics and Adolescent Medicine, 150,* 260–262.

Rawlings, J.S., Smith, F.R., & Garcia, J. (1993). Expected duration of hospital stay of low birth weight infants: Graphic depiction in relation to birth weight and gestational age. *Journal of Pediatrics, 123,* 307–309.

Reuss, M.L., Paneth, N., Pinto-Martin, J.A., et al. (1996). The relation of transient hypothyroxinemia in preterm infants to neurologic development at two years of age. *New England Journal of Medicine, 334,* 821–827.

Robertson, P.A., Sniderman, S.H., Laros, R.K., Jr., et al. (1992). Neonatal morbidity according to gestational age and birth weight from five tertiary care centers in the United States, 1983 through 1986. *American Journal of Obstetrics and Gynecology, 166,* 1629–1641.

Robinson, C., & Jackson, B. (1993). Continuity of care for medically fragile infants. In M. Krajicek & R. Tompkins (Eds.), *The medically fragile infant* (pp. 77–95). Austin, TX: PRO-ED.

Ross, G., Lipper, E.G., & Ald, P. (1990). Social competence and behavior problems in premature children at school age. *Pediatrics, 86,* 391–397.

Scanlon, J.W. (1994). The very-low-birth-weight infant. In G.B. Avery, M.A. Fletcher, & M.G. MacDonald (Eds.), *Neonatology: Pathophysiology and management in the newborn* (4th ed., 399–416). Philadelphia: Lippincott Williams & Wilkins.

Shankaran, S., Bauer, C.R., Bain, R., et al. (1996). Prenatal and perinatal risk and protective factors for neonatal intracranial hemorrhage. *Archives of Pediatric and Adolescent Medicine, 150,* 491–497.

Shankaran, S., Cepeda, E., Muran, G., et al. (1996). Antenatal phenobarbital therapy and neonatal outcome, I: Effect on intracranial hemorrhage. *Pediatrics, 97,* 644–648.

Shankaran, S., Papile, L., Wright, L.L., et al. (1997). The effect of antenatal phenobarbital therapy on neonatal intracranial hemorrhage in preterm infants. *New England Journal of Medicine, 71,* 466–471.

Skranes, J., Vik, T., Nilsen, G., et al. (1998). Can cerebral MRI at age 1 year predict motor and intellectual outcomes in very-low-birth-weight children? *Developmental Medicine and Child Neurology, 40,* 256–262.

Snyder, C.L., Gittes, G.K., Murphy, J.P., et al. (1997). Survival after necrotizing enterocolitis in infants weighing less than 1000 g: 25 years' experience at a single institution. *Journal of Pediatric Surgery, 32,* 434–437.

Suresh, G.K., Horbar, J.D., Kenny, M., et al. (2001). Major birth defects in very low birth weight infants in the Vermont Oxford Network. *Journal of Pediatrics, 139,* 366–373.

Tapia, J.L., Ramirez, R., Cifuentes, J., et al. (1998). The effect of early dexamethasone administration on bronchopulmonary dysplasia in preterm infants with respiratory distress syndrome. *Journal of Pediatrics, 132,* 48–52.

Tauman, R., & Sivan, Y. (2000). Duration of home monitoring for infants discharged with apnea of prematurity. *Biology of the Neonate, 78,* 168–173.

Thorpe, J.A., Ferrette-Smith, D., Gaston, L.A., et al. (1995). Combined antenatal vitamin K and phenobarbital therapy for preventing intracranial hemorrhage in newborns less than 34 weeks gestation. *Obstetrics and Gynecology, 86,* 1–8.

Tortorolo, G., Luciano, R., Papacci, P., et al. (1999). Intraventricular hemorrhage: Past, present and future, focusing on classification, pathogenesis and prevention. *Child's Nervous System, 15,* 652–661.

Valleur-Masson, D., Vodovar, M., Zeller, J., et al. (1993). Bronchopulmonary dysplasia: Course over 3 years in 88 children born between 1984 and 1988. *Archives of Pediatrics, 50,* 553–559.

Van Naarden, K., & Decoufle, P. (1999). Relative and attributable risks for moderate to profound bilateral sensorineural hearing impairment associated with lower birth weight in children 3 to 10 years old. *Pediatrics, 104,* 905–910.

Van Overmeire, B., Smets, K., Lecoutere, D., et al. (2000). A comparison of ibuprofen and indomethacin for closure of patent ductus arteriosus. *New England Journal of Medicine, 343,* 674–681.

Verma, R.P. (1995). Respiratory distress syndrome of the newborn infant. *Obstetrical and Gynecological Survey, 50,* 542–555.

Vohr, B., & Ment, L.R. (1996). Intraventricular hemorrhage in the preterm infant. *Early Human Development, 44,* 1–16.

Vohr, B.R., Wright, L.L., Dusick, A.M., et al. (2000). Neurodevelopmental and functional outcomes of extremely low birth weight infants in the National Institute of Child Health and Human Development Neonatal Research Network, 1993–1994. *Pediatrics, 105,* 1216–1226.

Volpe, J.J. (2001). *Neurology of the newborn* (4th ed.). Philadelphia: W.B. Saunders.

Wagner, C.L., Kramer, B.M., Kendig, J.W., et al. (1995). School-age follow-up of a single-dose prophylactic surfactant cohort. *Journal of Developmental and Behavioral Pediatrics, 16,* 327–332.

Walburn, K.S., Heermann, J.A., & Balsillie, L.J. (1997). Training in family-focused developmental care: Bridging the gap between traditional and family-centered care in the NICU. *Infants and Young Children, 10,* 46–56.

Watchko, J.F., & Claassen, D. (1994). Kernicterus in premature infants: Current prevalence and relationship to NICHD Phototherapy Study exchange criteria. *Pediatrics, 93,* 996–999.

Wells, J.T., & Ment, L.R. (1995). Prevention of intraventricular hemorrhage in preterm infants. *Early Human Development, 42,* 209–233.

Westrup, B., Kleberg, A., von Eichwald, K., et al. (2000). A randomized, controlled trial to evaluate the effects of the newborn individualized developmental care and assessment program in a Swedish setting. *Pediatrics, 105,* 66–72.

Wheater, M., & Renie, J.M. (2000). Perinatal infection is an important risk factor for cerebral palsy in very-low-birth-weight infants. *Developmental Medicine and Child Neurology, 42,* 364–367.

Yu, V.Y., & Bascain, M.B. (1994). Avoidance of red blood cell transfusion in an extremely preterm infant given recombinant human erythropoietin therapy. *Journal of Paediatrics and Child Health, 30,* 360–362.

II The Developing Child

7 Substance Abuse

A Preventable Threat to Development

Martha J. Wunsch, Charles J. Conlon, and Peter C. Scheidt

Upon completion of this chapter, the reader will:

- understand the impact of the disease of addiction on a woman and her fetus during pregnancy

- be able to describe the effects of prenatal exposure to alcohol, nicotine, and illicit drugs of abuse on the newborn

- be aware of the neurodevelopmental alterations in infancy associated with in utero exposure to drugs of abuse, including cocaine, opiates, marijuana, and phencyclidine

- be knowledgeable about the role of prevention and aware of the most effective multidisciplinary intervention strategies utilized in this area

Some chemicals that are teratogenic (capable of producing physical defects in the developing fetus) are also psychoactive substances with the potential for abuse and dependency. When a pregnant woman uses or becomes addicted to these substances, the potential for serious and adverse effects on the development of her child is of great concern. Data about the prevalence of illicit and legal substance use during pregnancy vary across studies, but the Center on Addiction and Substance Abuse (1996) estimated that among pregnant women, approximately 10% abuse alcohol, 20% smoke cigarettes, 10% use marijuana, about 1% use cocaine, and 0.5% use opiates including heroin. The prevalence of abuse of prescription drugs by pregnant women, such as benzodiazepines (prescribed to treat seizures), is not known.

In Pinellas County, Florida, urine samples from private and public prenatal clinics were screened for alcohol, opiates, cocaine and its metabolites, and cannabinoids (marijuana derivatives). The study revealed that 15% of women across all socioeconomic and racial classifications used some illicit psychoactive chemical or alcohol or tobacco during pregnancy (Chasnoff, Landress, & Barrett, 1990). In the California Perinatal Substance Exposure Study, alcohol use rates were fairly stable at 6%–12% across populations in the state, but rates of tobacco use and illicit drug use varied by social and demographic variables (Noble et al., 1997).

It should be emphasized that three quarters of individuals who abuse one substance are likely to abuse others as well (Center for Substance Abuse Treatment, 1991). With maternal use of multiple illicit and legal psychoactive substances, it is difficult to discriminate the specific effect on the fetus of each substance. Other confounding maternal factors associated with substance abuse during pregnancy include malnutrition, sexually transmitted diseases (STDs), and inadequate prenatal care. As a result, the following discussions must be read with the understanding that these effects are often complex and shared.

The biological effects of psychoactive substances on fetal development may be quite varied. Alcohol abuse during pregnancy and its effect on the fetus were clearly described in the 1970s. Fetal alcohol syndrome (FAS) is a delineated diagnosis resulting in neurobehavioral abnormalities including developmental delay, growth problems, and other physical effects. Intrauterine exposure to opioids such as heroin, methadone, or morphine may cause newborns to experience withdrawal symptoms, manifest at birth as extreme hyperarousal and jitteriness, but does not cause a dysmorphic syndrome as is seen in alcohol exposure. Possible teratogenic effects of cocaine on the fetus are less clear and extensively debated in the literature (Britt, Ingersoll, & Schnoll, 1999). Use of nicotine by the pregnant woman is clearly associated with growth restriction manifest by decreases in birth weight, but effects on neurodevelopment are unclear (American College of Obstetrics and Gynecology, 1993). Finally, among babies exposed to cannabis/marijuana during pregnancy, there is little evidence of adverse neurobehavioral or developmental effects (Cornelius et al., 1995). The specific effects of each chemical are discussed in detail later in this chapter.

The development of babies exposed in utero to these substances is also greatly confounded by the lifestyle of the drug addict. The disease of addiction may preclude provision of a safe, nurturing, and appropriate home. The pregnant woman may have been raised in a family affected by substance abuse and dependency, in which chaos may preclude the healthy emotional and psychological development of children. Furthermore, the woman may be in a relationship with a partner who is also affected by substance abuse or dependency.

This chapter examines the interaction of a woman, her addiction, and her pregnancy. It discusses the treatment needs of the addicted woman and her substance-exposed newborn. Finally, the chapter describes the known effects of fetal exposure to these drugs, a body of knowledge fraught with the confounding psychosocial, environmental, and genetic factors. What is clear, however, is that a child born to an addicted pregnant woman faces many more challenges than simply the possible teratogenic effects of psychoactive substances. The vignette outlined next illustrates how substance abuse and dependency affects the entire family for more than one generation. This case also illustrates the difference that a treatment intervention program can make in pregnancy outcome for two young mothers.

SHARON AND STELLA

Sharon is a 23-year-old woman incarcerated for possession of heroin and for public intoxication. Eight months ago she gave birth to a daughter, a 2,400-gram (5⅓-pound) full-term baby with signs of FAS. This was her fourth pregnancy in 7 years, and her addiction to heroin and alcohol has become more severe with each pregnancy. Sharon's mother was given custody of Sharon's three oldest children when Sharon was incarcerated. Sharon's partner, the father of her children, was judged unfit for custody because he had become physically abusive on multiple occasions while intoxicated. Her two oldest children are receiving services in school for learning and behavior disorders.

Sharon's family has been known to the social service agency in the community for many years. When she was 10 years old, Sharon and her younger sister Stella were placed in foster care after physical and sexual abuse occurred in their home. After their mother separated from her abusive boyfriend, a "heavy drinker," the girls were returned to her custody. Sharon had a history of marijuana, tobacco, and alcohol use beginning at age 12. She began failing classes in eighth grade and dropped out of school at tenth grade. She was first involved with the juvenile justice system at age 15 when she was arrested for being intoxicated in public. She became pregnant with her first child at 16 years old and left home to live with her boyfriend. Sharon was treated for substance abuse at age 19 and was abstinent from alcohol and other drugs for 6 months.

Sharon's mother learned about Sharon's alcoholism and drug abuse when Sharon was involved in the treatment program. Sharon's mother became very concerned when her younger daughter Stella began using alcohol and marijuana and failing in school at age 14. After Stella was involved in an automobile accident in which she was found to be legally intoxicated, Stella agreed to attend a multidisciplinary outpatient substance abuse treatment program with other adolescents. After an intensive period of treatment, she was able to return to school while maintaining contact with her substance abuse treatment program and attending Alcoholics Anonymous meetings. When Stella became pregnant at age 17, she again became involved with her treatment program and received case management services. Her drug screens were negative throughout pregnancy and at the time of delivery. She delivered a healthy, full-term daughter who weighed 3,800 grams (8½ pounds). Stella has subsequently graduated from high school and continues to maintain sobriety.

CHEMICAL DEPENDENCY: A DISEASE

If substance abuse is to be considered a preventable cause of developmental disability, health care professionals at all levels need to recognize and understand the process of addiction. The medical community recognizes substance abuse and dependency as a disease and clearly defines alcoholism as a model of addiction. Alcoholism is a chronic disease with genetic, psychosocial, and environmental factors influencing its development and manifestations. The disease is progressive and often fatal. It is characterized by impaired control over drinking; preoccupation with the drug; use of alcohol despite adverse consequences; and distortions in thinking, most notably denial (Morse & Flavin, 1992).

Like other chronic illnesses, substance abuse and dependency, also known as addiction, is a disease that waxes and wanes but gets worse over time. Though early in the disease process a woman may be able to stop or limit drinking or drug use during her pregnancy, she is more likely to abuse substances throughout later pregnancies. Furthermore, even if a pregnant or postpartum woman has remained abstinent during the pregnancy, return to substance abuse may occur after the birth under the stress of parenting. This can be frustrating for health care providers when carefully crafted care plans for mother and infant are "sabotaged" by the mother's active disease of addiction.

Family, twin, and adoption studies provide evidence that addiction has a significant genetic component (Anthenelli & Schuckit, 1998). Family studies comparing the risk of developing alcoholism in relatives of affected individuals with the rate of disease in the general population show an increased occurrence in biological relatives of alcoholics (Kendler et al., 1992). Thus, the infant born to the addicted woman has some predisposition to become the next generation affected by this disease, even if removed from the mother's care at birth. Typically, substance use begins with experimentation with using psychoactive chemicals in adolescence or young adulthood. Use continues and escalates because of the resultant euphoric, or positive, feelings. After a period of use, however, the pleasant effects may become less pronounced, and tolerance to the pleasant effects of the chemical develops. The motivation to continue use comes from both a desire to experience the pleasurable feelings and to avoid the unpleasant symptoms of withdrawal. The individual now becomes dependent on the drug (Jaffe, 1990).

Dependence on psychoactive substances can be physical or psychological; usually, it is a combination of the two. Physical dependency is a state in which there are withdrawal symptoms after cessation of drug use. The drug is then used to avoid these symptoms. Alcohol is an example of a drug that produces physical symptoms of withdrawal upon cessation. These range from nausea, vomiting, tremors, and irritability, to visual, auditory, and tactile **hallucinations**; seizures; and even death. Psychological symptoms reflect the perceived need for a chemical by the individual after use is stopped, often reflected by a change in mood or personality. Cocaine typically produces intense symptoms of psychological withdrawal, and addicts sometimes describe cocaine "calling them to use" during this withdrawal phase. After cessation of use, individuals may experience depression or dysphoria, which provides a further stimulus for resuming use (Jaffe, 1990). Nicotine is a drug with both physical withdrawal symptoms, such as irritability, headaches, gastrointestinal disturbances, and insomnia, and psychological withdrawal manifest by an intense desire to smoke that lingers for months or even years. Drug use may be triggered by emotions, by association with peers who use drugs, or by special situations (Jaffe, 1990). In reality, every psychoactive chemical has some degree of psychological withdrawal, for it has occupied a central and powerful role in the life of the user.

There is evidence that heavy use of a chemical may alter brain neurochemistry with permanent effects that drive continued dependency (Leshner, 1998). Psychoactive drugs produce these effects through the mesolimbic dopamine system in the brain. This is an area of the brain that mediates pleasure and reward in human behavior (Koob, 1996). After years of heroin use, some addicts require methadone maintenance to remain abstinent from abused opioids, reflecting a change in brain neurochemistry resulting from exposure to the drug.

The positive feelings associated with use of a chemical and the physical and psychological effects of withdrawal strongly deter cessation of drug use. This cycle of use, euphoria, withdrawal, and dependency interferes with appropriate and attentive parenting as the financial, emotional, and psychological resources necessary for effective parenting are diverted to obtaining, using, and recovering from drug use. Individuals with addiction often attempt to set limits on their use, but these usually fail. Pleas and reasoning about the effects of use on children and other family members are overpowered by the compulsion to use. This occurs even as affected individuals may face loss of employment, homelessness, and loss of custody of children.

A pregnant woman actively using these psychoactive substances, illicit or legal, is at risk for developing withdrawal at the time of birth. She may require medical treatment for withdrawal from alcohol, opiates, or other sedative/hypnotic drugs. Her newborn may display symptoms of intoxication or withdrawal. Though some infants do not have any symptoms of withdrawal, up to 90% require special handling or medical intervention during the first days or weeks of life (Tran, 1999). Both mother and child may have physical conditions that make early bonding difficult. Ideally, the addicted or alcoholic mother is in treatment and recovery at the time of the her child's birth. If she is not in treatment or recovery, her disease of addiction may result in devastating consequences to her and her child during a developmentally vulnerable time.

THE FAMILY AND SUBSTANCE ABUSE

The family dealing with substance abuse has difficulty nurturing its members and raising its children. Children whose parents abuse alcohol and other drugs are raised in homes where they are at biological, psychological, and environmental risk. In an extensive review of the literature, Johnson and Leff (1999) outlined the combination of risk factors affecting these children but noted that the single most potent factor is parental substance abuse. Parents who abuse alcohol and other drugs exert a very powerful influence on the family system because their behavior is unpredictable, manipulative, and frightening to other adults and children in the family. The drug addict or alcoholic may become angry and violent or sad and withdrawn and may project blame for problems onto other family members (Cermak, 1990, 1991). He or she will do anything to maintain access to alcohol and/or other drugs.

In an extensive review of the literature on children, Giglio and Kaufman (1990) emphasized that a parent who is high, drunk, or impaired by chemicals is unable to fulfill a role in the family system. Violence is common and is sometimes directed at the children. An infant in this environment is at increased risk for abuse and neglect, and older children may display their distress through physical or psychological symptoms. These children are at higher risk for school failure and subsequent delinquency, depression, and increased anxiety. In turn, they are more likely to have trouble with alcohol and other drugs themselves as they reach adolescence (Johnson & Leff, 1999).

EFFECTS OF PSYCHOACTIVE SUBSTANCES ON THE FETUS

The following sections discuss the specific effects of alcohol, opiates, cocaine, nicotine, and marijuana on the fetus during pregnancy.

Alcohol

Alcohol ingestion during pregnancy has been associated with a spectrum of physical and neurodevelopmental effects on the fetus (Astley & Clarren, 1996; Streissguth & Kanter, 1997). The diagnosis of fetal alcohol syndrome (FAS) is defined by four criteria: maternal drinking during pregnancy, a characteristic facial appearance, growth retardation, and brain damage (Table 7.1.) The effect on the central nervous system is seen in school-age children as difficulties with learning and behavior. If there are signs of neurodevelopmental problems without the other criteria for FAS, the term **alcohol-related neurodevelopmental disorder (ARND)** is often used (Stratton, Howe, & Battaglia, 1996).

The mechanism of injury to the fetal brain by alcohol has been studied in animal models as well as in children through the use of neuroimaging (Swayze et al., 1997). In addition to an overall reduction in brain size, there are specific areas of the brain that are most affected. The basal ganglia, associated with memory and cognition, may be affected as well as the cerebellum, an area that controls balance, gait, coordination, and some cognitive functions (Mattson, Riley, Sowell, et al., 1996; Sowell et al., 1996). Absence of the corpus callosum, the structure linking the right and left sides of the brain, is present in 7% of children with FAS, a rate 20 times greater than in the general population (Riley et al., 1995). Research in animal models implicates **free radicals** and other metabolites of alcohol as adversely affecting the differentiation and growth of neuronal cells in the developing brain (Chen & Sullik, 1996; Maier, Chen, & West, 1996; Michaelis & Michaelis, 1994).

The prevalence of FAS and ARND worldwide is difficult to estimate and appears to differ among populations. This reflects a number of factors, including maternal age, amount of alcohol consumed in a country, and genetic factors affecting fetal susceptibility. Estimates range from 1 to 5 in 1,000 live births depending on the population studied (Centers for Disease Control and Prevention, 1997). Overall, FAS and ARND account for about 5% of congenital anomalies and for 10%–20% of all cases of mild mental retardation (Spohr, Willms, & Stein-

Table 7.1. Diagnostic classification of fetal alcohol syndrome (FAS) and related disorders

Diagnosis	Criteria					
	Confirmed exposure to alcohol	Facial anomalies	Growth retardation	Central nervous system abnormalities	Cognitive abnormalities	Birth defects
FAS with confirmed maternal exposure	X	X	X	X		
FAS without confirmed maternal exposure		X	X	X		
Partial FAS with confirmed maternal exposure	X	X	Growth retardation OR central nervous system abnormalities OR cognitive abnormalities			
Alcohol-related birth defects (ARBD)	X					X
Alcohol-related neurodevelopmental disorder (ARND)	X			X	X	

From American Academy of Pediatrics, Committee on Substance Abuse and Committee on Children with Disabilities. (2000). Fetal alcohol syndrome and alcohol-related neurodevelopmental disorders. *Pediatrics, 106,* 359. This figure is an adaptation of Stratton, K., Howe, C., & Battaglia, F. (Eds.). (1996). *Fetal alcohol syndrome: Diagnosis, epidemiology, prevention, and treatment* (pp. 4–5). Washington DC: National Academy Press. Adapted by permission.

hausen, 1993), which surpasses the number of cases attributable to Down syndrome and fragile X syndrome. This makes FAS and ARND together the leading diagnosable cause of mental retardation.

FAS involves both prenatal and postnatal growth retardation (Lewis & Woods, 1994). Although children with FAS are typically born at term, about 80% have low birth weights (i.e., below the 10th percentile; American Academy of Pediatrics, Committee on Substance Abuse and Committee on Children with Disabilities, 1993). During infancy, about 70% of these children have severe feeding problems, often leading to **failure to thrive** (see Chapter 27). Children with FAS tend to remain thin and short in childhood but by late adolescence may have attained typical height and weight.

Characteristic facial features can help identify young children with FAS (Autti-Rämö, Gaily, & Granström, 1992; Clarren & Smith, 1978; Jones et al., 1973). They frequently have microcephaly (i.e., head circumferences below the 5th percentile), and their eyes are widely spaced with short eye slits. Their noses are short and upturned, the upper lips thin, and the groove in the midline of the lips **(philtrum)** flattened. Although the craniofacial characteristics diminish with time, the microcephaly remains (Spohr et al., 1993). Twenty to fifty percent of children with FAS also have congenital heart defects (most commonly ventricular septal defect), hemangiomas (benign tumors made up of blood vessels), genitourinary malformations, and/or minor joint and limb abnormalities (Bratton, 1995). During childhood, vision complications include **strabismus, nystagmus, astigmatism,** and **myopia** (see Chapter 10). Malformations of the middle ear lead to an increased risk of recurrent otitis media and resultant conductive hearing loss (see Chapter 11).

In the first 2 years of life, developmental delays become evident, particularly in the area of speech and language (Jacobson et al., 1993). Verbal learning may be most impaired by difficulties in encoding information, with less difficulty in memory recall (Mattson, Riley, Delia, et al., 1996). There is also **hypotonia** and associated motor delays. By school age, however, there is only subtle motor impairment, manifested as fine motor incoordination and clumsiness.

At school entry, children with FAS exhibit a wide range of IQ scores but, on average, exhibit mild mental retardation (Janzen, Nanson, & Block, 1995; Streissguth, Herman, & Smith, 1978; Streissguth, Randels, & Smith, 1991).

As part of the intellectual impairment, there are deficits in **executive function,** which is involved in planning, sequencing, self-monitoring, and goal-directed behaviors. These deficits can affect routine activities such as dressing (that requires sequencing skills), limit independence, hinder social interactions, and lead to adaptive behavior problems (Connor et al., 1999; Kopera-Frye, Dehaene, & Streissguth, 1996).

Children and young adults with FAS frequently manifest significant behavior and/or emotional disturbances. Some of these problems are the result of cognitive impairments, but others are a direct effect of alcohol on the developing brain (Kelly, Day, & Streissguth, 2000). These maladaptive behaviors may be profound, pervasive, and persistent; they may, in fact, be the principal factor determining outcome (American Academy of Pediatrics, Committee on substance Abuse and Committee on Children with Disabilities, 2000). Behavioral problems such as hyperactivity and impulsivity are common and differ from behavioral difficulties in other children with developmental delay. Children with FAS may have conduct disorders and may display oppositional-defiant behavior that results in poor social functioning into adulthood (Streissguth, Aase, et al., 1991; Streissguth, Barr, Sampson, et al., 1994). Other problems such as depression, substance abuse, involvement with the legal system, and inappropriate sexual behavior result in "secondary disabilities" in adolescents and adults with FAS (Streissguth & Kanter, 1997).

Children with ARND may have fewer intellectual and behavioral impairments than do children with FAS (Bratton, 1995). These children tend to have intellectual functioning in the borderline-average range and less severe behavior problems. They often demonstrate subtle impairments in executive function, memory, language, and fine motor skills. In school, they have particular difficulty with reading and math (Streissguth, Barr, Olson, et al., 1994). The effects of alcohol exposure on the fetus seem to lead to specific areas of impairment, with some variability. Therefore, it is of paramount importance that these children not be seen as having global impairments in the learning environment.

Opiates

Opium is a mixture of alkaloids derived from the seeds of the poppy, *Papaver somniferum*. Morphine comprises 10% of these alkaloids and can be converted chemically to heroin. Heroin was first manufactured in 1874 and was used medicinally until 1914, when it became recognized as a drug of abuse. It can be ingested, smoked, injected, or absorbed through mucous membranes. Most users administer heroin intravenously so that there is immediate onset of action. Its effects, which last about 2 hours, range from analgesia and sedation to feelings of well-being and euphoria. Continued use leads to the phenomenon of tolerance, in which increasingly higher doses are required to produce the desired effect. This leads to physical dependence (Jaffe, 1990).

In response to the need for treatment of heroin addiction, substance abuse treatment providers began giving methadone to support abstinence. Methadone was initially developed for use as a pain medication. It binds to opiate receptors, does not produce as much euphoria as other opiates, and blocks cravings for the opiate drugs. Even when on a methadone maintenance program, however, 50%–90% of individuals abuse other drugs, and some still fail attempts at abstinence (Glanz & Woods, 1993).

Heroin places women at significant risk for hepatitis, bacterial endocarditis (a serious infection of the heart that can be fatal if not treated with antibiotics in the hospital), and/or HIV infection from shared needles; syphilis and other STDs from prostitution; malnutrition from inadequate food intake; pulmonary edema; overdoses; and withdrawal reactions. Approximately 12%–30% of heroin addicts will become infected with the hepatitis B virus, 13%–25% will become infected with syphilis, and 3%–9% per year become HIV positive (Glanz & Woods, 1993).

Although the prevalence of heroin addiction declined in the 1990s, about 1 in 200 infants born each year are exposed in utero to heroin or to methadone (Glanz & Woods, 1993). The principal direct effect of both heroin and methadone on the fetus is growth retardation. Approximately 45% of infants born to mothers who abuse heroin have low birth weight compared with 25% of infants exposed to methadone and 15% of infants whose mothers were drug free during pregnancy (Glanz & Woods, 1993). There is also a twofold increased risk of prematurity and a fourfold increased risk of stillbirth. Heroin itself is not a teratogen, but some fetuses will be infected with syphilis, which can cause malformations. The most serious immediate risk to the fetus relates to the sharing of needles, which carries a significant chance of transmission of hepatitis B and HIV infection from the mother to the fetus. Infants born to mothers using heroin should receive hepatitis immune globulin to decrease the risk of developing hepatitis and antiretroviral drug therapy if the mother is HIV positive (see Chapter 8).

For a heroin-exposed newborn, the major concern is a severe withdrawal response or neonatal abstinence syndrome. Sixty to ninety-five percent of infants of mothers using heroin or methadone have withdrawal symptoms, and some of these infants may need pharmacological intervention (Tran, 1999). Onset is usually at 24–72 hours of age; treatment may need to be continued until 7–10 days of age; and infants may display subtle symptoms of withdrawal until age 6 months. Symptoms of withdrawal reflect dysregulation of the central nervous system and gastrointestinal tract and include irritability, tremors, sweating, stuffy nose, uncoordinated suck, diarrhea, vomiting, sleep disturbances, hypertonicity, and occasionally seizures (Wagner et al., 1998). Severe symptoms require treatment with an opioid such as tincture of opium or paregoric. Neonatal methadone withdrawal is more delayed than neonatal heroin withdrawal and also can be more severe because the body metabolizes methadone differently than heroin.

For some months after recovery, heroin- and methadone-exposed infants may show subtle neurobehavioral abnormalities, including an abnormal sleep pattern, decreased interactive behavior, resistance to cuddling, and decreased orientation to auditory and visual stimuli (van Baar & de Graaff, 1994).

Long-term effects of fetal opiate exposure may be associated with developmental abnormalities (Wagner et al., 1998). Gestational opiate exposure of fetal rat pups results in decreases in nucleic acid synthesis, protein production, and density of **cortical** neurons and neuronal processes (Malanga & Kosofsky, 1999). There have been reports of decreased head growth, but this finding is controversial. Early language development and motor maturity are often delayed. IQ scores generally are in the low-average range, and there is an increased risk of learning problems. Behavior disorders and inattention have also been reported in school-age children (Eyler & Behnke, 1999; van Baar & de Graaff, 1994). Well-controlled longitudinal studies of neurodevelopment associated with neonatal opiate exposure are about evenly divided between showing no differences and demonstrating adverse developmental effects. Potential effects are seriously confounded by the health status of the mother, polydrug use that almost always accompanies opiate use, and adverse environmental conditions. Thus, direct developmental effects of opiates are uncertain, but the benefits of prevention cannot be disputed.

Cocaine

Cocaine is both one of the most powerfully addictive and most commonly used illicit drugs. Fetal exposure to cocaine occurs in about 1%–3% of all pregnancies (Chiriboga, 1996). It has been associated with an increased risk of prematurity, placental abruption, low birth weight, and infantile neurobehavioral abnormalities. As cocaine is rarely used alone, however, it has been difficult to discriminate its long-term effects from those of other concurrently used drugs of abuse. As with alcohol abuse, there are also confounding prenatal, genetic, and environmental variables.

Cocaine addiction reached epidemic proportions in the 1980s when inexpensive and accessible "crack" became readily available (Abelson & Miller, 1985). Cocaine is a potent short-acting central nervous system **stimulant** that heightens the body's natural response to pleasure, creating feelings of euphoria. Cocaine (benzoylmethylecgonine) is available in two forms: a cocaine hydrochloride salt (the usual street preparation) and a purified alkaloidal base known as crack cocaine. Cocaine hydrochloride is soluble in water and is therefore readily absorbed when administered orally, intranasally, or intravenously (Farrar & Kearns, 1989). Conversely, crack is almost insoluble in water and is heat stable. It vaporizes at low temperatures, and smoking is the preferred route of administration. Cocaine affects brain chemistry principally by blocking the reuptake (and thus increasing the levels) of three **neurotransmitters:** norepinephrine, dopamine, and serotonin (Gonzalez & Campbell, 1994; Figure 7.1). Acute increases in norepinephrine result in constriction of blood vessels, leading to rapid heart rate and elevated blood pressure. Norepinephrine is also the likely source of the euphoria experienced following cocaine intake. Alterations in serotonin levels decrease appetite and the need for sleep. Dopamine stimulation results in hyperactivity and sexual arousal. Yet, long-term cocaine exposure ultimately leads to depletion of dopamine and the reverse effects (Hurt et al., 1995).

Cocaine is often used with other drugs of abuse; in one study, 47% of cocaine users also were heavy alcohol users and 14% used opiates (Davis et al., 1992). When used together, alcohol and cocaine produce a unique metabolite, cocaethylene, which is a more potent constrictor of blood vessels than cocaine alone (Snodgrass, 1994). In infants exposed in utero to both drugs, especially premature infants, there may be an increased risk for intracerebral hemorrhage and a stroke-like syndrome, but this has been debated in the literature.

Animal studies do not support a direct teratogenic effect of cocaine at levels similar to those ingested by humans. At higher doses, however, cocaine can alter neuronal migration and brain

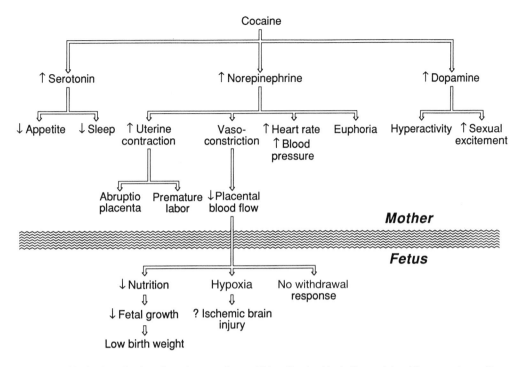

Figure 7.1. Mechanism of action of cocaine on mother and fetus. Cocaine blocks the reuptake of three neurotransmitters: norepinephrine, dopamine, and serotonin. The resultant increase in serotonin suppresses the appetite and the need for sleep in the mother, whereas the dopamine stimulation results in hyperactivity and sexual arousal. Increases in norepinephrine result in increased uterine contractions, predisposing the mother to placental abruption and premature labor. Norepinephrine also leads to a sense of euphoria and constricts blood vessels, leading to rapid heart rate and elevated blood pressure. Increased norepinephrine also results in decreased placental blood flow, predisposing the infant to intrauterine growth retardation and ischemic brain injury.

development (Wilkins et al., 1998). At levels similar to those found in humans, cocaine exposure early in gestation in the rat does lead to abnormalities of the heart, limbs, and genitourinary tract. These are thought to result from **vasoconstriction** and hypoxic-ischemic damage to the developing body organs (Keller & Snyder-Keller, 2000). There is controversy as to whether cocaine can cause similar abnormalities in children. Mice exposed to high doses of cocaine later in gestation have decreased brain size (Church et al., 1998). This is compatible with the finding of decreased head circumference in infants exposed to cocaine in utero. Late-gestation cocaine ingestion also leads to increased uterine contractility. This is consistent with the finding of an increased risk of placental abruptions, miscarriages, premature deliveries, and stillbirths in human fetuses exposed to cocaine (Levy & Koren, 1990; Table 7.2). There appears to be a dose–response effect of fetal cocaine exposure on fetal growth and neonatal neurobehavior abnormalities (Chiriboga, 1998).

In 2001, Frank et al. published a large, systematic review of studies on the effect of prenatal exposure to cocaine on growth, development and behavior in children under age 6 years. Thirty-six studies with information in the five domains of physical growth; cognition; language skills; motor skills; and behavior, attention, affect, and neurophysiology were analyzed. This review found no consistent negative association between prenatal cocaine exposure and physical growth, developmental test scores, and expressive or receptive language. Abnormalities found in motor development faded by 7 months of age and were associated with concurrent heavy tobacco use in pregnancy. The study also indicated that cocaine-exposed infants may have some differences in physiologic responses to stress, attentiveness, and emotional expressivity. The variation in instruments utilized across the studies that Frank et al. analyzed, however, make conclusions difficult.

Table 7.2.   Selected perinatal outcomes, according to whether the mother used cocaine

Outcome	Cocaine users (%)	Nonusers (%)	Adjusted relative risk
Birth weight less than 2,500 grams	28	6	2.8
Gestational age less than 37 weeks	29	9	2.4
Small for gestational age	29	9	3.4 for smokers, 2.1 for nonsmokers
Decreased head circumference	16	6	2.1 for smokers, 1.1 for nonsmokers
Placental abruption	4	1	4.5
Perinatal death	4	1	2.1

Newborn infants who have positive urine screens for cocaine may display symptoms such as irritability, restlessness, lethargy, poor feeding, abnormal sleep pattern, tremors, increased muscle tone, vomiting, and a high-pitched cry (Doberczak et al., 1988). The symptoms are usually displayed within 24–48 hours after birth and reflect autonomic instability. They are secondary to the continued presence of cocaine and its metabolites, including cocaethylene, in the infant's serum and are not a withdrawal syndrome. Because the newborn infant has decreased levels of plasma cholinesterase and is therefore unable to metabolize cocaethylene efficiently, symptoms may persist for up to 48–72 hours after birth.

Nicotine

Although the percentage of women smoking tobacco during pregnancy has declined since the 1980s, it remains a significant problem (Chiriboga, 1993; Ebrahim et al., 2000; Mathews, 1998). Cigarette tobacco smoke contains more than 4,000 different compounds. The major health and potentially developmental effects, however, result from nicotine in the particulate phase and carbon monoxide in the gas phase (Lee, 1998). Although there is no direct teratogenic effect, cigarette smoking increases the risk of miscarriage and low birth weight (Slotkin, 1998; Wheeler, 1993). The effect on fetal growth is dose related. There is a threefold increased risk of low birth weight with a one-pack-per-day habit and a sixfold increase with a two-packs-per-day intake (Fried, 1993). When smoking and high caffeine intake are combined, the effect is doubled; and when cigarettes and alcohol are used together, the effect on birth weight is quadrupled (Chiriboga, 1993).

Nicotine has also been demonstrated to affect brain development in sheep fetuses (Roy & Sabherwal, 1994) and rat pups. This may be relevant to the finding of decreased head circumferences of infants of mothers who smoked during pregnancy. Several studies have reported an inverse relationship between smoking and cognitive development, attention-deficit/hyperactivity disorder, behavior problems, and psychopathology (Weissman et al., 1999). In a study of cocaine and nicotine exposure, generalized hypotonia was increased in infants who had positive screens for urine cotinine (a product of nicotine) (Dempsey et al., 2000). Because of confounding factors associated with smoking, however, it is still controversial whether cigarette smoking during pregnancy actually causes long-term effects on development or behavior (Cornelius et al., 1995).

Marijuana

Although cocaine use during pregnancy is more common in women living in poverty, marijuana use is more prevalent in the middle class. Approximately half of all women 18–25 years of age have used marijuana at least once, 21% have used it during the past year, and 9% in the past month. Approximately 10% of women smoke marijuana during their pregnancy, more in the first trimester than the third (Richardson, Day, & McGauhey, 1993).

Marijuana can be smoked or ingested. It causes a mild euphoria and sleepiness and is not thought to be addictive. Adverse effects include impaired short-term memory, increased risk-taking behavior, decreased motivation, and altered interpersonal relations. Chronic use can lead to decreased coordination and visual tracking, respiratory problems, and a lack of motivation (Wheeler, 1993).

There is little information concerning the effects of marijuana on the fetus. What data exist suggest that there are no differences in miscarriage rate, Apgar scores, or fetal malformations in infants whose mothers smoked marijuana consistently during pregnancy and those whose mothers have not (Wheeler, 1993). Marijuana use, however, is associated with reduced gestational age and may decrease birth weight (Chiriboga, 1993).

If the mother has smoked marijuana in the hours prior to the onset of labor, the newborn may demonstrate a mild withdrawal response with tremor and an exaggerated startle response (Cornelius et al., 1995). This does not require treatment and subsides in a few days. Prenatal marijuana exposure does not seem to have an important impact on postnatal growth, but deleterious cognitive and attentional effects have been found in some preschool and early school-age samples (Walker, Rosenberg, & Balaban-Gil, 1999). When used during pregnancy in combination with cocaine, however, marijuana has been reported to be associated with subsequent impairment in abstract and visual reasoning (Griffith, Azuma, & Chasnoff, 1994).

PREVENTION OF AND INTERVENTION IN SUBSTANCE ABUSE DURING PREGNANCY

Experts in addiction medicine agree that there is no safe level of alcohol consumption during pregnancy. Public health efforts to label alcoholic beverages as dangerous during pregnancy and education about the effects of alcohol on the developing fetus are worthwhile in their support of women's efforts to cut down on drinking during pregnancy (Blume, 1998). It seems logical to encourage abstinence for women who are trying to conceive or who are pregnant (National Institute on Alcohol Abuse and Alcoholism, 2000).

Besides advocating abstinence, identifying women with substance abuse and encouraging them to enroll in a treatment program during pregnancy should be a major goal. Women are likely to enter substance abuse treatment as a result of a medical or psychological problem (Lanehart et al., 1996). Therefore, use of a screening instrument for substance abuse should be part of the routine medical examination for any woman but especially when she is entering into a prenatal care program. An open, accepting, and nonjudgmental approach during the substance abuse screening interview is most effective. After screening, high-risk prenatal patients should be referred to a substance abuse professional for further evaluation, referral, and treatment (Jansson et al., 1996).

The pregnant woman diagnosed with substance abuse addiction or alcoholism should immediately be offered intensive substance abuse treatment services. Given the nature of addiction within the family, a multidisciplinary approach utilizing many clinical and community resources is most successful. Affected mothers are unable to provide structured, safe, and nurturing environments for their children without case management and support from a team of physicians, social workers, substance abuse treatment professionals, educators, and psychologists (Howell, Heiser, & Harrington, 1999). Additional support should come from legal services, housing authority, social services, and educational institutions within the community (Lewis et al., 1997).

The needs of the pregnant woman can be visualized along a time line from entry into treatment, through the delivery of her infant, and into the nurturing drug-free environment that she must establish for her family as she recovers from her addiction. Upon entry into substance abuse treatment, the pregnant woman must be assessed for her medical needs (including drug withdrawal) and prenatal care. Her lifestyle as an addict or alcoholic may be chaotic (and may include homelessness), and she may need mental health treatment for depression, other psychiatric illness, or **posttraumatic stress disorder** (Howell et al., 1999; National Institute on Drug Abuse, 1999). She will also need support to develop appropriate interpersonal skills to manage the rest of her life, including possibly leaving an abusive relationship with the infant's father. She may also be faced with the legal consequences of her drug abuse.

Women may be afraid to seek substance abuse treatment services for fear of losing custody of their other children. Support and resolution of any pending child protective actions is an important component of care, as this issue will sabotage treatment if not addressed. Finally, survival issues such as housing (if treatment is not residential), transportation to clinics, groups, and appointments, and child care for her other children need attention if treatment is to be successful (Lewis et al., 1997).

When the baby is born, he or she may need intensive care nursery services. For example, the child may need medical care for withdrawal from opioid drugs, sedative hypnotic drugs, or alcohol. In addition, parenting education and development of a healthy mother–child bond are critical elements in postnatal care. Though the mother may not formally have her other children in treatment, they too may have educational, psychological, and medical issues that need to be addressed in creating a healthy family unit.

After stabilization in a substance abuse treatment program, the recovering woman will hopefully begin setting goals in the areas of permanent housing, employment, and reunification with any children who have been removed from her custody (Howard & Beckwith, 1997). She will, however, continue to require support in the areas of parenting, interpersonal skills, mental health, and basic survival. Maintenance of recovery from addiction is a lifelong process, and parenting responsibilities magnify the challenge.

INTERVENTION STRATEGIES FOR INFANTS AND CHILDREN OF SUBSTANCE-ABUSING MOTHERS

The ideal plan for intervention is to encourage the addicted mother to accept necessary treatment and provide social, financial, and medical supports to her family, as just discussed. The optimal outcome of treatment is for the mother to be healthy and capable of caring for the physical and psychological needs of her children. If this is not possible, however, the children should be placed in a foster home that has received training in caring for children with special health care needs. Many of these children qualify for early intervention services as infants and, as preschoolers, for Head Start programs. Early intervention and Head Start programs should strive to create a home–school partnership by providing home visits, maintaining frequent telephone contacts, and encouraging parents or guardians to visit and perform volunteer work at the program. The long-term effects of this kind of intervention are still unclear, but the short-term benefits have been encouraging in terms of gains in language acquisition and socialization skills (Dixon, Bresnahan, & Zuckerman, 1990).

In elementary school, the academic needs of the children are a function of their cognitive abilities and behavioral/emotional resources. The Salvin Special Education Center in Los Angeles is an example of an excellent school program that deals effectively with these issues. For stability, each child has the same teacher for 2 years and the same support team for at least 1 year. Class size is restricted to eight pupils, seat assignments and time schedules are fixed, overstimulation is minimized, and hands-on activities with frequent positive reinforcement are emphasized.

OUTCOME

Of all outcomes of substance abuse affecting the fetus, the outcomes of alcohol exposure have been most studied; and the results are not encouraging. Only about 30% of children with FAS were found to be in the care of their mothers through adolescence (Spohr et al., 1993; Spohr, Willms, & Steinhausen, 1994). For children who remained at home, one study found that 86% of the mothers had been cited for neglect and 52% for child abuse (Streissguth, Aase, et al., 1991). A significant number of mothers of children with FAS die from alcohol-related causes (e.g., cirrhosis, car accident, suicide, overdose) during the early years of the child's life (Abel & Sokol, 1987). Out-of-home placement of these children, however, is often difficult because of their extreme hyperactive and noncompliant behavior combined with limitations in intellectual and language skills. Some children with FAS have been assessed through adulthood (Streissguth, Randels, et al., 1991). Few are living independently, and alcohol abuse is quite frequent (Blum et al., 1990). Although in the past the outcome for these children has seemed bleak, it is likely that outcome can be significantly improved using a comprehensive intervention approach beginning in infancy (Streissguth & Kanter, 1997).

The long-term neurodevelopmental side effects of fetal exposure to opiates, cocaine, nicotine, and marijuana are less well delineated. Studies of methadone and recovering pregnant heroin addicts suggest that exposure to opioid drugs does not always imply teratogenicity (Harper et al., 1974). Rather, the lifestyle of the intravenous drug abuser is deleterious to the fetus. In the case of cocaine, information is conflicting. Nicotine causes problems with growth and perhaps neurological parameters such as tone. Marijuana use may cause a decrease in birth weight and gestational age and may be associated with a withdrawal syndrome at birth.

SUMMARY

The most effective way to prevent the prenatal insult of alcohol and other drugs is to treat affected women intensively and effectively for substance abuse. Untreated, this disease will worsen with each pregnancy. Treatment of the mother–child dyad is complex, expensive, and difficult but is worth the effort in prevention of the next affected pregnancy. The myriad issues these women and their children bring to health providers and health care systems can be overwhelming, but failure to intervene effectively is a tragedy in this preventable cause of developmental problems.

REFERENCES

Abel, E.L., & Sokol, R.J. (1987). Incidence of fetal alcohol syndrome and economic impact of FAS-related anomalies. *Drug and Alcohol Dependence, 19,* 51–70.

Abelson, H., & Miller, J. (1985). A decade of trends in cocaine use in the household population. *NIDA Research Monograph Series, 61,* 35–49.

American Academy of Pediatrics, Committee on Substance Abuse and Committee on Children with Disabilities. (1993). Fetal alcohol syndrome and fetal alcohol effects. *Pediatrics, 91,* 1004–1006.

American Academy of Pediatrics, Committee on Substance Abuse and Committee on Children with Disabilities. (2000). Fetal alcohol syndrome and alcohol-related neurodevelopmental disorders. *Pediatrics, 106,* 358–361.

American College of Obstetrics and Gynecology. (1993, May). Smoking and reproductive health. *AGOG Technical Bulletin, 180,* 1–5.

Anthenelli, R.M., & Schuckit, M.A. (1998). Genetic influences in alcoholism. In A.W. Graham & T.K. Schultz (Eds.), *Principles of addiction medicine* (2nd ed., pp. 17–35). Chevy Chase, MD: American Society of Addiction Medicine.

Astley, S.J., & Clarren, S.K. (1996). A case definition and photographic screening tool for the facial phenotype of fetal alcohol syndrome. *Journal of Pediatrics, 129,* 33–41.

Autti-Rämö, I., Gaily, E., & Granström, M.L. (1992). Dysmorphic features in offspring of alcoholic mothers. *Archives of Disabled Children, 67,* 712–716.

Blum, K., Noble, E.P., Sheridan, P.J., et al. (1990). Allelic association of human dopamine D_2 receptor gene in alcoholism. *Journal of the American Medical Association, 263,* 2055–2060.

Blume, S.B. (1998). Understanding addictive disorders in women. In A.W. Graham & T.K. Schultz (Eds.), *Principles of addiction medicine* (2nd ed., pp. 1173–1190). Chevy Chase, MD: American Society of Addiction Medicine.

Bratton, R.L. (1995). Fetal alcohol syndrome: How you can

help prevent it. Postgraduate medicine. *Fetal Alcohol Syndrome, 98*, 197–200.

Britt, G.C., Ingersoll, K.S., & Schnoll, S.H. (1999). Developmental consequences of early exposure to alcohol and drugs. In P.J. Ott, R.E. Tarter, & R.T. Ammerman (Eds.), *Sourcebook on substance abuse* (pp. 75–97). Needham Heights, MA: Allyn & Bacon.

Center for Substance Abuse Treatment. (1991). *Treatment improvement protocols for pregnant, substance using women.* Rockville, MD: Author.

Center on Addiction and Substance Abuse. (1996). *Substance abuse and the American woman.* New York: Columbia University.

Centers for Disease Control and Prevention. (1997). Surveillance for fetal alcohol syndrome using multiple sources. Atlanta, GA, 1981–1989. *MMWR, 46*, 1118–1120.

Cermak, T. (1990). *Evaluating and treating adult children of alcoholics: Vol. 1. Evaluation.* Minneapolis, MN: Johnson Institute.

Cermak, T. (1991). *Evaluating and treating adult children of alcoholics: Vol. 2. Treatment.* Minneapolis, MN: Johnson Institute.

Chasnoff, I., Landress, H.J., & Barrett, M.E. (1990). The prevalence of illicit drug or alcohol use during pregnancy and discrepancies in mandatory reporting in Pinellas County, Florida. *New England Journal of Medicine, 322*, 1202–1206.

Chen, S., & Sullik, K.K. (1996). Free radicals and ethanol-induced cytotoxicity in neural crest cells. *Alcoholism: Clinical and Experimental Research, 20*, 1071–1076.

Chiriboga, C.A. (1993). Fetal effects. *Neurologic Clinics, 11*, 707–728.

Chiriboga, C.A. (1996). Cocaine and the fetus: Methodological issues and neurological correlates. In R.J. Koukol & G.D. Olsen (Eds.), *Prenatal cocaine exposure* (pp. 1–21). Boca Raton, FL: CRC Press.

Chiriboga, C.A. (1998). Neurological correlates of fetal cocaine exposure. *Annals of the New York Academy of Sciences, 846*, 109–125.

Church, M.W., Jen, K.L., Pellizzon, M.A., et al. (1998). Prenatal cocaine, alcohol, and undernutrition differentially alter mineral and protein content in fetal rats. *Pharmacology, Biochemistry, and Behavior, 59*, 577–584.

Clarren, S.K., & Smith, D.W. (1978). The fetal alcohol syndrome. *New England Journal of Medicine, 298*, 1063–1067.

Connor, P.D., Streissguth, A.P., Sampson, P.D., et al. (1999). Individual differences in auditory and visual attention in fetal alcohol-affected adults. *Alcoholism: Clinical and Experimental Research, 23*, 1395–1402.

Cornelius, M.D., Taylor, P.M., Geva, D., et al. (1995). Prenatal tobacco and marijuana use among adolescents: Effects on offspring gestational age, growth, and morphology. *Pediatrics, 95*, 738–743.

Davis, E., Fennoy, I., Laraque, D., et al. (1992). Autism and developmental abnormalities in children with perinatal cocaine exposure. *Journal of the National Medical Association, 84*, 315–319.

Dempsey, D.A., Hajnal, B.L., Partridge, J.C., et al. (2000). Tone abnormalities are associated with maternal cigarette smoking during pregnancy in in-utero cocaine-exposed infants. *Pediatrics, 106*, 79–85.

Dixon, S.D., Bresnahan, K., & Zuckerman, B. (1990). Cocaine babies: Meeting the challenge of management. *Contemporary Pediatrics, 7*(6), 70–92.

Doberczak, T.M., Shanzer, S., Senie, R.T., et al. (1988). Neonatal neurologic and electroencephalographic effects of intrauterine cocaine exposure. *Journal of Pediatrics, 113*, 354–358.

Ebrahim, S.H., Floyd, L.R, Merritt, R.K., et al. (2000). Trends in pregnancy-related smoking rates in the United States, 1987–1996. *Journal of the American Medical Association, 283*, 361–366.

Eyler, F.D., & Behnke, M. (1999). Early development of infants exposed to drugs prenatally. *Clinics in Perinatology, 26*, 107–150.

Farrar, H.C., & Kearns, G.L. (1989). Cocaine: Clinical pharmacology and toxicology. *Journal of Pediatrics, 115*, 665–675.

Frank, D.A., Augustyn, M., Knight, W.G., et al. (2001). Growth, development and behavior in early childhood following prenatal cocaine exposure: A systematic review. *Journal of the American Medical Association, 285*, 1613–1625.

Fried, P.A. (1993). Prenatal exposure to tobacco and marijuana: Effects during pregnancy, infancy, and early childhood. *Clinical Obstetrics and Gynecology, 36*, 319–337.

Giglio, J.J., & Kaufman, E. (1990). The relationship between child and adult psychopathology in children of alcoholics. *International Journal of the Addictions, 25*, 263–290.

Glanz, J.C., & Woods, J.R., Jr. (1993). Cocaine, heroin, and phencyclidine: Obstetric perspectives. *Clinical Obstetrics and Gynecology, 36*, 279–301.

Gonzalez, N.M., & Campbell, M. (1994). Cocaine babies: Does prenatal exposure to cocaine affect development? *Journal of the American Academy of Child and Adolescent Psychiatry, 33*, 16–19.

Griffith, D.R., Azuma, S.D., & Chasnoff, I.J. (1994). Three-year outcome of children exposed prenatally to drugs. *Journal of the American Academy of Child and Adolescent Psychiatry, 33*, 20–27.

Harper, R.G., Solish, G.I., Purow, H.M., et al. (1974). The effect of a methadone treatment program upon pregnant heroin addicts and their newborn infants. *Pediatrics, 54*, 300–305.

Howard, J., & Beckwith, L. (1997). Issues in subject recruitment and retention with pregnant and parenting substance abusing women. In E.R. Rahdert (Ed.), Treatment for drug exposed women and their children. *NIDA Research Monograph Series, 166*, 68–86.

Howell, E.M., Heiser, N., & Harrington, M. (1999). A review of recent findings on substance abuse treatment for pregnant women. *Journal of Substance Abuse Treatment, 16*, 195.

Hurt, H., Brodsky, N.L., Betancourt, L., et al. (1995). Cocaine-exposed children: Follow-up through 30 months. *Journal of Developmental and Behavioral Pediatrics, 16*, 29–35.

Jacobson, J.L., Jacobson, S.W., Sokol, J.J., et al. (1993). Teratogenic effects of alcohol on infant development. *Alcoholism: Clinical and Experimental Research, 17*, 174–183.

Jaffe, J.H. (1990). Drug addiction and abuse. In A.G. Gilman, T.W. Rall, A.S. Nies, & P. Taylor (Eds.), *The pharmacological basis of therapeutics* (8th ed., pp. 522–573). Elmsford, NY: Pergamon.

Jansson, L.M., Svikis, D., Lee, J., et al. (1996). Pregnancy and addiction: A comprehensive care model. *Journal of Substance Abuse Treatment, 13*, 321–329.

Janzen, L.A., Nanson, J.L., & Block, G.W. (1995). Neuropsychological evaluation of preschoolers with fetal alcohol syndrome. *Neurotoxicology and Teratology, 17*, 273–279.

Johnson, J.L., & Leff, M. (1999). Children of substance abusers: An overview of research finding. *Pediatrics, 103*(5, Suppl.), 1089–1099.

Jones, K.L., Smith, D.W., Ulleland, C.N., et al. (1973). Pattern of malformation in offspring of chronic alcoholic mothers. *Lancet, 1*, 1267–1271.

Keller, R.W. Jr., & Snyder-Keller, A. (2000). Prenatal co-caine exposure. *Annals of the New York Academy of Sciences, 909,* 217–232.

Kelly, S.J., Day, N., & Streissguth, A.P. (2000). Effects of pre-natal alcohol exposure on social behavior in humans and other species. *Neurotoxicology and Teratology, 22,* 143–149.

Kendler, K.S., Heath, A.C., Neale, M.C., et al. (1992). A pop-ulation based twin study of alcoholism in women. *Journal of the American Medical Association, 268,* 1877–1882.

Koob, G.F. (1996). Drug addiction: The yin and yang of he-donic homeostasis. *Neuron, 16,* 893–896.

Kopera-Frye, K., Dehaene, S., & Streissguth, A.P. (1996). Impairments of number processing induced by prenatal al-cohol exposure. *Neuropsychologia, 34,* 1187–1196.

Lanehart, R.E., Clark, H.B., Rollings, J.P., et al. (1996). The impact of intensive case-managed intervention on sub-stance using pregnant and postpartum women. *Journal of Substance Abuse, 8,* 487–495.

Lee, M.J. (1998). Marihuana and tobacco use in pregnancy. *Obstetrics and Gynecology Clinics of North America, 25,* 65–83.

Leshner, A.I. (1998). What we know: Drug abuse is a brain disease. In A.W. Graham & T.K. Schultz (Eds.), *Principles of addiction medicine* (2nd ed., pp. xxix–xxxvi). Chevy Chase, MD: American Society of Addiction Medicine.

Levy, M., & Koren, G. (1990). Obstetric and neonatal effects of drugs of abuse. *Emergency Medicine Clinics of North America, 8,* 633–652.

Lewis, D.D., & Woods, S.E. (1994). Fetal alcohol syndrome. *American Family Physician, 50,* 1025–1032.

Lewis, R.A., Haller, D.L., Branch, D., et al. (1997). Reten-tion issues involving drug abusing women in treatment re-search. In E.R. Rahdert (Ed.), Treatment for drug exposed women and their children. *NIDA Research Monograph Se-ries, 166,* 110–122.

Maier, S.E., Chen, W., & West, J.R. (1996). The effects of timing and duration of alcohol exposure on development of the fetal brain. In E.L. Abel (Ed.), *Fetal alcohol syndrome: From mechanism to prevention* (pp. 27–30). Boca Raton, FL: CRC Press.

Malanga, C.J., & Kosofsky, B.E. (1999). Mechanisms of ac-tion of drugs of abuse on the developing fetal brain. *Clinics in Perinatology, 26,* 17–37.

Mathews, T.J. (1998). Smoking during pregnancy, 1990–96. *National Vital Statistics Reports, 47,* 1–12.

Mattson, S.N., Riley, E.P., Delia, D.C., et al. (1996). Verbal learning and memory in children with fetal alcohol syn-drome. *Alcoholism: Clinical and Experimental Research, 20,* 810–816.

Mattson, S.N., Riley, E.P., Sowell, E.R., et al. (1996). A de-crease in the size of the basal ganglia in children with fetal alcohol syndrome. *Alcoholism: Clinical and Experimental Re-search, 20,* 1088–1093.

Michaelis, E.K., & Michaelis, M.L. (1994). Cellular and mo-lecular bases of alcohol's teratogenic effects. *Alcohol Health and Research World, 18,* 17–21.

Morse, R.M., & Flavin, D.C. (1992). Joint Committee of the National Council on Alcoholism and Drug Dependence and the American Society of Addiction Medicine to study the definition and criteria for the diagnosis of alcoholism. *Journal of the American Medical Association, 268,* 1012–1014.

National Institute on Alcohol Abuse and Alcoholism. (2000, December). Fetal alcohol exposure and the brain. *Alcohol Alert* (50).

National Institute on Drug Abuse. (1999). *Drug abuse and addiction: 25 years of discovery to advance the health of the pub-lic. The sixth triennial report to Congress from the Secretary of Health and Human Services.* Bethesda, MD: Author.

Noble, A., Vega, W.A., Kolody, B., et al. (1997). Prenatal substance abuse in California: Findings from the Perinatal Substance Exposure Study. *Journal of Psychoactive Drugs, 29,* 43–53.

Richardson, G.A., Day, N.L., & McGauhey, P.J. (1993). The impact of prenatal marijuana and cocaine use on the infant and child. *Clinical Obstetrics and Gynecology, 36,* 302–318.

Riley, E.P., Mattson, S.N., Sowell, E.R., et al. (1995). Abnor-malities of the corpus callosum in children prenatally ex-posed to alcohol. *Alcoholism: Clinical and Experimental Re-search, 19,* 1198–1202.

Roy, T., & Sabherwal, U. (1994). Effects of prenatal nicotine exposure on the morphogenesis of the somatosensory cor-tex. *Neurotoxicology and Teratology, 16,* 411.

Slotkin, T.A. (1998). Fetal nicotine or cocaine exposure: Which one is worse? *Journal of Pharmacology and Experi-mental Therapeutics, 285,* 931–945.

Snodgrass, S.R. (1994). Cocaine babies: A result of multiple teratogenic influences. *Journal of Child Neurology, 9,* 227–233.

Sowell, E.R., Jernigan, T.L., Mattson, S.N., et al. (1996). Ab-normal development of the cerebellar vermis in children prenatally exposed to alcohol: Size reduction in lobules I–V. *Alcoholism: Clinical and Experimental Research, 20,* 31–34.

Spohr, H.-L., Willms, J., & Steinhausen, H.-C. (1993). Pre-natal alcohol exposure and long-term developmental con-sequences. *Lancet, 341,* 907–910.

Spohr, H.-L., Willms, J., & Steinhausen, H.-C. (1994). Fetal alcohol syndrome in adolescence. *Acta Paediatrica Scandi-navica, 404*(Suppl.), 19–26.

Stratton, K., Howe, C., & Battaglia, F. (Eds.). (1996). *Fetal alcohol syndrome: Diagnosis, epidemiology, prevention, and treatment.* Washington DC: National Academy Press.

Streissguth, A.P., Aase, J.M., Clarren, S.K., et al. (1991). Fetal alcohol syndrome in adolescents and adults. *Journal of the American Medical Association, 265,* 1961–1967.

Streissguth, A.P., Barr, H.M, Olson, C.H., et al. (1994). Drinking during pregnancy decreases word attack and arithmetic scores on standardized tests: Adolescent data from a population-based prospective study. *Alcoholism: Clinical and Experimental Research, 18,* 248–254.

Streissguth, A., Barr, H., Sampson, P.D., et al. (1994). Prena-tal alcohol and offspring development: The first 14 years. *Drug and Alcohol Dependence, 36,* 88–99.

Streissguth, A.P., Herman, C.S., & Smith, D.W. (1978). Sta-bility of intelligence in the fetal alcohol syndrome: A pre-liminary report. *Alcoholism: Clinical and Experimental Re-search, 2,* 165–170.

Streissguth, A., & Kanter, J. (Eds.). (1997). *The challenge of fetal alcohol syndrome: Overcoming secondary disabilities.* Se-attle: University of Washington Press.

Streissguth, A.P., Randels, S.P., & Smith, D.F. (1991). A test-retest study of intelligence in patients with fetal alcohol syndrome: Implications for care. *Journal of the American Academy of Child and Adolescent Psychiatry, 30,* 584–587.

Swayze, V.W., II, Johnson, V.P., Hanson, J.W., et al. (1997). Magnetic resonance imaging of brain anomalies in fetal al-cohol exposure. *Pediatrics, 99,* 232–240.

Tran, J.H. (1999). Treatment of neonatal abstinence syn-drome. *Journal of Pediatric Health Care, 13,* 295–300.

van Baar, A., & de Graaff, B.M.T. (1994). Cognitive devel-opment at preschool-age of infants of drug-dependent mothers. *Developmental Medicine and Child Neurology, 36,* 1063–1075.

Volpe, J.J. (1992). Effect of cocaine use on the fetus. *New England Journal of Medicine, 327,* 399–407.

Wagner, C.L., Katikaneni, L.D., Cox, T.H., et al. (1998).

The impact of prenatal drug exposure on the neonate. *Obstetrics and Gynecology Clinics of North America, 25,* 169–194.

Walker, A., Rosenberg, M., & Balaban-Gil, K. (1999). Neurodevelopmental and neurobehavioral sequelae of selected substances of abuse and psychiatric medications in utero. *Child and Adolescent Psychiatry Clinics of North America, 8,* 845–867.

Weissman, M.M., Warner, V., Wickramaratne, P.J., et al. (1999). Maternal smoking during pregnancy and psychopathology in offspring followed to adulthood. *Journal of the American Academy of Adolescent Psychiatry, 38,* 892–899.

Wheeler, S.F. (1993). Substance abuse during pregnancy. *Primary Care Clinics in Office Practice, 20,* 191–207.

Wilkins, A.S., Genova, L.M., Posten, W., et al. (1998). Transplacental cocaine exposure, 1: A rodent model. *Neurotoxicology and Teratology, 20,* 215–226.

8 HIV Infection in Children

Hans M.L. Spiegel and Andrew M. Bonwit

Upon completion of this chapter, the reader will:

- understand the biology, immunology, mode of transmission, and natural history of HIV infection
- be aware of developmental issues associated with pediatric HIV infection
- be knowledgeable about approaches to medical treatment
- understand the importance of family-centered, comprehensive programs of ongoing medical care, social services, and psychological support for children with HIV infection

Acquired immunodeficiency syndrome (AIDS) was first described in 1981. It presented as an unusual type of pneumonia, ***Pneumocystis carinii,*** in previously healthy men who were gay or who practiced intravenous substance abuse. As cases were investigated, the affected individuals were found to have severe deficiencies of the immune system, with marked decreases in CD4+ T-cells ("helper" T-lymphocytes, or white blood cells). Further studies identified a previously unknown **retrovirus** (a type of RNA virus that, unlike other RNA viruses, reproduces by transcribing itself into DNA), human immunodeficiency virus type 1 (HIV-1), as the infectious agent leading to the depletion of the patient's CD4+ T-cells and the clinical picture of AIDS.

AIDS is now seen as a much broader disease affecting men, women, and children alike. It is understood that HIV-1 can be transmitted through heterosexual as well as homosexual contact, through blood products, and from mother to child. Furthermore, there is evidence, based on HIV-1 gene mutation calculations, that the virus originated in Central Africa from a closely related chimpanzee retrovirus, SIVcpz, which probably crossed the species barrier during the 1930s (Gao et al., 1999; Korber et al., 2000). A related retrovirus, isolated from humans in the mid-1980s in West Africa (Clavel et al., 1986), has been named HIV-2. This virus is much less frequently transmitted from mother to child and causes a less severe form of AIDS. Although prevalent in West African countries, it is only occasionally encountered in the United States and Europe (Li et al., 1998). The remainder of the chapter focuses on HIV-1, which is designated as HIV in the text.

JEROME

Jerome is a 7-year-old who was found in retrospect to have been infected with HIV at birth. His mother had been using intravenous drugs of abuse but had not been tested for HIV. At the time of Jerome's birth in 1994, prenatal screening and perinatal treatment was not well established. His initial evaluation for HIV occurred at 6 months of age because of recurrent infections, diarrhea, and failure to thrive. Evaluation at that time revealed that Jerome had a severely suppressed immune system. His CD4+ T-cell count was 40 cells per cubic millimeter (normal is greater than 500 per cubic millimeter at his age), and only 3% instead of the normal of greater than 25% of total lymphocytes were CD4+. His plasma HIV viral load was 240,000 copies per milliliter.

Jerome was enrolled in an experimental multidrug protocol supported by the AIDS Clinical Trials Group of the National Institutes of Health. He was initially placed on the reverse transcriptase inhibitors zidovudine and lamivudine. He tolerated these well, and 2 weeks later a protease inhibitor, nelfinavir, was added to the drug regimen. On this therapy Jerome showed a reduction in plasma viral load to below the limits of detection (less than 400 copies per milliliter). After 5 months of therapy, his CD4+ lymphocyte count had increased to 1,490 cells per cubic millimeter, equaling 40% of his T-cells. Over the following years, his viral load has remained undetectable at almost every measurement, and he has remained clinically healthy. When he entered first grade, he was found to have some learning impairments but has done well in a general education classroom receiving special education supports.

Jerome's mother, who was HIV positive but did not have clinical symptoms, entered a drug treatment program and began antiretroviral therapy at the same time as her son. She has survived and is now working as a teacher's aide in a preschool program. She had another child in 1998. Her daughter, Tanya, received prenatal antiretroviral therapy and was delivered by cesarean section. Tanya had two negative virologic HIV tests at 1 and 4 months of age; at her 18-month checkup she had a negative HIV enzyme-linked immunosorbent assay (ELISA). Now 3 years old, Tanya's development has been entirely typical.

EPIDEMIOLOGY AND DIAGNOSIS OF PEDIATRIC HIV INFECTION

HIV infection has spread worldwide since it was identified more than 20 years ago, and the pandemic continues to evolve in magnitude and diversity (Cock & Weiss, 2000). HIV can now be found on every continent, and AIDS is a leading cause of death in many resource-poor countries ("Cause-Specific Adult Mortality," 2000; Pictet et al., 1998). In 2000, more than 5 million new cases of HIV infection were detected; 3 million people died from AIDS; and more than 36 million people were living with HIV or AIDS, two thirds of them in sub-Saharan Africa (Schwartlaender et al., 2000). Of those infected, almost 34 million were adults and 1.4 million were children younger than 15 years of age. About 90% of pediatric HIV infections originate from perinatal transmission of the virus (from mother to infant in the period around birth). The establishment of prenatal counseling and testing for HIV, the provision of perinatal antiretroviral prophylaxis, and the use of cesarean sections in appropriate cases has led to an overall reduction of the number of infected children in many developed countries. In the United States, voluntary screening of pregnant women for HIV infection has been integrated into routine prenatal care. As a result of these efforts, the incidence of mother-to-infant HIV transmission has declined from approximately 25% to 1%–2% in the United States and other developed countries (Lindegren, Steinberg, & Byers, 2000).

HIV infection can be diagnosed definitively in most infected infants by 1 month of age and in almost all by 6 months. Conversely, perinatal HIV infection can be reasonably excluded among children who have had two or more negative virologic HIV tests, one around 1 month of age and a second at 4 months of age or older (Dunn et al., 1995). There should also be documented loss of maternal antibodies (negative HIV ELISA) by 18 months.

BIOLOGY OF PEDIATRIC HIV INFECTION

HIV consists of a core structure covered by an envelope (Figure 8.1). The virus uses its envelope proteins to enter cells that have suitable surface receptors for "docking." The virus protein core, which then glides inside the cell, covers two tiny pieces of ribonucleic acid (RNA), the genetic material of HIV. One of these, the genetic code for an enzyme called *reverse transcriptase* (RT), is unique to retroviruses. Without the work of this enzyme and another critical

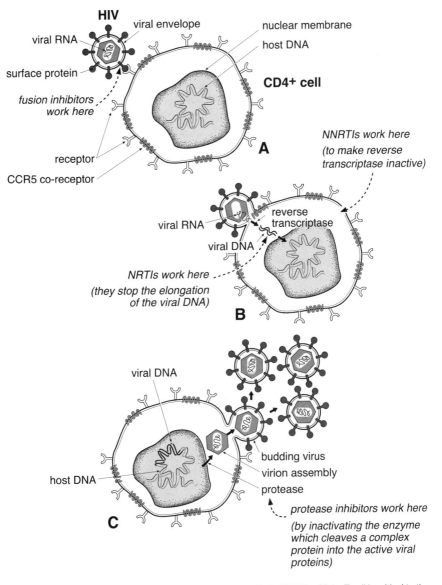

Figure 8.1. The HIV life cycle and destruction of CD4+ T-cells by HIV. The CD4+ T-cell is critical to the immune defense, and its destruction is the major cause of the progressive immunodeficiency disorder that is the hallmark of HIV infection. One mechanism of destruction involves HIV a) entering and b) replicating in the CD4+ cell and then c) budding from and damaging the cell membrane. (*Key:* NNRTIs, nonnucleoside reverse transcriptase inhibitors; NRTIs, nucleoside reverse transcriptase inhibitors.)

virus enzyme, called *integrase*, HIV could infect the cell but could not make progeny. Both enzymes are necessary for HIV to translate its RNA into deoxyribonucleic acid (DNA) and insert it into the DNA of the cell nucleus, a necessary step for viral replication. A third HIV enzyme, called *protease*, is required to tailor the proteins of HIV so that mature progeny can emerge from inside the infected cell. This life cycle provides the basis for antiretroviral therapy, which is described later.

Insights into the biology of HIV infection have been provided by a combination of sensitive methods that measure the HIV RNA concentrations in the plasma of infected patients (reported as viral load) and by treatment with new antiretroviral drugs that interrupt viral replication. Using these methods, researchers have been able to show that infected cells continuously produce HIV progeny at high rates, even when the patient is clinically asymptomatic. In untreated infected patients, approximately 10 billion virus particles are produced each day; every 6 hours about half of the particles in the plasma are replaced by new ones (Ho et al., 1995; Perelson et al., 1996). It has further been found that the patient's plasma HIV particle count gives an accurate indication of the infection in the rest of the body tissues. Therefore, it can be used to monitor the efficacy of treatment in eliminating the infection.

Without the help of antiretroviral agents, the immune system of infected patients is not able to eliminate or completely suppress the replication of HIV, but it can play a role in containing the virus. Adults who are newly infected with HIV have high plasma viral loads during the first 3–6 months after infection. Subsequently, there is a precipitous drop in the number of HIV particles to between 1,000 and 100,000 per milliliter of plasma. The patient's immune system has been shown to be the major force behind this decrease. Ultimately, however, the continuous production of HIV particles overwhelms the patient's immune system, leading to a progressive immunodeficiency, or AIDS. Infants have an immature immune system and thus have much higher initial viral loads during the acute HIV infection period than adults. Furthermore, it takes 2–3 years in children (rather than 3–6 months in adults) for viral load concentrations to decline to a stable level. A high viral load at 1 month of age is predictive of subsequent rapid disease progression.

In children infected with HIV, high-level viral replication leads to destruction of the CD4+ T-cells as well, which are essential for protecting the child against infectious diseases. Without treatment, even children who show slow disease progression will develop AIDS sooner than do adults who have been infected with HIV (Barnhart et al., 1996). The early use of the combination highly active antiretroviral therapy (HAART) to control HIV replication in infants immediately after diagnosis offers the best chance of significantly delaying the HIV infection from progressing to AIDS (Luzuriaga & Sullivan, 2000). It should be noted, however, that despite prolonged HAART, residual HIV will persist in a dormant state in CD4+ T-cells (Persaud et al., 2000) and that drug-resistant mutant HIV can develop.

CLINICAL MANIFESTATIONS OF PEDIATRIC HIV INFECTION

HIV infection can cause a wide spectrum of illnesses in children, depending on the degree of immune system dysfunction. A classification system has been developed to define the range of clinical and immunological findings (Tables 8.1 and 8.2). When first diagnosed with HIV infection, the child can be asymptomatic or the disease can present with nonspecific signs of a systemic infection. These signs include generalized lymph node swelling and enlargement of the liver, spleen, and/or parotid salivary glands. There may also be persistent fevers and episodes of common childhood bacterial and viral infections more frequently than expected. Oral yeast infection (*Candida albicans*/thrush) or symptoms of opportunistic infections such as pneumonia due to *Pneumocystis carinii* can be present. There may also be slowing or arrest of growth and development.

AIDS represents the most severe stage of the infection, when the patient's immune system is so severely weakened that overwhelming opportunistic infections and, more rarely, tumors can occur. The formal report of an AIDS diagnosis for a child younger than 13 years infected with HIV is still based on the diagnosis of one of the AIDS-defining illnesses included in Centers for Disease Control and Prevention (CDC) clinical category C or the diagnosis of lymphocytic interstitial pneumonitis, which is in CDC category B. Without adequate treatment of the underlying HIV infection and related opportunistic infections, children with AIDS die

Table 8.1. Pediatric human immunodeficiency virus (HIV) classification

	Clinical categories			
Immunologic categories	N: No signs/ symptoms	A: Mild signs/ symptoms	B: Moderate signs/ symptoms	C: Severe signs/ symptoms
1: No evidence of immunosuppression	N1	A1	B1	C1
2: Evidence of moderate immunosuppression	N2	A2	B2	C2
3: Severe immunosuppression	N3	A3	B3	C3

Note: Children whose HIV infection status is not confirmed are classified by using the above classifications with the letter *E* (for perinatally *e*xposed) before the appropriate classification code (e.g., EN2 for perinatally exposed with no signs/symptoms and evidence of moderate immunosuppression).

Clinical Category N characterizes children who are infected with HIV but remain asymptomatic.

Clinical Category A includes mildly symptomatic children who have enlargement of lymph nodes, liver, and spleen and recurrent infections of the middle ear and sinus cavities.

Clinical Category B includes moderately symptomatic children. Symptoms include but are not limited to low counts of various blood cell types (anemia, thrombocytopenia, or neutropenia), a single episode of serious bacterial infection (bacterial pneumonia, bone or joint infection, meningitis, bacteremia), chickenpox, herpes simplex oral infection, cardiomyopathy (abnormality of the heart muscle, leading to its relative weakness and widening of its chambers), and other conditions.

Clinical Category C includes children with severe symptoms such as multiple system bacterial infections or opportunistic infections that are considered to be AIDS indicator diseases, including tuberculosis, *Candida* infection of the esophagus, cryptococcal infection, *Pneumocystis carinii* pneumonia, B-cell lymphoma, and others.

Adapted from Centers for Disease Control and Prevention (CDC). (1994). 1994 revised classification system for human immunodeficiency virus infection in children less than 13 years of age. *MMWR, 43*(No. RR-12), 2.

(Langston et al., 2001). This dire outcome, however, was markedly altered in the late 1990s with the adaptation of HAART regimens for pediatric use and the development of specialized support programs for children with HIV infection and their families. Therapy adjustment of HAART has resulted in 40% of heavily pretreated patients maintaining an undetectable viral load after 9 months of therapy (Feingold et al., 2000). This treatment has converted HIV infection from a universally fatal disorder to a chronic illness with the potential for long-term survival.

The overall mortality rate from AIDS fell by 80% in developed countries between 1995 and 1998 as a result of HAART (Gortmaker et al., 2000). Unfortunately, this has not been the case in resource-poor countries such as those in sub-Saharan Africa. For children infected with

Table 8.2. Immunologic categories based on age-specific CD4+ T-cell counts and percentage of total lymphocytes

	Age of child					
	< 12 months		1–5 years		6–12 years	
Immunologic categories	µL	(%)	µL	(%)	µL	(%)
1: No evidence of immunosuppression	≥ 1,500	(≥ 25)	≥ 1,000	(≥ 25)	≥ 500	(≥ 25)
2: Evidence of moderate immunosuppression	750–1,499	(15–24)	500–999	(15–24)	200–499	(15–24)
3: Severe immunosuppression	< 750	(< 15)	< 500	(< 15)	< 200	(< 15)

Key: µL, microliters.

Adapted from Centers for Disease Control and Prevention (CDC). (1994). 1994 revised classification system for human immunodeficiency virus infection in children less than 13 years of age. *MMWR, 43*(No. RR-12), 4.

HIV in the southeast African country of Rwanda, the chance of survival to age 5 is only 38% as compared with 75% in the United States (Spira et al., 1999). The reason for the difference in survival is unavailability of HAART due to cost and lack of adequate health care services. As of 2002, the former is being addressed by some pharmaceutical companies that are pledging to provide HAART medication at markedly discounted prices to resource-poor countries.

Infections

Children infected with HIV who are immunocompromised are constantly at risk for developing opportunistic infections, those that almost never occur in a person with an intact immune system. The most common opportunistic infection is pneumonia secondary to infection with *Pneumocystis carinii*. Esophagitis (inflammation of the lining of the esophagus) caused by a fungal infection (*Candida albicans*) and disseminated infection secondary to *Mycobacterium avium* are late-stage manifestations in severely immunocompromised children.

Fortunately, in the United States the incidence of nearly all HIV-associated opportunistic infections has decreased significantly with the introduction of HAART. Opportunistic infections continue to occur only when the patient has a low CD4+ T-cell count; however, with an increasingly wider spectrum of possible opportunistic infections, the lower the CD4+ count drops (most commonly below 15% for all age groups). In addition, survival has also improved with the use of antibiotic prophylaxis against common opportunistic infections as well as vaccination against *Streptococcus pneumoniae* infection (Kaplan et al., 2000).

Children infected with HIV also have more frequent "common" bacterial infections that can lead to such severe complications as sepsis, meningitis, pneumonia, internal organ **abscesses,** and osteomyelitis (Hauger & Powell, 1990). In addition, less severe but still worrisome bacterial infections occur in more than a third of individuals, including chronic sinusitis, middle-ear infections (which can result in hearing loss), dental caries, and periodontal disease ("Natural History," 1994).

Finally, affected children are at risk for life-threatening illness from common childhood viral infections such as measles and chickenpox (Burroughs & Edelson, 1991). Other viral infections include cytomegalovirus (CMV) of the eye (which can lead to visual impairment) and recurrent episodes of herpes skin infections and cold sores (which can interfere with eating).

Neurodevelopmental Impairments

Severe neurodevelopmental impairments have fortunately become uncommon since the availability of HAART. There remain, however, more subtle impairments that place the child with HIV infection at increased risk for learning and attentional disorders by school entry (Grubman et al., 1995). Infants infected with HIV have been found to demonstrate lower mental and motor developmental indexes when compared with uninfected infants (Coplan et al., 1998; Knight et al., 2000). By early childhood, speech, language, and communication impairments may become evident (Davis-McFarland, 2000; Layton & Scott, 2000). Infants infected in utero appear to be more affected than do infants infected perinatally (Chase et al., 2000). By school age, IQ scores in children with HIV infection fall in the low-average range, statistically lower than in noninfected children born to infected mothers, even when controlling for maternal drug use, illness, and poverty (Fowler, 1994; Gay et al., 1995).

In the early years of AIDS, the outcome was much bleaker and is still dismal in resource-poor countries (Chase et al., 2000). Progressive encephalopathy is seen in as many as 20% of untreated infants infected with HIV (Cooper et al., 1998). In this condition, there is impaired brain growth, a decline in cognitive and neurobehavioral function, and progressive motor abnormalities. Cerebrospinal fluid HIV levels correlate with progression of the neurological condition, suggesting that viral replication occurs within the central nervous system (Angelini et al., 2000). Fortunately, HIV-associated encephalopathy can improve as a result of HAART, especially when the treatment regimen includes a protease inhibitor (Arendt et al., 2001; Rosenfeldt, Valerius, & Paerregaard, 2000; Sacktor et al., 2001; Suarez, Baril, et al., 2001; Suarez, Stankoff, et al., 2000; Tepper et al., 1998).

Failure to Thrive

Regardless of their HIV status, infants born to women infected with HIV have significantly lower mean birth weight and length compared with infants born to uninfected women. Yet, although postnatal growth in both height and weight remains below normal standards in children with HIV infection, it is not abnormal in their uninfected prenatally exposed peers. In symptomatic children infected with HIV, poor growth may result from inadequate dietary intake, gastrointestinal malabsorption, increased energy utilization, acute infections, and psychosocial stress (Myhre, Chadwick, & Yogev, 1996). Children who have HIV infection and show a poor growth rate have higher HIV viral loads (plasma HIV RNA levels) than infected children with a normal growth rate; suppression of HIV replication appears to have a favorable long-term effect on linear growth (Arpadi, 2000). New nutritional problems, however, are emerging with the more widespread use of HAART (discussed later), including fat redistribution (lipodystrophy) and insulin resistance (Miller, 2000).

Other Manifestations

Prior to HAART, the function of virtually every body organ could be affected by the virus. With the new therapeutic regimen, the incidence of cardiac involvement, including pericarditis, arrhythmias, and dilated cardiomyopathy, has significantly decreased (Pugliese et al., 2000). Evidence suggests that HIV-associated kidney disease also responds to HAART (Brook & Miller, 2001; Dellow et al., 1999; Viani et al., 1999). Treatment has also improved HIV-related anemia and platelet dysfunction (Aboulafia et al., 2000; Semba, Shah, & Vlahov, 2001).

INTERDISCIPLINARY CARE

To be effective, assessment and treatment of pediatric HIV infection must be interdisciplinary, child centered, family focused, and culturally sensitive. The disciplines involved may include pediatrics, psychology, mental health, education, nutrition, speech-language therapy, advocacy, and service coordination. Together the team can provide well-child care, anticipatory guidance for treatment of common childhood illnesses, modification of the immunization schedule, nutritional support, psychosocial support, and referral to early intervention/special education services. These teams are often located within a special immunology clinic in a children's hospital (Mok & Newell, 1995; Woodruff, Driscoll, & Sterzin, 1992). The various aspects of care are discussed in the following sections.

Antiretroviral Therapy

It is recommended that all infants under 1 year of age who are infected with HIV be treated with antiretroviral agents, regardless of clinical, immunologic, or virologic status. If this is not done, there is an increased risk for rapid progression of the disease. For an older child antiretroviral treatment is recommended 1) if the child has clinical symptoms associated with HIV infection (CDC clinical categories A, B, or C) or 2) if the child has evidence of immune suppression (CDC immune category 2 or 3 based on the CD4+ T-cell count). For the older child who is asymptomatic and has a normal immune status, there is a choice. The child can be treated immediately on diagnosis, or antiretroviral therapy can be temporarily postponed, especially if there is concern about medication adherence. If treatment is postponed, the child should be followed closely to identify an increasing HIV viral load, a declining CD4+ T-cell count, or the development of HIV-related clinical symptoms. Any of these signs should lead to the immediate onset of antiretroviral therapy (CDC, 1998; see http://www.hivatis.org/trtgdlns .html#Pediatric for the most recent guidelines).

As of 2002, three categories of antiretroviral drugs are approved for use in treating children with HIV: nucleoside reverse transcriptase inhibitors (NRTIs), non-nucleoside reverse transcriptase inhibitors (NNRTIs), and protease inhibitors (PIs). The basic goal of each class of drugs is to restrain HIV in the child's cells from making progeny. NRTIs interfere directly with the work of the crucial virus enzyme reverse transcriptase (RT). NNRTIs interfere indirectly with the function of RT by attaching to it. Blockers of the enzyme protease are used to inhibit viral replication. Clinical trials of a fourth class of enzyme-inhibiting drugs, integrase inhibitors, are being conducted as of 2002.

As of February 2002, the Food and Drug Administration has approved a total of 16 antiretroviral agents; 11 of these have been approved for use in children (marked with an asterisk):

NRTIs:

- zidovudine (AZT; Retrovir)*
- didanosine (ddI; Videx)*
- stavudine (d4T; Zerit)*
- zalcitabine (ddC; Hivid)
- lamivudine (3TC; Epivir)*
- abacavir (ABC; Ziagen)*
- tenofovir (TFV; Viread)

NNRTIs:

- nevirapine (NVP; Viramune)*
- efavirenz (EFV; Sustiva)*
- delavirdine (DLV; Rescriptor)

PIs:

- ritonavir (RTV; Norvir)*
- nelfinavir (NFV; Viracept)*
- amprenavir (APV; Agenerase)*
- lopinavir/ritonavir (LPV/rtv; Kaletra)*
- saquinavir (SQV; Invirase and, as soft-gel preparation, Fortovase)
- indinavir (IDV; Crixivan)

In addition to the drugs just listed that prevent viral replication once inside the cell, two new drug classes are being studied that prevent HIV from infecting the CD4+ T-cells in the first place: co-receptor inhibitors and fusion inhibitors. For HIV to infect a CD4+ T-cell, it must first attach to the CD4 protein. This enables the main HIV envelope protein to bind subsequently to the co-receptors on CD4+ T-cells (chemokine receptor 5 [CCR5] or occasionally chemokine receptor CXCR4). The HIV co-receptors normally bind important immune system proteins. Blocking the co-receptor with a co-receptor inhibitor drug does not harm the immune system but makes it impossible for HIV to dock onto the CD4+ T-cell and infect it. The second class of drugs being studied, fusion inhibitors, interferes with the normal mechanism that HIV uses to get into the cell after it binds to it. Both of these drug classes have been promising in clinical trials.

Adherence to Antiretroviral Medication Regimens

Strict adherence to antiretroviral medication regimens is crucial for achieving and maintaining an undetectable viral load in the blood. The shift to HAART for treating individuals infected with HIV, however, has increased adherence challenges. Estimates of average rates of sufficient adherence to antiretroviral therapy range only from 30% to 50% (Laurence, 2001; Watson & Farley, 1999). Unfortunately, adherence rates lower than 80% are associated with a detectable viral load in a majority of patients and lead to the development of drug-resistant mutant HIV. Principal factors associated with nonadherence are the poor palatability of the medication, the large number of pills, inconvenient dosing schedules, uncomfortable side effects, poor patient–parent–health care provider relationships, substance abuse problems of the patient or caregiver, and a poorly coordinated or inadequate system of health care. It is helpful to view adherence as a collaborative effort between the child, his or her family, and health care providers. Service coordinators, mental health counselors, peer educators, outreach workers, and other members of the multidisciplinary team may be able to address specific barriers to adherence (Chesney, 2000; Reddington et al., 2000).

Simplification of drug regimens, specific medication instructions, and continual follow-up are crucial to avoid treatment failure. Occasionally, postponing therapy while educating the child and family is the preferred option. Adherence to drug regimens is especially problematic for infants and young children because of their dependence on others for administration of the medication. Therefore, the ability and willingness of the child to take antiretroviral medication, as well as the commitment of the caregiver to treatment, need to be assessed.

For young children, poorly palatable liquid or powder formulations are necessary for administration of oral drugs but may decrease adherence to the drug regimen. Techniques to improve palatability include masking the taste of liquid medication with favorite foods or strong-flavored syrups, and dulling the taste buds with a Popsicle or coating the tongue with peanut butter before medication administration. For adolescents with HIV infection, adherence problems may result from denial or fear of HIV, misinformation about effectiveness of antiretroviral medication, distrust of the medical establishment, problems with low self-esteem, and unstructured lifestyles with a lack of family and social supports. Treatment regimens for adolescents must balance the goal of using a potent antiretroviral regimen with a realistic assessment of compliance issues.

Monitoring Antiretroviral Treatment

Once therapy is started it is important to both routinely monitor antiretroviral drug levels to ensure that they are therapeutic (and to monitor compliance) and to quantitate HIV RNA in plasma. Drug levels are measured in plasma using a technique called *tandem mass spectroscopy*. HIV viral load can be measured using an amplification technique (i.e., reverse-transcriptase polymerase chain reaction [RT-PCR] or nucleic acid sequence–based amplification [NASBA]) or a probe technique (i.e., branched DNA assay [b-DNA]). One assay type should be used consistently. It should be recognized that up to a fivefold variation in viral load can occur in samples obtained from the same patient during one day; only changes above this level should be considered clinically relevant.

In addition to viral and drug levels, viral resistance assays have become increasingly important for modification of the antiretroviral regimen when the given regimen does not completely suppress HIV viral replication. This involves one of three options: 1) identifying mutations of the patient's most frequent HIV population (genotypic assay), 2) studying the growth capacity of the patient's HIV isolates in the presence of the various drugs in the test tube (phenotypic assay), or 3) using extensive databases of phenotype-matched genotypes to predict the growth capacity of the patient's most frequent HIV population (called *virtual prediction of phenotype*).

After combination antiretroviral therapy (HAART) has been initiated, viral load should be assayed initially on a monthly basis to determine treatment response and subsequently at least every 3 months. A change in treatment can be considered if therapy does not result in a significant reduction of the child's initial plasma viral load. When choosing a new regimen, it is important to use antiretroviral drugs to which HIV is not cross-resistant and, if possible, to include new antiretroviral drug classes to which the patient has not been previously exposed. Antiretroviral treatment history and results from HIV-resistance testing should be used as guidance for changes of therapy. Treatment approaches should be continually reevaluated as more data become available from clinical trials of approved and investigational drugs.

Adverse Drug Reactions

Adverse drug reactions are responses to medication that are unintended, can be harmful to the patient, and occur even when the medication is given at the prescribed dosage. The most common (and usually mild) adverse drug effects are anemia, **neutropenia** (low white blood cell count), and **thrombocytopenia** (low platelet count). Anemia can be seen in up to 10% of children treated with AZT and in about 4% of children treated with ddI. Neutropenia is observed in 10% of children on AZT and about 25% of children on ddI but is usually unassociated with complications. Thrombocytopenia (defined as fewer than 100,000 platelets per cubic millimeter) is also relatively common as a consequence of antiretroviral therapy but is seen in 30% of untreated children with HIV infection as well.

Serious but uncommon adverse effects include pancreatitis, peripheral neuropathy, retinal depigmentation, lactic acidosis, and lipodystrophy. Pancreatitis has been linked to the use of ddI and less commonly to the use of d4T, ddC, and 3TC. Peripheral neuropathy (causing sharp pain or numbness in limbs) has also been associated with the use of the "d" series of NRTI drugs: ddI, d4T, and ddC. Retinal depigmentation (unassociated with visual impairment) is also associated with ddI therapy. Lipodystrophic syndrome (associated with fat redistribution and insulin resistance) has been seen in a few prepubertal children receiving HAART (Jaquet et al., 2000).

Management of Adverse Effects

It is important to determine whether an adverse effect is attributable to the antiretroviral agents, to other medications, to the HIV infection itself, or to other infections that may complicate the course of HIV infection. The physician must analyze the nature and severity of the toxicity and assess the need for each medication. Severe complications require discontinuation of the most suspect medication(s). In the case of milder complications, antiretroviral therapy can be continued provided there is frequent observation, monitoring, and evaluation. Moderately severe toxicities may require specific interventions such as the use of erythropoietin for anemia, granulocyte colony stimulating factor (G-CSF) for neutropenia, and/or intravenous immunoglobulin (IVIG) or corticosteroids for thrombocytopenia. When toxicity requires interruption of treatment, it is preferable to discontinue all antiretroviral agents simultaneously. This approach avoids single drug therapy and subtherapeutic drug levels, which can result in the growth of drug-resistant mutant HIV.

Immunizations

Children with HIV infection should receive immunizations against the common childhood illnesses. All children with HIV infection should receive the standard inactivated vaccines for diphtheria, pertussis, and tetanus (DPT or DaPT); *Haemophilus influenzae* Type B (HIB); and hepatitis B; as well as the yearly influenza A/B vaccine and the pneumococcal vaccine at 2 years of age. As recommended for all routine childhood polio vaccinations in the United States, the inactivated injectable polio vaccine (Salk, IPV) should be used instead of the live (Sabin) oral polio vaccine (Mueller & Pizzo, 1992). It should also be noted that when one family member has HIV infection, all members of that family who receive a polio vaccine should receive the killed vaccine in lieu of the live vaccine. This avoids the theoretical risk of polio infection in the immunocompromised household member passed on by a recipient of the live oral vaccine.

The use of the live measles, mumps, and rubella (MMR) vaccine in children with HIV infection is controversial. Most physicians believe that the risk to the child of measles, which can be fatal in children with HIV infection, outweighs the risk of the vaccine, except in children with severe immune dysfunction (as measured by low age-adjusted CD4+ T-cell counts). Although MMR is a live virus vaccine, there is no evidence of intra-family spread, so it can be safely given to siblings and family contacts of individuals infected with HIV. The varicella zoster (chickenpox) vaccine can be given to children with HIV who have no history of immune suppression or significant HIV-related complications.

It is important to be aware that despite immunization, children with HIV infection remain at risk for vaccine-preventable illnesses, as their immune system is unable to mount a competent response to the vaccine (Onorato, Markowitz, & Oxtoby, 1988; Tasker & Wallace, 2000). For children on successful HAART, however, improvements in immune responses to selected childhood vaccines have been shown (Berkelhamer et al., 2001). Therefore, in addition to active immunization, passive vaccines should be given when a child is exposed to certain viral illnesses. **Hyperimmune globulin** against hepatitis B, measles, or varicella zoster virus should be administered within 72 hours of exposure to these infections (Mueller & Pizzo, 1992). If the child contracts varicella or systemic herpes, acyclovir (Zovirax) should be used (Fletcher, 1992); if the child contracts CMV, ganciclovir (Cytovene) may be effective (Spector et al., 1995).

Pain Management

Children with HIV infection may experience pain from medical procedures as well as from symptoms associated with the infection. Local anesthetic cream (EMLA) has become very useful in reducing the child's anxiety with the repeated blood draws that are necessary for laboratory monitoring of antiretroviral therapy. In addition, HIV-related chronic pain symptoms, including arthralgias (joint pain), myalgias (muscle pain), pharyngitis (sore throat), esophagitis, and headaches, should be treated aggressively. The recommended approach to pain management uses a combination of pharmacological and nonpharmacological (e.g., relaxation) therapies. Inadequately treated chronic pain can manifest as depression, inactivity, and anorexia.

Nutritional Support

Nutritional counseling and the provision of nutritional supplements can improve the overall health of children with HIV infection as well as facilitate uptake of antiretroviral medications from the bowel. In contrast, malnutrition can severely weaken the cellular and humoral (antibody) immune response. If malnutrition is an issue and increased feeding by mouth is not practical, gastrostomy tube supplementation (see Chapter 27) can be used to improve weight and fat mass (Miller et al., 1995).

Developmental Assessment and Educational Programs

The neurodevelopment of children with HIV infection may be affected not only by the virus but also by other confounding environmental and biological factors, such as in utero exposure to drugs of abuse, prematurity, low birth weight, and failure to thrive (Johnson, 1993). Chaotic family environments and neglect may add to the adverse effects of HIV infection (Butler et al., 1991).

To identify neurodevelopmental delays as early as possible, children with HIV infection should receive developmental assessments at regular intervals. In general, infants with HIV infection should be evaluated by 2 months of age and then at least every 6 months for the first 2 years of life, if they remain asymptomatic. After 2 years of age, children with HIV infection should have a neurodevelopmental assessment at least yearly (Butler et al., 1991). If significant cognitive or motor impairments are identified, assessments should be more frequent.

In terms of educational services, children with HIV infection are covered by the Individuals with Disabilities Education Act Amendments of 1997 (PL 105-17). This makes them eligible for developmental testing and early intervention programs as infants (see Chapter 29) and for psychoeducational assessment and special education services at school age (see Chapter 30). Thus, children with HIV infection and developmental delay who are younger than 3 years of age should be referred to the local Child Find agency for entry into an early intervention program. Children ages 3–5 years should be referred to their county school committee for preschool special education services if they have a developmental delay or to Head Start if they are developing typically. School-age children may receive special education services if needed (Pizzo & Wilfert, 1999).

Disclosing HIV Status

Disclosing HIV status has been shown to be a long-term process that requires many discussions, must be age-appropriate, and should be done with outside psychological support (Nehring, Lashley, & Malm, 2000). The stigma of HIV infection creates many barriers to the parents' disclosing the diagnosis, even to their child who has the infection. Yet, not telling children about their HIV status for prolonged periods can contribute to poor emotional adjustment (Instone, 2000). Conversely, disclosing the diagnosis can help enhance medication adherence in children, who otherwise would question the need for ongoing drug treatment.

Many parents of children with HIV infection are concerned about the risk of disclosure of the child's or their own HIV status when enrolling the child in school. Most states now protect the family's right to confidentiality regarding HIV-related information. In many states, physicians cannot release HIV-related information on school health appraisal forms without specific parental consent. Most states also proscribe teachers or other educators from disseminating information about HIV infection should they receive the information in an informal manner (e.g., in a classroom discussion). In some school systems there have been attempts to obstruct the enrollment of children with HIV infection; however, on the basis of the Americans with Disabilities Act of 1990 (PL 101-336), the courts have protected children with HIV infection from discrimination.

Psychotherapy and Psychopharmacology

The treatment of psychological problems associated with HIV infection is a difficult but essential task. This may include both **psychotherapy** and psychoactive medication (Krener & Miller, 1989; Trad et al., 1994). Both individual and family therapy may be helpful. Some children may benefit from antidepressant medication, although potential drug interactions with HAART must be carefully considered. Effective treatment not only improves a child's or adolescent's overall quality of life but also leads to improved compliance with HAART regimens and reduced high-risk behaviors (e.g., unprotected sex, intravenous substance abuse).

Social Supports

As is the case of children with other chronic illnesses, the special service needs of the child with HIV infection impose a significant demand on the entire family (Brown, Lourie, & Pao, 2000). This is often accentuated by the need for medical care for HIV infection in one or both of the parents as well. In many cities, comprehensive family-centered programs of ongoing medical care, psychological support, and social services have been developed to improve care. At the core of these programs are interdisciplinary teams composed of professionals who plan with the parents and provide the care for the child with HIV infection. Important in this context is the minimization of unnecessary contact of the patient and family with the health care system by coordinating multiple services. Home-based services can be a key to health care and treatment compliance. In addition, services need to be well integrated within a community context, including regular communication with other health care providers such as AIDS clinics, visiting nurse services, and AIDS care agencies (Gerwitz & Gossart-Walker, 2000).

No single administrative system can be responsive to the many social, mental health, legal, and support service needs of children with HIV infection and their families (Oleske, 1994; Taylor-Brown & Garcia, 1995; Taylor-Brown & Kumetat, 1994; Taylor-Brown et al., 1998). Cross-disciplinary initiatives are needed among agencies that administer child welfare services, income supports, AIDS care, and children's mental health services at the national, state, and local levels. A more family-centered, coordinated approach to care has been created through funding by the Ryan White CARE Act Amendments of 2000 (PL 106-345). Additional legislative, educational, and advocacy initiatives, however, are needed to make managed care and welfare reform more responsive to the many needs of children and youth with HIV and their families (Salisbury, 2000).

Infection Control Issues at Home and School

It is reassuring to note that HIV transmission outside of sexual contact, blood transfusions, intravenous drug use, and vertical transmission (from mother to child before or during childbirth) is highly unlikely. No case of person-to-person transmission of HIV infection has ever been documented in child care centers or schools. The risk of transmission within a household also is thought to be extremely low. Even in health care settings, the risk of transmission is less than 1 in 250 for a health care worker who has been inadvertently stuck by a needle containing infected blood (Simonds & Rogers, 1992).

Given that the risk of HIV infection by school contact is negligible, there is no justification for excluding a child with HIV infection from a general school environment. No special precautions other than handwashing are needed in handling body fluids when no visible blood is present. If there are injuries that result in bleeding, surgical gloves should be worn when tending to wounds, and the blood should be washed off with soap and water. Blood spills should be cleaned with disinfectants, such as household bleach at a dilution of 1:10 to 1:100 (American Academy of Pediatrics, Task Force on Pediatric AIDS, 1988). With these few precautions, there is virtually no risk of HIV transmission in caring for a child with HIV infection. In fact, these universal precautions should be used with all blood spills in any school because not all children with HIV infection will have been identified and other blood-borne diseases may be present.

The major concern in a child care center or a school, in fact, is the risk to the child with HIV infection, who has a limited ability to fight infection. Risks may be minimized by identifying outbreaks of infectious diseases early so that treatment can be instituted. For example, during an outbreak of chickenpox or measles in a school, a child with HIV infection may require hyperimmune globulin (Dominguez, 2000; Spiegel & Mayers, 1991).

Permanency Planning

Children with HIV infection are at greater risk than usual for multiple placements outside the home because the adult caregivers in their lives may be incapacitated by AIDS-related complications or by substance abuse and unable to provide stable, consistent care. Parents who are intravenous drug users may place their children outside of the home voluntarily, or the children may be removed involuntarily. For parents abusing intravenous drugs who live with their children, HIV-related clinical symptoms rather than HIV status per se seem to be associated with retention. HIV-negative and asymptomatic HIV-positive parents are three times more likely to be living with their children than are HIV-positive parents with clinical symptoms. Parents with drug addiction who continue to live with their children are more likely to be female, to have health insurance, and to engage in no-risk or low-risk drug practices (Pilowsky et al., 2000).

HIV SERVICES IN RESOURCE-POOR COUNTRIES

The vast majority of new pediatric HIV infections occurs in resource-poor countries, which have few prevention and treatment programs (Tudor-Williams, 2000). High rates of perinatal transmission and of morbidity and mortality due to HIV infection have resulted. There is mounting evidence, however, that abbreviated and more affordable regimens of antiretroviral prophylaxis for the prevention of mother-to-child HIV transmission are highly effective. A number of countries have already initiated such prevention projects, some with international support. These programs provide voluntary counseling and testing in antenatal clinics; antiretroviral prophylaxis during pregnancy, labor, and after delivery; infant formula to prevent breast milk transmission of HIV; and protection against discrimination of mothers who decide not to breast-feed (Luo, 2000). In the absence of an effective HIV vaccine, using HIV prevention and providing new treatment regimens for infected individuals is of greatest importance. International funds are currently being generated to make antiretroviral drugs more available to patients with HIV infection in resource-poor countries.

OUTCOME

The outlook for children with HIV in the United States and other developed countries has changed dramatically since the mid-1990s. At that point, although the life span of children with HIV infection had improved, it was still considered a fatal disease. In the intervening years, the development of PI drugs and then HAART has converted HIV infection into more of a chronic disease. In addition, the perinatal treatment of women who have HIV infection has markedly reduced the risk of maternal to child transmission of the virus. In sum, fewer children are born with HIV infection, and those who are infected are expected to survive and to have much less of a risk of sustaining severe cognitive or motor disabilities. As their parents are also healthier, these children have improved psychosocial outcomes as well. Further advances in treatment are likely to result from the development of new antiretroviral drugs and the future use of immune-based therapies, such as therapeutic vaccination in children.

Despite this improved picture, major issues have yet to be addressed. Patient adherence to the HAART regimen continues to be a problem. Medication-related side effects (especially hepatitis and pancreatitis) are an unsolved problem. Accumulation of HIV with drug-resistant mutations in children with HIV infection who have received changing antiretroviral treatment regimens since birth can limit future treatment options. Much of the natural history and prognosis of long-term surviving children with HIV infection will need to be reassessed (Grubman et al., 1995). Above all, ongoing support of children with HIV infection, from both the public and the political decision makers, is essential in both the developed and the developing world.

SUMMARY

With the introduction of perinatal antiretroviral prophylaxis and the use of HAART for children, considerable progress has been made in understanding the dynamics of HIV infection and in advancing treatment and prevention. As a consequence, the rate of pediatric HIV infection in the United States has markedly declined, and survival of children with HIV infection has significantly improved. Although HIV infection remains a serious and still ultimately fatal infection, advances in therapy have changed it to a more chronic illness, with patients increasingly remaining in good health and having productive lives for many years. HIV infection in infants needs to be identified as early as possible, and the most current and comprehensive therapy, including medical treatment as well as expert individual and family support should be provided. Treatment is best delivered by an integrated interdisciplinary team of providers with expertise in HIV-related medical care, mental health, child development, and case management and social work. Public and political support for children with HIV infection is essential to maintain the progress already made and to advance therapeutic options.

REFERENCES

Aboulafia, D.M., Bundow, D., Waide, S., et al. (2000). Initial observations on the efficacy of highly active antiretroviral therapy in the treatment of HIV-associated autoimmune thrombocytopenia. *The American Journal of the Medical Sciences, 320,* 117–123.

American Academy of Pediatrics, Task Force on Pediatric AIDS. (1988). Pediatric guidelines for infection control of human immunodeficiency virus (acquired immunodeficiency virus) in hospitals, medical offices, schools, and other settings. *Pediatrics, 82,* 801–807.

Americans with Disabilities Act (ADA) of 1990, PL 101-336, 42 U.S.C. §§ 12101 *et seq.*

Angelini, L., Zibordi, F., Triulzi, F., et al. (2000). Age-dependent neurologic manifestations of HIV infection in childhood. *Neurological Sciences, 21,* 135–142.

Arendt, G., von Giesen, H.J., Hefter, H., et al. (2001). Therapeutic effects of nucleoside analogues on psychomotor slowing in HIV infection. *AIDS, 15,* 493–500.

Arpadi, S.M. (2000). Growth failure in children with HIV infection. *Journal of Acquired Immune Deficiency Syndrome, 25*(Suppl. 1), S37–S42.

Barnhart, H.X., Caldwell, M.B., Thomas, P., et al. (1996). Natural history of human immunodeficiency virus disease in perinatally infected children: An analysis from the Pediatric Spectrum of Disease Project. *Pediatrics, 97,* 710–716.

Beisel, W.R. (1996). Nutrition in pediatric HIV infection: Setting the research agenda. Nutrition and immune function: Overview. *Journal of Nutrition, 126*(Suppl.), 2611S–2615S.

Berkelhamer, S., Borock, E., Elsen, C., et al. (2001). Effect of highly active antiretroviral therapy on the serological response to additional measles vaccinations in human immunodeficiency virus-infected children. *Clinical Infectious Diseases, 32,* 1090–1094.

Brook, M.G., & Miller, R.F. (2001). HIV associated nephropathy: A treatable condition. *Sexually Transmitted Infections, 77,* 97–100.

Brown, L.K., Lourie, K.J., & Pao, M. (2000). Children and adolescents living with HIV and AIDS: A review. *Journal of Child Psychology and Psychiatry and Allied Disciplines, 41,* 81–96.

Burroughs, M.H., & Edelson, P.J. (1991). Medical care of the HIV-infected child. *Pediatric Clinics of North America, 38,* 45–67.

Butler, K.M., Husson, R.N., Balis, F.M., et al. (1991). Dideoxyinosine in children with symptomatic human immunodeficiency virus. *New England Journal of Medicine, 324,* 137–144.

Cause-specific adult mortality: Evidence from community-based surveillance—selected sites, Tanzania, 1992–1998. (2000). *MMWR, 49,* 416–419.

Centers for Disease Control and Prevention (CDC). (1994). 1994 revised classification system for human immunodeficiency virus infection in children less than 13 years of age. *MMWR, 43*(No. RR-12), 1–10.

Centers for Disease Control and Prevention (CDC). (1998). Guidelines for the use of antiretroviral agents in pediatric HIV infection. *MMWR, 47*(No. RR-4), 1–38. (See http://www.hivatis.org/trtgdlns.html#Pediatric for most recent guidelines.)

Chase, C., Ware, J., Hittelman, J., et al. (2000). Early cognitive and motor development among infants born to women infected with human immunodeficiency virus. Women and Infants Transmission Study Group. *Pediatrics, 106,* E25.

Chesney, M.A. (2000). Factors affecting adherence to antiretroviral therapy. *Clinical Infectious Diseases, 30*(1, Suppl. 2), S171–S176.

Clavel, F., Guetard, D., Brun-Vezinet, F., et al. (1986). Isolation of a new human retrovirus from West African patients with AIDS. *Science, 233,* 343–346.

Cock, K.M., & H.A. Weiss. (2000). The global epidemiology of HIV/AIDS. *Tropical Medicine and International Health, 5*(7), A3–A9.

Cooper, E.R., Hanson, C., Diaz, C., et al. (1998). Encephalopathy and progression of human immunodeficiency virus disease in a cohort of children with perinatally acquired human immunodeficiency virus infection. Women and Infants Transmission Study Group. *Journal of Pediatrics, 132,* 808–812.

Coplan, J., Contello, K.A., Cunningham, C.K., et al. (1998). Early language development in children exposed to or infected with human immunodeficiency virus. *Pediatrics, 102,* e8.

Davis-McFarland, E. (2000). Language and oral-motor development and disorders in infants and young toddlers with human immunodeficiency virus. *Seminars in Speech and Language, 21,* 19–34; quiz 34–35.

Dellow, E., Unwin, R., Miller, R., et al. (1999). Protease inhibitor therapy for HIV infection: The effect on HIV-associated nephrotic syndrome. *Nephrology, Dialysis, Transplantation, 14,* 744–747.

Dominguez, K.L. (2000). Management of HIV-infected children in the home and institutional settings. Care of children and infections control in schools, day care, hospital settings, home, foster care, and adoption. *Pediatric Clinics of North America, 47,* 203–239.

Dunn, D.T., Brandt, C.D., Krivine, A., et al. (1995). The sensitivity of HIV-1 DNA polymerase chain reaction in the neonatal period and the relative contributions of intra-uterine and intra-partum transmission. *AIDS, 9,* F7–F11.

Feingold, A.R., Rutstein, R.M., Meislich, D., et al. (2000). Protease inhibitor therapy in HIV-infected children. *AIDS Patient Care and STDs, 14,* 589–593.

Fletcher, C.V. (1992). Treatment of herpes virus infections in HIV-infected individuals. *Annals of Pharmacotherapy, 26,* 955–962.

Fowler, M.G. (1994). Pediatric HIV infection: Neurological and neuropsychologic findings. *Acta Paediatrica, 400* (Suppl.), 59–62.

Gao, F., Bailes, E., Robertson, D.L., et al. (1999). Origin of HIV-1 in the chimpanzee *Pan troglodytes troglodytes. Nature, 397,* 436–441.

Gay, C.L., Armstrong, F.D., Cohen, D., et al. (1995). The effects of HIV on cognitive and motor development in children born to HIV-seropositive women with no reported drug use: Birth to 24 months. *Pediatrics, 96*, 1078–1082.

Gewirtz, A., & Gossart-Walker, S. (2000). Home-based treatment for children and families affected by HIV and AIDS. Dealing with stigma, secrecy, disclosure, and loss. *Child and Adolescent Psychiatric Clinics of North America, 9,* 313–330.

Gortmaker, S., Hughes, M., Oyomopito, R., et al. (2000). *Impact of introduction of protease inhibitor therapy on reductions in mortality among children and youth infected with HIV-1* (Abstract 691). Seventh Conference on Retroviruses and Opportunistic Infections, San Francisco.

Grubman, S., Gross, E., Lerner-Weiss, N., et al. (1995). Older children and adolescents living with perinatally acquired human immunodeficiency virus infection. *Pediatrics 95,* 657–663.

Hauger, S.B., & Powell, K.R. (1990). Infectious complications in children with HIV infection. *Pediatric Annals, 19,* 421–436.

Ho, D.D., Neumann, A.U., Perelson, A.S., et al. (1995). Rapid turnover of plasma virions and CD4 lymphocytes in HIV-1 infection. *Nature, 373,* 123–126.

Individuals with Disabilities Education Act Amendments of 1997, PL 105-17, 20 U.S.C. §§ 1400 *et seq.*

Instone, S.L. (2000). Perceptions of children with HIV infection when not told for so long: Implications for diagnosis disclosure. *Journal of Pediatric Health Care, 14,* 235–243.

Jaquet, D., Levine, M., Ortega-Rodriguez, E., et al. (2000). Clinical and metabolic presentation of the lipodystrophic syndrome in HIV-infected children. *AIDS, 14,* 2123–2128.

Johnson, C.B. (1993). Developmental issues: Children infected with the human immunodeficiency virus. *Journal of Infants and Young Children, 6,* 1–10.

Kaplan, J.E., Hanson, D., Dworkin, M.S., et al. (2000). Epidemiology of human immunodeficiency virus-associated opportunistic infections in the United States in the era of highly active antiretroviral therapy. *Clinical Infectious Diseases, 30*(5, Suppl. 1), S5–S14.

Knight, W.G., Mellins, C.A., Levenson, R.L., et al. (2000). Effects of pediatric HIV infection on mental and psychomotor development. *Journal of Pediatric Psychology, 25*(8), 583–587.

Korber, B., Muldoon, M., Theiler, J., et al. (2000). Timing the ancestor of the HIV-1 pandemic strains. *Science, 288,* 1789–1796.

Krener, P., & Miller, F.B. (1989). Psychiatric response to HIV spectrum disease in children and adolescents. *Journal of the American Academy of Child and Adolescent Psychiatry, 28,* 596–605.

Langston, C., Cooper, E.R., Goldfarb, J., et al. (2001). Human immunodeficiency virus-related mortality in infants and children: Data from the Pediatric Pulmonary and Cardiovascular Complications of Vertically Transmitted HIV (P(2)C(2)) Study. *Pediatrics, 107,* 328–338.

Laurence, J. (2001). Adhering to antiretroviral therapies. *AIDS Patient Care and STDs, 15,* 107–108.

Layton, T.L., & Scott, G.S. (2000). Language development and assessment in children with human immunodeficiency virus: 3 to 6 years. *Seminars in Speech and Language, 21,* 37–46; quiz 46–47.

Li, Q., Tsang, B., Ding, L., et al. (1998). Infection with the human immunodeficiency virus type 2: Epidemiology and transmission (Review). *International Journal of Molecular Medicine, 2,* 573–576.

Lindegren, M.L., Steinberg, S., & Byers, R.H. (2000). Epi-demiology of HIV/AIDS in children. *Pediatric Clinics of North America, 47,* 1–20, v.

Luo, C. (2000). Achievable standard of care in low-resource settings. *Annals of the New York Academy of Sciences, 918*(4), 179–187.

Luzuriaga, K., & Sullivan, J.L. (2000). Viral and immuno-pathogenesis of vertical HIV-1 infection. *Pediatric Clinics of North America, 47,* 65–78.

Miller, T.L. (2000). Nutrition in paediatric human immunodeficiency virus infection. *The Proceedings of the Nutrition Society, 59,* 155–162.

Miller, T.L., Awnetwant, E.L., Evans, S., et al. (1995). Gastrostomy tube supplementation for HIV-infected children. *Pediatrics, 96,* 696–702.

Mok, J., & Newell, M.L. (Eds.). (1995). *HIV infection in children: A guide to practical management.* New York: Cambridge University Press.

Mueller, B.U., & Pizzo, P.A. (1992). Medical treatment of children with HIV infection. In A.C. Crocker, H.J. Cohen, & T.A. Kastner (Eds.), *HIV infection and developmental disabilities: A resource for service providers* (pp. 63–73). Baltimore: Paul H. Brookes Publishing Co.

Myhre, J.A., Chadwick, E.G., & Yogev, R. (1996). Failure to thrive in HIV-infected children: Incidence, prevalence, and clinical correlates. *Pediatric AIDS and HIV Infection, 7,* 83–90.

Natural history of vertically acquired human immunodeficiency virus-1 infection. The European Collaborative Study. (1994). *Pediatrics, 94,* 815–819.

Nehring, W.M., Lashley, F.R., & Malm, K. (2000). Disclosing the diagnosis of pediatric HIV infection: Mothers' views. *Journal of the Society of Pediatric Nurses, 5,* 5–14.

Oleske, J.M. (1994). The many needs of the HIV-infected child. *Hospital Practice (Office Edition), 29,* 81–87.

Onorato, I.M., Markowitz, L.E., & Oxtoby, M.J. (1988). Childhood immunization, vaccine-preventable diseases and infection with human immunodeficiency virus. *The Pediatric Infectious Disease Journal, 7,* 588–595.

Perelson, A.S., Neumann, A.U., Markowitz, M., et al. (1996). HIV-1 dynamics in vivo: Virion clearance rate, infected cell life-span, and viral generation time. *Science, 271,* 1582–1586.

Persaud, D., Pierson, T., Ruff, C., et al. (2000). A stable latent reservoir for HIV-1 in resting CD4+ T lymphocytes in infected children. *The Journal of Clinical Investigation, 105,* 995–1003.

Pictet, G., Le Coeur, S., M'Pele, P., et al. (1998). Contribution of AIDS to the general mortality in Central Africa: Evidence from a morgue-based study in Brazzaville, Congo. *AIDS, 12,* 2217–2223.

Pilowsky, D.J., Lyles, C.M., Cross, S.I., et al. (2001). Characteristics of injection drug using parents who retain their children. *Drug and Alcohol Dependence, 61,* 113–122.

Pizzo, P.A., & Wilfert, C.M. (1999). *Pediatric AIDS: The challenge of HIV infection in infants, children, and adolescents* (3rd. ed.). Philadelphia: Lippincott Williams & Wilkins.

Pugliese, A., Isnardi, D., Saini, A., et al. (2000). Impact of highly active antiretroviral therapy in HIV-positive patients with cardiac involvement. *The Journal of Infection, 40,* 282–284.

Reddington, C., Cohen, J., Baldillo, A., et al. (2000). Adherence to medication regimens among children with human immunodeficiency virus infection. *The Pediatric Infectious Disease Journal, 19,* 1148–1153.

Rosenfeldt, V., Valerius, N.H., & Paerregaard, A. (2000). Regression of HIV-associated progressive encephalopathy of childhood during HAART. *Scandinavian Journal of Infectious Diseases, 32,* 571–574.

Ryan White CARE Act Amendments of 2000, PL 106-345, 42 U.S.C. §§ 201 *et seq.*

Sacktor, N., Lyles, R.H., Skolasky, R., et al. (2001). HIV-associated neurologic disease incidence changes: Multicenter AIDS Cohort Study, 1990–1998. *Neurology, 56,* 257–260.

Salisbury, K.M. (2000). National and state policies influencing the care of children affected by AIDS. *Child and Adolescent Psychiatric Clinics of North America, 9*(2), 425–449.

Schwartlaender, B., Garnett, G., Walker, N., et al. (2000). AIDS in a new millennium. *Science, 289,* 64–66.

Semba, R.D., Shah, N., & Vlahov, D. (2001). Improvement of anemia among HIV-infected injection drug users receiving highly active antiretroviral therapy. *Journal of Acquired Immune Deficiency Syndrome, 26,* 315–319.

Simonds, R.J., & Rogers, M.F. (1992). Epidemiology of HIV infection in children and other populations. In A.C. Crocker, H.J. Cohen, & T.A. Kastner (Eds.), *HIV infection and developmental disabilities: A resource for service providers* (pp. 3–13). Baltimore: Paul H. Brookes Publishing Co.

Spector, S.A., Busch, D.F., Follansbee, S., et al. (1995). Pharmacokinetic, safety, and antiviral profiles of oral ganciclovir in persons infected with human immunodeficiency virus: A phase I/II study. AIDS Clinical Trials Group and Cytomegaolvirus Cooperative Study Group. *Journal of Infectious Diseases, 171,* 1431–1437.

Spiegel, H., & Mayers, A. (1991). Psychosocial aspects of AIDS in children and adolescents. *Pediatric Clinics of North America, 38,* 153–167.

Spira, R., Lepage, P., Msellati, P., et al. (1999). Natural history of human immunodeficiency virus type 1 infection in children: A five-year prospective study in Rwanda. Mother-to-Child HIV-1 Transmission Study Group. *Pediatrics, 104,* e56.

Suarez, S., Baril, L., Stankoff, B., et al. (2001). Outcome of patients with HIV-1–related cognitive impairment on highly active antiretroviral therapy. *AIDS, 15,* 195–200.

Suarez, S.V., Stankoff, B., Conquy, L., et al. (2000). Similar subcortical pattern of cognitive impairment in AIDS patients with and without dementia. *European Journal of Neurology, 7,* 151–158.

Tasker, S.A., & Wallace, M.R. (2000). Vaccination in HIV-infected Patients. *Current Infectious Diseases Reports, 2,* 245–256.

Taylor-Brown, S., & Garcia, A. (1995). Social workers and HIV-affected families: Is the profession prepared? *Social Work, 40,* 14–15.

Taylor-Brown, S., & Kumetat, S. H. (1994). Psychosocial aspects of pediatric human immunodeficiency virus and acquired immunodeficiency syndrome: Annotated literature review and call for research. *Journal of Developmental and Behavioral Pediatrics, 15,* S71–S76.

Taylor-Brown, S., Teeter, J.A., Blackburn, E., et al. (1998). Parental loss due to HIV: Caring for children as a community issue—the Rochester, New York experience. *Child Welfare, 77,* 137–160.

Tepper, V.J., Farley, J.J., Rothman, M.I., et al. (1998). Neurodevelopmental/neuroradiologic recovery of a child infected with HIV after treatment with combination antiretroviral therapy using the HIV-specific protease inhibitor ritonavir. *Pediatrics, 101,* e7.

Trad, P.V., Kentros, M., Solomon, G.E., et al. (1994). Assessment and psychotherapeutic intervention for an HIV-infected preschool child. *Journal of the American Academy of Child and Adolescent Psychiatry, 33,* 1338–1345.

Tudor-Williams, G. (2000). HIV infection in children in developing countries. *Transactions of the Royal Society of Tropical Medicine and Hygiene, 94,* 3–4.

Viani, R.M., Dankner, W.M., Muelenaer, P.A., et al. (1999). Resolution of HIV-associated nephrotic syndrome with highly active antiretroviral therapy delivered by gastrostomy tube. *Pediatrics, 104,* 1394–1396.

Watson, D.C., & Farley, J.J. (1999). Efficacy of and adherence to highly active antiretroviral therapy in children infected with human immunodeficiency virus type 1. *The Pediatric Infectious Disease Journal, 18,* 682–689.

Woodruff, G., Driscoll, P., & Sterzin, E.D. (1992). Providing comprehensive and coordinated services to children with HIV infection and their families: A transagency model. In A.C. Crocker, H.J. Cohen, & T.A. Kastner (Eds.), *HIV infection and developmental disabilities: A resource for service providers* (pp. 105–112). Baltimore: Paul H. Brookes Publishing Co.

9 Nutrition and Children with Disabilities

Leila T. Beker, Abigail F. Farber, and Colleen Comonitski Yanni

Upon completion of this chapter, the reader will:

- be able to describe basics of nutrition and components of a nutritional assessment
- understand the fundamental role of nutrition in the growth and development of children
- recognize the special nutritional needs and challenges of children with disabilities
- understand the importance of integrating nutritional interventions into each child's care plan

Good nutrition is important throughout life. Dietary choices can influence our health, altering the likelihood of obesity, hypertension, diabetes, and other disorders; they can even affect life-span. This influence begins even before birth. As noted in Chapter 6 children who experienced growth restriction in utero or who were born small for gestational age may continue to have growth deficits outside the womb. Nutrition carries its greatest influence during infancy and childhood, when the body is actively growing. Fortunately, for most children in developed countries, nutritional deficiencies are not a major concern. A typical diet provides all of the nutrients, minerals, and vitamins needed for typical growth and development. In children with disabilities, however, this may not be the case. For example, because of motor impairments, the child with cerebral palsy may have difficulty ingesting sufficient food, and the child with autism may have food selectivity that results in nutritional deficiencies. This chapter reviews basic aspects of nutrition and the nutritional needs of children with disabilities. It emphasizes the importance of including nutrition as part of the overall treatment program for these children (Cloud, 1999; Kozlowski, 1997; National Research Council, Subcommittee on the Tenth Edition of the RDAs, 1989).

SAM

Sam, now 24 months old, was a 28-week premature infant who weighed 950 grams (about 2 pounds) at birth. Although he had an initially rocky hospital course, he was able to double his weight on concentrated feedings within his first 2 months of life. When Sam was discharged at 3 months, his family was referred to a registered dietitian who met with them monthly for 4 months to adjust feeding volumes and texture to optimize his intake. He subsequently gained weight well. At Sam's 15-month checkup, however, his pediatrician became concerned about a fall-off in his weight gain and linear growth. Sam's early intervention specialist also noticed a change in his behavior, appearance, and interaction with caregivers. On a growth chart that corrected for the degree of prematurity, Sam's growth parameters previously had been above the 25th percentile but now plotted below the 10th percentile (Casey et al., 1991).

Sam was referred for nutrition reevaluation at 16 months. The dietitian measured his weight, length, arm circumference, and triceps skinfold thickness; results indicated that Sam's fatty tissue reserves were low and that his muscle mass was mildly depleted. Results from laboratory studies indicated that Sam was also anemic. A dietary history revealed that Sam's mother had switched him from an infant formula to cow's milk at 12 months based on the general recommendation to start cow's milk at that time. She was unaware that cow's milk contains no iron. This change, combined with Sam's refusal to eat meat-containing and other pureed (baby) foods, meant that he had limited dietary sources of calories, protein, and iron-containing foods. Sam was subsequently diagnosed with failure to thrive (FTT) and iron deficiency anemia. His mother was reassured that she was not to blame, and Sam was placed on a pediatric nutritional supplement that contained iron and an increased caloric density. In about 2 weeks, Sam's early intervention specialist reported that he seemed to have "perked up" and that his strength was returning. When Sam returned for a scheduled checkup 3 months later, his growth had started to accelerate.

TYPICAL GROWTH DURING CHILDHOOD

The average full-term newborn infant weighs 3.4 kilograms (about 7½ pounds); after an initial weight loss in the first week of life, he or she gains 20–30 grams (about an ounce) each day for several months. By 4–6 months of age, the infant's birth weight has doubled; by 12 months, it has tripled (Guo et al., 1991). After this period of rapid weight gain, growth slows to about 5 pounds per year until approximately 9–10 years of age, when the adolescent growth spurt begins (American Academy of Pediatrics [AAP], Committee on Nutrition, 1998; Ogden et al., 2002). Increase in length moves at a slower pace than weight, increasing by 50% during the first year of life, from an average of 50 centimeters (about 19½ inches) at birth, doubling by 4 years of age, and tripling by 13 years of age. Head circumference increases by 3 inches during the first year of life; brain weight doubles by 2 years of age (AAP Committee on Nutrition, 1998). Increase in head circumference parallels brain growth.

THE BASICS OF NUTRITION

Food contains carbohydrates, protein, and lipids (fat). These nutrients provide energy, allowing the cells in the body to do work (Johnson, 2000b). These substances are referred to as *macronutrients*. The energy produced is measured in kilocalories (kcal; the amount of heat needed to raise the temperature of one kilogram of water 1 degree Celsius). A gram of carbohydrate and a gram of protein yield 4 kcal, whereas 1 gram of fat provides 9 kcal. Carbohydrates are needed in sufficient amounts as a source of energy to spare protein, which can then be utilized for growth, muscle development, repair, and other metabolic activities (Ettinger, 2000; National Research Council, 1989). The other nutrients are water, vitamins, and minerals. They do not produce energy and are often referred to as *micronutrients* (Groff, Gropper, & Hunt, 2000; National Research Council, 1989). Vitamins are unique organic molecules that perform regulatory functions needed by the body to utilize the energy-producing nutrients and to allow cellular metabolic functions to take place (Combs, 2000; Groff et al., 2000). All six of these nutrient groups are found in foods in varying amounts. *Nutrient-dense foods* are those that provide a high quantity of essential nutrients in a relatively small quantity of kilocalories (Johnson, 2000b).

The recommended dietary allowances (RDA) of each nutrient are monitored by the Food and Nutrition Board (National Research Council, 1989). These recommendations are appropriate for the needs of most healthy individuals under usual environmental conditions and are periodically updated as more scientific data become available. However, they may not represent optimal recommendations for children with disabilities who have special health care needs (Cloud, 1999). The amount of food needed by a growing child is determined by using **anthropometrics** (measurements of body composition), laboratory, and medical evaluations. The appropriate foods in amounts that will meet these needs then become part of the meal plan or other nutrition support (e.g., tube feedings) developed by a dietitian.

The ability to maintain an ideal body weight depends on energy balance. In children, energy needs are based on body size and composition, level of physical activity, and growth pattern. Often, children with developmental disabilities have altered energy needs, leading to problems in estimating caloric requirements. For example, it is customary to use ideal weight for age and length for age, with the calorie levels suggested by the RDA (based on age and gender), to determine energy needs (National Research Council, 1989). The ideal body weight is determined by growth charts that have been developed from national surveys of healthy children by the National Center for Health Statistics (NCHS), part of the Centers for Disease Control and Prevention (CDC) (Hamill et al., 1979; Kuczmarski et al., 2000). For many children with disabilities, however, it may be difficult to accurately measure length and activity level may be either decreased or increased compared with typically developing children (Cloud, 1999), so the charts may overestimate or underestimate caloric needs. If energy intake is too great for the needs of the child, obesity results; if energy intake is insufficient, there is growth failure (Cloud, 1999; Dahl et al., 1996; National Research Council, 1989).

NUTRIENTS AND THEIR DEFICIENCIES

A healthy diet may supply all the essential nutrients and calories for typical growth and development during childhood. It should provide choices from each of the six major food groups with variety, balance, and moderation. The food guide pyramid (Figure 9.1) illustrates the dif-

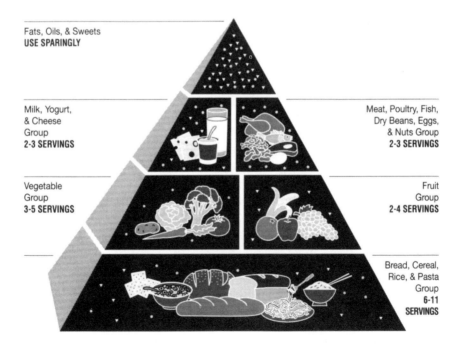

Figure 9.1. The food guide pyramid. (*Key:* □ fat [naturally occurring and added]; ∇ sugars [added]. These symbols show fat and added sugars in foods.) (From U.S. Department of Agriculture & U.S. Department of Health and Human Services. [2000]. *Dietary guidelines for Americans* [5th ed.]. Washington, D.C.: Author.)

ferent food groups and the suggested number of daily servings from each group. A child's diet is balanced over several days, not necessarily with every meal. Decisions about food choices have been made easier by the availability of food labeling information, mandated by the Nutrition Labeling and Education Act Amendments of 1993 (PL 103-80). This information provides consumer-friendly listings of all ingredients in descending order by weight. The following discussion focuses on the various nutrients that compose a healthful diet and the adverse effects of deficiencies.

Water

Water is second only to oxygen as essential for life. Water transports nutrients to and waste products from cells, helps regulate body temperature, and is involved in metabolic reactions. Our requirements for water are related to caloric consumption and average about 1 milliliter (⅕ teaspoon) of water per 1 kcal consumed in people of all ages. Thus, an infant needs to c onsume far larger amounts of water for weight than an older child does. In young infants, the average intake of fluid should be about 90–150 milliliters per kilogram of weight each day, or 1.5–2.5 ounces per pound of weight each day (AAP Committee on Nutrition, 1998). Most of an infant's water needs are met through breast milk or formula intake. In older infants and children, eating solid foods provides additional water. Water is lost through the skin and respiratory tract and by elimination in the feces and urine. Water is also important in the prevention of constipation. Although it is not necessary for a child to ingest all of the recommended calories needed each day, he or she must receive adequate fluid each day to avoid dehydration.

Carbohydrates

At least half of all calories should come from carbohydrates (Ettinger, 2000). Similar to fatty foods, high-carbohydrate foods are used as fuel and provide energy, as glucose, for brain metabolism. Carbohydrates also can be stored in muscle as glycogen and released as needed for energy (AAP Committee on Nutrition, 1998). There are two classes of carbohydrates: simple sugars and complex carbohydrates. **Lactose** (the sugar in milk) and sucrose (table sugar) are examples of simple sugars. They are rapidly absorbed and readily available for use as energy. Polysaccharides, or complex carbohydrates, are present in cereals, grains, potatoes, and corn. These starches are broken down slowly into simple sugars and dietary fibers.

Protein

After energy needs are met, the next most important macronutrient is protein. In children and adolescents without disabilities, protein should constitute about 10%–15% of the total calories ingested; in children with disabilities, 20% of total calories should come from protein (Cloud, 1999). High-protein foods include milk, cheese, meat, eggs, and fish. Following ingestion, protein is broken down into its constituent amino acids and nitrogen. Amino acids are involved in the synthesis of new tissue, hormones, enzymes, and antibodies; nitrogen is needed to keep existing tissue healthy. There are 20 amino acids, 9 of which are essential (histidine, isoleucine, leucine, lysine, methionine, phenylalanine, threonine, tryptophan, and valine) that must be supplied in the diet (National Research Council, 1989). The other, nonessential amino acids can be manufactured by the body in sufficient amounts. Under certain circumstances, such as in certain inborn errors of metabolism, normally nonessential amino acids may become essential (Groff et al., 2000). The quality of a specific protein depends on whether it contains all 9 essential amino acids. In general, animal protein contains essential amino acids in greater amounts and in better balance than plant protein. For example, egg protein is a complete protein; it contains all of the essential amino acids. In contrast, grains, beans, and seeds each contain limited amounts of an essential amino acid and are thus considered incomplete proteins. The relative requirements for various essential amino acids decrease with age as growth slows, and the overall requirement for protein also declines. A lack of protein in the diet, especially during infancy, can lead to a reduction in growth rate and muscle depletion. In an older child, protein malnutrition can lead to a failure to develop normal secondary sexual characteristics, such as pubic hair and breast tissue. An increased incidence of infections and poor digestion also may result because of deficiencies in certain enzymes (Groff et al., 2000).

Lipids

The third macronutrient group is composed of lipids (fat). Lipids are more calorically dense than carbohydrates and proteins and therefore are a very important source of energy. In addition, they are involved in the structure and function of biological membranes, hormones, and cellular signals (Groff et al., 2000). The long chain fatty acids linoleic (omega 6) and alpha-linolenic (omega 3) acid are essential because they cannot be synthesized in the body and are necessary for the formation of cellular membranes. Essential fatty acid deficiency is rare except in certain chronic diseases, such as cystic fibrosis and **celiac disease,** in which fatty acid absorption is impaired. A deficiency state increases the child's susceptibility to infection and bleeding and can lead to growth failure. Treatment of these disorders may involve formulas that are supplemented with essential and **medium chain fatty acids**.

Fats in food consist primarily of triglycerides, which have either **saturated** or **unsaturated** fatty acids attached. Saturated fats come principally from animal sources, whereas polyunsaturated fats come from vegetable sources. Animal fats also contain cholesterol. Foods high in fats include all fried foods, ice cream, nuts, and potato chips. Fats produce energy, give food its taste, and make us feel full.

Because cow's milk fat (butter) contains much less of the essential fatty acids than does human milk, infant formulas are made with modified skim milk and supplemented with vegetable oils to provide the essential fats. In one study, adequately nourished 4-month-old full-term infants who were fed formulas fortified with very long chain polyunsaturated fatty acids had better neurodevelopmental outcomes at 4 years of age compared with infants who were fed standard nonfortified formulas (Agostoni et al., 1995; Hack et al., 1991). Controversy continues regarding the value of adding very long chain fatty acids (i.e., docosahexaenoic acid [DHA] and eicospentaenoic acid [EPA]) to full-term infant formulas. Although commonly used in Europe, they have not been recommended for full-term infant formulas in the United States (Raiten, Talbot, & Waters, 1998).

Infants have an increased growth rate and require a higher percentage of calories from fat compared with older children. Breast milk and infant formulas contain 45%–55% energy in the form of fat; poor growth has been associated with a lower fat intake (Koletzko, 1997). It is generally recommended that full-term infants switch from breast milk or commercial infant formula to whole cow's milk around 1 year of age and continue the use of whole milk in the diet until 2 years of age (AAP Committee on Nutrition, 1998). In children older than 2 years of age, the fat content of the diet can come from more varied sources. For the underweight child, fat can provide supplemental calories; for the overweight child, it needs to be carefully monitored and regulated.

Studies in adult populations suggest that diets low in total fats, saturated fats, and cholesterol reduce the risk of coronary artery disease. Whether these recommendations are also appropriate for young children is controversial. Several professional organizations, however, recommend that for a child older than 2 years, no more than 30% of the child's calories should be derived from fat. Data from the Child and Adolescent Trial for Cardiovascular Health (Johnson, 2000a) suggest that lowering calories from fat to 30% of the diet does not cause any adverse effects on growth and development.

Fiber

Dietary fiber is the part of food that is not degraded in the digestive tract. Plants, including whole grains, fruits, and vegetables, are the primary sources of dietary fiber in our diet. One portion each of high-fiber cereal, bread, fresh fruit, and raw vegetables is recommended daily. Specifically, children older than 2 years should consume fiber equaling their age plus 5–10 grams per day (e.g., a 5-year-old should ingest 10–15 grams of fiber per day; Williams, Bollella, & Wynder, 1995) to a maximum of 35 grams per day (AAP Committee on Nutrition, 1998). Fiber induces water intake in the stool; promotes softer, more frequent, and bulkier stool; and helps prevent constipation (see Chapter 27). Excessive fiber, however, can delay gastric emptying and thus take up room in the small stomach of a child, potentially making it harder to consume all the calories and protein needed (Tolia, Ventimiglia, & Kuhns, 1997). It may interfere with the absorption of certain nutrients.

Vitamins

Although children need large quantities of fats, proteins, and carbohydrates for normal growth, they require only minute amounts of vitamins (Combs, 2000). Vitamins are used primarily as cofactors in metabolic reactions; they stimulate, or **catalyze,** the reactions without being used up (National Research Council, 1989). Although fresh foods contain them naturally, most processed foods in the United States are supplemented with vitamins. As long as the child eats a well-balanced and appropriately prepared diet, there should be no need for vitamin or mineral supplements, except for fluoride (AAP Committee on Nutrition, 1998). Children who have special nutritional stresses (e.g., premature infants, children who receive vegetarian or therapeutic restricted diets, children taking certain antiepileptic drugs), however, do require vitamin supplementation (Kozlowski, 1997). The body can store some fat-soluble vitamins so that a deficiency does not become evident until weeks or months after **undernutrition** has developed (Baer et al., 1997). Vitamin supplements, formulated for children, are available in liquid form, and vitamin and mineral combinations are available in chewable tablets and pills. Chewable tablets can be crushed and added to food, which may be useful for the child who needs dosing beyond infancy but cannot chew or swallow pills. Table 9.1 lists functions of selected vitamins and manifestations of states of deficiency and excess.

Minerals

Children and adults need various minerals to ensure appropriate body functioning. Some minerals are required in substantial amounts (e.g., calcium, magnesium, phosphorus). They compose 98% of the mineral content of the body and are required for the formation of bones and teeth and for normal muscle contraction (AAP Committee on Nutrition, 1998). A deficiency in any of these minerals can lead to brittle bones, **rickets,** poor muscle tone, and poor linear growth. Decreased use of bones due to paralysis or immobilization causes these minerals to be lost from the bones (Baer et al., 1997).

Minerals needed in smaller amounts include potassium, chloride, and sodium. These electrolytes maintain the body's fluid balance. An imbalance can result in nausea, muscle weakness, states of confusion, and seizures. Electrolyte imbalance is often associated with a gastrointestinal infection and concomitant dehydration.

Still other minerals are required only in minute amounts. These trace elements include copper, fluoride, iodine, iron, selenium, and zinc. Most are essential for the activation of certain enzymes. Except for iron deficiency, trace element deficiency states are rare. They can occur, however, 1) in children with malnutrition; 2) in premature infants on restricted diets; or 3) in children with ongoing medical conditions who have malabsorption, who are fed intravenously, or who require **dialysis.** Zinc deficiency results in growth failure, skin rashes, and impaired immunity against infections. Copper deficiency has been linked to anemia and weakened bones. Fluoride deficiency affects tooth integrity and bone strength. Iodine deficiency leads to hypothyroidism. Selenium deficiency has been associated with heart failure and neurological impairments (AAP Committee on Nutrition, 1998; Balint, 1998; Combs, 2000).

The most common trace mineral problem by far, however, is iron deficiency (de Benoist, 2001). Iron is an important constituent of hemoglobin, and its deficiency leads to anemia (Beard, 2001). Like Sam, infants may become anemic if they are fed whole cow's milk, which is both a poor source of dietary iron and may irritate the intestine, causing gastrointestinal blood loss. Older children who eat insufficient quantities of iron-containing foods are also at risk for developing iron-deficiency anemia. This is especially true for children who are raised on milk or formulas without iron supplementation or who do not eat enriched cereals. Iron-deficiency anemia occurs most frequently in children between 6 months and 3 years of age (AAP Committee on Nutrition, 1998). Affected children have impairments in temperature regulation, immunity against infections, cognitive development, and physical performance (Beard, 2001). Symptoms include irritability, listlessness, **anorexia,** diminished spontaneous activity, and decreased interest in the environment. Although scores on motor tests in children revert to normal after nutritional rehabilitation, there may be residual effects of early iron-deficiency anemia in areas of emotionality, cognitive processing, and attention (Pollitt, 2000). To avoid iron deficiency, beginning at 4–6 months of age, all full-term breast-fed infants should receive iron supplementation that provides 1 milligram per kilogram per day (AAP Committee on Nutrition, 1998). In addition, iron-fortified cereals should be introduced between 4 and 6 months of age (AAP Committee on Nutrition, 1998). For preterm infants, the recommendation is to begin iron supplements of 2 milligrams per kilogram per day to a maximum of 15 milligrams per day at 1–2 months of age or when birth weight is doubled, through age 12 months. It should be emphasized that treatment of iron deficiency requires replacement therapy and the identification of its underlying cause.

NONTRADITIONAL DIETS

To this point, this chapter has focused on the most common diets of children in developed countries who consume a wide variety of animal and plant foods. There are, however, a number of alternative diets. Some of these, such as vegetarian (plant-based) diets, are acceptable substitutes provided certain adjustments are made. Other novel diets, such as macrobiotic diets and **megavitamin therapy,** can be harmful to a child. Still others, such as certain elimination diets, may have no adverse effects but have benefits that remain unproven. This section touches on some of these nontraditional and novel diets.

Vegetarian Diets

A well-planned, balanced vegetarian diet with a vitamin supplement can meet all of the average child's nutritional requirements ("Position of the American Dietetic Association," 1995). Interest in vegetarian diets has increased for cultural, religious, philosophical, and health reasons. Vegetarians classify themselves as lacto-ovo-vegetarian (eat vegetables plus dairy products and eggs), lacto-vegetarian (eat no eggs), or vegan (eat plant foods only). People in many societies have practiced vegetarianism for centuries and have remained healthy, especially when they have supplemented their diet with milk or eggs. In older children and adults, vegan diets can be as nourishing as diets containing animal products, as long as individuals select their foods carefully and make sure that they receive sufficient calories and essential amino acids and vitamins. Advantages of a vegetarian diet include a lower incidence of obesity, coronary artery disease, hypertension, diabetes mellitus, and certain cancers ("Position of the American Dietetic Association," 1997).

When appropriately planned, vegan and lacto-ovo-vegetarian diets can be adequate for all stages of the life cycle, including pregnant and nursing mothers ("Position of the American Di-

Table 9.1. Food sources for selected minerals and vitamins: Their functions, deficiencies, and excess states

Macronutrient	Sources	Functions	Deficiency (and excess) states
Minerals			
Calcium	Dairy products (including breast milk), infant formula, canned sardines and salmon, tofu, broccoli, legumes, dark green leafy vegetables	Development and maintenance of healthy bones and teeth Blood clotting Nerve transmission and muscle contractions	Seizures, rickets, tetany (*Hypercalcemia*)
Iron	Red meats and organ meats (e.g., liver), dried fruits, molasses, legumes, dark green leafy vegetables	Component of hemoglobin Constituent of enzymes	Iron deficiency anemia, listlessness, fatigue, cognitive impairments, immune deficiency, spoon nails (*Possible tissue damage, fatal poisoning*)
Magnesium	Nuts, legumes, whole-grain breads and cereals, soybeans, dark green leafy vegetables	Conversion of carbohydrate, protein, and fat into energy Muscle contraction and relaxation and nerve transmission Synthesis of bone and teeth	Deficiency is associated with other illnesses, such as alcoholism, renal disease.
Phosphorus	Meats, especially organ meats; fish poultry; eggs; cheese; milk; peanut butter; soybeans	Component of bone Conversion of dietary carbohydrate, protein, and fat into energy Component of cell membranes Help in maintenance of acid–base balance in blood	Deficiency is rare; hyperphosphatemic rickets
Potassium	Most foods, vegetables, legumes, dried fruits, bananas, cantaloupe, apricots, citrus fruits, meats	Maintenance of water balance Formation of muscle tissue Activation of enzyme reaction	Muscle weakness (*Heart arrhythmia*)
Sodium	Table salt, monosodium glutamate, soy sauce, baking powder, cheese, milk, shellfish	Regulation of water and acid–base balance	Anorexia, nausea (*Stroke*)
Zinc	Meats, poultry, fish, organ meats, whole-grain breads and cereals	Induction of mineralization Production of protein Wound healing Maintenance of immune system	Acrodermatitis enteropathica (*Growth retardation, copper deficiency*)
Fat-soluble vitamins			
Vitamin A (retinol)	Fortified margarine, egg yolk, liver (*Sources of beta-carotene, precursor of vitamin A*: carrots, sweet potatoes, spinach, apricots, winter squash, cantaloupe, broccoli, dark green and yellow vegetables)	Essential for normal eyesight Normal body growth Infection fighting Enhancement of activity of immune system	Night blindness, poor dark adaptation, impaired growth, impaired immune function (*Increased intracranial pressure, anorexia*)

Vitamin	Functions	Sources	Deficiency (Toxicity)
Vitamin D (cholecalciferol)	Regulation of absorption and use of calcium and phosphorous, bone mineralization	Milk fortified with vitamin D, fish oils, exposure to sunlight	Rickets, osteomalacia (*Calcinosis, or calcification of soft tissues*)
Vitamin E (α-tocopherol)	Antioxidant Protection of cell membranes	Vegetable oil, seeds, wheat germ, nuts	Hemolytic disease in premature infant (*At levels greater than two times recommended daily allowance, interferes with vitamin K metabolism*)
Vitamin K (phylloquinone)	Regulation of normal blood clotting Activation of proteins needed for protein in bone	Green leafy vegetables, broccoli, turnip greens, romaine lettuce, cabbage	Hemorrhagic disease of newborn, prolonged bleeding time (*No known toxicity*)
Water-soluble vitamins			
Vitamin B₁ (thiamin) Vitamin B₂ (riboflavin) Vitamin B₃ (niacin)	Functioning of the heart and nervous system Conversion of carbohydrate into energy Maintenance of healthy skin Assistance in hormone synthesis	Whole-grain or enriched breads and cereals, dark green leafy vegetables, dairy products, eggs, fish, poultry, beef, veal, lamb, pork, organ meats, brewer's yeast, peanut butter	B_1: Beriberi—muscle weakness B_2: Cheilosis—lesions on outside of lips B_3: Pellagra—diarrhea, dermatitis, dementia (*No known toxicity with vitamins B_1, B_2, and B_3*)
Vitamin B₆ (pyridoxine)	Conversion of carbohydrates, fats, and protein into energy Aiding in the conversion of one amino acid to another	Meats, fish, poultry, bananas, navy beans, walnuts, green leafy vegetables	Seizures (*Neuropathy*)
Vitamin B₁₂ (cyanocobalamin)	Normal processing of carbohydrate, protein, and fat Formation of myelin sheath Essential for replacement and maintenance of all cells	Lean meats, poultry, fish, shellfish, milk, organ meats, cheese and eggs, fortified soy milk	Megaloblastic, or pernicious, anemia; ataxia (*No known toxicity*)
Folic acid	Formation of DNA and certain amino acids Formation of blood cells	Mushrooms; beef liver; beans; green leafy vegetables; orange juice; fortified bread, flour, and rice	Anemia; teratogenic effects on fetus, such as neural tube defects (*Excess can mask B_{12} deficiency.*)
Vitamin C (ascorbic acid)	Formation and maintenance of collagen Antioxidant Enhancement of absorption of iron Protection of folic acid	Citrus fruits and juices, Brussels sprouts, strawberries, broccoli, collard greens, cantaloupe, tomato juice	Scurvy

Sources: Balint, 1998; Mitchell, 1997.

etetic Association," 1997). Common hazards in these diets, however, include decreased energy consumption and deficiencies in vitamin B_{12}, vitamin D, calcium, and phosphorus in children younger than 5 years. These problems can be averted with knowledge, proper planning, and vigilance (Sanders, 1995).

The recommendation for breast milk in the first year of life also applies to healthy full-term vegetarian/vegan infants (AAP Committee on Nutrition, 1998). A plant-based diet can provide adequate nutrition for normal growth in infancy and childhood. Nutritional problems associated with vegetarian/vegan infants are usually due to the use of homemade formulas or to the improper use of adult commercial products during the first year of life (Mangels & Messina, 2001). Spoon foods should be introduced into the diet in a stepwise, age- and developmentally appropriate manner between ages 4 and 6 months. In place of animal-based sources, foods such as tofu, soy yogurt, pureed legumes, and some soy cheeses can be added between ages 7 and 10 months (Mangels & Messina, 2001). Multivitamin/mineral supplements for breast-fed vegan infants are the same as for omnivore infants, with the additional need of vitamin B_{12} from birth (Messina & Mangels, 2001).

Vegan toddlers and children need foods with high energy density. They should be offered three meals daily, as well as two to three snacks such as nut butters and hummus (Mangels & Messina, 2001). Commercially available soy-milk products are now fortified and help meet nutritional needs of this age group in the same way as cow's milk ("Position of the American Dietetic Association," 1997).

Organic Food Diets

Natural or organic food diets are not restricted in their content but in how the plants are grown or the animals raised. The U.S. Department of Agriculture has proposed a national standard definition for the term *organic*. To qualify as organic, plants must be grown in soil enriched with humus or compost in which no pesticides, herbicides, or inorganic fertilizers have been used. Animals must be reared on natural feeds and not treated with hormones or antibiotics. Although proponents of these diets laud their results, no long-term study has shown the nutritional superiority of organically grown crops over those grown under standard conditions. Nevertheless, concerns about hormones and additives may be valid and, for some individuals, are sufficient reason to buy only organic foods. One important consideration is that organically grown foods are more costly than standard foods.

Elimination Diets

Elimination diets are used to identify and manage food allergy (an abnormal immunological reaction to a particular food [Sicherer, 1999b]) or hypersensitivity. Five foods account for the majority of food allergies in children: cow's milk, soy, eggs, peanuts, and wheat (Sicherer, 1999b). Two types of elimination diets are common: 1) as a test to identify a food allergy and 2) as a treatment regimen to remove the offending allergen from the diet. There is good evidence that some individuals who have allergic symptoms (i.e., eczema, wheezing, gastrointestinal disturbances) in response to certain food proteins that they ingest benefit from their elimination. Peanut allergy has been associated with fatal **anaphylaxis** (an acute allergic response leading to shock); this allergy is not outgrown, and the treatment is to eliminate the allergic food from the diet (Sicherer, 1999a). A food challenge may be used to test whether the suspected food produces allergic reactions. The suspected food is presented to the patient in a systematic way that may be blinded (disguised) or open. The patient is closely monitored for reactions for a set period. It is imperative that emergency medical attention be immediately available to treat serious reactions that may occur during the food challenge (Sicherer, 1999a).

There is far less evidence, however, that ingestion of certain foods or food additives is a common cause of behavioral disturbances associated with learning disabilities or attention-deficit/hyperactivity disorder (ADHD). Yet, elimination diets have become quite popular as an alternative therapy for these disorders. In 1975, Dr. Benjamin Feingold published a book detailing his observations of the relationship among food additives, allergy, and behavior, which became the basis for the Feingold diet. Later, Feingold extended his elimination diet to proscribe all artificial colors and preservatives as well as foods that contain natural **salicylates** (aspirin-like compounds), and he expanded his treatment group to include children with hyperactivity and/or learning disabilities. The physiological basis for sensitivity to food additives remains obscure (Conners, 1989; Feingold, 1975). Many studies have attempted to prove or disprove the efficacy of the Feingold diet (Conners, 1989; Conners, Goyette, & Southwick, 1976; "Consensus Conference," 1982; Harley et al., 1978; Weiss, 1982; Wender, 1986). A small number of children, about 5%, did appear to respond, suggesting that elimination diets may be of some use. The majority of children tested, however, did not respond, and there is no current way of predicting the responders.

NUTRITIONAL DISORDERS

Nourishing the body requires 1) an adequate source of food, 2) the capability to digest it, and 3) the ability to transform the nutrients into absorbable molecules that can then be delivered to and utilized by the appropriate cells in the body (AAP Committee on Nutrition, 1998; Balint, 1998; Groff et al., 2000; Rogol, Clark, & Roemmich, 2000). When, as in developing countries, the signs of malnutrition are severe, they are more easily recognized (Balint, 1998). When nutritional deficiencies are milder, however, they are more difficult to identify and may cause nonspecific symptoms that are similar to other nonnutritional problems (Balint, 1998).

Children with disabilities are at particular risk for nutritional problems (Cloud, 1999; Hawdon et al., 2000; Kozlowski, 1997). Child-related nutritional issues include 1) altered nutrient needs, 2) altered energy needs (increased or decreased), 3) nutritional deficiencies, 4) poor appetite, 5) aberrant feeding skills, 6) malabsorption, 7) constipation/diarrhea, 8) drug–nutrient interactions, and 9) maladaptive behaviors (Baer & Harris, 1997; Sullivan et al., 2000). Caregiver-related factors include 1) a poor understanding or lack of knowledge of the nutritional problem, 2) difficulty in following complex dietary recommendations, 3) an inability to limit dietary intake, and 4) engaging in inappropriate feeding practices.

Failure to Thrive

To grow normally after birth, an infant must have adequate nutritional intake. Early signs of undernutrition include poor weight gain and a decrease in muscle and fatty tissue (Raynor et al., 1999). FTT is the clinical term that has been generally applied to an infant or young child who is failing to meet the standards for age in both growth and development; this FTT is a symptom, not a diagnosis (AAP Committee on Nutrition, 1998). Inadequate intake affects development not only directly (by causing deficits in nutrition to the brain) but also indirectly (by causing diminished physical energy for exploring and learning). In older children, undernutrition delays growth by first affecting growth tempo, resulting in a slowing of both weight gain and linear growth (Rogol et al., 2000; Sermet-Gaudelus et al., 2000; Zemel, Riley, & Stallings, 1997). FTT is most often caused by inadequate food intake resulting from environmental, developmental, or behavioral factors (Zlotkin, 1997). Raynor and Rudolf (2000) found that the majority of children with FTT in one community had inadequate food intake and that more than half had developmental disabilities. Traditionally, the origin of FTT was thought to be nonorganic (i.e., psychosocial/behavioral) or organic (i.e., biological). Blame was often directed toward poor maternal skills, often without the benefit of a full medical evaluation. It is now understood that organic and nonorganic factors are usually intertwined (Raynor et al., 1999). Although more common among the impoverished, FTT can occur in all socioeconomic strata. A child may have nonorganic FTT because he or she is offered an inadequate diet due to lack of food availability or lack of parental knowledge or involvement. Alternatively, the child may have behavior problems, including food refusal or selectivity. From an organic perspective, the child with a developmental disability may have multiple factors contributing to the risk of undernutrition (Manikam & Perman, 2000; Trier & Thomas, 1998). Medical conditions that place children at greater risk for FTT include pulmonary diseases (e.g., **bronchopulmonary dysplasia;** see Chapter 6), heart disease, HIV/AIDS, chromosome disorders (e.g., Down syndrome), cerebral palsy, cleft lip or palate, cystic fibrosis, gastrointestinal disorders, developmental disabilities, metabolic or endocrine disorders, and neurological disorders.

Ultimately, undernutrition may be the cause and the result of neurodevelopmental impairments. If it progresses, it can become malnutrition, in which case there is usually a reduced rate of growth in length and head circumference as well as in weight (Jeejeebhoy, 1998). Malnutrition is the leading cause of infant illness and death in the developing world. Although much less common in developed countries, it is a potential problem among individuals who do not have access to a balanced diet, who have restricted food choices, or who have chronic diseases or developmental disabilities (Zlotkin, 1997).

Malnutrition can severely affect the neurodevelopment of the young child (Brown & Pollitt, 1996; Suskind & Lewind-Suskind, 1993). In fact, it has been shown that infantile malnutrition can reduce brain cell count by as much as 20% (Crosby, 1991; Winick, 1979). It is surprising, therefore, that the brain is quite resilient to malnutrition and that psychoeducational rehabilitation can reduce the impact on cognitive development (DeLong, 1993). Adoption studies have confirmed that nutritional rehabilitation of malnourished infants combined with a psychosocially enriched environment can result in achievement of typical IQ scores (Colombo, de la Parra, & Lopez, 1992). This contrasts with children in control groups, who were raised in institutions or with their impoverished biological families, who have significant cognitive impairments.

In addition to the environment, the content of early supplementary feedings is important in determining outcome in children who have experienced malnutrition. In general, infants who received rehabilitation diets with a high protein/caloric content had better neurodevelopmental outcomes and catch-up growth than those who received supplements with low protein/caloric content did (Berry, Abrahamowicz, & Usher, 1997; Nichols, 1997).

Nutritional support for treatment of FTT or malnutrition includes increasing caloric density of foods and beverages for the child who can eat and swallow safely, offering education and counseling for caregivers regarding more nutritious food and beverage choices, and providing feeding strategies (Nichols, 1997; Raynor et al., 1999). Management of nutritional issues may include other feeding options such as tube feedings.

Obesity

Although undernutrition results in growth delay, excessive intake of food relative to the metabolic needs of the child leads to obesity. Thus, obesity is basically a disorder of energy balance in which there is chronic disequilibrium between energy intake and expenditure. Operationally, obesity is defined as weight in infancy in excess of 120% of median weight for height on NCHS growth charts (Maynard et al., 2001; Schonfeld-Warren & Warren, 1997); in childhood, a body mass index (BMI) above the 85th percentile for age; or, in adults, a BMI of 30 or greater. BMI levels of 25–29 are defined as overweight (Maynard et al., 2001). BMI is obtained by dividing weight in kilograms by height in meters squared (Barlow & Dietz, 1998). Using these criteria about one quarter of the general population in the United States is overweight, and 18% satisfy the criteria for obesity. Among school-age children (6–11 years), 13% of the population is obese (CDC NCHS, 1999). Obesity tends to follow children into adulthood, especially when there is a genetic predisposition. Eighty percent of obese teenagers become obese adults (Barlow & Dietz, 1998). The increase in prevalence of obesity suggests changes in nongenetic factors (AAP Committee on Nutrition, 1998).

Constipation

Constipation is a very common problem in children with developmental disabilities. It is defined as infrequent bowel movements of hard, dry stool (Cloud, 1999). Some of the contributing factors include generalized hypotonia and limited muscle function of the bowel, lack of physical activity, inadequate fluid intake, and inadequate dietary fiber. Certain long-term medications can also promote constipation. Although laxatives and enemas are often used to resolve the problem, simply adjusting the diet can help significantly (AAP Committee on Nutrition, 1998; Cloud, 1999). Additional dietary fiber can be added by replacing low-fiber foods with higher-fiber foods such as whole grains (instead of white bread), fiber-rich beverages, 1–2 tablespoons of unprocessed grain, or fiber supplements (e.g., Metamucil; Cloud, 1999). Increasing daily exercise also helps prevent constipation (Cloud, 1999). Finally, fluids must be provided in amounts appropriate for size. Table 9.2 contains general fluid requirements.

Diarrhea and Dehydration

Diarrhea may be acute or chronic, with many possible causes, such as infections, food intolerance, or medications (AAP Committee on Nutrition, 1998). From a nutritional perspective, when diarrhea occurs, prompt management is needed to prevent dehydration (AAP Committee on Nutrition, 1998). Dehydration involves the loss of adequate circulating fluid volume. The goal of therapy therefore is rehydration. Fortunately, commercially available oral rehydration solutions (e.g., Pedialyte, Ricelyte, Rehydrate, Resol) can be used effectively at the first signs of dehydration (AAP Committee on Nutrition, 1998). The sodium, glucose, and osmolarity (density) of these solutions are in a specific ratio to promote rehydration. In contrast, high-carbohydrate beverages that were used in the past to treat diarrhea may worsen the problem; thus, soft drinks, fruit juices, punches, and similar drinks should not be used (AAP Committee on Nutrition, 1998). After rehydration, children who have returned to their normal age-appropriate diet have done better than those who have been placed on a restricted diet to "rest" their bowel, such as the "BRATT" diet (banana, rice, applesauce, tea, and toast; AAP Committee on Nutrition, 1998). Any child who has severe or persistent diarrhea should be evaluated by his or her pediatrician in a timely fashion so that dehydration is prevented (AAP Committee on Nutrition, 1998). Signs of severe dehydration include lethargy with sunken eyes, a very dry mouth, and inability to drink.

Malabsorption/Lactose Intolerance

When diarrhea is due to a nutritional intolerance, such as lactose, it is accompanied by malabsorption symptoms that include cramping and flatulence (AAP Committee on Nutrition, 1998). To prevent these symptoms from occurring, foods containing lactose (e.g., dairy products) may be removed from the diet. Because this removal can leave gaps in consumption of total calories, protein, calcium, vitamin D, and other important nutrients, a safe substitute is needed. Options include using milk products that have been pretreated with **lactase** enzyme or with a different carbohydrate source. As another approach, fortified soy protein beverages that are lactose-free but contain nutrients similar to those found in milk can be

Table 9.2. Fluid requirements

Body weight	Fluid required
First 10 kg	100 cc/kg/day
11–20 kg	1000 cc + 50 cc/kg for each kg > 10 kg
> 20 kg	1500 cc + 20 cc/kg for each kg > 20 kg

Source: Nevin-Folino & Miller, 1999.

Key: 30 cubic centimeters (cc) = 1 ounce; 1 kilogram (kg) = 2.2 pounds.

used. In addition, oral dietary supplements such as Pediasure and Kindercal use a different source of carbohydrate while supplying other nutrients in amounts slightly more concentrated than in conventional cow's milk.

Dental Disease

Dental diseases that inhibit the intake of food also can have nutritional consequences that are far reaching (Boyd, Palmer, & Dwyer, 1998). Mouth pain from **periodontal disease** or **dental caries** can contribute to a child's refusal to eat. This emphasizes the importance of regular dental checkups (see Chapter 28; Boyd et al., 1998).

Drug–Nutrient Interactions

Certain long-term medications can contribute to a nutrient deficiency because of an interaction. Children with disabilities are more likely than typically developing children to be given long-term medication. These include drugs to manage seizures, hyperactivity, digestive problems, and behavioral/emotional issues. Many of these children are on several medications. These medications may alter the amount of specific nutrients needed and produce symptoms that are often associated with nutritional deficiencies. For example, if a child is receiving a certain antiepileptic medication, he or she may become deficient in folic acid, vitamin B_6, vitamin C, vitamin D, or phosphorus (Table 9.3).

Table 9.3.   Drug–nutrient interactions common to children with developmental disabilities

Medication class	Generic name (trade name)	Potential nutrient reactions
Antiepileptics	phenytoin (Dilantin) phenobarbital (Luminal) carbamazepine (Carbatrol, Tegretol) primidone (Mysoline)	• Decreased serum folic acid levels • Decreased vitamin D levels leading to decreased calcium absorption
	valproic acid (Depakene)	• Same as with other antiepileptics listed, plus possibly decreased carnitine levels in serum and tissue
Corticosteroids	prednisone	• Increased appetite • Sodium and fluid retention • Decreased calcium and phosphorus absorption • Occasional glucose intolerance
Diuretics	furosemide (Lasix) spironalactone (Aldactone)	• Increased excretion of potassium, calcium, and magnesium • Decreased carbohydrate tolerance • Fluid and electrolyte imbalance • Increased serum glucose
Anticonstipation agents	mineral oil milk of magnesia	• Interference with absorption of vitamins A, D, E, and K • With decreased absorption of vitamin D, possible impaired absorption of calcium and phosphorus • Long-term use: decreased thiamin, phosphate, calcium, and iron absorption
Antacids	omeprazole (Prilosec) ranitidine (Zantac) famotidine (Pepcid)	• Long-term use: decreased vitamin B_{12} and possibly anemia
Stimulants	dextroamphetamine (Dexedrine, DextroStat)	• Decreased appetite
	methylphenidate (Ritalin, Concerta, Metadate CD, Methylin)	• Poor growth

Source: Cloud, 1999.

DEVELOPMENTAL DISABILITIES WITH NUTRITIONAL ISSUES

Certain developmental disabilities are associated with specific nutritional issues. These include mental retardation, inborn errors of metabolism, autism, ADHD, cerebral palsy, and meningomyelocele (Isaacs et al., 1997). These are briefly discussed in the following sections.

Mental Retardation

In mental retardation, the issue is more often one of obesity rather than undernutrition. For example, although there may be feeding problems in infancy (Spender et al., 1996), the majority of children with Down syndrome become obese by adolescence (Kozlowski, 1997). Although the cause is not completely clear, it seems to relate to decreased metabolic rate due to shorter stature and decreased muscle tone (Cloud, 1999). Maintaining a normal weight for height requires an appropriate intake and increased physical activity (Kozlowski, 1997). Prader-Willi syndrome, another mental retardation disorder, is associated with compulsive eating and often with food stealing and hoarding behaviors. This points to the importance of behavioral and dietary support from early childhood combined with promotion of an active lifestyle through regular participation in sports and recreational activities (see Chapter 34).

Inborn Errors of Metabolism

Some of the most complex nutritional issues occur in inborn errors of metabolism. In disorders of amino acid and organic acid metabolism, special diets must be adhered to that restrict the intake of biochemical compounds that are toxic to the child (see Chapter 18). The need for a very restricted diet makes maintenance of normal growth difficult. As a result, many children with inborn errors of metabolism are at risk for undernutrition. There is a problem in remaining on the tightrope of not giving so much protein as to cause toxicity or too little as to cause undernutrition. These children require intensive follow-up in special metabolism clinics, where nutritionists play a crucial role in dietary planning (Pass et al., 2000).

Autism

A significant feature of autistic disorder is food selectivity. Children with autism may choose very few foods that they eat exclusively for some period. They may then switch to a completely different restricted food selection. The result may be an unbalanced diet, placing the children at risk for nutritional deficiencies and undernutrition. Their self-stimulatory behavior may also include **pica** (eating nonfood substances such as clay, paint, or starch), which increases the risk of lead poisoning and displaces adequate food intake (Isaacs et al., 1997). An evaluation of nutritional concerns should include anthropometric measurements to determine whether the child's growth curve is flattening; a dietary history to identify potential nutritional deficiencies; and blood studies including albumin, hemoglobin, and lead levels. Treatment should focus on nutritional counseling to provide needed supplements and behavior management approaches to increase the breadth of accepted foods and to decrease pica.

Attention-Deficit/Hyperactivity Disorder

ADHD and its treatment can affect nutrition (Callaghan, 1999). The physical hyperactivity may increase caloric needs, and stimulant medication often decreases appetite. The nutritional assessment should focus on following growth in weight and height. Nutritional supplements may be needed, especially at lunchtime, to provide needed calories. These can include Power-Bars, Carnation instant breakfast bars, and so forth. It is rare that the anorexia related to stimulants is severe enough to force their withdrawal. Restricting their use to school days during the school year, however, may allow maximum growth during treatment.

Cerebral Palsy

Growth failure is frequently observed among children with cerebral palsy. They are often smaller and lighter (weigh less for height) than typically developing children are. This is attributable to both nutritional and nonnutritional factors (Kong, Tse, & Lee, 1999). Inadequate intake of food is often cited as the most important factor (Hals, Svalastog, & Nilsen, 1996; Kozlowski, 1997; Krick et al., 1996); however, other issues may include involuntary movement (consuming energy), gastroesophageal reflux (resulting in vomiting; see Chapter 27), and interactions between drugs and nutrition (antiepileptic drug effects on vitamins). In terms of height gain, there appears to be growth suppression (Kong et al., 1999). Growth failure and undernutrition are not the inevitable outcome of cerebral palsy, however, and can often be corrected. Results from the Oxford Feeding Study (Sullivan et al., 2000) suggested that many children with cerebral palsy do not receive feeding and nutrition assessments and would benefit from them. Less commonly, issues of obesity arise because of inactivity.

Meningomyelocele

Obesity is a problem among individuals with meningomyelocele because of the inactivity engendered by paralysis below the neural tube defect. Just as with individuals who have Down syndrome, a weight control program is very important. Adaptive sports activities also should be stressed, including weight training and aerobic exercise (see Chapter 34). In addition, many children with meningomyelocele are allergic to latex (see Chapter 24). These children may thus have food sensitivity to banana, kiwi, avocado, and water chestnuts (Cloud, 1999).

NUTRITIONAL ASSESSMENT

It is imperative that high-risk children are nutritionally screened and appropriately referred for intervention (Baer & Harris, 1997). Sometimes, all that is needed is education and guidance; at other times, additional services are required. The initial screening process involves questionnaires and evaluations that provide baseline information on growth and eating habits, often provided by a nurse or other health care professional. If abnormalities are suspected, the screening is followed by referral for further assessment, intervention, monitoring, and reevaluation by appropriate medical professionals (Baer & Harris, 1997; "Position of American Dietetic Association," 1995). Table 9.4 describes questions to include in a feeding assessment that have important nutritional outcomes.

The nutritional assessment commonly begins with routine anthropometric measurements: height, weight, and head circumference (Rogol et al., 2000). Growth can be monitored using growth charts (Hamill et al., 1979; Zemel et al., 1997). The most recent growth charts have been developed by the NCHS and can be downloaded from the CDC's web site (http://www.cdc.gov/growthcharts); see also Ogden et al., 2002. Most children grow steadily and predictably, staying within one to two growth percentiles or channels over time (AAP Committee on Nutrition, 1998). In addition to the NCHS charts, a number of specialized growth charts are available for children with achondroplasia, cerebral palsy, Down syndrome, Marfan syndrome, spina bifida, Turner syndrome, and Williams syndrome. These charts reflect the growth of a particular subset of children so they can be compared with children who have the same disorder rather than with typically growing children (Cloud, 1999).

Anthropometric Measurements

Anthropometric measurements usually focus on height, weight, and head circumference. One can, however, measure skinfold thickness, arm circumference, and arm and leg length in children with disabilities when usual measurement procedures are inadequate. In measuring weight,

Table 9.4.   Questions to include in a feeding assessment

1.   What foods are eaten?
2.   How much food is eaten at each meal or snack?
3.   How frequent are meals and snacks?
4.   How are the foods prepared (e.g., baked, fried, broiled, boiled)?
5.   Are any commercial food supplements, vitamin/mineral preparations, or complementary or alternative remedies or practices used?
6.   Does the child eat nonfood items?
7.   Does the child self-feed?
8.   Are there problems with suck, swallow, or chew?
9.   Who feeds the child?
10.   What is the method of feeding?
11.   How long does feeding take per meal?
12.   Do certain foods cause gagging, aspiration, or vomiting?
13.   Are there any food allergies?
14.   Is there any food intolerance, such as to dairy products?
15.   What medication is the child receiving?
16.   Is food used as a reward, punishment, or pacifier?
17.   Is there a history of chronic constipation?
18.   What is the dietary and fluid intake?
19.   How much and what foods are offered versus those consumed?
20.   Are there mechanical eating issues?
21.   Is there evidence of gastroesophageal reflux (GER)?
22.   Are adequate calories, protein, and micronutrients ingested, based on an intake record?

Sources: Baer & Harris, 1997; Cloud, 1999; Thomas & Akobeng, 2000.

the major sources of error include poorly or inaccurately calibrated equipment, inconsistent weighing procedures, and inaccurate conversion of pounds to kilograms or vice versa (Zemel et al., 1997). Length measures, although more straightforward, may be inappropriate for a child with a condition that prevents proper positioning, such as **spastic** cerebral palsy with its associated spinal curvature and/or contractures (Cloud, 1999; Zemel et al., 1997). Here, arm or leg length measurements may need to be used (Kong et al., 1999). Bone age compared with chronological age may also help provide more information on the growth potential of the child (Kong et al., 1999). Growth charts that are age-dependent for height and weight of children with cerebral palsy have been developed but may have limited use when bone age is taken into account (Kong et al., 1999; Krick et al., 1996). Common sources of error in measuring head circumference include improper positioning of the measuring tape around the head, hairstyles or headwear, ears under the tape, and movement of the child's head (Zlotkin, 1997).

In addition to these routine measures, arm circumference and skinfold thickness can provide information on body composition that is not attainable from weight and length measurements alone. The triceps (upper arm) skinfold thickness is one of the most useful measurements. It is a good indicator of energy reserves, correlates well with total body fat stores, and reflects short-term fluctuations (Zemel et al., 1997). Subscapular (below shoulderblade) skinfold thickness is less sensitive to short-term fluctuations in body fat stores but better reflects long-term energy stores (Zemel et al., 1997). A combination of skinfold measurements can be used to estimate the percent body fat and lean body mass (Zemel et al., 1997). The mid-upper arm circumference reflects muscle, fat, and bone. This measurement provides a rapid index of malnutrition, especially if height and weight are unavailable (Cloud, 1999). In the child with a disability, body composition assessment becomes an essential component of nutritional assessment because linear growth is so often compromised (Zemel et al., 1997). Both upper arm length and lower leg length provide an alternative to length or stature measurements. Reference charts are available for assessing nutritional status in infants and children using these measures. For example, tibial (shin bone) length can be measured and compared with reference standards (Spender et al., 1989). If these measures fall outside the range of a child's gender and age norms, it suggests an unusual growth pattern that may be caused by a nutritional deficiency, developmental delay, or other conditions. In children who are nonambulatory, the upper arm is generally less severely affected than the lower leg (Zemel et al., 1997).

Accurate anthropometric measurements, taken periodically, provide information on the rate of growth of a child compared with reference norms. In addition, the values can be used to evaluate nutritional status. Serial weight, length, or other anthropometric measurements are needed when evaluating a child's growth (Balint, 1998). Changes in a child's growth pattern can identify under- and overnutrition. The most consistent finding and earliest sign of undernutrition is poor weight gain. If it is not treated, a slowing of linear growth is likely to follow.

Assessing Methods of Feeding

Assessment of feeding skills of the child with disabilities and his or her caregivers is an essential component of a nutritional assessment (Baer & Harris, 1997). Often undernutrition is associated with mechanical feeding problems (Thomas & Akobeng, 2000). Problems that interfere with food intake include tongue thrust, tonic bite reflex, tactile defensiveness, and lack of tongue lateralization (see Chapter 27). The child may also use maladaptive eating behaviors (e.g., food refusal, temper tantrums) to manipulate caregivers and control the environment. Clues provided by "following the food" can be very helpful in diagnosing the problem. For example, if an inadequate or inappropriate food intake is identified, then the reasons for these problems must be determined. By using food records, child- or caregiver-centered problems can be identified (Stevenson, 1995). With the identification of the problems, individualized intervention may be started that may include proper positioning, adaptive feeding equipment, behavior support, and individualized oral-motor therapy (Thomas & Akobeng, 2000).

Laboratory Measurements

Biochemical measures that relate to nutritional status can be useful in supporting the assessment. In addition, certain laboratory tests can be used to confirm a diagnosis or evaluate interventions (Table 9.5). For example, the hemoglobin/hematocrit level is a commonly used screening test for iron status because iron deficiency anemia can contribute to faltering growth.

INTERVENTIONS FOR NUTRITIONAL PROBLEMS

The goal of nutritional intervention is to provide adequate nourishment while enhancing the mealtime experience for the child and caregivers (Cloud, 1999). Treatment plans are based on the chronicity of the problem and focus on modifying the content and mode of delivery of the nutrition. Attention must be paid to underlying medical, neurodevelopmental, psychosocial,

Table 9.5.   Laboratory tests to confirm a diagnosis

Nutritional marker	Test
Protein status	Albumin, prealbumin, transferrin
Chemical rickets	Calcium, phosphorus, alkaline phosphatase
Iron status	Hemoglobin, hematocrit, ferritin
Plasma amino acids and urinary organic acids	Diagnosis of metabolic disorders

and economic factors (Ekvall, 1993). The child's unique metabolic needs, nutritional requirements, and ability to ingest or digest nutrients also must be considered. Table 9.6 provides caloric requirements for children with selected developmental disorders.

Liquid Oral Nutrition

In the first months of life, nutrition is provided as oral liquids. The AAP Committee on Nutrition (1998) has strongly recommended breast feeding for full-term infants as the exclusive source of nutrition during this period. It should be noted that most infants who are unable to breast-feed do well nutritionally with standard infant formula. Infants given formula, however, do not obtain the benefits provided by breast milk for host defense against infection and improved gastrointestinal function. The nutritional content of infant formula is regulated by the Food and Drug Administration (FDA) and is required to contain specific nutrients between minimum and maximum points. The formulation is designed to approximate human milk as closely as possible. Infant formulas are based either on cow's milk or on soy and then modified. Many types of specialized formulas are commercially available (see Chapter 27).

Some infants need caloric supplements, either because of a metabolic disturbance (e.g., an inborn error of metabolism) or because of increased requirements (e.g., prematurity). For the premature infant, 24 calories per ounce of formula may be necessary. Concentrating the formula further requires medical supervision as it increases the protein load to the kidneys. Breast milk also can be expressed and fortified to provide more calories per ounce for the premature infant. For inborn errors of metabolism, caloric density can be increased by adding carbohydrates (e.g., MJ 80056, Prophree) and/or fat (e.g., Microlipid). When these manipulations are done, distribution of calories needs to be monitored so that 7%–16% of calories come from protein, 30%–55% from fat, and 35%–65% from carbohydrates. Formula manufacturers (see Appendix D) maintain web sites that provide the most recent lists of formula products.

Solid Oral Nutrition

There is a natural developmental progression in a child's ability to handle solid (spoon) foods, starting with strained foods and progressing to more complex textures. Strained foods include pureed fruits and vegetables, Stage 1 commercial baby foods, and blenderized foods. Unfortunately, children with disabilities who have impaired oral-motor skills (e.g., children with cerebral palsy) may have difficulties handling even these smooth textures (Croft, 1992). This problem often can be overcome by using commercially available thickeners, such as Thick-It and Thick

Table 9.6.   Caloric requirements of children with selected disorders

Disorder	Factors	Daily caloric needs
Down syndrome	Genetic predisposition	Boys, ages 1–3 years: 16.1 kcal/cm; girls, ages 1–3 years: 14.3 kcal/cm
Cerebral palsy	Increased/decreased tone, increased/decreased movement	Ages 5–11 years: 13.9 kcal/cm for mild to moderate activity, 11.1 kcal/cm for inactivity
Meningomyelocele	Restricted activity, oromotor dysfunction	9–11 kcal/cm for maintenance, 7 kcal/cm for weight loss
Prader-Willi syndrome	Genetic predisposition	10–11 kcal/cm for maintenance, 8–9 kcal/cm for weight loss
Prematurity	Increased metabolic needs	Infants: 90–120 kcal/kg

Source: Cloud, 1999.

Note: Caloric needs are expressed as kilocalories (kcal) per centimeter (cm) of height or, for premature infants, as kcal per kilogram (kg) of body weight.

Key: 1 inch = 2.54 centimeters; 1 pound = 2.2 kilograms.

& Easy, or other foods such as dried baby cereal, instant potatoes, instant pudding, and ground cracker crumbs. These, of course, add calories and need to be factored into total daily intake.

Once a child is ready to progress from strained foods, the next stage is "junior foods" that introduce small lumps and some texture. These foods can be swallowed without chewing but do require some munching (see Chapter 27). Examples include mashed potatoes and Stage 2 baby food. Many of these foods can be prepared at home using a grinder or blender. As a child gains more experience and skills, he or she can tolerate more and more lumps and is ready for Stage 3 baby food. Finally, when the child is ready for finger feeding, foods such as macaroni or soft, cooked carrots can be introduced. Hard foods should be offered cautiously until the child has passed the stage of increased risk of choking, which usually lasts until 3–5 years (AAP Committee on Nutrition, 1998).

Enteral Feedings

Enteral, or tube, feedings may be required on a short-term basis for refeeding malnourished children or on a long-term basis for children who cannot safely ingest sufficient food to maintain adequate nutrition (Tawfik et al., 1997). Short-term enteral feedings generally involve the insertion of a nasogastric (nose to stomach) or a nasojejunal (nose to small intestine) tube. Long-term enteral feedings require the placement of **gastrostomy** or a jejunostomy feeding tube (see Chapter 27).

In planning tube feeding, the first objective is to establish tolerance to the feeding solution and to its rate of flow (Nardella, 1995). The tube feedings are started slowly and gradually advanced. It is prudent not to increase 24-hour volumes and concentrations simultaneously. Feedings are based on the nutritional requirements and gastrointestinal tolerance of the child, so the choice of formula must be individualized. There are many factors to consider in selecting a tube-feeding formula, including 1) nutrient and fluid requirements, 2) route of delivery (gastric, jejunal), 3) osmolality (concentration), 4) viscosity (thickness), 5) medical condition, 6) age of the child, 7) cost, 8) family lifestyle, and 9) feeding schedule.

For infants younger than 1 year of age, breast milk or a commercial infant formula is most appropriate for tube feeding. Standard infant commercial formulas or specialized casein hydrolysate formulas can be used. For children ages 1–10 years, specific tube-feeding formulas are available, such as Pediasure, and Kindercal (AAP Committee on Nutrition, 1998). Alternatively, some families choose to blenderize the meals, a process that is more economical but also more labor-intensive. Blenderized meals also increase the risk of an unbalanced diet and bacterial contamination. Furthermore, the thickness of the blenderized meals may impair flow through small-bore feeding tubes.

Parenteral Feeding

Rarely, children are unable to meet their nutritional needs enterally because of chronic diarrhea, congenital or acquired bowel abnormalities, or hypermetabolic states. An example is a former premature infant who has had a significant portion of the small bowel removed because of necrotizing enterocolitis (see Chapter 6). In these children, **parenteral nutrition** may be required for extended periods. This involves the delivery of a combination of water, electrolytes, carbohydrates, fats, protein, vitamins, and minerals through a central venous line. Although started in the hospital, these infusions can be delivered in the home once the child is medically stable. Close collaboration and monitoring by a team consisting of nutritional, medical, and home nursing professionals is essential. The most common complications are clotting of the venous line and infection. Rare complications include liver or pancreatic damage or worsening intestinal malfunction.

Weight Reduction in Obesity

Weight reduction is a difficult process. To be successful, management of obesity requires a multidisciplinary approach including a balanced low-calorie diet, behavior support program, exercise regimen, counseling, and parental education and involvement (Stockmyer et al., 2001; Willett, Dietz, & Colditz, 1999). The child and family both must be motivated to participate in the program.

Decreasing the rate of weight gain, maintaining weight while height increases, and/or achieving modest weight loss are reasonable goals. When weight reduction is the goal, it is important to monitor linear growth to make sure it does not "fall off" the growth chart (AAP Committee on Nutrition, 1998). A behavioral support program should be instituted that rewards the child for compliance and achievement of weight goals. Food craving as well as hoarding and stealing behaviors also may need to be addressed. In adolescents, issues of self-esteem should be explored. Appetite suppressant medication is not a usual part of a weight reduction program in children. Perhaps the most important issue in treatment of obesity is the maintenance of weight at a constant level while length/height increases. Weight management requires changes in lifestyle for the child and family; food must become a less prominent part of the child's life. A maintenance diet should be prescribed and the exercise program continued on a long-term basis.

NUTRITION AND A CHILD'S INDIVIDUAL CARE PLAN

Children with disabilities are at greater risk for nutritional problems and should be referred for a nutritional care plan. The type and extent of nutritional care the child needs ranges from education of the family to care provided by a multidisciplinary team of experts (Baer & Harris, 1997). All nutritional recommendations should be included in the formulation of an individualized family service plan (see Chapter 29) for the preschool-age child and into an individualized education program (see Chapter 30) for the school-age child. These plans emphasize parental involvement as essential for success (AAP Committee on Children with Disabilities, 1999; Baer & Harris, 1997; Isaacs et al., 1997).

The feeding plan should include nutritional goals and objectives (Baer & Harris, 1997). A written dietary prescription should identify the disability being treated (e.g., cerebral palsy), the specifics of the dietary modification (e.g., increased/decreased calories, modified food texture), and a list of restricted foods and permitted substitutions (Isaacs et al., 1997). The nutritional goal in Sam's case is to improve growth through 1) identification and use of an age-appropriate formula, 2) provision of nutritional education for his parents, 3) identification of community resources, and 4) monitoring of weight gain and growth through regular follow-up visits (Isaacs et al., 1997).

SUMMARY

Nutrition is intrinsic to good health as well as to the normal growth and development of all children. Children with developmental disabilities may have unique problems in the acquisition and maintenance of adequate nutrition. Inadequate nutrition may contribute to or exacerbate the developmental disability. Setting realistic nutritional goals through age-appropriate, culturally sensitive, team-based interventions benefits the child and caregiver and is vital to maximizing the child's well-being and developmental outcome.

REFERENCES

Agostoni, C., Trojan, S., Bellu, R., et al. (1995). Neurodevelopment quotient of healthy term infants at 4 months and feeding practice: The role of long-chain polyunsaturated fatty acids. *Pediatric Research, 38,* 262–266.

American Academy of Pediatrics (AAP), Committee on Children with Disabilities. (1999). Care coordination: Integrating health and related systems of care for children with special health care needs. *Pediatrics, 104,* 978–981.

American Academy of Pediatrics (AAP), Committee on Nutrition. (1998). *Pediatric nutrition handbook.* Elk Grove Village, IL: Author.

Baer, M., & Harris, A. (1997). Pediatric nutrition assessment: Identifying children at risk. *Journal of the American Dietetic Association, 97*(10, Suppl. 2), S107–S115.

Baer, M., Kozlowski, B., Blyler, E.M., et al. (1997). Vitamin D, calcium, and bone status in children with developmental delay in relation to anticonvulsant use and ambulatory status. *American Journal of Clinical Nutrition, 65,* 1042–1051.

Balint, J. (1998). Physical findings in nutritional deficiencies. *Pediatric Clinics of North America, 45,* 245–259.

Barlow, S., & Dietz, W. (1998). Obesity evaluation and treatment: Expert Committee recommendations. *Pediatrics, 102,* E29.

Beard, J.L. (2001). Iron biology in immune function: Muscle metabolism and neuronal function. *Journal of Nutrition, 131,* 568S–580S.

Berry, M.A., Abrahamowicz, M., & Usher, R.H. (1997). Factors associated with growth of extremely premature infants during initial hospitalization. *Pediatrics, 100,* 640–646.

Boyd, L., Palmer, C., & Dwyer, J.T. (1998). Managing oral health related nutrition issues of high risk infants and children. *Journal of Clinical Pediatric Dentistry, 23,* 31–36.

Brown, J.L., & Pollitt, E. (1996). Malnutrition, poverty, and intellectual development. *Scientific American, 284,* 38–43.

Callaghan, R.S. (1999). Appetite and weight in children treated for ADHD. *Journal of the American Academy of Child and Adolescent Psychiatry, 38,* 792–793.

Casey, P., Kraemer, H., Bernbaum, J., et al. (1991). Growth status and growth rates of a varied sample of low birth weight, preterm infants: A longitudinal cohort from birth to three years of age. *Journal of Pediatrics, 119,* 599–605.

Centers for Disease Control and Prevention, National Center for Health Statistics (NCHS). (1999). *Prevalence of overweight among children and adolescents: United States 1999.* Hyattsville, MD: Author.

Cloud, H. (1999). Developmental disabilities. In P.Q. Samour, K.K. Helm, C.E. Lang (Eds.), *Handbook of pediatric nutrition* (2nd. ed, pp. 293–314). Gaithersburg, MD: Aspen.

Colombo, M., de la Parra, A., & Lopez, I. (1992). Intellectual and physical outcome of children undernourished in early life is influenced by later environmental conditions. *Developmental Medicine and Child Neurology, 34,* 661–662.

Combs, G.F., Jr. (2000). Vitamins. In L.K. Mahan & S. Escott-Stump (Eds.), *Krause's food, nutrition, and diet therapy* (10th ed., pp. 110–152). Philadelphia: W.B. Saunders.

Conners, C.K. (1989). *Feeding the brain: How foods affect children.* New York: Kluwer Academic/Plenum Publishers.

Conners, C.K., Goyette, C.H., & Southwick, D.A. (1976). Food additives and hyperkinesis: A controlled double-blind experiment. *Pediatrics, 58,* 154–165.

Consensus conference: Defined diets and childhood hyperactivity. (1982). *Journal of the American Medical Association, 248,* 290–292.

Croft, R.D. (1992). What consistency of food is best for children with cerebral palsy who cannot chew? *Archives of Disease in Childhood, 67,* 269–271.

Crosby, W.M. (1991). Studies in fetal malnutrition. *American Journal of Diseases of Childhood, 145,* 871–876.

Dahl, M., Thommessen, M., Rasmussen, M., et al. (1996). Feeding and nutritional characteristics in children with moderate or severe cerebral palsy. *Acta Paediatrica, 85,* 697–701.

de Benoist, B. (2001). Introduction. *Journal of Nutrition, 131*(Suppl.), 564S.

DeLong, G.R. (1993). Effects of nutrition on brain development in humans. *American Journal of Clinical Nutrition, 57* (Suppl.), 286S–290S.

Ekvall, S.W. (1993). *Pediatric nutrition in chronic diseases and developmental disorders: Prevention, assessment, and treatment.* New York: Oxford University Press.

Ettinger, S. (2000). Macronutrients: Carbohydrates, protein, and lipids. In L.K. Mahan & S. Escott-Stump (Eds.), *Krause's food, nutrition, and diet therapy* (10th ed., pp. 31–66). Philadelphia: W.B. Saunders.

Feingold, B. (1975). *Why your child is hyperactive.* New York: Random House.

Groff, J.L., Gropper, S.S., & Hunt, S.M. (2000). *Advanced nutrition and human metabolism.* Belmont, CA: Wadsworth, Thomson Learning.

Guo, S., Roche, A.F., Fomon, S.J., et al. (1991). Reference data on gains in weight and length during the first two years of life. *Journal of Pediatrics, 119,* 355–362.

Hack, M., Breslau, N., Weissman, B., et al. (1991). Effect of very low birth weight and subnormal head size on cognitive abilities at school age. *New England Journal of Medicine, 325,* 231–237.

Hals, J.J.E., Svalastog, A., & Nilsen, H. (1996). Studies on nutrition in severely neurologically disabled children in an institution. *Acta Paediatrica, 85,* 1469–1475.

Hamill, P., Drizd, T., Johnson, C.L., et al. (1979). Physical growth: National Center for Health Statistics percentiles. *American Journal of Clinical Nutrition, 32,* 607–629.

Harley, J.P., Ray, R.S., Tomasi, L., et al. (1978). Hyperkinesis and food additives: Testing the Feingold hypothesis. *Pediatrics, 61,* 818–828.

Hawdon. J.M., Beauregard, N., & Slattery, J., et al. (2000). Identification of neonates at risk of developing feeding problems in infancy. *Developmental Medicine and Child Neurology, 42,* 235–239.

Isaacs, J.S., Cialone, J., Horsely, J.W., et al. (1997). *Children with special health care needs: A community nutrition pocket guide.* Chicago: Dietetics in Developmental and Psychiatric Disorders and the Pediatric Nutrition Practice Group of the American Dietetic Association and Ross Products Division, Abbott Laboratories.

Jeejeebhoy, K.N. (1998). Nutrition assessment. *Gastroenterology Clinics of North America, 27,* 347–369.

Johnson, R.K. (2000a). Can children follow a fat modified diet and have adequate nutrient intakes essential for optimal growth and development? *Journal of Pediatrics, 136,* 181–187.

Johnson, R.K. (2000b). Energy. In L.K. Mahan & S. Escott-Stump (Eds.), *Krause's food, nutrition, and diet therapy* (10th ed., pp. 19–30). Philadelphia: W.B. Saunders.

Koletzko, B. (1997). The importance of dietary lipids. In R.C. Tsang, S.H. Zlotkin, B.L. Nichols, et al. (Eds.), *Nutrition during infancy: Principles and practice* (2nd ed.). Cincinnati, OH: Digital Educational Publishing.

Kong, C.K., Tse, P.W., & Lee, W.Y. (1999). Bone age and linear skeletal growth of children with cerebral palsy. *Developmental Medicine and Child Neurology, 41,* 758–765.

Kozlowski, B.W. (1997). Nutrition of persons with developmental delays and disabilities. In M.K. Mitchell, *Nutrition across the life span* (pp. 416–451). Philadelphia: W.B. Saunders.

Krick, J., Murphy-Miller, P., Zeger, S., et al. (1996). Pattern of growth in children with cerebral palsy. *Journal of the American Dietetic Association, 97,* 680–685.

Kuczmarski, R.J., Ogden, C.L., Grummer-Strawn, L.M., et al. (2000, December 4). CDC growth charts: United States (Revised). *Advance Data*(314), 1–27. (DHHS Publication No. PHS 2000–1250).

Mangels, A.R., & Messina, V. (2001). Consideration in planning vegan diets: Infants. *Journal of the American Dietetic Association, 101,* 670–677.

Manikam, R., & Perman, J. (2000). Pediatric feeding disorders. *Journal of Clinical Gastroenterology, 30,* 34–46.

Maynard, L.M., Wisemandle, W., Roche, A.F., et al. (2001). Childhood body composition in relation to body mass index. *Pediatrics, 107,* 334–350.

Messina, V., & Mangels, A.R. (2001). Considerations in planning vegan diets: Children. *Journal of the American Dietetic Association, 101,* 661–669.

Mitchell, M.K. (1997). *Nutrition across the life span.* Philadelphia: W.B. Saunders.

Nardella, M.T. (1995). Practical tips on tube-feedings for children. *Nutrition Focus, 10,* 1–8.

National Research Council, Subcommittee on the Tenth Edition of the RDAs. (1989). *Recommended dietary allowances* (10th ed.). Washington, DC: National Academy Press.

Nevin-Folino, N., & Miller, M. (1999). Enteral nutrition. In P.Q. Samour, K.K. Helm, C.E. Lang (Eds.), *Handbook of pediatric nutrition* (2nd. ed., pp. 513–549). Gaithersburg, MD: Aspen.

Nichols, B.L. (1997). Managing growth faltering. In R.C. Tsang, S.H. Zlotkin, B.L. Nichols, et al. (Eds.), *Nutrition during infancy: Principles and practice* (2nd ed., pp. 21–36). Cincinnati, OH: Digital Educational Publishing.

Nutrition Labeling and Education Act Amendments of 1993, PL 103-80, 21 U.S.C. §§ 301 *et seq.*

Ogden, C.L., Kuczmarski, R.J., Flegal, K.M., et al. (2002). Centers for Disease Control and Prevention 2000 growth charts for the United States: Improvements to the 1977 National Center for Health Statistics version. *Pediatrics, 109,* 45–60.

Pass, K., Lane, P., Fernhoff, P.M., et al. (2000). US newborn screening system guidelines, II: Follow-up of children, diagnosis, management and evaluation. Statement of the Council of Regional Networks for Genetic Services (CORN). *Journal of Pediatrics, 137*(Suppl.), S1–S46.

Pollitt, E. (2000). Developmental sequel from early nutritional deficiencies: Conclusive and probability judgements. *Journal of Nutrition, 130*(Suppl.), 350S–353S.

Position of the American Dietetic Association: Nutrition services for children with special health care needs. (1995). *Journal of the American Dietetic Association, 95,* 809–812.

Position of the American Dietetic Association: Vegetarian diets. (1997). *Journal of the American Dietetic Association, 97,* 1317–1321.

Raiten, D., Talbot, J., & Waters, J. (Eds.). (1998). Assessment of nutrient requirements for infant formulas. *Journal of Nutrition, 129*(Suppl.), 2059S–2235S.

Raynor, P., & Rudolf, M.L.J. (2000). Anthropometric indices of failure to thrive. *Archives of Disease in Childhood, 82,* 364–365.

Raynor, P., Rudolf, M.L.J., Cooper, K., et al. (1999). A randomized controlled trial of special health interventionist for failure to thrive. *Archives of Disease in Childhood, 90,* 500–506.

Rogol, A., Clark, P., & Roemmich, J.N. (2000). Growth and pubertal development in children and adolescents: Effects of diet and physical activity. *American Journal of Clinical Nutrition, 72*(Suppl.), 521S–528S.

Sanders, T.A. (1995). Vegetarian diets and children. *Pediatric Clinics of North America, 42,* 955–965.

Schonfeld-Warren, M., & Warren, C.H. (1997). Pediatric obesity: An overview of etiology and treatment. *Pediatric Clinics of North America, 44,* 339–361.

Sermet-Gaudelus, I., Poisson-Salomon, A., Colomb, V., et al. (2000). Simple pediatric nutritional risk score to identify children at risk of malnutrition. *American Journal of Clinical Nutrition, 72,* 64–70.

Sicherer, S. (1999a). Food allergy: When and how to perform oral food challenges. *Pediatric Allergy and Immunology, 10,* 226–234.

Sicherer, S. (1999b). Manifestations of food allergy: Evaluation and management. *American Family Physician, 59,* 415–424.

Spender, Q., Cronk, C., Charney, E., et al. (1989). Assessment of linear growth of children with cerebral palsy: Use of alternative measures to height or length. *Developmental Medicine and Child Neurology, 31,* 206–214.

Spender, Q., Stein, A., Dennis, J., et al. (1996). An exploration of feeding difficulties in children with Down Syndrome. *Developmental Medicine and Child Neurology, 38,* 681–694.

Stevenson, R. (1995). Feeding and nutrition in children with developmental disabilities. *Pediatrics Annals, 24,* 255–260.

Stockmyer, C., Kuester, S., Ramsey, D., et al. (2001). National Nutrition Summit, May 30, 2000: Results of the obesity discussion groups. *Obesity Research, 9*(4, Suppl.), 41S–52S.

Sullivan, P., Lambert, B., Rose, M., et al. (2000). Prevalence and severity of feeding and nutritional problems in children with neurological impairment: Oxford Feeding Study. *Developmental Medicine and Child Neurology, 42,* 674–680.

Suskind, R.M., & Lewind-Suskind, L. (1993). *Textbook of pediatric nutrition.* New York: Raven Press.

Tawfik, R., Dickson, A., Clarke, M., et al. (1997). Caregivers' perceptions following gastrostomy in severely disabled children with feeding problems. *Developmental Medicine and Child Neurology, 39,* 746–751.

Thomas, A., & Akobeng, A. (2000). Technical aspects of feeding the disabled child. *Current Opinion in Clinical Nutrition and Metabolic Care, 3,* 221–225.

Tolia, V., Ventimiglia, J., & Kuhns, L. (1997). Gastrointestinal tolerance of a pediatric fiber formula in developmentally disabled children. *Journal of the American College of Nutrition, 16,* 224–228.

Trier, E., & Thomas, A.G. (1998). Feeding the disabled child. *Nutrition, 14,* 801–805.

U.S. Department of Agriculture & U.S. Department of Health and Human Services. (2000). *Dietary guidelines for Americans* (5th ed.). Washington, DC: Author.

Weiss, B. (1982). Food additives and environmental chemicals as sources of childhood behavior disorders. *Journal of the American Academy of Child and Adolescent Psychiatry, 21,* 144–152.

Wender, E.H. (1986). The food additive-free diet in the treatment of behavior disorders: A review. *Journal of Deviant Behavioral Pediatrics, 7,* 35–42.

Willett, W.C., Dietz, W.H., & Colditz, G.A. (1999). Guidelines for healthy weight. *New England Journal of Medicine, 341*, 427–434.

Williams, C., Bollella, M., & Wynder, E.L. (1995). A new recommendation for dietary fiber in childhood. *Pediatrics, 96*, 985–988.

Winick, M. (Ed.). (1979). *Nutrition: Pre- and postnatal development.* New York: Kluwer Academic/Plenum Publishers.

Zemel, B., Riley, E., & Stallings, V. (1997). Evaluation of methodology for nutritional assessment in children: Anthropometry, body composition and energy expenditure. *Annual Review of Nutrition, 17*, 211–235.

Zlotkin, S.H. (1997). Clinical skills for nutrition evaluation. In R.C. Tsang, S.H. Zlotkin, B.L. Nichols, et al. (Eds.), *Nutrition during infancy: Principles and practice* (2nd ed., pp. 1–20). Cincinnati, OH: Digital Educational Publishing.

10 Vision

Our Window to the World

Marijean M. Miller, Sheryl J. Menacker, and Mark L. Batshaw

Upon completion of this chapter, the reader will:

- be able to describe the anatomy and function of the eye

- know about common eye problems in children

- be aware of the tests used to determine visual acuity

- understand how a child typically develops visual skills

- know the definition and major causes of visual impairment in children

- recognize some of the ways in which the development of a child with visual impairment differs from that of a sighted child and some approaches to intervention

Impairment of sight in childhood can have detrimental effects on physical, neurological, cognitive, and emotional development. A severe visual impairment causes delays in walking and talking and affects behavior and socialization. Although it may occur as an isolated disability, visual impairment is often associated with other developmental disabilities, including mental retardation and cerebral palsy.

If visual loss is identified early, effective interventions can be instituted. Toward this goal, this chapter explores the embryonic development of the eye and its normal structure and function. It also examines **ocular** disorders and common visual problems of the child with disabilities. Finally, the effects of blindness on a child's development are discussed and educational resources for the blind are introduced.

ANN

Ann was born prematurely at 25 weeks' gestation. Ophthalmologic screening in the neonatal intensive care unit identified retinopathy of prematurity (ROP), but it was not severe enough to require laser treatment. After discharge she was followed at 3-month intervals by a pediatric ophthalmologist to determine if strabismus had developed or if she had an early need for glasses. At 1 year old, she was found to require glasses to treat myopia. When Ann was 2 years old, the ophthalmologist noted that her left eye began crossing, producing **amblyopia** (visual loss) in her left eye. By age 5, she required thick lenses with a −16.00 **diopter** prescription. Part-time patching of the good right eye along with the full-time wearing of glasses improved her vision so that it became equal in both eyes. The strabismus, however, worsened over time, and Ann eventually required eye muscle surgery at age 6. Now, at 11 years old, Ann has achieved a best corrected vision of 20/30 in each eye. Contact lenses will be tried as soon as she is ready to handle the lens care.

STRUCTURE OF THE EYE

In many ways, the structure of the eye is similar to that of a camera (Figure 10.1). In the eye, the thick, white fibrous covering called the **sclera** functions as the camera body. Like a shutter, the colored region, called the **iris,** responds to changes in light conditions by opening and closing. The **pupil** is the aperture in the center of the iris. Light rays entering the eye through the pupil are focused first by the **cornea,** the clear dome that covers and protects the iris, and then by the **lens,** which lies behind the pupil. The cornea is the most important refracting surface of the eye. The lens further focuses light rays toward the **retina,** the photographic film of the eye, which lines its inner surface. The retina records the image in an upside-down, reversed format and sends the image via the optic nerve to the brain for interpretation.

The round shape of the eye is maintained by two substances: the aqueous humor, a watery liquid in the anterior chamber, and the translucent, jelly-like **vitreous humor** that fills the posterior space between the lens and retina. The eye itself sits in a bony socket of the skull, the orbit, which provides support and protection. This space also is occupied by blood vessels, muscles that move the eye, a lacrimal gland that produces tears, and the optic nerve, which sends images from the eye to the brain. Additional protection for the eyeball is provided by the eyelids, eyelashes, and conjunctiva. Blinking the eyelids wipes dust and other foreign bodies from the surface of the eye. Eyelashes help to protect the eye from airborne debris. The conjunctiva, a thin, transparent layer covering the sclera, contains tiny nutritive blood vessels that give a "bloodshot" appearance to the eye when it is inflamed or infected (called *conjunctivitis*).

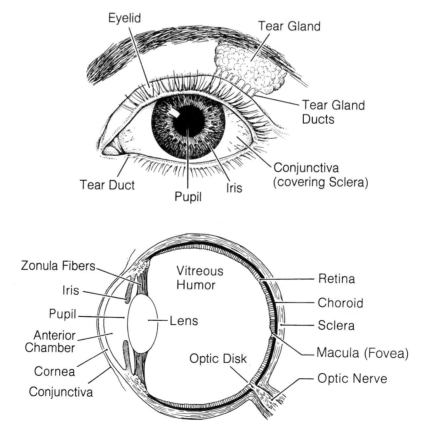

Figure 10.1.   The structure of the eye is similar to that of a camera.

OCULAR DEVELOPMENT

In the human embryo, the structures that will develop into eyes first appear at 4 weeks' gestation as two spherical bulbs at the side of the head (Figure 10.2). These bulbs gradually indent to form the optic cups. Three specialized cell layers in these cups subsequently develop into the various parts of the eye. By 7 weeks' gestation, when the embryo is only 1 inch long, the eyes have already assumed their basic form (Sadler, 1990). As fetal growth continues, the eyes gradually move from the side of the head to the center of the face.

Deviations from typical development can lead to a wide variety of ocular defects, ranging from **anophthalmia,** a lack of eyes, to subtle abnormalities such as irregularly shaped pupils. To understand the origin of ocular malformations, consider a **coloboma,** a cleft-like defect in the eye. Early in gestation, the developing eye is cup shaped. In order for it to become ball shaped, the edges of this optic cup come together at the base and form a "seam" that closes during the seventh week of gestation. A coloboma results from a defect in the closure of this seam. The location and extent of the defect may vary from the cosmetic problem of a keyhole-shaped pupil to a wedge split malformation of the optic nerve and retina, which often causes severe visual impairment (Cook, Sulik, & Wright, 1995; Olsen, 1997). As is true of most other ocular malformations, a coloboma can occur as an isolated defect or as part of a syndrome such as the chromosomal disorders trisomy 13 or trisomy 18 (see Table 10.1 and Appendix B). Approximately 15%–30% of children with small eyes and coloboma have the CHARGE association (see Appendix B; Warburg, 1983). It is called an *association* as the abnormalities all occur at the

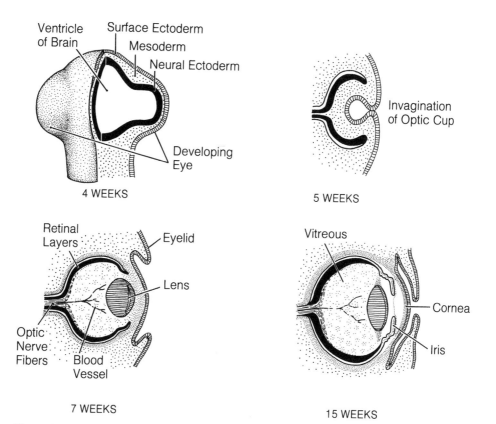

Figure 10.2. Embryonic development of the eye. The eyes first appear at 4 weeks' gestation as two spherical bulges at the side of the head. They indent in the next week to form the optic cups. By 7 weeks, the eyes have already assumed their basic form. The eye is completely formed by 15 weeks.

Table 10.1.   Selected genetic syndromes associated with eye abnormalities

Syndrome	Eye abnormality
Aicardi syndrome	Retinal abnormalities
CHARGE association	Coloboma, microphthalmia
Galactosemia	Cataracts
Homocystinuria	Dislocated lens, glaucoma
Hurler syndrome	Cloudy cornea
Lowe syndrome	Cataracts, glaucoma
Marfan syndrome	Dislocated lens
Osteogenesis imperfecta	Blue sclera, cataracts
Osteopetrosis	Cranial nerve palsies, optic atrophy
Stickler syndrome	Extreme myopia
Tuberous sclerosis	Retinal defects, iris depigmentation
Tay-Sachs disease	Cherry-red spot in macula, optic nerve atrophy
Trisomy 13, trisomy 18	Microphthalmia, coloboma
Zellweger syndrome	Cataracts, retinitis pigmentosa

Key: CHARGE association: **c**oloboma of the eye, congenital **h**eart defect, choanal **a**tresia, **r**etarded growth and development, **g**enital abnormalities, and **e**ar malformations with or without hearing loss.

same time of embryonic development and are therefore related. As part of this association, children have a cluster of characteristics that may include **c**oloboma of the eye, congenital **h**eart defect, choanal **a**tresia, **r**etarded growth and development, **g**enital abnormalities, and **e**ar malformations with or without hearing loss (Traboulsi, 1998).

Abnormalities occurring later in embryogenesis, when the eyes usually migrate closer together, may lead to abnormal widely spaced eyes, called **hypertelorism.** Finally, intrauterine infections (see Chapter 3) can cause **cataracts, glaucoma,** and/or **chorioretinitis** (an inflammation of the **choroid** and retinal layers of the eye), depending on when the infection occurs during development and which tissues are affected (Table 10.1).

DEVELOPMENT OF VISUAL SKILLS

As in the acquisition of language and motor skills, vision has developmental milestones (Friendly, 1993). Although the eyes have good optical clarity within days of birth, the visual system remains immature in many respects (Simons, 1993). Although infants will fixate briefly on a face soon after birth, steady fixation and tracking of a small target at near range is not expected until 3 months of age in term infants (Friendly, 1989). Although variable eye misalignments can be seen soon after birth, they should diminish in frequency over time, and the eyes should be absolutely straight by 3 months. By age 3–4 years, many children can sit and have vision objectively measured by identifying a series of pictures at a distance. The test result should be approximately 20/40 or better. (A visual acuity result of 20/40 means the child can see at 20 feet an object that a person with typical vision can see at 40 feet.) There also should be minimal vision difference between eyes, less than two test lines.

Amblyopia

Until age 8, the visual system remains immature (Daw, 1998; Gwiazda & Thorn, 1999) and susceptible to a unique type of visual regression called *amblyopia*. Here a "healthy" eye does not see well because it is "turned off" by the brain. Normally the brain receives input from both eyes, and information from each eye is precisely integrated. The result is fine depth perception (stereopsis) and eyes locked into proper alignment (Braddick & Atkinson, 1983). If inferior information is sent to the brain from one eye because it is out of focus (needing glasses because of a refractive error) or pointed out of alignment (strabismus), the child's brain chooses to use the clearer eye preferentially. The other eye is ignored even though it is anatomically normal and has the potential to see well (von Noorden, 1996). Unless the amblyopia is identified and treated before age 8, vision could permanently decrease even to the level of legal blindness. Other causes of amblyopia include a droopy eyelid **(ptosis)** and anatomical problems such as cataracts.

It has been estimated that amblyopia affects more than 2% of the general population and causes loss of vision in more people under age 45 than all other ocular diseases and trauma combined (von Noorden, 1996). With early recognition and treatment of the underlying cause of amblyopia, however, visual loss can be minimized or even completely restored (Eibschitz-Tsimhoni et al., 2000). The extent of visual impairment resulting from amblyopia ranges from mild to profound and depends on the underlying defect, the age of onset, and the delay in identification and treatment.

Because the visual system matures with age, the risk of developing amblyopia is greatest in early childhood and decreases as visual maturity is achieved (Kemper et al., 1999; Mills, 1999). Early treatment of amblyopia involves eliminating the cause, such as correcting a refractive error with glasses, surgically correcting ptosis, straightening the eyes, or removing a cataract (Spiritus, 1997). The other key step to treatment, however, involves making the brain use the amblyopic eye. Three techniques exist to force the brain to switch fixation to the amblyopic eye: patching, pharmacologic penalization, and optical penalization.

For a child with severe amblyopia, with vision worse than 20/100, the first line of treatment is patching: covering the good eye with an occlusive bandage patch. The daily patching treatment is continued until vision in the amblyopic eye improves or plateaus. Infants can be patched only briefly, whereas older children can be patched up to full waking hours. All children under treatment for amblyopia must be followed regularly by a pediatric ophthalmologist to determine the treatment dose and to avoid overtreatment of the good eye.

For moderate amblyopia, atropine penalization works well (The Pediatric Eye Disease Investigator Group, 2002; Wright, 1999). With pharmacologic penalization, the good eye vision is blurred by atropine eye drops, forcing the child to use the "lazy" eye for near activities (Chatzistefanou & Mills, 2000). Older children who refuse occlusive patching may benefit from pharmacologic penalization. The third treatment is optical penalization, whereby the eyeglass lens for the good eye is blurred for distance vision. Amblyopia must be identified and treated early because after age 9, it is unusual for intervention to significantly improve visual acuity (von Noorden, 1996; Woodruff et al., 1994).

Visual Development in Children with Disabilities

Many of the causes of developmental disabilities can also influence the visual system (Mervis et al., 2000). In fact, one half to two thirds of individuals with developmental disabilities have a significant ocular disorder. Processes governing eye motions, alignment, visual acuity, and visual perception may mature slowly, partially, or abnormally in these children. Refractive errors, ocular misalignment, and eye movement disorders are especially common (Simon, Calhoun, & Parks, 1998). Because of these associations, it is imperative that an examination by a pediatric ophthalmologist be included in the overall assessment for a child with a disability.

FUNCTION AND DISEASES OF THE EYE

This section describes the functions of the cornea, anterior chamber, lens, retina, optic nerves, visual cortex, and eye muscles, along with some of the common disorders that affect them.

The Cornea

The cornea focuses light on the retina, including the **fovea centralis.** This occurs in the following manner. When a person looks at a tree, for example, a series of parallel rays of light leave the tree and reach the dome-shaped surface of the cornea, where they are **refracted,** or bent, toward a focal point on the retina. The rays are further refracted by the lens and come into focus on the fovea, resulting in a sharp image that is transmitted to the brain (Figure 10.3). If the cornea is cloudy or deformed, however, the images will be blurred and indistinct. This requires prompt evaluation and treatment to avoid amblyopia. In infants, some causes of a cloudy cornea include birth trauma from a forceps delivery, congenital glaucoma, herpes infection, and certain inborn errors of metabolism.

The Anterior Chamber

The anterior chamber is a fluid-filled space located behind the cornea and in front of the iris. This area is like a water balloon with plumbing to maintain ocular pressure. The fluid called *aqueous humor* is made in the ciliary body just behind the iris and drains out of the eye in the angle where the cornea meets the iris through a spongelike meshwork to Schlemm's canal (Figure 10.4). If fluid drainage is obstructed or slowed, the pressure rises, a condition called *glaucoma*, which can injure the optic nerve and damage vision.

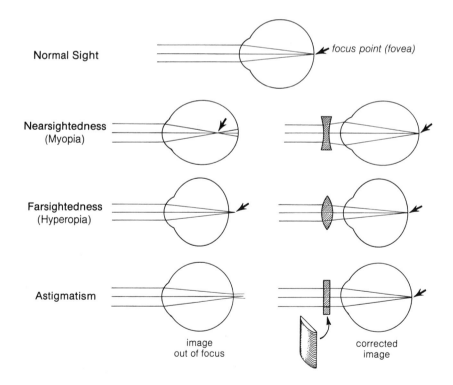

Figure 10.3. Refractive errors. If the eyeball is too long, images are focused in front of the retina (myopia). A concave lens deflects the rays, correcting the problem. If the eyeball is too short, the image focuses behind the retina and is again blurred (hyperopia). A convex lens corrects this. In astigmatism, the eyeball is the correct size, but typically the cornea is misshapen. A cylindrical lens is required to compensate.

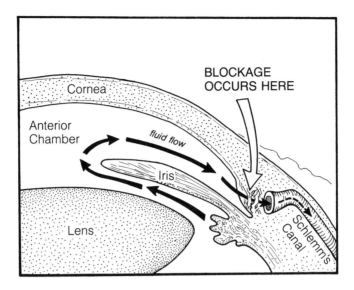

Figure 10.4. Glaucoma. Fluid normally drains from the anterior chamber through Schlemm's canal. A blockage in this passage leads to the accumulation of fluid and pressure, a condition called *glaucoma*.

Glaucoma

In congenital glaucoma, an abnormal membrane often covers the meshwork, blocking fluid outflow and raising pressure (Hitchings, 1997; Wagner, 1993). This condition must be repaired surgically; however, medication can be used to lower the pressure until surgery can be performed. In contrast, some cases of acquired glaucoma can be successfully treated with medications alone. Acquired glaucoma can result from an intrauterine infection, ROP, eye trauma, or chronic inflammation. Glaucoma also has been observed to develop in children with certain genetic syndromes and inborn errors of metabolism.

Glaucoma can be detected using a special instrument (a tonometer) that measures pressure by touching the cornea. (Because an adequate glaucoma examination cannot always be obtained in the office, a sedated pressure check or an examination under anesthesia may be necessary with some children.) Once glaucoma is diagnosed, effective monitoring and treatment are essential. Parents must bring their child in for frequent follow-up visits; at home, they must apply eye drops several times a day on a long-term basis.

Glaucoma causes approximately 4% of all blindness in children (Nelson, Calhoun, & Harley, 1991). The clinical signs and symptoms of congenital glaucoma include an enlarged, hazy cornea; excessive tearing; light sensitivity; and eye pain. Acquired glaucoma, however, may have few symptoms and be identified only during an eye examination. Early treatment results in successful preservation of vision in 90% of affected children (Franks & Taylor, 1989). Additional medications or surgery may be required over time, so the child needs to be followed carefully for signs of elevated intraocular pressure throughout life. Delayed treatment can result in blindness of the affected eye.

The Lens

The lens, the second refracting surface of the eye, is a translucent, globular body located behind the iris, about one third of the way between the cornea and retina. It is **convex** on both sides and is attached by **ciliary muscles** to the inside of the eye. Stretching or relaxing these muscles changes the shape of the lens, fine-tuning the focus to accommodate changes in the distance of an object from the eye (Figure 10.5). When light comes from a distant object, the rays are close together and well focused. Because little refraction is needed, the ciliary muscles tighten, pulling the lens so that it is stretched and minimally refracts the light rays (Figure 10.5). To see a nearby object, in which the rays are more dispersed, the ciliary muscles relax so that the lens assumes a more globular shape and has greater refractive power. As a person ages, the lens becomes less flexible and therefore less able to accommodate, causing near vision to become blurred (a condition termed **presbyopia**). Wearing bifocals or reading glasses helps to compensate for this loss of lens flexibility.

Cataracts

The major disorder affecting the lens is cataracts (Khater & Koch, 1998), which are defects in the clarity of the lens. Small cataracts often do not worsen or need to be removed. A dense central cataract larger than 3 millimeters, however, requires surgical removal. It appears as a white spot in the pupil and if untreated, will cause amblyopia (Figure 10.6). In the newborn nursery, pediatricians screen for cataracts using an instrument called a *direct ophthalmoscope*. This permits magnification of the pupil and retroillumination to look for black spots or irregularities that could indicate a cataract. Any child with a suspected cataract should see a pediatric ophthalmologist promptly. Although cataracts are primarily seen in adults, they also occur in about 1 in 250 infants, accounting for about 15% of blindness in children (Moore, 1994). A cataract may be an isolated abnormality or part of a syndrome or disease. For example, children with certain inborn errors of metabolism (e.g., galactosemia; see Chapter 18), congenital infections (e.g., rubella), and eye trauma may develop cataracts (Cassidy & Taylor, 1999).

In the case of a dense congenital cataract, surgery is needed soon after birth (Potter, 1993). Studies of children with congenital cataracts indicate that **binocular vision** develops during the first 3 months after birth. The better visual outcomes for children with severe, unilateral cataracts are found in those who have cataract surgery before 6 weeks of age (Birch & Stager, 1996). Children with dense, bilateral cataracts who have surgery after 2 months of age have poorer vision (amblyopia) and unsteady eyes (nystagmus; Lambert & Drack, 1996). The surgery is a procedure in which the contents of the lens are aspirated, leaving only some of the outer shell of the lens intact. The surgery is safe and can be performed as an outpatient procedure.

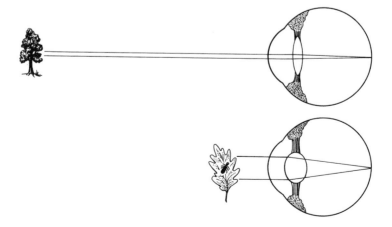

Figure 10.5. Accommodation. The lens changes shape to focus on a near or far object. The lens becomes thin and less refractive for distant objects and rounded and more refractive for near vision.

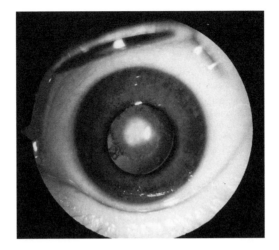

Figure 10.6. Photograph of a cataract, the white body seen through the pupil.

When the natural lens is removed by this surgery, one of the two refracting mechanisms of the eye is eliminated. To compensate for the loss of the natural lens, a contact lens, thick glasses, or a lens implant is used (Dahan, 2000; Hammil & Koch, 1999; Wright, 1997). Contact lenses are used in both very young and older children with unilateral or bilateral cataract extraction. Thick glasses are often employed for very young children with bilateral cataract extraction. Intraocular lens implants are generally reserved for children older than 2–3 years with unilateral cataract extraction. With the development of a foldable intraocular lens that allows smaller surgical incisions, however, intraocular lens implantation is considered in many clinical situations even for very young children with bilateral cataracts (Zwaan et al., 1998). Individual factors such as the size of the eye and the cause of the cataract are important to the surgical plan for a given child. The outcome for vision depends both on how long the cataract has affected vision prior to its removal and on how compliant the child and parents are with visual rehabilitation (i.e., patching for amblyopia and optical correction with contact lenses or glasses) following surgery.

The Retina

The retina is the light-sensitive "film" of the eye on which visual images are projected before transmission to the brain. Anatomically, the retina is like wallpaper inside the eyeball. The sclera and choroid are the tissues underlying the retina, providing support, protection, and nourishment (Figure 10.1). Within the retina are two types of **photoreceptor** cells: the **rods** and **cones.** Both respond to light by undergoing a chemical reaction.

For detailed vision, such as reading, seeing distant objects, and having color vision, cones are needed. They are located primarily in the fovea centralis, or **macula,** where central vision is processed. Each cone is sensitive to one of three distinct colors: red, green, or blue. The light from a colored object elicits a different response from each type of cone and leads to a patchwork pattern that is interpreted in the brain as shades of color. In the more peripheral or outside areas of the retina, rods predominate. Rods function in conditions of diminished light and are therefore necessary for night vision.

Nystagmus

Nystagmus is an unsteady jiggling of the eyes seen by observation or by eye movement recording (Tusa, 1999). Early-onset nystagmus in children may be caused by problems with the optic nerve or retina, which then sends an impaired or limited visual signal to the brain. A small optic nerve (optic nerve **hypoplasia**), absent macula (macular hypoplasia), or a variety of rod or cone abnormalities can result in nystagmus. Some children have idiopathic congenital nystagmus, in which there is no anatomic disorder (Neely & Sprunger, 1999).

The evaluation of children with nystagmus should include a comprehensive pediatric ophthalmologic examination. When the retina appears normal yet the vision is poor, an electroretinogram (ERG) may be suggested to test rod and cone function. If there is evidence of neurologic disease or if the nystagmus has atypical features such as rotatory or vertical components, then neurologic evaluation with neuroimaging should be considered (Brodsky, Baker, & Hamed, 1996; Gottlob, 1998).

Disorders of Photoreceptors: Color and Night Blindness

A number of disorders involve abnormalities in the rods or cones. The most common is color blindness, in which one of the three types of cones is either abnormal or missing from birth. Red–green color blindness, the most common form, is typically inherited as an X-linked trait and affects about 8% of men and 1% of women (Neitz & Neitz, 2000). Although affected individuals are able to correctly identify the color of common moderate-to-large objects, such as automobiles, solid colored carpets, and walls, they have great difficulty identifying colors in small objects and in the lines of a plaid pattern. When viewing traffic lights, the red and yellow lights are indistinguishable; however, the green traffic light falls on the blue side of the spectrum and appears white or colorless (Gordon, 1998). Congenital color blindness does not cause a decrease in vision. In contrast, acquired loss of color vision can be a sign of an optic nerve disorder, such as injury resulting from elevated intracranial pressure.

Other diseases can affect the cones or rods after birth. For example, a dietary deficiency of vitamin A may cause impairment of night vision, which may improve after replenishment of the vitamin (Haynes & Pulido, 1995). In retinitis pigmentosa (see Appendix B), a group of related genetic disorders, the rods and/or cones undergo a process of degeneration (Kimura, Drack, & Stone, 1995). Night blindness is usually the first symptom, followed by generalized visual impairment (Baumgartner, 2000). Certain inborn errors of metabolism (e.g., mitochondrial diseases) can be associated with retinal degeneration and reduction in side vision and night vision before vision is affected as measured by the eye chart.

Retinopathy of Prematurity

In infants, the most common cause of retinal damage is ROP. Nearly one quarter of infants weighing less than 2,500 grams at birth will develop some degree of ROP (Hussain, Clive, & Bhandari, 1999). The actual number of affected infants has increased because of the increase in survival among very low birth weight infants (Phelps, 1993).

ROP results from vascular damage to the retina. During the fourth month of gestation, retinal blood vessels start growing at the optic nerve in the back of the eye. By the ninth month, they have reached the furthest edges of the retina, near the front of the eye (Cook et al., 1995). In premature infants, this blood vessel growth is incomplete. In the catching-up process, a ridge can develop, with some blood vessels growing into the vitreous (toward the center of the eye) instead of along the back wall of the eye on the retinal surface. These abnormal blood vessels eventually die, and the resultant scar tissue can constrict, pulling on the retina. This pulling can lead to a retinal detachment and loss of vision. All infants weighing less than 1,500 grams at birth or with a gestational age of 28 weeks or less should be screened for ROP by an ophthalmologist in the nursery and upon discharge until the blood vessels are matured around 40 weeks from conception (Clemett & Darlow, 1999; "Screening Examination of Premature Infants," 1997). This is done using an indirect **ophthalmoscope** to examine the retina and surrounding tissue. If ROP becomes severe enough to make detachment possible, it is treated with either laser or **cryotherapy** to "tack down" the retina (Andrews, Hartnett, & Hirose, 1999). Despite treatment, many children with ROP will have visual impairments. These may include poor central vision, nearsightedness (myopia), strabismus, glaucoma, and even blindness (Figure 10.7; Quinn & Dobson, 1996). In addition, extremely low birth weight infants (those weighing less than 1,000 grams) sustain many neurologic insults, such as periventricular leukomalacia, that can worsen the impact of ROP on vision (Gosch et al., 1997).

The best way to prevent ROP is to delay delivery of a premature infant so that the retinal blood vessels have more time to mature (see Chapter 6). Other preventive measures include providing surfactant replacement therapy to mitigate the severity of hyaline membrane diseases (see Chapter 6) and to use the lowest concentrations of oxygen supplementation possible (Whitfill & Drack, 2000). Initial enthusiasm for using large doses of vitamin E, an antioxidant, as prophylaxis has diminished (Johnson et al., 1989).

Other Retinal Disorders

Other disorders that damage the retina include nonaccidental injury (e.g., shaken baby syndrome) that can cause retinal hemorrhages, scarring, and detachment of the retina; toxoplasmosis and other congenital infections; and certain inborn errors of metabolism such as Tay-Sachs disease, in which abnormal cellular material is deposited in the retina. Finally, retinal tumors, such as retinoblastoma, can lead to blindness in the affected eye.

The Optic Nerves

The surface of the retina contains more than 1 million optic nerve fibers that are connected to the rods and cones. The fibers come together at the back of the eye in an area called the optic disc (DeCarlo & Nowakowski, 1999). This region is also known as the blind spot because it contains nerve fibers but no rods or cones; therefore, no vision occurs when light rays are projected onto this area of the eye (Figure 10.1). One optic nerve emerges from behind each eye and begins its journey toward the brain. Some of the fibers from each nerve cross at a point

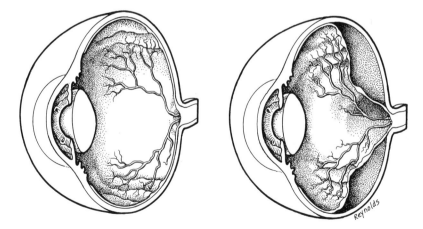

Figure 10.7.   Retinopathy of prematurity (ROP). Blood vessels in the retina proliferate (left). Eventually they stop growing, leaving a fibrous scar that contracts in the most severe cases and pulls the retina away from the back of the eye, causing blindness (right). (From Batshaw, M.L. [1991]. *Your child has a disability: A complete sourcebook of daily and medical care* [p. 165]. Baltimore: Paul H. Brookes Publishing Co.; reprinted by permission. Copyright © 1991 by M.L. Batshaw; illustrations copyright © 1991 by Lynn Reynolds. All rights reserved.)

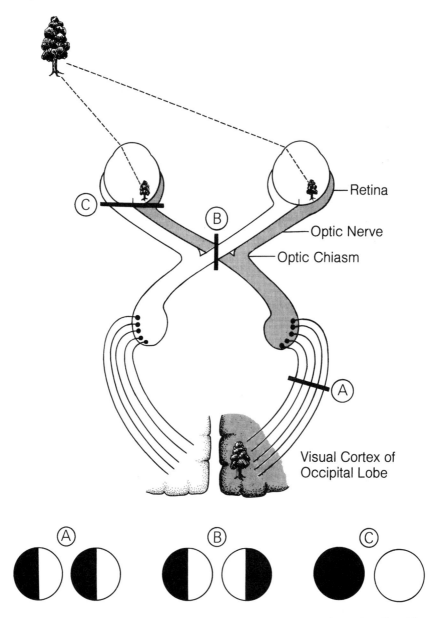

Figure 10.8.   The visual pathway. One optic nerve emerges from behind each eye. A portion of the fibers from each crosses at the optic chiasm. An abnormality at various points along the route (upper figure) will lead to different patterns of visual loss (shown as black areas in the lower figures). These are illustrated: A) abnormality at the cortical pathway; B) damage to the optic chiasm; C) retinal damage.

called the *optic chiasm* that rests within the skull just before the nerves enter the brain (Figure 10.8). Each optic nerve (at this point called a *tract*) continues through the cerebral hemisphere to the occipital (back) lobe of the brain (Figure 10.8). Because some nerve fibers from each eye cross to the opposite side, each eye sends information to both the right and left sides of the brain. Therefore, damage to the right or left optic tract at any point after the optic chiasm will cause defects in the visual fields of both eyes (Figure 10.8). By identifying the part of a visual field affected, an ophthalmologist often can determine where the damage has occurred.

The Visual Cortex

The visual cortex is the region of the occipital lobe responsible for receiving and decoding information sent by the eyes. The information is subsequently relayed to the temporal and parietal lobes. Damage to these areas can result in a type of visual loss called *cortical visual impairment* (CVI; previously called *cortical blindness*), which in children is most commonly caused by oxygen deprivation (hypoxia), infections of the central nervous system (**encephalitis**), traumatic brain injury (see Chapter 26), and hydrocephalus (Brodsky et al., 1996; Good et al., 1994; Lambert, 1995).

Cortical Visual Impairment

CVI is characterized by visual perceptual deficits in the setting of an ophthalmologic examination that is normal or has only minor abnormalities and is one of the most common causes of visual impairment in children in the developed world (Steinkuller et al., 1999). Advances in neonatal care have resulted in the survival of an increased number of infants who have sustained hypoxic-ischemic encephalopathy resulting in CVI. At the same time, advances in ophthalmology have resulted in a decrease in blindness from treatable causes. Together, these two factors have increased the proportion of blindness in children due to CVI (Brodsky et al., 1996). Although testing in infancy may indicate extremely poor vision in CVI, many children do recover some visual function (Huo et al., 1999; Lambert, 1995). Most do not bump into objects when walking and do not have visual self-stimulatory behavior, such as eye pressing, which is commonly associated with retinal blindness (Whiting et al., 1985). It is not fully understood why vision often improves in children with CVI, but it has been hypothesized that either alternate neuronal pathways or cortical areas take over some visual function. Brain imaging studies may help differentiate which children with CVI are most likely to improve (Casteels et al., 1997).

Delayed Visual Maturation (DVM)

It is important to differentiate CVI from delayed visual maturation (DVM) in the infant with visual inattention. Both groups show no response to visual stimuli in early infancy. Children with DVM, however, have normal gestational and birth histories, normal eye examinations, no cortical abnormalities, and usually only mild to moderate developmental delays (Brodsky et al., 1996; Mercuri et al., 1997). In DVM, improvement of visual function occurs spontaneously in infancy as the overall development of the child progresses. The cause of DVM is poorly understood (Russell-Eggitt, Harris, & Kriss, 1998).

The Eye Muscles

Six muscles direct the eye toward an object and maintain binocular vision (Figure 10.9). The four recti muscles lie along the upper, lower, inner, and outer portions of the eye. The horizontal recti muscles converge the eyes toward the nose for near activities or diverge the eyes to look at distance. The horizontal recti muscles also move the eyes into right and left gaze. The recti muscles above and below the eyes serve to elevate and lower the eyes and also have some rotational functions. The oblique muscles lie obliquely above and below the eye and serve primarily a rotational function with secondary functions contributing to movement of the eyes in the horizontal and vertical plane.

Three nerves originating in the **brain stem** control the movement of these six eye muscles. The oculomotor, or third, cranial nerve controls the majority of eye muscles. Two muscles are controlled by their own assigned nerve: The trochear, or fourth, cranial nerve controls the superior oblique muscle, and the abducens, or sixth, cranial nerve controls the lateral rectus muscles.

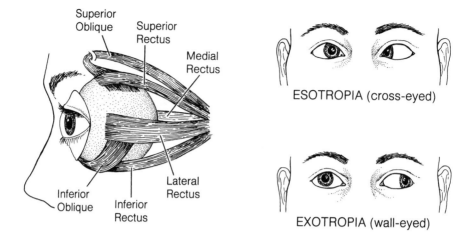

Figure 10.9.   The eye muscles. Six muscles move the eyeball. A weakness of one of these muscles causes strabismus. In esotropia, the eye turns in, whereas in exotropia, the eye turns out. Esotropia and exotropia of the left eye are illustrated.

The complex, coordinated movement of these eye muscles allows us to look in all directions without turning our heads and to maintain proper alignment of the eyes. The loss of this co-ordinated movement leads to misalignment of the eyes, or strabismus.

Strabismus

Overall, strabismus occurs in about 3%–4% of children. It occurs, however, in 15% of former premature infants and in 40% of children with cerebral palsy (Olitsky & Nelson, 1998). Two main forms of strabismus exist: **esotropia** (cross-eyed), in which the eyes turn in, and **exotropia** (wall-eyed), in which the eyes turn out (Figure 10.9). Esotropia is much more common. Strabismus may be apparent all the time or only intermittently, such as when the child tires. Recall that strabismus is a cause of amblyopia in children younger than age 8.

Misalignment of the eyes can result from an abnormality in eye focusing, in the nerves supplying the eye muscles, in the eye muscles themselves, or in the brain regions controlling eye movement (Wright, 1995). With regard to eye focusing, or **accommodation,** the eyes normally converge toward the nose to read a book (near vision). Children who are farsighted must do this same sort of accommodation for both distance and near vision. In some children, this focusing effort leads to esotropia after the age of 2, which can be improved by eyeglasses that correct the farsightedness. In contrast, cerebral palsy may alter the brain's signals to the eye muscles and cause strabismus. Here, corrective eye muscle surgery may be necessary to realign the eyes. This is also true for the child with hydrocephalus who may develop strabismus as a result of nerve palsy caused by increased intracranial pressure. Strabismus surgery can also be used to correct a head tilt that is caused by idiopathic congenital nystagmus. In such cases, a head posture is assumed so the child can use the null point of the nystagmus. Strabismus surgery can reposition the eyes so that this null point is in the head-straight position. Approximately 80% of children show good ocular alignment following surgery (Shauly, Miller, & Meyer, 1997).

REFRACTIVE ERRORS IN CHILDREN

As discussed previously, light entering the eye is focused by the cornea and lens. Under optimal conditions, the light rays are perfectly refracted onto the retina, resulting in a clearly focused image. If the eye is too long or if the refracting mechanisms of the eye are too strong, the focused image falls in front of the retina, and the picture is blurred (Figure 10.3). This is called *myopia*, or nearsightedness. If the eye is too short or the refracting mechanisms are too weak, the image is focused behind the retina, also producing a blurred image (Figure 10.3). In this instance, the person has **hyperopia**, or farsightedness. The other common refractive problem is astigmatism (Figure 10.3). Astigmatism typically occurs when the surface of the cornea has an elliptical rather than spherical shape. Because of this, light rays entering the eye do not focus on a single point and the image is blurred.

Farsightedness is the most common refractive error of childhood (Moore, 1997). The important difference between myopia and hyperopia is that with farsightedness, the eye can use its power of accommodation to further focus light rays onto the retina. As a result, most children with mild farsightedness require no correction and have excellent visual acuity. Hyperopia of more than 4 diopters often requires correction with glasses. (A diopter is a unit of light-bending power of a lens; it is the reciprocal of the distance in meters to the point where the rays intersect [Cole et al., 2001].) The accommodative load on the child to maintain sharp focus must be considered, especially in children with disabilities. With farsightedness greater than 4 diopters, the accommodative load may be so great that the child always has blurred vision except for those brief moments when something of exceptional interest triggers more complete accommodation effort and precise focus. Children with more than 6 diopters of hyperopia can develop both amblyopia and esotropia.

With myopia, the child sees clearly only at a near range. Severe myopia, such as that found in former premature infants who had ROP, may have a clear range of focus of only a few inches from the face. These children need eyeglass correction from infancy to expand their distance vision. Mild refractive errors, on the other hand, may not necessitate glasses if a child is functioning well. Both severe hyperopia and myopia, however, can impair the development of the visual system, causing amblyopia and affecting the child's interactions with the world.

In children with disabilities, even small refractive errors should be corrected to optimize performance. Furthermore, when there is a significant difference in refractive error between eyes, glasses must be prescribed to avert amblyopia in the eye more poorly in focus. In these cases, glasses promote equal clarity of the images focused on the retina of each eye and ultimately sent to the brain.

Glasses are also used to treat strabismus, especially when the eyes cross while accommodating for farsightedness. In this case, eyeglasses must be worn at all times. Glasses are successful if the eyes are straight while wearing the glasses, but the eyes will continue to turn inward when the glasses are removed. Over time, gradual changes in the prescription may allow good alignment even without glasses. Some children, however, will need glasses into adulthood or require strabismus surgery if the condition worsens. Less commonly, glasses are prescribed when the eyes turn out and the patient has myopia.

Eyeglasses can be prescribed even for the youngest infant and for the child with multiple disabilities. This is because a method exists for assessing refractive errors that relies completely on objective measures rather than on subjective input from the child. After instillation of eyedrops, which dilate the pupils and paralyze accommodation, the ophthalmologist views the child's eyes through a **retinoscope** (a magnifying light source) and can determine, using lenses of varying powers, the refractive error and the required correction. Eyeglasses can then be prescribed.

Eyeglasses in children should be made of polycarbonate plastic rather than of glass. Although plastic lenses scratch more easily, they are impact resistant, lighter, and last longer. For smaller children, frames with cable temples and spring hinges tend to fit best. Although teenagers may prefer contact lenses, the age at which the lenses can successfully be worn depends on the child's commitment and ability to accept responsibility for cleaning and inserting the lenses (Jurkus, 1996). Whether glasses or contacts are used, vision testing should be repeated at least once a year because the child's prescription is likely to change.

VISION TESTS

Assessing the visual function of children with developmental disabilities is critical in helping to determine the best interventions (Mackie et al., 1995). In experienced hands, vision testing can be quite informative even when the child is not able to or will not cooperate. Tests of visual function fall into two general categories: those based on an examiner's assessment through observation or eye charts and those using higher technology.

Assessing Visual Function through Acuity Charts and Observation

In early childhood, parental report may be the best indicator of visual function. In addition, many verbal and cooperative children can identify picture characters or symbols on an eye chart beginning at age 3–3½ years (Broderick, 1998). Several symbol tests exist: Allen pictures, LEA symbols, and the HOTV test (Hartmann et al., 2000). The goal is to engage the child with the most accurate test that can catch the child's interest. Often, several tests may be tried or the pictures sent home to practice until the true best effort assessment of vision can be obtained.

Older children can identify letters at distance. In nonverbal children, a matching game can be used in which the child points to the figure on a near card to show what he or she sees at distance. In a shy child, a near card alone can be used to assess vision. This is often inaccurate, however, unless the working distance is precisely measured and maintained during testing. Otherwise, holding the target a few inches too close will magnify the target and overestimate the vision (Figure 10.10; Ipata et al., 1994; Ottar, 1997).

Although it is easier to test visual acuity by showing characters one at a time rather than in groups, this tends to underestimate amblyopia because acuity is better for single symbols than for groups; this phenomenon is called the *crowding effect* (von Noorden, 1996). This problem is avoided by a method of visual acuity testing that uses a distance chart in which only the letters H, O, T, and V appear with black bars beside the letters, allowing characters to be shown individually (Cole et al., 2001; Jenkins et al., 1983). A card containing the letters H, O, T, and V is placed on the child's lap. As each letter is presented on the distance chart, the child is asked to point to the corresponding character on the lap card. This does not require familiarity with the alphabet but does entail comprehension, coordination, and cooperation on the part of the child. With all objective vision tests, the child is taught the test binocularly first and then the eyes are tested individually.

All children should be screened for cataracts in the newborn nursery, and the ability to fix and follow visually and to maintain proper eye alignment should be assessed in the first year of life. At approximately ages 3 and 5 years, objective vision screenings should be done in the pediatrician's office. Referral to a pediatric ophthalmologist is recommended whenever visual impairment is suspected, when the child fails the screening test, or when vision cannot be reliably tested.

When the child is an infant and vision cannot be measured by charts, the pediatric ophthalmologist can assess vision by the quality of behavioral responses (Leat, Westall, & Shute, 1998; Rydberg & Ericson, 1998; Simons, 1996). For example, the ophthalmologist can present a small toy to the child and can evaluate whether the visual following is steady and maintained on target. If the vision behavior is good, it is reported as CSM (central, steady, and maintained). If the infant cries when one eye is covered, this may indicate that vision in the other eye is impaired.

Another type of acuity testing, called *contrast sensitivity*, measures the minimal amount of contrast needed to resolve objects of various sizes from the background. In CVI or amblyopia, ordinary high-contrast visual acuity testing may show normal functioning, but contrast sensitivity testing often reveals abnormalities (Stout & Wright, 1995). Identifying decreased contrast sensitivity allows those involved in the child's care to choose high-contrast visual stimuli

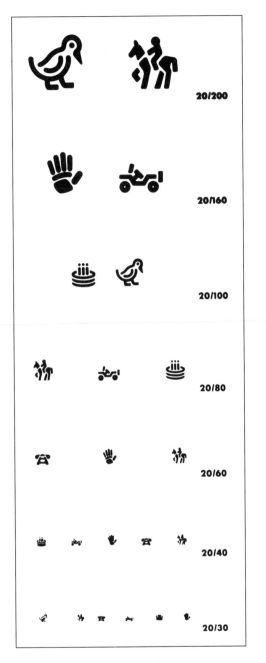

Figure 10.10. Allen Kindergarten Chart. The child names the various pictures down as far as he or she can go on a card held 18" away from the face. The smallest line that can be named indicates visual acuity. (Courtesy of Richmond Products, Inc.)

to best meet therapeutic, educational, and recreational needs. Several different charts and tests are available to assess contrast sensitivity in children.

In the older child who is noncompliant, it is also possible to make useful behavioral observations. For example, does the child appear to fixate on objects or people? Do the eyes wander aimlessly, have unusual motions, or remain directed in one position? Wandering eye motions, oscillations of the eyes, and eyes that always gaze in one direction are warning flags of significant visual dysfunction. Making good eye contact with the examiner as well as steadily fixating and following a face or toy, however, indicate the presence of some functional vision. (A lack of eye contact may be a function of behavior rather than vision, however, as in disorders on the autism spectrum.)

Assessing Visual Function through Higher Technology

Several techniques are available for testing visual function without relying on verbal responses or character recognition (Jackson & Saunders, 1999). These techniques include **optokinetic nystagmus (OKN),** preferential looking (PL), and electrophysiological testing (Mackie & McCulloch, 1995).

Optokinetic Nystagmus

The OKN response is determined by rotating a black-and-white striped drum in front of the child's eyes. Similar to the effect of watching a picket fence from a passing car, the child's eyes should jiggle back and forth as they follow the movement of one stripe and then quickly jerk back to fixate on another. OKN is an involuntary response that should be evident soon after birth (Boothe, Dobson, & Teller, 1985; Lewis, Maurer, & Brent, 1989). It is estimated that the minimum vision necessary for an OKN response is perception of fingers held in front of the eyes (Burde, Savino, & Trobe, 1985). OKN also may be employed to assess quality of visual acuity by using progressively thinner stripes and ascertaining the thinnest that produce a response. Although the presence of an OKN response is reassuring, its absence does not necessarily indicate poor visual function. It may simply be due to the child's inattention to stripes that are held too far away or moved too quickly (Friendly, 1989; Hoyt, 1986; Lewis et al., 1989). Despite its shortcomings, OKN testing is a quick, easy, inexpensive, and noninvasive method of evaluating visual function in infants, nonverbal children, and those with severe mental retardation.

Preferential Looking Techniques

PL testing relies on the fact that an infant or young child will preferentially fixate on a boldly patterned striped target rather than on an equally luminous blank target (Teller et al., 1986). In PL testing, the child is shown a series of cards containing a pattern of black-and-white stripes, or gratings, on one side and a blank gray target of equal luminance on the other side (Dobson et al., 1995). The stripe widths become progressively thinner on successive cards, creating finer gratings that require better visual resolution (Figure 10.11). The tester presents the cards at a predetermined distance and watches the child's fixation through a peephole in the center of each card. The finest set of stripes for which the child reliably looks to the patterned side is called the *grating visual acuity*.

Acuity card testing has been shown to correlate well with traditional estimates of visual acuity (Quinn, Berlin, & James, 1993). Despite the fact that it relies on the clinical judgment and possible bias of the tester, there is good interobserver agreement (Hertz & Rosenberg, 1992). The overall success rate for performing PL testing in children with developmental disabilities ranges from 82% to 99% (Bane & Birch, 1992; Hertz & Rosenberg, 1992). The testing may, however, overestimate visual acuity in children with amblyopia or underestimate visual acuity in children with eye movement abnormalities, and it requires some level of cooperation. In practice, PL testing requires a spacious quiet room and a trained technician. It is not generally used to estimate visual acuity; rather the test is employed to assess visual improvement in an infant undergoing amblyopia treatment or to detect differences in vision between eyes.

Figure 10.11.   Teller preferential looking cards. The infant is held, and a card is shown with a grating pattern on one side and a gray color on the other. The infant prefers the grating to a plain color. The sides are switched to ensure that the infant is looking at the pattern. Successively smaller gratings are shown until the infant no longer shows a preference, indicating that he or she cannot differentiate the stripes from the solid color. The smallest discriminable size determines the grating visual acuity. (Courtesy of Graham Quinn, M.D., Children's Hospital of Philadelphia.)

Electrophysiological Testing

Electrophysiological testing includes ERGs and visual evoked potentials to determine whether the vision problem lies primarily in the eyes or in the brain (Weleber & Palmer, 1991).

Electroretinogram   An ophthalmologist may decide to obtain an ERG when the retina looks normal but vision is absent or is very poor. An ERG is also useful in assessing poor night vision. The ERG tests retinal functioning by evaluating the quality of cone and rod response to light stimuli. It is particularly useful in demonstrating diseases of the retina such as retinitis pigmentosa, Leber's congenital **amaurosis** (see Appendix B), and cone–rod dystrophy. In ERG testing, modified contact lenses are placed on the corneas of the child after instillation of topical anesthetic drops. Depending on the type of equipment used, one to three electrodes are also affixed to the face and/or body. Lights are momentarily flashed in the child's eyes under different conditions while a computer analyzes the information received from the electrodes and from leads attached to the contact lenses. For the ERG to evaluate the retinal rods, which function in the dark, and the cones, which function in conditions of light, children are dark adapted prior to testing by sitting with their parents in a dark room for approximately 30 minutes. To obtain optimal cooperation and results in young or noncompliant children, sedation may be necessary.

Visual Evoked Potential   Visual evoked potential (VEP) testing may be considered once an ERG indicates that the retina is functioning normally. VEP testing is used to evaluate the pathway between the eye and the brain in children suspected of having CVI and to test visual acuity in infants and children with severe disabilities (Granet, Hertle, Quinn, et al., 1993; Iinuma, Lombroso, & Matsumiya, 1997). Pattern VEP testing for children, however, is available only at a few research centers, and flash VEP gives less information.

For the test, the child is seated in front of a computer screen on which checkerboard patterns or grated lines of various sizes are alternated at various rates. Scalp electrodes affixed to the back of the head receive impulses as the child watches the screen. Computer-analyzed results reflect activity in the visual cortex and are used to obtain an estimate of visual acuity. If the child's level of cooperation or attention precludes fixation on the screen, a bright light can be flashed into the child's eye as a stimulus for measuring VEP. This can ascertain the general integrity of the pathway between the eye and the brain but does not establish visual acuity.

There has been considerable controversy regarding the reliability of VEPs in predicting future visual functioning in children with CVI (Granet, Hertle, Breton, et al., 1992; Lambert, 1995). In addition, interpretation of VEP results must take into account that they may be inaccurate when evaluating children who have seizure disorders or nystagmus or who are under sedation (Hoyt, 1984).

BLINDNESS

Vision permits a child to extend learning beyond his or her body to the environment. Imperfect vision leads to imperfect perception of the world, and sensory deprivation, especially blindness in the developing child, can be particularly problematic.

The definition of blindness from a legal and federal educational standpoint is visual acuity of 20/200 or worse in the better eye with correction or a visual field that subtends to an angle of not greater than 20 degrees instead of the usual 105 degrees (Bishop, 1991; Individuals with Disabilities Education Act Amendments of 1997, PL 105-17). Individuals with low vision (partially sighted) are defined as having a visual acuity better than 20/200 but worse than 20/70 with correction (Buncic, 1987; Education for All Handicapped Children Act of 1975, PL 94-142). Both of these categories of students are considered to have visual impairments. Most people who are "legally blind" actually have considerable useful vision and may be able to distinguish light and dark or detect objects (20/500 to 20/800) or may even read large-print texts (20/200 to 20/500). Other people with blindness, however, do not even have light and dark perception. Associated visual deficits also must be considered when labeling someone as having a visual impairment. A child who has both a visual loss and reduced side vision after laser treatment for ROP will have more functional limitations than a child with visual loss alone of the same level will. To provide the best services to children with multiple disabilities and some degree of visual impairment, it is important to know the extent of limitations from the visual impairment (Jan & Freeman, 1998).

The overall incidence of blindness in children is about 1 in 3,000; 46% of these children were born blind, and an additional 38% lost their sight before 1 year of age (Foster, 1988). Children with severe visual impairments fall into four fairly evenly divided groups: individuals who are totally blind, those who have some light perception, those who can perform visual tasks with poor efficiency, and those who have enough vision to read large type (Buncic, 1987). The most common sites of the visual impairment are the retina (36%), the optic nerve and pathways to the brain (22%), the lens (17%), and the eye (16%; Nelson et al., 1991).

Causes of Blindness

In childhood, the causes of blindness are many and varied. The most common congenital causes are intrauterine infections and malformations. Malformations of the visual system range from colobomas of the retina (e.g., CHARGE association) to optic nerve abnormalities and cerebral malformations. Other causes of blindness include ROP, traumatic brain injury, anoxic events, severe eye infections, and tumors (Jacobson et al., 1998). Blindness is far more prevalent in developing countries, where nutritional disorders such as vitamin A deficiency and infections such as **trachoma,** measles, and tuberculosis are common (Foster & Johnson, 1990). Public health measures, including the use of silver nitrate drops at birth to prevent infections in infants' eyes and immunization programs, are gradually making inroads into this major health problem.

Identifying the Child with Severe Visual Impairment

Blindness can be an isolated disability or part of a condition involving multiple disabilities. For example, visual impairment caused by an inherited disorder such as albinism (in which there is a reduction in retinal pigment) may be an isolated finding, whereas CVI caused by hypoxia-ischemia in the newborn period is often associated with cerebral palsy and mental retardation. About half of all children with severe visual impairments have other associated developmental disabilities (Ferrell, 1998; Teplin, 1995).

Several clues may indicate that an infant has a severe visual impairment. The child will not visually fixate on a parent's face or show interest in following brightly colored objects. Parents also may notice abnormalities in the movement of the child's eyes, including wandering eye motions, nystagmus, or eyes that always gaze in one particular direction. In addition, the infant may not blink or cry when a threatening gesture is made or a bright light is shined in the eyes. Any of these findings should lead to a thorough examination by an ophthalmologist.

Developmental Variations in the Child with Severe Visual Impairment

One might expect severe visual impairment to result in lags in early childhood development. Being unable to establish eye contact with parents could have an impact on the infant's attachment and socialization skills. Preverbal communication, which is dependent on visual observation and imitation, could be delayed. Hypotonia and/or fear of movement combined with parental concern about injury might affect the development of motor skills in the child who is blind. Studies that have examined these issues have in fact found developmental delays, but the delays appear to be dependent on the amount of residual vision and the presence or absence of associated developmental disabilities (Hatton et al., 1997).

The early development of children with vision better than 20/500 and with no other severe associated impairments may approximate that of sighted children, whereas that of children with less than 20/500 visual acuity (or 20/800 in some studies) has shown significant lags in early developmental milestones (Figure 10.12). Children with early developmental lags, provided that they have no associated severe developmental disabilities (e.g., cerebral palsy, mental retardation, hearing impairment), test typically by school age (Ferrell, 1998). If there are associated impairments, however, the delays will persist (Ferrell, 1998; Teplin, 1995). The origin of the visual loss (eye, optic nerve, brain) does not seem to influence the degree of delay in milestone acquisition.

Even children with visual impairments who reach most early developmental milestones at a typical age show some deviance (Cass, Sonkesen, & McConachie, 1994; Dekker & Koole, 1992). Searching for dropped objects, crawling, and walking without support are all acquired later. There are also differences in the use of words and difficulty with pragmatics and pronouns (e.g., using "you" for "I"; Perez-Pereira & Conti-Ramsden, 1999). The child must learn to speak using auditory cues alone, which is a slow and painstaking process. The child also may imitate noises in the environment (e.g., cars, flushing toilets) rather than use words. In the child with average intelligence, speech and language become typical by school age. Speech, however, is accompanied by less body and facial "language," and conversation skills may be less developed.

In addition to developmental differences, there may be behavioral mannerisms that have been termed "blindisms." These self-stimulatory behaviors include eye pressing, blinking forcefully, gazing at lights, waving fingers in front of the face, rolling the head, and swaying the body (Good & Hoyt, 1989). Eye pressing seems to occur only in children with retinal disease, in whom it produces visual stimulation. Fortunately, most children with these mannerisms learn to inhibit them as they grow older. These behaviors may persist into adulthood, however, in individuals who also have mental retardation (Jan, 1991).

It is interesting to note that the child with congenital blindness may be unaware of having an impairment until 4–5 years of age. In the school-age child, however, social skills impairments may be related to social isolation and poor self-image. Therefore, inclusion in a program with typically developing children should include an agenda to promote socialization (Warren, 1994; Zell Sacks, Kekelis, & Gaylord-Ross, 1992).

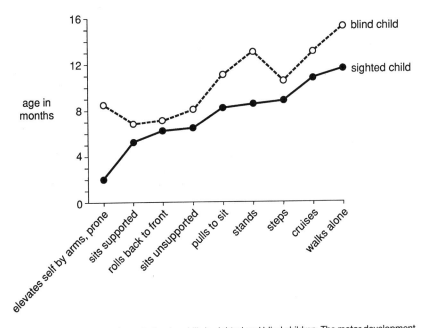

Figure 10.12. Age of attainment of motor skills in sighted and blind children. The motor development of a blind child is delayed. (From Fraiberg, S., with the collaboration of Fraiberg, L. [1977]. *Insights from the blind: Comparative studies of blind and sighted infants.* Copyright © 1977 by Selma Fraiberg; reprinted by permission of Perseus Books Group.)

Because the Bayley Scales of Infant Development–Second Edition (Bayley, 1993) and other infant developmental tests are based primarily on performance of visual skills, they may not be optimal in evaluating infants with severe visual impairment. Alternative non–visually based developmental scales can be used, including the Reynell-Zinkin Developmental Scales for Young Visually Handicapped Children (Reynell & Zinkin, 1979) and the Oregon Project (Brown, Simmons, & Methwin, 1994). The verbal subtests of the Wechsler Intelligence Scale for Children–Third Edition (WISC-III; Wechsler, 1991) can give a fairly accurate picture of the school-age child's intelligence and help in educational planning (Wodrich, 1997).

Early Intervention for the Infant and Young Child with Severe Visual Impairment

As soon as an infant is diagnosed with a severe visual impairment, he or she should be entered into an early intervention program. The early intervention staff should be trained in visual impairment education, and the team should include an orientation and mobility specialist (Fiedler, Best, & Bax, 1994; Harrison, 1993). The focus should be to increase skills in other senses, to improve body concept and awareness, and to promote locomotion and active exploration of the environment (Dietz & Ferrell, 1993; Zambone, 1989).

While awake, infants should be placed on the stomach rather than on the back to strengthen neck and trunk muscles (Moller, 1993). The young child with a severe visual impairment must explore the world through touch and sound (Niemann & Jacob, 2000; Pogrund, Fazzi, & Lampert, 1992). Therefore, parents and therapists should place or store toys at a height the child can reach. Textured and sound-producing toys are generally favored. If there is any usable vision, the child should be encouraged to take advantage of it. Bright colors should be used, and the child's vision and attention directed verbally toward them (Holbrook, 1995). It is very important for the parents, teachers, and therapists to give verbal cuing to provide the child with information prior to being touched/handled to eliminate any resistance to touch (tactile defensiveness; Warren, 1994).

The child's name should be used frequently to encourage inclusion in conversations and so that he or she will respond to questions in the absence of verbal cues. There also should be a verbal explanation before, during, and after a task is performed (Ferrell, 1985). While the child is moving from one space to another, the purpose of the move and the orientation of the space should be explained.

Orientation encompasses such skills as laterality and directionality. In terms of orientation and mobility, the child is first taught by an orientation and mobility specialist to locate familiar objects within the home and then progresses to travel outdoors. The child should be urged to walk despite the risks of scrapes and bruises. Poor peripheral vision (tunnel vision) is more of a problem in walking than the loss of central vision is. Any residual vision, however, is better than total absence of vision. The use of mobility aids for walking should be encouraged, including push toys (Sonksen, Petrie, & Drew, 1991).

The educational placement for a child depends on age, extent of visual impairment, and associated disabilities (Warren, 1994; Wheeler et al., 1997). For the infant, an early intervention program usually entails a once-per-week home-based program in which the early childhood educator or therapist trained in visual impairment visits and works with the parent to set up a stimulating environment. In addition to working on language and exploration, the teacher works on motor skills and stimulation of residual vision (Sonksen et al., 1991). By 2–3 years of age, the child is usually ready for a school-based program. Over the next few years, listening, concept development, conversation, and daily living skills (e.g., dressing, eating, personal hygiene) are emphasized. Literacy modality assessment can also begin at this time so that emergent literacy activities can be part of the child's educational program. Self-dressing should be encouraged by using loose clothing and Velcro straps to fasten shoes, pants, and shirts. Play and social skills training and behavior therapy for "blindisms" may also be a part of the program. It is important to create an attitude of stimulating all areas of sensory development, including visual skills in the child who has some residual vision. It is equally important that the parents and other caregivers do not perform too many tasks for the child so that he or she is encouraged to interact with the environment. Otherwise, the child will develop a distorted understanding of how the world works (Dietz & Ferrell, 1993).

Educating the School-Age Child with Severe Visual Impairment

By the time the child reaches school age, the extent of the visual loss is usually clear. A child with better than 20/200 vision should be able to read large-print books or use optical aids and devices to read regular print text. This child should be included in the general education classroom with the use of visual aids and resource help.

After a consideration of the learning modes of the child and the severity of the visual impairment, it may be determined that learning braille is appropriate for the child. Braille is a code formed from a series of raised dots on a page that are read from left to right. Visual efficiency, visual fatigue, prognosis for future visual loss or gain, and reading rates with a variety of materials are all factors to consider. Reading readiness for braille begins in kindergarten (Castellano & Kosman, 1997). Fine motor skills and tactile sensitivity are taught first. When the child is able to recognize small shapes, differentiate between rough and smooth, and follow a line of small figures across a page, the learning of the braille alphabet can begin (Swenson, 1999).

Children with severe visual impairments should also learn to type on a computer by fourth grade. No modifications are needed, except a computer mouse cannot be used. In addition, a vast assortment of books on tape are available from Recording for the Blind & Dyslexic (http://www.rfbd.org) and from bookstores and libraries. It is critical to make sure that the child has all of the appropriate equipment needed for learning and independence. With these tools, children with severe visual impairments and typical intelligence should be able to succeed in a general academic setting. They may, however, need certain specialized assistance and training in the use of braille, low vision devices, orientation and mobility aids, and so forth.

Assistive Technology

The computer age is greatly benefiting individuals with severe visual impairment. Voice recognition software permits individuals to input instructions to computer applications verbally. Conversely, various devices from calculators to computers produce voice messages, vocalize results of calculations, and so forth. There are even computers that convert printing into braille (Blenkhorn, 1997) and haptic interface technology that makes digital information tactile (Fritz & Barner, 1999). In addition, there is research on producing a visual prosthesis (Arno et al., 1999; Dobelle, 2000) analogous to the cochlear implant that is used in deafness (see Chapter 11).

Communities are also becoming more accessible to individuals with visual impairment with elevators that announce floors, stoplights that beep on green, ramps, and so forth. The classic mobility aid (tapping stick) is being replaced by devices with sophisticated laser/ultrasound wave processing and spatial hearing capacity (Bitjoka & Pourcelot, 1999; Shoval, Borenstein, & Koren, 1998), and Global Positioning System (GPS) software may soon permit individuals to be guided verbally to their destination.

Intervention for Children with Multiple Disabilities

The incidence of blindness in children with multiple developmental disabilities is more than 200 times that found in the general population (Warburg, Frederiksen, & Rattleff, 1979). One third of children with partial sight and two thirds of children with blindness have other developmental disabilities, the most common being mental retardation, hearing impairments, seizure disorders, and cerebral palsy. The majority of these children have two or more disabilities in addition to visual impairment (Curtis & Donlon, 1984; Teplin, 1995). Treatment of these children must address all the disabilities and use all the senses and abilities that remain. A multidisciplinary approach involving a range of educational and health care professionals is essential.

Outcome for Severe Visual Impairment

Outcome for the child with severe visual impairment depends on the amount of residual vision, the presence of associated disabilities, the motivation of the child and family, and the skills of the involved teachers and therapists. In general, less severe visual impairment and the absence of associated impairments predict typical development and good outcomes for independence and occupational success.

SUMMARY

Abnormalities of the visual system are among the many obstacles that children with developmental disabilities may face. The visual challenges encountered may range from minor to severe, transient to permanent, stable to progressive, and ocular to cortical. Children with developmental disabilities, as a group, are at higher risk for visual impairment than children in the general population are. Because the visual system is undergoing a process of maturation during childhood, early recognition of visual disorders is essential to ensure prompt treatment and to optimize visual outcome. Therefore, careful visual assessment is important for all children and can be performed regardless of a child's level of impairment or ability to cooperate. Outcome for children with visual impairments depends on the degree of the visual loss, developmental status, motivation of child and family, and skill of involved teachers and therapists.

REFERENCES

Andrews, A.P., Hartnett, M.E., & Hirose, T. (1999). Surgical advances in retinopathy of prematurity. *International Ophthalmology Clinics, 39,* 275–290.

Arno, P., Capelle, C., Wanet-Defalque, M.C., et al. (1999). Auditory coding of visual patterns for the blind. *Perception, 28,* 1013–1029.

Bane, M.C., & Birch, E.E. (1992). VEP acuity, FPL acuity, and visual behavior of visually impaired children. *Journal of Pediatric Ophthalmology and Strabismus, 29,* 202–209.

Batshaw, M.L. (1991). *Your child has a disability: A complete sourcebook of daily and medical care.* Baltimore: Paul H. Brookes Publishing Co.

Baumgartner, W.Z. (2000). Etiology, pathogenesis, and experimental treatment of retinitis pigmentosa. *Medical Hypotheses, 54,* 814–824.

Bayley, N. (1993). *The Bayley Scales of Infant Development–Second Edition manual.* San Antonio, TX: Psychological Corporation.

Birch, E.E., & Stager D.R. (1996). The critical period of surgical treatment of dense congenital unilateral cataract. *Investigative Ophthalmology and Visual Science, 37,* 1532–1538.

Bishop, V.E. (1991). Preschool visually impaired children: A demographic study. *Journal of Visual Impairment and Blindness, 85,* 69–74.

Bitjoka, L., & Pourcelot, L. (1999). New blind mobility aid devices based on the ultrasonic Doppler effect. *International Journal of Rehabilitation Research, 22,* 227–231.

Blenkhorn, P. (1997). A system for converting print into braille. *IEEE Transactions on Rehabilitation Engineering, 5,* 121–129.

Boothe, R.G., Dobson, V., & Teller, D.Y. (1985). Postnatal development of vision in human and nonhuman primates. *Annual Review of Neuroscience, 8,* 495.

Braddick, O., & Atkinson, J. (1983). The development of binocular function in infants. *Acta Ophthalmologica Supplement, 157,* 27–35.

Broderick, P. (1998). Pediatric vision screening for the family physician. *American Family Physician, 58,* 691–700, 703–704.

Brodsky, M.C., Baker, R.S., & Hamed, L.M. (1996). *Pediatric neuro-ophthalmology.* New York: Springer-Verlag.

Brown, L.B., Simmons, J.C., & Methwin, E. (1994). *Oregon project curriculum for visually impaired and blind preschool children (OPC).* Medford, OR: Jackson County Education Service District.

Buncic, J.R. (1987). The blind child. *Pediatric Clinics of North America, 34,* 1403–1414.

Burde, R.M., Savino, P.J., & Trobe, J.D. (1985). *Clinical decisions in neuro-ophthalmology.* St. Louis: Mosby.

Cass, H.D., Sonkesen, P.M., & McConachie, H.R. (1994). Developmental setback in severe visual impairment. *Archives of Disease in Childhood, 70,* 192–196.

Cassidy, L., & Taylor, D. (1999). Congenital cataract and multisystem disorders. *Eye, 13,* 464–473.

Casteels, I. Demaerel, P., Spileers, W., et al. (1997). Cortical visual impairment following perinatal hypoxia: Clinicoradiologic correlation using magnetic resonance imaging. *Journal of Pediatric Ophthalmology and Strabismus, 34,* 297–305.

Castellano, C., & Kosman, D. (1997). *The bridge to Braille: Reading and school success for the young blind child.* Baltimore: National Organization of Parents of Blind Children.

Chatzistefanou, K.I., & Mills, M.D. (2000). The role of drug treatment in children with strabismus and amblyopia. *Paediatric Drugs, 2,* 91–100.

Clemett, R., & Darlow, B. (1999). Results of screening low-birth-weight infants for retinopathy of prematurity. *Current Opinion in Ophthalmology, 10,* 155–163.

Cole, S.R., Beck, R.W., Moke, P.S., et al. (2001). The Amblyopia Treatment Index. *Journal of AAPOS, 5,* 250–254.

Cook, C.S., Sulik, K.K., & Wright, K.W. (1995). Embryology. In K.W. Wright (Ed.), *Pediatric ophthalmology and strabismus* (pp. 3–43). St. Louis: Mosby.

Curtis, W.S., & Donlon, E.T. (1984). A ten-year follow-up study of deaf-blind children. *Exceptional Child, 50,* 449–455.

Dahan, E. (2000). Intraocular lens implantation in children. *Current Opinion in Ophthalmology, 11,* 51–55.

Daw, N.W. (1998). Critical periods and amblyopia. *Archives of Ophthalmology, 116,* 502–505.

DeCarlo, D.K., & Nowakowski, R. (1999). Causes of visual impairment among students at the Alabama School for the Blind. *Journal of the American Optometric Association, 70,* 647–652.

Dekker, R., & Koole, F.D. (1992). Visually impaired children's visual characteristics and intelligence. *Developmental Medicine and Child Neurology, 34,* 123–133.

Dietz, S.J., & Ferrell, K.A. (1993). Early services for young children with visual impairment: From diagnosis to comprehensive services. *Infants and Young Children, 6,* 68–76.

Dobelle, W.H. (2000). Artificial vision for the blind by connecting a television camera to the visual cortex. *ASAIO Journal, 46,* 3–9.

Dobson, V., Quinn, G.E., Saunders, R.A., et al. (1995). Grating visual acuity in eyes with retinal residua of retinopathy of prematurity. *Archives of Ophthalmology, 113,* 1172–1177.

Education for All Handicapped Children Act of 1975, PL 94-142, 20 U.S.C. §§ 1400 *et seq.*

Eibschitz-Tsimhoni, M., Friedman, T., Naor, J., et al. (2000). Early screening for amblyogenic risk factors lowers the prevalence and severity of amblyopia. *Journal of the AAPOS, 4,* 194–199.

Ferrell, K.A. (1985). *Reach out and teach: Meeting the training needs of parents of visually and multiply handicapped young children.* New York: American Foundation for the Blind.

Ferrell, K. (1998). *Project PRISM: A longitudinal study of developmental patterns of children who are visually impaired* (Final report). Greeley: University of Northern Colorado, Division of Special Education.

Fiedler, A., Best, A., & Bax, M.C.O. (1994). *Clinics in developmental medicine: No. 128. Management of visual impairment in childhood.* Cambridge, England: Cambridge University Press.

Foster, A. (1988). Childhood blindness. *Eye, 2*(Suppl.), S27–S36.

Foster, A., & Johnson, G.J. (1990). Magnitude and causes of blindness in the developing world. *International Ophthalmology, 14,* 135–140.

Fraiberg, S. (with Fraiberg, L.). (1977). *Insights from the blind: Comparative studies of blind and sighted infants.* New York: Basic Books.

Franks, W., & Taylor, D. (1989). Congenital glaucoma: A preventable cause of blindness. *Archives of Disease in Childhood, 64,* 649–650.

Friendly, D.S. (1989). Visual acuity assessment of the pre-verbal patient. In S.J. Isenberg (Ed.), *The eye in infancy* (pp. 48–56). Chicago: Yearbook Medical Publishers.

Friendly, D.S. (1993). Development of vision in infants and young children. *Pediatric Clinics of North America, 40,* 693–704.

Fritz, J.P., & Barner, K.E. (1999). Design of a haptic data visualization system for people with visual impairments. *IEEE Transactions on Rehabilitation Engineering, 7,* 372–384.

Good, W.V., & Hoyt, C.S. (1989). Behavioral correlates of poor vision in children. *International Ophthalmology Clinics, 29,* 57–60.

Good, W.V., Jan, J.E., DeSa, L., et al. (1994). Cortical visual impairment in children. *Survey of Ophthalmology, 38,* 251–264.

Gordon, N. (1998). Colour blindness. *Public Health, 112,* 81–84.

Gosch, A., Brambring M., Gennat, H., et al. (1997). Longitudinal study of neuropsychological outcome in blind extremely-low-birthweight children. *Developmental Medicine and Child Neurology, 39,* 295–304.

Gottlob, I. (1998). Nystagmus. *Current Opinion in Ophthalmology, 9,* 32–38.

Granet, D.B., Hertle, R.W., Breton, M.E., et al. (1992, February 9–13). *The visual evoked response in infants with central visual impairment.* Poster session presented at the American Association for Pediatric Ophthalmology and Strabismus conference, Maui, HI.

Granet, D.B., Hertle, R.W., Quinn, G.E., et al. (1993). The visual evoked response in infants with central visual impairment. *American Journal of Ophthalmology, 116,* 437–443.

Gwiazda, J., & Thorn, F. (1999). Development of refraction and strabismus. *Current Opinion in Ophthalmology, 10,* 293–299.

Hammil, M.B., & Koch, D.D. (1999). Pediatric cataracts. *Current Opinion in Ophthalmology, 10,* 4–9.

Harrison, F. (1993). *Living and learning with blind children: A guide for parents and teachers of visually impaired children.* Toronto: University of Toronto Press.

Hartmann, E.E., Dobson, V., Hainline, L., et al. (2000). Preschool vision screening: Summary of a task force report. *Pediatrics, 106,* 1105–1112.

Hatton, D.D., Bailey, D.B., Burchinal, J.R., et al. (1997). Developmental growth curves of preschool children with vision impairments. *Child Development, 68,* 788–806.

Haynes, W.L., & Pulido, J.S. (1995). Infectious, inflammatory, and toxic diseases of the retina and vitreous. In K.W. Wright (Ed.), *Pediatric ophthalmology and strabismus* (pp. 541–544). St. Louis: Mosby.

Hertz, B.G., & Rosenberg, J. (1992). Effect of mental retardation and motor disability on testing with visual acuity cards. *Developmental Medicine and Child Neurology, 34,* 115–122.

Hitchings, R.A. (1997). Glaucoma. *Eye, 11,* 900–903.

Holbrook, M.C. (1995). *Children with visual impairments: A parents' guide.* Bethesda, MD: Woodbine House.

Hoyt, C.S. (1984). The clinical usefulness of the visual evoked response. *Journal of Pediatric Ophthalmology and Strabismus, 21,* 231.

Hoyt, C.S. (1986). Objective techniques of visual acuity assessment in infancy. *Australia and New Zealand Journal of Ophthalmology, 14,* 205.

Huo, R., Burden, S.K., Hoyt, C.S., et al.(1999). Chronic cortical visual impairment in children: Aetiology, prognosis and associated neurological deficits. *British Journal of Ophthalmology, 83,* 670–675.

Hussain, N., Clive, J., & Bhandari, V. (1999). Current incidence of retinopathy of prematurity, 1989–1997. *Pediatrics, 104,* e26.

Iinuma, K., Lombroso, C.T., & Matsumiya, Y. (1997). Prognostic value of visual evoked potentials (VEP) in infants with inattentiveness. *Electroencephalography and Clinical Neurophysiology, 104,* 165–170.

Individuals with Disabilities Education Act Amendments of 1997, PL 105-17, 20 U.S.C. §§ 1400 *et seq.*

Ipata, A.E., Cioni, G., Bottai, P., et al. (1994). Acuity card testing in children with cerebral palsy related to magnetic resonance images, mental levels and motor abilities. *Brain and Development, 16,* 195–203.

Jackson, A.J., & Saunders, K.J. (1999). The optometric assessment of the visually impaired infant and child. *Ophthalmic and Physiological Optics, 2,* S49–S62.

Jacobson, L., Fernall, E., Broberger, U., et al. (1998). Children with blindness due to retinopathy of prematurity: A population-based study. Perinatal data, neurological and ophthalmological outcome. *Developmental Medicine and Child Neurology, 40,* 155–159.

Jan, J.E. (1991). Head movements of visually impaired children. *Developmental Medicine and Child Neurology, 33,* 645–647.

Jan, J.E., & Freeman, R.D. (1998). Who is a visually impaired child? *Developmental Medicine and Child Neurology, 40,* 65–67.

Jenkins, P.F., Prager, P.C., Mazow, M.L., et al. (1983). Preliterate vision screening: A comparative study. *American Orthoptic Journal, 33,* 91.

Johnson, L., Quinn, G.E., Abbasi, S., et al. (1989). Effect of sustained pharmacologic vitamin E levels on incidence and severity of retinopathy of prematurity: A controlled clinical trial. *Journal of Pediatrics, 114,* 827–838.

Jurkus, J.M. (1996). Contact lenses for children. *Optometry Clinics, 5,* 91–104.

Kemper, A.R., Margolis, P.A., Downs, S.M., et al. (1999). A systematic review of vision screening tests for the detection of amblyopia. *Pediatrics, 104,* 1220–1222.

Khater, T.T., & Koch, D.D. (1998). Pediatric cataracts. *Current Opinion in Ophthalmology, 9,* 26–32.

Kimura, A.E., Drack, A.V., & Stone, E.M. (1995). Retinitis pigmentosa and associated disorders. In K.W. Wright (Ed.), *Pediatric ophthalmology and strabismus* (pp. 449–466). St. Louis: Mosby.

Lambert, S.R. (1995). Cerebral visual impairment. In K.W. Wright (Ed.), *Pediatric ophthalmology and strabismus* (pp. 801–805). St. Louis: Mosby.

Lambert, S.R., & Drack, A.V. (1996). Infantile cataracts. *Survey of Ophthalmology, 40,* 427–458.

Leat, S.J., Westall, C., & Shute, R. (1998). *Assessing children's vision: A handbook.* Woburn, MA: Butterworth-Heinemann Medical.

Lewis, T.L., Maurer, D., & Brent, H.P. (1989). Optokinetic nystagmus in normal and visually deprived children: Implications for cortical development. *Canadian Journal of Psychology, 43,* 121–140.

Mackie, R.T., & McCulloch, D.L. (1995). Assessment of visual acuity in multiply handicapped children. *British Journal of Ophthalmology, 79,* 290–296.

Mackie, R.T., McCulloch, D.L., Saunders, K.J., et al. (1995). Comparison of visual assessment tests in multiply handicapped children. *Eye, 9,* 136–141.

Mercuri, E., Atkinson, L., Braddick, O., et al. (1997). The aetiology of delayed visual maturation: Short review and personal findings in relation to magnetic resonance imaging. *European Journal of Pediatric Neurology, 1,* 31–34.

Mervis, C.A., Yeargin-Allsopp, M., Winter, S., et al. (2000). Aetiology of childhood vision impairment, Metropolitan Atlanta, 1991–93. *Paediatric and Perinatal Epidemiology, 14,* 70–77.

Mills, M.D. (1999). The eye in childhood. *American Family Physician, 60,* 907–916, 918.

Moller, M.A. (1993). Working with visually impaired children and their families. *Pediatric Clinics of North America, 40,* 881–890.

Moore, B.D. (1994). Pediatric cataracts: Diagnosis and treatment. *Optometry and Vision Science, 71,* 168–173.

Moore, B.D. (1997). *Eye care for infants and young children.* Woburn, MA: Butterworth-Heinemann Medical.

Neely, D.E., & Sprunger, D.T. (1999). Nystagmus. *Current Opinion in Ophthalmology, 10,* 320–326.

Neitz, M., & Neitz, J. (2000). Molecular genetics of color vision and color vision defects. *Archives of Ophthalmology, 118,* 691–700.

Nelson, L.B., Calhoun, J.H., & Harley, R.D. (1991). *Pediatric ophthalmology* (3rd ed.). Philadelphia: W.B. Saunders.

Niemann, S., & Jacob, N. (2000). *Helping children who are blind: Family and community support for children with low vision.* Berkeley, CA: Hesperian Foundation. (Available from the publisher, 1919 Addison Street, Suite 304, Berkeley, CA 94704; http://www.hesperian.org)

Olitsky, S.E., & Nelson, L.B. (1998). Common ophthalmologic concerns in infants and children. *Pediatric Clinics of North America, 45,* 993–1012.

Olsen, T.W. (1997). Visual acuity in children with colobomatous defects. *Current Opinion in Ophthalmology, 8,* 63–67.

Ottar, W.L. (1997). The ABCs of visual acuity assessment. *Insight, 22,* 81–87.

The Pediatric Eye Disease Investigator Group (PEDIG). (2002). A randomized trial of atropine vs. patching for treatment of moderate amblyopia in children. *Archives of Ophthalmology, 120,* 268–278.

Perez-Pereira, M., & Conti-Ramsden, G. (1999). *Language development and social interaction in blind children.* Philadelphia: Psychology Press.

Phelps, D.L. (1993). Retinopathy of prematurity. *Pediatric Clinics of North America, 40,* 705–714.

Pogrund, R.L., Fazzi, D.L., & Lampert, J.S. (Eds.). (1992). *Early focus: Working with young blind and visually impaired children and their families.* New York: American Foundation for the Blind.

Potter, W.S. (1993). Pediatric cataracts. *Pediatric Clinics of North America, 40,* 841–854.

Quinn, G.E., Berlin, J.A., & James, M. (1993). The Teller acuity card procedure: Three testers in a clinical setting. *Ophthalmology, 100,* 488–494.

Quinn, G.E., & Dobson, V. (1996). Outcome of prematurity and retinopathy of prematurity. *Current Opinion in Ophthalmology, 7,* 51–56.

Reynell, J., & Zinkin, K. (1979). *Reynell-Zinkin Developmental Scales for Young Visually Handicapped Children (RZS).* Wood Dale, IL: Stoelting.

Russell-Eggitt, I., Harris, C.M., & Kriss, A. (1998). Delayed visual maturation: An update. *Developmental Medicine and Child Neurology, 40,* 130–136.

Rydberg, A., & Ericson, B. (1998). Assessing visual function in children younger than 1 1/2 years with normal and subnormal vision: Evaluation of methods. *Journal of Pediatric Ophthalmology and Strabismus, 35,* 312–319.

Sadler, T.W. (1990). *Langman's medical embryology* (6th ed.). Philadelphia: Lippincott Williams & Wilkins.

Screening examination of premature infants for retinopathy of prematurity: A joint statement of the American Academy of Pediatrics, the American Association for Pediatric Ophthalmology and Strabismus, and the American Academy of Ophthalmology. (1997). *Pediatrics, 100*(2), 273–274. (Available from American Academy of Ophthalmology, Post Office Box 7424, San Francisco, CA 94120; http://www.aao.org)

Shauly, Y., Miller, B., & Meyer, E. (1997). Clinical characteristics and long-term postoperative results of esotropia and myopia. *Journal of Pediatric Ophthalmology and Strabismus, 34,* 357–364.

Shoval, S., Borenstein, J., & Koren, Y. (1998). The NavBelt: A computerized travel aid for the blind based on mobile robotics technology. *IEEE Transactions on Biomedical Engineering, 45,* 1376–1386.

Simon, J.W., Calhoun, J.H., & Parks, M.M. (1998). *A child's eyes: A guide to pediatric primary care.* Gainesville, FL: Triad.

Simons, K. (Ed.). (1993). *Early visual development normal and abnormal.* New York: Oxford University Press.

Simons, K. (1996). Preschool vision screening: Rationale, methodology, and outcome. *Survey of Ophthalmology, 41,* 3–30.

Sonksen, P.M., Petrie, A., & Drew, K.J. (1991). Promotion of visual development of severely visually impaired babies: Evaluation of a developmentally based programme. *Developmental Medicine and Child Neurology, 33,* 320–335.

Spiritus, M. (1997). Detection, prevention, and rehabilitation of amblyopia. *Current Opinion in Ophthalmology, 8,* 11–16.

Steinkuller, P.G., Du, L., Gilbert C., et al. (1999). Childhood blindness. *Journal of AAPOS, 3,* 26–32.

Stout, A.U., & Wright, K.W. (1995). Pediatric eye examination. In K.W. Wright (Ed.), *Pediatric ophthalmology and strabismus* (pp. 63–72). St. Louis: Mosby.

Swenson, A.M. (1999). *Beginning with Braille: Firsthand experiences with a balanced approach to literacy.* New York: American Foundation for the Blind.

Teller, D.Y., McDonald, M., Preston, K., et al. (1986). Assessment of visual acuity in infants and children: The acuity card procedure. *Developmental Medicine and Child Neurology, 28,* 779.

Teplin, S. (1995). Visual impairments in infants and young children. *Infants and Young Children, 8,* 18–50.

Traboulsi, E.I. (1998). Colobomatous microphthalmia, anophthalmia, and associated malformation syndromes. In E.I. Traboulsi (Ed.), *Genetic diseases of the eye* (pp. 67–68). New York: Oxford University Press.

Tusa, R.J. (1999). Nystagmus: Diagnostic and therapeutic strategies. *Seminars in Ophthalmology, 14,* 65–73.

von Noorden, G.K. (1996). *Binocular vision and ocular motility* (5th ed.). St. Louis: Mosby.

Wagner, R.S. (1993). Glaucoma in children. *Pediatric Clinics of North America, 40,* 855–867.

Warburg, M. (1983). Ocular coloboma and multiple congenital anomalies: The CHARGE association. *Ophthalmic Paediatrics and Genetics, 3,* 189–199.

Warburg, M., Frederiksen, P., & Rattleff, J. (1979). Blindness among 7,720 mentally retarded children in Denmark. *Clinics in Developmental Medicine, 73,* 56–67.

Warren, D.H. (1994). *Blindness and children: An individual differences approach.* New York: Cambridge University Press.

Wechsler, D. (1991). *Wechsler Intelligence Scale for Children* (3rd ed.). San Antonio, TX: Psychological Corporation.

Weleber, R.G., & Palmer, E.A. (1991). Electrophysiological evaluation of children with visual impairment. *Seminars in Ophthalmology, 6,* 161–168.

Wheeler, L.C., Griffin, H.D., Taylor, R.J., et al. (1997). Educational intervention strategies for children with visual impairments with emphasis on retinopathy of prematurity. *Journal of Pediatric Health Care, 11,* 275–279.

Whitfill, C.R., & Drack, A.V. (2000). Avoidance and treatment of retinopathy of prematurity. *Seminars in Pediatric Surgery, 9,* 103–105.

Whiting, S., Jan, J.E., Wong, P.K., et al. (1985). Permanent cortical visual impairment in children. *Developmental Medicine and Child Neurology, 27,* 730–739.

Wodrich, D.L. (1997). *Children's psychological testing: A guide for nonpsychologists* (3rd ed.). Baltimore: Paul H. Brookes Publishing Co.

Woodruff, G., Hiscox, F., Thompson, J.R., et al. (1994). Factors affecting the outcome of children treated for amblyopia. *Eye, 8,* 627–631.

Wright, K.W. (Ed.). (1995). *Pediatric ophthalmology and strabismus.* St. Louis: Mosby-Year Book.

Wright, K.W. (1997). Pediatric cataracts. *Current Opinion in Ophthalmology, 8,* 50–55.

Wright, K.W. (1999). *Pediatric ophthalmology for pediatricians.* Philadelphia: Lippincott Williams & Wilkins.

Zambone, A.M. (1989). Serving the young child with visual impairments: An overview of disability impact and intervention needs. *Infants and Young Children, 2,* 11–23.

Zell Sacks, S., Kekelis, L.S., & Gaylord-Ross, R.J. (Eds.). (1992). *The development of social skills by blind and visually impaired students: Exploratory studies and strategies.* New York: American Foundation for the Blind.

Zwaan, J., Mullaney, P.B., Awad, A., et al. (1998). Pediatric intraocular lens implantation. Surgical results and complications in more than 300 patients. *Ophthalmology, 105,* 112–118.

11 Hearing

Sounds and Silences

Gilbert R. Herer, Carol A. Knightly, and Annie G. Steinberg

Upon completion of this chapter, the reader will:

- be able to describe the anatomy of the ear
- know the different types of hearing losses and their causes
- be aware of various hearing tests and their uses
- understand the multidimensional aspects of the assessment of a child with a hearing loss
- understand the treatment options for the child with a hearing loss
- be able to discuss the educational options and potential outcomes for the child with a hearing loss

The sense of hearing is integral to one of the most fundamental of human activities: the use of language for communication. It is through hearing that the child acquires a linguistic system to both transmit and receive information, express thoughts and feelings, learn, and influence the behaviors of their parents and peers. Problems with hearing can negatively affect a child in the areas of language/speech and social-emotional development and in learning in school. Therefore, early identification and intervention for the child with hearing problems are imperative. This chapter reviews the human auditory system, hearing impairment and its effects on the development of a child's communication skills, and various approaches to treatment/education of children with hearing loss.

JIMMY

Jimmy, a healthy 8½-pound baby boy, was screened in the newborn period before hospital discharge using both transient evoked otoacoustic emissions (TEOAE) and screening auditory brainstem response (SABR) methods. He did not pass either of these tests or the re-screening done 4 weeks later and was referred for a diagnostic auditory brainstem evoked response (ABR) test. This revealed that Jimmy had no measurable responses in his left ear and a sloping mild to severe sensorineural (40–90 dB) hearing loss from 1,000 through 4,000 Hz in his right ear.

Several interventions were initiated, including taking earmold impressions in preparation for hearing aid use, helping his parents enroll in an information and education program about hearing loss, and providing a medical evaluation to explore the origin of the hearing loss. The medical evaluation found that Jimmy had no family history or any other apparent risk factor for hearing loss. An intrauterine cytomegalovirus (CMV) infection was diagnosed (see Chapter 3), however, and because this is known to be accompanied by a progressive hearing loss, audiological evaluations were recommended every 3 months.

By 4½ months of age, Jimmy was fitted with behind-the-ear aids that included an FM system. Although his left ear showed no response, it also was fitted for amplification because of the possibility of his having some low frequency hearing that was not measurable by testing. The FM hearing aid system allowed his parents to wear a wireless lapel microphone and broadcast their speech directly to Jimmy's aids from various places in a room, thus stimulating his hearing with minimum environmental interference. Jimmy, his mother, and his older brother (who has normal hearing) were seen for weekly treatment sessions designed to demonstrate age-appropriate auditory and speech-language activities that could be carried out at home, to provide continuing information about hearing loss, and to offer parental support.

Jimmy was enrolled in an early intervention program at 14 months of age and received weekly home visits by a speech-language pathologist until age 2 when he was enrolled in a local preschool program. Jimmy's parents began using cued speech to accompany their spoken language when Jimmy was 8 months old and read stories, just as they did with his older brother. Until age 3, Jimmy's language skills progressed well, except for some difficulty in pronouncing high-frequency consonant sounds like /s/ and /ch/. Shortly after his third birthday, however, Jimmy lost all hearing. After a 3-month evaluation, he was deemed an appropriate candidate for a cochlear implant in the right ear; the procedure was uneventful, and he has made significant gains in speech-language development.

Jimmy's story illustrates the array of needs of a child born with a severe hearing loss. These include 1) early detection through universal newborn hearing screening; 2) immediate audiological evaluation to identify the type, configuration, and extent of the hearing loss; 3) use of hearing aids by 4 months of age; 4) comprehensive medical assessment in search of an origin of the hearing loss and possible related medical problems; 5) parent education, support, and involvement; 6) appropriate intervention based on the child's age and development; 7) frequent hearing, hearing aid, and speech-language assessments; and 8) immediate response to any changes in hearing status or family needs.

DEFINING SOUND

When we hear a sound, we are actually processing and interpreting a pattern of vibrating air molecules. An initial vibration sets successive rows of air molecules into motion in oscillating concentric circles, or waves. This movement of the molecules is described in terms of the **frequency** with which the oscillations occur and the amplitude of the oscillations from the resting point (Figure 11.1).

The frequency of a sound is perceived as **pitch** and is measured in cycles per second or hertz (Hz). The more cycles that occur per second, the higher the frequency, or pitch, of the sound. Middle C on the musical scale is 256 Hz, whereas the ring of a cellular telephone is approximately 2,000 Hz. The human ear can detect frequencies ranging from 20 Hz to 20,000 Hz, but is most sensitive to sounds in the 500 to 6,000 Hz range, in which most of the sounds of speech occur (Bluestone, Stool, & Kenna, 1996).

The amplitude of the molecular oscillation is perceived as the loudness, or intensity, of the sound and is measured in decibels (dB). The softest sound an individual with normal hearing can usually detect is defined as 0 dB hearing level (HL). A whisper is about 20 dB HL, typical conversation is at about 40 dB HL, and a shout close by can be 70 dB HL. (HL norms were established by the American National Standards Institute [ANSI] in 1969.) A lawn mower or chain saw is measured at about 100 dB HL (Northern & Downs, 2002).

Speech, however, does not occur at a single intensity or frequency. In general, vowel sounds are low frequency in nature and more intense, whereas consonants, particularly the voiceless consonants (e.g., /s/, /sh/, /t/, /th/ as in *thin*, /k/, /p/, /h/), are composed of higher

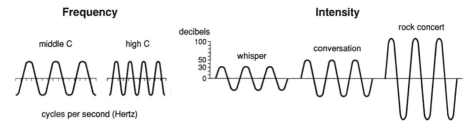

Figure 11.1. Frequency and intensity of sound waves. The frequency of a sound, or its pitch, is expressed as cycles per second, or hertz (Hz). Middle C is 256 Hz; one octave higher (high C) is 512 Hz. Intensity of sound is expressed as decibels (dB) and varies from a whisper at 30 dB to a rock concert at 100 dB or more.

frequencies and are the least intense (Figure 11.2). Furthermore, during a conversation, the speaker will change the intensity of speech by talking in a louder or softer voice to express emotion or emphasis. This can adversely affect an individual with a hearing loss, especially if the loss is not consistent at all frequencies. If an individual has a high-frequency hearing loss but normal hearing in the low-frequency region, that individual will be able to hear speech (because of the relative loudness of vowels) but may not be able to understand it because of the softness of voiceless consonants. The person may hear only parts of words and therefore would find it difficult to follow a conversation.

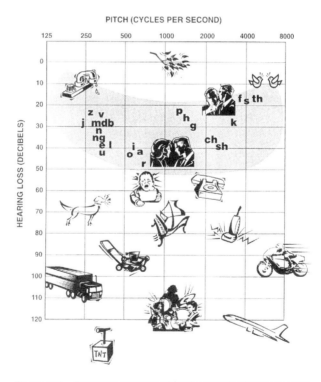

Figure 11.2. Frequency spectrum of familiar sounds plotted on a standard audiogram. The shaded area contains most of the sound elements of speech. (From Northern, J.L., & Downs, M.P. [2002]. *Hearing in children* [5th ed., p. 18]. Philadelphia: Lippincott Williams & Wilkins. Copyright © Lippincott Williams & Wilkins; reprinted by permission.)

THE HEARING SYSTEM

The anatomical mechanism for hearing is a complex system (B.C.J. Moore, 1995). It is divided into a peripheral auditory mechanism, which starts at the external ear and ends at the auditory nerve, and a central auditory system, which extends from the auditory nerve to the brain. A disorder in the peripheral system results in a hearing loss, whereas a central auditory problem interferes with the interpretation of what is heard.

The peripheral auditory system is divided into the external, middle, and inner ear. The external ear includes the **auricle** and the ear canal (Figure 11.3). The auricle channels sound into the ear canal and thence to the middle ear. The ear canal in adults is roughly 1½–2 inches long. The skin along the lateral portion of the canal contains hair and glands that produce **cerumen** (ear wax) and function together to limit foreign bodies from entering the canal.

At the end of the ear canal lies the eardrum, or tympanic membrane, which separates the external ear from the middle ear. The tympanic membrane is attached to the first of a series of small bones of the middle ear—the malleus, incus, and stapes—which are collectively called the **ossicles.** The end of the ossicular chain, the stapes footplate, is attached by ligaments to the oval window, which serves as the boundary between the middle ear and the bony housing of the inner ear, the cochlea.

The **eustachian tube** is also part of the middle ear. This tube runs from the floor of the middle-ear space down to the **nasopharynx.** The eustachian tube is usually closed but opens during a swallow or yawn, allowing a small amount of air from the nasopharynx into the middle ear to equalize its air pressure with that in the external canal, as well as provide a new supply of oxygen for the mucous membrane lining of the middle ear.

When sound waves strike the tympanic membrane, the membrane vibrates and thus sets the ossicular chain into motion. Because the tympanic membrane has a larger surface area than the oval window and because the ossicles act as a lever system, the incoming sound pressure is amplified by about 30 dB.

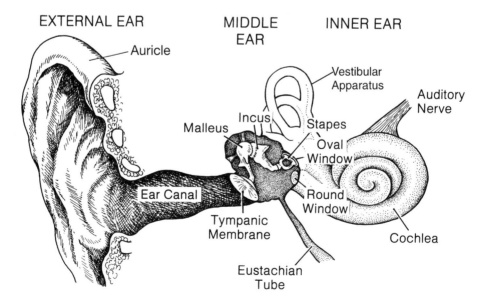

Figure 11.3.   Structure of the ear. The middle ear is composed of the tympanic membrane, or eardrum, and the three ear bones: the malleus, the incus, and the stapes. The stapes footplate lies on the oval window, the gateway to the inner ear. The inner ear contains the cochlea and the vestibular (balance) apparatus, collectively called the *labyrinth.*

The inner ear is composed of the **vestibular system** and the **cochlea.** The vestibular system houses the sensory organ of balance, whereas the cochlea houses the organ of hearing. The cochlea is a snail-shaped structure, approximately 35 millimeters in length, which is divided into three fluid-filled chambers by the membranous labyrinth (Figure 11.4). The actual end organ of hearing, the **organ of Corti,** is housed on the floor of the interior chamber, or basilar membrane of the scala media, and runs the entire length of the cochlea.

The organ of Corti consists of multiple rows of delicate hair cells that are the actual receptors for the auditory nerve. The cochlea is arranged **tonotopically;** that is, hair cells located at the base of the cochlea, near the oval window, respond more specifically to high-frequency sounds (above 2,000 Hz), whereas those in the middle and top respond more to gradually lower-frequency sounds (Figure 11.5). The organ of Corti converts the mechanical energy arriving from the middle ear into electrical energy, or the nerve impulse. As the ossicular chain is set into motion by the vibrating tympanic membrane, the movement is transmitted through the chambers of the cochlea and results in release of neurotransmitters from the hair cells. This generates a nerve impulse that is transmitted via the ascending auditory pathway to the brain. Most of the nerve impulses from the right cochlea cross over to ascend the left central auditory pathway to the left portion of the brain, and vice versa for impulses from the left ear. However, a small portion of impulses from the right and left cochlea ascend on their respective sides (Figure 11.6).

The organizational structure of the auditory nerve itself is orderly, much like the tonotopic arrangement of the cochlea. The individual nerve fibers leave the cochlea via the spiral ganglion and then wrap around one another to form the auditory nerve, with the fibers from the **basal** end of the cochlea (which respond to high-frequency sounds) located around the outside and the fibers from the **apical** end (which respond to low-frequency sounds) arranged nearer the center of the nerve. About half of the fibers respond to frequencies greater than 2,000 Hz, yielding hearing that is most sensitive for higher-pitched sounds.

From the inner ear, sound is carried to the auditory cortex in the temporal lobe of the brain. The route from ear to cortex involves at least four neural relay stations (Figure 11.6).

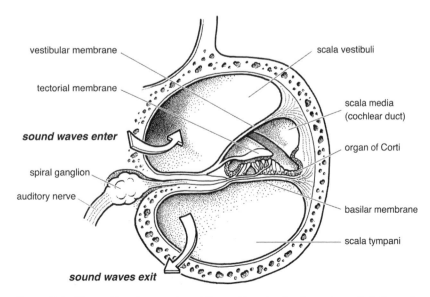

Figure 11.4. The cochlea. Cross-section of the cochlea, showing the scala vestibuli, the scala media, the scala tympani, and the organ of Corti.

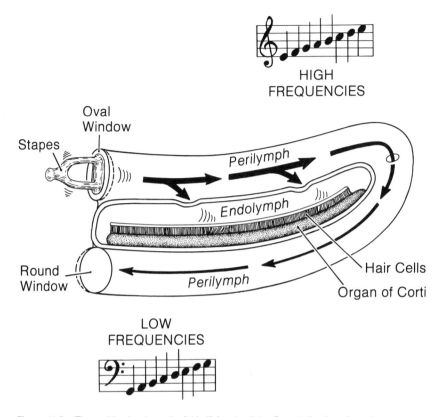

Figure 11.5. The cochlea has been "unfolded" for simplicity. Sound vibrations from the stapes are transmitted as waves in the perilymph. This leads to the displacement of hair cells in the organ of Corti. These hair cells lie above and attach to the auditory nerve, and the impulses generated are fed to the brain. High-frequency sounds stimulate hair cells close to the oval window, whereas low-frequency sounds stimulate the end of the organ. The sound wave in the perilymph is rapidly dissipated through the round window, and the cochlea is ready to accept a new set of vibrations.

The final destination is the auditory cortex, where sound can be associated with other sensory information and memory to permit perception and interpretation. The auditory cortex is not needed to perceive sound, but it is needed to interpret language.

EMBRYOLOGIC DEVELOPMENT OF THE HEARING APPARATUS

Knowledge of the development of auditory structures can be helpful in predicting and diagnosing hearing loss if the clinician recognizes syndromes that are associated with altered ear development, such as in CHARGE association or in Waardenburg syndrome (see Appendix B). In addition, if the timing of a prenatal insult or possible fetal injury is close to the timing of ear development, the clinician should also suspect hearing loss.

The differentiation of the normal hearing apparatus from the three primitive cell types—the ectoderm, mesoderm, and endoderm—begins in the first weeks of life (Romand, 1992). By 4½ weeks, a tubular extension known as the endolymphatic duct can be recognized as the early vestibular portion of the labyrinth; and by 6 weeks, three outpockets have an arch-shaped configuration and represent the early derivatives of the semicircular canals (i.e., part of the vestibular system). Although sensory end-organ cells are visible by the seventh week, maturation of the sensory cells in the cochlea does not occur until the fifth month. The middle ear has

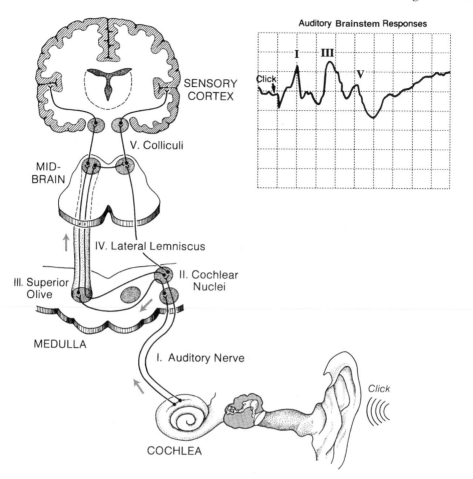

Figure 11.6. The auditory pathway and auditory brainstem responses (ABR). The auditory nerve carries sounds to the cochlear nuclei in the medullary portion of the brainstem. Here, most impulses cross over to the superior olivary body and then ascend to the opposite inferior colliculus and ultimately the sensory cortex, where the sound is perceived. The function of this pathway can be measured by ABR. Each wave corresponds to a higher level of the pathway (denoted by Roman numerals in the pathway and in the reporting of ABRs). Shaded arrows indicate the direction of travel of the nerve impulse along the pathway.

a different developmental process, with the tympanic cavity and auditory tube derived from an endodermal-lined pouch between the first and second branchial arches and the ossicles derived from these arches. By the 15th week, the form of the ear is completed, and the cartilaginous structures begin to ossify over the ensuing 4 months. The auricle begins to develop by the third or fourth week of gestation (Figure 11.7) and by the 20th week has an adult configuration but continues to develop until the seventh year of life.

DEFINING HEARING LOSS

Normal hearing requires intact functioning of both the peripheral and central components of the auditory pathway. The location and nature of the dysfunction in the auditory pathway will determine the degree and type of the hearing loss. Because it is through hearing that a child develops the comprehension of speech, a hearing loss commonly affects both the receptive and

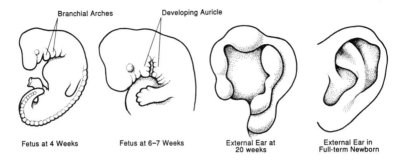

Figure 11.7. Embryological development of the ear, showing stages from the 4 weeks' gestation to the newborn period. The ear is functional by 20 weeks' gestation.

expressive development of spoken language. This is particularly true if the hearing loss occurs prior to 2 years of age, during the period of most rapid language acquisition. When hearing is impaired, the child typically compensates through the use of vision. This can consist of close observation of the visual environment, speechreading for those who are able to do so, or use of a sign language.

Terms that describe the degree of loss for a person with a bilateral loss (both ears) include *deaf* or *hard of hearing*. The former is often reserved for individuals with profound losses greater than 70 dB HL that result in severe oral speech and language delay or that prevent the understanding of spoken language through hearing. Using hearing aids, children with this degree of loss may hear only the rhythm of speech, their own voice, and environmental sounds (Northern & Downs, 2002). They are also more likely to use sign language as a means of communication. *Hard of hearing* is a term frequently used for children with losses in the better ear of 25–70 dB HL who benefit greatly from amplification through hearing aids and who communicate primarily through spoken language. Some refer to children with hearing loss as hearing-impaired regardless of the degree of loss (Northern & Downs, 2002). Although special educators use person-first language when referring to students with auditory disabilities (e.g., *a child who is hard of hearing*), the Deaf community has preferred the term *deaf child*.

Other descriptors of degree of hearing loss are *slight, mild, moderate, severe,* and *profound*. Each of these terms is often accompanied by specific threshold levels of loss in the frequency region for speech, that is, the average threshold loss for 500 Hz, 1,000 Hz, and 2,000 Hz. These terms are meant to convey the extent of loss in one ear (unilateral) or for both ears (bilateral) and are useful in explaining to parents how much of speech their child can hear. Each child's capacities do vary as a consequence of listening circumstances. These descriptive terms, therefore, may only partially explain the listening experiences of a particular child. For example, a child with a mild hearing loss in both ears may encounter as much difficulty in listening as one with a moderate loss. The impact of the different levels of hearing loss is discussed later in the section called "Degrees of Hearing Loss."

Types of Hearing Loss

Dysfunction of the external or middle ear causes a conductive hearing loss. If the cochlea or auditory nerve malfunctions, a sensorineural hearing loss results. Occasionally, the term sensorineural is broken down further into the terms *sensory hearing loss*, implicating the cochlea, and *neural hearing loss*, implicating the auditory nerve. A mixed hearing loss indicates that there are both conductive and sensorineural components to the loss.

The effect of a hearing loss on speech and language depends on a number of variables, including severity, age at onset, age at discovery, and age at intervention. Hearing losses acquired after language has been well established usually have less of an impact on language and speech skills and later academic achievement than do hearing losses occurring in infancy. However, findings (Yoshinaga-Itano et al., 1998) of infants identified prior to 6 months of age and provided with hearing aids/intervention immediately demonstrate that language development can be within normal limits by age 3 years. Hearing loss may affect one ear (unilateral loss) or both ears (bilateral loss). Although it is more subtle, unilateral hearing loss can have a significant impact on communication, interpersonal relationships, and the educational achievement of the child. Progressive hearing losses can be insidious and challenging to recognize early (Levi, Tell, & Feinwesser, 1993).

Prevalence and Incidence of Hearing Loss

Approximately 10%–15% of children who receive hearing screenings at school fail the screenings; however, the majority of these children have a transient conductive hearing loss. A 1996 estimate of prevalence in the United States reported that slightly fewer than 1 million or 1.3% of children younger than 18 years have a hearing impairment (Adams, Hendershot, & Marano, 1999). One frequently reported estimate is that approximately 1 in 1,000 infants is born with a severe to profound hearing loss and that this incidence doubles during infancy and childhood (Kvaerner & Arnesen, 1994). Inconsistencies in assessing the incidence of hearing impairment in childhood result from the lack of clear parameters for and definitions of hearing impairment. The specific age of onset of hearing impairment is often difficult to determine, particularly between birth and 2½ years because the early identification of hearing loss has only recently begun to be addressed by universal newborn hearing screening programs. Nevertheless, outcome data from a few reports of such programs show incidences ranging from 1.4 to 3.1 per 1,000 births, including newborns with both sensorineural and conductive hearing losses (Finitzo, Albright, & O'Neal, 1998; Herer, 2001; Kanne, Schaefer, & Perkins, 1999; Mason & Herrmann, 1998; Vohr et al., 1998). One of these studies of more than 25,000 newborns, for example, shows an overall incidence rate of 2.2 per 1,000 births as follows: 0.97 per 1,000 with bilateral sensorineural loss, 0.46 per 1,000 with bilateral conductive loss, 0.46 per 1,000 with unilateral sensorineural loss, and 0.27 per 1,000 with unilateral conductive loss (Herer, 2001). If these few studies are supported by additional reports, it appears that most sensorineural hearing losses in children are present at birth, highlighting the need for the earliest possible identification and intervention.

Causes of Hearing Loss

The determination of the cause of hearing loss is often complicated by a delay in diagnosis and because the specific contributing factors are often unknown. Hearing losses present at birth are described as congenital, regardless of causation, whereas those that develop after birth are described as acquired. Hereditary (genetic) origins, albeit congenital, may not be revealed until later in life.

Hearing loss in children can occur as a result of hereditary factors, an event or injury in utero, perinatal circumstances, or an occurrence after birth (Parving & Hauch, 1994). Traditionally, the literature has reported that the cause of hearing loss is approximately one third genetic, one third acquired, and one third unknown (Peckham, 1986). A more recent report, however, indicated that at least half of hearing loss in children is caused by genetic factors, with approximately 80% being nonsyndromic and due to autosomal recessive inheritance (Cohn et al., 1999). The relatively few other children with genetic causes, therefore, have hearing loss as part of a spectrum of physical and/or developmental disorders. For children with a hearing loss of nongenetic origin, it is estimated that approximately one third have additional disabilities. Nongenetic hearing loss (congenital or acquired) can result from prenatal and postnatal infections; anoxia; prematurity; prenatal and postnatal exposures to ototoxic agents (e.g., certain antibiotics); and physical trauma. Because middle-ear infections have been shown to contribute to so many cases of acquired conductive hearing loss (Bluestone & Klein, 1995), they are discussed in some detail later in this chapter.

Genetic Causes

Hereditary hearing loss occurs in approximately 1 in 2,000 children. As mentioned previously, in approximately 80% of children with hereditary hearing loss, the hearing loss is inherited in an autosomal recessive way (see Chapter 1) and is not associated with a syndrome; that is, hearing loss is the child's sole disability. About half of all childhood nonsyndromic autosomal recessive hearing losses are caused by mutations in the connexin 26 (Cx26) gene (GJB2/DFNB1), which makes it the most common type of hereditary hearing loss (Cohn et al., 1999). Siblings of a child with nonsyndromic autosomal recessive hearing loss can be affected as well (McKusick, 1998). Other hereditary disorders can affect the formation or function of any part of the hearing mechanism (Gorlin, Toriello, & Cohen, 1995; Wolf, Spencer, & Gleason, 2002). There are more than 70 documented inherited syndromes associated with deafness, some of which manifest later in life. Table 11.1 describes some of the most common genetic disorders associated with hearing loss.

Cleft palate, in which the roof of the mouth fails to close during embryological development, is a malformation with associated conductive hearing loss. It has a multifactorial inheritance pattern and an incidence of about 1 in 900. It may occur alone or together with cleft lip. Of children with a cleft palate, 50%–90% are susceptible to significant and persistent middle-ear infections (Muntz, 1993). Because of the absence of closure of the palate, the tensor veli palati muscle does not have a normal midline attachment and functions poorly in opening the eustachian tube, predisposing the child to middle-ear involvement (Potsic et al., 1995). Many

Table 11.1. Examples of genetic disorders associated with hearing loss

Syndrome	Inheritance pattern	Type of hearing loss	Other characteristics
Treacher Collins syndrome	Autosomal dominant	Conductive or mixed	Abnormal facial appearance, deformed auricles, defects of ear canal and middle ear
Waardenburg syndrome	Autosomal dominant	Sensorineural, stable	Unusual facial appearance, irises of different colors, white forelock, absent organ of Corti
Bardet-Biedl syndrome	Autosomal recessive	Sensorineural, progressive	Retinitis pigmentosa, mental retardation, obesity, extra fingers or toes
Usher syndrome	Autosomal recessive	Sensorineural; progressive in type III	Retinitis pigmentosa; central nervous system effects, including vertigo, loss of sense of smell, mental retardation, epilepsy; half have psychosis
CHARGE association	Sporadic (i.e., noninherited)	Mixed, progressive	Eye, gastrointestinal, and other malformations
Down syndrome	Chromosomal	Conductive; occasionally sensorineural	Small auricles, narrow ear canals, high incidence of middle-ear infections
Trisomy 13, trisomy 18	Chromosomal	Sensorineural	Central nervous system malformations
Cleft palate	Multifactorial	Conductive	Cleft lip

Key: CHARGE association: **c**oloboma, congenital **h**eart defect, choanal **a**tresia, **r**etarded growth and development, **g**enital abnormalities, and **e**ar malformations with or without hearing loss.

children with cleft palate, therefore, develop a conductive hearing loss, and some exhibit sensorineural impairment as well. Close monitoring of hearing in a child with cleft palate is important. Also, surgical **myringotomy** and pressure-equalization tube insertions (described later) are often necessary to remediate the middle-ear condition and conductive hearing loss of a child who has or who had a cleft palate (see Chapter 12).

Pre-, Peri-, and Postnatal Factors and Prematurity

Environmental exposures to viruses, bacteria, and other toxins such as drugs prior to or following birth can result in hearing loss. During delivery or in the newborn period, a number of other complications such as hypoxia may cause damage to the hearing mechanism, particularly the cochlea (Razi & Das, 1994). Neonatal hyperbilirubinemia and intracranial hemorrhage also have been associated with subsequent sensorineural hearing loss. Premature infants, especially those born weighing less than 1,500 grams (3⅓ pounds), have an increased susceptibility to all three of these problems. Of these infants, 2%–5% will demonstrate significant hearing loss (Herregard et al., 1995; Weisglas-Kuperus et al., 1993). (See Chapters 5 and 6 for further discussion of neonatal complications and prematurity, respectively.)

Infections

Infections, both intrauterine and those acquired following birth, are common causes of hearing loss. A mother who contracts rubella during the first trimester of pregnancy has about a 30% risk of bearing an infant who has a severe to profound sensorineural hearing loss, microcephaly, cardiac malformations, retinal abnormalities, and other disabilities (Bale, 1992). Other infections during pregnancy, including toxoplasmosis, herpes virus, syphilis, and cytomegalovirus (CMV), may cause similar hearing losses (Henderson & Weiner, 1995; Veda, Tokugawa, & Kusuhara, 1992). The most prevalent of these is CMV, with an incidence of 5–25 per 1,000 newborn infants (Hanshaw, 1994). Among children with clinically detectable CMV at birth, 80% have nervous system sequelae, including hearing loss. As many as 90% of CMV infections, however, are thought to be subclinical (Schildroth, 1994). Among children with subclinical CMV, only 5%–15% will develop central nervous system manifestations; however, these children are still at risk for late-onset hearing loss that is usually symmetrical and may worsen over time (Fowler et al., 1997; Williamson et al., 1992).

Infections of infancy and childhood also can lead to a sensorineural hearing loss. Bacterial meningitis carries a 10% risk of hearing loss from damage to the cochlea (Fortnum & Davis, 1993). The hearing loss may progress further if the weakened cochlea degenerates. Among the viral diseases of childhood, unilateral hearing loss has been reported after mumps, whereas bilateral involvement has occurred after measles and chickenpox (Nussinovitch, Volovitz, & Varsano, 1995).

Middle-Ear Disease

The most common type of hearing impairment is a mild conductive hearing loss secondary to a chronic middle-ear disease or **effusion** (Kessner, Snow, & Singer, 1974). Such hearing loss often goes undiagnosed, may fluctuate due to the middle-ear condition, and usually does not result in a permanent hearing loss. Middle-ear infection (acute otitis media) is most common in very young children, with 76%–95% of all children having at least one middle-ear infection during their first 2 years of life (Shapiro & Bluestone, 1995). Members of certain ethnic groups, especially African Americans, Native Americans, and the Inuit, appear to be at greater risk than usual to develop recurrent or chronic otitis media (Bluestone & Klein, 1995; Roberts et al., 2000). This increased prevalence may be due to reduced access to health care and exposure to other sick children in the child care setting, and it underscores the importance of rapid detection and treatment of middle-ear disease.

Although some children with otitis media are asymptomatic, in most cases, fever or irritability is the first sign of an infection. The older child may pull at the external ear, or fluid may drain from the ear. Hearing may be obviously decreased, and the child may have an unsteady gait. On examination with an otoscope, the eardrum looks red and opaque rather than white and translucent. Fluid, or effusion, is usually present behind the eardrum. Pneumatic otoscopy, or the use of an insufflation bulb to detect the degree of movement of the tympanic membrane, reveals stiffness and decreased mobility; the diagnosis can be supported by **tympanometry** (discussed later) that shows a flat rather than tented or peaked pattern.

Trauma

A blow to the skull, resulting in trauma to the cochlea, may lead to a sensorineural hearing loss (Zimmerman et al., 1993). Such a blow, however, can also cause damage to the ossicles and/or blood in the middle ear, resulting in a conductive hearing loss. Mild to moderate sensorineural hearing losses also may result from traumatic noise levels. In children and adolescents, sources of excessive impact noise include firecrackers, fireworks, and air guns. Transient or permanent sensorineural hearing loss may occur also with exposure to very loud sound over time. For example, using stereo headphones at high-intensity levels; playing in school bands; and attending rock concerts, where noise levels may exceed 100–110 dB are each highly suspect for causing permanent or temporary hearing loss (Montgomery & Fujikawa, 1992). Any sustained noise level above 90 dB is potentially damaging to the cochlea and should be avoided (Brookhouser, Worthington, & Kelly, 1992). Three warning signals of a noise hazardous area are having to shout to be understood within 3 feet of the listener; experiencing ringing (i.e., tinnitus) in ears after leaving the noisy area; and hearing only muffled/softer sounds for about 1–2 hours following the noise exposure.

Ototoxic Agents

Certain antibiotics used to treat severe bacterial infections may be toxic to the cochlea (Aran, 1995). This is especially true of the following aminoglycosides when administered intravenously: neomycin, kanamycin, gentamicin, vancomycin, and tobramycin (listed in descending order of toxicity). They destroy the outer row of hair cells in the cochlea. Fortunately, physicians can monitor blood levels of the antibiotics during treatment to avoid the development of toxic levels. Other drugs that can damage the inner ear include diuretics, nonsteroidal anti-inflammatory drugs, and chemotherapeutic agents.

IDENTIFICATION OF HEARING LOSS

There is often considerable delay in identifying a child with hearing impairment (Coplan, 1987; Van Naarden, Decoufle, & Caldwell, 1999). Many parents suspect a hearing loss before the child's first birthday. Although it is now possible to reliably test auditory system function hours after birth, the average age of a child at the time of identification of a significant hearing loss is 2½ years (Goldberg, 1996), with the average initiation of appropriate intervention at 3½ years. Many factors are involved in this delay of diagnosis. In general, the more severe the hearing loss and the greater its association with other disabilities, the earlier identification of the loss occurs. The reported age of identification of severe to profound congenital hearing loss in children in the United States ranges from younger than 6 months of age to 16–18 months of age (Stein et al., 1995). This delay in part is the consequence of hearing loss being a silent disability; it is not usually accompanied by pain, fever, or physical abnormalities. During the first 6 months of life, development occurs on the foundation of a nonverbal and prelinguistic communication system and after that, on a visual gestural system as well. Only when expectations of and demands for verbal communication are placed on the child does the sensory impairment become more obvious. Furthermore, although children with sudden-onset hearing loss (e.g., secondary to meningitis) may become frustrated and angry, infants or young children who are completely deaf may not appear upset.

The importance of early identification of hearing loss (until recently usually defined as occurring before 2 years of age) is analogous to the need for early detection of a vision loss. The brain pathways for both of these senses are still immature at birth and develop normally only when stimulated early. Evidence has indicated that identification and intervention prior to age 6 months, regardless of degree of hearing loss, can lead to typical communicative development by age 3 (Yoshinaga-Itano et al., 1998). These findings support the conventional wisdom that amplification should be used as early as possible. This vital intervention step, coupled with continual parental guidance and support, gives the child the maximum opportunity to utilize residual hearing in the acquisition of speech and language skills during the critical early stage of development. In addition, some professionals recommend augmenting auditory input with visual forms of communication in the early years, including cued speech and/or sign language (discussed later).

Hearing Milestones for Detecting Hearing Loss

There are specific milestones that are helpful in detecting a hearing loss. The hearing mechanism is functional by 20 weeks' gestation, particularly for low-pitched sound, making it quite likely that the fetus has an appreciation of and the ability to distinguish familiar from nonfamiliar sounds. It has been shown that a newborn will suck preferentially to the recorded voice of his or her mother. The infant also will awaken from sleep specifically to the loud voice of his or her parent (Northern & Downs, 2002).

The newborn clearly prefers to listen to speech as opposed to other environmental sounds, just as the infant prefers to fixate visually on a face rather than an object. By 2 months of age, the typically developing infant can distinguish vowel from consonant sounds, and by 4 months, the infant shows a preference for speech patterns that have varied rhythm and stress (Northern & Downs, 2002). He or she prefers listening to prolonged discourse rather than to repetitive baby talk. During this early period, an infant with normal hearing can be seen orienting its body toward a familiar sound source from its right or left.

Up to 5 months of age, the speech sounds an infant makes are not influenced by the sounds that he or she hears. This is why the early babbling of infants from different countries sounds alike. After 5 months of age, however, the infant's babbling starts to imitate the parents' speech patterns (Gopnik, Meltzoff, & Kuhl, 1999; Northern & Downs, 2002). Thus, the babbling of an infant with French-speaking parents becomes different from that of an infant with English-speaking parents. For all hearing children, however, listening to spoken language during early life is a critical prerequisite for the typical development of speech. This is likely to explain why children who acquire a hearing loss after learning to speak have both better speech and better command of the language spoken in their community than do children with congenital deafness. Helen Keller was an example of a child who lost hearing (and vision) as a result of meningitis at 18 months of age and ultimately developed effective speech, presumably because her brain had been exposed to spoken language in her early life.

Signs of Hearing Impairment

With the usual milestones in mind, the variations in development seen in deaf infants are easier to understand. An early sign of severe hearing loss is a sleeping infant who does not awaken to loud noises. Even an infant who is deaf, however, may react to the vibration alone, leading family members to assume that he or she has actually heard the sound. Between 3 and 4 months of age, infants who are deaf coo and laugh normally, yet babbling seems to be delayed

(Oller & Eilers, 1988). In children with unaffected hearing, babbling noises become more varied and eventually are attached to meanings (e.g., the babble "dadadadada" becomes the word "Dada"), whereas the vocalizations of infants who are deaf show less variety in articulation and are less likely to become meaningful and recognizable words. Between the ages of 5 months and 17 months, although hearing infants increase their repertoire of consonant sounds, their deaf counterparts demonstrate a reduction in consonant variety (Stoel-Gammon & Otomo, 1986). It is this failure to develop comprehensible speech that leads parents to suspect a hearing loss.

Receptive language also lags in children with hearing loss. By 4 months of age, the hearing child generally orients his or her head or body toward parents' voices; the child with a hearing loss may or may not do this, depending on the severity and configuration of the loss. By 8 to 9 months, a direct head turn (right or left) to locate the parent's voice or a familiar sound can be observed in an infant with typical hearing but not in one with a severe to profound loss. At around 12 months of age, infants receive verbal instructions accompanied by gestures, such as waving "bye-bye." The deaf child of this age may seem to understand the message because he or she can often figure out the command by watching mouth movements, following gestures, and understanding the context. For example, a deaf toddler may get his or her jacket when others do, whether or not he or she has understood "Get your coat." By about 16 months of age, the hearing child responds to more complex instructions by words alone. The child with an undiagnosed hearing loss, however, may have great difficulty in doing this and may stop following instructions unless they can be inferred from context or are accompanied by gestures. This failure to respond to verbal instructions may lead parents to suspect a hearing loss but also can be misperceived as an oppositional or behavior disorder. Hearing children with mental retardation also are delayed in the achievement of these language milestones. In children with mental retardation, however, speech, motor, and cognitive skills are similarly delayed, whereas the child with hearing impairment has slow development of speech and language skills but usually has typical development of other abilities.

Hearing Screening

Screening for hearing loss can facilitate early identification (McCormick, 1995). As with any screening procedure, hearing screening is designed to separate those individuals with a higher risk of the target condition (hearing loss) from the general population (Johnson, Benson, & Seaton, 1997). An individual either passes a screening or is referred for diagnostic evaluation. Although a screening alerts the professional to the possibility of hearing loss, the diagnostic evaluation serves to confirm whether a hearing loss is present and provides additional information regarding the type, extent, and configuration of the hearing loss. Some groups of children, such as premature infants; those with complicated pre-, peri-, and postnatal periods; those requiring hospitalization at birth in a newborn intensive care nursery; and children with family histories of deafness, should be screened routinely for signs of hearing loss. In 1982, the Joint Committee on Infant Hearing first published risk factors for hearing loss, including 1) a positive family history of hearing loss; 2) congenital perinatal infection, such as rubella or syphilis; 3) bacterial meningitis; 4) congenital malformations of the head and neck; 5) prematurity with a birth weight of less than 1,500 grams; 6) anoxia; and 7) hyperbilirubinemia requiring exchange transfusion. Other factors added since 1982 by the Joint Committee include 1) admission to the neonatal intensive care unit for greater than 48 hours (Fortnum & Davis, 1997); 2) in utero infection such as CMV (Littman et al., 1995); 3) stigmata (visible physical characteristics) associated with syndromes known to include hearing loss and with syndromes associated with progressive hearing loss, such as neurofibromatosis; 4) neurodegenerative disorders or sensory motor neuropathies; 5) head trauma; and 6) persistent otitis media with effusion for at least 3 months (Stool et al., 1994).

Evaluating the hearing of children who meet these risk criteria identifies only about half of children with hearing impairments. The 1993 National Institutes of Health (NIH) consensus statement sought to improve identification of all children by advising universal newborn screening by 3 months of age. A 1997 report by the National Institute on Deafness and Other Communication Disorders (a division of the NIH) that is considered an undated supplement to the 1993 consensus statement recommended universal hearing screening before hospital discharge. The Joint Committee on Infant Hearing's Year 2000 Position Statement endorsed the screening of all infants using objective, physiologic measures during hospital birth admission. It also recommended that newborns birthed at alternative places or at home be screened before 1 month of age. Furthermore, the Joint Committee advised that newborns who do not pass screening/rescreening have audiological and medical evaluations to confirm hearing loss before age 3 months. It also urged that intervention for those with permanent hearing loss occur before 6 months of age. For infants who pass newborn screening and have risk factors for auditory disorders, the Joint Committee recommended periodic audiological and medical evaluations for 3 years so that prompt identification and intervention can ensue.

In addition to observing the guidelines found in the NIH consensus (1993) and the Joint Committee (2000) statements, clinicians should monitor the achievement of developmental language milestones and obtain a hearing test for any child who appears to have delays in speech and/or language development. A child's hearing can be tested at any age, even within 24 hours of birth, so parental concern should prompt an immediate referral for testing.

Screening Infants Younger than 6 Months of Age

In infants up to age 6 months, behavioral observation **audiometry** (BOA) can help detect a hearing loss but cannot determine precisely the degree of impairment nor its type (Northern & Downs, 2002). BOA relies upon the subjective observation of an infant's reactions to a variety of sound stimuli in a structured situation. It is efficient, does not require specialized equipment, and can be a useful initial screening method. Limitations include possible tester bias, rapid extinction of responses, and wide variations of reactions in infants younger than 6 months. Observable responses to sound include but are not limited to fluttering of eyes during light sleep states, changes in breathing patterns, variations in sucking behavior, startle to loud sounds, and body orientation to the sound source. Observable responses usually occur in response to sounds that are familiar to the infant, such as the mother's voice or favorite toys that produce sounds. Starting at 4 months of age, infants begin to locate familiar sounds by turning their heads toward the sound source (emanating from about 3 feet to the right or left side of the head). Head-turn location of sounds becomes quicker and more direct as the infant reaches age 6 months and older.

Generally, the stimulus required to elicit a response, even in a child with typical hearing sensitivity, must be rather intense, often in the range of 80–90 dB. Thus, a positive response serves only to rule out a severe or profound hearing loss but does not distinguish among lesser degrees or unilateral hearing loss or between conductive and sensorineural hearing loss. Furthermore, the absence of a response does not necessarily mean that the child has a hearing loss. Infants do adjust to repeated loud environmental noise, and this habituation limits the interpretation of BOA.

Because of these circumstances, the NIH consensus statement endorses evoked otoacoustic emissions (EOAE) and/or screening auditory brainstem response (SABR) testing as preferred methods of screening for hearing loss in infants (Meredith et al., 1994). These screening methods can be used whether the infant is awake or asleep. EOAE testing is a rapid, noninvasive, computer-managed, and inexpensive method of assessing cochlear function based on the cochlea's capability of not only transmitting sound to the brain but also generating low-level sound that is transmitted from the cochlea to the outer ear canal (Champlin, 1996;

Glattke et al., 1995). In this test, the infant's ear canal is sealed with a plastic probe that includes a microphone and a receiver. Clicks or tones of various frequencies are introduced into the ear canal, and the microphone records responses that are evoked from the cochlea, specifically from its outer hair cells. Of course, each ear is tested separately. If a hearing loss exists that is greater than about 30 dB, no response is obtained. Either the screening equipment used or the examiner makes the pass/refer decision based upon preset criteria. An occasional limitation of EOAE procedures is that the stimulus intensity and response may be reduced in the presence of vernix (a waxy substance from the birthing process found in the ear canals of some newborns) or middle-ear fluid (Brass & Kemp, 1994).

The other newborn screening method is SABR. It is a version of diagnostic ABR audiometry (American Speech-Language-Hearing Association [ASHA], 1989; Stein et al., 1995). Like EOAE testing, the SABR procedure does not require the infant's cooperation. Unlike EOAE testing, which assesses only the cochlea, ABR testing assesses the auditory neural pathway as well. EEG sensors are affixed at various sites on the newborn's head. Using external or ear canal insert earphones, tones or clicks are presented separately to each ear, stimulating bursts of neural activity from the auditory pathway within the brainstem. The electrodes detect this activity, and a computer averages the responses from the auditory nerve and activity in the auditory brainstem pathway. A pass/refer decision is made at the conclusion of the SABR either by the screening equipment or by the screener.

If a newborn does not pass EOAE and/or SABR before hospital discharge, a rescreen within 1 month is usually performed (using either method). If an infant does not pass this latter rescreen, the expected protocol is to refer the infant for diagnostic ABR audiometry within several weeks.

Diagnostic ABR audiometry is a highly sensitive test for both hearing loss and neural disruption of the auditory pathway (McClelland et al., 1992). It explores threshold loss, usually across the 1,000–4,000 Hz range, and activity in the auditory brainstem pathway. In infants, the ABR waveform is composed of three distinct waves, numbered I, III, and V (Figure 11.6), that represent successively higher levels of the ascending auditory pathway. An absence of waveform at a given intensity suggests a hearing loss, whereas the complete absence of a particular wave suggests an abnormality at a particular location of the brain pathway.

Hearing Tests

In addition to hearing screening, both EOAE and ABR measurements can be used as part of a diagnostic battery of audiology tests for infants, toddlers, and young children and are particularly useful in assessing older children with severe developmental disabilities who are unable to respond to conventional audiometric testing (Gorga et al., 1995; Richardson, Williamson, & Lenton, 1995). These methods of assessment, nevertheless, should be considered part of the battery of tests available to evaluate children with hearing losses or other auditory disorders. The methods are especially useful, therefore, when coupled with behavioral hearing testing (Gravel, 1994). Behavioral hearing testing is performed to 1) determine whether there is a hearing loss; 2) differentiate a conductive from a sensorineural hearing loss; 3) determine the configuration of the hearing loss in each ear (i.e., the degree of the hearing impairment at specific frequencies); and 4) estimate the clarity with which speech sounds can be discriminated. The age of the child need not interfere with the successful completion of behavioral audiological assessment, although the methodology and specific techniques must be modified for the developmental age of the child (Gans & Gans, 1993).

Testing Children with Developmental Ages from 6 Months to 2½ Years

Between 6 months and 2½ years of age, as a child's responses to auditory stimuli become more predictable, visual reinforcement audiometry (VRA) can be used to assess hearing sensitivity

(Gravel & Traquina, 1992; J.M. Moore, 1995). VRA enables identification of the magnitude and configuration of the hearing loss. Tones or other sounds are presented through loudspeakers (i.e., in soundfield), and information is limited to responses from the better hearing ear (in cases of asymmetrical hearing loss). This method does not provide ear-specific information as both of the child's ears are uncovered and receive the sound information together.

VRA uses visual reinforcers to elicit consistent responses to auditory stimuli. Typically, the child is seated on the parent's lap in the middle of a sound-treated audiometric booth. At a 90-degree angle to one side of the child is a loudspeaker. Above the speaker is a darkened Plexiglas box that contains an animated toy. To establish conditioning, an acoustic stimulus (e.g., a tone, a voice) is presented from the speaker and at the same time the box above the speaker is illuminated to reveal an animated toy inside. Thus, the child is conditioned to associate the presence of the sound with the pleasurable experience of viewing the toy. Once the child has gained an awareness of the relationship between the acoustic stimulus and the visual reward, the box is not illuminated until the child responds by turning toward the sound in anticipation of viewing the toy.

Conditioned orienting response (COR) audiometry differs from VRA in that it requires the child not only to show an awareness of the stimuli but also to localize the sound source. In this case, speakers are usually placed at 45-degree angles to the front of the child and the Plexiglas boxes containing the toys are positioned above or near each speaker. After conditioning, the child must turn toward the correct speaker before receiving reinforcement. COR audiometry can also be used with earphones to obtain ear-specific information.

Testing Children with Developmental Ages Greater than 2½ Years

Conditioned play audiometry can be used for testing children generally between the ages of 2½ and 4 years. In this approach, the child usually wears earphones and is conditioned to perform a play task whenever the stimulus is heard. For example, the child may stack blocks, put rings on a peg, or perform some other motor task in response to hearing the auditory stimulus. By about 4 years of age, the child can respond to requests to press a button or to raise a hand in response to the stimulus. If conditioning of the child is successful, audiometric testing results are as complete as from a mature child or adult, although all preschool children require developmentally appropriate reinforcement and praise.

When a child's hearing is assessed via loudspeakers or earphones (i.e., air conduction; Figure 11.8a) and a hearing loss is identified, it is not possible to determine whether the loss is conductive or sensorineural. The sounds must then also be presented through a bone conduction vibrator placed on the mastoid bone behind the ear (Figure 11.8b). Whereas air conduction testing involves the contribution of the external, middle, and inner ear, bone conduction testing essentially bypasses the external and middle ear and stimulates the inner ear directly. Therefore, if the child demonstrates a hearing loss by air conduction but hearing is normal by bone conduction, the hearing loss is conductive in nature. Likewise, if the child evidences hearing loss of equal magnitude by air and bone conduction, the hearing loss is sensorineural (Figure 11.9).

Assessing Middle-Ear Function

To evaluate objectively the function of the middle-ear system, immittance measures (assessing the resistance and compliance of the system) are used. Any significant change to these characteristics of the middle-ear system can affect transmission of sound energy to the cochlea (Page et al., 1995). Immittance tests include tympanometry and acoustic reflex measures. Tympanometry assesses middle-ear pressure, tympanic membrane compliance, mobility of the ossicles, and eustachian tube function. Acoustic reflex measurements assess the contraction of the muscle tendon attached to the head of the stapes when a very loud sound enters the cochlea. In tym-

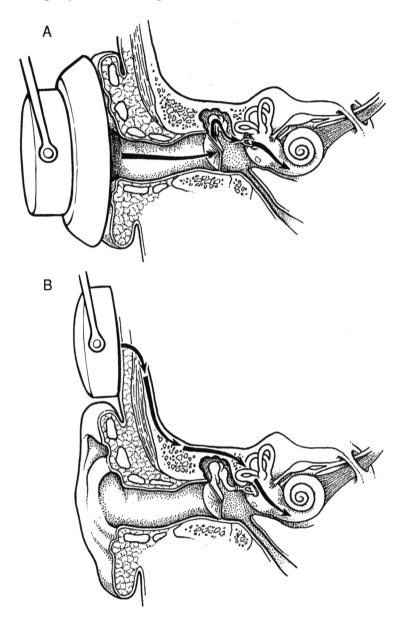

Figure 11.8.   Approaches to testing air and mastoid bone conduction of sound. A) In air conduction, the sound comes through the ear canal and middle ear to reach the inner ear. B) In bone conduction, the sound bypasses the external and middle ear and for the most part comes directly to the inner ear.

panometry, an ear probe presenting a steady tone is placed in the ear canal. Varying amounts of air pressure (positive, negative, or atmospheric) are sent through the probe to the eardrum. A microphone in the probe measures intensity differences of the tone as the air pressure changes. The air pressure–intensity relationships are plotted graphically and can show normal function in the middle-ear system or various problems within it (Figure 11.10). Acoustic reflex measurements provide an assessment of the functional integrity of the afferent auditory and efferent facial nerves (Hall & Baer, 1993).

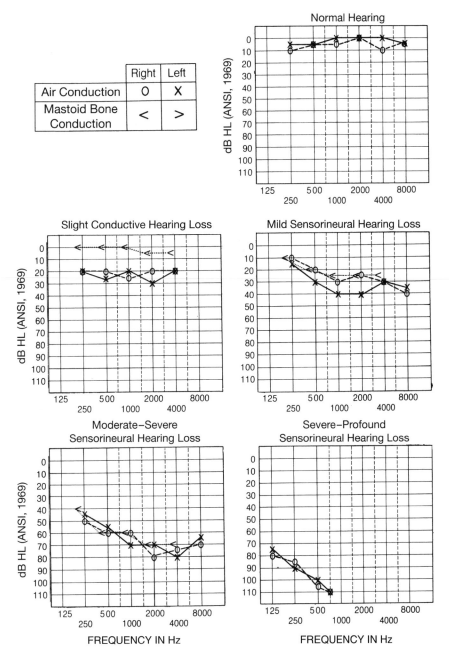

Figure 11.9. Audiograms showing normal hearing and various degrees of hearing loss. Note that in all cases shown, both ears are equally affected. In a conductive hearing loss, bone conduction is found to be better than air conduction because it bypasses the external and the middle ear where the problem exists. In sensorineural hearing loss, bone and air conduction produce similar results because the problem is within the inner ear and/or auditory nerve. The range of hearing loss is as follows: slight, 15–25 dB (decibels) HL (hearing level); mild, 25–30 dB; moderate, 30–50 dB; severe, 50–70 dB; profound, 71 dB HL and greater. (*Key:* ANSI, American National Standards Institute; Hz, hertz.) (Courtesy of Brad Friedrich, Ph.D.)

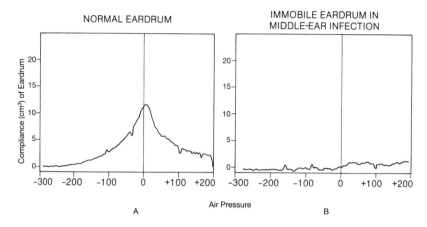

Figure 11.10. Tympanogram. The zero point represents atmospheric air pressure. The positive and negative numbers indicate that positive or negative pressures (relative to atmospheric pressure) have been applied to the eardrum. The compliance values are determined by the intensity of the probe tone at the various pressures and are influenced by the presence or absence of middle-ear pathology. A) A normal tent-shaped tympanogram. B) During otitis media (middle-ear infection), a flattened function may be obtained. (*Key:* cm³, cubic centimeters.) (Courtesy of Brad Friedrich, Ph.D.)

Assessing Cortical Function

In order to assess how well the brain receives auditory messages and interprets or retains what is heard, complex psycholinguistic tests are used (Martin et al., 1994). These address central auditory processing disorders, which are most often diagnosed in older children (i.e., older than 7 years of age) and adults (for whom test norms exist) with learning disabilities (see Chapter 22) or traumatic brain injury (see Chapter 26). Children with hearing impairments should not be administered these psycholinguistic tests, as the tests themselves degrade the incoming auditory signals. It would be impossible to determine whether a poor score on a specific test was the result of a true central auditory processing disorder or a combination of degradation of the incoming signal by the test procedure and the individual's own hearing loss.

Degrees of Hearing Loss

In general, the degree of hearing loss is meant to predict the difficulty the child will have in understanding speech through hearing alone and, therefore, in acquiring language and information through hearing. Typically, many believe that the more severe the bilateral hearing loss, the more the individual is apt to rely on vision for receiving information; the less severe the loss, the more effective amplification is likely to be. However, these are generalizations; many individuals with hearing loss are exceptions. Many variables other than the degree of hearing loss affect a child's acquisition of language and educational progress. These include age of onset, frequency configuration of the hearing loss, speech discrimination, general intelligence, and family support, among others. It is therefore not possible to state definitively the educational and therapeutic interventions appropriate for all children evidencing a specific degree of hearing loss.

Degree of hearing loss is categorized from slight to profound (Chan, 1994). A slight loss ranges from 15 to 25 dB HL (at 500–2,000 Hz); a mild loss, from 25 to 30 dB HL; a moderate loss, from 30 to 50 dB HL; a severe loss, from 50 to 70 dB HL; and a profound loss, 71 dB HL and greater (Northern & Downs, 2002). Although most often described in one of these categories, the degree of hearing loss can be better understood as a continuum. Albeit convenient, generalizations of ranges of hearing levels often result in misperceptions of the consequences of the loss. For example, a so-called mild bilateral hearing loss has potentially serious implications for the language and emotional development of a preverbal child, whereas a similar loss in an adolescent may have less of an impact (Crandell, 1993). A description of the functional impact of the hearing loss is the best measure of the degree of hearing loss for a specific child and should accompany any interpretation of audiometric testing.

Although not completely accurate, the degree of hearing loss frequently is determined by measuring and averaging the minimum response levels at three different frequencies (500 Hz, 1,000 Hz, and 2,000 Hz). A slight loss is usually associated with a middle-ear infection and typically has no significant effect on development, especially if the loss is transitory. The child may have difficulty, however, hearing faint or distant speech, missing up to 10% of speech when the teacher is at a distance of greater than 3 feet or when the classroom is noisy (Anderson & Matkin, 1991). Some clinicians believe that intermittent or recurrent slight hearing loss can be more confusing to a child than a consistent loss to which the child most often can accommodate. A slight loss should be monitored, and if there is evidence of problems in school or in social interactions, a hearing aid or personal FM amplification system may be necessary. At the minimum, children with slight hearing loss should be seated in the front of the classroom and may need academic supports.

A mild hearing loss is commonly associated with chronic otitis media but can reflect sensorineural loss as well. A child with a mild bilateral loss typically has difficulty hearing distant sounds or soft speech, missing 25%–40% of speech at typical conversational loudness. The child has difficulty perceiving the unvoiced consonants /s/, /p/, /t/, /k/, /th/ as in *thin*, /f/, and /sh/, which are soft, high-frequency sounds. As a result, the child may miss some of the content of class and home discussions and confuse forms of language that depend on these sounds (e.g., plurals, possessives). In addition, if there is a significant loss in the low frequencies, the child may have difficulty discriminating differing tones and the stress patterns of speech. Hearing aid use is often a consideration for a child with a mild loss in each ear.

A child with a moderate bilateral hearing loss begins to be aware of sounds starting at the level of average conversational speech. This amount of loss affects the ability to hear even loud conversation without intervention. In the absence of amplification, a child with a severe loss in both ears misses almost all conversation. Nonetheless, no assumptions can be made about the vocabulary, speech production, or voice quality of children with these degrees of hearing loss. Learning difficulties often result, however, from the significantly reduced auditory input associated with a moderate or severe hearing loss. Academic supports, hearing aids and classroom amplification, speech-language therapy, tutoring, and possibly special education services (see Chapter 30) should be considered based on the needs of the individual child.

Functionally, a child with a profound bilateral hearing loss may hear close, loud environmental sounds without amplification but not speech of typical conversational volume. Even with amplification, certain consonant sounds are likely to be missed. If the loss occurs before 2 years of age, language and speech may not develop spontaneously unless identification/intervention is begun prior to 6 months (Yoshinaga-Itano et al., 1998).

A child with a profound loss may react to very loud sounds, but aided hearing is essential for contact with the auditory world. The child with this extent of hearing loss has little awareness of tonal patterns; although amplification may help the child to distinguish rhythm, accent, and patterns of speech and to recognize environmental sounds, he or she may not comprehend speech without visual input (e.g., sign language, cued speech).

Spoken language is not the sole language option available to children with profound hearing impairments and their families. Visual communication strategies, including but not limited to sign language and cued speech, can be very important to individuals with significant hearing loss. Signed languages are accessible to the child with a hearing impairment, and many families opt to raise their child in a signing environment to foster the development of language with or in the absence of strong speech or speechreading skills. The need for visual communication is not limited to children with profound deafness. Some children with severe losses have enough difficulty in receiving and processing information auditorily that they benefit from visual communication as well.

TREATMENT OF MIDDLE-EAR DISEASE

If hearing is tested during a middle-ear infection (acute otitis media), a mild or moderate conductive hearing loss may be found. If the infection is chronic, occurring 6 or more times in 12 months, and is accompanied by hearing loss, this loss may affect speech and language development in a preschooler and scholastic achievement in a school-age child. An ordinary middle-ear infection usually clears up within a week or two. If the infection persists or recurs often, however, it may cause a sensorineural component to the hearing loss. This loss may be of a mixed type; that is, it may comprise a conductive loss caused by middle-ear conditions and a sensorineural loss caused by damage to the organ of Corti from bacterial toxins (Brookhouser, Worthington, & Kelly, 1993). Therefore, aggressive medical treatment and follow-up of middle-ear infections, especially of the chronic type, are now standard practice and involve the use of an antibiotic, usually amoxicillin or ampicillin, for 1 week. Although decongestants have been used in the past, experimental studies indicate that they make little difference in the duration or outcome of a middle-ear infection and are no longer recommended (Bluestone & Klein, 1995). Clinical improvement generally occurs in 48–72 hours, but the ears should be rechecked in 1–2 weeks to make certain that the fluid is gone. Children with a history of chronic middle-ear problems may also need their hearing checked after a course of treatment.

Following otitis media, monitoring for less common complications such as the formation of a **cholesteatoma** or the development of **mastoiditis** should occur. A cholesteatoma can develop during chronic otitis media in which severe retraction or perforation of the tympanic membrane has occurred (Potsic et al., 1995). Under these conditions, skin tissue lining the ear canal can migrate through the perforated eardrum into the middle ear, forming a mass. If not surgically removed, this cholesteatoma can destroy the ossicles, erode the temporal bone, or invade the meninges.

Mastoiditis involves the extension of middle-ear infection into the mastoid air cells of the temporal bone, which contains the cochlea. It can lead to a permanent sensorineural hearing loss by damaging the cochlea. Treatment involves antibiotics and if those are unsuccessful, surgical drainage of the abscessed mastoid air cells. Although a major cause of hearing loss in the pre-antibiotic era (i.e., before 1950), mastoiditis is now very uncommon in the United States.

These complications point to the importance of aggressive treatment and follow-up of middle-ear disease. If the infection is recurrent or persistent, it often must be treated with a 1- to 2-month course of antibiotics. This is particularly true if the first infection occurred before 6 months of age, if there have been three episodes of otitis media within a 6-month period, or if the child has had fluid in the middle ear for at least 3 months.

Surgical Management of Middle-Ear Disease

If antibiotics are not effective in treating persistent fluid in the middle ear (chronic otitis media), an otolaryngology (ear, nose, and throat) surgeon may need to perform a myringotomy, a minor surgical procedure in which an incision is made in the eardrum and the fluid is suctioned from the middle-ear system. The surgeon may also insert a pressure-equalization tube in the incision (Figure 11.11). This tube serves in place of the often malfunctioning eustachian tube, equalizing the pressure between the middle ear and the ear canal, permitting clean air to enter the middle-ear space helping its mucous tissue lining to rebound, and allowing the fluid in the middle-ear cavity to drain. A tube will generally remain in the eardrum for at least 6 months, after which time it usually falls out and the eardrum closes over the incision. Recent evidence indicates that immediate insertion of tubes in a group of children younger than age 3 compared with tube placement up to 9 months later in another group in the same age range did not improve outcomes at age 3 on measures of communicative abilities (Paradise et al., 2001). However, children age 4 and older with chronic otitis media requiring tube placement can show subsequent speech and language problems (Gravel & Wallace, 1992). These findings may reflect children with longer periods of chronic otitis media and possible greater hearing loss. The use of tubes has significantly reduced the risk of permanent hearing loss in children with chronic otitis media (Briggs & Luxford, 1994). There is also some evidence that removal of the adenoids (but not the tonsils) decreases the occurrence of recurrent middle-ear infections in children who have enlarged adenoids (Bluestone & Klein, 1995). Therefore, the procedures of myringo-

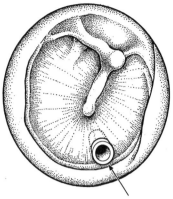

pressure-equalization tube

Figure 11.11. The procedure of myringotomy and tube placement involves the surgical incision of the tympanic membrane. The effusion is withdrawn, and a plastic tube is then inserted through the opening to permit ongoing drainage of fluid and equilibration of air pressure.

tomy and pressure-equalization tube placement may be combined with an adenoidectomy. These surgery procedures, often done in the morning with the patient discharged later in the day, require general anesthesia; complications are rare but include infection and bleeding.

INTERVENTION FOR HEARING LOSS

The diagnosis of permanent hearing impairment in an infant or child can have a profound psychological impact on the family (Gregory, 1995). Yet, it is during this diagnostic period that parents must make treatment decisions that will affect the life and the language of the child and family. Successful passage through this stage requires the coping mechanisms of the immediate and extended family, the child's adaptability, and especially nonjudgmental and knowledgeable professional support.

Parents need to make informed decisions by being presented with substantial information that can come from their child's pediatrician, other health care providers, organizations concerned with hearing loss, other parents of children with hearing impairment, and their local school system. Parents are often upset about their child's newly identified hearing loss during and especially following the diagnostic period. However, they want complete information even though they may not have a frame of reference yet to understand it all (Davis, 1999). They also need "anytime" access to caring professionals (e.g., physicians, audiologists, educators) who are responsible for their child's evaluation, treatment, and intervention/education. Having often-repeated questions answered provides parents with a comfort level of knowledge and support, allows them to make informed decisions, and enables them to focus their energies in positive directions. Their anxiety and stress can be abated greatly within this framework of information and decision making (Luterman & Kurtzer-White, 1999).

Professionals' views about hearing loss often affect the information, treatment options, and recommendations presented to parents (Densham, 1995). When a child has a loss ranging from mild to severe, the language and speech choices will focus on a variety of aural/oral intervention methodologies. When a child has a profound loss (i.e., is deaf), however, his or her family will want to learn about the positions of both the aural/oral and Deaf communities. A bitter controversy has existed since the mid-1800s about the recommended approach for communication with and education of deaf infants and children. There continues to exist a heated debate among proponents of oralism, who emphasize the development of speech, speechreading, and the use of residual hearing, and advocates for the use of visually accessible forms of communication including manual sign language and total communication (use of sign language and speech). Proponents of the oral/aural approach argue that access to sign language will limit a child's comfort and presence in the "hearing world" and thereby lessen the likelihood that the child will learn to speak and later integrate into that world. Supporters of manual communication argue that sign language allows the child access to communication and that it aids in the development of meaningful language at the earliest possible age. Those advocating total communication believe that teaching and using spoken language and sign language simultaneously with deaf infants, toddlers, and children supports the learning of both symbol systems and affords the opportunity for early language learning as well as eventual access to the language/speech of the hearing world. Spoken language, a key component of preschool curricula, is closely aligned with the development of preliteracy skills in children younger than 3 years (van Kleek, 1998). Studies of the phonological development of children with hearing impairments have generally found that these children develop the same phonological rules as hearing children (Kuder, 1997). Some argue, however, that total communication teaching is more often predominantly sign language without accompanying spoken language and that it is too difficult for a child with a profound hearing loss to learn several language systems at the same time.

Parents often encounter ardent proponents of one of these positions and are further polarized by endorsements of specific interventions. The intensity of the argument and the lack of scientific basis for specific recommendations often made to parents have impeded the objective examination of options, obstacles, and outcomes (Rushmer, 1994).

Early Intervention

Once the diagnosis of hearing impairment has been made, the infant or child should be referred for assessment in a multidisciplinary, comprehensive early intervention program (Moore-Brown & Montgomery, 2001; O'Hare, Grigor, & Cowan, 1993; see Chapter 29). Guidelines for early intervention have been reauthorized in Part C of the Individuals with Disabilities Education Act (IDEA) Amendments of 1997 (PL 105-17) (formerly Part H). The original legislation (the Education for All Handicapped Children Act of 1975, PL 94-142) addressed the school-age population, and the Education of the Handicapped Act Amendments of 1986 (PL 99-457) added children birth to age 5. Hearing loss has been one of the categories listed in the law since its inception (Brannen et al., 2000). Following the diagnosis, parents need support in resolving possible conflicting expert opinions about which language-learning system their child should undertake. Regardless of the language approach, the goals for successful intervention include family adaptation to and acceptance of the child's special communication needs and the provision of a linguistically accessible home and school environment that enhances the child's self-esteem (Ramkalawan & Davis, 1992). Optimally, programs should be flexible in their orientation and include family supports and integration with community services. Parent education materials, support groups, and national information centers are now available to assist parents in selecting an appropriate intervention site and a language acquisition strategy.

The regulations for IDEA '97 (Assistance to States for the Education of Children with Disabilities, 2001) have strengthened the role of parents and expanded the opportunities for parents and public agency staff to work in partnership at the state and local level. According to Brannen et al., the regulations also require that individualized education program (IEP) teams consider the following for a child who is deaf or hard of hearing:

The language and communication needs, opportunities for direct communications with peers and professional personnel in the child's language and communication mode, academic level and full range of needs, including opportunities for direct instruction in the child's language and communication mode; and whether the child needs assistive technology devices and services (Brannen et al., 2000, Appendix A, p. 20)

Lastly, the student should be present (when possible), and the parents must participate when decisions about transition services are made (Moore-Brown & Montgomery, 2001).

Amplification

Amplification (e.g., hearing aids, assistive listening devices) is an important part of the services required by the child with hearing loss (Alpiner & McCarthy, 1993; McCracken & Bamford, 1995). Hearing aids can be used by children of any age and should be fitted as soon as a persistent or a permanent hearing loss has been identified, even if all of the information about the hearing loss is not yet available. Assistive listening devices, such as FM systems, are often used in conjunction with hearing aids in difficult listening situations, such as the classroom (Madell, 1992). Recent technological advances, however, have produced all-in-one hearing aid–FM combinations that can be used as the primary amplification option. Audiologists find these systems particularly useful in fitting infants recently identified with hearing losses. A parent can wear a lapel microphone and thus speak to the infant from anywhere in the room. This situation provides the most favorable signal-to-noise ratio for the infant and most important, provides him or her with the constant vocal stimulation often found between parents and their awake infant.

Audiologists are responsible for the appropriate fitting of amplification devices. The selection and utilization of amplification for children, particularly preverbal children, differs significantly from the procedures used in adult fittings (Palmer, 1994). First, the selection of hearing aids for a child is an ongoing process that extends far beyond the identification of hearing loss and the initial fitting of an amplification device. Second, the settings of the system are subject to change as new information regarding the hearing loss and responses to amplification are obtained by frequent audiological evaluations of the young child. Moreover, the degree of hearing loss is not the only consideration in determining a child's candidacy for amplification. Profiles of the child's existing speech and language skills, intellectual ability, commonly encountered listening situations, and school performance are all important factors in determining the appropriateness of hearing aid use and its specific fitting.

Hearing aids have three components: a microphone that changes the acoustic signal into electrical energy, one or more amplifiers that increase the intensity of the electrical signal, and a receiver that converts the electrical signal back to an amplified acoustical signal. The amplified sound is channeled into the ear canal through an earmold. The hearing aid is powered by a battery, and the loudness of the aid can be adjusted by the volume control. Children's hearing aids also should permit direct audio input to allow coupling to an FM system, should have tamper-resistant battery compartments to prevent swallowing of the batteries, and should have a cover for the volume dial to prevent inadvertent changing of the setting.

Hearing aids can be adjusted to the specific characteristics of a hearing loss, providing amplification to the frequency region where the hearing loss exists. Four categories of hearing aids exist: behind-the-ear (BTE) aids, in-the-ear (ITE) aids, body aids, and bone conduction aids.

BTE hearing aids (Figure 11.12), because of their casing size, can accommodate more circuitry and controls, allowing for more fitting flexibility than an ITE hearing aid permits. This flexibility is especially important if audiometric information is incomplete or if the possibility of progressive hearing loss exists; that is, adjustments in the child's hearing aid can be made more easily and rapidly. The relatively recent development of programmable hearing aids has permitted the user to modify the aid's settings based on listening environments. Such devices

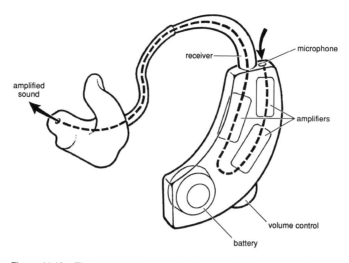

Figure 11.12. The components of a behind-the-ear (BTE) hearing aid. The aid consists of a microphone, a battery power supply, an amplifier, and a receiver that projects the amplified sound through the earmold into the ear canal.

may be beneficial to older children and adolescents who might otherwise reject standard aids in certain situations.

The microphone on an ITE hearing aid benefits from its location relative to the pinna (i.e., the auricle) that directs sound toward the microphone. As the child grows and ear canal sizes change, however, the aid will need to be recased at a cost. In addition, the relatively smaller size of an ITE hearing aid limits the controls that can be built in and therefore the flexibility of the aid. The advantage of ITE hearing aids is primarily cosmetic. These aids are used in older children and adolescents who are likely to reject the more visible hearing aids and who are less likely to misplace or lose the device.

Body hearing aids are less frequently used now than in the past. Initially, body aids provided more power with less acoustical feedback than BTE hearing aids. This circumstance is no longer usual due to improved electronic and acoustic modifications with BTE hearing aids. The chest-level placement of the microphone in a body aid is also a disadvantage. The child's body can act as a baffle against receiving sound, and clothing may rub on the microphone, causing interference. Body hearing aids are the least cosmetically appealing of the four types, and noncompliance is a significant factor with older children.

Bone conduction hearing aids can be used with children who have long-term conductive hearing loss or who have chronic middle-ear drainage into the external ear canal. The latter condition would prevent use of an ITE hearing aid or an earmold with a BTE instrument. The receiver of the bone conduction hearing aid is actually a vibrator approximately 1 inch in size. The vibrator is attached to a headband that holds it in place, usually on the mastoid. The speech signal is then sent via bone conduction to the cochlea, in much the same way that bone conduction testing is performed.

Binaural fittings are preferred with children, unless there are contraindications to fitting both ears such as structural abnormalities or the absence of any usable hearing in an ear. In cases of asymmetrical hearing loss in adults, binaural amplification has on occasion been shown to improve speech understanding in the poorer ear. The same phenomenon is likely to be true in children. Close monitoring of the child's use of binaural amplification must be followed in cases of significant asymmetry.

Although hearing aids are valuable tools, it is important to understand that they do not correct hearing loss in the same way that glasses correct vision loss. Hearing aids simply make sounds louder; they do not make sounds clearer, nor do they selectively amplify speech or other necessary sounds. Therefore, when sensorineural hearing loss is present, the child may have difficulty understanding what is said, even when the hearing aids provide sounds that are comfortably loud. The individual and family must be counseled regarding realistic expectations from amplification, as well as the importance of speech and language therapy and the need to modify the child's listening environment. Even with technological advances, some children derive limited auditory benefit or report disturbing background noise when using hearing aids. In such instances, careful assessment of hearing aids and circumstances is necessary to determine whether continued hearing aid use would be beneficial.

Surgical Interventions for Sensorineural Hearing Loss

Cochlear implantation is an elective surgical procedure approved by the Food and Drug Administration in 1990 for use in children who are deaf and do not benefit from amplification (Miyamoto, 1995; NIH Consensus Development Panel, 1995; Young, 1994). A cochlear implant is a prosthetic device that electrically stimulates the cochlea via an electrode array surgically implanted in the inner ear. The reasoning behind the use of a cochlear implant is that many auditory nerve fibers remain functional even when the hair cells in the cochlea are damaged or reduced in number.

The device provides auditory information via four components: a microphone, a signal processor that electronically encodes incoming sounds, a receiver, and the implanted electrodes (Figure 11.13). The sound is received by the microphone, converted into its electrical equivalent, and sent by the transmitter to the signal processor. The processor transforms the signal into individually programmed electrical information. This information is sent to the implanted receiver and then through the electrodes that have been surgically threaded into the cochlea. These electrodes can stimulate nerve fibers at different locations along the cochlea. Various multichannel multiple electrode implant devices are currently available that provide different patterns of electrode excitation. The purpose of each device, of course, is to provide the listener with as many speech feature cues as possible.

The information perceived by a child using a cochlear implant does not imitate normal hearing (Manrique et al., 1995). Use of cochlear implants, however, does improve detection of environmental and speech sounds as well as speech patterns, recognition, and production (Coerts & Mills, 1995). A number of variables influence the progress and improvement children achieve with a cochlear implant. Some of these are the device, processing strategies, surviving neurons, age at implantation, length of deafness, mode of communication, educational environment, medical/surgical issues, training, additional disabilities, and family commitment (Osberger, Maso, & Sam, 1993; Robbins et al., 1995; Waltzman & Shapiro, 1999). Large individual differences in postimplant success are found among prelingually deaf children that could not be predicted from preimplant information (Pisoni, 2000; Pisoni et al., 1997). Nevertheless, reviews have summarized significant overall improvement in language development and speech production by children with profound hearing losses using multichannel cochlear implants (Robbins, 2000; Svirsky & Chin, 2000; Waltzman & Cohen, 2000).

Parents, other family members, and caregivers are core participants in the process of a child's cochlear implant consideration, selection, and postimplant intervention regimen. These individuals need to be fully informed about a number of significant issues when a child is being considered for an implant. Parents' understanding of these issues will help them make informed decisions, as well as recognize the important commitments they will have to make if their child receives the implant (Waltzman & Shapiro, 1999). Further advances in cochlear implant technology are anticipated.

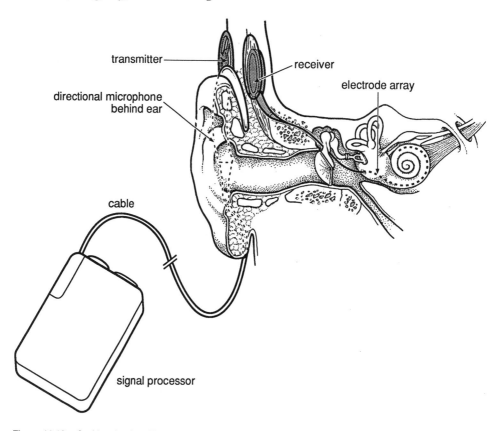

Figure 11.13.   Cochlear implant. The device has four components: a microphone to capture sound, a signal processor that electronically encodes the incoming sounds, a receiver, and the electrodes that have been surgically threaded through the cochlea. The electrodes stimulate nerve fibers along the cochlea, and the child perceives sound.

Communication and Education

Communication and education are inextricably linked for the child with a hearing impairment because educational curricula are language based (Volterra et al., 1995). Without adequate language skills, a child with a hearing impairment is at a functional disadvantage in all academic arenas. The goal of the speech-language pathologist, the educational audiologist, and the educator should be the facilitation of optimal communication, utilizing whatever is most beneficial for the individual child based on his or her cognitive, attentional, and sensory profile and other related variables, including family preferences (Kelly, Kelly, & Jones, 1993). The two factors most predictive of the educational achievement of persons with deafness are language development and educational opportunities (Kuder, 1997).

To improve communication for a child with hearing loss, education and intervention should focus on developing listening skills and all aspects of language, including syntax and grammar, increasing speech or sign language production, and expanding vocabulary. The educational achievement of students with deafness is weakest in the areas of reading and writing (Kuder, 1997). Many believe that literacy experiences should be an intrinsic component of education and intervention and that preliteracy experiences must begin with infants/toddlers (Moore-Brown & Montgomery, 2001). The roles of different interventionists are variable and dependent on the context of the service provision. Some speech-language pathologists, teachers of children with hearing loss, and educational audiologists, for example, work in the classroom along with a teacher or special educator; some work in conjunction with preschool programs for children with hearing loss; and still others work as independent contractors either in school-linked consultations or as providers of education/therapy sessions at the homes of infants/toddlers. The variety of available services is likely dependent on the child's age, his or her degree of hearing and communication impairment, the local and regional educational philosophy, and other factors such as the family's financial resources (Kvam, 1993). Collaborative interventions are the most supportive for families (ASHA, 1990).

Speech-language pathology service models often incorporate a specific type of communication modality, according to the preference of the clinician, center, school, or family. Ideally, parents and professionals should review the child's development and arrive at a consensus regarding a common modality for all environments to support the achievement of the child's potential. Different language-learning options include oralism, cued speech, an English-based sign system, American Sign Language (ASL), total communication, and the bilingual-bicultural approach (discussed later; Dolman, 1992).

Most hearing children enter public school with the ability to process and integrate spoken information. They have mastered sentence patterns; have a fairly extensive vocabulary; and are ready to read, write, and compute. Children with a hearing impairment have the same ability to learn, and they must experience a linguistically rich environment in order to learn. It is the responsibility of the school to provide such an environment for the child and sufficient information for the caregivers to also provide a linguistically rich home environment (California Department of Education, 2000; Schwartz, 1996).

Infants, toddlers, and preschool children with all degrees of hearing loss may have a variety of possible service delivery systems available to them in most urban, suburban, and exurban communities. These services can range from home visits by interventionists, to provision of services in a special preschool, to enrollment in a regular preschool with education/therapy services brought to the child in that environment. With the advent of universal newborn hearing screening in birthing hospitals, parents of infants determined to have hearing loss may immediately seek assistance from their school district (Moore-Brown & Montgomery, 2001).

In general, children of school age with mild and moderate to severe hearing losses will be enrolled in general education classrooms in community schools. Consultation and collaboration services from speech-language pathologists, educational audiologists, teachers of children with hearing loss and other interventionists are brought to the child's classroom. On occasion, the child may leave the general education classroom for individual or small group sessions and at times may spend part of a day in a special class for intensive small group instruction. Aural/oral language teaching is usually employed as the mode of communication in these learning environments, coupled with the child's use of individually worn hearing aids and/or a classroom FM amplification system.

An infant-toddler program should provide service coordination by a knowledgeable professional; appropriate assessment in all areas of development, design of an individual family service plan (see Chapter 29), assistance with parent–child interactions, modeling and demonstration of speech and language experiences, information to help families decide on communication modes and educational methods, emotional support, direct instruction to the child (if warranted), and transition services beginning at $2\frac{1}{2}$ years of age.

A well-defined preschool program is characterized by a communication-based, developmentally appropriate preschool curriculum, comprehensive services for children 3–5 years of age, a multidisciplinary team approach, program options, parental training and support, interagency cooperation, involvement of deaf or hearing impaired role models, in-service training for professionals and support personnel, and transition planning when the child reaches age 5 or 6 for admission to school.

School-age children with severe to profound hearing losses may follow the same educational format just described, but there is likely to be some or significant variations in public school environments. Young school-age children with this degree of loss may spend most school days in a special classroom taught by a teacher of children with hearing loss, with other service providers coming into the classroom or taking a child or children out for individualized instruction. This self-contained class may mix with children without hearing losses for some academic subjects or for other school activities. Parents need to be alert to their children's need to have equal access to the core curriculum expected for the grade level. The children grouped in a specific classroom are usually taught exclusively by a specific language method, such as aural-oral, a sign system, or total communication, depending upon the method selected by their parents. As children with all degrees of hearing loss (mild to profound) reach middle school age, they can be found more often in general education classes with hearing children and receiving various types of in-class support, including note-takers and sign interpreters. Experience with same-age peers is critical for academic and social reasons. Other school options for children with severe to profound hearing loss include private schools as well as state schools for the deaf. Deaf and hearing impaired students in elementary and secondary school programs should be provided instruction in the local school district's adopted core curriculum (Assistance to States, 2001; Moore-Brown & Montgomery, 2001). In addition, the students should receive instruction in specialized curriculum areas such as Deaf studies; use of assistive technology, including TTY/telecommunications devices; ASL; speech and speech reading; auditory training; social skills; and career and vocational education. Content and performance standards in each of these areas must be developed by the education staff. Modifications and accommodations for each curricular area should be addressed at the IEP meetings at least yearly. It is important that the students have the full range of activities, including after-class and extracurricular options with appropriate accommodations (e.g., sign language interpreters; Assistance to States, 2001). Transition from high school to adult life is also a responsibility of the school system. For students who are deaf or hearing impaired, transition planning is the lifeline to adulthood. (See Chapter 30 for more information on transition planning.)

Language-Learning Options

Various language-learning methods are available to children with hearing loss. Aural/oral educational methods emphasize the teaching of listening skills, speechreading, and speech articulation. Many clinicians and educators who utilize these approaches believe that sign language use will inhibit speech development. Some oral approaches include cued speech, which utilizes a limited number of hand shapes to express phonetic sounds with spoken language; and unimodal speech, which emphasizes the training of residual hearing without reliance on visual stimuli.

English-oriented sign systems are intended to facilitate the learning of English by combining ASL vocabulary, coined signs, and fingerspelling (letter-for-letter spelling of whole words) in an attempt to represent English sentence structure. Proponents of total communication incorporate aural/oral and manual communication modes such as listening skills, speechreading, English-oriented signing or ASL, gesture/mime, and anything that facilitates the child's comprehension of what is spoken and/or signed. Advocates of the bilingual-bicultural approach propose that children must first be immersed in ASL so that they have full access to and can acquire the meaningful use of a language before they can attain a less available (spoken) language (Wood, 1992). ASL has been shown to have its own unique grammatical patterns and is structurally different from a spoken language, as it is visually received and spatially expressed. Furthermore, ASL is not English in any way; it is a different language within a different culture (Gallimore & Woodruff, 1996). Establishing ASL as the first language is almost impossible if the child has hearing parents, unless they turn over the care of their child to a surrogate deaf parent (Seal, 1997). If the infant is born into a Deaf culture, however, then he or she could learn spoken English as a second language in late elementary or middle school. If this bilingual-bicultural approach follows the same principles as other second language learning, then the higher the linguistic development in the first language, the better the acquisition of the second language (Shiff-Myers, 1992). There are, however, no efficacy studies of these bilingual models for deaf or hearing impaired students at this time (Seal, 1997).

Remediation and education for a deaf child goes beyond amplification and speech-language therapy. Deafness is an inability to hear, not an inability to speak or to learn. Not only does a child who is unable to hear fail to develop speech and spoken language in a typical fashion, but he or she also misses interpersonal interactions and world knowledge that is transmitted auditorily. Educators and interventionists, therefore, must address this larger communication issue and reduce the information gaps that exist.

Section 504 of the Rehabilitation Act of 1973 (PL 93-112; see Chapter 30) requires accommodations for all people with disabilities. More specifically, however, IDEA '97 mandates early intervention and a free appropriate public education for all infants and children who have hearing impairments. The public school system is responsible for all programs, services, and safeguards (Moore-Brown & Montgomery, 2001). Mandated services include but are not limited to hearing assessment, hearing aid fittings, speech-language therapy, and special education. Services should begin shortly after the diagnostic assessment, with home visits by early intervention specialists as well as center-based services with other families and children. Education includes both specialized instruction and related services necessary for the student to benefit from the instruction; therefore, ongoing in-school intervention sessions (e.g., speech-language therapy, occupational therapy) and audiology services are part of the school day. Perhaps the most important consideration is the matter of "appropriateness," or what is often referred to as the *least restrictive environment* for the child with a hearing impairment. Although some view inclusion with hearing children as the least restrictive alternative for a deaf child, for example, others maintain that a deaf residential or day school is in fact less restrictive than a setting in which deaf students face a constant communicative challenge in interaction with hearing students both in the classroom and in extracurricular activities. Advocates of inclusive programs suggest that decisions be made using multiple factors (Seal, 1997). It is most important in this matter to consider the needs of each individual child for such decision making. Successful inclusion is dependent on many factors, including supportive administrators and teachers, the sharing of specialized knowledge, dynamic assessment of student progress from year to year, and a full spectrum of options so that different choices can be made as conditions change (Brannen et al., 2000; Montgomery, 1997; Seal, 1997; Schwartz, 1996).

Supportive Therapy

Hearing impairment exerts a tremendous influence on important aspects of child rearing (Cohen, 1994; Medwid & Weston, 1995). First, parents must learn how to communicate with their child who is hearing impaired beyond using the early nonverbal and prelinguistic modes (Densham, 1995). Frustration and discomfort may accompany efforts to communicate because of the limits of what can be expressed and understood. Without the availability of verbal explanations, parents of deaf children often find it difficult to establish early behavioral expectations; however, the same may not be so for parents of children with moderate to severe losses. In addition, the sense of self and self-esteem of a child who is deaf (and his or her family) is often deeply affected by perceptions and beliefs about hearing impairment that are held by family and community members (Hindley et al., 1994). Family dynamics often shift due to the increased need for parental involvement in the early intervention and ongoing treatment of the child who has a hearing impairment, mild or severe. Supporting the family in their adaptation to their child's hearing loss involves the use of multimodal therapies, including behavior management, supportive-expressive family therapy, and most important, the facilitation of family communication and dialogue (Greenberg & Kusche, 1993).

OUTCOME

A wide range of audiological, familial, linguistic, social, and environmental factors can affect speech development; English literacy; language competence; social development; and ultimately, educational outcome and career options. These factors include age of onset and severity of hearing loss, family response and resources, age of exposure to a language system, psychosocial supports, and the nature of other disabling or comorbid conditions (Schilling & DeJesus, 1993).

Formulating a prognosis for the child's ultimate language, educational, and psychosocial development based on any single variable, however, is not possible with the current level of knowledge. Instead, the focus should be on the early identification of hearing loss and the prompt initiation of individually tailored and carefully monitored education, habilitation, and rehabilitation efforts.

SUMMARY

Hearing loss can be temporary or permanent, conductive or sensorineural, congenital or acquired. It can affect one or both ears and may exist alone or with other disabilities. Regardless of the degree or the cause of the hearing loss, it is important for the professional working with children who have a hearing impairment to understand the anatomy and physiology of the hearing mechanism and the impact of the hearing loss on the perception and processing of spoken language.

Hearing loss in childhood offers a unique opportunity to witness adaptation to perceptual impairment and human resilience in the face of a disruption in communication channels. The child's and family's innate strengths, capacities, and vulnerabilities must be viewed within a larger social, linguistic, educational, cultural, and environmental context. Hearing impairment need not impede typical development, place an individual at a functional disadvantage, or alter ultimate outcome. Clinicians who wish to address the needs of the child with a hearing impairment must recognize and make recommendations based on the unique needs of the individual child and family.

REFERENCES

Adams, P.F., Hendershot, G.E., & Marano, M.A. (1999). Current estimates from the National Health Interview Survey, 1996. *Vital and Health Statistics, 10*(200), 93.

Alpiner, J.G., & McCarthy, P.A. (1993). *Rehabilitative audiology: Children and adults.* Philadelphia: Lippincott Williams & Wilkins.

American National Standards Institute (ANSI). (1969). *Specifications for audiometers* (ANSI S3.6–1969). New York: Author.

American Speech-Language-Hearing Association (ASHA). (1989). Audiologic screening of infants who are at risk for hearing impairment. *Asha, 31,* 89–92.

American Speech-Language-Hearing Association (ASHA). (1990). Roles of speech-language pathologists in service delivery to infants, toddlers, and their families. *Asha, 32* (Suppl. 2), 4.

Anderson, K.L., & Matkin, N.D. (1991). Hearing conservation in the public schools revisited. *Seminars in Hearing, 12,* 340–364.

Aran, J.M. (1995). Current perspectives on inner ear toxicity. *Otolaryngology—Head and Neck Surgery, 112,* 133–144.

Assistance to States for the Education of Children with Disabilities, 300 C.F.R. § 300 (2001).

Bale, J.F., Jr. (1992). Congenital infections and the nervous system. *Pediatric Clinics of North America, 39,* 669–690.

Bluestone, C.D., & Klein, J.O. (1995). *Otitis media in infants and children* (2nd ed.). Philadelphia: W.B. Saunders.

Bluestone, C.D., Stool, S.E., & Kenna, M.A. (1996). *Pediatric otolaryngology* (3rd ed.). Philadelphia: W.B. Saunders.

Brannen, S.J., Cooper, E.B., Dellegrotto, J.T., et al. (2000). *Developing educationally relevant IEPs: A technical assistance document for speech-language pathologists.* Rockville, MD: American Speech-Language-Hearing Association.

Brass, D., & Kemp, D.T. (1994). The objective assessment of transient evoked otoacoustic emission in neonates. *Ear and Hearing, 15,* 371–377.

Briggs, R.J., & Luxford, W.M. (1994). Correction of conductive hearing loss in children. *Otolaryngologic Clinics of North America, 27,* 607–620.

Brookhouser, P.E., Worthington, D.W., & Kelly, W.J. (1992). Noise-induced hearing loss in children. *Laryngoscope, 102,* 645–655.

Brookhouser, P.E., Worthington, D.W., & Kelly, W.J. (1993). Middle ear disease in young children with sensorineural hearing loss. *Laryngoscope, 103,* 371–378.

California Department of Education. (2000). *Guidelines for program standards for deaf and hard of hearing.* Sacramento: Author.

Champlin, C.A. (1996). Physiologic measures of auditory and vestibular function. In F. Martin & J.G. Clark (Eds.), *Hearing care for children.* Needham Heights, MA: Allyn & Bacon.

Chan, K.H. (1994). Sensorineural hearing loss in children: Classification and evaluation. *Otolaryngologic Clinics of North America, 27,* 473–486.

Coerts, J., & Mills, A. (1995). Spontaneous language development of young deaf children with a cochlear implant. *Annals of Otology, Rhinology, and Laryngology, 166*(Suppl.), 385–387.

Cohen, L.H. (1994). *Train go sorry: Inside a deaf world.* Boston: Houghton Mifflin.

Cohn, L.S., Kelley, P.M., Fowler, T.W., et al. (1999). Clinical studies of families with hearing loss attributable to mutations in the connexin 26 gene (GJB2/DFNB1). *Pediatrics, 103,* 546–550.

Coplan, J. (1987). Deafness: Ever heard of it? Delayed recognition of permanent hearing loss. *Pediatrics, 79,* 206–213.

Crandell, C.C. (1993). Speech recognition in noise by children with minimal degrees of sensorineural hearing loss. *Ear and Hearing, 14,* 210–216.

Davis, A. (1999). Paper presented at the annual convention of the American Speech-Language-Hearing Association, San Francisco.

Densham, J. (1995). *Deafness, children and the family: A guide to professional practice.* Brookfield, VT: Ashgate.

Dolman, D. (1992). Some concerns about using whole language approaches with deaf children. *American Annals of the Deaf, 137,* 278–282.

Education for All Handicapped Children Act of 1975, PL 94-142, 20 U.S.C. §§ 1400 *et seq.*

Education of the Handicapped Act Amendments of 1986, PL 99-457, 20 U.S.C. §§ 1400 *et seq.*

Finitzo, T., Albright, K., & O'Neal, J. (1998). The newborn with hearing loss: Detection in the nursery. *Pediatrics, 102,* 1452–1460.

Fortnum, H., & Davis, A. (1993). Hearing impairment in children after bacterial meningitis: Incidence and resource implications. *British Journal of Audiology, 27,* 43–52.

Fortnum, H., & Davis, A. (1997). Epidemiology of permanent child hood hearing impairment in Trent Region, 1985–1993. *British Journal of Audiology, 21,* 409–446.

Fowler, K.B., McCollister, F.P., Dahle, A.J., et al. (1997). Progressive and fluctuating sensorineural hearing loss in children with asymptomatic congenital cytomegalovirus infection. *The Journal of Pediatrics, 130,* 624–630.

Gallimore, L., & Woodruff, S. (1996). The bilingual-bicultural (bi-bi) approach: A professional point of view. In S. Schwartz (Ed.), *Choices in deafness* (2nd ed., pp. 89–116). Bethesda, MD: Woodbine House.

Gans, D., & Gans, K.D. (1993). Development of a hearing test protocol for profoundly involved multi-handicapped children. *Ear and Hearing, 14,* 128–140.

Glattke, T.J., Pafitis, I., Cummiskey, C., et al. (1995). Identification of hearing loss in children and young adults using measures of transient otoacoustic emission reproducibility. *American Journal of Audiology, 4,* 71–86.

Goldberg, D. (1996). Early intervention. In F. Martin & J.G. Clark (Eds.), *Hearing care for children.* Needham Heights, MA: Allyn & Bacon.

Gopnik, A., Meltzoff, A.H., & Kuhl, P.K. (1999). *The scientist in the crib: Minds, brains and how children learn.* New York: William Morrow & Co.

Gorga, M.P., Stover, L., Bergman, B.M., et al. (1995). The application of otoacoustic emissions in the assessment of developmentally delayed patients. *Scandinavian Audiology, 41*(Suppl.), 8–17.

Gorlin, R.L., Toriello, H.V., & Cohen, M.M., Jr. (1995). *Hereditary hearing loss and its syndromes.* New York: Oxford University Press.

Gravel, J. (1994). Auditory assessment of infants. *Seminars in Hearing, 15,* 100–113.

Gravel, J.S., & Traquina, D.N. (1992). Experience with the audiologic assessment of infants and toddlers. *International Journal of Pediatric Otorhinolaryngology, 23,* 59–71.

Gravel, J.S., & Wallace, I.F. (1992). Listening and language at 4 years of age: Effects of early otitis media. *Journal of Speech and Hearing Research, 35,* 588–595.

Greenberg, M.T., & Kusche, C.A. (1993). *Promoting social and emotional development in deaf children: The PATHS project.* Seattle: University of Washington Press.

Gregory, S. (1995). *Deaf children and their families.* New York: Cambridge University Press.

Hall, J.W., III, & Baer, J.E. (1993). Current concepts in hearing assessments of children and adults. *Comprehensive Therapy, 19,* 272–280.

Hanshaw, J.B. (1994). Congenital cytomegalovirus infection. *Pediatric Annals, 23,* 124–128.

Henderson, J.L., & Weiner, C.P. (1995). Congenital infection. *Current Opinion in Obstetrics and Gynecology, 7,* 130–134.

Herer, G.R. (2001, April). [Universal newborn hearing screening program outcomes for four years]. Unpublished data reported at the annual meeting of the California Speech-Language-Hearing Association, Monterey.

Herregard, E., Karjalainen, S., Martikainen, A., et al. (1995). Hearing loss at the age of 5 years of children born preterm: A matter of definition. *Acta Paediatrica, 84,* 1160–1164.

Hindley, P.A., Hill, P.D., McGuigan, S., et al. (1994). Psychiatric disorder in deaf and hearing impaired children and young people: A prevalence study. *Journal of Child Psychology and Psychiatry and Allied Disciplines, 35,* 917–934.

Individuals with Disabilities Education Act (IDEA) Amendments of 1997, PL105-17, 20 U.S.C. §§ 1400 *et seq.*

Johnson, C.D., Benson, P.V., & Seaton, J.B. (1997). *Educational audiology handbook.* San Diego: Singular Publishing Group.

Joint Committee on Infant Hearing. (1982). Position statement. *Asha, 24,* 1017–1018.

Joint Committee on Infant Hearing. (2000). Year 2000 position statement. *American Journal of Audiology, 9,* 9–29.

Kanne, T.J., Schaefer, L., & Perkins, J.A. (1999). Potential pitfalls of initiating a newborn hearing screening program. *Archives of Otolaryngology—Head and Neck Surgery, 125,* 28–32.

Kelly, D.P., Kelly, B.J., & Jones, M.L. (1993). Attention deficits in children and adolescents with hearing loss: A survey. *American Journal of Diseases of Children, 147,* 737–741.

Kessner, D.M., Snow, C.K., & Singer, J. (1974). *Assessment of medical care for children: Vol. 3. Contrasts in health status: An analysis of contrasting forms of delivery.* Washington, DC: National Academy Press.

Kuder, S.J. (1997). *Teaching students with language and communication disabilities.* Needham Heights, MA: Allyn & Bacon.

Kvaerner, K.J., & Arnesen, A.R. (1994). Hearing impairment in Oslo born children 1989–1991: Incidence, etiology, and diagnostic delay. *Scandinavian Audiology, 23,* 233–239.

Kvam, M.H. (1993). Hard-of-hearing pupils in ordinary schools: An analysis based on interviews with integrated hard-of-hearing pupils and their parents and teachers. *Scandinavian Audiology, 22*, 261–267.

Levi, H., Tell, L., & Feinwesser, M. (1993). Progressive hearing loss in hard-of-hearing children. *Audiology, 32*, 132–136.

Littman, T., Demmler, G., Williams, et al. (1995). Congenital asymptomatic cytomegalovirus infection and hearing loss. *Abstracts for the Association for Research in Otorhinolaryngology, 19*, 40.

Luterman, D., & Kurtzer-White, E. (1999). Identifying hearing loss: Parents' needs. *American Journal of Audiology, 8*, 13–18.

Madell, J.R. (1992). FM systems as primary amplification for children with profound hearing loss. *Ear and Hearing, 13*, 102–107.

Manrique, M., Paloma, V., Cervera-Paz, F.J., et al. (1995). Pitfalls in cochlear implant surgery in children. *Advances in Oto-Rhino-Laryngology, 50*, 45–50.

Martin, W.K., Schwegler, J.W., Gleeson, A.L., et al. (1994). New techniques of hearing assessment. *Otolaryngologic Clinics of North America, 27*, 487–510.

Mason, J.A., & Herrmann, K.R. (1998). Universal infant hearing screening by automated auditory brainstem response measurement. *Pediatrics, 101*, 221–228.

McClelland, R.J., Watson, D.R., Lawless, V., et al. (1992). Reliability and effectiveness of screening for hearing loss in high risk neonates. *British Medical Journal, 304*, 806–809.

McCormick, B. (1995). *The medical practitioner's guide to paediatric audiology.* New York: Cambridge University Press.

McCracken, W.M., & Bamford, J.M. (1995). Auditory prostheses for children with multiple handicaps. *Scandinavian Audiology, 41*(Suppl.), 51–60.

McKusick, V.A. (1998). *Mendelian inheritance in man: A catalog of human genes and genetic disorders* (12th ed.). Baltimore: The Johns Hopkins University Press.

Medwid, D.K., & Weston, D.C. (1995). *Kid-friendly parenting with deaf and hard of hearing children.* Washington, DC: Gallaudet University Press.

Meredith, R., Stephens, D., Hogan, S., et al. (1994). Screening for hearing loss in an at-risk neonatal population using evoked otoacoustic emissions. *Scandinavian Audiology, 23*, 187–193.

Miyamoto, R.T. (1995). Cochlear implants. *Otolaryngologic Clinics of North America, 28*, 287–294.

Montgomery, J.K. (1997) Inclusion in the secondary school. In L. Power-deFur & F.P. Orelove (Eds.), *Inclusive education: Practical implementation of the least restrictive environment* (pp. 181–192). Gaithersburg, MD: Aspen Publications.

Montgomery, J.K., & Fujikawa, S. (1992). Hearing thresholds of students in the second, eighth and twelfth grades. *Language, Speech, and Hearing Services in Schools, 23*, 61–63.

Moore, B.C.J. (1995). *Hearing.* San Diego: Academic Press.

Moore, J.M. (1995). Behavioural assessment procedures based on conditioned head-turn responses for auditory detection and discrimination with low-functioning children. *Scandinavian Audiology, 41*(Suppl.), 36–42.

Moore-Brown, B.J., & Montgomery, J.K. (2001). *Making a difference for America's children: Speech-language pathologists in public schools.* Eau Claire, WI: Thinking Publications.

Muntz, H.R. (1993). An overview of middle ear disease in cleft palate children. *Facial Plastic Surgery, 9*, 177–180.

National Institute on Deafness and Other Communication Disorders. (1997). *Recommendations of NIDCD Working Group on early identification of hearing impairment on acceptable protocols for use in state-wide universal newborn screening programs.* Bethesda, MD: NIDCD Clearinghouse.

National Institutes of Health (NIH). (1993). Early identification of hearing impairment in infants and young children: Conference statement. *International Journal of Pediatric Otorhinolaryngology, 27*, 215–227.

NIH Consensus Development Panel. (1995). Cochlear implants in adults and children. *Journal of the American Medical Association, 274*, 1955–1961.

Northern, J.L., & Downs, M.P. (2002). *Hearing in children* (5th ed.). Philadelphia: Lippincott Williams & Wilkins.

Nussinovitch, M., Volovitz, B., & Varsano, I. (1995). Complications of mumps requiring hospitalization in children. *European Journal of Pediatrics, 154*, 732–734.

O'Hare, A.E., Grigor, J., & Cowan, D. (1993). Screening and assessment of childhood deafness: Experience from a centralized multi-disciplinary service. *Child: Care, Health and Development, 19*, 239–249.

Oller, D.K., & Eilers, R.E. (1988). The role of audition in infant babbling. *Child Development, 59*, 441–466.

Osberger, M.J., Maso, M., & Sam, L.K. (1993). Speech intelligibility of children with cochlear implants, tactile aids, or hearing aids. *Journal of Speech and Hearing Research, 36*, 186–203.

Page, A., Kramer, S., Novak, J., et al. (1995). Tympanometric screening in elementary school children. *Audiology, 34*, 6–12.

Palmer, C.V. (1994). Variables to consider when interpreting the impact of monaural amplification. *Journal of the American Academy of Audiology, 5*, 286–290.

Paradise, J.L., Feldman, H.M., Campbell, T.F., et al. (2001). Effect of early or delayed insertion of tympanostomy tubes for persistent otitis media on developmental outcomes at the age of three years. *New England Journal of Medicine, 344*, 1179–1187.

Parving, A., & Hauch, A.M. (1994). The causes of profound hearing impairment in a school for the deaf: A longitudinal study. *British Journal of Audiology, 28*, 63–69.

Peckham, C.S. (1986). Hearing impairment in childhood. *British Medical Bulletin, 42*, 145–149.

Pisoni, D.B. (2000). Cognitive factors and cochlear implants: Some thoughts on perception, learning, and memory in speech perception. *Ear and Hearing, 21*, 70–78.

Pisoni, D.B., Svirsky, M.A., Kirk, K.I., et al. (1997). *Looking at the "Stars": A first report on the intercorrelations among measures of speech perception, intelligibility and language development in pediatric cochlear implant users.* Paper presented at the fifth International Cochlear Implant Conference, New York.

Potsic, W.P., Handler, S.D., Wetmore, R.F., et al. (1995). *Primary care pediatric otolaryngology* (2nd ed.). Andover, NJ: J. Michael Ryan Publishing.

Ramkalawan, T.W., & Davis, A.C. (1992). The effects of hearing loss and age of intervention on some language metrics in young hearing-impaired children. *British Journal of Audiology, 26*, 97–107.

Razi, M.S., & Das, V.K. (1994). Effects of adverse perinatal events on hearing. *International Journal of Pediatric Otorhinolaryngology, 30*, 29–40.

Rehabilitation Act of 1973, PL 93-112, 29 U.S.C. §§ 701 et seq.

Richardson, M.P., Williamson, T.J., & Lenton, S.W. (1995). Otoacoustic emissions as a screening test for hearing impairment in children. *Archives of Disease in Childhood, 72*, 294–297.

Robbins, A. (2000). Language development. In S.B. Waltzman & N.L. Cohen (Eds.), *Cochlear implants.* New York: Thieme Medical Publishers.

Robbins, A.M., Osberger, M.J., Miyamoto, R.T., et al. (1995). Language development in young children with cochlear implants. *Advances in Oto-Rhino-Laryngology, 50,* 160–166.

Roberts, J., Burchinal, M.R., Jackson, S., et al. (2000). Otitis media in early childhood in relation to preschool language and school readiness skills among black children. *Pediatrics, 106,* 725–735.

Romand, R. (Ed.). (1992). *Development of auditory and vestibular systems* (2nd ed.). New York: Elsevier.

Rushmer, N. (1994). Supporting families of hearing impaired infants and toddlers. *Seminars in Hearing, 15,* 160–172.

Schildroth, A. (1994). Congenital cytomegalovirus and deafness. *American Journal of Audiology, 3,* 27–38.

Schilling, L.S., & DeJesus, E. (1993). Developmental issues in deaf children. *Journal of Pediatric Health Care, 7,* 161–166.

Schwartz, S. (Ed.). (1996). *Choices in deafness* (2nd ed.). Bethesda, MD: Woodbine House.

Seal, B.C. (1997). Educating students who are deaf and hard of hearing. In L. Power-deFur & F.P. Orelove (Eds.), *Inclusive education: Practical implementation of the least restrictive environment* (pp. 259–271). Gaithersburg, MD: Aspen Publishers.

Shapiro, A.M., & Bluestone, C.D. (1995). Otitis media reassessed: Up-to-date answers to some basic questions. *Postgraduate Medicine, 97,* 73–76, 79–82.

Shiff-Myers, N.B. (1992). Considering arrested language development and language loss in the assessment of second language learners. *Language, Speech, and Hearing Services in Schools, 23,* 28–33.

Stein, L., Kraus, N., McGee, T., et al. (1995). New developments in the clinical application of auditory evoked potentials with children with multiple handicaps. *Scandinavian Audiology, 41*(Suppl.), 18–30.

Stoel-Gammon, C., & Otomo, K. (1986). Babbling development of hearing-impaired and normally hearing subjects. *Journal of Speech and Hearing Disorders, 51,* 33–41.

Stool, S.E., Berg, A.O., Berman, S., et al. (1994). *Managing otitis media with effusion in young children: Quick reference guide for clinicians* (AHCPR Publication 94-D623). Rockville, MD: U.S. Department of Health and Human Services, Public Health Service, Agency for Health Care Policy and Research.

Svirsky, M.A., & Chin, S.B. (2000). Speech production. In S.B. Waltzman & N.L. Cohen (Eds.). *Cochlear implants.* New York, Thieme Medical Publishers.

Van Kleek, A. (1998). Preliteracy domains and stages: Laying the foundations for beginning reading. *Journal of Children's Communication Development, 20,* 33–51.

Van Naarden, K., Decoufle, P., & Caldwell, K. (1999). Prevalence and characteristics of children with serious hearing impairment in metropolitan Atlanta, 1991–1993. *Pediatrics, 103,* 570–575.

Veda, K., Tokugawa, K., & Kusuhara, K. (1992). Perinatal viral infections. *Early Human Development, 29,* 131–135.

Vohr, B.R., Carty, L.M., Moore, P.E., et al. (1998). The Rhode Island Hearing Assessment Program: Experience with statewide hearing screening (1993–1996). *The Journal of Pediatrics, 133,* 353–357.

Volterra, V., Pace, C., Penacchi, B., et al. (1995). Advanced learning technology for a bilingual education of deaf children. *American Annals of the Deaf, 140,* 402–409.

Waltzman, S.B., & Cohen, N.L. (2000). *Cochlear implants.* New York: Thieme Medical Publishers.

Waltzman, S.B., & Shapiro, W.H. (1999). Cochlear implants in children. *Trends in Amplification, 4,* 143–162.

Weisglas-Kuperus, N., Baerts, W., de Graaf, M.A., et al. (1993). Hearing and language in preschool very low birthweight children. *International Journal of Pediatric Otorhinolaryngology, 26,* 129–140.

Williamson, W.D., Demmler, G.J., Percy, A.K., et al. (1992). Progressive hearing loss in infants with asymptomatic congenital cytomegalovirus infection. *Pediatrics, 89,* 862–866.

Wolf, B., Spencer, R., & Gleason, T. (2002). Hearing loss is a common feature of symptomatic children with profound biotinidase deficiency. *The Journal of Pediatrics, 140,* 242–246.

Wood, D. (1992). Total communication in the education of deaf children. *Developmental Medicine and Child Neurology, 34,* 266–269.

Yoshinaga-Itano, C., Sedey, A.L., Coulter, D.K., et al. (1998). Language of early- and later-identified children with hearing loss. *Pediatrics, 102,* 1161–1171.

Young, N.M. (1994). Cochlear implants in children. *Current Problems in Pediatrics, 24,* 131–138.

Zimmerman, W.D., Ganzel, T.M., Windwill, I.M., et al. (1993). Peripheral hearing loss following head trauma in children. *Laryngoscope, 103,* 87–91.

12 Communication

Speech and Language

Sheela Stuart

Upon completion of this chapter, the reader will:

- be able to describe the different elements of speech and of language
- understand the typical course of language development
- be familiar with the biological processes that underlie speech and language
- know the major types of speech and language disorders and their causes
- be aware of the methods of speech and language assessment
- recognize the treatment alternatives for these communication disorders

As humans one of the major means of participating in our lives is through communication. We complain, calm, greet, request, inform, question, praise, compliment, argue, demand, order, correct, beg, invite, cajole (and so the list continues). Although there are many different elaborate, sophisticated, versatile, and creative ways of communicating, the means most frequently used is talking. Therefore, families herald a child's first words with joy, and when there is a problem in the development of his or her ability to talk, anxiety abounds. The following letter is an example of this type of situation.

LETTER FROM A WORRIED GRANDMOTHER

Dear Children's Hospital Professionals: My grandson, David, is 2½ years old. Although as a baby he cooed and babbled and began walking at 12 months, he has never talked. He often grunts and points to things he wants and recently has begun to consistently make a few sounds for "mama," "daddy," "up," "bow wow," and "cup." He has never been seriously ill and has only had some colds, but we had been afraid these had caused problems with his hearing. However, he recently received a complete audiological evaluation and he hears perfectly. (These results were a bit puzzling, as he frequently does not respond when we talk to him.)

His pediatrician also recommended that David be evaluated by a speech-language pathologist. During this evaluation, the therapist played with David while she made a video-tape recording of this part of the session. She also tried to get him to say words and imitate animal sounds that she made, and they spent some time looking in the mirror while she tried to get him to imitate facial expressions. She also asked him to look at some pictures in a book and do some things she requested (point to the picture of the baby, put the block in the box, behind the bear, and so forth) In addition, she used a long interview sheet and asked David's mother about many things such as how he plays, what he does to interact with his parents and with other children, whether he follows directives, and so forth. In her report, the speech-language pathologist indicated she had used these instruments: the

Rossetti Infant-Toddler Language Scale, the Preschool Language Scale–3, and the MacArthur Communicative Development Inventories. Her reported conclusion was that David's receptive language was at approximately the 18- to 20-month level.

Although we know what we were told, we do not understand it. Our family handles things much better if we know what's going on. What causes this type of problem? Will David eventually talk? My daughter is considering having a second child. Is this type of problem likely to occur a second time? Is there anything in addition to the therapy we can do? Thank you in advance for your help.

Sincerely,
A Worried Grandmother

This chapter provides information that addresses these questions. The various aspects that compose talking (speech and language) and their development are described. There also is a discussion of the underlying causes that result in disorders of speech and language. Finally, the focus of therapy and compensatory approaches for overcoming communication disorders are described.

COMPONENTS OF COMMUNICATION

Communication has been studied by many different professionals, including linguists, psychologists, anthropologists, literature scholars, speech-language pathologists, neuropsychologists, and even engineers and biologists. Because each profession's interest in communication comes from a different perspective, the resulting information includes a variety of terminology and at times contrasting viewpoints (Hegde, 2001).

Regardless of the perspective, however, it is agreed that the human brain is the underlying mechanism that supports and coordinates the separate processes of communication. The brain also is a dynamic organ that functions in a varying manner depending upon the age, personal experiences, and even the gender of the individual (Shaywitz et al., 1995).

The brain includes interconnected pathways between areas that regulate, integrate, and formulate communicative messages. Many of the specific functions related to hearing, speech, and language are found in the cerebrum (cerebral cortex). The frontal lobe of the cerebrum has the primary motor area and Broca's speech production area. The temporal lobe contains the primary auditory area and Wernicke's speech comprehension area. The occipital lobe is concerned with vision, and the parietal lobe is concerned with somatesthetic (bodily) sensations.

The **neural network** that interconnects the many brain regions makes it possible for auditory, visual, and conceptual brain regions that serve speech and language functions to differ, at least slightly, from one person to the next (Ojemann, 1991). It is useful to understand some general information about the complex activities of producing speech and understanding language. For example, a person hearing the word "cup" has the signal transmitted along the auditory pathways, which then sends the signal to Wernicke's area, where neurons that correspond to that particular combination of sounds are activated. Neurons are then activated to store a visual picture of a cup, and other neurons store concepts about how cups are used.

Expressive language starts with the production of single words and then progresses to their organization according to a complex set of rules stored in various areas of the brain. If a person wishes to name the object *cup*, he or she would first activate the internal visual picture of a cup (e.g., shape, uses, materials used for cups). These ideas would be channeled through the speech area of the brain (Broca's area) located in the frontal lobe. Here, these thoughts are converted into patterns of motor movement, then transmitted to the motor strip located in the frontal lobe, where impulses for muscle movement needed to produce the sound /kŭp/ are transmitted (Hegde, 2001).

To answer David's grandmother's questions, it is necessary to summarize the basic components that, directed by the brain, provide the ability to listen and talk. Figure 12.1 outlines the components of human communication: hearing, speech (voice and **articulation**), language (including form, which consists of **phonology** and **grammar,** and function, which consists of **semantics** and **pragmatics**), and **fluency** (rhythm and emphasis).

Hearing

To develop typical speech, children must perceive speech sounds. Normal hearing (see Chapter 11) is also vital so that children have an active model and can monitor and modify what they say. Hearing related to speech and language includes being able to perceive the sounds (auditory perception) and being able to decode the different sounds for meaning (auditory processing).

Speech

Speech is the production of articulated sounds and syllables (Nicolosi, Harryman, & Kresheck, 1996). The areas composing speech are *voice* (used to produce the sounds) and *articulation* (used to shape the sounds). A brief description of voice and articulation follows.

Voice is the sound source for producing words (talking). Breath from the lungs is channeled through the larynx and provides the power source to set the vocal folds vibrating, producing sound. Regular opening and closing of the vocal folds results in a normal voice, which can be varied for pitch and loudness. After the sound is produced, it moves through the throat, nose, and mouth. This process is called **resonance.** Individual variations of resonance contribute to personal voice quality. Once voice is produced, the voice sounds must be shaped into specific speech sounds. This process is called *articulation.*

Articulation is the shaping of voice sounds into specific sound patterns by a series of rapid movements of various structures in the mouth including the tongue and lips (forming shapes and coming together or moving apart). A single speech sound is called a **phoneme.** Phonemes are combined to make syllables and words. Changes in one phoneme can drastically alter the meaning of a word; for example, changing a first phoneme from /s/ to /h/ makes "sit" become "hit."

Language

Language is a set of rules regarding form (comprising phonology and grammar) and function (comprising semantics and pragmatics). These rules govern use of words to express information (Nicolosi et al., 1996). *Form* consists of the rules that govern the way in which sounds and words are combined to transmit meaning. Within the area of language form, there are rules for phonology and for grammar. *Phonology* incorporates the rules for combining types of phonemes (i.e., consonants and vowels), pauses, and stress to form words. Languages (e.g., French, Japanese) vary from one another in the common use or not of phonemes, pauses, and stress (Hegde, 2001). *Grammar* incorporates rules for using the smallest meaningful units of language (**morphemes**) and word order (syntax) to convey specific information. Each morpheme supplies meaning (e.g., /s/ at the end of a word in English can signal plural). *Syntax* consists of the rules governing the order of words used to accomplish different communication functions (e.g., questions, statements, commands). Using different word order can drastically change meaning. For example, in English, using a verb as the first word signals a question, as in "Is he here?" whereas placing the pronoun first, as in "He is here," indicates a statement of fact.

Function comprises rules governing the use of specific words to convey meaning (semantics) and use of specific words to accomplish communicative functions within personal interactions (pragmatics). *Semantics* is the study of meaning conveyed by various words, phrases, and sentences. This area is related to cognitive processing involving referents to concepts and

COMMUNICATION

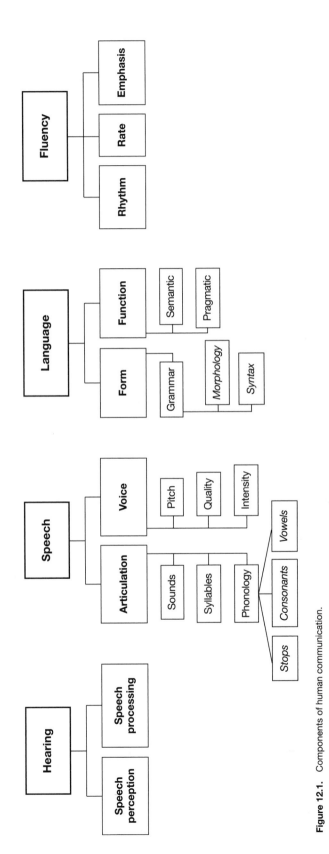

Figure 12.1. Components of human communication.

mental imagery. Semantics also involves memory and listener response. Researchers in children's language acquisition have developed semantic categories (Gleason, 1993; Owens, 1996) to determine a child's semantic development: possession (e.g., "mine"), nomination (e.g., "doggie"), and agent–action (e.g., "Mama go"). *Pragmatics* is the study of rules for use of language in personal interactions and social situations. Simply put, these rules are guidelines for what to say and when to say it. Halliday (1975) developed pragmatic categories for children's language development: instrumental (satisfying needs/wants; e.g., "Water, please?"), regulatory (commanding; e.g., "Stop it!"), and interactional (engaging others; e.g., "Let's play").

Fluency

Achieving the goal of communication through talking also requires that a child produce words in a particular easy, fluid manner. This process is called fluency. *Fluency* is the joining of sounds, syllables, words, and phrases within oral language without hesitations or repetitions. This involves rate, rhythm, and emphasis. *Rhythm* and *rate* describe the way a speaker produces one word following another. Words that are produced too fast or too slowly or that are grouped too closely together and pauses within a meaningful sequence are examples of interruptions of rhythm and rate that decrease intelligibility and listener comfort. *Emphasis* involves variations in tone, pitch, and loudness that are made to convey meaning; these variations contribute to a speaker's ability to talk fluently.

TYPICAL DEVELOPMENT OF SPEECH AND LANGUAGE

After this review of the specific parts involved in talking, it is easier to understand the complexity of this skill and appreciate the typical development of communication, speech, and language in children. Infants hear in utero (Querleu & Renard, 1981) and are affected by what they have heard before birth. For example, infants prefer their mothers' voices to those of strangers (DeCasper & Fifer, 1980), and 4-day-old infants have been found to distinguish between utterances in their native language and those of another language (Mehler et al., 1988).

All infants start as preintentional communicators (relying on crying and movement to express needs and wants), then become intentional communicators (relying on vocalization, gestures, and facial expression), and finally learn to use language to communicate. Language is a tool that children learn to use to interact within their environment and to maintain better social contact (Owens, 1996). Research (cross-sectional and longitudinal methods) has provided broad patterns of stages of communication function and language acquisition. At first, an infant cries because he or she is wet, for example, not because he or she wants to make the caregiver do something. From the perspective of communication function, the infant's initial communication is unintentional. This is called the *prelocutionary* stage, which starts at birth and continues to approximately 8 months. During this time, the caregiver responds to the infant's cry and in doing so begins to assist the infant in learning to become an intentional communicator. At 8–12 months, the infant enters the *illocutionary* stage. During this period, the infant uses conventional gestures or vocalizations to communicate his or her intentions. This stage is characterized by differentiated interactions in which the infant's behavior becomes more coordinated and focused to achieve a goal (e.g., obtaining a bottle or the mother's attention). By 12 months or later, the child enters the *locutionary* stage in which words accompany or replace gestures. In this stage, the child's intent becomes encoded in language. Pointing develops within a shared attention context, vocalization occurs with pointing, and finally naming emerges within vocalization (e.g., child points at a dog and says "bow wow"; Hegde, 2001; Owens, 1996).

Researchers of children's language acquisition focus on babbling as a significant initial expressive behavior. This commonly begins at approximately 6 months of age. The infant produces strings of consonant-vowel combinations such as "bababa" or "nanana." Babbling increases between 4 and 10 months and becomes more varied and complex, with new sounds being added (Owens, 1996; Sachs, 1993). The first words are produced around 12 months and are related to the child's world of objects and events (e.g., toys, animals, food; Owens, 1992).

By 18 months of age, most children begin to produce two-word utterances and semantic development greatly expands. Generally the first two-word utterances do not have grammatical features but they can be understood in the context of the production; for example, "Mommy eat" may mean *Mommy is eating* or *Please Mommy, eat this so I don't have to.*

In the third year, semantic ability continues to develop and grammar emerges. Children produce phrases that are longer and demonstrate initial word-order rules (e.g., "Daddy go bye-bye car"). During the preschool years, children continue to acquire vocabulary and master morphemes (e.g., /s/ for plurals, /əd/ for past tense). Often, a child learns several aspects of language at the same time. For example, new sentence forms are learned at the same time that vocabulary is expanding and pragmatic aspects (when to use a particular word with a particular person) are being mastered. By the age of 5 or 6, the majority of children have acquired basic language form and function (Hegde, 2001).

COMMUNICATION DISORDERS

The grandmother's brief description of David's levels of communicative functioning indicates that he has delays in both speech and language development. She also mentions some of the standardized instruments and techniques used to evaluate and make the determination of a communication disorder by the speech-language pathologist. Parental report, direct observation of spontaneous communication, and communicative interaction within specific tasks provide an opportunity to gather and analyze data using systematic methods. The final measurement of a child's communication skills is based on a combination of measures and approaches

Table 12.1. Indications for speech-language evaluation

Age for referral	Indications for referral
Birth to 6 months	Does not respond to environmental sounds or voices
3–4 months	Does not gesture or make sounds to indicate he or she wants you to do something
	Has no interactive eye gaze
1 year	Does not follow simple commands or understand simple questions (e.g., "Roll the ball," "Kiss the doll," "Where's your shoe?")
	Does not say 8–10 words spontaneously
	Does not identify three body parts on self or doll
2 years	Does not use some one- to two-word questions (e.g., "Where kitty?" "Go bye-bye?" "What's that?")
	Does not use at least 50 understandable, different words
	Does not refer to self by name or pronoun (e.g., "me," "mine")
3 years	Does not understand differences in meaning (e.g., *go/stop, in/on, big/little, up/down*)
	Does not respond to *wh-* questions (e.g., who, what, where)
	Does not tell you about something in two- to three-word "sentences"
4 years	Has difficulty learning new concepts and words
	Still echoes speech
	Has unclear speech
	Does not explain events

used to probe many parameters of communicative competency. A child's approximate level of functioning is then compared with the norms of development for his or her chronological age. In David's case, **receptive language** skills are approximately 10–12 months behind and expressive language skills 18 months behind those normed for his chronological age. Table 12.1 provides some of the indications that there is a need for referral for speech and language assessment, and Table 12.2 lists some commonly used tests of speech and language skills.

Cultural Considerations

The United States of America is becoming an increasingly diverse society, so when evaluating any communication disorder, it is important that the speech-language pathologist utilize information regarding the child's cultural and familial background. Although English is the dominant language of the United States, many children grow up in homes in which English is not the dominant language. Spanish, Navajo, Haitian Creole, Chinese, Korean, Russian, and hundreds of other languages are spoken in the United States. As these children are involved in a bilingual experience that includes either simultaneous or successive language acquisition, specific considerations in evaluating both speech and language development emerge.

In addition, English is spoken with a variety of dialects. For example, African Americans in the United States often use a characteristic dialect that is called *African American English* (AAE; Owens, 1996). Not all African Americans speak AAE, but it is important to realize that this dialect has a systematic language rule system. Use of it is not deviant or improper English. Similarly, in bilingual and dialect language environments, differences in linguistic or pragmatic rules may not be errors. Children acquiring language within these diverse influences

Table 12.2. Frequently used measures of speech and language skills

Test	Ages	Description
Bankson-Bernthal Phonological Process Survey Test (Bankson & Bernthal, 1990)	2–16 years	Identifies error patterns according to distinctive features and phonological processes
Peabody Picture Vocabulary Test–Third Edition (PPVT-III; Dunn & Dunn, 1997)	2½–40 years	Tests receptive vocabulary
MacArthur Communicative Development Inventories (Fenson et al., 1993)	Birth to 12 months	Develops a profile of communicative behaviors in words and gestures
MacArthur Communicative Development Inventories (Fenson et al., 1993)	12–36 months	Develops a profile of communicative behaviors in words and sentences
Expressive One-Word Picture Vocabulary Test–Revised (Gardner, 1990)	2–15 years	Tests expressive vocabulary
Goldman-Fristoe Test of Articulation–2 (GFTA-2; Goldman & Fristoe, 2000)	2–16 years	Assesses articulation of consonant sounds
The Rossetti Infant-Toddler Language Scale (Rossetti, 1990)	Birth to 36 months	Develops a profile of communicative behaviors in six areas: interaction-attachment, pragmatics, gesture, play, language comprehension, and language expression
Clinical Evaluation of Language Fundamentals–Third Edition (CELF-3; Semel, Wiig, & Secord, 1995)	6–21 years	Has multiple subtests of expressive and receptive language, tapping grammar semantics, phonology, sentence recall, and paragraph comprehension; Spanish version available
Clinical Evaluation of Language Fundamentals–Preschool (CELF–Preschool; Wiig, Secord, & Semel, 1992)	3–6 years	Contains multiple subtests of receptive language, tapping semantics, morphology, syntax, and expressive language and assessing phonology, sentence recall, and auditory memory
Preschool Language Scale–3 (PLS-3; Zimmerman, Steiner, & Pond, 1992)	Birth to 6 years	Has subscales on auditory comprehension and expressive communication; Spanish version available

present a diagnostic challenge for clinicians, who must determine whether the variations are merely differences or are disorders. Ideally, the services of a bilingual speech-language pathologist will be available. Regardless, it is imperative to include input from a native speaker and to acknowledge diverse language influences when reporting assessment results.

Delays and disorders can occur in any one or a combination of specific areas (e.g., voice, articulation, fluency, resonance, receptive and expressive language). These difficulties are often associated with genetic, neurological, structural, physiological, emotional, psychological, and/or cognitive disorders, but they may also be merely a matter of late maturity. As a result, the calculated prevalence of communication disorders depends on definitions, levels of impairment, populations screened, and so forth.

Some general demographics for speech and language disorders are as follows: The National Center for Health Statistics (Adams, Hendershot, & Marano, 1999) reported that 16 in every 1,000 children younger than 18 have a chronic speech disorder. The U.S. Department of Education (1999) reported that in the 1997–1998 school year, 1,065,074 children ages 6–21 in public schools (20% of all children covered by Part B of the Individuals with Disabilities Education Act Amendments of 1997, PL 105-17) received services for speech or language disorders. Tomblin et al. (1997) estimated the overall prevalence of specific language impairment in kindergarten-age children to be 7% (the prevalence estimates were 8% for boys and 6% for girls).

Speech Disorders

Speech disorders are caused by problems in making sounds correctly. They may involve any of the previously discussed components of speech: voice, resonance, articulation, and fluency. *Voice disorders* are discussed in terms of abnormalities of pitch, loudness, softness, and hoarseness. They occur as a result of changes (often injuries) to the laryngeal apparatus. Frequent sources of injury include viral infections or polyps on the vocal cords, abuse of the vocal folds (e.g., by screaming, shouting, singing, or altering pitch), and neurological injuries (e.g., paralysis of one or both vocal folds). *Resonance disorders* are discussed in terms of abnormal amounts of nasality (hypernasality = too much, hyponasality = too little). Hypernasality occurs because the soft and/or hard palate do not close the space between the mouth and nose and thereby allow too much nasal resonance. Causes include a cleft of the palate(s) or a soft palate that does not move properly. Hyponasality occurs when something obstructs airflow and resonance in the nasal area. Causes include enlarged **adenoids,** septal deviation in the nose, and chronic congestion.

Once the sound is produced, it is shaped by the oral mechanism (cheeks, tongue, lips, teeth, soft and hard palates, and jaw) in sequential, rapid, coordinated movements that result in the production of phonemes. There is a developmental progression in the ability to articulate phonemes. In English, the correct articulation of sounds involves stopping the airflow by bringing parts of the oral mechanism together and then releasing. The sounds /p/ and /b/ may be correctly produced by 12–24 months, but sounds such as /r/ and /l/ may take the child up to age 6 years to produce correctly (Goldman & Fristoe, 2000). Sound patterns such as vowel-consonant or consonant-vowel-consonant also require practice to produce the sounds correctly in different positions within words. Some children produce a simpler sound in place of a more difficult sound or omit the sound entirely (e.g., "wabbit" for "rabbit"; "du" for "duck"). The child's ability to correct these types of errors depends on the interaction of their hearing (listening to others produce the sounds and self-monitoring their productions) and oral-motor skills (coordinating accurate placement of tongue, lips, and jaw). As children progress in their development of articulatory skills, unfamiliar listeners have an easier time understanding them. As a rule of thumb, an unfamiliar listener may expect to understand approximately 25% of what a 1-year-old says, 50% of what a 2-year-old says, and 100% of what a 4-year-old says.

It is important to note that even though understanding increases with age, not all sounds are always produced accurately, even by age 4 years.

Articulation difficulties are most frequently due to problems in learning or in oral-motor movement. Problems in learning involve being able to identify a sound and remember to produce it in the proper manner within a word. Problems in oral-motor movement are classified in two ways: **Dysarthria** is the inability of the muscles to move to their proper position due to neuromotor control issues; **dyspraxia** is an interruption in the ability to program the position of the speech musculature and sequence these movements.

Hesitations; pauses; repetition of initial sounds, syllables, or words; and interjections of nonspeech sounds are all examples of disruptions of fluency and rhythm. Typically developing children and adults all have some disfluencies within their communication but do not find them overly upsetting. *Stuttering* consists of abnormalities in fluency that have a developmental pattern of increasing severity that are psychologically upsetting to the speaker. Research in speech-language pathology has not definitely defined a single reason for stuttering. Certain neurological conditions (e.g., traumatic brain injury; see Chapter 26) can result in very dysfluent speech, and certain environmental, psychological, and emotional situations can result in dysfluent behaviors. The chief indicator of a communication disorder is the speaker's personal reaction to these dysfluent behaviors (e.g., frustration, shame, withdrawal), which may signal a need for early identification and careful efforts to support the child's confidence in his or her speaking ability (Leung & Robson, 1990).

Language Disorders

There are two major categories of language disorders: acquired (arising after the child has typically developing language) and congenital (present from birth). The most frequent type of acquired language disorder results from traumatic brain injury, but a rare cause of acquired language disorder is Landau-Kleffner syndrome (Paquier, Van Dongen, & Loonen, 1992; see Appendix B). In this syndrome, the child's initial language skills develop typically but then deteriorate, with a loss of the ability to process complex auditory signals such as speech. Affected children manifest symptoms that simulate autism (see Chapter 20 for further discussion of autism).

Congenital language disorders result in a child's experiencing a delay in the acquisition of language skills. There are many causes, with hearing loss being the first consideration. The degree of the hearing loss is directly correlated with the delay in language development. Even a mild hearing loss, when combined with a home environment that does not offer intensive language learning, can result in a delay in language acquisition.

Other causes contributing to congenital language disorders include genetic (Lai, Fisher, & Hurst, 2001), neurological, physiological, and psychological variations in the child. These affect how the child is able to listen to talking within the environment, analyze it, associate it with a multitude of experiences, and use his or her communication system to respond and/or imitate.

Research into language disorders is being pursued by several professions, including neuropsychology, speech-language pathology, and genetics. Each is searching for a means of better classifying language disorders and developing specific therapeutic strategies. Through the use of imaging techniques and electroencephalogram (EEG), efforts to link specific language dysfunction, epilepsy, and cognitive and behavioral disturbances have been pursued (Cordle, 1997; Jayakar, 1997). Fisher et al. (1998) reported a study involving a family in which approximately half of the members are affected with a severe speech and language disorder that appears to be transmitted as an autosomal dominant trait. Future investigation may offer insight into the molecular genetics of the developmental process that culminates in speech and language. This obviously has implications for David's grandmother's question regarding the possibility of his sibling's also experiencing a communication disorder.

Speech-language pathologists continue to focus on an in-depth understanding of ways in which these variations affect the learning of language. Often, however, the aforementioned variations result in an underlying inability to rapidly process the ever changing auditory stimuli that surrounds the child, despite the child's having normal hearing. This inability is called a fundamental processing impairment (Anderson, Brown, & Tallal, 1993). When the child has a fundamental processing impairment, learning of meanings, sound combinations, and specific order of words is disordered. As a result, the internal models of language that the child obtains (on which he or she bases imitations) are flawed.

The brief description of David's levels of functioning indicates that he has delays in learning both speech and language. It is most important to answer his grandmother's questions regarding outcome (e.g., "Will David eventually talk?") with a delineation of the factors involved. Research indicates that two very important contributors to recovery from a communication disorder are early identification and intervention. Two additional factors, the specific disease or condition causing the communication impairment and the severity of the communication impairment, help in determining the extent of recovery (Bashir & Scavuzzo, 1992). In David's case, there is a good likelihood that he will talk. The first step has been taken (early identification and assessment), and plans are in place for intervention services. Outcome is improved because his hearing is within normal limits; there is no known trauma, congenital anomaly, or disease process; his language delay is moderate (comprehending at the 18- to 20-month level at 2½ years of age); and he has some word approximations.

TREATMENT FOR COMMUNICATION DISORDERS

A very important first step in addressing any communication disorder is a speech and language evaluation. This provides a profile of the areas of strength and needs that will guide the overall plan for intervention. Speech-language therapy generally follows one of three models of service delivery: preventive, remedial, or compensatory. Speech-language treatment for David will be remedial. The speech-language pathologist will use clinical observations, results of the interview scales, and David's performance on standardized tests to identify David's level of communicative functioning, language skills (receptive and expressive), and phonological development. Comparing this information with speech-language skills observed in typically developing children of the same chronological age will identify specific items that are not present in David's communicative functioning. These impairments will be the basis for long-term goals in the intervention plan. When there are several areas of need, such as receptive/expressive language and specific speech sound development, goals are designed to assist in eventually developing all areas. Speech-language therapy sessions may initially focus on one area; when a level of development is reached in that area, intervention is begun on the next area. Another approach is to design therapy activities to simultaneously address several areas. To the extent possible, the final target of treatment is *typical communicative interaction* within all activities of daily life.

David has delays in speech and language development. Treatment goals for him include his gaining an understanding of more words and sentence meanings and expanding the number of words he says. It will also be important that he use these new words to participate in a variety of interactions in different situations. Initial emphasis *will not* be on his making every sound in each word correctly but instead on facilitating his developing language that is maximally useful. Although all language behaviors are generally useful, some have more immediate value within a child's everyday life. The names of siblings, pets, foods, toys, and frequent activities are most meaningful to the child and his or her family and are more likely to be produced at home and maintained over time (Hegde, 2001).

As can be seen in David's case, the many decisions involved in designing an intervention program are directly related to the child and his or her personal needs. The frequency, place, and manner in which therapy is provided depend on the age, type, and severity of the child's impairment. David may have therapy in an infant-toddler program. In infant-toddler or early intervention programs, professionals provide individual sessions in the natural environment in which the child feels most comfortable (e.g., the child's home, child care, preschool settings). In addition to individual sessions, professionals teach the family and other care providers specific activities and programs to use on a daily basis. Intervention begins at the level most likely to promote initial communication skills. This means that intervention may focus on developing intentional communication skills rather than on using actual speech or language. This type of intervention is common for children whose underlying medical condition includes multiple disorders and/or cognitive impairments (e.g., Down syndrome). At birth, these children are determined to be at high risk for communication disorders and receive speech-language services of the preventive service model type. Programs of this type emphasize facilitating development to lessen the probability and/or severity of speech-language delays.

These types of intervention programs are very different from those used for a child with a mild articulation disorder. Such a child may receive individual therapy once per week at an outpatient clinic or as a specialized part of his or her school program. Upon school entry, children with communication disorders may receive individual speech-language therapy sessions two to four times weekly, and the speech-language pathologist may consult with their classroom teacher. For successful intervention, these approaches require integration of therapy and practice in daily activities by families, teachers, and other caregivers.

Response to therapy (time needed to improve and overall level of improvement) also depends on the individual child's communication disorder. Studies of children with specific language impairments (and no other concomitant disorder) reveal variable progress (Bashir & Scavuzzo, 1992). The majority of children made substantial improvements, but most retained subtle impairments that persisted into adulthood (Aram & Hall, 1989). Children with a communication disorder associated with a general cognitive impairment may improve with therapy but are not expected to surpass their general cognitive level. Other examples of variable improvement correlated with coexisting conditions include children with autism. These children may start to develop language to the single-word vocabulary stage but may then experience a plateau in language development. Although they may make some gains in communication skills as a result of therapy, most continue to have severe expressive language delays (Harris et al., 1991; Siegel, 1996).

The third intervention strategy is a compensatory therapeutic approach in which strategies and supports are designed for children to bypass their communicative limitations. This approach most frequently is used in addition to remedial intervention services focusing on continued improvement in speech and language development. The next section provides a brief overview of compensatory therapy.

AUGMENTATIVE AND ALTERNATIVE COMMUNICATION

Augmentative and alternative communication (AAC) encompasses compensatory approaches that provide a means of communicating as a supplement to verbal communication. These systems are designed for children who are unable to use speech as their primary communication method. AAC "attempts to compensate (either temporarily or permanently) for the impairment and disability patterns of individuals with severe expressive communication disorders" (i.e., people who have severe speech-language and writing impairments; ASHA, 1989, p. 107).

AAC systems have the fundamental goal of being as natural and functional as possible (Stuart, 2000). Even when it seems likely that oral speech may eventually develop, AAC is still often used to prevent delayed communication development and to support communicative participation in daily activities (Beukelman & Mirenda, 1998).

There are two categories of AAC systems: unaided and aided. Unaided communication systems use only the physical body for communication. Sign language, gestures, vocalizations, and facial expressions are examples of unaided communication methods. Aided communication methods require additional tools or equipment to convey a message. Typewriters, communication boards, pen and paper, tangible objects placed on corrugated form board, and computers with voice output can all be used in aided communication methods. Although aided communication systems are physically cumbersome, they have the advantage of being easily understood by most listeners. Unaided systems usually require familiarity with the person using AAC and some additional learning (e.g., sign language) to be successful in assisting the person in communication.

Most children's AAC systems have many parts that can be used in a variety of situations with different activities, listeners, and environments. Children may rely on their voice output communication aids to participate in telephone calls to relatives, circle time at school, and singing at a birthday party. They may use their symbol boards to express needs and wants (e.g., positioning, request for drink), and they may use head nods, facial expressions, and vocalizations with family and friends.

Although the design and strategies used may vary greatly, AAC has been found to be successful with children who have communication disorders with a wide variety of underlying causes such as autism, cerebral palsy, developmental delay, and Down syndrome and temporary causes such as trauma or **intubation** following surgery.

SUMMARY

The ability to communicate provides a primary means of participating in our lives and the lives of others. Therefore, disorders of communication have a profound impact on the very essence of our being. Returning to the case example, David's grandmother has reason to be worried, but she also has reason to be optimistic. David has received a speech-language evaluation, and a plan is in place for him to receive therapy designed to address his delays. With appropriate therapy and maturation, he is most likely to talk, although he may have associated learning disabilities and residual impairments.

REFERENCES

Adams, P.F., Hendershot, G.E., & Marano, M.A. (1999, October). Current estimates from the National Health Interview Survey, 1996. National Center for Health Statistics. *Vital and Health Statistics, 10*(200), 93.

American Speech-Language-Hearing Association (ASHA). (1989). Competencies for speech-language pathologists providing services in augmentative communication. *Asha, 31*, 107–110.

Anderson, K.C., Brown, C.P., & Tallal, P. (1993). Developmental language disorders: Evidence for a basic processing deficit. *Current Opinion in Neurology and Neurosurgery, 6*, 98–106.

Aram, D.M., & Hall, N.E. (1989). Longitudinal follow-up of children with preschool communication disorders: Treatment implications. *School Psychology Review, 18*, 487–501.

Bankson, N.B., & Bernthal, J.E. (1990). *Bankson-Bernthal Phonological Process Survey Test.* Chicago: Riverside.

Bashir, A.S., & Scavuzzo, A. (1992). Children with language disorders: Natural history and academic success. *Journal of Learning Disabilities, 25*, 53–65.

Beukelman, D.R., & Mirenda, P. (1998). *Augmentative and alternative communication: Management of severe communica-* tion disorders in children and adults (2nd ed.). Baltimore: Paul H. Brookes Publishing Co.

Cordle, J.M. (1997). Neuropsychological assessment of language disorders. *International Pediatrics, 3*(12), 151–154.

DeCasper, A.J., & Fifer, W.P. (1980). Of human bonding: Newborns prefer their mothers' voices. *Science, 208,* 1174–1176.

Dunn, L.M., & Dunn, L.M. (1997). *Peabody Picture Vocabulary–Third Edition (PPVT-III).* Circle Pines, MN: American Guidance Service.

Fenson, L., Dale, P., Reznick, J.S., et al. (1993). *MacArthur Communicative Development Inventories (CDI).* San Diego: Singular Publishing Group.

Fisher, S.E., Vargha-Khadem, F., Watkins, K.E., et al. (1998). Localisation of a gene implicated in a severe speech and language disorder. *Nature Genetics, 18,* 168–170.

Gardner, M.F. (1990). *Expressive One-Word Picture Vocabulary Test–Revised.* Novato, CA: Academic Therapy Publications.

Gleason, J.B. (1993). *The development of language* (3rd ed.). New York: Macmillan.

Goldman, R., & Fristoe, M. (2000). *Goldman-Fristoe Test of Articulation–2.* Circle Pines, MN: American Guidance Service.

Halliday, M. (1975). *Learning how to mean: Explorations in the development of language.* New York: Arnold.

Harris, S.L., Handelman, J.S., Gordon, R., et al. (1991). Changes in cognitive and language functioning of preschool children with autism. *Journal of Autism and Developmental Disorders, 21,* 281–290.

Hegde, M.N. (2001). *Introduction to communicative disorders* (3rd ed.). Austin, TX: PRO-ED.

Individuals with Disabilities Education Act Amendments of 1997, PL 105-17, 20 U.S.C. §§ 1400 *et seq.*

Jayakar, P. (1997). Neurophysiology of language disorders. *International Pediatrics, 3*(12), 146–150.

Lai, C.S., Fisher, S.E., & Hurst, J.A. (2001). A forkhead-domain gene is mutated in a severe speech and language disorder. *Nature, 413,* 519–523.

Leung, A.K., & Robson, W.L. (1990). Stuttering. *Clinical Pediatrics, 29,* 498–502

Mehler, J., Jusczyk, P., Lambertz, G., et al. (1988). A precursor of language acquisition in young infants. *Cognition, 29,* 143–178.

Nicolosi, L., Harryman, E., & Kresheck, J. (1996). *Terminology of communication disorders: Speech-language-hearing* (4th ed.). Philadelphia: Lippincott Williams & Wilkins.

Ojemann, G.A. (1991). Cortical organization of language. *Journal of Neuroscience, 11,* 2281–2287.

Owens, R.E. (1992). *Language development: An introduction* (3rd ed.). New York: Macmillan.

Owens, R.E., Jr. (1996). *Language development: An introduction* (4th ed.). Needham Heights, MA: Allyn & Bacon.

Paquier, P.F., Van Dongen, H.R., & Loonen, C.G. (1992). The Landau-Kleffner syndrome or "acquired aphasia with convulsive disorder": Long-term follow-up of 6 children and a review of the recent literature. *Archives of Neurology, 49,* 354–359.

Querleu, D., & Renard, K. (1981). Les perceptions auditives du fœtus humain [Auditory perception of the human fetus]. *Médecine et hygiene, 39,* 2101–2110.

Rossetti, L. (1990). *The Rossetti Infant-Toddler Language Scale.* East Moline, IL: LinguiSystems.

Sachs, J. (1993). The emergence of intentional communication. In J. Gleason (Ed.), *The development of language* (3rd ed., pp. 39–64). New York: Macmillan.

Semel, E., Wiig, E.H., & Secord, W.A. (1995). *Clinical Evaluation of Language Fundamentals–Third Edition* (CELF-3). San Antonio, TX: The Psychological Corporation.

Shaywitz, B.A., Shaywitz, S.E., Pugh, K.R., et al. (1995). Sex differences in the functional organization of the brain for language. *Nature, 373,* 607–609.

Siegel, B. (1996). *The world of the autistic child: Understanding and treating autistic spectrum disorders.* New York: Oxford University Press.

Stuart, S. (2000). Understanding the storytelling of older adults for AAC system design. *Augmentative and Alternative Communication, 16,* 1–12.

Tomblin, J.B., Records, N.L., Buckwalter, P., et al. (1997). Prevalence of specific language impairment in kindergarten children. *Journal of Speech, Language, and Hearing Research, 40,* 1245–1260.

U.S. Department of Education. (1999). *To assure the free appropriate public education of all Americans: Twenty-first annual report to Congress on the implementation of the Individuals with Disabilities Education Act.* Washington, DC: Author.

Wiig, E.H., Secord, W., & Semel, E. (1992). *Clinical Evaluation of Language Fundaments–Preschool (CELF-Preschool).* San Antonio, TX: The Psychological Corporation.

Zimmerman, I.L., Steiner, V.G., & Pond, R.E. (1992). *Preschool Language Scale–3 (PLS-3).* San Antonio, TX: The Psychological Corporation.

13 The Brain and Nervous System

Normal and Abnormal Development

Robert F. Keating, Caple A. Spence, and David Lynch

Upon completion of this chapter, the reader will:

- be able to trace the embryonic development of the central nervous system and understand potential deviations

- be aware of the structure and function of the neuron, the functional unit of the central nervous system

- understand the anatomy of the brain and the function and interactions of its parts

- be knowledgeable about the functions of the peripheral nervous system and the autonomic nervous system

- be able to describe the origin and function of cerebrospinal fluid and its associated blockage in hydrocephalus

- be aware of current and future trends in radiographic investigation of the central nervous system

Long viewed as an incredibly complex computer, the central nervous system (CNS) is considerably more complicated than any machine made to date (Tanaka & Gleeson, 2000). Each component of the nervous system controls some aspect of behavior and affects our interaction with the world around us. An impairment of any part of this system makes us less able to adapt to the environment and can lead to disorders as diverse as mental retardation, learning disabilities, cerebral palsy, meningomyelocele, and epilepsy (Lequin & Barkovich, 1999). This chapter provides an overview of the interrelationships between the individual elements of the CNS. It also illustrates examples of abnormal development and its effects upon the child.

DEVELOPMENT OF THE CENTRAL NERVOUS SYSTEM

By the 3rd week of gestation, the CNS begins its elaborate development, starting out as a 1.5-millimeter–long thin plate of ectoderm (the outer cell layer of the embryo). This elongated collection of cells subsequently differentiates into outer and inner layers that becomes the shoe shaped body called the **neural plate** (Figure 13.1). The neural plate then extends in a head-to-tail direction; because its cells grow at a greater rate than the surrounding tissue, they begin to overgrow their immediate location and fold over to become the **neural fold** (Figure 13.1).

At this time, the CNS looks like a closed tubular structure with a tail and a head. The tail portion is the forerunner of the spinal cord, whereas the broader head portion will form the

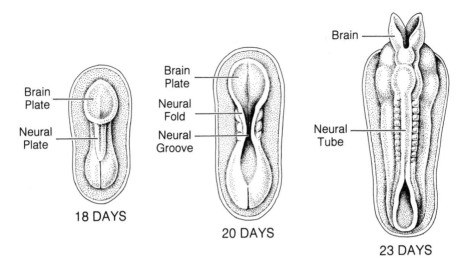

Brain

Brain
Plate

Brain
Plate

Neural
Fold

Brain
Plate

Neural
Plate

Neural
Groove

Neural
Tube

18 DAYS

20 DAYS

23 DAYS

Figure 13.1. Development of the central nervous system (CNS) during the first month of fetal life. This is a longitudinal view showing the gradual closure of the neural tube to form the spinal column and the rounding up of the head region to form the primitive brain.

brain. The hollow tube will persist as the ventricular system of the mature brain. Incomplete closure of the neural tube, most commonly seen in the lumbosacral (lower back) regions, will result in spinal malformations called *dysraphisms* (Drolet, 2000; Manning, Jennings, & Madsen, 2000; Muenke & Cohen, 2000). These neural tube defects include meningomyelocele and anencephaly (see Chapter 24; Botto et al., 1999).

In contrast to the rest of the spinal cord, the tail portion is formed by a process known as canalization, in which neural cells congregate at the end of the spinal canal and then resorb at their center, forming a canal. Abnormalities at this point can lead to a tethered spinal cord, whereby the cord's normal ascent after birth is restricted. This leads the child to experience back pain and lower-extremity discomfort during accelerated growth periods (McLone & La Marca, 1997). If untreated, a tethered cord may result in scoliosis; decreased lower-extremity strength, tone, and sensation; and bowel and bladder dysfunction. Prophylactic detethering, a neurosurgical procedure, may offer considerable benefit (Byrne et al., 1995).

At 5 weeks' gestation, three distinct bulges form in the forward region of the neural tube. These will become the prosencephalon (the **forebrain,** containing the **cerebral hemispheres,** basal ganglia, and diencephalon, or thalamus), the mesencephalon (the midbrain region), and the rhombencephalon (the hindbrain, containing the cerebellum and **brainstem**) (ten Donkelaar, 2000; Figure 13.2). These parts of the brain begin to bend into their adult shape approximately 5 weeks after fertilization. Eventually, the cerebral hemispheres rest on top of the brainstem, and the cerebellum lies behind it. The cerebellum is the last part of the CNS to be formed and is still immature at birth (Figure 13.2).

Between the 2nd and 3rd month of gestation, the formation of the face and cleavage of the hemispheres occurs. An error at this stage results in a condition termed *holoprosencephaly.* Occurring in 6–12 per 100,000 births, this condition is associated with a wide range of malformations (Kinsman, Plawner, & Hahn, 2000). The facial characteristics range from the child having a single eye to the eyes being narrowly spaced. The child may have a cleft palate and lip or may have a single incisor rather than a full complement of teeth. Brain malformations reflect the lack of division of the cerebral hemispheres (Golden, 1999). Frequently, the degree of facial abnormalities correlates with the severity of the brain malformation and associated cognitive impairments. Holoprosencephaly can be caused by a mutation in the sonic hedgehog

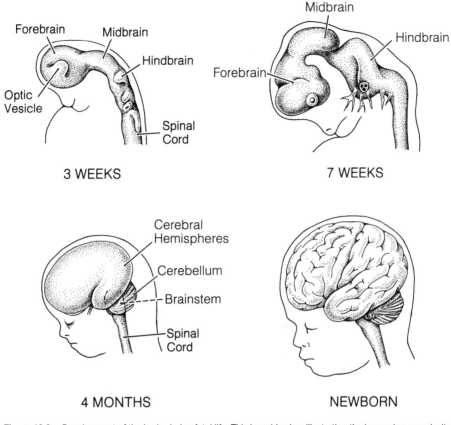

Figure 13.2. Development of the brain during fetal life. This is a side view illustrating the increasing complexity of the brain over time. The forebrain, or prosencephalon, develops into the cerebral hemispheres; the midbrain, or mesencephalon, into the brainstem; and the hindbrain, or rhombencephalon, into the cerebellum. Although all brain structures are formed by 4 months, the brain grows greatly in size and complexity during the final months of prenatal development.

(SHH) gene, which is involved in early brain development (Muenke et al., 1994). Holoprosencephaly can, however, also be part of a chromosomal disorder or can have unclear origin.

The central cavities of the brain also develop at this time and include the lateral, third, and fourth ventricles. The cerebral hemispheres contain the lateral ventricles, the third ventricle forms at the level of the diencephalon, and the fourth ventricle is contained within the hindbrain. All of these cavities initially communicate with a central canal inside the spinal cord. As the brain develops, however, this site of communication normally becomes obliterated. If there is a Chiari malformation (as usually occurs in meningomyelocele; see Chapter 24), however, hydrocephalus develops, in which the normal cerebrospinal fluid (CSF) pathway is obstructed (Shuman, 1995; Figure 24.6b). This can also lead to the reestablishment of the central canal as an alternative CSF pathway (Heiss et al., 1999). In severe cases this may result in the formation of syringomyelia (a cavity within the spinal cord), which is marked clinically by muscle atrophy and loss of pain sensation and can lead to paralysis and scoliosis (Hanieh et al., 2000). In some cases, it can be treated through a neurosurgical procedure (Hida et al., 1999).

Once formed, the ventricles are filled with fluid produced by the **choroid plexus.** This structure, which resembles a cluster of grapes, is formed between 44 and 48 days of gestation and hangs from the ceiling of the **lateral ventricles.** As the ventricles fill with CSF, the pressure normally opens the foramen of Magendie, an outlet from the fourth ventricle. An obliteration of this outlet or stenosis (narrowing) of the aqueduct of Sylvius (which connects the third ventricle to the spinal cord; Figure 13.3) can also lead to the development of hydrocephalus.

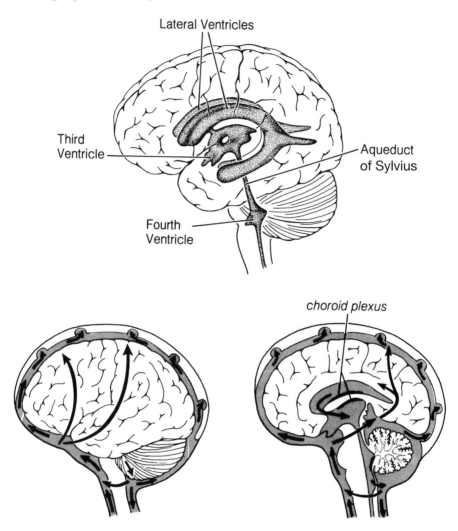

Figure 13.3. The ventricular system of the brain. The major parts of the ventricular system are shown (top). The flow of cerebrospinal fluid (CSF) is shown (bottom). The fluid is produced by the choroid plexus in the roof of the lateral and third ventricles. Its primary route is through the aqueduct of Sylvius, into the fourth ventricle, and then into the spinal column, where it is absorbed. A secondary route is around the surface of the brain. A blockage, most commonly of the aqueduct of Sylvius, leads to hydrocephalus. (Lower illustrations redrawn by permission from Milhorat, T.H. [1972]. *Hydrocephalus and the cerebrospinal fluid.* Philadelphia: Lippincott Williams & Wilkins. Copyright 1972, The Williams & Wilkins Co., Baltimore.)

DEVELOPMENT OF THE CORTICAL NEURON

By the time the fetus is 3 months old, all of the basic brain structures are in place. Yet, internally, enormous changes continue to occur, especially at the level of the neuron, the basic functional unit of the CNS (Leventer & Harvey, 1998).

Neuronal Proliferation and Migration

Between 3 and 5 months' gestation, neurons originally arising from the intermediate layer of the neural tube rapidly divide (proliferate) and then migrate radially into the outer cell layers of the brain (the marginal zone) to form the cortex (Figure 13.4; Pomeroy & Klim, 2000). If proliferation of the neurons is inhibited during this critical period, the fetus will develop a small brain, or microcephaly. The process of neuronal migration is complicated and depends

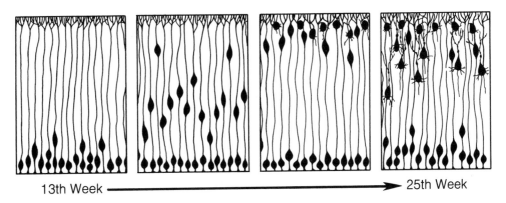

13th Week ⟶ 25th Week

Figure 13.4. Growth of nerve cells in the cortex between 3 and 6 months' gestation. The cell bodies climb toward the upper layers of the cortex and sprout dendrites. There is an increase both in the number of cells and in the complexity of their projections.

upon proper timing of gene expression. It also depends on the orientation of neurons, which is aided by scaffolding provided by surrounding **glial cells** (Walsh, 2000). From a single cell layer, six separate layers are formed that define the mature cortex. Any interruption or error in this process can result in an incomplete or disordered cortical architecture, called *dysplasia* (Uher & Golden, 2000). A variety of cortical dysplasias may be manifested by these errors, including schizencephaly, lissencephaly (see Appendix B), polymicrogyria, and **heterotopias.** In schizencephaly, there is a complete lack of development of a portion of the germinal zone and thereby the cerebral wall, leaving seams or clefts. Lissencephaly, or "smooth brain," is associated with **agyria,** the near or complete absence of convolutions (Reiner, 2000). Polymicrogyria is characterized by a great number of small grooves in the cortical surface, rendering its appearance like that of a wrinkled chestnut. Neuronal heterotopias are the least severe of the migrational disturbances. They involve collections of nerve cells that prematurely stop their migration in the subcortical white matter during radial migration from the periventricular germinal zones. Except for heterotopias, migration defects are rare and are usually associated with severe mental retardation and seizures (Duchowny, Jayakar, & Levin, 2000; Lagae, 2000). Heterotopias, however, have been associated with learning disabilities. Numerous teratogens (substances capable of producing defects in the fetus) have been implicated in disrupting normal neuronal proliferation and migration. These include maternal exposure to antiepileptic drugs, alcohol, and irradiation, as well as fetal exposure to intrauterine infections.

Neuronal Differentiation and Organization

The neuron is similar to other cells in that it has a cell body consisting of a nucleus and cytoplasm. Unlike other cells, however, it has a long process called an *axon*, which extends from the cell body, and many, shorter, jutting processes called *dendrites* (Figure 13.5). The axon carries impulses away from the nerve cell body, often for a distance of greater than 1 meter. Dendrites receive impulses from other neurons and carry them a short distance toward the cell body. The size and shape of dendrites may change with neuronal activity, suggesting that these changes represent the anatomical basis of memory.

As the brain begins to organize by 5 months' gestation (a process that continues into early childhood) the axons and dendrites grow and differentiate. The major developmental features of this organizational period include 1) the establishment and differentiation of neurons; 2) the attainment of proper alignment, orientation, and layering of cortical neurons; 3) the elaboration of dendrites and axons; 4) the establishment of synaptic contacts; and 5) cell death and selective elimination of neuronal processes and **synapses.**

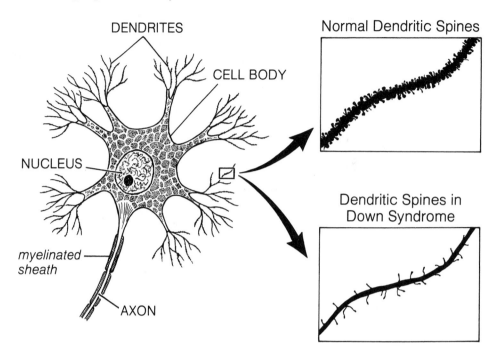

Figure 13.5. Illustration of a nerve cell, showing its component elements. The enlargements show the minute dendritic spines that increase the number of synapses or junctures among nerve cells. Note the diminished size and number of dendritic spines in a child with Down syndrome.

As the neuron develops, growing axons are able to recognize various molecules that are on the surface of and that are diffusing away from other axons and cells and use these as cues to navigate the circuitous pathway to their final destination. These axons need sensory abilities to perceive this guidance information, distinguishing the correct pathway from the incorrect one. In addition, axons need to move forward, sometimes rapidly, make turns, avoid obstacles, and stop when the target is reached. These guidance functions—sensory, motor, and integrative—are all contained within the specialized tip of a growing axon, the growth cone (Sanes, Reh, & Harris, 2000).

During neuronal differentiation, the primitive neurons begin to express their distinctive physical and biochemical features. This arborization is much like the growth of a tree from a sapling. It even involves pruning, such that new connections are established while others are abolished. For example, in the visual cortex, the formation of synapses is most rapid between 2 and 4 months after term, a time critical for the development of visual function. Maximum synaptic density is attained at 8 months of age, when elimination of synapses begins; by age 11 months, approximately 40% of synapses have been lost (Volpe, 2001).

The overproduction of synapses early in development and selective elimination at a later time appears to be a basic strategy of neuronal development. It is now established that this regressive event is crucial for brain development, enhancing both cognitive capacity and **plasticity** (Volpe, 2001). In conditions such as Down syndrome, fragile X syndrome, and certain inborn errors of metabolism (see Chapters 16, 17, and 18, respectively), there are defects during this organizational period (Sarnat, 1991).

As axons grow toward their respective dendritic targets, the dendrites respond by increasing the number of spines, or projections, along their surface (Figure 13.5). The spines increase the surface area of the dendrites, permitting more elaborate and sophisticated communication between neurons. In fact, increased dendritic outgrowth has been associated with enhanced memory. In contrast, deficient development of the dendritic arborization has been observed in individuals with cognitive impairments, most prominently in Down syndrome (Huttenlocher, 1991).

Nerve impulses are transmitted from one neuron to another across a synaptic cleft. Here, the terminal of the axon of one neuron almost touches either the dendrite or the cell body of another neuron. For information to be passed on, nerve impulses must cross this space. This is accomplished with the help of a chemical bridge, called a *neurotransmitter,* which permits the conversion of the electrical energy of a nerve impulse into chemical energy that can cross the synaptic cleft. At the other side the impulse is reconverted to electrical energy so that it can continue on its journey from the brain to another body organ.

The mechanism for neurotransmission is as follows. Each neuron is specialized to utilize one of a number of neurotransmitters. Common neurotransmitters include dopamine, acetylcholine, serotonin, GABA (gamma-aminobutyric acid), glutamate, norepinephrine, and substance P. The neurotransmitter is stored in pouches called *presynaptic vesicles* that abut the synaptic membrane (Figure 13.6). It is released when a depolarizing electrical current passes through the presynaptic neuron. Upon stimulation by the electrical impulse, the pockets open and release the neurochemical into the synaptic cleft. The neurotransmitter then diffuses to a receptor at the postsynaptic membrane of the adjacent neuron where it exerts an excitatory or inhibitory influence (Kandel, Schwartz, & Jessell, 2000). Synaptic communication is also aided by the surrounding glial cells. The impulse then continues on to distant neurons, producing a cascade of excitatory or inhibitory neural impulses. Thus, a single neuron's **depolarization** may affect countless other neurons and is responsible for the coordination and "fine tuning" that permits complex thoughts and actions. Abnormalities in neurotransmitters have been found in children with autism (see Chapter 20), attention-deficit/hyperactivity disorder (ADHD; see Chapter 21), and certain inborn errors of metabolism (see Chapter 18). Synaptic neurotransmission is also important because many of the drugs used to treat seizures, movement disorders, depression, and ADHD act by altering specific neurotransmitters or their receptors.

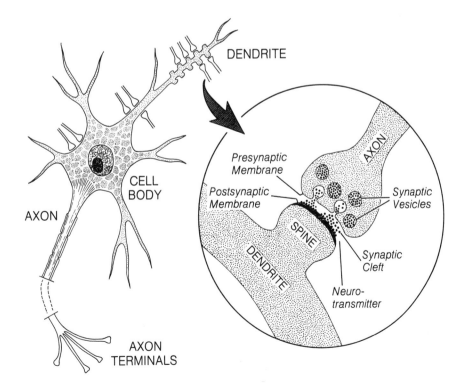

Figure 13.6. Central nervous system (CNS) synapse. The enlargement shows the abutting of an axon against a dendritic spine. The space separating the two is the synaptic cleft. Neurotransmitter bundles are released into the cleft from vesicles in the presynaptic membrane. These permit transmission of an impulse across the juncture.

Myelination

The neurons of the brain and spinal cord form two distinct regions of the CNS called the *gray matter* and the *white matter.* The gray matter contains the nerve cell bodies, appearing grayish in color. The white matter is made up of axons sheathed with a protective covering called *myelin* that promotes the rapid conduction of nerve impulses. During fetal life, most of the axons have no myelin coating. They gradually develop this glistening casing after birth. Effective **myelination** is necessary for the development of voluntary gross and fine motor movement and the suppression of primitive reflexes. Myelination is usually complete by 18 months of age, around the time a child can run (Volpe, 2001). Deficient myelin formation has been found in a number of conditions including prematurity, congenital hypothyroidism, and malnutrition (Porter & Tennekoon, 2000; Rodriguez-Pena et al., 1993).

THE MATURE CENTRAL NERVOUS SYSTEM: BRAIN AND SPINAL CORD

The brain and the spinal cord comprise the mature CNS and have five main components: the cerebral hemispheres, basal ganglia, thalamus, brainstem, cerebellum, and spinal cord (Crossman & Neary, 2000; Goldberg, 2000).

The Cerebral Hemispheres

During embryonic development the prosencephalon gives rise to a left and right cerebral hemisphere. Each consists of an outer cerebral cortex, subcortical white matter, and deep masses of gray matter, collectively called the *basal ganglia.* Within each hemisphere is a fluid-filled cavity called the *lateral ventricle.* The hemispheres are joined together by a band of fibers called the **corpus callosum** that permits the exchange of information between the two hemispheres (Figure 13.7a–b). Various conditions may lead to partial formation of the corpus callosum or, in more severe cases, complete failure resulting in agenesis of the corpus callosum. The importance of this exchange is emphasized by the results of a surgical procedure called a **corpus callosotomy.** In this operation, a portion of the corpus callosum is cut in an attempt to control a severe seizure disorder (McInerney et al., 1999; Shimizu & Maehara, 2000). It has proven quite effective in decreasing the spread of seizure activity but in some adults has resulted in a decline in language and visual-perceptual skills and in manual dexterity (Funnell, Corballis, & Gazzaniga, 1999). This is presumed to occur because the operation interferes with interhemispheric exchange of information (see Chapter 25; Sorenson et al., 1997).

During early fetal life the surface of the cerebral hemispheres is smooth. As the complexity of the brain increases during the third trimester, however, involutions called *fissures* and **sulci** appear. Fissures, which are deeper than sulci, are visible earlier during development and separate each hemisphere into four functional areas or lobes. The frontal lobe occupies the front, or anterior, third of the hemisphere; the parietal lobe sits in the middle-upper part of the hemisphere; the temporal lobe is in the lower-middle region; and the occipital lobe takes up the back, or posterior, quarter of each hemisphere (Figure 13.7c). The regions lying between the sulci are called *convolutions,* or **gyri.** Some gyri show little variation in location and contour from one person to another, whereas others show considerable variability.

The surface of the cerebral hemisphere is called the cortex and is composed principally of nerve cell bodies. Below this gray matter lie the nerve fibers, or white matter. The cerebral cortex initiates motion and thought processes. Each cortical lobe is responsible for particular activities and functions.

The Frontal Lobe

The frontal lobe controls both voluntary motor activity and important aspects of cognition (Brodal, 1998). Within the frontal lobe the different areas of the body are represented topo-

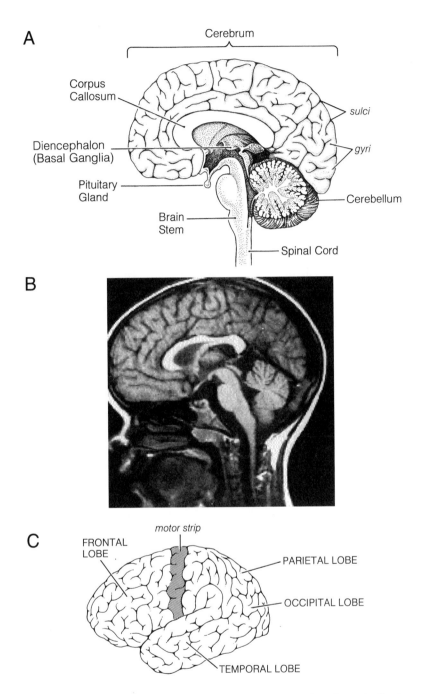

Figure 13.7. A) Lateral view of the brain showing the component elements: cerebral hemispheres, diencephalon, cerebellum, brainstem, and spinal cord. B) Lateral view of brain by magnetic resonance imaging (MRI) scan. Note the excellent reproduction of the structures of the brain. C) Side view of the left hemisphere. The cortex is divided into four lobes: frontal, parietal, temporal, and occipital. The motor strip, lying at the back of the frontal lobe, is highlighted. It initiates voluntary movement and is damaged in spastic cerebral palsy.

graphically along a strip called the *primary motor cortex*. The tongue and the larynx, or voice box, are controlled from the lowest point, followed in an upward sequence by the face, hand, arm, trunk, thigh, and foot (Figure 13.8). The tongue, larynx, and hand occupy a particularly large area along this strip due to the complexity of speech and fine motor activity.

Once the motor strip initiates a nerve impulse, it passes down the **pyramidal (cortico-spinal) tract** that connects the cortex with the spinal cord. Reaching the spinal cord, the impulse passes across a synapse to an anterior horn cell. This neuron relays the transmission via its axon to a peripheral nerve that connects to an appropriate muscle. The muscle subsequently contracts in response to the original signal from the motor cortex. In **spinal muscular atrophy** of childhood (Werdnig-Hoffmann disease), the motor neurons die, resulting in hypotonia and weakness (see Chapter 15; Andersson & Rando, 1999; Cole & Siddique, 1999; Talbot, 1999).

Conversely, if there is damage to either the motor cortex or the pyramidal tract, increased tone in the form of spasticity results. In spasticity, the underlying involuntary muscle contractions controlled by the brainstem and spinal cord are no longer inhibited by pyramidal tract activity. As a result, voluntary movement becomes less fluid, as is seen in cerebral palsy and other movement disorders (see Chapter 23). Therapeutic approaches to spasticity include measures that manipulate neurotransmitters to reduce tone. For example, the drug baclofen, which increases the activity of GABA, an inhibitory neurotransmitter, has been administered into the spinal column using an implantable pump in individuals with cerebral palsy to decrease spasticity (see Chapter 23; Butler & Campbell, 2000).

Damage to the motor cortex can also lead to seizures that begin as focal twitchings and can generalize to involve large muscle groups (Jacksonian epilepsy; see Chapter 25). The frontal lobe has also been implicated in promoting abstract thinking. With functional imaging techniques (discussed later), the frontal lobe has been identified as the origin of executive function (Barkley, 2000; Pineda et al., 1998). This high-level abstract thinking involves planning and organizing for future activities and is deficient in children with ADHD and learning disabilities (see Chapter 22; Lazar & Frank, 1998).

The Parietal Lobe

Vision, hearing, touch, pain, smell, and temperature sensation all reside in distinct areas in the parietal lobe. In addition, the parietal lobe contributes to the integration of other stimuli, promoting a "whole" impression from various sensory inputs. The primary sensory projection cortex that receives information from the skin and membranes of the body and face is located

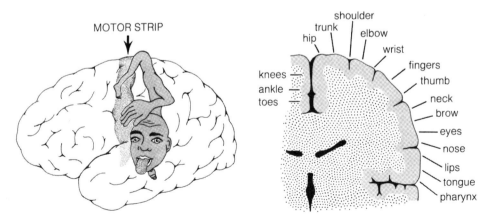

Figure 13.8. The motor strip. This cartoon shows a representation of body parts at various points on the strip. Note that the areas representing facial and hand muscles are very large. This is because of the intricate control necessary for speech and fine motor coordination. A cross-section of the motor strip is shown to the right.

in the somatosensory area. From the thalamus, this area receives fibers that convey touch and proprioceptive (muscle, joint, and tendon) sensations from the opposite side of the body. Irritative lesions of this area may produce paresthesias (e.g., numbness, pins-and-needles sensation) on the opposite side of the body. A destructive lesion (such as a tumor) in this area produces impairment in sensibility, such as difficulty localizing or measuring the intensity of painful stimuli. There is also evidence that the visual-perceptual problems experienced by children with learning disabilities and the difficulties in performing fine motor tasks found in children with ADHD may be related to abnormalities in this region (Vaidya et al., 1998).

The Temporal Lobe

The temporal lobe is primarily involved in communication and sensation. The dominant hemisphere (the left side in more than 90% of people) is responsible for producing and comprehending speech as well as contributing to the memory of auditory and visual experiences. It receives input from each ear, and there is point-to-point projection of the cochlea upon the acoustic area of the temporal lobe. Within the base of the temporal lobe rest two structures, the hippocampus and amygdala, that serve special cognitive functions. The hippocampus plays an important role in memory and allows for the rapid learning of new information. The amygdala is involved in sensory processing and emotions and is part of the general-purpose "fight or flight" defense response control system.

Temporal lobe dysfunction can contribute to a number of disorders, the two most common being receptive aphasia and complex partial seizures (Parry-Fielder et al., 1997). In **receptive aphasia,** the temporal lobe may have been damaged by a tumor, vascular insufficiency, or traumatic injury (Van Hout, 1997). The individual is unable to understand spoken words but is able to speak, frequently in an unintelligible fashion (see Chapter 12). Irritation of the region in or near the primary auditory receptive area may cause buzzing or roaring sensations. A unilateral lesion in this area may cause only mild hearing loss, but bilateral lesions can result in deafness. Complex partial seizures also arise in the temporal lobe (Bourgeois, 1998). Before the seizure begins, the individual may experience a déjà vu, or flashback, phenomenon, caused by stimulation of this area of the brain. The patient may also have visual hallucinations, hear bizarre sounds, or appreciate olfactory **auras,** which again emanate from the temporal lobe (see Chapter 25).

Treatment of refractory complex partial seizures may involve surgical removal of the seizure focus (Cross, 1999). Although adults who undergo this neurosurgical procedure often sustain some language loss, children appear less likely to experience this complication. This suggests that the child's brain is more flexible than the adult brain, such that the nondominant hemisphere can take over some of the language functions of the damaged area. In fact, children as old as 6 years have undergone total dominant hemispherectomies (removal of most of the left hemisphere for intractable generalized seizures) who have been able to recover speech function, presumably by incorporating other cortical locations in a new functional role (Chugani & Muller, 1999; deBode & Curtiss, 2000; Neville & Bavelier, 1998). This is known as **plasticity** (Vicari et al., 2000).

The Occipital Lobe

The primary visual receptive cortex is located in the occipital lobe. The right occipital lobe receives impulses from the right half of each retina, whereas the left visual cortex receives impulses from the left half of each retina. The upper portion of this cortical area represents the upper half of each retina, whereas the lower portion represents the lower half. Irritation of the visual cortex can produce such visual hallucinations as flashes of light, rainbows, brilliant stars, or bright lines. Destructive lesions can cause defects in the visual fields on the opposite side without destruction of macular (central) vision.

Visual stimuli are first interpreted in the visual-receptive area. The image is processed further in another part of the occipital lobe before being passed on to the temporal and parietal lobes. Here the location in space and the identity of the object are further determined. In both the temporal and parietal lobes, the image is related to what has been heard and felt so that an interpretation can be made. Cortical visual impairment (cortical blindness) may result from severe damage to the occipital region (Huo et al., 1999). In this condition despite a normal visual apparatus and pathway, the occipital lobe does not receive the image and the person appears to be functionally blind (see Chapter 10).

Interconnections

The white matter of the adult cerebral hemispheres contains myelinated nerve fibers of many sizes. Some of these fibers serve to connect various regions of the brain. The most important of these interconnections is the **corpus callosum,** a large arrangement of fibers that connects portions of one hemisphere with corresponding parts of the opposite cerebral hemisphere (Figure 13.7a–b).

A second type of interconnection is formed by projection fibers, which connect the cerebral cortex with lower portions of the brain or the spinal cord. As an example, the internal capsule is a type of projection fiber that projects from the cortex to the distant peripheral muscle. Destructive lesions such as tumors or stroke may compress or destroy the internal capsule and the pyramidal tract it contains, resulting in hemiplegia (spasticity and weakness) on the other side of the body.

Finally association fibers connect the various portions of a cerebral hemisphere. Short association fibers, or U fibers, connect adjacent gyri. Those fibers located in the deeper portions of the white matter are termed *intracortical fibers*, and those just beneath the cortex are called *subcortical fibers*. Long association fibers connect more widely separated areas.

The Basal Ganglia and Thalamus

Deep beneath the cortical surface resides the diencephalon (Figures 13.7a and 13.9) with the adjacent basal ganglia and related structures. In humans, this primitive part of the brain modulates instructions from the motor cortex in directing voluntary movement (Roberts, 1992). In lower vertebrates it directly controls motor activity. Anatomically, the basal ganglia include the caudate nucleus and the putamen (together called the *corpus striatum*), the globus pallidus, and other gray areas at the base of the forebrain. Together, the putamen and the globus pallidus form the lentiform nucleus. The caudate nucleus is separated from the lentiform nucleus and thalamus by the internal capsule. Functionally, these collections of neurons together with their fibrous connections and neurotransmitters form an associated motor system. Damage to the basal ganglia produces various movement disorders. Although voluntary movement is possible, it may be exaggerated in a twisting, squirming pattern called **choreoathetosis.** Alternately, there may be dystonic posturing or rigidity. These manifestations can be seen in children with dyskinetic cerebral palsy (see Chapter 23; Cote & Crutcher, 2000).

Immediately adjacent to the basal ganglia is the thalamus. All sensory input connecting with the cortex detours through the thalamus. The thalamus is believed to act as a gateway for the cerebral cortex and has also been implicated in a variety of movement disorders as well as in absence seizures (previously called *petit mal seizures;* see Chapter 25). The thalamus is also thought to be part of an integral neuronal network concerned with cognitive functions, especially language.

The Brainstem

In contrast to the voluntary actions controlled by the cerebral hemispheres, the brainstem controls more reflexive and involuntary activities. It is comprised of three distinct areas (midbrain,

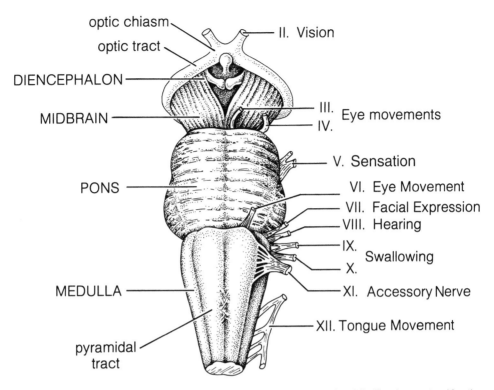

Figure 13.9. The three regions of the brainstem are shown: midbrain, pons, and medulla. The placement and function of 11 of the 12 cranial nerves are illustrated. (The first cranial nerve [smell] is not shown. It lies in front of the second cranial nerve, below the frontal lobe.) Note that the pyramidal tract runs from the cortex (not shown) into the brainstem. The pyramidal fibers cross over in the medulla. Thus, the right hemisphere controls left-side movement, and the left hemisphere controls right-side movement.

pons, and medulla) and connects the cerebral hemispheres to the spinal cord (Figure 13.9). Within it are the 12 cranial nerves that control functions such as smell, vision, hearing, swallowing, and articulation (Klemm & Vertes, 1990). These nerves also affect facial expression, eye and tongue movements, salivation, and even breathing. In addition to the cranial nerve nuclei, the brainstem is composed of a vast array of fiber tracts bringing messages into and out of the brain. The corticospinal (pyramidal) tracts provide for the passage of neural impulses from the cortex to the spinal cord. Conversely, there are tracts bringing sensory information into the brain via the thalamus. Therefore, any abnormality in this region affects function in distant locations. Children with cerebral palsy often have damage to the brainstem or to pathways that end in the brainstem; this damage thus offers an explanation for the high incidence of excessive salivation, swallowing problems, strabismus, and speech disorders (see Chapter 23).

The Cerebellum

The cerebellum (Figure 13.7a–b) resides in back of and immediately below the cerebral hemispheres and coordinates voluntary muscle activity. Its principal role is to dampen skeletal muscular activity by providing for the smooth transition between activation of **agonist** muscles (that work together) and inhibition of their counterpart antagonist muscles. Normal muscle coordination requires that the functions of the cerebellum be integrated with those of the cerebral hemispheres and the basal ganglia. Although voluntary movement can occur without the cerebellum, such movement is erratic and uncoordinated. This gait is known as ataxic and may be seen with cerebellar tumors, with progressive neurologic disorders (e.g., ataxia **telangiectasia**), as a side effect of medication, or with inebriation (Menkes & Sarnat, 2000). The cerebellum may also have some influence on cognitive function through interconnections with the prefrontal cortex (Diamond, 2000). Cerebellar abnormalities have been found in children with autism.

The Spinal Cord

The spinal cord transmits motor and sensory messages from the brain to the rest of the body. In addition to permitting voluntary movement, the spinal cord acts to provide protective reflex arcs in both the upper and lower extremities, such as the deep tendon reflex elicited when the knees are tapped. The spinal cord is an elongated, cylindrical mass of nerve tissue that is continuous with the brain stem at its upper end and occupies the upper two thirds of the adult spinal canal within the vertebral column (Figure 13.10). It widens laterally in the neck and lower back regions. These enlargements correspond to the origins of the nerves of the upper and lower extremities. The nerves of the brachial plexus originate at the **cervical** enlargement; the nerves of the lumbosacral plexus arise from the **lumbar** enlargement. Injury to the brachial plexus may occur during a difficult vaginal delivery resulting in weakness of the upper extremity (Dodds & Wolfe, 2000).

The spinal cord is divided into approximately 30 segments—8 cervical (neck), 12 thoracic (chest), 5 lumbar (lower back), 5 sacral (pelvic), and a few small coccygeal (tailbone) segments—that correspond to attachments of groups of nerve roots. Individual segments vary in length; they are about twice as long in the midthoracic region as in the cervical or upper lumbar area.

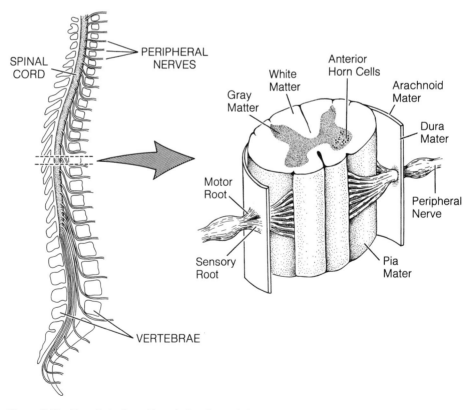

Figure 13.10.   The spinal column. The spinal cord extends from the neck to the lower back. It is protected by the bony vertebrae that form the spinal column. The enlargement to the right shows a section of the cord taken from the upper-back region. Note that the meninges (the dura, arachnoid, and pia mater) surrounding the cord and the peripheral nerve on its way to a muscle. This nerve contains both motor and sensory components. The spinal cord, like the brain, has both gray and white matter. The gray matter consists of various nerve cells, the most important of which are the anterior horn cells. These are destroyed in polio. The white matter contains nerve fibers wrapped in myelin, which gives the cord its glistening appearance.

There are no sharp boundaries between segments within the cord itself. Each segment contributes to four roots: a ventral (front) and a dorsal (back) root of the left half and a similar pair of the right half; each root is made up of many individual **rootlets.** The dorsal nerve roots allow sensory input to ascend to the brainstem, whereas the ventral roots deliver motor input from the brainstem to the appropriate muscle.

If the spinal cord is damaged (e.g., because of trauma or a congenital malformation such as meningomyelocele), messages from the brain are short-circuited before they reach the peripheral nerves below the area of abnormality. The result may be the loss of both sensation and movement in the affected limbs. This flaccid paralysis may involve the legs (paraplegia) or all extremities (quadriplegia) depending on the level of the damage.

THE PERIPHERAL NERVOUS SYSTEM

The peripheral nerves allow neural impulses to continue from the CNS (brain and spinal cord) to the distant muscle end plates. These nerve tracts have both motor and sensory fibers that run in opposite directions. Motor, or **efferent,** fibers transmit neural impulses from the brain to the muscle to initiate movement. Sensory, or **afferent,** fibers carry signals from the muscle to the brain that indicate the position of a joint and the tone of the muscle following the movement. Hyperexcitability of sensory neurons in the patient with cerebral palsy contributes to spasticity. There are also a number of hereditary neuropathies that interfere with the **peripheral nervous system** (Ouvrier, 1996).

The regeneration capacity of the peripheral nervous system differs substantially from that of the CNS. Although the CNS is now considered capable of regeneration, the ease of repair in the peripheral nervous system is far greater. This ability to promote the regrowth of peripheral nerves is responsible for the success seen in the neural reconstruction for brachial plexus palsy. At present, the success rate ranges from 60% to 90% for reestablishing meaningful neurological function in children undergoing a neural reconstruction (Xu, Cheng, & Gu, 2000).

Voluntary movement is controlled by the **somatic** component of the peripheral nervous system. Complex coordination between the motor and sensory system is necessary to ensure normal muscle tone. An imbalance can lead to increased or decreased muscle tone. Injury to motor neurons will affect voluntary as well as reflex activities of the involved muscle.

Involuntary activities involving control of the cardiovascular, digestive, endocrine, urinary, respiratory, and reproductive systems are undertaken by the **autonomic** nervous system. Control of these functions begins in the diencephalon and terminates in the end organs. In contrast to the graded response with voluntary movement demonstrated by the somatic nervous system, the autonomic nervous system involves an on/off type of control. The best example of this is the "fight or flight" response (Figure 13.11). When a person feels threatened physically or psychologically, several physiological changes take place simultaneously. The pupils dilate, the hair stands on end, and the functioning of the digestive system is suspended so that blood can be diverted to more important areas, such as the brain. Heart rate and blood pressure increase, and the air passages of the lung expand in size. All of these changes prepare the individual to react to the emergency.

Although the autonomic nervous system works involuntarily in maintaining **homeostasis,** there are nonetheless voluntary adjustments that come from the cerebral cortex to modulate these effects. This is perhaps best illustrated by the development of bowel and bladder control. In an infant, when the bladder or bowel fills, the outlet muscles release automatically, and the infant urinates or defecates. Between the ages of 12 and 18 months, however, the child gradually gains control over these functions. The cerebral cortex begins to send inhibitory signals to reduce the normal autonomic nervous system reflexive activity. As any parent knows only too well, however, this coordination and fine tuning may take months to master. Individuals who

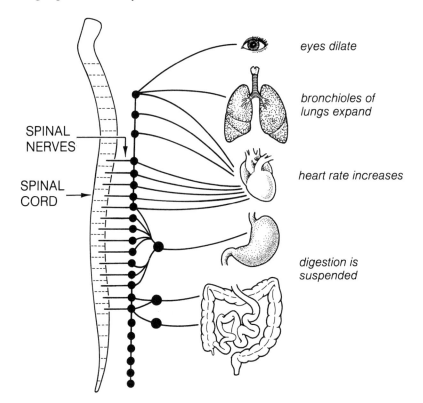

SPINAL
NERVES

SPINAL
CORD

eyes dilate

*bronchioles of
lungs expand*

heart rate increases

*digestion is
suspended*

Figure 13.11.   Autonomic nervous system. These nerves control such involuntary motor activities as breathing, heart rate, and digestion. This system is involved in "fight or flight" reactions.

have sustained damage to either the corticospinal tracts or the spinal cord are unable to inhibit the autonomic nervous system in this way (Low, 1994). This explains the great difficulty that children with cerebral palsy or meningomyelocele or those who have sustained a traumatic brain injury (see Chapter 26) may have in controlling bladder and bowel function.

CEREBROSPINAL FLUID AND HYDRODYNAMIC BALANCE

Long considered simply an aqueous environment for the suspension of the brain, CSF is now known to perform many additional functions. In addition to physically supporting the neural elements and serving to buffer the brain and spinal cord from excessive motion, CSF acts to provide nutritional support as well as to remove excessive hormones and neurotransmitters. CSF may also serve as a "relief valve," adjusting its volume when there are increases in intracranial pressure. Furthermore, its hydrodynamic properties no doubt influence the formation of the brain.

Approximately a pint of CSF is produced each day by the choroid plexus and arachnoid granulations in the brain. This fluid moves throughout the lateral and third ventricles and communicates with the fourth ventricle via the aqueduct of Sylvius (Figure 13.3). At the level of the fourth ventricle, the CSF exits at the foramina of Luschka and Magendie to circulate over the surface of the brain as well as over the spinal cord and its **meningeal** coverings. Removal of CSF occurs at the arachnoid granulations over the superior surface of the brain, which act as a one-way valve and allow CSF to move into the blood stream.

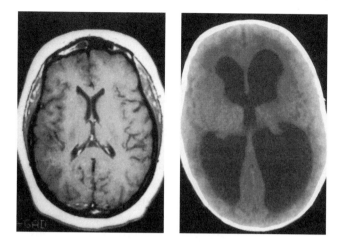

Figure 13.12. Normal computed tomography (CT) scan (left) and CT scan showing hydrocephalus (right). In the image to the right, note the rounded appearance of the frontal horns (top) as well as the differentially enlarged occipital horns (bottom). This is known as *culpocephaly* and is frequently in patients with spina bifida.

Should an imbalance develop between production and absorption of CSF, hydrocephalus may ensue (Figure 13.12). As mentioned previously, this buildup of CSF within the ventricles may be caused by an obstruction of CSF flow within the ventricles (frequently at the aqueduct of Sylvius) or at the exit foramina (Luschka or Magendie). This is known as a noncommunicating hydrocephalus; in contrast, communicating hydrocephalus is caused by an obstruction at the level of the arachnoid granulations. In addition to inadequate absorption, it is also possible to have an oversupply of CSF, as is seen in the setting of a tumor of the choroid plexus. This may overwhelm the ability of the arachnoid granulation to absorb the fluid.

When fluid builds up inside the skull of an infant, the **sutures** (the joints connecting the skull bones) expand and dissipate the increased pressure, at the expense of an increase in head circumference and may present in a bulging fontanelle. The same situation in the older child whose sutures have closed, however, may quickly lead to headache, vomiting, lethargy, and **focal neurological changes.** This buildup of fluid can be life threatening at any age and is considered a medical emergency.

When hydrocephalus occurs, it is necessary to restore the balance between production and absorption of CSF. This is often accomplished by performing a shunting procedure that increases the removal of CSF. The shunt's objective is to bypass the obstruction, whether at the level of the arachnoid granulations or within the ventricular system. This usually involves the diversion of CSF from the head to another site, preferably the abdomen. The complication rate from this procedure is low, and the long-term outcome reasonably good. Once placed, however, numerous obstacles remain in maintaining a working shunt and avoiding infection. Many children require shunt revisions as a result of these problems. Despite present-day imperfections, the management of hydrocephalus has been simplified and often allows for a near-typical lifestyle.

IMAGING THE BRAIN

In the 1990s, considerable advances in neuroradiological investigation permitted a better understanding of the living brain (Inder & Huppe, 2000; Zimmerman, Gibby, & Carmody,

2000). High-speed computed tomography (CT) scans, which are produced from multiple, thin-cut X rays, have become a mainstay for the evaluation of the child with hydrocephalus, trauma, craniofacial disorders, new-onset seizures, or tumors of the brain and skull (Maytal et al., 2000). The inherent strength of CT resides in its excellent bone definition. Three-dimensional CT now routinely provides sophisticated three-dimensional reconstruction of complex skull base disorders, whereas CT angiography offers good resolution in characterizing blood vessel or flow abnormalities with additional information from adjacent bony structures.

Despite the strengths of CT scanning, magnetic resonance imaging (MRI) has surpassed all other modalities for evaluating brain structure (Rivkin, 2000). It is particularly useful in evaluating developmental brain abnormalities and epilepsy (Gaillard, 2000). Although CT scans have offered increasing resolution with each successive generation of machines, soft tissue (e.g., white versus gray matter) definition remains inferior to that obtained from MRI. MRI exploits subtle magnetic differences in water and other molecules of the brain to evaluate regions in great anatomical detail. A variant approach, called diffusion-weighted (DW) MRI is the only technique that permits a noninvasive assessment of water molecular diffusion, which reflects tissue configuration at a microscopic level. Therefore, this technique appears to be particularly useful in identifying brain abnormalities. MRI can also be used to perform magnetic resonance spectroscopy to detect metabolic abnormalities in the brain, as is seen in certain inborn errors of metabolism. MRI scanning, which uses no radiation, is safe and usually provides superior resolution to CT scanning. It is, however, more expensive and time consuming than CT scanning and more difficult to perform under emergency situations. It also provides slightly different information, so in some instances CT and MRI are complementary.

Additional neuroradiological approaches are now available for assessing the functional state of the CNS. Single photon emission computed tomography (SPECT) and positron emission tomography (PET) are techniques that demonstrate metabolically active regions in the brain. A radioactively labeled compound, most commonly glucose, is injected into the bloodstream and SPECT or PET is then used to assess its selective uptake up in various brain regions. This has been used to diagnose strokes, tumors, and brain injury following head trauma (Abdel-Dayem et al., 1998) and to predict gross motor development in children with cerebral palsy (Yim et al., 2000). These modalities have also been employed in the evaluation of seizure disorders prior to surgery (Chugani & Chugani, 1999; So, 2000). In this instance, the studies can differentiate areas that are functionally hyperactive secondary to seizure activity from those that are hypoactive as a result of structural lesions.

Another approach to functional imaging is functional MRI (fMRI). This combines the excellent resolution of MRI with the capacity to study the effects of attention and activity (such as reading or movement) on brain function (Baving, Laucht, & Schmidt, 1999; Rubia et al., 1999). It can also be used to determine efficacy of medication on these activities. This technique affords significantly superior resolution to PET and will most likely supplant it in the future.

SUMMARY

The nervous system is composed of central and peripheral elements. The CNS (the brain and spinal cord) undergoes elaborate development and differentiation during embryogenesis and is at risk for innumerable malformations. Some of these mistakes may contribute to developmental disabilities. Meningomyelocele, hydrocephalus, and cerebral palsy are a few examples. As an improved understanding of the pathogenesis of developmental disabilities unfolds, better therapeutic avenues will be forthcoming.

REFERENCES

Abdel-Dayem, H.M., Abu-Judeh, H., Kumar, M., et al. (1998). SPECT brain perfusion abnormalities in mild or moderate traumatic brain injury. *Clinical Nuclear Medicine, 23*, 309–317.

Andersson, P.B., & Rando, T.A. (1999). Neuromuscular disorders of childhood. *Current Opinion in Pediatrics, 11*, 497–503.

Barkley, R.A. (2000). Genetics of childhood disorders: XVII. ADHD, Part 1: The executive functions and ADHD. *Journal of the American Academy of Child and Adolescent Psychiatry, 39*, 1064–1068.

Baving, L., Laucht, M., & Schmidt, M.H. (1999). Atypical frontal brain activation in ADHD: Preschool and elementary school boys and girls. *Journal of the American Academy of Child and Adolescent Psychiatry, 38*, 1363–1371.

Botto, L.D., Moore, C.A., Khoury, M.J., et al. (1999). Neural-tube defects. *New England Journal of Medicine, 341*, 1509–1519.

Bourgeois, B.F. (1998). Temporal lobe epilepsy in infants and children. *Brain and Development, 20*, 135–141.

Brodal, P. (1998). *The central nervous system: Structure and function* (2nd ed.). New York: Oxford University Press.

Butler, C., & Campbell, S. (2000). Evidence of the effects of intrathecal baclofen for spastic and dystonic cerebral palsy. AACPDM Treatment Outcomes Committee Review Panel. *Developmental Medicine and Child Neurology, 42*, 634–645.

Byrne, R.W., Hayes, E.A., George, T.M., et al. (1995). Operative resection of 100 spinal lipomas in infants less than 1 year of age. *Pediatric Neurosurgery, 23*, 182–186; discussion 187.

Chugani, H.T., & Chugani, D.C. (1999). Basic mechanisms of childhood epilepsies: Studies with positron emission tomography. *Advances in Neurology, 79*, 883–891.

Chugani, H.T., & Muller, R.A. (1999). Plasticity associated with cerebral resections. *Advances in Neurology, 81*, 241–250.

Cole, N., & Siddique, T. (1999). Genetic disorders of motor neurons. *Seminars in Neurology, 19*, 407–418.

Cote, L., & Crutcher, M.D. (2000). The basal ganglia. In E.R. Kandel, J.H. Schwartz, & T.M. Jessell (Eds.), *Principles of neural science* (4th ed., pp. 853–867). New York: McGraw-Hill.

Cross, J.H. (1999). Update on surgery for epilepsy. *Archives of Disease in Childhood, 81*, 356–359.

Crossman, A.R., & Neary, D. (2000). *Neuroanatomy: An illustrated colour text* (2nd ed.). Philadelphia: Churchill Livingstone.

de Bode, S., & Curtiss, S. (2000). Language after hemispherectomy. *Brain and Cognition, 43*(1–3), 135–138.

Diamond, A. (2000). Close interrelation of motor development and cognitive development and of the cerebellum and prefrontal cortex. *Child Development, 71*, 44–56.

Dodds, S.D., & Wolfe, S.W. (2000). Perinatal brachial plexus palsy. *Current Opinion in Pediatrics, 12*, 40–47.

Drolet, B.A. (2000). Cutaneous signs of neural tube dysraphism. *Pediatric Clinics of North America, 47*, 813–823.

Duchowny, M., Jayakar, P., & Levin, B. (2000). Aberrant neural circuits in malformations of cortical development and focal epilepsy. *Neurology, 55*, 423–428.

Funnell, M.G., Corballis, P.M., & Gazzaniga, M.S. (1999). A deficit in perceptual matching in the left hemisphere of a callosotomy patient. *Neuropsychologia, 37*, 1143–1154.

Gaillard, W.D. (2000). Structural and functional imaging in children with partial epilepsy. *Mental Retardation and Developmental Disabilities Research Reviews, 6*, 220–226.

Goldberg, S. (2000). *Clinical neuroanatomy made ridiculously simple* (2nd ed.). Miami, FL: Medmaster.

Golden, J.A. (1999). Towards a greater understanding of the pathogenesis of holoprosencephaly. *Brain and Development, 21*, 513–521.

Hanieh, A., Sutherland, A., Foster, B., et al. (2000). Syringomyelia in children with primary scoliosis. *Child's Nervous System, 16*, 200–202.

Heiss, J.D., Patronas, N., DeVroom, H.L., et al. (1999). Elucidating the pathophysiology of syringomyelia. *Journal of Neurosurgery, 91*, 553–562.

Hida, K., Iwasaki, Y., Koyanagi, I., et al. (1999). Pediatric syringomyelia with Chiari malformation: Its clinical characteristics and surgical outcomes. *Surgical Neurology, 51*, 383–390; discussion 390–391.

Huo, R., Burden, S.K., Hoyt, C.S., et al. (1999). Chronic cortical visual impairment in children: Aetiology, prognosis, and associated neurological deficits. *British Journal of Ophthalmology, 83*, 670–675.

Huttenlocher, P.R. (1991). Dendritic and synaptic pathology in mental retardation. *Pediatric Neurology, 7*, 79–85.

Inder, T.E., & Huppe, P.S. (2000). In vivo studies of brain development by magnetic resonance techniques. *Mental Retardation and Developmental Disabilities Research Reviews, 6*, 59–67.

Kandel, E.R., Schwartz, J.H., & Jessell, T.M. (Eds.). (2000). *Principles of neural science* (4th ed.). New York: McGraw-Hill.

Kinsman, S.L., Plawner, L.L., & Hahn, J.S. (2000). Holoprosencephaly: Recent advances and new insights. *Current Opinion in Neurology, 13*, 127–132.

Klemm, W.R., & Vertes, R.P. (Eds.). (1990). *Brainstem mechanisms of behavior.* New York: John Wiley & Sons.

Lagae, L. (2000). Cortical malformations: A frequent cause of epilepsy in children. *European Journal of Pediatrics, 159*, 555–562.

Lazar, J.W., & Frank, Y. (1998). Frontal systems dysfunction in children with attention-deficit/hyperactivity disorder and learning disabilities. *The Journal of Neuropsychiatry and Clinical Neurosciences, 10*, 160–167.

Lequin, M.H., & Barkovich, A.J. (1999). Current concepts of cerebral malformation syndromes. *Current Opinion in Pediatrics, 11*, 492–496.

Leventer, R.J., & Harvey, A.S. (1998). Cortical malformations: A significant cause of paediatric neurological morbidity. *Journal of Paediatric Child Health, 34*(1), 6–8.

Low, P.A. (1994). Autonomic neuropathies. *Current Opinion in Neurology, 7*, 402–406.

Manning, S.M., Jennings, R., & Madsen, J.R. (2000). Pathophysiology, prevention, and potential treatment of neural tube defects. *Mental Retardation and Developmental Disabilities Research Reviews, 6*, 6–14.

Maytal, J., Krauss, J.M., Novak, G., et al. (2000). The role of brain computed tomography in evaluating children with new onset of seizures in the emergency department. *Epilepsia, 41*, 950–954.

McInerney, J., Siegel, A.M., Nordgren, R.E., et al. (1999). Long-term seizure outcome following corpus callosotomy in children. *Stereotactic and Functional Neurosurgery, 73*(1–4), 79–83.

McLone, D.G., & La Marca, F. (1997). The tethered spinal cord: Diagnosis, significance, and management. *Seminars in Pediatric Neurology, 4,* 192–208.

Menkes, J.H., & Sarnat, H.B. (Eds.). (2000). *Child neurology* (6th ed.). Baltimore: Lippincott Williams & Wilkins.

Muenke, M., & Cohen, M.M., Jr. (2000). Genetic approaches to understanding brain development: Holoprosencephaly as a model. *Mental Retardation and Developmental Disabilities Research Reviews, 6,* 15–21.

Muenke, M., Gurrieri, F., Bay, C., et al. (1994). Linkage of a human brain malformation, familial holoprosencephaly, to chromosome 7 and evidence for genetic heterogeneity. *Proceedings of the National Academy of Sciences of the United States of America, 91,* 8102–8106.

Neville, H.J., & Bavelier, D. (1998). Neural organization and plasticity of language. *Current Opinion in Neurobiology, 8,* 254–258.

Ouvrier, R.A. (1996). Hereditary neuropathies in children: The contribution of the new genetics. *Seminars in Pediatric Neurology, 3,* 140–151.

Parry-Fielder, B., Nolan, T.M., Collins, K.J., et al. (1997). Developmental language disorders and epilepsy. *Journal of Paediatric Child Health, 33*(4), 277–280.

Pineda, D., Ardila, A., Rosselli, M., et al. (1998). Executive dysfunctions in children with attention deficit hyperactivity disorder. *International Journal of Neuroscience, 96,* 177–196.

Pomeroy, S.L., & Klim, J.Y.H. (2000). Biology and pathobiology of neuronal development. *Mental Retardation and Developmental Disabilities Research Reviews, 6,* 41–46.

Porter, B.E., & Tennekoon, G. (2000). Myelin and disorders that affect the formation and maintenance of this sheath. *Mental Retardation and Developmental Disabilities Research Reviews, 6,* 47–59.

Reiner, O. (2000). The unfolding story of two lissencephaly genes and brain development. *Molecular Neurobiology, 20,* 143–156.

Rivkin, M.J. (2000). Developmental neuroimaging of children using magnetic resonance techniques. *Mental Retardation and Developmental Disabilities Research Reviews, 6,* 68–80.

Roberts, P.A. (1992). *Neuroanatomy* (3rd ed.). New York: Springer-Verlag.

Rodriguez-Pena, A., Ibarrola, N., Iniguez, M.A., et al. (1993). Neonatal hypothyroidism affects the timely expression of myelin-associated glycoprotein in the rat brain. *Journal of Clinical Investigation, 91,* 812–818.

Rubia, K., Overmeyer, S., Taylor, E., et al. (1999). Hypofrontality in attention deficit hyperactivity disorder during higher-order motor control: A study with functional MRI. *American Journal of Psychiatry, 156,* 891–896.

Sanes, D.H., Reh, T.A., & Harris, W.A. (Eds.). (2000). *Development of the central nervous system.* San Diego: Academic Press.

Sarnat, H.B. (1991). Cerebral dysplasias as expressions of altered maturational processes. *Canadian Journal of Neurological Sciences, 18,* 196–204.

Shimizu, H., & Maehara, T. (2000). Neuronal disconnection for the surgical treatment of pediatric epilepsy. *Epilepsia, 41*(Suppl. 9), S28–S30.

Shuman, R.M. (1995). The Chiari malformations: A constellation of anomalies. *Seminars in Pediatric Neurology, 2,* 220–226.

So, E.L. (2000). Integration of EEG, MRI, and SPECT in localizing the seizure focus for epilepsy surgery. *Epilepsia, 41*(Suppl. 3), S48–S54.

Sorenson, J.M., Wheless, J.W., Baumgartner, J.E., et al. (1997). Corpus callosotomy for medically intractable seizures. *Pediatric Neurosurgery, 27,* 260–267.

Talbot, K. (1999). Spinal muscular atrophy. *Journal of Inherited Metabolic Diseases, 22,* 545–554.

Tanaka, T., & Gleeson, J.G. (2000). Genetics of brain development and malformation syndromes. *Current Opinion in Pediatrics, 12,* 523–528.

ten Donkelaar, H.J. (2000). Major events in the development of the forebrain. *European Journal of Morphology, 38,* 301–308.

Uher, B.F., & Golden, J.A. (2000). Neuronal migration defects of the cerebral cortex: A destination debacle. *Clinical Genetics, 58,* 16–24.

Vaidya, C.J., Austin, G., Kirkorian, G., et al. (1998). Selective effects of methylphenidate in attention deficit hyperactivity disorder: A functional magnetic resonance study. *Proceedings of the National Academy of Sciences of the United States of America, 95,* 14494–14499.

Van Hout, A. (1997). Acquired aphasia in children. *Seminars in Pediatric Neurology, 4,* 102–108.

Vicari, S., Albertoni, A., Chilosi, A.M., et al. (2000). Plasticity and reorganization during language development in children with early brain injury. *Cortex, 36,* 31–46.

Volpe, J.J. (2001). *Neurology of the newborn* (4th ed). Philadelphia: W.B. Saunders.

Walsh, C.A. (2000). Genetics of neuronal migration in the cerebral cortex. *Mental Retardation and Developmental Disabilities Research Reviews, 6,* 34–40.

Waxman, S.G., & de Groot, J. (1995). *Correlative neuroanatomy* (22nd ed.). Norwalk, CT: Appleton and Lange.

Xu, J., Cheng, X., & Gu, Y. (2000). Different methods and results in the treatment of obstetrical brachial plexus palsy. *Journal of Reconstructive Microsurgery, 16,* 7–20; discussion 420–422.

Yim, S.Y., Lee, I.Y., Park, C.H., et al. (2000). A qualitative analysis of brain SPECT for prognostication of gross motor development in children with cerebral palsy. *Clinical Nuclear Medicine, 25*(4), 268–272.

Zimmerman, R.A., Gibby, W.A., & Carmody, R. (2000). *Neuroimaging: Clinical and physical principles.* New York: Springer-Verlag.

14 Muscles, Bones, and Nerves

The Body's Framework

Arabella I. Leet, John P. Dormans, and Laura L. Tosi

Upon completion of this chapter, the reader will:

- be aware of the structure and function of bones, muscles, and nerves

- understand how the different structures composing the musculoskeletal system work together to produce movement

- learn the basic principles of the musculoskeletal physical exam

- know some of the more common musculoskeletal and neuromuscular diseases of childhood and their treatments

- recognize that the impairment caused by neuromuscular deformity can be lessened through the efforts of the health care team

Although the brain initiates the commands for movement, nothing would happen if motor neurons, nerves, neuromuscular junctions, muscles, bones, and joints did not respond in a coordinated manner to these signals. Together, these components make up the musculoskeletal and neuromuscular systems and are responsible for our physical strength and movement. Signals from the brain travel down the spinal cord to the peripheral nerves and to the neuromuscular junctions, signaling the muscles to contract. The muscles attach to bones via tendons and produce movement through the joints. Joints are made from the ends of two different bones attached to each other via ligaments. As the bones move and the framework of the body changes, signals are sent back to the brain giving information about the position of the body in space. Without this complex, integrated system, we would be immobile. This chapter explores how these systems function and examines what can go wrong.

THE MUSCULOSKELETAL SYSTEM

The musculoskeletal system is composed of bone, muscles, and joints, as well as their associated **ligaments** and **tendons,** which work together to permit movement. Impairments within this system are a major cause of disability in childhood.

Common Musculoskeletal Terms

Before discussing how the musculoskeletal system works, it is important to define the terms used to describe different kinds of movement. These terms are illustrated in Figure 14.1.

Flexion refers to the bending of a limb or body part forward through one or more joints. **Extension,** the opposite of flexion, means to straighten, or bend back. When a part of the body

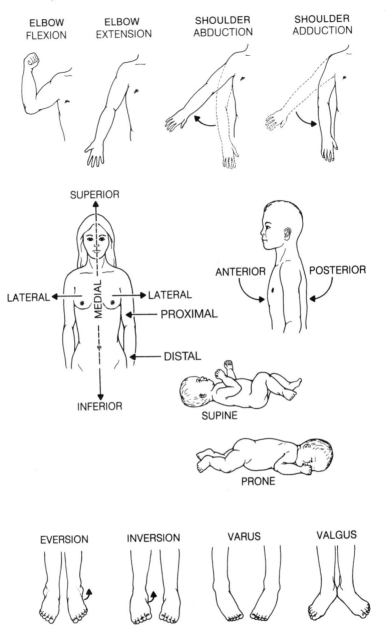

Figure 14.1. Various types of movements and postures.

moves away from the midline of the body, this movement is called **abduction;** movement toward the midline is called **adduction.** The midline also is called the **median plane;** the outer parts of the body are the **lateral** sections. **Anterior** refers to the front of a flat surface, whereas **posterior** is the rear or underneath part. Thus, the chest is anterior, whereas the back is posterior. The word **superior** means up or above; **inferior** means below. The head is superior to and the feet are inferior to the shoulders. For the extremities, **proximal** means toward the center of the body, and **distal** means away from the center of the body. The hands are distal, and the shoulders are proximal.

Supine refers to the position of being on one's back, whereas **prone** describes the position of lying on one's stomach. A foot is **everted** when the sole faces outward, or away from the midline, and **inverted** when the sole turns inward. **Varus** denotes a condition in which the distal body part is angled toward the midline of the body. The opposite of varus is **valgus,** in which the distal body part is angled away from the midline. Varus or valgus may be normal or abnormal. An example of varus is to have "bowed legs," which is the nonmedical term for varus of the knees (genu varum); "knock-knees" describes the state of valgus of the knees (genu valgum).

    Equinus refers to a condition in which the foot is pointed down; a child with equinus of the foot will walk on tiptoes. **Dislocation** refers to the complete displacement of one **articular** (joint) surface from its opposing surface. **Subluxation** is an incomplete or partial dislocation of a joint.

    Spasticity is a state of increased muscle tone and is often a major feature of children with pyramidal (spastic) cerebral palsy (see Chapter 23). **Athetosis** refers to random, writhing, involuntary movements, especially in the hands; it can be seen in individuals with certain forms of cerebral palsy. **Ataxia** implies an incoordination of muscular movement such as walking, usually resulting from abnormalities in the cerebellum. If a movement disorder prevents full range of motion around a joint, a **contracture,** or a fixed loss of joint motion, develops.

Orthopedic Management of the Child with a Disability

Optimizing musculoskeletal function for a child with a disability is vitally important. If a child uses a wheelchair to ambulate, then he or she must be able to sit for a prolonged period in a comfortable position to participate in school and play. If **scoliosis** (spinal curvature) causes loss of sitting balance or if a foot contracture does not allow the legs to be positioned in a wheelchair, then function may be lost. Maximizing a child's functional level and maintaining that function throughout childhood are the goals of **orthopedic** management.

    Although different musculoskeletal disorders are associated with various orthopedic problems, a general philosophy of care for any child, regardless of the specific disability, is to promote function (Birch, 1998). Helping families have realistic goals for their child is the first step in this process. To accomplish this, it is necessary to assess the child and predict the maximal level of function that he or she may attain. Many families are most concerned about walking ability; however, children may still lead very productive lives with wheelchair ambulation. A more important final goal of interventions may be that a child can perform independent transfers or can achieve good sitting posture. Children do not benefit from surgery on their legs to help with walking if it will not eventually be possible for them to walk, as is the case for a child with a thoracic meningomyelocele (spina bifida; see Chapter 24).

    In the initial assessment, it is important to discuss the physical and/or occupational therapy programs the child is enrolled in and the adaptive equipment he or she uses. Next, the types of interventions to maximize function are considered. For example, would additional therapy or orthotics (e.g., braces, splints), or even surgery, allow the child to perform better in functional activities? Following this assessment, the health team designs and implements a therapy program. Reassessment is provided at regular intervals to ensure continued progress. Children's bodies change with growth, and in children with neuromuscular disabilities, these changes can lead to new deformities or impairments that need to be addressed to prevent loss of function. All too often children are seen who have not had continuity of care and present with hips that are dislocated or spines that are curved to such a degree that treatment is very difficult, and the opportunity to intervene with less aggressive management has been lost.

Physical Examination of the Musculoskeletal System

The musculoskeletal physical exam in children can be challenging because children may not be cooperative or able to follow instructions. The exam is best performed with the child undressed and either in an examining gown or in shorts. Young children are sometimes easier to examine in their parent's lap at first, where they become accustomed to being examined. They can then be moved more easily to the examining table.

If the child can walk, observing the gait pattern is very valuable. During normal gait, the head and trunk should be level, with minimal sway from side to side. It is helpful to listen to the sound of the feet on the floor. Each footstep should be even, like a metronome, with equal pauses between foot strikes. Watch to see whether the child can maintain balance while standing on one leg and swinging through the opposite leg. The leg that is swinging through should clear the ground, and the foot should not drag; each step should be large enough to allow for forward progression of the body. More complex gait patterns can be better studied using videotape or computerized gait analysis.

If the child crawls, his or her ability to get up on all fours and move in a reciprocal (right then left) pattern should be documented. If the child is unable to crawl, it is still important to document whether he or she can sit independently and how he or she sits. Is the head held independently and the back straight? Are the limbs straight or contracted?

Children with disorders that cause an imbalance of the muscles around the spine can develop a significant spinal curvature. Curves from side to side are called *scoliosis*, whereas excessive roundness to the back is called **kyphosis;** the opposite of kyphosis is *lordosis*, an inward curve of the spine. Because spinal curves are best managed when they are still small, the spine of a child who is at particular risk (e.g., a child with spastic cerebral palsy, meningomyelocele, or muscular dystrophy) should be examined regularly. Early clues suggesting scoliosis are unequal heights of the shoulders or a slanting of the waist. The ribs attach to the thoracic (upper) spine and may follow the curve of the vertebrae, causing a rib rise or "rib hump" when the child bends forward. School screening examinations for scoliosis are designed to look for these physical exam findings to detect scoliosis as early as possible.

The hips, knees, and ankles should be examined for range of motion. Loss of motion in a joint can result from many causes. For example, bone abnormalities in the opposing surfaces of a joint or contractures (shortening of the soft tissue around a joint) can limit motion. Often an X ray of the joint is helpful in distinguishing between these two possibilities.

The hip exam, like the spine exam, should be performed often, as early treatment of hip problems is easier than later treatment. The examiner should be able to abduct (spread apart) the hips easily and symmetrically. Loss of hip abduction may indicate a hip dislocation or subluxation (Figure 14.2a). Another easy way to assess whether the hip is dislocated is to look at the knee heights with the hips and knees flexed and the ankles together. If the knee heights are unequal, called a positive Galeazzi test, the hip may be dislocated or the legs may be of unequal length for some other reason (Figure 14.2b).

The knee joint must be straight for standing but must flex to 90 degrees for comfortable sitting and flex even farther for easy stair climbing. Tightness of the hamstring muscles can

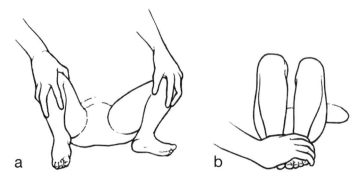

a   b

Figure 14.2.   a) Abduction of the hip is reduced or lost when the hip is dislocated. Whenever the hips cannot be abducted fully or symmetrically hip dislocation needs to be ruled out. b) A Galeazzi sign measures the differences in height of the femurs and can be caused by a dislocated hip or by a difference in limb length.

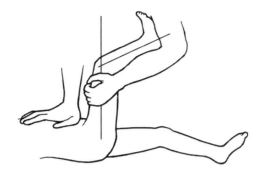

Figure 14.3. With the hip flexed to 90 degrees, the ability of the knee to extend is measured. A knee flexion contracture or tightness of the hamstring muscles can cause loss of extension of the knee in this position.

limit knee movement; the popliteal angle (Figure 14.3) helps monitor the range of knee motion. The ankle should be examined for *plantarflexion* (foot down) and *dorsiflexion* (foot up). The ability to dorsiflex beyond a neutral position (90 degrees) is important for both walking and sitting and should be tested with the knee both extended and flexed. The goal for every child is to maintain the feet in a *plantargrade* (flat on the floor) position and to maintain as much flexibility in the feet as possible.

Other important aspects of the musculoskeletal exam involve studying the rotation of the lower extremities. There are three possible areas (thigh, shin, and foot) where an internal twist can occur, causing the child to walk with a toe-in ("pigeon-toed") gait. There can be an internal twist in the femur bone, described as increased femoral anteversion. Anteversion can be assessed with the child prone by palpating or by looking at the amount of internal rotation (Figure 14.4) compared with external rotation. If there is more internal rotation than external rotation, the femur is anteverted. If the leg appears to turn in when there is no discernible increase in femoral anteversion, then testing for internal tibial torsion (internal rotation in the tibia, or shin bone) can be performed by measuring the foot–thigh angle (Figure 14.5). Finally, internal rotation of the forefoot (metatarsus adductus) can also cause intoeing and can be best demonstrated by loss of the straight inside border of the foot. The foot instead appears c-shaped or bean shaped. If this internal foot position is accompanied by loss of ankle dorsiflexion in an otherwise typical child, then the diagnosis of **clubfoot** (discussed later) is likely.

Figure 14.4. The child pictured is prone (lying on the stomach), and the legs are rotated in internal rotation (remember, the child is face down). Loss of external rotation accompanied by increased internal rotation is consistent with increased femoral anteversion. The test for loss of internal rotation in the hip also is useful to determine if the hip is irritable from synovitis, which can occur in juvenile rheumatoid arthritis (JRA).

The upper extremities should also be examined for range of motion of the shoulders, elbows, and hands. The arms should be able to be placed above the head. The elbows should straighten fully. All fingers should be able to be straightened and brought out of the palm fully. The hands should be tested for feeling, as occasionally sensation may be diminished. Testing the ability of the child to grasp an object and place it in a desired spot demonstrates selective control, a skill necessary to operate hand controls.

Abnormal physical exam findings are often followed by X rays of the involved areas, which can help detect limits in movement caused by bony deformity. X rays are helpful in detecting the shapes of bone but are a poor gauge of the quality of bone. Almost one third of the bone must be involved before changes are detectable by X ray.

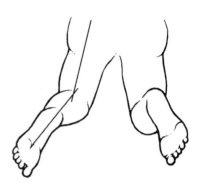

Figure 14.5. The angle made by the foot and thigh helps determine whether there is rotation in the tibia, or shin bone. This angle is called, appropriately, the *thigh–foot angle*.

Components of the Musculoskeletal System

Bone

The bones of the skeleton form the internal scaffolding of the body. They range in size from the ½-inch–long bones of the finger **(phalanges)** to the thigh bone **(femur),** which is roughly 18 inches long in adults. Some bones, such as the skull, are flat; others, such as the femur, are tubular. Even though bones are hard and immobile, they are a dynamic organ system contributing not only to structural support but also to the blood and metabolic systems of the body. And just as the body depends on the skeleton for support, the skeletal system relies on the body for its maintenance and growth.

The height of a child increases because of growth of the spine and the long, tubular bones of the lower extremities. To understand how this occurs, it is helpful first to examine the structure of a bone. For example, the femur consists of 1) a shaft, or **diaphysis,** composed mostly of dense cortical bone; 2) spongy, upper and lower portions called **metaphyses,** composed mostly of **cancellous** (spongy) bone; 3) the ends of the bone, called the **epiphyses;** and 4) growth plates, or **physes,** that separates the metaphyses and epiphyses (Figure 14.6). Surrounding the bone is a tough, fibrous layer called the **periosteum.** Calcium crystals embedded in a protein compound make up about two thirds of bone. The remainder is composed of living cells. It is the mineral and protein mixture that lends strength to the bone. The central core, the *bone marrow,* is where blood cells are formed. Weaving through the bone's structure are blood vessels that supply oxygen and nutrients necessary for growth.

New bone originates at the level of the growth plate. Here, cartilage cells are laid down and form the matrix for later bone formation. The matrix is converted to bone by specialized bone-forming cells called **osteoblasts.** These cells contain calcium and gradually transform the cartilage into bone. This process is called **endochondral ossification.** As both ends of the long bone lengthen, the child grows taller (Figure 14.6).

As growth takes place and the bone is subject to different stresses, the bone responds by changing its shape, a process called *remodeling.* These changes usually increase the tensile strength and stability of the bone, making it less susceptible to fracture. Remodeling and growth involve formation of new bone by the osteoblasts as well as the breakdown and resorption (uptake) of bone by **osteoclasts.** The osteoblasts produce **osteoid** that **calcifies** or crystallizes; the osteoclasts remove the crystals from already-formed bone and return the calcium to

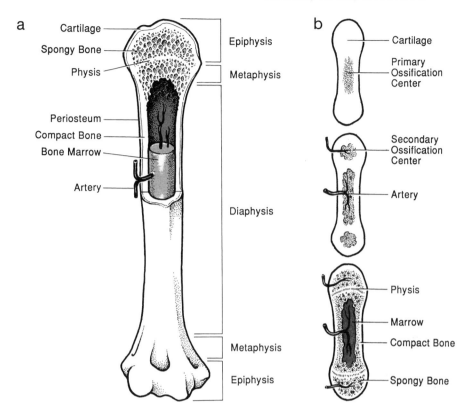

Figure 14.6. a) The structure of a typical long bone, the humerus. New bone arises from the physis, and the arm lengthens. The upper portion of the bone is the metaphysis, and the shaft is the diaphysis. The bone marrow, which produces blood cells, lies in the center of the shaft. Surrounding the bone is a fibrous sheath, the periosteum. The surface of the bone facing the joint space is covered by articular cartilage. b) The long bone starts off as a mass of cartilage in fetal life. Gradually the center is invaded by osteoblasts. These cells lay down minerals that form bone. The ossification centers spread and the bone enlarges. After birth, further bone growth occurs only from the physis.

the bloodstream. Thus a part of the bone is constantly disappearing as new bone is being laid down in its place. On average, a section of a child's bone lasts about a year and is then replaced by new bone. In an adult, the reshaping continues even though growth has stopped. The average bone segment of an adult lasts about 7 years. In other words, bone is a living organ that constantly grows and reshapes in response to physiological stresses.

Joints

A joint is the connection between two or more bones, such as at the knee. A joint is composed of 1) the epiphysis and cartilage of the two connecting bones; 2) the small, lubricated space between the cartilage ends, called the *joint cavity*; and 3) the ligaments, tendons, and muscles that bind the bones together and make the joint stable (Figure 14.7).

Joints may be immobile, partly mobile, or completely mobile. The sutures of the skull are examples of immobile joints. The wrist and hand are composed of both slightly mobile joints and completely mobile joints. Mobile joints include hinge, pivot, and ball-and-socket types. The knee most closely resembles a hinge joint that can flex and extend (Figure 14.7). At this joint, movement of 145 degrees back and forth is normally possible. At the elbow, which is a pivot and hinge joint, rotation as well as hinge movement occurs. The hip, a ball-and-socket joint, can move in all three planes, allowing flexion/extension, rotation, and adduction/abduction.

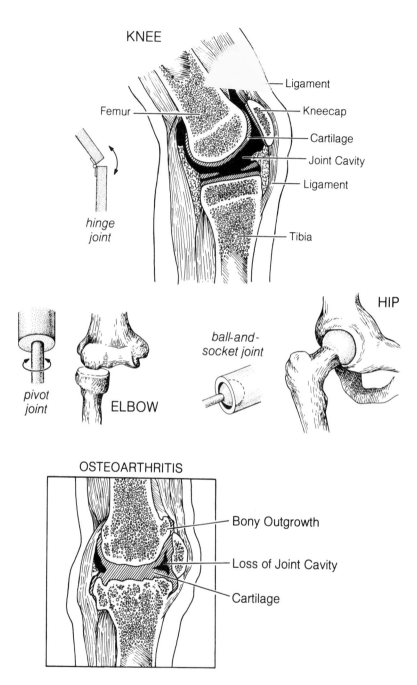

Figure 14.7. Joints. A typical knee joint is compared with an arthritic knee joint. Usually, there is a lubricated joint cavity separating the femur and tibia bones. Muscles cross the joint attached to the ligaments. In the diseased joint, the cartilage is abnormal and has disappeared in places, and there may be fusion of the opposing bones. This severely limits movement. Several different types of joints are also illustrated: hinge (knee), pivot (elbow), and ball-and-socket (hip).

The ends of the bones that make up a joint are covered with a shiny coat of cartilage (articular cartilage) that forms the surface of the joint. The cartilage receives nourishment from the *synovial fluid* contained inside the joint. Specialized synovial cells can be found in joints and are responsible for producing joint fluid. Inflammation of the synovial cells (synovitis) causes an excess production of joint fluid and expansion of the synovial cells.

Ligaments and Tendons

Ligaments are the fibrous tissues that attach one bone to another across a joint, providing stability to the joint. (Figure 14.7). Tendons, which attach muscles to bones, are similar in composition and function to ligaments but have looser fibers (Figure 14.8). Tendons enable muscles to exert forces across the bones and joints, allowing movement. Both ligaments and tendons are flexible and resilient and are essential to keeping joints moving properly. In comparison with bone, these tissues have a more limited capacity to regenerate. Thus damage to tendons or ligaments (all too common in sports injuries) might require surgical repair.

Muscle

The main function of skeletal muscle is to contract by shortening and thus produce movement of the limbs across joints. Cells called *muscle fibers* comprise muscle. Muscle fibers' contractile machinery consists of two proteins, **actin** and **myosin** (Figure 14.8), which form highly organized subunits called **sarcomeres.** These subunits are stimulated to contract by nerve impulses. Smooth movement requires the coordination of all of the muscle groups around a joint. Most joints have attached muscles that pull in different directions. **Antagonist** muscles oppose one another in the movement of a joint, whereas **agonist** muscles pull together to produce movement. For example, when the arm is flexed, the biceps contracts, as does the **brachialis;** the triceps, however, relaxes (Figure 14.8). If both muscle groups contracted simultaneously, the arm

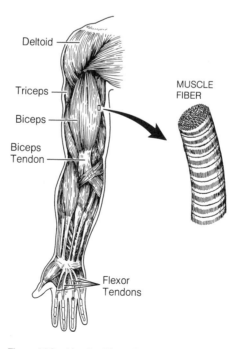

Deltoid

Triceps

Biceps

Biceps Tendon

MUSCLE FIBER

Flexor Tendons

Figure 14.8. Muscles. The major muscles in the arm. Note that the biceps and triceps are antagonists. The enlargement shows a muscle fiber, which is the unit of muscle tissue.

would be held stiffly in an isometric contraction. Thus, when the brain tells the arm to move, it actually sends a number of messages that tell some muscles to contract and others to relax.

COMMON DISEASES OF BONES, MUSCLES, AND JOINTS

Malformations of the Bone

A malformation is a defect that results from an intrinsically (often inherited) abnormal developmental process. Two examples of bone malformation syndromes are achondroplasia and **osteopetrosis.**

Achondroplasia

Achondroplasia is the most common form of disproportionate short stature ("dwarfism"). The disorder occurs as the result of a mutation in the gene for fibroblast growth factor receptor 3 (Matsui, Yasui, & Kimura, 1998). This mutation is inherited in an autosomal dominant pattern, although three quarters of individuals with achondroplasia have a spontaneous mutation for the disease (Tanaka, 1997). Individuals with achondroplasia have smaller limbs than predicted based on the size of their trunk. Although motor development is often delayed, cognitive development is usually unimpaired.

A serious musculoskeletal complication of achondroplasia is *spinal stenosis* (narrowing of the spinal column), causing spinal cord compression, hydrocephalus, and apneic episodes. Anticipatory care, which may involve decompression spinal surgery, is essential to allow the child to lead a full and productive life (Hunter et al., 1998). A less severe but much more common complication, tibial bowing, also may often require surgical correction. Evaluation for disorders that may require rehabilitative therapy (e.g., physical therapy, occupational therapy, speech-language pathology) and adaptive equipment is also recommended (American Academy of Pediatrics, Committee on Genetics, 1995). Attempts to increase height may also be considered. Controversial therapies include surgical limb lengthening and the use of human growth hormone (Ramaswami et al., 1999). Both of these treatments are considered experimental.

Osteopetrosis

Osteopetrosis is an autosomal recessively inherited disorder with an incidence of about 1 in 200,000 births. It is caused by an abnormality of the osteoclasts, resulting in the failure of bone resorption (Carolino, Perez, & Popa, 1998; Gerritsen et al., 1994). As a result, the bone becomes very dense, and the bone marrow space becomes very narrow. This results in severe anemia because the space for blood cell production is reduced. There is also growth failure and progressive thickening of the bones of the skull, with eventual impingement of the cranial nerves that emerge through holes in the skull, which may cause progressive vision and hearing loss. If untreated, most children with the disorder die in the first decade of life. Since the late 1990s, bone marrow transplantation has been used to provide normal osteoclasts. This intervention has been shown to reverse many of the symptoms and to permit prolonged survival (Fasth & Porras, 1999) but may be complicated by problems such as **graft versus host disease.**

Deformities of Bone

Unlike a malformation, a deformity does not involve an abnormality in the developmental process. Instead, normally formed bone is deformed as a result of external forces. Two of the more common extremity deformities seen at birth are clubfoot and **developmental dislocation of the hip (DDH).** Both are thought to be multifactorial in nature, having both genetic and environmental influences (see Chapter 1). Bony deformities also may develop after birth.

For example, in cerebral palsy, muscle imbalance due to spasticity can cause contractures, dislocations of joints, or scoliosis (Dormans, 1993).

Clubfoot

Clubfoot occurs in about 1 in 1,000 births and affects twice as many males as females (Bleck, 1993). It may be an isolated deformity without a known cause (idiopathic), or it may be part of a generalized neurological disorder such as cerebral palsy or meningomyelocele. It can result from an abnormality or arrest of embryonic development or from lack of room during intrauterine development (called a *postural clubfoot*). Clubfeet can be detected on some prenatal ultrasounds of the fetus.

At approximately the 9th week of gestation, the typical fetal foot appears clubbed; but by the 11th week the foot assumes a more functional position. One theory asserts that if there is a developmental arrest at 9 weeks, clubfoot results (Coleman, 1993). "Fetal packing" can also contribute to the formation of clubfoot, particularly when there are multiple births or decreased amniotic fluid production. In these situations, the fetus may have little room to move, and the foot may get stuck in one position for prolonged periods of time and become deformed.

The clubfoot deformity, or talipes equinovarus, actually has three components: equinus of the foot, varus of the heel, and forefoot adduction. One or both feet may be affected in idiopathic clubfoot. Treatment should start at birth with serial casting (Blakeslee, 1997; Ikeda, 1992). Surgical correction, if needed, is usually carried out at 4–6 months. This approach leads to a positive outcome for 60%–95% of children with clubfoot.

Developmental Dislocation of the Hip

Although clubfoot is more common in boys, DDH occurs more frequently in girls (Coleman, 1994). It results from a disruption of the normal ball-and-socket relationship between the femoral head and the **acetabulum** (hip socket; Figure 14.9). DDH ranges in severity from acetabular dysplasia, in which the acetabulum is shallow and does not hold the femoral head well;

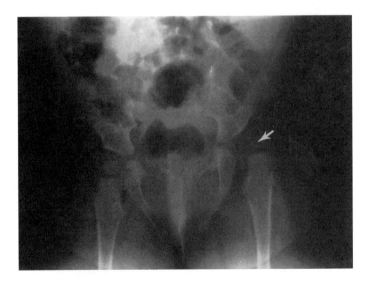

Figure 14.9.   Developmental dislocation of the hip (DDH). The arrow points to the left proximal femoral epiphysis that is dislocated from the acetabulum. (Courtesy of Dr. Sandra Kramer, Department of Pediatric Radiology, The Children's Hospital of Philadelphia.)

to subluxation, in which the head slips partially out of the acetabulum; to dislocation, in which there is a complete loss of contact between the femoral head and the acetabulum. DDH was once called *congenital dislocation of the hip*. It is now known, however, that the disorder may occur gradually after birth. In most infants, successful treatment is achieved with a Pavlik harness that is worn for 3–6 months (Song & Lapinsky, 2000). This holds the hip in flexion and abduction, keeping the femoral head securely in place and allowing for better formation of the joint (Crawford, Mehlman, & Slovek, 1999). Use of the Pavlik harness often negates the need for corrective surgery, so making the diagnosis as soon as possible is of the utmost importance, because nonsurgical treatment is most successful before 6 months of life.

Diseases of the Bone Matrix

If sufficient force is brought to bear against a bone, it will break (Figure 14.10). The most common causes of fractures in typically developing children are household, automobile, and playground accidents; sports injuries; and physical abuse. In some children with disabilities, however, a fracture can occur with little or no trauma, even from being lifted out of bed. These are called *pathological fractures* and can be associated with significant weakness of the bone (e.g., *osteogenesis imperfecta* [OI], *Ehlers-Danlos syndrome* [EDS]), a nutritional or metabolic deficiency (e.g., rickets), a secondary effect of a medication (e.g., steroids, antiepileptic drugs), weakness from disuse (e.g., cerebral palsy), or an invasion of bone (e.g., tumor). In each of these cases, the underlying medical condition causes the bone to be more brittle than usual and thereby more susceptible to fracture (Sambrook & Jones, 1995; Shaw et al., 1994). This brittleness, or **osteopenia,** results from too little or abnormal bony matrix, the mineral content and structural elements of bone. The mechanisms of some of these underlying medical conditions are described next.

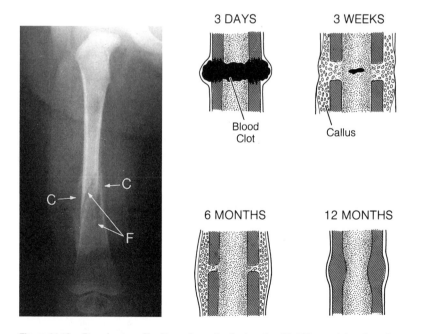

Figure 14.10. Bone fracture. The X ray shows the fracture line (F). This was taken 3 weeks after the accident, and callus formation can be seen (C). The mechanism of healing is outlined to the right. Initially, there is bleeding from the bone and surrounding soft tissues damaged in the accident. Soon this blood clot is invaded by osteoblasts that lay down bony tissue, forming a callus. In addition, the covering of the bone, the periosteum, lays down new bone. By 6 months, the bones are almost fused, but the bone structure is still enlarged. At 12 months, fusion is complete, and the bone is strong and looks fairly normal. Further reshaping over time will make all signs of fracture disappear.

Osteogenesis Imperfecta

OI causes bones to be brittle; children with this disorder have frequent fractures. OI has an incidence in the population of 1 in 20,000 births. It results from a defect in the COL1A1 and COL1A2 genes, which normally provide the message for formation of type 1 collagen, which is found in bone and other tissues (Kocher & Shapiro, 1998). Type 1 collagen is essential for building the scaffold in which bone mineral is laid down. If the scaffold is weak, then so too is the bone. Blue sclera (the part of the eye that is normally white) and poor dentition, along with fractures and bone deformity, are the most common characteristics of OI. It can, however, present as a continuum, ranging from very mild disease, with just a few fractures, to severe involvement, with multiple fractures, poor growth, and significant deformity (Paterson, 1997). The clinical diagnosis of OI is supported by a skin biopsy to test for the underlying genetic defect (Minch & Kruse, 1998).

Orthopedic care has been the mainstay of management of OI and involves measures to prevent fractures, to treat acute fractures, and to correct bony deformities. Placing rods inside the bones for support at the time of a fracture or in conjunction with *osteotomies* (surgical cuts through the bone to correct deformities) can improve the bone alignment and help prevent future fractures. Deformity of the spine occurs in 40%–80% of individuals with OI. Because thoracic curves can decrease lung capacity (Widemann et al., 1999), orthopedic consultation is recommended for monitoring curve progression and treatment with spine fusion if necessary (Engelbert et al., 1998). With modern medical care, life expectancy and quality of life have been improving for children with severe OI (Paterson, Ogston, & Henry, 1996).

A number of novel treatments for OI are being tested. One involves long-term cyclic intravenous administration of pamidronate (Aredia), a medication that stops bone resorption and thereby increases bone density. Children given this medication for 1–5 years had fewer fractures and increased growth (Glorieux et al., 1998). Bone marrow transplantation, performed in a small number of children with the most severe forms of OI, decreased the number of fractures but failed to prevent them from occurring altogether (Horwitz et al., 1999). Finally, because OI is caused by a genetic error in collagen metabolism, gene therapy to replace the incorrect message for collagen holds considerable promise for a future cure (Forlino & Marini, 2000).

Ehlers-Danlos Syndrome

EDS, like OI, includes a spectrum of disease (Raff & Byers, 1996) involving a defect in type 1 collagen (Burrows, 1999). It is characterized by hypermobility of the skin, extreme joint laxity, easy bruisability, and skin and bone fragility. Eight types of EDS have been characterized, each with its own constellation of clinical features. Orthopedic care of children with joint laxity and pain may prompt the diagnosis of EDS. Many children with EDS develop scoliosis that can be managed with cautious bracing and surgical intervention. Orthopedic treatment of joint problems related to hyperlaxity of joints can be challenging because laxity may recur over time.

Acquired Causes of Brittle Bones

Some antiepileptic drugs, especially phenytoin (Dilantin) and phenobarbital (Luminal), have been found to cause vitamin D deficiency or to interfere with the utilization of vitamin D. This places nonambulatory children with seizure disorders at increased risk for fractures. Nonambulatory children with cerebral palsy or meningomyelocele also tend to have frail bones, resulting from disuse and associated with severe reductions in bone mineral density (Quan et al., 1998). Fractures also may occur in children who have leukemia or osteosarcoma or other tumors that invade the bone and weaken its internal structure (Roebuck, 1999; Wall et al., 1996). Children with pathological fractures may present with swelling and increased warmth of the fractured extremity; this can occasionally be confused with *osteomyelitis* (an infection of the bone). Because children with disabilities are at increased risk for fractures, weight-bearing activities are important for the maintenance of bone density, which in turn helps to decrease fractures. Thus, having children stand is extremely important as the bone has internal receptors that recognize weight-bearing activity and send signals to make bones stronger in response. Children who cannot stand independently can use standing frames to build up their bones.

Treatment of Fractures

For proper healing to occur, fractures must be aligned properly and held immobile. If the bone fragments are only minimally displaced, then a cast can be used to hold the bone. Casts are made of plaster or of fiberglass (the lighter and stronger of the two, but more difficult to shape). The cast stabilizes the bone fragments, which makes the child more comfortable and holds the bones in satisfactory position and alignment. If the ends of the bones are not close together, a surgical procedure may be necessary to align the bones. This often involves using devices such as pins, screws, plates, or rods to hold the bone in position.

Healing takes place by a process called *callus formation* (Figure 14.10). The **callus** begins as a blood clot, the result of bleeding from blood vessels inside and around the bone. This stimulates the formation of cartilage within the blood clot at the fracture site. In a few weeks, osteoblasts start to lay down new bone on the cartilage framework. After 4–6 weeks, healing has usually progressed to the point that the cast can be removed and there can be a gradual return of function. The remodeling process, however, continues. Eventually, the bulging callus remodels and disappears, and by 6–12 months the bone appears normal on an X ray (Morrissy, 1990). Children have physes that can be damaged when a bone is broken. The Salter-Harris classification describes the involvement of the fracture with the growth plate and on a 1–5 scale classifies the increasing possibility of growth plate injury caused by the fracture (Salter & Harris, 1963).

Disorders of Muscle

Disorders of muscle can involve voluntary and involuntary muscle function. Voluntary muscles are essential for movement and respiration, whereas involuntary muscles control cardiac function. Two examples of inherited muscle disorders are muscular dystrophies and congenital myopathies.

Muscular Dystrophies

The muscular dystrophies are actually a group of muscle disorders, the best known of which is Duchenne muscular dystrophy (DMD). DMD is an X-linked recessive disorder caused by a deficiency in the production of dystrophin, a component of the plasma membrane of muscle fibers. Without dystrophin, muscle cannot function and degenerates. Dystrophin is also found in the brain, and its deficiency is associated with cognitive impairments (Mehler, 2000). DMD has a lifetime incidence of about 1 in 3,000 males (Roland, 2000). Children with DMD appear typical at birth. During early childhood, however, they develop muscle weakness and characteristic enlargement of the calves that is called **pseudohypertrophy** (Dubowitz, 2000). Blood drawn from children with DMD shows marked elevation in levels of **creatine kinase.** Most children are no longer able to ambulate by 12–14 years of age. Once a child needs a wheelchair, the risk of progressive scoliosis is significant. These curves should be surgically straightened and fused early to prevent a decrease in respiratory function and to prevent loss of sitting balance.

Ideally, care is provided by a multidisciplinary team consisting of a pediatrician, physical therapist, occupational therapist, orthopedic surgeon, physiatrist, neurologist, and social worker. Such clinics have been supported throughout the country by the Muscular Dystrophy Association (see Appendix D). These clinics use multimodal treatment that includes rehabilitation therapy, orthopedic surgery, medication, educational planning, and family counseling. Rehabilitative therapy is directed at minimizing contractures, maximizing muscle strength, and compensating for weakness (Kakulas, 1999). Therapists should encourage the child to avoid the use of a wheelchair as long as possible and to be involved in an active exercise program. Passive stretching and night splints may delay contractures. Self-care skills also should be stressed and maintained, and the child may need to use assistive devices in self-care to maintain independence (see Chapter 33).

Prednisone (a steroid medication) has been shown to prolong walking ability in patients with DMD but has significant side effects, including excessive weight gain, irritability, and osteoporosis (Tawil, 1999). Deflazacort, a related compound, is being tested as a treatment that reduces these side effects (Reitter, 1995). Transplantation of myoblasts (muscle stem cells) from a healthy donor has had only limited success because of immunologic rejection of the tissue, poor survival of the transplant, and limited ability of the transplanted cells to migrate into other muscle tissues (Qu & Huard, 2000; Skuk et al., 2000). Research is focusing on better techniques for muscle transplantation and the development of gene therapy (Urtizberea, 2000). Despite current treatment efforts, DMD is usually fatal during young adulthood as a result of either cardiac or respiratory failure. Becker muscular dystrophy is a less severe form of muscular dystrophy; some normal dystrophin is produced, leading to prolonged survival (Tsao & Mendell, 1999).

Congenital Myopathies

Congenital myopathies are another group of childhood muscle diseases, marked by decreased muscle tone and strength (Dubowitz, 1995). Children with congenital myopathies are distinguished from those with muscular dystrophies because their levels of creatine kinase are normal or only mildly elevated. They also have a different pattern of abnormalities on muscle biopsy. There are many forms of congenital myopathies, and the causes of most remain unknown. A fair amount is known, however, about one group of congenital myopathies, called **mitochondrial myopathies** (Wallace, 2000). Mitochondria are small cellular organelles that are inherited maternally. They have their own circular DNA (see Chapter 1). Mitochondria serve as the cell's power plants by converting certain nutritional elements into a chemical that contains high-energy phosphate groups that are used by the cell in metabolic processes. This conversion involves a complex series of enzymatic steps, and a deficiency in any of the enzymes in this pathway impairs energy production. Because muscles use enormous amounts of energy to contract, one result of a mitochondrial defect is muscle weakness. Some children with mitochondrial disorders have catastrophic illnesses beginning at birth and leading to death in the first months of life. Others have milder disorders that impair typical muscle function. At this time, there is no specific medical therapy for these disorders.

Disorders of Joints

A common disorder of joints is **arthritis.** Actually, arthritis is a group of disorders, each with its own characteristics and challenges. In general, however, arthritis involves damage to the cartilage comprising the joint. With joint damage, inflammation occurs, and over time cartilage wears away, exposing the underlying bones in the joint, which grind against each other (Figure 14.7), resulting in pain and loss of motion.

Although **osteoarthritis** (wear-and-tear arthritis) most commonly occurs in adults, it can also affect children. For example, a child with spastic cerebral palsy who develops a dislocation of the hip may, over the years, develop painful arthritis of the hip (Gabos et al., 1999). To lessen the risk of arthritis and pain, surgery is directed at preventing or correcting the dislocation. With cerebral palsy and other neuromuscular diseases, arthritis occurs because the joints are not normal in shape and are not able to move through a normal arc of motion. If the contact between the two bones making up a joint is reduced, there is less cartilage over which to distribute the forces across the joint; and the cartilage will wear down faster than usual. Also, movement is very important to the nourishment of cartilage. The concept that continuous passive motion (CPM) across a joint nourishes cartilage has lead to the use of CPM machines to move joints after traumatic cartilage injury. Children who have diseases of the musculoskeletal system may not move as often or as much as other children secondary to decreased functional status or contractures, making physical therapy to achieve full ranges of motion vitally important to their care.

Juvenile Rheumatoid Arthritis

Autoimmune disease can cause inflammation of the synovium (synovial cells), increased joint fluid, and arthritic changes in childhood. Three forms of juvenile rheumatoid arthritis (JRA) exist: systemic, polyarticular (involving many joints), and pauciarticular (involving few joints). Twenty percent of all JRA is systemic. Girls and boys are affected equally and, as the name implies, have constitutional signs of disease, including fevers, rash, fluid around the lungs (pleural effusion) and heart (pericardial effusion), and enlargement of the liver and spleen. Unlike adult forms of rheumatoid arthritis, the blood work for rheumatologic markers (e.g., antinuclear antibody, rheumatoid factor) is often normal. Approximately 40% of children with JRA have the pauciarticular form (involving four or fewer joints), and 40% have polyarticular JRA. Pauciarticular JRA is associated with inflammation of the eye (the anterior uvea) that can lead to blindness if not treated. Thus, all children with this diagnosis must see an ophthalmologist for periodic slitlamp examination. Polyarticular JRA affects girls twice as often as boys. These children can also show constitutional signs, including fever, growth retardation, anemia, and enlargement of the spleen and lymph nodes. A latex fixation test is positive in approximately 15% of children and is associated with less severe disease. Treatment for JRA includes aspirin and nonsteroidal anti-inflammatory drugs (NSAIDs), as well as systemic steroid use for severe disease or steroid injection to treat isolated involved joints. Physical therapy is important to maintain joint motion, and as a last resort, joint replacement may be necessary.

THE NEUROMUSCULAR SYSTEM

For a muscle to produce movement across a joint, a signal begins in the brain, passes through the spinal cord to an **anterior horn cell,** then to a peripheral nerve, and ends at a neuromuscular junction. The electrical impulse then jumps the gap (synapse) at this junction using the neurotransmitter acetylcholine. The message then passes to the muscle fiber, stimulating it to contract or relax, and movement results. A defect anywhere in the neuromuscular system leads to weakness and decreased movement (Menkes, 1995).

Diseases of the Anterior Horn Cells

Polio

The poliomyelitis virus selectively destroys anterior horn cells of the brain or spinal cord, creating a functional gap between the central nervous system and the peripheral nerves. Paralysis occurs below the part of the brainstem and/or spinal cord that has been damaged by the infection. **Polio** has not been a significant health problem in the United States since the polio vaccine was introduced in 1955 by Dr. Jonas Salk. Later, Dr. Albert Sabin developed an oral vaccine that is used worldwide. Polio is still seen in developing countries. Treatment includes bracing and tendon lengthenings and transfers when necessary to maintain function. It is hoped that like smallpox, polio will be eliminated on a global basis in the next few years.

Spinal Muscular Atrophy

Spinal muscular atrophy (SMA) is caused by a congenital and progressive loss of the anterior horn cells in the spinal cord and results in muscle weakness and atrophy (Strober & Tennekoon, 1999). The disease, inherited in an autosomal recessive pattern, affects about 1 in 20,000 children. The gene for this disorder has been identified as the survival of motor neuron (SMN) gene (Jablonka et al., 2000; Lefebvre et al., 1998). The severity of the muscle weakness correlates with the amount of SMN protein produced (Gendron & MacKenzie, 1999; Talbot, 1999). Diagnosis of the disorder now rests with a blood study that can identify mutations in the SMN gene and also permit prenatal diagnosis (Stewart et al., 1998; Wirth, 2000).

Infants with the most severe form of SMA (previously called Werdnig-Hoffmann disease) have low muscle tone; other forms are milder and more difficult to detect. Muscle biopsy shows atrophy and degeneration of muscle fibers. The characteristic physical signs are wasting, weakness, and loss of deep tendon reflexes of voluntary muscles (Iannaccone, 1998). Muscle weakness is symmetric, with proximal muscles being more involved than distal muscle groups. Children with the disease may have weak muscles around the trunk resulting in poor trunk control and respiratory difficulty, although they often can use a keyboard for typing with relative ease. There is also cranial nerve involvement, which may interfere with feeding and speech. Unlike muscular dystrophy, there is no involvement of the heart; and individuals with SMA appear to have typical intelligence.

Care for children with SMA involves aggressive respiratory therapy to prevent pneumonia and ongoing monitoring of respiratory capacity (Barois & Estournet-Mathiaud, 1997). Occupational therapy and speech-language therapy may be helpful with feeding and speech issues. As the disease progresses, oxygen or home ventilation may be required (Bach, Niranjan, & Weaver, 2000; Bach et al., 1998). The muscle imbalance and weakness in the trunk can also produce significant scoliosis that is very difficult if not impossible to control with a brace. Because scoliosis can reduce respiratory capacity, the spine should be fused while the child is still relatively small. Once scoliosis begins to progress, surgery becomes increasingly difficult and eventually impossible in the face of respiratory deterioration (Phillips et al., 1990).

Rehabilitative care centers on developing methods of seating and trunk support so the child can use his or her hands for functions other than sitting balance. A cure for SMA is not yet possible, but antiapoptotic and neurotropic agents that enhance the survival of neurons or that stimulate growth of nerve endings, respectively, are being investigated (Miller, 1999; Robertson et al., 2000). This includes the use of thyrotropin-releasing factor (Tzeng et al., 2000). Gene therapy and gene activation approaches are also being explored (Hofmann et al., 2000).

Arthrogryposis

Arthrogryposis refers to the presence of multiple joint contractures at the time of birth. It can be a primary neuropathic defect called *arthrogryposis multiplex congenita* or *multifactorial*, caused by many things, including problems with the fetus or the intrauterine environment (Hall, 1997).

In arthrogryposis multiplex congenita, the primary defect involves a loss of anterior horn cells, resulting in the partial paralysis of muscles during intrauterine life (Gordon, 1998). It can be inherited as an X-linked or autosomal recessive disorder, and candidate genes have been localized at chromosome regions Xq, 11p15.5, and 5qter (Shohat et al., 1997; Zori et al., 1998).

Secondary causes of arthrogryposis may be neuropathic, affecting the brain, spinal cord, or peripheral nerves, or may be musculoskeletal, representing abnormalities of the muscles, such as maternal or fetal myasthenia gravis (discussed later; Brueton et al., 2000; Polizzi, Huson, & Vincent, 2000) or congenital muscular dystrophies or myopathies (Swoboda et al., 1997; Vardon et al., 1998; Vielhaber et al., 2000). Arthrogryposis can also result from limits of space within the uterus or defects of the uterine environment. In all of these cases, there is lack of fetal movement resulting in the limbs' being stuck in one position and becoming deformed.

Children with arthrogryposis are stiff and have many joint contractures. Creases in the skin are lost; instead, small dimples can be seen in the skin over the joints. The upper extremities tend to be in a classic posture of internal rotation at the shoulders, extension of the elbows and flexion at the wrists. The lower extremities show **rigid** flexion and internal rotation at the hips, stiffness in the knees, and clubfeet. The proximal muscles of the trunk are less involved than with SMA. Like children with SMA, children with arthrogryposis have typical intelligence; maximizing their function helps them to be very active members of society.

Children with arthrogryposis can present with many orthopedic problems that require surgical interventions, including scoliosis, hip dislocation, and clubfoot (Akazawa et al., 1998; Sodergard et al., 1997). In addition, joints can be released or bone alignment changed surgically to increase function (Yingsakmongkol & Kumar, 2000). Physical and occupational therapy are helpful in maintaining joint motion and maximizing functional development. In secondary causes of arthrogryposis, there may also be medical problems associated with the underlying condition that must be addressed.

Diseases of the Peripheral Nerves

The peripheral nerves connect the spinal column to the muscles. Disorders of the peripheral nervous system lead to paralysis of the muscles, either localized or generalized depending on where the problem resides. With the exception of Guillain-Barré syndrome, these disorders are uncommon in children.

Guillain-Barré Syndrome

Guillain-Barré syndrome, a heterogeneous acute inflammatory peripheral neuropathy, presents clinically as an ascending paralysis that typically occurs 1–2 weeks after an acute respiratory or gastric illness. It has been associated with *Campylobacter jejuni* infection (a type of bacterial infection); the pathological mechanism appears to involve the antibodies produced to combat the infection (Asbury, 2000; Ho & Griffin, 1999). The antigens produced by the infection mimic the antigens of the peripheral nerves; as a result, the body's defense mechanism (through antibodies or antigens) attacks its own nerve cells inadvertently (Hughes et al., 1999; Vedeler, 2000).

Over the course of 1–2 weeks, the affected individual begins to have weakness in the legs and difficulty walking or using stairs (Jones, 2000). Proximal muscles are involved more than distal; one third of patients require ventilatory support because of paralysis of the respiratory muscles. Guillain-Barré syndrome has a mortality rate of 2%–5% and should be considered a medical emergency (Pascuzzi & Fleck, 1997).

Diagnosis can be made on the basis of history, elevated protein in the spinal fluid without cells, and electromyographic changes showing a decrease in nerve conduction velocity. A normal magnetic resonance imaging scan of the spine rules out other spinal cord pathology. It is treated by supportive care and rehabilitative therapy. Immunotherapy also appears to be helpful, specifically high-dose intravenous immunoglobulin and **plasmapheresis** (a process whereby blood plasma is removed from a vein, dialyzed, or cleansed, and then reinfused; Hadden & Hughes, 1999). The weakness abates and strength returns slowly over the next few months, with 85% of patients being able to walk within 6 months.

Diseases of the Neuromuscular Junction

The peripheral nerves end at the neuromuscular junction. For a nerve impulse to "jump" across the synapse separating the nerve and muscle, it requires a chemical neurotransmitter (see Chapter 13). Impaired neurotransmitter activity prevents the impulse from generating muscle movement.

Myasthenia Gravis

Myasthenia gravis is the classic example of a disorder of the neuromuscular junction. There are both acquired and inherited forms of myasthenia. The rare inherited form presents in infancy and results from a mutation affecting a subunit of the acetylcholine neurotransmitter receptors on skeletal muscles (Engel et al., 1993). As a result, there is a 70%–90% reduction in the number of functional acetylcholine receptors. In the absence of these receptors, the neurotransmitter is unable to stimulate the muscle.

Individuals with the more common acquired form of myasthenia experience an autoimmune phenomenon akin to Guillain-Barré syndrome that targets the acetylcholine receptor on the skeletal muscle rather than the nerve (Anlar, 2000). As a consequence, nerve impulses do not effectively bridge the neuromuscular junction and muscles do not receive a signal to contract. This form of disease occurs more commonly in girls and young women.

Unusual fatigability of voluntary muscles is the main characteristic of both forms of myasthenia. A muscle may be strong with the first effort at contraction but rapidly weakens. Myasthenia often affects the muscles of the face first, with droopy eyelids or indistinct speech. It may then progress to involve other muscle groups, interfering with eating, walking, or even breathing. Because the weakness increases with repeated muscle contractions, a person with myasthenia gravis usually feels stronger in the morning and increasingly weakens as the day progresses.

Treatment of acquired myasthenia has been directed at both removing the offending antibody and increasing the level of acetylcholine in the synaptic cleft (Lisak, 1999). The immunological approach has employed corticosteroid medication, immunoglobulin, plasmapheresis, and the surgical removal of the thymus gland (thymectomy). Plasmapheresis is used on an emergency basis in an individual with myasthenia gravis who is having difficulty breathing because of weak respiratory muscles. Yet, unlike Guillain-Barré syndrome, which is a self-limited postinfectious disease, myasthenia gravis is a lifelong illness; thus, plasmapheresis usually is not a permanent solution (Qureshi & Suri, 2000). A permanent solution involves thymectomy (Kogut et al., 2000). The thymus, a small gland resting under the sternum or breast plate, plays an important role in the autoimmune response; lymphocytes that initiate this response develop in this gland. Immunosuppression with aziathioprine, glucocorticoids, or cyclosporine (Sandimmune) is used in patients who do not respond very well to thymectomy (Harvard & Fonseca, 1990). Although most individuals continue to require immunosuppression, the proportion of individuals achieving long-term remission increases after thymectomy. It should be noted that because immune cells that develop in the thymus early in life serve a critical surveillance function, removal of the thymus may increase the risk of cancer and the susceptibility to some infections (Genkins, Sivak, & Tartter, 1993).

Immune therapy is not helpful in congenital myasthenia (Engel, 1999). Here, treatment requires increasing neurotransmitter levels in the synaptic cleft by using a medication called *pyridostigmine* (Mestinon). This drug delays the breakdown of acetylcholine so that more of this neurochemical is available to aid in the transmission of the nerve impulse. Strength improves within minutes of taking this drug, and improvement lasts about 4 hours. This drug is also used in acquired myasthenia in combination with immune therapy. Overall, using these various treatment approaches, individuals with myasthenia can lead quite typical lives.

SUMMARY

The musculoskeletal and neuromuscular systems support the physical structure of the body and help carry out movement. Diseases affecting these systems can have a huge impact on a child's functional capacity and independence. The challenge to treatment is first to determine the highest level of function a child can attain realistically. Then, a team is assembled involving family members, primary care physicians, therapists, surgeons, and rehabilitative specialists. Each member of the team brings insights from a different perspective to help the child gain function. This may involve a combination of therapies, including bracing, seating systems, adaptive equipment, and, when necessary, surgery. The treatment efforts may need to be short- or long-term. Many of the disorders are under active investigation to develop new treatment approaches, including the repair of genetic material, development of more effective medications, and improvement of surgical techniques.

REFERENCES

Akazawa, H., Oda, K., Mitani, S., et al. (1998). Surgical management of hip dislocation in children with arthrogryposis multiplex congenita. *Journal of Bone and Joint Surgery: British Volume, 80,* 636–640.

American Academy of Pediatrics, Committee on Genetics. (1995). Health supervision for children with achondroplasia. *Pediatrics, 95,* 443–451.

Anlar, B. (2000). Juvenile myasthenia: Diagnosis and treatment. *Paediatric Drugs, 2,* 161–169.

Asbury, A.K. (2000). New concepts of Guillain-Barré syndrome. *Journal of Child Neurology, 15,* 183–191.

Bach, J.R., Niranjan, V., & Weaver, B. (2000). Spinal muscular atrophy type 1: A noninvasive respiratory management approach. *Chest, 117,* 1100–1105.

Bach, J.R., Rajaraman, R., Ballanger, F., et al. (1998). Neuromuscular ventilatory insufficiency: Effect of home mechanical ventilator use versus oxygen therapy on pneumonia and hospitalization rates. *American Journal of Physical Medicine and Rehabilitation, 77,* 8–19.

Barois, A., & Estournet-Mathiaud, B. (1997). Respiratory problems in spinal muscular atrophies. *Pediatric Pulmonology, 16*(Suppl.), 140–141.

Birch, J.G. (1998). Orthopedic management of neuromuscular disorders in children. *Seminars in Pediatric Neurology, 5,* 78–91.

Blakeslee T.J. (1997). Congenital idiopathic talipes equinovarus (clubfoot). Current concepts. *Clinics in Podiatric Medicine and Surgery, 14,* 9–56.

Bleck, E.E. (1993). Club foot. *Developmental Medicine and Child Neurology, 35,* 927–931.

Brueton, L.A., Huson, S.M., Cox, P.M., et al. (2000). Asymptomatic maternal myasthenia as a cause of the Pena-Shokeir phenotype. *American Journal of Medical Genetics, 92,* 1–6.

Burrows, N.P. (1999). The molecular genetics of the Ehlers-Danlos syndrome. *Clinical and Experimental Dermatology, 24,* 99–106.

Carolino, J., Perez, J.A., & Popa, A. (1998). Osteopetrosis. *American Family Physician, 57,* 1293–1296.

Coleman, S.S. (1993). *Complex foot deformities in children.* Philadelphia: Lea & Febiger.

Coleman, S.S. (1994). Developmental dislocation of the hip: Evolutionary changes in diagnosis and treatment. *Journal of Pediatric Orthopedics, 14,* 1–2.

Crawford, A.H., Mehlman, C.T., & Slovek, R.W. (1999). The fate of untreated developmental dislocation of the hip: Long-term follow-up of eleven patients. *Journal of Pediatric Orthopedics, 19,* 641–644.

Dormans, J.P. (1993). Orthopaedic management of children with cerebral palsy. *Pediatric Clinics of North America, 40,* 645–657.

Dubowitz, V. (1995). *Muscle disorders in childhood* (2nd ed.). Philadelphia: W.B. Saunders.

Dubowitz, V. (2000). Congenital muscular dystrophy: An expanding clinical syndrome. *Annals of Neurology, 47,* 143–144.

Engel, A.G. (1999). Congenital myasthenic syndromes. *Journal of Child Neurology, 14,* 38–41.

Engel, A.G., Hutchinson, D.O., Nakano, S., et al. (1993). Myasthenic syndromes attributed to mutations affecting the epsilon subunit of the acetylcholine receptor. *Annals of the New York Academy of Sciences, 681,* 496–508.

Engelbert, R.H., Pruijs, H.E., Beemer, F.A., et al. (1998). Osteogenesis imperfecta in childhood: Treatment strategies. *Archives in Physical Medicine and Rehabilitation, 79,* 1590–1594.

Fasth, A., & Porras, O. (1999). Human malignant osteopetrosis: Pathophysiology, management and the role of bone marrow transplantation. *Pediatric Transplantation, 3*(Suppl. 1), 102–107.

Forlino, A., & Marini, J.C. (2000). Osteogenesis imperfecta: Prospects for molecular therapeutics. *Molecular Genetics and Metabolism, 71*(1–2), 225–232.

Gabos, P.G., Miller, F., Galban, M.A., et al. (1999). Prosthetic interposition arthroplasty for the palliative treatment of end-stage spastic hip disease in nonambulatory patients with cerebral palsy. *Journal of Pediatric Orthopedics, 19,* 796–804.

Gendron, N.H., & MacKenzie, A.E. (1999). Spinal muscular atrophy: Molecular pathophysiology. *Current Opinion in Neurology, 12,* 137–142.

Genkins, G., Sivak, M., & Tartter, P.I. (1993). Treatment strategies in myasthenia gravis. *Annals of the New York Academy of Sciences, 681,* 603–608.

Gerritsen, E.J., Vossen, J.M., van Loo, I.H., et al. (1994). Autosomal recessive osteopetrosis: Variability of findings at diagnosis and during the natural course. *Pediatrics, 93,* 247–253.

Glorieux, F.H., Bishop, N.J., Plotkin, H., et al. (1998). Cyclic administration of Pamidronate in children with severe osteogenesis imperfecta. *New England Journal of Medicine, 14,* 947–952.

Gordon, N. (1998). Arthrogryposis multiplex congenita. *Brain Development, 20,* 507–511.

Hadden, R.D., & Hughes, R.A. (1999). Treatment of immune-mediated inflammatory neuropathies. *Current Opinion in Neurology, 12,* 573–579.

Hall, J.G. (1997). Arthrogryposis multiplex congenita: Etiology, genetics, classification, diagnostic approach, and general aspects. *Journal of Pediatric Orthopaedics: Part B, 6,* 159–166.

Harvard, C.W., & Fonseca, A. (1990). New treatment approaches to myasthenia gravis. *Drugs, 39,* 66–73.

Ho, T., & Griffin, J. (1999). Guillain-Barré syndrome. *Current Opinion in Neurology, 12,* 389–394.

Hofmann, Y., Lorson, C.L., Stamm, S., et al. (2000). Htra2-beta 1 stimulates an exonic splicing enhancer and can restore full-length SMN expression to survival motor neuron 2 (SMN2). *Proceedings of the National Academy of Sciences of the United States of America, 97,* 9618–9623.

Horwitz, E.M., Prockop, D.J., Fitzpatrick, L.A., et al. (1999). Transplantability and therapeutic effects of bone marrow-derived mesenchymal cells in children with osteogenesis imperfecta. *Nature Medicine, 5,* 309–313.

Hughes, R.A., Hadden, R.D., Gregson, N.A., et al. (1999). Pathogenesis of Guillain-Barré syndrome. *Journal of Neuroimmunology, 100*(1–2), 74–97.

Hunter, A.G., Bankier, A., Rogers, J.G., et al. (1998). Medical complications of achondroplasia: A multicentre patient review. *Journal of Medical Genetics, 35,* 705–712.

Iannaccone, S.T. (1998). Spinal muscular atrophy. *Seminars in Neurology, 18,* 19–26.

Ikeda, K. (1992). Conservative treatment of idiopathic clubfoot. *Journal of Pediatric Orthopedics, 12,* 217–223.

Jablonka, S., Rossoll, W., Schrank, B., et al. (2000). The role of SMN in spinal muscular atrophy. *Journal of Neurology, 247*(Suppl 1.), 137–142.

Jones, H.R., Jr. (2000). Guillain-Barré syndrome: Perspectives with infants and children. *Seminars in Pediatric Neurology, 7,* 91–102.

Kakulas, B.A. (1999). Problems and solutions in the rehabilitation of patients with progressive muscular dystrophy. *Scandinavian Journal of Rehabilitation Medicine, 39*(Suppl.), 23–37.

Kocher, M.S., & Shapiro, F. (1998). Osteogenesis imperfecta. *The Journal of the American Academy of Orthopaedic Surgeons, 6,* 225–236.

Kogut, K.A., Bufo, A.J., Rothenberg, S.S., et al. (2000). Thoracoscopic thymectomy for myasthenia gravis in children. *Journal of Pediatric Surgery, 35,* 1576–1577.

Lefebvre, S., Burglen, L., Frezal, J., et al. (1998). The role of the SMN gene in proximal spinal muscular atrophy. *Human Molecular Genetics, 7,* 1531–1536.

Lisak, R.P. (1999). Myasthenia gravis. *Current Treatment Options in Neurology, 1,* 239–250.

Matsui, Y., Yasui, N., Kimura, T., et al. (1998). Genotype phenotype correlation in achondroplasia and hypochondroplasia. *The Journal of Bone and Joint Surgery: British Volume, 80,* 1052–1056.

Mehler, M.F. (2000). Brain dystrophin, neurogenetics and mental retardation. *Brain Research: Brain Research Reviews, 32,* 277–307.

Menkes, J.H. (1995). *Textbook of child neurology* (5th ed.). Philadelphia: Lippincott Williams & Wilkins.

Miller, R.G. (1999). Carrell-Krusen Symposium invited lecture. Clinical trials in motor neuron diseases. *Journal of Child Neurology, 14,* 173–179.

Minch, C.M., & Kruse, R.W. (1998). Osteogenesis imperfecta: A review of basic science and diagnosis. *Orthopedics, 21,* 558–567, 568–569.

Morrissy, R.T. (1990). *Lovell and Winter's pediatric orthopaedics* (4th ed.). Philadelphia: Lippincott Williams & Wilkins.

Pascuzzi, R.M., & Fleck, J.D. (1997). Acute peripheral neuropathy in adults: Guillain-Barré syndrome and related disorders. *Neurologic Clinics, 15,* 529–547.

Paterson, C.R. (1997). Osteogenesis imperfecta and other heritable disorders of bone. *Bailliere's Best Practice and Research: Clinical Endocrinology and Metabolism, 11,* 195–213.

Paterson, C.R., Ogston, S.A., & Henry, R.M. (1996). Life expectancy in osteogenesis imperfecta. *British Medical Journal, 312,* 351.

Phillips, D.P., Roye, D.P., Farcy J.P., et al. (1990). Surgical treatment of scoliosis in a spinal muscular atrophy population. *Spine, 15,* 942–945.

Polizzi, A., Huson, S.M., & Vincent, A. (2000). Teratogen update: Maternal myasthenia gravis as a cause of congenital arthrogryposis. *Teratology, 62,* 332–341.

Qu, Z., & Huard J. (2000). Matching host muscle and donor myoblasts for myosin heavy chains improves myoblast transfer therapy. *Gene Therapy, 7,* 428–437.

Quan, A., Adams, R., Ekmark, E., et al. (1998). Bone mineral density in children with myelomeningocele. *Pediatrics, 102,* E34.

Qureshi, A.I., & Suri, M.F. (2000). Plasma exchange for treatment of myasthenia gravis: Pathophysiologic basis and clinical experience. *Therapeutic Apheresis, 4,* 280–286.

Raff, M.L., & Byers, P.H. (1996). Joint hypermobility syndromes. *Current Opinion in Rheumatology, 8,* 459–466.

Ramaswami, U., Rumsby, G., Spoudeas, H.A., et al. (1999). Treatment of achondroplasia with growth hormone: Six years of experience. *Pediatric Research, 46,* 435–439.

Reitter, B. (1995). Deflazacort vs. prednisone in Duchenne muscular dystrophy: Trends of an ongoing study. *Brain and Development, 17*(Suppl.), 36–43.

Robertson, G.S., Crocker, S.J., Nicholson, D.W., et al. (2000). Neuroprotection by the inhibition of apoptosis. *Brain Pathology, 10,* 283–292.

Roebuck, D.J. (1999). Skeletal complications in pediatric oncology patients. *Radiographics, 19,* 873–885.

Roland, E.H. (2000). Muscular dystrophy. *Pediatrics in Review, 21,* 233–237, 238.

Salter, R.B., & Harris, W.R. (1963). Injuries involving the epiphyseal plate. *Journal of Bone and Joint Surgery, American Volume, 45,* 587–622.

Sambrook, P.N., & Jones, G. (1995). Corticosteroid osteoporosis. *British Journal of Rheumatology, 34,* 8–12.

Shaw, N.J., White, C.P., Fraser, W.D., et al. (1994). Osteopenia in cerebral palsy. *Archives of Disease in Childhood, 71,* 235–238.

Shohat, M., Lotan, R., Magal, N., et al. (1997). A gene for arthrogryposis multiplex congenita neuropathic type is linked to D5S394 on chromosome 5qter. *American Journal of Human Genetics, 61,* 1139–1143.

Skuk, D., Goulet, M., Roy, B., et al. (2000). Myoblast transplantation in whole muscle of nonhuman primates. *Journal of Neuropathology and Experimental Neurology, 59,* 197–206.

Sodergard, J., Hakamies-Blomqvist, L., Sainio, K., et al. (1997). Arthrogryposis multiplex congenita: Perinatal and electromyographic findings, disability, and psychosocial outcome. *Journal of Pediatric Orthopedics: Part B, 6,* 167–171.

Song, K.M., & Lapinsky, A. (2000). Determination of hip position in the Pavlik harness. *Journal of Pediatric Orthopedics, 20,* 317–319.

Stewart, H., Wallace, A., McGaughran, J., et al. (1998). Molecular diagnosis of spinal muscular atrophy. *Archives of Disease in Children, 78,* 531–535.

Strober, J.B., & Tennekoon, G.I. (1999). Progressive spinal muscular atrophies. *Journal of Child Neurology, 14,* 691–695.

Swoboda, K.J., Specht, L., Jones, H.R., et al. (1997). Infantile phosphofructokinase deficiency with arthrogryposis: Clinical benefit of a ketogenic diet. *Journal of Pediatrics, 131,* 932–934.

Talbot, K. (1999). Spinal muscular atrophy. *Journal of Inherited Metabolic Disease, 22,* 545–554.

Tanaka, H. (1997). Achondroplasia: Recent advances in diagnosis and treatment. *Acta Paediatrica Japonica, 39,* 514–520.

Tawil, R. (1999). Outlook for therapy in the muscular dystrophies. *Seminars in Neurology, 19,* 81–86.

Tsao, C.Y., & Mendell, J.R. (1999). The childhood muscular dystrophies: Making order out of chaos. *Seminars in Neurology, 19,* 9–23.

Tzeng, A.C., Cheng, J., Fryczynski, H., et al. (2000). A study of thyrotropin-releasing hormone for the treatment of spinal muscular atrophy: A preliminary report. *American Journal of Physical Medicine and Rehabilitation, 79,* 435–440.

Urtizberea, J.A. (2000). Therapies in muscular dystrophy: Current concepts and future prospects. *European Neurology, 43,* 127–132.

Vardon, D., Chau, C., Sigodi, S., et al. (1998). Congenital rapidly fatal form of nemaline myopathy with fetal hydrops and arthrogryposis. A case report and review. *Fetal Diagnosis and Therapy, 13,* 244–249.

Vedeler, C.A. (2000). Inflammatory neuropathies: Update. *Current Opinion in Neurology, 13,* 305–309.

Vielhaber, S., Feistner, H., Schneider, W., et al. (2000). Mitochondrial complex I deficiency in a female with multiplex arthrogryposis congenita. *Pediatric Neurology, 22,* 53–56.

Wall, J.E., Kaste, S.C., Greenwald, C.A., et al. (1996). Fractures in children treated with radiotherapy for soft tissue sarcoma. *Orthopedics, 19,* 657–664.

Wallace, D.C. (2000). Mitochondrial defects in cardiomyopathy and neuromuscular disease. *American Heart Journal, 139*(2, Pt. 3), S70–S85.

Widemann, R.F., Bitan, F.D., Laplaza, F.J., et al. (1999). Spinal deformity, pulmonary compromise, and quality of life in osteogenesis imperfecta. *Spine, 24,* 1673.

Wirth, B. (2000). An update of the mutation spectrum of the survival motor neuron gene (SMN1) in autosomal recessive spinal muscular atrophy (SMA). *Human Mutation, 15,* 228–237.

Yingsakmongkol, W., & Kumar, S.J. (2000). Scoliosis in arthrogryposis multiplex congenita: Results after nonsurgical and surgical treatment. *Journal of Pediatric Orthopedics, 20,* 656–661.

Zori, R.T., Gardner, J.L., Zhang, J., et al. (1998). Newly described form of X-linked arthrogryposis maps to the long arm of the human X chromosome. *American Journal of Medical Genetics, 78,* 450–454.

III Developmental Disabilities

15 Mental Retardation

Mark L. Batshaw and Bruce Shapiro

Upon completion of this chapter, the reader will:

- know the developmental milestones of childhood
- understand the definition and implications of the term *mental retardation*
- be aware of the various causes of mental retardation
- know the advantages and disadvantages of the principal intelligence tests used with children
- recognize the various interventions in mental retardation
- be aware of the different levels of functioning and independence that individuals with mental retardation can achieve

At birth, a newborn responds in an involuntary way to the environment. Over the next few years, a combination of brain growth and learning experiences enables the child to move from complete dependence on his or her parents to active participation in the world. This development occurs in a sequential fashion. Yet, some of the steps are steeper than others, and some children do not achieve all of them. This chapter discusses the principles of typical and delayed development. It also identifies different causes of mental retardation and reviews approaches to intervention.

EARLY DEVELOPMENT

Development is an ongoing process that begins with embryogenesis and continues throughout childhood. This process is tightly linked to the maturation of the central nervous system. Consequently, the most rapid development corresponds to the time of fastest brain growth, the first few years of life (see Chapter 13). As an example, motor development progresses from head to foot, or in a **cephalocaudal** fashion. Thus, a child first gains head control, then sits, then crawls, and finally walks. Furthermore, development follows a typical sequence. Children usually roll before sitting, sit before crawling, and crawl before walking. Their sequential development permits the assessment of infants and young children. By comparing rates of attaining developmental milestones with norms, professionals can identify those children with atypical development or developmental delay.

When discussing early developmental milestones (birth to 3 years), four major types of skills are usually considered: language, social-adaptive, gross motor, and fine motor. Language, the best predictor of future intellectual functioning, is further broken down into expressive and receptive skills (see Chapter 12). The early developmental history of Tyrone, a child born of an uncomplicated pregnancy, illustrates the typical sequence of developmental milestones children master as they grow from birth to 2 years of age (Table 15.1).

Table 15.1. Development in the first 2 years of life (approximate ages of skill attainment)

Month	Gross motor	Fine motor	Language	Social-adaptive

1	Has partial head control
	Primitive reflexes
	  predominate
		Clenches fists	Alerts to sound
			Makes small sounds
				Fixates objects and
				  follows 90°

2	Has good head control Lifts chin in prone			Follows 180° Smiles responsively

3	Lifts chest off bed
	Has less prominent
	  primitive reflexes
		Holds hands open
		Reaches toward
		  objects
		Pulls at clothing
			Coos	Follows 360°
				Recognizes mother

4	Makes swimming
	  movements
		Hands go to midline	Laughs aloud
			Produces different sounds
			  for different needs
				Shakes rattle
				Anticipates food
				Belly laughs

5	Rolls over stomach to
	  back
	Holds head erect
			Orients toward sound
			Gives a "raspberry"
				Frolics when played
				  with

6	Has anterior propping
	  response
		Transfers objects
		Holds bottle
		Has palmar grasp
			Babbles
			Recognizes friendly and
			  angry voices
				Looks after lost toy
				Enjoys mirror play

7	Bounces when standing with support Sits without support	Feeds self cookie	Imitates noise Responds to name	Drinks from cup

8	Has lateral propping
	  responses
		Rings bell
		Has radial raking
		  grasp
			Uses nonspecific "ma-ma"
			Understands "no"
				Has separation anxiety
				Tries to gain attention

9	Crawls		Recognizes familiar words	Mouths objects
10	Stands with support	Plays with bell Claps	Says specific "Da-da," "Ma-ma"	Waves "bye-bye" Plays Pat-a-cake
11	Cruises around objects	Uses pincer grasp	Follows gesture command	

12	Makes first steps	Throws objects
		Puts objects in
		  containers
			Says two or three specific
			  words
				Aids in dressing
				Turns papers
				Takes turns

15	Climbs up stairs	Marks with pencil	Follows one-step commands Speaks four to six words Identifies one body part	Indicates when wet Spoon-feeds Builds tower with blocks Gives kisses Imitates chores

18	Runs stiffly
	Handedness is
	  determined
		Plays constructively
		  with toys
		Scribbles
		Imitates lines
		Places objects in
		  formboard
			Follows two-step
			  commands
			Points to one picture in
			  book
			Uses 10 words
				Places formboard
				Turns pages
				Engages in parallel play
				Takes off shoes
				Does puzzles

24	Walks up/down steps,
	  both feet on each step
		Imitates vertical lines	Uses "I"
			Identifies four body parts
			Can form three-word
			  sentences
			Says "yes" and "no"
				Puts on and takes off
				  shoes
				Plays alongside other
				  children
				Is negativistic
				Uses fork
				Indicates toileting needs

Language Skills

From birth, Tyrone began to explore the world with his eyes. If his mother was persistent, she could hold his attention for a few seconds. He responded to loud noises by stopping his movement for an instant and then returning to his seemingly purposeless movements. When Tyrone was 2 months old, he rewarded his parents' attention with a smile.

As a newborn, Tyrone communicated his needs mainly by crying. As time went on, he developed more complex communication skills. He cooed in the third month and gave a "raspberry" in the fourth. Tyrone also started to turn his head toward a voice, as if to take part in a conversation. In the sixth month, he started making babbling sounds. Four weeks later, he tried to imitate the sounds his parents made and responded to his name with a smile and a turn of the head. By the time Tyrone was 8 months old, he understood the command "no," although understanding it did not ensure consistent compliance. He began saying "dada" to everything and everyone in sight. At 11 months, Tyrone spoke a few specific words ("mama," "bye") and could follow a simple command if it was accompanied by a gesture.

In comparison with his motor skills, which were simply being refined during the second year of life, Tyrone's language skills exploded. At 15 months, he had a six-word vocabulary and used jargon (word-like sounds that do not carry meaning) all of the time. He also closed the door or sat down when asked, without a gesture as a guide. When he was 18 months old, Tyrone could point to different parts of his body when asked to name them. He spoke unintelligible monologues, interspersing the jargon with real words. His vocabulary was about 18 words. By 2 years of age, he could name some pictures in a book, followed two-step commands such as "Take the bell and put it on the table," and referred to himself as "I." His vocabulary was now greater than 50 words. By age 3, he could put together three-word sentences and had a vocabulary of about 250 words.

Social-Adaptive Skills

In addition to gaining motor and language skills, Tyrone developed the ability to relate to the important people in his life and to differentiate some of their emotional responses. By the time he was 2 months old, Tyrone started to distinguish his mother from other people, giving her big smiles. During his fourth month, he began to laugh. By 6 months, he would reach for his bottle when it was brought into sight.

Tyrone's social interactions also became more sophisticated. Before he was a year old, he could play Peekaboo and Pat-a-cake, wave "bye-bye," and throw a ball. During his second year, Tyrone started to help push his arms through a shirt and take off most of his clothes. He also began to play alongside other children but did not yet want to share with them. When he was separated from his parents, he became upset. By age 2, he became quite independent, feeding himself with a spoon and fork. Like his communication skills, his social skills had become much more refined.

Gross Motor Development

As is generally true of children, Tyrone's activity during the first 3 months of life reflected the influence of primitive reflexes. When Tyrone's mother stroked the side of his lips, he rooted, or turned toward her. When she placed her breast at his lips, he began to suck vigorously. If Tyrone turned his head to the right, his right arm and leg extended involuntarily while his left arm and leg flexed into a "fencer" reflex. He usually held his hands in a closed position and when pried open, his fingers automatically grasped his mother or father's fingers.

By 2 months, Tyrone began to gain some control over his movements. For example, when pulled to a sitting position, he managed to hold his head upright for a few seconds before it fell to rest on his chest. Also, when placed face down, Tyrone turned his head to one side or the other, which allowed him to breathe more comfortably.

As Tyrone grew, his actions became more purposeful. He was able to roll over from stomach to back at 4 months of age. To perform this action, his brain had to suppress certain primitive reflexes. If Tyrone had cerebral palsy, the primitive reflexes would have persisted and interfered with rolling (see Chapter 23).

Continuing to develop on schedule, Tyrone next progressed to sitting up without support at 7 months of age. He then began the evolution to walking. At 8 months, he could stand when held, bearing weight on his feet. Then, at 9 months, he began to crawl, alternating his legs. He was also able to move from a crawling to a seated position. He was able to pull himself up to a standing position at 10 months and started to walk around objects while hanging on to them, or cruise, at 11 months. At last, at 12 months, Tyrone took his first independent step. Five months later, he was running, and by 2 years of age, he could jump and walk up steps.

Fine Motor Development

Tyrone's fine motor development paralleled his gross motor development. During his first 2–3 months, he could do very little with his hands because they were usually closed tightly. Once they remained opened at 3 months, he started to reach toward his colorful mobile and pull at his clothing. In the fourth month, he would clasp his hands together and then put them in his mouth, often chortling as he did this.

By 5 months of age, Tyrone could transfer objects from one hand to the other. This gave him slightly more independence; he could feed himself a cookie and hold a bottle. Over the next few months, he started to explore his environment actively, reaching out and examining anything in sight. For example, at 8 months, if placed near a bell, Tyrone would grab and ring it until one of his parents substituted a quieter instrument. When he could crawl, at 9 months, he explored all of the nooks and crannies of his house. At 10 months, his pincer grasp (i.e., using his thumb and forefinger) was refined and enabled him to pick up small objects. These objects usually ended up in his mouth, whether they were edible or not. When he reached 18 months of age, he could scribble with a pencil.

DEVELOPMENTAL DELAY

In the medical field, the term *developmental delay* is most commonly used as a temporary diagnosis in young children at risk for developmental disabilities. In this context, it indicates a failure to achieve age-appropriate neurodevelopmental milestones (Petersen, Kube, & Palmer, 1998). To illustrate, consider the story of Daniel, whose mother, Marina, noticed many signs in his early development that indicated atypical development. (In the following paragraphs, the typical ages for these developmental milestones are indicated in parentheses after the age at which Daniel achieved them.)

As an infant, Daniel showed little interest in his environment and was not very alert. He would sit in an infant seat for hours without complaint. Although Marina tried to breast-feed him, his suck was weak, and he frequently regurgitated his formula. He was floppy and had poor head control. His cry was high-pitched, and he was difficult to comfort.

In social and motor development, Daniel lagged behind the norm. In language skills, he did not start babbling until 13 months (6 months). He smiled at 5 months (2 months) and was not very responsive to his parents' attention. In terms of gross motor development, Daniel could hold his head up at 4 months (1 month), roll over at 8 months (5 months), and sit up at 14 months (6 months). He transferred objects from one hand to the other at 14 months (5 months).

When given the Bayley Scales of Infant Development–Second Edition (BSID-II; Bayley, 1993) at 16 months, Daniel's mental age was found to be 7 months, and he received a Mental Developmental Index (MDI; similar to an IQ score) of less than 50. He progressed from an early intervention program to a special preschool program, and prior to school entry at age 6,

Daniel was retested on the fourth edition of the Stanford-Binet Intelligence Scale (Terman & Merrill, 1985). His score indicated a mental age of 2 years, 8 months, and an IQ score of 40. Concomitant impairments in adaptive behavior were demonstrated by the Vineland Adaptive Behavior Scales (VABS; Sparrow, Balla, & Cicchetti, 1984).

Developmental delay is recognized by the failure to meet age-appropriate expectations based on the typical sequence of development. In the first months of life, delayed development can be indicated by a lack of visual or auditory response, an inadequate suck, and/or floppy or spastic muscle tone. Later in the first year, lack of language and motor delays in sitting and walking may suggest developmental delay. When a child continues to show significant delays in all developmental spheres, mental retardation is the likely diagnosis. Unfortunately, some medical practitioners continue to use the term *developmental delay* long after the diagnosis of mental retardation can be made. Although developmental delay is the most common presenting concern in children who turn out to have mental retardation, sensory impairments, autism, or cerebral palsy, it does not always indicate a developmental disability. Isolated mild delays in expressive language (particularly in boys) or gross motor abilities usually resolve over time. These mild early delays, however, often signal an increased risk of the child being a slow learner or having a learning disability that will become evident by school age.

EARLY IDENTIFICATION

Parents usually seek an evaluation for developmental delay once their child fails to meet specific developmental milestones. In early infancy, these include a lack of responsiveness, unusual muscle tone or posture, and feeding difficulties. Between 6 and 18 months of age, motor delay is the most common complaint. Language and behavior problems are the common concerns after 18 months.

Early identification of atypical development is more likely to occur with more severe impairments (Daily, Ardinger, & Holmes, 2000). In order to facilitate early identification, all children should receive developmental screening as part of their routine pediatric care (Gilbride, 1995). Unfortunately, too many children live in poverty and receive medical care episodically or move so frequently that follow-up records are unavailable to make this goal achievable. Even when followed in a clinic, there may be little time for the staff to take a developmental history or to perform a developmental screening test. Furthermore, the available developmental screening tests themselves (e.g., the Denver II; Frankenburg et al., 1992) are not sufficiently sensitive to detect many developmental disabilities.

It is important to emphasize that screening tests are not designed to supplant a formal neurodevelopmental and psychological assessment. They are meant to be used in asymptomatic populations to identify individuals at risk. The usefulness of a screening instrument is determined by its ability to appropriately classify children who do or do not have significant developmental delays, that is, its sensitivity and specificity, respectively. Sensitivity is measured by the true positive rate. Specificity is measured by the true negative rate. The ideal screening instrument would detect all of the children who require further assessment and none of those who do not. Unfortunately, many screening instruments misclassify too many children (i.e., have too many false positives and false negatives) to be clinically useful.

Given these difficulties, the best approach to early identification is multifaceted. Infants at high risk (e.g., those with prematurity, maternal substance abuse, perinatal insult) should be registered in newborn follow-up programs in which they are evaluated periodically for developmental lags during the first 2 years of life and entered in early intervention programs if appropriate. All parents should be educated to look for and report delays in the typical development sequence. Clinic staff and physicians should routinely note developmental milestones, much like they note height and weight. In addition, children should receive a developmental screening battery and tests of vision and hearing every 6–12 months during early childhood (Shapiro, 1996).

If there is evidence of a significant developmental lag over time, the child should then be sent for a comprehensive evaluation (Curry et al., 1997). Ideally, the evaluation should include an examination by a neurodevelopmental or behavioral pediatrician or a pediatric neurologist, by a clinical psychologist, and by a social worker. Depending on the child's age and impairments, he or she also may need to be seen for early intervention assessment by an early childhood educator, speech-language pathologist, audiologist, and psychologist. If the child displays motor impairments, physical and occupational therapists should also be involved. Following the assessment, an individualized family service plan (IFSP) is developed in the context of an early intervention program (see Chapter 29).

MENTAL RETARDATION

Defining Mental Retardation

Although the definition of mental retardation (and even the use of the term) is controversial, there is general agreement that a person with mental retardation must have significantly subaverage intellectual functioning and impairment in adaptive abilities (Table 15.2). Despite this general agreement, disagreements over the details of these definitions have arisen for biological and philosophical reasons.

IQ Scores

The first controversial issue involves IQ scores. The definition of mental retardation relates to an interpretation of typical intellectual functioning. The average level of intellectual functioning in a population corresponds to the apex of a bell-shaped curve. Two standard deviations on either side of the mean encompass 95% of a population sample and approximately define the range of typical intellectual functioning (Figure 15.1). By definition, the average intelligence quotient, or IQ score, is 100, and the standard deviation (a statistical measure of dispersion from the mean) of most IQ tests is 15 points. Historically, a person scoring more than 2 standard deviations below the mean, or below 70, has been considered to have mental retardation.

Statisticians, however, point out that there is a measurement variance of approximately 5 points in assessing IQ by most psychometric tests. In other words, repeated testing of the same

---

Table 15.2. Diagnostic criteria for mental retardation (MR)

A. Significantly subaverage intellectual functioning: an IQ score of approximately 70 or below on an individually administered IQ test (for infants, a clinical judgment of significantly subaverage intellectual functioning).

B. Concurrent deficits or impairments in present adaptive functioning (i.e., the person's effectiveness in meeting the standards expected for his or her age by his or her cultural group) in at least two of the following areas: communication, self-care, home living, social/interpersonal skills, use of community resources, self-direction, functional academic skills, work, leisure, health, and safety.

C. The onset is before age 18 years.

. . . .

Code based on degree of severity reflecting level of intellectual impairment:

317	**Mild Mental Retardation:**	IQ level 50–55 to approximately 70
318.0	**Moderate Mental Retardation:**	IQ level 35–40 to 50–55
318.1	**Severe Mental Retardation:**	IQ level 20–25 to 35–40
318.2	**Profound Mental Retardation:**	IQ level below 20–25
319.	**Mental Retardation, Severity Unspecified:**	when there is a strong presumption of Mental Retardation but the person's intelligence is untestable by standard tests

From DIAGNOSTIC AND STATISTICAL MANUAL OF MENTAL DISORDERS: DSM-IV-TR (p. 46) by APA. Copyright 2001 by AM PSYCHIATRIC ASSN (DSM). Reproduced with permission of AM PSYCHIATRIC ASSN (DSM) in the format Textbook via Copyright Clearance Center.

individual will produce scores that vary by as much as 5 points (American Psychiatric Association [APA], 2000). Thus, it has been proposed that the demarcation of mental retardation be changed from an IQ score of 70 to a range of 65–75, using the presence or absence of significant impairments in adaptive skills to confirm the diagnosis. Using this schema, mental retardation would be diagnosed in an individual with an IQ score between 70 and 75 who exhibits significant impairments in adaptive behavior, whereas it would not be diagnosed in an individual with an IQ of 65–70 who does not have impairments in adaptive skills.

Beyond any measurement variability, a more fundamental concern of some theorists is the underlying value of an IQ score. Gardner (1983) challenged the dichotomous (verbal versus performance) structure of intelligence assessed by most IQ tests. He proposed that intelligence comprises a wider range of abilities, not only the traditional linguistic and logical-mathematical skills, but musical, spatial, bodily-kinesthetic, and interpersonal characteristics as well. This approach has not gained wide acceptance as it does not have a clear neuropsychological or neuroanatomical basis. And, although it is acknowledged that a single IQ score averages a person's cognitive abilities and may not capture all forms of intelligence, there is evidence that a significantly subnormal IQ score is a meaningful predictor of future cognitive functioning.

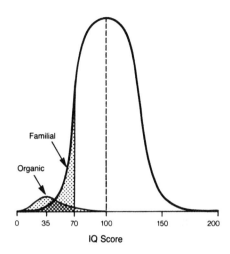

Figure 15.1. Bimodal distribution of intelligence. The mean IQ score is 100. An IQ score of less than 70, or 2 standard deviations below the mean, can indicate mental retardation (MR). The second, smaller curve takes into account individuals who have mental retardation because of birth trauma, infection, inborn errors, or other organic causes. This explains why more individuals have severe to profound mental retardation than are predicted by the familial curve alone. (Reprinted with permission from Zigler, E. [1967]. Familial retardation: A continuing dilemma. *Science, 155,* 292, Figure 1. Copyright 1967 by the American Association for the Advancement of Science.)

Yet, it must be emphasized that cognitive functioning is not always uniform across all neurodevelopmental domains. An example is found in the study by Wang and Bellugi (1993) comparing neuropsychological testing results in children with Down syndrome and Williams syndrome. Although the Full-Scale IQ scores on the Wechsler Intelligence Scale for Children–Revised (Wechsler, 1974) in both groups were similar, the pattern of cognitive strengths and weaknesses was very different. The individuals with Williams syndrome had much stronger skills in language but much poorer visual-perceptual abilities than did the children with Down syndrome.

Finally, there are the concerns over predictive validity and cultural bias. Infant psychological tests are notoriously poor predictors of adult IQ scores, although they clearly differentiate severe impairments from typical functioning. And, cultural bias has been suggested as one explanation for differences in IQ scores found among individuals from various racial, ethnic, and socioeconomic groups.

Adaptive Impairments

Individuals with mental retardation not only must have limitations in their intellectual abilities but also must be impaired in their ability to adapt or function in daily life. Earlier definitions of mental retardation did not elaborate on the specifics of these adaptive impairments. The American Association on Mental Retardation (AAMR; Luckasson et al., 1992) and the APA (2000), however, have defined mental retardation as including at least two of the following impairments in adaptive behavior: communication, self-care, home living, social/interpersonal skills, use of community resources, self-direction, functional academic skills, work, leisure, health, and safety (Table 15.2).

Degrees of Mental Retardation

There is also controversy about defining the levels of mental retardation. The APA's *Diagnostic and Statistical Manual of Mental Disorders, Fourth Edition, Text Revision* (DSM-IV-TR; 2000), subdivides mental retardation into four degrees of severity. An individual is classified as having mild mental retardation if his or her IQ score is 50 to approximately 70; moderate retardation, IQ 35 to approximately 50; severe retardation, IQ 20 to approximately 35; and profound retardation, IQ below 20–25 (Table 15.2; APA, 2000). This classification has met with widespread acceptance in the medical community, although it has also been suggested that mental retardation should be simply dichotomized into mild (IQ score of 50 to approximately 70) and severe (IQ score below 50). This is based on the discrete biological division between mild retardation and the more severe forms of mental retardation, with different etiologies and outcomes. This dichotomy has not been widely accepted for clinical purposes because the medical, educational, and habilitative needs are quite different between individuals with moderate and profound retardation.

AAMR takes a different approach in defining the degree of severity of mental retardation, relying not on IQ scores but rather on the patterns and intensity of support needed (i.e., requiring intermittent, limited, extensive, or pervasive support; Luckasson et al., 1992). This definition marks a philosophical shift from an emphasis on degree of impairment to a focus on the abilities of individuals to function in an inclusive environment. This shift is controversial, as it assumes that adaptive behaviors can be independent of cognition and does not provide clear guidelines for establishing diagnostic eligibility of children with IQ scores in the upper limits of the range connoting mental retardation (MacMillan, Gresham, & Siperstein, 1995). This chapter (as well as the others in the book) uses the APA's categories in discussing medical issues and the AAMR's categories in discussing educational and other interventions, emphasizing the capabilities rather than the impairments of individuals with mental retardation.

A final controversy concerns the continued use of the rather pejorative term *mental retardation*. In a sense, this term is like the word *cancer*. Both carry appropriate meanings—intellectual disability and neoplastic growth, respectively. Both, however, also carry stigmas that are no longer warranted—the need for segregation and the assumption of rapid death, respectively. Furthermore, both of these terms encompass subgroups of disorders with different causes, biological origins, and outcomes. For example, an infant diagnosed with mental retardation caused by a nutritional deficit may grow up to have typical intelligence if treated appropriately, whereas a child with Down syndrome (see Chapter 16) will retain his or her genetically based intellectual disability despite intensive intervention. Perhaps it would be better to discard the term *mental retardation* altogether. Already there is a host of new terms waiting to be anointed, including *intellectual disability*, *cognitive disability*, and *learning disability*. As of 2002, however, AAMR has tabled proposed name changes in deference to the wide legal usage (for entitlements) of the term *mental retardation*, which cannot easily be changed.

It is likely that in the future, novel approaches to neuropsychological testing combined with new medical tests, including neuroimaging and DNA studies, will profile an individual's cognitive strengths and challenges and their biological origin more precisely. This may lead to more appropriate terms and prove helpful in developing new intervention strategies that may include neurotransmitter medication, gene therapy, and/or stem cell transplantation. In sum, the concept of mental retardation is in a period of transition. The final resolution of the name, definition, and subtyping may not be determined for a number of years.

Domains of Disability

Another way of classifying mental retardation and other developmental disabilities is to use the *terminology in disability classification* developed by the National Center for Medical Rehabilitation Research (Hogan, Rogers, & Msall, 2000; Lollar, Simeonsson, & Nanda, 2000). This model defines five domains: pathophysiology, impairment, functional limitation, disability, and societal limitation (Table 15.3). *Pathophysiology* focuses on the cellular, structural or functional events resulting from injury, disease, or genetic abnormality that underlies the developmental disability. *Impairment* refers to the losses that result from the pathophysiological event. *Functional limitation* describes the restriction or lack of ability to perform a normal function. *Disability* is the inability to perform or limitation in performing activities. *Societal limitations* focus on barriers to full participation in society. Table 15.3 illustrates how this system could be applied to a child with Down syndrome. The advantage of this approach is that it leads directly from diagnosis to treatment and focuses on how to overcome limitations. It also acknowledges the change in emphasis in the diagnosis of mental retardation from impairment and functional limitations to disability and societal limitations. This is consistent with the move from focusing on the intensity of the disability (e.g., severe mental retardation) to focusing on the intensity of support needed to function in society (e.g., mental retardation requiring extensive support). This approach is also in keeping with the process for developing an individualized education program (IEP) for a school-age child (see Chapter 30).

Prevalence of Mental Retardation

Based on the previous discussion, the prevalence of mental retardation depends on the definition used, the method of ascertainment, and the population studied (Fernell, 1996; Roeleveld, Zielhuis, & Gabreels, 1997; Strømme & Valvatne, 1998). Approximately 1.5 million people between the ages of 5 and 65 years in the United States were receiving services for mental retardation in 1993 (Centers for Disease Control and Prevention, 1996). According to statistics and based on the DSM-IV-TR (APA, 2000) definition, 2.5% of the population could be predicted to have mental retardation, and another 2.5% superior intelligence (Figure 15.1). Of individuals with mental retardation, the IQ scores of 85% should fall 2–3 standard deviations below the mean, in the range of mild mental retardation. If individuals who score low on IQ tests because of cultural or social disadvantage are excluded from the count of those with mild mental retardation, however, the prevalence is about half these predictions, somewhere between 0.8% and 1.2% (McLaren & Bryson, 1987). Whatever the prevalence, mental retardation appears to peak at 10–14 years of age, acknowledging that children with mild impairments are identified significantly later than those with more severe impairments.

Overall, mental retardation occurs more frequently in boys than in girls. The ratio of males to females is about 2:1 in mild mental retardation and 1.5:1 in severe mental retardation (Chiurazzi & Oostra, 2000). This is thought to be principally the consequence of X-linked disorders, of which 95 have been described, the most prominent being fragile X syndrome (see Chapter 17; Feldman, 1996; Gecz & Mulley, 2000; Neri & Chiurazzi, 1999).

The prevalence of severe mental retardation has not changed appreciably since the 1940s and is approximately 0.3%–0.5% of the population (Aicardi, 1998; Roeleveld et al., 1997). This is likely a result of the natural balance between improved health care and the emergence of new diseases. For example, although the morbidity rate of premature infants weighing

Table 15.3.   Relationship between domain and treatment in a child with Down syndrome

Condition	Impairment	Functional limitations	Disability	Societal limitations	Treatment
Trisomy 21	Global developmental delay	Mental retardation	Learning skills below expectation for age and adaptive skills below age level	Inclusion in general education classroom	Special education

1,500–2,500 grams has declined markedly, there is improved survival of much smaller premature infants, weighing less than 1,000 grams, who have a relatively high prevalence of disability (see Chapter 6; Hack & Fanaroff, 2000). Prenatal diagnosis has been associated with a decrease in the number of births of children with Down syndrome, and neonatal screening and early dietary management have helped to eradicate mental retardation caused by phenylketonuria (PKU; see Chapter 18). Both of these preventive measures have been counterbalanced, however, by maternal PKU, the increased prevalence of prenatal exposure to drugs of abuse (including alcohol; see Chapter 7), and congenital human immunodeficiency virus infection (see Chapter 8). In addition, many of the causes of severe mental retardation result from genetic or congenital brain malformations that, as of 2002, can neither be anticipated nor treated.

Overall, the recurrence risk in families with one child who has severe mental retardation of unknown origin is 3%–9% (Crow & Tolmie, 1998; Louhiala, 1995). Recurrence risk for mental retardation of known origin, however, varies according to the cause. A family whose child has mental retardation following neonatal meningitis does not have a significantly increased risk of having future affected children, whereas a woman who has had one child with fetal alcohol syndrome (FAS) has a 30%–50% risk of having other affected children if she continues to drink during pregnancy. The risk of recurrent Down syndrome ranges from less than 1% for trisomy 21 to more than 10% for a balanced translocation (see Chapter 1; Mikkelsen, Poulsen, & Tommerup, 1989; Wolff et al., 1989). If the cause of mental retardation is a Mendelian disorder (see Chapter 1) such as neurofibromatosis (an autosomal dominant trait), Hurler syndrome (an autosomal recessive trait), or fragile X syndrome (an X-linked trait), the recurrence risk ranges from 0% to 50%, depending on the inheritance pattern of the specific disorder.

Associated Impairments

Although mild mental retardation is frequently an isolated disability, severe mental retardation is often accompanied by associated impairments that further limit the child's adaptive abilities and adversely affect outcome. The prevalence of these associated impairments correlates with the severity of the retardation (Cascella, 1999; Fuller & Sabatino, 1998; Pellock & Morton, 2000; Steffenburg, Hagberg, & Kyllerman, 1995; Steffenburg, Hagberg, Viggedal, et al., 1995). These associated impairments (Table 15.4) include cerebral palsy, sensory impairments, seizure disorders, communication impairments, feeding difficulties, behavior/psychiatric disorders, and attention-deficit/hyperactivity disorder (ADHD). More than half of children with severe mental retardation and one quarter of children with mild mental retardation have sensory impairments, of which vision impairments, especially strabismus and refractive errors, are the most common. Speech-language impairments beyond those related to the cognitive impairment also are frequent. Approximately 20% of children with severe mental retardation have cerebral palsy, which may also be associated with feeding problems and failure to thrive (see Chapter 27). Seizure disorders also occur in about 20% of children with mental retardation (Airaksinen et al., 2000). Finally, psychiatric and behavior disorders such as mood disorders

Table 15.4. Percentages of children with mental retardation (MR) who have associated developmental disabilities

Associated disability	Severe MR (%)	Mild MR (%)
None	17	63
Cerebral palsy	19	6
Seizure disorders	21	11
Sensory impairments	55	24
Psychological/behavioral	50	25

From Kiely, M. (1987). The prevalence of mental retardation. *Epidemiologic Reviews, 9,* 194; adapted by permission of Oxford University Press.

(see Chapter 19), pervasive developmental disorders (see Chapter 25), and self-injurious behavior (see Chapter 31) occur in up to half of children with mental retardation (Dykens, 2000; Vig & Jedrysek, 1999). In considering intervention strategies, identifying these additional impairments and working toward their treatment is essential (Sunder, 1997).

Associated impairments may make distinguishing mental retardation from other developmental disabilities difficult. Certain distinguishing features, however, usually exist (Table 15.5). In isolated mental retardation, language and nonverbal reasoning skills are significantly delayed, whereas gross motor skills tend to be less affected. Conversely, in cerebral palsy, motor impairments are more prominent than cognitive impairments are. In communication disorders, expressive and/or receptive language skills are more delayed than motor and nonverbal reasoning skills are (Cascella, 1999). In pervasive developmental disorders, social skills impairments and atypical behaviors are superimposed on cognitive (especially communication) impairments (Vig & Jedrysek, 1999). In some instances, repeated assessments may be necessary to determine the primary developmental disability.

Causes of Mental Retardation

The **epidemiology** of mental retardation suggests that there are two overlapping populations: Mild mental retardation is associated with lower socioeconomic status and less stimulating environments; severe mental retardation is more typically linked to a biological cause (Hou, Wang, & Chuang, 1998; Strømme, 2000). There is often, however, an interaction between nature and nurture. For example, a child may have an initial biological insult (e.g., intrauterine growth retardation) that is compounded by environmental variables (e.g., poor nutrition, parental neglect). Mothers who never finished high school are four times more likely to have children with mild mental retardation than are women who completed high school (Drews et al., 1995). The explanation for this is unclear but may involve a genetic component (i.e., inheritance of a cognitive impairment) and socioeconomic factors (e.g., poverty, undernutrition). Although African American children appear to be more than twice as likely to have mild mental retardation than Caucasian children are, at least half of the mental retardation is attributable to poverty or other adverse social conditions and is likely to be remediable (Yeargin-Allsopp et al., 1995). For example, application of early intervention services to high-risk infants who are also at socioeconomic risk has resulted in improved cognitive outcomes (Ramey & Ramey, 1998; Ramey, Ramey, & Friedlander, 1999).

The specific origins of mild mental retardation are currently identifiable in less than 50% of individuals (Aicardi, 1998). Cultural and social factors play an important role here. The most common biological causes are genetic syndromes with multiple minor congenital anomalies (e.g., velocardiofacial syndrome), fetal deprivation, perinatal insults (e.g., asphyxia, infection), intrauterine exposure to drugs of abuse (especially alcohol), and X-chromosome abnormalities

Table 15.5. Developmental delays in various developmental disabilities during preschool years

| Disorder | Developmental area | | | |
	Motor	Language	Nonverbal reasoning	Social-adaptive
Mental retardation	Variable	2	2	2
Autism	N/A	3	Variable	3
Cerebral palsy	3	Variable	Variable	2
Deafness	N/A	2	N/A	Variable
Blindness	1	N/A	Variable	1

Key: 3, severe impairment; 2, moderate impairment; 1, mild impairment; N/A, not affected.

(e.g., Klinefelter syndrome; Agostoni, 2000; Matilainen et al., 1995). Although definite genetic causes are less common (5% versus 47% in severe mental retardation), familial clustering is frequent (Gillberg, 1998).

In children with severe mental retardation, a biological origin of the condition can be identified in about three quarters of cases (Aicardi, 1998). The most common diagnoses are fragile X syndrome, Down syndrome, and FAS, which together account for almost one third of all identifiable cases of severe mental retardation (Table 15.6; Macmillan, 1998; Moser, 1995).

One way of dividing the biological origins of mental retardation is by their timing in the developmental sequence (Crocker, 1989). In general, the earlier the problem exists, the more severe its consequences. This is consistent with finding a prenatal cause in about three quarters of individuals with an identifiable cause of severe mental retardation (Gillberg, 1998). Chromosomal disorders (e.g., Down syndrome), nonchromosomal dysmorphic syndromes (e.g., Rubinstein-Taybi syndrome), and abnormalities of brain development (e.g., lissencephaly) that affect early embryogenesis are the most common and severe (see Chapter 1). In addition, 10% are attributable to single-gene defects (e.g., inborn errors of metabolism; see Chapter 18). Together, these groups of genetically based causes of mental retardation account for more than two thirds of identifiable causes of mental retardation and encompass more than 500 disorders (McKusick, 1998). Insults occurring in the first and second trimesters as a result of substance abuse (e.g., FAS), infections (e.g., cytomegalovirus; see Chapter 3), and other pregnancy problems (e.g., intrauterine growth retardation; see Chapter 3) occur in 10% of cases. Fetal deprivation in the third trimester due to placental damage, preeclampsia, or hemorrhage (see Chapter 4) and problems in the perinatal period (see Chapter 5) now account for less than 10% of cases of severe mental retardation. Five percent are the result of postnatal brain damage, most commonly brain infections and traumatic brain injury (see Chapter 26).

Table 15.6. Identifiable etiologies in children with severe mental retardation

Etiology	% of total
Chromosomal disorders	22
Genetic syndromes	21
Developmental brain abnormalities	9
Inborn errors of metabolism or neurodegenerative disorders	8
Congenital infections	4
Familial retardation	6
Perinatal causes	4
Postnatal causes	5
Unknown	21

Source: Strømme & Hagberg, 2000.

Medical Diagnostic Testing

No single method exists for detecting all causes of mental retardation (Shevell et al., 2000). As a result, diagnostic testing should be based on the medical history and a physical examination (Majnemer & Shevell, 1995; Shevell, 1998). For example, a child with an unusual facial appearance or multiple congenital anomalies should be referred to a geneticist. Even minor anomalies may be worth pursuing with high-resolution chromosomal banding, fluorescent *in situ* hybridization, and chromosome painting (Flint et al., 1995; Moss et al., 1999). A male with unusual physical features and/or a family history of mental retardation should probably have molecular genotyping for fragile X syndrome. A child with a progressive neurological disorder will need extensive metabolic investigation; a child with seizure-like episodes should have an electroencephalogram. These tests, however, should not be seen as screening tools to be used in all children with mental retardation. Finally, children with abnormal head growth or asymmetrical neurological findings warrant a neuroimaging procedure such as magnetic resonance imaging (MRI; Levy & Hyman, 1993).

Although these are the most common reasons for performing diagnostic tests, it now seems clear that some children with subtle physical or neurological findings also may have determinable biological origins of their mental retardation. It has been shown that about 6% of unexplained mental retardation can be accounted for by microdeletions (very minute chromosomal abnormalities) that require extensive testing to identify (Flint et al., 1995; McFadden & Friedman, 1997). In addition, MRI scans have been found to document a significant number of subtle markers of cerebral dysgenesis in children with mental retardation (Majnemer & Shevell, 1995).

How intensively the physician investigates the cause of a child's mental retardation is based on a number of factors. First, what is the degree of mental retardation? One is less likely to find a cause in a child with mild mental retardation than in a child with severe retardation. Second, is there a specific diagnostic path to follow? If there is a medical history, a family history, or physical findings pointing to a specific cause, a diagnosis is more likely to be made. Conversely, in the absence of these indicators, it is difficult to choose specific tests to perform. Third, are the parents planning on having additional children? If so, one would be more likely to intensively seek disorders for which prenatal diagnosis or a specific early treatment option is available. Finally, and most importantly, what are the parents' wishes? Some parents have little interest in searching for the cause and focus exclusively on treatment. Others are so focused on obtaining a diagnosis that they have difficulty accepting intervention until a cause has been found. Both extremes and everything in between must be respected, but supportive guidance should be provided in the context of parent education.

Psychological Testing

The routine evaluation for mental retardation should include an individual intelligence test. The most commonly used test in infants is the BSID-II (Bayley & Bayley, 1993). For children older than 2 years, the fourth edition of the Stanford-Binet Intelligence Scale (Terman & Merrill, 1985), the Wechsler scales (Wechsler, 1989, 1991), and the Kaufman Assessment Battery for Children (K-ABC; Kaufman & Kaufman, 1983) are most commonly used (Table 15.7; Wodrich, 1997).

Table 15.7. Psychometric tests (IQ tests) used in diagnosing mental retardation (MR)

Name of test	Age range	Description
Bayley Scales of Infant Development–Second Edition (BSID-II; Bayley, 1993)	1–42 months	Verbal, motor, and behavior scales. Measures sensory motor development. Limited predictability of future development. Also gives motor development index and behavior rating scale.
Kaufman Assessment Battery for Children (K-ABC; Kaufman & Kaufman, 1983)	2–12 years	A theory-driven measure of intelligence that focuses on the assessment of processing styles—sequential and simultaneous processing
Stanford-Binet Intelligence Scale, Fourth Edition (Terman & Merrill, 1985)	2 years–adult	Designed for measuring verbal reasoning, abstract visual reasoning, quantitative, and short-term memory skills. Few motor tasks.
Wechsler Preschool and Primary Scale of Intelligence–Revised (WPPSI-R; Wechsler, 1989)	3–7 years	General intelligence scale for young children. Information, similarities, arithmetic, vocabulary, comprehension, sentences, object assembly, picture completion, geometric design, block design, animal pegs, and mazes. Focuses on motor and processing skills.
Wechsler Intelligence Scale for Children–Third Edition (WISC-III; Wechsler, 1991)	6–17 years	Standard measure of intelligence in children. Subtests: information, similarities, arithmetic, vocabulary, comprehension, digit span, picture completion, picture arrangement, block design, object assembly, symbol search, coding, and mazes. Focuses on approach to problem solving.

Source: Wodrich, 1997.

Infant Developmental Tests

The BSID-II is used to assess language, visual problem-solving skills, behavior, fine motor skills, and gross motor skills of children between 1 month and 42 months of age. An MDI and a Psychomotor Development Index (PDI; a measure of motor competence) score are derived from the results. Less commonly used infant tests include the Battelle Developmental Inventory (Newborg et al., 1984) and the Mullen Scales of Early Learning (Mullen, 1989).

In infants and young children with typical development, there is substantial variability in IQ scores on repeated cognitive testing and consequently poor predictive validity until around 10 years of age. Accuracy is enhanced if repeated testing confirms a stable rate of cognitive development. The predictive value of infant tests is further limited because they are primarily dependent on nonlanguage items, whereas language skills remain the best predictors of future IQ scores (Bayley, 1958). These tests do permit the differentiation of infants with severe mental retardation from typically developing infants but are less helpful in distinguishing between a typical child and one with mild mental retardation (Maisto & German, 1986). In general, however, there is less variability seen with cognitive growth in children with mental retardation, so predictive validity is enhanced compared with children with typical development.

Intelligence Tests in Children

One of the most established of the psychological tests used in children older than 18 months is the Stanford-Binet Intelligence Scale, Fourth Edition (Terman & Merrill, 1985). It comprises 15 subtests that assess four areas of intelligence: verbal abilities, abstract/visual thinking, quantitative reasoning, and short-term memory. This permits the evaluator to determine, using some caution, areas of relative strength and weakness (Wodrich, 1997).

The most commonly used psychological tests for children older than 3 years of age are the Wechsler scales. The Wechsler Preschool and Primary Scale of Intelligence–Revised (WPPSI-R; Wechsler, 1989) is used for children with mental ages of 3–7 years. The Wechsler Intelligence Scale for Children–Third Edition (WISC-III; Wechsler, 1991) is used for children who function above a 6-year mental age. Both scales contain a number of subtests in verbal and performance skills. Although children with mental retardation usually score below average on all subscale scores, they occasionally score in the typical range in one or more performance areas. Overall, the Stanford-Binet and Wechsler scales are quite accurate in predicting adult IQ scores when given to school-age children. The evaluator, however, must ensure that situations that may lead to falsely low IQ scores do not confound the test performance. Conditions such as motor impairments, communication disorders, sensory impairments, speaking a language other than English, extremely low birth weight, or severe sociocultural deprivation may invalidate certain intelligence tests, require modification of others, and always involve caution in interpretation.

Tests of Adaptive Functioning

As noted in the DSM-IV-TR (2000) definition of mental retardation, in addition to testing intelligence, adaptive skills also should be measured. The most commonly used test of adaptive behavior is the VABS (Sparrow et al., 1984). This test involves semistructured interviews with parents and/or caregivers and teachers that assess adaptive behavior in four domains: communication, daily living skills, socialization, and motor skills. The test has three forms, with 244–577 items. Other tests of adaptive behavior (Wodrich, 1997) include the Woodcock-Johnson Scales of Independent Behavior (Bruininks et al., 1996) and the AAMR Adaptive Behavior Scale. There is usually (but not always) a good correlation between scores on the intelligence and adaptive scales (Bloom & Zelko, 1994). Adaptive abilities, however, are more responsive to intervention efforts than is the IQ score. They are also more variable, which may relate to the underlying condition and to environmental expectations. For example, although individuals with Prader-Willi syndrome have stability of adaptive skills through adulthood, individuals with fragile X syndrome may have increasing impairments over time (Dykens, Hodapp, Ort, et al., 1993; Dykens, Hodapp, Walsh, et al., 1992).

Treatment Approaches

The most useful treatment approach for children with mental retardation consists of multimodal efforts directed at many aspects of the child's life—education, social, and recreational activities; behavior problems; and associated impairments (American Academy of Pediatrics, Committee on Children with Disabilities, 1999). Support for parents, siblings, and other family members is also important (see Chapters 2 and 36).

Educational Services

Education is the single most important discipline involved in intervention for children with mental retardation and their families (see Chapters 29 and 30). The achievement of good outcomes in an educational program is dependent on the interaction of the student and teacher. Educational programs must be relevant to the child's needs and address the child's individual strengths and challenges. The child's developmental level and his or her requirements for support and goals for independence provide a basis for establishing an IFSP or an IEP.

Leisure and Recreational Needs

In addition to education, the child's social and recreational needs should be addressed (Dattilo & Schleien, 1994). In the ideal world, children with mental retardation would participate as equals in all recreation and leisure activities. Although young children with mental retardation are not usually excluded from play activities, adolescents frequently do not have opportunities for appropriate social interaction and often are not competitive in extracurricular sports activities. Yet, participation in sports should be encouraged as it offers many benefits, including weight management, development of physical coordination, maintenance of cardiovascular fitness, and improvement of self-image (see Chapter 34; Dykens, Rosner, & Butterbaugh, 1998; Halle, Gabler-Halle, & Chung, 1999). Social activities are equally important. These include dances, trips, dating, and other typical recreational events.

Behavior Therapy

Although most children with mental retardation do not have behavior disorders, these problems do occur with a greater frequency in this population than among children with typical development (Fraser & Rao, 1991; King et al., 1997). To facilitate the child's socialization, significant behavior problems must be addressed (Walker, 1993). Behavior problems may result from inappropriate parental expectations, organic problems, and/or family difficulties. Alternatively, they may represent attempts by the child to communicate, gain attention, or avoid frustration. In assessing the behavior, one must consider whether it is inappropriate for the child's mental age rather than for his or her chronological age. When intervention is needed, an environmental change, such as a more appropriate classroom environment, may improve certain behavior problems. For some children, behavior management techniques (see Chapter 31) and/or the use of medication may be appropriate.

Use of Medication

Medication is not useful in treating the core symptoms of mental retardation; no drug has been found to improve intellectual function. Medication may be helpful, however, in treating associated behavior and psychiatric problems. These drugs are generally directed at specific symptom complexes, including ADHD (e.g., methylphenidate [Ritalin]); self-injurious behavior (e.g., risperidone [Risperdal]); aggression (e.g., carbamazepine [Tegretol]); and depression (e.g., fluoxetine [Prozac]; Aman, 1997; Madrid, State, & King, 2000; Santosh & Baird, 1999). These drugs are discussed in detail in Chapters 19 and 21. Before long-term therapy with any psychopharmacological agent is initiated, a short trial should be conducted. Even if a medication proves successful, its use should be reevaluated at least yearly to assess the need for continued treatment.

Treating Associated Impairments

Any associated impairments—cerebral palsy; sensory impairments; seizure disorders; speech disorders; pervasive developmental disorders; and other disorders of language, behavior, and perception—must also be treated to achieve an optimal outcome for the child. This may require ongoing physical therapy, occupational therapy, speech-language therapy, adaptive equipment, eyeglasses, hearing aids, medication, and so forth. Failure to adequately identify and treat these problems may hinder successful **habilitation** and result in difficulties in the home, school, or neighborhood environment.

Family Counseling

Many families adapt well to having a child with mental retardation, but some have difficulty (Scorgie & Sobsey, 2000). Among the factors that have been associated with family coping skills are stability of the marriage, age of the parents, parental self-esteem, number of siblings, socioeconomic status, degree of disability, parental expectations and acceptance of the diagnosis, supportive extended family members, and availability of community programs and respite care services. In families in which the emotional demands of having a child with mental retardation is great, family counseling should be an integral part of the treatment plan.

Periodic Reevaluation

The needs of the child and his or her family change over time. As the child grows, more information must be provided to parents, goals must be reassessed, and programming will need to be adjusted. A periodic review should include information about the child's health status as well as his or her functioning at home, at school, and in other environments. Other information, such as formal psychological or educational testing, may be needed. Reevaluation should be undertaken at routine intervals, at any time the child is not meeting expectations, and when he or she is moving from one service provision system to another. This is especially true during adolescence and in the transition to adulthood, when fewer services may be available (see Chapter 37).

OUTCOME

Outcome for an individual with mental retardation depends on the underlying cause; the degree of retardation; the presence of associated medical and developmental disabilities; the capabilities of the family; and the supports, services, and training provided to the child and family. As adults, many people with mental retardation requiring intermittent support are able to gain economic and social independence with functional literacy. They may need periodic assistance, however, especially under social and economic stress. Most marry and live successfully in the community, either independently or in supervised settings (APA, 2000). Life expectancy is not adversely affected.

For individuals with mental retardation requiring limited support, the goals of education are to enhance adaptive abilities, "survival" academics, and vocational skills so that these individuals are better able to live in the adult world. Contemporary gains including supported employment have benefited these individuals the most. Supported employment challenges the view that prerequisite skills must be taught before there can be successful vocational adaptation. Instead, individuals are trained by a coach to do a specific job in the setting in which the person is to work. This bypasses the need for a sheltered workshop experience and has resulted in successful work adaptation in the community for many people with mental retardation. Outcome studies have documented the effectiveness of this approach. People with mental retardation requiring limited support (e.g., individuals with Down syndrome) generally live at home or in a supervised setting in the community.

As adults, people with mental retardation requiring extensive to pervasive support may perform simple tasks in supervised settings. These individuals, however, may have associated impairments such as cerebral palsy and sensory impairments that further limit their adaptive functioning. Yet, most people with this level of mental retardation are able to live in the community. Some individuals with severe medical problems, behavioral disturbances, or disrupted families, however, live in such settings as foster homes, alternative living units, group homes, nursing homes, residential schools, and institutions. Life span appears to be shortened in these individuals (Hollins et al., 1998).

SUMMARY

Development is a step-by-step process that is linked to the maturation of the central nervous system. With mental retardation, development is altered so that intellectual and adaptive skills are impaired. In most cases of mild mental retardation, the underlying cause is unclear. In three quarters of individuals with severe retardation, however, there is a definable cause. The vast majority of people with mental retardation require only intermittent support and are often able to achieve economic and social independence. The early identification of a developmental delay is important to ensure appropriate treatment and to enable the child to develop and use all of his or her capabilities. Treatment should be multimodal, supporting the educational, mental and physical health, adaptive behavior, and communication skills of individuals with mental retardation.

REFERENCES

Agostoni, C. (2000). Chromosomal rearrangements and mental retardation. *Pediatric Research, 47*(Pt. 1), 429.

Aicardi, J. (1998). The etiology of developmental delay. *Seminars in Pediatric Neurology, 5,* 15–20.

Airaksinen, E.M., Matilainen, R., Mononen, T., et al. (2000). A population-based study on epilepsy in mentally retarded children. *Epilepsia, 41,* 1214–1220.

Aman, M.G. (1997). Recent studies in psychopharmacology in mental retardation. In N. Bray (Ed.), *International review of research in mental retardation* (Vol. 21, pp.113–146). San Diego: Academic Press.

American Academy of Pediatrics, Committee on Children with Disabilities. (1999). Care coordination: Integrating health and related systems of care for children with special health care needs. *Pediatrics, 104*(4, Pt. 1), 978–981.

American Psychiatric Association. (2000). *Diagnostic and statistical manual of mental disorders* (4th ed., Text rev.). Washington, DC: Author.

Bayley, N. (1958). Value and limitations of infant testing. *Children, 5,* 129–133.

Bayley, N. (1993). *Bayley Scales of Infant Development: Second edition manual.* San Antonio, TX: The Psychological Corporation.

Bloom, A.S., & Zelko, F.A. (1994). Variability in adaptive behavior in children with developmental delay. *Journal of Clinical Psychology, 50,* 261–265.

Bruininks, R.H., Woodcock, R.W., Weatherman, R.F., et al. (1996). *Scales of Independent Behavior–Revised (SIB-R).* Chicago: Riverside.

Cascella, P.W. (1999). Communication disorders and children with mental retardation. *Child and Adolescent Psychiatric Clinics of North America, 8*(1), 61–75.

Centers for Disease Control and Prevention. (1996). State-specific rates of mental retardation—United States, 1993. *MMWR, 45*(3), 61–65.

Chiurazzi, P., & Oostra, B.A. (2000). Genetics of mental retardation. *Current Opinion in Pediatrics, 12,* 529–535.

Crocker, A.C. (1989). The causes of mental retardation. *Pediatric Annals, 18,* 623–635.

Crow, Y.J., & Tolmie, J.L. (1998). Recurrence risks in mental retardation. *Journal of Medical Genetics, 35,* 177–182.

Curry, C.J., Stevenson, R.E., Aughton, D., et al. (1997).

Evaluation of mental retardation: Recommendations of a consensus conference. *American College of Medical Genetics. American Journal of Medical Genetics, 72,* 468–477.

Daily, D.K., Ardinger, H.H., & Holmes, G.E. (2000). Identification and evaluation of mental retardation. *American Family Physician, 61,* 1059–1067, 1070.

Dattilo, J., & Schleien, S.J. (1994). Understanding leisure services for individuals with mental retardation. *Mental Retardation, 32,* 53–59.

Drews, C.D., Yeargin-Allsopp, M., Decoufle, P., et al. (1995). Variation in the influence of selected sociodemographic risk factors for mental retardation. *American Journal of Public Health, 85,* 329–334.

Dykens, E.M. (2000). Psychopathology in children with intellectual disability. *Journal of Child Psychology and Psychiatry and Allied Disciplines, 41,* 407–417.

Dykens, E.M., Hodapp, R.M, Ort, S.I., et al. (1993). Trajectory of adaptive behavior in males with fragile X syndrome. *Journal of Autism and Developmental Disorders, 23,* 135–145.

Dykens, E.M., Hodapp, R.M., Walsh, K., et al. (1992). Profiles, correlates and trajectories of intelligence in individuals with Prader-Willi syndrome. *Journal of the American Academy of Child and Adolescent Psychiatry, 31,* 1125–1130.

Dykens, E.M., Rosner, B.A., & Butterbaugh, G. (1998). Exercise and sports in children and adolescents with developmental disabilities: Positive physical and psychosocial effects. *Child and Adolescent Psychiatric Clinics of North America, 7*(4), 757–771.

Feldman, E.J. (1996). The recognition and investigation of X-linked learning disability syndromes. *Journal of Intellectual Disability Research, 40,* 400–411.

Fernell, E. (1996). Mild mental retardation in schoolchildren in a Swedish suburban municipality. Prevalence and diagnostic aspects. *Acta Paediatrica, 85,* 584–588.

Flint, J., Wilkie, A.O.M., Buckle, V.J., et al. (1995). The detection of subtelomeric chromosomal rearrangements in idiopathic mental retardation. *Nature Genetics, 9,* 132–140.

Frankenburg, W.K., Dodds, J.B., Archer, P., et al. (1992). *Denver II* (2nd ed.). Denver, CO: Denver Developmental Materials.

Fraser, W.I., & Rao, J.M. (1991). Recent studies of mentally handicapped young people's behavior. *Journal of Child Psychology and Psychiatry and Allied Disciplines, 32,* 79–108.

Fuller, C.G., & Sabatino, D.A. (1998). Diagnosis and treatment considerations with comorbid developmentally disabled populations. *Journal of Clinical Psychology, 54,* 1–10.

Gardner, H. (1983). *Frames of mind: The theory of multiple intelligences.* New York: Basic Books.

Gecz, J., & Mulley, J. (2000). Genes for cognitive function: developments on the X. *Genome Research, 10,* 157–163.

Gilbride, K.E. (1995). Developmental testing. *Pediatrics in Review, 16,* 338–345.

Gillberg, C. (1998). Mental retardation. In J. Aicardi (Ed.), *Clinics in developmental medicine: Nos. 115–118. Diseases of the nervous system in childhood* (2nd ed., pp. 822–826). Cambridge, England: Cambridge University Press.

Hack, M., & Fanaroff, A.A. (2000). Outcomes of children of extremely low birthweight and gestational age in the 1990s. *Seminars in Neonatology, 5,* 89–106.

Halle, J.W., Gabler-Halle, D., & Chung, Y.B. (1999). Effects of a peer-mediated aerobic conditioning program on fitness levels of youth with mental retardation: Two systematic replications. *Mental Retardation, 37,* 435–448.

Hogan, D.P., Rogers, M.L., & Msall, M.E. (2000). Functional limitations and key indicators of well-being in children with disability. *Archives of Pediatrics and Adolescent Medicine, 154,* 1042–1048.

Hollins, S., Attard, M.T., von Fraunhofer, N., et al. (1998). Mortality in people with learning disability: Risks, causes, and death certification findings in London. *Developmental Medicine and Child Neurology, 40,* 50–56.

Hou, J.W., Wang, T.R., & Chuang, S.M. (1998). An epidemiological and aetiological study of children with intellectual disability in Taiwan. *Journal of Intellectual Disability Research, 42*(Pt. 2), 137–143.

Kaufman, A.S., & Kaufman, N.L. (1983). *Kaufman Assessment Battery for Children (K-ABC).* Circle Pines, MN: American Guidance Service.

Kiely, M. (1987). The prevalence of mental retardation. *Epidemiologic Reviews, 9,* 194–218.

King, B.H., State, M.W., Shah, B., et al. (1997). Mental retardation: A review of the past 10 years, Part I. *Journal of the American Academy of Child and Adolescent Psychiatry, 36,* 1656–1663.

Levy, S.E., & Hyman, S.L. (1993). Pediatric assessment of the child with developmental delay. *Pediatric Clinics of North America, 40,* 465–477.

Lollar, D.J., Simeonsson, R.J., & Nanda, U. (2000). Measures of outcomes for children and youth. *Archives of Physical Medicine and Rehabilitation, 81*(12, Suppl. 2), S46–S52.

Louhiala, P. (1995). Risk indicators of mental retardation: Changes between 1967 and 1981. *Developmental Medicine and Child Neurology, 37,* 631–636.

Luckasson, R., Coulter, D.L., Polloway, E.A., et al. (1992). *Mental retardation: Definition, classification, and systems of supports* (9th ed.). Washington, DC: American Association on Mental Retardation.

Macmillan, C. (1998). Genetics and developmental delay. *Seminars in Pediatric Neurology, 5,* 39–44.

MacMillan, D.L., Gresham, F.M., & Siperstein, G.N. (1995). Heightened concerns over the 1992 AAMR definition: Advocacy versus precision. *American Journal on Mental Retardation, 100,* 87–97.

Madrid, A.L., State, M.W., & King, B.H. (2000). Pharmacologic management of psychiatric and behavioral symptoms in mental retardation. *Child and Adolescent Psychiatric Clinics of North America, 9*(1), 225–243.

Maisto, A.A., & German, M.L. (1986). Reliability, predictive validity, and interrelationships of early assessment indices used with developmentally delayed infants and children. *Journal of Clinical Child Psychiatry, 15,* 547–554.

Majnemer, A., & Shevell, M.I. (1995). Diagnostic yield of the neurologic development of the developmentally delayed child. *Journal of Pediatrics, 127,* 193–199.

Matilainen, R., Airaksinen, E., Mononen, T., et al. (1995). A population-based study on the causes of mild and severe mental retardation. *Acta Paediatrica, 84,* 261–266.

McFadden D.E., & Friedman, J.M. (1997). Chromosome abnormalities in human beings. *Mutation Research, 396*(1–2), 129–140.

McKusick, V.A. (1998). *Mendelian inheritance in man: A catalog of human genes and genetic disorders* (12th ed.). Baltimore: The Johns Hopkins University Press.

McLaren, J., & Bryson, S.E. (1987). Review of recent epidemiological studies of mental retardation: Prevalence, associated disorders, and etiology. *American Journal on Mental Retardation, 92,* 243–254.

Mikkelsen, M., Poulsen, H., & Tommerup, N. (1989). Genetic risk factors in human trisomy 21. In T.J. Hassold & C.J. Epstein (Vol. Eds.), *Progress in clinical and biological research: Vol. 311. Molecular and cytogenetic studies of nondisjunction: Proceedings of the Fifth Annual National Down Syndrome Society Symposium, held in New York, NY, December 1–2, 1988* (pp. 183–197). New York: Wiley Liss.

Moser, H.W. (1995). A role for gene therapy in mental retardation. *Mental Retardation and Developmental Disabilities Research Reviews, 1,* 4–6.

Moss, E.M., Batshaw, M.L., Solot, C.B., et al. (1999). Psychoeducational profile of the 22q11.2 microdeletion: A complex pattern. *Journal of Pediatrics, 134,* 193–199.

Mullen, E. (1989). *Mullen Scales of Early Learning.* Cranston, RI: T.O.T.A.L. Child.

Neri, G., & Chiurazzi, P. (1999). X-linked mental retardation. *Advances in Genetics, 41,* 55–94.

Newborg, J., Stock, J.R., Wnek, L., et al. (1984). *Battelle Developmental Inventory (BDI).* Chicago: Riverside.

Pellock, J.M., & Morton, L.D. (2000). Treatment of epilepsy in the multiply handicapped. *Mental Retardation and Developmental Disabilities Research Reviews, 6,* 309–323.

Petersen, M.D., Kube, D.A., & Palmer, F.B. (1998). Classification of developmental delays. *Seminars in Pediatric Neurology, 5,* 2–14.

Ramey, C.T., & Ramey, S.L. (1998). Prevention of intellectual disabilities: Early interventions to improve cognitive development. *Preventive Medicine, 27,* 224–232.

Ramey, S.L., Ramey, C.T., & Friedlander, M.J. (Eds.). (1999). Early intervention. *Mental Retardation and Developmental Disabilities Research Reviews, 5,* 1–100.

Roeleveld, N., Zielhuis, G.A., & Gabreels, F. (1997). The prevalence of mental retardation: A critical review of recent literature. *Developmental Medicine and Child Neurology, 39,* 125–132.

Santosh, P.J., & Baird, G. (1999). Psychopharmacotherapy in children and adults with intellectual disability. *Lancet, 354,* 233–242.

Scorgie, K., & Sobsey D. (2000). Transformational outcomes associated with parenting children who have disabilities. *Mental Retardation, 38,* 195–206.

Shapiro, B.K. (1996). Neurodevelopmental assessment of infants and young children. In A.J. Capute & P.J. Accardo (Eds.), *Developmental disabilities in infancy and childhood: Vol. I. Neurodevelopmental diagnosis and treatment* (2nd ed., pp. 311–322). Baltimore: Paul H. Brookes Publishing Co.

Shevell, M.I. (1998). The evaluation of the child with a global developmental delay. *Seminars in Pediatric Neurology, 5,* 21–26.

Shevell, M.I., Majnemer, A., Rosenbaum, P., et al. (2000). Etiologic yield of subspecialists' evaluation of young children with global developmental delay. *Journal of Pediatrics, 136,* 593–598.

Sparrow, S., Balla, D., & Cicchetti, D. (1984). *Vineland Adaptive Behavior Scales.* Circle Pines, MN: American Guidance Service.

Steffenburg, U., Hagberg, G., & Kyllerman, M. (1995). Active epilepsy in mentally retarded children, II: Etiology and reduced pre- and perinatal optimality. *Acta Paediatrica, 84,* 1153–1159.

Steffenburg, U., Hagberg, G., Viggedal, G., et al. (1995). Active epilepsy in mentally retarded children: I. Prevalence and additional neuroimpairments. *Acta Paediatrica, 84,* 1147–1152.

Strømme, P. (2000). Aetiology in severe and mild mental retardation: A population-based study of Norwegian children. *Developmental Medicine and Child Neurology, 42,* 76–86.

Strømme, P., & Hagberg, G. (2000). Aetiology in severe and mild mental retardation: A population-based study of Norwegian children. *Developmental Medicine and Child Neurology, 42,* 76–86.

Strømme, P., & Valvatne, K. (1998). Mental retardation in Norway: Prevalence and sub-classification in a cohort of 30,037 children born between 1980 and 1985. *Acta Paediatrica, 7,* 291–296.

Sunder, T.R. (1997). Meeting the challenge of epilepsy in persons with multiple handicaps. *Journal of Child Neurology, 12*(Suppl. 1), S38–S43.

Terman, L.M., & Merrill, M.A. (1985). *Stanford-Binet Intelligence Scale: Manual for the fourth revision.* Chicago: Riverside.

Vig, S., & Jedrysek, E. (1999). Autistic features in young children with significant cognitive impairment: Autism or mental retardation? *Journal of Autism and Developmental Disorders, 29,* 235–248.

Walker, G.R. (1993). Noncompliant behavior of people with mental retardation. *Research in Developmental Disabilities, 14,* 87–105.

Wang, P.P., & Bellugi, U. (1993). Williams syndrome, Down syndrome, and cognitive neuroscience. *American Journal of Diseases of Childhood, 147,* 1246–1251.

Wechsler, D. (1974). *Wechsler Intelligence Scale for Children–Revised.* San Antonio, TX: The Psychological Corporation.

Wechsler, D. (1989). *Wechsler Preschool and Primary Scale of Intelligence–Revised.* San Antonio, TX: The Psychological Corporation.

Wechsler, D. (1991). *Wechsler Intelligence Scale for Children* (3rd ed.). San Antonio, TX: The Psychological Corporation.

Wodrich, D.L. (1997). *Children's psychological testing: A guide for nonpsychologists* (3rd ed.). Baltimore: Paul H. Brookes Publishing Co.

Wolff, G., Back, E., Arleth, S., et al. (1989). Genetic counseling in families with inherited balanced translocations: Experience with 36 families. *Clinical Genetics, 35,* 404–416.

Yeargin-Allsopp, M., Drews, C.D., Decoufle, P., et al. (1995). Mild mental retardation in black and white children in metropolitan Atlanta: A case-control study. *American Journal of Public Health, 85,* 324–328.

Zigler, E. (1967). Familial retardation: A continuing dilemma. *Science, 155,* 292–298.

16 Down Syndrome

Nancy J. Roizen

Upon completion of this chapter, the reader will:

- recognize the physical characteristics of Down syndrome
- understand the medical complications of this disorder
- know the typical cognitive, developmental, and behavioral characteristics of a child with Down syndrome
- understand approaches to intervention

Down syndrome was one of the first symptom complexes associated with mental retardation to be identified as a syndrome. In fact, evidence of the syndrome dates back to ancient times. Archaeological excavations have revealed a skull from the 7th century A.D. that displays the physical features of an individual with Down syndrome. Portrait paintings from the 1500s depict children with a Down-like facial appearance. In 1866, Dr. John Langdon Down, for whom the syndrome is named, published the first complete physical description of Down syndrome, including the similarity of facial features among affected individuals. In 1959, researchers identified the underlying chromosomal abnormality (an additional chromosome 21) that causes Down syndrome (Lejeune, Gautier, & Turpin, 1959).

JASON

In most ways, Jason is like all of the other 8-year-olds in the neighborhood. He plays soccer, skates, swims, is a Boy Scout, and is in the second grade. Jason has a great sense of humor and is a bit mischievous. His mother makes every effort to provide him with a balance of social and academic opportunities. But Jason has had experiences that most of the other children have not. He has had operative procedures in his ears, a hernia repair, and surgical correction of his congenital heart defect. He has a unilateral hearing loss that was discovered on auditory brainstem response (ABR) testing when he was 2 years of age. He is nearsighted and recently began to wear glasses. In addition, Jason has attention-deficit/hyperactivity disorder (ADHD), which has improved on methylphenidate (Ritalin). In his school, Jason was the first child with Down syndrome to be included in the general education kindergarten. His reading skills are at a pre-primer level. His most recently revealed medical challenge was obstructive sleep apnea. This resolved with the removal of his adenoids.

CHROMOSOMAL ABNORMALITIES

Three types of chromosomal abnormalities can lead to Down syndrome: trisomy 21 (which accounts for about 95% of individuals with the disorder), translocation (4%), and mosaicism (1%). Trisomy 21 results from nondisjunction, most commonly during meiosis I of the egg (see Chapter 1). Translocation Down syndrome involves the attachment of the long arm of an extra chromosome 21 to chromosome 14, 21, or 22. Mosaic trisomy implies that some, but not all, cells have the defect. This results from nondisjunction during mitosis of the fertilized egg.

Studies indicate that children with translocation Down syndrome do not differ cognitively or medically from those with trisomy 21 (Johnson & Abelson, 1969). Children with mosaic Down syndrome, perhaps because their trisomic cells are interspersed with normal cells, typically score 10–30 points higher on IQ tests and have fewer medical complications than do children with translocation or trisomy 21 Down syndrome (de Moreira et al., 2000; Fishler & Koch, 1991).

PREVALENCE

The prevalence of Down syndrome births has decreased from 1.33 per 1,000 to 0.92 per 1,000 since the 1970s, presumably as a result of prenatal diagnosis and termination of a significant number of affected pregnancies (Olsen et al., 1996; Wortelboer et al., 2000). In definitions of prevalence, maternal age has been consistently linked to Down syndrome. At 20 years of age, women have about a 1 in 2,000 chance of having a child with trisomy 21; at 45 years of age, the likelihood increases to 1 in 20 (Figure 2.2; Trimble & Baird, 1978). There is no increased risk of translocation Down syndrome with increased maternal age, but one third of individuals with this type of Down syndrome inherit the translocation from a parent who is a carrier (Jones, 1996). Chromosome analysis can identify parents who are at risk of producing other children with translocation Down syndrome. Although trisomic Down syndrome occurs in more males (59%) than females (41%), translocation Down syndrome more often occurs in females (74%; Staples et al., 1991). The reason for these phenomena is unclear.

CAUSE

When an individual has three copies of a critical region on chromosome 21 (Figure 16.1), he or she will present with the clinical features of Down syndrome. Although it is not known how three copies of this region produce this syndrome, researchers believe that defects on a closely

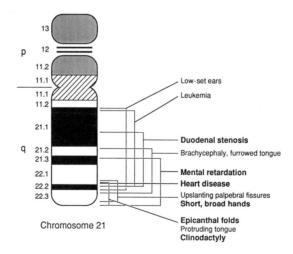

Figure 16.1. The critical region for the Down syndrome phenotype is on the long arm (q11.1–q22.3) of chromosome 21. Specific malformations are noted as being localized to the bracketed regions. The most clear associations are shown in boldface. (From Epstein, C.E. [Ed.]. [1991, January 17–18]. *The morphogenesis of Down syndrome* [Proceedings of the National Down Syndrome Society Conference on Morphogenesis and Down Syndrome, New York; p. 44]. Copyright © 1991 John Wiley & Sons, Inc. This material is used by permission of John Wiley & Sons, Inc.)

related group of genes together contribute to the clinical picture; this condition is called a *contiguous gene syndrome* (Korenberg et al., 1994; Sinet et al., 1994). Two of these genes, for example, code for the enzyme DYRK (dual specificity tyrosine phosphorylation-related kinase) and *myo*-inositol, which play an important role in how neuronal pathways are formed (Becker & Joost, 1999; Berry et al., 1999). Although the underlying mechanism remains unclear, much has been learned about the embryology and neuropathology of Down syndrome. It is likely that the trisomy causes malformations as a result of incomplete rather than deviant development of the embryo. For example, although the heart may be normally formed, the wall separating the two sides of the heart may not close completely. Similarly, the separation of the trachea and esophagus may be incomplete, resulting in a **tracheoesophageal fistula** (an area of connection between the two).

Examination of the brain tissue of individuals with Down syndrome reveals multiple developmental abnormalities, including delayed myelination, fewer neurons, decreased synaptic density, and decreased acetylcholine neurotransmitter receptors (Florez et al., 1990; Zigman, Silverman, & Wisniewski, 1996). Furthermore, a gene for amyloid, an abnormal protein found in the brain of individuals with Alzheimer's disease, is located on chromosome 21, which may explain why adults with Down syndrome are at an increased risk for developing Alzheimer's disease.

EARLY IDENTIFICATION

Typically, women 35 years of age and older are offered prenatal diagnostic testing for Down syndrome. In addition, most obstetricians utilize a blood screening test for determining whether prenatal diagnosis for Down syndrome is indicated in younger women (see Chapter 2; Rose, 1996; Wald, Watt, & Hackshaw, 1999). Identification of Down syndrome prior to birth enables the physician to provide genetic counseling to the family and, if the pregnancy is continued to term, appropriate medical evaluation of the newborn infant.

Because of the distinctive pattern of physical features, infants with Down syndrome can be identified fairly easily at birth. An index developed by Rex and Preus (1982) based on eight physical features predicts Down syndrome with an accuracy rate of 75%. These characteristics include three palm print (dermatoglyphic) patterns, Brushfield spots (colored speckles in the iris of the eye), ear length, internipple distance, neck skinfold, and widely spaced first toes. Individuals with XXXY, XXXXY, and XXXX syndromes (see Chapter 2), however, bear a physical resemblance to individuals with Down syndrome in the newborn period (Jones, 1996). Therefore, all children suspected of having Down syndrome should have a chromosomal analysis to ensure correct diagnosis and to provide accurate genetic counseling about future pregnancies.

MEDICAL COMPLICATIONS IN DOWN SYNDROME

Children with Down syndrome have an increased risk of abnormalities in almost every organ system (Roizen, 1996). A knowledge of the possible complications enables the caregiver to evaluate the child for the more common disorders and increase vigilance for less common medical problems (Table 16.1).

Congenital Heart Disease

In one study of newborns with Down syndrome, two thirds were found by echocardiogram to have congenital heart defects, the most common being endocardial cushion defect (resulting in a connection between the **atria,** or upper chambers, and **ventricles,** or lower chambers), ventric-

Table 16.1.   Medical complications in Down syndrome

Disorder	% affected
Congenital heart defect	66
Endocardial cushion defect	19
Ventricular septal defect	15
Atrial septal defect	14
Other	18
Ophthalmic disorders (often more than 1)	60
Refractive errors	35
Strabismus	27
Nystagmus	20
Blepharitis	9
Tear duct obstruction	6
Cataracts	5
Ptosis	5
Hearing loss	66
Endocrine abnormalities	50–90
Subclinical hypothyroidism	30–50
Overt hypothyroidism	4
Diabetes	0.4
Growth problems	50–90
Obesity	60
Short stature	50–90
Orthopedic abnormalities	16
Subclinical atlantoaxial subluxation	15
Symptomatic atlantoaxial subluxation	1
Dental problems, periodontal disease malocclusion	60–100
Gastrointestinal malformations	5
Celiac disease	5
Epilepsy	6
Leukemia	0.01
Skin conditions	50
Alzheimer's disease after 40 years	15–20

ular septal defect (a connection between the two lower chambers), and atrial septal defect (a connection between the two upper chambers; Marino & Pueschel, 1996; Wells et al., 1994). A major complication of congenital heart disease is pulmonary vascular obstructive disease. This leads to increased back pressure in the arteries that connect the heart to the lungs and results in congestive heart failure. Progression of this potentially fatal complication is more rapid in children with Down syndrome than in children with the same heart defects and normal chromosomes (Suzuki et al., 2000).

Sensory Impairments

Vision and hearing problems occur with increased frequency in children with Down syndrome. A survey of 77 randomly selected children with Down syndrome found that more than 60% had ophthalmic disorders requiring treatment or monitoring. The most common of these disorders were refractive errors, strabismus (crossed eyes), nystagmus (jiggling of the eyes), blepharitis (inflammation of the eyelids), tear duct obstruction, cataracts, and ptosis (droopy eyelids) (Roizen, Mets, & Blondis, 1994). In children with no ophthalmic abnormalities observed during general pediatric checkups, 35% actually had an identifiable disorder when examined by an ophthalmologist. Thus, in the first few weeks of life, and subsequently at periodic intervals, all children with Down syndrome should receive an ophthalmological examination (da Cunha & Moreira, 1996).

Hearing loss occurs in approximately two thirds of children with Down syndrome. It can be conductive (bone conduction of sound), sensorineural (involving the cochlea or auditory nerve), or combined, and it can be unilateral or bilateral (see Chapter 11; Roizen et al., 1993). Conductive hearing problems result from a combination of narrow throat structures and a subtle immune deficiency that predisposes these children to recurrent ear infections. Chapman et al. (1998) estimated that 10% of the language impairment in children with Down syndrome is accounted for by the hearing impairments. These children also may develop sleep apnea (brief periods of arrested breathing during sleep) as a consequence of upper airway obstruction from enlarged tonsils and adenoids (Stebbens et al., 1991).

Endocrine Abnormalities

Congenital hypothyroidism due to poor development of the thyroid gland is found in 1 in 141 infants with Down syndrome, a rate about 28 times that seen in the general population (Fort et al., 1984; Karlsson et al., 1998; Prasher, 1999). In addition, 30%–40% of older children with Down syndrome manifest subclinical hypothyroidism with a normal thyroxine (thyroid hormone) level but an elevated level of thyroid stimulating hormone. In one study, 7% of children with an elevated thyroid stimulating hormone level were found to ultimately develop overt hypothyroidism thought to be due to autoimmune thyroiditis (Rubello et al., 1995). Diabetes occurs in 1 in 250 children with Down syndrome, more than twice the usual prevalence (Anwar, Walker, & Frier, 1998; Ohyama et al., 2000).

In terms of growth patterns, children with Down syndrome tend to be lightweight for their height during the first year of life. During the next few years, however, the children gain relatively more weight than height, and by early childhood, half are overweight (Rubin et al., 1998). Yet, compared with children of the same size, they have similar activity levels and consume fewer calories (Luke et al., 1994). The mechanism for the obesity therefore appears to be a lower resting metabolic rate; children with Down syndrome require fewer calories to gain weight (Ulrich et al., 2001).

In addition to being overweight, individuals with Down syndrome have short stature. The average adult height is 5 feet in males and 4½ feet in females with the syndrome (Toledo et al., 1999). A few studies have examined the effect of growth hormone in children with Down syndrome and documented accelerated short-term growth (Annerén et al., 1999). It remains unclear, however, whether the eventual height of children with Down syndrome treated with growth hormone will be significantly increased. There also is a need for further assessment of the safety (including concerns about leukemia) and ethical ramifications of growth hormone treatment before it is more commonly used in children with Down syndrome.

Orthopedic Problems

Children with Down syndrome have an increased prevalence of orthopedic problems that are probably related to abnormally loose ligaments. These include atlantoaxial subluxation, or partial dislocation of the upper spine (Figure 16.2); hip dislocation; patellar instability; and flat feet. These children also can develop juvenile rheumatoid arthritis (see Chapter 14; Pueschel & Pueschel, 1992).

Atlantoaxial subluxation is the most controversial and perplexing of these problems, occurring in approximately 15% of children with Down syndrome (American Academy of Pediatrics [AAP], Committee on Sports Medicine and Fitness, 1995; Frost et al., 1999). Only 1% of children with Down syndrome become symptomatic, however, and the subluxation rarely leads to paralysis (Pueschel, Scola, & Pezzullo, 1992). Symptoms of subluxation include easy fatigability, difficulties in walking, abnormal gait, neck pain, limited neck mobility, **torticollis**

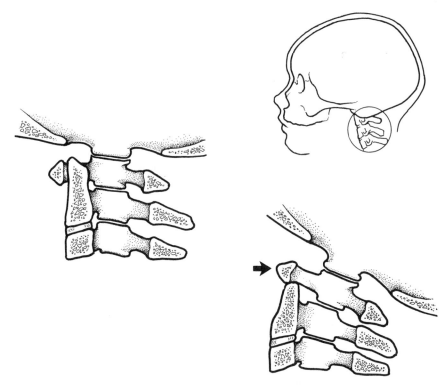

Figure 16.2. Children with Down syndrome are at risk of developing subluxation (partial dislocation) of the atlantoaxial or atlanto-occipital joint, as shown in this illustration (right side). A typical neck region is shown for comparison (left side). This subluxation predisposes these children to spinal injury with trauma. This abnormality can be detected by X ray or magnetic resonance imaging scan of the neck.

(painful head tilt), a change in hand function, the new onset of urinary retention or incontinence, incoordination and clumsiness, sensory impairments, and spasticity (AAP Committee on Sports Medicine and Fitness, 1995).

Dental Problems

The most serious dental problem is early-onset periodontal disease that can rapidly progress (Hennequin et al., 1999). This involves both gingivitis (gum inflammation) and regression of the jaw bone that anchors the teeth (see Chapter 28). The periodontal disease is a manifestation of the general low resistance to infection in children with Down syndrome. In addition to having periodontal disease, almost all children with Down syndrome have malocclusions (abnormal contact of opposing teeth), and many have a variety of dental anomalies, including fused teeth, microdontia (small teeth), and missing teeth. In the majority of these children, primary and permanent teeth erupt later than usual. Interestingly, dental caries occurs less often in children with Down syndrome than in the general population (Pueschel & Pueschel, 1992); the reason for this is unclear but is probably related to differences in immunity and tooth shape.

Gastrointestinal Malformations

Gastrointestinal malformations are found in approximately 5% of children with Down syndrome. Most of these abnormalities present with symptoms in the newborn period such as poor feeding, vomiting, or aspiration pneumonia. The malformations include stenosis (narrowing) or **atresia** (blockage) of the duodenum (3%), **imperforate** (closed) anus (0.9%), Hirschsprung disease (congenitally enlarged colon; 0.5%), tracheoesophageal fistula (an abnormal connection between the trachea and esophagus) or esophageal atresia (0.4%), and pyloric stenosis (narrowing of the stomach outlet; 0.3%) (Pueschel & Pueschel, 1992). Recently, celiac disease (sensitivity to wheat and other grains) has been found in 1%–7% of children with Down syndrome (Carlsson et al., 1998; Pueschel et al., 1999; Zachor, Mroczek-Musulman, & Brown, 2000).

Epilepsy

Epilepsy occurs in 6% of individuals with Down syndrome (Johannsen et al., 1996). This is more common than in the general population but about average for children with moderate mental retardation. Seizure types include generalized tonic-clonic (55% of all seizures in children with Down syndrome), infantile spasms (13%), myoclonic (6%), atonic plus tonic-clonic (6%), and simple partial (6%; see Chapter 25). The age of onset of seizures has a bimodal distribution, occurring most commonly in individuals younger than 3 years and older than 13. Sixty-two percent of the seizures have an identifiable cause, the most common being infections and hypoxia resulting from congenital heart disease (Stafstrom et al., 1991). Infantile spasms have a better outcome in children with Down syndrome than in children who do not have Down syndrome (Stafstrom & Konkol, 1994).

Hematologic Disorders

Although there is little information about the specific mechanisms of the abnormalities, almost every cellular element of the **hematopoietic** (blood) system has been found to be at risk for an abnormality in Down syndrome. For example, erythrocytosis (too many red blood cells) can be found in the newborn. Therefore, a complete blood count is indicated at birth for infants with Down syndrome. Platelets may be either increased or decreased (Pueschel & Pueschel, 1992). Although these hematologic abnormalities rarely lead to severe problems, children with Down syndrome have a 1 in 150 risk of developing leukemia as compared with 1 in 2,800 in children without Down syndrome (Avet-Loiseau, Mechinaud, & Harousseau, 1995; Chang et al., 2000).

Skin Conditions

Several skin conditions, mostly of immune origin, are observed more frequently in individuals with Down syndrome than in the general population. Some of these conditions noticeably affect the appearance, and therefore the quality of life, of the child, and thus require treatment. By puberty, half or more of these individuals will experience atopic dermatitis (eczema), cheilitis (inflammation of the lips), ichthyosis (dry and scaly skin), onychomycosis (fungal infection of the nails), seborrheic dermatitis (dandruff), vitiligo (patches of depigmentation), and/or xerosis (dryness of eyes) (Ercis, Balci, & Atakan, 1996; Nomura, 1999; Schepis et al., 1997; Velthuis & Nijenhuis, 1995). Less common are syringomas (sweat gland cysts) and **alopecia** (hair loss) (Pueschel & Pueschel, 1992; Scherbehske et al., 1990).

NEURODEVELOPMENTAL AND BEHAVIOR IMPAIRMENTS

Infants with Down syndrome typically have central hypotonia (floppiness without weakness); consequently, gross motor skills are delayed. On the average, most children with Down syndrome do not sit up until 11 months of age or walk until 19 months (Winders, 1997). The early developmental milestones of boys with Down syndrome tend to occur slightly later than those of girls (Melyn & White, 1973). Although continued progress in the gross motor area is slow, significant physical disabilities are rare. Children with Down syndrome learn to run, ride bicycles, and participate in sports (see Chapter 34).

In the first 2 years of life, children with Down syndrome, primarily because of their social responsiveness, appear to have fewer cognitive impairments than they actually have (Brown et al., 1990). By 2 years of age, however, significant language delays become evident; children with Down syndrome often do not speak their first word until 18 months of age (Kumin, 1996). Their receptive language is generally better than their expressive language. Even after children with Down syndrome speak in sentences, problems with intelligibility interfere with effective communication. Therefore, speech therapy that addresses the development of expressive speech and intelligibility is needed for many years (Chapman et al., 1991; Chapman et al., 1998; Kumin, 1996; Miller, Leddy, & Leavitt, 1999). Formal psychological testing at school age shows that 85% of children with Down syndrome have IQ scores that range from 40 to 60 (Connolly, 1978), which label them as having mild to moderate mental retardation. Although these children generally have poor verbal short-term memory skills, their visual-motor skills are relatively strong (Wang, 1996). This cognitive pattern is consistent with functional neuroimaging studies that reveal impairments within and between the frontal and parietal lobes of the brain, including the inferior frontal gyrus, which contains Broca's speech area (see Chapter 12; Horwitz et al., 1990).

Children with Down syndrome are stereotyped as being amiable and happy. Temperament studies, however, have shown them to have profiles comparable to typically developing children (Chapman & Hesketh, 2000). In addition, a survey of 261 children with Down syndrome found the following prevalence of behavior and psychiatric disorders: aggressive behavior (7%), ADHD (6%), oppositional disorder (5%), stereotypic behavior (3%), elimination difficulties (2%), phobias (2%), autism (1%), eating disorders (1%), self-injurious behavior (1%), and Tourette syndrome (0.4%) (Collacott et al., 1998; Cuskelly & Dadds, 1992; Kerbeshian & Burd, 2000; Myers & Pueschel, 1991). A second study found an even higher frequency of pervasive developmental disorders (7%) in children with Down syndrome (Kent et al., 1999).

Some individuals with Down syndrome may experience a deterioration of cognitive or psychological functioning in adolescence, often manifested as worsening of behavior or academic performance. Many times, this deterioration can be attributed to unrecognized hypothyroidism or depression. If such diagnoses are confirmed, medical and psychiatric treatment can reverse these problems. It appears, however, that virtually all individuals with Down syndrome older than 50 have pathological plaques and tangles in their brain, which are the hallmarks of Alzheimer's disease. Yet, even in adults with Down syndrome who have a decline in function, a mental health disorder such as anxiety, depression, or **obsessive-compulsive disorder** accounts for more than half (55%) of the cases; about one fifth (21%) have Alzheimer's disease (Janicki & Dalton, 1999; Pearlson et al., 1998).

The educational program of the child with Down syndrome needs to provide the optimal environment for learning. Thus, a balance of inclusion in learning environments with typical children and therapeutic interventions need to be planned for each child (see Chapter 30). The plan needs to consider the child's opportunities for socialization in the home and community and his or her developmental and educational strengths and needs. Such plans need to be reviewed and altered as needed at regular intervals.

EVALUATION AND TREATMENT

Several of the aforementioned medical conditions occur with sufficient frequency that all children with Down syndrome should be evaluated for them. These include congenital heart disease, ophthalmic disorders, hearing loss, celiac disease, and hypothyroidism (Saenz, 1999; van Allen, Fung, & Jurenka, 1999). An outline of the suggested periodic evaluation of children with Down syndrome is shown in Figure 16.3.

Figure 16.3. Recommendations for preventive health care for children and adolescents with Down syndrome. (*Sources:* American Academy of Pediatrics, Committee on Genetics, 2001; Cohen for the Down Syndrome Medical Interest Group, 1999.)

	Infancy						Early childhood					Late childhood					Adolescence			
Age (in months / in years)	1	2	4	6	9	12	15	18	24	3	4	5	6	8	10	12	14	16	18	21
History	•[1]	•[1]	•[1]	•	•	•	•[2]	•[2]	•[2]	•[2]	•[2]	•	•	•	•	•	•[3]	•[3]	•[3]	•[3]
Measurements	•[4]	•	•	•	•	•	•	•	•	•	•	•	•	•	•	•	•	•	•	•
Developmental/ behavioral assessment	•	•	•	•	•	•	•[5]	•	•	•	•	•[6]	•	•[6]	•	•[6]	•	•[6]	•	•
Physical exam	•[7]	•[7]	•[7]	•[7]	•[7]	•[7]	•[7]	•[7]	•[8]	•[8]	•[8]	•	•[8]	•	•[8]	•	•	•	•[0]	•[9]
Procedures																				
Karyotype	•																			
Thyroid screen	•		•			•				•	•	•	•	•	•	•	•	•	•	•
Complete blood count	•[10]																			
Echocardiogram	•[11]																			
Neck X rays										•[12]										
Celiac panel									•											
Sensory																				
Vision	O[13]	S	S	S	S	S	S	S	O	O	O	O	O	O	O	O	O	O	O	O
Hearing	O[14]	S	S	O	S	S	O	S	O	O	O	O	O	O	O	O	O	O	O	O
Consultation																				
Cardiology	•																			
Ophthalmology			•			•				•	•						•	•	•	•
Ear, nose, and throat			•[15]							•	•						•	•	•	•
Genetic	•																			
Down syndrome clinic			•			•				•	•	•	•	•	•	•	•	•	•	•
Dental									•	•	•	•	•	•	•	•	•	•	•	•
Referrals																				
Early intervention	•————————————————▶																			
Supplemental Security Income (SSI)	•					•													•	
State mental retardation agency	•——▶																			
Anticipatory guidance[16]	•	•	•	•	•	•	•	•	•	•	•	•	•	•	•	•	•[17]	•	•	•

• = to be performed   S = subjective, by history   O = objective, by a standard testing method

1. Special attention to gastrointestinal/cardiac systems
2. Special attention to sleep/behavior problems
3. Special attention to thyroid, seizures
4. Based on growth curves developed for Down syndrome (Cronk et al., 1988)
5. Special attention to speech evaluation begins at this time.
6. Psychoeducational evaluation
7. Check tympanic membrane
8. Neurological exam regarding atlantoaxial instability
9. GYN exam
10. Special attention to increased platelets
11. Even in absence of murmur
12. Earlier, if having surgery
13. Must see red reflex to rule out cataracts
14. Neonatal screening, auditory brainstem response (ABR)
15. Depending on view of tympanic membrane
16. Information on medical problems, educational programs, tax deductions, SSI, local services, wills, vaccinations (including hepatitis)
17. Information on vocational programs, sexuality, independent living, hepatitis vaccine

Congenital heart disease in children with Down syndrome may be difficult to identify based on physical findings alone as it is not always accompanied by a cardiac murmur nor does it commonly produce a "blue baby" (Wells et al., 1994). Yet, because children with Down syndrome tend to develop pulmonary vascular disease sooner than other children with the same defect do, early identification and treatment are essential. Although children with Down syndrome were once considered poor risks for cardiac surgery, data now indicate that they have a similar outcome as other children with the same heart defect (Malec et al., 1999). The one exception is complete atrioventricular septal defect, which has a higher overall surgical mortality in children with Down syndrome (Reller & Morris, 1998). A cardiac evaluation, including an echocardiogram, is the standard of care for the newborn with Down syndrome.

Within the first 6 months of life, all children with Down syndrome need an ophthalmologic evaluation to identify cataracts and strabismus (see Chapter 10). Subsequently, these children should be evaluated annually or semiannually to detect refractive errors and other ophthalmic disorders (Roizen et al., 1994).

Clarification of the hearing status of infants with Down syndrome requires an ABR test (see Chapter 11). An initial ABR test is recommended at birth to demonstrate the child's baseline hearing status and to rule out unilateral hearing loss (Joint Committee on Infant Hearing, 2000). It also can determine whether a hearing loss is conductive or sensorineural (Roizen et al., 1993). Because these children are at increased risk for recurrent middle-ear infections, leading to conductive hearing loss, hearing evaluation should be repeated every 6 months until age 3 and annually thereafter (Cohen for the Down Syndrome Medical Interest Group, 1999; Joint Committee on Infant Hearing, 2000).

If there is the suspicion of sleep apnea, a **polysomnogram** (sleep study) should be performed (Levanon, Tarasiuk, & Tal, 1999). If the diagnosis is confirmed and found to be associated with enlarged adenoids, antibiotic treatment is used and the adenoids are subsequently removed surgically (Lefaivre et al., 1997). If the adenoidectomy does not correct the mechanical obstruction, further surgical procedures (e.g., **tracheostomy** to bypass the obstruction) or sleeping with continuous positive airway pressure to keep the airway open may be necessary.

As with all newborns, children with Down syndrome are routinely screened for congenital hypothyroidism (see Chapter 18). In addition, they should have thyroid function tests performed at 4–6 months of age, at 1 year, and then annually (AAP Committee on Genetics, 2001). More frequent thyroid function tests are indicated if the child displays accelerated weight gain, behavior problems, plateauing of height, or an unexpected lack of cognitive progress. If there is laboratory evidence of hypothyroidism, treatment with thyroxine (thyroid hormone) is indicated. It is now recommended that children with Down syndrome also be screened for celiac disease at 24 months using a celiac panel (Carlsson et al., 1998).

Because of the high prevalence of periodontal disease, daily cleaning of teeth should begin as soon as they erupt. As with all children, regular dental visits should also begin at this time. Orthodontic intervention is needed by most children with Down syndrome and becomes possible when a child is able to cooperate with and tolerate the therapy.

The evaluation of children for atlantoaxial subluxation by X-ray studies is customarily done on entrance to preschool and sometimes prior to elective surgery. If the child participates in Special Olympics activities (see Chapter 34), an additional radiograph is usually obtained at that time to make sure that subluxation has not developed, placing the child at increased risk for sports injuries. Signs and symptoms of spinal cord compression, such as the onset of weakness in gait, torticollis, neck pain, or bowel and bladder incontinence, indicate the need for further testing (AAP Committee on Sports Medicine and Fitness, 1995). Children with radiologic findings indicating neck instability of an unacceptable degree and children with symptomatic subluxation are treated surgically with a neck fusion.

Several other medical problems, such as diabetes and leukemia, occur more frequently in children with Down syndrome than in the general population. Although screening for these disorders is not routinely done, it is appropriate to lower the threshold for evaluation for individuals with Down syndrome. The clinician also should be alert to symptoms of psychiatric illness (e.g., depression) and refer the individual for appropriate evaluation and treatment when indicated (see Chapter 19).

EARLY INTERVENTION

The parents of a newborn with Down syndrome should be made aware of a variety of services, including early intervention educational programs (see Chapter 29), local and national parent support/advocacy programs such as the National Down Syndrome Society and the National Down Syndrome Congress (see Appendix D), respite care options, and Supplemental Security Income (see Chapter 38). Children with Down syndrome have a long history of involvement in early intervention programs; studies of this early intervention indicate improved motor and developmental function (Guralnick, 1997).

As there is no cure for Down syndrome and the cognitive and medical problems may significantly interfere with a child's function, parents are vulnerable to the recommendations of proponents of alternative therapies. Alternative therapies have included mixtures of vitamins, minerals, and hormones; cell therapy or injections of fetal lamb brains; and, most recently, Piracetam, a stimulant drug. Scientifically designed studies of vitamin, mineral, and cell therapies for children with Down syndrome have not shown improvement in appearance, growth, health, or developmental function (Bennett et al., 1983; Smith et al., 1984; Van Dyke et al., 1990). Piracetam is a member of a class of drugs thought to enhance cognitive function, but a study in children with Down syndrome taking the drug revealed no improvements in behavioral or cognitive function (Lobaugh et al., 2001).

OUTCOME

Since the 1970s, the prognosis for a productive and positive life experience for individuals with Down syndrome has increased substantially, largely due to the efforts of parent advocacy groups (Carr, 1994, 1995; Hassold & Patterson, 1998; Pueschel, 1996). Previously, physicians would often endorse or even recommend institutionalization for newborn infants with Down syndrome and sometimes would hesitate to recommend life-saving cardiac and gastrointestinal surgery. Now, when a child is born with Down syndrome, the physician routinely refers the family to early intervention programs and parent support groups and performs surgery as a matter of course (Haslam & Milner, 1992). Children with Down syndrome were among the first children with disabilities to be mainstreamed in the public schools and thus have been the pioneers in the trend toward inclusion.

Life expectancy and quality of life for individuals with Down syndrome also have improved greatly since the 1980s (Friedman, 2001; Leonard et al., 2000; Strauss & Eyman, 1996; Yang, Rasmussen, & Friedman, 2002). In the first 5 years of life, 87% of children with Down syndrome without congenital heart disease survive, as do 76% of those with congenital heart disease (Baird & Sadovnick, 1987). Life expectancy tables indicate that more than half of individuals with Down syndrome will survive into their fifties and that 13.5% will still be alive at age 68 years (Baird & Sadovnick, 1989; Hijii et al., 1997).

With the introduction in the 1980s of supported employment (in which individuals have a job coach), adults with Down syndrome often hold real jobs with better pay and benefits and good working conditions (Kingsley & Levitz, 1994; Nadel & Rosenthal, 1995). To succeed in supported employment, the person needs to have a healthy sense of self-esteem that is nurtured from early childhood, the ability to complete tasks without assistance, a willingness to separate emotionally from parents and family members, and access to personal recreational activities (Pueschel, 1996; Turnbull & Turnbull, 1985; Unruh, 1994). All of these should be goals of educational programs for individuals with Down syndrome.

SUMMARY

Down syndrome is a disorder characterized by a recognizable pattern of physical features, an increased risk for specific medical problems, and mental retardation requiring intermittent to limited support. As children with Down syndrome are usually identified at birth, the early intervention system frequently has them as their youngest enrollees. Although much remains to be learned and done, the educational and medical systems are probably more knowledgeable and comfortable with the special needs of children with Down syndrome than with any other single diagnostic disability group.

The AAP Committee on Genetics (2001) and the Down Syndrome Medical Interest Group (Cohen, 1999) have proposed standards of medical care that include periodic monitoring for medical problems that occur frequently in children with Down syndrome. With optimal audiologic, cardiac, endocrinologic, ophthalmologic, and orthopedic functioning, children with Down syndrome have the opportunity for good health and developmental functioning.

REFERENCES

American Academy of Pediatrics (AAP), Committee on Genetics. (2001). Health supervision for children with Down syndrome. *Pediatrics, 107,* 442–449.

American Academy of Pediatrics (AAP), Committee on Sports Medicine and Fitness. (1995). Atlantoaxial instability in Down syndrome: Subject review. *Pediatrics, 96,* 151–154.

Annerén, G., Tuvemo, T., Carlsson-Skwirut, C., et al. (1999). Growth hormone treatment in young children with Down's syndrome: Effects on growth and psychomotor development. *Archives of Disease in Childhood, 80,* 334–338.

Anwar, A.J., Walker, J.D., & Frier, B.M. (1998). Type I diabetes mellitus and Down's syndrome: Prevalence, management and diabetic complications. *Diabetes Medicine, 15,* 160–163.

Avet-Loiseau, H., Mechinaud, F., & Harousseau, J.-L. (1995). Clonal hematologic disorders in Down syndrome: A review. *Journal of Pediatric Hematology and Oncology, 17,* 19–24.

Baird, P.A., & Sadovnick, A.D. (1987). Life expectancy in Down syndrome. *Journal of Pediatrics, 110,* 849–854.

Baird, P.A., & Sadovnick, A.D. (1989). Life tables for Down syndrome. *Human Genetics, 82,* 291–292.

Becker, W., & Joost, H.G. (1999). Structural and functional characteristics of DYRK: A novel subfamily of protein kinases with dual specificity. *Progress in Nucleic Acid Research and Molecular Biology, 62,* 1–17.

Bennett, F.C., McClelland, S., Kriegsmann, E.A., et al. (1983). Vitamin and mineral supplementation in Down's syndrome. *Pediatrics, 72,* 707–713.

Berry, G.T., Wang, Z.J., Dreba, S.F., et al. (1999). In vivo brain myo-inositol levels in children with Down syndrome. *Journal of Pediatrics, 135,* 94–97.

Brown, F.R., Greer, M.K., Aylward, E.H., et al. (1990). Intellectual and adaptive functioning in individuals with Down syndrome in relation to age and environmental placement. *Pediatrics, 85,* 450–452.

Carlsson, A., Axelsson, I., Borulf, S., et al. (1998). Prevalence of IgA-antigliadin antibodies and IgA-antiendomysium antibodies related to celiac disease in children with Down syndrome. *Pediatrics, 101,* 272–275.

Carr, J. (1994). Long-term-outcome for people with Down's syndrome. *Journal of Child Psychology and Psychiatry and Allied Disciplines, 35,* 429–439.

Carr, J.H. (1995). *Down's syndrome: Children growing up.* New York: Cambridge University Press.

Chang, M., Raimondi, S.C., Ravindranath, Y., et al. (2000). Prognostic factors in children and adolescents with acute myeloid leukemia (excluding children with Down syndrome and acute promyelocytic leukemia): Univariate and recursive partitioning analysis of patients treated on Pediatric Oncology Group (POG) Study 8821. *Leukemia, 14,* 1201–1207.

Chapman, R.E., Schwartz, S.E., & Kay-Raining Bird, E. (1991). Language skills of children and adolescents with Down syndrome, I: Comprehension. *Journal of Speech, Language, and Hearing Research, 34,* 1106–1120.

Chapman, R.E., Seung, H.-K., Schwartz, S.E. et al. (1998). Language skills of children and adolescents with Down syndrome, II: Production deficits. *Journal of Speech, Language, and Hearing Research, 41,* 861–873.

Chapman, R.S., & Hesketh, L.J. (2000). Behavioral phenotype of individuals with Down syndrome. *Mental Retardation and Developmental Disabilities Research Reviews, 6,* 84–95.

Cohen, W.I., for the Down Syndrome Medical Interest Group. (1999). Health care guidelines for individuals with Down syndrome: 1999 revision (Down syndrome preventive medical checklist). *Down Syndrome Quarterly, 4,* 1–15.

Collacott, R.A., Cooper, S.A., Branford, D., et al. (1998). Behaviour phenotype for Down's syndrome. *British Journal of Psychiatry, 172,* 85–89.

Connolly, J.A. (1978). Intelligence levels on Down's syndrome children. *American Journal of Mental Deficiency, 83,* 193–196.

Cronk, C.E., Crocker, A.C., Pueschel, S.M., et al. (1988). Growth charts for children with Down syndrome: 1 month to 18 years of age. *Pediatrics, 81,* 102–110.

Cuskelly, M., & Dadds, M. (1992). Behavioral problems in children with Down's syndrome and their siblings. *Journal of Child Psychology and Psychiatry and Allied Disciplines, 33,* 749–762.

da Cunha, R.P., & Moreira, J.B. (1996). Ocular findings in Down's syndrome. *American Journal of Ophthalmology, 122,* 236–44.

de Moreira, L.M., San Juan, A., Pereira, P.S., et al. (2000). A case of mosaic trisomy 21 with Down's syndrome signs and normal intellectual development. *Journal of Intellectual Disability Research, 44,* 91–96.

Epstein, C.E. (Ed.). (1991). *The morphogenesis of Down syndrome* [Proceedings of the National Down Syndrome Society Conference on Morphogenesis and Down Syndrome, New York]. New York: John Wiley & Sons.

Ercis, M., Balci, S., & Atakan, N. (1996). Dermatological manifestations of 71 Down syndrome children admitted to a clinical genetics unit. *Clinical Genetics, 50,* 317–320.

Fishler, K., & Koch, R. (1991). Mental development in Down syndrome mosaicism. *American Journal on Mental Retardation, 96,* 345–351.

Florez, J., del Arco, C., Gonzalez, A., et al. (1990). Autoradiographic studies of neurotransmitter receptors in the brains of newborn infants with Down syndrome. *American Journal of Medical Genetics, 7*(Suppl.), 301–305.

Fort, P., Lifshitz, F., Bellisario, R., et al. (1984). Abnormalities of thyroid functioning in infants with Down syndrome. *Journal of Pediatrics, 104,* 545–549.

Friedman, J.M. (2001). Racial disparities in median age at death of persons with Down syndrome: United States, 1968–1997. *MMWR, 50,* 463–465.

Frost, M., Huffer, W.E., Sze, C.I., et al. (1999). Cervical spine abnormalities in Down Syndrome. *Clinical Neuropathology, 18,* 250–259.

Guralnick, M.J. (Ed.). (1997). *The effectiveness of early intervention.* Baltimore: Paul H. Brookes Publishing Co.

Haslam, R.H.A., & Milner, R. (1992). The physician and Down syndrome: Are attitudes changing? *Journal of Child Neurology, 71,* 304–310.

Hassold, T.J., & Patterson, D. (Ed.). (1998). *Down syndrome: A promising future, together.* New York: Wiley-Liss.

Hennequin, M., Faulks, D., Veyrune, J.-L., et al. (1999). Significance of oral health in persons with Down syndrome: A literature review. *Developmental Medicine and Child Neurology, 41,* 275–283.

Hijii, T., Fukushige, J., Igarashi, H., et al. (1997). Life expectancy and social adaptation in individuals with Down syndrome with and without surgery for congenital heart disease. *Clinical Pediatrics, 36,* 327–332.

Horwitz, B., Schapiro, M.B., Grady, C.L., et al. (1990). Cerebral metabolic pattern in young adult Down's syndrome subjects: Altered intercorrelations between regional rates of glucose utilization. *Journal of Mental Deficiency Research, 34,* 237–252.

Janicki, M.P., & Dalton, A.J. (1999). *Dementia, aging, and intellectual disabilities: A handbook.* Philadelphia: Brunner/Routledge.

Johannsen, P., Christensen, J.E., Goldstein, H., et al. (1996). Epilepsy in Down syndrome: Prevalence in three age groups. *Seizure, 5,* 121–125.

Johnson, R.C., & Abelson, R.B. (1969). Intellectual, behavioral, and physical characteristics associated with trisomy, translocation, and mosaic types of Down's syndrome. *American Journal of Mental Deficiency, 73,* 852–855.

Joint Committee on Infant Hearing. (2000). Year 2000 position statement: Principles and guidelines for early hearing detection and intervention programs. *Pediatrics, 106,* 798–817.

Jones, K.L. (1996). *Smith's recognizable patterns of human malformation* (5th ed.). Philadelphia: W.B. Saunders.

Karlsson, B., Gustafsson, J., Hedov, G., et al. (1998). Thyroid dysfunction in Down's syndrome: Relation to age and autoimmunity. *Archives of Diseases in Childhood, 79,* 242–245.

Kent, L., Evans, J., Paul, M. et al. (1999). Comorbidity of autistic spectrum disorders in children with Down syndrome. *Developmental Medicine and Child Neurology, 41,* 153–158.

Kerbeshian, J., & Burd, L. (2000). Comorbid Down's syndrome, Tourette syndrome and intellectual disability: Registry prevalence and developmental course. *Journal of Intellectual Disability Research, 44,* 60–67.

Kingsley, J., & Levitz, M. (1994). *Count us in: Growing up with Down syndrome.* Orlando, FL: Harcourt Brace & Co.

Korenberg, J.R., Chen, X.N., Schipper, C.R., et al. (1994). Down syndrome phenotypes: The consequences of chromosomal imbalance. *Proceedings of the National Academy of Sciences of the United States of America, 91,* 4997–5001.

Kumin, L. (1996). Speech and language skills in children with Down syndrome. *Mental Retardation and Developmental Disabilities Research Reviews, 2,* 109–115.

Lefaivre, J.F., Cohen, S.R., Burstein, F.D., et al. (1997). Down syndrome: Identification and surgical management of obstructive sleep apnea. *Plastic Reconstructive Surgery, 99,* 629–37.

Leonard, S., Bower, C., Petterson, B., et al. (2000). Survival of infants born with Down's syndrome. *Paediatric Perinatal Epidemiology, 14,* 163–171.

Lejeune, J., Gautier, M., & Turpin, R. (1959). Etude des chromosomes somatiques de neuf enfants mongoliens. *Comptes Rendus de l'Académie de Sciences, 248,* 1721–1722.

Levanon, A., Tarasiuk, A., & Tal, A. (1999). Sleep characteristics in children with Down syndrome. *Journal of Pediatrics, 134,* 755–760.

Lobaugh, N.J., Karaskov, V., Rombough, V., et al. (2001). Piracetam therapy does not enhance cognitive functioning in children with Down syndrome. *Archives of Pediatric and Adolescent Medicine, 155,* 442–448.

Luke, A.H., Roizen, N.J., Sutton, M., et al. (1994). Energy expenditure in Down syndrome. *Journal of Pediatrics, 125,* 829–836.

Malec, E., Mroczek, T., Pajak, J., et al. (1999). Results of surgical treatment of congenital heart defects in children with Down's syndrome. *Pediatric Cardiology, 20,* 351–354.

Marino, B., & Pueschel, S.M. (Eds.). (1996). *Heart disease in persons with Down syndrome.* Baltimore: Paul H. Brookes Publishing Co.

Melyn, M.A., & White, D.T. (1973). Mental and developmental milestones of noninstitutionalized Down's syndrome children. *Pediatrics, 52,* 542–545.

Miller, J.F., Leddy, M., & Leavitt, L.A. (Eds.). (1999). *Improving the communication of people with Down syndrome.* Baltimore: Paul H. Brookes Publishing Co.

Myers, B.A., & Pueschel, S.M. (1991). Psychiatric disorders in persons with Down syndrome. *Journal of Nervous and Mental Diseases, 179,* 609–613.

Nadel, L., & Rosenthal, D. (1995). *Down syndrome: Living and learning in the community.* New York: John Wiley & Sons.

Nomura, K. (1999). Ichthyosis and psoriasis in a patient with Down syndrome. *Journal of Dermatology, 26,* 538–540.

Ohyama, Y., Utsugi, T., Uchiyama, T., et al. (2000). Prevalence of diabetes in adult patients with Down's syndrome living in a residential home. *Diabetes Care, 23,* 705–706.

Olsen, C.L., Cross, P.K., Gensburg, L.J., et al. (1996). The effects of prenatal diagnosis, population aging, and changing fertility rates on the live birth prevalence of Down syndrome in New York State, 1983–1992. *Prenatal Diagnosis, 16,* 991–1002.

Pearlson, G.D., Breiter, S.N., Aylward, E.H., et al. (1998).

MRI brain changes in subjects with Down syndrome with and without dementia. *Developmental Medicine and Child Neurology, 40,* 326–334.

Prasher, V.P. (1999). Down syndrome and thyroid disorders: A review. *Down's Syndrome: Research and Practice, 6,* 25–42.

Pueschel, S.M. (1996). Young people with Down syndrome: Transition from childhood to adulthood. *Mental Retardation and Developmental Disabilities Research Reviews, 2,* 90–95.

Pueschel, S.M., & Pueschel, J.K. (Eds.). (1992). *Biomedical concerns in persons with Down syndrome.* Baltimore: Paul H. Brookes Publishing Co.

Pueschel, S.M., Romano, D., Failla, P., et al. (1999). A prevalence study of celiac disease in persons with Down syndrome residing in the United States of America. *Acta Paediatrica, 88,* 953–956.

Pueschel, S.M., Scola, F.H., & Pezzullo, J.C. (1992). A longitudinal study of atlanto-dens relationships in asymptomatic individuals with Down syndrome. *Pediatrics, 89,* 1194–1198.

Reller, M.D., & Morris, C.D. (1998). Is Down syndrome a risk factor for poor outcome after repair of congenital heart defects? *Journal of Pediatrics, 132,* 738–741.

Rex, A.P., & Preus, M. (1982). A diagnostic index for Down syndrome. *Journal of Pediatrics, 100,* 903–906.

Roizen, N.J. (1996). Down syndrome and associated medical disorders. *Mental Retardation and Developmental Disabilities Research Reviews, 2,* 85–89.

Roizen, N.J., Mets, M.B., & Blondis, T.A. (1994). Ophthalmic disorders in children with Down syndrome. *Developmental Medicine and Child Neurology, 36,* 594–600.

Roizen, N.J., Wolters, C., Nicol, T., et al. (1993). Hearing loss in children with Down syndrome. *Journal of Pediatrics, 123,* S9–S12.

Rose, N.C. (1996). Pregnancy screening and prenatal diagnosis of fetal down syndrome. *Mental Retardation and Developmental Disabilities Research Reviews, 2,* 80–84.

Rubello, D., Pozzan, G.B., Casara, D., et al. (1995). Natural course of subclinical hypothyroidism in Down's syndrome: Prospective study results and therapeutic considerations. *Journal of Endocrinologic Investigation, 17,* 35–40.

Rubin, S.S., Rimmer, J.H., Chicoine, B., et al. (1998). Overweight prevalence in persons with Down syndrome. *Mental Retardation, 36,* 175–181.

Saenz, R.B. (1999). Primary care of infants and young children with Down syndrome. *American Family Physician, 59,* 381–390, 392, 395–396.

Schepis, C., Barone, C., Siragusa, M., et al. (1997). Prevalence of atopic dermatitis in patients with Down syndrome: A clinical survey. *Journal of the American Academy of Dermatology, 365,* 1019–1021.

Scherbehske, J.M., Benson, P.M., Rotchford, J.P., et al. (1990). Cutaneous and ocular manifestations of Down syndrome. *Journal of the American Academy of Dermatology, 22,* 933–938.

Sinet, P.M., Theophile, D., Rahmani, Z., et al. (1994). Mapping of the Down syndrome phenotype on chromosome 21 at the molecular level. *Biomedicine and Pharmacotherapy, 48,* 247–252.

Smith, G.F., Spiker, D., Peterson, C.P., et al. (1984). Use of megadoses of vitamins with minerals in Down syndrome. *Journal of Pediatrics, 105,* 228–234.

Stafstrom, C.E., & Konkol, R.J. (1994). Infantile spasms in children with Down syndrome. *Developmental Medicine and Child Neurology, 36,* 576–585.

Stafstrom, C.E., Patxot, O.F., Gilmore, H.E., et al. (1991). Seizures in children with Down syndrome: Etiology, characteristics and outcome. *Developmental Medicine and Child Neurology, 33,* 191–200.

Staples, A.J., Sutherland, G.R., Haan, E.A., et al. (1991). Epidemiology of Down syndrome in South Australia, 1960–89. *American Journal of Human Genetics, 49,* 1014–1024.

Stebbens, V.A., Dennis, J., Samuels, M.P., et al. (1991). Sleep related upper airway obstruction in a cohort with Down's syndrome. *Archives of Disease in Childhood, 66,* 1333–1338.

Strauss, D., & Eyman, R. (1996). Mortality of people with mental retardation in California with and without Down syndrome, 1986–1992. *American Journal on Mental Retardation, 100,* 643–653.

Suzuki, K., Yamaki, S., Mimori, S., et al. (2000). Pulmonary vascular disease in Down's syndrome with complete atrioventricular septal defect. *American Journal of Cardiology, 86,* 434–437.

Toledo, C., Alembik, Y., Aguirre Jaime, A., et al. (1999). Growth curves of children with Down syndrome. *Annals of Genetics, 42,* 81–90.

Trimble, B.K., & Baird, P.A. (1978). Maternal age and Down syndrome: Age-specific incidence rates by single-year intervals. *American Journal of Medical Genetics, 2,* 1–5.

Turnbull, A.P., & Turnbull, H.R. (1985). Developing independence. *Journal of Adolescent Health Care, 6,* 108–119.

Ulrich, D.A., Ulrich, B.D., Angulo-Kinzler, R.M., et al. (2001). Treadmill training of infants with Down syndrome: Evidence-based developmental outcomes. *Pediatrics, 108,* e84.

Unruh, J.F. (1994). *Down syndrome: Successful parenting of children with Down syndrome.* Eugene, OR: Fern Ridge Press.

van Allen, M.I., Fung J., & Jurenka, S.B. (1999). Health care concerns and guidelines for adults with Down syndrome. *American Journal of Medical Genetics, 89,* 100–110.

Van Dyke, D.C., Lang, D.J., van Duyne, S., et al. (1990). Cell therapy in children with Down syndrome: A retrospective study. *Pediatrics, 85,* 79–84.

Velthuis, P.J., & Nijenhuis M. (1995). Treatment of onychomycosis with terbinafine in patients with Down syndrome. *British Journal of Dermatology, 133,* 144–146.

Wald, N.J., Watt, H.C., & Hackshaw, A.K. (1999). Integrated screening for Down's syndrome based on tests performed during the first and second trimesters. *New England Journal of Medicine, 341,* 461–467.

Wang, P. (1996). A neuropsychological profile of Down syndrome: Cognitive skills and brain morphology. *Mental Retardation and Developmental Disabilities Research Reviews, 2,* 102–108.

Wells, G.L., Barker, S.E., Finley, S.C., et al. (1994). Congenital heart disease in infants with Down's syndrome. *Southern Medical Journal, 87,* 724–727.

Winders, P.C. (Ed.). (1997). *Gross motor skills in children with Down syndrome: A guide for parents and professional.* Bethesda, MD: Woodbine House.

Wortelboer, M.J.M., De Wolf, B.T., Verschuuren-Bemelmans, C.C., et al. (2000). Trends in live birth prevalence of Down syndrome in the Northern Netherlands 1987–96: The impact of screening and prenatal diagnosis. *Prenatal Diagnosis, 20,* 709–713.

Yang, Q., Rasmussen, S.A., & Friedman, J.M. (2002). Mortality associated with Down's syndrome in the USA from 1983 to 1997: A population-based study. *Lancet, 359,* 1019–1025.

Zachor, D.A, Mroczek-Musulman, E., & Brown, P. (2000). Prevalence of celiac disease in Down syndrome in the United States. *Journal of Pediatric Gastroenterology and Nutrition, 31,* 275–279.

Zigman, W., Silverman, W., & Wisniewski, H.M. (1996). Aging and Alzheimer's disease in Down syndrome: Clinical and pathological changes. *Mental Retardation and Developmental Disabilities Research Reviews, 2,* 73–79.

17 Fragile X Syndrome

Gretchen A. Meyer and Mark L. Batshaw

Upon completion of this chapter, the reader will:

- understand this most frequent inherited cause of mental retardation
- recognize its different clinical presentations in boys and girls
- be aware of the behavior and cognitive impairments associated with the syndrome
- know the underlying molecular genetic abnormalities and the diagnostic tests available
- be familiar with intervention strategies for individuals with this disorder
- understand issues concerning outcome

Fragile X syndrome is the most frequently diagnosed inherited cause of mental retardation. Understanding of this unique genetic condition has increased exponentially in recent years. The first reported cases of fragile X syndrome were described by Martin and Bell (1943). They described 11 males and 2 females in two generations of a family who had a number of similar clinical symptoms. The affected men had severe mental retardation, language impairments, and behavior problems, whereas the women had mild mental retardation and a "highly nervous temperament." Over subsequent decades, researchers have learned that this disorder is a form of X-linked mental retardation (mental retardation that is inherited and occurs more frequently and more severely in boys; Lehrke, 1972; Sutherland, 1977). Furthermore, scientists now know that individuals with fragile X syndrome have an abnormality of the X chromosome that causes the bottom tip of the long arm to become constricted and threadlike. This is known as a "fragile" site. In 1991, the underlying gene defect, an abnormality in the fragile X mental retardation gene (named FMR1), was discovered by Verkerk et al. In 1993, Verheij et al. investigated the consequences of an FMR1 gene defect on bodily function, particularly on brain development. They found that the gene product of FMR1 is a protein that has been called the *FMR1 protein*, or FMRP. Thus, it is now assumed that the genetic defect causes a decrease in FMRP, which is highly important for neurologic development and function (Feng et al., 1995; Verheij et al., 1993). The identification of FRMP and the study of its location and function in the brain have provided a mechanism by which neuroscientists can gain an understanding of the neuronal processes involved in learning and memory (Brown et al., 2001; Darnell et al., 2001).

TONY, JEAN, AND SYLVIA

Tony was 4 years old when his parents first learned that he had fragile X syndrome. He had been referred to a specialist because of speech and language delay, marked hyperactivity, and self-stimulatory behavior. Extensive testing revealed that he also had mild mental retardation. A family history revealed that Tony's maternal uncle, 16-year-old Vincent, attends a school for teenagers with special needs and is reading at the first-grade level. Tony's mother, Sylvia, reports having been excessively shy as a young girl, and although only 36 years old, she is already having symptoms of menopause. Tony has a 9-year-old sister, Jean, who is receiving resource assistance at school for a non–language-based learning disability and has particular difficulty with learning math facts. In addition, Jean has social anxiety and has trouble making and keeping friends.

A DNA test for fragile X syndrome was done on all four members of this family; Sylvia was found to have 120 CGG repeats (repetitive triplets of specific nucleotide bases); Vincent had 1,500; Jean, 430; and Tony, 1,000. Tony was enrolled in a small, structured preschool program that focuses on language development and uses behavior management techniques. Tony recently began taking dextroamphetamine (Dexedrine), which has significantly decreased his hyperactivity. Jean is also coping better; in addition to receiving services at school, she is seeing a counselor who is helping her overcome her shyness and social anxiety.

PREVALENCE

Fragile X syndrome represents one third of all X-linked causes of mental retardation and 40% of X-linked causes of learning disability (Feldman, 1996). Studies suggest that 1 in 4,000 males and 1 in 6,000 females have a full mutation for fragile X syndrome (de Vries et al., 1997; Turner et al., 1996). However, when one considers the prevalence in individuals who do not have mental retardation but who have learning disabilities and/or emotional problems, the number may actually be much higher, particularly in girls. Of unaffected females in the general population, 0.33–0.5 per 100 carry a premutation for fragile X syndrome (Reiss et al., 1994). Mazzocco et al. (1998) indicated that nearly 0.6% of preschool children evaluated for speech delay may have a fragile X full mutation. Individuals with fragile X syndrome account for up to 1.1% of children receiving special education services (Crawford et al., 1999; Meadows et al., 1996) and 4.9% of children receiving special education supports for mental retardation of various degrees (Mila et al., 1997). Fragile X syndrome may also account for a sizable percentage of avoidant, anxious, or schizoid personality disorders in females (Franke et al., 1996).

THE GENETICS OF FRAGILE X SYNDROME

Although fragile X syndrome is an X-linked disorder (see Chapter 1), the transmission of fragile X syndrome from parent to offspring is more complex than the transmission of other X-linked disorders (Nolin et al., 1996). The typical genetic mutation in fragile X syndrome is an expanded section of DNA on the X chromosome. The sequence of DNA that is repeated in excess consists of a series of three nucleotide bases, cytosine-guanine-guanine (CGG), also known as a *triplet repeat*. Although all individuals have CGG repetition to some degree, when there is a marked increase in the number of CGG repeats, a "fragile site" may be visible on the chromosome at the FMR1 site (Xq27.3; Eberhart & Warren, 1996). There are at least four known fragile sites on the X chromosome. Only two of these, however, have been associated with developmental disabilities: the fragile X syndrome gene site (Xq27.3) and a nearby fragile XE site, a much less common cause of mental retardation (Crawford et al., 1999; Mulley et al., 1995).

The fragile X mental retardation gene (FMR1) typically has 6–50 repeats of the CGG triplet. Individuals who are capable of transmitting the mutation to their offspring but are clinically unaffected are called *carriers* and have between 50 and 200 CGG repeats. These carriers are said to have a *premutation*. Clinically affected individuals (both males and females) generally have 200–3,000 CGG repeats and are said to have a *full mutation*. All mothers of children with fragile X syndrome have been shown to be carriers. Thus, new mutations must occur exceedingly rarely (to escape detection), or they occur only in males.

A feature of the FMR1 is a unique inheritance pattern known as *genomic imprinting*. Genomic imprinting implies that the expression or nonexpression of a gene mutation is influenced by which parent passes it on. For example, if the FMR1 mutation is passed from an unaffected male with a premutation to his daughter, the daughter will also have a premutation and be an unaffected carrier. These fathers are known as *transmitting males* and generally have between 50 and 150 repeats. Surprisingly, however, the daughters of fully affected males (with a full mutation) have a premutation only and are clinically unaffected. Thus, the number of CGG repeats gets smaller (undergoes contraction) rather than larger (undergoes expansion). In contrast, when females with a premutation or a full mutation pass the defect on to their offspring, the CGG region nearly always undergoes expansion, frequently from a premutation to a full mutation (Nolin et al., 1996). Thus, the expression of fragile X syndrome depends on which parent passes on the trait.

In a female carrier of the fragile X mutation, the larger the number of triplet repeats, the more unstable the fragile X site (Eichler et al., 1994). Because contraction does not occur when a mother carries the trait, a female with a full mutation will always pass on a full mutation to her children. The chance that a female with a premutation will bear a child with a full mutation depends primarily on the number of maternal CGG repeats (Table 17.1; Fisch et al., 1995). In this way, the mutation in a particular family expands further (through maternal transmission), resulting in increasing severity of clinical manifestations with each generation. This genetic phenomenon is known as *anticipation*.

Counseling should be offered to individuals with fragile X syndrome and their families by a knowledgeable genetics expert because of the extremely complex nature of this inherited disorder. In addition to this counseling from the genetics specialist, the child's primary physician should take time to discuss the basics of this disorder with the parents in a supportive way. Many parents will experience guilt, particularly the parent through whom the genetic abnormality was transmitted. All professionals who interact with the family must be cognizant of this reaction and offer reassurance that no one is to blame for errors that exist within one's chromosomes.

CLINICAL FINDINGS IN AFFECTED MALES

Once fragile X syndrome was identified as a discrete entity, it soon became clear that affected men have certain characteristic physical features (Bailey & Nelson, 1995; Hagerman & Cronister, 1996). These include a long, narrow face; prominent jaw and forehead; large, protruding ears; high, arched palate; hyperextensible joints; flat feet; and mitral valve prolapse. Almost all of these men have markedly enlarged testicles **(macroorchidism)**, frequently not apparent until puberty. Some of these physical characteristics are subtle during childhood and become more pronounced with age, making early identification difficult based on physical features alone. At school age, an affected boy generally has a somewhat enlarged head; protruding ears; and a high, arched palate (Table 17.2). Boys with fragile X syndrome tend to be hypotonic (have low muscle tone) and often lack coordination. Although they grow rapidly during childhood, they have short stature as adults.

In addition to having unusual physical features, males with fragile X syndrome manifest impairments in cognitive abilities and communication skills. Developmental delays are evident in infancy; these boys typically begin to walk at 19 months and speak at 26–30 months (Dykens, 1995; Freund et al., 1995). More than 80% of young boys with fragile X syndrome have IQ scores in the range of mild to moderate mental retardation. Boys without mental retardation usually have a mosaic pattern (see Chapter 1); at least some cells in the body do not contain the mutation. Typically, boys with a premutation do not have mental retardation, although those who have repeat numbers in

Table 17.1. Risk of expansion to full mutation in children born to women with the fragile X premutation

Number of CGG copies in mother	Risk of expansion to full mutation in offspring
50–59[a]	20%
60–69[a]	17%
70–79	39%
80–89	76%
90–99	89%
>99	≥99%

Source: Fisch et al., 1995.
[a]No significant difference in risk between 50–59 and 60–69 repeats.

the upper premutation range often have some degree of cognitive impairment or learning disability (Hagerman et al., 1996; Steyaert et al., 1996). Some studies have described a decline in IQ over time; this appears to be a slowing in rate of development rather than a loss of skills (Hagerman, 1995; Maes et al., 1994; Wright-Talamante et al., 1996). The exact trajectory of developmental rate and the cause of the apparent cognitive decline are still unknown (Bailey, 1998).

Learning is easier for boys and men with fragile X syndrome when all parts of a task are presented at once, for these individuals have a cognitive skill known as simultaneous processing (Maes et al., 1994). In contrast, sequential processing (multiple-step tasks involving memorizing parts rather than the whole) is challenging for them. Daily living skills are also relatively strong in contrast to their communication and socialization skills (Dykens, 1995; Dykens, Hodapp, & Evans, 1994; Fisch et al., 1996).

Table 17.2. Physical findings in males with fragile X syndrome

Physical feature	% of males affected
Prepubertal boy	
Large, protruding ears	75
Hyperextensible joints	73
Single palmar creases	51
Flat feet	50
High, arched palate	50
Strabismus	44
Epicanthal folds	40
Macrocephaly	31
Macroorchidism	3
Adult male	
Long ears	80
Macroorchidism	80
Mitral valve prolapse	55
Hyperextensible joints	30

Source: Hagerman & Cronister, 1996.

Finally, individuals with fragile X syndrome often have a delightful sense of humor, which may help them tremendously with social interactions (Hagerman & Cronister, 1996).

Speech and language delays are usually present from the preschool period (Reiss et al., 1995). When speech does develop, it tends to be **echolalic** (parrot-like), cluttered (rushed and poorly articulated), and perseverative. Word-finding difficulties and irrelevant associations are also problematic, especially when the child is anxious. Moreover, boys with fragile X syndrome generally have difficulties with auditory memory and receptive language (Ferrier et al., 1991; Sudhalter et al., 1990).

In addition, a behavioral phenotype, seemingly unique to fragile X syndrome, is evident. In fully affected males, this behavioral pattern includes **stereotypies** such as hand flapping (present in 85% of individuals), lack of eye contact (90%), tactile defensiveness (76%), hyperactivity (73%), inattention (95%), aggression (25%), and anxiety (64%; Baumgardner, Reiss, & Freund, 1995; Hagerman & Cronister, 1996; Hatton et al., 1999; Lachiewicz et al., 1994). Some of these behaviors are similar to those seen in children with pervasive developmental disorders (see Chapter 20). Although less than 7% of children with autism have been found to have the fragile X syndrome mutation, a significant percentage of individuals with fragile X syndrome (15%–28%) meet American Psychiatric Association (1987, 1994, 2000) diagnostic criteria for autism (Bailey et al., 1998a; Bailey, 2000; Feinstein & Reiss, 1998; Hessl et al., 2001; Turk & Cornish, 1998). In the past, researchers have disagreed as to whether a true relationship exists between autism and fragile X syndrome (Einfeld, Tonge, & Turner, 1999; Franke et al., 1996; Klauck et al., 1997; Meyer et al., 1997). Nevertheless, it is important to note that some children with fragile X syndrome may have autistic-like behaviors, whereas others may have frank autism. For this reason, it is recommended that all patients diagnosed with a pervasive developmental disorder be tested for fragile X syndrome.

CLINICAL FINDINGS IN AFFECTED FEMALES

Among females with a mutation of FMR1, 70% have the premutation (fewer than 200 CGG repeats) and, like Sylvia, do not manifest significant physical, cognitive, or behavioral abnormalities (Reiss et al., 1993). The other 30% have a full mutation (more than 200 CGG repeats) and, like Jean, show a varied spectrum of symptoms (Abrams et al., 1994; Sobesky et al., 1996;

Taylor et al., 1994). In general, women with the full mutation may look typical or may have only a slightly altered physical appearance, with a narrow face and large ears (Riddle et al., 1998).

The cognitive profile of women with the full mutation is also much more variable and less severe than that seen in males with fragile X syndrome. About half of the women have typical intellectual functioning but may exhibit non–language-based learning disabilities. The other half have mental retardation, usually mild (Hagerman & Cronister, 1996). The variance in cognitive impairment is a result of females' usually having a second, nonmutated X chromosome, which produces FMRP. All women with a full mutation demonstrate characteristic weaknesses in visuospatial-perceptual skills, executive function, mathematics, and sequential processing (Bennetto et al., 2001; Cornish, Munir, & Cross, 1998). Like males with fragile X syndrome, affected females have strengths in simultaneous processing, verbal memory, and reading (Lachiewicz, 1995). They also often have an unusual speech pattern, which may be perseverative and cluttered (Reiss et al., 1995).

The behavioral phenotype seen in females with the FMR1 gene mutation is quite similar to that seen in affected males, although it may be less severe (Hagerman & Cronister, 1996). Girls with fragile X syndrome tend to be shy and withdrawn, with poor eye contact and stereotypic mannerisms (e.g., hand flapping). Other features include hyperactivity, inattention, tactile defensiveness, and perseverative tendencies. Psychiatric disorders have been diagnosed in 20%–60% of adult females with the full mutation, the most common diagnoses being depression, schizoid personality disorder, avoidant personality disorder, and anxiety disorder (Franke et al., 1996; Sobesky et al., 1994). Frequently, females with a premutation, despite being clinically unaffected in other areas, manifest significant levels of shyness and anxiety (Freund, Reiss, & Abrams, 1993). This is of import because when evaluating a young child with developmental delay, a history of excessive shyness in the mother may be enough to warrant testing for fragile X syndrome. Women with a premutation also have an increased risk of experiencing premature ovarian failure (menopause prior to the age of 40; Allingham-Hawkins et al., 1999; Murray, 2000).

ORIGINS OF ABNORMALITIES

FMR1, the site of the gene mutation in fragile X syndrome, encodes a protein that has been dubbed the fragile X mental retardation protein (FMRP) and that appears to be an important protein regulating brain development (Abrams & Reiss, 1995; Small & Warren, 1995; Tassone et al., 2000). When FMR1 contains the mutation seen in fragile X syndrome, the result is decreased or absent production of FMRP (Eberhart & Warren, 1996; Hoogeveen & Oostra, 1997). Studies have revealed that the highest concentrations of FMRP in the brain are found in the caudate nucleus (which governs affect, impulse control, and executive function), the thalamus (which is involved in sensory integration), the cerebellum (which is involved in motor planning), the hippocampus (which directs memory and attention), and the superior temporal gyrus (which directs language) (see Chapter 13; Devys, Lutz, & Rouyer, 1993). Abnormalities in these regions are associated with the specific behavioral phenotype and cognitive impairments of fragile X syndrome. This has been confirmed through neuroimaging and neuropathology studies of people with fragile X syndrome (Jakala et al., 1997; Schapiro et al., 1995).

Many of the physical characteristics of fragile X syndrome, such as hyperextensible joints and mitral valve prolapse, are likely to be related to connective tissue abnormalities. The long face, prominent jaw, and macroorchidism are likely be related to hypothalamic dysfunction. Reproductive problems (premature ovarian failure and increased **twinning** rate) found in carrier females with a premutation are particularly surprising given that these women should theoretically have normal FMRP levels. However, a study found that individuals with a premutation for FMR1 have a fivefold increase in FMR1 messenger RNA levels compared with controls, whereas individuals with a full mutation for FMR1 have significantly decreased levels of

FMR1 messenger RNA (Tassone et al., 2000). One hypothesis is that increased levels of FMR1 messenger RNA may reduce the total number of oocytes produced in developing female fetus.

A number of the cognitive and behavioral findings in humans have been reproduced in a "knockout" mouse model of fragile X syndrome. Knockout mice are created by deleting the FMR1 gene in mouse embryos (Willems, Reyniers, & Oostra, 1995). These mice have enlarged testes and visuospatial abnormalities similar to males with fragile X syndrome. This is further evidence that the absence of FMR1 is likely to be the underlying cause of the neurodevelopmental abnormalities in fragile X syndrome. What is most promising is that this animal model can be used to investigate the stage(s) of development during which FMRP is essential for normal brain development.

DIAGNOSING FRAGILE X SYNDROME

Until 1991, when the fragile X gene defect was identified, the diagnosis could only be confirmed when the well-known fragile site was detected on the long arm of the X chromosome (Xq27.3). A special culture medium deficient in folic acid was necessary in order to induce this fragility. This technique was quite effective at identifying affected males, but it was expensive and could be done only in specialized laboratories. Furthermore, carrier women and transmitting males were not identified in this way because they do not express the fragile site on the X chromosome. Despite these limitations, chromosome analysis can still be useful in identifying other chromosomal anomalies and thus may be a useful adjunct to DNA testing in some individuals.

Since the identification of the triplet CGG repeat expansion in the FMR1 gene, blood tests utilizing DNA have been developed. They are much more sensitive and specific and are less costly than chromosome analysis by karyotype. Southern blot analysis (Figure 17.1) has the advantage of being able to detect mosaic patterns as well as carrier females (Rousseau, Heitz, & Biancalana, 1991). Its disadvantage is that it cannot detect the precise number of CGG copies present. The polymerase chain reaction (PCR) can be completed much more rapidly than Southern blot analysis (24–48 hours versus 1–2 weeks) and can identify precisely the

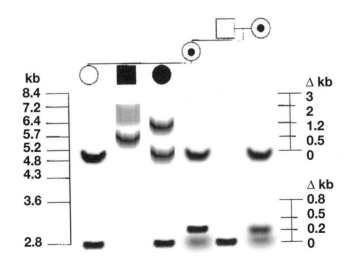

Figure 17.1. Southern blot fragile X analysis. Normal DNA fragment sizes are 2.8 kilobase pairs (kb) for males and 2.8 kb and 4.8 kb (methylated) in females. *(Key:* ○ unaffected female, (two normal-sized fragments); ■ male with a full mutation (no normal fragment and an elongated, methylated fragment); ● female with a full mutation (normal 2.8 kb fragment and an elongated, methylated fragment); ⊙ carrier female (slightly elongated, unmethylated fragment); □ unaffected male; ⊙ carrier female.)

number of CGG copies present (Brown et al., 1993). The use of one or both of these DNA tests allows detection of 99% of patients with a premutation or full mutation of FMR1. Only the extremely rare patient with a point mutation at Xq27.3 rather than the typical trinucleotide repeat expansion will be missed with these methods (Quan et al., 1995).

In 1995, a blood antibody test that seeks the presence of FMRP and can be used to detect individuals with the full mutation was developed (Willemsen et al., 1995). More recently, another test showing the presence or absence of FMRP using hair root analysis has been described (Willemsen et al., 1999). Efficacy of these two tests, however, is not yet known. Prenatal testing is widely available and can be performed by amniocentesis or chorionic villus sampling followed by DNA analysis (Castellvi-Bel et al., 1995).

INTERVENTION STRATEGIES

Children with fragile X syndrome should receive all routine pediatric care, including immunizations (American Academy of Pediatrics, Committee on Genetics, 1996). In addition, serial physical examinations should be done to identify the presence of medical complications related to fragile X syndrome. These include ophthalmic disorders, orthopedic abnormalities, serous otitis media, mitral valve prolapse, seizure disorders, and macroorchidism.

Ophthalmic disorders in fragile X syndrome include strabismus, myopia, ptosis, and nystagmus. The most common of these is strabismus; if present, refraction or patching may help prevent the development of amblyopia. Orthopedic abnormalities relate to the underlying connective tissue abnormality and include flat feet, scoliosis, and loose joints; orthotics may occasionally be useful, but surgery is rarely needed. Recurrent middle-ear infections are common in fragile X syndrome and may require antibiotic prophylaxis or, if persistent, surgical aspiration and placement of pressure-equalization tubes. In cases of recurrent ear infections or serous otitis media, it is critical that the child's hearing status be monitored closely. Serous fluid in the middle ear can cause a fluctuating hearing loss that may further impair the child's language skills and attention span. If there is a heart murmur, an echocardiogram should be obtained. If mitral valve prolapse is detected, antibiotic prophylaxis should be considered prior to surgical or dental procedures. Seizures occur in 20% of affected individuals and are most commonly complex partial or generalized tonic-clonic types. Although the development of seizures can be frightening, the seizures generally respond well to antiepileptic drugs (see Chapter 25; Wisniewski et al., 1991). If properly treated, the seizures need not dramatically alter the life of the child or family. Macroorchidism may become evident before adolescence in some boys with fragile X syndrome; parents should be reassured that this does not require treatment or lead to any symptoms, including precocious puberty.

Educational and therapeutic intervention strategies for boys with the full mutation and resultant fragile X syndrome are directed at the various cognitive, communicative, and behavior impairments they exhibit. Most often, their needs are best met through an individualized education program (IEP; see Chapter 30). Because children with fragile X syndrome have difficulties with organization skills, auditory memory, and inattention, a structured learning environment is helpful. Verbal instructions should be concrete and clear, with visual cues given whenever possible. Given these children's strength in visual memory, a multisensory approach when learning new skills is more effective than a purely auditory approach. Computer learning also may be helpful in promoting visual learning and attention. A sight word approach to reading rather than an emphasis on phonics is recommended. Children with fragile X syndrome learn arithmetic best when manipulatives and visual associations are utilized. For the development of daily living skills, a behavior-based (shaping) technique seems to work well (see Chapter 31). Speech-language therapy is essential to helping children with fragile X syndrome improve listening skills, auditory memory, ability to follow directions, and the social rules of language (pragmatics). In addition, many of these children benefit from formal social skills training. Occupational therapy may be indicated to assist a child whose joint laxity is interfering with self-help or handwriting skills. In severe cases, assistive technology should be included.

The educational needs of girls with fragile X syndrome depend on the degree and type of cognitive impairments. Those with mental retardation will benefit from a similar approach to the one just described for boys. Girls with typical development but who have learning disabilities require appropriate special education services to address individual weaknesses in math and sequential processing. Frequently, the most disabling features of fragile X syndrome in women are the anxiety and shyness. These can be severe enough to greatly impair functioning in the classroom and in social activities outside the home. When these symptoms are present, counseling to address shyness, social anxiety, and poor social skills is a critical component of an effective multidisciplinary treatment program.

No medication is yet available to treat the primary genetic defect or lack of FMRP in tissues. Folic acid has been proposed as a treatment for fragile X syndrome based on the finding that in the laboratory, it prevents the fragility of the X chromosome. Although its use remains controversial, researchers have found that a subset of children with fragile X syndrome demonstrate improvements in attention, concentration, and speech when taking folic acid (Hagerman & Cronister, 1996). Medications prescribed to address specific behavioral and psychiatric characteristics have proven very effective and should be considered on an individual basis. Stimulants have been effective in treating hyperactivity and inattention. Other classes of medications, such as serotonin reuptake inhibitors, are being used successfully for obsessive-compulsive behaviors, anxiety, social inhibition, and depression (Hagerman et al., 1994).

Studies in the mouse model utilizing medications to reactivate the silent FMR1 gene are still in their infancy. Further identification of the nature and timing of FMRP production and function may lead to the development of gene therapy for fragile X syndrome.

OUTCOME

Outcome in fragile X syndrome is dependent primarily on the degree of impairment experienced by an individual. Males with a full mutation tend to have mental retardation requiring limited to extensive support indefinitely. Furthermore, they tend to be less independent than would be predicted based on their cognitive abilities because of their associated communicative, behavior, and social skills impairments. Females with a full mutation may succeed in society without support or may require supervision, depending on the degree of clinical involvement. The most prominent long-term problem facing females with the full mutation is the development of psychiatric disorders (Einfeld et al., 1999). Shyness and social anxiety superimposed on mild cognitive impairments can significantly interfere with independence. Fertility is normal in males and females with a full mutation and in males with a premutation. Females with a premutation often experience fertility problems and/or premature ovarian failure. Longevity in both males and females is likely to be normal.

SUMMARY

Fragile X syndrome is the most common inherited cause of mental retardation. It is an X-linked disorder in which most affected boys present with a characteristic pattern of physical, cognitive, and behavior impairments, whereas a fraction of carrier girls manifest less severe symptoms. Because of an expansion of a triplet base pair repeat, CGG, the X chromosome becomes fragile and the FMR1 gene is inactivated. This results in decreased or absent production of FMRP, a protein important in early brain development. Although there is currently no specific treatment for this disorder, special education, behavior management techniques, social skills training, and pharmacotherapy can improve outcome for affected individuals.

REFERENCES

Abrams, M.T., & Reiss, A.L. (1995). The neurobiology of fragile X syndrome. *Mental Retardation and Developmental Disabilities Research Reviews, 1,* 269–275.

Abrams, M.T., Reiss, A.L., Freund, L.S., et al. (1994). Molecular-neurobehavioral association in females with the fragile X full mutation. *American Journal of Medical Genetics, 51,* 317–327.

Allingham-Hawkins, D.J., Babul-Hirji, R., Chitayat, D., et al. (1999). Fragile X premutation is a significant risk factor for premature ovarian failure: The International Collaborative POF in Fragile X Study. Preliminary data. *American Journal of Medical Genetics, 83,* 322–325.

American Academy of Pediatrics, Committee on Genetics. (1996). Health supervision for children with fragile X syndrome. *Pediatrics, 98,* 297–300.

American Psychiatric Association. (1987). *Diagnostic and statistical manual of mental disorders* (3rd rev. ed.). Washington, DC: Author.

American Psychiatric Association. (1994). *Diagnostic and statistical manual of mental disorders* (4th ed.). Washington, DC: Author.

American Psychiatric Association. (2000). *Diagnostic and statistical manual of mental disorders* (4th ed., Text rev.). Washington, DC: Author.

Bailey D.B., Jr. (1998). Early developmental trajectories of males with fragile X syndrome. *American Journal on Mental Retardation, 103,* 29–39.

Bailey D.B., Jr. (2000). Early development, temperament, and functional impairment in autism and fragile X syndrome. *Journal of Autism and Developmental Disorders, 30,* 49–59.

Bailey, D.B., Jr., Mesibov, G.B., Hatton, D.D., et al. (1998). Autistic behavior in young boys with fragile X syndrome. *Journal of Autism and Developmental Disorders, 28,* 499–508.

Bailey, D.B., Jr., & Nelson, D. (1995). The nature and consequences of fragile X syndrome. *Mental Retardation and Developmental Disabilities Research Reviews, 1,* 238–244.

Baumgardner, T.L., Reiss, A.L., & Freund, L.S. (1995). Specification of the neurobehavioral phenotype in males with fragile X syndrome. *Pediatrics, 95,* 744–752.

Bennetto, L., Pennington B.F., Porter, D., et al. (2001). Profile of cognitive functioning in women with the fragile X mutation. *Neuropsychology, 15,* 290–299.

Brown, V., Jin, P., Ceman, S., et al. (2001). Microarray identification of FMRP-associated brain mRNAs and altered mRNA translational profiles in Fragile X syndrome. *Cell, 107,* 477–487.

Brown, W.T., Houck, G.E., Jr., Jeziorowska, A., et al. (1993). Rapid fragile X carrier screening and prenatal diagnosis using a nonradioactive PCR test. *Journal of the American Medical Association, 270,* 1569–1575.

Castellvi-Bel, S., Mila, M., Soler, A., et al. (1995). Prenatal diagnosis of fragile X syndrome: (CGG)n expansion and methylation of chorionic villus samples. *Prenatal Diagnosis, 15,* 801–807.

Cornish, K.M., Munir, F., & Cross, G. (1998). The nature of the spatial deficit in young females with Fragile-X syndrome: A neuropsychological and molecular perspective. *Neuropsychologia, 36,* 1239–1246.

Crawford, D.C., Meadows, M.L., Newman, J.L., et al. (1999). Prevalence and phenotype consequences of FRAXA and FRAXE alleles in a large, ethnically diverse, special education-needs population. *American Journal of Human Genetics, 64,* 495–507.

Darnell, J.C., Jensen, K.B., Jin, P., et al. (2001). Fragile X mental retardation protein targets G quartet mRNAs important for neuronal function. *Cell, 107,* 489–499.

de Vries, B.B.A., van den Ouweland, A.M.W., Mohkamsing, S., et al. (1997). Screening and diagnosis for the fragile X syndrome among the mentally retarded: An epidemiological and psychological survey. *American Journal of Human Genetics, 61,* 660–667.

Devys, D., Lutz, Y., & Rouyer, N. (1993). The FMR-1 protein is cytoplasmic, most abundant in neurons, and appears normal in carriers of a fragile X premutation. *Nature Genetics, 4,* 335–340.

Dykens, E.M. (1995). Adaptive behavior in males with fragile X syndrome. *Mental Retardation and Developmental Disabilities Research Reviews, 1,* 281–284.

Dykens, E.M., Hodapp, R.M., & Evans, D.W. (1994). Profiles and development of adaptive behavior in children with Down syndrome. *American Journal on Mental Retardation, 98,* 580–587.

Eberhart, D.E., & Warren, S.T. (1996). The molecular basis of fragile X syndrome. *Cold Spring Harbor Symposia on Quantitative Biology, 61,* 679–687.

Eichler, E.E., Holden, J.A., Popovich, B.W., et al. (1994). Length of uninterrupted CGG repeats determines instability in the FMR1 gene. *Nature Genetics, 8,* 88–94.

Einfeld, S., Tonge, B., & Turner, G. (1999). Longitudinal course of behavioral and emotional problems in fragile X syndrome. *American Journal of Medical Genetics, 87,* 436–439.

Feinstein, C., & Reiss, AL. (1998). Autism: The point of view from fragile X studies. *Journal of Autism and Developmental Disorders, 28,* 393–405.

Feldman, E.J. (1996). The recognition and investigation of X-linked learning disability syndromes. *Journal of Intellectual Disability Research, 40,* 400–411.

Feng, Y., Zhang, F., Lokey, L.K., et al. (1995). Translational suppression by trinucleotide repeat expansion at FMR1. *Science, 268,* 731–734.

Ferrier, L.J., Bashir, A.S., Meryash, D.L., et al. (1991). Conversational skills of individuals with fragile X syndrome: A comparison with autism and Down syndrome. *Developmental Medicine and Child Neurology, 33,* 776–788.

Fisch, G.S., Simensen, R., Tarleton, J., et al. (1996). Longitudinal study of cognitive abilities and adaptive behavior levels in fragile X males: A prospective multicenter analysis. *American Journal of Medical Genetics, 64,* 356–361.

Fisch, G.S., Snow, K., Thibodeau, S.N., et al. (1995). The fragile X premutation in carriers and its effect on mutation size in offspring. *American Journal of Human Genetics, 56,* 1147–1155.

Franke, P., Maier, W., Hautzinger, M., et al. (1996). Fragile X carrier females: Evidence for a distinct psychopathological phenotype? *American Journal of Medical Genetics, 64,* 334–339.

Freund, L.S., Peebles, C.D., Aylward, E., et al. (1995). Preliminary report on cognitive and adaptive behaviors of preschool aged males with fragile X. *Developmental Brain Dysfunction, 8,* 242–251.

Freund, L.S., Reiss, A.L., & Abrams, M.T. (1993). Psychiatric disorders associated with fragile X in the young female. *Pediatrics, 91,* 321–329.

Hagerman, R.J. (1995). Molecular and clinical correlations in fragile X syndrome. *Mental Retardation and Developmental Disabilities Research Reviews, 1,* 276–280.

Hagerman, R.J., & Cronister, A. (Eds.). (1996). *Fragile X syndrome: Diagnosis, treatment, and research* (2nd ed.). Baltimore: The Johns Hopkins University Press.

Hagerman, R.J., Fulton, M.J., Leaman, A., et al. (1994). Fluoxetine therapy in fragile X syndrome. *Developmental Brain Dysfunction, 7,* 155–164.

Hagerman, R.J., Stanley, L.W., O'Conner, R., et al. (1996). Learning-disabled males with a fragile X CGG expansion in the upper premutation size range. *Pediatrics, 97,* 122–126.

Hatton, D.D., Bailey, D.B., Jr., Hargett-Beck, M.Q., et al. (1999). Behavioral style of young boys with fragile X syndrome. *Developmental Medicine and Child Neurology, 41,* 625–632.

Hessl, D., Dyer-Friedman J., Glaser, B., et al. (2001). The influence of environmental and genetic factors on behavior problems and autistic symptoms in boys and girls with Fragile X syndrome. *Pediatrics, 108,* e88.

Hoogeveen, A.T., & Oostra, B.A. (1997). The fragile X syndrome. *Journal of Inherited Metabolic Disorders, 20,* 139–151.

Jakala, P., Hanninen, T., Ryynanen, M., et al. (1997). Fragile X: Neuropsychological test performance, CGG triplet repeat lengths and hippocampal volumes. *Journal of Clinical Investigation, 100,* 331–338.

Klauck, S.M., Munstermann, E., Bieber-Martig, B., et al. (1997). Molecular genetic analysis of the FMR-1 gene in a large collection of autistic patients. *Human Genetics, 100,* 224–229.

Lachiewicz, A.M. (1995). Females with fragile X syndrome: A review of the effects of an abnormal FMR1 gene. *Mental Retardation and Developmental Disabilities Research Reviews, 1,* 292–297.

Lachiewicz, A.M., Spiridigliozi, G.A., Gullion, C.M., et al. (1994). Aberrant behaviors of young boys with fragile X syndrome. *American Journal on Mental Retardation, 98,* 567–579.

Lehrke, R. (1972). Theory of X-linkage of major intellectual traits. *American Journal of Mental Deficiency, 76,* 611–619.

Maes, B., Fryns, J.P., Van Walleghem, M., et al. (1994). Cognitive functioning and information processing of adult mentally retarded men with fragile-X syndrome. *American Journal of Medical Genetics, 50,* 190–200.

Martin, J.P., & Bell, J. (1943). A pedigree of mental defect showing sex-linkage. *Journal of Neurology and Psychiatry, 6,* 154–157.

Mazzocco, M.M.M., Myers, G.F., Hamner, J.L., et al. (1998). The prevalence of the FMR1 and FMR2 mutations among preschool children with language delay. *Journal of Pediatrics, 132,* 795–801.

Meadows, K.L., Pettay, D., Newman, J., et al. (1996). Survey of the fragile X syndrome and the fragile XE syndrome in a special education needs population. *American Journal of Medical Genetics, 64,* 428–443.

Meyer, G.A., Blum, N., Hitchcock, W., et al. (1997). Absence of the CGG trinucleotide repeat in females diagnosed with pervasive developmental disorder. *Journal of Pediatrics, 133,* 363–365.

Mila, M., Sánchez, A., Badenas, C., et al. (1997). Screening for FMR1 and FMR2 mutations in 222 individuals from Spanish special schools: Identification of a case of FRAXE-associated mental retardation. *Human Genetics, 100,* 503–507.

Mulley, J.C., Yu, S., Loesch, D.Z., et al. (1995). FRAXE and mental retardation. *Journal of Medical Genetics, 32,* 162–169.

Murray, A. (2000). Premature ovarian failure and the FMR1 gene. *Seminars in Reproductive Medicine, 18,* 59–66.

Nolin, S.L., Lewis, F.A., III, Ye, L.L., et al. (1996). Familial transmission of the FMR1 CGG repeat. *American Journal of Human Genetics, 59,* 1252–1261.

Quan, F., Zonana, J., Gunter, K., et al. (1995). An atypical case of fragile X syndrome caused by a deletion that includes the FMR1 gene. *American Journal of Human Genetics, 56,* 1042–1051.

Reiss, A.L., Abrams, M.T., Greenlaw, R., et al. (1995). Neurodevelopmental effects of the FMR1 full mutation in humans. *Nature Medicine, 1,* 159–167.

Reiss, A.L., Freund, L., Abrams, M.T., et al. (1993). Neurobehavioral effects of the fragile X premutation in adult women: A controlled study. *American Journal of Human Genetics, 52,* 884–894.

Reiss, A.L., Kazazian, H.H., Jr., Krebs, C.M., et al. (1994). Frequency and stability of the fragile X premutation. *Human and Molecular Genetics, 3,* 393–398.

Riddle, J.E., Cheema, A., Sobesky, W.E., et al. (1998). Phenotype involvement in females with the FMR1 gene mutation. *American Journal on Mental Retardation, 102,* 590–601.

Rousseau, F., Heitz, D., Biancalana, V., et al. (1991). Direct diagnosis by DNA analysis of the fragile X syndrome of mental retardation. *New England Journal of Medicine, 325,* 1673–1681.

Schapiro, M.B., Murphy, D.G.M., Hagerman, R.J., et al. (1995). Adult fragile X syndrome: Neuropsychology, brain anatomy and metabolism. *American Journal of Medical Genetics, 60,* 480–493.

Small, K., & Warren, S.T. (1995). Analysis of FMRP, the protein deficient in fragile X syndrome. *Mental Retardation and Developmental Disabilities Research Reviews, 1,* 245–250.

Sobesky, W.E., Pennington, B.F., Porter, D., et al. (1994). Emotional and neurocognitive deficits in fragile X. *American Journal of Medical Genetics, 51,* 378–384.

Sobesky, W.E., Taylor, A.K., Pennington, B.F., et al. (1996). Molecular/clinical correlations in females with fragile X. *American Journal of Medical Genetics, 64,* 340–345.

Steyaert, J., Borghgraef, M., Legius, E., et al. (1996). Molecular-intelligence correlations in young fragile X males with a mild CGG repeat expansion in the FMR1 gene. *American Journal of Medical Genetics, 64,* 274–277.

Sudhalter, V., Cohen, I.L., Silverman, W., et al. (1990). Conversational analyses of males with fragile X, Down syndrome, and autism: Comparison of the emergence of deviant language. *American Journal on Mental Retardation, 94,* 431–441.

Sutherland, G.R. (1977). Fragile sites on human chromosomes: Demonstration of their dependence on the type of tissue culture medium. *Science, 197,* 265–266.

Tassone, F., Hagerman, R.J., Taylor, A.K., et al. (2000). Elevated levels of FMR1 mRNA in carrier males: A new mechanism of involvement in the fragile X syndrome. *American Journal of Human Genetics, 66,* 6–15.

Taylor, A.K., Safanda, J.F., Fall, M., et al. (1994). Molecular predictors of cognitive involvement in female carriers of fragile X syndrome. *Science, 271,* 507–514.

Turk, J., & Cornish, K. (1998). Face recognition and emotion perception in boys with fragile-X syndrome. *Journal of Intellectual Disability Research, 42,* 490–499.

Turner, G., Webb, T., Wake, S., et al. (1996). Prevalence of fragile X syndrome. *American Journal of Medical Genetics, 64,* 196–197.

Verheij, C., Bakker, C.E., de Graaff, E., et al. (1993). Characterization and localization of the FMR-1 gene product associated with fragile X syndrome. *Nature, 363,* 722–724.

Verkerk, A.J.M.H., Pieretti, M., Sutcliffe, J.S., et al. (1991). Identification of a gene (FMR1) containing a CGG repeat coincident with a breakpoint cluster region exhibiting length variation in fragile X syndrome. *Cell, 65,* 905–914.

Willems, P.J., Reyniers, E., & Oostra, B.A. (1995). An animal model for fragile X syndrome. *Mental Retardation and Developmental Disabilities Research Reviews, 1,* 298–302.

Willemsen, R., Anar, B., De Diego Otero, Y., et al. (1999). Noninvasive test for fragile X syndrome, using hair root analysis. *American Journal of Human Genetics, 65,* 98–103.

Willemsen, R., Mohkamsing, S., de Vries, B., et al. (1995). Rapid antibody test for fragile X syndrome. *Lancet, 345,* 1147–1148.

Wisniewski, K.E., Segan, S.M., Miezejeski, C.M., et al. (1991). Fragile-X syndrome: Neurological, electrophysiological and neuropathological abnormalities. *American Journal of Medical Genetics, 38,* 476–480.

Wright-Talamante, C., Cheema, A., Riddle, J.E., et al. (1996). A controlled study of longitudinal IQ changes in females and males with fragile X syndrome. *American Journal of Medical Genetics, 64,* 350–355.

18 PKU and Other Inborn Errors of Metabolism

Mark L. Batshaw and Mendel Tuchman

Upon completion of this chapter, the reader will:

- understand the term *inborn error of metabolism*
- know the differences among a number of these inborn errors, including amino acid disorders; organic acidemias; fatty acid oxidation defects; and mitochondrial, peroxisomal, and lysosomal storage diseases
- identify the clinical symptoms and diagnostic tests associated with these disorders
- know which of these disorders have newborn screening tests available
- recognize different approaches to treatment
- understand the outcome and range of developmental disabilities associated with inborn errors of metabolism

To receive adequate nutrition, the food we eat must be broken down into fats, proteins, and carbohydrates and then metabolized by hundreds of enzymes that work to maintain equilibrium in body functions. Approximately 1 in 2,500 children are born with a deficiency in an enzyme that normally catalyzes an important biochemical reaction in the cells (Applegarth et al., 2000). These children are said to have an **inborn error of metabolism.** The enzyme deficiency can result in the accumulation of a toxic **substrate** (chemical compound) behind the enzyme block or lead to a deficiency of a product normally produced by the deficient enzyme (Figure 18.1). The result may be organ damage (principally the brain) or even death. For example, children with phenylketonuria (PKU) have a deficiency in the enzyme that normally converts the amino acid phenylalanine to tyrosine. A deficiency of this enzyme, phenylalanine hydroxylase, leads to the toxic accumulation of phenylalanine, which if untreated leads to mental retardation (Figure 18.1). In contrast, in children with congenital adrenal hypoplasia, an enzyme deficiency leads to decreased production of **steroid** hormones, which are essential for normal body growth. Fortunately, for both of these disorders, newborn screening tests and early treatment have permitted affected children to grow up with their intellectual and body functioning intact. Not all inborn errors of metabolism are as effectively treated, however, because of delays in diagnosis or lack of adequate intervention. This chapter provides examples of inborn errors of metabolism to explain diagnostic and therapeutic advances that are improving the outcome of these disorders.

LISA

Lisa was discharged from the hospital at 3 days of age. Her parents were surprised and upset to be called back a week later, after doctors reported that Lisa had a positive PKU screening test. Amino acid studies confirmed the diagnosis, and Lisa was placed on low-phenylalanine

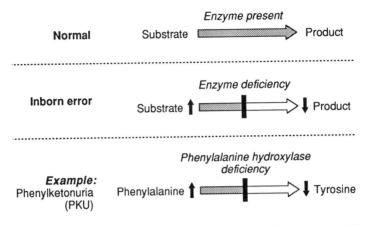

Figure 18.1.   Inborn errors of metabolism are genetic disorders involving an enzyme deficiency. This enzyme block leads to the accumulation of a toxic substrate and/or the deficient synthesis of a product needed for normal body function. In phenylketonuria (PKU) there is a toxic accumulation of phenylalanine behind the deficient enzyme, phenylalanine hydroxylase.

formula. Her parents could hardly believe there was a problem because Lisa looked and acted well and achieved her developmental milestones on time. The visits to the metabolism clinic were difficult reminders of her "silent disorder." Once Lisa entered elementary school, she began resisting the restrictions on her diet, and her parents had difficulty maintaining good metabolic control. Lisa was born in 1970, when the importance of strict dietary control was not widely known. She stopped her diet at 7 years of age. Psychometric testing at 10 years of age showed that she had an IQ score of 85. Despite learning difficulties in school, she graduated from high school and began a clerical job. She soon became pregnant but was not placed back on a low-phenylalanine diet. Her child was born with microcephaly, and at age 5, has mental retardation requiring limited supports. Fortunately, Lisa's younger sister Barbara, who also has PKU, has had a better outcome. Barbara has remained on the low-phenylalanine diet continuously and intends to remain on the diet through her pregnancies.

DARNEL

Darnel babbled at 6 months and sat without support shortly thereafter. His parents became concerned by 1 year, however, when he had made no further progress. If anything, he seemed less steady in sitting and was uninvolved with his surroundings. His pediatrician worried that Darnel might have autism. By 18 months, there were graver concerns. Darnel was no longer able to roll over; he was very floppy and did not appear to respond to light or sound. His pediatrician referred Darnel to a genetics clinic, where an extensive workup eventually diagnosed Tay-Sachs disease. Over the next 3 years, Darnel slipped into an unresponsive condition and required tube feeding. He finally succumbed to aspiration pneumonia. As a result of the diagnosis, his mother was able to undergo prenatal diagnosis in subsequent pregnancies. She now has two unaffected children and underwent one termination of an affected fetus.

TYPES OF INBORN ERRORS OF METABOLISM

Inborn errors of metabolism are a relatively newly discovered group of diseases. PKU was one of the first disorders identified, described by Fölling in 1934. About 300 additional disorders have been identified since the 1950s, and a number of new ones are described each year (Scriver

Table 18.1. Examples of inborn errors of metabolism

Type I: Silent disorders
Phenylketonuria (PKU)
Congenital hypothyroidism

Type II: Disorders presenting in acute metabolic crisis
Urea cycle disorders (ornithine transcarbamylase [OTC] deficiency)
Organic acidemias (multiple carboxylase deficiency)

Type III: Disorders with progressive neurological deterioration
Tay-Sachs disease
Gaucher disease
Metachromatic leukodystrophy

et al., 1995). The majority of these enzyme deficiencies are inherited as autosomal recessive traits, although a few are transmitted as X-linked disorders or through mitochondrial DNA (see Chapter 1). Prenatal diagnosis is available for most of them (see Chapter 2).

Inborn errors of metabolism can be divided into those that are clinically "silent," those that produce acute toxicity, and those that cause progressive neurological damage (Table 18.1). Among silent disorders are certain amino acid (e.g., PKU) and hormone (e.g., congenital hypothyroidism) abnormalities. Disorders producing acute toxicity include certain inborn errors of amino acid, organic acid, fatty acid, mitochondrial, and carbohydrate metabolism (Burlina, Bonafe, & Zacchello, 1999; Burton, 1998). Inborn errors of metabolism causing progressive neurological disorders include peroxisomal and lysosomal storage disorders. The names of the disorders are often derived from their deficient enzyme (e.g., ornithine transcarbamylase [OTC] deficiency, an inborn error of amino acid metabolism). Silent disorders such as PKU do not manifest life-threatening crises, but if untreated lead to brain damage and developmental disabilities. These disorders contrast with inborn errors that cause acute symptoms, such as OTC deficiency, that may be life threatening in infancy. In both cases, an affected child is generally protected in utero because maternal circulation can remove the toxic substrate or provide the missing product. After birth, however, the infant must rely on his or her own metabolic pathways, and if they are abnormal, toxicity occurs rapidly or over time depending on the severity of the defect. In progressive neurological disorders, there is the gradual accumulation, beginning in utero, of large molecules that cannot cross the cell membranes or the placenta. These molecules are stored in the cells of various body organs, including the brain, where they ultimately destroy the neurons, leading to neurological deterioration.

CLINICAL MANIFESTATIONS

The clinical manifestations of the various inborn errors of metabolism fall along a continuum. Silent disorders do not manifest such symptoms as lethargy, coma, or regression of skills. Instead, affected children develop very slowly; they are typically not identified as having mental retardation until later in childhood.

Life-threatening crises characterize the second group of inborn errors of metabolism. Infants with these disorders appear to be unaffected at birth, but by a few days of age, they develop vomiting, respiratory distress, and lethargy before slipping into coma. These symptoms, however, mimic those observed in other severe newborn illnesses (see Chapter 5) such as sepsis (blood-borne infection), intracerebral hemorrhage, cardiopulmonary abnormalities, and gastrointestinal obstruction, which can make correct diagnosis difficult. If specific metabolic testing of the blood and urine are not performed, the disease will go undetected. Undiagnosed and untreated, virtually all affected children will die quickly. One study reported that 60% of children with inborn errors of the **urea** cycle had at least one sibling who died before it was correctly diagnosed in a subsequent affected child (Batshaw et al., 1982). Even with heroic treatment, which may include dialysis to "wash out" the toxin, many infants do not survive, and severe developmental disabilities are common in those who do (Msall et al., 1984).

In children with neonatal-onset disease, DNA analysis typically shows mutations that cause the absence of the enzyme or formation of a nonfunctional enzyme. Enzyme activity levels are generally undetectable (see Chapter 1). Some children with the same inborn error of metabolism, however, have less severe mutations that produce enzymes that are only partially dysfunctional. These children have later onset of clinical signs and more variable symptoms. Here, symptoms of behavioral changes and cyclical vomiting and lethargy are often provoked in childhood by excessive protein intake or intercurrent infections (Trifiletti & Packard, 1999). Although these children have a better outcome than those with neonatal-onset disease do, they remain at risk for life-threatening metabolic crises throughout life. And although their developmental disabilities may be less severe than those in children with neonatal-onset disease, children with later onset rarely escape without some residual impairments, ranging from attention-deficit/hyperactivity disorder (ADHD) to mental retardation.

The third clinical presentation of inborn errors of metabolism is as neurodegenerative disorders (Clarke, 1999; Vadasz & Epstein, 1995). Examples include lysosomal storage disorders, such as Tay-Sachs disease (Kaplan, 1998), Batten disease (Bennett & Hofmann, 1999), Hurler syndrome (Cleary & Wraith, 1995), and metachromatic leukodystrophy (Powers & Rubio, 1995); mitochondrial disorders such as Leigh syndrome (deLonlay-Debeney et al., 2000; Loeffen et al., 2000); and peroxisomal disorders, including adrenoleukodystrophy and Zellweger syndrome (Raymond, 1999). In these disorders, there is a progressive loss of motor and cognitive skills beginning in early childhood, resulting in a nonresponsive state by the preschool years and commonly ending in death in infancy or childhood (Kaback et al., 1993). In the case of Tay-Sachs disease, for example, the affected child appears to develop typically until 3–6 months of age, at which point skill development is arrested. For the next 1–2 years, the child gradually loses all skills; begins having seizures; and exhibits decreased muscle tone, vision, hearing, and cognition. Death usually results from malnutrition or from aspiration pneumonia. Unfortunately, no effective treatment currently exists for this group of disorders, although organ transplantation and gene therapy offer some hope for the future (Guffon et al., 1998).

MECHANISM OF BRAIN DAMAGE

The causes of brain damage in the various inborn errors of metabolism are not completely understood. Research, however, is starting to provide some clues that may eventually lead to improved treatment. For example, thyroid hormone has been found to be necessary for the normal growth of neurons, their processes, and surrounding myelin in the brain. A thyroid hormone deficiency is thought to lead to poor postnatal brain growth and resultant microcephaly (Rodriguez-Pena et al., 1993).

Neurotoxins appear to play a role in certain other metabolic disorders. In nonketotic hyperglycinemia, an inborn error of amino acid metabolism, there is an accumulation of glycine leading to uncontrolled seizures (Lu et al., 1999). Glycine appears to produce excitotoxicity at a neurotransmitter receptor, leading to the influx of calcium ions and water into the neuron. This causes swelling of the neuron and, eventually, cell death. Experimental drugs are being tested to partially block receptor overstimulation (Hamosh et al., 1998). In Lesch-Nyhan syndrome, caused by a defect in **purine** metabolism, deficits in the dopamine neurotransmitter system are associated with self-injurious behavior (Ernst, Zametkin, & Matochik, 1996).

In some disorders, more than one neurotoxin may be involved. Scientists believe that in inborn errors of the urea cycle (another group of amino acid disorders, which includes OTC deficiency), the accumulating toxin, ammonia, directly causes the nerve cells to swell and also indirectly causes **excitotoxic** damage to the brain (Batshaw, 1994). If children are rescued from the ammonia-induced coma within a few days, the neurotoxic effect can be arrested and outcome can be fairly good (Msall et al., 1984). If coma is prolonged, however, irreversible brain damage occurs (Batshaw et al., 1993).

ASSOCIATED DISABILITIES

The toxic accumulation of metabolic substrates or deficient synthesis of essential products results in a spectrum of developmental disabilities in children with inborn errors of metabolism. The most common are mental retardation and cerebral palsy. However, there are also rather unique impairments in certain inborn errors. These are sometimes associated with distinctive pathological features, which may eventually permit a better understanding of brain development and function. For example, boys with the X-linked Lesch-Nyhan syndrome exhibit choreoathetosis (a form of dyskinetic cerebral palsy; see Chapter 23) and compulsive, self-injurious behavior (Matthews et al., 1999; Nyhan, 1997). Children with glutaric acidemia type I, an **organic acidemia,** have **dystonic cerebral palsy** associated with calcifications in their basal ganglia (Baric et al., 1998). In Zellweger syndrome, a disorder of the **peroxisome,** children exhibit multiple malformations more commonly associated with chromosomal disorders, including an abnormal facial appearance, kidney cysts, and congenital heart defects (FitzPatrick, 1996).

DIAGNOSTIC TESTING

A child with developmental disabilities of unknown origin should be referred for metabolic evaluation if he or she has any of the following signs or symptoms: cyclical behavioral changes, vomiting and lethargy, enlargement of the liver or spleen, evidence of neurological deterioration, and/or a suggestive family history. Available tests can lead to a correct diagnosis and possibly improved therapy and outcome. Even in untreatable disorders, knowledge of the diagnosis may permit effective genetic counseling. A metabolic evaluation is not recommended, however, for all children with mental retardation.

Diagnoses of inborn errors of metabolism rely primarily on blood and urine tests to detect accumulation of toxins. The most common tests performed include blood tests for ammonia, lactic acid, carnitine, and amino acids and urine tests for organic acids. The metabolic evaluations are individualized based on the specific biochemical pathway that is suspected to be defective (Winter, 1993). OTC deficiency, the most common inborn error of the urea cycle, illustrates one such defective pathway (Figure 18.2). When protein is broken down into its component amino acids, if the amino acids are metabolized, ammonia is normally released. The ammonia is then converted into the nontoxic product urea through the five enzymatic steps in the urea cycle (OTC is the second enzyme). Urea is then excreted in the urine. If any one of these five enzymes is deficient, ammonia will accumulate and can cause severe neurological symptoms (Batshaw, 1994). To diagnose this disorder, levels of ammonia and amino acids are measured in blood, and orotic acid is measured in the urine. Many other inborn errors of amino acid and organic acid metabolism can be identified using similar blood and urine tests.

Lysosomal storage disorders are typically diagnosed by measuring the suspected deficient enzyme activity in the blood. Neuroimaging studies (e.g., magnetic resonance imaging [MRI] with magnetic resonance spectroscopy [MRS], computed tomography [CT] scan), electroencephalogram (EEG), and other neurophysiological measures (e.g., nerve conduction velocity, electromyography) may also prove helpful in diagnosing these disorders.

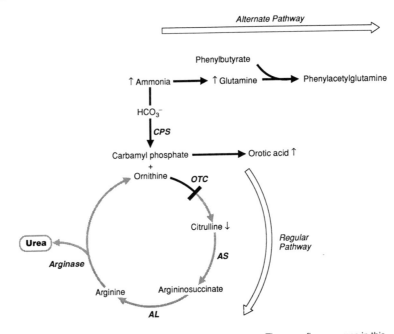

Figure 18.2.   The urea cycle and alternate pathway therapy. There are five enzymes in this cycle that convert toxic ammonia, a breakdown product of protein, to nontoxic urea, which is excreted in the urine. The enzymes, shown in boldface italic type, are CPS (carbamyl phosphate synthetase), OTC (ornithine transcarbamylase), AS (argininosuccinate synthetase), AL (argininosuccinate lyase), and arginase. Inborn errors at each step of the urea cycle have been described, with the most common being OTC deficiency. In OTC deficiency, behind the block there is accumulation of orotic acid, ammonia, and glutamine and deficient production of citrulline. Treatment has been directed at providing an alternate pathway for waste nitrogen excretion by giving the drug sodium phenylbutyrate, which combines with glutamine to form phenylacetylglutamine, a nontoxic product that can be excreted in the urine. This results in a decrease in the accumulation of ammonia.

NEWBORN SCREENING

Because individual inborn errors of metabolism are rare (usually occurring in fewer than 1 in 10,000 births) and their diagnosis is easily missed, efforts have been directed at developing newborn screening methods for the detection of the more common and treatable disorders. Rapid diagnosis and treatment is important to achieve a good outcome. As a result, screening efforts have focused on newborns. The first newborn screening test was developed for PKU in 1959 (Guthrie & Susi, 1963). It was successful in detecting more than 90% of affected children. Subsequently, methods have been established for testing for other inborn errors of metabolism, including congenital hypothyroidism, galactosemia, homocystinuria, biotinidase deficiency, maple syrup urine disease, fatty acid oxidation defects, as well as certain other genetic disorders not associated with developmental disabilities, including cystic fibrosis, sickle cell anemia, and alpha$_1$-antitrypsin deficiency (a disorder affecting liver and lungs). This testing, now usually done by tandem mass spectrometry, is offered to families in the newborn nurseries; the specific inborn errors of metabolism tested for vary among states (Seashore, 1998).

To perform the test, a few drops of blood are taken from the infant's heel and placed on filter paper. The blood sample is mailed to the screening laboratory, where the staff can obtain results within a few days. Although these tests have proved to be remarkably effective, parents should be reminded that the tests can detect only a fraction of the inborn errors of metabolism that cause developmental disabilities. Parents might incorrectly assume that these tests are diagnostic for mental retardation.

THERAPEUTIC APPROACHES

Diagnosis is most valuable if it leads to effective treatment. Figure 18.3 illustrates the varying approaches to treating inborn errors of metabolism. These methods include 1) limiting intake of a potentially toxic substrate, 2) supplying the deficient product, 3) stimulating an alternate metabolic pathway to eliminate a toxin, 4) providing a vitamin co-factor to enhance residual enzyme activity, 5) providing enzyme replacement therapy, 6) transplanting an organ containing the deficient enzyme, 7) using gene therapy, and 8) using other therapies and emerging technologies. Each of these approaches is illustrated by specific disorders in Table 18.2.

Limiting Intake of a Potentially Toxic Substrate

A relatively straightforward way to correct an inborn error of metabolism is to establish dietary restrictions that limit the child's intake of a potentially toxic substrate. For example, children with PKU are placed on a phenylalanine-restricted diet in order to prevent the phenylalanine accumulation that causes brain damage (Wappner et al., 1999). This involves using a special phenylalanine-restricted formula and low-protein foods. One study showed that the IQ scores of children who began this treatment in the first month of life were around 100, whereas the scores of those initially treated later in childhood were 20–50 points lower (Table 18.3; Hanley, Linsao, & Netley, 1971).

Scientists initially thought that only those children with PKU younger than 6 years needed to follow a phenylalanine-restricted diet. For older children, the high cost and rejection of this rather unpleasant and restrictive diet made continuation difficult. Initial studies to determine whether children with PKU experienced a loss in intellectual functioning following dietary discontinuation suggested that IQ scores did not decline over time (Waisbren et al., 1987). In a subsequent study, however, researchers found that children with PKU who maintained the diet through age 10 actually experienced a modest gain in IQ scores compared with children who stopped the diet at age 6. The differences in IQ scores between the two groups

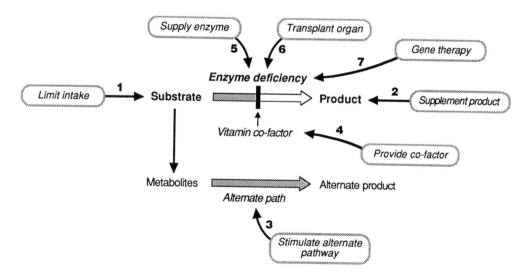

Figure 18.3. Approaches to treatment of inborn errors of metabolism. Treatment can be directed at 1) limiting the intake of a potentially toxic compound, 2) supplementing the deficient product, 3) stimulating an alternate metabolic pathway, 4) providing a vitamin co-factor to activate residual enzyme activity, 5) supplying the enzyme itself, 6) transplanting a body organ containing the deficient enzyme, and 7) gene therapy.

Table 18.2. Examples of treatment approaches for inborn errors of metabolism

Approaches	Disorder	Specific treatment
Restrict diet	Phenylketonuria (PKU)	Phenylalanine restriction
	Maple syrup urine disease	Branch chain amino acid restriction
	Galactosemia	Galactose restriction
Supplement deficient product	Congenital hypothyroidism	Synthroid
	Glycogen storage disease	Cornstarch
	Urea cycle disorders (except argininemia)	Arginine
Stimulate alternate pathway	Urea cycle disorders	Sodium phenylbutyrate
	Organic acidemias	Carnitine
	Isovaleric acidemia	Glycine
	Wilson disease	Penicillamine
Supply vitamin co-factor	Multiple carboxylase deficiency	Biotin
	Homocystinuria	Pyridoxine
	Methylmalonic acidemia	Vitamin B_{12}
Replace enzyme	Severe combined immunodeficiency (SCID)	PEG-ADA
	Gaucher disease	Glucocerebrosidase
Transplant organ	Metachromatic leukodystrophy	Bone marrow
	Ornithine transcarbamylase (OTC) deficiency	Liver
	Tyrosinemia	Liver
	Glycogen storage disease	Liver
Use gene therapy	SCID	Retrovirus gene transfer
Use other therapies/ emerging technologies	Inhibit pathway: tyrosinemia	NTBC
	Use substrate deprivation: PKU	Recombinant enzyme

were statistically significant (Michals et al., 1988). Thus, metabolic specialists now suggest that the phenylalanine-restricted diet be continued indefinitely.

PKU poses a serious complication for women of childbearing age (Rouse et al., 2000). At one time, women with PKU had mental retardation and did not often bear children. Most treated women with PKU have typical intelligence and can bear children. Most of them, however, have stopped following the phenylalanine-restricted diet. Unexpectedly, almost all of the children born to these women were found to have mental retardation and congenital abnormalities, including congenital heart disease, cleft lip and palate, esophageal atresia, and genitourinary abnormalities. These children, however, do not have PKU; they are only carriers. Instead, the mental retardation is caused by the effect of the mother's high phenylalanine levels on the developing brain. Studies have indicated that lowering the phenylalanine levels in the pregnant mother with PKU significantly improves the chances for typical development of offspring. As a result, it is now advised that women with PKU resume the phenylalanine-restricted diet prior to conception or at least as soon as they discover that they are pregnant (Rouse et al., 2000).

Supplying the Deficient Product

Some children with inborn errors of metabolism are given replacements for the enzyme product they are missing. For example, children with congenital hypothyroidism receive a thyroid supplement to compensate for the thyroid hormone they lack. This treatment, if administered early, effectively corrects the metabolic disorder, and children treated in the first months of life

Table 18.3.   Results of treating phenylketonuria (PKU) diagnosed at various stages

	Number of children by age at diagnosis (months)				
	Birth–2	2–6	6–12	12–24	24+
Number of cases	38	6	11	19	20
IQ score					
90+	27	0	0	1	2
80–89	6	3	0	2	1
70–79	4	1	3	2	0
Less than 70	1	2	8	14	17
Mean IQ score	93.5	71.6	54.5	55.5	40.8

From Hanley, W.B., Linsao, L.S., & Netley, C. (1971). The efficiency of dietary therapy for phenyketonuria. Reprinted from *CMAJ* 1971:104 Page 1089 by permission of the publisher. © 1971 Canadian Medical Association.

develop typical intelligence (LaFranchi, 1999), although as with children who have PKU, they have some residual impairments in attention and learning (Rovet, 1999).

Stimulating a Detour

Physicians are able to treat some metabolic disorders by stimulating an alternative pathway that detours around the enzymatic block. For example, children with inborn errors of the urea cycle cannot convert toxic ammonia, a byproduct of protein breakdown, to nontoxic urea. Treatment by dietary protein restriction alone has proved unsuccessful as the level of restriction required to prevent an accumulation of ammonia is insufficient for sustained growth or prolonged survival (Shih, 1976). A novel approach is to use the drug sodium phenylbutyrate to stimulate an alternate pathway for ammonia excretion. By providing a detour around the enzyme block and converting the ammonia to an alternate nontoxic product, phenylacetylglutamine, instead of urea (Figure 18.2), this drug allows the majority of children with these disorders to survive, although many have developmental disabilities (Feillet & Leonard, 1998).

Providing a Vitamin Co-factor to Activate Residual Enzyme Activity

For a few inborn errors, providing large doses of a vitamin co-factor results in amplification of residual enzyme activity and clinical improvement. This approach has been most effective in treating children with an organic acidemia called *multiple carboxylase deficiency* (Dupuis et al., 1999). These children, who develop symptoms of acidosis and coma because of a defect in their enzyme holocarboxylase synthetase, can show marked improvement if **biotin** is provided at a very high (but nontoxic) dose. Similar vitamin therapy can also help children with certain forms of another organic acidemia called *methylmalonic aciduria* (using vitamin B$_{12}$) and an amino acid disorder called *homocystinuria* (using vitamin B$_6$; Fowler, 1998). Vitamin therapy has unfortunately spawned a "quick-fix" approach to treating everything from cancer, to Down syndrome, to schizophrenia, although there is no evidence that megavitamin therapy is effective in treating these disorders (Nutrition Committee of the Canadian Paediatric Society, 1990). Thus, although rare diseases teach us much about normal body chemistry, they have also been used inappropriately to advocate for unproven therapies in unrelated disorders.

Providing Enzyme Replacement Therapy

The previously discussed methods of therapy use indirect approaches to improve the child's condition. Supplying the missing enzyme is a direct approach to actually treat the inborn error. Injections of a synthetic enzyme have proved successful in treating the lysosomal storage disorder

Gaucher disease, which is associated with the accumulation of glucocerebroside in cells of the liver, spleen, and bone marrow (with severe infantile Gaucher disease, the enzyme accumulates in the brain as well). Individuals who receive biweekly injections of the deficient enzyme show marked improvements, including significant shrinkage of the liver and spleen (MacKenzie, Amato, & Clarke, 1998). This enzyme, however, cannot cross the blood–brain barrier, making replacement therapy ineffective for those children with severe infantile Gaucher disease.

Although replacement therapy seems ideal for those with the milder form of Gaucher disease, it is not without problems. As of 2002, the necessary synthetic enzyme is the most expensive drug in the world. In addition, the enzyme must be injected at frequent intervals throughout the individual's life, and antibodies can develop against the foreign protein, just as insulin resistance develops in some individuals with diabetes.

Transplanting an Organ Containing the Deficient Enzyme

Some deficient enzymes can be replaced by transplanting a body organ that contains the enzyme. For example, bone marrow transplantation has been attempted in individuals with certain lysosomal and peroxisomal storage disorders, including juvenile metachromatic leukodystrophy, adrenoleukodystrophy, and Hurler syndrome. These disorders, marked by dementia, physical deterioration, and early death, are caused by the deficiency of enzymes found in many body organs, including bone marrow cells. In a few affected children, bone marrow transplantation has resulted in the arrest of or improvement in symptoms (Guffon et al., 1998; Krivit, Peters, & Shapiro, 1999).

In addition to bone marrow transplants, liver transplantation has been used to treat certain inborn errors of amino acid metabolism, most notably OTC deficiency and hereditary tyrosinemia, with associated biochemical correction and improvement in symptoms (Whittington et al., 1998). Organ transplantation, however, is a very expensive procedure with significant mortality and morbidity, and transplant recipients require immunosuppression therapy throughout life.

Using Gene Therapy

In theory, the ideal treatment for an inborn error of metabolism would involve the insertion of a normal gene to compensate for a defective one. This insertion would allow for the production of a normal enzyme, thereby permanently correcting or curing the disorder. In human experiments, however, initial gene therapy trials that began in the early 1990s have been less successful; efficacy and duration have been limited (Barranger, Rice, & Swaney, 1999; Friedmann, 1997; Lemoine & Vile, 1998; Lyon & Gorner, 1995).

Using Other Therapies and Emerging Technologies

Novel therapies for inborn errors of metabolism have been developed since the 1990s. Some have been used in patients, whereas others have only been tested in laboratory animals. One example is the inhibition of a pathway that leads to the formation of toxic products in hereditary tyrosinemia type I (Lindstedt et al., 1992). NTBC, an herbicide derivative, was found in affected children to inhibit tyrosine degradation, preventing the formation of a toxic compound that is suspected to cause kidney disease and liver disease and cancer. Another example of innovative therapy is substrate deprivation, which has shown promise in animal models of PKU (Sarkissian et al., 1999) and lysosomal storage disorders (Abe et al., 2000; Jeyakumar et al., 2001). In PKU, the use of a recombinant enzyme to degrade phenylalanine in the intestine before its absorption could reduce the phenylalanine load and allow less severe dietary restriction. In lysosomal storage disorders, inhibition of glycosphingolipid synthesis would have the analogous effect of reducing lysosomal products that are toxic to the brain.

OUTCOME

The range of outcomes in inborn errors of metabolism varies enormously. In disorders such as PKU that can be detected by newborn screening, affected children have generally done well. Their intellectual functioning generally falls within the typical range, if somewhat lower than that of their parents; they are, however, at increased risk for having learning disabilities and ADHD (Weglage et al., 1995). Less optimistic outcomes occur in inborn errors of amino acid and organic acid metabolism that are not detected early. Although these children are surviving longer, many manifest mental retardation and cerebral palsy (Msall et al., 1984). Among children with metabolic disorders associated with progressive neurological disorders, such as lysosomal storage diseases, there has not been significant improvement in mortality or morbidity.

A 1995 study attempted to evaluate the overall effectiveness of therapies for 65 inborn errors of metabolism (Treacy, Childs, & Scriver, 1995) by examining a number of parameters: longevity, reproductive ability, growth, intelligence, and ability to work independently (Figure 18.4). The study showed that about half of the disorders were completely or partially ameliorated by treatment.

SUMMARY

Although inborn errors of metabolism are rare, their consequences are often devastating. Fortunately, therapy is effective for a number of these disorders. Affected children, however, often must continue treatment for the rest of their lives, which may prove difficult to accomplish. For therapy to succeed, it must be started early. Researchers continue to look for new therapeutic strategies for these diseases. It is hoped that these new therapeutic approaches will continue to improve the outcome for children with these disorders.

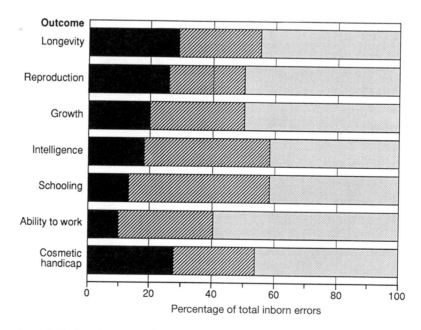

Figure 18.4. An outcome study (Treacy, Childs, & Scriver, 1995) showed that about half of individuals with inborn errors of metabolism have benefited from therapy approaches in terms of improved longevity, reproduction, growth, intelligence, or ability to hold a job as adults. (*Key:* ■ prevented adverse effects; ▨ modified adverse effects; ▫ unchanged adverse effects.)

REFERENCES

Abe, A., Gregory, S., Lee, L., et al. (2000). Reduction of globotriaosylceramide in Fabry disease mice by substrate deprivation. *Journal of Clinical Investigation, 105*, 1563–1571.

Applegarth, D.A., Toone, J.R., & Lowry, R.B. (2000). Incidence of inborn errors of metabolism in British Columbia, 1969–1996. *Pediatrics, 105*, e10.

Baric, I., Zschocke, J., Christensen, E., et al. (1998). Diagnosis and management of glutaric aciduria type I. *Journal of Inherited Metabolic Disease, 21*, 326–340.

Barranger, J.A., Rice, E.O., & Swaney, W.P. (1999). Gene transfer approaches to the lysosomal storage disorders. *Neurochemical Research, 24*, 601–615.

Batshaw, M.L. (1994). Inborn errors of urea synthesis: A review. *Annals of Neurology, 35*, 133–141.

Batshaw, M.L., Brusilow, S., Waber, L., et al. (1982). Treatment of inborn errors of urea synthesis: Activation of alternative pathways of waste nitrogen synthesis and excretion. *New England Journal of Medicine, 306*, 1387–1392.

Batshaw, M.L., Robinson, M.B., Hyland, K., et al. (1993). Quinolinic acid in children with congenital hyperammonemia. *Annals of Neurology, 34*, 676–681.

Bennett, M.J., & Hofmann, S.L. (1999). The neuronal ceroid-lipofuscinoses (Batten disease): A new class of lysosomal storage diseases. *Journal of Inherited Metabolic Disease, 22*, 535–544.

Burlina, A.B., Bonafe, L., & Zacchello, F. (1999). Clinical and biochemical approach to the neonate with a suspected inborn error of amino acid and organic acid metabolism. *Seminars in Perinatology, 23*, 162–173.

Burton, B.K. (1998). Inborn errors of metabolism in infancy: A guide to diagnosis. *Pediatrics, 102*, e69.

Charrow, J., Esplin, J.A., Gribble, T.J., et al. (1998). Gaucher disease: Recommendations on diagnosis, evaluation, and monitoring. *Archives of Internal Medicine, 158*, 1754–1760.

Clarke, J.T.R. (1999). *A clinical guide to inherited metabolic diseases*. Cambridge, England: Cambridge University Press.

Cleary, M.A., & Wraith, J.E. (1995). The presenting features of mucopolysaccharidosis type IH (Hurler syndrome). *Acta Paediatrica, 84*, 337–339.

deLonlay-Debenney, P., von Kleist-Retzow, J.C., Hertz-Pannier, L., et al. (2000). Cerebral white matter disease in children may be caused by mitochondrial respiratory chain deficiency. *Journal of Pediatrics, 136*, 209–214.

Dupuis, L., Campeau, E., Leclerc, D., et al. (1999). Mechanism of biotin responsiveness in biotin-responsive multiple carboxylase deficiency. *Molecular Genetics and Metabolism, 66*, 80–90.

Ernst, M., Zametkin, A.J., & Matochik, J.A. (1996). Presynaptic dopaminergic deficits in Lesch-Nyhan disease. *New England Journal of Medicine, 334*, 1568–1572.

Feillet, F., & Leonard, J.V. (1998). Alternative pathway therapy for urea cycle disorders. *Journal of Inherited Metabolic Disease, 21*(Suppl. 1), 101–111.

FitzPatrick, D.R. (1996). Zellweger syndrome and associated phenotypes. *Journal of Medical Genetics, 33*, 863–868.

Fölling, A. (1934). Excretion of phenylalanine in urine: An inborn error of metabolism associated with mental retardation. *Hoppe-Seyler's Zeitschrift für Physiologische Chemie, 227*, 169–176.

Fowler, B. (1998). Genetic defects of folate and cobalamin metabolism. *European Journal of Pediatrics, 157*(Suppl. 2), S60–S66.

Friedmann, T. (1997). Overcoming the obstacles to gene therapy. *Scientific American, 276*, 96–101.

Guffon, N., Souillet G., Maire, I., et al. (1998). Follow-up of nine patients with Hurler syndrome after bone marrow transplantation. *Journal of Pediatrics, 133*, 119–125.

Guthrie, R., & Susi, A. (1963). A simple method for detecting phenylketonuria in large populations of newborn infants. *Pediatrics, 32*, 338–343.

Hamosh, A., Maher, J.F., Bellus, G.A., et al. (1998). Long-term use of high-dose benzoate and dextromethorphan for the treatment of nonketotic hyperglycinemia. *Journal of Pediatrics, 132*, 709–713.

Hanley, W.B., Linsao, L.S., & Netley, C. (1971). The efficiency of dietary therapy for phenylketonuria. *Canadian Medical Association Journal, 104*, 1089.

Jeyakumar, M., Norflus, F., Tifft, C.J., et al. (2001). Enhanced survival in Sandhoff disease mice receiving a combination of substrate deprivation therapy and bone marrow transplantation. *Blood, 97*, 327–329.

Kaback, M., Lim-Steele, J., Dabholkar, D., et al. (1993). Tay-Sachs disease: Carrier screening, prenatal diagnosis, and the molecular era. An international perspective, 1970 to 1993. *Journal of the American Medical Association, 270*, 2307–2315.

Kaplan, F. (1998). Tay-Sachs disease carrier screening: A model for prevention of genetic disease. *Genetic Testing, 2*, 271–292.

Krivit, W., Peters, C., & Shapiro, E.G. (1999). Bone marrow transplantation as effective treatment of central nervous system disease in globoid cell leukodystrophy, metachromatic leukodystrophy, adrenoleukodystrophy, mannosidosis, fucosidosis, aspartylglucosaminuria, Hurler, Maroteaux-Lamy, and Sly syndromes, and Gaucher disease type III. *Current Opinion in Neurology, 12*, 167–176.

LaFranchi, S. (1999). Congenital hypothyroidism: Etiologies, diagnosis, and management. *Thyroid, 9*, 735–740.

Lemoine, N.R., & Vile, R.G. (Eds.). (1998). *Understanding gene therapy*. New York: Springer-Verlag.

Lindstedt, S., Holme, E., Lock, E.A., et al. (1992). Treatment of hereditary tyrosinaemia type I by inhibition of 4-hydroxyphenylpyruvate dioxygenase. *Lancet, 340*, 813–817.

Loeffen, J.L., Smeitink, J.A., Trijbels, J.M., et al. (2000). Isolated complex I deficiency in children: Clinical, biochemical and genetic aspects. *Human Mutation, 15*, 123–134.

Lu, F.L., Wang, P.J., Hwu, W.L., et al. (1999). Neonatal type of nonketotic hyperglycinemia. *Pediatric Neurology, 20*, 295–300.

Lyon, J., & Gorner, P. (1995). *Altered fates: Gene therapy and the retooling of human life*. New York: W.W. Norton.

MacKenzie, J.J., Amato, D., & Clarke, J.T. (1998). Enzyme replacement therapy for Gaucher's disease: The early Canadian experience. *Canadian Medical Association Journal, 159*, 1273–1278.

Matthews, W.S., Solan, A., Barabas, G., et al. (1999). Cognitive functioning in Lesch-Nyhan syndrome: A 4-year follow-up study. *Developmental Medicine and Child Neurology, 41*, 260–262.

Michals, K., Azen, C., Acosta, P., et al. (1988). Blood phenylalanine levels and intelligence of 10-year-old children with PKU in the national collaborative study. *Journal of the American Dietetic Association, 88*, 1226–1229.

Msall, M., Batshaw, M.L., Suss, R., et al. (1984). Neurologic outcome in children with inborn errors of urea synthesis: Outcome of urea-cycle enzymopathies. *New England Journal of Medicine, 310*, 1500–1505.

Nutrition Committee of the Canadian Paediatric Society. (1990). Megavitamin and megamineral therapy in childhood. *Canadian Medical Association Journal, 143,* 1009–1013.

Nyhan, W.L. (1997). The recognition of Lesch-Nyhan syndrome as an inborn error of purine metabolism. *Journal of Inherited Metabolic Disease, 20,* 171–178.

Powers, J.M., & Rubio, A. (1995). Selected leukodystrophies. *Seminars in Pediatric Neurology, 2,* 200–210.

Raymond, G.V. (1999). Peroxisomal disorders. *Current Opinion in Pediatrics, 11,* 572–576.

Rodriguez-Pena, A., Ibarrola, N., Iniguez, M.A., et al. (1993). Neonatal hyperthyroidism affects the timely expression of myelin-associated glycoprotein in the rat brain. *Journal of Clinical Investigation, 91,* 812–818.

Rouse, B., Matalon, R., Koch, R., et al. (2000). Maternal phenylketonuria syndrome: Congenital heart defects, microcephaly, and developmental outcomes. *Journal of Pediatrics, 136,* 57–61.

Rovet, J.F. (1999). Congenital hypothyroidism: Long-term outcome. *Thyroid, 9,* 741–748.

Sarkissian, C.N., Shao, Z., Blain, F., et al. (1999). A different approach to treatment of phenylketonuria: Phenylalanine degradation with recombinant phenylalanine ammonia lyase. *Proceedings of the National Academy of Sciences of the United States of America, 96,* 2339–2344.

Seashore, M.R. (1998). Tandem spectrometry in newborn screening. *Current Opinion in Pediatrics, 10,* 609–614.

Scriver, C.R., Kaufman, S., Eisensmith, R.C., et al. (1995). The hyperphenylalaninemias. In C.R. Scriver, A.L. Beaudet, et al. (Eds.), *The metabolic and molecular bases of inherited disease* (7th ed., pp. 1015–1076). New York: McGraw-Hill.

Shih, V.E. (1976). Hereditary urea-cycle disorders. In S. Grisolia, R. Baguena, & F. Mayor (Eds.), *The urea cycle* (pp. 367–414). New York: John Wiley & Sons.

Treacy, E., Childs, B., & Scriver, C.R. (1995). Response to treatment in hereditary metabolic disease: 1993 survey and 10-year comparison [Review]. *American Journal of Human Genetics, 56,* 359–367.

Trifiletti, R.R., & Packard, A.M. (1999). Metabolic disorders presenting with behavioral symptoms in the school-aged child. *Child and Adolescent Psychiatry Clinics of North America, 8,* 791–806.

Vadasz, A.G., & Epstein, L.G. (1995). Degenerative central nervous system disease. *Pediatrics in Review, 116,* 426–431.

Waisbren, S.E., Mahon, B.E., Schnell, R.R., et al. (1987). Predictors of intelligence quotient and intelligence quotient change in persons treated for phenylketonuria early in life. *Pediatrics, 79,* 351–355.

Wappner, R., Cho, S. Kronmal, R.A., et al. (1999). Management of phenylketonuria for optimal outcome: A review of guidelines for phenylketonuria management and a report of surveys of parents, patients, and clinic directors. *Pediatrics, 104,* e68.

Weglage, J., Pietsch, M., Fünders, B., et al. (1995). Neurological findings in early treated phenylketonuria. *Acta Paediatrica, 84,* 411–415.

Whittington, P.F., Alonso, E.M., Boyle, J.T., et al. (1998). Liver transplantation for the treatment of urea cycle disorders. *Journal of Inherited Metabolic Disease, 21,* 112–118.

Winter, S.C. (1993). Diagnosing metabolic disorders: One step at a time. *Contemporary Pediatrics, 10,* 35–63.

19 Dual Diagnosis

Mental Retardation and Psychiatric Disorders

Mark Reber

Upon completion of this chapter, the reader will:

- understand why individuals with mental retardation have a relatively high prevalence of psychiatric disorders

- be able to describe the types and symptoms of psychiatric disorders among people with mental retardation

- be able to discuss interventions for children who have a dual diagnosis of mental retardation and a psychiatric disorder

The burden of intellectual disability is unfortunately not limited to slowness in learning, to social stigma, or even—for those with genetic syndromes and multiple disabilities—to associated medical problems. Children with mental retardation also experience a higher rate of psychiatric disorders than typically developing children do. These disorders can, in turn, have a negative impact on learning, development, and social adaptation, particularly if they go unrecognized and untreated. The presence of mental retardation, moreover, often alters the symptomatic presentation of psychiatric disorders and makes accurate diagnosis more difficult. It is a distinct challenge for parents and people who work with children with mental retardation to be alert to the possible presence of a psychiatric disorder and obtain diagnosis and treatment.

ANNETTE

Annette is an 11-year-old girl with Down syndrome who lives with her parents and her typically developing 6-year-old brother. She attended an early intervention program from age 6 months to 3 years, then a special preschool program to age 6, and then a special education class in elementary school that permitted her to be included in regular education classes with a modified curriculum. Although she had several friends, she was shy, often speaking in a whisper. Her only behavior problems were hyperactivity, some rocking in her seat, and sometimes intruding into other children's physical space. She would cry, however, when feeling overwhelmed or confused. When Annette moved up with her age-mates to the local middle school, she was placed in a self-contained life-skills class. She had some difficulty adjusting to the new, larger building and missed her friends. Her parents noticed that she no longer looked forward to going to school, generally seemed less happy, and occasionally had tears in her eyes when she got off the school bus. For the first time, teachers were reporting noncompliant behavior, including some angry calling out and refusal to follow directions. When later questioned by a psychiatrist, Annette's parents recalled that their daughter seemed less energetic, more sluggish, and more irritable. She fought more with her brother and no longer seemed to enjoy her favorite videos and computer games.

Annette also started to have tantrums "at the drop of a hat." She would scream in response to minor frustration and occasionally "fall out" and cry for extended times. She also started to wake during the night, sometimes staying awake for hours. The school reported that her behavior in the classroom had become unmanageable. Previously noncompliant on occasion, she now screamed and threw things if required to do certain tasks. The school recommended a multidisciplinary team evaluation to consider a more restrictive placement and referred the family to a psychiatrist.

After obtaining the above history and learning of a family history of depression and possible bipolar disorder in several maternal relatives, the psychiatrist conducted a play interview with Annette. She kept her gaze downward; looked sad most of the time; and played in a passive, unenthusiastic manner. After ascertaining from the pediatrician that Annette's thyroid studies were normal, the psychiatrist diagnosed major depressive disorder and started Annette on the antidepressant medication fluoxetine (Prozac). The psychiatrist scheduled several follow-up appointments with the family to monitor the effect of the medication and to give Annette's parents advice on managing their daughter's tantrums. The psychiatrist also recommended that Annette's parents and school staff provide opportunities for Annette to maintain contact with her friends from elementary school and that she take part in social activities, such as a Girl Scouts, that accommodate children with disabilities.

In about 3 weeks, Annette's mood and sleep started to improve; she appeared happier and played games she had previously enjoyed. Her head-banging during tantrums also stopped, but tantrums at school continued. She developed new behavior problems: She became much more hyperactive and began hitting and pushing other children. The school recommended a transfer to a full-time special education placement for children with severe behavior problems. The psychiatrist, however, thinking that the fluoxetine was having a disinhibiting effect on Annette, changed her antidepressant medication to paroxetine (Paxil) and added clonidine (Catapres) for hyperactivity. The psychiatrist also requested that the school defer any plans to transfer Annette while these medicines were being tried and recommended obtaining the services of a behavioral psychologist, who could suggest classroom interventions for Annette. The psychologist conducted a behavior analysis, which showed that the tantrums were enabling Annette to avoid tasks she did not like. Some tasks were modified, a reward-based program was implemented, and a one-to-one aide was assigned to Annette. As a result, she was able to stay in her present classroom, and her tantrums became much less frequent at school and at home.

THE CONCEPT OF DUAL DIAGNOSIS

In the case presented, Annette had two diagnoses: mental retardation and major depression. Since the mid-1980s, the term **dual diagnosis** has come to be used for the presence of a psychiatric disorder in a person with mental retardation (Lovell & Reiss, 1993). This conceptualization of coexisting developmental and psychiatric diagnoses has been an advance in clinical practice because it precludes the simplistic attribution of any behavioral or emotional disturbance to the individual's mental retardation, and it requires that a search for a second (psychiatric) diagnosis be undertaken. As one can tell from the case of Annette, however, providing a psychiatric diagnosis does not automatically account for all of the problems a child may experience, nor does it translate simply into effective intervention. The process of sorting out the complexities of neurodevelopmental, psychological, environmental, and specific biological contributions to a person's symptoms and making a reliable diagnosis is difficult, even for experienced clinicians. Individuals with dual diagnosis are, moreover, an extremely heterogeneous group of people, and individual differences can variably affect outcomes.

A HISTORICAL PERSPECTIVE

The development of intelligence tests in the early 20th century permitted people with mental retardation to be reliably distinguished from individuals with mental illness. During most of the next 70 years, mental retardation and mental illness were regarded as separate, possibly mutually exclusive conditions. Professionals debated whether people with mental retardation could become mentally ill, wondering whether the presence of cognitive impairment precluded the development of the psychological mechanisms that were viewed as the cause of emotional disorders (Scheerenberger, 1987). In the 1960s and 1970s, when behavioral psychologists developed specific techniques to manage aberrant behaviors and teach skills to people with mental retardation, they tended to attribute symptoms exclusively to maladaptive learning and environmental effects. Even among advocates for people with disabilities, there was historically a bias against adding the further stigma of mental illness to that of mental retardation (Harris, 1995).

It is thus only since the 1980s or 1990s that the concept of dual diagnosis has gained acceptance in the community of professionals, advocates, and family members who serve the interests of people with mental retardation. Several phenomena have made this change possible: the establishment of an objective and reliable system for making diagnoses in psychiatric practice, the development of instruments to assess and measure psychiatric symptoms in people with mental retardation, advancement and refinement in the use of psychotropic medications, and the inclusion of mental health practitioners on interdisciplinary teams that evaluate and manage care for individuals with mental retardation.

Of these trends, the one most germane to the concept of dual diagnosis is the increased reliability of psychiatric evaluations. Since the mid-1970s, the leadership of the American and international psychiatric communities, with the support of extensive epidemiologic and clinical research, has developed guidelines for defining, describing, and diagnosing mental disorders. Specific psychiatric disorders are now identified by patterns of psychological, behavioral, and biological symptoms that cluster and may be associated with a particular course of illness. Thus, an episode of major depression is defined in the *Diagnostic and Statistical Manual of Mental Disorders, Fourth Edition, Text Revision* (DSM-IV-TR), of the American Psychiatric Association (2000) by nine specifically described symptoms, five of which (including depressed mood or loss of pleasure) must be present for a 2-week period for the diagnosis to be made. Exclusionary criteria might also have to be met. For example, recent bereavement would rule out the diagnosis of major depression if the symptoms were attributable to appropriate grieving.

PREVALENCE AND CAUSES OF PSYCHIATRIC DISORDERS IN MENTAL RETARDATION

In their landmark study of the epidemiology of childhood psychiatric disorders on the Isle of Wight, Rutter, Graham, and Yule (1970) found emotional disturbances in 7%–10% of typically developing children. Yet, 30%–42% of children with mental retardation demonstrated psychiatric disorders (Rutter et al., 1970). In a Swedish study, Gillberg et al. (1986) found that 57% of children and adolescents with mild mental retardation and 64% with severe mental retardation met diagnostic criteria for a psychiatric disorder. Additional studies have confirmed these results, indicating a four- or fivefold increase in the prevalence of psychiatric disorder in children with mental retardation and the absence of any decline in frequency with age (Borthwick-Duffy, 1994; Bregman, 1991; Koller et al., 1983).

In general, it can be said that children both with and without mental retardation are at risk for the same types of psychiatric disorders. Certain maladaptive behavior disorders, however— **stereotypic movement disorder** (i.e., repetitive, self-stimulating, nonfunctional motor behavior, which may include self-injurious behavior [SIB]) and pica (i.e., the persistent ingesting of nonfood items)—are found principally among individuals with severe to profound levels of intellectual disability.

In some cases, the cause of psychiatric disorders in individuals with mental retardation is the direct result of a biochemical abnormality. For example, in Lesch-Nyhan syndrome (see Appendix B), an inborn error of metabolism, abnormalities in the dopamine neurotransmitter system cause affected individuals to exhibit a compulsive form of SIB (Zimmerman, Jinnah, & Lockhart, 1998). In other cases, conditions that affect the developing brain and cause mental retardation are risk factors for psychiatric disorder. Among such conditions are prenatal exposure to alcohol sufficient to cause fetal alcohol syndrome or alcohol-related neurodevelopmental disorder (see Chapter 7), congenital infections such as rubella (which is associated with autism), and perinatal or neonatal hypoxic-ischemic encephalopathy (see Chapter 5). The increased risk of psychiatric disturbance in neurobiological disorders may be attributable to nonspecific factors such as irritability, affective instability, distractibility, and communication impairments (Feinstein & Reiss, 1996). Risk may also increase in the presence of conditions such as epilepsy, developmental language disorders, and sensory impairments, which are independently associated with an increased incidence of psychiatric disorders.

The cause of most psychiatric disorders among children with mental retardation is likely, however, to be a complex interaction among biological (including genetic), environmental, and psychosocial factors. For example, a young man who has sustained a significant traumatic brain injury (see Chapter 26) with resulting cognitive impairment may become depressed because of a combination of neurotransmitter alterations induced by the brain injury, a familial predisposition to depression, his parents' grief, and his own despair over loss of previous abilities.

When one considers the psychosocial contribution to the cause of psychiatric disorders, the chronic stress and limited opportunities inherent in the life experiences of most children with mental retardation cannot be overemphasized. Phenomena such as ridicule and rejection by peers and society at large; repeated experience of failure at school; limited opportunities to participate in the recreational, social, cultural, and community learning experiences of peers; confused and prejudicial responses to emerging sexuality; and foreclosed or vague future plans all tend to make a person feel ashamed, inadequate, dependent, and without self-esteem (Feinstein & Reiss, 1996). It also has been suggested that the kinds of family dysfunction and social adversity that can contribute to emotional disturbances in typically developing children have a greater impact on children with mental retardation because of their limited understanding and problem-solving abilities, greater need for support, and temperaments that make them less able to cope with such stress. Their family structures, in turn, may be more fragile because of the experience of having a child with mental retardation (Corbett, 1985). Limited availability of or access to community resources and services may increase stress on families and exacerbate minor emotional disturbances. Finally, individuals with mental retardation often experience genuine powerlessness, which greatly increases psychosocial distress. Individuals with severe impairments in particular may have difficulty communicating needs and desires that thus places them at increased risk for emotional and sexual exploitation and abuse (McCreary & Thompson, 1999).

PSYCHIATRIC DIAGNOSES

The following sections describe symptoms of several major psychiatric diagnoses and severe behavior disorders that may present in young people with mental retardation.

Mood Disorders

Mood disorders have been well described in individuals with mental retardation (Johnson et al., 1995; Sovner & Pary, 1993). Researchers estimate that 5%–15% of individuals with mental retardation, compared with 2%–5% of the general population, have mood disorders. There are three significant syndromes of disturbed mood: **dysthymia, major depression,** and **mania.** People who experience mania are also prone to episodes of depression and are diagnosed with **bipolar disorder** (manic depression).

Dysthymia is characterized in DSM-IV-TR by 2 years (1 year in children and adolescents) of chronic, low-grade depressive symptoms that lead to significant functional impairments (American Psychiatric Association, 2000; Jancar & Gunaratne, 1994). These symptoms are typically of a lesser magnitude than those required for a diagnosis of major depression but can go unrecognized because of their chronicity and can cause significant psychosocial morbidity.

Major depression, a common diagnosis, can present as a single episode or a repetitive series of discrete episodes. Prominent symptoms include emotional withdrawal, diminished interest in activities of daily living, problems with sleep and appetite, poor concentration, feelings of worthlessness, inappropriate guilt, and recurrent thoughts of death or suicide. When severe, major depression can be associated with **psychosis** and suicidal behavior. Although vulnerability to depression has a hereditary component, a depressive episode is commonly precipitated by life stresses.

Bipolar disorder is a condition in which a person has episodes of mania and may also experience depression. Mixed states of agitated depression, or dysphoric mania, also occur. During a manic phase, an individual experiences an altered state of mood and behavior for a distinct period of time. Symptoms include an elevated, expansive, or irritable mood. For example, an individual might have inflated self-esteem, decreased need for sleep, excessive or pressured talking, distractibility, a feeling that one's thoughts are racing, and excessive involvement in pleasurable activities that have potentially harmful consequences (e.g., promiscuous sexual behavior). During a depressed phase, a person may experience all of the symptoms of major depression. In a mixed state, a person may show signs of both depression (depressed mood, feelings of worthlessness) and mania (increased energy, racing thoughts) or rapidly alternate between manic and depressive phases. Bipolar disorder appears to have a strong hereditary component, and a gene locus has been reported in certain families (Byerley et al., 1995).

Syndromes of disturbed mood may be hidden or overlooked in people with mental retardation (Hardan & Sahl, 1999; Johnson et al., 1995). Sleep or appetite problems often go unnoticed, and fluctuations in such symptoms as noncompliance, social withdrawal, aggressiveness, irritability, self-injury, or crying spells are often assumed to be components of an individual's personality rather than signs of a psychiatric disorder. Because criteria for diagnosing mood disorders depend in part on a person's ability to report on what he or she is feeling, observable signs need to be given more weight in making the diagnosis in nonverbal people who require extensive support. In 1999, Matson et al. made suggestions for diagnosing depression using an assessment scale with such individuals. The key to the diagnosis of mood disorders in all individuals with mental retardation is recognizing changes from previous levels of functioning or the episodic nature of recurrent symptoms (Myers, 1998; Pary, Levitas, & Hurley, 1999).

Anxiety Disorders

Anxiety disorders, among the most common psychiatric conditions, are associated with feelings of emotional uneasiness, arousal, fear, and a need to escape. For an anxiety disorder to be diagnosed, these feelings and associated symptoms must be severe enough to disrupt normal daily functioning. DSM-IV-TR designates a broad range of anxiety disorders, including specific **phobia,** separation anxiety disorder, social phobia (also called *social anxiety disorder*), **panic disorder,** generalized anxiety disorder, and obsessive-compulsive disorder (OCD). The literature on anxiety disorders among children and adolescents with mental retardation is somewhat sparse, but there is evidence that prevalence is as high as 25%, at least for significant anxiety symptoms (Feinstein & Reiss, 1996).

Phobias, or excessive fear in the presence of certain objects or situations, can occur in children with intellectual disability much as they do in typically developing children. Phobias must be distinguished, however, from normal childhood fears, with the child's developmental age taken into consideration. Similarly, separation anxiety disorder, which involves developmentally inappropriate and excessive anxiety upon separation from the home or attachment figures, must be distinguished from persisting, appropriate **separation anxiety** in the presence of delays in emotional development. Social phobia, which is characterized by extreme discomfort in social situations where the person is subjected to the scrutiny of others, is an unsurprising disorder in children and adolescents with mental retardation, given the social stress to which they are routinely exposed. Socially avoidant behavior with anxiety may also be associated with certain mental retardation syndromes, such as fragile X syndrome (see Chapter 17) and velocardiofacial syndrome (see Appendix B).

The occurrence of OCD, an anxiety disorder with a neurobiological origin involving the basal ganglia and frontal lobe circuits (see Chapter 13), has been recognized with increasing frequency in people with mental retardation (Bodfish et al., 1995). Individuals with OCD have recurrent and persistent thoughts or ideas that may be quite bizarre but cannot be suppressed, even when the individual is aware of their inappropriate nature. Often these obsessive thoughts are associated with compulsive behaviors or repetitive rituals, such as compulsive touching, counting, or excessive hand washing. Obsessive-compulsive symptoms are increased in individuals with pervasive developmental disorders (PDDs; see Chapter 20) and Prader-Willi syndrome (see Appendix B) and can be associated with SIB. In people with lower levels of cognitive functioning, compulsions may be extremely difficult to distinguish from stereotypic mannerisms.

Psychosis

The classical symptoms of psychosis—confused thinking, **delusions,** and hallucinations—may be seen in many psychiatric disorders, including **schizophrenia,** severe depression, mania, and **delirium.** (Delirium is the sudden onset of confusion associated with traumatic brain injury, drug toxicity, or severe medical disorders such as encephalitis that acutely affect brain function.)

Schizophrenia is the most common cause of persistent psychotic symptoms. It is a chronic condition, typically characterized by a deterioration in functional level; prominent hallucinations; delusions (i.e., false beliefs that are often quite bizarre); incoherence; catatonia (i.e., muscle rigidity and stupor); and grossly inappropriate emotional expression. An individual must exhibit these symptoms for at least 6 months to receive a diagnosis of schizophrenia. The more severe manifestations are usually preceded by a period of social withdrawal, apparent loss of skills, peculiar behaviors, altered thought and speech, poor self-care, lack of initiative, and odd ideas. Schizophrenia is extremely rare in prepubertal children, usually having its onset in the second and third decades of life. In individuals with severe levels of intellectual disability, behavior deterioration and disorganization may be the only presenting symptoms.

Concern has been raised by a number of authors about the risk of misdiagnosing people with mental retardation as psychotic because they exhibit so-called "bizarre behaviors" (Myers, 1999; Sovner & Hurley, 1999). Talking out loud to oneself, intense involvement in fantasy, and having imaginary friends can be developmentally appropriate behaviors that should not be otherwise interpreted.

Pervasive Developmental Disorders

PDDs involve poor reciprocal social interactions, difficulty with communication, and impaired imagination (according to one's mental age). It is estimated that one fourth of the individuals with severe to profound levels of intellectual disability have a PDD (see Chapter 20; Bregman, 1991).

Attention-Deficit/Hyperactivity Disorder

Children with mental retardation are diagnosed as having attention-deficit/hyperactivity disorder (ADHD; see Chapter 21) if they exhibit hyperactivity, impulsivity, and inattentiveness that are developmentally inappropriate for age or developmental level and associated with marked functional impairments. The occurrence of ADHD in individuals with mental retardation is two to four times the prevalence in typically developing children (Benson & Aman, 1999; Gillberg et al., 1986). Thus, as many as one in five children with mental retardation may have ADHD. When compared with children with mental retardation without ADHD, children with mental retardation and ADHD have higher levels of fidgeting and off-task behavior in classroom settings (Handen, McAuliffe, et al., 1994). When rated by their mothers, they have higher scores than children with mental retardation without ADHD on measures of depression, delinquency, anxiety, psychosis, and immature social development. When compared with typically developing children with ADHD, however, children with mental retardation and ADHD have been found to be characteristically less aggressive (Benson & Aman, 1999).

ADHD is diagnosed by direct observation of the child, parent report, and standardized rating scales. Pearson and Aman (1994) have suggested that these scales can be used without adjusting for a child's IQ or mental age. Given the high prevalence of ADHD in children with mental retardation and the deleterious impact of ADHD on a child's learning and social development (see Chapter 21), it is extremely important that this diagnosis not be overlooked.

Adjustment Disorders

Acute, time-limited reactions to stress are classified in DSM-IV-TR as **adjustment disorders** and defined by anxiety or disturbances in conduct or mood (American Psychiatric Association, 2000). These maladaptive reactions to an identifiable stressful event include mildly disturbed emotions or behaviors that lead to short-term functional impairment. An example would be a child's persistent anxiety and tearfulness after a hospitalization for medical illness. Adjustment disorder with anxious mood is diagnosed as long as the child's symptoms are not sufficiently severe to meet criteria for other anxiety disorders. Although not proven, it seems likely that these disorders are more common in individuals with mental retardation because of these individuals' exposure to increased levels of stress and decreased adaptability.

Posttraumatic Stress Disorder

An individual may experience a stressor that is severe enough to involve the threat of serious harm or death and that is associated with feelings of intense fear or helplessness. If the individual subsequently develops recurrent and intrusive recollections of the stressful event (flashbacks), nightmares, and intense emotional distress in situations or at times that remind the individual of the trauma, then he or she is diagnosed as having posttraumatic stress disorder (PTSD; Ryan, 1994). Diagnosis of this disorder often depends on a description of symptoms, such as flashbacks, which may be difficult to elicit from a person with mental retardation who has limited verbal skills. As a result, the prevalence of PTSD among children and adolescents with mental retardation is unclear. As these individuals are prone to victimization, however, the disorder is probably not uncommon. Symptoms of PTSD may follow rape, sexual molestation, physical abuse, or a terrifying situation that is beyond the individual's capacity to understand or a caregiver's ability to explain. In all instances, efforts must be made to try to determine the cause and nature of the traumatic event and to protect the child from its recurrence.

Conduct Disorders

Children with conduct disorders display aggressive, destructive, and rule-violating behaviors in repetitive and persistent patterns. These behaviors include bullying, intimidating others, initiating fights, setting fires, deliberately destroying other people's property, stealing, and truancy. Children tend to have conduct disorders when there are models for this kind of behavior in their families or communities, inadequate educational and extracurricular programming in their schools, social neglect or abuse, or detrimental peer influences.

The term *conduct disorder*, which is defined as the violation of social norms and rules, should not be used to describe the behaviors of someone who does not comprehend the nature of such rules. It is often more accurate to speak of children and adolescents with mental retardation as exhibiting conduct problems: episodic aggressive, destructive, and disruptive behavior. It is estimated that 12%–45% of individuals with mental retardation have conduct problems (Bregman, 1991). These problems often result from an inability to verbalize feelings combined with poor impulse control (Lovell & Reiss, 1993), as well as from certain temperamental factors, such as irritability and instability of mood. Depression, pain, fear, and impaired communication skills may also lead to conduct problems in children and adolescents with mental retardation. It is important to interpret a child's behaviors in light of the child's mental age. For example, tantrums that usually disappear after the preschool years may persist into adolescence and lead to aggressive and destructive behavior in some children with more severe cognitive impairment. Many people with aggressive and destructive behaviors have coexisting mood and anxiety disorders.

Substance Abuse Disorders

People with mental retardation appear to have lower rates of drug and alcohol abuse than the general population (Christian & Poling, 1999). There is some suggestion, however, that people who are dually diagnosed are more likely than people with mental retardation only to develop substance abuse problems (see Chapter 7; Longo, 1997). The same genetic, family, and emotional factors that place typically developing adolescents at risk for substance abuse also influence those with mental retardation. In addition, immature judgment, impulsiveness, and a desire for social acceptance may lead individuals with mental retardation to experiment with alcohol or other drugs of abuse (Tyas & Rush, 1993).

There is, however, no evidence that the prior use of psychoactive drugs, such as stimulant medications for ADHD, increases the risk of later substance abuse. The best treatment for substance abuse is prevention through education, starting in elementary school. Once an alcohol or other drug abuse problem does arise, however, the individual should be immediately referred to competent substance abuse specialists.

Maladaptive Behavior Disorders

Some individuals with severe to profound levels of intellectual disability develop behavioral symptoms that are qualitatively different from those seen in people without developmental disabilities. These symptoms, which include repetitive self-stimulating behavior, SIB, and pica, rarely occur in typically developing children.

Individuals who engage in SIB generally display a specific pattern for producing injury. They may bang their heads, bite their hands, pick at their skin, hit themselves with their fists, or poke their eyes. They may do this once or twice a day, in association with tantrums, or as often as several hundred times an hour. Tissue destruction, infection, internal injury, loss of vision, and even death may result. These behaviors may be accompanied by additional repetitive, stereotyped behaviors, such as hand waving and body rocking. When these repetitive behaviors interfere with activities of daily living or result in significant injury to the individual, a diagnosis of stereotypic movement disorder with SIB is made.

Although serious SIB occurs in fewer than 5% of people with mental retardation, these behaviors cause enormous distress to the individuals and their caregivers, can result in severe body injury, and may lead to residential placement with the separation of the individual from the family and from other community contacts. Some children with SIB also demonstrate severe aggressive behavior toward their caregivers or peers.

SIB is a puzzling and disturbing phenomenon that prompts one to ask why these individuals hurt themselves. Although no simple answer exists, there is evidence for both environmental and biological causes, in a context of enormous individual variation (Buitelaar, 1993; Mace & Mauk, 1995; Schroeder et al., 1999). Some children exhibit SIB as a result of environmental events (i.e., **operant control;** Loschen & Osman, 1992). For example, a girl who is nonverbal may demonstrate head banging that is reinforced once she learns that this action captures the attention she craves. In addition to attention, other environmental factors that can reinforce this behavior include access to desired items (e.g., food), avoidance of task demands (e.g., chores), and certain sensory effects (e.g., bright lights from eye pressing; Mace & Mauk, 1995). The inference that the sensations produced through self-induced painful stimulation may somehow be gratifying has led to the notion that SIB plays a role in regulating physiologic states, such as arousal. Guess and Carr (1991) have proposed a biobehavioral model in which the regulation of normal sleep, wake, and arousal patterns is delayed or disturbed in some individuals. These individuals then develop stereotypic movements and SIB as a way to self-regulate arousal in under- or overstimulating environments; they ultimately also get environmental reinforcement for the behavior. Other biological factors are suggested by the increased prevalence of SIB in certain genetic syndromes, including de Lange syndrome, Lesch-Nyhan syndrome, Prader-Willi syndrome, and Rett disorder (see Appendix B). Psychiatric disorders such as autism, depression, mania, and schizophrenia are also risk factors for SIB. General medical conditions and medication side effects can be acute precipitants of SIB. For example, a painful middle-ear infection may lead to head banging. Evaluating any individual for the cause of SIB demands the systematic testing of a broad range of behavioral and biomedical hypotheses (Sternberg, Taylor, & Babkie, 1994).

Although the brain mechanisms underlying most forms of SIB remain unknown, several neurotransmitters are thought to be involved. These include dopamine, which mediates certain reinforcement systems in the brain; serotonin, depletion of which is sometimes associated with violent behavior; gamma-aminobutyric acid (GABA), an inhibitory neurotransmitter; and opioids, the brain's natural painkillers (Verhoeven et al., 1999). As of 2002, there is no effective pharmacologic therapy for SIB that has been derived from studies of these neurotransmitter systems. Targeting them, however, can be one rationale for choosing certain psychotropic medications when attempting to treat SIB that has a prominent biologic component.

Pica, the persistent craving and ingesting of nonfood items, is a typical behavior of toddlers. When children older than 2 years display pica, however, professionals should explore the possibility that the child has a psychiatric disorder or a nutritional deficiency. It should be noted that pica in older children can also be a typical behavior of people with severe to profound levels of intellectual disability. Irrespective of the cause, pica can seriously affect a child's well-being. It can result in toxicity from ingested materials such as medications or lead-containing plaster or paint chips. It also can cause physical damage to the individual's gastrointestinal tract. Behavior management techniques (see Chapter 31) have been found to be the most effective intervention for pica (Johnson, Hunt, & Siebert, 1994).

ASSOCIATED MEDICAL PROBLEMS

It is important to note that many of the symptoms of a psychiatric disorder can actually be caused by a variety of medical disorders and treatments. For example, hypothyroidism, common in individuals with Down syndrome, can cause emotional disturbances that present as anxiety or depression. In excessive (and sometimes therapeutic) dosages, drugs used to treat associated impairments such as epilepsy can cause symptoms of hyperactivity or depression (Alvarez, 1998). Careful evaluation for medical conditions or drug reactions should be a part of any assessment of new-onset behavioral or psychiatric symptoms.

EVALUATION

Psychiatric needs can be met only if parents, teachers, and other staff who work with children with disabilities are attuned to the possible existence of emotional disturbances. Ideally, the referral for evaluation should be made to mental health professionals (e.g., psychiatrists, psychologists, social workers) with specific training, experience, and expertise in the psychiatric disorders of children with mental retardation and other developmental disabilities. Often this requires referral to a specialized tertiary care center with a multidisciplinary team. Less experienced mental health professionals who undertake such evaluations should have access to consultation from a specialized center.

The mental health professional first takes a detailed history of the current symptoms and problematic behaviors from parents or other caregivers. For example, identification of recent changes in sleep pattern, appetite, or mood provides important evidence of depression. In addition, an individual and family medical history should be obtained. The family history may reveal, for example, other members with depression. A review of the individual's past medical and psychological assessments may indicate prior behavior or psychiatric problems. Following the history taking, an interview is conducted posing both structured and open-ended questions to the child and parents. If impairments in communication and cognitive skills are significant, the professional can still gain important information from the direct observation of the child both alone and in the presence of the parents (King et al., 1994).

The evaluation should also focus on the social system in which the psychiatric disorder occurs. Thus, the professional should evaluate the current level of family functioning by assessing 1) family members' ability to cope with the child's psychiatric disorder and therapy; 2) their current morale, problem-solving abilities, external social supports, and practical resources (e.g., finances, insurance); 3) the system of beliefs that sustains their efforts; and 4) the stability of the parents' relationship. It is important to understand how individual family members are reacting and adjusting to the child's underlying developmental disability as well as any current mental health problems (see Chapter 36).

Following the comprehensive interview, the child may be referred for psychological testing or behavioral assessment. Although standardized behavior rating scales are available for use in people with mental retardation, they are insufficient by themselves as diagnostic tools. The range of developmental levels and behavioral baselines exhibited by these individuals may not be able to be covered by a single, structured psychological testing instrument. These instruments are important, however, for confirming or adding to information obtained from the history and interview. They can also be extremely helpful in measuring changes that occur during the course of intervention (Aman, Burrow, & Wolford, 1995; Demb et al., 1994; Linaker & Helle, 1994; Reiss & Valenti-Hein, 1994).

Standardized rating scales may be combined with a functional behavior analysis. This type of assessment is most useful for children with severe behavioral abnormalities for which specific family or behavior therapies are being considered. Behavior analysis provides direct observation of the child in a natural setting, yielding a clear description of the abnormal behavior itself and its antecedents and consequences (see Chapter 31).

After the evaluations have been completed, the professional can begin to work to formulate an intervention plan based not only on the psychiatric diagnosis but also on the developmental level of the child, accompanying medical conditions, the family's strengths and weaknesses, and the needs and limitations of the settings where the child spends his or her time.

INTERVENTION

The foundation for treating a child or adolescent with both mental retardation and a psychiatric disorder is a comprehensive plan that addresses habilitation and education, the child's emotional needs, social stressors, the family's need for support, and the specific psychiatric diagnosis and behavior problems. Implementing such a plan involves interdisciplinary teamwork incorporating various approaches, including special education programs, rehabilitation therapy, psychotherapy, behavior therapy, and pharmacological management.

Special Education Programs

Because the educational setting can help other interventions, it is essential that the school be part of the therapy program and that collaboration and communication among teachers, parents, and therapists be encouraged. Children with dual diagnosis are eligible, by reason of their developmental disability, for special education services under the Individuals with Disabilities Education Act Amendments of 1997 (PL 105-17) and have the right to be educated in the least restrictive environment (see Chapter 30). Because problems with behavior or specific psychiatric symptoms (e.g., mood swings, aggression) may be the main obstacle to placement in more inclusive environments, it is important for psychiatric disorders to be diagnosed and behavior problems to be specifically addressed in a child's individualized education program.

The basic instructional approach, as with all children with developmental disabilities, should be individualized and based on a comprehensive understanding of the child's strengths and weaknesses. Emphasis on language and communication, problem-solving skills, attention and motivation, and self-instruction benefits children with dual diagnosis. Many of these children's difficulties with aggression, tantrums, and poor frustration tolerance can be treated by improving these children's ability to communicate their feelings and needs and to solve interpersonal problems. Classroom approaches that have been successful with typically developing children with ADHD (see Chapter 21) can be used with children with mental retardation who have ADHD. School psychologists should be involved in active consultation to special education teachers, providing behavior analyses on which specific behavior management plans can be based as well as **psychoeducational** assessments.

Children with severe emotional and behavior problems are often best served in small classes with a high teacher–student ratio, where teachers and assistants can record data on specific behaviors, implement behavior management programs, and provide emotional support. Many children can then move on to inclusion in general education classrooms, where they can benefit from broader social contacts and the behavioral modeling of other students.

In secondary school, especially in the later years when the curriculum is focused on transition to adult life, particular attention needs to be paid to the limitations imposed by psychiatric illness. Adolescents and young adults with dual diagnosis need more intensive and longer supervision in community and work settings and more careful planning for their transition to community living and adult services. Their individualized transition plans should reflect their emotional needs. Adapting to life after school is a major challenge for all individuals with mental retardation, but this period is fraught with particular risk for those with psychiatric disorders.

Rehabilitation Therapy

Rehabilitation therapy programs can have a positive impact on the child with dual diagnosis. There is evidence that language impairments significantly contribute to the development of certain behavior problems. Some aggressive and self-injurious behaviors have been linked to the inability to communicate needs, and teaching functional communication skills has been shown to decrease SIB. Thus, speech-language therapy and training in augmentative and alternative communication systems (see Chapter 12) may be an important part of the therapy program. Similarly, if the child has a physical disability, the pain from contractures, an inability to ambulate, or difficulty reaching for desired objects may lead to behavior and mood alterations. Physical and occupational therapy may result in an improvement in motor function, with associated improvement in behavior and mood.

Psychotherapy

There is ample evidence that psychotherapy (individual, group, and family) can benefit a child or adolescent with dual diagnosis, if it is adapted to the child's mental age and communication abilities (Hollins, Sinason, & Thompson, 1994; Nezu & Nezu, 1994; Sigman, 1985). Goals of therapy are to relieve symptoms and help the child to understand the nature of his or her disability and associated feelings and to gain a recognition of and appreciation for his or her strengths. Psychotherapy, particularly group work, can also enhance social skills and help the child deal with stigmatization, rejection, peer pressure, and attempts at exploitation (American Academy of Child and Adolescent Psychiatry, 1999). Regrettably, individuals with mental retardation are seriously underserved with this treatment, despite the fact that psychotherapy can provide a supportive relationship, help restore self-esteem, and enhance the capacity to recognize and master emotional conflicts and solve problems. Psychotherapy also can be added to behavior therapy and pharmacotherapy when these approaches have not adequately resolved symptoms or improved quality of life. Ideally, the therapist should have expertise in working with individuals with mental retardation.

Behavior Therapy

Behavior therapy is perhaps the most widely researched therapeutic intervention for children and adolescents with mental retardation (see Chapter 31). There is extensive literature supporting the effectiveness of behavioral approaches in psychiatric disorders (National Institutes of Health, 1989). When used in conjunction with comprehensive assessment, accurate medical and psychiatric diagnoses, and programmatic intervention, behavior therapy is among the most powerful available interventions. As with psychotherapy and pharmacotherapy, however, it should be implemented only under the supervision of licensed professionals who have been specifically trained in this methodology (see Chapter 31).

Pharmacological Management

Since the 1970s, pharmacotherapy has become an established mode of treatment for psychiatric disorders in children and adolescents (Baumeister, Todd, & Sevin, 1993; Campbell & Cueva, 1995a, 1995b; Reiss & Aman, 1998; Santosh & Baird, 1999). Although most guidelines for using psychoactive medicines come from studies performed with adults without mental retardation, a few well-controlled studies of the efficacy of pharmacological treatment of psychiatric disorders among children with and without mental retardation have been conducted. It appears that typically developing children and children with mental retardation respond to drug treatments for psychiatric disorders in much the same way. The only exception to this rule is that individuals with mental retardation may respond at lower dosages than their typically developing peers and may be more sensitive to certain side effects, such as disinhibition and movement disorders.

There has historically been concern about the overuse or inappropriate use of psychoactive medications with individuals with mental retardation because of incidents in the 1950s involving the abuse of major tranquilizers for the purpose of behavior control in residential institutions (Aman & Singh, 1988). Now, appropriate use of pharmacotherapy assumes that a comprehensive medical and psychiatric evaluation has been completed, a psychiatric diagnosis has been made, and the medication has been selected because of its known effects in relieving target symptoms associated with the psychiatric diagnosis. As indicated previously, the use of medicine should be only one part of a comprehensive intervention plan (American Academy of Child and Adolescent Psychiatry, 1999). Generally speaking, it is impossible to predict whether a particular medicine will be helpful to a specific patient or whether side effects may prove to be intolerable to that individual. In the clinical situation, even medicines that have been appropriately selected are used empirically, with ongoing monitoring to determine whether they have the intended salutary effect and continue to be tolerated by the patient.

The primary use of antidepressant medication is to treat major depression and dysthymia. Many studies in adults without mental retardation support their use in depressive disorders. Emslie et al. (1997) demonstrated the effectiveness of fluoxetine (Prozac) in treating depression in children and adolescents in a scientifically sound, placebo-controlled study. Other studies have shown that sertraline (Zoloft) and fluvoxamine (Luvox) can treat depression in typically developing children (Ambrosini et al., 1999; Apter et al., 1994). These three medications are newer antidepressants called selective **serotonin reuptake inhibitors** (SSRIs). Other SSRIs are paroxetine (Paxil) and citalopram (Celexa). Although there have been no large studies of the treatment of depression with these agents in children and adolescents with mental retardation, there have been enough reported cases to demonstrate that these medicines have a good side-effect profile and can be safely used with these individuals (Sovner et al., 1998). It has thus become standard practice to use SSRIs when pharmacologic treatment of depression is needed in youth with mental retardation.

Antidepressants are, however, useful for more than depression. A number of studies have shown that SSRIs significantly reduce obsessive-compulsive behaviors in otherwise typical adults and children with OCD, as does clomipramine (Anafranil), an older tricyclic antidepressant with potent effects on the neurotransmitter serotonin. These medications have therefore been used to treat obsessive-compulsive and other repetitive behaviors, such as SIB and aggression, in children and adults with mental retardation (Bodfish & Madison, 1993; Cook et al., 1992; Davanzo et al., 1998; Garber et al., 1992; Lewis et al., 1996).

Stimulant medications such as methylphenidate (Ritalin, Concerta, Metadate, Methylin), dextroamphetamine (Dexedrine, DextroStat), and mixed amphetamine salts (Adderall) are the primary pharmacologic treatments for ADHD in typically developing children (see Chapter 21). They have also been proven effective in reducing hyperactivity, impulsivity, and distractibility in children with mental retardation requiring intermittent to limited support (Aman et al., 1993; Handen, Janosky, et al., 1994). Side effects, including appetite suppression, sleep disturbance, irritability, and worsening of stereotypies, are generally mild and well tolerated among these individuals. These medications may be less effective and less tolerated among children with severe levels of intellectual disability. Another type of medication, clonidine (Catapres) has been used as a second-line treatment for ADHD, with some positive effects in typically developing children (Connor, Fletcher, & Swanson, 1999). Clonidine has been used with people with mental retardation to treat ADHD and **tics** and to reduce hyperarousal and hyperactivity in fragile X syndrome (Hagerman, 1996b). Side effects that may limit clonidine's use are sedation and lowering of heart rate and blood pressure.

Bipolar mood disorders are complicated to treat with medication because separate treatments are needed for manic and depressive episodes and to maintain mood stability between episodes. **Antipsychotic medications** also are frequently needed to control mania and treat psychotic thought processes, which can arise during both manic and depressed phases. Lithium and the anticonvulsants divalproex sodium (Depakote) and carbamazepine (Tegretol) are used to treat mania and to maintain mood stability. They can have significant side effects, which are usually tolerated because of the severity of the disorders they are used to treat, but they require careful monitoring. Side effects of lithium include increased urination, tremor, gastrointestinal disturbance, and impaired functioning of the thyroid gland. Divalproex sodium and carbamazepine can cause sedation and can affect the concentration of certain blood cells and the functioning of the liver. There is also some evidence that lithium is useful for reducing aggressive behavior (Alessi et al., 1994; Campbell, Kafantaris, & Cueva, 1995). Carbamazepine and divalproex sodium have also been used in this nonspecific manner, but their primary use in people with mental retardation is for seizures and bipolar disorder. When antidepressants are used to treat depression in bipolar disorder, care must be taken to limit their duration of use because they can destabilize mood and even induce manic episodes.

Antipsychotic medications are indicated for the treatment of psychotic disorders such as mania and schizophrenia. Their use has been subject to considerable debate when they are prescribed for individuals with mental retardation with the goal of treating behavior problems such as aggression, irritability, noncompliance, and self-injury. Although these medications may be appropriate for use in treating self-injury and other stereotypic behavior (Aman, 1993; Baumeister, Sevin, & King, 1998), they should not be used to control noncompliant behavior. This is a form of chemical restraint and is not ethically defensible when given to an individual who cannot understand and consent to this use and who poses no immediate threat to the safety of self or others.

Several of these antipsychotic drugs carry a significant risk of serious side effects, especially when used on a long-term basis. Among these side effects is **tardive dyskinesia,** a condition involving involuntary movements. Because tardive dyskinesia is occasionally masked by the drug that causes the disorder, it might not be observed until the medication is decreased or withdrawn. The abnormal movements occur around the mouth and face but can also involve the limbs and trunk. These movements can be incapacitating and disfiguring. They may stop, diminish, or persist indefinitely after cessation of the medication. Newer medications—atypical antipsychotics such as risperidone (Risperdal), olanzapine (Zyprexa), quetiapine (Seroquel), and clozapine (Clozaril)—are thought to be less likely to cause movement disorders and are better tolerated than the older medications (Leucht et al., 1999). Clozapine has been shown to treat psychosis in adults with mental retardation (Buzan et al., 1998), and risperidone has been shown to be useful in reducing aggression and SIB in these individuals (Cohen, Ihrig, & Lott, 1998). Two major controlled studies of risperidone have been completed and show significant reduction in disruptive behavior in children and adolescents with mental retardation (Aman et al., 2000; Turgay et al., 2000).

Other potentially useful pharmacological agents for treating SIB and aggression include **opiate antagonists** and **beta-adrenergic blockers** (Aman, 1993; Fraser et al., 1998; Osman & Loschen, 1992; Sandman et al., 1998). The use of opiate antagonists such as naltrexone (Trexan, REVIA) is based on a hypothesis linking certain subtypes of SIB to the release of endogenous opiate-like substances into the central nervous system. Opiates are highly reinforcing, and this hypothesis postulates that SIB occurs often in certain individuals because it is reinforced by the release of opiate-like substances. Opiate antagonists block the chemical effects of opiates. Studies of the use of these agents for SIB have not, however, demonstrated consistent results. Other agents that have shown some usefulness in decreasing aggressive and impulsive behaviors are beta-adrenergic blockers such as propranolol (Inderal). These medications have an unclear mechanism of action but are relatively safe when used and monitored appropriately and can be helpful for some individuals with sudden, impulsive violent outbursts.

Several principles are important to consider when psychoactive medications are being used as part of a comprehensive intervention plan. First, the psychiatric disorder and symptoms must be correctly identified and periodically reevaluated. Second, medications should be used at the lowest effective dosage. Third, an adequate trial (in terms of period of time and amount) of one medication should occur before switching to a new drug. Fourth, polypharmacy, or the use of multiple medications for the same condition, should be avoided if possible. Exceptions to this rule do exist, particularly with bipolar disorder and when an individual has multiple symptoms that do not respond sufficiently to a single medication. Because of the complexity in adjusting dosage and assessing side effects, individuals receiving multiple psychoactive drugs must be carefully monitored, with ongoing attention to the risk–benefit ratio. Finally, decisions about starting, changing, or adding medications should be made only after careful explanation of anticipated benefits and potential harmful effects to the family and, if developmentally appropriate, the child (Towbin, 1995). Carefully used pharmacotherapy has become an integral part of the management of psychiatric disorders in individuals with dual diagnosis. (See Appendix C for more information on commonly used medications.)

SUMMARY

When compared with their typically developing peers, children and adolescents with mental retardation are at increased risk of developing psychiatric disorders. The reasons for this are multiple and interactive, deriving in part from brain dysfunction, psychosocial adversity, associated medical disorders, and genetic factors. The types of psychiatric disorders experienced by individuals with mental retardation are the same as those found in the general population, but symptomatic presentation may be altered and diagnosis may be more difficult because of cognitive and linguistic limitations. Children with dual diagnosis benefit from multimodal intervention, including special education, rehabilitation, psychotherapy, behavior therapy, and pharmacotherapy. Intervention is most effective when parents and caregivers are alert to the possibility of a psychiatric disorder, when prompt referral is made to a mental health professional with experience in mental retardation, and when a multidisciplinary team is involved in the child's care.

REFERENCES

Alessi, N., Naylor, M.W., Ghaziuddin, M., et al. (1994). Update on lithium carbonate therapy in children and adolescents. *Journal of the American Academy of Child and Adolescent Psychiatry, 33*, 291–304.

Alvarez, N. (1998). Barbiturates in the treatment of epilepsy in people with intellectual disability. *Journal of Intellectual Disability, 42*(Suppl. 1), 16–23.

Aman, M.G. (1993). Efficacy of psychotropic drugs for reducing self-injurious behavior in the developmental disabilities. *Annals of Clinical Psychiatry, 5*, 171–188.

Aman, M.G., Burrow, W.H., & Wolford, P.L. (1995). The Aberrant Behavior Checklist Community: Factor validity and effect of subject variables for adults in group homes. *American Journal on Mental Retardation, 100*, 293–294.

Aman, M.G., Findling, R.L., Derivan, A.T., et al. (2000, May 13–17). *Risperidone versus placebo for severe conduct disorder in children with mental retardation.* Paper presented at the annual meeting of the American Psychiatric Association, Chicago.

Aman, M.G., Kern, R.A., McGee, E.E., et al. (1993). Fenfluramine and methylphenidate in children with mental retardation and ADHD. *Journal of the American Academy of Child and Adolescent Psychiatry, 32*, 851–859.

Aman, M.G., & Singh, N.N. (Eds.). (1988). *Psychopharmacology of the developmental disabilities.* New York: Springer-Verlag.

Ambrosini, P.J., Wagner, K.D., Biederman, J., et al. (1999). Multicenter open-label sertraline study in adolescent outpatients with major depression. *Journal of the American Academy of Child and Adolescent Psychiatry, 38*, 566–572.

American Academy of Child and Adolescent Psychiatry (1999). Practice parameters for the assessment and treatment of children, adolescents and adults with mental retardation and comorbid mental disorders. *Journal of the*

American Academy of Child and Adolescent Psychiatry, 38 (Suppl. 12), 5S–31S.

American Psychiatric Association. (2000). *Diagnostic and statistical manual of mental disorders* (4th ed., Text rev.). Washington, DC: Author.

Apter, A., Ratzoni, G., King, R.A., et al. (1994). Fluvoxamine open-label treatment of adolescent inpatients with obsessive-compulsive disorder or depression. *Journal of the American Academy of Child and Adolescent Psychiatry, 33*, 342–348.

Baumeister, A.A., Sevin, J.A., & King, B.H. (1998). Neuroleptic medications. In S. Reiss & M.G. Aman (Eds.), *Psychotropic medications and developmental disabilities: The international consensus handbook* (pp. 133–150). Columbus: The Ohio State University, Nisonger Center for Mental Retardation and Developmental Disabilities.

Baumeister, A.A., Todd, M.E., & Sevin, J.A. (1993). Efficacy and specificity of pharmacological therapies for behavioral disorders in persons with mental retardation. *Clinical Neuropharmacology, 16*, 271–294.

Benson, B.A., & Aman, M.G. (1999). Disruptive behavior disorders in children with mental retardation. In H.C. Quay & A.E. Hogan (Eds.), *Handbook of disruptive behavior disorders* (pp. 559–578). New York: Kluwer Academic/Plenum Publishers.

Bodfish, J.W., Crawford, T.W., Powell, S.B., et al. (1995). Compulsions in adults with mental retardation: Prevalence, phenomenology, and comorbidity with stereotypy and self-injury. *American Journal on Mental Retardation, 100*, 183–192.

Bodfish, J.W., & Madison, J.T. (1993). Diagnosis and fluoxetine treatment of compulsive behavior disorder of adults with mental retardation. *American Journal on Mental Retardation, 98*, 360–367.

Borthwick-Duffy, S.A. (1994). Epidemiology and prevalence of psychopathology in people with mental retardation. *Journal of Consulting and Clinical Psychology, 62,* 17–27.

Bregman, J.D. (1991). Current developments in the understanding of mental retardation, Part II: Psychopathology. *Journal of the American Academy of Child and Adolescent Psychiatry, 30,* 861–872.

Buitelaar, J.K. (1993). Self-injurious behavior in retarded children: Clinical phenomena and biological mechanisms. *Acta Paedopsychiatrica, 56,* 105–111.

Buzan, R.D., Dubovsky, S.L., Firestone, D., et al. (1998). Use of clozapine in 10 mentally retarded adults. *Journal of Neuropsychiatry and Clinical Neuroscience, 10,* 93–95.

Byerley, W., Holik, J., Hoff, M., et al. (1995). Search for a gene predisposing the manic depression on chromosome 21. *American Journal of Medical Genetics, 60,* 231–233.

Campbell, M., & Cueva, J.E. (1995a). Psychopharmacology in child and adolescent psychiatry: A review of the past seven years, part I. *Journal of the American Academy of Child and Adolescent Psychiatry, 34,* 1124–1132.

Campbell, M., & Cueva, J.E. (1995b). Psychopharmacology in child and adolescent psychiatry: A review of the past seven years, part II. *Journal of the American Academy of Child and Adolescent Psychiatry, 34,* 1262–1272.

Campbell, M., Kafantaris, V., & Cueva, J.E. (1995). An update on the use of lithium carbonate in aggressive children and adolescents with conduct disorder. *Psychopharmacology Bulletin, 31,* 93–102.

Christian, L., & Poling, A. (1997). Drug abuse in persons with mental retardation: A review. *American Journal on Mental Retardation, 102,* 126–136.

Cohen, S.A., Ihrig, K., Lott, R.S., et al. (1998). Risperidone for aggression and self-injurious behavior in adults with mental retardation. *Journal of Autism and Developmental Disorders, 28,* 229–233.

Connor, D.F., Fletcher, K.E., & Swanson, J.M. (1999). A meta-analysis of clonidine for symptoms of attention-deficit hyperactivity disorder. *Journal of the American Academy of Child and Adolescent Psychiatry, 38,* 1551–1559.

Cook, E., Rowlett, R., Jaselskis, C., et al. (1992). Fluoxetine treatment of children and adults with autistic disorder and mental retardation. *Journal of the American Academy of Child and Adolescent Psychiatry, 31,* 739–745.

Corbett, J.A. (1985). Mental retardation: Psychiatric aspects. In M. Rutter & L. Hersov (Eds.), *Child and adolescent psychiatry: Modern approaches* (2nd ed., pp. 661–678). Oxford, England: Blackwell Scientific Publications.

Davanzo, P.A., Belin, T.R., Widawski, M.H., et al. (1998). Paroxetine treatment of aggression and self-injury in persons with mental retardation. *American Journal on Mental Retardation, 102,* 427–437.

Demb, H.B., Brier, N., Huron, R., et al. (1994). The adolescent behavior checklist: Normative data and sensitivity and specificity of a screening tool for diagnosable psychiatric disorders in adolescents with mental retardation and other developmental disabilities. *Research in Developmental Disabilities, 15,* 151–165.

Emslie, G.J., Rush, A.J., Weinberg, W.A., et al. (1997). Double-blind placebo-controlled trial of fluoxetine in depressed children and adolescents. *Archives of General Psychiatry, 54,* 1031–1037.

Feinstein, C., & Reiss, A.L. (1996). Psychiatric disorder in mentally retarded children and adolescents: The challenges of meaningful diagnosis. *Child and Adolescent Psychiatric Clinics of North America, 5,* 827–852.

Fraser, W.I., Ruedrich, S., Kern, M., et al. (1998). Beta-adrenergic blockers. In S. Reiss & M.G. Aman (Eds.), *Psychotropic medications and developmental disabilities: The inter-national consensus handbook* (pp. 271–289). Columbus: The Ohio State University, Nisonger Center for Mental Retardation and Developmental Disabilities.

Garber, H.J., McGonigle, J.J., Slomka, G.T., et al. (1992). Clomipramine treatment of stereotypic behaviors and self-injury in patients with developmental disabilities. *Journal of the American Academy of Child and Adolescent Psychiatry, 31,* 1157–1160.

Gillberg, C., Persson, E., Grufman, M., et al. (1986). Psychiatric disorders in mildly and severely mentally retarded urban children and adolescents: Epidemiological aspects. *British Journal of Psychiatry, 149,* 68–74.

Guess, D., & Carr, E. (1991). Emergence and maintenance of stereotypy and self-injury. *American Journal on Mental Retardation, 96,* 299–320.

Hagerman, R.J. (1996b). Medical follow-up and pharmacotherapy. In R.J. Hagerman & A. Cronister (Eds.), *Fragile X syndrome: Diagnosis, treatment, and intervention* (2nd ed., pp. 283–331). Baltimore: The Johns Hopkins University Press.

Handen, B.L., Janosky, J., McAuliffe, S., et al. (1994). Prediction of response to methylphenidate among children with ADHD and mental retardation. *Journal of the American Academy of Child and Adolescent Psychiatry, 33,* 1185–1193.

Handen, B.L., McAuliffe, S., Janosky, J., et al. (1994). Classroom behavior and children with mental retardation: Comparison of children with and without ADHD. *Journal of Abnormal Child Psychology, 22,* 267–280.

Hardan, A., & Sahl, R. (1999). Suicidal behavior in children and adolescents with developmental disorders. *Research in Developmental Disabilities, 20,* 287–296.

Harris, J.C. (1995). *Developmental neuropsychiatry* (Vol. II). New York: Oxford University Press.

Hollins, S., Sinason, V., & Thompson, S. (1994). Individual, group and family psychotherapy. In N. Bouras (Ed.), *Mental health in mental retardation.* Cambridge, England: Cambridge University Press.

Individuals with Disabilities Education Act Amendments of 1997, PL 105-17, 20 U.S.C. §§ 1400 *et seq.*

Jancar, J., & Gunaratne, I.J. (1994). Dysthymia and mental handicap. *British Journal of Psychiatry, 164,* 691–693.

Johnson, C.R., Handen, B.L., Lubetsky, M.J., et al. (1995). Affective disorders in hospitalized children and adolescents with mental retardation: A retrospective study. *Research in Developmental Disabilities, 16,* 221–231.

Johnson, C.R., Hunt, F.M., & Siebert, M.J. (1994). Discrimination training in the treatment of pica and food scavenging. *Behavior Modification, 18,* 214–229.

King, B.H., DeAntonio, C., McCracken, J.T., et al. (1994). Psychiatric consultation in severe and profound mental retardation. *American Journal of Psychiatry, 151,* 1802–1808.

Koller, H., Richardson, S.W., Katz, M., et al. (1983). Behavioral disturbance since childhood in a 5-year birth cohort of all mentally retarded young adults in a city. *American Journal of Mental Deficiency, 87,* 386–395.

Leucht, S., Pitschel-Walz, G., Abraham, D., et al. (1999). Efficacy and extrapyramidal side-effects of the new antipsychotics olanzapine, quetiapine, risperidone and sertindole compared to conventional antipsychotics and placebo. A meta-analysis of randomized controlled trials. *Schizophrenia Research, 34,* 51–68.

Lewis, M.H., Bodfish, J.W., Powell, S.B., et al. (1996). Clomipramine treatment for self-injurious behavior of individuals with mental retardation: A double-blind comparison with placebo. *American Journal on Mental Retardation, 100,* 654–655.

Linaker, O.M., & Helle, J. (1994). Validity of the schizophrenia diagnosis of the Psychopathology Instrument For Mentally Retarded Adults (PIMRA): A comparison of schizophrenic patients with and without mental retardation. *Research in Developmental Disabilities, 15,* 473–486.

Longo, L.P. (1997). Alcohol abuse in persons with developmental disabilities. *The Habilitative Mental Healthcare Newsletter, 16,* 61–64.

Loschen, E.L., & Osman, O.T. (1992). Self-injurious behavior in the developmentally disabled: Assessment techniques. *Psychopharmacology Bulletin, 28,* 433–438.

Lovell, R.W., & Reiss, A.L. (1993). Dual diagnoses: Psychiatric disorders in developmental disabilities. *Pediatric Clinics of North America, 40,* 579–592.

Mace, F.C., & Mauk, J.E. (1995). Bio-behavioral diagnosis and treatment of self-injury. *Mental Retardation and Developmental Disabilities Research Reviews, 1,* 104–110.

Matson, J.L., Rush, K.S., Hamilton, M., et al. (1999). Characteristics of depression as assessed by the Diagnostic Assessment for the Severely Handicapped-II (DASH-II). *Research in Developmental Disabilities, 20,* 305–313.

McCreary, B.D., & Thompson, J. (1999). Psychiatric aspects of sexual abuse involving persons with developmental disabilities. *Canadian Journal of Psychiatry, 44,* 350–355.

Myers, B.A. (1998). Major depression in persons with moderate to profound mental retardation: Clinical presentations and case illustrations. *Mental Health Aspects of Developmental Disabilities, 1,* 57–68.

Myers, B.A. (1999). Psychiatric disorders mimicking psychotic disorders in people with mental retardation. *Mental Health Aspects of Developmental Disabilities, 2,* 113–121.

National Institutes of Health. (1989). Treatment of destructive behaviors in persons with developmental disabilities. *NIH Consensus Development Conference Statement, 7(9),* 1–14.

Nezu, C.M., & Nezu, A.M. (1994). Outpatient psychotherapy for adults with mental retardation and concomitant psychopathology: Research and clinical imperatives. *Journal of Consulting and Clinical Psychology, 62,* 34–42.

Osman, O.T., & Loschen, E.L. (1992). Self-injurious behavior in the developmentally disabled: Pharmacological treatment. *Psychopharmacology Bulletin, 28,* 439–449.

Pary, R.J., Levitas, A.S., & Hurley, A.D. (1999). Diagnosis of bipolar disorder in persons with developmental disabilities. *Mental Health Aspects of Developmental Disabilities, 2,* 37–49.

Pearson, D.A., & Aman, M.G. (1994). Ratings of hyperactivity and developmental indices: Should clinicians correct for developmental level? *Journal of Autism and Developmental Disorders, 24,* 395–411.

Reiss, S., & Aman, M.G. (Eds.). (1998). *Psychotropic medications and developmental disabilities: The international consensus handbook.* Columbus: The Ohio State University, Nisonger Center for Mental Retardation and Developmental Disabilities.

Reiss, S., & Valenti-Hein, D. (1994). Development of a psychopathology rating scale for children with mental retardation. *Journal of Consulting and Clinical Psychology, 62,* 28–33.

Rutter, M., Graham, P., & Yule, W. (1970). *A neuropsychiatric study in childhood.* London: Spastics International.

Ryan, R. (1994). Posttraumatic stress disorder in persons with developmental disabilities. *Community Mental Health Journal, 30,* 45–54.

Sandman, C.A., Thompson, T., Barrett, R.P., et al. (1998). Opiate blockers. In S. Reiss & M.G. Aman (Eds.), *Psychotropic medications and developmental disabilities: The international consensus handbook* (pp. 291–302). Columbus: The Ohio State University, Nisonger Center for Mental Retardation and Developmental Disabilities.

Santosh, P.J., & Baird, G. (1999). Psychopharmacotherapy in children and adults with intellectual disability. *Lancet, 354,* 233–242.

Scheerenberger, R.C. (1987). *A history of mental retardation: A quarter century of promise.* Baltimore: Paul H. Brookes Publishing Co.

Schroeder, S.R., Reese, R.M., Hellings, J., et al. (1999). The causes of self-injurious behavior and their clinical implications. In N.A. Wieseler & R.H. Hanson (Eds.), *Challenging behavior of persons with mental health disorders and severe developmental disabilities* (pp. 65–87). Washington, DC: American Association on Mental Retardation.

Sigman, M. (1985). Individual and group psychotherapy with mentally retarded adolescents. In M. Sigman (Ed.), *Children with emotional disorders and developmental disabilities* (pp. 259–276). New York: Grune & Stratton.

Sovner, R., & Hurley, A.D. (1999). Facts and fictions concerning mental illness in people with mental retardation and developmental disabilities. In N.A. Wieseler & R.H. Hanson (Eds.), *Challenging behavior of persons with mental health disorders and severe developmental disabilities* (pp. 89–99). Washington, DC: American Association on Mental Retardation.

Sovner, R., & Pary, R.J. (1993). Affective disorders in developmentally disabled persons. In J.L. Matson & R.P. Barrett (Eds.), *Psychopathology in the mentally retarded* (pp. 87–147). Needham Heights, MA: Allyn & Bacon.

Sovner, R., Pary, R.J., Dosen, A., et al. (1998). Antidepressants. In S. Reiss & M.G. Aman (Eds.), *Psychotropic medications and developmental disabilities: The international consensus handbook* (pp. 179–200). Columbus: The Ohio State University, Nisonger Center for Mental Retardation and Developmental Disabilities.

Sternberg, L., Taylor, R.L., & Babkie, A. (1994). Correlates of interventions with self-injurious behavior. *Journal of Intellectual Disability Research, 38,* 475–485.

Towbin, K.E. (1995). Evaluation, establishing the treatment alliance, and informed consent. *Child and Adolescent Psychiatric Clinics of North America, 4,* 1–14.

Turgay, A., Snyder, R., Fisman, S., et al. (2000, October 24–29). *Risperidone versus placebo for conduct disorder and other disruptive behavior disorders in children with subaverage IQ.* Paper presented at the 47th annual meeting of the American Academy of Child and Adolescent Psychiatry New York.

Tyas, S., & Rush, B. (1993). The treatment of disabled persons with alcohol and drug problems: Results of a survey of addiction services. *Journal of Studies on Alcohol, 54,* 275–282.

Verhoeven, W.M., Tuinier, S., van den Berg, Y.W., et al. (1999). Stress and self-injurious behavior; hormonal and serotonergic parameters in mentally retarded subjects. *Pharmacopsychiatry, 32,* 13–20.

Zimmerman, A.W., Jinnah, H.A., & Lockhart, P.J. (1998). Behavioral neuropharmacology. *Mental Retardation and Developmental Disabilities Research Reviews, 4,* 26–35.

20 Pervasive Developmental Disorders

Kenneth E. Towbin, Joyce E. Mauk, and Mark L. Batshaw

Upon completion of this chapter, the reader will:

- be familiar with the three central features of autism and of the spectrum of pervasive developmental disorders

- understand the differences between autistic disorder, Asperger disorder, pervasive developmental disorder-not otherwise specified, childhood disintegrative disorder, and Rett disorder

- know how to distinguish pervasive developmental disorders from other developmental disabilities

- be familiar with interventions for and outcomes with the pervasive developmental disorders

The term *pervasive developmental disorders* (PDDs) includes autistic disorder, Asperger disorder, pervasive developmental disorder-not otherwise specified (PDD-NOS), Rett disorder, and childhood disintegrative disorder (CDD; Bauer, 1995; Berney, 2000; Cohen & Volkmar, 1997; Rapin, 1997; Towbin, 1997a). The primary feature of all PDDs is impairment in social reciprocity. In addition, impairments in communication and restricted behaviors such as repetitive behaviors, narrow interests, rituals, or stereotypies (repetitive simple movements, e.g., hand flapping) are usually present. Limitations in social motivation and emotional recognition result in profound limitations in play skills.

PDDs are neurogenetic disorders and may coexist with other developmental disabilities such as mental retardation, inattention, hyperactivity, and epilepsy (Charman, 1999). Although PDDs are usually regarded as lifelong, advances in defining the underlying impairments and in developing novel treatment approaches have improved outcomes.

AMANDA

Amanda was the first child born to her parents and was a quiet, easy baby who ate vigorously and slept well. She was active and her parents remember her as contented. She reached her early motor milestones "on time," but her mother became concerned when Amanda had not yet begun to say "Mama" or "Dada" by 12 months. Her mother also noticed how unaffected Amanda was by the approach of unfamiliar adults. In fact, Amanda did not even have much reaction when her mother came to pick her up from child care. At 18 months the pediatrician found that Amanda was quite healthy physically but was worried that she only babbled and had no words. She did not even point or use gestures such as lifting her arms up to request "up." She held only brief eye contact with the pediatrician as compared with other 18-month-olds.

By 24 months, Amanda was fascinated by ceiling fans and watched them for 15–20 minutes at a time. She used "Mama" and "Dada" and a few other single words but was not putting any words together. At her child care center, the staff members commented that Amanda kept to herself and would become aggressive when other children approached her. She most enjoyed playing with beads and spent time sorting them by colors. She did not engage in interactive play with the other children, and she resisted sitting with them during circle time. In addition, Amanda did not point to objects that interested her, and her mother reported that she had a difficult time getting Amanda's attention.

Although Amanda's hearing was normal, a speech-language evaluation at 30 months revealed significant delays in expressive language, moderate delays in receptive language, and hardly any use of gestures, eye contact, or facial expression. In her play, Amanda continued to be interested in tiny beads and pieces of cloth, which she would carry around. She did not request things of her parents but would cry or whine to get their attention. She rarely approached those around her. She remained to the side, watching for long periods of time before moving off to do her own thing. When injured, Amanda did not seek her mother out for consolation, and she showed a high tolerance for pain. She occasionally flopped on her mother's lap for affection but in general did not like being held. By 36 months Amanda referred to herself as "Man" and began to use some two-word phrases such as "Man juice!" Her voice was strained and had an unusual pitch. She did use certain phrases, but these were scripted, as if lifted verbatim and with proper intonation from videotapes or television programs. At 4 years she did not respond reliably to verbal requests by her mother or maintain eye contact. On evaluation, Amanda was diagnosed with autistic disorder.

CENTRAL CHARACTERISTICS OF PERVASIVE DEVELOPMENTAL DISORDERS

PDDs are marked by three central characteristics: impairments in social reciprocity, communication impairments, and behavioral abnormalities (Jordan, 1999; Rodier, 2000; Volkmar, 1998).

Impairments in Social Reciprocity

When child development specialists talk about social development, they refer to maturation of the understanding of other people and the ability to engage in the "give-and-take" of social interactions. These abilities draw on a variety of skills, such as social perception, social knowledge, and social functioning. Social perception includes picking up on the nonverbal aspects of social communication. Social knowledge involves knowing about feelings, intentions, and belief states of others. Social functioning includes the capacity to relate to others, to be aware of others' emotions, to engage others in mutually enjoyable ways, and to use language and nonverbal skills during social interactions. In sum, social abilities hinge on understanding one's own emotions, interests, wishes, and experiences and on "reading" and comprehending the feelings, experiences, and motives of others. Sometimes these aptitudes are referred to as *social skills*. These skills involve an amazing variety of verbal and nonverbal messages, some obvious but many subtle, including nuanced facial expression, vocal inflection, gestures, social intention, and emotional tone. Although human beings have an inherent desire to engage with others, everyone is not equally endowed with social perceptivity, grace, and skill. Some people have extraordinary social abilities, whereas others are inept; most people are somewhere between these extremes.

Having an impairment in social learning means that a child has difficulties learning conventional social interchange (Travis & Sigman, 1998). The impediment can result from problems employing signals for social purposes (expression) and/or perceiving the signals that others produce (reception). It follows that PDDs have been regarded as disorders of *social communication*, meaning that they are disabilities in communicating within a social context. When viewed in this context, communication means more than mere vocabulary and grammar; it refers to all types of information that are passed between two people.

Early clinical descriptions promoted the idea that individuals with PDDs lack *any* social reciprocity. A common misconception remains that an individual with these conditions must be entirely unresponsive to social overtures. The modern view has cleared up this misconception considerably. Individuals with PDDs exhibit severe disabilities in initiating, responding to, and maintaining social interactions, but they may be highly responsive to specific individuals or situations (Grossman, Carter, & Volkmar, 1997). What they exhibit are unusual *patterns* of relating. Their impairments are particularly prominent in nonverbal communication, such as using eye contact, gestures, and voice inflection for communicative purposes. Moreover, these individuals have significant impairments in *integrating* verbal and nonverbal components of communication.

It should be emphasized, however, that the range of skills in social motivation, emotional recognition, and social knowledge in individuals with PDDs is very broad. Those who have the least social motivation appear comparatively aloof, typically not responding to and actively avoiding the attempts of others to initiate social contact. Individuals with more motivation generally respond to efforts to interact but do so awkwardly and are limited in their responses or depend on another person to continue the interaction. Individuals with PDDs who are considered the most motivated make repeated but clumsy social overtures that are primarily one-sided; these individuals appear to have very limited ability to recognize social misperceptions or errors and are almost indifferent to the effect of these misperceptions on their communication partners or those around them.

Communication Impairments

All PDDs involve communication impairments, but the degree helps to define the different syndromes (Gillberg, 1999; Rapin & Dunn, 1997; Wilkinson, 1998). In children with autistic disorder, the development of language is both severely delayed and deviant or unusual, hindering both expressive and receptive communication. Speech may be impoverished, poorly articulated, and sparse. Cooing and babbling may develop in the first 6 months of life but then may be lost. Speech may develop late or not at all (Prizant, 1996).

When expressive language does develop in children with PDDs, the first word is often spoken between 2 and 3 years of age. It becomes quickly evident, however, that language pragmatics are impaired (see Chapter 12). Early speech in PDDs may be idiosyncratic and echolalic rather than creative and spontaneous. The echolalia may be immediate (e.g., repetition of the last part of a question) or delayed (e.g., repetition of stock phrases, songs, or long commercial jingles). Although children with PDDs may seem to understand what they are saying, these children may be just parroting what they have heard. There is often confusion of personal pronouns (using "you" to refer to oneself) and verbal perseveration (dwelling on a specific subject). Abnormalities of prosody may be evident; these children's voices are often high pitched, with unusual speech rhythm and intonation, which makes their speech sound singsongy, monotonous, or pedantic. In higher-functioning children with PDDs or in children with Asperger disorder, the echolalia may disappear by school entry, accompanied by a marked increase in spontaneous vocabulary. Their basic difficulties with pragmatics, however, remain.

Receptive language also may be impaired in children with PDDs. Children with autistic disorder may respond to brief phrases but find it very difficult to understand more complex commands. As infants, they tend not to engage in imitation or do so only in a mechanical way. They learn better with visual, rather than auditory, cues and have sensory processing difficulties (Minshew & Goldstein, 1998). Eye contact, body posture, gestures, and other nonverbal aspects of communication are also severely impaired. Although other aspects of language may improve over time, nonverbal communication impairments remain prominent, unless specific behavioral interventions are provided to address these issues (Frea, 1995).

Behavioral Abnormalities

The work of children is play, and children with PDDs have profound limitations in their core capacities for play or pretending. Instead, their play behavior is typically marked by restricted, perseverative, and stereotyped patterns, interests, and activities (Kraijer, 2000; Lewis & Bodfish, 1998; Turner, 1999). Although children with PDDs have prolonged attention spans for rituals, they seem incapable of focusing on interacting with others. Strict adherence to routines are common, including a rigid insistence on eating at the same time each day or eating a restricted menu of foods, sitting in exactly the same position at the table, placing objects in a particular location, or touching every doorknob one passes. Young children with PDDs may show intense attachment to an unusual object such as a piece of string rather than to a cuddly item such as a teddy bear. They may not use toys in their intended manner but may focus instead on a part of a toy, such as the wheels on a toy truck, which they may spin endlessly. A common form of play is to line objects up in rows. Shiny surfaces, rotating fans, and people's hair or beards may fascinate young children with autistic disorder. They focus on these objects to the exclusion of other activities such as make-believe games.

Frequently, children with PDDs become upset and have intense temper tantrums if anything interrupts these daily routines, rituals, and preoccupations. Stereotyped movements and self-stimulating behaviors, such as pacing, spinning, running in circles, drumming, flipping light switches, rocking, hand waving, arm flapping, and toe walking are common. Self-injurious behavior such as gouging, self-biting, and head banging may also occur, especially among children with PDDs who also have severe mental retardation. Other behavior problems associated with PDDs include sleep disturbances (decreased need for sleep and frequent awakenings, especially in younger children), short attention span, rapid mood changes, hyperactivity, phobias, and aggressiveness (Richdale, 1999). Unusual responses to sensory input are also common. These include insensitivity to pain or heat and overreaction to environmental noises, touch, or odors. For example, although the child may appear "deaf" to parental questions or commands, he or she may cover the ears and scream when close to a vacuum cleaner. Food selectivity, food refusal, or resistance to certain food textures may lead to compromised nutrition or constipation.

THE PERVASIVE DEVELOPMENTAL DISORDERS

Five conditions are considered to belong to the category of PDDs: autistic disorder, Asperger disorder, PDD-NOS, CDD, and Rett disorder (American Psychiatric Association [APA], 2000). The term *autism spectrum disorders* is often used to describe the subcategories autistic disorder, Asperger disorder, and PDD-NOS.

Autistic Disorder

The most widely known of the PDDs is autistic disorder. Historically speaking, it is also a "new" condition. The term *autism* was first coined in 1943 by Leo Kanner, a child psychiatrist, who observed a pattern of social aloofness and "preservation of sameness" in a series of young children. Kanner believed this condition was a result of biological forces and outlined many of the features associated with aloofness and "needs for sameness" that we observe today. Other features from Kanner's initial papers, however, have not held up upon further investigation including the intellectual "giftedness" of individuals with autistic disorder. Rather than resorting to highly subjective or excessively vague impressions, clinicians now rely on the specific definitions provided by the *Diagnostic and Statistical Manual of Mental Disorders, Fourth Edition, Text Revision* (DSM-IV-TR; APA, 2000; see Table 20.1), or on the *International Statistical Classification of Diseases and Related Health Problems* (ICD-10; World Health Organization, 1992–1994). Nevertheless, these criteria provide only a guideline, and experience in evaluating affected children is essential in making the diagnosis.

Asperger Disorder

At about the same time that Leo Kanner was collecting his series of patients, Hans Asperger was observing boys in Austria who displayed similar features (Asperger, 1944/1991). These children displayed impairments in social interaction and reciprocity, were unable to conform to social demands, and had restricted interests and repetitive behaviors. But, unlike children with autistic disorder, children with Asperger disorder did not have severely impaired development of language. The obstacles to exchanging information between Europe and America during the 1940s prevented Kanner and Asperger from learning of each other's work. It was only in 1981 that Lorna Wing published observations in English of a series of patients whom she suggested had features similar to those in Asperger's account. Over the next decade a flurry of work produced reliable diagnostic criteria for this disorder (Attwood & Wing, 1997; Schopler, Mesibov, & Kunce, 1998; Volkmar, Klin, & Pauls, 1998). Some investigators view Asperger disorder (or syndrome) as a high-functioning form of autistic disorder (Gillberg, 1998), whereas others (Klin, Volkmar, & Sparrow, 2000) consider this disorder distinct from high-functioning autism. Further investigation into the genetics and course of these disorders will be needed to decide which hypothesis is correct. The average age at diagnosis for Asperger disorder is around 11 years (Howlin & Asgharian, 1999; Klin et al., 1995) as compared with autistic disorder, which is generally diagnosed before 5 years of age.

    Individuals with Asperger disorder share many behavioral and social features of autistic disorder but do not have the same impairments in language or cognition (Attwood & Wing,

Table 20.1.   Diagnostic criteria for autistic disorder

A.   A total of six (or more) items from the following groups:

Group 1[a]	Group 2[b]	Group 3[c]
1. Marked impairment in the use of multiple nonverbal behaviors such as eye-to-eye gaze, facial expression, body postures, and gestures to regulate social interaction	1. Delay in, or total lack of, the development of spoken language (not accompanied by an attempt to compensate through alternative modes of communication such as gesture or mime)	1. Encompassing preoccupation with one or more stereotyped and restricted patterns of interest that is abnormal either in intensity or focus
2. Failure to develop peer relationships appropriate to developmental level	2. In individuals with adequate speech, marked impairment in the ability to initiate or sustain a conversation with others	2. Apparently inflexible adherence to specific, nonfunctional routines or rituals
3. A lack of spontaneous seeking to share enjoyment, interests, or achievements with other people (e.g., by a lack of showing, bringing, or pointing out objects of interest)	3. Stereotyped and repetitive use of language or idiosyncratic language	3. Stereotyped and repetitive motor mannerisms (e.g., hand or finger flapping or twisting, complex whole-body movements)
4. Lack of social or emotional reciprocity	4. Lack of varied, spontaneous make-believe play or social imitative play appropriate to developmental level	4. Persistent preoccupation with parts of objects

B.   Delays or abnormal functioning in at least one of the following areas with onset prior to age 3 years:
1. Social interaction
2. Language as used in social communication
3. Symbolic or imaginative play

C.   The disturbance is not better accounted for by Rett disorder or childhood disintegrative disorder.

  [a]Qualitative impairments in social interaction, as manifested by at least two criteria from Group 1.

  [b]Qualitative impairments in communication as manifested by at least one criterion from Group 2.

  [c]Restricted, repetitive, and stereotyped patterns of behavior, interests, and activities, as manifested by at least one criterion from Group 3.

1997; Klin et al., 2000). The pattern of neuropsychological skills and weaknesses in children with the more narrowly defined Asperger disorder are characterized by significantly stronger verbal skills compared with nonverbal or "gestalt learning" abilities. Such children display a strong aptitude for rote learning, spelling, and vocabulary but much poorer performance in concept formation, flexible problem solving, and complex verbal or reading comprehension. Some children have hyperlexia and are able to decode words before age 5, but they usually have much less ability to comprehend what they have "read." Although the spoken language of children with Asperger disorder may superficially appear typical, they cannot use their vocabulary in flexible, socially adaptive ways and often sound pedantic. These kinds of difficulties are referred to as semantic and pragmatic language impairments. Children with Asperger disorder also have severe impairments in their core abilities to recognize and express nonverbal aspects of communication such as eye contact and body position. People with Asperger disorder also often exhibit weakness in motor coordination skills.

Older children with Asperger disorder may exhibit unusual activities and interests in maps, sports statistics, train schedules, and so forth. Some of these preoccupations may prove to be adaptive and lead to future careers, such as in computing. The social ineptitude, however, often prevents these individuals from developing friendships and other long-term personal relationships (Bashe & Kirby, 2001; Grandin, 1995; Grandin & Scariano, 1996; Williams, 1992).

Pervasive Developmental Disorder-Not Otherwise Specified

PDD-NOS has been a source of confusion and frustration for clinicians and parents alike. The term has been applied under different circumstances; as a result it does not convey the same meaning across clinicians or situations. Unlike autistic disorder or Asperger disorder, PDD-NOS has been a necessary but vague designation that does not have specific criteria. It has been most commonly used to describe children who have a syndrome that resembles autistic disorder or Asperger disorder but is different in some important way (Towbin, 1997b). Some clinicians apply the term when the age of onset cannot be firmly placed prior to age 3 years (a DSM-IV-TR requirement for the diagnosis of autistic disorder). Others use this diagnosis when a child "looks too good" or when his or her symptoms are "too mild" to satisfy the criteria for autistic disorder but shares some features. Still others have used this term when there are clear impairments in social learning but the features of other PDDs are not completely satisfied. Although it is not appropriate, sometimes this diagnosis has been given in preference to autistic disorder because a clinician believes that it is more palatable to parents, will cause the parents less distress, or is not stigmatizing. It is likely that more specific and reliable criteria for PDD-NOS will be proposed and perhaps subtypes identified. Most likely this will be a designation for children who clearly exhibit a social learning disorder but do not fully meet the language or restricted pattern criteria for autistic disorder or Asperger disorder.

Childhood Disintegrative Disorder

CDD is a very rare condition in which all aspects of development proceed typically until age 3–5 years, then skills rapidly decline (Hendry, 2000; Malhotra & Gupta, 1999). This affects language, social reciprocity, play, motor skills, and often bowel and bladder control. Eventually, the decline stabilizes, leaving the patient with a clinical picture closely resembling autistic disorder. It is important in making a diagnosis to observe a decline that is significant (e.g., for language regression, a loss in the capacity to form sentences) and a loss of acquired skills. The progressive course of this disorder necessitates that these children be evaluated for metabolic and neurodegenerative diseases. No single neurobiological mechanism has been identified for CDD, and some researchers believe that causes are diverse (Volkmar et al., 1997).

Rett Disorder

Rett disorder is an X-linked dominant disorder (almost exclusively affecting girls) with clinical onset between 6 and 18 months of age. It is caused by mutations in the gene MeCP2, which codes for the methyl-CpG-binding protein 2 (Amir et al., 1999), important in early brain development. This progressive neurological disorder is characterized by loss of purposeful hand use, progressive spasticity of the lower extremities, seizures, acquired microcephaly, and mental retardation (Ellaway & Christodoulou, 1999; Hagberg, 1995). Individuals often appear to develop typically during the first year of life, although in retrospect, there may have been subtle neurodevelopmental abnormalities present in infancy. At variable ages older than 1 year, children with Rett disorder experience rapid deterioration of behavior, language, and mental status; lose purposeful hand movements; and develop ataxia and seizures. A prominent feature is continuous "handwashing" movements, often accompanied by hyperventilation. By 6 years of age, an affected girl generally has mental retardation requiring extensive to pervasive support, spasticity, and seizures. The condition then stabilizes over a period of many years. Although its early presentation may be indistinguishable from autistic disorder, the particular characteristics of Rett disorder usually become evident in the preschool years. It can be diagnosed by mutation analysis of the MeCP2 gene.

PREVALENCE

The general population prevalence describes how many individuals in the population have a condition at a specific point in time. Fombonne's (1999) extensive meta-analysis relying on the most current definitions reported an aggregate rate for all of the PDDs of 7.2 per 10,000. In a carefully constructed study of the entire preschool population served by the National Health Service Trust in Staffordshire, England, Chakrabarti and Fombonne (2001) reported rates of 16.8 per 10,000 for autistic disorder; 8.4 per 10,000 for Asperger disorder; and 36.1 per 10,000 for PDD-NOS. These contemporary studies offer rates that are increased over those previously reported (Bryson & Smith, 1998; Fombonne, 1999). Despite a variety of news reports implying an epidemic of autism (Maugh, 1999), it is likely that this does not represent a true increase in prevalence. Rather, fewer affected children are being misdiagnosed. This is a consequence of a diagnostic system that now includes Asperger disorder and clinicians who have a lower threshold for making the diagnosis in children with borderline symptoms and improved methods of detection (Mangravite, 2001; Webb et al., 1997).

CAUSE

It now seems clear that PDDs are the product of developmental brain abnormalities with a significant genetic influence. This stands in contrast to a history in the field of attributing social learning, parenting, and adverse environmental circumstances as causes of the disorder. It appears unlikely that autism is the result of infections, adverse nutrition, or maternal stress.

Genetics

The genetic evidence in autism is compelling and comes from both twin studies and more extensive family studies. They show that the rate of autism is much greater among identical twins (70%–90%) than among fraternal twins (0%; Folstein & Rutter, 1977). Family studies also demonstrate much higher rates of autism (3%) among siblings of children with autism than in the general population (less than 0.1%). In addition, if one child in the family has autism, the parents' risk of having a second child with a PDD is about 5%–7% (Cook, 1998; Lamb et al., 2000; Piven, 1997; Smalley, 1997; Turner, Barnby, & Bailey, 2000).

It should be emphasized, however, that these rates are not as high as would be predicted by Mendelian genetics (see Chapter 1). Thus, it may be that environmental factors influence gene expression. In addition, as the definition of PDDs has broadened, the concordance rates have increased. A family member may have just one or partial features of a PDD, such as a highly rigid temperament, language delay, pragmatic language impairments, or stereotyped patterns of behavior (Bailey et al., 1998; Mesibov, Adams, & Klinger, 1998). This has led investigators to suggest that autistic disorder may be a contiguous gene disorder, that is, the end product of 4–10 closely situated genes acting together (Rutter, 2000). Cook et al. (1997) suggested a possible link to a serotonin-transporter gene, and further investigation has supported this hypothesis (Maestrini et al., 1999). More recently, an association with defects in the HOXA1 gene on chromosome 7 was reported (Rodier, 2000). This gene affects the transcription of other genes early in embryonic development (see Chapter 13). Rodier (2000) and Ingram et al. (2000) reported the presence of the HOXA1 allele in approximately 40% of people with autistic disorder, double the rate in the general population, suggesting that this gene may predispose individuals to autistic disorder. Another gene on chromosome 7 coding for WNT2, a factor influencing early embryonic neuronal development, has also been associated with autistic disorder in family studies (Wassink et al., 2001). Other work points to chromosome 13 (Barrett et al., 1999) and a region on chromosome 15 (q11–q13) (Wassink & Piven, 2000) as sites for further exploration.

Neurobiology

Neurobiological studies of autistic disorder have focused on neurochemistry, neuropathology, and neuroimaging (Rapin & Katzman, 1998; Trottier, Srivastava, & Walker, 1999). Serotonin has been the most important neurotransmitter system to be implicated so far in studies of autistic disorder. Approximately 30% of individuals with autistic disorder have elevated blood serotonin levels (Schain & Freedman, 1961). Further evidence in support of the importance of serotonin comes from the effects of experimental manipulation of its amino acid precursor, tryptophan. McDougle et al. (1996) reported increased symptoms in six adults with autistic disorder following tryptophan depletion. In an effort to learn more about serotonin synthesis throughout childhood, Chugani et al. (1999) used a radiolabeled tryptophan tracer to study serotonin synthesis in children with autistic disorder, a control group of unaffected siblings, and a second control group of children with epilepsy. Control children showed an increase in serotonin synthesis between the ages of 2 and 5 years, with a decline toward adult values from 5 to 14 years of age. Consonant with these researchers' previous findings (Chugani et al., 1997) of elevated serotonin synthesis in three adult men with autistic disorder, the children with autistic disorder displayed continued high levels of production of serotonin (Chugani et al., 1999). Similar investigations of the neurotransmitters norepinephrine and dopamine have not demonstrated significant differences comparing individuals in a control group with individuals with autistic disorder (Anderson & Hoshino, 1997). In addition, no differences have been found in the precursors or metabolites of endogenous opioids in cerebrospinal fluid, blood, and urine comparing individuals in a control group and people with autistic disorder (Anderson & Hoshino, 1997).

Neuropathology studies of autism have revealed heavier and larger brains when matched to controls (Bauman & Kemper, 1994). Regions related to the limbic system (which is involved in emotions) are most affected, with reduced neuron size and increased density (Bauman & Kemper, 1994). The greatest increase in cell density was found in the amygdala, a region known to be critical for processing fear and emotional memory. Outside of the limbic system, the other areas found to have significant abnormalities are the cerebellum and inferior olive (Bauman & Kemper, 1994).

The use of structural magnetic resonance imaging (MRI) has consistently identified larger brain volumes in people with autistic disorder (Filipek et al., 1999; Haznedar et al., 2000; Rumsey & Ernst, 2000). Courchesne et al. (2001), Eliez and Reiss (2000), and Manes et al. (1999) have reported increased amounts of white matter in the cerebellum and cerebral cortex and increased amounts of gray matter in the cortex in the youngest children with autistic disorder. As the children advanced toward middle childhood, white matter growth declined and these elevated volumes were no longer evident. It appeared as if the normal pattern of growth in white matter after 2 years of age did not occur in these individuals. With regard to the cerebellum, a smaller volume of gray matter (the area containing neuronal cell bodies) was found in the younger subjects, particularly in comparison with the increase in white matter. This pattern suggests that white and gray matter growth stalls at about 3 years of age and that by middle childhood a pattern of relatively typical white matter volume and smaller gray matter cerebellar volume is observed. This points to the potential abnormal action of genes that control myelination, dendritic connections, and creation of synapses. Rather than connections in the brain being shaped by experience and learning, there may be "growth without guidance" in neuronal migration and in the development and connections of synapses (Courchesne et. al, 2001).

Functional neuroimaging has also suggested that the amygdala, right somatosensory cortex, orbitofrontal cortex, and cingulate gyri each provide a segment in the chain of events necessary for social cognition (Adolphs, 2001; Baron-Cohen et al., 2000). Additional work suggests that the medial frontal gyri are important for verbal tasks related to understanding the mental state of another person (Fletcher et al., 1995). Research also suggests that individuals with high-functioning autism and Asperger disorder display abnormal processing of facial recognition in the fusiform gyri, located in the inferior temporal gyri (Schultz et al., 2000), and significantly decreased function in the amygdala (Baron-Cohen et al., 2000; Baron-Cohen et al., 1999).

Complications During Delivery

Considerable thought has been given to whether birth complications predispose certain individuals to having PDDs. There is not yet uniform agreement, but some evidence suggests an association between PDDs and birth trauma. It appears more likely, however, that autism predisposes the fetus to complications at delivery rather than that problems in delivery cause autism. Some investigators believe that delivery complications are a more important factor for children born to families without any genetic history for PDDs than in circumstances when there is genetic loading toward autism. In sum, complications in delivery alone are not a likely cause of autism (Bolton et al., 1997; Burd et al., 1999).

Vaccinations

Concern has been expressed about a possible relationship between the measles, mumps, and rubella (MMR) vaccine and autistic disorder. Population-based studies have shown that there is no correlation between the vaccination and the subsequent development of autistic disorder (Afzal, Minor, & Schild, 2000; Halsey, Hyman, & the Conference Writing Panel, 2001; Taylor et al., 1999). There are also reports of onset of autism-like disorders following diphtheria, pertussis, and tetanus (DPT) vaccination, but data are not sufficient to support a causative role (Howson, Howe, & Fineberg, 1991; Stratton, Howe, & Johnson, 1993).

EARLY IDENTIFICATION OF AUTISTIC DISORDER

By definition, the symptoms of autistic disorder must be manifest by 3 years of age. Yet, this does not necessarily mean that the diagnosis is made by this age; some children may not be diagnosed until school entry. Studies have shown that even when parents express a concern early, there is often a 2- to 3-year lag before a firm diagnosis is made (Mars, Mauk, & Dowrick, 1998). As with many other disorders, the more severe the symptoms, the earlier the diagnosis.

The core symptoms of delay in language development, aberrant behavior, and lack of socialization are the most common parental concerns. Infants with autistic disorder often make poor eye contact and are irritable and stiffen when held. In the first and second years of life, they may be unresponsive, are generally difficult to care for, and have frequent temper tantrums. Speech may not develop, and commands will not be followed.

Although autistic disorder is generally not diagnosed before 2–3 years, systematic review of early videotapes demonstrates prelinguistic communication abnormalities, such as lack of response to name, disinterest in faces, and inattention to voices, even before 12 months of age (Mars et al., 1998; Werner et al., 2000). Furthermore, parent questionnaires, such as the Checklist for Autism in Toddlers (CHAT; Baron-Cohen et al., 1996), often retrospectively reveal impairments in pretend play, declarative pointing, joint-attention, social interest, and social play as early as 18 months of age (Baron-Cohen, Allen, & Gillberg, 1992).

During the preschool years, severe disruptive behaviors may emerge, including aggression, hyperactivity, and self-injury. At this time, affected children often manifest stereotypies, social withdrawal, and emotional lability to a degree that the diagnosis is seriously considered. Even children with the milder PDD-NOS or Asperger disorder have poorly developed social imitation skills, and pretend play is usually absent.

Diagnosing a PDD in a young child relies on parental and educational observations. Early developmental milestones are delayed, especially in language and social-adaptive skills. Unusual behaviors may also be evident, and parental responses on one of the autism questionnaires are usually suggestive of the diagnosis. No medical diagnostic tests can rule in or out the diagnosis. The diagnosis of this syndrome basically relies on satisfying the DSM-IV-TR criteria for a PDD.

DISTINGUISHING PERVASIVE DEVELOPMENTAL DISORDERS FROM OTHER DISABILITIES

It is important to differentiate autistic disorder from other childhood developmental disorders such as mental retardation, childhood schizophrenia, sensory impairments, communication disorders, and neurodegenerative disorders.

Usually, autistic disorder can be distinguished from mental retardation by its characteristic social and behavior problems and by a somewhat different pattern of cognitive impairments (Vig & Jedrysek, 1999), but doing so can be difficult, especially when both a PDD and mental retardation are present and severe. Children with autistic disorder typically do not respond to social overtures and actively avoid social interactions, whereas children with mental retardation generally enjoy social contacts (Njardvik, Matson, & Cherry, 1999). In addition, children with autistic disorder tend to have an IQ profile in which nonverbal (or performance) scores are higher than verbal scores. For Asperger disorder, this pattern is reversed (Klin et al., 2000). Looking for a disparity in IQ and social adaptive functioning can be a useful screen for a possible PDD (Volkmar et al., 1993). Some children with autistic disorder have unusually good musical, mathematical, or visuospatial abilities, combined with excellent rote visual or auditory memory skills. These are often called "splinter skills." These same children, however, may have severe impairments in other cognitive areas. Examples of splinter skills include being able to calculate in one's head large numbers or days of the week from the past or in the future. Individuals with such skills have been called "savants." In contrast, children with mental retardation usually have uniform delays in language, cognitive, and visual-perceptual skills. It must be acknowledged, however, that many children with autistic disorder also have mental retardation, and many individuals with severe mental retardation display features of autism, such as stereotyped movements and self-injurious behavior.

PDDs may also be confused with severe psychiatric disorders, such as childhood schizophrenia (APA, 2000). Drawing distinctions between these conditions is particularly challenging, because individuals with onset of schizophrenia before adolescence often have a history of developmental delays in early childhood. If a child has the characteristic features of a PDD, then the diagnosis of schizophrenia can be made *only* if he or she has very prominent hallucinations and/or delusions. These symptoms, however, can be difficult to single out in very young children. In children who meet the criteria for schizophrenia of having prominent hallucination/delusion for at least a month, this diagnosis takes precedence over a PDD. Taking a developmental history with close attention paid to social milestones and reciprocity in social interactions is particularly important in making these distinctions. A child with a PDD can have hallucinations or delusions, but when they arise they are usually short-lived and occur with environmental stressors.

Children with sensory impairments may also demonstrate features associated with autism. For example, congenital blindness often is associated with eye-poking behaviors and impaired interpersonal skills (Hobson, Lee, & Brown, 1999). Children with blindness, however, do not have the global language disorder that typifies children with autistic disorder. Severe to profound hearing impairment also may mimic autistic disorder because of inconsistent responses to verbal commands and social situations (Peterson & Siegal, 1997). Social interactions and cognition, however, are usually unaffected. It is therefore important to test vision and hearing in children with a suspected PDD.

Similarly, children with developmental language disorders may display shyness, echolalia, and some social withdrawal, but they typically do not show other behaviors typical of autistic disorder, including stereotyped utterances, abnormal social interactions, bizarre behaviors, and absence of a desire to communicate (Rapin, 1998).

Neurodegenerative disorders, such as Tay-Sachs disease (see Chapter 18), may initially present with features of autistic disorder. They must also be differentiated from Rett disorder and CDD.

When children are evaluated, it is crucial that the assessment be comprehensive enough to consider PDDs. It is common for children with PDDs to be misdiagnosed as having attention-deficit/hyperactivity disorder (ADHD), obsessive compulsive disorder, or oppositional defiant disorder before a more detailed assessment of social functioning has been obtained. Any child who exhibits signs of such disorders, especially in the context of a language disability or problems in relating to peers, deserves a comprehensive developmental evaluation to detect a PDD.

EVALUATION OF THE CHILD WITH A PERVASIVE DEVELOPMENTAL DISORDER

The assessment of children who are suspected of having a PDD requires time, collaboration among health care and educational professionals, and knowledge of the disorder. The evaluation follows directly from the diagnostic criteria that focus on impairments in social reciprocity and language and restricted patterns of behavior (Filipek et al., 1999). The diagnosis is based on history as much as on current functioning (American Academy of Pediatrics, Committee on Children with Disabilities, 2001b).

In general, the evaluation team should include a physician (pediatrician with expertise in autism, neurodevelopmental pediatrician, child psychiatrist, or child neurologist), a developmental psychologist, and a speech-language pathologist with early childhood expertise. The team evaluation should include 1) a detailed developmental history with particular attention to social development, 2) a hearing assessment, 3) a test of language development, 4) a measurement of overall cognitive functioning (IQ testing), 5) a basic neurological examination, 6) a general medical evaluation with blood studies, 7) an electroencephalogram (EEG), 8) a family medical history, and 9) an evaluation of current family functioning and circumstances. Additional assessments by an occupational therapist, physical therapist, and/or geneticist may be needed depending on the individual.

A competent evaluation relies on observations made over multiple times and in different settings. This is particularly important in the case of children who have language or anxiety disorders, cognitive limitations, attentional deficits, or disruptive behaviors. For such children, meeting strangers in novel settings and being asked to do new things can affect functioning. With more familiarity and time, the novelty of the experience declines and the findings are more reliable.

Rating scales are often used during the evaluation and can assist clinicians in organizing their observations. Commonly used rating scales include the following:

- Autism Behavior Checklist (ABC; Krug, Arick, & Almond, 1980; see also Gillberg, Nordin, & Ehlers, 1996)
- Autism Diagnostic Observation Schedule–Generic (ADOS-G ; Lord et al., 2000)
- Autism Diagnostic Interview–Revised (ADI-R; Lord, Rutter, & LeCouteur, 1994)
- Modified Checklist for Autism in Toddlers (M-CHAT; Robins et al., 2001)
- Childhood Autism Rating Scale (CARS; Schopler, Reichler, & Renner, 1986)
- Screening Tool for Autism in Two-Year-Olds (STAT; Stone, Coonrod, & Ousley, 2000)

Medical testing generally is not helpful; there are no specific screening tests for PDDs. However, if the history suggests developmental regression (e.g., CDD, Rett disorder) or the physical examination supports a neurological disorder (e.g., tuberous sclerosis) or a genetic syndrome (e.g., Angelman syndrome), these conditions should be explored. Evidence of regression may prompt a metabolic/genetic evaluation, and an unusual appearance may lead to chromosomal testing. Other nonspecific findings may also warrant study. For example, a very large or small head circumference may prompt a brain imaging scan.

ASSOCIATED CONDITIONS IN PERVASIVE DEVELOPMENTAL DISORDERS

Mental Retardation

Two thirds to three quarters of individuals with autistic disorder also have mental retardation. There appears to be a correlation between the severity of autism symptoms and the degree of mental retardation. Conversely, the prevalence of autistic disorder rises with increasing severity of mental retardation. On the one hand, it is logical that a condition severe enough to impede language and social development might also affect cognitive functioning. On the other hand, it is not clear why mental retardation is so prominent in disorders of social learning. This close relationship between these two developmental disabilities creates difficulties in separating the conditions. For example, stereotypies and self-stimulatory behaviors are evident in 15% of people with severe mental retardation (Rogers, 1998).

The close connection between mental retardation and autistic disorder also complicates the diagnostic process. In a child with mental retardation, determining whether social development is on par with the rest of the child's development or is delayed even more than other domains of development requires a careful assessment. Particular care is necessary when a child's level of cognitive development is less than 24 months because of the difficulty in making a valid estimate of the child's overall social development.

Epilepsy

Epilepsy occurs in 25%–30% of individuals with autistic disorder (Giovanardi Rossi, Posar, & Parmeggiani, 2000; Tuchman, 2000). One striking feature is that in people with autistic disorder, seizures are as likely to begin in adolescence as in infancy. In otherwise ordinary children with epilepsy, the onset of seizures in adolescence is rare. No one type of epilepsy is specifically associated with autistic disorder.

An epilepsy syndrome termed *Landau-Kleffner syndrome*, however, can present with symptoms that simulate a PDD (Mantovani, 2000). It is characterized clinically by deterioration in language skills in a preschooler who has previously shown typical expressive and receptive language development (Ballaban-Gil & Tuchman, 2000). There are also behavioral abnormalities, including hyperactivity, distractability, aggressiveness, and social withdrawal. Landau-Kleffner syndrome is associated either with seizures or with a specific abnormal EEG pattern. MRI scans have been normal, but positron emission tomography (PET) metabolic scans have shown abnormalities in the temporal lobes of the brain.

Medical and Genetic Disorders Associated with Autistic Disorder

A number of genetic disorders have been associated with a high rate of autism (Rutter et al., 1997). In some of these disorders, the elevated rate may be an artifact, as these conditions are commonly associated with severe mental retardation. Therefore, this chapter focuses on only four genetic disorders that have specific features thought to be associated with autistic disorder: tuberous sclerosis, Tourette syndrome, Angelman syndrome, and fragile X syndrome. It should be emphasized that taken together, these conditions are present in less than 10% of all individuals with autistic disorder (Meyer et al., 1998).

Tuberous Sclerosis

Tuberous sclerosis is an autosomal dominant disorder caused by a defect in the TSC2 gene that codes for the protein tuberin. It results in characteristic skin lesions (depigmented ash leaf spots) and benign growths **(tubers)** in the brain (Crino & Henske, 1999). Its most prominent clinical features are mental retardation and epilepsy, but the rate of PDDs is also strikingly high, with almost half of all individuals with tuberous sclerosis being affected (Smalley, 1998). Conversely, about 1%–4% of individuals with PDDs are likely to have tuberous sclerosis.

Tourette Syndrome

Tourette syndrome is an autosomal dominant tic condition. These quick motor movement discharges most commonly present as facial grimaces often accompanied by vocal sounds that may be as simple as throat clearing or sniffing or as complex as whole words or phrases. Most affected children have typical intellectual function, but there is a high prevalence of ADHD. Recent reports suggest that the prevalence of Tourette syndrome is higher than would be predicted by chance alone in people with PDDs. These studies report rates of 4%–30% (Stern & Robertson, 1997).

Angelman Syndrome

The genetic condition Angelman syndrome features severe motor and intellectual retardation, ataxia, hypotonia, jerky movements, epilepsy, absence of speech, and unusual facies characterized by a large, open-mouth expression. Many of the children show features of autistic disorder. Angelman syndrome has a prevalence of about 1 in 12,000 and is caused by a deletion in chromosome 15q11–q13 (Steffenburg et al., 1996). It has been found to be transmitted genetically by **uniparental disomy** (genomic imprinting), and the underlying defect is a mutation in the UBE3A gene (Laan, van Haeringen, & Brouwer, 1999). This gene is preferentially expressed in human brain (hippocampus and cerebellar cells), regions implicated in the neuropathology of autistic disorder (Veenstra-VanderWeele et al., 1999).

Fragile X Syndrome

At one time fragile X syndrome, the most prevalent known cause of inherited mental retardation (see Chapter 17), was believed to be a common genetic cause of autistic disorder. Reported rates of autism among individuals with fragile X ranged up to 60%. But upon further scrutiny, unreliable methods used to make the diagnosis of autistic disorder and to collect subjects may have influenced these results. In addition, many of these subjects also had severe mental retardation. As described previously, the difficulty in diagnosing autistic disorder in people with mental retardation can produce inaccurate results.

Further study of females with fragile X syndrome who have higher IQs has suggested a unique behavioral phenotype (Mazzocco et al., 1997). Gaze avoidance, perseverative behaviors, restricted interests, language abnormalities, difficulties with modulating sensory input, and inattention with hyperactivity are common, yet the vast majority of individuals with fragile X have social interest and typical appreciation of others' emotions (Feinstein & Reiss, 1998). The overlap of these features with autistic disorder, especially in those individuals with a mental retardation, means that there is a risk of overdiagnosis of autistic disorder. More rigorous investigations have recently reported estimates that closer to 4%–5% of individuals with fragile X syndrome have autistic disorder (Feinstein & Reiss, 1998).

TREATMENT APPROACHES

Supporting children with PDDs can be frustrating for families and other caregivers. Treatment must be intensive, continuous, and multidisciplinary (Hurth et al., 1999; Murray-Slutsky & Paris, 2000; Volkmar et al., 1999). Sir Michael Rutter (1985a, 1985b), an eminent British child psychiatrist, outlined goals of autism treatment that remain applicable: 1) fostering development, 2) promoting learning, 3) reducing rigidity and stereotypy, 4) eliminating maladaptive behaviors, and 5) alleviating family distress. A comprehensive approach usually requires a combination of educational programs, behavioral supports, social and pragmatic language skills training, and family support. Also, there are specific circumstances under which to include pharmacotherapy.

Educational Programs

The mainstay of treatment for PDDs is education (Cumine, Leach, & Stevenson, 2000). This should start as soon as the diagnosis is made. In autistic disorder, this generally means enrollment in an early intervention program in the preschool period (Dawson & Osterling, 1997; Ozonoff & Cathcart, 1998; Rogers, 1996). An educational setting that has experience in teaching children with these disorders is extremely important (Hurth et al., 1999). It is now evident that all successful early intervention programs for children with autistic disorder take into account the influence of environmental stimulation, structure the teaching environment purposely and to a high degree, and present materials in a planned, predictable manner (Hurth et al., 1999; Schreibman, 2000). There are, however, diverse approaches to providing educational services ranging from discrete trial training (e.g., the Lovaas [1987] method), to traditional behavioral (e.g., applied behavior analysis), to social-pragmatic, to developmental (e.g., Prizant & Wetherby, 1998). The current state of knowledge does not permit endorsement of one particular method.

For school-age children, autistic disorder is included as a special category of educational disability under the Individuals with Disabilities Education Act Amendments of 1997 (PL 105-17). This law mandates that specific academic goals relate both to the child's cognitive and functional level and that the educational program be provided in the least restrictive environment. This last provision has led to controversy regarding inclusion versus a specialized educational setting for children with autistic disorder. For high-functioning older children with autistic disorder or Asperger disorder, inclusion may be very appropriate (Simpson & Myles, 1998). For younger and lower-functioning children with autistic disorder, inclusion may be a future goal or a starting point. With either choice, some interaction with typically developing peers can be helpful.

One of the commonly used traditional behavior curricula in special education programs for children with PDDs is TEACCH (Treatment and Education of Autistic and related Communication handicapped Children). TEACCH is a comprehensive educational approach that includes classroom teaching, parent training, and other support services (Cox & Schopler, 1993; Panerai, Ferrante, & Caputo, 1997). It can also be adapted to a home-based model that has been shown to be effective (Ozonoff & Cathcart, 1998). The approach is eclectic and involves the use of behavioral strategies to reinforce communication and social interaction. It also heavily emphasizes the parents' role as co-therapists.

Individualized educational programming based on the discrete trial practices of Lovaas has been very popular (Lovaas, 1987). Lovaas developed and reported on a model of intensive (40 hours per week), comprehensive, one-to-one teaching. This therapy relies on the introduction, prompting, and reinforcement of a behavior. The curriculum includes hundreds of individual lessons to teach specific language, academic, and social behaviors. Treatment is generally initiated at 2 years of age. Goals of the first year of treatment include developing language; increasing social behavior; promoting cooperative play; and decreasing excessive rituals, tantrums, and aggressive behavior. In the second year, treatment focuses on expressive and abstract language and interactive play with peers. In his initial study, Lovaas reported an almost 50% recovery rate (i.e., the children did not need special support services or aids in a general classroom) with significant gains in IQ scores, preacademic skills, and adaptive functioning (discussed in Lovaas, 1993). Skepticism with the Lovaas method, however, has focused on the claims of success, explicit intensity of the intervention, demands for highly specific training, and the expense (Gresham & MacMillan, 1998). One study, in fact, showed gains in IQ during the early childhood period independent of the Lovaas intervention (Stone et al., 1999).

Behavioral Support

An important goal of educating children with PDDs is to teach them skills that extend their ability to communicate and socialize with others. Sometimes specific behaviors can interfere with this adaptation. When these arise, it is important to recognize that maladaptive behaviors may emerge from a need or urge that the child cannot communicate more directly. A principle of teaching children with PDDs is that behavior carries meaning and should not be presumed to be a random act. The procedures that grow out of this principle consider the origin of the behavior, teach more effective ways to achieve a similar result (e.g., comfort, communication), and extend behaviors that increase social adaptability. Any setting in which children with PDDs are taught should include professionals with skills in understanding, teaching, and shaping the behavior of its students. These tasks are as important as the educational program (Coucouvanis, 1997; Maurice, Green, & Luce, 1996). They are critical to understanding the barriers that thwart building skills in communication, social interactions, and self-care. Behavioral support can be helpful in establishing daily routines, extinguishing self-injurious, aggressive, or destructive behaviors, and responding to tantrums (Howlin, 1998; Koegel, Koegel, & Dunlap, 1996; Koegel & Koegel, 1995). There are an increasing number of helpful materials for teachers dealing with behavioral supports (see, e.g., Koegel et al., 1996; see Chapter 31).

Social and Pragmatic Language Skills Training

Research has shown that all communication attempts in young individuals with autistic disorder should be rewarded socially or in other ways to foster language development (Carr et al., 1995). Sign language can be attempted but is often difficult for these children, who may have poor fine motor skills and impairments in processing visual signals. Low-tech augmentative and alternative communication strategies (see Chapter 12), such as the Picture Exchange Communication System (PECS; Frost & Bondy, 1994) can be effective (Liddle, 2001). Art and music therapy has also been used in attempts to communicate nonverbally with these children (Schleien, Mustonen, & Rynders, 1995; Wimpory, Chadwick, & Nash, 1995).

For older and higher-functioning children, an important objective of intervention is the promotion of social and pragmatic language skills (Quill, 2000). These skills can make the difference in the individual's ability to attain independent living, employment, and higher education. Encouraging social and pragmatic language development can be accomplished through a variety of approaches including "social stories," inclusion in the general education classroom (see Chapter 30), individual and small-group speech-language services, social skills training groups, supervised social group experiences, and tutoring by typical peers (Rogers, 2000). There is some suggestion, however, that individuals with PDDs do not generalize rehearsal in a group to other settings unless specific direction is given to promote this. Moreover, these techniques may not bridge the gap between social interactions and social relationships (Bauminger & Kasari, 2000). Therefore, educational objectives should help a child use a new social skill in a variety of settings with different people and situations until that skill has been mastered (Coyne et al., 1999). An integrated approach infuses pragmatic language and social skills training into each classroom activity and time period rather than pulling children out of class.

Family Support

It was once thought that individuals with autistic disorder and other PDDs have no interest in or ability to relate to others, including family members. This is not true; family members can have vital and trusting relationships with individuals who have social learning disorders. It is common for individuals with PDDs to be attached to family members and more comfortable in their presence.

The specific role family members play in the life of a child or young adult with a PDD will depend on that individual's skills and limitations (Janzen, 2000). For almost all children with PDDs, parents are the most important resource for learning about other people and for fostering social interactions. Beyond this, parents are crucial for implementing appropriate behavior programs and being advocates for their child's optimal educational placement throughout the year, including summers. Parents take on the role of interpreting the world and buffering their children from experiences that are excessively taxing or stimulating. And, parents are primarily responsible for assembling a team of experts to assist them in keeping their child healthy, finding optimal educational programs, monitoring progress, and making important life decisions.

Siblings also may be quite influential. Many children with PDDs relate to siblings as their first and primary child relationships. Play with siblings can teach a child with a PDD how to take turns, share, and become more flexible in interactions with other people. In addition, an older sibling can be a guide when parents are unable to help. A younger sibling can provide social opportunities that may be more appropriate for the child with a PDD. A sibling helps parents understand how a typical child develops and learns; this can bring into sharper focus the difficulties or obstacles facing the child with a PDD. Having a sibling with autistic disorder, however, may produce different demands than having a sibling with another chronic medical condition. Siblings have a harder time comprehending autism and often do not understand the explanations offered by parents (Glasberg, 2000).

Medications

Medications play only a modest supporting role in the general treatment of PDDs, and there is no medication that affects the core features of these disorders (Tanguay, 2000). Treatment with medication requires intense monitoring by an experienced medical professional. Side effects are often a problem because these children can be sensitive to otherwise insignificant changes in their world. For this reason, medication is not for every child with a PDD, nor should it be considered casually. It is most helpful to consider medication under two circumstances. The primary case is when an individual has symptoms that have not responded to a proper educational environment or behavioral treatment. The second situation is when symptoms severely hamper participating at school or managing at home, when symptoms pose a risk to the child or other's safety, or when a child is distressed constantly.

Medication may be useful for some specific symptoms (see Chapter 19 and Appendix C; Buitelaar & Willemsen-Swinkels, 2000). Aggression, agitation, and self-injurious behaviors have been treated with atypical neuroleptic drugs such as risperidone (Risperdal), clozapine (Clozaril), and olanzapine (Zyprexa) (Arnold et al., 2000; McDougle, Kresch, & Posey, 2000; see Appendix C). These drugs act by blocking dopamine receptors. Other drugs used for treating severe aggression include drugs with anticonvulsant or mood-stabilizing properties such as carbamazepine (Tegretol) and valproic acid (Depakene, Depakote); the anti-anxiety drug buspirone (BuSpar); or another mood-stabilizing drug, lithium. Ritualistic behaviors, stereotyped movements, anxiety, and difficulties in making transitions may decrease with serotonin reuptake inhibitors (SRIs) such as fluoxetine (Prozac), paroxetine (Paxil), sertraline (Zoloft), fluvoxamine (Luvox), and clomipramine (Anafranil) (McDougle, Scahill, et al., 2000). Decreasing anxiety may also lead to more socialization and have some modest beneficial effect on language. Some children with hyperactivity or inattention respond well to methylphenidate (e.g., Ritalin, Concerta), dextroamphetamine (e.g., Dexedrine) or dextroamphetamine /amphetamine (Adderall), but these drugs also can increase self-stimulatory behavior, irritability, and social withdrawal (Aman & Langworthy, 2000; Tsai, 1999). The antihypertensive agent, clonidine (Catapres), has shown some short-term success in controlling hyperactivity and sleep problems, but it does little to improve attention (Riddle et al., 1999). Opioid inhibitors (e.g., naltrexone [Trexan, REVIA]) have also shown weak efficacy in the treatment of self-injurious behavior and hyperactivity in individuals with autistic disorder.

Alternative Medicine, Nutritional Supplements, and Controversial Therapies

Considerable attention is being paid to alternative medicine and nutritional supplements for treatment of PDDs (American Academy of Pediatrics, Committee on Children with Disabilities, 2001a). Usually such attention is a sign that traditional medicine has not produced as much benefit as anyone would like. The problem with these nontraditional approaches is that they rarely have been studied in a scientific manner. Testimonials about the success of a treatment may exist, but it can be hard to know whether the active intervention or something else was instrumental in the improvement. Thus, it is hard to recommend any of the currently used alternative medicine or nutritional supplements. People still use them, however, so certain guidelines have been proposed: 1) The therapy should not compromise the child's attendance at his or her optimal school program and should not delay entry into a program; 2) it should not be too expensive; and 3) it should be safe and noninvasive.

One example of nontraditional therapy is the use of secretin, a peptide hormone that stimulates pancreatic secretion. A hypothesis was put forth that secretin could reverse abnormal intestinal permeability and thereby affect the abnormal central neurotransmitter metabolism in autistic disorder (Horvath et al., 1999). A number of controlled, double-blinded studies, however, could not replicate the initial report of beneficial effects (Chez et al., 2000; Coniglio et al., 2001; Dunn-Geier et al., 2000; Owley et al., 1999, Sandler et al., 1999). In a similar vein, there was the conjecture that corticosteroids might prove useful. The rationale was that certain forms of autistic disorder might arise from an autoimmune disease (Burger & Warren, 1998; Furlano et al., 2001; Gupta, 2000; van Gent, Heijnen, & Treffers, 1997), but there is little reliable data to support this hypothesis (DelGiudice-Asch et al., 1999).

LIVING WITH A CHILD WITH A PERVASIVE DEVELOPMENTAL DISORDER

Just as the family influences the child with PDD, so such a child powerfully influences the family (Kephart, 1998). For many, the child brings out the best in the family. Each member may become more aware of the others and appreciate one another's positive attributes more strongly. Life with a child who has a PDD can bring a family closer together and promote deep and mutually satisfying relationships. Parents often find support from their extended family, school, religious community, and neighborhoods.

But having a child with a PDD also can be a significant challenge for parents and siblings. Living with a child who may not be constitutionally able to return affection, empathy, or consideration can be draining. These tensions and pressures can amplify any disharmony that has existed in a relationship prior to the entry of the child with a PDD. Siblings can have more difficulty adapting to their family and peer group. They may also find it harder to achieve developmental tasks of independence and effect a healthy separation from their family. Having a child with a PDD increases the chances of family members' becoming depressed or harboring guilt about not doing enough for the child who has a PDD. In addition, living with a child with a PDD can consume a great deal of energy and time. This can reduce the time available for other relationships among family members. It can also leave little time to spend with friends, neighbors, and extended family and for recreational and community activities, work, and other emotionally refreshing activities.

It is helpful for parents to seek consultation from professionals who are knowledgeable about PDDs and about the effect that such disorders can have on a family. Sometimes family members benefit from attending family therapy, talking with clergy or mental health professionals, or participating in family support groups. There is no one best way for this work to proceed. It may be conducted in the context of the family, with couples, or with individuals.

OUTCOME

Outcome for a child with a PDD is closely linked to his or her language abilities and intelligence (Bryson & Smith, 1998; Harris & Handleman, 2000; Nordin & Gillberg, 1998). One fifth to one half of children with autistic disorder experience regression of skills during the first to third year of life, followed by a period of plateauing and then improvement (Davidovich et al., 2000). Approximately half of all children with autistic disorder acquire language and learn to communicate with useful speech (Howlin, 1997; Smith, Belcher, & Juhrs, 1997). The classic behavioral features of autism tend to recede somewhat over time. Behavior may deteriorate, however, in adolescence, but behavioral support (see Chapter 31) and medications may be helpful. Historically, most adults with autistic disorder have remained dependent to some degree and do not have successful work experiences. A larger number of more mildly affected individuals with Asperger disorder or PDD-NOS are now being identified, however, and these people tend to have better outcomes (Gonzalez et al., 1993). It is increasingly recognized that major barriers to social function may be related to a lack of opportunity or instruction rather than just to intrinsic impairments (Holmes & Schopler, 1998).

SUMMARY

Autistic disorder and the other PDDs are neuropsychological disorders with a genetic basis that present in infancy or early childhood. They are characterized by abnormalities in communication, social interaction, activities, and interests. Children with autistic disorder are more likely to have associated mental retardation and severe communication impairments. Individuals with Asperger disorder or PDD-NOS have a better outcome but still may have substantial difficulties, particularly in interpersonal relationships. Remarkable advances in early recognition and intervention have had a positive impact on outcome and quality of life for individuals with these conditions. Individualized, multidimensional treatment is the standard of care and can produce notable improvements.

REFERENCES

Adolphs, R. (2001). The neurobiology of social cognition. *Current Opinion in Neurobiology, 11,* 231–239.

Afzal, M.A., Minor, P.D., & Schild, G.C. (2000). Clinical safety issues of measles, mumps and rubella vaccines. *Bulletin of the World Health Organization, 78,* 199–220.

Aman, M.G., & Langworthy, K.S. (2000). Pharmacotherapy for hyperactivity in children with autism and other a pervasive developmental disorders. *Journal of Autism and Developmental Disorders, 30,* 451–459.

American Academy of Pediatrics, Committee on Children with Disabilities. (2001a). Counseling families who choose complementary and alternative medicine for their child with chronic illness or disability. *Pediatrics, 107,* 598–601.

American Academy of Pediatrics, Committee on Children with Disabilities. (2001b). The pediatrician's role in the diagnosis and management of autistic spectrum disorder in children. *Pediatrics, 107,* 1221–1226.

American Psychiatric Association. (2000). *Diagnostic and statistical manual of mental disorders* (4th ed., Text rev.). Washington, DC: Author.

Amir, R.E., Van den Veyver, I.B., Wan, M., et al. (1999). Rett syndrome is caused by mutations in X-linked MECP2, encoding methyl-CpG-binding protein 2. *Nature Genetics, 23,* 185–188.

Anderson, G.M., & Hoshino, Y. (1997). Neurochemical studies of autism. In D.J. Cohen & F.R. Volkmar (Eds.), *Handbook of autism and pervasive developmental disorders* (2nd ed., pp. 325–343). New York: John Wiley & Sons.

Arnold, L.E., Aman, M.G., Martin, A., et al. (2000). Assessment in multisite randomized clinical trials of patients with autistic disorder: The Autism RUPP Network. Research Units on Pediatric Psychopharmacology. *Journal of Autism and Developmental Disorders, 30,* 99–111.

Asperger, H. (1991). 'Autistic psychopathy' in childhood (U. Frith, Trans.). In *Autism and Asperger syndrome* (pp. 37–92). Cambridge, England: Cambridge University Press. (Reprinted from *Archiv für Psychiatrie und Nervenkrankheiten, 117,* 76–136 [1944])

Attwood, T., & Wing, L. (1997). *Asperger's syndrome: A guide for parents and professionals.* London, England: Jessica Kingsley Publishers.

Bailey, A., Palferman, S., Heavey, L., et al. (1998). Autism: The phenotype in relatives. *Journal of Autism and Developmental Disorders, 28,* 369–392.

Ballaban-Gil, K., & Tuchman, R. (2000). Epilepsy and epileptiform EEG: Association with autism and language disorders. *Mental Retardation and Developmental Disabilities Research Reviews, 6,* 300–308.

Baron-Cohen, S., Allen, J., & Gillberg, C. (1992). Can autism be detected at 18 months?: The needle, the haystack and the CHAT. *British Journal of Psychiatry, 161,* 839–843.

Baron-Cohen, S., Cox, A., Baird, G., et al. (1996). Psychological markers in the detection of autism in infancy in a large population. *British Journal of Psychiatry, 168,* 158–163.

Baron-Cohen, S., Ring, H.A., Bullmore, E.T., et al. (2000). The amygdala theory of autism. *Neuroscience and Biobehavioral Reviews, 24,* 355–364.

Baron-Cohen, S., Ring, H.A., Wheelwright, S., et al. (1999). Social intelligence in the normal and autistic brain: An fMRI study. *European Journal of Neuroscience, 11,* 1891–1898.

Barrett, S., Beck, J.C., Bernier, R., et al. (1999). An autosomal genomic screen for autism. Collaborative linkage study of autism. *American Journal of Medical Genetics, 88,* 609–615.

Bashe, P.R., & Kirby, B.L. (2001). *The Oasis guide to Asperger syndrome: Advice, support, insights and inspiration.* New York: Crown.

Bauer, S. (1995). Autism and the pervasive developmental disorders. *Pediatrics in Review, 16,* 130–136, 168–176.

Bauman, M.L., & Kemper, T.L. (Eds.). (1994). *The neurobiology of autism.* Baltimore: The Johns Hopkins University Press.

Bauminger, N., & Kasari, C. (2000). Loneliness and friendship in high functioning children with autism. *Child Development, 71,* 447–456.

Berney, T.P. (2000). Autism: An evolving concept. *British Journal of Psychiatry, 176,* 20–25.

Bolton, P.F., Murphy, M., MacDonald, H., et al. (1997). Obstetric complications in autism: Consequences or causes of the condition? *Journal of the American Academy of Child and Adolescent Psychiatry, 36,* 272–281.

Bryson, S.E., & Smith, I.M. (1998). Epidemiology of autism: Prevalence, associated characteristics, and implications for research and service delivery. *Mental Retardation and Developmental Disabilities Research Reviews, 4,* 97–103.

Buitelaar, J.K., & Willemsen-Swinkels, S.H. (2000). Autism: Current theories regarding its pathogenesis and implications for rational pharmacotherapy. *Paediatric Drugs, 2*(1), 67–81.

Burd, L., Severud, R., Kerbeshian, J., et al. (1999). Prenatal and perinatal risk factors for autism. *Journal of Perinatal Medicine, 27,* 441–450.

Burger, R.A., & Warren, R.P. (1998). Possible immunogenetic basis for autism. *Mental Retardation and Developmental Disabilities Research Reviews, 4,* 137–141.

Carr, E.G., Levin, L., McConnachie, G., et al. (1995). *Communication-based intervention for problem behavior: A user's guide for producing positive change.* Baltimore: Paul H. Brookes Publishing Co.

Chakrabarti, S., & Fombonne, E. (2001). Pervasive developmental disorders in preschool children. *Journal of the American Medical Association, 285,* 3093–3099.

Charman, T. (1999). Autism and the pervasive developmental disorders. *Current Opinion in Neurology, 12,* 155–159.

Chez, M.G., Buchanan, C.P., Bagan, B.T., et al. (2000). Secretin in autism: A two part clinical investigation. *Journal of Autism and Developmental Disorders, 30,* 87–94.

Chugani, D.C., Muzik, O., Behen, M., et al. (1999). Developmental changes in brain serotonin synthesis capacity in autistic and nonautistic children. *Annals of Neurology, 45,* 287–295.

Chugani, D.C., Muzik, O., Rothermel, R., et al. (1997). Altered serotonin synthesis in the dentatothalamocortical pathway in autistic boys. *Annals of Neurology, 42,* 666–669.

Cohen, D.J., & Volkmar, F.R. (Eds.). (1997). *Handbook of autism and pervasive developmental disorders* (2nd ed.). New York: John Wiley & Sons.

Coniglio, S.J., Lewis, J.D., Lang, C., et al. (2001). A randomized, double-blind, placebo-controlled trial of single-dose intravenous secretin as treatment for children with autism. *Journal of Pediatrics, 138,* 649–655.

Cook, E.H., Jr. (1998). Genetics of autism. *Mental Retardation and Developmental Disabilities Research Reviews, 4,* 113–120.

Cook, E.H., Jr., Courchesne, R., Lord, C., et al. (1997). Evidence of linkage between the serotonin transporter and autistic disorder. *Molecular Psychiatry, 2,* 247–250.

Coucouvanis, J.(1997). Behavioral intervention for children with autism. *Journal of Child and Adolescent Psychiatric Nursing, 10*(1), 37–44.

Courchesne, E., Karns, C.M., Davis, H.R., et al. (2001). Unusual brain growth patterns in early life in patients with autistic disorder: An MRI study. *Neurology, 57,* 245–254.

Cox, R.D., & Schopler, E. (1993). Aggression and self-injurious behaviors in persons with autism: The TEACCH (Treatment and Education of Autistic and related Communications Handicapped Children) approach. *Acta Paedopsychiatrica, 56,* 85–90.

Coyne, P., Nyberry, C., Vandenburg, M., et al. (1999). *Developing leisure time skills for persons with autism: A practical approach for home, school and community.* Arlington, TX: Future Horizons.

Crino, P.B., & Henske, E.P. (1999). New developments in the neurobiology of the tuberous sclerosis complex. *Neurology, 53,* 1384–1390.

Cumine, V., Leach, J., & Stevenson, G. (2000). *Resource materials for teachers. Autism in the early years: A practical guide.* London: David Fulton.

Davidovich, M., Glick, L., Holtzman, G., et al. (2000). Developmental regression in autism: Maternal perception. *Journal of Autism and Developmental Disorders, 30,* 113–120.

Dawson, G., & Osterling, J. (1997). Early intervention in autism. In M.J. Guralnick (Ed.), *The effectiveness of early intervention* (pp. 307–326). Baltimore: Paul H. Brookes Publishing Co.

DelGiudice-Asch, G., Simon, L., Schmeidler, J., et al. (1999). Brief report: A pilot open clinical trial of intravenous immunoglobulin in childhood autism. *Journal of Autism and Developmental Disorders, 29,* 157–161.

Dunn-Geier, J., Ho, H.H., Auersperg, E., et al. (2000). Effect of secretin on children with autism: A randomized controlled trial. *Developmental Medicine and Child Neurology, 42,* 796–802.

Eliez, S., & Reiss, A.L. (2000). MRI neuroimaging of childhood psychiatric disorders: A selective review. *Journal of Child Psychology and Psychiatry and Allied Disciplines, 41,* 679–694.

Ellaway, C., & Christodoulou, J. (1999). Rett syndrome: Clinical update and review of recent genetic advances. *Journal of Paediatrics and Child Health, 35,* 419–426.

Feinstein, C., & Reiss, A.L. (1998). Autism: The point of view from fragile X studies. *Journal of Autism and Developmental Disorders, 28,* 393–405.

Filipek, P.A., Accardo, P.J., & Baranek, G.T., et al. (1999). The screening and diagnosis of autistic spectrum disorders. *Journal of Autism and Developmental Disorders, 29,* 439–484.

Fletcher, P.C., Happé, F., Frith, U., et al. (1995). Other minds in the brain: A functional imaging study of "theory of mind" in story comprehension. *Cognition, 57,* 109–128.

Folstein, S., & Rutter, M. (1977) Infantile autism: A genetic study of 21 twin pairs. *Journal of Child Psychology, Psychiatry, and Allied Disciplines, 18,* 297–321.

Fombonne, E. (1999). The epidemiology of autism: A review. *Psychological Medicine, 29,* 769–786.

Frea, W.D. (1995). Social-communicative skills in higher-functioning children with autism. In R.L. Koegel & L.K. Koegel (Eds.), *Teaching children with autism: Strategies for initiating positive interactions and improving learning opportunities* (pp. 53–66). Baltimore: Paul H. Brookes Publishing Co.

Frost, L., & Bondy, A. (1994). *PECS: The Picture Exchange Communication System training manual.* Cherry Hill, NJ: Pyramid Educational Consultants.

Furlano, R.I, Anthony A., Day, R., et al. (2001). Colonic CD8 and γδ T-cell infiltration with epithelial damage in children with autism. *Journal of Pediatrics, 138,* 366–372.

Gillberg, C. (1998). Asperger syndrome and high-functioning autism. *British Journal of Psychiatry, 172,* 200–209.

Gillberg, C. (1999). Neurodevelopmental processes and psychological functioning in autism. *Development and Psychopathology, 11,* 567–587.

Gillberg, C., Nordin, V., & Ehlers, S. (1996). Early detection of autism: Diagnostic instruments for clinicians. *European Child and Adolescent Psychiatry, 5*(2), 67–74.

Giovanardi Rossi, P., Posar, A., & Parmeggiani, A. (2000). Epilepsy in adolescents and young adults with autistic disorder. *Brain Development, 22,* 102–106.

Glasberg, B.A. (2000). Development of siblings understanding of autism spectrum disorders. *Journal of Autism and Developmental Disorders, 30,* 143–156.

Gonzalez, N.M., Alpert, M., Shay, J., et al. (1993). Autistic children on follow-up: Change of diagnosis. *Psychopharmacology Bulletin, 29,* 353–358.

Grandin, T. (1995). *Thinking in pictures: And other reports from my life with autism.* New York: Bantam Doubleday Dell.

Grandin, T., & Scariano, M.M. (1996). *Emergence: Labeled autistic.* New York: Warner Books.

Gresham, F.M., & MacMillan, D.L. (1998). Early intervention project: Can its claims be substantiated and its effects replicated? *Journal of Autism and Developmental Disorders, 28,* 5–14.

Grossman, J.B., Carter, A., & Volkmar, F.R. (1997). Social behavior in autism. *Annals of the New York Academy of Sciences, 807,* 440–454.

Gupta, S. (2000). Immunological treatments for autism. *Journal of Autism and Developmental Disorders, 30,* 475–479.

Hagberg, B. (1995). Rett syndrome: Clinical peculiarities and biological mysteries. *Acta Paediatrica, 84,* 971–976.

Halsey, N.A., Hyman, S.L., & the Conference Writing Panel. (2001). Measles-mumps-rubella vaccine and autistic spectrum disorder: Report from the New Challenges in Childhood Immunizations conference convened in Oak Brook, Illinois, June 12–13, 2000. *Pediatrics, 107,* E84.

Harris, S.L., & Handleman, J.S. (2000). Age and IQ at intake as predictors of placement for young children with autism: A four- to six-year follow-up. *Journal of Autism and Developmental Disorders, 30,* 137–142.

Haznedar, M.M., Buchsbaum, M.S., Wei, T.C., et al. (2000). Limbic circuitry in patients with autism spectrum disorders studied with positron emission tomography and magnetic resonance imaging. *American Journal of Psychiatry, 157,* 1994–2001.

Hendry, C.N. (2000). Childhood disintegrative disorder: Should it be considered a distinct diagnosis? *Clinical Psychology Review, 20,* 77–90.

Hobson, R.P., Lee, A., & Brown, R. (1999). Autism and congenital blindness. *Journal of Autism and Developmental Disorders, 29,* 45–56.

Holmes, D.L., & Schopler, E. (1998). *Autism through the lifespan: The Eden model.* Woodbine House.

Horvath, K., Papadimitriou, J.C., Rabsztyn, A., et al. (1999).

Gastrointestinal abnormalities in children with autistic disorder. *Journal of Pediatrics, 135,* 559–563.

Howlin, P. (1997). *Autism: Preparing for adulthood.* London: Routledge.

Howlin, P. (1998). Practitioner review: Psychological and educational treatments for autism. *Journal of Child Psychology and Psychiatry and Allied Disciplines, 39,* 307–322.

Howlin, P., & Asgharian, A. (1999). The diagnosis of autism and Asperger syndrome: Findings from a survey of 770 families. *Developmental Medicine and Child Neurology, 41,* 834–839.

Howson, C.P., Howe, C.J., & Fineberg, H.V. (Eds.). (1991). *Adverse effects of pertussis and rubella vaccines: A report of the Committee to Review the Adverse Consequences of Pertussis and Rubella Vaccines.* Washington, DC: National Academy Press.

Hurth, J., Shaw, E., Iseman, S., et al. (1999). Areas of agreement about effective practices among programs serving very young children with autism spectrum disorders. *Infants and Young Children, 12,* 17–26.

Individuals with Disabilities Education Act Amendments of 1997, PL 105-17, 20 U.S.C. §§ 1400 *et seq.*

Ingram, J.L., Stodgell, C.J., Hyman, S.L., et al. (2000). Discovery of allelic variants of HOXA1 and HOXB1: Genetic susceptibility to autism spectrum disorders. *Teratology, 62,* 393–405.

Janzen, J. (2000). *Autism: Facts and strategies for parents.* The Psychological Corporation.

Jordan, R. (1999). *Autistic spectrum disorders: An introductory handbook for practitioners.* London: David Fulton.

Kanner, L. (1943). Autistic disturbances of affective contact. *Nervous Child, 2,* 217–250.

Kephart, B. (1999). *A slant of sun: One child's courage.* New York: Quill.

Klin, A., Volkmar, F., & Sparrow, S. (Eds.). (2000). *Asperger syndrome.* Guilford Press.

Klin, A., Volkmar, F.R., Sparrow, S.S., et al. (1995). Validity and neuropsychological characterization of Asperger syndrome: Convergence with nonverbal learning disabilities syndrome. *Journal of Child Psychology and Psychiatry and Allied Disciplines, 36,* 1127–1140.

Koegel, L.K., Koegel, R.L., & Dunlap, G. (Eds.). (1996). *Positive behavioral support: Including people with difficult behavior in the community.* Baltimore: Paul H. Brookes Publishing Co.

Koegel, R.L., & Koegel, L.K. (Eds.). (1995). *Teaching children with autism: Strategies for initiating positive interactions and improving learning opportunities.* Baltimore: Paul H. Brookes Publishing Co.

Kraijer, D. (2000). Review of adaptive behavior studies in mentally retarded persons with autism/pervasive developmental disorder. *Journal of Autism and Developmental Disorders, 30,* 39–47.

Krug, D.A., Arick, J., & Almond, P. (1980). Behavior checklist for identifying severely handicapped individuals with high levels of autistic behavior. *Journal of Child Psychology and Psychiatry, 21,* 221–229.

Laan, L.A., van Haeringen, A., & Brouwer, O.F. (1999). Angelman syndrome: A review of clinical and genetic aspects. *Clinical Neurology and Neurosurgery, 103,* 161–170.

Lamb, J.A., Moore, J., Bailey, A., et al. (2000). Autism: Recent molecular genetic advances. *Human Molecular Genetics, 9,* 861–868.

Lewis, M.H., & Bodfish, J.W. (1998). Repetitive behavior disorders in autism. *Mental Retardation and Developmental Disabilities Research Reviews, 4,* 80–89.

Liddle, K. (2001). Implementing the picture exchange communication system (PECS). *International Journal of Language and Communication Disorders, 36*(Suppl.), 391–395.

Lord, C., Risi, S., Lambrecht, L., et al. (2000). The Autism Diagnostic Observation Schedule–Generic: A standard measure of social and communication deficits associated with the spectrum of autism. *Journal of Autism and Developmental Disorders, 30,* 205–223.

Lord, C., Rutter, M., & LeCouteur, A. (1994). Autism Diagnostic Interview–Revised: A revised version of a diagnostic interview for caregivers of individuals with possible pervasive developmental disorders. *Journal of Autism and Developmental Disorders, 24,* 659–685.

Lovaas, O.I. (1987). Behavioral treatment and normal intellectual and educational functioning in autistic children. *Journal of Consulting and Clinical Psychology, 55,* 3–9.

Lovaas, O.I. (1993). The development of a treatment-research project for developmentally disabled and autistic children. *Journal of Applied Behavior Analysis, 26,* 617–630.

Maestrini, E., Lai, C., Marlow, A., et al. (1999). Serotonin transporter (5-HTT) and gamma-aminobutyric acid receptor subunit beta3 (GABRB3) gene polymorphisms are not associated with autism in the IMGSA families. The International Molecular Genetic Study of Autism Consortium. *American Journal of Medical Genetics, 88,* 492–496.

Malhotra, S., & Gupta, N. (1999). Childhood disintegrative disorder. *Journal of Autism and Developmental Disorders, 29,* 491–498.

Manes, F., Piven, J., Vrancic, D., et al. (1999). An MRI study of the corpus callosum and cerebellum in mentally retarded autistic individuals. *The Journal of Neuropsychiatry and Clinical Neurosciences, 11,* 470–474.

Mangravite, D.N. (2001). Regarding autism. *Journal of Pediatrics, 138,* 147–148.

Mantovani, J.F. (2000). Autistic regression and Landau-Kleffner syndrome: Progress or confusion? *Developmental Medicine and Child Neurology, 42,* 349–353.

Mars, A.E., Mauk, J.E., & Dowrick, P.W. (1998). Symptoms of pervasive developmental disorders as observed in prediagnostic home videos of infants and toddlers. *Journal of Pediatrics, 132,* 500–504.

Maugh, T. (1999, April 16). State study finds sharp rise in autism rate. *Los Angeles Times,* p. 3.

Maurice, C., Green, G., & Luce, S. (Eds.). (1996). *Behavioral intervention for young children with autism: A manual for parents and professionals.* Austin, TX: PRO-ED.

Mazzocco, M.M., Kates, W.R., Baumgardner, T.L., et al. (1997). Autistic behaviors among girls with Fragile X syndrome. *Journal of Autism and Developmental Disorders, 27,* 415–436.

McDougle, C.J., Kresch, L.E., & Posey, D.J. (2000). Repetitive thoughts and behavior in pervasive developmental disorders: Treatment with serotonin reuptake inhibitors. *Journal of Autism and Developmental Disorders, 30,* 427–436.

McDougle, C.J., Naylor, S.T., Cohen, D.J., et al. (1996). Effects of tryptophan depletion in drug-free adults with autistic disorder. *Archives of General Psychiatry, 53,* 993–1000.

McDougle, C.J., Scahill, L., McCracken, J.T., et al. (2000). Research Units on Pediatric Psychopharmacology (RUPP) Autism Network. Background and rationale for an initial controlled study of risperidone. *Child and Adolescent Psychiatric Clinics of North America, 9,* 201–224.

Mesibov, G.B., Adams, L.W., & Klinger, L.G. (1998). *Clinical child psychology library. Autism: Understanding the disorder.* New York: Kluwer Academic/Plenum Publishers.

Meyer, G.A., Blum, N.J., Hitchcock, W., et al. (1998). Absence of the fragile X CGG trinucleotide repeat expansion in girls diagnosed with a pervasive developmental disorder. *Journal of Pediatrics, 133,* 363–365.

Minshew, N.J., & Goldstein, G. (1998). Autism as a disorder

of complex information processing. *Mental Retardation and Developmental Disabilities Research Reviews, 4*, 129–136.

Murray-Slutsky, C., & Paris, B.A. (2000). *Exploring the spectrum of autism and pervasive developmental disorders: Intervention strategies.* San Antonio, TX: Therapy Skill Builders.

Njardvik, U., Matson, J.L., & Cherry, K.E. (1999). A comparison of social skills in adults with autistic disorder, pervasive developmental disorder not otherwise specified, and mental retardation. *Journal of Autism and Developmental Disorders, 29*, 287–295.

Nordin, V., & Gillberg, C. (1998). The long-term course of autistic disorders: Update on follow-up studies. *Acta Psychiatrica Scandinavica, 97*, 99–108.

Owley, T., Steele, E., Corsello, C., et al. (1999). A double-blind, placebo-controlled trial of secretin for the treatment of autistic disorder. *Medscape General Medicine, 6*, E2.

Ozonoff, S., & Cathcart, K. (1998). Effectiveness of a home program intervention for young children with autism. *Journal of Autism and Developmental Disorders, 28*, 25–32.

Panerai, S., Ferrante, L., & Caputo, V. (1997). The TEACCH strategy in mentally retarded children with autism: A multidimensional assessment. Pilot study: Treatment and Education of Autistic and Communication Handicapped children. *Journal of Autism and Developmental Disorders, 27*, 345–347.

Peterson, C.C., & Siegal, M . (1997). Domain specificity and everyday biological, physical, and psychological thinking in normal, autistic, and deaf children. *New Directions in Child Development, 75*, 55–70.

Piven, J. (1997). The biological basis of autism. *Current Opinion in Neurobiology, 7*, 708–712.

Prizant, B.M. (1996). Brief report: Communication, language, social, and emotional development. *Journal of Autism and Developmental Disorders, 26*, 73–178.

Prizant, B.M., & Wetherby, A.M. (1998). Understanding the continuum of discrete-trial traditional behavioral to social-pragmatic developmental approaches in communication enhancement for young children with autism/PDD. *Seminars in Speech and Language, 19*, 329–52, quiz 353, 424.

Quill, K.A. (2000). *DO-WATCH-LISTEN-SAY: Social and communication intervention for children with autism.* Baltimore: Paul H. Brookes Publishing Co.

Rapin, I. (1997). Autism. *New England Journal of Medicine, 337*, 97–104.

Rapin, I. (1998). Understanding childhood language disorders. *Current Opinion in Pediatrics, 10*, 561–566.

Rapin, I., & Dunn, M. (1997). Language disorders in children with autism. *Seminars in Pediatric Neurology, 4*, 86–92.

Rapin, I., & Katzman, R. (1998). Neurobiology of autism. *Annals of Neurology, 43*, 7–14.

Richdale, A. (1999). Sleep problems in autism: Prevalence, cause and intervention. *Developmental Medicine and Child Neurology, 41*, 60–66.

Riddle, M.A., Bernstein, G.A., Cook, E.H., et al. (1999). Anxiolytics, adrenergic agents, and naltrexone. *Journal of American Academy of Child and Adolescent Psychiatry, 38*, 546–556.

Robins, D.L., Fein, D., Barton, M.L., et al. (2001). The modified checklist for autism in toddlers: An initial study investigating the early detection of autism and pervasive developmental disorders. *Journal of Autism and Developmental Disorders, 31*, 131–144.

Rodier, P.M. (2000). The early origins of autism. *Scientific American, 282*(2), 56–63.

Rogers, S.J. (1996). Brief report: Early intervention in autism. *Journal of Autism and Developmental Disorders, 26*, 243–246.

Rogers, S.J. (1998). Neuropsychology of autism in young children and its implications for early intervention. *Mental Retardation and Developmental Disabilities Research Reviews, 4*, 104–112.

Rogers, S.J. (2000). Interventions that facilitate socialization in children with autism. *Journal of Autism and Developmental Disorders, 30*, 399–410.

Rumsey, J.M., & Ernst, M. (2000). Functional neuroimaging of autistic disorders. *Mental Retardation and Developmental Disability Research Reviews, 6*, 171–179.

Rutter, M. (1985a). Infantile autism and other pervasive developmental disorders. In M. Rutter & L. Hersov (Eds.), *Child and adolescent psychiatry: Modern approaches* (pp. 545–566). Oxford, England: Blackwell Scientific.

Rutter, M. (1985b). The treatment of autistic children. *Journal of Child Psychology and Psychiatry and Allied Disciplines, 26*, 193–214.

Rutter, M. (2000). Genetic studies of autism: From the 1970s into the millennium. *Journal of Abnormal Child Psychology, 28*, 3–14.

Rutter, M., Bailey, A., Simonoff, E., et al. (1997). Genetic influences in autism. In D.J. Cohen & F.R. Volkmar (Eds.). *Handbook of autism and pervasive developmental disorders* (2nd ed., pp. 370–387). New York: John Wiley & Sons.

Sandler, A.D., Sutton, K.A., DeWeese, J., et al. (1999). Lack of benefit of a single dose of synthetic human secretin in the treatment of autism and pervasive developmental disorder. *New England Journal of Medicine, 341*, 1801–1806.

Schain, R.J., & Freedman, D.X. (1961). Studies on 5 hydoxyindole metabolism in autistic and other mentally retarded children. *Journal of Pediatrics, 58*, 315–320.

Schleien, S.J., Mustonen, T., & Rynders, J.E. (1995). Participation of children with autism and nondisabled peers in a cooperatively structured community art program. *Journal of Autism and Developmental Disorders, 25*, 397–413.

Schopler, E., Mesibov, G.B., & Kunce, L. (Eds.). (1998). *Asperger syndrome or high functioning autism?* New York: Kluwer Academic/Plenum Publishers.

Schopler, E., Reichler, R.J., & Renner, B.R. (1986). *The Childhood Autism Rating Scale (CARS) for diagnostic screening and classification of autism.* New York: Irvington.

Schreibman, L. (2000). Intensive behavioral/psychoeducational treatments for autism: Research needs and future directions. *Journal of Autism and Developmental Disorders, 30*, 373–379.

Schultz, R.T., Gauthier, I., Klin, A., et al. (2000). Abnormal ventral temporal cortical activity during face discrimination among individuals with autism and Asperger syndrome. *Archives of General Psychiatry, 57*, 331–340.

Simpson, R., & Myles, B. (Eds.). (1998). *Educating children and youth with autism: Strategies for effective practice.* Austin, TX: PRO-ED.

Smalley, S. (1997). Genetic influences in childhood-onset psychiatric disorders: Autism and attention-deficit/hyperactivity disorder. *American Journal of Human Genetics, 60*, 1276–1282.

Smalley, S.L. (1998). Autism and tuberous sclerosis. *Journal of Autism and Developmental Disorders, 28*, 407–414.

Smith, M.D., Belcher, R.G., & Juhrs, P.D. (1997). *A guide to successful employment for individuals with autism.* Baltimore: Paul H. Brookes Publishing Co.

Steffenburg, S., Gillberg, C.L., Steffenburg, U., et al. (1996). Autism in Angelman syndrome: A population-based study. *Pediatric Neurology, 14*, 131–136.

Stern, J.S., & Robertson, M.M. (1997). Tics associated with autistic and pervasive developmental disorders. *Neurologic Clinics, 15*, 345–355.

Stone, W.L., Coonrod, E.E., & Ousley, O.Y. (2000). Brief report: Screening Tool for Autism in Two-Year-Olds (STAT). Development and preliminary data. *Journal of Autism and Developmental Disorders, 30*, 607–612.

Stone, W.L., Ousley, O.Y., Hepburn, S.L., et al. (1999). Patterns of adaptive behavior in very young children with autism. *American Journal on Mental Retardation, 104*, 187–199.

Stratton, K.R., Howe, C.J., & Johnston, R.B., Jr. (Eds.). (1993). *Adverse events associated with childhood vaccines: Evidence bearing on casuality*. Washington, DC: National Academy Press.

Tanguay, P.E. (2000). Pervasive developmental disorders: A 10-year review. *Journal of the American Academy of Child and Adolescent Psychiatry, 39*, 1079–1095.

Taylor, M., Miller, E., Farrington, C.P., et al. (1999). Autism and measles, mumps, and rubella vaccine: No epidemiological evidence for a causal association. *Lancet, 353*, 2026–2029.

Towbin, K.E. (1997a). Autism and Asperger's syndrome. *Current Opinion in Pediatrics, 9*, 361–366.

Towbin, K.E. (1997b). Pervasive developmental disorder not otherwise specified. In D.J. Cohen & F.R. Volkmar (Eds.), *Handbook of autism and pervasive developmental disorders* (2nd ed., pp. 123–147). New York: John Wiley & Sons.

Travis, L.L., & Sigman, M. (1998). Social deficits and interpersonal relationships in autism. *Mental Retardation and Developmental Disabilities Research Reviews, 4*, 65–72.

Trottier, G., Srivastava, L., & Walker, C.D. (1999). Etiology of infantile autism: A review of recent advantages in genetic neurobiological research. *Journal of Psychiatry and Neuroscience, 24*, 103–115.

Tsai, L.Y. (1999). Psychopharmacology in autism. *Psychosomatic Medicine, 61*, 651–665.

Tuchman, R. (2000). Treatment of seizure disorders and EEG abnormalities in children with autism spectrum disorders. *Journal of Autism and Developmental Disorders, 30*, 491–495.

Turner, M. (1999). Annotation: Repetitive behaviour in autism. A review of psychological research. *Journal of Child Psychology and Psychiatry and Allied Disciplines, 40*, 839–849.

Turner, M., Barnby, G., & Bailey, A. (2000). Genetic clues to the biological basis of autism. *Molecular Medicine Today, 6*, 238–244.

Van Gent, T., Heijnen, C.J., & Treffers, P.D. (1997). Autism and the immune system. *Journal of Child Psychology and Psychiatry and Allied Disciplines, 38*, 337–349.

Veenstra-VanderWeele, J., Gonen, D., Leventhal, B.L., et al. (1999). Mutation screening of the UBE3A/E6-AP gene in autistic disorder. *Molecular Psychiatry, 4*, 64–67.

Vig, S., & Jedrysek, E. (1999). Autistic features in young children with significant cognitive impairment: Autism or mental retardation? *Journal of Autism and Developmental Disorders, 29*, 235–248.

Volkmar, F. (Ed.). (1998). *Autism and pervasive developmental disorders* (Cambridge Monographs in Child and Adolescent Psychiatry). Cambridge, England: Cambridge University Press.

Volkmar, F.R., Carter, A., Sparrow, S.S., et al. (1993). Quantifying social development in autism. *Journal of the American Academy of Child and Adolescent Psychiatry, 32*, 627–632.

Volkmar, F., Cook, E.H., Jr., Pomeroy, J., et al. (1999). Practice parameters for the assessment and treatment of children, adolescents, and adults with autism and other pervasive developmental disorders. American Academy of Child and Adolescent Psychiatry Working Group on Quality Issues. *Journal of the American Academy of Child and Adolescent Psychiatry, 38*(12, Suppl.), 32S–54S.

Volkmar, F.R., Klin, A., Marans, W., et al. (1997). Childhood disintegrative disorder. In D.J. Cohen & F.R. Volkmar (Eds.), *Handbook of autism and pervasive developmental disorders* (2nd ed., pp. 47–60). New York: John Wiley & Sons.

Volkmar, F.R., Klin, A., & Pauls, D. (1998). Nosological and genetic aspects of Asperger syndrome. *Journal of Autism and Developmental Disorders, 28*, 457–463.

Wassink, T.H., & Piven, J. (2000). The molecular genetics of autism. *Current Psychiatry Reports, 2*, 170–175.

Wassink, T.H., Piven, J., Vieland, V.J., et al. (2001). Evidence supporting WNT2 as an autism susceptibility gene. *American Journal of Medical Genetics, 105*, 406–413.

Webb, E.V., Lobo, S., Hervas, A., et al. (1997). The changing prevalence of autistic disorder in a Welsh health district. *Developmental Medicine and Child Neurology, 39*, 150–152.

Werner, E., Dawson, G., Osterling, J., et al. (2000). Brief report: Recognition of autism spectrum disorder before one year of age. A retrospective study based on home videotapes. *Journal of Autism and Developmental Disorders, 30*, 157–162.

Wilkinson, K.M. (1998). Profiles of language and communication skills in autism. *Mental Retardation and Developmental Disabilities Research Reviews, 4*, 73–79.

Williams, D. (1992). *Nobody nowhere: The extraordinary autobiography of an autistic*. New York: Times Books.

Wimpory, D., Chadwick, P., & Nash, S. (1995). Brief report: Musical interaction therapy for children with autism. An evaluative case study with two-year follow-up. *Journal of Autism and Developmental Disorders, 25*, 541–552.

Wing, L. (1981). Asperger's syndrome: A clinical account. *Psychological Medicine, 11*, 115–129.

World Health Organization. (1992–1994). *International statistical classification of diseases and related health problems (ICD-10)*. Geneva: Author.

21 Attention Deficits and Hyperactivity

Mark A. Stein, Lisa A. Efron,
Wendy B. Schiff, and Marianne Glanzman

Upon completion of this chapter, the reader will:

- be familiar with the characteristics of attention-deficit/hyperactivity disorder
- be aware of some of the causes of inattention and hyperactivity
- understand the components of the diagnostic process
- know the different approaches to management
- be aware of the natural history and outcomes for this disorder

Attention-deficit/hyperactivity disorder (ADHD) is one of the most common reasons for referral to pediatricians, educational specialists, and child mental health professionals (Goldman et al., 1998). It is a neurobehavioral syndrome that begins in early childhood and is diagnosed in individuals who display developmentally inappropriate levels of inattention or hyperactivity with impairments in adaptive functioning at home, at school, and/or in social situations. Treatment improves academic, social, and adaptive functioning (Pelham & Gnagy, 1999). It is anticipated, though not proven, that comprehensive management can lead to improved long-term outcomes for children with ADHD (Ingram, Hechtman, & Morgenstern, 1999).

JASON AND ELIZABETH

Jason, 7 years old, is in second grade. His teacher reports that Jason is having great difficulty learning to read. He also is quite disruptive in class, frequently not listening to directions, getting out of his seat, making silly comments, and talking out of turn. Similar problems were reported by his first-grade teacher, but these difficulties were attributed to his adjusting to the new school, as he had attended a Montessori kindergarten. His parents and soccer coach have also noticed that Jason has problems with following directions and paying attention. Jason was adopted shortly after birth, so no family history is available. He has, however, always had a "difficult" temperament. He was a colicky baby with poor sleep patterns. As a preschooler, he was demanding and exhausted all those around him. His parents and teachers feel that he requires much more attention than other children his age do.

Elizabeth is a 12-year-old sixth grader. She did well in the first few years of elementary school, but her grades have steadily declined since fourth grade. Although she spends hours doing her homework, she still seems unprepared for class and has difficulty keeping up with her schoolwork. She is well liked by her teachers and has several close friends, but recently her parents have become concerned that her self-esteem is suffering. She has made comments about being stupid and seems to be having increasing difficulty getting her assignments completed on time. She is described as frequently staring into space. Her mother has a history of mild depression, but otherwise there is no family history of psychiatric disorders or ADHD.

Although very different from one another, both Jason and Elizabeth have ADHD. Comprehensive evaluations revealed that Jason had ADHD, combined type, and a learning disability in reading, though he was intellectually gifted, and that Elizabeth met criteria for the predominantly inattentive subtype of ADHD and had average to above-average intellectual abilities with a relative strength in her verbal compared with nonverbal, perceptual abilities. Although stimulant medication is likely to be helpful for both of them, they will require different approaches to treatment. Elizabeth is at risk primarily for academic failure and will require additional counseling for self-esteem and performance anxiety issues as well as a "504 plan" (discussed later) and study skills instruction. She takes medication only for the hours when she is at school or is completing homework. Jason, on the other hand, is at significant risk for both academic and behavioral difficulties and requires medication on weekends and during school vacations as well. His psychosocial treatment focuses on the development of a consistent behavior management plan at home and school, with a daily report card and an intensive summer camp program that emphasizes sports and social skills instruction. At school, he receives resource room teaching for reading and language arts and meets with the school counselor for a weekly social skills group.

A HISTORY OF ATTENTION-DEFICIT/HYPERACTIVITY DISORDER

Since the early 1900s, a plethora of terms has been used to refer to individuals with attention problems or hyperactivity. These have included Post-encephalitic Syndrome, Minimal Brain Damage, Minimal Brain Dysfunction, Hyperkinetic Reaction of Childhood, Hyperactivity, Attention Deficit Disorder with or without Hyperactivity and most recently, Attention-Deficit/Hyperactivity Disorder (American Psychiatric Association [APA], 1994). Since the 1970s, the diagnostic nomenclature has changed several times, reflecting evolving views of the most salient features of the disorder as well as changing conceptualizations of the presumed origin (Swanson et al., 1998). At first, hyperactivity was considered the most important feature. In the 1970s, attention deficits, rather than hyperactivity, were considered primary. In the 1990s, the importance of impulsivity in influencing outcome was recognized. A growing understanding of the underlying biological and neuropsychological mechanisms will clarify how inattention/distractibility and hyperactivity/impulsivity are or are not related and how they contribute to the specific symptoms and impairments in a given individual.

DIAGNOSIS AND ADHD SUBTYPES

ADHD is a neurobehavioral syndrome; there are no currently available medical or psychological tests to make the diagnosis. Instead, the diagnosis depends on an experienced clinician who can evaluate whether clinically significant ADHD symptoms are present; decide whether they result in significant impairment; and determine that these symptoms are not the result of another psychiatric, medical, or social condition. The current diagnostic criteria that define the disorder consist of two major clusters of symptoms: inattention and hyperactivity/impulsivity (APA, 2000). These criteria are shown in Table 21.1.

Attention-Deficit/Hyperactivity Disorder, Combined Type

Children who display a significant number of symptoms (six or more) from each of the symptom clusters are said to have ADHD, combined type, provided that the symptoms were evident

Table 21.1. Diagnostic criteria for attention-deficit/hyperactivity disorder (ADHD)

At least six symptoms of *inattention* or at least six symptoms of *hyperactivity/ impulsivity* lasting 6 months:

I. Symptoms of inattention
1. Often fails to give attention to detail or makes careless mistakes
2. Often has difficulty sustaining attention
3. Often does not seem to listen
4. Often does not follow through on instruction and fails to finish tasks
5. Often has difficulty organizing tasks and activities
6. Often avoids or dislikes tasks that require sustained mental effort
7. Often loses things
8. Is often easily distracted
9. Is often forgetful

II. Symptoms of hyperactivity/impulsivity
1. Often fidgets or squirms
2. Often leaves seat when remaining seated is expected
3. Often runs about or climbs excessively in inappropriate situations
4. Often has difficulty engaging in activities quietly
5. Is often "on the go" or "driven by a motor"
6. Often talks excessively
7. Often blurts out answers before questions have been completed
8. Often has difficulty awaiting turn
9. Often interrupts or intrudes on others

From DIAGNOSTIC AND STATISTICAL MANUAL OF MENTAL DISORDERS: DSM-IV-TR (p. 92) by AMERICAN PSYCHIATRIC ASSOCIATION. Copyright 2000 by AM PSYCHIATRIC ASSN (DSM). Reproduced with permission of AM PSYCHIATRIC ASSN (DSM) in the format Textbook via Copyright Clearance Center.

before age 7, have persisted for at least 6 months, occur across settings, represent an impairment, and cannot be accounted for by another disorder. In addition to having a short attention span, impulsivity, and hyperactivity, affected children also display a low frustration tolerance, a lack of or inconsistent motivation for all but the most stimulating activities, a tendency to become bored easily, and a relative inability to recognize future consequences of behavior and thus modify behavior in response to previous mistakes. ADHD, combined type, is the most common form of ADHD and the subtype about which the most is known (Barkley, 1998b).

Attention-Deficit/Hyperactivity Disorder, Predominantly Inattentive Type

The second most common subtype, ADHD, predominantly inattentive type, includes individuals who do not display significant levels of hyperactivity but who have significant problems in maintaining attention. Some children with ADHD, combined type, "grow out" of their hyperactive symptoms and in adolescence meet criteria for ADHD, predominantly inattentive type. For those who never displayed hyperactive or impulsive symptoms, some evidence suggests that the specific nature of inattention in this subtype may differ from the inattention shown by those with the combined subtype. A "slow" cognitive tempo is characteristic in the predominantly inattentive subtype of ADHD. The ratio of girls to boys with this subtype is slightly higher than for the other subtypes, and this subtype is usually identified at a later age. The pattern of psychiatric comorbidity also differs from that of ADHD, combined type, with fewer disruptive behavior disorders among individuals with the predominantly inattentive subtype and their relatives. Educational impairments are the most prominent difficulty experienced by individuals with this kind of ADHD (Barkley, 1998b; McBurnett, Pfiffner, & Ottolini, 1999).

Attention-Deficit/Hyperactivity Disorder, Predominantly Impulsive/Hyperactive Type

The third subtype, ADHD, predominantly impulsive/hyperactive type, was first identified in the DSM-IV (APA, 1994) and refers to children who do not display significant levels of attention problems in the presence of hyperactivity and impulsivity. This subtype is generally used to describe young children believed to be at risk for ADHD, combined type, who have not yet reached the age at which significant attention problems are evident. Little is known about the developmental course of this subtype or its response to treatment. One study, however, suggested that this group displays impairments similar to those of individuals with ADHD, combined type (Lahey et al., 1998).

Attention-Deficit/Hyperactivity Disorder, Not Otherwise Specified

Finally, the label ADHD, not otherwise specified, can be used for individuals who have significant functional impairment from the symptoms of ADHD but who may not meet the strict criteria for the number of symptoms or the age of onset. Any of the subtypes can be used with the phrase *in partial remission* when symptoms are present but have improved such that the individual no longer meets the strict criteria for diagnosis.

PREVALENCE AND EPIDEMIOLOGY

For a variety of reasons that have been insufficiently analyzed, there has been a significant increase worldwide in the number of individuals diagnosed and treated for ADHD (Robinson et al., 1999). It is unclear whether this increase represents changes in the diagnostic classification system, improved identification, an actual increase in the number of symptomatic children, or all three. Particularly dramatic has been the increase in the use of stimulant medication in the United States (Safer & Zito, 1999).

Studies suggest that ADHD continues to be both over- and underdiagnosed (Angold et al., 2000). Although diagnostic practices, service utilization, and prevalence rates differ widely across and within cultures, when similar diagnostic procedures are utilized ADHD has been detected in 2%–9% of children (Wolraich et al., 1996). The combined and predominantly impulsive/hyperactive subtypes of ADHD are more common in boys. This is especially true in clinical settings, in which the male to female ratio ranges from 9:1 to 3:1 (Sharp et al., 1999). The predominantly inattentive subtype has a more equal gender ratio. Although there has been increased interest in studying ADHD in females and across various age groups, the vast majority of knowledge of the disorder comes from studies of elementary school–age boys.

CAUSES OF ATTENTION-DEFICIT/HYPERACTIVITY DISORDER

Brain damage caused by prenatal insults or postnatal brain infection was identified as a cause of ADHD in the 20th century; it is now recognized, however, that acquired brain damage is not the cause of ADHD in the vast majority of affected children. In addition, although social factors, such as inadequate parenting or poverty, may influence the functioning and severity of symptoms in children who have ADHD, such factors are not believed to play a causal role in the disorder itself.

Heredity

The most common etiological factor in the development of ADHD is heredity, which is thought to account for cause in approximately 80% of the cases. Siblings of children with ADHD are between 5 and 7 times more likely to be diagnosed with ADHD than are children from unaffected families. Each child of a parent with ADHD has a greater than 50% chance of having ADHD. When an identical twin has ADHD, the other twin also had ADHD in 55%–92% of cases (Cook, 1999).

Three genes have been hypothesized to relate to susceptibility to ADHD: the D4 dopamine receptor gene, the dopamine transporter gene (DAT1), and the D2 dopamine receptor gene (Cook, 1999; Swanson et al., 2000). In molecular genetic studies of ADHD families, a specific allele (variant) of each of these genes has been found to occur at an unexpectedly high frequency in individuals with ADHD. This suggests that specific alleles of these genes may confer increased susceptibility to ADHD. The genes thus far identified do not account for the majority of ADHD symptoms, however, suggesting that other yet unidentified genes also confer susceptibility (or protection). The dopamine-related genes that have been identified are very active in the prefrontal cortex and in the basal ganglia, particularly the striatum (see Chapter 13). These same regions of the brain have been shown to be related to ADHD symptoms and stimulant medication effects in neuroimaging studies. The first replicated molecular genetic finding associated with ADHD is the 10-copy repeat allele of the dopamine transporter gene (Cook, Stein, & Leventhal, 1997).

Other Causes

Although it appears that the most common cause of ADHD is genetic, other conditions known to affect brain development may result in ADHD symptoms or may increase the risk in those who are genetically predisposed. These include 1) prenatal exposure to cigarette smoking, lead, alcohol, and possibly cocaine; 2) prematurity and/or intrauterine growth retardation; 3) brain infections; and 4) inborn errors of metabolism. Chromosomal disorders, such as X-linked abnormalities (e.g., Klinefelter syndrome, Turner syndrome; see Chapter 1), and certain other genetic syndromes, such as neurofibromatosis type I, Williams syndrome, fragile X syndrome (see Chapter 17), and Tourette syndrome, are associated with attention problems or with overactivity/impulsivity (Accardo, 1999; Mercugliano, Power, & Blum, 1999). In addition, there appears to be an increased incidence of a variety of complications during labor, delivery, and infancy in children with nonfamilial ADHD, although how the complications relate specifically to ADHD is unclear (Sprich-Buckminster et al., 1993).

Structural and Functional Differences in the Brain

Multiple lines of evidence suggest that subtle structural and functional differences exist in the brains of individuals with ADHD (Glanzman, 2000; Shaywitz et al., 1999). The frontal lobe of the brain serves as the "executive center," processing incoming stimuli and coordinating appropriate cognitive, emotional, and motor responses. Evidence indicates that the frontal lobe in individuals with ADHD may be compromised in its role of processing incoming stimuli and coordinating appropriate cognitive, emotional, and motor responses, either intrinsically or because of altered communication with other brain regions. In particular, it is thought that dopamine and norepinephrine are involved because the stimulants that are helpful in treating the symptoms of ADHD are known to increase the availability of these neurotransmitters in the frontal lobe. It is hypothesized that the cerebellum and basal ganglia (including the striatum and the globus pallidus) may also be involved because these areas are critical to motor planning, behavioral inhibition, and motivation (Corkum, Tannock, & Moldofsky, 1998). These brain regions have direct and indirect connections to the frontal lobes.

Neuroimaging studies, particularly magnetic resonance imaging, have found that the frontal lobe, cerebellum, and basal ganglia are all smaller and presumably less active in subjects with ADHD than in controls (Aylward et al., 1996; Castellanos et al., 2001; Filipek et al., 1997; Rubia et al., 1999; Semrud-Clikeman et al., 2000; Shaywitz et al., 1999; Vaidya et al., 1998). Further, in preliminary studies using functional magnetic resonance imaging, methylphenidate, the most commonly prescribed drug for ADHD, enhances activity of these hypoactive regions

(Lou et al., 1989; Vaidya et al., 1998) in subjects with ADHD. Methylphenidate has been shown to bind to the dopamine transporter in both in vitro and in vivo animal studies. In resting positron emission tomography metabolic studies with adults who do not have ADHD, methylphenidate has been shown to be taken up primarily in the striatum (Volkow et al., 1998).

Methylphenidate blockade of the dopamine transporter increases the levels of extracellular dopamine in healthy adults (Volkow et al., 2001). Thus, a working hypothesis is that ADHD is characterized by hypoactive frontal-striatal-cerebellar pathways that are functionally enhanced by increasing dopaminergic transmission with stimulant medication. Studies have indicated that adults with ADHD have elevated levels of the striatal dopamine transporter, though it is not clear whether this is also true in children and whether this is an important abnormality or merely the brain's adaptation to a different, more primary abnormality (Dougherty et al., 1999; Dresel et al., 2000; Krause et al., 2000).

CLINICAL COURSE

ADHD can be diagnosed at any age, but the symptom presentation often differs with age. During the preschool years, excessive activity level and impulsivity are typically the most prominent symptoms. This is often accompanied by "intense" temperament, movement from one activity to another, and impulsive aggression toward peers. However, given the high activity level and short attention span of the typical preschooler, only preschoolers severely affected with ADHD will differ sufficiently from the developmental norm to fully meet the criteria for the disorder. Children who present in the preschool period should be carefully assessed for developmental language, cognitive, sensory, and pervasive developmental disorders, all of which can impair the ability to communicate, contributing to disruptive behavior that may mimic ADHD.

Upon starting school, children are confronted with a more structured environment and increased demands for sustained attention. It is during the early school years that many children with ADHD begin experiencing significant impairments in functioning, leading to the diagnosis. Problems with listening and compliance, task completion, work accuracy, and fitting in with the peer group are common concerns of parents and teachers. In adolescence, observable hyperactivity may decline significantly, although teenagers with ADHD may report subjective feelings of restlessness. Concerns often focus on work completion, organization, and following rules. Approximately 70% of children with ADHD diagnosed early in childhood continue to meet the criteria for the disorder in adolescence, although some will meet criteria for ADHD, not otherwise specified, because of a reduced number of symptoms (Barkley, 1998a).

ASSOCIATED IMPAIRMENTS

Deficits in Executive Function

Although ADHD is defined and diagnosed based on the presence of observed behavior, neuropsychological investigations suggest that deficits in executive functioning may underlie the characteristic observed behaviors (Mercugliano, 1999b). Executive functions include sustaining and shifting attention, organizing and prioritizing incoming information, planning, self-monitoring, and inhibiting responses. One of the important processes that allows an individual to carry out his or her executive functions is verbal working memory, or the ability to maintain information in one's thoughts while it is being manipulated. This is clearly an important skill if one is to comprehend in a coherent fashion what is heard or read and may underlie the attentional deficits characteristic of ADHD. Similarly, the ability to inhibit responding until all information is considered is a skill that, when deficient, may result in impulsivity, inflexibility, and affective lability. Barkley (1998c) has developed a theory in which the neuropsychological and behavioral features of ADHD are combined into a broader conceptualization of ADHD as a deficit in self-regulation.

Academic Underachievement

Academic underachievement is often the primary concern of parents of school-age children with ADHD. School is usually a difficult environment for such children, owing to the symptoms of ADHD, and is sometimes further exacerbated by comorbid learning disabilities (see the section called "Other Associated Conditions" and Chapter 22). Learning problems occur on a spectrum of severity in association with ADHD. Although perhaps only 10%–40% of children with ADHD have a learning disorder that meets the criteria for a specific learning disability, the vast majority of children with ADHD will have impairments in their academic skills demonstrated as academic underachievement relative to their intellectual abilities. Difficulty reading (involving word attack skills, comprehension, or both) is the most well-documented academic weakness associated with ADHD. Although the specific prevalence of actual reading disability among students with ADHD is unclear because of variability in how each diagnosis is made, it is estimated to be 30% (Fletcher, Shaywitz, & Shaywitz, 1999). Many children with ADHD also have significant problems with the mechanics and organization of writing, although these problems have received little scientific scrutiny.

Children with ADHD generally have difficulty with the reliable processing of auditory information (Mercugliano, 1999b). This may be related to the underlying neuropsychological characteristic of weak verbal working memory. Although not well studied, there appears to be a high rate of pragmatic language difficulties in children with ADHD, even among those who do not meet criteria for a diagnosis of a developmental language disorder (Camarata & Gibson, 1999). Pragmatic language refers to the use of language for appropriate communicative purposes. As classrooms are generally busy, active, language-rich environments, it is no wonder that children with ADHD struggle with both the listening and the participation required for optimal academic achievement.

Given the extent of academic difficulties that a child with ADHD may encounter, making the school aware of the child's diagnosis is important; in this way classroom and homework accommodations can be made and supports can be provided. Identifying the individual's strengths, both in and outside of school, and capitalizing on those strengths is a critical component of effective treatment. Most children with ADHD benefit from extra assistance and specific accommodations (e.g., extended time for exams, a nondistracting environment, assistance with organizational and study skills, frequent home–school communication to prevent small issues from becoming overwhelming) in the general education classroom.

Impairment in Adaptive Skills

Children with ADHD often display marked impairments in their performance of adaptive skills (Roizen et al., 1994). These skills include a variety of daily living, communication, and social skills that are necessary for self-sufficiency. For example, during interview, the mother of an 11-year-old boy who was referred for reevaluation of ADHD poignantly asked, "When do I have to stop being Nick's brain?"

As a result of the impairments in key adaptive skills that children with ADHD experience, many parents of children with ADHD often decide that it is easier to perform the skill for the child than to have the child complete the task by him or herself. Unfortunately, this strategy fosters dependency and increases parent–child conflicts. When a child's adaptive skills are impaired, it is useful for parents to develop an "adaptive prescription," which often includes a behavior management plan (see Chapter 31) in combination with exposure to environments that encourage the performance of adaptive skills (e.g., summer camp, job).

In addition, children with ADHD often have social difficulties with peers or adults. Many children with ADHD have difficulty "reading" the nuances of social behavior or inhibiting impulsive responses. They may react excessively or overly negatively to the behavior of others, leading other children to enjoy "pushing their buttons" to get a reaction. Children with ADHD, predominantly inattentive type, may be ignored and may not initiate social interactions.

Developmental Coordination Disorder

Children with ADHD may have poor coordination of fine or gross motor skills, compromising their ability to effectively participate in sports, leading to further social isolation (Blondis & Opacich, 1999). For these reasons, the child with ADHD often experiences peer rejection or victimization, especially in less structured settings such as the lunchroom and playground. The result can be a severe blow to the child's self-esteem and the development of significant anxiety about performance in group situations. Children with ADHD may have sufficiently impaired fine motor skills as to be diagnosed with comorbid developmental coordination disorder, which appears to be a predictor of worse outcome in adulthood compared with having ADHD alone (Gillberg, 2001; Rasmussen & Gilberg, 2000).

Sleep Difficulties

Research has supported a link between ADHD and sleep disturbances (Corkum et al., 1999; Corkum et al., 1998; Stein, 1999). Using parental report, Corkum et al. (1999) found that 86% of unmedicated children with ADHD experienced at least one sleep problem, compared with 96% of children with ADHD receiving stimulant medication, 83% of controls with psychiatric disorders, and 55% of typically developing controls. Along these lines, Stein (1999) found that insomnia and nocturnal enuresis (bedwetting) occurred at least once per week in 20%–50% of children with ADHD and nightly in 5%–30% of the sample. More recently, a study using the Multiple Sleep Latency Test demonstrated that children with ADHD were more tired during the day and more likely to fall asleep (Lecendreux et al., 2000).

Accidental and Nonaccidental Injury

Children with ADHD are at greater risk than the general population for accidental and nonaccidental injuries (DiScala et al., 1998). Because of their difficult behaviors, these children are at increased risk for physical abuse at the hands of caregivers. An increase in risk-taking behaviors also increases the likelihood of accidental injuries from falls and motor vehicle versus pedestrian accidents. These can lead to traumatic brain injury with severe and long-term consequences (see Chapter 26). Finally, as drivers, adolescents and young adults with ADHD have been found to have a significantly increased risk for experiencing negative driving-related outcomes, including increased rates of motor vehicle accidents, resulting injuries, and moving violations (Barkley et al., 1993; Woodward, Fergusson, & Horwood, 2000). These negative outcomes do not seem to be related to a lack of knowledge about appropriate driving behavior but rather an inability to exercise the necessary motor and attentional control (Barkley, Murphy, & Kwasnik, 1996). Preliminary evidence suggests that stimulant treatment may improve the driving performance of young adults with ADHD (Cox et al., 2000).

OTHER ASSOCIATED CONDITIONS

Numerous medical, psychiatric, and social conditions lead to symptoms that can mimic or coexist with ADHD (Pearl, Weiss, & Stein, 2001; Tables 21.2 and 21.3). These conditions must be identified in the course of an evaluation for ADHD because they are different disorders that require different treatment.

Table 21.2. Ruling out conditions that can mimic attention-deficit/hyperactivity disorder (ADHD)

Disorder/problem	Test or procedure to rule out
Vision or auditory problems	Vision or hearing screen, motor exam
Fine or gross motor impairments	Neurological examination, Developmental Test of Visual-Motor Integration–Third Revision (Beery, 1989), occupational therapy evaluation
Poor nutrition	Physical exam, history, blood count
Sleep deprivation	Physical examination, history, sleep diary, actigraph (objective measure of movement and sleep latency)
Absence seizures	History, electroencephalogram (EEG)
Thyroid disease	History, physical exam, thyroid function tests
Medication side effects	History
Syndromes (e.g., fragile X, fetal alcohol, Williams)	Physical examination, history, genetic tests
Poor fit between child and expectations; chaotic home or school environment	Knowledge of child, family, and school (but also consider psychosocial adversity comorbid with ADHD; see Table 21.3)
Mental retardation or borderline normal IQ score	Wechsler Intelligence Scale for Children–Third Edition (WISC-III; Wechsler, 1991)
Pervasive developmental disorders	Screening instrument, such as one of the following:
	Pre-Linguistic Autism Diagnostic Observation Schedule (PL-ADOS; DiLavore, Lord, & Rutter, 1995)
	Autism Screening Instrument for Educational Planning–Second Edition (ASIEP-2; Krug, Arick, & Almond, 1993)
	Autism Diagnostic Interview–Revised (ADI-R; Lord, Rutter, & LeCouteur, 1994)
	Autism Diagnostic Observation Schedule–WPS Edition (ADOS-WPS; Lord et al., 1999)
	Modified-Checklist for Autism in Toddlers (M-CHAT; Robins et al., 2001)
	The Childhood Autism Rating Scale (CARS; Schopler, Reichler, & Renner, 1986)
	Children's Atypical Development Scale (Stein et al., 1994)
	Screening Tool for Autism in Two-Year-Olds (Stone, Coonrod, & Ousley, 2000)

   In addition, several conditions can coexist with ADHD; these are frequently referred to as *comorbid conditions* or *comorbidities*. These conditions need to be identified because they may require additional treatment or may in other ways influence the treatment or clinical course of ADHD. The majority of children who present for evaluations at ADHD specialty clinics have a comorbid condition (Brown, 2000; Bussing, Zima, & Berlin, 1998; Pliszka, Carlson, & Swanson, 1999). Approximately one third of children referred to specialty clinics display additional disruptive behavior disorders, such as oppositional defiant disorder (characterized by noncompliance and defiance of authority) or conduct disorder (characterized by more serious antisocial behaviors). Estimates of mood disorders in children with ADHD vary considerably from study to study, ranging from 14% to 83% (Broitman, Robb, & Stein, 1999). Childhood bipolar dis-

Table 21.3.   Identifying conditions comorbid with attention-deficit/hyperactivity disorder (ADHD)

Common comorbid conditions	Signs or symptoms	Test or procedure to rule out
Oppositional defiant disorder	Argues, has poor compliance	History and rating scales
Conduct disorder	Violates rules, steals	History and rating scales
Learning disorders	Has poor school achievement	Wechsler Intelligence Scale for Children–Third Edition (WISC-III; Wechsler, 1991) and one of the following: Wechsler Individual Achievement Test (WIAT; Wechsler, 1992) Woodcock-Johnson–Revised Tests of Achievement (Woodcock & Johnson, 1989)
Communication disorders	Exhibits language dysfunction	Various tests depending on age, such as one of the following: Peabody Picture Vocabulary Test–Third Edition (PPVT-III; Dunn & Dunn, 1997) MacArthur Communicative Development Inventories (Fenson et al., 1993) Expressive One-Word Picture Vocabulary Test–Revised (Gardner, 1990) Clinical Evaluation of Language Fundamentals–Third Edition (CELF-3; Semel, Wiig, & Secord, 1995)
Developmental coordination disorder	Has poor fine motor skills	Neurodevelopmental examination
Tic disorders	Experiences motor and/or vocal tics	History and examination
Depression and anxiety disorders	Displays sadness, irritability, fears, worries, or somatic complaints	Observation and depression inventory, such as one of the following: Beck Depression Inventory (Beck, 1987) Children's Depression Inventory (Kovacs, 1983) Multidimensional Anxiety Scale for Children (MASC; March, 1999)
Personality disorders	Has a variety of symptoms depending on specific disorder and age	Personality inventory such as the Minnesota Multiphasic Personality Inventory–Adolescent (MMPI-A; Butcher et al., 1992)
Psychosocial adversity (e.g., child abuse)	May exhibit worsened functioning	History; interview; observation suggestive of parental mental health disorder, severe family stress, or abuse/neglect

order is just beginning to be studied and conceptualized; as a result, there is much controversy about its prevalence in ADHD, though estimates range from approximately 10% to 20%. Conversely, the vast majority of children diagnosed with bipolar disorder meet criteria for ADHD. Children with bipolar disorder are likely to be chronically highly irritable, with intermittent explosiveness and some signs of disordered thinking. They tend to have significant aggression and are at risk for additional problems including anxiety and conduct disorders (Pliszka et al., 1999). Anxiety disorders occur in approximately 25% of children with ADHD and may include separation anxiety, generalized anxiety, phobias, or obsessive-compulsive disorder. There is much debate about the prevalence of learning disorders in children with ADHD, and estimates range from 10% to 40% depending on which test and criteria for learning disabilities are utilized. As noted in the section on associated impairments, learning problems occur on a spectrum of severity in association with ADHD. Although perhaps only

10%–40% of children with ADHD have a learning impairment that meets criteria as a learning disability, the vast majority have deficiencies in academic skills demonstrated as academic underachievement relative to their intellectual abilities (Ingersoll & Goldstein, 1993). Likely contributors to the differing findings of comorbid conditions are how these disorders are defined and how patients are selected for study. At the very least, these prevalence estimates highlight the importance of a comprehensive evaluation.

EVALUATION

ADHD is a complex disorder with symptoms that can affect an individual's functioning in a variety of ways. Without a thorough evaluation, important problems may be missed and treatment may be ineffective or inappropriate. Evaluation must include an assessment of the symptoms of ADHD; an evaluation of different conditions that might cause the same symptoms; an assessment of comorbid conditions; and an evaluation of any associated medical, psychosocial, or learning issues that may not reach the threshold for a specific diagnosis but may nonetheless influence the treatment plan.

To cover these four areas, a comprehensive history, physical/neurological examination, and some academic evaluation must be completed. The history, generally taken from the parents, with the child's participation depending on age, includes current status and concerns; previous treatments and their effects; prenatal and perinatal events; medical history; developmental, psychiatric, and behavioral histories; educational course; social and family circumstances; and a biological family history for ADHD symptoms and associated disorders. The medical examination should focus on growth parameters and physical signs of sensory, genetic, chronic medical, and neurologic disorders, as well as mental status, informal communicative ability and insight, and motor skills.

Psychological testing (including intellectual and achievement measures) should focus on the careful assessment of learning disabilities and areas of academic weakness that may not meet criteria for a learning disability but for which additional support may allow the child to make better academic progress. This should include particularly careful assessments of reading mechanics and comprehension and writing. With increasing recognition of the importance of neuropsychological characteristics of ADHD, evaluators are more commonly including tests of verbal and visual memory and processing efficiency, which can be useful in identifying reasons for intellectual-achievement discrepancies and can inform choices about educational remediation strategies. (For reviews of psychoeducational and neuropsychological testing in ADHD, see Gordon and Barkley, 1998, and Trapani, 1999. For a review of psychoeducational tests, see Wodrich, 1997.)

The evaluation may be conducted by a team or a series of individuals, but because of the comprehensive nature of the information required, usually more than one individual is involved. Most families benefit from having one primary person who acts as the case coordinator. He or she is responsible for formulating the diagnosis and communicating the findings and recommendations to the family. Evaluations can be conducted by primary care physicians or by pediatric subspecialists (e.g., pediatrician, developmental-behavioral pediatrician, neurologist, psychiatrist, psychologist) who are familiar with the range of mimic and coexisting conditions associated with this disorder. Additional professionals such as educators and speech-language and occupational therapists may also be asked to provide input.

Structured methods for obtaining information about symptoms of ADHD and related conditions, comparing the level of symptoms with those in age- and gender-matched peers, and assessing the level of functional impairment can be facilitated by the use of **standardized rating scales** and interview formats. In addition, rating scales designed for teachers allow the required collection of information from more than one setting and provide an inventory of ADHD symptom frequencies and for judging severity relative to the child's classmates. Structured diagnostic interviews are most often used in psychiatric and research settings as they are quite time-consuming and require training for standardized administration. Commonly used structured diagnostic interviews include the Diagnostic Interview for Children and Adolescents–Revised (DICA-R; Reich, Leacock, & Shanfeld, 1995), and the NIMH Diagnostic Interview Schedule for Children, Version IV (Shaffer et al., 2000). Commonly used rating scales for parents and teachers to assess ADHD and comorbidity symptoms include the Child Behavior Checklist for Ages 4–18 (CBCL/4–18; Achenbach, 1991a), the Teacher's Report Form for Ages 5–18 (Achenbach, 1991b), and the Behavior Assessment System for Children (BASC; Reynolds & Kamphaus, 1992). Commonly used rating scales to specifically assess ADHD symptoms include the ADHD Rating Scale–IV (DuPaul et al., 1998), the Conners Rating Scale–Revised (Conners, 1997), the ADD-H Comprehensive Teacher's Rating Scale (ACTeRS; Ullman et al., 1996). (For a review of these measures, see Chapter 2 in Mercugliano et al., 1999.)

TREATMENT

Treatment of ADHD by health, mental health, and educational professionals may include education about ADHD for the child, parents, and teachers; counseling; educational interventions; and medication. In general, individualized, multimodal treatment offers the best chance for improved functioning in most children because of the variety of aspects of life that are affected by ADHD.

Empowering the Child, Parent, and Teacher

Perhaps the most important role of clinicians that evaluate and care for a child with ADHD is to empower parents and teachers, and the child as well, to learn as much as possible about ADHD in an ongoing fashion so that parents and teachers can be effective decision makers and advocates throughout the child's life. Parents come to the clinician with a range of abilities and background knowledge, and the clinician must tailor the discussion and educational recommendations to their needs. Likewise, teachers may be more or less knowledgeable about ADHD and skilled in the classroom strategies that may help a child with ADHD succeed. Finally, family members and teachers who do not understand the neuropsychological underpinnings of ADHD may assume that the child with ADHD is undisciplined, unmotivated, or willfully disruptive.

National support and advocacy organizations, mail-order catalogs, books and videotapes, and parent support groups (see Appendix D) can often provide the foundation upon which parents, teachers, siblings, and children with ADHD continue to learn about ADHD and gain insight into its effect on their lives and classrooms and acquire the skills to cope with it. Increasingly, important materials are available on video- and audiotape and in other languages so that parents with limited reading skills in English may also have access to this information.

Psychosocial Interventions

Psychosocial interventions may take the form of parent training in behavior management strategies, family therapy, social skills training, individual therapy, and school consultation (Pelham & Gnagy, 1999). These approaches are particularly useful for targeting the associated impairments in ADHD, such as noncompliance and poor social skills. The appropriate type of psychosocial treatment is determined by the child's age, developmental level, and presenting problems.

Behavior management techniques (e.g., contingency management, **positive reinforcement, time-out**) are the foundation for most parent training and school consultation (see Chapter 31). Such services are important for preschool and school-age children. Parents and teachers can learn a variety of strategies to help manage ADHD behaviors. These strategies generally emphasize the importance of providing immediate and consistent positive consequences for appropriate behavior and negative consequences for inappropriate behavior. Parent training in such skills can be done individually or in group settings. Many different training programs are available for parents of children who display a range of externalizing behaviors (e.g., oppositional defiant disorder, conduct disorder), and these programs have demonstrated short-term effectiveness (McMahon & Wells, 1998). Research also supports the use of behavior interventions in the classroom (DuPaul & Stoner, 1994; Pelham & Gnagy, 1999; Wells et al., 2000). Adolescents can benefit from problem-solving interventions provided in the context of a collaborative relationship with parents and a therapist.

In contrast, there is little data to support the use of individual psychotherapy in treating the core symptoms of ADHD, although it may be very helpful in treating coexisting mood, anxiety, and self-esteem issues, particularly as children approach adolescence. Cognitive therapy approaches that help individuals to change distorted and/or self-defeating thought and behavior patterns and coaching to assist individuals to implement practical, effective self-management strategies have become important components of counseling for adults with ADHD, although it is not clear that a child with ADHD generalizes these strategies to the situations in which they are needed (Pelham & Gnagy, 1999; Wilens et al., 1999). An important area for intervention research is how to blend externally provided behavior management strategies and self-provided cognitive/coaching strategies in a developmentally appropriate fashion so that children with ADHD have the best chance to become adolescents and adults who have the self-confidence, motivation, and ability to increasingly self-manage their daily lives.

Family therapy does not directly affect the core symptoms of ADHD but may be important in assisting parents who have differing views of the child's difficulties and of how to manage these difficulties come to agreement on a consistent approach. It may also be helpful in assisting families in meeting all members' needs equitably when the demands of caring for a child with ADHD disrupt marital, parent–child, and sibling relationships.

Social skills interventions, often conducted in school or other group settings, provide children who have impaired social skills with direct instruction and controlled opportunities to practice adaptive social behaviors. Examples of targets for intervention may include initiating a conversation; joining a social group or game in progress; responding to others' social overtures; and handling social conflicts, teasing, and bullying in more emotionally neutral and productive ways. Meaningful behavioral change, particularly in the area of social skills, is most likely to occur when intervention approaches are conducted in naturalistic settings (e.g., in the home or school rather than in a clinic). For example, DuPaul and Stoner (1994) have described several approaches to school-based interventions for children with ADHD. Because peer victimization and social isolation are such important issues for many children with ADHD, it is fortunate that the importance of investigation of this phenomenon and its remediation has been recognized (Lindsay & Whitman, 1999; Mercugliano et al., 1999).

Jensen, Martin, and Cantwell (1997) have suggested that ADHD be further subtyped based on the presence of aggression or anxious behavior because these characteristics have a significant influence on treatment. Children with ADHD and aggressive behavior appear to be at the greatest risk for a poor outcome and require the most intensive psychosocial and medical interventions. Because ADHD comorbid with anxiety may be associated with a less robust response to stimulant medication and an increased risk for stimulant side effects, psychosocial intervention is particularly important for individuals with ADHD and anxiety (Pliszka et al., 1999).

Educational Interventions

Appropriate school programs are extremely important for children with ADHD, many of whom have coexisting learning disabilities. Even children without a specific learning disability may experience frequent frustration in their attempts to master new material and therefore require some educational assistance. Children with ADHD often require substantial repetition, yet are bored by it, and resist it. A well-trained teacher who is interested in providing special help and an educational program suited to the needs of the child is invaluable. The teacher may need to use behavior management techniques to maintain the child's attention on tasks and improve behavior, teach the child organizational skills, and modify classwork or assignments in light of the child's learning weaknesses or disabilities. Environmental modification may also help. For example, a child who is easily distracted can be moved away from a window or noisy hallway and seated next to the teacher or blackboard. A child who frequently talks to friends in class may do better when not sitting near those friends or when sitting by positive role models. A child who leaves books needed for homework assignments at school is more likely to have the opportunity to complete assignments if a second set of books is kept at home. Hands-on activities in contrast to listening activities tend to increase academic engagement. Preteaching of concepts to be learned individually or in a small group and subsequent review is often helpful. Tutoring outside of school is useful in some cases, especially to ensure that basic concepts that serve as building blocks for more advanced work are learned thoroughly.

When children with ADHD need more educational assistance than is provided in the general education classroom, they may qualify for accommodations within their general classes or in special education settings under either the Individuals with Disabilities Education Act (IDEA) Amendments of 1997 (PL 105-17) or Section 504 of the Rehabilitation Act of 1973 (PL 93-112; see Chapter 30). Having ADHD does not guarantee a student an IEP, but a student with ADHD may qualify for an IEP if he or she has a learning disability, emotional disturbance, or other health impairment. If a student with ADHD does not need modified educational materials, but rather needs assistance or accommodations in order to be successful with the regular educational materials, he or she is likely eligible for a 504 plan. This type of plan provides for accommodations such as regular home–school communication, extra supervision to ensure that the student understands and follows through on instructions, modifications of testing time or format, a quiet environment, an extra set of materials at home, and technological assistance such as tape recorders and word processors (Latham & Latham, 1999; Mercugliano et al., 1999).

Pharmacological Treatment

Medication is often used to treat children with ADHD. Stimulant medications are the most effective and most commonly prescribed medications for ADHD (Bennett et al., 1999; Powers, 1999). Other medications, such as the alpha-2-adrenergic **agonists,** antidepressants, and neuroleptics, may be used with children with ADHD who do not benefit from stimulants, who have significant side effects from stimulants, or who have a comorbid condition that is better treated by one of these medications. Although combinations of these medications are sometimes used, there is little research available concerning the efficacy and safety of combined pharmacological treatment in ADHD.

Stimulant Medication

Children with disruptive behavior problems and overactivity have been treated with stimulant medications for more than 60 years, and these medications remain the most frequently studied and recommended treatment for ADHD (American Academy of Pediatrics, Subcommittee on Attention-Deficit/Hyperactivity Disorder and Committee on Quality Improvement, 2001; Swanson et al., 1993; Wigal et al., 1999). In the 1990s, 1%–3% of children in the United States received a stimulant medication for ADHD (Safer & Malever, 2000; Safer & Zito, 1999). More than 11 million stimulant prescriptions per year are written. There appears to be a significant mismatch, however, between symptoms and treatment. One study showed that one quarter of the children with confirmed ADHD were not receiving drug therapy (Angold et al., 2000). The study also found that more than half of the children who were on stimulant medication did not come close to meeting the diagnostic criteria for ADHD. These findings suggest that more needs to be learned about the variations between the symptoms and diagnosis of ADHD, about the nature of recommendations and treatments from different clinicians, and about the factors that influence service delivery.

Mechanism of Action   Stimulant medications interact with the biogenic amine (dopamine, norepinephrine, and serotonin) transporters, leading to increased availability of these neurotransmitters, although the predominant effect is on dopamine. The methylphenidate stimulants (Ritalin, Ritalin-SR, Metadate, Metadate ER, Metadate CD, Methylin, Methylin ER, Concerta) differ slightly in mechanism of action from the amphetamine (Dexedrine, DextroStat, Adderall) stimulants (Mercugliano, 1999a; Solanto, 1984; Solanto, 1998). The methylphenidate stimulants predominantly block the dopamine transporter, leading to increased synaptic dopamine. To a small degree, they also increase the release of the biogenic amines, primarily dopamine, that have already been incorporated into storage vesicles. Amphetamines increase the release of biogenic amines to a greater degree, are less specific for dopamine, release newly synthesized transmitters, and may specifically increase the release of dopamine by causing the dopamine transporter to work in reverse (Sulzer et al., 1995). Recent evidence suggests that manipulating the dopamine transporter may also have effects on serotonin neurotransmission (Gainetdinov et al., 1999). Pemoline (Cylert), the only stimulant in a third category of stimulants, is rarely used because reports have linked it to severe liver failure (Rosh et al., 1998; Marotta & Roberts, 1998).

Beneficial Effects   Stimulant drugs are most effective in school-age children and adolescents with typical intelligence. They are somewhat less effective in children with mental retardation (Handen et al., 1992; Handen et al., 1991; see Chapter 19). Although they are also effective in children younger than age 6, side effects may be more common (Handen et al., 1999). Adults with ADHD also respond favorably to stimulant treatment, although the effectiveness is slightly less than in children. Characteristics such as gender, family income, functionality of the family, and parents' marital status do not predict treatment response (Spencer et al., 1996; Wigal et al., 1999). The safety and efficacy of stimulant medications have been well established in hundreds of controlled studies (Swanson et al., 1993), though the studies have been short-term (usually 6–8 weeks). These drug trials have demonstrated that stimulant medications reduce or normalize symptoms of ADHD in more than 70% of those treated (Wigal et al., 1999). Stimulants improve attention and performance on many tasks. In addition, stimulants have been found to improve academic productivity and accuracy, improve parent–child interactions, and decrease aggression. The effect of stimulants on academic performance is less strong than that on behavior, with only about half of the children showing significant academic improvement (Rapport et al., 1994). It should be noted, however, that response to stimulant treatment is not diagnostic of ADHD because individuals with other psychiatric or developmental disorders, as well as controls, display similar effects when given stimulant medication (Klein & Wender, 1995; Rapaport et al., 1978).

Side Effects   Decreased appetite is reported in about 80% of children, but it is often mild and limited to daytime hours, with intake increasing in the evening. About 10%–15% of children have substantial weight loss and may require caloric supplementation. Growth velocity slows during continuous treatment with stimulants, but long-term effects are generally minimal, and, in fact, may relate to growth alterations in ADHD itself as opposed to an effect of the medication (Spencer, Biederman, & Wilens, 1998).

A common adverse effect is **rebound,** that is, the development of a temporary worsening of symptoms, including irritability, increased activity, and/or mood swings, when the drug wears off. This phenomenon is seen in about 30% of school-age children (Johnston et al., 1988). It is more likely to occur with the short-acting forms of stimulant medication (e.g., Ritalin) than with the longer-acting formulations (i.e., Metadate, Concerta, Ritalin-SR). It is best treated by shortening the gap between medication doses, adding a dose, or switching to a longer-acting medication.

Tics, which are brief, repetitive movements (e.g., eye blinks, throat clearing) that resemble nervous habits, have been reported in approximately 10% of children treated with stimulants (Lipkin, Goldstein, & Adesman, 1994). These are common in children and sometimes may be worsened by stimulants. Fortunately, these stimulant-induced tics usually subside with time, after the dosage is reduced, or when treatment is discontinued. In rare cases, tics that appear to have been induced by stimulants do not resolve or may even worsen over time. Given that Tourette syndrome, stuttering, chronic motor tics, and obsessive-compulsive disorder appear to have an underlying genetic relationship, it is likely that individuals with a history of transient tics or an individual or family history of one of these disorders are at increased risk for this side effect. Although tics or a personal or family history of tics are listed as contraindications to stimulant use, most experienced clinicians feel that this is overly restrictive (discussed later).

Other stimulant side effects include insomnia; headache; stomachache; mild elevations of pulse or blood pressure; and rarely, activation of mania or psychosis. Gastrointestinal and emotional side effects may subside after several days to a few weeks, but if they do not, modifications in the treatment regimen should be made. Elevations of pulse or blood pressure outside of the normal range for age should prompt a search for underlying medical problems that may be exacerbated by stimulants because the medication rarely causes significant cardiovascular effects by itself. For example, a rapid pulse may occur in a child who starts stimulants on a background of excessive caffeine intake, and hypertension may occur in a child with previously undiagnosed renal abnormalities, whose blood pressure was high-normal prior to stimulant exposure. Stimulants should not be used, however, in the presence of anorexia, current substance abuse, mania, psychosis, severe anxiety, unaddressed major depression, or an untreated severe tic disorder.

Potential for Substance Abuse   Children and adolescents with ADHD who take stimulant medication do not report euphoria, and physiologic and psychological dependence is rare. The potential for abuse may increase in adolescents and adults. According to a U.S. General Accounting Office Report (2001), however, diversion of stimulants to others is a larger problem than stimulant abuse by individuals with ADHD is. The slow entrance of oral methylphenidate into the brain was initially thought to explain its low potential for abuse, but this is not certain (Volkow et al., 2001). Because of concerns about the potential for stimulants to be abused, in the United States these medications are classified as controlled substances by the Drug Enforcement Agency. This means that prescriptions cannot be refilled or telephoned in and that the number of pills dispensed at one time is limited.

There has been concern that adolescents or adults may abuse methylphenidate or dextroamphetamine by injecting it or taking it intranasally to produce a high. Long-acting slow-release forms in which the medication is mixed with other substances makes this less likely to occur. There has also been concern that the use of methylphenidate to treat ADHD increases the risk for later substance abuse. Long-term follow-up studies, however, have not supported this concern (Hechtman, Weiss, & Pearlman, 1984). In fact, several studies suggest stimulant medication use decreases the risk of later substance abuse in children with ADHD (Biederman, Wilens, et al., 1999; Paternite et al., 1999).

Initiating and Monitoring Therapy   Stimulant therapy is often started with a low dosage (approximately 0.3 milligrams per kilogram of body weight of immediate-release methylphenidate or slightly less of the amphetamine stimulants) that is increased every 3–7 days until an adequate response is evident or significant side effects develop. The initial drug trial may be done in a blinded fashion, with the teacher filling out daily to weekly behavior rating forms without knowing the child's medication regimen. Comparison of 1 week on and 1 week off medication is often sufficient to demonstrate both positive and side effects. Stimulants do not need to build up in the body; improvements in behavior are often reported the very first day that medication is taken.

Dosing should relate to the time course and severity of ADHD. For a child who primarily struggles with attention problems in school, medication on school days only may be sufficient. For some children, homework completion requires similar medication levels as during school; for others, the lack of distraction from classmates means that homework can be completed adequately on less or no medication. A child with moderate to severe impulsivity, inattention, and social problems may require dosing 7 days per week.

There is not a consistent relationship between weight or age and clinical response. Heavier adolescents or adults, however, may require higher dosages. Therefore, it is best to try several different dosages until a clinical response is evident or significant side effects develop. Only if this approach fails should an alternative stimulant or a different class of medication be used. Overall, the amphetamine stimulants are similarly effective to methylphenidate (Pliszka et al., 2000); however approximately 25%–35% of children respond better to one type of stimulant than the other (Greenhill et al., 1966), though there is no way yet to predict the best medication for a given individual. Thus, the other stimulant category should be tried if a variety of dosages of the first results in suboptimal effects or problematic side effects.

Decisions regarding after-school, weekend, and summer dosages need to be made on an individual basis, balancing the benefits the child receives from the medication with the side effects he or she may experience. For example, if a child experiences a decrease in the rate of growth during treatment, it may be necessary to stop the medication on weekends and over the summer to allow for "catch-up" growth. Similarly, a child with mild inattentive-type ADHD may not require summer treatment.

School achievement, behavior, relationships, mood, vital signs, and growth velocity should be monitored at baseline and at regular intervals (at least every 3–6 months in addition to well-child visits) to ensure continued beneficial responses and the absence of significant adverse effects. No specific blood test is indicated as part of the monitoring, though some children show mild decreases in white blood cell numbers while taking methylphenidate. Appetite suppression may require the use of caloric and vitamin/mineral supplements (see Chapter 9) as it is virtually impossible for children to meet their recommended dietary allowances of nutrients on less than three meals per day. Some children with ADHD are poor eaters and/or have poor growth at baseline; these children require particularly close nutritional follow-up. With such children, it may be wise to consider underlying gastrointestinal disorders (see Chapters 9 and 27), such as gastroesophageal reflux, constipation, and food allergy/intolerance, among others. Laboratory monitoring of the ferritin level may reveal low iron stores, and fasting zinc levels may also be low. Both of these findings have been linked to symptoms that may interfere with attention and school functioning (Halterman et al., 2001; Toren et al., 1996).

Formulations of Stimulant Medication   The most commonly used stimulants are methylphenidate and amphetamines. Several new stimulant formulations and novel delivery systems are in the process of entering the market.

Both categories of commonly used stimulants come in short-acting (3- to 4-hour) and sustained-release (6- to 12-hour) formulations, and both take about a half hour to begin acting. Clearly, one of the major disadvantages of the short-acting stimulants is the need for taking a dose at school, which may be stigmatizing for the child. Multiple dosing also increases the likelihood of missing doses.

The sustained release form of methylphenidate (Ritalin-SR) lasts up to 6 hours, but it takes longer to take effect and generally its effects are more variable than short-acting Ritalin. The newer long-acting methylphenidate preparations were developed to provide more consistent 8-hour coverage (Greenhill, Findling, & Swanson, 2002). Concerta, the only 12-hour form of methylphenidate, was released in 2000 and has become very useful in this age of after-school activities and after-school care (Pelham, Gnagy, & Burrows-Maclean, 2001; Wolraich et al., 2001). It is coated with a small amount of methylphenidate for immediate release; as the capsule moves through the gastrointestinal tract and water is absorbed, the gel in the bottom of the capsule expands and pushes the drug out of a laser-drilled hole at the top of the capsule. This ingenious device is particularly useful for the older child or adolescent who has homework in the late afternoon and only wants to take one pill a day. It is also useful in younger children whose behavior problems associated with ADHD continue throughout the day. It has low abuse potential because the capsule is difficult to break open, and the contents would have to undergo a complex extraction process to obtain pure methylphenidate.

Amphetamine formulations include Dexedrine 5-milligram tablets, which last approximately 4–5 hours, and Dexedrine Spansules (available as 5-, 10-, and 15-milligram capsules), which last about 6 hours. Dexedrine, however, is perceived to have higher abuse potential due to its street-drug value as "speed." Another stimulant, Adderall (available as 5-, 10-, 20-, and 30-milligram capsules), is a combination of the salts of dextro- and levo-amphetamine and has similar effects and duration (5–7 hours) as the Dexedrine Spansule. It is flexible to use because dosage and duration are directly related, and it comes in several different-sized double-scored tablets.

Stimulant Use in Adolescents and Young Adults   Stimulant medications may actually be more rather than less important in treating ADHD symptoms in adolescents and young adults than in younger children. These symptoms place the teenager at increased risk for impulsive actions and risk-taking behaviors (leading to, e.g., poor driving records; Nada-Raja et al., 1997). Adolescents typically respond well to stimulant medication. Compliance with the treatment regimen, however, can be difficult, especially if the adolescent does not acknowledge that he or she has ADHD or is not actively involved in medical treatment. Teenagers can be reluctant to take medication due to lack of acceptance or understanding of the diagnosis or embarrassment related to a perceived stigma associated with the disorder and its treatment. The recent availability of Concerta, which permits a single daily dose of medication to be given at home, should also help. Some teenagers (and younger school-age children) are noncompliant because they feel dysphoric (sad) on medication but cannot adequately express this. If a teenager has had education from parents, clinicians, or teachers about the dangers of mixing drugs, the result may be that he or she is noncompliant with medication for ADHD when using recreational drugs.

Stimulant Use in Preschoolers   Few studies have been conducted on the efficacy and safety of stimulant medication in preschool-age children (Musten et al., 1997). Given limited study, it is possible that medication response is more variable in this group (Spencer et al., 1996). Therefore, stimulants should be considered only in extreme cases in children younger than age 5. This should be done after environmental interventions (e.g., preschool staff and parent training, classroom accommodations) have been tried without sufficient success in controlling ADHD symptoms. Of concern is the finding that there is increased stimulant medication use in younger children despite this decreased efficacy (Zito et al., 2000). This suggests the need to better understand whether this reflects an increase in the prevalence of the symptoms in this age group and, if so, possible causes or whether this represents an increased rate of medication treatment.

Outcome of Stimulant Treatment   Although the short-term benefits of stimulants are clear and the side effects are generally mild, many questions remain about the long-term efficacy of stimulants. Studies generally have failed to show significant improvement in behavioral outcome or academic achievement (Gillberg et al., 1997; Ingram et al., 1999). Many methodologic problems, however, make these results suspect. Several more carefully executed long-term studies are currently in progress.

Treatment of Stimulant Nonresponders

A minority of children with ADHD will not benefit from stimulants or will have adverse side effects that preclude their use. Children should try two or more different stimulant medications before trying a second-line medication, as there is some likelihood of response to the second stimulant (Pliszka et al., 2000). Moreover, nonstimulants have been studied much less and may have a less beneficial effect than stimulant medications (Spencer et al., 1996).

    Antidepressants   Several types of antidepressants have been found to be effective in treating children with ADHD. The tricyclic antidepressants desipramine (Norpramin), imipramine (Tofranil), and nortriptyline (Pamelor) have been the most extensively studied. These drugs work by inhibiting the metabolism of dopamine and norepinephrine so that higher levels are maintained in the brain. In general, when tricyclic antidepressants are compared with placebo and stimulants, they are found to be more effective than placebo but slightly less effective than stimulants in improving attention span, improving teacher ratings of behavior, and decreasing impulsivity (Spencer et al., 1996). About two thirds of children with ADHD who do not respond to a stimulant will improve with a tricyclic antidepressant (Biederman et al., 1989).

    Unlike stimulants, tricyclic antidepressants must be administered continuously to be effective. Tricyclics also have more problematic side effects, and there is a significant risk of overdose. Cardiovascular (arrhythmias), neurologic (tingling, incoordination, tremors), and anticholinergic (constipation, blurred vision, dry mouth) effects limit their use. Drug levels in blood should be checked to avoid toxicity as there can be large differences across individuals in metabolism of these medications (Green, 1995). EKGs must be obtained at baseline and monitored for cardiovascular changes. A few cases of sudden death, presumably from cardiac arrhythmias, have occurred in children taking desipramine, although the association is not certain (Green, 1995).

    Other types of antidepressants may also be effective in treating children with ADHD. As with the tricyclic antidepressants, bupropion (Wellbutrin), a chemically distinct antidepressant that blocks the reuptake of dopamine and norepinephrine, has been shown to be almost as effective as stimulants (Barrickman et al., 1995; Cantwell, 1998). It may be particularly useful for adolescents with conduct disorder, substance abuse concerns, and/or comorbid depression (Riggs et al., 1998). Bupropion can, however, increase the risk of seizures and should be used cautiously in children with a previous history of a seizure disorder. Venlafaxine (Effexor), also a chemically distinct antidepressant that blocks serotonin and norepinephrine reuptake, has shown some benefit in treating ADHD in uncontrolled studies (Adler et al., 1995; Findling et al., 1996; Hedges et al., 1995). Selective serotonin reuptake inhibitor (SSRI) antidepressants such as fluoxetine (Prozac), sertraline (Zoloft), and paroxetine (Paxil) may be helpful for comorbid depression or anxiety, but they have not been shown to have positive effects on core ADHD symptoms and may actually increase impulsivity.

    Alpha-2-adrenergic Agents   Another medication group used to treat ADHD is the alpha-2-adrenergic agents, which includes clonidine (Catapres) and guanfacine (Tenex). These medications can reduce hyperactivity but may also reduce attention and alertness. Sometimes, these medications cause depressed mood and irritability (Hunt, Capper, & O'Connell, 1990). Originally used as antihypertensives, they can also cause postural hypotension (low blood pressure upon sudden rising from a lying or seated position) and resultant fainting. Unlike stimulants, these medications should not be stopped abruptly, as this can result in rebound hypertension. Combining a stimulant medication during the day with clonidine at night has been used to treat sleep disturbances, which may be exacerbated by stimulants (Prince et al., 1996). There have been a few reports, however, of clonidine in combination with stimulants being associated with a fatal cardiac arrhythmia (Cantwell, Swanson, & Connor, 1997). There is controversy regarding these reported fatalities because they could also be ascribed to other factors (Fenichel & Lipicky, 1995; Popper, 1995). Until more studies have been conducted, however, combinations of these medications should be used cautiously. It may be wise to monitor blood pressure, pulse (especially in the arm), and EKG when the stimulant is taking effect and the clonidine has worn off, as this is when the arrhythmia has generally occurred.

A promising nonstimulant medication for ADHD, tomoxetine (Atomoxetine), a selective noradrenergic reuptake inhibitor, was in clinical trials as of 2002 (Michelson, Faries, & Wernicke, 2001; Spencer et al., 1998). Tomoxetine is a long-acting medication that does not require dosing in school, and it shows promise in that it does not appear to have the side effects that are associated with stimulants.

Stopping Medication

Throughout childhood, it is important for the child to undergo periodic "drug holidays" to see if medication is still required. These are recommended yearly, either in October or in the spring rather than the summer or the start of school, depending on individual circumstances. Rarely is more than 1 week off medication needed to determine if the medication is still needed and effective for a child with disruptive behavior. It is best to run these periods off medication as a partially blinded trial, with teachers filling out behavior rating scales before and after the change. For children with purely academic issues, a longer trial may be needed, with evaluation before and after the school day and homework completion. Many children with ADHD, however, require medication as long as they are in an educational setting. This means they may continue the use of stimulants in college. Some adults have benefited from continued treatment after entry into the workplace, depending on the severity of symptoms and their job requirements.

Multimodal Treatment

Satterfield, Satterfield, and Schell (1987) provided encouraging data on the value of an intensive multimodal ADHD treatment program that combines medication and psychosocial treatment. Youth who participated in their treatment program were followed for 3 years and were found to display better adjustment than those who had received stimulant medication alone. Subsequently, the National Institute of Mental Health (NIMH) and the U.S. Department of Education sponsored a multisite study to evaluate the 2-year effectiveness of combined pharmacological and psychosocial treatments ("Moderators and Mediators of Treatment Response," 1999; "Special Section," 2001).

Results revealed that medication was the most effective treatment in targeting the core symptoms of ADHD; combined treatment had no added benefit in reducing ADHD symptoms in children with isolated ADHD. Children in the combined group, however, were able to be maintained on lower dosages of medication compared with children in the medication-only group. Combined treatment had advantages over other groups in improving comorbid ADHD symptoms, including oppositional and aggressive behavior, problems with parent–child relationships, and social skills impairments. Surprisingly, the behavioral intervention was particularly effective in children with anxiety. Finally, medication management was more effective than community treatment, despite the fact that two thirds of the latter group were prescribed medication (at lower dosages than the children in the medication-only group) to target their ADHD symptoms. In a follow-up analysis of the role of comorbidity in treatment effects, it became clearer that psychosocial intervention and medication were each similarly effective in children with ADHD and anxiety, whereas combined treatment was superior to either alone when children had either a comorbid externalizing disorder or the combination of anxiety and an externalizing disorder (Jensen et al., 2001). Taken together, these results clarify the ways in which medication and psychosocial interventions affect ADHD symptoms and highlight the benefits of a standardized approach to medication management and follow-up. Future research will seek to determine the impact of multimodal treatment on other outcomes and whether these findings can be applied to usual practice settings.

Controversial Therapies

There are numerous nonconventional treatments for ADHD. Among these, elimination diets that prohibit additives and salicylates (the Feingold diet), allergenic substances, or both have received the most controlled study, suggesting that approximately 5%–15% of subjects respond, that the response rate may be higher in preschoolers, and that irritability and sleep problems may be most responsive (Baumgaertel, 1999; Mercugliano et al., 1999). Systematic flaws in early studies related to the Feingold diet were numerous. In addition, it appears that a substantial percentage of diet responders react to artificial additives and some allergenic substances, and few studies addressed both. Other studies that investigated the effects of allergenic foods found that the majority of children reacted to additives as well as some allergenic foods (Arnold, in press; Boris & Mandel, 1994; Carter et al., 1993), suggesting that more limited studies would underestimate the percentage of positive responders.

Systematic studies of the role of sugar challenges do not indicate that they substantially influence behavior in the paradigms used, though these do not address chronically high versus low sugar diets. Conners (1993) showed that a sugar challenge after a breakfast with sufficient protein actually improved academic performance, whereas a sugar challenge after a purely carbohydrate breakfast was detrimental. Supplements of vitamins, minerals, and/or neurotransmitter precursors have not been widely studied, but most studies have shown negative results. Megadoses (greater than tenfold the required amount) of vitamins or minerals can have important negative health effects and are not indicated. Essential fatty acids, which serve as precursors to cell membrane structural and signaling compounds (e.g., cell membrane phospholipids, prostaglandins, cytokines), have been shown to be low in children with ADHD compared with controls in multiple different laboratories. Treatment trials of essential fatty acid supplements, however, have been negative (Voigt et al., 2001). Other alternative therapies have received too little study to be reviewed. Parents cannot assume that "natural" therapies are safe and should discuss any they are considering with their child's clinician. In recognition that more families are turning to alternative therapy, more research and information is becoming available to clinicians.

Treatment of Attention-Deficit/ Hyperactivity Disorder and Comorbid Disorders

Tic Disorders

Tourette syndrome is defined by 1) waxing and waning multiple motor tics; 2) vocal tic; and 3) onset in childhood (before age 18 years). There is a high prevalence of ADHD (often identified prior to the onset of the tics) in individuals with Tourette syndrome. The alpha-2-adrenergic agonists are often the first type of medication used to treat tic disorders with associated ADHD because they may improve both hyperactivity and tics (Hunt et al., 1995). Some of these children's ADHD symptoms, however, will improve more when given stimulants or antidepressants than when administered clonidine or guanfacine (Singer et al., 1995). It had been thought that the use of stimulants in children with ADHD and tics or Tourette syndrome was contraindicated because the stimulants would worsen the tics. This has turned out not to be true for all children (Castellanos et al., 1997; Gadow et al., 1995). Thus, if other treatment strategies fail and ADHD is a more functionally relevant problem for the child than the tics, a judicious trial of stimulants may be warranted. The tricyclic antidepressants have been used effectively to treat ADHD in these children without exacerbating the tics (Singer et al., 1995). Finally, combinations of medications are sometimes used in children with ADHD and comorbid tics—a stimulant for ADHD, an alpha-agonist or neuroleptic for tic suppression and an antidepressant/antianxiety agent for the also commonly associated obsessive-compulsive or other internalizing symptoms.

Internalizing Disorders

Children with ADHD may also experience depression or anxiety disorders. Studies comparing children with ADHD alone with children with ADHD and comorbid internalizing disorders have suggested that stimulants may be less effective in the latter group (Pliszka, 1999). The Multimodal Treatment Study ("Moderators and Mediators of Treatment Response," 1999), however, did not find this. Thus, stimulants remain the first-line medication for treating the symptoms of ADHD in children with ADHD and anxiety or mood symptoms. Bupropion, tricyclic antidepressants, or potentially venlafaxine or tomoxetine may be more effective, however, at treating both disorders with a single medication. Otherwise, a combination of stimulants with an antianxiety or antidepressant agent may be required. Combination of psychotropic medications is increasingly common in children treated in psychiatric settings (Zarin et al., 1997), although there is no controlled study as yet on the safety and efficacy of this practice. The most commonly used antidepressants are the SSRIs, bupropion, and venlafaxine; an SSRI or buspirone (BuSpar) may be used for anxiety. The newer atypical antidepressants mirtazapine (Remeron) and nefazodone (Serzone) are yet to be studied for their potential role in children with ADHD and comorbid internalizing disorders. Bipolar disorder may differ from other mood disorders in that mood stabilization may be necessary before ADHD symptoms can be improved with other medications (Biederman, Mick, et al., 1999).

Conduct Disorder

The diagnostic features of conduct disorder include "a repetitive and persistent pattern of behavior in which the basic rights of others or major age-appropriate societal norms or rules are violated" (APA, 2000, p. 98). Conduct disorder is not easy to treat as an isolated problem, and comorbid ADHD makes its management even more complicated. A multimodal approach is indicated (e.g., medication, counseling, behavior therapy). Interestingly, some symptoms of conduct disorder may be responsive to stimulant therapy. With such therapy, there appears to be a significant diminution in a range of antisocial behaviors, including provocative, aggressive, and mean behaviors; lying; and cheating (Klein et al., 1997). Abuse potential of the stimulants, however, is greatest in this group of children. There is a significant rate of comorbid depression with conduct disorder as well, so bupropion or tricyclic antidepressants may be useful. These drugs have the additional advantages of round-the-clock coverage and absence of abuse potential, which is critical because conduct disorder is not exclusively an in-school issue.

Seizure Disorders

Approximately 20% or more of children with epilepsy have ADHD, a percentage that increases to 30% when the side effects of antiepileptic drugs are considered (Gross-Tsur, Manor, & van deer Meere, 1997). There has been a concern that stimulant medication may be detrimental in these children because of the risk of lowering the seizure threshold and increasing seizure frequency. Studies (e.g., Gross-Tsur et al., 1997), however, suggest that stimulants are both effective in treating the symptoms of ADHD and do not increase seizure activity in patients whose seizures are under good control. In patients who have poorly controlled seizures, there was an increase in seizure activity, so stimulants should not be used with such children. Although antidepressants can also theoretically decrease the seizure threshold, this seems clinically meaningful primarily for bupropion. Antiepileptic metabolism may be altered by certain medications used for the treatment of ADHD (typically tricyclics but not stimulants), so anticonvulsant levels may need to be rechecked after the initiation of ADHD medications.

OUTCOME

Most symptoms of ADHD diminish between ages 10 and 25 years; hyperactivity declines more rapidly than does impulsivity or inattentiveness (Hill & Schoener, 1996; Ingram et al., 1999). In 40% of individuals, however, ADHD symptoms persist into adulthood (Weiss & Hechtman, 1986). Even for those individuals whose symptoms no longer meet the criteria for ADHD, subclinical difficulty with sustained attention and/or impulsivity may persist. College-age students with ADHD continue to complain of difficulty with the organization, planning, and self-management required for longer-term projects. Young adults may express concerns about completing projects; handling job stress; interacting with work colleagues; and juggling the demands of marriage, family, and work. In general, adults with persistent symptoms complete less formal schooling, have lower-status jobs, and have higher rates of antisocial behavior (Mannuzza et al., 1998; Thompson et al., 1996; Wilens, Biederman, & Mick, 1998).

For a small, but significant, subgroup of affected individuals, ADHD is associated with severe antisocial behavior and substance abuse, significantly affecting their clinical course in adolescence and adulthood (Mannuzza et al., 1998). Although there has been concern that stimulants may increase the risk of substance abuse in these individuals, the reverse has actually been found (Biederman, Wilens, et al., 1999).

Among patients whose symptoms decrease during adolescence, the outcome is similar to those of their peers in terms of occupational achievement, social function, and drug and alcohol use, but not academic achievement (Mannuzza et al., 1988). The best indicators of outcome are high intelligence, a strong family support structure, and the lack of comorbid conditions.

SUMMARY

Advances in molecular genetics and functional brain imaging have resulted in an improved understanding of the origin and pathophysiology of ADHD. Several studies suggest the importance of the neurotransmitter dopamine in specific brain systems. As the biological and cognitive mechanisms that underlie ADHD are delineated and the social and economic factors related to provision of treatment services are better understood, it is hoped that more effective interventions and service delivery models can be developed. It will be important, though complicated, to determine whether the current trend of increasing medication use in this disorder reflects a change in the prevalence or severity of the disorder itself or a change in the pattern of its management. With increased understanding and utilization of an individual's unique strengths and ways to treat his or her weaknesses, perhaps many of the complications of ADHD secondary to social and academic failure can be prevented.

Specifically, it is anticipated that the development of school-based interventions, monitored medication, improved access to quality child mental health services, and further collaboration between specialists and primary care providers will be important components of the innovative and effective approaches to providing care to this important population of children with disabilities.

REFERENCES

Accardo, P. (1999). A rational approach to the medical assessment of the child with attention-deficit/hyperactivity disorder. *Pediatric Clinics of North America, 46,* 845–856.

Achenbach, T.M. (1991a). *Manual for the Child Behavior Checklist/4–18 and 1991 Profile.* Burlington, VT: University of Vermont, Department of Psychiatry.

Achenbach, T.M. (1991b). *Manual for the Teacher's Report Form and 1991 Profile.* Burlington, VT: University of Vermont, Department of Psychiatry.

Adler, L.A., Resnick, S., Kunz, M., et al. (1995). Open-label trial of venlafaxine in adults with attention deficit disorder. *Psychopharmacology Bulletin, 31,* 785–788.

American Academy of Pediatrics, Subcommittee on Attention-Deficit/Hyperactivity Disorder and Committee on Quality Improvement. (2001). Clinical practice guideline: Treatment of the school-aged child with attention-deficit/hyperactivity disorder. *Pediatrics, 108,* 1033–1044.

American Psychiatric Association. (1994). *Diagnostic and statistical manual of mental disorders* (4th ed.). Washington, DC: Author.

American Psychiatric Association. (2000). *Diagnostic and statistical manual of mental disorders* (4th ed., Text rev.). Washington, DC: Author.

Angold, A., Erkanli, A., Egger, et al. (2000). Stimulant treatment for children: A community perspective. *Journal of the American Academy of Child and Adolescent Psychiatry, 39,* 975–984.

Arnold, L.E. (in press). Treatment alternatives for attention deficit/hyperactivity disorder. In P.S. Jensen & J. Cooper (Eds.), *Diagnosis and treatment of ADHD: An evidence-based approach.* Washington, DC: American Psychological Press.

Aylward, E.H., Reiss, A.L., Reader, M.J., et al. (1996). Basal ganglia volumes in children with attention-deficit hyperactivity disorder. *Journal of Child Neurology, 11,* 112–115.

Barkley, R.A. (1998a). Developmental course and adult outcome. In R.A. Barkley, *Attention-deficit hyperactivity disorder: A handbook for diagnosis and treatment* (2nd ed., pp. 186–224). New York: Guilford Press.

Barkley, R.A. (1998b). Primary symptoms, diagnostic criteria, prevalence, and gender differences. In R.A. Barkley, *Attention-deficit hyperactivity disorder: A handbook for diagnosis and treatment* (2nd ed., pp. 56–96). New York: Guilford Press.

Barkley, R.A. (1998c). A theory of ADHD: Inhibition, executive functions, self-control, and time. In R.A. Barkley, *Attention-deficit hyperactivity disorder: A handbook for diagnosis and treatment* (2nd ed., pp. 225–260). New York: Guilford Press.

Barkley, R.A., Guevremont, D.C., Anastopoulos, A.D., et al. (1993). Driving-related risks and outcomes of attention deficit hyperactivity disorder in adolescents and young adults: A 3- to 5-year follow-up survey. *Pediatrics, 92,* 212–218.

Barkley, R.A., Murphy, K.R., & Kwasnik, D. (1996). Motor vehicle driving competencies and risks in teens and young adults with attention deficit hyperactivity disorder. *Pediatrics, 98,* 1089–1095.

Barrickman, L.L., Perry, P.J., Allen, A.J., et al. (1995). Bupropion versus methylphenidate in the treatment of attention-deficit hyperactivity disorder. *Journal of the American Academy of Child and Adolescent Psychiatry, 34,* 649–657.

Baumgaertel, A. (1999). Alternative and controversial treatments for attention-deficit/hyperactivity disorder. *Pediatric Clinics of North America, 46,* 977–992.

Beck, A.T. (1987). *Beck Depression Inventory (BDI).* San Antonio, TX: The Psychological Corporation.

Beery, K.E. (1989). *Developmental Test of Visual-Motor Integration (VMI)* (3rd rev.). Chicago: Riverside.

Bennett, C.F., Brown, R.T., Craver, J., et al. (1999). Stimulant medication for the child with attention-deficit/hyperactivity disorder. *Pediatric Clinics of North America, 46,* 929–944.

Biederman, J., Baldessarini, R.J., Wright, V., et al. (1989). A double-blind placebo controlled study of desipramine in the treatment of ADD, I: Efficacy. *Journal of the American Academy of Child and Adolescent Psychiatry, 28,* 777–784.

Biederman, J., Mick, E., Prince, J., et al. (1999). Systematic chart review of the pharmacologic treatment of comorbid attention deficit hyperactivity disorder in youth with bipolar disorder. *Journal of Child and Adolescent Psychopharmacology, 9,* 247–256.

Biederman, J., Wilens, J., Mick, E., et al. (1997). Is ADHD a risk factor for psychoactive substance use disorders?: Findings from a four-year prospective follow-up study. *Journal of the American Academy of Child and Adolescent Psychiatry, 36,* 21–29.

Biederman, J., Wilens, T., Mick, E., et al. (1999). Pharmacotherapy of attention-deficit/hyperactivity disorder reduces risk for substance use disorder. *Pediatrics, 104,* e20.

Blondis, T., & Opacich, K. (1999). Developmental coordination disorder and ADHD. In P.J. Accardo, T.A. Blondis, B.Y. Whitman, & M.A. Stein (Vol. eds.), *Pediatric habilitation series: Vol. 10. Attention deficits and hyperactivity in children and adults: Diagnosis, treatment, management* (2nd rev. ed., pp. 265–288). New York: Marcel Dekker.

Boris, M., & Mandel, F.S. (1994). Foods and additives are common causes of the attention deficit hyperactive disorder in children. *Annals of Allergy, 72,* 462–468.

Broitman, M., Robb, A., & Stein, M.A. (1999). Paying attention to mood symptoms in children with ADHD. In P.J. Accardo, T.A. Blondis, B.Y. Whitman, & M.A. Stein (Vol. eds.), *Pediatric habilitation series: Vol. 10. Attention deficits and hyperactivity in children and adults: Diagnosis, treatment, management* (2nd rev. ed., pp. 325–344). New York: Marcel Dekker.

Brown, T.E. (Ed.). (2000). *Attention-deficit disorders and comorbidities in children, adolescents, and adults.* Washington, DC: American Psychiatric Press.

Bussing, R., Zima, B.T., & Berlin, T.R. (1998). Variations in ADHD treatment among special education students. *Journal of the American Academy of Child and Adolescent Psychiatry, 37,* 968–976.

Butcher, J.N., Williams, C.L., Graham, J.R., et al. (1992). *Minnesota Multiphasic Personality Inventory–Adolescent (MMPI-A).* Minneapolis: University of Minnesota Press.

Camarata, S.M., & Gibson, T. (1999). Pragmatic language deficits in attention-deficit hyperactivity disorder (ADHD). *Mental Retardation and Developmental Disabilities Research Reviews, 5,* 207–214.

Cantwell, D.P. (1998). ADHD through the lifespan: The role of bupropion in treatment. *Journal of Clinical Psychiatry, 59*(Suppl. 4), 92–94.

Cantwell, D.P., Swanson, J., & Connor, D.F. (1997). Case study: Adverse response to clonidine. *Journal of the American Academy of Child and Adolescent Psychiatry, 36,* 539–544.

Carter, C.M., Urbanowicz, M., Hemsley, R., et al. (1993). Effects of a few food diet in attention deficit disorder. *Archives of Disease in Childhood, 69,* 564–568.

Castellanos, F.X., Giedd, J.N., Berquin, P.C., et al. (2001). Quantitative brain magnetic resonance imaging in girls with ADHD. *Archives of General Psychiatry, 58,* 289–295.

Castellanos, F.X., Giedd, J.N., Elia, J., et al. (1997). Controlled stimulant treatment of ADHD and comorbid Tourette's syndrome: Effects of stimulant and dose. *Journal of the American Academy of Child and Adolescent Psychiatry, 36,* 589–596.

Conners, C.K. (1993). Nootropics and foods. In J.S. Werry & M.G. Aman (Eds.), *Practitioner's guide to psychoactive drugs for children and adolescents* (pp. 373–389). New York: Plenum.

Conners, C.K. (1997). *Conner's Rating Scales–Revised.* North Tonawanda, NY: Multi-Health Systems.

Cook, E.H., Jr. (1999). Genetics of attention-deficit hyperactivity disorder. *Mental Retardation and Developmental Disabilities Research Reviews, 5,* 191–198.

Cook, E.H., Jr., Stein, M.A., & Leventhal, B.L. (1997). Family based association of attention deficit/hyperactivity disorder and the dopamine transporter. In K. Blum & E.P.

Noble (Eds.), *Handbook of psychiatric genetics* (pp. 297–309). Boca Raton, FL: CRC Press.

Corkum, P., Moldofsky, H., Hogg-Johnson, S., et al. (1999). Sleep problems in children with attention-deficit/hyperactivity disorder: Impact of subtype, comorbidity, and stimulant medication. *Journal of the American Academy of Child and Adolescent Psychiatry, 38,* 1285–1293.

Corkum, P., Tannock, R., & Moldofsky, H. (1998). Sleep disturbances in children with attention-deficit/hyperactivity disorder. *Journal of the American Academy of Child and Adolescent Psychiatry, 37,* 637–646.

Cox, D.J., Merkel, R.L., Kovatchev, B., et al. (2000). Effect of stimulant medication on driving performance of young adults with attention-deficit hyperactivity disorder: A preliminary double-blind placebo controlled trial. *The Journal of Nervous and Mental Disease, 188,* 230–234.

DiLavore, P., Lord, C., & Rutter, M. (1995). Pre-Linguistic Autism Diagnostic Observation Schedule (PL-ADOS). *Journal of Autism and Developmental Disorders, 25,* 355–379.

DiScala, C., Lescohier, I., Barthel, M., et al. (1998). Injuries to children with attention deficit hyperactivity disorder. *Pediatrics, 102,* 1415–1421.

Dougherty, D.D., Bonab, A.A., Spencer, T.J., et al. (1999). Dopamine transporter density in patients with attention deficit hyperactivity disorder. *Lancet, 354,* 2132–2133.

Dresel, S., Krause, J., Krause, K.-H., et al. (2000). Attention deficit hyperactivity disorder: Binding of [99mTc]TRODAT-1 to the dopamine transporter before and after methylphenidate treatment. *European Journal of Nuclear Medicine, 27,* 1518–1524.

Dunn, L.M., & Dunn, L.M. (1981). *Peabody Picture Vocabulary Test–Third Edition (PPVT-III).* Circle Pines, MN: American Guidance Service.

DuPaul, G.J., Power, T.J., Anastopoulos, A.D., & Reid, R. (1998). *ADHD Rating Scale-IV: Checklists, norms, and clinical interpretation.* New York: Guilford Press.

DuPaul, G.J., & Stoner, G. (1994). *ADHD in the schools: Assessment and intervention strategies.* New York: Guilford Press.

Fenichel, R.R., & Lipicky, R.J. (1995). Combination products as first-line pharmacotherapy. *Archives of Internal Medicine, 155,* 117.

Fenson, L., Dale, P., Reznick, J.S., et al. (1993). *MacArthur Communicative Development Inventories (CDI).* San Diego: Singular Publishing Group.

Filipek, P.A., Semrud-Clikeman, M., Steingard, R.J., et al. (1997). Volumetric MRI analysis comparing subjects having attention-deficit hyperactivity disorder with normal controls. *Neurology, 48,* 589–601.

Findling, R.L., Schwartz, M.A., Flannery, D.J., et al. (1996). Venlafaxine in adults with attention-deficit/hyperactivity disorder: An open clinical trial. *Journal of Clinical Psychiatry, 57,* 184–189.

Fischer, M., Barkley, R.A., Edelbrock, C.S., et al. (1990). The adolescent outcome of hyperactive children diagnosed by research criteria, II: Academic attentional and neuropsychological statues. *Journal of Consulting and Clinical Psychology, 58,* 580–588.

Fletcher, J.M., Shaywitz, S.E., & Shaywitz, B.A. (1999). Comorbidity of learning and attention disorders: Separate but equal. *Pediatric Clinics of North America, 46,* 885–897.

Gadow, K.D., Sverd, J., Sprafkin, J., et al. (1995). Efficacy of methylphenidate for attention-deficit hyperactivity disorder in children with tic disorder. *Archives of General Psychiatry, 52,* 444–455.

Gainetdinov, R.R., Wetsel, W.C., Jones, S.R., et al. (1999). Role of serotonin in the paradoxical calming effect of psychostimulants on hyperactivity. *Science, 283,* 397–401.

Gardner, M.F. (1990). *Expressive One-Word Picture Vocabulary Test–Revised.* Novato, CA: Academic Therapy Publications.

Gillberg, D. (2001). Attention-deficit/hyperactivity disorder with comorbid developmental coordination disorder: Long-term outcome in a community sample. *The ADHD Report, 9(2),* 5–12.

Gillberg, C., Melander, H., von Knorring, A., et al. (1997). Long-term stimulant treatment of children with attention-deficit hyperactivity disorder: A randomized, double-blind, placebo-controlled trial. *Archives of General Psychiatry, 54,* 857–864.

Glanzman, M. (2001). An update on the pathophysiology of ADHD. In B.T. Rogers, T.R. Montgomery, T.M. Lock, & P.J. Accardo (Eds.), *Attention deficit hyperactivity disorder: The clinical spectrum* (pp. 1–14). Timonium, MD: York Press.

Goldman, L., Genel, M., Bezman, R., et al. (1998). Diagnosis and treatment of attention-deficit/hyperactivity disorder in children and adolescents. *Journal of the American Medical Association, 279,* 1100–1107.

Gordon, M., & Barkley, R.A. (1999). Tests and observational measures. In R.A. Barkley, *Attention-deficit hyperactivity disorder: A handbook for diagnosis and treatment* (2nd ed., pp. 294–311). New York: Guilford Press.

Green, W.H. (1995). The treatment of attention-deficit hyperactivity disorder with nonstimulant medications. *Child and Adolescent Psychiatric Clinics of North America, 4,* 169–195.

Greenhill, L.I., Abikoff, H.B., Arnold, L.E., et al. (1996). Medication treatment strategies in the MTA study: Relevance to clinicians and researchers. *Journal of the American Academy of Child and Adolescent Psychiatry, 35,* 1304.

Greenhill, L.L., Findling, R.L., & Swanson, J.M. (2002). A double-blind, placebo-controlled study of modified-release methylphenidate in children with attention-deficit/hyperactivity disorder. *Pediatrics, 109,* e39.

Gross-Tsur, V., Manor, O., van der Meere, J., et al. (1997). Epilepsy and attention deficit hyperactivity disorder: Is methylphenidate safe and effective? *Journal of Pediatrics, 130,* 40–44.

Halterman, J.S., Kaczorowski, J.M., Aligne, C.A., et al. (2001). Iron deficiency and cognitive achievement among school-aged children and adolescents in the United States. *Pediatrics, 107,* 1381–1386.

Handen, B.L., Breaux, A., Janosky, J., et al. (1992). Effects and noneffects of methylphenidate in children with mental retardation and ADHD. *Journal of the American Academy of Child and Adolescent Psychiatry, 31,* 455–461.

Handen, B.L., Feldman, H., Gosling, A., et al. (1991). Adverse side effects of methylphenidate among mentally retarded children with ADHD. *Journal of the American Academy of Child and Adolescent Psychiatry, 30,* 241–245.

Handen, B.L., Feldman, H.M., Lurier, A., et al. (1999). Efficacy of methylphenidate among preschool children with developmental disabilities and ADHD. *Journal of the American Academy of Child and Adolescent Psychiatry, 38,* 805–812.

Hechtman, L., Weiss, G., & Perlman, T. (1984). Hyperactives as young adults: Past and current substance abuse and antisocial behavior. *American Journal of Orthopsychiatry, 54,* 415–425.

Hedges, D., Reimherr, F.W., Rogers, A., et al. (1995). An open trial of venlafaxine in adult patients with attention deficit hyperactivity disorder. *Psychopharmacology Bulletin, 31,* 779–783.

Hill, J.C., & Schoener, E.P. (1996). Age-dependent decline of attention deficit hyperactivity disorder. *American Journal of Psychiatry, 153,* 1143–1146.

Hunt, R.D., Capper, L., & O'Connell, P. (1995). Clonidine in child and adolescent psychiatry. *Journal of Child and Adolescent Psychopharmacology, 1,* 87–102.

Individuals with Disabilities Education Act Amendments of 1997, PL 105-17, 20 U.S.C. §§ 1400 *et seq.*

Ingersoll, G., & Goldstein, S. (1993). *Attention deficit disorder and learning disabilities: Realities, myths and controversial treatments.* New York: Doubleday Broadway.

Ingram, S., Hechtman, L., & Morgenstern, G. (1999). Outcome issues in ADHD: Adolescent and adult long-term outcome. *Mental Retardation and Developmental Disabilities Research Reviews, 5,* 243–250.

Jensen, P.S., Hinshaw, S.P., Kraemer, H.C., et al. (2001). ADHD comorbidity findings from the MTA study: Comparing comorbid subgroups. *Journal of the American Academy of Child and Adolescent Psychiatry, 40,* 147–158.

Jensen, P.S., Martin, D., & Cantwell, D.P. (1997). Comorbidity in ADHD: Implications for research, practice, and DMS-V. *Journal of the American Academy of Child and Adolescent Psychiatry, 36,* 1065–1079.

Johnston, C., Pelham, W.E., Hoza, J., et al. (1988). Psychostimulant rebound in attention deficit disordered boys. *Journal of the American Academy of Child and Adolescent Psychiatry, 27,* 806–810.

Klein, R.G., Abikoff, H., Klass, E., et al. (1997). Clinical efficacy of methylphenidate in conduct disorder with and without attention deficit hyperactivity disorder. *Archives of General Psychiatry, 54,* 1073–1080.

Klein, R., & Wender, P. (1995). The role of methylphenidate in psychiatry. *Archives of General Psychiatry, 52,* 429–433.

Kovacs, M. (1983). *Children's Depression Inventory.* North Tonawanda, NY: Multi-Health Systems.

Krause, K.-H., Dresel, S.H., Krause, J., et al. (2000). Increased striatal dopamine transporter in adult patients with attention deficit hyperactivity disorder: Effects of methylphenidate as measured by single photon emission computed tomography. *Neuroscience Letters, 285,* 107–110.

Krug, D.A., Arick, J., & Almond, P.J. (1993). *Autism Screening Instrument for Educational Planning–Second Edition (ASIEP-2).* Austin, TX: PRO-ED.

Lahey, B.B., Pelham, W.E., Stein, M.A., et al. (1998). Validity of DSM-IV attention-deficit/hyperactivity disorder for younger children. *Journal of the American Academy of Child and Adolescent Psychiatry, 37,* 695–702.

Latham, P.A., & Latham, P.S. (1998). Legal issues. In P.J. Accardo, T.A. Blondis, B.Y. Whitman, & M.A. Stein (Vol. eds.), *Pediatric habilitation series: Vol. 10. Attention deficits and hyperactivity in children and adults: Diagnosis, treatment, management* (2nd rev. ed., pp. 613–631). New York: Marcel Dekker.

Lecendreux, M., Konofal, E., Bouvard, M., et al. (2000). Sleep and alertness in children with ADHD. *Journal of Child Psychology and Psychiatry and Allied Disciplines, 41,* 803–812.

Lindsay, R.L., & Whitman, B.Y. (1999). Social skill development in children with attentional problems. In P.J. Accardo, T.A. Blondis, B.Y. Whitman, & M.A. Stein (Vol. eds.), *Pediatric habilitation series: Vol. 10. Attention deficits and hyperactivity in children and adults: Diagnosis, treatment, management* (2nd rev. ed., pp. 535–550). New York: Marcel Dekker.

Lipkin, P.H., Goldstein, I.J., & Adesman, A.R. (1994). Tics and dyskinesias associated with stimulant treatment in attention-deficit hyperactivity disorder. *Archives of Pediatric and Adolescent Medicine, 148,* 859–886.

Lord, C., Rutter, M., & LeCouteur, A. (1994). Autism Diagnostic Interview–Revised: A revised version of a diagnostic interview for caregivers of individuals with possible pervasive developmental disorders. *Journal of Autism and Developmental Disorders, 24,* 659–685.

Lord, C., Rutter, M., DiLavore, P.C., & Risi, S. (1999). Autism Diagnostic Observation Schedule–WPS Edition (ADOS-WPS). Los Angeles: Western Psychological Services.

Lou, H.C., Henriksen, L., Bruhn, P., et al. (1989). Striatal dysfunction in attention deficit and hyperkinetic disorder. *Archives of Neurology, 46,* 48–52.

Mannuzza, S., Klein, R.G., Bessler, A., et al. (1998). Adult psychiatric status of hyperactive boys grown up. *American Journal of Psychiatry, 155,* 493–498.

Mannuzza, S., Klein, R.G., Bonagura, N., et al. (1988). Hyperactive boys almost grown up, II: Status of subjects without a mental disorder. *Archives of General Psychiatry, 45,* 13–18.

March, J. (1999). *Multidimensional Anxiety Scale for Children (MASC).* North Tonawanda, NY: Multi-Health Systems.

Marotta, P.J., & Roberts, E.A. (1998). Pemoline hepatotoxicity in children. *Journal of Pediatrics, 132,* 894–897.

McBurnett, K., Pfiffner, L.J., & Ottolini, Y.L. (1999). Types of ADHD in DSM-IV. In P.J. Accardo, T.A. Blondis, B.Y. Whitman, & M.A. Stein (Vol. eds.), *Pediatric habilitation series: Vol. 10. Attention deficits and hyperactivity in children and adults: Diagnosis, treatment, management* (2nd rev. ed., pp. 229–240). New York: Marcel Dekker.

McMahon, R.J., & Wells, K.C. (1998). Conduct problems. In E.J. Mash & R.A. Barkley (Eds.), *Treatment of childhood disorders* (2nd ed., pp. 111–217). New York: Guilford Press.

Mercugliano, M. (1999a). Neurochemistry of ADHD. In P.J. Accardo, T.A. Blondis, B.Y. Whitman, & M.A. Stein (Vol. eds.), *Pediatric habilitation series: Vol. 10. Attention deficits and hyperactivity in children and adults: Diagnosis, treatment, management* (2nd rev. ed., pp. 59–72). New York: Marcel Dekker.

Mercugliano, M. (1999b). What is ADHD? *Pediatric Clinics of North America, 46,* 831–843.

Mercugliano, M., Power, T.J., & Blum, N.J. (1999). *The clinician's practical guide to attention-deficit/hyperactivity disorder.* Baltimore: Paul H. Brookes Publishing Co.

Michelson, D., Faries, D., & Wernicke, J. (2001). Atomoxetine in the treatment of children and adolescents with attention-deficit/hyperactivity disorder: a randomized, placebo-controlled, dose-response study. *Pediatrics, 108,* e83.

Moderators and mediators of treatment response for children with attention-deficit/hyperactivity disorder: The Multimodal Treatment Study of children with attention-deficit/hyperactivity disorder. (1999). *Archives of General Psychiatry, 56,* 1088–1096.

Musten, L.M., Firestone, P., Pisterman, S., et al. (1997). Effects of methylphenidate on preschool children with ADHD: Cognitive and behavioral functions. *Journal of the American Academy of Child and Adolescent Psychiatry, 36,* 1407–1415.

Nada-Raja, S., Langley, J.D., McGee, R., et al. (1997). Inattentive and hyperactive behaviors and driving offenses in adolescents. *Journal of the American Academy of Child and Adolescent Psychiatry, 36,* 515–522.

Paternite, C., Loney, J., Salisbury, H., et al. (1999). Childhood inattention-overactivity, aggression, and stimulant medication history as predictors of young adult outcome. *Journal of Child and Adolescent Psychopharmacology, 9,* 169–184.

Pearl, P., Weiss, R., & Stein, M.A. (2001). Medical mimics.

In J. Wasserstein (Ed.), *ADHD in adults: Brain mechanisms and behavior* (pp. 97–112). New York: New York Academy of Sciences.

Pelham, W.E., Jr., & Gnagy, E.M. (1999). Psychosocial and combined treatments for ADHD. *Mental Retardation and Developmental Disabilities Research Reviews, 5,* 225–236.

Pelham, W.E., Gnagy, E.M., Burrows-Maclean, L. et al. (2001). Once-a-day Concerta methylphenidate versus three-times daily methylphenidate in laboratory and natural settings. *Pediatrics, 107,* e105.

Pliszka, S.R., Browne, R.C., Olvera, R.L., et al. (2000). A double-blind, placebo-controlled study of Adderall and methylphenidate in the treatment of attention-deficit/hyperactivity disorder. *Journal of the Academy of Child and Adolescent Psychiatry, 39,* 619–626.

Pliszka, S.R., Carlson, C.L., & Swanson, J.M. (1999). *ADHD with comorbid disorders: Clinical assessment and management.* New York: Guilford Press.

Popper, C.W. (1997). Antidepressants in the treatment of attention-deficit/hyperactivity disorder. *Journal of Clinical Psychiatry, 58,* 14–29.

Powers, C.A. (1999). The pharmacology of drugs used for the treatment of attention deficit hyperactivity disorder. In P.J. Accardo, T.A. Blondis, B.Y. Whitman, & M.A. Stein (Vol. eds.), *Pediatric habilitation series: Vol. 10. Attention deficits and hyperactivity in children and adults: Diagnosis, treatment, management* (2nd rev. ed., pp. 477–511). New York: Marcel Dekker.

Prince, J.B., Wilens, T.E., Biederman, J., et al. (1996). Clonidine for sleep disturbances associated with ADHD: A systematic chart review of 62 cases. *Journal of the American Academy of Child and Adolescent Psychiatry, 35,* 599–605.

Rapaport, J., Buchsbaum, M., Zahn, T.P., et al. (1978). Dextroamphetamine: Cognitive and behavioral effects in normal prepubertal boys. *Science, 199,* 560–563.

Rapport, M.D., Denney, M.A., DuPaul, G.J., et al. (1994). Attention deficit disorder and methylphenidate: Normalization rates, clinical effectiveness, and response prediction in 76 children. *Journal of the American Academy of Child and Adolescent Psychiatry, 33,* 882–893.

Rasmussen, P., & Gilberg, C. (2000). Natural outcome of ADHD with developmental coordination disorder at age 22 years: A controlled, longitudinal, community-based study. *Journal of the American Academy of Child and Adolescent Psychiatry, 39,* 1424–1431.

Rehabilitation Act of 1973, PL 93-112, 29 U.S.C. §§ 701 et seq.

Reich, W., Leacock, N., & Shanfeld, K. (1995). *Diagnostic Interview for Children and Adolescents–Revised.* St. Louis, MO: Washington University, Division of Child Psychiatry.

Reynolds, C., & Kamphaus, R. (1992). *Behavioral Assessment System for Children (BASC).* Circle Pines, MN: American Guidance Service.

Riggs, P.A., Leon, S.L., Mikulich, S.K., et al. (1998). An open trial of bupropion for ADHD in adolescents with substance abuse disorders and conduct disorder. *Journal of the American Academy of Child and Adolescent Psychiatry, 37,* 1271–1278.

Robins, D.L., Fein, D., Barton, M.L., et al. (2001). The Modified Checklist for Autism in Toddlers: An initial study investigating the early detection of autism and pervasive developmental disorders. *Journal of Autism and Developmental Disorders, 31,* 131–144.

Robinson, L.M., Sclar, D.A., Skaer, T.L., et al. (1999). National trends in the prevalence of attention-deficit/hyperactivity disorder and the prescribing of methylphenidate among school-age children. *Clinical Pediatrics, 38,* 209–217.

Roizen, N.J., Blondis, T.A., Irwin, M., et al. (1994). Adaptive functioning in children with attention-deficit hyperactivity disorder. *Archives of Pediatric and Adolescent Medicine, 148,* 1137–1142.

Rosh, J.R., Dellert, S.F., Narkewicz, M., et al. (1998). Four cases of severe hepatotoxicity associated with pemoline: Possible autoimmune pathogenesis. *Pediatrics, 101,* 921–923.

Rubia, K., Overmeyer, S., Taylor, E., et al. (1999). Hypofrontality in attention deficit hyperactivity disorder during higher-order motor control: A study with functional MRI. *American Journal of Psychiatry, 156,* 891–896.

Safer, D.J., & Malever, M. (2000). Stimulant treatment in Maryland public schools. *Pediatrics, 106,* 533–539.

Safer, D.J., & Zito, J.M. (1999). Psychotropic medications for ADHD. *Mental Retardation and Developmental Disabilities Research Reviews, 5,* 237–242.

Satterfield, J.H., Satterfield, B.T., & Schell, A.M. (1987). Therapeutic interventions to prevent delinquency in hyperactive boys. *Journal of the American Academy of Child and Adolescent Psychiatry, 26,* 56–64.

Schopler, E., Reichler, R.J., & Renner, B.R. (1986). *The Childhood Autism Rating Scale (CARS): For diagnostic screening and classification of autism.* New York: Irvington.

Semel, E., Wiig, E.H., & Secord, W.A. (1995). *Clinical Evaluation of Language Fundaments–Third Edition* (CELF-3). San Antonio, TX: The Psychological Corporation.

Semrud-Clikeman, M., Steingard, R.J., Filipek, P., et al. (2000). Using MRI to examine brain-behavior relationships in males with attention deficit disorder with hyperactivity. *Journal of the American Academy of Child and Adolescent Psychiatry, 39,* 477–484.

Shaffer, D., Fisher, P., Lucas, C., Dulcan, M.K., & Schwab-Stone, M.E. (2000). NIMH Diagnostic Interview Schedule for Children, Version IV (NIMH DISC-IV): Description, differences from previous versions, and reliability of some common diagnoses. *Journal of the American Academy of Child and Adolescent Psychiatry, 39,* 28–38.

Sharp, W., Walter, J.M., Marsh, W.L., et al. (1999). ADHD in girls: Clinical comparability of a research sample. *Journal of the American Academy of Child and Adolescent Psychiatry, 38,* 40–47.

Shaywitz, G.A., Fletcher, J.M., Pugh, K.R., et al. (1999). Progress in imaging attention deficit hyperactivity disorder. *Mental Retardation and Developmental Disabilities Research Reviews, 5,* 185–190.

Singer, H.S., Brown, J., Quaskey, S., et al. (1995). The treatment of attention-deficit hyperactivity disorder in Tourette's syndrome: A double-blind placebo controlled study with clonidine and desipramine. *Pediatrics, 95,* 74–81.

Solanto, M.V. (1984). Neuropharmacological basis of stimulant drug action in attention deficit disorder with hyperactivity: A review and synthesis. *Psychological Bulletin, 95,* 387–409.

Solanto, M.V. (1998). Neuropsychopharmacological mechanisms of stimulant drug action in attention-deficit hyperactivity disorder: A review and integration. *Behavioural Brain Research, 94,* 127–152.

Special section. (2001). *Journal of the American Academy of Child and Adolescent Psychiatry, 40,* 134–196.

Spencer, T., Biederman, J., & Wilens, T. (1998). Growth deficits in children with attention deficit hyperactivity disorder. *Pediatrics, 102,* 501–506.

Spencer, T., Biederman, J., Wilens, T., et al. (1996). Pharmacotherapy of attention-deficit hyperactivity disorder across the life cycle. *Journal of the American Academy of Child and Adolescent Psychiatry, 35,* 409–432.

Sprich-Buckminster, S., Biederman, J., Milberger, S., et al. (1993). Are perinatal complications relevant to the manifestations of ADD?: Issues of comorbidity and familiarity. *Journal of the American Academy of Child and Adolescent Psychiatry, 32*, 1032–1037.

Stein, M.A. (1999). Unraveling sleep problems in treated and untreated children with ADHD. *Journal of Child and Adolescent Psychopharmacology, 9*, 157–168.

Stein, M.A., Szumowski, E., Sandoval, R., et al. (1994). Psychometric properties of the Children's Atypical Development Scale. *Journal of Abnormal Child Psychology, 22*, 167–175.

Stone, W.L., Coonrod, E.E., & Ousley, O.Y. (2000). Brief report: Screening Tool for Autism in Two-Year-Olds (STAT): Development and preliminary data. *Journal of Autism and Developmental Disorders, 30*, 607–612.

Sulzer, D., Chen, T.-K., Lau Y.Y., et al. (1995). Amphetamine redistributes dopamine from synaptic vesicles to the cytosol and promoes reverse transport. *Journal of Neuroscience, 15*, 4102–4108.

Swanson, J.M., Flodman, P., Kennedy, J., et al. (2000). Dopamine genes and ADHD. *Neuroscience and Biobehavioral Reviews, 24*, 21–25.

Swanson, J., McBurnett, K., Wigal, T., et al. (1993). Effects of stimulant medication on children with attention deficit disorder: A review of reviews. *Exceptional Children, 60*, 154–162.

Swanson, J., Sergeant, J.A., Taylor, E., et al. (1998). Attention-deficit hyperactivity disorder and hyperkinetic disorder. *Lancet, 351*, 429–433.

Thompson, L.L., Riggs, P.D., Mikulich, S.K., et al. (1996). Contribution of ADHD symptoms to substance abuse problems and delinquency in conduct-disordered adolescents. *Journal of Abnormal Child Psychology, 24*, 325–347.

Toren, P., Eldar, S., Sela, B.-A., et al. (1996). Zinc deficiency and attention-deficit hyperactivity disorder. *Biological Psychiatry, 40*, 1308–1310.

Trapani, C. (1999). Psychoeducational assessment of children and adolescents with attention deficit hyperactivity disorder. In P.J. Accardo, T.A. Blondis, B.Y. Whitman et al., (Vol. eds.), *Pediatric habilitation series: Vol. 10. Attention deficits and hyperactivity in children and adults: Diagnosis, treatment, management* (2nd rev. ed., pp. 197–214). New York: Marcel Dekker.

Ullman, R., Sleator, S., Sprague, R., & MetriTech Staff. (1996). *Manual for the Comprehensive Teacher's Rating Scale: Parent Form.* Champaign, IL: MetriTech.

U.S. General Accounting Office. (2001, September). *Attention disorder drugs: Few incidents of diversion or abuse identified by schools* (Publication No. GAO-01-1011). Retrieved January 22, 2002, from http://www.gao.gov.

Vaidya, C.J., Austin, G., Kirkorian, G., et al. (1998). Selective effects of methylphenidate in attention deficit hyperactivity disorder: A functional magnetic resonance study. *Proceedings of the National Academy of Sciences of the United States of America, 95*, 14494–14499.

Voigt, R.G., Llorente, A.M., Jensen, C.L., et al. (2001). A randomized, double-blind, placebo-controlled trial of docosahexaenoic acid supplementation in children with attention deficit/hyperactivity disorder. *Journal of Pediatrics, 139*, 189–196.

Volkow, N.D., Wang, G.-J., Fowler, J.S., et al. (1998). Dopamine transporter occupancies in the human brain induced by therapeutic doses of oral methylphenidate. *American Journal of Psychiatry, 155*, 1325–1331.

Volkow, N.D., Wang, G.-J., Fowler, J.S., et al. (2001). Therapeutic doses of oral methylphenidate significantly increase extracellular dopamine in the human brain. *Journal of Neuroscience, 21*(RC121), 1–5.

Wechsler, D. (1991). *Wechsler Intelligence Scale for Children* (3rd ed.). San Antonio, TX: The Psychological Corporation.

Wechsler, D. (1992). *Wechsler Individual Achievement Test.* San Antonio, TX: The Psychological Corporation.

Weiss, G., & Hechtman, L. (1986). *Hyperactive children grown up.* New York: Guilford Press.

Wells, K.C., Pelham, W.E., Kotkin, R.A., et al. (2000). Psychosocial treatment strategies in the MTA study: Rationale, methods, and critical issues in designing and implementation. *Journal of Abnormal Child Psychology, 28*, 483–505.

Wigal, T., Swanson, J.M., Regino, R., et al. (1999). Stimulant medications for the treatment of ADHD: Efficacy and limitations. *Mental Retardation and Developmental Disabilities Research Reviews, 5*, 215–224.

Wilens, T., Biederman, J., & Mick, E. (1998). Does ADHD affect the course of substance abuse? *American Journal on Addiction, 7*, 156–63.

Wilens, T.E., McDermott, S.P., Biederman, J., et al. (1999). Cognitive therapy in the treatment of adults with ADHD: A systematic chart review of twenty-six cases. *Journal of Cognitive Psychotherapy, 13*, 215–226.

Wodrich, D.L. *Children's psychological testing: A guide for nonpsychologists* (3rd ed.). Baltimore: Paul H. Brookes Publishing Co.

Wolraich, M.L., Greenhill, L.L., Pelham, W., et al. (2001). Randomized, controlled trial of OROS methylphenidate once a day in children with attention-deficit/hyperactivity disorder. *Pediatrics, 108*, 883–891.

Wolraich, M.L., Hannah, J.N, Pinnock, T.Y., et al. (1996). Comparison of diagnostic criteria for attention-deficit hyperactivity disorder in a country-wide sample. *Journal of the American Academy of Child and Adolescent Psychiatry, 35*, 319–324.

Woodcock, R.W., & Johnson, M.B. (1989). *Woodcock–Johnson–Revised Tests of Achievement.* Allen, TX: DLM.

Woodward, L.J., Fergusson, D.M., & Horwood, J. (2000). Driving outcomes of young people with attentional difficulties in adolescence. *Journal of the American Academy of Child and Adolescent Psychiatry, 39*, 627–634.

Zarin, D.A., Suarez, A.P., Pincus, H.A., et al. (1999). Clinical and treatment characteristics of children with attention-deficit/hyperactivity disorder in psychiatric practice. *Journal of the American Academy of Child and Adolescent Psychiatry, 37*, 1262–1270.

Zito, J.M., Safer, D.J., dosReis, S., et al. (2000). Trends in the prescribing of psychotropic medications to preschoolers. *Journal of the American Medical Association, 23*, 1025–1030.

22 Specific Learning Disabilities

Bruce Shapiro, Robin P. Church, and M.E.B. Lewis

Upon completion of this chapter, the reader will:

- know the definitions of the term *specific learning disability*
- be aware of impairments associated with specific learning disabilities
- recognize some of the methods of early identification
- be aware of some intervention strategies
- be knowledgeable about the range of outcomes for children with specific learning disabilities

A child may have difficulty learning for many reasons. Mental retardation, cerebral palsy, seizure disorders, receptive/expressive language disorders, and hearing and vision impairments all can interfere with learning. This chapter focuses on children whose difficulty with learning is not primarily the result of any of these disorders. These children instead appear to have an impairment in some aspect of language and/or visual-perceptual development that interferes with learning. Specific reading disability, or **dyslexia,** is the principal focus of discussion as it is both the most common specific learning disability (SLD) and the one about which the most is known.

DONALD: A CHILD WITH DYSLEXIA

Donald developed typically as a young child and seemed as bright and alert as his sisters, although he began to talk somewhat later than they had. In kindergarten, however, he was found to have learning difficulties. He had particular problems learning the alphabet and the sound of each letter. On a test of early reading skills, he scored well below average in knowledge of the alphabet, phoneme awareness, and early word recognition skills, although his math skills fell within the average range. In first grade, Donald entered a general education class and soon began to fail. He could not learn phonics, and his spelling errors seemed bizarre. Yet, he learned to add and subtract easily. Donald went through a battery of tests that identified specific reading disability in the presence of superior intellectual function—his Full-Scale IQ score on the Wecshler Intelligence Scale for Children–Third Edition (WISC-III; Wecshler, 1991) was 120.

The school decided to keep Donald in a general education class with an itinerant special education teacher providing extra help. This approach was not effective, however, and Donald fell further behind the other children in language arts. He started misbehaving in school and avoiding going to school, using headaches as an excuse. At the end of first grade, his reading was more than 1 year delayed, whereas his arithmetic skills were well above an age-appropriate level.

When he entered second grade, Donald was anxious and unhappy. During that year, however, he attended a general education class but went to a reading resource room daily for

45 minutes. In the resource room, Donald and only five other children worked with a reading specialist who used a structured phonics approach to learning to read. Donald also worked with a speech and language specialist who focused on phoneme awareness skills. His parents also worked with him at night. He remained a poor reader, but he could feel the excitement of gaining new knowledge. He developed friendships with the other children in the resource room, although his less sensitive schoolmates continued to tease him.

At the end of second grade, Donald was retested and found to have made substantial progress during the previous school year. He remained a little more than a year behind in reading, but his rate of learning had accelerated. He continued to attend the resource room daily for another year. By this time, he excelled in mathematics, which helped to offset his difficulty with reading and spelling. He still found school difficult, but he stopped avoiding it. His behavior problems also faded. With the continued support of his teachers and parents, Donald is likely to have a good outcome.

MARIA: A CHILD WITH DYSGRAPHIA AND DYSCALCULIA

Maria is a 12-year-old who attends a general education class but has received resource services since second grade. Although Maria has always maintained adequate grades, especially in reading, her teachers have noted her struggle with note taking, completing written assignments, and copying from the board. Maria also has had difficulty in arithmetic instruction, finding it impossible to memorize math facts and apply them to problem solving. These weaknesses with writing and math (**dysgraphia** and **dyscalculia,** respectively) were documented in a comprehensive educational assessment when Maria was in fourth grade. The evaluator predicted that Maria's impairments in written expression would have an increasing impact on her academic functioning upon middle school entry because more writing and study strategies would be required. This has proven to be the case.

The WISC-III showed a Verbal IQ score of 105 and a Performance IQ score of 90. On educational testing the evaluator noted that Maria displayed a high degree of frustration whenever she had to contend with written demands or math calculations. This had begun to manifest itself both in the classroom, with a falling attendance rate, and at home, with more frequent complaints of stomachaches and headaches.

Maria's parents and the school agreed that staff would provide Maria with specific resource assistance in organization and study skills. She began using a computer for longer written assignments and a computer-based graphic organizer to order her thoughts. Maria also was assigned a buddy to take notes for her whenever she could not keep up with the demands of the written work. In addition, teachers were advised not to penalize her for spelling errors but rather to require her to correct them. During math class, she was allowed to use a calculator for basic math operations.

Maria's difficulties seem manageable because the school staff has been willing to be flexible and creative in accommodating her needs. Since this program was implemented, Maria's attendance has improved and her increasing willingness to attempt more difficult assignments has met with success. As she progresses through middle school and enters high school, she will continue to need assistance in organizing her study skills, in using computers for word processing, and in developing math coping strategies. Given these compensations, her prognosis is good.

DEFINING SPECIFIC LEARNING DISABILITIES

The Individuals with Disabilities Education Act (IDEA) of 1997 (PL 105-17) defines *specific learning disability* as

> A disorder in one or more of the basic psychological processes involved in understanding or in using language, spoken or written, which disorder may manifest in imperfect ability to listen, think, speak, read, write, spell, or do mathematical calculations. (§ 602[26][a])

The term *specific learning disability* replaces such older terms as *perceptual disabilities, brain injury, minimal brain dysfunction, dyslexia,* and *developmental aphasia.* The term, however, excludes learning problems that are the result of visual, hearing, or motor disabilities; of mental retardation; of emotional disturbance; or of environmental, cultural, or economic disadvantage.

Unfortunately, there are several problems with this definition in the federal legislation. First, it fails to define the core features of SLD. The definition does not provide guidelines regarding what the "basic psychological processes" of learning are or how marked an "imperfect ability" to learn must be to constitute a disability. It is a definition of exclusion; all other possible causes for the learning problems must be eliminated. This is problematic because SLDs can coexist with other conditions, most notably attention-deficit/hyperactivity disorder (ADHD; Mayes, Calhoun, & Crowell, 2000; see Chapter 21). Visual, hearing, or motor disabilities; mental retardation; emotional disturbance; and environmental, cultural, or economic disadvantage were excluded from the definition to prevent "double dipping" from existing federal programs that deal with those issues. It is clear, however, that a child with SLD may also have one of these other conditions. Finally, this definition does not address origin or the response to treatment (Shapiro & Gallico, 1993).

The way this definition has been operationalized is also problematic. The common approach for diagnosing SLD has been to document a severe discrepancy between ability and achievement. This is done by demonstrating a significant difference between the child's potential to learn, or IQ score, and his or her actual educational achievement (Gregg & Scott, 2000; Wallach & Butler, 1994). Evidence now suggests, however, that this discrepancy approach has poor sensitivity and specificity in discriminating students with specific reading disability from those with low IQ scores and poor reading (Lyon, 1996). In one study, this approach correctly identified less than half of children who were currently receiving special education services, particularly underidentifying young and African American students (Shapiro, 1996). In fact, children with high IQ scores who have specific reading disability do not differ from those with lower IQ scores in reading skills (Siegel, 1998). Discrepancy formulas also have shown poor validity in projecting the child's later school performance in reading. Only 17% of children classified as having specific reading disability in first grade on the basis of ability–achievement discrepancy remained in this classification by sixth grade (Shaywitz et al., 1992). In addition, the discrepancy model incorrectly assumes that IQ scores measure the basic skills involved in the various SLDs. In many studies, the discrepancy formula was no better in identifying SLD than simply applying a criterion of low achievement (Fletcher et al., 1994). For all of these reasons, there is now serious doubt about the utility and validity of the discrepancy concept for specific reading disability. It is less clear whether the discrepancy model has better classification abilities for other SLDs (Berninger & Abbott, 1994; Lyon, 1994; Lyon et al., 1993).

In an attempt to deal with these limitations, the National Joint Committee on Learning Disabilities proposed the following amended definition:

> Learning disability is a generic term that refers to a heterogeneous group of disorders manifested by significant difficulties in the acquisition and use of listening, speaking, reading, writing, reasoning, or mathematical abilities. These disorders are intrinsic to the individual and are presumed to be due to a dysfunction of the central nervous system. Even though a learning disability may occur concomitantly with other disabling conditions (e.g., sensory impairment, mental retardation, social and emotional disturbance) or environmental influences (e.g., cultural differences, insufficient/inappropriate instruction), it is not the direct result of those conditions or influences. (Hammill, 1990, pp. 77–78)

This definition has a number of advantages: It emphasizes the heterogeneous nature of SLDs, it recognizes that the impairments extend beyond childhood, it acknowledges cultural disadvantage, and it states that there can be comorbidity with other developmental disabilities. This is consistent with the findings of MacMillan, Gresham, and Bocian (1998), who noted that students whose learning disabilities were first identified in school constituted an extremely heterogeneous group. MacMillan et al. also showed a discrepancy between criteria specified in state regulations and what school teams used to classify students with learning disabilities.

PREVALENCE

The U.S. Department of Education, National Center for Education Statistics (2000), reported that of the more than 6 million students receiving special education services during the 1998–1999 school year, slightly less than half (2.8 million) were classified as having SLD. This represents approximately 5% of the total school-age population. The size of this category has more than doubled since its original creation in 1977, with a particular acceleration in the 1990s. Although this expansion may represent early or improved diagnosis, it also may be a consequence of a certain amount of overdiagnosis or of the inclusion of children with more subtle learning problems in a category previously reserved for students with more obvious disabilities. It should be emphasized, too, that prevalence figures depend on the definition of disability. Because the definition of SLD is problematic, it follows that prevalence figures may be unreliable and vary from author to author or study to study (Francis et al., 1996).

Another area of dispute is whether gender affects the prevalence of SLDs. Studies traditionally have suggested a four- to fivefold increased prevalence of SLDs among boys. However, because girls manifest attention and learning problems differently from boys and tend not to exhibit oppositional-defiant behavior, some have suggested that girls may be underidentified as having SLD, and that the actual gender ratio may be closer to 1:1 (Shaywitz, Shaywitz, & Fletcher, 1990). Others have questioned these findings and raised concerns about the definition of SLD that was used, the recruitment methods for the study, and the statistical power to prove "no difference."

SUBTYPES OF SPECIFIC LEARNING DISABILITIES

Just as there are different definitions of SLDs, so too are there different approaches to subtyping the disorder. The Office of Education (1977), now known as the U.S. Department of Education, specified seven areas in which a child might exhibit SLD: oral expression, written expression, listening comprehension, basic reading skills, reading comprehension, math calculation, and math reasoning. One approach to subtyping SLDs is to differentiate an impairment in a single academic area (e.g., reading) from a combined disability (e.g., a reading disability associated with impairments in spelling and/or written expression) or a global learning problem (e.g., reading, writing, and mathematics; Gross-Tsur, Manor, & Shalev, 1996). Unfortunately, this subdivision is incomplete as it focuses on functional areas and does not address the underlying impairments. Another approach has been to grade learning impairments from mild to severe (Shafrir & Siegel, 1994). This is useful but also incomplete as it does not take into account the biological underpinnings of SLDs. A third approach attempts to define the processes involved in a function and classifies SLDs according to the abnormality in the learning process. For example, the Yale University Learning Disability Research Center (Lyon, 1995) proposed three subtypes of reading disability: one based on phonological impairment, a second based on phonological and short-term memory impairments, and a third based on general cognitive impairment. SLDs in written expression have been grouped into those involving a language disorder, those involving a spatial disorder, those involving memory and attention impairments, and those involving motor impairments. As of 2002, no subtypes of SLDs have been experimentally validated. The current classification by behavioral phenotype is not likely to yield biologically meaningful subtypes. As knowledge of the neurobiology of SLDs increases, it is likely that these subgroupings will be modified further to reflect their biological bases. A meaningful classification will then result.

SPECIFIC READING DISABILITY

Mechanisms

Specific reading disability is by far the most common form of SLD, accounting for approximately 80% of affected children (Flynn & Rabar, 1994; Roush, 1995). Theoretically, any defect in the processing or interpretation of written words can lead to specific reading disability. Efficient reading depends on rapidly, accurately, and fluently decoding and recognizing the phonemes (speech sounds) of single words (Lyon & Chhabra, 1996; Talcott et al., 2000; Wolf, Bowers, & Biddle, 2000). Phonological awareness includes phoneme awareness (the understanding that speech is made up of discrete sounds) as well as a metacognitive understanding of word boundaries within spoken sentences, of syllable boundaries within spoken words, and of how to isolate these phonemes to establish their location within syllables and words (Clark & Uhry, 1995). Phonological awareness manifests in the ability to analyze and manipulate sounds within syllables (e.g., to count, delete, and reorder them). If a child does not realize that syllables and words are composed of phonemes and that these segments can be divided according to their acoustic boundaries, reading will be slow, labored, and inaccurate and comprehension will be poor (Fletcher et al., 1994; Lyon, 1995). This may result from impaired rapid sequential processing across both auditory and visual modalities (Kraus et al., 1996; Nagarajan et al., 1999; Shaywitz, 1998; Tallal et al., 1996). A second possible mechanism may be a defect in **phonetic** representation in working memory, wherein the child can understand the syntactic structure of a sentence but is unable to maintain it in working memory long enough to comprehend the meaning (Mann, 1994).

Taking these findings into account, the International Dyslexia Association proposed a biologically based definition of specific reading disability:

> A specific language-based disorder of constitutional origin characterized by difficulties in single word decoding, usually reflecting insufficient phonological processing. These difficulties in single word decoding are often unexpected in relation to age and other cognitive and academic abilities; they are not the result of a generalized developmental disability or sensory impairment. Dyslexia is manifest by variable difficulty with different forms of language, often including, in addition to problems with reading, a conspicuous problem with acquiring proficiency in writing and spelling. (Lyon, 1995, p. 9)

Genetics

Since the turn of the 20th century, it has been hypothesized that SLDs are heritable (Thomas, 1905). Often several members of a family have specific reading disability, and the underlying phonological processing impairments in this disorder appear to be highly heritable (Pennington & Gilger, 1996). Studies of identical twins have found that more than half of reading performance impairments are a consequence of heritable influences (DeFries & Alarcon, 1996; Wolff et al., 1995). Furthermore, the recurrence rate of reading disability in susceptible families has been found to be 35%–45%, suggesting that a single gene may be involved (Pennington, 1995). Scarborough (1998) found that 23%–65% of children who have a parent with dyslexia are reported to have the disorder. Wolff and Melngailis (1994) found that the risk for reading impairment was 51% if one parent was affected and 75% if two were. They noted that the severity of the specific reading disability was greater with two affected parents. Genetic studies using linkage and association techniques have shown a relationship between specific reading disability and loci on chromosomes 2, 6, and 15 (Fagerheim et al., 1999; Hodgson, 1998; Smith et al., 1998).

Children with certain genetic syndromes also may have an increased risk of manifesting a particular type of learning disability, although less commonly specific reading disability (Light & DeFries, 1995). For example, girls with Turner syndrome and fragile X syndrome (see Chapters 1 and 17, respectively) and boys with Klinefelter syndrome (see Chapter 1) tend to have visual-perceptual learning disabilities (Pennington et al., 1985; Reiss & Freund, 1990). Casey et al. (2000) studied parents of children with Tourette syndrome and found that these parents showed language-based learning problems. Children with neurofibromatosis, type I (see Appendix B), have both visual-perceptual and language-based learning disabilities (Cutting, Koth, & Denckla, 2000; Denckla, 1996).

Neuroanatomy

To understand the neurological impairments underlying specific reading disability, the normal neural pathways involved in reading must be explained. When one reads, the visual pathways of both eyes pass the print image (written language) to the visual cortex in the occipital lobes of the brain (Figure 13.7). From here, the information is transferred forward to the left angular gyrus of the temporal lobe and to Wernicke's area, which both appear to be critical for phonological coding (i.e., the translation of written language into its speech sound equivalents; Rumsey, 1996). Data from the right occipital (visual) cortex cross over to the left through the corpus callosum and are interpreted in the dominant left temporal lobe of the brain (Hynd et al., 1995; Hynd et al., 1990). Consistent with evidence that the left temporal lobe is a center for phonemic analysis of spoken language, there is typically an asymmetry, with structures being larger on the left than on the right.

Investigations of the neural underpinnings of SLDs have focused on specific reading disability. Two broad approaches have been used for these investigations. The first focuses on brain structure. These studies use neuropathology or neuroimaging (computed tomography or magnetic resonance imaging) to quantify structures and are based on the assumption that brain structure reflects brain function. One shortcoming of this approach is that one cannot distinguish between the observed differences being the cause or the result of different brain functioning. Structural studies in adults with dyslexia have found abnormal nests and connections of cells (termed **ectopias** and *architectonic dysplasias*) that would have occurred during early brain development. These include abnormal cells in the visual system; abnormalities in the corpus callosum; and, possibly, reversal of normal brain asymmetry (see Shapiro, 2001).

In contrast to neuropathological studies, functional approaches allow us to view the brain at work. Function imaging studies are based on the hypothesis that working brain areas are more active than nonworking areas. These techniques use oxygen consumption, radioisotope binding, magnetic fields, or surface electrical activity to demonstrate functional differences. Functional neuroimaging is still being developed, and consistent findings have not resulted.

Although functional neuroimaging studies have not yielded consistent findings, they support a general involvement of the posterior temporal and nearby occipital and parietal regions in dyslexia (Fiez & Petersen, 1998; Lyon & Rumsey, 1996). They also suggest that dyslexia is a complex disorder with impairments that extend beyond phonological processing (Figure 22.1). These findings suggest that reading involves the simultaneous activation of multiple associated cortical regions in a neural network involved in language and visual processing and in attention and planning. A defect anywhere in the network would be expected to result in specific reading disability. This supports the idea that subtypes of reading disability are associated with specific neurocognitive impairments in phonological decoding, visual processing, and so forth (Georgiewa et al., 1999; Shaywitz et al., 1998; see also Rumsey & Eden, 1998). Using positron emission tomography scans, Horwitz, Rumsey, and Donohue (1998) demonstrated the anatomical disconnection in the brains of dyslexics of the left angular gyrus from other brain regions that are part of the normal reading network.

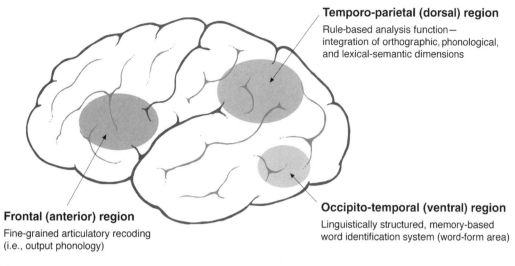

Temporo-parietal (dorsal) region
Rule-based analysis function—
integration of orthographic, phonological,
and lexical-semantic dimensions

Frontal (anterior) region
Fine-grained articulatory recoding
(i.e., output phonology)

Occipito-temporal (ventral) region
Linguistically structured, memory-based
word identification system (word-form area)

Figure 22.1. An overview of the major reading circuits defined by functional neuroimaging studies. (From Pugh, K.R., Mencl, W.E., Jenner, A.R., et al. [2000]. Functional neuroimaging studies of reading and reading disability [developmental dyslexia]. *Mental Retardation and Developmental Disabilities Research Reviews, 6,* 209. Copyright © 2000 Wiley-Liss, Inc. Adapted by permission of Wiley-Liss, Inc., a subsidiary of John Wiley & Sons, Inc.)

IMPAIRMENTS ASSOCIATED WITH SPECIFIC LEARNING DISABILITIES

Donald's case is unusual in that he has an isolated specific reading disability. One quarter to one half of children with SLDs have additional impairments that interfere with school functioning. These may include executive function impairments, ADHD, social skills impairments, and emotional and behavior disorders (Capute, Accardo, & Shapiro, 1994). These behavior and emotional problems may be externalizing (e.g., aggression, oppositional-defiant behavior) or internalizing (e.g., shyness, depression). Failure to detect and treat these additional impairments is a common reason for failed intervention programs (Kube & Shapiro, 1996).

As comorbid conditions may adversely affect outcome, it may be most appropriate to categorize children not only on the basis of their learning impairments but also according to comorbid conditions (McConaughy, Mattison, & Peterson, 1994; McKinney, 1987, 1989; Pennington, 1991; Rock, Fessler, & Church, 1996).

Impairments in Executive Functions

According to Pennington (1991), executive functions involve the ability to maintain an appropriate problem-solving set of procedures for attaining a future goal. This includes the ability to inhibit or defer a response; to formulate a sequential, strategic plan of action; and to encode relevant information in memory for future use (Welsh & Pennington, 1988). These meta-cognitive abilities are necessary for organizational skills, planning, future-oriented behavior, maintaining an appropriate problem-solving set of procedures, impulse control, selective attention, vigilance, inhibition, and creativity in thinking (Denckla & Reader, 1993). These abilities involve an awareness of what skills, strategies, and resources are needed to perform a task effectively. They also require the ability to use self-regulatory mechanisms to ensure the successful completion of a task. Yet students with SLDs are often impulsive rather than reflective when presented with a problem-solving task. This failure to consider alternative solutions often results in errors or poor quality in the solution (Lyon & Krasnegor, 1996). Executive functions become essential in middle school to complete homework and long-term projects, to sustain attention during lectures, and to set future goals. Disruption in this organization and control of behavior often manifests itself as disruption in the classroom.

Memory Impairments

Impairments in the ability to listen, remember, and repeat auditory stimuli have been associated with reading disability. The holding of information in immediate and working memory is essential to learning to read. A number of studies (see Clark & Uhry, 1995) comparing children with equivalent IQ scores but low or high reading abilities have reported impairments in the poor readers on the Digit Span subtest of the WISC-III. Executive dysfunction coupled with memory deficits may adversely affect the student's ability to choose the appropriate strategy for solving a problem. As a result, the student's ability to use cognitive behavioral techniques may be limited because he or she cannot remember a sequence of problem-solving steps.

Attention-Deficit/Hyperactivity Disorder

Approximately one third of children with SLDs also have ADHD, making this the most common comorbid condition (Light & DeFries, 1995; Shaywitz, Fletcher, & Shaywitz, 1995; Shaywitz & Shaywitz, 1991). Studies have found that the prevalence of ADHD in children with SLDs is higher than the prevalence of SLDs in children with ADHD (see Schulte, Conners, & Osborne, 1999). The symptoms typically include inattention, impulsivity, and hyperactivity (see Chapter 21).

Social Skills Impairments

Some children with SLDs may have perceptually based impairments in social skills. Such children tend to be socially isolated, may have few close friends, and infrequently participate in social activities. In turn, they are often overlooked or rejected by their peers because of their odd behavior and poor school and/or athletic performance. Teachers tend to rate these children as having social adjustment difficulties and being easily led. There may be many reasons for these problems, including poor social comprehension, inability to take the perspective of others, poor pragmatic language skills, and misinterpretation of body language (Shapiro & Gallico, 1993).

Emotional and Behavior Disorders

Although associated impairments may represent endogenous biological conditions, they also may result from the child's external experiences of school failure (Fessler, Rosenberg, & Rosenberg, 1991; Gallico, Burns, & Grob, 1988; Spafford & Grosser, 1993). Children with SLDs can exhibit a range of emotional and behavior disturbances, including conduct disorders, withdrawal, poor self-esteem, and depression. These individuals are less likely to take pride in their successes and more likely to be overcome by their failures. More than one third of students with SLDs receive a failing grade in one or more courses each school year. These children often exhibit chronic frustration and anxiety as they attempt to meet the demands of skill-based tasks such as phonological decoding, comprehension, spelling, and math. This school failure, combined with social skills impairments, may lead to peer rejection, poor self-image, and withdrawal from participation in school activities (Bender & Wall, 1994; McKinlay, Ferguson, & Jolly, 1996). Eventually, these children may avoid going to school all together or act out in class to obtain the attention they do not receive through good grades. The overall dropout rate of children with SLDs is twice that found in the general population (U.S. Department of Education, Office of Special Education Programs, 1991).

HEALTH PROBLEMS SIMULATING SPECIFIC LEARNING DISABILITIES

Some children who do not have SLDs may demonstrate learning differences in school as a consequence of another developmental disability, a chronic illness, or psychosocial problems. If these children are misdiagnosed as having SLDs, efforts directed solely at treating the learning problem will have limited success. Instead, the underlying problem must be identified and addressed. Once this problem has been treated, the learning problem may well improve or disappear.

For example, if a child has an unidentified sensory impairment, learning is likely to be impaired. The provision of hearing aids to a child with hearing loss or of glasses to the child with visual impairment may lead to a significant improvement in school performance. Children with epilepsy (see Chapter 25) also may have problems in school resulting either from poorly controlled seizures or from side effects of antiepileptic drugs. Modifying the drug regimen may significantly improve both attention and learning. Children with psychiatric disorders also may fail in school. The use of psychotropic drugs and psychotherapy often leads to significantly improved school performance, although some of these drugs can have an adverse effect on attention. (For specific information on medication side effects, see Appendix C.)

An increased incidence of learning problems also has been described in children with such chronic illnesses as diabetes (Rovet et al., 1993), acquired immunodeficiency syndrome (Armstrong, Seidel, & Swales, 1993; see Chapter 8), cancer (Brown & Madan-Swain, 1993), and chronic kidney and liver disease (Hobbs & Sexson, 1993). In these situations, SLD may exist, but learning difficulties also may result from other causes such as physiological derangement, excessive school absences, attention impairments, or depression. A secondary learning problem rather than a primary SLD is suggested if learning improves once the medical condition is brought under control (Sexson & Madan-Swain, 1993).

Acute disorders such as meningitis, encephalitis, and traumatic brain injury (TBI) also can result in the subsequent development of learning problems. TBI is the most common of these and is an increasingly recognized cause of behavior and learning problems in children (see Chapter 26). The injury may result in either temporary or permanent neurological impairments. Affected children present special challenges in the classroom as a result of the evolving nature of their recovery (Savage & Wolcott, 1994). During the acute phase of recovery, disorders of attention and other executive functions, higher language skills, and behavior are common. Because of this, TBI has been identified as a separate category of disability under IDEA '97 (see Chapter 30), to distinguish it from SLDs and other related disorders. When recovery is completed, some children with TBI may have residual SLDs.

Finally, psychosocial influences may affect the child's ability to learn. A child who is hungry cannot pay attention or learn well (Durkin, 1989). A child who comes from a home that does not value learning rarely achieves well in school. And a home beset with family problems or abuse is a poor setting in which to encourage the child's school performance (Coles, 1987; Maslow, 1970). Improvement in these psychosocial areas would likely result in improved school performance but has proven very difficult to achieve.

ASSESSMENT PROCEDURES

Ideally, assessment is undertaken to explain the reasons for a student's difficulty in the classroom and to propose a method of therapy. It should delineate a student's areas of strength and challenges and permit the development of a comprehensive plan that would optimize his or her academic function. Often assessment is used as a method of determining eligibility for special education services. It is an interdisciplinary process that seeks to identify an educationally disabling condition, delineate other important factors that modify the student's learning abilities, and set learning goals and objectives in an individualized education program (IEP; see Chapter 30).

Simply looking at the discrepancy between potential and actual achievement can lead to misclassification of students. The whole process that the student uses in producing a response is a vital part of understanding his or her relative strengths and weaknesses. Evaluators need to use procedures for assessment that give more information than a simple statistic as an indicator of a student's abilities. If this does not occur, inappropriate treatment recommendations can result. Labeling a test-taker as a "low achiever" does no service to the student. Well-documented strengths and challenges lead to a more serviceable IEP (Swanson, 1996).

Psychological and educational tests are the mainstay of assessment for SLDs in school-age children. However, a complete medical, behavioral, educational, and social history also should be taken to consider confounding variables that may simulate or worsen SLD (Shapiro & Gallico, 1993). After it is determined that no other physical or emotional disorder is responsible for the learning problem, a comprehensive psychoeducational evaluation that assesses cognitive, visual-perceptual, and linguistic processes should be performed. In addition, the implementing regulations of IDEA '97 require assessment of the following seven academic areas: oral expression, listening comprehension, written expression, basic reading skills, reading comprehension, mathematical calculation, and mathematical reasoning. This assessment theoretically permits the diagnosis of an ability–achievement discrepancy and a strategy for intervention. As noted previously, though, the validity of this discrepancy approach is now being questioned (Hooper, 1996).

Although the definition of SLD assumes that the impairments have resulted despite an adequate educational program, it should be acknowledged that not all schools are equal. Some schools have extremely high rates of underachievement for many reasons. Diagnosing SLD in a child who underachieves in this situation is difficult and open to question.

Assessment of cognitive functioning should include areas relevant to discrimination, generalization, motor behavior, general information, vocabulary, induction, comprehension, sequencing, detail recognition, analogies, abstract reasoning, memory, and pattern completion (Table 22.1; Salvia & Ysseldyke, 1995). This is accomplished using intelligence tests such as the WISC-III or the Kaufman Assessment Battery for Children (K-ABC; Kaufman & Kaufman, 1983). The Woodcock-Johnson III (WJ III) Tests of Cognitive Abilities (Woodcock, McGrew, & Mather, 2001) may offer supplemental information about cognitive function.

The WISC-III is divided into six verbal and seven performance subtests, none of which requires reading or spelling. These subtests consist of a series of increasingly difficult questions ranging from a 6- to 16-year-old level. On each subtest, the child is asked to perform up to the level at which he or she consistently fails. Each subtest is then scored, with 10 being an average score. It is possible to determine a child's strengths and challenges by examining the subtest scores. The verbal subtests of the WISC-III include Information, Comprehension, Arithmetic, Similarities, Vocabulary, and Digit Span. The performance subtests include Picture Completion, Picture Arrangement, Block Design, Object Assembly, Coding, Symbol Search, and Mazes (which is optional). The child with SLD may have a scattering of abilities (Branch, Cohen, & Hynd, 1995; Stanford & Hynd, 1994). For example, the examiner may find specific strengths in verbal areas or particular challenges in the visual performance area. Such information is helpful in setting up an IEP.

The K-ABC is designed to measure both intelligence and achievement through mental processing and achievement scales. It yields five global scales: Sequential Processing, Simultaneous Processing, Mental Processing Composite, Achievement, and Nonverbal. (See Wodrich, 1997, for more information on the WISC-III and K-ABC.)

Methods for assessing executive functioning vary and are reviewed in Table 22.1. These tasks challenge the child to tolerate boredom, to operate independently, and to generate active plans to solve puzzles or problems. Such tasks tap the child's ability to initiate problem-solving activities, to maintain sustained attention, to inhibit off-track behavior, and to organize and carry out successful and flexible problem-solving strategies (Campione, 1989; Denckla & Reader, 1993; Haywood & Wingenfeld, 1992; Palincsar, Brown, & Campione, 1991). Dynamic assessment, as described by Swanson (1996), provides an estimate of the stability of information processing potential. This involves measuring a child's performance with examiner assis-

Table 22.1. Commonly used tests for evaluating cognitive and executive functioning

Test	Description/contents	Areas assessed
California Verbal Learning Test—Children's Version (Delis & Fridlund, 1994)	Lists of unrelated words; for ages 5–16 years	Amount of verbal information learned and how it is learned
Behavior Rating Inventory of Executive Function (Gioia et al., 2000)	86-item questionnaire available in parent and teacher forms with eight discrete clinical scales and two validity scales; for ages 5–18 years	Inhibition, initiation, organization of materials, attention shift, working memory, monitoring, emotional control, planing/organization, negativity, and inconsistency of responses
Gordon Diagnostic System (Gordon, 1983)	Computerized activity in which child must react to stated stimuli and not to other stimuli; for ages 4–16 years	Vigilance and inhibition of impulsivity
Wisconsin Card Sorting Test (Grant & Berg, 1993)	Patterns that must be recognized and categorized by attributes that shift and change; for ages 6½–89 years	Perseveration and abstract reasoning
Test of Variables of Attention (Greenberg, 1990)	Computerized activity in which child must react to stated stimuli and not react to others; for ages 6–19 years	Inhibition of impulsivity and selective attention
Kaufman Assessment Battery for Children (K-ABC; Kaufman & Kaufman, 1983)	Five global scales; for ages 2½–12½ years	Sequential processing, simultaneous processing, mental processing, achievement, and nonverbal tasks
NEPSY (Korkman, Kirk, & Kemp, 1998)	27 subtests that assess a wide range of neuropsychological abilities in 3- to 12-year olds	Impairment in five functional domains: attention and executive functions, language, sensorimotor functions, visuospatial processing, memory and learning
Wide Range Assessment of Memory and Learning (WRAML; Sheslow & Adams, 1990)	Nine subtests that assess aspects of memory in 5- to 17-year-olds	Verbal memory, visual memory, learning, and general memory
Wechsler Intelligence Scale for Children–Third Edition (WISC-III; Wechsler, 1991)	Six verbal and six performance subscales; for ages 6–17 years	General information, verbal comprehension, abstract reasoning, memory, spatial abilities
Woodcock-Johnson III (WJ III) Tests of Cognitive Abilities (Woodcock, McGrew, & Mather, 2001)	Six clusters on standard battery and twenty on extended battery; for ages 2–90 years	Verbal ability, thinking ability, cognitive efficiency, phonemic awareness, working memory, delayed recall, comprehension-knowledge, long term retrieval, visual-spatial thinking, auditory processing, fluid reasoning, processing speed, short-term memory, broad attention, cognitive fluency, executive processes, and knowledge

tance and allows for performance to be modified in an effort to understand learning potential (Carlson & Wiedl, 1978; Haywood & Wingenfeld, 1992). These measures of processing are designed to capture subtle differences in children with and without learning disabilities.

These tests are usually combined with tests of visual perception, language, and academic achievement (Table 22.2). Tests that measure visual-perceptual abilities include the Bender Visual-Motor Gestalt Test (Bender, 1946) and the Goodenough-Harris Drawing Test (also called the Draw-A-Man Test; Harris, 1963). Language functioning may be tested by the Clinical Evaluation of Language Fundamentals–Third Edition (CELF-III; Semel, Wiig, & Secord, 1995). Finally, there is a group of academic achievement tests, the most prominent of which are the Woodcock-Johnson III (WJ III) Tests of Achievement (Woodcock et al., 2001), that measure oral reading/comprehension, written language, and mathematics. In addition to

Table 22.2. Commonly used tests for evaluating achievement and related abilities

Test	Description/contents
Visual perceptual tests	
Bender Visual-Motor Gestalt Test (Bender, 1946)	Task: copy nine drawings; measures visual-perceptual skills and eye–hand coordination
Developmental Test of Visual Motor Integration–Fourth Edition (Beery & Buktenica, 1997)	Task: copy 24 geometric forms; scoring system revised for the fourth edition; applicable through age 17 years
Goodenough-Harris Drawing Test (Draw-A-Man Test; Harris, 1963)	Task: draw a person; points given for number of body parts, accuracy, and detail, measuring visual-perceptual skills and self-image for ages 3–15 years
Comprehensive academic achievement tests	
Kaufman Test of Educational Achievement (Kaufman & Kaufman, 1985)	Measures word recognition and comprehension, math calculation and reasoning, and spelling; for grades 1–12
Peabody Individualized Achievement Test–Revised (PIAT-R; Markwardt, 1989)	Measures word recognition and comprehension, math calculation and reasoning, spelling, and written expression; for grades 1–12
Wechsler Individual Achievement Test–Second Edition (WIAT-II; Wechsler, 2001)	Empirically linked to the Wechsler intellectual ability tests; measures achievement from 4 years through adulthood. Subtests include oral language, listening comprehension, written expression, spelling, pseudoword decoding, word reading, reading comprehension, numerical operations, and mathematics reasoning.
Woodcock-Johnson III (WJ III) Tests of Achievement (Woodcock, McGrew, & Mather, 2001)	In 11 subtests, measures achievement from kindergarten through graduate school in word recognition, reading fluency, reading comprehension, calculation, math fluency, applied math reasoning, spelling, writing fluency, written expression, oral expression, and listening comprehension; for ages 2–90 years
Standardized tests of reading	
Nelson-Denny Reading Test (Brown, Bennett, & Hanna, 1985)	Assesses reading skills and comprehension; for ages 9–16 years
Stanford Diagnostic Reading Test–Fourth Edition (Karlsen, Madden, & Gardner, 1996)	Assesses reading in six levels from grades 1.5–13; subtests assess phonetic analysis, vocabulary, comprehension, and scanning
Gates-MacGinitie Reading Tests (MacGinitie et al., 2000)	Presents vocabulary words and stories, with questions to assess reading comprehension; for kindergarten through grade 12
Test of Early Reading Achievement–Third Edition (TERA-3; Reid, Hresko, & Hammill, 2001)	Assesses knowledge of contextual meaning, the alphabet, and print conventions; for ages 3–8 years
Gray Oral Reading Test–Fourth Edition (GORT-4; Wiederholt & Bryant, 2001)	Assesses a variety of reading skills, including oral reading rate and accuracy and oral reading comprehension; for ages 6–18 years
Standardized tests of math	
KeyMath–Revised (Connolly, 1998)	Measures basic math concepts, operations, and applications; for kindergarten through grade 9
Standardized tests of written expression	
Test of Written Language–3 (TOWL-3; Hammill & Larsen, 1999)	Uses both an essay analysis format (mechanics, language, and construction) and traditional test formats (style, spelling, vocabulary, logical sentences, sentence combining) to assess written language; for grades 2–12
Test of Written Spelling–4 (TWS-4; Larsen, Hammill, & Moats, 1999)	Assesses spelling of phonetically regular and irregular words; for grades 1–12

offering broad academic clusters, the WJ III Tests of Achievement provide three additional cross-academic clusters: Academic Skills, Academic Fluency, and Academic Applications. The Wecshler Individualized Achievement Test–Second Edition (WIAT-II; Wechsler, 2001) is another broad-ranging test of educational achievement that assesses oral language and listening comprehension in addition to assessing reading, mathematics, and written language.

The results of the combined psychoeducational testing indicate the child's IQ score, executive functioning, visual-perceptual and language abilities, and levels of achievement in various academic areas. From these findings, coupled with reports about the child's classroom performance and the parents' perceptions of the child's educational capabilities, an IEP is developed. Although federal legislation no longer requires psychoeducational testing to be repeated every 3 years, periodic reassessment of cognitive and executive functions is warranted if the student is failing to progress. Annual assessment of academic subjects, however, is important to determine the progress the child has made and the effectiveness of the program.

INTERVENTION STRATEGIES

The primary goal of intervention is to facilitate the acquisition and expression of the knowledge needed for effective performance in the workplace. The objectives are to achieve academic competence, treat associated impairments, and prevent adverse mental health outcomes. This requires the cooperation of educators, health care professionals, and families. If children with specific reading disability are not provided with an intervention program composed of instruction in phonological awareness, sound–symbol relations, and contextual reading skills before the third grade, at least three quarters of these children will show little improvement in reading throughout their later school years (Shaywitz & Shaywitz, 1991). If given intensive remediation, however, improvement can occur (Lovett & Steinbach, 1997).

In addition to treating the core SLD, intervention strategies also need to focus on associated cognitive, attentional, perceptual, and sensory impairments. Immaturity, lack of motivation, and poor impulse control also must be considered in determining the child's needs for remediation (Bakker, 1992). Intervention must recognize the developmental changes that occur as the student ages. It must be sensitive to the changing demands of the curriculum, the typical developmental challenges faced by the child, and the effects of maturation and intervention on the academic abilities of the student. Successful interventions must not be withdrawn prematurely.

Professionals continue to debate the most effective intervention strategies. A major consideration is whether to teach to the child's abilities (i.e., compensation/circumvention strategies) or to the disabilities (i.e., remedial strategies). Little evidence supports the superiority of one approach over the other. It is generally agreed, however, that there must be a combination of instructional and cognitive interventions (Deshler, Ellis, & Lenz, 1995).

Instructional and Other Types of Interventions

The following is a review of some interventions in reading, writing, mathematics, and other areas.

Reading

Reading proficiency depends on phonological processing and alphabetical mapping. Phonics instruction, however, is different from phonological awareness training. Clark and Uhry (1995) defined *phonics* as a low level of rote knowledge of the association between letters and sounds; *phonological awareness* is an oral language ability that can be measured in different ways. As mentioned previously, phonological awareness includes higher-level metacognitive understandings of word boundaries within spoken sentences, of syllable boundaries in spoken words, and of how to isolate the phonemes and establish their location within syllables and words. Regardless of the method chosen, the major goal of reading instruction is to improve phonological awareness so that there is effective word recognition and comprehension of meaning. Reading activities focus on helping the child gain print awareness and become attuned to the sound characteristics of language (phoneme awareness) and letter–sound relationships (the alphabetic principle).

In elementary school, reading instruction includes methods designed to increase skills in acquiring vocabulary, using syntax, and understanding meaning (Maggart & Zintz, 1993; Newby, Recht, & Caldwell, 1993). Explicit phonics training programs teach individual **grapheme**–phoneme correspondences before they teach the blending these sounds together to form syllables and words. The cornerstone of these programs is the Orton-Gillingham approach (Gillingham & Stillman, 1997; Orton, 1937; Sheffield, 1991). Newer remedial programs adapted from this method are commonly used today with students with reading disabilities. Examples of such programs include Alphabetic Phonics (Cox, 1985), Recipe for Reading (Traub & Bloom, 1975), and the Wilson Reading System (Wilson, 1988). For students who have difficulty with sounds, a program that stresses the oral-motor characteristics of speech, such as the Lindamood Phoneme Sequencing Program for Reading, Spelling, and Speech (LiPS) can be useful (Lindamood & Lindamood, 1998).

Along with knowledge of phonics, a rapid sight vocabulary (words recognized on sight, without sounding them out phonetically) is essential to efficient reading. Different word recognition strategies include analysis of sound (phonics or phonetics), analysis for structure (visual configuration), and use of memory skills to recognize words as total entities (whole-word approach). Comprehension strategies center on developing the ability to draw meaning from text, often using a sequence of books that introduces words and concepts in a gradual progression. An example of a program designed to deliver this kind of systematic direct instruction is Project READ (Calfee & Henry, 1986).

On April 13, 2000, the National Reading Panel released its report on scientific research–based reading instruction (National Institute of Child Health and Human Development, 2000). This report articulates the most effective approaches to teaching reading to all students including those at risk of reading failure. The panel identified the following essential components to a sound reading program: phoneme awareness skills; phonics skills; fluency, accuracy, speed, and expression; reading comprehension strategies to enhance understanding; teacher education; and computer technology.

As students progress to middle and high school, the reading process must connect with other skills needed for mastering content-related matter in subjects such as social studies, geography, higher-level mathematics, and sciences. Study, organizational, and problem-solving skills must blend with the processing skills involved in obtaining meaning from words, sentences, charts, maps, books, poetry, and dramatic or narrative literature. Meaning is easier to teach in the elementary and middle grades than in high school, when it may become buried in nuances of language, such as humor, sarcasm, and metaphor (Englert & Hiebert, 1984).

Many students with a reading disability need an adjustment in the curriculum (Lewis, 1993). Some methods of teaching reading such as Orton-Gillingham and Fernald (Denning, 1990; Silberberg, Iverson, & Goins, 1975) employ multisensory approaches (Birsh, 1999) for the remediation of difficulties in efficient sound–symbol processing. Other approaches include whole language (reinforcing a spectrum of language arts; Edelsky, Atwerger, & Flores, 1991); thematics (utilizing content areas conceptually; Lewis, 1993); literature-based methods (using trade books to build on basal program skills); individualized reading programs (using trade books and alternative literature forms to build personal reading; Fielding & Roller, 1992); and language experience (having students generate their own reading material; Tierney, Readence, & Dishner, 1995). An approach that emphasizes functional skills involves the use of materials involved in daily living (e.g., forms, notices, directions).

As more is known about the neuropsychological impairments of specific reading disability, it is likely that new methods will emerge that focus on the underlying brain impairments. One example of such an experimental approach has been reported by Tallal et al. (1996). Based on evidence that certain children with language-based reading disabilities have difficulty discriminating rapidly successive phonetic elements and nonspeech sound stimuli, computer games have been designed to improve these temporal processing skills (Merzenich et al., 1996).

Writing

Students with dysgraphia have specific disabilities in processing and reporting information in written form. Writing is firmly connected to reading and spelling because comprehension and exposition of these skills are demonstrated through production of written symbols as indicators of understanding. Although writing is a representation of oral language (Maggart & Zintz, 1993), it also must convey meaning without the benefit of vocal intonation or stress. This makes additional demands on the writer.

Problems in writing may result from either an inability to manipulate a pen and paper to produce a legible representation of ideas or an inability to express oneself on paper. Word processors can assist children who have disabilities related to the manipulation of the writing implements (Bain, Bailet, & Moats, 1991). Remedial and instructional techniques helpful with problems of written expression include the use of open-ended sentences (Mercer, Hughes, & Mercer, 1985), probable passages (a strategy used to draw on a student's prior knowledge of a topic while incorporating writing into a basic reading lesson; Wood, 1984), journal keeping (Beach & Anson, 1993; Taylor, 1991), modified writing systems using rebuses or other symbols (Newcomer, Nodine, & Barenbaum, 1988), and newspapers and other print media to demonstrate various writing styles and organizational models.

Writing is also a sociocultural endeavor, representing a cognitive process learned through dialogic interactions, expressing the social and cultural perspectives of the student (Englert, 1992). The difficulties that a student with SLD may have with social perception and awareness of cultural aspects of personal development may influence the written product as well as the writing process.

Content area literacy calls for connections between reading and writing (Mason, 1989; Vacca & Vacca, 1993). Study skills and organization of written materials so that they are retrievable for later use are both vital elements to the success of the student with SLD (Barr et al., 1991).

Mathematics

Students whose SLDs center around arithmetic functioning are diagnosed as having dyscalculia, as was the case with Maria. This problem involves an inability to perform basic math operations (i.e., addition, subtraction, multiplication, division) or to apply those operations to daily situations. For some children with this disorder, a calculator may prove helpful as an aid. Often, however, the problem is in understanding the abstract concepts of mathematical usage. When students with dyscalculia have only written math problems to solve, the concepts remain vague, but when functional applications (e.g., involving money or time) and manipulatives are used the student can connect the concepts to their practical applications and demonstrate greater understanding (Schwartz & Budd, 1983). Thus, teaching may focus on the use of money in fast-food restaurants (e.g., making change), grocery shopping (e.g., comparing prices per unit of weight), banking (e.g., balancing a checkbook, calculating interest), cooking (e.g., measurement), and transportation (e.g., reading, keeping to schedules).

Hutchinson (1992) and Montague (1992) have demonstrated the effectiveness of an approach that emphasizes executive functions for solving mathematical word problems and complex operations (i.e., multiplication). This approach involves rehearsal, practice, and mastery of math skills, in combination with corrective and positive feedback throughout the process of instruction. A metacognitive approach can give students with dyscalculia hope for greater success and facility in progressing to higher and more complex mathematical operations (Desoete, Roeyers, & Buysse, 2001; Hutchinson, 1990; Keeler & Swanson, 2001; Montague & Bos, 1986).

For many students with mathematical disabilities, the more abstract levels of mathematics, such as algebra, geometry, and calculus, may remain mysteries forever; however, these students can still gain facility with basic mathematical facts used in daily life (Mercer, 1991). Many schools teach students how and when to use calculators so that more complex problems can be simplified or homework checked for accuracy. In addition, the computer is now a common part of a school's equipment, and computer-assisted instruction in mathematics may provide opportunities for practice and reinforcement (Okolo, 1992).

Social Skills Training

The maintenance of self-esteem and development of social skills are very important in preventing adverse mental health outcomes in a child with SLD (Meltzer et al., 1998; Vaughn et al., 1998; Wachelka & Katz, 1999). The teacher can encourage this by giving the child special jobs in the classroom and by supporting participation in extracurricular activities such as sports, scouting, music, drama, arts and crafts, and so forth. Social skills training also can be provided in a group setting using role-playing techniques and in summer camp programs.

Counseling

Counseling may be required to treat underlying psychological disorders. This can be provided individually or in groups. Family-centered counseling also may be appropriate. Issues to be discussed may include homework, behavior management techniques, parental expectations, and the child's self-esteem. Families also should be provided a source of information about SLDs, support groups, and their legal rights and responsibilities in the education of their child.

Vocational Training and Career Education

Vocational training, which usually begins in high school, consists of counseling, assessment, and training in the hands-on skills that future jobs require. The U.S. Department of Labor (1992) publishes competencies determined to be necessary for employment. These Secretary's Commission on Achieving Necessary Skills (SCANS) reports have been translated into curriculum areas that deemphasize specific job-related tasks while teaching general competencies that cross all job markets. Programs for adolescents with SLDs need to carefully consider these issues if they are to adequately prepare young adults for employment. The design of these programs becomes part of the student's IEP as an individualized transition plan (ITP; see Chapter 30).

Vocational training for students with SLDs begins with realistic counseling resulting from a comprehensive assessment of abilities and aptitudes. Without appropriately directed training, students are at risk to become unable to support themselves in an independent manner as adults (Michaels, 1994). If vocational rehabilitative services are delayed until adulthood, they are less likely to be effective (Dowdy, Smith, & Nowell, 1992).

Career and technology education is equally important if students are to be ready for the jobs that are available in the new millennium. Career education should be an objective of educational programming from the primary grades. Even as adults, individuals with SLDs have poor retention of verbal instructions and other problems that may interfere with effectiveness in their jobs. They also may be hesitant to ask questions and seek assistance. Social immaturity, clumsiness, and poor judgment may make social interactions more difficult. The skills taught in career education are those required to overcome these impairments and enhance success in the work environment, be it the classroom or the adult job market. Cooperation, respect, responsibility, teamwork, organization, and how to seek information to solve one's problems are part of career education (U.S. Department of Labor, 1992).

Medication

Although SLDs cannot be "cured" through the use of medication, certain associated impairments that affect learning, such as ADHD (see Chapter 21) and behavior and emotional disorders, can be improved with the use of psychoactive drugs (Forness et al., 1992). If any of these drugs is used, its effectiveness must be monitored carefully. Medication should never be a substitute for sound educational programming.

Nontraditional Treatment Approaches

Because there is no cure for SLDs, it is not surprising that a host of nontraditional therapies have gained advocates from time to time. The most commonly used of these approaches have been directed at correcting underlying perceptual impairments. These treatment methods include optometric approaches (Hoyt, 1990) and sensory integration techniques (Hoehn & Baumeister, 1994). Neither has been proved effective.

OTHER INTERVENTION ISSUES

Homework

Taking into account weekends and summer vacations, students spend less than one fifth of their waking hours in school. Thus, planning for successful educational interventions requires open and ongoing communication between home and school. Influences within the community, recreational and leisure choices, family resources, and expectations all must be factored into the educational plan. Accommodations then can be made so that assignments are meaningful and appropriately challenging without being too demanding and so that beneficial routines at home can be established. The home and school should be able to function in partnership so that the hours spent at home do not lead to tension among family members or misunderstanding of the teacher's intent in providing the home assignment. This may require training the parent to set up a workable system and schedule at home (Kay et al., 1994). Students with SLDs often feel that homework is an imposition, providing no personal fulfillment or advancement (Nicholls, McKenzie, & Shufro, 1994), so individualization and creative use of assignments is essential for homework to fulfill its reinforcing purpose. Techniques to facilitate homework performance include parents' reading and reviewing difficult material with the child and teachers' minimizing the need for boring exercises, such as copying. Homework should be limited to a specific time allotment and ideally, should be completed in a fixed area of the home that is quiet, organized, and stocked with needed supplies.

Teacher Work Force

Critical teacher shortages, particularly in special education, are affecting education practices such as inclusion. According to Bandeira de Mello and Broughman (1996), substantial numbers of teachers and administrators will be retiring before 2010 without a ready supply of adequately prepared, certified teachers to replace them. Although there may be a national commitment toward lowering the student–teacher ratio, this ratio is ultimately affected by the ability to meet the projected demands for teachers (Gerald & Hussar, 1996). The availability of a sufficient number of well-trained teachers continues to be among the most critical factors facing students with learning disabilities.

Periodic Reevaluations

The treatment programs for SLDs are complex, and many potential gaps exist. Furthermore, the child is a developing organism whose needs and abilities change from year to year. Therefore, ongoing monitoring is essential. The goal of periodic reassessments is to evaluate parent–child relationships, psychosocial issues, and academic progress. Reassessment is also an opportunity to convey new information to the family and ensure that they are obtaining appropriate resources. Finally, it is a time for retesting the child and revising the educational program. These reevaluations should occur yearly, usually in the spring, so that planning for the next school year can occur.

EARLY IDENTIFICATION OF LEARNING DISABILITIES

The age at which a child is identified as having SLD is a function of many issues: the type of disability, its severity, associated medical problems, the child's intelligence, parental concerns, and school surveillance methods (Richards & Hammitte, 1993). In general, the more severe or global the disability, the earlier it will be detected. Parental concern, often resulting from another family member's having SLD, also may lead to early identification. A medical history of a condition (e.g., prematurity) that places the child at increased risk for developing SLD may also lead to early diagnosis. By contrast, intellectually gifted children may be identified later because their cognitive abilities often compensate for their SLDs during elementary school.

Because the diagnosis of SLD from a federal legislative perspective is based on discrepancy formulas, the identification of an affected child traditionally has occurred after school entry. Yet, studies have shown that the core symptoms of SLDs are present from the preschool years (Catts, 1991; Scanlon & Vellutino, 1996; Scarborough, 1998). They may manifest in the preschool years as delays in language, attention, and behavior and may be associated with impairments in social interactions, impulse control, and motor skills (Reynolds, Elksnin, & Brown, 1996). The most prominent predictor of SLDs in preschool children appears to be weakness in the comprehension of semantics and syntax (Scarborough, 1998). Conversely, strengths in phoneme awareness and verbal memory are predictors of good reading ability. Scarborough (1990) found that 2-year-olds who later developed reading disabilities had decreased length of utterances, syntactic complexity, and pronunciation accuracy. By age 3, these children showed weaknesses in receptive vocabulary and object naming; by age 5 they had impairments in phonological awareness and letter–sound knowledge.

Unfortunately, the items most commonly asked on traditional school readiness education tests (e.g., The Metropolitan Readiness Tests–Sixth Edition [MRT6; Nurss & McGauvran, 1995], Pediatric Examination of Educational Readiness [PEER]) are not good predictors of which students will develop SLD (Badian et al., 1990). Other tests of language and memory function, employing grapheme–phoneme associations and rapid retrieval from long-term memory, appear to be more helpful in early identification of specific reading disability (Badian, 1995; Badian et al., 1990). Measures of phonological awareness include the Lindamood Auditory Conceptualization Test (Lindamood & Lindamood, 1979), the Test of Awareness of Language Segments (Sawyer, 1987), the Test of Phonological Awareness (Torgesen & Bryant,

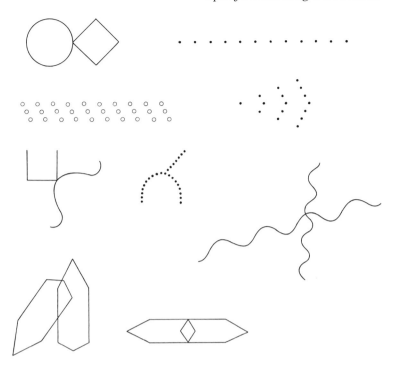

Figure 22.2. Figures used in the Bender Visual Motor Gestalt Test of visual-perceptual abilities. The individual is asked to copy the nine figures. (From Bender, L. [1946]. *Instructions for
the use of Visual Motor Gestalt Test, plate I.* New York: American Orthopsychiatric Association; reprinted by permission. Copyright © 1946 by Lauretta Bender and The American Orthopsychiatric Association, Inc.)

1994), and The Comprehensive Test of Phonological Processing (Wagner, Torgesen, &
Rashotte, 1999). Other useful tests include measures of verbal short-term memory, such as the
Digit Span subtest of the WISC-III, and comparisons of memory for rote material with memory for meaningful material. Rapid automatic recall of information can be measured by the
Rapid Automatized Naming Test (Denckla & Rudel, 1976). Impairments in both short-term
auditory memory and retrieval of phonological information also have been good predictors of
future learning disabilities (Brady et al., 1994; Felton & Wood, 1989; Stone & Brady, 1993).

Impairments in visual-perceptual skills are more difficult to diagnose in the preschool period than are language delays. Tests, however, can indicate problems in drawing and understanding shape concepts. For example, a 3-year-old should be able to draw a circle and a cross
and match colors. A 4-year-old typically can draw a stick figure, and a 6-year-old should be able
to copy a number of the pictures in the Bender Visual Motor Gestalt Test (Figure 22.2; Bender,
1946). Many kindergarten and first-grade teachers believe that difficulty with certain perceptual-
motor tasks, such as tying shoes and skipping, are red flags in predicting poor academic success. Other visual-perceptual signs, however, may not emerge until a child is older than 7 years
of age. For example, although letter reversal is common in children with SLDs, it is not uncommon for typically developing children younger than 7 years of age to reverse letters such
as *b* for *d*. Although an inability to distinguish right from left may be a marker for SLDs, an average child does not accomplish this task consistently until 6 years of age. Other so-called soft
neurological signs, such as difficulty with rapid alternating movements, do not become apparent
until after 6 years of age, and their importance in diagnosing SLD at any time is questionable.

OUTCOME

Long-term outcome appears to depend less on the specific method used to help the student than on the severity of the SLD, the age at diagnosis and intervention, the IQ score, the presence of a comorbid condition, the socioeconomic status of the family, the child's motivation to learn, and family support systems (Gottesman, 1991; Satz et al.,1998). For example, children with comorbid conditions such as ADHD have a less optimistic outcome than individuals with an isolated SLD. By middle and secondary school, students with comorbid conditions may have acquired "learned helplessness," lacking confidence in their own ability to solve learning and social problems independently (Bryan, 1986). They also are at greater risk for making poor choices in their postsecondary education, employment, and independent living. In one study, during the years following high school, only 5% had professional- or managerial-level jobs (Brown, Aylward, & Keogh, 1996).

Adolescence is often a time when even children with SLDs who have learned to compensate for their disabilities may experience difficulty (Shaywitz et al., 1999). Some children are able to compensate for organizational and study skills impairments during elementary school. Matters, however, tend to deteriorate during middle school when students encounter changing class schedules and the need for time management, organization of materials, and completion of multiple assignments and long-term projects (Shapiro & Gallico, 1993). In addition, the demands for sustained attention are greater as classes increase in duration and complexity. If intervention is not provided, these students may show dramatic worsening of behavior and academic performance in high school.

As adults, the outcome for most individuals with an isolated SLD is good (Kurzweil, 1992). Although they may never perform at grade level, most gain the academic skills required for everyday activities. Some students who do not achieve this functional literacy during traditional education may still do so as young adults. Academic preparation of students with SLDs is permitting more and more students to pursue post-secondary education (Gajar, 1992; Shaw & Shaw, 1989). However, the average college student with specific reading disability reads only at about a tenth-grade level (Hughes & Smith, 1990). These students also read more slowly, make more spelling errors, and acquire less information from texts. They tend to have difficulty in writing essays, completing heavy reading assignments, scoring well on timed tests, and learning foreign languages (Denckla, 1993). Many colleges now offer adjustments to program load and schedules as well as tutorial and other support services, which have permitted students with SLDs to complete college at an increasing rate (Brinckerhoff, Shaw, & McGuire, 1992; Durlak, Rose, & Bursuck, 1994; Scott, 1994; Spillane, McGuire, & Norlander, 1992; Vogel & Adelman, 1992).

SUMMARY

SLD is a disorder in which a healthy child with typical intelligence fails to learn adequately in one or more school subjects. The underlying cause of the most common of these disorders, specific reading disability, appears to be an impairment in phonological decoding. Neuroimaging and neuropathological studies in specific reading disability suggest developmental abnormalities in the temporal, parietal, and occipital lobes of the brain. There also appears to be a significant genetic component. Early detection of SLD is important because, untreated, the child may develop secondary emotional and behavior problems that hinder progress. If SLD is suspected, a psychoeducational evaluation should be performed to identify areas of strengths and weaknesses. Then the education team can develop an IEP, which must be assessed at the end of each year and appropriate changes made. No one treatment method is best for all children, so a trial-and-error approach may be needed to find the most useful method. Career and vocational education should be integrated into the general educational program and included as an ITP within the IEP. Although the individual with SLD usually carries his or her learning impairment into adulthood, outcome is often good.

REFERENCES

Armstrong, F.D., Seidel, J.F., & Swales, T.P. (1993). Pediatric HIV infection: A neuropsychological and educational challenge. *Journal of Learning Disabilities, 26*, 92–103.

Badian, N.A. (1995). Predicting reading ability over the long term: The changing roles of letter naming, phonological awareness, and orthographic processing. *Annals of Dyslexia, 45*, 79–96.

Badian, N.A., McAnulty, G.B., Duffy, F.H., et al. (1990). Prediction of dyslexia in kindergarten boys. *Annals of Dyslexia, 40*, 152–169.

Bain, A.M., Bailet, L.L., & Moats, L.C. (1991). *Written language disorders: Theory into practice.* Austin, TX: PRO-ED.

Bakker, D.J. (1992). Neuropsychological classification and treatment of dyslexia. *Journal of Learning Disabilities, 2*, 102–109.

Bandeira de Mello, M.V., & Broughman, S.R. (1996). *1993–94 schools and staffing survey: Selected results* (NCES No. 96-312). Washington, DC: U.S. Department of Education, National Center for Education Statistics.

Barr, R., Kamil, M.L., Mosenthal, P.B., et al. (Eds.). (1991). *Handbook of reading research* (Vol. II). New York: Longman.

Beach, R., & Anson, C.M. (1993). Using peer-dialogue journals to foster response. In G. Newell & R.K. Durst (Eds.), *The role of discussion and writing in the teaching and learning of literature* (pp. 204–205). Norwood, MA: Christopher-Gordon Publishers.

Beery, K.E., Buktenica, N.A. (1997). *Developmental Test of Visual Motor Integration–Fourth Edition.* Columbus, OH: Modern Curriculum Press.

Bender, L. (1946). *Instructions for the use of Visual Motor Gestalt Test, plate 1.* New York: American Orthopsychiatric Association.

Bender, W.N., & Wall, M.E. (1994). Social-emotional development of students with learning disabilities. *Learning Disabilities Quarterly, 17*, 323–341.

Berninger, V.W. & Abbott, R.D. (1994). Redefining learning disabilities: Moving beyond aptitude–achievement discrepancies to failure to respond to validated treatment protocols. In G.R. Lyon (Ed.), *Frames of reference for the assessment of learning disabilities: New views on measurement issues* (pp. 163–183). Baltimore: Paul H. Brookes Publishing Co.

Birsh, J.R. (Ed.). (1999). *Multisensory teaching of basic language skills.* Baltimore: Paul H. Brookes Publishing Co.

Brady, S., Fowler, A., Stone, B., et al. (1994). Training phonological awareness: A study with inner-city kindergarten children. *Annals of Dyslexia, 44*, 26–59.

Branch, W.G., Cohen, M.J., & Hynd, G.W. (1995). Academic achievement and attention-deficit/hyperactivity disorder in children with left- or right-hemisphere dysfunction. *Journal of Learning Disabilities, 28*, 35–43, 64.

Brinckerhoff, L.C., Shaw, S.F., & McGuire, J.M. (1992). Promoting access, accommodations, and independence for college students with learning disabilities. *Journal of Learning Disabilities, 25*, 417–429.

Brown, F.R., Aylward, E., & Keogh, B.K. (Eds.). (1996). *Diagnosis and management of learning disabilities: An interdisciplinary lifespan approach* (3rd ed.). San Diego: Singular Publishing Group.

Brown, J.I., Bennett, J.M., & Hanna, G.S. (1985). *The Nelson-Denny Reading Test.* Chicago: Riverside.

Brown, R.T., & Madan-Swain, A. (1993). Cognitive, neuropsychological, and academic sequelae in children with leukemia. *Journal of Learning Disabilities, 26*, 74–90.

Bryan, T.H. (1986). Self-concept and attributions of the learning disabled. *Learning Disability Focus, 1*, 82–89.

Calfee, R., & Henry, M. (1986). Project READ: An inservice model for training classroom teachers in effective reading instruction. In J.V. Hoffman (Ed.), *Effective teaching of reading: Research and practice* (pp. 199–229). Newark, DE: International Reading Association.

Campione, J.C. (1989). Assisted assessment: A taxonomy of approaches and an outline of strengths and weaknesses. *Journal of Learning Disabilities, 22*, 151–165.

Capute, A.J., Accardo, P.J., & Shapiro, B.K. (Eds.). (1994). *Learning disabilities.* New York: Spectrum Publications.

Carlson, J.S., & Wiedl, K.H. (1978). Use of testing-the-limits procedures in the assessment of intellectual capabilities in children with learning difficulties. *American Journal of Mental Deficiency, 82*, 559–564.

Casey, M.B., Cohen, M., Schuerholz, L.J., et al. (2000). Language-based cognitive functioning in parents of offspring with ADHD comorbid for Tourette syndrome or learning disability. *Developmental Neuropsychology, 17*, 85–110.

Catts, H.W. (1991). Early identification of dyslexia: Evidence from a follow-up study of speech-language impaired children. *Annals of Dyslexia, 41*, 163–177.

Clark, D.B., & Uhry, J.K. (1995). *Dyslexia: Theory and practice of remedial instruction* (2nd ed.). Timonium, MD: York Press.

Coles, G. (1987). *The learning mystique: A critical look at learning disabilities.* New York: Fawcett.

Connolly, A.J. (1998). *KeyMath–Revised.* Circle Pines, MN: American Guidance Service.

Cox, B.A. (1985). Alphabetic phonics: An organization and expansion of Orton-Gillingham. *Annals of Dyslexia, 35*, 187–198.

Cutting, L.E., Koth, L.W., & Denckla, M.B. (2000). How children with neurofibromatosis Type I differ from "typical" learning disability clinic attenders: Nonverbal learning disability revisited. *Developmental Neuropsychology, 17*, 29–47.

DeFries, J.C., & Alarcon, M. (1996). Genetics of specific reading disability. *Mental Retardation and Developmental Disabilities Research Reviews, 2*, 39–47.

Delis, D., & Fridlund, A. (1994). *The California Verbal Learning Test–Children's Version.* San Antonio, TX: The Psychological Corporation.

Denckla, M.B. (1993). The child with developmental disabilities grown up: Adult residua of childhood disorders. *Neurology Clinics, 11*, 105–125.

Denckla, M.B. (1996). Neurofibromatosis type 1: A model for the pathogenesis of reading disability. *Mental Retardation and Developmental Disabilities Research Reviews, 2*, 48–53.

Denckla, M.B., & Reader, M.J. (1993). Education and psychosocial interventions: Executive dysfunction and its consequences. In R. Kurlan (Ed.), *Handbook of Tourette's syndrome and related tic and behavioral disorders* (pp. 431–451). New York: Marcel Dekker.

Denckla, M.B., & Rudel, R.G. (1976). Rapid automatized naming (R.A.N.): Dyslexia differentiated from other learning disabilities. *Neuropsychologia, 14,* 471–479.

Denning, E.M. (1990). *A comparison of nonoral and an oral method of teaching reading association skills to children with language learning disabilities.* Unpublished doctoral dissertation, The Johns Hopkins University, Baltimore.

Deshler, D.D., Ellis, E.S., & Lenz, B.K. (Eds.). (1995). *Teaching adolescents with learning disabilities: Strategies and methods* (2nd ed.). Denver, CO: Love Publishing.

Desoete, A., Roeyers, H., & Buysse, A. (2001). Metacognition and mathematical problem solving in grade 3. *Journal of Learning Disabilities, 34,* 435–449.

Dowdy, C.A., Smith, T.E.C., & Nowell, C.H. (1992). Learning disabilities and vocational rehabilitation. *Journal of Learning Disabilities, 25,* 442–447.

Durkin, D. (1989). *Teaching them to read.* Needham Heights, MA: Allyn & Bacon.

Durlak, C.M., Rose, E., & Bursuck, W.D. (1994). Preparing high school students with learning disabilities for the transition to postsecondary education: Teaching the skills of self-determination. *Journal of Learning Disabilities, 27,* 51–59.

Edelsky, C., Atwerger, B., & Flores, B. (1991). *Whole language: What's the difference?* Portsmouth, NH: Heinemann.

Englert, C.S. (1992). Writing instruction from a sociocultural perspective: The holistic, dialogic, and social enterprise of writing. *Journal of Learning Disabilities, 25,* 153–172.

Englert, C.S., & Hiebert, E.H. (1984). Children's developing awareness of text structure in expository material. *Journal of Educational Psychology, 76,* 65–74.

Fagerheim, T., Raeymaekers, P., Tonnessen, F.E., et al. (1999): A new gene (DYX2) for dyslexia is located on chromosome 2. *Journal of Medical Genetics, 36,* 664–669.

Felton, R.H., & Wood, F.B. (1989). Cognitive deficits in reading disability and attention deficit disorder. *Journal of Learning Disabilities, 22,* 3–22.

Fessler, M.A., Rosenberg, M.S., & Rosenberg, L.A. (1991). Concomitant learning disabilities and learning problems among students with behavioral/emotional disorders. *Behavioral Disorders, 16,* 97–106.

Fielding, L., & Roller, C. (1992). Making difficult books accessible and easy books acceptable. *Reading Teacher, 45,* 678–685.

Fiez, J.A., & Petersen, S.E. (1998). Neuroimaging studies of word reading. *Proceedings of the National Academy of Sciences of the United States of America, 95,* 914–921.

Fletcher, J.M., Shaywitz, S.E., Shankweiler, D., et al. (1994). Cognitive profiles of reading disability: Comparisons of discrepancy and low achievement definitions. *Journal of Educational Psychology, 86,* 6–23.

Flynn, J.M., & Rabar, M.H. (1994). Prevalence of reading failure in boys compared with girls. *Psychology in Schools, 31,* 66.

Forness, S.R., Swanson, J.M., Cantwell, D.P., et al. (1992). Stimulant medication and reading performance: Follow-up on sustained dose in ADHD boys with and without conduct disorders. *Journal of Learning Disabilities, 25,* 115–123.

Francis, D.J., Shaywitz, S.E., Stuebing, K.K., et al. (1996). Developmental lag versus deficit models of reading disability: A longitudinal, individual growth curves analysis. *Journal of Educational Psychology, 88,* 3–17.

Gajar, A. (1992). Adults with learning disabilities: Current and future research priorities. *Journal of Learning Disabilities, 25,* 507–519.

Gallico, R.P., Burns, T.J., & Grob, C.S. (1988). *Emotional and behavioral problems in children with learning disabilities.* Boston: College-Hill.

Georgiewa, P., Rzanny, R., Hopf, J.M., et al. (1999). FMRI during word processing in dyslexic and normal reading children. *Neuroreport, 10,* 3459–3465.

Gerald, D., & Hussar, W. (1996). *Projections of education statistics to 2006* (NCES No. 96–661). Washington, DC: U.S. Department of Education, National Center for Education Statistics.

Gillingham, A., & Stillman, B.W. (1997). *The Gillingham manual: Remedial training for children with specific disabilities in reading, spelling, and penmanship* (8th ed.). Cambridge, MA: Educators Publishing Service.

Gioia, G.A., Isquith, P.K., Guy, S.C., et al. (2000). *Behavior Rating Inventory of Executive Function.* Odessa, FL: Psychological Assessment Resources.

Gordon, M. (1983). *Gordon Diagnostic System.* DeWitt, NY: Gordon Systems.

Gottesman, R.L. (1991). Prognosis: The adult with a learning disability. *Seminars in Neurology, 11,* 64–74.

Grant, D., & Berg, F. (1993). *Wisconsin Card Sorting Test.* Odessa, FL: Psychological Assessment Resources.

Greenberg, L. (1990). *Test of Variables of Attention.* Minneapolis, MN: Attention Technology Systems.

Gregg, N., & Scott, S.S. (2000). Definition and documentation: Theory, measurement, and the courts. *Journal of Learning Disabilities, 33,* 5–13.

Gross-Tsur, V., Manor, O., & Shalev, R.S. (1996). Developmental dyscalculia: Prevalence and demographic features. *Developmental Medicine and Child Neurology, 38,* 25–33.

Hammill, D.D. (1990). On defining learning disabilities: An emerging consensus. *Journal of Learning Disabilities, 23,* 74–84.

Hammill, D.D., & Larsen, S.C. (1996). *Test of Written Language–3 (TOWL-3).* Austin, TX, PRO-ED.

Harris, D.B. (1963). *Children's drawings as measures of intellectual maturity: A revision and extension of the Goodenough Draw-A-Man Test.* New York: Harcourt, Brace & Co.

Haywood, H.C., & Wingenfeld, S.A. (1992). Interactive assessment as a research tool. *Journal of Special Education, 26,* 253–268.

Hobbs, S.A., & Sexson, S.B. (1993). Cognitive development and learning in the pediatric organ transplant recipient. *Journal of Learning Disabilities, 26,* 104–113.

Hodgson, S.V. (1998). The genetics of learning disabilities. *Developmental Medicine and Child Neurology, 40,* 137–140.

Hoehn, T.P., & Baumeister, A.A. (1994). A critique of the application of sensory integration therapy to children with learning disabilities. *Journal of Learning Disabilities, 27,* 338–350.

Hooper, S.R. (1996). Subtyping specific reading disabilities: Classification approaches, recent advances, and current status. *Mental Retardation and Developmental Disabilities Research Reviews, 2,* 14–20.

Horwitz, B., Rumsey, J.M., & Donohue, B.C. (1998). Functional connectivity of the angular gyrus in normal reading and dyslexia. *Proceedings of the National Academy of Sciences of the United States of America, 95,* 8039–8044.

Hoyt, C.S. (1990). Irlen lenses and reading difficulties. *Journal of Learning Disabilities, 23,* 624–627.

Hughes, C.A., & Smith, J.O. (1990). Cognitive and academic performance of college students with learning disabilities: A synthesis of the literature. *Learning Disabilities Quarterly, 13,* 66–79.

Hutchinson, N.L. (1990). *Problem representation and algebra problem solving of students with LD.* Paper presented at the Council for Exceptional Children International Conference, Toronto.

Hutchinson, N.L. (1992). The challenges of componential analysis: Cognitive and metacognitive instruction in mathematical problem solving. *Journal of Learning Disabilities, 25,* 249–252.

Hynd, G.W., Hall, J., Novey, E.S., et al. (1995). Dyslexia and corpus callosum morphology. *Archives of Neurology, 52,* 32–38.

Hynd, G.W., Semrud-Clikeman, M., Lorys, A.R., Novey, E.S., & Eliopulos, D. (1990). Brain morphology in developmental dyslexia and attention deficit disorder/hyperactivity: Morphometric analysis of MRI. *Archives of Neurology, 47,* 919–926.

Individuals with Disabilities Education Act Amendments of 1997, PL 105-17, 20 U.S.C. §§ 1400 *et seq.*

Karlsen, B., Madden, R., & Gardner, E.F. (1996). *Stanford Diagnostic Reading Test–Fourth Edition.* San Antonio, TX: The Psychological Corporation.

Kaufman, A.S., & Kaufman, N.L. (1983). *Kaufman Assessment Battery for Children (K-ABC).* Circle Pines, MN: American Guidance Service.

Kaufman, A.S., & Kaufman, N.L. (1985). *Kaufman Test of Educational Achievement.* Circle Pines, MN: American Guidance Service.

Kay, P.J., Fitzgerald, M., Paradee, C., et al. (1994). Making homework work at home: The parent's perspective. *Journal of Learning Disabilities, 27,* 550–561.

Keeler, M.K., & Swanson, H.L. (2001). Does strategy knowledge influence working memory in children with math disabilities? *Journal of Learning Disabilities, 34,* 418–434.

Korkman, M., Kirk, U., & Kemp, S. (1998). *NEPSY: A developmental neuropsychologic assessment.* San Antonio, TX: The Psychological Corporation.

Kraus, N., McGee, T.J., Carrell, T.D., et al. (1996). Auditory neuropshysiologic responses and discrimination deficits in children with learning problems. *Science, 273,* 971–973.

Kube, D.A., & Shapiro, B.K. (1996). Persistent school dysfunction: The impact of hidden morbidity and suboptimal therapy. *Clinical Pediatrics, 35,* 571–576.

Kurzweil, S.R. (1992). Developmental reading disorder: Predictors of outcome in adolescents who received early diagnosis and treatment. *Journal of Developmental and Behavioral Pediatrics, 13,* 399–404.

Larsen, S.C., Hammill, D.D., & Moats, L.C. (1999). *Test of Written Spelling–4 (TWS-4).* Austin, TX: PRO-ED.

Lewis, M.E.B. (1993). *Thematic methods and strategies for learning disabled students.* San Diego: Singular Publishing Group.

Light, J.G., & DeFries, J.C. (1995). Comorbidity of reading and mathematics disabilities: Genetic and environmental etiologies. *Journal of Learning Disabilities, 28,* 96–106.

Lindamood, C.H., & Lindamood, P.C. (1979). *Lindamood Auditory Conceptualization Test (LAC).* Chicago: Riverside.

Lindamood, P., & Lindamood, P.C. (1998). *Lindamood phoneme sequencing program for reading, spelling, and speech.* Austin, TX: PRO-ED.

Lovett, M.W., & Steinbach, K.A. (1997). The effectiveness of remedial programs for reading disabled children of different ages: Does the benefit decrease for older children? *Learning Disability Quarterly, 20,* 189–210.

Lyon, G.R. (Ed.). (1994). *Frames of reference for the assessment of learning disabilities: New views on measurement issues.* Baltimore: Paul H. Brookes Publishing Co.

Lyon, G.R. (1995). Toward a definition of dyslexia. *Annals of Dyslexia, 45,* 3–27.

Lyon, G.R. (1996). Learning disabilities. In E.J. Mash & R.A. Barkley (Eds.), *Child psychology* (pp. 390–435). New York: Guilford Press.

Lyon, G.R., & Chhabra, V. (1996). The current state of science and the future of specific reading disability. *Mental Retardation and Developmental Disabilities Research Reviews, 2,* 2–9.

Lyon, G.R., Gray, D.B., Kavanagh, J.F., et al. (Eds.). (1993). *Better understanding learning disabilities: New views from research and their implications for education and public policies.* Baltimore: Paul H. Brookes Publishing Co.

Lyon, G.R., & Krasnegor, N.A. (Eds.). (1996). *Attention, memory, and executive function.* Baltimore: Paul H. Brookes Publishing Co.

Lyon, G.R., & Rumsey, J.M. (Eds.). (1996). *Neuroimaging: A window to the neurological foundations of learning and behavior in children.* Baltimore: Paul H. Brookes.

MacGinitie, W.H., MacGinitie, R.K., Maria, K., et al. (2000). *Gates-MacGinitie Reading Tests–Fourth Edition (Forms S and T).* Chicago: Riverside.

MacMillan, D.L., Gresham, F.M., & Bocian, K.M. (1998). Discrepancy between definitions of learning disabilities and school practices: An empirical investigation. *Journal of Learning Disabilities, 31,* 314–326.

Maggart, Z.R., & Zintz, M. (1993). *The reading process: The teacher and the learner* (6th ed.). Dubuque, IA: William C. Brown.

Mann, V. (1994). Phonological skills and the prediction of early reading problems. In N.C. Jordan & J. Goldsmith-Phillips (Eds.), *Learning disabilities: New directions for assessment and intervention* (pp. 67–84). Needham Heights, MA: Allyn & Bacon.

Markwardt, F. (1989). *Peabody Individual Achievement Test–Revised (PIAT-R).* Circle Pines, MN: American Guidance Service.

Maslow, A. (1970). *Motivation and personality.* New York: HarperCollins.

Mason, J.M. (Ed.). (1989). *Reading and writing connections.* Needham Heights, MA: Allyn & Bacon.

Mayes, S.D., Calhoun, S.L., & Crowell, E.W. (2000). Learning disabilities and ADHD: Overlapping spectrum disorders. *Journal of Learning Disabilities, 33,* 417–424.

McConaughy, S.H., Mattison, R.E., & Peterson, R.L. (1994). Behavior/emotional problems of children with serious emotional disturbance and learning disabilities. *School Psychology Review, 23,* 81–98.

McKinlay, I., Ferguson, A., & Jolly, C. (1996). Ability and dependency in adolescents with severe learning disabilities. *Developmental Medicine and Child Neurology, 38,* 48–58.

McKinney, J.D. (1987). Research on conceptually and empirically derived subtypes of specific learning disabilities. In M.C. Wang, M.C. Reynolds, & H.J. Walberg (Eds.), *Handbook of special education: Research and practice* (Vol. 11, pp. 253–282). Elmsford, NY: Pergamon.

McKinney, J.D. (1989). Longitudinal research on the behavioral characteristics of children with learning disabilities. *Journal of Learning Disabilities, 22,* 141–150.

Meltzer, L., Roditi, B., Hauser, R.F., Jr., et al. (1998). Perceptions of academic strategies and competence in students with learning disabilities. *Journal of Learning Disabilities, 31,* 437–451.

Mercer, C.D. (1991). *Students with learning disabilities* (4th ed.). Upper Saddle River, NJ: Merrill.

Mercer, C.D., Hughes, C.A., & Mercer, A.R. (1985). Learning disabilities definitions used by state education departments. *Learning Disability Quarterly, 8,* 45–55.

Merzenich, M.M., Jenkins, W.M., Johnston, P., et al. (1996). Temporal processing deficits of language learning impaired children ameliorated by training. *Science, 271,* 77–81.

Michaels, C.A. (1994). *Transition strategies for persons with learning disabilities.* San Diego: Singular Publishing Group.

Montague, M. (1992). The effects of cognitive and metacognitive strategy instruction on the mathematical problem solving of middle school students with learning disabilities. *Journal of Learning Disabilities, 25,* 230–248.

Montague, M., & Bos, C.S. (1986). The effect of cognitive strategy training on verbal math problem solving performance of learning disabled adolescents. *Journal of Learning Disabilities, 19,* 26–33.

Nagarajan, S., Mahncke, H., Salz, T., et al. (1999). Cortical auditory signal processing in poor readers. *Proceedings of the National Academy of Sciences of the United States of America, 96,* 6483–6488.

National Institute of Child Health and Human Development (2000). *Report of the National Reading Panel: Teaching children to read. An evidence-based assessment of the scientific research literature on reading and its implications for reading instruction.* Retrieved January 8, 2002, from http://www.nichd.nih.gov/publications/nrp/smallbook.htm

Newby, R.F., Recht, D., & Caldwell, J. (1993). Empirically tested interventions for subtypes of reading disabilities. In M.G. Tramontana & S.R. Hooper (Eds.), *Advances in child neuropsychology* (Vol. 2, pp. 201–232). New York: Springer-Verlag.

Newcomer, P., Nodine, B., & Barenbaum, E. (1988). Teaching writing to exceptional children: Reaction and recommendations. *Exceptional Children, 54,* 559–564.

Nicholls, J.G., McKenzie, M., & Shufro, J. (1994). Schoolwork, homework, life's work: The experience of students with and without learning disabilities. *Journal of Learning Disabilities, 27,* 562–569.

Nurss, J.R., & McGauvran, M.E. (1995). *Metropolitan Readiness Tests–Sixth Edition (MRT6).* San Antonio, TX: The Psychological Corporation.

Office of Education. (1977). Assistance to states for education for handicapped children: Procedures for evaluating specific learning disabilities. *Federal Register, 42*(250), 62082–62085.

Okolo, C.M. (1992). The effects of computer-based attribution retraining on the attributions, persistence, and mathematics computation of students with learning disabilities. *Journal of Learning Disabilities, 25,* 327–334.

Orton, S.T. (1937). *Reading, writing, and speech problems in children: A presentation of certain types of disorders in the development of the language faculty.* New York: W.W. Norton.

Palincsar, A., Brown, A., & Campione, J. (1991). Dynamic assessment. In H.L. Swanson (Ed.), *Handbook on the assessment of learning disabilities: Theory, research and practice* (pp. 75–94). Austin, TX: PRO-ED.

Pennington, B.F. (1991). Genetics of learning disabilities. *Seminars in Neurology, 11,* 28–34.

Pennington, B.F. (1995). Genetics of learning disabilities. *Journal of Child Neurology, 10,* 69–77.

Pennington, B.F., Gilger, J.W. (1996). How is dyslexia transmitted? In C.H. Chase G.D. Rosen, & G.F. Sherman (Eds.), *Developmental dyslexia: Neural, cognitive, and genetic mechanisms* (pp. 41–61). Timonium, MD: York Press.

Pennington, B.F., Heaton, R.K., Karzmark, P., et al. (1985). The neuropsychological phenotype in Turner syndrome. *Cortex, 21,* 391–404.

Pugh, K.R., Mencl, W.E., Jenner, A.R., et al. (2000). Functional neuroimaging studies of reading and reading disability (developmental dyslexia). *Mental Retardation and Developmental Disabilities Research Reviews, 6,* 207–213.

Reid, D.K., Hresko, W., & Hammill, D. (2001). *Test of Early Reading Ability–Third Edition (TERA-3).* Austin, TX: PRO-ED.

Reiss, A.L., & Freund, L. (1990). Fragile X syndrome. *Biological Psychiatry, 27,* 223–240.

Reynolds, A.M., Elksnin, N., & Brown, F.R., III. (1996).

Specific reading disabilities: Early identification and long-term outcome. *Mental Retardation and Developmental Disabilities Research Reviews, 2,* 21–27.

Richards, S., & Hammitte, D.J. (1993). The assessment of preschoolers in reference to the learning disabilities label. *Learning Disabilities Forum, 18,* 27–30.

Rock, E.E., Fessler, M.A., & Church, R.P. (1996). The concomitance of learning disabilities and emotional/behavioral disorders: A conceptual model. *Journal of Learning Disabilities, 30,* 245–265.

Roush, W. (1995). Arguing over why Johnny can't read. *Science, 267,* 1896–1898.

Rovet, J.F., Ehrlich, R.M., Czuchta, D., et al. (1993). Psychoeducational characteristics of children and adolescents with insulin-dependent diabetes mellitus. *Journal of Learning Disabilities, 26,* 7–22.

Rumsey, J. (1996). Developmental dyslexia: Anatomic and functional neuroimaging. *Mental Retardation and Developmental Disabilities Research Reviews, 2,* 28–38.

Rumsey J.M., & Eden G. (1998). Functional neuroimaging of developmental dyslexia. Regional cerebral blood flow in dyslexic men. In B.K. Shapiro, P.J. Accardo, & A.J. Capute (Eds.), *Specific reading disability: A view of the spectrum* (pp. 37–62). Timonium, MD: York Press.

Salvia, J., & Ysseldyke, J.E. (1995). *Assessment* (6th ed.). Boston: Houghton Mifflin.

Satz, P., Buka, S., Lipsitt, L., et al. (1998). The long-term prognosis of learning disabled children. In B.K. Shapiro, P.J. Accardo, & A.J. Capute (Eds.), *Specific reading disability: A view of the spectrum* (pp. 223–250). Timonium, MD: York Press.

Savage, R.C., & Wolcott, G.F. (Eds.). (1994). *Educational dimensions of acquired brain injury.* Austin, TX: PRO-ED.

Sawyer, D.J. (1987). *Test of Awareness of Language Segments.* Austin, TX: PRO-ED.

Scanlon, D.M., & Vellutino, F.R. (1996). Prerequisite skills, early instruction, and success in first-grade reading: Selected results from a longitudinal study. *Mental Retardation and Developmental Disabilities Research Reviews, 2,* 54–63.

Scarborough, H.S. (1990). Very early language deficits in dyslexic children. *Child Development, 61,* 1728–1743.

Scarborough, H.S. (1998): Early identification of children at risk for reading disabilities. In B.K. Shapiro, P.J. Accardo, & A.J. Capute (Eds.), *Specific reading disability: A view of the spectrum* (pp. 75–120). Timonium, MD: York Press.

Schwartz, S.E., & Budd, D. (1983). Mathematics for handicapped learners: A functional approach for adolescents. In E. Meyer, G.A. Vergason, & B.P. Whelan (Eds.), *Promising practices for exceptional children: Curriculum implications* (pp. 321–340). Denver, CO: Love Publishing.

Schulte, A.C., Conners, C.K., & Osborne, S.S. (1999). Linkages between attention deficit disorders and reading disability. In D.D. Duane (Ed.), *Reading and attention disorders: Neurobiological correlates* (pp. 161–184). Timonium, MD: York Press.

Scott, S.S. (1994). Determining reasonable academic adjustments for college students with learning disabilities. *Journal of Learning Disabilities, 27,* 403–412.

Semel, E., Wiig, E.H., & Secord, W. (1995). *Clinical evaluation of language fundamentals* (3rd ed.). San Antonio, TX: The Psychological Corporation.

Sexson, S.B., & Madan-Swain, A. (1993). School reentry for the child with chronic illness. *Journal of Learning Disabilities, 26,* 115–125, 137.

Shafrir, U., & Siegel, L.S. (1994). Subtypes of learning disabilities in adolescents and adults. *Journal of Learning Disabilities, 27,* 123–134.

Shapiro, B.K. (1996). The prevalence of specific reading disability. *Mental Retardation and Developmental Disabilities Research Reviews, 2,* 10–13.

Shapiro, B.K. (2001). Specific reading disability: A multiplanar view. *Mental Retardation and Developmental Disabilities Research Reviews, 7,* 13–20.

Shapiro, B.K., & Gallico, R.P. (1993). Learning disabilities. *Pediatric Clinics of North America, 40,* 491–505.

Shaw, S.F., & Shaw, S.R. (1989). Learning disabilities and college programming: A bibliography. *Journal of Postsecondary Education and Disability, 6,* 77–85.

Shaywitz, B.A., Fletcher, J.M., & Shaywitz, S.E. (1995). Defining and classifying learning disabilities and attention-deficit/hyperactivity disorder. *Journal of Child Neurology, 10*(Suppl.), S50–S57.

Shaywitz, B.A., & Shaywitz, S.E. (1991). Comorbidity: A critical issue in attention deficit disorder. *Journal of Child Neurology, 6*(Suppl.), S13–S22.

Shaywitz, S.E. (1998). Dyslexia. *New England Journal of Medicine, 338,* 307–312.

Shaywitz, S.E., Escobar, M.D., Shaywitz, B.A., et al. (1992). Evidence that dyslexia may represent the lower tail of a normal distribution of reading ability. *New England Journal of Medicine, 326,* 145–150.

Shaywitz, S.E., Fletcher, J.M., Holahan, J.M., et al. (1999). Persistence of dyslexia: The Connecticut Longitudinal Study at adolescence. *Pediatrics, 104,* 1351–1359.

Shaywitz S.E., Shaywitz B.A., & Fletcher J.M., et al. (1990). Prevalence of reading disability in boys and girls: Results of the Connecticut Longitudinal Study. *Journal of the American Medical Association, 264,* 998–1002.

Shaywitz, S.E., Shaywitz, B.A., Pugh, K.R., et al. (1998). Functional disruption in the organization of the brain for reading in dyslexia. *Proceedings of the National Academy of Sciences of the United States of America, 95,* 2636–2641.

Sheffield, B.B. (1991). The structured flexibility of Orton-Gillingham. *Annals of Dyslexia, 41,* 41–54.

Sheslow, D., & Adams, W. (1990). *Wide Range Assessment of Memory and Learning.* Wilmington, DE: Wide Range, Inc.

Siegel, L.S. (1998). The discrepancy formula: Its use and abuse. In B.K. Shapiro, P.J. Accardo, & A.J. Capute (Eds.), *Specific reading disability: A view of the spectrum* (pp. 123–135). Timonium, MD: York Press.

Silberberg, N.E., Iverson, I.A., & Goins, J.T. (1975). Which reading method works best? *Journal of Learning Disabilities, 6,* 547–556.

Smith, S.D., Brower, A.M., Cardon, L.R., et al. (1998): Genetics of reading disability: Further evidence for a gene on chromosome 6. In B.K. Shapiro, P.J. Accardo, & A.J. Capute (Eds.), *Specific reading disability: A view of the spectrum* (pp. 63–74). Timonium, MD: York Press.

Spafford, C.S., & Grosser, G.S. (1993). The social misperception syndrome in children with learning disabilities: Social causes versus neurological variables. *Journal of Learning Disabilities, 26,* 178–189, 198.

Spillane, S.A., McGuire, J.M., & Norlander, K.A. (1992). Undergraduate admission policies, practices, and procedures for applicants with learning disabilities. *Journal of Learning Disabilities, 25,* 665–670, 677.

Stanford, L.D., & Hynd, G.W. (1994). Congruence of behavioral symptomatology in children with ADD/H, ADD/WO, and learning disabilities. *Journal of Learning Disabilities, 27,* 243–253.

Stone, B., & Brady, S. (1993, October). *Evidence for basic phonological deficits in less-skilled readers.* Paper presented at the International Association for Research on Learning Disabilities conference, Boston.

Swanson, H.L. (1996). Classification and dynamic assessment of children with learning disabilities. *Focus on Exceptional Children, 28,* 9.

Talcott, J.B., Witton, C., McLean, M.F., et al. (2000). From the cover: Dynamic sensory sensitivity and children's word decoding skills. *Proceedings of the National Academy of Sciences of the United States of America, 97,* 2952–2957.

Tallal, P., Miller, S.L., Bedi, G., et al. (1996). Language comprehension in language-learning impaired children improved with acoustically modified speech. *Science, 271,* 81–84.

Taylor, D.F. (1991). Literature letters and narrative response: Seventh and eighth graders write about their reading. In J. Feeley, D. Strickland, & S. Wepner (Eds.), *Process reading and writing: A literature-based approach.* New York: Teachers College Press.

Thomas, C. (1905). Congenital word-blindness and its treatment. *Ophthalmoscope, 3,* 380–385.

Tierney, R.J., Readence, J.E., & Dishner, E.K. (1995). *Reading strategies and practices: A compendium.* Needham Heights, MA: Allyn & Bacon.

Torgesen, J.K., & Bryant, B.R. (1994). *Test of Phonological Awareness.* Austin, TX: PRO-ED.

Traub, N., & Bloom, F. (1975). *Recipe for reading.* Cambridge, MA: Educators Publishing Service.

U.S. Department of Education, National Center for Education Statistics. (2000). Table 53—Children 0 to 21 years old served in federally supported programs for the disabled, by type of disability: 1976–77 to 1998–99. In *Digest of education statistics, 2000* (p. 65; NCES No. 2001-034). Washington, DC: U.S. Government Printing Office.

U.S. Department of Education, Office of Special Education Programs. (1991). *Youth with disabilities: How are they doing? The first comprehensive report from the National Longitudinal Transition Study of Special Education Students.* Menlo Park, CA: SRI International.

U.S. Department of Labor, Secretary's Commission on Achieving Necessary Skills (SCANS). (1992). *Learning a living: A blueprint for high performance. A SCANS report for AMERICA 2000.* Washington, DC: U.S. Government Printing Office.

Vacca, R.T., & Vacca, J.A.L. (1993). *Content area reading* (4th ed.). New York: HarperCollins.

Vaughn, S., Elbaum, B.E., Schumm, J.S., et al. (1998). Social outcomes for students with and without learning disabilities in inclusive classrooms. *Journal of Learning Disabilities, 31,* 428–436.

Vogel, S.A., & Adelman, P.B. (1992). The success of college students with learning disabilities: Factors related to educational attainment. *Journal of Learning Disabilities, 25,* 430–441.

Wachelka, D., & Katz, R.C. (1999). Reducing test anxiety and improving academic self-esteem in high school and college students with learning disabilities. *Journal of Behavioral Therapy and Experimental Psychiatry, 30,* 191–198.

Wagner, R.K., Torgesen, J.K., & Rashotte, C.A. (1999). *Comprehensive Test of Phonological Processing.* Austin, TX: PRO-ED.

Wallach, G., & Butler, K. (Eds.). (1994). *Language learning disability in school age children and adolescents: Some underlying principles and applications.* Columbus, OH: Charles E. Merrill.

Wechsler, D. (1991). *Wechsler Intelligence Scale for Children–Third Edition (WISC-III).* San Antonio, TX: The Psychological Corporation.

Wechsler, D. (2001). *Wechsler Individual Achievement Test–Second Edition (WIAT-II).* San Antonio, TX: The Psychological Corporation.

Welsh, M.C., & Pennington, B.F. (1988). Assessing frontal lobe functioning in children: Views from developmental psychology. *Developmental Neuropsychology, 4*, 199–230.

Wiederholt, J.L., & Bryant, B.R. (2001). *Gray Oral Reading Test–Fourth Edition (GORT-4)*. Austin, TX: PRO-ED.

Wilson, B.A. (1988). *Wilson Reading System program overview*. Millbury, MA: Wilson Language Training.

Wodrich, D.L. (1997). *Children's psychological testing: A guide for nonpsychologists* (3rd ed.). Baltimore: Paul H. Brookes Publishing Co.

Wolf, M., Bowers, P.G., & Biddle, K. (2000). Naming-speed processes, timing, and reading: A conceptual review. *Journal of Learning Disabilities, 33*, 387–407.

Wolff, P.H., & Melngailis, I. (1994). Family patterns of developmental dyslexia: Clinical findings. *American Journal of Medical Genetics, 54*, 121–131.

Wolff, P.H., Melngailis, I., Obregon, M., et al. (1995). Family patterns of developmental dyslexia, Part II: Behavioral phenotypes. *American Journal of Medical Genetics, 60*, 494–505.

Wood, K. (1984). Probable passages: A writing strategy. *The Reading Teacher, 37*, 496–499.

Woodcock, R.W., McGrew, K.S., & Mather, N. (2001). *Woodcock-Johnson III Complete Battery (WJ III)*. Chicago: Riverside.

23 Cerebral Palsy

Louis Pellegrino

Upon completion of this chapter, the reader will:

- understand the causes of cerebral palsy

- be aware of some early clues to the diagnosis of cerebral palsy

- know the various types of cerebral palsy and their characteristics

- understand how cerebral palsy is diagnosed

- know the sensory, cognitive, and medical problems commonly associated with cerebral palsy

- understand the role of primitive reflexes and automatic movement reactions in motor function and dysfunction

- recognize habilitation as an interdisciplinary strategy to maximize function for children with cerebral palsy

- be knowledgeable about the prognoses for the different forms of cerebral palsy

Cerebral palsy is a disorder of movement and posture that is caused by a nonprogressive abnormality of the immature brain. Although the brain continues to grow into early adulthood, the crucial events of its development occur during intrauterine life and early childhood. Disturbances in the usual unfolding of this process can result in cerebral palsy and may also produce several associated disabilities, including mental retardation, seizures, visual and auditory impairments, learning difficulties, and behavior problems.

JAMAL

Jamal is a 15-month-old boy who was seen by his primary pediatrician for a routine well-child checkup. Jamal's mother expressed concern that her son was not yet walking. The pediatrician had documented some modest delays in motor development at Jamal's 12-month office visit but had attributed these delays to the fact that Jamal was born 3 months prematurely. Jamal's mother had delivered him vaginally following spontaneous onset of labor at 27 weeks' gestation. This spontaneous labor was probably caused by chorioamnionitis, an infection of the membranes surrounding the fetus. Jamal's birth weight was 1 pound, 10 ounces. He required ventilator support for 5 days, and at 2 weeks of age, an ultrasound study of the brain demonstrated a possible abnormality of the white matter of the brain.

As of his 12-month well-child checkup, Jamal had been sitting on his own for about 2 months. The pediatrician had explained to Jamal's mother that based on age adjusted for prematurity, Jamal began sitting at an adjusted age of 7 months. This was only slightly delayed compared with the expected age of sitting independently. Jamal's leg muscles were also a little stiff, and he sat slouched forward, but his pediatrician knew that many premature infants have mild, temporary abnormalities of muscle tone (known as transient **dystonia** of prematurity) that resolve by 15–18 months of age.

At this 15-month visit, Jamal was sitting well but still sat with a slouch. He could crawl stiffly on all fours but was not yet pulling up to a standing position. Jamal showed a pronounced tendency to keep his legs stiffly extended with his toes pointed and feet crossed at the ankles (scissoring). His pediatrician was concerned that Jamal was showing signs of cerebral palsy.

CAUSES OF CEREBRAL PALSY

Until the 1980s, it was thought that most cases of cerebral palsy resulted from "birth asphyxia" (hypoxic-ischemic encephalopathy; see Chapter 5), which is usually defined as a disruption of blood flow **(ischemia)** and oxygen supply (hypoxia) to the brain as a consequence of problems encountered at the time of birth (Harum et al., 1999). It is now clear, however, that only a small fraction of cases of cerebral palsy result from this cause (Moster et al., 2001; Nelson & Ellenberg, 1986); prematurity and problems during intrauterine development account for the majority (Croen et al., 2001; Scher et al., 1991). Although children with cerebral palsy are more likely to have had difficult deliveries, this appears to be the result of preexisting brain abnormalities rather than the cause of them.

Research suggests that children who develop cerebral palsy unrelated to postnatal infection or trauma tend to fall into one of two groups: those born at full term and those born prematurely (Table 23.1). Although the overall prevalence of cerebral palsy has remained fairly constant for many years at 1.4–2.4 cases per 1,000 in the population (Cummins et al., 1993; Hagberg et al., 1996; Stanley et al., 1993), the proportion of former premature infants among all children with cerebral palsy has steadily increased to 40%–50% since the 1970s (Cummins et al., 1993). As of 2000, this trend seems to be leveling off (Hagberg et al., 1996; Meberg & Broch, 1995). Infants with a birth weight of less than 1,500 grams (3⅓ pounds) are especially vulnerable, although it should be emphasized that the vast majority of low birth weight infants do not develop cerebral palsy (Grether, Nelson, & Emery, 1996). Prematurity-related cerebral palsy is most often caused by injury to the white matter of the brain as a result of periventricular leukomalacia (PVL; Figure 6.6) or intraventricular hemorrhage (IVH; see Figure 5.7 and Chapter 6).

The second group of children with cerebral palsy includes those born at term. Compared with those born prematurely, these children are more often small for gestational age or have malformations inside and outside the central nervous system (CNS), suggesting a problem with early fetal development (Krageloh-Mann et al., 1995). In addition, if a full-term infant experiences severe birth asphyxia, he or she may develop cerebral palsy, especially the athetoid or dystonic types, which reflects damage to deep brain structures (e.g., the basal ganglia). In the past, high bilirubin in the immediate postnatal period resulted in a condition called *kernicterus*, which also caused athetoid cerebral palsy. Improvements in the care of infants, however, have made this condition rare in developed countries (see Chapter 5).

A number of brain imaging techniques are available to help define the anatomical correlates of cerebral palsy (Barnes, 1992). Ultrasonography is used for fetal and neonatal screening and can distinguish large malformations of the brain and abnormalities related to brain hemorrhage (i.e., IVH, PVL). Computed tomography (CT) and especially magnetic resonance imaging (MRI) provide more detailed resolution of anatomical structures than ultrasound and may help to define the cause of cerebral palsy. New techniques, such as positron emission tomography (PET) and single photon emission computed tomography (SPECT), complement CT and MRI by providing information about brain metabolic function, which in some cases is abnormal even when brain structure appears to be normal (Chugani, 1993).

Table 23.1. Causes, types, and consequences of cerebral palsy: percentages among pre-term and full-term infants with cerebral palsy

	% of cerebral palsy cases	
	Preterm	Full term
Cause		
Prenatal	8	33
Perinatal	54	28
Unknown	38	39
Types of cerebral palsy		
Hemiplegic	22	44
Diplegic	66	29
Quadriplegic	7	10
Other	5	17
Consequences		
Nonambulatory	39	38
Mental retardation	39	44
Epilepsy	26	36
Severe visual impairment	18	14
Hydrocephalus	23	5

Source: Hagberg et al., 1996.

TYPES OF CEREBRAL PALSY

Cerebral palsy is often classified according to the type of motor impairment that predominates (Figure 23.1; Blair & Stanley, 1985), with spastic cerebral palsy being the most common type. Cerebral palsy is further categorized according to the distribution of limbs involved. In *spastic hemiplegia,* one side of the body is more affected than the other; usually, the arm is more affected than the leg. Because the motor neurons that control one side of the body are located in the opposite cerebral cortex, a right-side **hemiplegia** implies damage to or dysfunction of the left side of the brain, and vice versa. In **spastic diplegia,** the legs are more affected than the arms. This is the type of cerebral palsy most frequently associated with prematurity (and is the type that Jamal exhibits). In **spastic quadriplegia,** all four limbs and usually the trunk and muscles that control the mouth, tongue, and pharynx are affected. The severity of the motor impairment in spastic quadriplegia implies wider cerebral dysfunction and worse outcome than for the other forms of spastic cerebral palsy. Individuals with spastic quadriplegia often have mental retardation, seizures, sensory impairments, and medical complications.

Dyskinetic cerebral palsy is characterized by abnormalities in muscle tone that involve the whole body. Changing patterns of tone from hour to hour and day to day are common. These children may exhibit rigid muscle tone while awake and normal or decreased tone while asleep. Involuntary movements are often present, though are sometimes difficult to detect, and are the hallmark of this type of cerebral palsy. Rapid, random, jerky movements (chorea) and slow, writhing movements (athetosis) are seen in **athetoid cerebral palsy,** a subtype of dyskinetic cerebral palsy (when seen together, these movements are called choreoathetosis). In **dystonic cerebral palsy,** another subtype of dyskinetic cerebral palsy, rigid posturing centered in the trunk and neck is characteristic.

Ataxic cerebral palsy is characterized by abnormalities of voluntary movement involving balance and position of the trunk and limbs in space. For children who can walk, this is noted most especially as a wide-based, unsteady gait. Difficulties with controlling the hand and arm during reaching (causing overshooting or past-pointing) and problems with the timing of motor movements are also seen. Ataxic cerebral palsy may be associated with increased or decreased muscle tone.

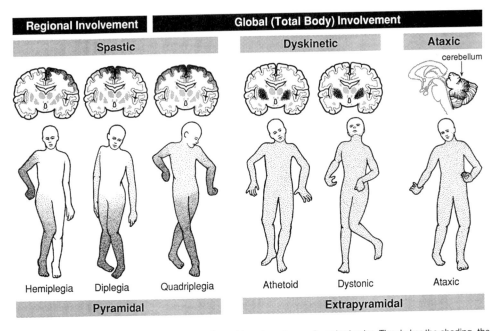

Figure 23.1. Different regions of the brain are affected in various forms of cerebral palsy. The darker the shading, the more severe the involvement.

The term **mixed cerebral palsy** is used when more than one type of motor pattern is present and should be used only when one pattern does not clearly predominate over another. The term *total body cerebral palsy* is sometimes used to emphasize that certain types of cerebral palsy (dyskinetic, ataxic, mixed, and spastic quadriplegia) involve the entire musculoskeletal system to a greater or lesser degree; other forms of spastic cerebral palsy (diplegia, hemiplegia) are localized to particular regions of the body. The terms *pyramidal* (i.e., spastic) and *dyskinetic* (i.e., nonspastic) cerebral palsy also are often applied; *pyramidal* implies abnormalities in the brain pathways originating in the cerebral gray matter, called the *corticospinal (pyramidal) pathways*, and *dyskinetic* implies pathological involvement of the basal ganglia or cerebellum. The physiological mechanisms suggested by these terms are presumptive and, in some cases, controversial (Young, 1994); thus, the clinically descriptive terms *spastic, dyskinetic, ataxic,* and *mixed* are preferred.

EARLY DIAGNOSIS OF CEREBRAL PALSY

Certain groups of newborns at high risk, especially infants who were born weighing less than 1,500 grams, multiple gestations, and small-for-gestational-age infants, merit close neurodevelopmental monitoring to detect cerebral palsy early (Cummins et al., 1993; Petterson, Stanley, & Henderson, 1990). Screening tests, such as the Denver II (Frankenburg et al., 1992), which have traditionally been used by pediatricians to screen infants in developmental follow-up programs, often fail to detect cerebral palsy during the first 12 months of life (Nickel, Rencken, & Gallenstein, 1989). For this reason, a number of neuromotor tests have been developed to evaluate the quality of movement skills in young infants (Darrah, Piper, & Watt, 1998; Paban & Piper, 1987; Piper et al., 1992). These instruments assess the presence of normal movement patterns and the absence of primitive reflexes and abnormal tone.

In addition to these formal tests, a group of behavioral symptoms may suggest cerebral palsy. Children with cerebral palsy may sleep excessively, be irritable when awake, have weak cries and poor sucks, and show little interest in their surroundings. Their resting position is also different. Instead of lying in a semiflexed position, they may lie in a floppy, rag-doll way; alternatively, they may have markedly increased tone and lie in an extended, arched position, called **opisthotonos.**

When examining such a child, a physician looks for abnormalities in muscle tone and deep tendon reflexes (DTRs). Muscle tone may be increased, decreased, or variable. It also may be asymmetrical because one side of the body may be more affected than the other side. Also, DTRs such as the knee jerk may be too brisk, or the child may have tremors, or **clonus,** in the arms and legs.

The persistence of **primitive reflexes** is also a sign of cerebral palsy. Primitive reflexes are typically seen only in the first 6–12 months of life. Their persistence beyond this time interferes with the expression of what are called **automatic** (or **protective**) **movement reactions,** which are necessary for such motor skills as sitting, standing, and walking. As a result, the child with cerebral palsy does not attain motor skills at the appropriate age. Although motor development is significantly delayed in children with cerebral palsy, cognitive and language skills may progress at more typical rates. Thus, a discrepancy between the rates of motor and intellectual development is another clue to the existence of cerebral palsy.

As children with cerebral palsy grow from infancy to 2 years of age, other signs become evident. Typically, 3-month-olds hold their hands open most of the time. In a child with cerebral palsy, the hands often remain clenched in fists. Also, a child does not typically show hand preference until around 18 months of age, whereas a child with spastic hemiplegia may do so before 6 months of age. This suggests that one side of the child's body is weaker than the other side. As the child grows, this may become more obvious because the spastic limbs atrophy, becoming smaller in circumference and length.

Not all of these signs are found in every infant with cerebral palsy, and not all infants who have these signs develop cerebral palsy (Allen & Caputo, 1989; Nelson & Ellenberg, 1982). Diagnostic errors are greatest in the group of children who exhibit mild abnormalities. For example, slightly more than half of infants suspected to be at high risk for cerebral palsy at 12 months of age are considered neurologically unimpaired by 2 years of age (Piper et al., 1988).

Primitive Reflexes

One of the chief diagnostic signs of cerebral palsy, as noted previously, is the persistence of primitive reflexes. These reflexes cause changes both in muscle tone and in movement of the limbs. They are called *primitive* because they are present in early life (in some cases during intrauterine development) and because they are controlled by the primitive regions of the nervous system: the spinal cord, the labyrinths of the inner ear, lower brain areas, and the brain stem. As the cortex matures, these reflexes are gradually suppressed and integrated into voluntary movement patterns. During early infancy, such primitive reflexes as the **Moro** and **tonic neck reflexes** dominate movement; by 12 months of age, integration of the primitive reflexes should be complete (Caputo, 1986).

This is not true of the child with cerebral palsy. In such a child, primitive reflexes are stronger than usual and often last into adult life (especially in dyskinetic cerebral palsy). In a previously unaffected child, primitive reflexes may reemerge following traumatic brain injury (see Chapter 26) or during a coma.

There are many primitive reflexes, three of which are discussed in this section: the **asymmetrical tonic neck reflexes (ATNR),** the **tonic labyrinthine reflex (TLR),** and the **positive support reflex (PSR).** Each of these significantly affects posture and movement, and each is elicited by a different stimulus (Caputo et al., 1978; Illingworth, 1987).

The ATNR is stimulated by the active or passive rotation of the head. When the head is turned, the ATNR causes the arm and leg on the same side as the chin to extend further while the opposite arm and leg become more flexed (Figure 23.2). Changes in muscle tone may occur

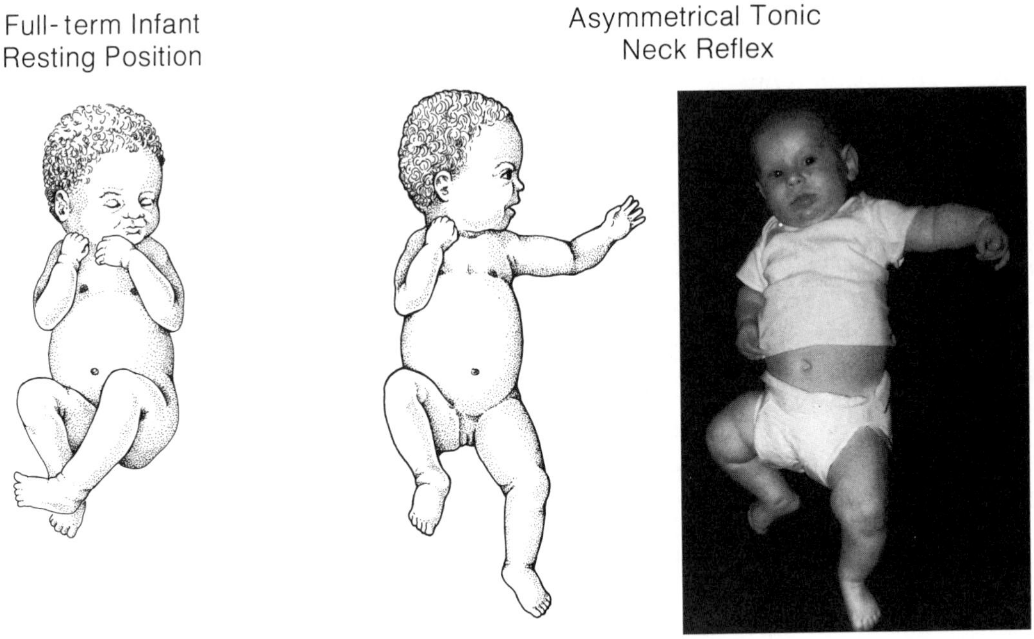

Full-term Infant
Resting Position

Asymmetrical Tonic
Neck Reflex

Figure 23.2. Asymmetrical tonic neck reflex (ATNR), or fencer's response. As the head is turned, the arm and leg on the same side as the chin extend, and the other arm and leg flex.

in the trunk as well. Thus, the ATNR causes an increase in muscle tone and also frequently brings about a change in position. Infants younger than 3 months of age typically show the ATNR. Yet, even in infancy, a child can overcome the reflex (i.e., flex and move the arm once it is reflexively extended). Children with cerebral palsy often cannot; they remain in the extended position until the head turns and releases the reflex. This predicament illustrates the obligatory nature of the primitive reflexes in cerebral palsy.

The TLR is stimulated by the position of the labyrinth inside the inner ear. The response is present at birth, more notable in prematurely born infants, and seen in some children with cerebral palsy. It is typically integrated by 4 months of age. When the child is lying on his or her back and the neck is extended, the legs extend and the shoulders retract, or pull back (Figure 23.3). When the child is lying on his or her stomach and the neck is flexed, the hips and knees flex while the shoulders protract, or roll forward. Flexing or extending the neck in either position may modify the response (e.g., flexing the neck when the infant is on his or her back may decrease extensor tone in the trunk and legs; extending the neck may enhance these responses). When the reflex is present but is not as strong (in many newborn infants and some children with cerebral palsy), muscle tone may change without any change in the position of the limbs.

A third primitive reflex is the PSR. When the balls of the feet touch a firm surface, the child extends the legs (Figure 23.4). This reflex enables the typical newborn infant to support weight while standing. The increased response in a child with cerebral palsy, however, leads to a rigid extension of the legs and feet. Rather than helping, this reflex interferes with standing and walking.

Because these primitive reflexes result in changes in muscle tone and in position of the limbs, their persistence interferes with the development of voluntary motor activity. For example, for an infant to be able to roll over (typically accomplished at 4–5 months of age), the ATNR must be fairly well suppressed. If the ATNR persists, as the infant turns his or her head,

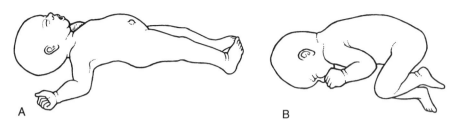

Figure 23.3. Tonic labyrinthine reflex (TLR). a) When the child is in the supine position with the head slightly extended, retraction of the shoulders and extension of the legs is observed. b) The opposite occurs when the infant is in the prone position with the head slightly flexed.

the extended arm and leg hinder the start of the roll. Once the roll is begun, the flexed arm of the strong ATNR prevents its completion.

A similar problem occurs with the TLR and sitting. For a child to sit independently, equilibrium reactions must be present. These reactions require constant, fine changes in muscle tone to maintain balance. If a strong TLR is present, changes in the position of the head cause patterns of flexion and extension throughout the body that are incompatible with maintaining equilibrium and balance in a sitting position, and the child falls over.

Automatic Movement Reactions

As primitive reflexes diminish in intensity in the typically developing child, **postural reactions,** also known as automatic movement reactions, are developing (Figure 23.5). Some of the more important of these reactions include righting, equilibrium, and protective reactions, all of which enable the child to have more complex voluntary movement and better control of posture.

Up to 2 months of age, an infant's head tilts passively in the same direction that the body is leaning. By 3 months of age, however, the infant should be able to compensate and hold the head upright even if the body is tilted. This is called head righting.

Before 5 months of age, if a child is placed in a sitting position and starts to fall forward, he or she will tumble over without trying to regain balance. At 5 months, when the child be-

Positive Support Reflex

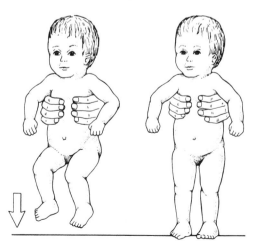

Figure 23.4. Positive support reflex (PSR). As the infant is bounced, the legs straighten to support the body weight.

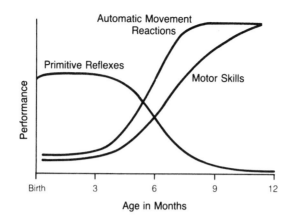

Figure 23.5. Relationship of primitive reflexes, automatic movement reactions, and motor skills. (From Capute, A.J., Accardo, P.J., Vining, E.P.G., et al. [1978]. *Primitive reflex profile* [p. 10]. Baltimore: University Park Press; adapted by permission.)

gins to fall forward, he or she will push out the arms to prevent the fall. This is called the anterior protective (or propping) response. By 7 months, a similar response, the lateral protective response, occurs when the child starts to fall sideways (Capute et al., 1978). Combined, these equilibrium reactions enable the child to sit and move comfortably by automatically compensating when the center of gravity is shifted. In children with cerebral palsy, not only do the primitive reflexes persist, but also the development of the automatic movement reactions may lag behind or never occur.

Walking

Many children with cerebral palsy first come to professional attention because of delayed walking. This developmental milestone has a powerful intrinsic meaning for parents and professionals alike. Most adults know that children begin walking at about 1 year of age, and there is an implicit understanding that a child's first steps mark the transition from infancy to toddlerhood. When a child does not make this transition at the expected time, it is more difficult to ignore than other delays in development.

To walk, a child must be able to maintain an upright posture, move forward in a smoothly coordinated manner, and demonstrate protective responses for safety when falling. Even a child with the mildest form of cerebral palsy has difficulty attaining the continuous changes in muscle tone that are required for typical walking. The child's walk or gait is affected in many ways. Scissoring, the most common gait disturbance, occurs because of increased tone in the muscles that control adduction (movement toward the midline) and internal rotation of the hips. Toe walking results from an equinus position of the feet (Figure 23.6) and increased extensor tone in the legs. In children without cerebral palsy, a protective reaction called the *parachute response* develops by 10 months of age. This is analogous to the anterior protective response and is manifest by forward extension of the arms when falling forward. Children with cerebral palsy have delayed or absent development of this response, which makes walking inherently unsafe.

ASSOCIATED IMPAIRMENTS IN CEREBRAL PALSY

All children with cerebral palsy have problems with movement and posture. Many also have other impairments associated with damage to the CNS (Table 23.1). The most common associated disabilities are mental retardation, visual impairments, hearing impairments, speech-

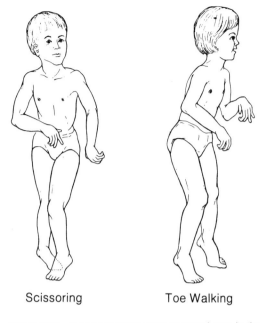

Scissoring   Toe Walking

Figure 23.6. Scissoring results from increased tone in the muscles that control adduction and internal rotation of the hip. Toe walking is due to an equinus position of the feet and increased extensor tone in the legs.

language disorders, seizures, feeding and growth abnormalities, and behavior and emotional disorders.

Assessment of intellectual functioning in children with cerebral palsy may be difficult because most tests of cognition require motor or verbal responses. Even taking this into account, approximately one half to two thirds of children with cerebral palsy have mental retardation, and many of those with average intelligence exhibit some degree of perceptual impairment and learning disability. The type of cerebral palsy influences the risk and degree of mental retardation. Hemiplegia, the most common type of cerebral palsy, is associated with the best intellectual outcome; more than 60% of children with hemiplegia have average intelligence. Spastic diplegia, the form of cerebral palsy associated with prematurity, also has a fairly good intellectual outcome. Less than 30% of individuals with the total body forms of cerebral palsy, however, have average intelligence.

Visual impairments are also common and diverse in children with cerebral palsy (Black, 1982; Schenk-Rootlieb et al., 1992). The premature infant may have severe visual impairment caused by retinopathy of prematurity (see Chapter 10). Nystagmus, or involuntary oscillating eye movements, may be present in the child with ataxia. Children with hemiplegia may present with homonomous hemianopsia, a condition causing loss of one part of the visual field. Strabismus, or squint, is seen in many children with cerebral palsy. Children with cerebral palsy are also more prone to hyperopia (farsightedness) than children without cerebral palsy are (Sobrado et al., 1999).

Hearing, speech, and language impairments are also common, occurring in about 30% of children with cerebral palsy. Children with congenital rubella or other intrauterine viral infections often have high-frequency hearing loss (see Chapter 11). Dyskinetic cerebral palsy is associated with articulation problems, as choreoathetosis affects tongue and vocal cord movements. Expressive or receptive language disorders are commonly observed among children with cerebral palsy who do not have mental retardation and may be a harbinger of a learning disability, such as specific reading disability (see Chapter 22).

Forty to fifty percent of children with cerebral palsy also develop seizures (Aksu, 1990; Delgado et al., 1996). Children with spastic hemiplegia and spastic quadriplegia are especially prone to develop epilepsy, whereas children with spastic diplegia have a lower incidence of seizures. Partial seizures are the predominant form in hemiplegia; generalized tonic-clonic seizures predominate in other types of cerebral palsy. Children with spastic quadriplegia also have an increased incidence of infantile spasms, a form of epilepsy that is difficult to treat and tends to have a poor prognosis for long-term seizure control and developmental outcome (see Chapter 25; Hadjipanayis, Hadjichristodoulou, & Youroukos, 1997).

Feeding and growth difficulties are often present in children with cerebral palsy (Azcue et al., 1996; Stallings et al., 1993) and may be secondary to a variety of problems, including hypotonia, weak suck, poor coordination of the swallowing mechanism, tonic bite reflex, hyperactive gag reflex, and exaggerated tongue thrust (Jones, 1989; Reilly, Skuse, & Poblete, 1996). These problems may lead to poor nutrition and may require the use of alternative feeding methods, such as tube feeding (Rempel, Colwell, & Nelson, 1988). Although these interventions may improve nutritional status, they may complicate other problems, such as the management of gastroesophageal reflux (see Chapter 27; Heine, Reddihough, & Catto-Smith, 1995).

Finally, behavior and emotional disorders play an important role in the lives of children with cerebral palsy and their families. Behavior disorders may range from attention-deficit/hyperactivity disorder (ADHD) to self-injurious behavior. Early intervention programs and agencies such as the United Cerebral Palsy Associations (see Appendix D) can provide invaluable support and training for preschool children and their families (see Chapter 31 for information on intervention for behavior disorders).

HABILITATION

Cerebral palsy is a lifelong disability that has different functional implications at different stages of the life cycle (McCuaig & Frank, 1992). For families and professionals involved in the care of children with cerebral palsy, the ultimate goal of any treatment or intervention is to maximize functioning while minimizing any disability-related disadvantages. This is accomplished by recognizing the specific abilities and needs of the individual child as they occur within the context of his or her family and community. Habilitation is an intervention strategy that is family focused and community based. Ideally, it is conceived and implemented as a comprehensive program designed to facilitate adaptation to and participation in an increasing number and variety of societal environments, including home, school, clinic, child care, neighborhood, and day treatment programs (Pellegrino, 1995). The ultimate goal of intervention is to enhance participation in these environments and to afford access to new environments in a manner that is mutually satisfying for the individual and the community.

Traditional models of multidisciplinary and interdisciplinary care recognize the need for the involvement of many different professionals in the care of the child with cerebral palsy but may be cumbersome and costly and often place inappropriate emphasis on the clinic setting and professional priorities. Interdisciplinary care works best when family members and professionals interact across a variety of environments and keep the goals of habilitation firmly in mind. This is best accomplished under the direction of a care or service coordinator. The care coordinator's job is to keep the "big picture" in mind and to represent the child's best interest to everyone involved. The care coordinator may be a social worker, nurse practitioner, teacher, physician, or a member of a number of other disciplines; the key requirements of the role are regular contact with the family and mobility across environments (e.g., home, school, clinic).

PREVENTING IMPAIRMENT: MANAGING THE MUSCULOSKELETAL COMPLICATIONS OF CEREBRAL PALSY

Orthotics: Braces and Splints

Orthotic devices, including braces and splints, are integrated into the habilitation plans of physical and occupational therapists in an effort to maintain adequate range of motion, prevent contractures at specific joints, provide stability, and control involuntary movements that interfere with function (Nuzzo, 1980). Contractures may develop when muscles consistently have increased tone and remain in shortened positions for prolonged periods of time. **Orthoses** are generally used to maintain a specific group of muscles in a lengthened or less contracted state so that the function of the joint is improved (see Chapter 14).

One of the most commonly prescribed orthotics is a short leg brace that prevents permanent shortening of the heel cords, sometimes decreasing the need for an operation to lengthen the Achilles, or ankle, tendon. This brace usually consists of a plastic splint worn inside the shoe, called a molded ankle-foot orthosis, or MAFO (Figure 33.2; Sankey, Anderson, & Young, 1989).

A variety of splints may be used to improve hand function. In the resting hand splint, the thumb is held in an abducted (away from the midline) position and the wrist in a neutral or slightly extended position. This helps the child keep his or her hand open to prevent a deformity from developing. Other splints are designed to position the arm and hand in such a way as to reduce tone and allow greater functional gains during therapy (Figure 33.1).

Most pediatric braces and splints are custom-made from plastics that are molded directly on the child, so they must be monitored closely and modified as the child grows or changes abilities. A type of brace called a *body splint* is made of a flexible, porous material and controls abnormal tone and involuntary movements by stabilizing the trunk and limbs (Blair et al., 1995).

The use of casts has become increasingly popular as an adjunct to more traditional methods of managing spasticity (Hanson & Jones, 1989; Smith & Harris, 1985). Tone-reducing, or inhibitive, casts are made for arms or legs and can be designed either for immobilization or to be used during weight-bearing activities. Benefits of inhibitive casting include improved gait and weight bearing, increased range of motion, and improved functional hand use (Bertoti, 1986; Smelt, 1989; Yasukawa, 1990). Casts position the limbs so that spastic muscles are in lengthened positions, being gently stretched. Serial application of casts (serial casting) can allow the therapist to increase range of motion gradually when contractures are present. After maximal range and position have been achieved, a cast is worn intermittently to maintain the improvement.

Positioning

Proper positioning geared to the age and functional status of the child is often a key intervention in addressing the tone and movement abnormalities associated with cerebral palsy. A variety of adaptive devices are available to this end (Perin, 1989). Static positioning devices, including sidelyers, prone wedges, and standers (Figure 23.7), may be used to promote skeletal alignment, to compensate for abnormal postures, or to prepare the child for independent mobility. For children who must sit for extended periods or who use a wheelchair for mobility, a carefully designed seating system becomes an all-important component of their habilitation. Careful attention to functional seating may also have long-term benefits in the prevention of contractures and joint deformities related to spasticity (Myhr et al., 1995).

Other devices, including scooters, tricycles, and wheelchairs, provide the child with the means to move independently within the environment and increase opportunities for exploratory play and social interaction.

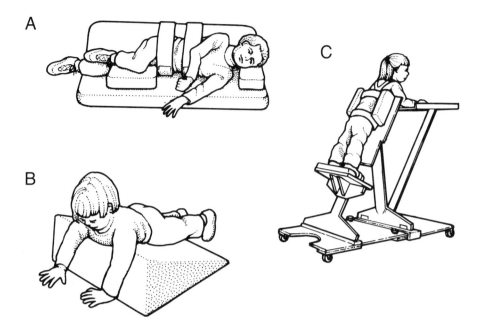

Figure 23.7.   a) Child in sidelyer, b) child in prone wedge, and c) child in prone standing device.

Oral Medication

Orally administered medications have shown limited usefulness in improving muscle tone in children with spasticity and rigidity (Pranzatelli, 1996). No drug has proved helpful for treating choreoathetosis. Both carbidopa-levodopa (Sinemet) and trihexyphenidyl (Artane), medications used in **Parkinson's disease,** have been helpful for some children with dystonic cerebral palsy. The medications most commonly used to control spasticity and rigidity are diazepam (Valium), baclofen, and dantrolene (Dantrium). Diazepam and its derivative compounds, lorazepam (Ativan) and clonazepam (Klonopin), have been used most frequently. They affect brain control of muscle tone, beginning within half an hour after ingestion and lasting about 4 hours. Withdrawal of these drugs should be gradual, as physical dependency can develop. Side effects include drowsiness and excessive drooling, which may interfere with feeding and speech.

Baclofen has been most commonly used to treat adults with multiple sclerosis and traumatic damage to the spinal cord. Drowsiness, nausea, headache, and low blood pressure are the most common side effects of the oral form of the medication in children with cerebral palsy. About 10% of children treated with baclofen experience side effects unpleasant enough to necessitate discontinuation of the medication. Care must be taken when stopping the medication to gradually taper it, as rapid withdrawal can lead to severe side effects, including hallucinations (Glenn & White, 1990).

Dantrolene works on muscle cells directly, as a calcium channel blocker, to inhibit their contraction. About half of the children with spasticity who were treated with this drug in one study showed modest improvement (Joynt & Leonard, 1980). It is usually given two to three times daily. Side effects include drowsiness, muscle weakness, and increased drooling. A rare side effect of this drug is severe liver damage, so liver function tests should be performed periodically.

Although a variety of additional medications are becoming available for the treatment of spasticity in children with cerebral palsy, most cause problematic side effects similar to those described for diazepam, baclofen, and dantrolene, and none are clearly superior to these medications (Coward, 1994; Young, 1994).

Nerve Blocks, Motor Point Blocks, and Botulinum Toxin

In contrast to medication therapy, which has both generalized effects and side effects, several injectable agents are available that can be used to target spasticity in particular muscle groups. Local anesthetic agents injected into the nerves that supply spastic muscles produce a temporary, reversible conduction block and are used for diagnostic purposes (Bleck, 1987). More long-lasting effects are achieved by injecting chemical agents, such as diluted alcohol or phenol, which denature muscle and nerve protein at the point of injection (Koman, Mooney, & Smith, 1996). Direct injections of denaturing agents into motor nerves, called **nerve blocks,** are sometimes used but carry the risk of sensory loss due to damaged sensory nerve fibers that are bundled together with motor fibers. A **motor point block** effectively interrupts the nerve supply at the entry site to a spastic muscle without compromising sensation. The main side effect of the procedure is localized pain that may persist for a few days after the injection. Inhibition of spasticity lasts for 4–6 months, and the procedure can be repeated after the initial effect has worn off. This temporary reduction of spasticity allows for more effective application of physical therapy to improve range of motion and function and may make it possible to postpone orthopedic surgery.

Injectable botulinum toxin (Botox) has been introduced as an alternative to motor point blocks, and has largely supplanted alcohol and phenol in many clinical applications (Bhakta et al., 2000; Calderon-Gonzalez et al., 1994; Cosgrove, Corry, & Graham, 1994; Denislic & Meh, 1995; Koman et al., 2001; Koman et al., 1993; Wissel et al., 1999). Botulinum toxin is produced by the bacterium that causes **botulism** and is among the most potent neurotoxins known. It works by irreversibly blocking the nerve–muscle junction. When the toxin is absorbed into the general circulation (as with botulism), death may result from paralysis of respiratory muscles. Small quantities, however, can be safely injected directly into spastic muscles without significant spread of the toxin into the bloodstream. This results in weakening of the muscle and reduction of spasticity for 3–6 months (the antispastic effects of the injections dissipate over time). Several studies have demonstrated significant short-term benefit of botulinum toxin for decreased spasticity, improved range of motion, improved patterns of gait, and increased mobility (Bentivoglio & Albanese, 1999; Simpson, 1997). Serious side effects have not occurred. Use of this modality in the legs has produced fairly consistent benefits, especially for the improvement of equinus gait (toe walking); results for its use in the arms have been mixed (Corry et al., 1997; Eames et al., 1999; Friedman et al., 2000; Koman et al., 2000; Sutherland et al., 1999). The main advantage of botulinum toxin over motor point blocks is its relative ease of administration with less pain and discomfort. The main disadvantage is the high cost of the drug and incomplete information regarding the long-term risks and benefits of treatment. Clarification of the specific clinical indications for botulinum toxin injections is also needed.

Neurosurgery

Selective posterior rhizotomy has become an accepted treatment option for the reduction of spasticity in selected children with severe lower extremity involvement, especially spastic diplegia (Abbott, 1996; Park, Phillips, & Peacock, 1989). In spasticity, the deep tendon (or stretch) reflex is overactive. This reflex has a motor (efferent) component and a sensory (afferent) component (Figure 23.8). When a muscle is stretched rapidly, special sensory organs in the muscle (called **muscle spindles**) send nerve impulses via the afferent nerve fibers to the spinal cord. Impulses are then directed from the spinal cord through the efferent nerve fibers, which end in the muscle and stimulate it to contract, thus completing a feedback loop and

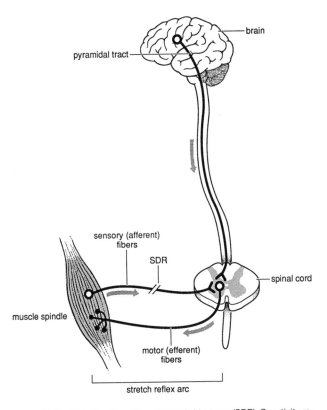

Figure 23.8. Selective dorsal (or posterior) rhizotomy (SDR). Spasticity results from an overactive stretch reflex. When a muscle is stretched, sensory organs (muscle spindles) initiate nerve impulses that are transmitted via sensory (afferent) fibers to the spinal cord. This signal is then modified by input from the pyramidal tract in the brain and relayed back to the muscle via motor (efferent) fibers, causing the muscle to contract. In spastic cerebral palsy, the pyramidal tract is impaired, leading to increased muscle contraction. In SDR, the stretch reflex is interrupted by cutting afferent fibers that supply the muscles that exhibit the greatest degree of spasticity. This results in a decrease in muscle tone.

counteracting the original stretch. In selective dorsal (or posterior) rhizotomy (SDR), the specific afferent fibers (or rootlets) that appear to make the greatest contribution to spasticity are found by observing which rootlets, when stimulated directly with electrical current in the operating room, result in the largest spastic motor response. These specific rootlets are then cut. Because only carefully selected rootlets are cut, touch and position senses remain intact. Postoperatively, spasticity is reduced but is associated with variable degrees of muscle weakness. Functional improvement in sitting, standing, and walking has been reported in some studies (Abbott, Forem, & Johann, 1989; Berman, Vaughan, & Peacock, 1990; Peacock & Staudt, 1990), but others suggest that long-term functional gains may be disappointing (McLaughlin et al., 1998).

A newer neurosurgical procedure allows for the direct delivery of antispasticity medication into the spinal fluid (intrathecal) space, where it can inhibit motor nerve conduction at the level of the spinal cord (Albright, 1996a, 1996b; Albright et al., 1998; McLaughlin et al., 1998; Prats, 1997). A disk-shaped pump is placed beneath the skin of the abdomen, and a catheter is tunneled below the skin around to the back, where it is inserted through the lumbar spine into the intrathecal space. The intrathecal medication most often used is baclofen, which is stored in a reservoir in the disk that can be refilled with a needle inserted into the reservoir through the skin. The medication is delivered at a continuous rate that is computer controlled and adjustable. Because the drug is delivered directly to its site of action (the cerebrospinal fluid), much lower dosage may be used to achieve benefit, with less risk of side effects. Improvements in lower extremity, upper extremity, and even oral-motor function have been observed. The main benefit of the method is dramatic reduction in spasticity and adjustable dosing (Albright, 1997). The main disadvantages are fairly common though usually manageable side effects, including hypotonia (low muscle tone), increased seizures in individuals with known epilepsy, sleepiness, and nausea/vomiting (Gilmartin et al., 2000). Complications related to mechanical failures and infection and the need for intensive and reliable medical follow-up are also significant concerns.

Some other neurosurgical procedures that were used in the past to treat cerebral palsy, including placement of cerebellar or dorsal column stimulators, have largely fallen out of favor due to a lack of efficacy and the presence of significant complications (Davis et al., 1987; Hugenholtz et al., 1988; Park & Owen, 1992).

Orthopedic Surgery

Because of the abnormal or asymmetrical distribution of muscle tone, children who have cerebral palsy are susceptible to the development of joint deformities (Dormans, 1993). The most common of these result from permanent shortening or contracture of one or more groups of muscles around a joint, which limits joint mobility. Orthopedic surgery is done to increase the range of motion by lengthening a tendon, by cutting through muscle or tendon (release), or by moving the point of attachment of a tendon on bone. For example, a partial release or transfer of the hip adductor muscles may improve the child's ability to sit and walk and may lessen the chances of a hip dislocation (Binder & Eng, 1989). A partial hamstring release, involving the lengthening or transfer of muscles around the knee, also may facilitate sitting and walking. A lengthening of the Achilles tendon at the ankle improves walking (Figure 23.9). All of these procedures require the use of a cast or splint for 6–8 weeks after surgery and a brace at night for at least several more months (Bleck, 1987).

More complicated orthopedic procedures may be required for correction of a dislocated hip (Cooke, Cole, & Carey, 1989; Scrutton, 1989). If this is diagnosed when there is a partial dislocation (called **subluxation**), release of the hip adductor muscles alone can be effective (Figure 23.10; Moreau et al., 1979). If the head of the femur is dislocated more than one third to one half of the way out of a hip joint socket, a more complex procedure, a varus derotational osteotomy, may be necessary. In this operation, the angle of the femur (the thigh bone) is changed surgically to place the head of the femur back into the hip socket (Figure 23.11). In

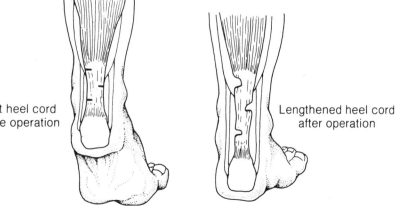

Tight heel cord
before operation

Lengthened heel cord
after operation

Figure 23.9. Achilles tendon lengthening operation. When the heel cord is tight, the child walks on his or her toes. Surgery lengthens the heel cord and permits a more flat-footed gait.

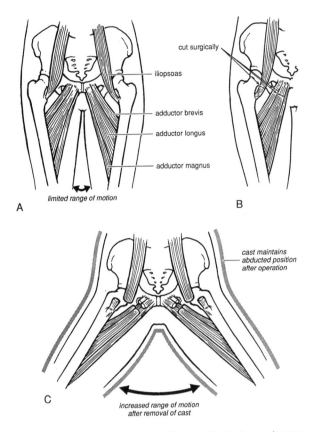

Figure 23.10. Adductor tenotomy. This operation is done to improve scissoring (Figure 23.6) and to prevent hip dislocation caused by contractures of the adductor muscles in the thigh (A). In this procedure, the iliopsoas, adductor brevis, and adductor longus muscles are cut, leaving the adductor magnus intact (B). The child is then placed in a cast for 6–8 weeks to maintain a more open (abducted) position (C). The muscles eventually grow together in a lengthened position, allowing improved sitting and/or walking.

some cases, the hip socket also must be reshaped to ensure that the hip joint remains functional. In some cases, muscle releases or lengthening are performed at the same time as these bony procedures.

Before performing surgery, the orthopedist should be careful to evaluate and explain to the parents and the child both the potential risks and benefits of an operation. Computerized gait analysis conducted prior to surgical intervention to improve ambulation has become increasingly common. Precise measurements obtained through motion analysis, force plates, and electromyography offer detailed information relating to specific abnormalities at each lower extremity joint as well as the muscle activity that controls motion through all phases of the gait (Cahan et al., 1990; Russman & Gage, 1989). Such precise definition is not possible through clinical observation alone. Preoperative gait analysis helps to determine exactly which procedures are likely to be successful. Postoperative analysis can provide an objective measure of outcome.

Besides treating contractures and dislocations, orthopedic surgeons also are involved in the care of scoliosis, a complication of both spastic and nonspastic forms of cerebral palsy. If untreated, a spinal curvature can interfere with sitting, walking, and self-care skills. If severe enough, it also can affect lung capacity and respiratory efforts. Treatment of significant scoliosis ranges from a molded plastic jacket or a chair insert to invasive surgery to straighten the

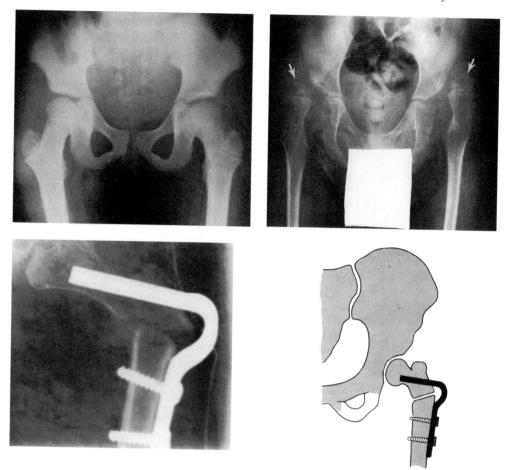

Figure 23.11. Dislocation of the hip. The upper X rays (frontal view) show a normal hip (left X ray) and a hip dislocated on both sides (right X ray). The arrows indicate the points of dislocation. The lower pictures show the results of a varus derotational osteotomy to correct the left-hip dislocation. The femur has been cut and realigned so that it now fits into the acetabulum. Pins, which are later removed, hold the bone in place until it heals.

spine as much as possible. This surgery involves using rods and wires to hold the spine in an improved alignment while bone graft material fuses the spine in position (Figure 23.12; Bulman et al., 1996). With an improved surgical technique called a *Luque procedure*, scoliosis surgery now is being pursued more aggressively (Ferguson & Allen, 1988).

PREVENTING DISABILITY: PROMOTING OPTIMAL FUNCTION

Early Intervention Services

The key to success in any therapy program is the consistency of its delivery and the early involvement of parents so that they can learn to effectively manage their child at home (Miller et al., 1995). Legislation governing public education for children with disabilities has provided guidelines and financial incentives for the development of statewide early intervention systems. Parents are encouraged to participate actively in planning and implementing services and in developing competence in advocacy for their child. Programs are individualized according to the specific needs of the family and may include a combination of consultative, home-based, or center-based intervention (see Chapter 29).

Therapy Options

The most common method of physical and occupational therapy for the young child with cerebral palsy is **neurodevelopmental therapy (NDT),** an approach designed to provide the child with sensorimotor experiences that enhance the development of normal movement patterns (see Chapter 33; Bobath, 1980; Perin, 1989). An individualized program of positioning, therapeutic handling, and play is developed for the child. Program goals include the normalization of tone and the improved control of movement during functional activities (see Chapter 33).

A controversial approach to treating children with cerebral palsy is called **patterning** (Zigler, 1981). Patterning involves putting the child through a series of exercises designed to improve "neurological organization." Three to five volunteers simultaneously manipulate the child's limbs and head for hours daily in patterns that are supposed to simulate prenatal and infantile movement of typically developing children. Proponents believe that if a child repeats certain motions frequently enough, undamaged brain cells will be reprogrammed to take over the functions of the damaged cells. The American Academy of Pediatrics (1982; American Academy of Pediatrics, Committee on Children with Disabilities, 1999) has stated its opposition to this treatment, as it has found no evidence to support the treatment's effectiveness. In addition, the regimen prescribed is so demanding and restrictive that it places considerable stress on the child, parents, and siblings (Matthews, 1988).

Figure 23.12. Treatment of scoliosis may require a spinal fusion. This X ray shows improved scoliosis following a Luque procedure. During this surgery, the position of the spine is improved using metal hooks, rods, and wires while bone graft material fuses the spine in position.

Functional Mobility and Equipment

One of the greatest concerns of parents is whether their child will ever walk. Early factors that may predict prognosis for ambulation include the type of cerebral palsy, age of independent sitting, postural reactions, and tonic reflex activity. A diagnosis of hemiplegia or ataxia and attainment of independent sitting by 2 years of age generally predict eventual ability to walk distances. A diagnosis of spastic quadriplegia or absence of postural reactions and obligatory persistence of primitive reflexes at 2 years of age carries a poor prognosis for ambulation (Trahan & Marcoux, 1994; Watt, Robinson, & Grace, 1989). Treatment interventions commonly used for ambulation training include a combination of physical therapy, assistive devices such as walkers or crutches, orthotics, and surgery. For children with limited walking skills, wheelchairs are essential for maximizing mobility and function (Hulme et al., 1987; Schultz-Hurlburt & Tervo, 1982).

A wheelchair with a solid seat and back is usually recommended. Some children, however, have difficulty using this type of chair unless modifications are made. The addition of head and trunk supports or a tray may be needed for the child who lacks postural control due to low tone. The child with limited head control or with feeding difficulties may benefit from a high-backed chair that can be tilted back 10 to 15 degrees (Figure 23.13a). This helps to maintain the child's body and head in proper alignment.

Special seating cushions or custom-molded inserts that conform to the contours of the body can offer necessary support for the child with orthopedic deformities such as scoliosis (Katz, Liebertal, & Erken, 1988). Motorized wheelchairs can enhance the independence of children who are able to use them. Although these usually have an easily manipulated joystick for controlling both speed and direction (Figure 23.13b), other types of switches are available for children who cannot control their hand movements.

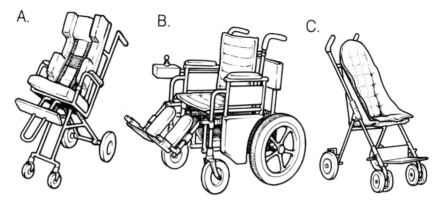

Figure 23.13. Wheelchairs. a) High-backed, tilting chair with lateral inserts and head supports. b) Motorized wheelchair with joystick control. c) Supportive collapsible stroller.

Special supportive strollers are an alternative to wheelchairs for mobility within the community or for the young child whose potential for ambulation has yet to be determined. These are lightweight and collapsible yet support the back and keep the hips properly aligned (Figure 23.13c).

Walkers, crutches, and canes may be appropriate for the child with milder forms of cerebral palsy. Walkers are available with or without wheels and offer a stable base of support to the child who can maintain correct positional alignment while in a standing position (Logan, Byers-Hinkley, & Ciccone, 1990). They are, however, difficult to maneuver around obstacles or over rough terrain. Crutches and canes are easier to maneuver but require considerable strength, endurance, and balance for functional use. They are recommended rarely.

Car seats are essential to the safety of all children who ride in automobiles. Several manufacturers offer adapted car seats that meet federal safety guidelines as well as provide proper support for the child with cerebral palsy. Often these models include a base that allows the seat to be used as a stroller or a positioning chair outside of the car. Car beds and special straps are also available for children who have more severe disabilities or who require these special adaptations temporarily (e.g., following surgery).

Physical Activity and Sports

Physical exercise is important to strengthen muscles and bones, enhance motor skills, and prevent contractures. In addition, the social and recreational aspects of organized physical activities can be highly beneficial (see Chapter 34; Humphrey, 1985). Many popular activities, including swimming, dancing, and horseback riding, can be modified so that children with cerebral palsy can participate (Jones, 1987). In addition, the Special Olympics has enabled thousands of children and young adults with intellectual disabilities to take part in various sporting events. The rewards of engaging in competitive sports are invaluable for enhancing self-esteem and providing a sense of belonging to a peer group. Parents and professionals should encourage all children to participate in whatever physical activities their interests, motivation, and capabilities allow.

Assistive Technology

Assistive technology devices are often an important part of the habilitation plan for children with cerebral palsy. The technology involved may be as simple as Velcro or as complex as the computer chip. Although it is often true that the simplest intervention is the best, it cannot be denied that the computer has become the hero of assistive technology. Computers can be used to control the environment, provide a lifeline with the outside world, enable a person to work at home, facilitate artificial speech and sight, and provide entertainment (Cole & Dehadashti, 1990; Desch, 1986; Levy, 1983; Treviranus & Tannock, 1987). The real potential of this technology to improve the quality of life for children with disabilities is just beginning to be realized. Enthusiasm for its use is tempered by problems with access related to the cost and availability of durable hardware and well-designed software (see Chapter 33).

School

For many children with cerebral palsy, entry into school represents the first major step into the wider community. Difficulties are often encountered in accommodating the physical, nutritional, and medical needs of these children at school. Whereas motor impairments tend to receive the most attention in the early years after the diagnosis of cerebral palsy, associated disabilities such as learning disabilities, attention and behavior problems, mental retardation, and sensory impairments tend to come to the fore in elementary school. For many children, these associated problems, rather than their motor disability, put them at greatest disadvantage relative to their peers.

The special education model has long been used to address the educational issues of children with special needs. Children with cerebral palsy have traditionally been segregated into classrooms with designations such as "multiply disabled" and "orthopedically impaired," sometimes without proper regard for their cognitive skills. The trend is now, however, toward inclusion in general education classrooms, which under ideal circumstances can accommodate the needs of children with a range of abilities. Inclusive environments require significant collaboration between the general and special education models and work best when a team of educators and paraprofessionals is associated with each classroom (see Chapter 30).

JAMAL'S HABILITATION PLAN

Jamal was referred by his pediatrician to a neurodevelopmental specialist, who confirmed the diagnosis of cerebral palsy, specifically spastic diplegia. Early ultrasound studies demonstrated equivocal white matter abnormalities; an MRI of the brain confirmed the presence of bilateral PVL.

Jamal was also referred to a pediatric orthopedic surgeon, who obtained X rays of the hips: There was no evidence of hip subluxation or dislocation. Jamal's family was asked to come for follow-up every 6 months to allow close monitoring for the first signs of subluxation. Although Jamal did not show evidence of permanent contractures, he consistently maintained his feet in equinus; the orthopedist prescribed MAFOs to be worn most of the day.

Finally, Jamal was referred for early intervention services and has been receiving 2 hours of physical therapy each week. His therapist feels that Jamal has a good prognosis for walking but is concerned that Jamal's braces may not prevent the development of contractures at the Achilles tendon. She suggested that Jamal's family discuss the option of botulinum toxin injections to the calf muscles with the orthopedic surgeon. She also told Jamal's family that once Jamal was walking more, he would need hinged (articulating) braces that provide flexibility for the ankle movement needed with walking while giving support to prevent contractures.

OUTCOME

Outcome is most simply defined in terms of longevity. Although most children with cerebral palsy will live to adulthood, their projected life expectancy is somewhat less than that of the general population (Crichton, Mackinnon, & White, 1995; Hutton, Cooke, & Pharoah, 1994).

Outcome varies for each type of cerebral palsy. A child with mild left hemiplegia probably will have a typical lifespan, whereas a child with spastic quadriplegia may not live beyond age 40 (Strauss & Shavelle, 1998). Children with very severe impairments, measured in terms of functional characteristics, have the poorest outcome. For example, children who cannot lift their heads and are fed via gastrostomy tube may not survive to adulthood (Strauss, Shavelle, & Anderson, 1998). Excess mortality for people with cerebral palsy may also be due to factors not directly connected with the cerebral palsy itself. Rates of mortality due to breast cancer, brain tumors, circulatory and digestive diseases, and accidents are higher for people with cerebral palsy than for the general population, suggesting that inadequate medical surveillance and psychosocial issues may play roles in excess mortality (Strauss, Cable, & Shavelle, 1999).

Outcome may also be defined in terms of functional outcome and ability to participate in a variety of environments (O'Grady, Crain, & Kohn, 1995). In this sense, outcome becomes a complex function of a child's profile of abilities and disabilities within a specific set of environmental circumstances. Outcome is also a matter of perception. A child who is unlikely to walk may have a "worse prognosis" than a child who will eventually walk; yet, he or she may have better functional mobility because of an excellent wheelchair, a supportive family, and an accessible community. Judgments about outcome are also biased by an understandable tendency to emphasize mobility issues when developing habilitation plans for children with cerebral palsy. Yet, when asked, parents often identify communication and socialization as the functional areas of greatest concern to them. A child's ability to successfully participate in society is probably more strongly related to cognitive strengths than to physical ability.

Although about 40% of the individuals who have cerebral palsy have average intelligence, most of these individuals still have difficulty leading completely typical lives (Murphy, Molnar, & Lankasky, 1995). Studies suggest that employability is not related solely to the degree of disability but to a variety of other factors including family support, quality of educational programs, and the availability of community-based training and technical support (Russman & Gage, 1989). In a study of young adults with cerebral palsy (van der Dussen, et al., 2001), 75% were fully independent with activities of daily living, 90% moved independently indoors, and 70% moved independently outdoors. The study also found that 77.5% of these individuals had adequate communication for telephone conversation, 30% lived with their parents, 12.5% lived with a partner, and 32.5% lived alone. In addition, 53% had some form of secondary education, but only 36.3% had paid employment. It is hoped that these figures will improve as a result of federal mandates (e.g., the Americans with Disabilities Act [ADA] of 1990, PL 101-336), which define the rights of people with disabilities and are making inroads into societal perceptions of disability. Once society recognizes that functional outcomes are related as much to societal conditions as they are to the characteristics of a particular child with a disability, society's perception of outcome will undergo a major shift. Ultimately, strengthening supports to families, improving schools, increasing opportunities for employment, and changing attitudes about disabilities in society at large may do as much for children with cerebral palsy as traditional therapy and medical interventions.

SUMMARY

Cerebral palsy is a developmental disability that results from damage to or dysfunction of the developing brain. The impairments associated with cerebral palsy are nonprogressive but permanent. Varying degrees of ability related to functional mobility, daily living skills, and communication/socialization skills result from these impairments. Habilitation is an interdisciplinary strategy that seeks to maximize function and minimize the disadvantage a person experiences as a consequence of disability or societal circumstances. Efforts founded on the principles articulated in the ADA will create new opportunities for greater participation and enhanced quality of life for people with cerebral palsy.

REFERENCES

Abbott, R. (1996). Sensory rhizotomy for the treatment of childhood spasticity. *Journal of Child Neurology, 11*(Suppl. 1), S36–S42.

Abbott, R., Forem, S., & Johann, M. (1989). Selective posterior rhizotomy for the treatment of spasticity: A review. *Child's Nervous System, 5,* 337–346.

Aksu, I. (1990). Nature and prognosis of seizures in patients with cerebral palsy. *Developmental Medicine and Child Neurology, 32,* 661–668.

Albright, A. (1996a). Baclofen in the treatment of cerebral palsy. *Journal of Child Neurology, 11,* 77–83.

Albright, A. (1996b). Intrathecal baclofen in cerebral palsy movement disorders. *Journal of Child Neurology, 11*(Suppl. 1), S29–S35.

Albright, A. (1997). Baclofen in the treatment of cerebral palsy. *Journal of Child Neurology, 11,* 77–83.

Albright, A., Barry, M., Painter, M., et al. (1998). Infusion of intrathecal baclofen for generalized dystonia in cerebral palsy. *Journal of Neurosurgery, 88,* 73–76.

Allen, M., & Capute, A. (1989). Neonatal neurodevelopmental examination as a predictor of neuromotor outcome in premature infants. *Pediatrics, 83,* 498–506.

American Academy of Pediatrics. (1982). Joint policy statement: The Doman-Delacato treatment of neurologically handicapped children. *Pediatrics, 70,* 810–811.

American Academy of Pediatrics, Committee on Children with Disabilities. (1999). The treatment of neurologically impaired children using patterning. *Pediatrics, 104,* 1149–1151.

Americans with Disabilities Act (ADA) of 1990, PL 101-336, 42 U.S.C. §§ 12101 *et seq.*

Azcue, M., Zello, G., Levy, L., et al. (1996). Energy expenditure and body composition in children with spastic quadriplegic cerebral palsy. *Journal of Pediatrics, 129,* 870–876.

Bhakta, U.T., Ives, H.L., Allgar, V., et al. (2000). Randomized double-blind placebo-controlled trial of the effect of botulinum toxin on walking in cerebral palsy. *Archives of Disease in Childhood, 83,* 481–487.

Barnes, P.D. (1992). Imaging of the central nervous system in pediatrics and adolescence. *Pediatric Clinics of North America, 39,* 743–776.

Bentivoglio, A., & Albanese, A. (1999). Botulinum toxin in motor disorders. *Current Opinion in Neurology, 12,* 447–456.

Berman, B., Vaughan, C., & Peacock, W. (1990). The effect of rhizotomy on movement in patients with cerebral palsy. *American Journal of Occupational Therapy, 44,* 511–516.

Bertoti, D. (1986). Effect of short-leg casting on ambulation in children with cerebral palsy. *Physical Therapy, 66,* 1522–1529.

Binder, H., & Eng, G. (1989). Rehabilitation management of children with spastic diplegic cerebral palsy. *Archives of Physical Medicine and Rehabilitation, 70,* 482–489.

Black, P. (1982). Visual disorders associated with cerebral palsy. *British Journal of Ophthalmology, 66,* 46–52.

Blair, E., Ballantyne, J., Horsman, S., et al. (1995). A study of a dynamic proximal stability splint in the management of children with cerebral palsy. *Developmental Medicine and Child Neurology, 37,* 544–554.

Blair, E., & Stanley, F. (1985). Intraobserver agreement in the classification of cerebral palsy. *Developmental Medicine and Child Neurology, 25,* 615–622.

Bleck, E.E. (1987). *Clinics in developmental medicine: Vol. 99/100. Orthopaedic management of cerebral palsy* (2nd ed.). Cambridge, England: Cambridge University Press.

Bobath, B. (1980). *Clinics in developmental medicine: Vol. 75. A neurophysiological basis for the treatment of cerebral palsy* (2nd ed.). Cambridge, England: Cambridge University Press.

Bulman, W., Dormans, J., Ecker, M., et al. (1996). Posterior spinal fusion for scoliosis in patients with cerebral palsy: A comparison of Luque rod and unit rod instrumentation. *Journal of Pediatric Orthopedics, 16,* 314–323.

Cahan, L., Adams, J., Perry, J., et al. (1990). Instrumented gait analysis after selective dorsal rhizotomy. *Developmental Medicine and Child Neurology, 32,* 1037–1043.

Calderon-Gonzalez, R., Calderon-Sepulveda, R., Rincon-Reyes, M., et al. (1994). Botulinum toxin A in management of cerebral palsy. *Pediatric Neurology, 10,* 284–288.

Capute, A. (1986). Early neuromotor reflexes in infancy. *Pediatric Annals, 15,* 217–218.

Capute, A., Accardo, P., Vining, E., et al. (1978). *Primitive reflex profile.* Baltimore: University Park Press.

Chugani, H.T. (1993). Positron emission tomography scanning applications in newborns. *Clinics in Perinatology, 20,* 395–409.

Cole, E., & Dehadashti, P. (1990). Interface design as a prosthesis for an individual with brain injury. *SIGCHI (Special Interest Group on Computer and Human Interaction) Bulletin, 22,* 28–32.

Cooke, P., Cole, W., & Carey, R. (1989). Dislocation of the hip in cerebral palsy: Natural history and predictability. *Journal of Bone and Joint Surgery, British Volume, 71,* 441–446.

Corry, I.S., Cosgrove, A.P, Walsh, E.G., et al. (1997). Botulinum toxin A in the hemiplegic upper limb: A double-blind trial. *Developmental Medicine and Child Neurology, 39,* 185–193.

Cosgrove, A.P., Corry, I.S., & Graham, H.K. (1994). Botulinum toxin in the management of the lower limb in cerebral palsy. *Developmental Medicine and Child Neurology, 36,* 386–396.

Coward, D.M. (1994). Tizanidine: Neuropharmacology and mechanism of action. *Neurology, 44*(Suppl. 9), S6–S11.

Crichton, J.U., Mackinnon, M., & White, C.P. (1995). The life-expectancy of persons with cerebral palsy. *Developmental Medicine and Child Neurology, 37,* 567–576.

Croen, L.A., Grether, J.K., Curry, C.J., et al. (2001). Congenital abnormalities among children with cerebral palsy: More evidence of prenatal antecedents. *Journal of Pediatrics, 138,* 804–810.

Cummins, S. K., Nelson, K. B., Grether, J. K., et al. (1993). Cerebral palsy in four northern California counties, births 1983 through 1985. *Journal of Pediatrics, 123,* 230–237.

Darrah, M., Piper, M., & Watt, M. (1998). Assessment of gross motor skills of at-risk infants: Predictive validity of the Alberta Infant Motor Scale. *Developmental Medicine and Child Neurology, 40,* 485–491.

Davis, R., Schulman, J., Nanes, M., et al. (1987). Cerebellar stimulation for spastic cerebral palsy: Double-blind quantitative study. *Applied Neurophysiology, 50,* 451–452.

Delgado, M., Schulman, J., Nanes, M., et al. (1996). Discontinuation of antiepileptic drug treatment after two seizure-free years in children with cerebral palsy. *Pediatrics, 97,* 192–197.

Denislic, M., & Meh, D. (1995). Botulinum toxin in the treatment of cerebral palsy. *Neuropediatrics, 26,* 249–252.

Desch, L. (1986). High technology for handicapped children: A pediatrician's viewpoint. *Pediatrics, 77,* 71–87.

Dormans, J. (1993). Orthopedic management of children with cerebral palsy. *Pediatric Clinics of North America, 3,* 645–652.

Eames, N., Baker, R., Hill, N., et al. (1999). The effect of botulinum toxin A on gastrocnemius length: Magnitude and duration of response. *Developmental Medicine and Child Neurology, 41,* 226–232.

Ferguson, R., & Allen, B.J. (1988). Considerations in the treatment of cerebral palsy patients with spinal deformities. *Orthopedic Clinics of North America, 19,* 419–425.

Frankenburg, W., Dodds, J., Archer, P., et al. (1992). The Denver II: A major revision and restandardization of The Denver Developmental Screening Test. *Pediatrics, 89,* 91–97.

Friedman, A., Diamond, M., Johnston, M., et al. (2000). Effects of botulinum toxin A on upper limb spasticity in children with cerebral palsy. *American Journal of Physical Medicine and Rehabilitation, 79*(1), 53–59.

Gilmartin, R., Bruce, D., Storrs, B., et al. (2000). Intrathecal baclofen for management of spastic cerebral palsy: Multicenter trial. *Journal of Child Neurology, 15,* 71–77.

Glenn, M.B., & White, J. (Eds.). (1990). *The practical management of spasticity in children and adults.* Philadelphia: Lea & Febiger.

Grether, J., Nelson, K., & Emery, E. (1996). Prenatal and perinatal factors and cerebral palsy in very low birth weight infants. *Journal of Pediatrics, 128,* 407–414.

Hadjipanayis, A., Hadjichristodoulou, C., & Youroukos, S. (1997). Epilepsy in patients with cerebral palsy. *Developmental Medicine and Child Neurology, 39,* 659–663.

Hagberg, B., Hagberg, G., Olow, I., et al. (1996). The changing pattern of cerebral palsy in Sweden, VII: Prevalence and origin in the birth year period 1987–90. *Acta Paediatrica, 85,* 954–960.

Hanson, C., & Jones, L. (1989). Gait abnormalities and inhibitive casts in cerebral palsy. *Journal of the American Podiatric Medical Association, 79,* 53–59.

Harum, K.H., Hoon, A.H., Jr., Kato, G.J., et al. (1999). Homozygous factor-V mutation as a genetic cause of perinatal thrombosis and cerebral palsy. *Developmental Medicine and Child Neurology, 41,* 777–780.

Heine, R.G., Reddihough, D.S., & Catto-Smith, A.G. (1995). Gastro-esophageal reflux and feeding problems after gastrostomy in children with severe neurological impairment. *Developmental Medicine and Child Neurology, 37,* 320–329.

Hugenholtz, H., Humphreys, P., McIntyre, W., et al. (1988). Cervical spinal cord stimulation for spasticity in cerebral palsy. *Neurosurgery, 22,* 707–714.

Hulme, J., Shaver, J., Acher, S., et al. (1987). Effects of adaptive seating devices on the eating and drinking of children with multiple handicaps. *American Journal of Occupational Therapy, 41,* 81–89.

Humphrey, F. (1985). Therapeutic recreation. In D.A. Umphred (Ed.), *Neurological rehabilitation* (Vol. 3, pp. 653–662). St. Louis: Mosby.

Hutton, J., Cooke, T., & Pharoah, P. (1994). Life expectancy of children with cerebral palsy. *British Medical Journal, 309,* 4315.

Illingworth, R. (1987). *The development of the infant and young child: Normal and abnormal* (9th ed.). Philadelphia: Churchill Livingstone.

Jones, J.A. (Ed.). (1987). *Training guide to cerebral palsy sports* (3rd ed.). Champaign, IL: Human Kinetics.

Jones, P. (1989). Feeding disorders in children with multiple handicaps. *Developmental Medicine and Child Neurology, 31,* 404–406.

Joynt, R., & Leonard, J.J. (1980). Dantrolene sodium suspension in treatment of spastic cerebral palsy. *Developmental Medicine and Child Neurology, 22,* 755–767.

Katz, K., Liebertal, M., & Erken, E. (1988). Seat insert for cerebral-palsied children with total body involvement. *Developmental Medicine and Child Neurology, 30,* 222–226.

Koman, L.A., Brashear, A., Rosenfeld, S. et al. (2001). Botulin toxin type A neuromuscular blockade in the treatment of equinus foot deformity in cerebral palsy: A multicenter, open-label clinical trial. *Pediatrics, 108,* 1062–1071.

Koman, L., Mooney, J.F., & Smith, B. (1996). Neuromuscular blockade in the management of cerebral palsy. *Journal of Child Neurology, 11,* S23–S28.

Koman, L.A., Mooney, J.F., III, Smith, B., et al. (1993). Management of cerebral palsy with botulinum A toxin: Preliminary investigation. *Journal of Pediatric Orthopaedics, 13,* 489–495.

Koman, L.A., Mooney, J.F., III, Smith, B.P., et al. (2000). Botulinum toxin type A neuromuscular blockade in the treatment of lower extremity spasticity in cerebral palsy: A randomized, double-blind, placebo-controlled trial. *Journal of Pediatric Orthopedics, 20,* 108–115.

Krageloh-Mann, I., Petersen, D., Hagberg, G., et al. (1995). Bilateral spastic cerebral palsy: MRI pathology and origin. Analysis from a representative series of 56 cases. *Developmental Medicine and Child Neurology, 37,* 379–397.

Levy, R. (1983). Interface modalities of technical aids used by people with disability. *American Journal of Occupational Therapy, 37,* 761–765.

Logan, L., Byers-Hinkley, K., & Ciccone, C. (1990). Anterior versus posterior walkers: A gait analysis study. *Developmental Medicine and Child Neurology, 32,* 1044–1048.

Matthews, D. (1988). Controversial therapies in the management of cerebral palsy. *Pediatric Annals, 17,* 762–764.

McCuaig, M., & Frank, G. (1992). The able self: Adaptive patterns and choices in independent living for a person with cerebral palsy. *American Journal of Occupational Therapy, 45,* 224–234.

McLaughlin, J., Bjornson, K., Astley, S., et al. (1998). Selective dorsal rhizotomy: Efficacy and safety in an investigator-masked randomized clinical trial. *Developmental Medicine and Child Neurology, 40,* 220–232.

Meberg, A., & Broch, H. (1995). A changing pattern of cerebral palsy: Declining trend for incidence of cerebral palsy in the 20-year period 1970–89. *Journal of Perinatal Medicine, 23,* 395–402.

Miller, F., Bacharach, S., Boos, M., et al. (1995). *Cerebral palsy: A complete guide for caregiving.* Baltimore: The Johns Hopkins University Press.

Moreau, M., Drummond, D., Rogala, E., et al. (1979). Natural history of the dislocated hip in spastic cerebral palsy. *Developmental Medicine and Child Neurology, 21,* 744–753.

Moster, D., Lie, R.T., Irgens, L.M., et al. (2001). The association of Apgar score with subsequent death and cerebral palsy: A population-based study in infants. *Journal of Pediatrics, 138,* 798–803.

Murphy, K., Molnar, G., & Lankasky, K. (1995). Medical and functional status of adults with cerebral palsy. *Developmental Medicine and Child Neurology, 37,* 1075–1084.

Myhr, U., von Wendt, L., Norrlin, S., et al. (1995). Five-year follow-up of functional sitting position in children with cerebral palsy. *Developmental Medicine and Child Neurology, 37,* 587–596.

Nelson, K.B., & Ellenberg, J.H. (1982). Children who "outgrew" cerebral palsy. *Pediatrics, 69,* 529–536.

Nelson, K.B., & Ellenberg, J.H. (1986). Antecedents of cerebral palsy: Multivariate analysis of risk. *New England Journal of Medicine, 315,* 81–86.

Nickel, R., Rencken, C., & Gallenstein, J. (1989). The infant motor screen. *Developmental Medicine and Child Neurology, 31,* 35–42.

Nuzzo, R. (1980). Dynamic bracing: Elastics for patient with cerebral palsy, muscular dystrophy and myelodysplasia. *Clinical Orthopaedics and Related Research, 148,* 263–273.

O'Grady, R., Crain, L., & Kohn, J. (1995). The prediction of long-term functional outcomes of children with cerebral palsy. *Developmental Medicine and Child Neurology, 37,* 997–1005.

Paban, M., & Piper, M. (1987). Early predictors of one-year neurodevelopmental outcome for "at risk" infants. *Physical and Occupational Therapy in Pediatrics, 7,* 17–34.

Park, T.S., & Owen, J.H. (1992). Surgical management of spastic diplegia in cerebral palsy. *New England Journal of Medicine, 326,* 745–749.

Park, T.S., Phillips, L.H., & Peacock, W.J. (1989). *Management of spasticity in cerebral palsy and spinal cord injury* (Vol. 4). Philadelphia: Hanley & Belfus.

Peacock, W., & Staudt, L. (1990). Spasticity in cerebral palsy and the selective posterior rhizotomy procedure. *Journal of Child Neurology, 5,* 179–185.

Pellegrino, L. (1995). Cerebral palsy: A paradigm for developmental disabilities. *Developmental Medicine and Child Neurology, 37,* 834–839.

Perin, B. (1989). Physical therapy for the child with cerebral palsy. In J.S. Tecklin (Ed.), *Pediatric physical therapy* (pp. 68–105). Philadelphia: Lippincott Williams & Wilkins.

Petterson, B., Stanley, F., & Henderson, D. (1990). Cerebral palsy in multiple births in Western Australia: Genetic aspects. *American Journal of Medical Genetics, 37,* 346–351.

Piper, M., Mazer, B., Silver, K., et al. (1988). Resolution of neurological symptoms in high-risk infants during the first two years of life. *Developmental Medicine and Child Neurology, 30,* 26–35.

Piper, M., Pinnell, L., Darrah, J., et al. (1992). Construction and validation of the Alberta Infant Motor Scale (AIMS). *Canadian Journal of Public Health, 83*(Suppl.), S46–S50.

Pranzatelli, M. (1996). Oral pharmacotherapy for the movement disorders of cerebral palsy. *Journal of Child Neurology, 11*(Suppl.), S13–S22.

Prats, A. (1997). Intrathecal baclofen infusion for the treatment of spasticity in children with cerebral palsy. *International Pediatrics, 12,* 239–241.

Reilly, S., Skuse, D., & Poblete, X. (1996). Prevalence of feeding problems and oral motor dysfunction in children with cerebral palsy: A community survey. *Journal of Pediatrics, 129,* 877–882.

Rempel, G., Colwell, S., & Nelson, R. (1988). Growth in children with cerebral palsy fed via gastrostomy. *Pediatrics, 82,* 857–862.

Russman, B., & Gage, J. (1989). Cerebral palsy. *Current Problems in Pediatrics, 19,* 65–111.

Sankey, R., Anderson, D., & Young, J. (1989). Characteristics of ankle-foot orthoses for management of the spastic lower limb. *Developmental Medicine and Child Neurology, 31,* 466–470.

Schenk-Rootlieb, A.J.F., van Nieuwenhuizen, O., van der Graaf, Y., et al. (1992). The prevalence of cerebral visual disturbance in children with cerebral palsy. *Developmental Medicine and Child Neurology, 34,* 473–480.

Scher, M.S., Belfar, H., Martin, J., et al. (1991). Destructive brain lesions of presumed fetal onset: Antepartum causes of cerebral palsy. *Pediatrics, 88,* 898–906.

Schultz-Hurlburt, B., & Tervo, R. (1982). Wheelchair users at a children's rehabilitation center: Attributes and management. *Developmental Medicine and Child Neurology, 24,* 54–60.

Scrutton, D. (1989). The early management of hips in cerebral palsy. *Developmental Medicine and Child Neurology, 31,* 108–116.

Simpson, D. (1997). Clinical trials of botulinum toxin in the treatment of spasticity. *Muscle and Nerve, 6*(Suppl.), 169–175.

Smelt, H. (1989). Effect of an inhibitive weight-bearing mitt on tone reduction and functional performance in a child with cerebral palsy. *Physical and Occupational Therapy in Pediatrics, 9,* 53–80.

Smith, L., & Harris, S. (1985). Upper extremity inhibitive casting for a child with cerebral palsy. *Physical and Occupational Therapy in Pediatrics, 5,* 71–79.

Sobrado, P., Suarez, J., Garcia-Sanchez, F., et al. (1999). Refractive errors in children with cerebral palsy, psychomotor retardation, and other non-cerebral palsy neuromotor disabilities. *Developmental Medicine and Child Neurology, 41,* 396–403.

Stallings, V.A., Charney, E.B., Davies, J.C., et al. (1993). Nutrition-related growth failure of children with quadriplegic cerebral palsy. *Developmental Medicine and Child Neurology, 35,* 126–138.

Stanley, F.J., Blair, E., Hockey, A., et al. (1993). Spastic quadriplegia in Western Australia: A genetic epidemiological study, I. Case population and perinatal risk factors. *Developmental Medicine and Child Neurology, 35,* 191–201.

Strauss, D., Cable, W., & Shavelle, R. (1999). Causes of excess mortality in cerebral palsy. *Developmental Medicine and Child Neurology, 41,* 580–585.

Strauss, D., & Shavelle, R. (1998). Life expectancy of adults with cerebral palsy. *Developmental Medicine and Child Neurology, 40,* 369–375.

Strauss, D., Shavelle, R., & Anderson, T. (1998). Life expectancy of children with cerebral palsy. *Pediatric Neurology, 18,* 143–149.

Sutherland, D., Kaufman, K., Wyatt, M., et al. (1999). Double-blind study of botulinum A toxin injections into the gastrocnemius muscle in patients with cerebral palsy. *Gait and Posture, 10,* 1–9.

Trahan, J., & Marcoux, S. (1994). Factors associated with the inability of children with cerebral palsy to walk at six years: A retrospective. *Developmental Medicine and Child Neurology, 36,* 787–795.

Treviranus, J., & Tannock, R. (1987). A scanning computer access system for children with severe physical disabilities. *American Journal of Occupational Therapy, 41,* 733–738.

van der Dussen, L., Nieuwstraten, W., Roebroeck, M., et al. (2001). Functional level of young adults with cerebral palsy. *Clinical Rehabilitation, 15,* 84–91.

Watt, J., Robinson, C., & Grace, M. (1989). Early prognosis for ambulation of neonatal intensive care survivors with cerebral palsy. *Developmental Medicine and Child Neurology, 31,* 766–773.

Wissel, J., Heinen, F., Schenkel, A., et al. (1999). Botulinum toxin A in the management of spastic gait disorders in children and young adults with cerebral palsy: A randomized, double-blind study of "high dose" versus "low-dose" treatment. *Neuropediatrics, 30,* 120–124.

Yasukawa, A. (1990). Upper extremity casting: Adjunct treatment for a child with hemiplegic cerebral palsy. *American Journal of Occupational Therapy, 44,* 512–520.

Young, R.R. (1994). Spasticity: A review. *Neurology, 44* (Suppl.), S12–S20.

Zigler, E. (1981). A plea to end the use of patterning treatment for retarded children. *American Journal of Orthopsychiatry, 51,* 388–390.

24 Neural Tube Defects

Gregory S. Liptak

Upon completion of this chapter, the reader will:

- be able to define the terms *spina bifida* and *meningomyelocele*
- know the incidence and multifactorial causes of neural tube defects
- be knowledgeable about the effects of meningomyelocele on the spinal cord and brain
- understand the variability and secondary effects of meningomyelocele
- understand strategies for intervention, the need for multidisciplinary care, and goals for independence

Neural tube defects (NTDs) are a group of malformations of the spinal cord, brain, and vertebrae. The resulting disorders vary in severity according to their location, the extent of bony opening, and the exposure of spinal cord or brain. The three major NTDs are **encephalocele,** anencephaly, and spina bifida. Encephalocele is a malformation of the skull that allows a portion of the brain, which is usually malformed, to protrude. The vast majority of encephaloceles occur in the occipital, or back, region of the brain (Adetioloye, Dare, & Oyelami, 1993). Affected children have mental retardation, hydrocephalus (excess fluid in the cavities of the brain), spastic diplegia (a form of cerebral palsy), and/or seizures. Encephaloceles also occur in the frontal area, such as the forehead, and may even appear as a mass in the nose or orbit (eye socket). The following factors are associated with a better outcome in children with encephaloceles: 1) no associated abnormalities of the brain (e.g., hydrocephalus, abnormal cell migration); 2) no other physical abnormalities (Bannister et al., 2000); 3) frontal rather than occipital location (Hoving, 2000); 4) head circumference in the normal range (rather than too small or too large); and 5) less brain tissue in the sac (Martinez-Lage et al., 1996). Anencephaly indicates an even more severe congenital malformation of the skull and brain in which no neural development occurs above the brainstem (the most primitive part of the brain). About half of fetuses with anencephaly are spontaneously aborted; those who are live born rarely survive infancy.

The most common NTD is spina bifida, which is a split of a section of the **vertebral arches.** This split may be isolated or occur with a protruding meningeal sac that may contain a portion of the spinal cord. The most common form of spina bifida, **spina bifida occulta,** is also the most benign. Approximately 10% of the general population has this hidden separation of the vertebral arches. Individuals with spina bifida occulta do not have 1) abnormalities visible on their back, 2) a sac or protruding spinal cord, or 3) any symptoms.

A related form of spina bifida is occult spinal dysraphism (OSD). In this condition the infant is born with a visible abnormality on the lower back. This may be a birthmark (especially a reddish area called a *hemangioma* or a *flame nevus*), tufts of hair, a dermal sinus (opening in the skin), or a small lump (containing a fatty benign tumor called a **lipoma**). Although many otherwise normal infants are born with a small, midline sacral dimple, if the dimple is not in the middle, is above the sacral region, is large, or does not have a visible bottom, it, too, may be associated with OSD. In OSD, the underlying spinal cord may be connected to the surface through a sinus (opening) that exposes it to bacteria, thereby increasing the risk of infection, especially meningitis. The spinal cord itself may be tied down (tethered) to surrounding tissue, or it may be split (termed *diastematomyelia* and *diplomyelia*, respectively; Dias & Pang, 1995). These defects can lead to subsequent neurological damage as the child grows. Therefore, babies who have these stigmata should have an evaluation of the underlying soft tissue and spinal cord. This can be accomplished by ultrasound (Kriss & Desai, 1998) or magnetic resonance imaging (MRI) scan. Although the issue is somewhat controversial, most clinicians believe that surgical treatment to correct the OSD should be performed early, even in asymptomatic infants, to prevent progressive neurological damage (Satar et al., 1995).

A final form of spina bifida (and the one most commonly associated with this term) is meningomyelocele. Some individuals are born with a membranous sac covering the spinal cord, called a **meningocele.** In this case, the spinal cord itself is not entrapped and these children usually have no symptoms. When the sac is associated with a malformed spinal cord, the condition is called *meningomyelocele* (or *myelomeningocele*). This disorder is associated with a complex array of symptoms that includes flaccid or spastic paralysis (Mazur, Stillwell, & Menelaus, 1986), sensory loss below the lesion of the spinal abnormality, and hydrocephalus. Most meningomyeloceles are open, and a portion of the spinal cord is visible at birth as an open sac overlying part of the vertebral column. Children with meningomyelocele typically have associated abnormalities of the brain, including abnormal migration of neurons (Bannister, Russell, & Rimmer, 1998; Bartonek & Saraste, 2001; Christensen & Rand-Hendriksen, 1998). These abnormalities may manifest clinically as difficulties with learning, worse-than-expected walking, and dysfunction/spasticity of the upper limbs. Because of its profound effects, meningomyelocele has been called the most complex congenital malformation compatible with life.

This chapter focuses on meningomyelocele. It discusses approaches to treatment, the effects of the condition on psychosocial and cognitive development, and the psychological and economic stress that can affect families of children with this disorder.

JESSICA

Jessica was born at term to her 20-year-old mother, who had not received prenatal care. At the time of birth, a thoracic-level spina bifida with meningomyelocele was evident. This was surgically closed at 2 days of age, and a **ventriculoperitoneal shunt** was inserted at 8 days of age to correct the hydrocephalus associated with her Chiari II malformation.

During her first year of life, Jessica received weekly in-home early intervention services that included physical therapy and an early childhood development program. She made good progress; at 12 months, she was speaking several single words, sitting independently, and crawling about commando style by propelling herself with her arms. A month later, she began to stand in a parapodium (an external flexible skeleton). Because of recurrent urinary tract infections that did not respond to preventive antibiotics and **catheterization, a vesicostomy** was placed surgically at age 18 months to allow urine to drain continuously into her diaper.

By 3 years of age, Jessica was independently using the parapodium for mobility. At age 4, she suddenly developed headaches, vomiting, and lethargy and was diagnosed as having a ventricular shunt blockage. This was corrected surgically, and although she had a brief period of neurological deterioration, she subsequently recovered well.

Prior to school entry at age 6, psychoeducational testing was performed, which indicated that she had typical intelligence (an IQ score of 90) but learning impairments. She was placed in an inclusive class with a teacher's aide and resource help in reading and arithmetic. She was successful in her clean intermittent catheterization (CIC) and bowel programs, and her improved continence gave her confidence in interacting with other children.

During her school years, she has had several medical setbacks related to recurrent urinary tract infections and scoliosis. She ultimately required a bladder augmentation procedure and a spinal fusion. Despite this, she has done well. Now at age 20, she attends a community college, where she is majoring in psychology. She uses a wheelchair for mobility and self-administers a saline enema every other day to maintain bowel continence. She catheterizes herself four times a day and is generally dry between catheterizations. She, however, has a limited social life and still depends on her family for transportation. She is now learning to drive through the state office of vocational rehabilitation, which should greatly increase her independence.

PREVALENCE OF NEURAL TUBE DEFECTS

The prevalence of NTDs varies remarkably among countries. In the United States, the prevalence of meningomyelocele is approximately 60 in 100,000 births; of encephalocele, 10 in 100,000; and of anencephaly, 20 in 100,000 (Olney & Mulinare, 1998). In Wales and Ireland, the prevalence is 3 to 4 times higher; in Africa it is much lower (Feuchtbaum et al., 1999; McDonnell 1999; Rankin et al., 2000). This variability is a reflection of genetic influences in certain ethnic groups and environmental factors. Remarkably, females are affected three to seven times as frequently as males, except in sacral-level NTDs, in which the occurrence is equal (Hall et al., 1988). The incidence also increases with maternal age and with lower socioeconomic status.

The prevalence of NTDs is falling worldwide as a result of a number of factors. Developed countries are now using maternal serum testing to screen prenatally for NTDs (Roberts et al., 1995). Approximately 50% of couples, upon learning that they are carrying an affected fetus, choose to terminate the pregnancy (Forrester & Merz, 2000). However, individuals in certain ethnic groups such as Latinos (who often have a strong Catholic religious background) tend to eschew abortion (Hendricks, Simpson, & Larsen, 1999). In addition, the association of NTDs with folic acid deficiency has caused obstetricians to generally recommend folic acid supplementation during pregnancy. The decline in the incidence of NTDs, however, preceded these innovations, suggesting that other factors, including improved nutrition, may be operative (Shurtleff & Lemire, 1995). In the 1990s, the overall incidence of NTDs was only half what it was in the 1960s (Stevenson et al., 2000). In addition to the decrease in prevalence, there is an increase in survival with improved medical care in many countries. This has resulted in an increased population of adolescents and adults with meningomyelocele (Dillon et al., 2000; Hook, 1982). Thus, the need arises to address the transition of these individuals from adolescence to adulthood (see Chapter 37) and to provide adult services.

THE ORIGIN OF NEURAL TUBE DEFECTS

The malformation causing NTDs occurs by 26 days after fertilization of the egg during the period of neurulation (Figure 24.1; Copp, Fleming, & Greene, 1998), the first step in the formation of the central nervous system (CNS; see Chapter 13). During this time, the neural groove folds over to become the neural tube, which develops into the spinal cord and vertebral arches. During this process, if a portion of the neural groove does not close completely, an NTD results and the spinal cord is malformed. There may be as little as 2 days separating the risk of developing anencephaly from that of forming a meningomyelocele. Although the mechanism of neural tube closure is not fully understood, it does not simply work like a zipper but has multiple sites of closure (Van Allen et al., 1993). Each of these sites may be under separate genetic control with differential sensitivity to environmental factors (Golden & Chernoff, 1995; Urui & Oi, 1995).

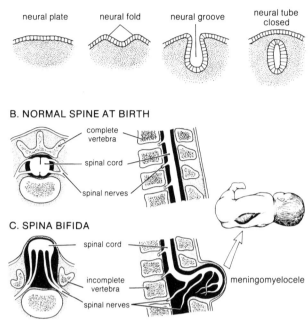

Figure 24.1. Neural tube development and spina bifida with meningomyelocele. a) The typical formation of the neural tube (i.e., the precursor of the spinal column) during the first month of gestation. b) Complete closure of the neural groove has occurred, and the vertebral column and spinal cord appear normal in the cross-section on the left and in the longitudinal section on the right. c) Incomplete closure of an area of the spine is called *spina bifida* and may be accompanied by a meningomyelocele, a sac-like abnormality of the spinal cord. As nerves do not normally form below this malformation, the child is paralyzed below (or caudal to) that point.

The causes of NTDs remain uncertain. Both environmental and genetic factors play a role, but their interaction appears to be complex (Hall & Solehdin 1998). For example, in mice, mutations of more than 50 different genes (Juriloff & Harris, 2000) as well as multiple environmental factors can lead to defects of the neural tube (Juriloff & Harris, 1998). Most of these genes, however, do not have homologous (parallel) expression in humans (Graf & Oleinik, 2000). However, mutations in PAX3, a transcription control gene involved in closure of the body axis (Baldwin et al., 1995), have been particularly associated with the development of NTDs in mice and also in some families with multiple children having NTDs (Chatkupt et al., 1995; Lakkis et al., 1999; Li et al., 1999; Scott et al., 1994; van der Put et al., 1995). Abnormalities of 5,10-methylene tetrahydrofolate reductase (MTHFR), an enzyme involved in the conversion of the amino acid homocysteine to methionine, also predispose humans to NTDs. Supplementation with its co-factor, folic acid (also called *folate*), reduces the risk of NTDs in affected families (Daly et al., 1995; Steegers-Theunissen, 1995). Abnormalities in PAX3 or MTHFR, however, account for only a small percentage of NTDs in humans (Botto & Yang, 2000; Johnson et al., 1999). The suggestion has been made that at least some of the genes responsible for NTDs are also related to neural crest cells because a higher-than-expected occurrence of abnormalities of the neural crest, such as white streaks in the hair, are found in individuals with NTDs (Nye et al., 1999).

Other conditions that have been associated with the development of NTDs include 1) chromosomal disorders (trisomies 13 and 18; see Appendix B), 2) maternal exposure to the antiepileptic drugs valproic acid (Depakene, Depakote) and carbamazepine (Tegretol) and to the acne medication isotretinoin (Accutane; Davis, Peters, & McTavish, 1994), 3) excessive maternal use of alcohol, 4) maternal exposure to hyperthermia (e.g., the use of saunas, high fever), and 5) maternal diabetes (Sadler, Robinson, & Msall, 1995). Excessive free radical formation has been suggested as a teratogenic factor in a number of these predisposing conditions (Shurtleff & Lemire, 1995). Maternal obesity has also been associated with the development of NTDs in offspring (Shaw, Velie, & Schaffer, 1996). For example, the risk of having a child with spina bifida is doubled if the body mass index (BMI; see Chapter 9) is greater than 29 kilograms per meters squared. Risks have also been found to vary by ethnicity and gender of the child. For example, obese Latina women who have daughters are 8 times more likely to have a child with meningomyelocele than nonobese Caucasian women who have sons (Shaw et al., 2000). As with single-gene defects, these environmental conditions account for only a small percentage of NTDs in humans.

It is unclear whether the neural damage in NTDs results simply from the malformed spinal cord or from a combination of malformation and the inflammatory effects of chronic exposure of the open cord to amniotic fluid. In one study, intrauterine surgery was performed on sheep fetuses that had an induced spina bifida. The open spine was covered with a patch so that it would be protected from prolonged exposure to potentially corrosive amniotic fluid (Meuli et al., 1995). After birth, these sheep were found to have less neural damage than the control group did. Experimental trials of prenatal surgery have also been performed in human fetuses who were diagnosed prenatally with meningomyelocele. The results of these studies indicated that prenatal surgery does not improve leg or bladder function. Infants born after the surgery, however, have less severe Chiari II malformations (discussed later) and resultant hydrocephalus and have less need for ventricular shunting (Bruner et al., 1999; Holzbeierlein et al., 2000; Sutton et al., 1999; Tulipan, Bruner, et al., 1999; Tulipan, Hernanz-Schulman, et al., 1999). One of the implications of these findings is that the development of Chiari II malformations is related to low pressure in the hindbrain secondary to cerebrospinal fluid (CSF) leakage from the back. Closing the back prior to birth increases the pressure in the hindbrain and prevents or lessens the occurrence of the Chiari II malformation. The failure of prenatal surgery to improve neurological functioning of the legs and bladder suggests either that inflammation of exposed tissue is not an important factor or that the surgery is currently being performed too late to prevent this damage from occurring. Premature delivery of the infant and maternal complications (bleeding and infection) remain major risks with this procedure. The risks and benefits of prenatal surgery have not been sufficiently evaluated to consider the surgery standard medical practice (Bannister, 2000).

PREVENTION OF NEURAL TUBE DEFECTS USING FOLIC ACID SUPPLEMENTATION

Although this chapter focuses on the treatment of children with meningomyelocele, it is important to recognize that prevention is possible based on the strong link between NTDs and folic acid deficiency. Although the mechanism of action of the vitamin folic acid is unclear, it may protect against NTDs in its role as a free radical scavenger (Chatkupt et al., 1994). Couples who have had one child with an NTD have a recurrence risk about 30 times higher (i.e., 3 in 100) than that of the general population. If these women take folic acid (4 milligrams per day) at or before conception and continue this supplementation for the first 3 months of the pregnancy, their recurrence risk is reduced by 70% (MRC Vitamin Study Research Group, 1991). Women who have an NTD or have a first-degree relative with an NTD also should take 4 milligrams per day around the time of conception.

Studies also have shown that daily supplemental doses of folic acid can reduce the incidence of new cases of NTDs in the general population by more than 50% (Bower & Stanley, 1992; Werler, Shapiro, & Mitchell, 1993). In a prospective study conducted in China, the group that received daily folic acid, 0.4 mg given periconceptionally, had a rate of NTDs of 1 per 1,000 births compared with a rate of 4.8 per 1,000 in the control group (Berry et al., 1999). As a result, it is now recommended that all women who are contemplating a pregnancy take 0.4 milligrams (400 micrograms) of supplemental folic acid per day while they are trying to conceive and during the first 12 weeks of pregnancy (American Academy of Pediatrics, Committee on Genetics, 1999; Centers for Disease Control, 1992; Daly et al., 1995; Manning, Jennings, & Madsen, 2000). Yet, only about one third of women who are planning a pregnancy take folic acid around the time of conception ("Knowledge and Use of Folic Acid," 1997; Schader & Corwin, 1999) and half of all pregnancies in the United States are unplanned ("Folate Status," 2000). To address this problem, since 1998 certain food staples in the United States (e.g., bread, flour) have been made with grain fortified with synthetic folic acid, which is better absorbed than the naturally occurring vitamin (Honein et al., 2001). The amount of folic acid in a typical diet, even with this fortification, however, is not sufficient to optimally prevent NTDs, so individual supplements are important in women of childbearing age. (It is intriguing to note that folic acid supplementation may also help to reduce the prevalence of heart disease in the general population because it decreases levels of the amino acid homocysteine, which has been associated with heart disease [Boushey et al., 1995; Motulsky, 1996].)

PRENATAL DIAGNOSIS

NTDs can be diagnosed prenatally by several methods (see Chapter 1; Main & Mennuti, 1986). Most obstetricians first measure levels of alpha-fetoprotein (AFP) in the mother's serum during the 16th–18th week of pregnancy (Bock, 1992; Candenas et al., 1995). AFP is a chemical typically found in fetal spinal fluid. In the presence of an open meningomyelocele, encephalocele, or anencephaly, AFP leaks from the open spine into the amniotic fluid. From here some AFP will enter the maternal circulation, where it can be detected in minute amounts. Because other conditions in both mother and fetus can lead to elevated AFP levels, maternal serum AFP (MSAFP) is used only as a screening test for NTDs. After a positive AFP screen has been obtained, a high-resolution ultrasound is used to detect specific abnormalities of the fetal head and back consistent with an NTD (Babcock, 1995; Ennever & Lave, 1995). If abnormalities are observed on ultrasound or an NTD is suspected even in the face of a normal ultrasound, amniocentesis is performed. The levels of two substances in the amniotic fluid, AFP and an enzyme specific for NTDs called acetylcholinesterase (ACH) that can be found in fetal CSF, are then measured. The presence of ACH in the amniotic fluid suggests leakage from an open spinal cord. The combination of elevated levels of AFP and ACH with abnormal ultrasonographic findings makes the diagnosis of an NTD in the fetus quite certain. Chromosomal analysis of the amniotic fluid is also performed to rule out chromosomal syndromes, such as trisomy 13, that are associated with NTDs. Even if a family is not considering a therapeutic abortion if an NTD is detected, obtaining a prenatal diagnosis can help the parents plan for the special needs of their child. For example, they may opt to deliver their child via cesarean section at a center with a neonatal intensive care unit and to have the back lesion closed early, precautions that some believe may decrease the severity of paralysis (Liu et al., 1999; Merrill et al., 1998; Shurtleff et al., 1994).

TREATMENT OF A MENINGOMYELOCELE IN THE NEWBORN PERIOD

When an infant is born with a meningomyelocele, the first two priorities are to prevent a spinal cord infection and to protect exposed spinal nerves and associated structures from physical injury. Both of these goals can be accomplished by the surgical closure of the defect within the first few days of life (Charney et al., 1985). In addition, a shunting procedure is often required shortly after the back closure to prevent CSF (which can no longer leak from an open meningomyelocele) from accumulating and causing progressive hydrocephalus (McLone, 1992).

PRIMARY NEUROLOGICAL IMPAIRMENTS IN CHILDREN WITH MENINGOMYELOCELE

The malformation leading to meningomyelocele can affect the entire CNS (Dahl et al., 1995; Gilbert et al., 1986). Table 24.1 illustrates some of the brain abnormalities commonly found in children with meningomyelocele.

Table 24.1. Malformations of the brain frequently seen in children with meningomyelocele

Malformation	Prevalence (%)
Dysplasia of cerebral cortex	92
Displaced nerve cells	44
Small gyri with abnormal layers	40
Abnormalities of layers	24
Profound primitive development	24
Small gyri with normal layers	12
Malformations of the brainstem	76
Malformations of the cerebellum	72

Source: Gilbert et al. (1986).

These include multiple disorders of the cranial nerve nuclei (e.g., the visual gaze centers of the brain can be affected, leading to strabismus; Lennerstrand, Gallo, & Samuelsson, 1990); excessive fluid or splitting of the spinal cord above the primary lesion, resulting in additional motor impairment (Dias & Pang, 1995); and diffuse changes in the brain's cortex from migration defects that are associated with cognitive impairments. The primary neurological abnormalities, however, are paralysis, loss of sensation, and a Chiari II malformation with associated hydrocephalus.

Paralysis and Loss of Sensation

The extent of motor paralysis and sensory loss in meningomyelocele depends on the location of the defect in the spinal cord (Figure 24.2), as sensory and motor function below that point are typically impaired. Children with defects at the chest (T, or thoracic) or upper back (L1–L2, or first or second lumbar) level have paralysis that affects the legs and causes variable weakness and sensory loss in the abdomen and lower body region (Figure 24.3). Children with defects at L3 typically can flex their hips and extend their knees, but their ankles and toes are paralyzed. Children with low back (L4 or L5) lesions usually can flex their hips, extend their knees, and flex their ankles but typically have weak or absent ankle extension, toe flexion, and hip extension. Children with sacral (low back–buttocks) lesions usually have only mild weakness of their ankles or toes. A number of different systems have been developed to classify the severity of neurological impairments in individuals with meningomyelocele to make an accurate prognosis (Bartonek, Saraste, & Knutson, 1999; Oi & Matsumoto, 1992). Classification based solely on motor level fails to predict functional abilities such as ambulatory status in many individuals (Bartonek & Saraste, 2001). Factors such as ventriculitis (infection of the cerebral ventricles), multiple episodes of shunt failure, joint contractures, previous surgeries, obesity, and types of bracing all affect ambulation.

All individuals with meningomyelocele experience a loss of sensation that is more marked on the back of the legs than on the front. Furthermore, most affected children lose sensa-

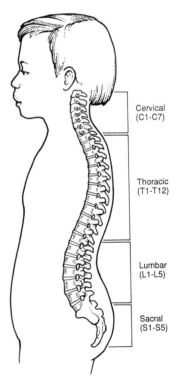

Figure 24.2. The vertebral column is divided into 7 neck (cervical), 12 chest (thoracic), 5 back (lumbar), and 5 lower-back (sacral) vertebrae. Meningomyelocele most commonly affects the thoracolumbar region.

Cervical (C1-C7)

Thoracic (T1-T12)

Lumbar (L1-L5)

Sacral (S1-S5)

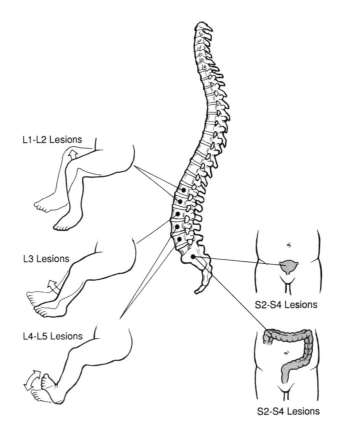

Figure 24.3. Diagram showing where movement, sensation, and bladder and bowel function are usually controlled in the spinal cord. Meningomyelocele at these levels usually prevents typical functioning at and below the levels shown.

tion around the anus, genitalia, and feet. The loss of motor and sensory function is not always symmetrical; one side may have better motor function or sensation than the other (Figure 24.4).

Chiari Malformation and Hydrocephalus

Almost all children with meningomyelocele above the sacral level have a Chiari type II (previously called *Arnold-Chiari*) malformation of the brain (Griebel, Oakes, & Worley, 1991; Rauzzino & Oakes, 1995). In this abnormality, the brainstem and part of the cerebellum are displaced downward toward the neck, rather than remaining within the skull (Figure 24.5), as if the spinal cord had been pulled downward prior to birth. Symptoms and signs of spinal cord compression from the malformation include difficulty swallowing, choking, hoarseness, breathholding spells, apnea (periodic brief respiratory arrests), disordered breathing during sleep, stiffness in the arms, and opisthotonos (holding the head arched backward). There have been rare sudden deaths from cardiorespiratory arrest (Charney et al., 1987; Kirk, Morielli, & Brouillette, 1999). If symptoms of compression develop, they can be treated surgically by a decompression procedure, in which the lower back of the skull and the arches of some of the cervical (neck) vertebral bodies are removed to provide additional space for the brainstem. This provides short-term benefit, but the long-term effectiveness remains uncertain (Park et al., 1983; Pollack et al., 1996; Pollack et al., 1992; Worley, Schuster, & Oakes, 1996). Children with more severe symptoms, such as vocal cord paralysis, and children who have been symptomatic for a longer period (e.g., months) have poorer outcomes following decompressive surgery.

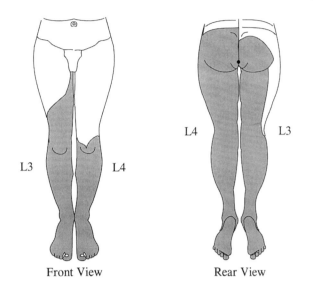

L3   L4

Front View

L4   L3

Rear View

Figure 24.4. Sensory loss (shaded areas) in a child with L3- to L4-level meningomyelocele. The back of legs has more loss than the front. Asymmetry of sensory or motor loss is common; sensory loss may not completely correlate with loss of motor function.

Disordered breathing during sleep occurs frequently in individuals with meningomyelocele and has been called the "missed diagnosis" (Kirk et al., 1999). It may be the result of obstructive sleep apnea, central apnea, or central hypoventilation (Kirk et al., 2000). Disordered sleep can cause children to be tired during the day, interfering with their ability to function in school. A formal sleep study can help differentiate among the various problems that can cause disordered breathing during sleep. In this procedure, the child sleeps overnight in a specialized hospital laboratory where sleep patterns are assessed by videotape, and respiratory rate, heart rate, electroencephalogram (EEG) pattern, and other vital signs can be monitored. The treatment depends on the nature of the breathing disorder identified by this study. For example, tonsillectomy with adenoidectomy may help if the upper airway is obstructed. If there is an underlying central apnea, surgery to provide posterior fossa decompression of the Chiari II malformation may be performed, although this is not always effective. A significant proportion of children with severe breathing disorders that do not respond to the above measures will require continuous positive airway pressure or bilevel positive airway pressure during sleep, or even tracheostomy with mechanical ventilation.

Associated with the Chiari II malformation is hydrocephalus (Table 24.2). This complication occurs in 60%–95% of children with meningomyelocele and is most common in thoracolumbar lesions (Griebel et al., 1991). Hydrocephalus develops as a result of an abnormal CSF flow pattern, leading to an enlargement of the ventricular system of the brain. It can be diagnosed by neuroimaging studies: ultrasonography in the prenatal period and in infancy, and computed tomography (CT) or MRI in older children.

Hydrocephalus is treated with a surgically implanted shunt. Shunting diverts CSF from the enlarged ventricular system to another place in the body where it can be better absorbed. The most common type, a ventriculoperitoneal shunt, drains fluid into the child's abdominal cavity (Figure 24.6). Shunts to the pleural space (surrounding the lungs) may be used as an alternative. Neither of these types of shunts necessitates prophylactic antibiotics prior to dental procedures. Shunts to the atrium of the heart, however, do require antibiotic prophylaxis and can result in inflammation of the kidney (nephritis) and chronic embolization to the lungs. As a result, ventriculo-atrial shunts are rarely used now.

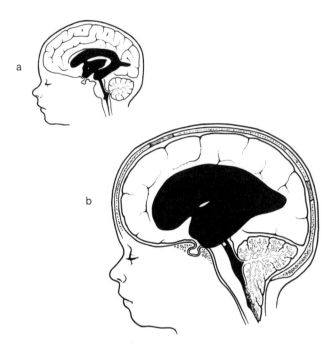

Figure 24.5. a) The typical brain, with ventricles of normal size (shaded area). b) In the Chiari II malformation and hydrocephalus (shaded area), the brainstem and part of the cerebellum are displaced downward toward the neck region, which can cause symptoms such as difficulty swallowing and hoarseness.

Any of the shunts can become blocked or infected, especially during the first year of life. By 2–3 years of age, approximately half of the shunts inserted have failed and been replaced surgically (Liptak & McDonald, 1985–1986). In infants, signs of a blocked shunt include excessive head growth and a tense **anterior fontanelle** ("soft spot") on the forehead. In children older than 2 years, the skull bones will have fused. As the pressure builds up inside the head, a blocked shunt will result in symptoms of lethargy, headache, vomiting, and irritability. This increased intracranial pressure can also lead to paralysis of the sixth cranial nerve (VI), with resultant strabismus and double vision, or paralysis of upward gaze (the inability to look upward). A child with an infected shunt can display symptoms similar to those seen in shunt blockage but will also have a fever and an elevated white blood cell count. Signs and symptoms of a

Table 24.2. Degree of paralysis in meningomyelocele and functional implications

Degree of paralysis	Hydrocephalus (%)	Mobility status	
		Childhood	Adulthood
Thoracic (T1–T12) or high lumbar (L1, L2)	90	Will require extensive orthosis like parapodium, reciprocal gait orthosis, or HKAFO[a]	Typically use wheelchairs; community ambulation rare
Lumbar (L3, L4)	80	Will ambulate with less extensive orthotics, using crutches	Most use wheelchairs; community ambulation is uncommon
Low lumbar (L5) and sacral (S1–S4)	65	Will ambulate with minimal or no bracing, with or without crutches	Most continue to be community ambulators

From Charney, E.B. (1997). Myelomeningocele. In M.W. Schwartz et al. (Eds.), *Pediatric primary care: A problem-oriented approach* (3rd ed., p. 812). St. Louis: Mosby; reprinted by permission.

[a]HKAFO, hip-knee-ankle-foot orthosis.

blocked shunt can mimic those of a tethered cord or Chiari malformation. Therefore, whenever a child with a meningomyelocele develops new neurological symptoms, especially deterioration of physical or cognitive function, a blocked or infected shunt should be investigated. More subtle symptoms of a partial shunt failure include a change in personality, decline in school performance, or weakness of the arms or legs (Mataro et al., 2000).

Early recognition of shunt failure or infection is critical, as both complications can be life threatening. A child who develops new neurological symptoms should be evaluated immediately for shunt failure. If a blocked shunt is suspected, the physician may order a neuroimaging study (CT or MRI) to determine if the ventricles have increased in size as well as radiographs of the shunt system (shunt series) to determine if the tubing is broken or kinked. To detect increased intracranial pressure, a neurosurgeon may insert a needle into the shunt tubing to measure CSF pressure. If the shunt is found to be obstructed, the blocked portion will be replaced surgically with a new catheter and/or valve.

As an interim measure to treat shunt failure, the oral medications acetazolamide (Diamox), furosemide (Lasix), or dexamethasone (Decadron) have been given (Carrion et al., 2001). These drugs inhibit CSF production and thereby lower intracranial pressure until surgery can be performed. Their prolonged use, however, is not useful and may be harmful (Whitelaw, Kennedy, & Brion, 2001). If the shunt is infected, the child also needs to receive intravenous antibiotics. In addition, it may be necessary to remove the infected shunt surgi-

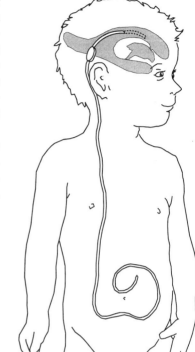

Figure 24.6. Ventriculoperitoneal shunt, which has been placed for hydrocephalus. A plastic tube is inserted into one of the lateral ventricles and connected to a one-way valve. Another tube runs under the skin from the valve to the abdominal cavity. Enough extra tubing is left in the abdomen to uncoil as the child grows.

cally and, after antibiotic treatment, replace it with a new one (Kulkarni et al., 2001). It is important to emphasize that the individual with hydrocephalus will almost always require a working shunt throughout his or her life. In some children, however, a new surgical procedure called endoscopic third ventriculostomy may obviate the need for ventricular shunts (Kim, Wang, & Cho, 2000). This technique involves placing a hole in the floor of one of the ventricles to drain CSF within the brain. Its safety and effectiveness in the treatment of children with hydrocephalus associated with NTDs is still uncertain.

ASSOCIATED IMPAIRMENTS AND MEDICAL COMPLICATIONS

The combination of an NTD, hydrocephalus, and other malformations of the brain leads to associated developmental disabilities and places the child at risk for a number of medical complications. These associated disabilities include mobility impairment, cognitive impairments, seizure disorders, and visual impairment. Medical complications include musculoskeletal abnormalities, spinal curvatures and humps, urinary and bowel dysfunction, skin sores, weight and stature abnormalities, sexual dysfunction, and allergy to latex. These are discussed further next. Many of these disabilities and medical complications can be prevented or their impact lessened by painstaking clinical care and monitoring by the family, the child, and health care professionals.

Mobility Impairments

The higher the level of the meningomyelocele and the greater the muscle weakness, the more ambulation will be impaired (McDonald, 1995). Even children with low-level lesions (L4 and below), however, are likely to have significant impairment in mobility. Many infants with meningomyelocele have delayed rolling and sitting skills. Most affected infants, regardless of their level of lesion, learn to belly crawl commando style as their first means of mobility. Infants with strong voluntary hip flexion and some knee movement may eventually assume the all-fours crawl but often do not until after 1 year of age.

Children with sacral lesions generally learn to walk well by 2 or 3 years of age with bracing at the ankles or no bracing at all. Children with mid-lumbar (L3) paralysis often require crutches and bracing up to the hip (Table 24.2). Children with thoracic or high lumbar (L1 and L2) paralysis may eventually stand upright and walk but only with support of the hips, knees, and ankles. This support may be provided by extensive bracing and/or mobility devices such as a parapodium, a reciprocal gait orthosis (Guidera et al., 1993), or a hip-knee-ankle-foot orthosis (HKAFO) used in combination with crutches or a walker.

As children with L3 and L4 lesions approach adolescence and their center of gravity and relative strength change, most will rely increasingly on wheelchairs for mobility (Table 24.2; Hunt & Poulton, 1995; McDonald et al., 1991). Because most children with meningomyelocele will not become effective community ambulators, the supplemental or primary use of a wheelchair should be considered at least by early adolescence as it offers the advantages of speed, efficiency, and attractiveness (Liptak et al., 1992).

The likelihood of ambulation is a function not only of the location of the lesion and associated muscle weaknesses but also of the cognitive functioning of the child, complications including joint contractures and shunt infections, the involvement of the parents, and the therapy program. Children with high-level paralysis are more likely to stand upright and walk, at least for exercise, if they have average IQ scores, regular ambulation therapy, and parents who are committed to carrying out walking therapy at home (Charney, Melchionni, & Smith, 1991). For children with a high-level lesion and mental retardation, walking may not be a realistic goal, and wheelchair training should start early. Motorized wheelchairs can be used beginning at a 24-month developmental level (McDonald, 1995). Formal gait analysis using video cameras and sensors linked to computers may help analyze the gait and guide subsequent orthopedic management, including surgery and bracing (Ounpuu et al., 2000). Whether this technology compared with conventional evaluation leads to improved outcome is not clear.

Cognitive Impairments

Approximately three quarters of children with meningomyelocele have IQ scores that fall within the low-average range (Friedrich et al., 1991). Most of the remaining one quarter have mild mental retardation. The few children with meningomyelocele who have severe mental retardation usually have had a complicating brain infection resulting from an infected shunt or prenatal hydrocephalus. Prenatal hydrocephalus begins in the first trimester of pregnancy and is associated with a head circumference at birth that is well above the 95th percentile (Brumfield et al., 1995).

Although the majority of children with meningomyelocele have typical intellectual function, they tend to show significant impairments in perceptual skills, organizational abilities, attention span, speed of motor response, memory, and hand function (Snow, 1994; Wills et al., 1990). By school age, many children with meningomyelocele and hydrocephalus are diagnosed with a nonverbal learning disability (see Chapter 22; Rourke, 1995; Williamson, 1987). These children typically have better reading than math skills. In addition to the learning disability, they often have impairments in executive function that have an impact on education, social, and self-help skills. Executive function skills include the ability to plan, initiate, sequence, sustain, inhibit competing responses, and pace work (Fletcher et al., 1996). For example, the child may know the steps involved in self-catheterization but may have difficulty planning and carrying out the process. In addition, Davidovitch et al. (1999) reported that one third of children with meningomyelocele have attention-deficit/hyperactivity disorder; about 30% of these children respond to stimulant medication (see Chapter 21).

Because children with meningomyelocele are at increased risk for multiple developmental disabilities, they should be referred to an early intervention program in infancy (see Chapter 29). This should be followed by a formal psychoeducational evaluation prior to school entry to identify strengths and weaknesses and to develop an individualized education program (IEP; see Chapter 30; Rowley-Kelly & Reigel, 1993).

Seizure Disorders

Approximately 15% of individuals with meningomyelocele develop a seizure disorder (Noetzel, 1989). The seizures usually are generalized tonic-clonic and respond well to antiepileptic medication (see Chapter 25). If a new type of seizure develops or if seizure frequency increases, however, a blocked shunt or shunt infection should be suspected and investigated.

Visual Impairments

Strabismus is present in about 20% of children with meningomyelocele and often requires surgical correction. Visual impairments can result from abnormalities of the visual gaze center in the brain or from increased intracranial pressure caused by a malfunctioning ventricular shunt (see Chapter 10).

Musculoskeletal Abnormalities

With partial or total paralysis, muscle imbalances and lack of mobility may lead to deformities around joints (Westcott et al., 1992). This can occur even prior to birth. For example, children with meningomyelocele may develop a clubfoot (see Chapter 14) or calcaneus deformity as a result of the foot being pressed against the uterine wall stuck in one position. Treatment of clubfoot involves serial casting during the first 3–4 months of life to gradually straighten the deformity. Corrective surgery can then follow at 4 months to 1 year of age (Swank & Dias, 1992). Other ankle and foot deformities may require surgical intervention to facilitate proper foot placement in shoes. Bracing is used to help maintain proper positioning of joints and should be monitored to minimize the occurrence of skin breakdown over bony prominences (e.g., decubitus ulcers of the elbow or buttocks).

Muscle imbalance and lack of movement also can lead to hip deformities. Surgical correction is controversial and may be appropriate only for those children with low lumbar paralysis who have the potential for functional ambulation (Roberts & Evans, 1993; Sherk et al., 1991). In general, surgery should be used to improve function and not for cosmetic reasons (Karol, 1995). It should be noted that loss of muscle strength and inactivity predispose affected children to fractures. These pathological fractures may also occur after orthopedic surgery, especially following prolonged casting (Parsch, 1991). All individuals with spina bifida should receive adequate calcium and vitamin D in order to minimize osteoporosis and the susceptibility to pathological fractures. This is especially true if the child is taking antiepileptic drugs that interfere with calcium and vitamin D metabolism. In addition, weight-bearing activities should be encouraged whenever possible. Following surgical procedures, steps should be taken to prevent deep vein thrombosis, which predispose the individual to pulmonary emboli (Bernstein et al., 1989). Lastly, as individuals with spina bifida age, they may develop arthritis of the hips or knees secondary to abnormal sensation and gait (Nagarkatti, Banta, & Thomson, 2000).

Spinal Curvatures and Humps

Almost 90% of children with a meningomyelocele above the sacral level have spinal curvatures and/or humps (Mayfield, 1991). These deformities include scoliosis (a spinal curvature), kyphosis (a spinal hump; Figure 24.7), and **kyphoscoliosis** (a combination of both conditions). Scoliosis and kyphosis may be present before birth (congenital) or develop in later in childhood (acquired). If untreated, spinal deformities may eventually interfere with sitting and walking and even decrease lung capacity. Scoliosis greater than 25 degrees requires an orthotic support (a molded plastic shield-like orthotic jacket). Despite this, the curvature often progresses, and surgery may be necessary (Mayfield, 1991). Surgical correction involves a spinal fusion with bone grafts. This often requires two surgical procedures, one through the front and one from the back. The procedures use metal rods (internal fixation) and wires (Luque procedure; Figure 23.12) for stabilization of the spinal column (Vivani et al., 1993). More recently, the two-stage procedure has been successfully replaced by a single frontal (anterior) approach in some children whose curve is less than 75 degrees in the absence of abnormalities of the spinal cord (Sponseller et al., 1999). Children with congenital rather than developmental scoliosis or kyphosis generally respond poorly to orthotic treatment and require spinal fusion at younger ages.

Kyphosis is usually located in the thoracic spine and may measure as much as 80 to 90 degrees at birth. The hump on the spine may be rigid and worsen over time. Surgical removal of the deformity is accomplished by an operation called a *kyphectomy*. This procedure has a high rate of complications and recurrences in infancy (Mayfield, 1991), but when performed in school-age children, it has been quite effective (Lintner & Lindseth, 1994).

Some evidence indicates that tethering of the spinal cord (discussed later) may lead to rapidly progressive scoliosis. Surgery to untether the cord may halt or even reverse the progression of the curve in individuals whose curves are less than 50 degrees at the time of surgery (Pierz et al., 2000). In addition, a significant number of individuals with spina bifida will have an abnormal fluid collection in the spinal cord or even thinning (hypoplasia) of the cord (Mos-

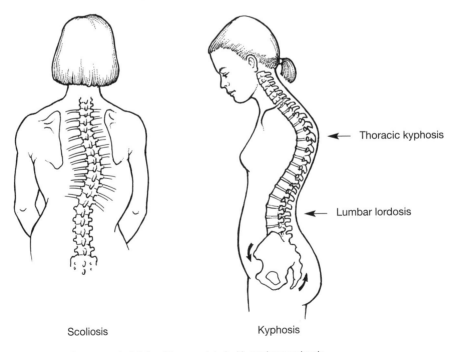

Scoliosis   Kyphosis

Figure 24.7.   Common spinal deformities associated with meningomyelocele.

kowitz et al., 1998). Because spinal surgery fuses the bones of the spine, making subsequent neurological surgery especially challenging, many centers obtain an MRI scan of the spine on all individuals prior to surgery for kyphosis or scoliosis. In this way they can identify tethering or cavities in the spinal cord that might require surgery prior to the orthopedic procedure.

Urinary Dysfunction

Because the bladder, the urinary outlet (urethra), and rectum are all controlled by nerves that leave the spinal cord in the lower sacrum (Figure 24.3), bladder and bowel dysfunction are present in virtually all children with meningomyelocele. Even children with sacral lesions and normal leg movement typically have bladder and bowel problems. In addition, these children have a higher incidence of malformations of the kidneys, including horseshoe kidney and absent kidney (Hulton et al., 1990).

The bladder has two major functions: 1) to store urine that has been produced by the kidney and 2) to empty the urine once the bladder is full. Children with meningomyelocele often have difficulty with both functions and are consequently incontinent (Vereecken, 1992). In addition, the inability to completely empty the bladder of urine may predispose the child to infections of the bladder and/or kidneys. The combination of a tight bladder outlet and increased tone in the bladder also may produce kidney damage over time (Anderson & Travers, 1993).

To detect early structural damage, the urinary tract is imaged using ultrasonography at regular intervals beginning in infancy. Ultrasound examination permits detection of malformations and abnormal functioning of the bladder and urinary outlet (MacKinnon, Roberts, & Searles, 2000).

Bladder function also may be evaluated using a cystometrogram, a procedure in which fluid is injected into the bladder and pressure is measured. If elevated pressure is found, it must be reduced to avoid permanent kidney damage (Sutherland & Gonzales, 1999). For many years, surgeons performed an **ileostomy,** a procedure in which urine is diverted from the bladder, through the abdominal wall, and into an external collection vessel (Krahn & Johnson, 1993). Now, reducing bladder pressure is accomplished by teaching CIC, and surgery can usually be avoided (Baskin, Kogan, & Benard, 1990). In CIC, the individual or his or her parents are taught to insert a clean, but not sterile, catheter (tube) through the urethra and into the bladder. This commonly is done at least four times a day to drain urine. When CIC is performed correctly, urine does not accumulate, become infected, or flow back into the kidneys. In some infants, however, this is not successful and a surgical procedure called a vesicostomy is performed. Here an opening through the abdominal wall and into the bladder is produced, allowing urine to drain directly into the diaper. This procedure often is temporary. When the child is older, the vesicostomy is closed surgically and he or she begins a CIC program.

In addition to assessing bladder pressure, the infant also is monitored for the occurrence of urinary infections, which occur in at least half of individuals with meningomyelocele. If these happen frequently, long-term prophylactic oral antibiotics such as cephalexin (Keflex) or trimethoprim/sulfamethoxazole (Bactrim or Septra) may be given to prevent infections. Alternatively, antibiotics can be instilled directly into the bladder through the catheter.

Attempts to achieve urinary continence are generally begun at 3–4 years of age. For a catheterization program to be successful, the parents and child must adhere to the recommendations. In addition, medications may be of use: oxybutynin chloride (Ditropan) can be given orally or instilled into the bladder to diminish bladder wall contractions; and pseudoephedrine (Sudafed) or imipramine (Tofranil) may be given orally to enhance storage of urine. About 70% of children who receive a combination of CIC and medications achieve continence during elementary school. Children also can be taught to monitor the pressure inside their bladders at home (Andros et al., 1998; Damaser et al., 1999). This technique can help with the early identification of changes in bladder function.

If CIC and medication are unsuccessful in producing continence, a surgical intervention may be undertaken. One method is to inject a silicone-like material around the urethra using an endoscope. This mechanically narrows the urethral opening, thereby improving continence (Guys et al. 1999). Another approach is a bladder augmentation procedure in which the bladder capacity is increased using a flap of bowel or stomach (Cher & Allen, 1993). A third procedure is an appendicovesicostomy, in which the appendix is used to connect the bladder to the abdominal wall, permitting catheterization through the appendix (Keating, Rink, & Adams, 1993). These approaches may be used in combination.

"Volitional" voiding is also possible using an artificial urinary sphincter that surrounds the urethra and stays closed to prevent leakage of urine. A bulb mechanism is placed in the scrotum or labia majora; when it is squeezed, fluid drains out of the artificial sphincter allowing urine to drain from the bladder. This system, however, has been plagued by complications such as erosion of the skin around the bulb and poor compliance leading to overdistension of the bladder and resultant kidney damage (Kryger et al., 1999). Yet, for a select group of highly motivated individuals, the artificial sphincter can permit volitional voiding (Jumper et al., 1990).

Finally, as the risk of bladder cancer is increased, adults with meningomyelocele probably should be monitored annually with endoscopy of the bladder and cytologic analysis of the cells from the urine (Game et al., 1999; Shaw & Lewis, 1999).

Bowel Dysfunction

Bowel problems in children with meningomyelocele are related to uncoordinated propulsive action of the intestines, ineffectual closure of the anus, and lack of rectal sensation (Agnarsson et al., 1993). Constipation is common and may be interspersed with periods of overflow diarrhea. Lack of sensation and failure of anal function also lead to soiling that can be socially devastating.

Attempts at bowel management can begin as soon as the child starts eating solids by encouraging foods that are high in fiber. Between 2½ and 4 years of age, timed potty sitting can be tried after every meal to take advantage of the postfeeding gastrocolic (propulsive) reflex. If, after several months, bowel control has not been achieved, parents may be instructed to administer one or more of the following medications that will facilitate more complete bowel emptying: 1) a daily laxative such as lactulose (a complex sugar), Miralax (an agent that keeps water in the stool), or senna (e.g., Senokot); 2) a fiber supplement such as psyllium (e.g., Metamucil); or 3) a nightly rectal suppository such as bisacodyl (e.g., Dulcolax), or daily enemas using water (Liptak & Revell, 1992). Two newer surgical procedures, one that connects the appendix to the colon (Malone procedure) and another that provides a direct connection between the abdominal wall and the colon (cecostomy), allow irrigation of the colon on a regular basis (antegrade [forward-flowing] colonic enema, or ACE). The cecostomy can be performed either in the operating room or in an interventional radiology suite. These approaches have been shown to be successful in children for whom more conventional bowel techniques have failed (Aksnes et al., 2002; Chait et al., 1997; De Peppo et al., 1999; Leibold, Ekmark, & Adams, 2000; Roberts et al., 1999; Squire et al., 1993; Webb et al., 1998).

For a select group of older children with low-level (sacral) meningomyeloceles who have rectal sensation, biofeedback training may be used to improve rectal function (Benninga et al., 1994). In this training technique, children use a balloon pressure transducer connected to a visible pressure monitor to optimize rectal function, including coordinating efforts to expulse stool.

Skin Sores

Skin sores or decubitus ulcers frequently occur in children with meningomyelocele, whose weight-bearing surfaces (e.g., feet, buttocks) are not sensitive to pain (Wood et al., 1993). These children may sustain injuries that they do not feel, often resulting in a skin sore. This problem becomes more frequent during adolescence and, if not caught early, the decubitus ulcer may require prolonged hospitalizations for **debridement** (removal of dead tissue), skin grafting, and intravenous antibiotics. Therefore, the best treatment is prevention. Certain common-sense rules should be followed: 1) Have the child use sunscreen to prevent sunburn; 2) replace tight-fitting shoes or braces; 3) have the child avoid hot baths; 4) give the child protective foot covering for swimming; and 5) do not let the young child crawl about on rough or hot surfaces.

For children in wheelchairs, pressure sores on the buttocks or coccyx (tail bone) can be prevented by modifying the wheelchair with an adaptive seating system. For example, some systems can be molded to the shape of the child, or special foam-filled cushions (e.g., Jay cushion) can be used to establish a better fit. Experiments are being conducted with cushions that hydraulically change their shape throughout the day, thereby changing the pressure patterns. Individuals can minimize prolonged pressure by performing regular wheelchair pushups to relieve pressure and by frequently changing position. Small skin sores should be treated by alleviating pressure and using saline-soaked dressings or artificial skin preparations such as Tegaderm or Vigilon. If ulcers do not heal in a reasonable time, an underlying infection may be present, requiring surgical debridement and intravenous antibiotic treatment. Many new coverings have been tried without clear advantage. The most important rule is that the only thing that should not be placed on a pressure sore is the child!

Weight and Stature Abnormalities

Children with meningomyelocele, particularly those with thoracic to L2 lesions, are at increased risk for obesity as a result of their decreased activity/energy expenditure (Polito et al., 1995). About two thirds of these children are significantly overweight. Attention should be directed at increasing involvement in physical activities such as stretching exercises, aerobic conditioning (e.g., wheelchair sports), and strength training (e.g., lifting free weights). Exercise should be combined with dietary restrictions of sweets and fats (Duncan & Ogle, 1995). Affected children also are likely to have short stature. This results from a combination of failure of growth of the legs, spinal curves, and, occasionally, a deficiency of growth hormone (Hochhaus, Butenandt, & Ring-Mrozik, 1999; Rotenstein, Adams, & Reigel, 1995).

Sexual Dysfunction

Although three quarters of adult males with meningomyelocele can have erections (Diamond, Rickwood, & Thomas, 1986), most do not have control of them. Penile implants, injection or application of prostaglandin prior to coitus (Kim & McVary, 1995), the use of vacuum devices (Chen et al., 1995), and sildenafil (Viagra; Palmer, Kaplan, & Firlit, 1999) can help males achieve volitional erections that allow intercourse. There may be the additional problem of retrograde ejaculation, in which the semen is discharged into the bladder. Despite this, two thirds of males with spina bifida have sufficient sperm in their ejaculate to permit fatherhood using artificial insemination or in vitro fertilization (Hultling et al., 2000). Although there are a number of sexual and reproductive health issues relating to meningomyelocele, in a survey of young adults with spina bifida, 95% stated they had inadequate knowledge about these problems (Sawyer & Roberts, 1999).

Females with meningomyelocele have normal fertility and, if sexually active, should use the same precautions as the general population. They have approximately a 4% risk of having a child with an NTD (McDonald, 1995). Although many of these women are able to experience orgasm during sexual intercourse, they usually have decreased genital sensation and less sexually stimulated lubrication. As a result, frequent intercourse without adequate lubrication can lead to vaginal sores. Precocious puberty (e.g., breast development 1–2 years before usual) is a common occurrence in females who have meningomyelocele with hydrocephalus due to a disorder of the hypothalamus (a part of the brain that controls certain endocrine hormones; Elias & Sadeghi-Nejad, 1994). This can be treated with leuprolide (Lupron), a synthetic sex hormone (Kappy, Stuart, & Perelman, 1988). Women with meningomyelocele who become pregnant benefit from close monitoring during gestation. Problems such as recurrent urinary tract infections, persistent decubitus ulcers, back pain or slipped disk, and difficult vaginal delivery secondary to hip contractures may occur. Although these are concerns, it is important to note that most women with meningomyelocele have good pregnancy outcomes with relatively few complications (Arata et al., 2000; Powell & Garvey, 1994).

Allergy to Latex

More than half of all children with meningomyelocele develop an allergy to latex in childhood (Pearson, Cole, & Jarvis, 1994). Although the reason for this is unclear, the allergy seems to be more common in children who have had frequent surgical procedures (Ellsworth et al., 1993). The risk of allergy increases as the child gets older (Mazon et al., 2000). This allergic reaction can be life threatening (Dormans et al., 1995). Latex allergy can be diagnosed by a clear history of an allergic reaction to latex, by skin testing, or by immunoassay blood testing (Nieto et al., 2000). As a result of the high incidence of allergy to latex in these children, all surgical procedures, including dental procedures, should occur in latex-free settings. Some centers give antianaphylaxis medications prior to operations to children who demonstrate severe latex sensitivity even in a supposedly latex-free environment. Early contact of the infant with latex should be avoided, if possible, in an effort to prevent the development of allergy (Emans, 1992). Catheterization should be performed with nonlatex catheters, and nonlatex gloves should be used during care. Toys that contain significant amounts of latex, such as balloons and rubber balls, should be avoided, as should latex products that come into contact with the skin, such as Band-Aids and ACE bandages. Rarely, children allergic to latex will have sensitivities to certain foods, such as bananas, water chestnuts, avocados, and kiwi fruit.

Neurological Deterioration

If a child's strength, bowel and bladder function, or daily living skills deteriorate, a cause should be sought. The origin of the deterioration may be a malfunctioning or blocked ventricular shunt; a tethered spinal cord; or, rarely, swelling in (syrinx, syringomyelia, or hydromyelia) or splitting of the spinal cord (diastematomyelia or diplomyelia). A tethered spinal cord may result from 1) scarring at the site of the initial surgery to close the back, 2) scoliosis, or 3) the pressure of a lipoma (Liptak, 1996, 1998; Yamada et al., 1995). Pressure or stretch on the tethered cord leads to poor circulation and diminished motor functioning. The Chiari II malformation may become symptomatic, too, leading to difficulty swallowing, hoarseness, weakness of the arms, or difficulty with respiration.

All children who present with neurological deterioration first should be evaluated for structure and function of the ventricular shunt. This involves imaging of the head (e.g., CT, MRI) with or without plain radiographic imaging of the shunt from head to abdomen (to look for a break in the tubing). In addition, the posterior fossa and spinal cord should be evaluated by a MRI of the head with a flow study (to look for Chiari II malformation and to look for tethered, swollen, or split cord, respectively; Levy, 1999) and a MRI of the spine. If identified early, each of these problems can be addressed successfully. A blocked shunt can be replaced, a tethered cord released, a lipoma removed, and a posterior fossa decompressed. Treatment of syringomyelia (syrinx or hydromyelia), however, is more controversial and often less rewarding (Ergun et al., 2000).

EDUCATIONAL PROGRAMS

Referral to an early intervention program should occur by 6 months of age (see Chapter 29). Sensorimotor assessment during the child's first year should include evaluations of range of motion of joints, muscle tone, strength and bulk, sensation, movement skills, postural control, and sensory integration skills (Williamson, 1987). Treatment should focus on maintaining range of motion, enhancing strength, and moving toward standing and ambulation. Because of the considerable variability in the degree of motor delay among these children, individualized intervention plans must be developed. Adaptive equipment should be provided as needed (see Chapter 33).

As the child moves toward school entry, it is important to perform psychoeducational testing. This permits the identification of the child's cognitive strengths and challenges, realistic expectations that will optimize the child's learning, and development of an IEP for school (Hurley, 1993). Physical therapy should be provided as part of the school program. Yearly reassessments will permit modification of the program based on the child's changing needs (see Chapter 30; Rowley-Kelly & Reigel, 1993; Thompson, 1997).

PSYCHOSOCIAL ISSUES FOR THE CHILD

During the preschool years, the achievement of independence (Erikson, 1959) may be thwarted by problems with mobility and bladder and bowel control. A sense of industry that develops in the school-age child may be reduced by the child's learning impairments as well as by his or her inability to compete with peers in sports. Difficulty in the school environment may exacerbate a preexisting poor self-image that many of these children have as a result of their physical disabilities. The feeling of being different can impair the establishment of peer relationships in both school and community (Hayden, 1985). The child's self-esteem also may be lowered if he or she must continue to wear diapers or care for an ostomy. During adolescence, lower self-esteem may relate to a poor body image and difficulty in dealing with sexual changes and feelings (Blum et al., 1991; Rinck, Berg, & Hafeman, 1989). Problems for the young adult with meningomyelocele may include increasing social isolation, a realization that the disability is permanent, and sexual dysfunction. Social outcomes, such as behavior problems, do not necessarily relate to the severity of physical impairment but are interrelated with functional status, such as scholastic achievement (Hommeyer et al., 1999). Helping a child cope with a disability requires 1) insight into the issues faced by the child, such as the developmental stages of Erickson (1959); 2) knowledge of the strengths and weaknesses of the child, such as a temperament characterized by shyness (social anxiety); 3) a strategy for dealing with the issues (e.g., behavior supports); and 4) support to carry out the strategies. Children require encouragement and support from adults. This assumes that families have sufficient financial and emotional resources to cope with their child's condition, which is not always the case. Efforts should be made to maximize the child's self-management, allowing the child to be as independent as possible in his or her own care. Providing safe, structured opportunities to learn socialization (e.g., arranging trips to the movies, the mall, and fast-food restaurants with friends) can be helpful in boosting an adolescent's self-esteem.

Some studies have found a higher-than-expected rate of depression in individuals with meningomyelocele. Signs of depression include lack of interest in usual activities, sadness, change in appetite, difficulty sleeping, anxiety, and decreased activity. Medical problems such as an adverse reaction to medication, problems with the ventricular shunt, and infections, however, can cause similar symptoms and must be ruled out. Many individuals with meningomyelocele develop learned helplessness; they feel that unpleasant or **aversive** stimuli cannot be controlled. As a result they cease trying to remedy an aversive circumstance, even if they are capable of exerting some influence. This contributes to depressive feelings. Depression should be recognized and brought to the attention of an appropriate mental health professional. A multimodal approach including counseling, exercise programs, and medications (especially selective serotonin reuptake inhibitors, e.g., paroxetine [Paxil], fluoxetine [Prozac]) is usually effective.

INTERDISCIPLINARY MANAGEMENT

The goals of therapy are to improve functioning and independence and to prevent or correct secondary physical or emotional problems. This generally involves surgical intervention, adaptive equipment, special education services, and psychosocial support for the child and family (see Chapter 36). As a result of the complexity of the resultant disabilities, an interdisciplinary approach to treating the child with meningomyelocele is essential (McDonald, 1995). The team of health care professionals should include a physician (e.g., neurodevelopmental pediatrician, pediatric neurologist, or physiatrist) with particular interest and expertise in the care of meningomyelocele; a nurse specialist; physical and occupational therapists; a social worker; consulting orthopedic, urological, and neurosurgeons; and an **orthotist.** Other team members or consultants may include a psychologist, plastic surgeon, dentist, special educator, speech-language pathologist, genetic counselor, and financial counselor. The services that the child needs and receives should be coordinated by a designated service coordinator (or case manager). Efforts should be made to empower the child and family by involving them in the design of a management plan that is both appropriate and realistic.

The successful development of the child with meningomyelocele is largely dependent on how well the family is able to meet the needs of the child. This requires emotional and behavioral supports, realistic expectations, special education services, and coordinated community services. The care of a child with meningomyelocele is expensive. Direct medical expenses have been estimated to total more than $100,000 over the individual's lifetime (Waitzman, Romano, & Scheffler, 1994); indirect costs, such as loss of parental income and decreased productivity of the affected individual, are estimated to total $250,000 over the life span (Centers for Disease Control, 1990). Therefore, one of the priorities of care is to provide financial counseling to families.

OUTCOME

The survival rate of children with meningomyelocele has improved dramatically. In the 1950s survival to adulthood was less than 10% (Dunne & Shurtleff, 1986; Hunt & Poulton, 1995; Steinbok et al., 1992); in the 1990s, about 85% of children with meningomyelocele survived to adulthood. This improved survival has resulted from many factors, including the use of ventriculoperitoneal shunts to control hydrocephalus and the prevention of kidney damage by CIC and urological surgery (McLone, 1989).

Outcome data for adults are incomplete, and the population is quite heterogeneous. In one center, Hunt (1990, 1999) found that half the individuals with meningomyelocele were still able to walk 50 yards or more in adulthood. Half also were able to maintain urinary and bowel continence. Overall, 12% had minimal disabilities, with average IQ scores, community ambulation, and well-managed continence; 52% had moderate disability with borderline normal IQ scores and the ability to attend to toilet needs independently and to use and transfer from a wheelchair. Severe disability involving mental retardation, incontinence, and dependence for most self-help skills was found in 37% of the individuals and was most related to a history of shunt infections or shunt failure.

SUMMARY

In meningomyelocele, an overlying sac protruding from the spine contains a malformed spinal cord and leads to the most complex birth defect compatible with life. Paralysis and loss of sensation occur below the level of the spinal cord defect, usually associated with hydrocephalus. Numerous disabilities arise as a consequence of this condition, including paralysis, musculoskeletal abnormalities, bowel and bladder incontinence, impotence, obesity, and cognitive impairments, including nonverbal learning disorders. Meningomyelocele, however, should be considered a nonprogressive condition, and any deterioration in function should lead to a search for a treatable cause, such as a blocked ventricular shunt or a tethered spinal cord. Advances in surgical and medical care have enhanced the survival and physical well being of individuals with meningomyelocele but have not completely corrected the associated impairments. To help an individual with meningomyelocele reach his or her potential, professionals must advocate for the child and family in the areas of education and psychosocial adjustment while providing integrated, high-quality health care.

REFERENCES

Adetioloye, V.A., Dare, F.O., & Oyelami, O.A. (1993). A ten-year review of encephalocele in a teaching hospital. *International Journal of Gynaecology and Obstetrics, 41*, 241–249.

Agnarsson, U., Warde, C., McCarthy, G., et al. (1993). Anorectal function of children with neurological problems, I: Spina bifida. *Developmental Medicine and Child Neurology, 35*, 893–902.

Aksnes, G., Diseth, T.H., Helseth, A., et al. (2002). Appendicostomy for antegrade enema: Effects on somatic and psychosocial functioning in children with meningomyelocele. *Pediatrics, 109*, 484–489.

American Academy of Pediatrics, Committee on Genetics. (1999). Folic acid for the prevention of neural tube defects. *Pediatrics, 104*, 325–327.

Anderson, P.A., & Travers, A.H. (1993). Development of hydronephrosis in spina bifida patients: Predictive factors and management. *British Journal of Urology, 72*, 958–961.

Andros, G.J., Hatch, D.A., Walter, J.S., et al. (1998). Home bladder pressure monitoring in children with myelomeningocele. *The Journal of Urology, 160*, 518–521.

Arata, M., Grover, S., Dunne, K., et al. (2000). Pregnancy outcome and complications in women with spina bifida. *The Journal of Reproductive Medicine, 45*, 743–748.

Babcock, C.J. (1995). Ultrasound evaluation of prenatal and neonatal spina bifida. *Neurosurgery Clinics of North America, 6*, 203–218.

Baldwin, C.T., Hoth, C.F., Macina, R.A., et al. (1995). Mutations in PAX3 that cause Waardenburg syndrome type I: Ten new mutations and review of the literature. *American Journal of Medical Genetics, 58*, 115–122.

Bannister, C.M. (2000). Suggested goals for intrauterine surgery for the repair of myelomeningoceles. *European Journal of Pediatric Surgery, 10*(Suppl. 1), 42.

Bannister, C.M., Russell, S.A., & Rimmer, S. (1998). Pre-natal brain development of fetuses with a myelomeningocele. *European Journal of Pediatric Surgery, 8*(Suppl. 1), 15–17.

Bannister, C.M., Russell, S.A., Rimmer, S., et al. (2000). Can prognostic indicators be identified in a fetus with an encephalocele? *European Journal of Pediatric Surgery, 10* (Suppl. 1), 20–23.

Bartonek, A., & Saraste, H. (2001). Factors influencing ambulation in myelomeningocele: A cross-sectional study. *Developmental Medicine and Child Neurology, 43*, 253–260.

Bartonek, A., Saraste, H., & Knutson, L.M. (1999). Comparison of different systems to classify the neurological level of lesion in patients with myelomeningocele. *Developmental Medicine and Child Neurology, 41*, 796–805.

Baskin, L.S., Kogan, B.A., & Benard, F. (1990). Treatment of infants with neurogenic bladder dysfunction using anticholinergic drugs and intermittent catheterisation. *British Journal of Urology, 66*, 532–534.

Benninga, M.A., van der Hoeven, C.W., Wijers, O.B., et al. (1994). Treatment of fecal incontinence in a child with sacral agenesis: The use of biofeedback training. *Developmental Medicine and Child Neurology, 36*, 518–527.

Bernstein, M.L., Esseltine, D., Azouz, E.M., et al. (1989). Deep venous thrombosis complicating myelomeningocele: Report of three cases. *Pediatrics, 84*, 856–859.

Berry, R.J., Li, Z., Erickson, J.D., et al. (1999). Prevention of neural-tube defects with folic acid in China. China–U.S. Collaborative Project for Neural Tube Defect Prevention. *New England Journal of Medicine, 341*, 1485–1490.

Blum, R.W., Resnick, M.D., Nelson, R., et al. (1991). Family and peer issues among adolescents with spina bifida and cerebral palsy. *Pediatrics, 88*, 280–285.

Bock, J.L. (1992). Current issues in maternal serum alpha-fetoprotein screening. *American Journal of Clinical Pathology, 97*, 541–554.

Botto, L.D., & Yang, Q. (2000). 5,10-Methylenetetrahydrofolate reductase gene variants and congenital anomalies: A HuGE review. *American Journal of Epidemiology, 151*, 862–877.

Boushey, C.J., Beresford, S.A.A., Owens, G.S., et al. (1995). A quantitative assessment of plasma homocysteine as a risk factor for vascular disease. *Journal of the American Medical Association, 274*, 1049–1057.

Bower, C., & Stanley, F.J. (1992). Periconceptional vitamin supplementation and neural tube defects: Evidence from a case-control study in Western Australia and a review of recent publications. *Journal of Epidemiology and Community Health, 46*, 157–161.

Brumfield, C.G., Aronin, P.A., Cloud, G.A., et al. (1995). Fetal myelomeningocele: Is antenatal ultrasound useful in predicting neonatal outcome? *Journal of Reproductive Medicine, 40*, 26–30.

Bruner, J.P., Tulipan, N., Paschall, R.L., et al. (1999). Fetal surgery for myelomeningocele and the incidence of shunt-dependent hydrocephalus. *Journal of the American Medical Association, 282*, 1819–1825.

Candenas, M., Villa, R., Fernandez Collar, R., et al. (1995). Maternal serum alpha-fetoprotein screening for neural tube defects: Report of a program with more than 30,000 screened pregnancies. *Acta Obstetricia et Gynecologica Scandinavica, 74*, 266–269.

Carrion, E., Hertzog, J.H., Medlock, M.D., et al. (2001). Use of acetazolamide to decrease cerebrospinal fluid production in chronically ventilated patients with ventriculopleural shunts. *Archives of Disease in Childhood, 84*, 68–71.

Centers for Disease Control. (1990). Economic burden of spina bifida: United States, 1980–1990. *MMWR, 38*(15), 264–267.

Centers for Disease Control. (1992). Recommendations for

the use of folic acid to reduce the number of cases of spina bifida and other neural tube defects. *MMWR, 41*(RR-14), 1–7.

Chait, P.G., Shandling, B., Richards, H.M., et al. (1997). Fecal incontinence in children: Treatment with percutaneous cecostomy tube placement—a prospective study. *Radiology, 203,* 621–624.

Charney, E.B. (1997). Meningomyelocele. In M.W. Schwartz, T.A. Curry, A.J. Sargent, et al. (Eds.), *Pediatric primary care: A problem-oriented approach* (3rd ed., p. 812). St. Louis: Mosby.

Charney, E.B., Melchionni, J.B., & Smith, D.R. (1991). Community ambulation by children with meningomyelocele and high level paralysis. *Journal of Pediatric Orthopaedics, 11,* 579–582.

Charney, E.B., Rorke, L.B., Sutton, L.N., et al. (1987). Management of Chiari II complications in infants with MM. *Journal of Pediatrics, 111,* 364–371.

Charney, E.B., Weller, S.C., Sutton, L.N., et al. (1985). Management of the newborn with meningomyelocele: Time for a decision making process. *Pediatrics, 75,* 58–64.

Chatkupt, S., Hol, F.A., Shugart, Y.Y., et al. (1995). Absence of linkage between familial neural tube defects and PAX3 gene. *Journal of Medical Genetics, 32,* 200–204.

Chatkupt, S., Skurnick, H.H., Jagg, L.M., et al. (1994). Study of genetics, epidemiology, and vitamin usage in familial spina bifida in the United States in the 1990s. *Neurology, 44,* 65–70.

Chen, J., Godschalk, M.F., Katz, P.G., et al. (1995). Combining intracavernous injection and external vacuum as treatment for erectile dysfunction. *The Journal of Urology, 153,* 1476–1477.

Cher, M.L., & Allen, T.D. (1993). Continence in the myelodysplastic patient following enterocystoplasty. *The Journal of Urology, 149,* 1103–1106.

Christensen, B., & Rand-Hendriksen, S. (1998). Betydningen av assosierte misdannelser i sentralnervesystemet ved myelomeningocele [The significance of associated malformations of the central nervous system in myelomeningocele] [Abstract]. *Tidsskrift for den Norske Laegeforening, 118,* 4232–4234.

Copp, A.J., Fleming, A., & Greene, N.D.E. (1998). Embryonic mechanisms underlying the prevention of neural tube defects. *Mental Retardation and Developmental Disabilities Research Reviews, 4,* 264–268.

Dahl, M., Ahlsten, G., Carlson, H., et al. (1995). Neurological dysfunction above cele level in children with spina bifida cystica: A prospective study to three years. *Developmental Medicine and Child Neurology, 37,* 30–40.

Daly, L.E., Kirke, P.N., Malloy, A., et al. (1995). Folate levels and neural tube defects: Implications for prevention. *Journal of the American Medical Association, 274,* 1698–1702.

Damaser, M.S., Brzezinski, K., Walter, J.S., et al. (1999). Estimating detrusor pressure at home in pediatric patients with myelomeningocele. *The Journal of Urology, 162,* 1410–1414.

Davidovitch, M., Manning-Courtney, P., Hartmann, L.A., et al. (1999). The prevalence of attentional problems and the effect of methylphenidate in children with myelomeningocele. *Pediatric Rehabilitation, 3,* 29–35.

Davis, R., Peters, D.H., & McTavish, D. (1994). Valproic acid: A reappraisal of its pharmacological properties and clinical efficacy in epilepsy. *Drugs, 47,* 332–372.

De Peppo, F., Iacobelli, B.D., De Gennaro, M., et al. (1999). Percutaneous endoscopic cecostomy for antegrade colonic irrigation in fecally incontinent children. *Endoscopy, 31,* 501–503.

Diamond, D.A., Rickwood, A.M., & Thomas, D.G. (1986). Penile erections in myelomeningocele patients. *British Journal of Urology, 58,* 434–435.

Dias, M.S., & Pang, D. (1995). Split cord malformations. *Neurosurgery Clinics of North America, 6,* 339–358.

Dillon, C.M., Davis, B.E., Duguay, S., et al. (2000). Longevity of patients born with myelomeningocele. *European Journal of Pediatric Surgery, 10*(Suppl. 1), 33–34.

Dormans, J.P., Templeton, J., Schreiner, M.S., et al. (1995). Intraoperative latex anaphylaxis in children: Early detection, treatment, and prevention. *Contemporary Orthopaedics, 30,* 342–347.

Duncan, C.C., & Ogle, E.M. (1995). Spina bifida. In B. Goldberg (Ed.), *Sports and exercise for children with chronic health conditions* (pp. 79–88). Champaign, IL: Human Kinetics.

Dunne, K.B., & Shurtleff, D.B. (1986). The adult with meningomyelocele: A preliminary report. In R.L. McLaurin (Ed.), *Spina bifida* (pp. 38–51). New York: Praeger.

Elias, E.R., & Sadeghi-Nejad, A. (1994). Precocious puberty in girls with myelodysplasia. *Pediatrics, 93,* 521–522.

Ellsworth, P.I., Merguerian, P.A., Klein, R.B., et al. (1993). Evaluation and risk factors of latex allergy in spina bifida patients: Is it preventable? *The Journal of Urology, 150,* 691–693.

Emans, J.B. (1992). Allergy to latex in patients who have myelodysplasia. *Journal of Bone and Joint Surgery, 74*(A), 1103–1109.

Ennever, F.K., & Lave, L.B. (1995). Parent preferences and prenatal testing for neural tube defects. *Epidemiology, 6,* 8–16.

Ergun, R., Akdemir, G., Gezici, A.R., et al. (2000). Surgical management of syringomyelia-Chiari complex. *European Spine Journal, 9,* 553–557.

Erikson, E.H. (1959). Identity and the life cycle. *Psychological Issues, 1,* 1–171.

Feuchtbaum, L.B., Currier, R.J., Riggle, S., et al. (1999). Neural tube defect prevalence in California (1990–1994): Eliciting patterns by type of defect and maternal race/ethnicity. *Genetic Testing, 3,* 265–272.

Fletcher, J.M., Brookshire, B.L., Landry, S.H., et al. (1996). Attentional skills and executive functions in children with early hydrocephalus. *Developmental Neuropsychology, 12,* 53–76.

Folate status in women of childbearing age—United States, 1999. (2000). *MMWR, 49* (42), 962–965.

Forrester, M.B., & Merz, R.D. (2000). Prenatal diagnosis and elective termination of neural tube defects in Hawaii, 1986–1997. *Fetal Diagnosis and Therapy, 15,* 146–151.

Friedrich, W.N., Lovejoy, M.C., Shaffer, J., et al. (1991). Cognitive abilities and achievement status of children with myelomeningocele: A contemporary sample. *Journal of Pediatric Psychology, 16,* 423–428.

Game, X., Villers, A., Malavaud, B., et al. (1999). Bladder cancer arising in a spina bifida patient [Electronic version]. *Urology, 54,* 923.

Gilbert, J.N., Jones, K.L., Rorke, L.B., et al. (1986). Central nervous system anomalies associated with meningomyelocele, hydrocephalus, and the Arnold-Chiari malformation: Reappraisal of theories regarding the pathogenesis of posterior neural tube closure defects. *Neurosurgery, 18,* 559–564.

Golden, J., & Chernoff, G.F. (1995). Multiple sites of anterior neural tube closure in humans: Evidence from anterior neural tube defects (anencephaly). *Pediatrics, 95,* 506–510.

Graf, W.D., & Oleinik, O.E. (2000). The study of neural tube defects after the Human Genome Project and folic acid fortification of foods. *European Journal of Pediatric Surgery, 10*(Suppl. 1), 9–12.

Griebel, M.L., Oakes, W.J., & Worley, G. (1991). The Chiari malformation associated with meningomyelocele. In H.L. Rekate (Ed.), *Comprehensive management of spina bifida* (pp. 67–92). Boca Raton, FL: CRC Press.

Guidera, K.J., Smith, S., Raney, E., et al. (1993). Use of the reciprocating gait orthosis in myelodysplasia. *Journal of Pediatric Orthopography, 13*, 341–348.

Guys, J.M., Simeoni-Alias, J., Fakhro, A., et al. (1999). Use of polydimethylsiloxane for endoscopic treatment of neurogenic urinary incontinence in children. *The Journal of Urology, 162*, 2133–2135.

Hall, J.G., Friedman, J.M., Kenna, B.A., et al. (1988). Clinical, genetic, and epidemiological factors in neural tube defects. *American Journal of Human Genetics, 43*, 827–837.

Hall, J.G., & Solehdin, F. (1998). Genetics of neural tube defects. *Mental Retardation and Developmental Disabilities Research Reviews, 4*, 269–281.

Hayden, P.W. (1985). Adolescents with meningomyelocele. *Pediatrics in Review, 6*, 245–252.

Hendricks, K.A., Simpson, J.S., & Larsen, R.D. (1999). Neural tube defects along the Texas–Mexico border, 1993–1995. *American Journal of Epidemiology, 149*, 1119–1127.

Hochhaus, F., Butenandt, O., & Ring-Mrozik, E. J. (1999). One-year treatment with recombinant human growth hormone of children with meningomyelocele and growth hormone deficiency: A comparison of supine length and arm span. *Journal of Pediatric Endocrinology and Metabolism, 12*, 153–159.

Holzbeierlein, J., Pope, J.C., IV, Adams, M.C., et al. (2000). The urodynamic profile of myelodysplasia in childhood with spinal closure during gestation. *The Journal of Urology, 164*, 1336–1339.

Hommeyer, J.S., Holmbeck, G.N., Wills, K.E., et al. (1999). Condition severity and psychosocial functioning in preadolescents with spina bifida: Disentangling proximal functional status and distal adjustment outcomes. *Journal of Pediatric Psychology, 24*, 499–509.

Honein, M.A., Paulozzi, L.J., Mathews, M.S., et al. (2001). Impact of folic acid fortification of the US food supply on the occurrence of neural tube defects. *Journal of the American Medical Association, 285*, 2981–2986.

Hook, E.B. (1982). Incidence and prevalence as measures of the frequency of birth defects. *American Journal of Epidemiology, 116*, 743–747.

Hoving, E.W. (2000). Nasal encephaloceles. *Child's Nervous System, 16*, 702–706.

Hultling, C., Levi, R., Amark, S.P., et al. (2000). Semen retrieval and analysis in men with myelomeningocele. *Developmental Medicine and Child Neurology, 42*(10), 681–684.

Hulton, S.A., Thomson, P.D., Milner, L.S., et al. (1990). The pattern of congenital renal anomalies associated with neural tube defects. *Pediatric Nephrology, 4*, 491–492.

Hunt, G.M. (1990). Open spina bifida: Outcome for a complete cohort treated unselectively and followed into adulthood. *Developmental Medicine and Child Neurology, 32*, 108–118.

Hunt, G.M. (1999). The Casey Holter lecture. Non-selective intervention in newborn babies with open spina bifida: The outcome 30 years on for the complete cohort. *European Journal of Pediatric Surgery, 9*(Suppl. 1), 5–8.

Hunt, G.M., & Poulton, A. (1995). Open spina bifida: A complete cohort reviewed 25 years after closure. *Developmental Medicine and Child Neurology, 37*, 19–29.

Hurley, A.D. (1993). Conducting psychological assessments. In F.L. Rowley-Kelly & D.H. Reigel (Eds.), *Teaching the student with spina bifida* (pp. 107–123). Baltimore: Paul H. Brookes Publishing Co.

Johnson, W.G., Stenroos, E.S., Heath, S.C., et al. (1999). Distribution of alleles of the methylenetetrahydrofolate reductase (MTHFR) C677T gene polymorphism in familial spina bifida. *American Journal of Medical Genetics, 87*, 407–412.

Jumper, B.M., McLorie, G.A., Churchill, B.M., et al. (1990). Effects of the artificial urinary sphincter on prostatic development and sexual function in pubertal boys with meningomyelocele. *The Journal of Urology, 144*, 438–442.

Juriloff, D.M., & Harris, M.J. (1998). Animal models of neural tube defects. *Mental Retardation and Developmental Disabilities Research Reviews, 4*, 254–263.

Juriloff, D.M., & Harris, M.J. (2000). Mouse models for neural tube closure defects. *Human Molecular Genetics, 9*, 993–1000.

Kappy, M.S., Stuart, T., & Perelman, A. (1988). Efficacy of leuprolide therapy in children with central precocious puberty. *American Journal of Diseases of Children, 142*, 1061–1064.

Karol, L.A. (1995). Orthopedic management in myelomeningocele. *Neurosurgery Clinics of North America, 6*, 259–268.

Keating, M.A., Rink, R.C., & Adams, M.C. (1993). Appendicovesicostomy: A useful adjunct to continent reconstruction of the bladder. *The Journal of Urology, 149*, 1091–1094.

Kim, E.D., & McVary, K.T. (1995). Topical prostaglandin-E1 for the treatment of erectile dysfunction. *The Journal of Urology, 153*, 1828–1830.

Kim, S.K., Wang, K.C., & Cho, B.K. (2000). Surgical outcome of pediatric hydrocephalus treated by endoscopic III ventriculostomy: Prognostic factors and interpretation of postoperative neuroimaging. *Child's Nervous System, 16*, 161–168; discussion 169.

Kirk, V.G., Morielli, A., & Brouillette, R.T. (1999). Sleep-disordered breathing in patients with myelomeningocele: The missed diagnosis. *Developmental Medicine and Child Neurology, 41*, 40–43.

Kirk, V.G., Morielli, A., Gozal, D., et al. (2000). Treatment of sleep-disordered breathing in children with myelomeningocele. *Pediatric Pulmonology, 30*, 445–452.

Knowledge and use of folic acid by women of childbearing age—United States, 1997. (1997). *MMWR, 46* (31), 721–723.

Krahn, C.G., & Johnson, H.W. (1993). Cutaneous vesicostomy in the young child: Indications and results. *Urology, 41*, 558–563.

Kriss, V.M., & Desai, N.S. (1998). Occult spinal dysraphism in neonates: Assessment of high-risk cutaneous stigmata on sonography. *AJR. American Journal of Roentgenology, 171*, 1687–1692.

Kryger, J.V., Spencer Barthold, J., & Fleming, P., et al. (1999). The outcome of artificial urinary sphincter placement after a mean 15-year follow-up in a paediatric population. *BJU International, 83*, 1026–1031.

Kulkarni, A.V., Rabin, D., Lamberti-Pasculli, M., et al. (2001). Repeat cerebrospinal fluid shunt infection in children. *Pediatric Neurosurgery, 35*, 66–71.

Lakkis, M.M., Golden, J.A., O'Shea, K.S., et al. (1999). Neurofibromin deficiency in mice causes exencephaly and is a modifier for Splotch neural tube defects. *Developmental Biology, 212*, 80–92.

Leibold, S., Ekmark, E., & Adams, R.C. (2000). Decision-making for a successful bowel continence program. *European Journal of Pediatric Surgery, 10*(Suppl. 1), 26–30.

Lennerstrand, G., Gallo, J.E., & Samuelsson, L. (1990). Neuro-ophthalmological findings in relation to CNS lesions in patients with myelomeningocele. *Developmental Medicine and Child Neurology, 32,* 423–431.

Levy, L.M. (1999). MR imaging of cerebrospinal fluid flow and spinal cord motion in neurologic disorders of the spine. *Magnetic Resonance Imaging Clinics of North America, 7,* 573–587.

Li, J., Liu, K.C., Jin, F., et al. (1999). Transgenic rescue of congenital heart disease and spina bifida in Splotch mice. *Development, 126,* 2495–2503.

Lintner, S.A., & Lindseth, R.E. (1994). Kyphotic deformity in patients who have a myelomeningocele. *Journal of Bone and Joint Surgery, 76*(A), 1301–1307.

Liptak, G.S. (1996). Tethered spinal cord: Update of an analysis of published articles. *European Journal of Pediatric Surgery, 5,* 21–23.

Liptak, G.S. (1998). Controversies in the treatment of neural tube defects with neurological deterioration. *Mental Retardation and Developmental Disabilities Research Reviews, 4,* 296–301.

Liptak, G.S., & McDonald, J. (1985–1986). Ventriculoperitoneal shunts in children with hydrocephalus: Factors affecting shunt survival. *Pediatric Neuroscience, 12,* 289–293.

Liptak, G.S., & Revell, G.M. (1992). Management of bowel dysfunction in children with spinal cord disease or injury by means of the enema continence catheter. *Journal of Pediatrics, 120,* 190–194.

Liptak, G.S., Shurtleff, D.B., Bloss, J.W., et al. (1992). Mobility aids in children with high-level meningomyelocele: Parapodium versus wheelchair. *Developmental Medicine and Child Neurology, 34,* 787–796.

Liu, S.L., Shurtleff, D.B., Ellenbogen, R.G., et al. (1999). 19-year follow-up of fetal myelomeningocele brought to term. *European Journal of Pediatric Surgery, 9*(Suppl. 1), 12–14.

MacKinnon, A.E., Roberts, J.P., & Searles, J. (2000). Day-care ultrasound avoids urodynamics. *European Journal of Pediatric Surgery, 10*(Suppl. 1), 24–25.

Main, D.M., & Mennuti, M.T. (1986). Neural tube defects: Issues in prenatal diagnosis and counselling. *Obstetrics and Gynecology, 67,* 1–16.

Manning, S.M., Jennings, R., & Madsen, J.R. (2000). Pathophysiology, prevention and potential treatment of neural tube defects. *Mental Retardation and Developmental Disabilities Research Reviews, 6,* 6–14.

Martinez-Lage, J.F., Poza, M., Sola, J., et al. (1996). The child with a cephalocele: Etiology, neuroimaging, and outcome. *Child's Nervous System, 12,* 540–550.

Mataro, M., Poca, M.A., Sahuquillo, J., et al. (2000). Cognitive changes after cerebrospinal fluid shunting in young adults with spina bifida and assumed arrested hydrocephalus. *Journal of Neurology, Neurosurgery, and Psychiatry, 68,* 615–621.

Mayfield, J.K. (1991). Comprehensive orthopedic management in meningomyelocele. In H.L. Rekate (Ed.), *Comprehensive management of spina bifida* (pp. 113–163). Boca Raton, FL: CRC Press.

Mazon, A., Nieto, A., Linana, J.J., et al. (2000). Latex sensitization in children with spina bifida: Follow-up comparative study after two years. *Annals of Allergy, Asthma and Immunology, 84,* 207–210.

Mazur, J.M., Stillwell, A., & Menelaus, M. (1986). The significance of spasticity in the upper and lower limbs in myelomeningocele. *Journal of Bone and Joint Surgery, British Volume, 68,* 213–217.

McDonald, C.M. (1995). Rehabilitation of children with

spinal dysraphism. *Neurosurgery Clinics of North America, 6,* 393.

McDonald, C.M., Jaffe, K.M., Mosca, V.S., et al. (1991). Ambulatory outcome of children with myelomeningocele: Effect of lower extremity muscle strength. *Developmental Medicine and Child Neurology, 33,* 482–490.

McDonnell, R.J., Johnson, Z., Delaney, V., et al. (1999). East Ireland 1980–1994: Epidemiology of neural tube defects. *Journal of Epidemiology and Community Health, 53,* 782–788.

McLone, D.G. (1989). Spina bifida today: Problems adults face. *Seminars in Neurology, 9,* 169–175.

McLone, D.G. (1992). Continuing concepts in the management of spina bifida. *Pediatric Neurosurgery, 18,* 254–256.

Merrill, D.C., Goodwin, P., Burson, J.M., et al. (1998). The optimal route of delivery for fetal meningomyelocele. *American Journal of Obstetrics and Gynecology, 179,* 235–240.

Meuli, M., Meuli-Simmen, C., Hutchins G.M., et al. (1995). In utero surgery rescues neurological function at birth in sheep with spina bifida. *Nature Medicine, 1,* 142–147.

Moskowitz, D., Shurtleff, D.B., Weinberger, E., et al. (1998). Anatomy of the spinal cord in patients with meningomyelocele with and without hypoplasia or hydromyelia. *European Journal of Pediatric Surgery, 8*(Suppl. 1), 18–21.

Motulsky, A.G. (1996). Nutritional ecogenetics: Homocysteine-related arteriosclerotic vascular disease, neural tube defects, and folic acid. *American Journal of Human Genetics, 58,* 17–20.

MRC Vitamin Study Research Group. (1991). Prevention of neural tube defects: Results of the Medical Research Council Vitamin Study. *Lancet, 338,* 131–137.

Nagarkatti, D.G., Banta, J.V., & Thomson, J.D. (2000). Charcot arthropathy in spina bifida. *Journal of Pediatric Orthopedics, 20,* 82–87.

Nieto, A., Mazon, A., Estornell, F., et al. (2000). The search of latex sensitization in spina bifida: Diagnostic approach. *Clinical and Experimental Allergy, 30,* 264–269.

Noetzel, M.J. (1989). Meningomyelocele: Current concepts of management. *Clinics in Perinatology, 16,* 311–329.

Nye, J.S., McLone, D.G., Charrow, J., et al. (1999). Neural crest anomaly syndromes in children with spina bifida. *Teratology, 60,* 179–189.

Oi, S., & Matsumoto, S. (1992). A proposed grading and scoring system for spina bifida: Spina Bifida Neurological Scale (SBNS). *Child's Nervous System, 8,* 337–342.

Olney, R., & Mulinare, J. (1998). Epidemiology of neural tube defects. *Mental Retardation and Developmental Disabilities Research Reviews, 4,* 241–246.

Ounpuu, S., Thomson, J.D., Davis, R.B., et al. (2000). An examination of the knee function during gait in children with myelomeningocele. *Journal of Pediatric Orthopedics, 20,* 629–635.

Palmer, J.S., Kaplan, W.E., & Firlit, C.F. (1999). Erectile dysfunction in spina bifida is treatable. *Lancet, 354,* 125–126.

Park, T.S., Hoffman, H.J., Hendrick, E.B., et al. (1983). Experience with surgical decompression of the Arnold-Chiari malformation in young infants with myelomeningocele. *Neurosurgery, 13,* 147–152.

Parsch, K. (1991). Origin and treatment of fractures in spina bifida. *European Journal of Pediatric Surgery, 1,* 298–305.

Pearson, M.L., Cole, J.S., & Jarvis, W.R. (1994). How common is latex allergy?: A survey of children with myelodysplasia. *Developmental Medicine and Child Neurology, 36,* 64–69.

Pierz, K., Banta, J., Thomson, J., et al. (2000). The effect of tethered cord release on scoliosis in myelomeningocele. *Journal of Pediatric Orthopedics, 20,* 362–365.

Polito, C., DelGaizo, G., DiManso, D., et al. (1995). Children with myelomeningocele have shorter stature, greater body weight, and lower bone mineral content than healthy children. *Nutrition Research, 15,* 161–162.

Pollack, I.F., Kinnunen, D., & Albright, A.L. (1996). The effect of early craniocervical decompression on functional outcome in neonates and young infants with myelodysplasia and symptomatic Chiari II malformations: Results from a prospective series. *Neurosurgery, 38,* 703–710.

Pollack, I.F., Pang, D., Albright, A.L., et al. (1992). Outcome following hindbrain decompression of symptomatic Chiari malformations in children previously treated with myelomeningocele closure and shunts. *Journal of Neurosurgery, 77,* 881–888.

Powell, B., & Garvey, M. (1984). Complications of maternal spina bifida. *Irish Journal of Medical Science, 153,* 20–21.

Rankin, J., Glinianaia, S., Brown, R., et al. (2000). The changing prevalence of neural tube defects: A population-based study in the north of England, 1984–96. Northern Congenital Abnormality Survey Steering Group. *Paediatric and Perinatal Epidemiology, 14,* 104–110.

Rauzzino, M., & Oakes, W.J. (1995). Chiari II malformation and syringomyelia. *Neurosurgery Clinics of North America, 6,* 293–309.

Rinck, C., Berg, J., & Hafeman, C. (1989). The adolescent with meningomyelocele: A review of parent experiences and expectations. *Adolescence, 24,* 699–710.

Roberts, A., & Evans, G.A. (1993). Orthopedic aspects of neuromuscular disorders in children. *Current Opinion in Pediatrics, 5,* 379–383.

Roberts, H.E., Moore, C.A., Cragan, J.D., et al. (1995). Impact of prenatal diagnosis on the birth prevalence of neural tube defects, Atlanta, 1990–1991. *Pediatrics, 96,* 880–883.

Roberts, J.P., Broadley, P., Searles, J., et al. (1999). Percutaneous tube caecostomy for antegrade continence enema (ACE). *European Journal of Pediatric Surgery, 9*(Suppl 1.), 47–48.

Rotenstein, D., Adams, M., & Reigel, D.H. (1995). Adult stature and anthropomorphic measurement of patients with myelomeningocele. *European Journal of Pediatrics, 154,* 398–402.

Rourke, B. (1995). *Syndrome of nonverbal learning disabilities: Neurodevelopmental manifestations.* New York: Guilford Press.

Rowley-Kelly, F.L., & Reigel, D.H. (Eds.). (1993). *Teaching the student with spina bifida.* Baltimore: Paul H. Brookes Publishing Co.

Sadler, L.S., Robinson, L.K., & Msall, M.E. (1995). Diabetic embryopathy: Possible pathogenesis. *American Journal of Medical Genetics, 55,* 363–366.

Satar, N., Bauer, S.B., Shefner, J., et al. (1995). The effects of delayed diagnosis and treatment in patients with an occult spinal dysraphism. *The Journal of Urology, 154,* 754–758.

Sawyer, S.M., & Roberts, K.V. (1999). Sexual and reproductive health in young people with spina bifida. *Developmental Medicine and Child Neurology, 41,* 671–675.

Schader, I., & Corwin, P. (1999). How many pregnant women in Christchurch are using folic acid supplements in early pregnancy? *The New Zealand Medical Journal, 112,* 463–465.

Scott, J.M., Weir, D.G., Molloy, A., et al. (1994). Folic acid metabolism and mechanisms of neural tube defects. *Ciba Foundation Symposium, 181,* 180–187.

Shaw, G.M., Todoroff, K., Finnell, R.H., et al. (2000). Spina bifida phenotypes in infants or fetuses of obese mothers. *Teratology, 61,* 376–381.

Shaw, G.M., Velie, E.M., & Schaffer, D. (1996). Risk of neural tube defect-affected pregnancies among obese women.

Journal of the American Medical Association, 275, 1093–1096.

Shaw, J., & Lewis, M.A. (1999). Bladder augmentation surgery—what about the malignant risk? *European Journal of Pediatric Surgery, 9*(Suppl. 1), 39–40.

Sherk, H.H., Uppal, G.S., Lane, G., et al. (1991). Treatment versus non-treatment of hip dislocations in ambulatory patients with meningomyelocele. *Developmental Medicine and Child Neurology, 33,* 491–494.

Shurtleff, D.B., & Lemire, R.J. (1995). Epidemiology, etiologic factors, and prenatal diagnosis of open spinal dysraphism. *Neurosurgery Clinics of North America, 6,* 183–193.

Shurtleff, D.B., Luthy, D.A., Nyberg, D.A., et al. (1994). Meningomyelocele: Management in utero and post natum. *Ciba Foundation Symposium, 181,* 270–280.

Snow, J.H. (1994). Memory functions for children with spina bifida: Assessment in rehabilitation and exceptionality. *Pediatrics, 1,* 20–27.

Sponseller, P.D., Young, A.T., Sarwark, J.F. (1999). Anterior only fusion for scoliosis in patients with myelomeningocele. *Clinical Orthopedics and Related Research, 364,* 117–124.

Squire, R., Kiely, E.M., Ransley, P.G., et al. (1993). The clinical application of the Malone antegrade colonic enema. *Journal of Pediatric Surgery, 28,* 1012–1015.

Steegers-Theunissen, R.P. (1995). Folate metabolism and neural tube defects: A review. *European Journal of Obstetrics, Gynecology, and Reproductive Biology, 61,* 39–48.

Steinbok, P., Irvine, B., Cochrane, D.D., et al. (1992). Long-term outcome and complications of children born with meningomyelocele. *Child's Nervous System, 8,* 92–96.

Stevenson, R.E., Allen, W.P., Pai, G.S., et al. (2000). Decline in prevalence of neural tube defects in a high-risk region of the United States. *Pediatrics, 106,* 677–683.

Sutherland, R.W., & Gonzales, E.T. (1999). Current management of the infant with myelomeningocele. *Current Opinion in Urology, 9,* 527–531.

Sutton, L.N., Adzick, N.S., Bilaniuk, L.T., et al. (1999). Improvement in hindbrain herniation demonstrated by serial fetal magnetic resonance imaging following fetal surgery for myelomeningocele. *Journal of the American Medical Association, 282,* 1826–1831.

Swank, M., & Dias, L. (1992). Myelomeningocele: A review of the orthopaedic aspects of 206 patients treated from birth with no selection criteria. *Developmental Medicine and Child Neurology, 34,* 1047–1052.

Thompson, S. (1997). *The source for nonverbal learning disorders,* East Moline, IL: LinguiSystems, Inc.

Tulipan, N., Bruner, J.P., Hernanz-Schulman, M., et al. (1999). Effect of intrauterine myelomeningocele repair on central nervous system structure and function. *Pediatric Neurosurgery, 31,* 183–188.

Tulipan, N., Hernanz-Schulman, M., Lowe, L.H., et al. (1999). Intrauterine myelomeningocele repair reverses preexisting hindbrain herniation. *Pediatric Neurosurgery, 31,* 137–142.

Urui, S., & Oi, S. (1995). Experimental study of embryogenesis of open spinal dysraphism. *Neurosurgery Clinics of North America, 6,* 195–202.

Van Allen, M.I., Kalousek, D.K., Chernoff, G.F., et al. (1993). Evidence for multi-site closure of the neural tube in humans. *American Journal of Medical Genetics, 47,* 723–743.

van der Put, N.M.J., Steegers-Theunissen, R.P.M., Frosst, P., et al. (1995). Mutated methylenetetrahydrofolate reductase as a risk factor for spina bifida. *Lancet, 346,* 1070–1071.

Vereecken, R.L. (1992). Bladder pressure and kidney function in children with myelomeningocele. *Paraplegia, 30,* 153–159.

Vivani, G.R., Raducan, V., Bednar, D.A., et al. (1993). Anterior and posterior spinal fusion: Comparison of one-stage and two-stage procedures. *Canadian Journal of Surgery, 36,* 468–473.

Waitzman, N.J., Romano, P.S., & Scheffler, R.M. (1994). Estimates of the economic costs of birth defects. *Inquiry, 31,* 188–205.

Webb, H.W., Barraza, M.A., Stevens, P.S., et al. (1998). Bowel dysfunction in spina bifida—an American experience with the ACE procedure. *European Journal of Pediatric Surgery, 8*(Suppl. 1), 37–38.

Werler, M.M., Shapiro, S., & Mitchell, A.A. (1993). Periconceptional folic acid exposure and risk of occurrent neural tube defects. *Journal of the American Medical Association, 269,* 1257–1261.

Westcott, M.A., Dynes, M.C., Remer, E.M., et al. (1992). Congenital and acquired orthopedic abnormalities in patients with myelomeningocele. *Radiographics, 12,* 1155–1173.

Whitelaw, A., Kennedy, C.R., & Brion, L.P. (2001). Diuretic therapy for newborn infants with posthemorrhagic ventricular dilatation (Cochrane Review). *Cochrane Database of Systematic Reviews, 2,* CD002270.

Williamson, G.G. (Ed.). (1987). *Children with spina bifida: Early intervention and preschool programming.* Baltimore: Paul H. Brookes Publishing Co.

Wills, K.E., Holmbeck, G.N., Dillon, K., et al. (1990). Intelligence and achievement in children with meningomyelocele. *Journal of Pediatric Psychology, 15,* 161–176.

Wood, J.M., Evans, P.E., Schallreuter, K.U., et al. (1993). A multicenter study of direct current for healing of chronic stage II and stage III decubitus ulcers. *Archives of Dermatology, 129,* 999–1009.

Worley, G., Schuster, J.M., & Oakes, W.J. (1996). Survival at 5 years of a cohort of newborn infants with myelomeningocele. *Developmental Medicine and Child Neurology, 38,* 816–822.

Yamada, S., Iacono, R.P., Andrade, T., et al. (1995). Pathophysiology of tethered cord syndrome. *Neurosurgery Clinics of North America, 6,* 311–324.

25 Epilepsy

Steven Weinstein

Upon completion of this chapter, the reader will:

- understand the physiological basis of seizures
- know how to recognize their differing manifestations
- be able to distinguish seizures from other paroxysmal events
- understand what is involved in the medical evaluation and therapy of seizure disorders
- be able to respond to family concerns about prognosis

Seizures occur frequently in childhood, with as many as 1 in 10 children having at least one event (Hauser, 1994; Kurtz, Tookey, & Ross, 1998). During the first years of life, the most common cause of an isolated seizure is a fever. Other acute seizures may be precipitated by acute illness (e.g., a metabolic disturbance, toxin ingestion), during an acute central nervous system infection (e.g., meningitis, encephalitis), or following a traumatic brain injury (Huang, Chang, & Wang, 1998). These individual provoked seizures must be distinguished from the condition of recurrent seizures, termed *epilepsy*. Thus, epilepsy is a chronic neurological condition of recurrent seizures occurring with or without other brain abnormalities.

JUANITA

Juanita's first seizure was a generalized tonic-clonic seizure. It was not associated with fever and occurred when she was 5 years old. A second seizure happened 2 weeks later. No immediate precipitant or neurological abnormality could be found. Juanita's electroencephalogram (EEG), however, was abnormal, showing focal spike and sharp waves. She was placed on carbamazepine (Tegretol) to control the seizures, but despite adequate levels of the medication, her seizures continued. Her family had difficulty coping with the problem, and they found it hard to give her the support and encouragement they knew she needed. Juanita felt ostracized at school; she was self-conscious about her disability and developed few friendships. Valproate (Depakote) was soon added to the carbamazepine, and her seizures became less frequent. Juanita's pediatrician, however, had difficulty achieving the desired drug level. Sometimes it was too high, and Juanita was lethargic; at other times, it was too low, and she had seizures. Finally, the right dosage was obtained and her seizures came under good control. When emotional problems for Juanita and her family persisted, they were referred to a social worker for family counseling. Juanita began to feel better about herself. Her parents developed ways of coping with her illness and began to handle the situation more effectively. At 8 years of age, Juanita is doing well in school. She now attends Brownie Girl Scouts and dancing classes; although still shy, she is making friends.

WHAT IS EPILEPSY AND WHAT IS A SEIZURE?

The word *epilepsy* is derived from a Greek word meaning *take hold of* or *to seize* (Reynolds, 2000). Indeed, the unusual behaviors observed during a seizure have led to the depiction of the patient as being "possessed." In earlier ages, individuals with epilepsy were shunned or exorcised in an attempt to let out the evil spirits. Although science and society have advanced, the stigma of epilepsy remains, and we still struggle to deal with these primitive perceptions (Reynolds, 2000).

Epilepsy is a chronic neurological condition with recurrent seizures that are an expression of an underlying brain abnormality. In contrast, a *seizure* really involves an abnormal **hypersynchronous** electrical discharge (excessive concurrent firing) of a cortical neuronal network (composed of cells on the surface of the brain). This results in the interruption of usual brain-generated electrical signals, leading to an abrupt change in the person's behavior. The seizure discharges and associated behaviors evolve over time, with a relatively rapid end and subsequent return to baseline (Shorvon, 2000). This evolution is useful in differentiating seizures from nonepileptic paroxysmal events (spells that abruptly interrupt the child's behavior but are not seizures), which superficially resemble epileptic seizures but are not associated with EEG abnormalities. This distinction is important because the causes of and treatments for each are different.

It should also be emphasized that the term *seizure* is not synonymous with *epilepsy*. A single seizure (one event of hypersynchronous electrical discharge) does not qualify an individual for the diagnosis of epilepsy. Indeed, the circumstances surrounding a first-time single seizure may have been so unique or have occurred during a specific developmental window such that it is unlikely to recur. The best example of this is a single **febrile** seizure in the preschool-age child. In contrast, epilepsy is an expression of a *chronic* neurological condition (brain dysfunction) of which one manifestation is recurrent seizures.

What Causes Seizures?

It is important to note that an acute brain insult has the potential to trigger a seizure in anyone. Not everyone, however, will suffer a seizure when presented with the same insult. This differing responsiveness is the result of genetic and acquired predisposition and of structural and chemical brain interactions (Briellmann et al., 2001; Prasad, Prasad, & Stafstrom, 1999). Together these factors establish the **seizure threshold** (the level of brain vulnerability that produces seizures in response to known or unknown triggers; Frucht et al., 2000). Because children with epilepsy are not continuously seizing, however, episodic and transitory internal and external influences that lower the seizure threshold must exist. Furthermore, the stage of brain development influences this threshold altering the probability of a seizure resulting from a triggering event at a specific age. The change in brain structure and function over time may explain why some children appear to grow into as well as outgrow epilepsy (Sillanpää, 2000).

Brain Development and the Origins of Epilepsy

Understanding brain development is important in studying epilepsy (Moshé, 2000b). It is within the context of the brain's orderly formation and any subsequent damage (and associated repair mechanisms) that seizures as well as behavioral, motor, and cognitive abnormalities may occur. This development is a dynamic process that continues beyond intrauterine life and, as has been recently shown, persists even into old age (Gage, 2002). Not only does the brain undergo visually obvious alterations in brain structure, but there are also developmental changes in brain chemistry, both in terms of what neurotransmitters are released and how other cells respond to them (Kriegstein, Owens, & Avoli, 1999). Alterations in normal brain development, structure, or chemistry can disrupt the subsequent cascade of normal brain maturation (Lowenstein & Alldredge, 1998). In addition, reparative mechanisms following certain brain injuries can potentially lead to the production of abnormal neuronal networks that predispose to seizure activity (Cole, 2000). (See Chapter 26 for a discussion of seizures following traumatic brain injury.)

Neuronal Transmission and Seizures

Neurons and supporting glial cells are connected in networks, with individual cells generating an electrical charge. As with batteries, chemical changes within the neuron generate direct current electrical fields, with superimposed rapid alternating current changes. A gradient of **ionic** concentrations (e.g., sodium, potassium, chloride) across the cell membrane produces internal electrical negativity that, when altered, allows for the transfer of information from one neuron to another. This resting electrical potential can be perturbed, leading to a discharge or firing (action potential) and the release of ions and neurotransmitters, which produce communication within connected network neurons. The probability that this will occur is influenced by a number of factors, such as the neighboring environment (the electrolyte concentration outside the cell) and the intrinsic qualities of the specific cell.

Neurotransmitters can be either inhibitory (making neurons less likely to fire) or excitatory (making neurons more likely to discharge). In response to the neurotransmitter, the postsynaptic neuron (the neuron receiving the signal) may then undergo chemical and electrical changes influencing other cells. As there are many connections between individual neurons, the likelihood of any neuron's being recruited to fire results from the summation of excitatory and inhibitory influences of neighboring neurons. This process is essential for typical brain functioning, producing interaction between cells and allowing motor, sensory, and memory processes to occur (Kandel, Schwartz, & Jessell, 2000).

During a seizure, the network begins to fire abnormally, producing an early, seemingly excessively synchronous discharge. At times this occurs with the simultaneous involvement or subsequent recruitment of an increasingly larger population of surrounding cortical neurons. The abnormal firing will continue until it is extinguished by inhibitory neurochemical influences or until the excitatory neurochemicals are depleted. The seizure usually subsides in seconds to minutes but in some instances will not stop spontaneously, producing a condition called *status epilepticus* (discussed later).

The area of the brain triggering the seizure determines its initial manifestations. When not producing seizures, the involved region has a variety of specific functions, such as vision, sensation, motor activity, or memory. As a result, the initial **ictal** activity (i.e., electrical hypersynchronous discharge in the brain) produces signs and symptoms typical of the brain area from which it arises. This is a simple partial seizure (discussed later) and may produce unusual sensations, an aura (a subjective sensation that precedes or marks the beginning of a seizure), or abnormal motor activity (e.g., jerking, assuming an abnormal posture). As the electrical discharge spreads within the brain, the clinical expression changes. As additional neurons are recruited, there is a progressive alteration of consciousness that is frequently associated with **automatisms** (e.g., staring, fumbling, picking at clothing) and is known as a complex partial seizure (discussed later). When the entire brain becomes maximally involved, the result is a generalized tonic-clonic seizure (discussed later; Risinger, 2000).

The ability of the brain to confine the abnormal electrical discharge to a limited area (called *surround inhibition*) and its capacity to extinguish the seizure perhaps explain the limited spread and duration of most seizures. The promotion of surround inhibition is yet another target for intervention. Some children, however, have defective inhibitory abilities. This results in consistent electrical spread, leading to recurrent tonic-clonic events and status epilepticus. The child's developmental age, underlying brain pathology, nature of the seizure trigger, presence of antiepileptic drugs (AEDs), and genetic background all influence the potential for developing status epilepticus (Prasad et al., 1999).

Do Seizures Hurt the Brain?

The consequences of these electrical events and the associated clinical seizures are hotly debated (Camfield, 1997; Wasterlain, 1997). Although the frequently observed cyanosis (blueness from ineffective breathing) in tonic-clonic seizures is frightening, it is the chemical changes in the brain during the seizure that are of the greatest theoretical concern. Overexcitation of neurons from specific amino acids are of particular concern. These changes may increase the likelihood of additional seizures and possibly lead to cognitive and behavioral abnormalities.

Children with epilepsy frequently have concomitant learning and behavior difficulties that are often attributed to either the seizures or the AED used to treat them. Evidence is accumulating, however, that these difficulties may actually predate the onset of the seizures, and that both the seizures and cognitive impairments are manifestations of the same underlying brain abnormality (Austin et al., 2001). This does not rule out that possibility that additional adverse effects may result from recurrent prolonged seizures (status epilepticus) or from very frequent shorter seizures. It is also unlikely that AEDs help to protect the brain from the process of pathological reorganization (epileptogenesis; Shinnar & Berg, 1994).

CLASSIFICATION OF SEIZURES AND EPILEPSY SYNDROMES

Seizures are commonly categorized as either having an apparently *generalized* onset (simultaneously involving widely spread cortical regions over both brain hemispheres) or having a *partial* onset (starting in one limited brain region with variable degrees of spread). This distinction is important in guiding the diagnostic evaluation and prescribing appropriate therapy. Yet, confusion often arises in classification for a number of reasons: 1) The onset of the seizure is often not observed, 2) the child has no memory of the event, 3) the seizure spread is extremely rapid and the focal signs may be lost among the associated dramatic behaviors, and 4) the parents may be overwhelmed by the experience and unable to discern the subtleties of the seizure presentation. Fortunately, the nature of the seizure onset can often be inferred by the **interictal** (between-seizure) EEG (Panayiotopoulos, 1999a). In addition, after additional experience with the seizures, parents and other caregivers become better observers.

The International League Against Epilepsy has attempted to improve communication among physicians and patients with a classification system for both seizures and epilepsy syndromes. The next sections do not precisely follow this system but describe the major events that may be witnessed (Delgado-Escueta et al., 1999).

Seizure Types

Seizures with Primarily Altered Consciousness

Primarily Generalized Seizures   Primarily generalized seizures do not have a recognizable focus of onset; large areas of each cortex (see Chapter 13) appear to be simultaneously affected. During a generalized seizure, the child may have a paucity of activity (*absence seizures*) or at times vigorous abnormal motor behaviors (myoclonic, **atonic,** and tonic-clonic seizures). The underlying cause is often a metabolic disorder or a genetic predisposition, leading to neurochemical or receptor alterations in cortical neurons or glia (Seyfried, Todorova, & Poderycki, 1999). Similar mechanisms underlie certain unusual familial epilepsies called *channelopathies* (a genetic abnormality in a "gate" that controls ion flow into the neuron; Bate & Gardiner, 1999). The regulation of ion channels (e.g., sodium, potassium, possibly calcium) is impaired, resulting in altered neurochemical transmission. This predisposes the child to febrile convulsions and to other generalized seizures (Singh et al., 1999).

Absence Seizures (Primarily Generalized Seizures)   Absence seizures (previously called *petit mal*; Table 25.1) are among the most benign seizure types and appear to arise simultaneously in broad regions of the brain (generalized). They are often inherited, and the onset is usually between 3 and 12 years of age. They have a different underlying neurochemical basis than other seizures. Although most seizures are associated with both behavioral and electrical hyperexcitability, absence seizures appear to be inhibitory in nature (Parker et al., 1998). The neurochemical origin of absence epilepsy appears to involve excessive activity of the inhibitory neurotransmitter GABA (gamma-aminobutyric acid; Hu, Banerjee, & Snead, 2000). Scientific support for this mechanism includes the observation that vigabatrin (discussed later), an AED that increases GABA activity, increases absence seizures (Parker et al., 1998).

The absence seizure is characterized by a brief (usually less than 30 seconds) behavioral arrest with impaired consciousness during which time a typical 3-hertz spike and wave discharge occurs on EEG. The child may continue to perform a simple activity such as walking or looking at something, but he or she is unable to rapidly respond to a novel situation such as reading. Rarely is the behavior arrest just a motionless blank stare; there is usually a glazed eye appearance, associated eye blinks, and/or changes in head and extremity tone. Unlike simple daydreaming, however, absence seizures cannot be interrupted by verbal or tactile (touch) stimulation (Loiseau, 1992). Furthermore, they may evolve into generalized tonic-clonic seizures (Mayville, Fakhoury, & Abou-Khalil, 2000). Untreated, these episodes can occur hundreds of times during the day and may significantly interfere with learning. In addition, absence seizures can be a physical hazard as the child may continue walking, unaware, into a busy street or down steps, and become injured. If absence seizures last longer (more than 30 seconds) or are associated with prominent motor activity, they may be but one aspect of an epilepsy syndrome, such as juvenile myoclonic epilepsy (JME) or atypical absence epilepsy (both discussed later).

Simple and Complex Partial Seizures

Partial seizures are the most common type of seizure disorder, accounting for almost 60% of all cases (Eriksson & Koivikko, 1997). Partial seizures may arise not only in the motor control centers of the brain but also in areas involved in sensory, behavioral, and cognitive functions (Figure 25.1). These seizures often start with auras and/or abrupt unprovoked alterations in behavior. Given that most children will have a single region of seizure onset, these feelings/behaviors will be stereotyped with little variation from one episode to another. This helps to distinguish them from other nonseizure phenomena for which typically a provocation can be identified (e.g., temper tantrum). When the electrical event is limited to a small region of one cortical hemisphere, with maintenance of normal alertness, it is categorized as a *simple seizure*. If the event is merely sensory in nature, it is called an *aura*. If the seizure spreads to the other hemisphere, altering consciousness, it is called a *complex partial seizure* (previously called *psychomotor* or *temporal lobe seizure*). This type of seizure may occur with or without subsequent evolution, or **secondary** generalization, into a tonic-clonic motor seizure.

Table 25.1. Comparison of complex partial seizures and absence seizures

	Complex partial	Absence
Incidence	Common	Uncommon
Duration	30 seconds to 5 minutes	Less than 30 seconds
Frequency of occurrence	Occasional	Multiple times daily
Aura	Yes	No
Consciousness	Partial amnesia and confusion	Immediate return to consciousness
EEG pattern	Focal	Generalized

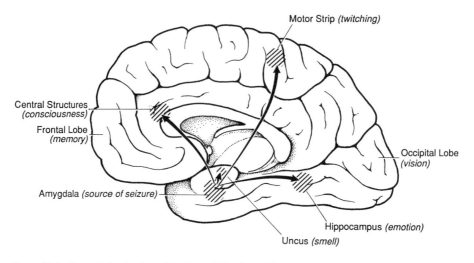

Figure 25.1. Spread of a simple partial seizure. A simple partial seizure may begin anywhere—in this case in the amygdala of the temporal lobe. The initial feature may be the child's smelling an unusual odor. The seizure may stop there or project out to the hippocampus, which might trigger feelings of fearfulness or abdominal queasiness. Memory and visual perception may be affected if the frontal or occipital lobe is involved. The seizure might ultimately extend to the motor strip, resulting in twitching of a limb, which may spread to other limbs or to central structures (causing loss of consciousness), thus becoming a complex partial seizure. Finally, the seizure may cross the corpus callosum to the other cerebral hemisphere and thus be converted from a partial to a generalized seizure.

During a complex partial seizure, the abnormal electrical disturbance in the brain causes the child's movements to become purposeless and slowed. Even though motor activity may be diminished, there is frequently eye blinking, lip smacking, facial grimacing, groaning, chewing, unbuttoning and buttoning of clothing, or other motor automatisms. In addition, depending upon the site of seizure onset, the child may on occasion appear agitated. The seizures associated with agitation occur frequently during sleep and can be misinterpreted as night terrors or, if during the day, as aberrant behavior. Violent, directed aggression rarely occurs, but due to confusion the child may strike out at someone who comes too close during the seizure or **postictal** period. The signs and symptoms of complex partial seizures are caused by the brain's impaired ability to rapidly plan motor activities and process environmental stimuli; the signs also provide clues to the region of seizure onset (Risinger, 2000).

Seizures with Prominent Motor Manifestations

Seizures that involve motor manifestations are caused by a different mechanism than what causes absence seizures. Rather than being inhibitory, these seizures involve mechanisms of excessive excitation of the neuronal network (McCormick & Contreras, 2001). It is postulated that specific channels are opened by the excitatory amino acids glutamate and aspartate, leading to an influx of calcium in amounts that exceed the normal protective buffering mechanisms and potentially cause neuronal damage (discussed later). Attempts at inhibiting this mechanism underlie certain of the new AEDs. These motor events, like seizures that primarily alter consciousness, can arise focally (partial seizure) or diffusely (primarily generalized seizure) and can be either brief or prolonged.

Myoclonic and Atonic Seizures   The briefest types of seizures with motor components include *myoclonic* and *atonic seizures.* Myoclonic seizures are lightning motor attacks, with sudden flexion or bending backward of the upper torso and head (Commission on Classification and Terminology of the International League Against Epilepsy, 1989). Some are subtle with just head nodding, whereas others appear to abruptly pull the child over. Myoclonic seizures, atonic seizures (which involve loss of muscle tone), and any other type of seizure that leads to an abrupt loss of posture compose a group called *drop seizures*. As consciousness is transiently impaired during these events, there is no attempt to protect oneself during the fall. Thus, there is a risk of the head striking the ground, and children with these kinds of seizures should wear a protective helmet throughout the day. Following these brief seizures, the child immediately regains consciousness, often crying, seemingly not in pain but upset by the sudden disruption. In infants, the seizures can occur in flurries of jerks with varying duration, frequently upon arousal and are categorized as *infantile spasms* (discussed later).

Tonic-Clonic Seizures   The tonic-clonic seizure (involving stiffening and shaking) is the most frightening seizure to observe and is what the public generally calls a *grand mal seizure* (Shorvon, 2000). It may arise focally (a partial seizure) or diffusely from both hemispheres (a generalized seizure). Clonic (repetitive jerking occurring at a regular rate) and tonic (sustained stiffening) seizures often occur within the same event. Clonic activity may be the initial manifestation of the seizure or may follow an aura or a tonic seizure. On occasion the seizure may spread from one portion of the brain to a contiguous area, producing a spread of the shaking to other body parts (called a *Jacksonian seizure*). Tonic seizures may also start in one area of the body (a partial seizure), or they may occur bilaterally, involving the trunk and extremities (a generalized seizure). If focal in onset, tonic or clonic seizures can be followed by a period of weakness on the initially involved body side (called *Todd's paralysis*). This may be misinterpreted by parents as a stroke (Szabó & Lüders, 2000).

Tonic-clonic seizures are the most common seizure type in children, accounting for about one quarter of seizures in individuals of any age (Kotagal, 2000). During the seizures observers frequently hear raspy respirations or see no respiratory effort at all and may mistakenly assume that the tongue has been swallowed. Tonic-clonic seizures are often associated with a unusual cry, cyanosis (blueness), and incontinence following the event. A period of sleep is required for recovery, and the individual usually has no memory of the event.

Status Epilepticus

Prolonged seizures (*status epilepticus*) occur infrequently with any seizure type but deserve special consideration. Such seizures have the potential to be life threatening and/or to lead to permanent pathological changes within the brain's structural organization. Status epilepticus is a "single seizure or cluster of seizures that is sufficiently prolonged or repeated at sufficiently brief intervals to produce an unvarying and enduring epileptic condition" (Gastaut, 1982). Although this definition does not establish a precise duration, most clinicians consider 15–30 minutes of continuous seizing or repetitive seizures without a full return of consciousness to represent status epilepticus (Lowenstein, 1999). There is evidence from animal models that irreversible changes in brain structure may occur as a result of status epilepticus (Fujikawa, Shinmei, & Cai, 2000). Death, however, is a rare consequence (Lhatoo et al., 2001). Status epilepticus should be considered a medical emergency and requires immediate diagnostic and therapeutic intervention (Moshé, 1998).

In terms of precipitants, status epilepticus can occur in a previously healthy infant or child as a result of hypoxic-ischemic injury (see Chapter 5), trauma, infection of the brain, stroke, and metabolic and toxic derangements. In a child known to have epilepsy, low AED levels can precipitate status epilepticus, whereas fever, migraine, meningitis or encephalitis, or toxin or chemical ingestion may produce seizures in otherwise typical children. Chronic brain disorders such as brain tumors, malformations, vascular anomalies, and progressive neurological disorders can also lead to episodes of status epilepticus. Finally, in some cases the cause remains unknown (Mizrahi & Clancy, 2000). In the emergency room, the physician will evaluate the child to exclude acute causes of the prolonged seizure; frequently a follow-up visit to a neurologist is indicated to exclude other underlying chronic disorders that could precipitate future episodes of status epilepticus.

Febrile Seizures

Febrile seizures are the most commonly witnessed seizures during childhood. They occur in approximately 5% of all children who are between the ages of 3 months and 5 years; they rarely appear at an older age (Nelson & Ellenberg, 1978; Figure 25.2). Febrile convulsions are generally seen with temperature elevations above 39 degrees Celsius (102 degrees Fahrenheit). Those that occur with lower temperatures are associated with an increased risk of subsequent febrile seizures (Berg et al., 1998). Upper respiratory illnesses, middle-ear infections, **gastroenteritis,** immunizations, and viruses associated with skin rashes (e.g., roseola) are known precipitants. Greater than 80% of all febrile seizures are brief, symmetric tonic or clonic-tonic-clonic events that occur once during an illness. These are called *simple febrile seizures;* in contrast, *complex febrile seizures* are prolonged, focal, and/or recurrent during a single illness (Hirtz, 1997). Complex febrile seizures are frequently of unknown cause, but a more aggressive evaluation than for simple febrile seizures may be undertaken to exclude a chronic encephalopthy or an acute central nervous system infection (e.g., meningitis, encephalitis).

After the first fever-provoked seizure, the risk of subsequent febrile seizures is 30%–50% depending upon the child's age at the time of the first seizure, a family history of febrile convulsions, and the intensity of the fever (Berg et al., 1992). The risk of developing epilepsy (recurrent seizures) by school age in a typically developing child is 1% following simple febrile seizures and 2%–3% following complex febrile seizures (Nelson & Ellenberg, 1976). The risk of developing epilepsy by adulthood may be somewhat higher (Berg & Shinnar, 1996). As many as 30%–50% of adults with intractable epilepsy due to scarring of the inner temporal lobe (a condition called *mesial temporal sclerosis*) have a history of febrile seizures (Bower et al., 2000). In addition, the risk of future epilepsy is increased in a child with a preexisting developmental disability (e.g., mental retardation, see Chapter 15; cerebral palsy, see Chapter 23) or with a family history of epilepsy (Nelson & Ellenberg, 1976). Risk should not influence the decision to treat (or not treat) with AEDs after a febrile seizure; although medications may pre-

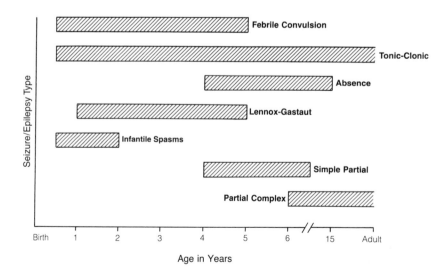

Figure 25.2.   Common ages of occurrence of various types of seizures.

vent subsequent febrile seizures, AEDs do not prevent the development of future epilepsy (Knudsen, 2000).

Benign Neonatal Convulsions

Neonates with seizures usually have significant brain or systemic disorders. There is a small subset of infants with seizures, however, who do not have a major illness; these infants are said to have benign neonatal convulsions. In this disorder the infant typically has seizures around the fifth day of life, but initial onset of seizures can occur anytime in the first 6 months of life. If there is a family history of other infants' having had a similar disorder, the underlying cause may be a channelopathy (Moulard, Buresi, & Malafosse, 2000). Regardless of the presence or absence of a family history, infants with benign neonatal convulsions subsequently develop normally, although a positive family history increases the risk of their subsequently developing epilepsy.

Epilepsy Syndromes

Epilepsy syndromes are seizure disorders characterized by specific clinical features and characteristic EEG findings. A constellation of information defines an epilepsy syndrome, including 1) age and genetic background, 2) neurological signs and symptoms, 3) clinical course, and 4) EEG findings (Wolf, 1994). A number of these syndromes are described next.

Benign Partial Seizures

If a seizure arises from one brain region, there is concern that an underlying structural abnormality (e.g., brain tumor) exists in that region. If brain imaging (e.g., magnetic resonance imaging [MRI], computed tomography [CT]; described later) fails to reveal any pathology, however, it is possible that the child actually has a benign epilepsy syndrome. Typically these seizures have their onset around the age of school entry and disappear by adolescence (Okumura et al., 2000). Rolandic epilepsy is the most common benign epilepsy syndrome of childhood. The seizures typically start in the region of the cortex that controls tongue, face, and hand movement and most commonly occur at sleep onset or arousal. When starting in sleep they may appear as a secondarily generalized tonic-clonic seizure, the partial onset having been unobserved (Lerman, 1992). Partial seizures that emanate from the occipital lobe frequently are associated with visual disturbances and can occasionally be triggered by entering or leaving a well-lit room. At night these seizures can simulate a migraine-like event, with vomiting and severe headache (Carballo et al., 2000). These benign partial epilepsy syndromes demonstrate a strong familial basis, with 30%–40% of near relatives having seizures (Neubauer, 2000). Usually these syndromes are unassociated with long-term sequelae (Fejerman, Caraballo, & Tenembaum, 2000).

Infantile Spasms and Other Myoclonic Epilepsy Syndromes

As mentioned before, **myoclonus** involves a sudden, brief, shock-like contraction of muscle. Not all involuntary muscle contractions, however, are myoclonus, and not all myoclonus represents an epileptic phenomenon. When myoclonus does have an epileptic basis, it is more often a reflection of a serious underlying disease (e.g., Tay-Sachs disease). A rare, transient, benign form of myoclonic epilepsy that occurs early in infancy is responsive to AEDs and does not lead to long-term cognitive impairments (Lin et al., 1998). This condition is strongly associated with a family history of epilepsy and has an EEG pattern that shows spike and polyspike and wave discharges.

A common myoclonic epilepsy is termed *infantile spasms*. It typically develops between 4 and 8 months of age, is difficult to control with AEDs, and often has a poor outcome (Shields,

2000). The seizures occur in flurries of flexor, extensor, or mixed jerks, typically occurring upon arousal but also sporadically throughout wakefulness. The jerks may happen in isolation, or they can occur with altered consciousness as a part of a complex partial seizure (which is termed a *facilitated spasm*; Kubota et al., 1999). The affected infant is generally lethargic, has poor visual fixation, and shows a plateauing or loss of developmental milestones. More than three quarters of these infants have a defined underlying disorder (Tramonte & Barron, 1998). The most common cause of infantile spasm is tuberous sclerosis (see Appendix B), but other etiologies include brain malformations (e.g., lissencephaly, Aicardi syndrome; see Appendix B), genetic syndromes (e.g., Down syndrome, see Chapter 15; PEHO syndrome [*p*rogressive encephalopathy with *e*dema, *h*ypsarrhythmia, and *o*ptic atrophy], see Riikonen, 2001), and inherited metabolic disorders (e.g., nonketotic hyperglycinemia; biotinidase deficiency, see Appendix B). Perinatal events causing brain injury, such as birth asphyxia and congenital infections (e.g., cytomegalovirus, see Chapter 3), also can predispose the infant to the development of infantile spasms. Infantile spasms frequently evolve into Lennox-Gastaut syndrome (described later).

A small percentage of infants have cryptogenic infantile spasms (i.e., infantile spasms caused by an underlying disorder that cannot be identified by present diagnostic techniques) and respond rapidly to therapy, do not develop Lennox-Gastaut syndrome, have normal development prior to spasm onset, and can have a good outcome. The EEGs of both spasm groups (cryptogenic and noncryptogenic) show hypsarrhythmia (a markedly disorganized EEG). Therapy aims to both normalize the EEG pattern and prevent further seizures.

Treatment with adrenocorticotropic hormone (ACTH), prescribed as an intramuscular gel preparation, often stops the spasms within days or weeks (Riikonen, 2000). AEDs have also been used as therapy, including valproate (Depakene, Depakote), phenobarbital (Luminal), lamotrigine (Lamictal), topiramate (Topamax), or clonazepam (Klonopin), and pyridoxine (vitamin B_6; Ito, 1998). A new AED, vigabatrin (Sabril), has also been found to be helpful in controlling infantile spasms, especially those associated with tuberous sclerosis (Jambaque et al., 2000). Although vigabatrin is available in Europe, the Food and Drug Administration (FDA) has not approved this drug for use in the United States because of its potential for producing myelin abnormalities (seen in numerous animal models) and retinal toxicity (seen in humans; Harding et al., 2000). In rare instances of infantile spasms, a single seizure focus can be identified and surgically removed (Shields et al., 1999).

Juvenile Myoclonic Epilepsy

JME can present as childhood absence seizures but is more commonly manifested in the adolescent as morning myoclonus. Medical attention for JME is frequently not sought until the child has a generalized tonic-clonic seizure following sleep deprivation or alcohol ingestion (Pedersen & Petersen, 1998). JME is a benign genetic disorder; there is neither an underlying brain disorder nor subsequent cognitive decline. The diagnosis of JME, however, is problematic. It is frequently underrecognized, leading to treatment with the wrong medication. Drugs used to treat generalized rather than partial seizures are indicated in JME (Montalenti et al., 2001; Wallace, 1998). In addition, the diagnosis commits the patient to a lifelong need for an AED.

Atypical Absence Epilepsy Syndromes

The onset of absence epilepsy syndromes is either in childhood or adolescence and may be the first sign of JME. Beyond the brief staring spells that are typical of absence seizures, these syndromes may be associated with generalized tonic-clonic seizures or with prominent myoclonus. Although still classified as forms of childhood absence epilepsy, atypical absence epilepsy syndromes have a worse prognosis (Wolf, 1992). These seizure types may also be present in Lennox-Gastaut and Landau-Kleffner syndromes.

Childhood Epileptic Degenerations with
Prominent Nocturnal Electroencephalographic Abnormality

Lennox-Gastaut Syndrome   In Lennox-Gastaut syndrome, which is associated with progressive encephalopathy, there are severe cognitive impairments and behavior disturbances. This syndrome is associated with the presence of multiple types of seizures, often evolving from infantile spasms, that occur throughout the day (Rantala & Putkonen, 1999). The seizure pattern involves tonic events during sleep coexisting with a mixture of daytime absence, drop (including myoclonic), tonic-clonic, and complex partial seizures. The EEG shows epileptiform activity that tends to be most frequent and widespread during non–rapid eye movement (NREM) sleep. Treatment of Lennox-Gastaut syndrome is difficult; and both seizure and EEG resolution appear to be necessary for improved cognitive and behavioral outcomes. There is some evidence that treatment with steroid medication is useful.

Landau-Kleffner Syndrome   In Landau-Kleffner syndrome and in acquired epileptic aphasia, both of which are also associated with progressive encephalopathy, the child experiences an isolated loss of language skills. The disorder is manifest by an auditory agnosia (inability to distinguish different sounds), language regression (or, rarely, inability to attain language skills), and behavioral disturbances that may resemble autism (see Chapter 20; Tuchman, 1997). Clinically evident seizures may not even be part of this syndrome's expression, but when the child is in NREM sleep the EEG pattern is similar to that seen during a seizure (Rossi et al., 1999). As with Lennox-Gastaut syndrome, treatment is difficult; again, seizure and EEG resolution seem to be necessary for improved outcomes, and steroid medication may be useful.

Conditions that Mimic Epilepsy

Not all paroxysmal events have an epileptic basis. A generalization is that if a behavior can be triggered, interrupted or modified by external stimuli, then it probably is not a seizure. Examples include sleep disorders, movement disorders, behavior disturbances, syncope (fainting), migraine, pseudoseizures (Bye et al., 2000), and systemic disorders such as gastroesophageal reflux (see Chapter 27). Exceptions to this rule include parasomnias, febrile-induced seizures in infancy, and reflex epilepsy (e.g., induced by flickering lights or other specific sensory changes) in older children.

Sleep Disorders

Most motor events during sleep are a part of normal sleep activity. These include the random jerks of the extremities or eyes that occur during active (rapid eye movement) sleep, when the child is dreaming. More pronounced jerking occurs at sleep onset and may awaken the child or anyone sleeping in the same bed. Benign **sleep myoclonus** of infancy, an uncommon symmetric and pronounced jerking of extremities that resembles a generalized clonic seizure, can occur in newborns and infants during sleep but ceases on arousal (Pachatz, Fusco, & Vigevano, 1999). The EEG is normal during this behavior, which stops by a few months of age with no long-term consequences.

Other, more complex motor behaviors may occur 1–2 hours after sleep onset or occasionally upon arousal. These **parasomnias** and include night terrors, somniloquy (sleep talking), sleepwalking, and bruxism (teeth grinding; Laberge et al., 2000). Rarely, nocturnal frontal lobe seizures are misinterpreted as a parasomnia, and a video EEG recording is required to distinguish between the two (Lombroso, 2000; Zucconi et al., 1997). During a parasomnia, the eyes are open and the child appears awake but the EEG shows a normal sleep rhythm. These parasomnia episodes may last as long as 15–30 minutes, and the parent may be unable to end the spell or rouse the child during this time. Rarely, treatment with medication such as diazepam (Valium) is necessary if the behavior is significantly disruptive to family life.

Movement Disorders

Tics   Involuntary movements during wakefulness usually represent a disorder of function of the basal ganglia (see Chapter 13). The most common of these are tics, which are small stereotypic jerks of a body part or involuntary vocalizations that wax and wane over time and in different circumstances. Motor tics typically involve the head and neck and may include facial twitches, head shaking, eye blinking, and shoulder shrugging. Vocal tics are characterized by coughing, humming, sniffing, repetitive grunting, or other sounds.

The most severe tic disorder is Tourette syndrome and occurs in approximately 1 in 2,000 children (Robertson, 2000). The criteria for diagnosis of Tourette syndrome include motor tics in combination with vocal tics and a duration of symptoms greater than 1 year (American Psychiatric Association, 2000). Repetitive tics may occasionally resemble partial or myoclonic seizures. Tics, however, are not associated with loss of consciousness and can be suppressed temporarily, suggesting that they are under partial voluntary control. The EEG of Tourette syndrome may have nonspecific abnormalities of background activity but rarely shows epileptiform features (Krumholz et al., 1983).

Dystonias   Less common than tics are *dystonias*. These involve slower movements with fixed abnormal postures of the trunk, head, or extremities. Dystonia may be seen as a side effect of certain medications, in one form of cerebral palsy, in some inborn errors of metabolism (e.g., mitochondrial disorders, organic acidemias, Wilson disease; see Appendix B), or in a genetic syndrome (e.g., Huntington disease; torsion dystonia, see Saunders-Pullman, Braun, & Bressman, 1999).

Stereotypies   A third group of disordered movements, termed *stereotypies*, consists of repetitive complex behaviors such as head banging, hand flapping, rocking, and teeth grinding. Stereotypies may be seen in 4% of preschool children (Foster, 1998), but they are most commonly associated with certain developmental disabilities, including blindness (see Chapter 10), severe mental retardation (see Chapter 15), and pervasive developmental disorders (see Chapter 20) (Bodfish et al., 2000).

Behavior Disorders

Behaviors associated with apparent altered consciousness can occur during sleep and wakefulness and may simulate seizures. Brief staring spells (daydreaming or "spacing out") are most commonly a sign of inattention rather than of seizure activity. These staring spells rarely interrupt an active behavior and lack the subtle motor changes seen with absence or complex partial seizures (Bye et al., 2000).

Temper tantrums and rage attacks may also resemble seizures (Gordon, 1999). During these episodes the child cries, yells, throws him- or herself on the floor, and lashes out at nearby people. Occasionally sweating, pallor, and dilated pupils (probably a consequence of an adrenaline surge), as well as post-event sleepiness, can be observed. Tantrums can be distinguished from seizures by the presence of a behavioral provocation, the absence of stereotypic behaviors that occur consistently with each event, and the presence of movements that are either directed at a person or too coordinated or rapid to occur during the confused state of a seizure.

Syncopal Episodes

Syncope (fainting) is caused by a brief decrease in blood supply to the brain. It can be the result of an abnormal heart rate, blood pressure, or cerebral blood flow. It occurs typically in response to postural changes or as a consequence of vagal nerve reflexes that slow the heart rate (Boehm et al., 2001). Predisposing factors include blood drawing (or anxiety about the procedure), viral illness, being overheated, fasting, hyperventilating, or engaging in highly emotional activities (e.g., rock concerts, evangelical gatherings, funerals). Syncopal episodes occur most commonly in adolescent girls, and there is usually a family history of syncope.

Fainting may mimic an atonic seizure but has a somewhat different clinical picture. The child first feels dizzy (lightheaded) and then becomes pale and sweaty. Everything then goes dark, and the child slips to the floor gradually (not forcefully as in a seizure). It is not unusual for the child to have abnormal eye movements and stiffening with or without jerking at this point. Recovery is usually within seconds and without amnesia. An EEG is not indicated following a fainting spell; if performed the test will be normal. In some instances a cardiac evaluation is indicated, especially to exclude an electrical disturbance of the heart (e.g., prolonged corrected QT [QTc] intervals) that can result in life-threatening arrhythmias (Ilhan et al., 1999).

Breath holding is a common nonepileptic cause of loss of consciousness that can be confused with seizures in infants ages 6–18 months. Breath-holding episodes are often precipitated by unexpected pain, anger, or frustration. This leads to prolonged crying and the eventual arrest of breathing out. This arrest may last close to a minute and may be associated with blueness of the lips, back arching, and loss of consciousness (Breningstall, 1996). The breath-holding spell ends with a sudden gasping for breath and rapid neurological recovery. Prolonged episodes can be associated with brief generalized convulsive movements followed by lethargy. Very rarely, episodes of status epilepticus have been precipitated by breath-holding spells (Kuhle et al., 2000). Breath-holding spells associated with a very brief crying duration and pallor (rather than cyanosis) may indicate a cardiac evaluation to rule out an arrhythmia. It is usually inappropriate to treat breath-holding spells with AEDs; however, there is increasing evidence that treatment with iron supplements decreases the number of spells, especially if the child is anemic (Mocan et al., 1999).

Migraines

The headache, vomiting, and lethargy seen in migraine headaches can simulate a seizure state, and the neurological events produced by migraine are at times difficult to distinguish from a partial seizure (Andermann & Zifkin, 1998). Most often these symptoms include visual loss on one side of the visual field, disturbances in one eye, and/or visual distortion in both eyes (sometimes part of Alice in Wonderland syndrome; Panayiotopoulos, 1999b). Occasionally there may be sensory changes around the mouth and in the hand, hemiparesis (weakness on one side of the body), aphasia (inability to speak), and/or confusion (Neinstein & Milgrom, 2000). These neurological symptoms of migraine are produced by an electrical change in the brain that is called *spreading depression*. The symptoms also appear to be associated with a transient decrease in cerebral blood flow (Goadsby, 2001).

The adult description of a migraine as a unilateral throbbing headache with nausea, vomiting, and photophobia is atypical in children, especially in preadolescents. In children, the headaches are more likely to be diffuse and difficult to describe, although they do produce nausea and vomiting. A period of sleeping and occasionally vomiting alleviate the symptoms. There is often a family history of migraine (Hernandez-Latorre & Roig, 2000). As there are no specific medical tests to diagnose migraine, typically the diagnosis is made after excluding other possibilities.

Other Systemic Disorders

Provoked events produced by systemic disorders represent a small subset of nonseizure paroxysmal behaviors. One example is the benign but frightening hypotensive-hyporesponsive-pallid reaction that may follow an immunization shot within 48 hours. This reaction involves an abrupt episode of loss of muscle tone and responsiveness associated with either pallor or blueness (DuVernoy & Braun, 2000). Other provoked events include rigors (shaking) associated with high fever (Tal et al., 1997) and tonic extension of the upper body to relieve gastroesophageal reflux (Werlin et al., 1980) or upper airway difficulties (Greene, Kang, & Fahn, 1995).

Pseudoseizures (Psychogenic Seizures)

Pseudoseizures, or psychogenic seizures, are behaviors that result from a significant disturbance of emotion or behavior. These spells may help the child obtain attention or avoid a task (Andriola & Ettinger, 1999). Pseudoseizures can be extremely difficult to distinguish from frontal lobe or other complex partial seizures. The quality of the movements and the typically rapid return to normal, however, arouses suspicion that these events may be nonepileptic in nature. A careful history and evaluation is necessary before accepting pseudoseizures as the diagnosis. Continuous video EEGs to capture spontaneous spells, EEGs with simultaneous provocative suggestion techniques, or placebo or drug administration to induce the spell have been used in the most difficult cases (Wyllie et al., 1999). This practice of inducing a spell, however, raises certain ethical dilemmas because of the lack of informed consent. Even in the presence of a normal EEG during a spell (especially if occurring during sleep), a frontal lobe seizure can be difficult to distinguish from a pseudoseizure.

DIAGNOSING SEIZURE DISORDERS

The evaluation of a child who has suffered a first seizure involves obtaining a description of the seizure that includes the sleep–wake status of child, initial signs/symptoms and their evolution over time, and postictal status (e.g., any transient neurological impairments following the seizure). Predisposing factors also should be explored such as behavioral changes the day prior to the event; sleep activity the prior evening and morning; and exposure to an acute infection, trauma, or drugs (recreational, prescribed, or accidentally ingested). A physical and neurological examination is then performed to look for the presence of an acute illness or, alternatively, factors suggestive of a chronic neurological disorder. If the child is well and has fully recovered from the seizure, then additional studies are unlikely to be revealing or helpful in deciding therapy. Some physicians may, however, choose to pursue further medical evaluations in order to a rule out possible underlying disorders, to alleviate parental anxiety, and/or to address medical and legal concerns. Typically this includes determinations of blood glucose and electrolytes, a complete blood count, and possibly an EEG and an MRI scan (Berg, Testa, et al., 2000). Certainly if the child remains neurologically impaired after the seizure, these tests should be performed to exclude a significant underlying disease. Additional studies could include a spinal tap (lumbar puncture), screening tests for inborn errors of metabolism (e.g., plasma amino acids, urinary organic acids), and chromosome analyses. Although it is unclear whether there is value in doing these studies after a first seizure, once epilepsy (recurrent seizures) is being considered, this approach is warranted to detect an underlying condition that may be treatable (Hirtz et al., 2000).

Electroencephalogram

The EEG is most often performed during an interictal period (between seizures) to demonstrate disturbances in brain electrical activity that are more frequently found in patients with a seizure disorder (Fisch, 1999). In this study, electrodes pasted to the head at set points record voltage changes that are generated by neuronal networks resting below the electrodes. Deviations from normal background patterns for age that are confined to one hemisphere or to one area of the brain are suggestive of a partial seizure disorder. EEG changes that are more generalized can represent a diffuse chronic encephalopathy (as may be seen in severe mental retardation or an untreated inborn error of metabolism), a global change resulting from a recent seizure, or a dose of medication. Specific interictal waveforms that stand out from the background (*spikes and sharp waves*) are seen more often in patients with epilepsy. These abnormal waveforms between seizures are focal in individuals who have partial seizures and diffuse in those who have generalized seizures. From the clinical descriptions of the seizures and the EEG profile, a specific seizure type can often be defined.

Whereas the EEG during wakefulness is important in defining the presence of a chronic encephalopathy, light sleep (following sleep deprivation or induced with medication) increases the likelihood of seeing the spikes and sharp waves most commonly associated with epilepsy (Fountain, Kim, & Lee, 1998). Hyperventilation and photic stimulation (with strobe lights) may also be performed to elicit changes found in certain absence and complex partial seizure syndromes (Hennessy & Binnie, 2000). Other interventions (e.g., asking the child to read, exposing the child to specific sounds, startling the child) may be attempted to trigger seizures if the parental observations are suggestive of reflex-induced seizures.

The optimal EEG captures the event of concern, for only then can it be stated with some assurance that it is or is not a seizure (Provini et al., 1999). With a seizure the stereotyped nature of the behavior across spells usually leads to the correct diagnosis. Most of the time, however, the behavior of concern is not captured during the EEG recording. In these instances the interictal EEG can still be helpful by showing spiking activity (Neufeld et al., 2000).

If nothing is known about the patient other than that a seizure has occurred, the risk of the child's having a second seizure can be estimated as 30%–55%. The presence of an abnormal EEG with spikes following this first seizure increases that recurrence risk to about 40%–70%, whereas the presence of a normal EEG is associated with a recurrence risk of approximately 20%–40%.

Although an EEG is not essential to determine the need for therapy after the first seizure (Gilbert & Buncher, 2000), it may suggest that the event was epileptic in nature. It also establishes a baseline that can be used to assess electrographic deterioration in the event that the seizure heralds a progressive neurological disorder. In addition, EEG may suggest the site of seizure onset, allowing the area of interest to be studied using neuroimaging techniques. Finally, it may suggest a particular epilepsy syndrome. This is helpful in predicting the future course of the disorder and in choosing an AED for treatment.

Special circumstances can dictate the urgent performance of the EEG. Acute, unexplained changes in alertness, cognition, or motor behaviors can occasionally be attributed to epilepsy. A prolonged lethargic state following unexpected episode of status epilepticus, especially during a febrile illness, can prompt an early EEG to exclude findings suggestive of encephalitis. Children in intensive care units can also benefit from EEG monitoring to follow the level of encephalopathy and discover unrecognized seizures when the child is heavily sedated or in a coma (Ross, Blake, & Whitehouse, 1999).

Follow-up EEGs are often of greater interest to the parents than to the doctor. The family would like to see the EEG normalize as evidence that their child is improving (Andersson et al., 1997). The interictal spikes, however, rarely disappear, even when the child's seizures are under good AED control. Absence epilepsies represent a particular challenge because the electrographic abnormality (and possibly seizures) may persist even though parents report that the episodes have disappeared (Appleton & Beirne, 1996). Only in rare epilepsy syndromes (e.g., Landau-Kleffner syndrome, infantile spasms) does the neurologist treat the between-seizure spikes. Therefore, there is usually no medical reason to routinely follow the EEG in a child who is seizure free. If the seizures are increasing or are changing in nature or if the underlying condition is worsening, however, a follow-up EEG may be helpful.

The decision to discontinue AEDs may provide another reason to perform a repeat EEG. If the EEG continues to demonstrate severe abnormalities of background activity and abundant spikes and waves, then the recurrence risk of a seizure following drug withdrawal is substantial (Andersson et al., 1997). If the EEG has totally normalized, however, the chances for recurrence are less. EEG abnormalities during drug withdrawal suggest continued risk for seizures (Verrotti et al., 2000). Subtle changes on the EEG may not be predictive one way or the other.

Under some circumstances prolonged EEG monitoring (electrodes left in place for 1 or more days) may be useful. This is done when it is necessary to record a spell electrographically to determine whether it is epileptic (Bye et al., 2000) or to suggest the site of seizure onset as part of an evaluation before epilepsy surgery. These recordings can be accomplished in the home with an ambulatory recorder. If it is important to have a visual recording of the child's behavior during the seizure as well as record the electrical pattern, a 24-hour video EEG may be performed in the hospital. After the suspected site of onset has been identified, video EEG with prolonged invasive monitoring with electrodes on or within the brain may also be utilized during a presurgical intervention (Jayakar, 1999). This technique precisely defines the site of seizure onset and maps normal brain functions of the area to be removed during surgery. This may avoid or limit damage to the speech and motor areas of the brain during surgery.

Brain Imaging Techniques

Until the 1970s the only way to examine the brain was to X-ray the skull, looking for bony abnormalities or fractures. Since then there has been a proliferation of new technologies that have revolutionized our ability to visualize the brain in the diagnosis and treatment of epilepsy: computed tomography (CT), magnetic resonance imaging and functional MRI (MRI and fMRI, respectively), positron emission tomography (PET), single photon emission computed tomography (SPECT), magneto-electroencephalography (MEG); and magnetic resonance spectroscopy (MRS).

CT was the first of these techniques to be developed and its inventor won the Nobel Prize in Physiology or Medicine. It combines X-ray techniques with computer technology to create serial images (slices) of the brain. It is often the first brain imaging test to be used after an initial seizure, especially one associated with trauma. This is because it is more rapid than MRI and is particularly good at picking up skull injuries, calcifications, and brain hemorrhages. In contrast to CT, MRI uses the intrinsic magnetic characteristics of the molecules of the brain rather than X-rays to produce images. It is better than CT in defining structural abnormalities such as aneurysms and differentiating gray and white matter and their abnormalities. MRI scans can identify brain atrophy, developmental brain malformations, small tumors and evidence of inborn errors of metabolism. MRI is most likely to yield positive findings in children with uncontrolled epilepsy, with more than one type of seizure, or with other developmental disabilities (Berg, Testa, et al., 2000).

CT and MRI examine brain structure, whereas the other brain imaging studies listed focus on abnormalities in brain blood flow and metabolism. PET and SPECT scans require injection of small amounts of radioactive material. SPECT has the advantage of utilizing commercially available reagents, whereas PET requires rapidly decaying tracers that must be produced on site by a cyclotron, an extremely expensive piece of equipment that is not widely available. PET images reveal metabolic activity of the brain, and SPECT maps blood flow to areas in proportion to their metabolic activity. These two techniques can assist in localizing a seizure focus by identifying areas of the brain that have decreased blood flow between seizures and increased blood flow during a seizure (Gaillard, 2000). The techniques can also help to examine neurotransmitter function and identify abnormalities in neurotransmitter receptors that occur in certain inborn errors of metabolism.

Other rapidly developing technologies, including MRS, fMRI, and MEG, have the potential to demonstrate brain activity without the need for radioactive tracers (Gaillard et al., 2000). MRS, which can be done as part of a routine MRI scan, is being used to identify certain metabolic derangements in the brain, as occur in mitochondrial disorders and other inborn errors of metabolism, that can cause seizures. As of 2002, fMRI is primarily a research tool; using MRI technology and advanced imaging processing, fMRI examines changes in blood flow during brain activation activities such as reading or moving a limb. Abnormal brain activation occurs at a seizure focus and can be identified. MEG is another currently experimental noninvasive modality that may permit an additional window on brain function by measuring magnetic activity of the cortex to produce three-dimensional localization of a seizure focus, which is especially important prior to epilepsy surgery (Ebersole, 1999).

INTERVENTION DURING A SEIZURE

The need for intervention during a seizure by parents or professionals depends on the seizure type and duration. Repeated absence seizures require no immediate action, provided that the episode of repeated seizures stops within 15 minutes. Tonic-clonic seizures, however, require simple, common-sense first aid procedures (Berg et al., 2001). The child should be placed on the floor or a bed and turned to one side to prevent choking or aspirating on vomit. The child should not, however, be tightly restrained. Clothing should be loosened around the neck. Fingers, tongue blades, spoons, or other instruments should not be inserted between the child's teeth to prevent "swallowing of the tongue," which is physically impossible. Cardiopulmonary resuscitation efforts should generally be avoided because they are unnecessary and can lead to the "rescuer" suffering bitten fingers and the child sustaining loosened teeth and vomiting and/or aspirating the vomit. Normally, emergency medical services (i.e., 911 in most locations of the United States) need to be called only if the seizure lasts more than 5–10 minutes, which is uncommon in children. The Epilepsy Foundation (2000–2001) has suggested that an ambulance be called if the child is not known to have had prior seizures, if the child has an intercurrent illness, if a second seizure occurs, or if consciousness is not immediately regained following the seizure. Furthermore, if the seizure occurs with fever or trauma, urgent care should be sought. Otherwise, the child should be attended until fully awake and alert and then allowed to nap. The child often needs reassurance and comforting and should be encouraged to resume activities after recovering fully. Parents should be notified and the details of the seizure explained. It is ideal to have a treatment plan in the school nurse's office outlining these interventions in advance of a seizure occurring in a child with epilepsy and to have a similar plan available to other adults caring for the child (e.g., child care, sport or community activities, summer camp).

ANTIEPILEPTIC DRUGS

The decision to treat a child who has seizures with AEDs, which manipulate neurotransmitter activity and ionic channels, thus influencing seizure activity, requires a balancing of potential benefits and risks. This includes considering whether the recurrence risk is high and whether control will alter biological outcome. In addition, social concerns and potential side effects of the seizures and AEDs must be evaluated. The first consideration, however, is making a correct diagnosis. Diagnostic studies may assist in clarifying the nature of the spell and the recurrence risk. Absolutely certain assessment of recurrence, unfortunately, can only be made after a subsequent seizure has already occurred. Because of this uncertainty, ultimately the decision to treat or not depends on the parents' and physician's assessment of the risk of seizures (biological and social) versus the risk associated with the AED (Greenwood & Tennison, 1999).

The optimal AED should prevent all seizures from occurring without producing side effects (Fisher et al., 2000b). At the most, one dose each day should be required, and the AED should improve or cure the underlying disorder. Unfortunately, present therapies do not meet these criteria. As a rule, multiple doses of medication are required to keep peak blood AED levels (in the hour or two after dosage) from becoming too high and producing toxic effects while keeping trough levels (in the hour or two before the next dose) high enough to prevent seizures from occurring. Furthermore, current AEDs do not improve the underlying condition that causes the seizures.

The definition of successful seizure control often differs among children, their parents, other caregivers, and physicians. Children generally do not like taking the medication or having side effects, so they want fewer and lower doses of AED. Teachers want the children to be seizure free and without medication side effects so that they can concentrate and learn. There must also be agreement between parent and physician as to whether the desired outcome is seizure freedom or a substantial reduction in seizure activity as this decision may affect the medication regimen or the choice of surgery.

How Antiepileptic Drugs Work

AEDs work by interfering with the physiological mechanisms that lead to seizures. There are numerous channels on neurons that allow the flow of ions (e.g., calcium, potassium, sodium) into and out of cells. These channels are opened and closed by excitatory (glutamate) and inhibitory (GABA) neurotransmitters that are released from nearby cells. The older AEDs phenytoin (Dilantin) and carbamazepine (Tegretol) block the high-frequency voltage-dependent sodium channels. Several newer AEDs (felbamate [Felbatol] and lamotrigine [Lamictal]) also block this channel but also inhibit excitatory neurotransmission. Valproate (Depakene, Depakote) and topiramate (Topamax) have even a wider range of potential mechanisms. Valproate blocks voltage-dependent sodium channels and calcium currents while also influencing GABA. Topiramate blocks sodium channels, opens chloride channels, and interferes with glutamate transmission. Other AEDs, such as barbiturates, benzodiazepines, vigabatrin (Sabril), tiagabine (Gabitril), and gabapentin (Neurontin), primarily increase inhibitory mechanisms. The mechanism of action of some drugs, such as levetiracetam (Keppra), is not yet known. This raises the possibility that additional mechanisms of action of AEDs are yet to be discovered (Moshé, 2000a; Willmore, 2000).

The Advantages of Monotherapy

AEDs are probably best utilized singly, that is, as monotherapy (Guberman, 1998). Use of multiple drugs carries the potential for biochemical interactions, with one drug increasing or decreasing the metabolism of the other in the child's body or brain, thus possibly decreasing efficacy and/or increasing side effects. It has also been observed that when too many AEDs are taken together, not only are patients more likely to be drowsy, but also seizure control may actually decrease. Drug interactions can also occur with medications taken for other conditions, and certain foods (e.g., grapefruit) can affect the metabolism of some drugs. In severe seizures that are unresponsive to a single medication, an additional drug may be required, but this should be done with caution (Leppik, 2000).

Choosing an Antiepileptic Drug

After an assessment of the risks and benefits of using an AED, the specific medication or group of medications is chosen based on the seizure type, age of the child, and specific epilepsy disorder. The willingness of the parents and child to tolerate specific potential side effects must also be considered (Bourgeois, 2000). Once a particular drug is decided upon, additional choices remain: generic versus brand-name drug, capsule versus liquid, and so forth. The generic drug (if available) will be cheaper, but it may not have the same formulation. This can affect the drug's absorption and metabolism (Besag, 2000). In addition, an identical drug from one manufacturer may come packaged in many forms: a syrup (rapidly absorbed but with quickly disappearing effects), sprinkles (easily administered, delayed in absorption, and longer lasting), or pills/capsules. Sustained-release pill/capsule formulations are easier for the patient to take as fewer doses a day are required. In addition, these formulations can potentially be more effective in controlling seizures by maintaining a more stable blood level of the medication throughout the day. Care must taken when switching from one formulation of a drug to another; it cannot be automatically assumed that drug levels and seizure control will remain stable. Obtaining a blood level of the AED after the switch will help identify a potential problem.

Availability of New Antiepileptic Drugs

Between 1978 and 1993 no new AEDs were introduced. During that period of time the most commonly used AEDs were phenobarbital, phenytoin, carbamazepine (Tegretol), ethosuximide (Zarontin), and valproate. Since the mid-1990s, however, eight new AEDs have been approved by the Food and Drug Administration in the United States: felbamate (Felbatol), gabapentin (Neurontin), lamotrigine (Lamictal), levetiracetam (Keppra), oxcarbazepine (Trileptal), tiagabine (Gabitril), topiramate (Topamax), and zonisamide (Zonegran). In addition, new sustained-release formulations of older drugs have decreased toxicity: carbamazepine (Tegretol XR, Carbatrol), and valproate (Depakote ER). Even intravenous drugs used to treat status epilepticus have undergone reformulation (e.g., fosphyenytoin [Cerebyx], which is closely related to phenytoin; rectal gel preparation of diazepam [Diastat]). These newer medications have increased both the options and the complexity of AED therapy. The major advantage of the new drugs is that they may be more specific in their action and therefore can theoretically be more effective at a lower dosage and have fewer side effects. (See Appendix D for more information on preparations available, dosages, and side effects.)

Side Effects

Most AEDs do not work solely on the neurons that trigger seizures. They alter neurochemistry diffusely throughout the brain. Indeed, the nonspecific nature of treatment is demonstrated by the fact that AEDs may also be prescribed for conditions that affect behavior and emotions. These include mood disorders (e.g., bipolar disorder), aggression, pain, and migraines (Backonja, 2000; Mitchell et al., 1993; Nemeroff, 2000). In addition to treating behavior and emotional symptoms, AEDs can produce them as side effects (Harbord, 2000). More commonly, however, side effects of AEDs affect motor and cognitive aspects of brain function. These side effects include sleepiness, decreased attention and memory, dysphasia (difficulty producing speech), ataxia (unstable gait), and diplopia (double vision). These side effects may occur transiently when a new drug is started or dosage is increased, or they may persist and require the discontinuation of the medication.

Concern About Learning Impairments

There is an additional concern that AEDs may have an adverse effect on learning that may persist long after the drug has been discontinued. This issue was raised by a study of phenobarbital in children with febrile seizures (Farwell et al., 1990). The children in the study were found to have subtle cognitive impairments that persisted for 6 months after drug cessation. Because the study was halted at this point, questions were raised about whether these changes would persist and for how long. This concern of persisting cognitive impairments was supported by animal data demonstrating continuing behavioral effects following early phenobarbital exposure. Virtually all AEDs, especially at high dosages, have the potential to cause cognitive impairments during treatment, but long-term effects, especially of the newer medications, have not been studied to date (Kwan & Brodie, 2001).

Effects on Other Body Systems

Medication administration requires gastrointestinal absorption, dissolution in the blood, and eventual exposure of other body organs to the drug. As a result, side effects of AEDs can involve many organs in addition to the brain. There can be gastrointestinal irritation (e.g., stomach discomfort), bone marrow suppression (leading to low white and red blood cell counts), liver dysfunction (e.g., as revealed by elevated liver function tests), kidney stones, pancreatitis (i.e., inflammation of the pancreas), cardiac arrhythmia or decreased heart contractility, and dermatological changes (e.g., hair loss, coarsening of facial features, gum overgrowth, skin changes). Certain AEDs taken during pregnancy can increase the risk of having a child with a neural tube defect or other birth defect (see Chapter 3).

Other side effects are hormonal/metabolic in nature and are more common with long-term therapy. These include abnormal calcium and vitamin D metabolism (see Chapter 9) that may be severe enough to increase the risk of fractures or rickets; weight gain or loss; in females, polycystic ovaries leading to impaired fertility; and decreased thyroid hormone level.

Many of the medication side effects are dosage related, so decreasing the prescribed amount of AED can lead to elimination of adverse effects. Sometimes, however, the side effects are independent of dosage and probably reflect genetic differences in the metabolism or sensitivity of the patient to the drug. In these instances, if the side effects are severe, the AED should be stopped (Harden, 2000).

Allergic Responses

Allergic responses to AEDs can also occur, resulting from an immune response to the drug. An acute life-threatening response (anaphylaxis) or slowly evolving delayed reactions (delayed hypersensitivity) can occur. Thus, when a rash occurs while a child is on an AED, it is important to determine whether the rash is attributable to the drug or to unrelated factors. If the child has been taking the medication for a prolonged period of time without side effects, a careful search for other triggers of the rash should be undertaken before considering stopping the drug. If the rash occurs early in the course of therapy, however, the medication is usually stopped and an alternative AED is chosen. Caution is necessary following any drug reaction as there can be allergic cross-reactivity between a number of the AEDs. Cross-reactivity has been found for phenobarbital, carbamazepine (all formulations), phenytoin, fosphenytoin, and possibly oxcarbazepine. Thus, if the child is allergic to one of these drugs, it should be assumed he or she will be allergic to the others in this group. For the most part these reactions cannot be anticipated, and parents should be counseled to be wary of their occurrence and what to do in the event of a reaction.

Learning About Side Effects

The *Physician's Desk Reference* manual on prescription drugs (published annually by Medical Economics Company) and the package inserts from medications typically list 2–3 pages of potential side effects for each AED. When an AED is being selected, it is reasonable to decide which of the more common side effects the child and family is willing to consider tolerating. Furthermore, because there are presently many alternates, if there are considerable side effects, it is fairly straightforward to change medications.

Determining Dosage

The usual approach in determining AED dosage is to use the lowest dosage that is effective in controlling the seizures and does not produce unacceptable side effects. This is achieved by starting at a low dosage of a single AED and gradually increasing it as necessary. Some practitioners aim to achieve a blood level within a particular range. This therapeutic range is a range of blood levels that will have the desired effect (seizure control) without toxicity for most children. These published norms, however, may not always be useful for decision making for the individual child. Some children can either achieve seizure control or have side effects with levels below this range. Similarly, other children require dosages above the therapeutic range to control their seizures, yet these children never experience side effects.

How quickly the drug dosage is increased after it is first started depends on the severity and frequency of the seizures as well as the metabolism of the medication. The newer AEDs appear to have fewer side effects overall but if increased rapidly, can still produce side effects or toxicity significant enough to require their discontinuation. This is an argument for a gradual increase in dosage of a new medication.

Monitoring Drug Therapy

After starting an AED, parents and physicians need to be attuned to changes in the child's well-being. Some practitioners require routine blood tests, including drug levels, complete blood counts, and liver function tests. They argue that this monitoring will provide early evidence of toxicity, demonstrate compliance (by maintenance of therapeutic blood levels), and provide information on how rapidly a child metabolizes a medication (Glauser & Pippenger, 2000). Other physicians suggest that routine blood studies are not necessary (Camfield & Camfield, 2000). They note that if the patient is clinically doing well, any blood abnormality is likely to be incidental and will resolve spontaneously. They feel that finding an abnormal level only leads to parental anxiety and child discomfort. Although there is some argument about the importance of routine testing, there is general agreement that these blood tests should be obtained if there are breakthrough seizures (seizures while on AEDs) or clinical signs of drug toxicity.

Deciding When Drug Therapy Should Be Started

Drug therapy is usually started when a child is diagnosed with epilepsy. Because the diagnosis requires the occurrence of multiple seizures over time, an AED may not be started at the time of the first seizure, and, in the case of febrile seizures, it may never be started despite multiple seizure episodes. No drug always works, and all AEDs have a risk of side effects. Furthermore, treating the child who has had an initial seizure may not be necessary. Without therapy the majority of these children will not have a second seizure. In addition, the process of brain remodeling following the first prolonged seizure is probably independent of seizure recurrence (Jensen, 1999). Thus, even if there are no further seizures, continuation of network reorganization could still lead to cognitive and behavior abnormalities.

The National Perinatal Collaborative Project in the 1960s followed more than 50,000 pregnant women, neurologically assessing their infants after birth, at 4 and 12 months of age, and finally at school age. In this study, children who experienced seizures had similar cognitive outcomes as their unaffected siblings and controls. Children who were suspected or found to be neurologically abnormal prior to the first seizure, however, did have significantly more scatter in cognitive development than did unaffected siblings or controls (Ellenberg, Hirtz, & Nelson, 1986; Ellenberg & Nelson, 1978). It has also been found that children with newly diagnosed epilepsy have a higher incidence of behavioral, social, and academic difficulties compared with unaffected siblings and controls (Austin et al., 2001). This suggests that preexisting brain dysfunction places a child at risk both for epilepsy and behavior/learning difficulties rather than that epilepsy causes these problems (Glaser, 1983).

Yet, some concern persists that seizures induce brain damage. As noted previously, children who have had febrile seizures are more likely to develop mesial temporal sclerosis (affecting the hippocampus, which is important in memory and new learning) and associated complex partial seizures later in life (Berg, Shinnar, et al., 2000). To study this issue further, animal models have been developed in which repetitive electrical shocks are administered to the hippocampus, resulting in the appearance of chronic spontaneous seizures (simulating partial complex seizures in humans). Microscopic changes were found in the brains of these animals. Interestingly, adult animals were more likely to show these pathological changes than immature animals were. The implications of these findings are being debated actively. Some argue that epileptogenesis is caused by recurrent seizures, whereas others hold that an underlying brain abnormality causes both the seizures and any associated neurological and behavioral disturbances.

Given these concerns, but recognizing that a majority of patients do not have a second seizure, what are the risks of not providing an AED early? Evidence in both children and adults suggests that following a small number of untreated seizures, the percentage of patients whose seizures will be controlled with AEDs is the same as if the drug had been started after the first seizure. Therefore, from a biological perspective, there is no rush to start long-term AEDs, although issues such as the ability to drive, safety (e.g., preventing traumatic falls from drop seizures), social stigma (e.g., dealing with incontinence following a seizure), and parental fear (e.g., of a seizure resulting in injury or death) may influence that decision.

There can be a compromise between starting prophylactic (preventive) therapy and doing nothing. A benzodiazepine (e.g., diazepam, clonazepam, lorazepam [Ativan]) can be administered at times of presumed high seizure risk for a given child, such as during a febrile illness in a young child who has had a previous febrile seizure, during long trips with the attendant sleep deprivation, or during other situations in which there has been a history of consistent seizure appearance. Diazepam can be given rectally (Diastat), and lorazepam can be given under the tongue if the child is alert enough to safely have something in the mouth. Even if the drug does not prevent the seizure from occurring, the drug may shorten the seizure's duration, decrease its intensity, or prevent a second seizure. The advantage of this approach is that although the medication is not given on a daily basis, it may still have a reasonable likelihood of success during at-risk periods. The disadvantages include the child's becoming sedated, hyperactive, or unsteady following the use of these acute medications. These drugs can also slow breathing, so the caregivers should be aware of how to intervene if there is respiratory compromise. It should be emphasized that this approach cannot be used if the seizure is random in its appearance.

Deciding When Drug Therapy Can Be Stopped

In the past, AED treatment was prescribed for life. There are, however, significant concerns regarding the long-term use of AEDs, including 1) potential teratogenicity during pregnancy; 2) establishment of a poor self-image of being chronically ill; and 3) cost in time and money for medications, doctor's visits, and laboratory monitoring. Now every attempt is made to stop the drug after a seizure-free interval. Overall, after an individual has been seizure-free for 2 years, the risk of seizure recurrence after medication is stopped is about 25%–35% (Caviedes & Herranz, 1998). The risk is higher in 1) children with developmental disabilities, 2) children with identified structural brain abnormalities, 3) children who require more than one AED to achieve seizure control, and 4) adolescents presenting with seizures for the first time. In most children the EEG is helpful in deciding whether to stop therapy. The presence of a normal EEG suggests that it is safe to stop AEDs, whereas an abnormal EEG points to increased uncertainty for seizure recurrence if AEDs are stopped. As mentioned previously, the chance of seizure recurrence can be significantly decreased but never truly eliminated.

OTHER ANTIEPILEPTIC THERAPIES

A number of antiepileptic therapies do not rely on medication. Some are old therapies that have recently gained favor based on new research findings (e.g., ketogenic diet, epilepsy surgery); others are preventive approaches involving vitamin and mineral supplementation and lifestyle changes that have been found to be helpful. In addition, there are alternative therapies that have not been tested scientifically and should be viewed with concern. Finally, there is the promise of new approaches to treating seizures in the future. These various therapies are briefly discussed in the sections that follow.

Ketogenic Diet

The ketogenic diet represents an alternative method to treat epilepsy for some patients. Although controlled studies are lacking, the existing studies indicate that 16% of patients stop seizing and that 56% have a significant reduction in seizures while on a ketogenic diet (Hemingway et al., 2001). The mechanism of action of the diet involves forcing the brain to utilize fat rather than carbohydrates for energy and altering neurotransmitters.

To be effective, the ketogenic diet requires weighing and calculating the amounts of nutrients in all the foods the child eats. The sugars/carbohydrates from any medications must also be considered in the calculations. In addition, the urine must be monitored to assure adequate spillage of ketones (from which the diet gets its name), a by-product of fat metabolism. The ketogenic diet is severely restrictive and not very tasty. Short-term side effects include metabolic acidosis and electrolyte disturbances, uric acid kidney stones, and diarrhea/vomiting. The diet, similar to AED therapy, can be stopped after the child has a period of being seizure free.

Surgical Interventions

Surgical interventions are also available to treat epilepsy. In fact, the only "cure" for epilepsy is removal of the seizure focus from the brain. This has been most successfully accomplished in complex partial seizures arising from the mesial temporal lobe (Wiebe et al., 2001). Another operation, hemispherectomy, involves the removal of most of one side of the brain. It is used for seizures that arise from multiple foci in one side of the brain and for progressive unilateral disorders, such as Rasmussen encephalitis or Sturge-Weber syndrome (see Appendix B). In addition to these "curative" surgical procedures, palliative surgical interventions are also available. These include corpus callosotomy for treating drop seizures and electrical stimulation of the vagus nerve or, rarely, the thalamus for intractable mixed seizures that have an onset that cannot be localized to one area or that arise from both hemispheres. Complications of surgical interventions include bleeding, infection, and harm to the eloquent (speech) cortex.

The decision to perform surgery generally follows the failure of the child's seizures to respond to AEDs. This decision is complicated, however, by the recent introduction of many new AEDs. Determining how many drugs should be tried without success before considering surgery is difficult. By the third or fourth drug failure, however, the likelihood of completely controlling the seizures with medication is estimated to be only 10% (Bourgeois, 2000). The timing of surgery is not only driven by how many and how severe the seizures are but also by the seizures' impact on the child's life and family dynamics.

Nonspecific Interventions

There are also certain nonspecific interventions that might be used to decrease seizure occurrence. These include ensuring that the child obtains regular, reasonable amounts of sleep and avoids sedative medications. These strategies help because many forms of epilepsy are exacerbated by drowsiness. Infection and/or fever can also trigger seizures, so appropriate handwashing, avoidance of contact with people who have viral illnesses, and aggressive fever control should be undertaken. Finally, it is important to identify and avoid or alter specific triggers that provoke seizures. The most common of these are the ovulatory cycle in females and flashing lights for the child with photic-induced seizures. In deciding whether a potential trigger is really a precipitant, it must be remembered how many times that event has occurred without precipitating a seizure.

Vitamins and Minerals

High dosages of supplemental vitamins and minerals are generally not necessary for a child with epilepsy. Rare cases of pyridoxine dependency/deficiency can require high dosages of vitamin B_6; certain other disorders of metabolism are treated with a combination of vitamins and nutritional supplements. All females (with or without epilepsy) who are capable of child-bearing, however, should receive folate supplements to minimize the risks of spina bifida (see Chapter 24) in a future pregnancy. For the child with seizures, supplementation with a multi-vitamin with calcium may be useful in preventing osteoporosis. Megadoses of the B and E vitamins or supplemental carnitine are not indicated for the typical child with epilepsy (Baxter, 1999).

Alternative Medicine

Various homeopathic and herbal remedies exist to attempt to treat epilepsy, but none have been proven efficacious (Danesi & Adetunji, 1994). These interventions, although often labeled "natural," are not necessarily harmless. As a rule of thumb, in considering the use of an alternative therapy, it should not 1) carry a significant risk of increasing seizure activity, 2) compromise any therapy already in place, such as AEDs, 3) be harmful to the child's general health, or 4) be costly.

Future Therapeutic Approaches

A number of research therapies may find use in the future. In animal studies reservoirs are being implanted into areas of the brain affected by seizures, permitting AEDs to be infused directly into the seizure focus (Stein et al., 2000). Electrical stimulators are being implanted into the thalamus to alter the pathways that lead from this organ to broad regions of the cerebral cortex (Velasco et al., 2000). The use of transcranial magnetic brain stimulation is also being tested (Ziemann et al., 1998).

In addition, in the future medical intervention is likely to shift from treating the symptom (seizures) of the brain disorder to treating the underlying dysfunction. Gene therapy may allow the introduction of new genes into patients with specific mutations (e.g., channelopathies) that lead to epilepsy. Agents may be developed that are given immediately after a brain injury to interrupt abnormal reorganization of neural networks. Stem cell implantation into the brain, with the provision of appropriate growth factors, may allow the replacement of destroyed networks. Finally, microchip implantation may permit the creation of a "bionic" part of the brain that assumes those functions lost in the seizure focus.

MULTIDISCIPLINARY INTERVENTION

The care of the child with epilepsy involves more than just medical or surgical treatment of the seizures. Education, psychosocial support, and involvement of the entire family are all critical to effective management for the child (Kwong, Wong, & So, 2000). For these reasons, it is wise for a child with seizures that are difficult to control to be followed at a comprehensive epilepsy center. These multidisciplinary clinics are staffed with a team of neurologists, nurses, psychologists, social workers, and other therapists working together. For families living at a distance from an epilepsy center, the center's staff can work with the local pediatrician as consultants in helping to ensure good seizure control.

Educational Programs

From an educational perspective, the student's basic needs are dictated by his or her cognitive and learning abilities (Bulteau et al., 2000). In addition, teachers must be alert for signs of difficulty attributable to seizures or their treatment. The child with absence seizures who suddenly begins to do poorly in class may have unrecognized increased seizure activity. Alternatively, new or worsening school problems may develop as a result of side effects to an increased AED dosage or a switch to a new medication (Fisher et al., 2000a). Behavioral side effects may include fatigue, inattention, irritability, and aggression. Teachers and parents must be alert to these signs, for they may indicate the need to check drug levels or to change the dosage schedule. Alternatively, these nonspecific features may point to intercurrent illness, peer problems, new learning difficulties, or the need to reevaluate the entire educational program. Children with epilepsy are covered by IDEA '97 legislation under "other health impairments" and can receive special education and related services (see Chapter 30).

There are also the psychological side effects of a child having a seizure in class. For example, bowel and bladder incontinence during a tonic-clonic seizure may cause the child intense embarrassment. For the child whose seizures are under good control and who has no known daytime seizures, there is no reason to discuss his or her epilepsy with the class. This will simply identify the child as different and subject to being stigmatized. Parents who are worried about a seizure occurring in class may request a classroom discussion about seizures. This can be done without identifying the specific child (Coleman & Fiedler, 1999). On the other hand, if the student is likely to have seizures in the classroom, the best approach is anticipatory education of classmates about seizures so that they know what to expect and can be helpful (Epilepsy Foundation, 2000–2001). A towel and a fresh change of clothing can be kept in the nurse's office for children who have poorly controlled tonic-clonic seizures that are associated with incontinence.

Psychosocial Issues

Seizures have a significant impact upon the child and his or her family (Fisher et al., 2000a, 2000b). Although most children have infrequent seizures and the total time of ictal activity is a tiny fraction of their lives, the disorder and its treatment may become all consuming for the family. The uncertainty of when the seizure will strike next may be what causes such distress. The child with epilepsy must be educated about the cause of the seizures. Even if seizures become rare after achieving proper medication dosage, full discussion is appropriate.

In addition, the social stigma attached to epilepsy may need to be addressed with the child and family (Schoenfeld et al., 1999). Yet, surveys find that the self-perception of a person with epilepsy is far worse than how others see this person (Arnston et al., 1986). Some children with seizure disorders have low self-esteem and depression, leading to absenteeism in school and overdependence on their parents. Unfortunately, these self-esteem concerns can lead to social isolation. When this is combined with subtle impairments in memory or learning, school failure may result. Although the seizures themselves or the social reaction to them are major concerns for families, it is actually the associated brain dysfunction (cognitive, behavior, and motor impairment) that is ultimately more problematic. Unlike a seizure, which is a time-limited episode, these disabilities are persistent and affect daily functioning.

The issue of sports has been controversial (Steinhoff et al., 1996). At one time, children with epilepsy were precluded from participation in many sports; now it is thought that most sports are permissible once seizures are well controlled (Nakken, 1999; see Chapter 34). Most clinicians continue to recommend that children with epilepsy avoid heavy contact sports such as tackle football as well as unusually dangerous activities such as rock climbing and scuba diving. Of course, the routine safety precautions recommended for all children should be taken.

Similarly, family vacations and camping trips need not be curtailed in the child with well-controlled seizures. Excessive fatigue, however, should be avoided, as it may precipitate a seizure, and the family should travel with an adequate supply of the AED and a written prescription or the doctor's and pharmacist's telephone numbers in case the medicine is misplaced or stolen. The decision for the child to wear a medical identification bracelet or necklace optimally should be made with the child's assent; its value is considerably diminished if it is felt to be stigmatizing.

The family structure and routine should be kept intact as much as possible, and it is important not to overprotect the child. Care should be taken, however, to use common-sense precautions, especially if the seizures are poorly controlled. These include having the child take showers rather than baths (unless attended), having him or her not lock the bathroom door, and supervising the child when he or she is working near a stove or on a ladder. When using a babysitter, parents need to provide careful instruction for seizure recognition, first aid, and a plan of action if a seizure occurs.

There may also be significant financial issues for the family regarding the cost of medications, doctor visits, laboratory tests, hospitalizations, and time off work (Begley et al., 2000). (See Chapter 38 for a discussion of health care financing and different funding options for families.) Families may have to make decisions as to where they can live and what jobs they can accept based on their concerns for the care of their children. As the child moves toward adulthood, independence should be encouraged as much as possible (see Chapter 37). This includes fostering independent living, driving, and the pursuit of appropriate job opportunities; addressing concerns about insurance; and dealing with altered fertility rate and potential teratogenic effects of AEDs.

Advocacy

Organizations such as the American Epilepsy Society, the Epilepsy Foundation, and the International League against Epilepsy; numerous other societies and medical centers across the world; and self-help groups advocate for acceptance of individuals with epilepsy in society. Governments are lobbied, businesses and school personnel educated, and children and families counseled in order to better provide the needed resources for children with epilepsy (see Appendix D).

OUTCOME

Most children with seizure disorders have normal intelligence scores (Dodson, 2001). There has been controversy as to whether repeated seizures or chronic AED treatment can lead to subtle brain injury, limiting the child's potential over time. Repeated IQ tests, however, have not shown a decline in intellectual abilities, unless the child is overmedicated, is exposed to certain AEDs that carry higher risk of cognitive impairment, or has had a very prolonged episode of status epilepticus.

Prognosis mostly depends on the seizure type and the underlying brain pathology. For example, the average IQ score for children with absence seizures is in the normal range, whereas children with Lennox-Gastaut syndrome have mental retardation. Yet, prognosis depends not solely on intelligence but also on how the child and family handle this chronic illness. If the seizures come under control easily and drug side effects are few, the family is likely to cope well. If the seizures prove resistant to treatment and drug side effects are many, these stresses may interfere with the functioning of both the child and family.

If psychosocial issues and subtle impairments in memory and learning are approached in an effective manner, the prognosis is generally good. Because most seizures remit during child-

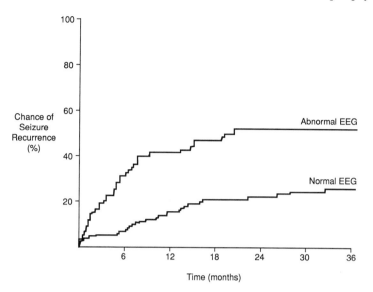

Figure 25.3. Percentage risk of seizure recurrence in the 3 years following a first non-febrile seizure. Overall, about 40% of children were found to have a second seizure. However, although those with normal electroencephalographs (EEGs) had a 26% chance of recurrence, those with abnormal EEG patterns had a 56% chance of recurrence. (From Shinnar, S., Berg, A.T., Moshé, S.L., et al. [1990]. Risk of seizure recurrence following a short unprovoked seizure in childhood: A prospective study. Reproduced with permission from *Pediatrics,* Vol. 85, Page 1079, Copyright 1990.)

hood, it is critical to encourage each child to achieve his or her maximal potential. For those whose epilepsy is but one feature of a multiple disability disorder, the eventual outcome is more commonly a function of the other disabilities than of the seizures.

What Are the Chances of Outgrowing Epilepsy?

About 70% to 80% of children with epilepsy achieve control of their seizures with the first or second AED tried. Two thirds remain seizure free during a 5-year follow up period; and almost the same percentage can be successfully weaned from their AED after 2 years of being seizure free (Figure 25.3; MacDonald et al., 2000). These generalizations, however, are somewhat misleading because they may not include all of the childhood seizure syndromes. These statements also overrepresent the more severe cases that are followed in epilepsy clinics, and the statistics do not deal with medication compliance issues or provide long-term follow-up (across several decades). Finally, epilepsy is not a homogeneous disorder; even within families with a genetic form of epilepsy, there is variability of seizure expression.

SUMMARY

Epilepsy is a chronic neurological condition that involves recurrent seizures as an expression of an underlying brain abnormality. The seizures themselves are merely manifestations of abnormal electrical discharges within the brain. Generalized seizures include those classified as tonic-clonic, absence, myoclonic, and atonic. Partial seizures are defined as simple or complex, depending on whether there is loss of consciousness. Seizures may occur singly or in combination and may start in the newborn period, in infancy, or in later childhood. For about half of affected children, the seizures are an isolated disability. Most can be controlled by a single

AED, and these children can lead almost typical lives. For a child with multiple disabilities, the prognosis is generally more a function of the other disabilities than of the seizures. A key problem with the condition is uncertainty regarding outcome. Will there be more seizures after the initial one? Do recurrent seizures cause biologic harm? Will medication prevent subsequent seizures without toxicity? If so, when can the medication be stopped? New medications and approaches to care provide hope for the future, but some degree of uncertainty is likely to remain.

REFERENCES

American Psychiatric Association. (2000). *Diagnostic and statistical manual of mental disorders* (4th ed., Text rev.). Washington, DC: Author.

Andermann, F., & Zifkin, B. (1998). The benign occipital epilepsies of childhood: An overview of the idiopathic syndromes and of the relationship to migraine. *Epilepsia, 39* (Suppl. 4), S9–S23.

Andersson, T., Braathen, G., Persson, A., et al. (1997). A comparison between one and three years of treatment in uncomplicated childhood epilepsy: A prospective study, II. The EEG as predictor of outcome after withdrawal of treatment. *Epilepsia, 38,* 225–232.

Andriola, M.R., & Ettinger, A.B. (1999). Pseudoseizures and other nonepileptic paroxysmal disorders in children and adolescents. *Neurology, 53*(5, Suppl. 2), S89–S95.

Appleton, R.E., & Beirne, M. (1996). Absence epilepsy in children: The role of EEG in monitoring response to treatment. *Seizure, 5,* 147–148.

Arnston, P., Droge, D., Norton, R., et al. (1986). The perceived psychosocial consequences of having epilepsy. In S. Whitman, B.P. Herman (Eds.), *Psychopathology in epilepsy: Social dimensions* (pp. 143–161). New York: Oxford University Press.

Austin, J.K., Harezlak, J., Dunn, D.W., et al. (2001). Behavior problems in children before first recognized seizures. *Pediatrics, 107,* 115–122.

Backonja, M.M. (2000). Anticonvulsants (antineuropathics) for neuropathic pain syndromes. *The Clinical Journal of Pain, 16*(2, Suppl.), S67–S72.

Bate, L., & Gardiner, M. (1999). Genetics of inherited epilepsies. *Epileptic Disorders,1,* 7–19.

Baxter, P. (1999). Epidemiology of pyridoxine dependent and pyridoxine responsive seizures in the UK. *Archives of Disease in Childhood, 81,* 431–433.

Begley, C.E., Famulari, M., Annegers, J.F., et al. (2000). The cost of epilepsy in the United States: An estimate from population-based clinical and survey data. *Epilepsia, 41,* 342–351.

Berg, A.T., Darefsky, A.S., Holford, T.R., et al. (1998). Seizures with fever after unprovoked seizures: An analysis in children followed from the time of a first febrile seizure. *Epilepsia, 39,* 77–80.

Berg, A.T., & Shinnar, S. (1996). Unprovoked seizures in children with febrile seizures: Short-term outcome. *Neurology, 47,* 562–568.

Berg, A.T., Shinnar, S., Hauser, W.A., et al. (1992). A prospective study of recurrent febrile seizures. *New England Journal of Medicine, 327,* 1122–1127.

Berg, A.T., Shinnar, S., Levy, S.R., et al. (2000). How well can epilepsy syndromes be identified at diagnosis?: A reassessment 2 years after initial diagnosis. *Epilepsia, 41,* 1269–1275.

Berg, A.T., Shinnar, S., Levy, S.R., et al. (2001). Defining early seizure outcomes in pediatric epilepsy: The good, the bad and the in-between. *Epilepsy Research, 43,* 75–84.

Berg, A.T., Testa, F.M., Levy, S.R., et al. (2000). Neuroimaging in children with newly diagnosed epilepsy: A community-based study. *Pediatrics, 106,* 527–532.

Besag, F.M. (2000). Is generic prescribing acceptable in epilepsy? *Drug Safety, 23*(3), 173–182.

Bodfish, J.W., Symons, F.J., Parker, D.E., et al. (2000). Varieties of repetitive behavior in autism: Comparisons to mental retardation. *Journal of Autism and Developmental Disorders,30,* 237–243.

Boehm, K.E., Morris, E.J., Kip, K.T., et al. (2001). Diagnosis and management of neurally mediated syncope and related conditions in adolescents. *The Journal of Adolescent Health, 28,* 2–9.

Bourgeois, B. (2000). *Presidential symposium.* American Epilepsy Society.

Bower, S.P., Kilpatrick, C.J., Vogrin, S.J., et al. (2000). Degree of hippocampal atrophy is not related to a history of febrile seizures in patients with proved hippocampal sclerosis. *Journal of Neurology, Neurosurgery, and Psychiatry, 69,* 733–738.

Breningstall, G.N. (1996). Breath-holding spells. *Pediatric Neurology, 14,* 91–97.

Briellmann, R.S., Jackson, G.D., Torn-Broers, Y., et al. (2001). Causes of epilepsies: Insights from discordant monozygous twins. *Annals of Neurology, 49,* 45–52.

Bulteau, C., Jambaque, I., Viguier, D., et al. (2000). Epileptic syndromes, cognitive assessment and school placement: A study of 251 children. *Developmental Medicine and Child Neurology, 42,* 319–327.

Bye, A.M., Kok, D.J., Ferenschild, F.T., et al. (2000). Paroxysmal non-epileptic events in children: A retrospective study over a period of 10 years. *Journal of Paediatrics and Child Health, 36,* 244–248.

Camfield, P.R. (1997). Recurrent seizures in the developing brain are not harmful. *Epilepsia, 38,* 735–737.

Camfield, P.R., & Camfield, C.S. (2000). Treatment of children with "ordinary" epilepsy. *Epileptic Disorders, 2,* 45–51.

Carballo, R., Cersosimo, R., Medina, C., et al. (2000). Panayiotopoulos-type benign childhood occipital epilepsy: A prospective study. *Neurology, 55,* 1096–1100.

Caviedes, B.E., & Herranz, J.L. (1998). Seizure recurrence and risk factors after withdrawal of chronic antiepileptic therapy in children. *Seizure, 7,* 107–114.

Cole, A.J. (2000). Is epilepsy a progressive disease?: The neurobiological consequences of epilepsy. *Epilepsia, 41* (Suppl. 2), S13–S22.

Coleman, H., & Fielder, A. (1999). Epilepsy education in schools. *Paediatric Nursing, 11*(9), 29–32.

Commission on Classification and Terminology of the International League Against Epilepsy. (1989). Proposal for revised classification of epilepsies and epileptic syndromes. *Epilepsia, 30,* 388–399.

Danesi, M.A., & Adetunji, J.B. (1994). Use of alternative medicine by patients with epilepsy: A survey of 265 epileptic patients in a developing country. *Epilepsia, 35,* 344–351.

Delgado-Escueta, A.V., Wilson, W.A., Olsen, R.W., et al. (1999). New waves of research in the epilepsies: Crossing into the third millennium. In A.V. Delgado-Escueta, W.A. Wilson, R.W. Olsen, et al. (Vol. eds.), *Advances in neurology series: Vol. 79. Jasper's basic mechanisms of the epilepsies* (3rd ed., pp. 3–58). Philadelphia: Lippincott Williams & Wilkins.

Dodson, W.E. (2001). Epilepsy, cerebral palsy, and IQ. In J.M. Pellock, W.E. Dodson, & B.F.D. Bourgeois (Eds.), *Pediatric epilepsy and therapy* (pp. 613–627). New York: Demos Medical.

DuVernoy, T.S., & Braun, M.M. (2000). Hypotonic-hyporesponsive episodes reported to the Vaccine Adverse Event Reporting System (VAERS), 1996–1998. *Pediatrics, 106,* e52.

Ebersole, J.S. (1999). Non-invasive pre-surgical evaluation with EEG/MEG source analysis. *Electroencephalography and Clinical Neurophysiology Supplement, 50,* 167–174.

Ellenberg, J.H., Hirtz, D., & Nelson, K.B. (1986). Do seizures cause intellectual deterioration? *New England Journal of Medicine, 314,* 1085–1088.

Ellenberg, J.H., & Nelson, K.B. (1978). Febrile seizures and later intellectual performance. *Archives of Neurology, 35,* 17–21.

Epilepsy Foundation. (2000–2001). *Making our schools seizure smart.* Retrieved January 11, 2002, from http://www.efa.org/answerplace/teachers/intro.html

Eriksson, K.J., & Koivikko, M.J. (1997). Prevalence, classification, and severity of epilepsy and epileptic syndromes in children. *Epilepsia, 38,* 1275–1282.

Farwell, J.R., Lee, Y.J., Hirtz, D.G., et al. (1990). Phenobarbital for febrile seizures: Effects on intelligence and on seizure recurrence. *New England Journal of Medicine, 322,* 364–369.

Fejerman, N., Caraballo, R., & Tenembaum, S.N. (2000). Atypical evolutions of benign localization-related epilepsies in children: Are they predictable? *Epilepsia, 41,* 380–390.

Fisch, B.J. (1999). *Fisch and Spehlmann's EEG primer: Basic principles of digital and analog EEG* (3rd rev. ed.). New York: Elsevier Science.

Fisher, R.S., Vickrey, B.G., Gibson, P., et al. (2000a). The impact of epilepsy from the patient's perspective, I: Descriptions and subjective perceptions. *Epilepsy Research, 41,* 39–51.

Fisher, R.S., Vickrey, B.G., Gibson, P., et al. (2000b). The impact of epilepsy from the patient's perspective, II: Views about therapy and health care. *Epilepsy Research, 41,* 53–61.

Foster, L.G. (1998). Nervous habits and stereotyped behaviors in preschool children. *Journal of the American Academy of Child and Adolescent Psychiatry, 37,* 711–717.

Fountain, N.B., Kim, J.S., & Lee, S.I. (1998). Sleep deprivation activates epileptiform discharges independent of the activating effects of sleep. *Journal of Clinical Neurophysiology, 15,* 69–75.

Frucht, M.M., Quigg, M., Schwaner, C., et al. (2000). Distribution of seizure precipitants among epilepsy syndromes. *Epilepsia, 41,* 1534–1539.

Fujikawa, D.G., Shinmei, S.S., & Cai, B. (2000). Seizure-induced neuronal necrosis: Implications for programmed cell death mechanisms. *Epilepsia, 41*(Suppl. 6), S9–S13.

Gage, F.H. (2002). Neurogenesis in the adult brain. *Journal of Neuroscience, 22,* 612–613.

Gaillard, W. (2000). Structural and functional imaging in children with partial epilepsy. *Mental Retardation and Developmental Disabilities Research Reviews, 6,* 220–226.

Gaillard, W.D., Bookheimer, S.Y., & Cohen, M. (2000). The use of fMRI in neocortical epilepsy. *Advances in Neurology, 84,* 391–404.

Gastaut, H. (1982). Classification of status epilepticus. In A.V. Delgado-Escueta, R.J. Porter, & C.G. Wasterlain (Eds.), *Status epilepticus: Mechanisms of brain damage and treatment.* New York: Raven Press.

Gilbert, D.L., & Buncher, C.R. (2000). An EEG should not be obtained routinely after first unprovoked seizure in childhood. *Neurology, 54,* 635–641.

Glaser, G.H. (1983). Medical complications of status epilepticus. *Advances in Neurology, 34,* 395–398.

Glauser, T.A., & Pippenger, C.E. (2000). Controversies in blood-level monitoring: Reexamining its role in the treatment of epilepsy. *Epilepsia, 41*(Suppl. 8), S6–S15.

Goadsby, P.J. (2001). Migraine, aura, and cortical spreading depression: Why are we still talking about it? *Annals of Neurology, 49,* 4–6.

Gordon, N. (1999). Episodic dyscontrol syndrome. *Developmental Medicine and Child Neurology, 41,* 786–788.

Greene, P., Kang, U.J., & Fahn, S. (1995). Spread of symptoms in idiopathic torsion dystonia. *Movement Disorders, 10,* 143–152.

Greenwood, R.S., & Tennison, M.B. (1999). When to start and stop anticonvulsant therapy in children. *Archives of Neurology, 56,* 1073–1077.

Guberman, A. (1998). Monotherapy or polytherapy for epilepsy? *The Canadian Journal of Neurological Sciences, 25,* S3–S8.

Harbord, M.G. (2000). Significant anticonvulsant side-effects in children and adolescents. *Journal of Clinical Neuroscience, 7,* 213–216.

Harden, C.L. (2000). Therapeutic safety monitoring: What to look for and when to look for it. *Epilepsia, 41*(Suppl. 8), S37–S44.

Harding, G.F., Wild, J.M., Robertson, K.A., et al. (2000). Electro-oculography, electroretinography, visual evoked potentials, and multifocal electroretinography in patients with vigabatrin-attributed visual field constriction. *Epilepsia, 41,* 1420–1431.

Hauser, W.A. (1994). The prevalence and incidence of convulsive disorders in children. *Epilepsia, 35*(Suppl. 2), S1–S6.

Hemingway, C., Freeman, J.M., Pillas, D.J., et al. (2001). The ketogenic diet: A 3- to 6-year follow-up of 150 children enrolled prospectively. *Pediatrics, 108,* 898–905.

Hennessy, M.J., & Binnie, C.D. (2000). Photogenic partial seizures. *Epilepsia, 41*(1), 59–64.

Hernandez-Latorre, M.A, & Roig, M. (2000). Natural history of migraine in childhood. *Cephalalgia, 20,* 573–579.

Hirtz, D.G. (1997). Febrile seizures. *Pediatrics in Review, 18,* 5–8.

Hirtz, D., Ashwal, S., Berg, A., et al. (2000). Practice parameter: Evaluating a first nonfebrile seizure in children. Report of the Quality Standards Subcommittee of the American Academy of Neurology, the Child Neurology Society, and the American Epilepsy Society. *Neurology, 55,* 616–623.

Hu, R.Q., Banerjee, P.K., Snead, O.C., III. (2000). Regulation of gamma-aminobutyric acid (GABA) release in cerebral cortex in the gamma-hydroxybutyric acid (GHB) model of absence seizures in rat. *Neuropharmacology, 39,* 427–439.

Huang, C.-C., Chang, Y.-C., & Wang, S.-T. (1998). Acute symptomatic seizure disorders in young children: A population study in Southern Taiwan. *Epilepsia, 39,* 960–964.

Ilhan, A., Tuncer, C., Komsuoglu, S.S., et al. (1999). Jervell and Lange-Nielsen syndrome: Neurologic and cardiologic evaluation. *Pediatric Neurology, 21,* 809–813.

Ito, M. (1998). Antiepileptic drug treatment of West syndrome. *Epilepsia, 39*(Suppl. 5), S38–S41.

Jambaque, I., Chiron, C., Dumas, C., et al. (2000). Mental

and behavioural outcome of infantile epilepsy treated by vigabatrin in tuberous sclerosis patients. *Epilepsy Research, 38*, 151–160.

Jayakar, P. (1999). Invasive EEG monitoring in children: When, where, and what? *Journal of Clinical Neurophysiology, 16*, 408–418.

Jensen, F.E. (1999). Acute and chronic effects of seizures in the developing brain: Experimental models. *Epilepsia, 40*(Suppl. 1), S51–S58.

Kandel, E.R., Schwartz, J.H., & Jessell, T.M. (Eds.). (2000). *Principles of neural science* (4th ed.). New York: McGraw-Hill.

Knudsen, F.U. (2000). Febrile seizures: Treatment and prognosis. *Epilepsia, 41*, 2–9.

Kotagal, P. (2000). Tonic-clonic seizures. In H.O. Lüders & S. Noachtar (Eds.), *Epileptic seizures: Pathophysiology and clinical semiology* (pp. 425–432). New York: Churchill Livingstone.

Kriegstein, A.R., Owens, F.F., & Avoli, M. (1999). Ontogeny of channels, transmitters and epileptogenesis. In A.V. Delgado-Escueta, W.A. Wilson, R.W. Olsen, et al. (Vol. eds.), *Advances in neurology series: Vol. 79. Jasper's basic mechanisms of the epilepsies* (3rd ed., pp. 145–159). Philadelphia: Lippincott Williams & Wilkins.

Krumholz, A., Singer, H.S., Niedermeyer, E., et al. (1983). Electrophysiological studies in Tourette's syndrome. *Annals of Neurology, 14*, 638–641.

Kubota, T., Aso, K., Negoro, T., et al. (1999). Epileptic spasms preceded by partial seizures with a close temporal association. *Epilepsia, 40*, 1572–1579.

Kuhle, S., Tiefenthaler, M., Seidl, R., et al. (2000). Prolonged generalized epileptic seizures triggered by breath-holding spells. *Pediatric Neurology, 23*, 271–273.

Kurtz, Z., Tookey, P., & Ross, E. (1998). Epilepsy in young people: 23 year followup of the British national child development study. *British Medical Journal, 316*, 339–342.

Kwan, P., & Brodie, M.J. (2001). Neuropsychological effects of epilepsy and antiepileptic drugs. *Lancet, 357*, 216–222.

Kwong, K.L., Wong, S.N., & So, K.T. (2000). Parental perception, worries and needs in children with epilepsy. *Acta Paediatrica, 89*, 593–596.

Laberge, L., Tremblay, R.E., Vitaro, F., et al. (2000). Development of parasomnias from childhood to early adolescence. *Pediatrics, 106*(1, Pt. 1), 67–74.

Leppik, I.E. (2000). Monotherapy and polypharmacy. *Neurology, 55*(11, Suppl. 3), S25–9.

Lerman, P. (1992). Benign partial epilepsy with centrotemporal spikes. In J. Roger, M. Bureau, C. Dravet, et al. (Eds.), *Epileptic syndromes in infancy, childhood and adolescence* (2nd ed., pp. 189–200). London: John Libbey & Co. Ltd.

Lhatoo, S.M., Johnson, A.L., Goodridge, D.M., et al. (2001). Mortality in epilepsy in the first 11 to 14 years after diagnosis: Multivariate analysis of a long-term, prospective, population-based cohort. *Annals of Neurology, 49*, 336–344.

Lin, Y., Itomi, K., Takada, H., et al. (1998). Benign myoclonic epilepsy in infants: Video-EEG features and long-term follow-up. *Neuropediatrics, 29*, 268–271.

Loiseau, P. (1992). Childhood absence epilepsy. In J. Roger, M. Bureau, C. Dravet, et al. (Eds.), *Epileptic syndromes in infancy, childhood and adolescence* (2nd ed., pp. 135–150). London: John Libbey & Co. Ltd.

Lombroso, C. (2000). Pavor nocturnas of proven epileptic origin. *Epilepsia, 41*, 1221–1226.

Lowenstein, D.H. (1999). Status epilepticus: An overview of the clinical problem. *Epilepsia, 40*(Suppl. 1), S3–S8.

Lowenstein, D.H., & Alldredge, B.K. (1998). Status epilepticus. *New England Journal of Medicine, 338*, 970–976.

MacDonald, B.K., Johnson, A.L., Goodridge, D.M., et al. (2000). Factors predicting prognosis of epilepsy after presentation with seizures. *Annals of Neurology, 48*, 833–841.

Mayville, C., Fakhoury, T., & Abou-Khalil, B. (2000). Absence seizures with evolution into generalized tonic-clonic activity: Clinical and EEG features. *Epilepsia, 41*, 391–394.

McCormick, D., & Contreras, D. (2001). On the cellular and network bases of epileptic seizures. *Annual Review of Physiology, 63*, 815–846.

Mitchell, W.G., Zhou, Y., Chavez, J.M., et al. (1993). Effects of antiepileptic drugs on reaction time, attention, and impulsivity in children. *Pediatrics, 91*, 101–105.

Mizrahi, E.M., & Clancy, R.R. (2000). Neonatal seizures: Early-onset seizure syndromes and their consequences for development. *Mental Retardation and Developmental Disabilities Research Reviews, 6*, 229–241.

Mocan, H., Yildiran, A., Orhan, F., et al. (1999). Breath holding spells in 91 children and response to treatment with iron. *Archives of Disease in Childhood, 81*, 261–262.

Montalenti, E., Imperiale, D., Rovera, A., et al. (2001). Clinical features, EEG findings and diagnostic pitfalls in juvenile myoclonic epilepsy: A series of 63 patients. *Journal of the Neurological Sciences, 184*, 65–70.

Moshé, S.L. (1998). Brain injury with prolonged seizures in children and adults. *Journal of Child Neurology, 13*(Suppl. 1), S3–S6.

Moshé, S.L. (2000a). Mechanisms of action of anticonvulsant agents. *Neurology, 55*(5, Suppl. 1), S32–S40.

Moshé, S.L. (2000b). Seizures early in life. *Neurology, 55* (Suppl. 1), S15–S20.

Moulard, B., Buresi, C., & Malafosse, A. (2000). Study of the voltage-gated sodium channel beta 1 subunit (SCN1B) in the benign familial infantile convulsion syndrome (BFIC). *Human Mutation, 16*, 139–142.

Nakken, K.O. (1999). Physical exercise in outpatients with epilepsy. *Epilepsia, 40*, 643–651.

Neinstein, L., & Milgrom, E. (2000). Trauma-triggered migraine and acute confusional migraine. *The Journal of Adolescent Health, 27*, 119–124.

Nelson, K.B., & Ellenberg, J.H. (1976). Predictors of epilepsy in children who have experienced febrile seizures. *New England Journal of Medicine, 295*, 1029–1033.

Nelson, K.B., & Ellenberg, J.H. (1978). Prognosis in children with febrile seizures. *Pediatrics, 61*, 720–727.

Nemeroff, C.B. (2000). An ever-increasing pharmacopoeia for the management of patients with bipolar disorder. *Journal of Clinical Psychiatry, 61*(Suppl. 13), 19–25.

Neubauer, B.A. (2000). The genetics of rolandic epilepsy. *Epileptic Disorders, 2*(Suppl. 1), S67–S68.

Neufeld, M.Y., Chistik, V., Vishne, T.H., et al. (2000). The diagnostic aid of routine EEG findings in patients presenting with a presumed first-ever unprovoked seizure. *Epilepsy Research, 42*, 197–202.

Okumura, A., Hayakawa, F., Kato, T., et al. (2000). Early recognition of benign partial epilepsy in infancy. *Epilepsia, 41*, 714–717.

Pachatz, C., Fusco, L., & Vigevano, F. (1999). Benign myoclonus of early infancy. *Epileptic Disorders, 1*, 57–61.

Panayiotopoulos, C.P. (1999a). *Current problems in epilepsy series: Vol. 15. Benign childhood partial seizures and related epileptic syndromes*. London: John Libbey & Co. Ltd.

Panayiotopoulos, C.P. (1999b). Visual phenomena and headache in occipital epilepsy: A review, a systematic study and differentiation from migraine. *Epileptic Disorders, 1*, 205–216.

Parker, A.P., Agathonikou, A., Robinson, R.O., et al. (1998). Inappropriate use of carbamazepine and vigabatrin in typical absence seizures. *Developmental Medicine and Child Neurology, 40,* 517–519.

Pedersen, S.B., & Petersen, K.A. (1998). Juvenile myoclonic epilepsy: Clinical and EEG features. *Acta Neurologica Scandinavica, 97,* 160–163.

Prasad, A.N., Prasad, C., & Stafstrom, C.E. (1999). Recent advances in the genetics of epilepsy: Insights from human and animal studies. *Epilepsia, 40,* 1329–1352.

Provini, F., Plazzi, G., Tinuper, P., et al. (1999). Nocturnal frontal lobe epilepsy. A clinical and polygraphic overview of 100 consecutive cases. *Brain, 122,* 1017–1031.

Rantala, H., & Putkonen, T. (1999). Occurrence, outcome, and prognostic factors of infantile spasms and Lennox-Gastaut syndrome. *Epilepsia, 40,* 286–289.

Reynolds, E.H. (2000). The ILAER/IBE/WHO global campaign against epilepsy: Bringing epilepsy "out of the shadows." *Epilepsy and Behavior, 1,* S3–SS8.

Riikonen, R.S. (2000). Steroids of vigabatrin in the treatment of infantile spasms? *Pediatric Neurology, 23,* 403–408.

Riikonen, R. (2001). The PEHO syndrome. *Brain Development, 23,* 765–769.

Risinger, M.W. (2000). Noninvasive ictal electroencephalography in humans. In H.O. Lüders & S. Noachtar (Eds.), *Epileptic seizures: Pathophysiology and clinical semiology* (pp. 32–48). New York: Churchill Livingstone.

Robertson, M.M. (2000). Tourette syndrome, associated conditions and the complexities of treatment. *Brain, 123* (Pt. 3), 425–462.

Ross, C., Blake, A., & Whitehouse, W.P. (1999). Status epilepticus on the paediatric intensive care unit: The role of EEG monitoring. *Seizure, 8,* 335–338.

Rossi, P.G., Parmeggiani, A., Posar, A., et al. (1999). Landau-Kleffner (LKS): Long-term follow-up and links with electrical status epilepticus during sleep (ESES). *Brain Development, 21,* 90–98.

Saunders-Pullman, R., Braun, I., & Bressman, S. (1999). Pediatric movement disorders. *Child and Adolescent Clinics of North America, 8,* 747–765.

Schoenfeld, J., Seidenberg, M., Woodard, A., et al. (1999). Neuropsychological and behavioral status of children with complex partial seizures. *Developmental Medicine and Child Neurology, 41,* 724–731.

Seyfried, T.N., Todorova, M.T., & Poderycki, M.J. (1999). Experimental models of multifactorial epilepsies: The EL mouse and mice susceptible to audiogenic seizures. In A.V. Delgado-Escueta, W.A. Wilson, R.W. Olsen, et al. (Vol. eds.), *Advances in neurology series: Vol. 79. Jasper's basic mechanisms of the epilepsies* (3rd ed., pp. 297–290). Philadelphia: Lippincott Williams & Wilkins.

Shields, W.D. (2000). Catastrophic epilepsy in childhood. *Epilepsia, 41*(Suppl. 2), S2–S6.

Shields, W.D., Shewmon, D.A., Peacock, W.J., et al. (1999). Surgery for the treatment of medically intractable infantile spasms: A cautionary case. *Epilepsia, 40,* 1305–1308.

Shinnar, S., & Berg, A.T. (1994). Does antiepileptic drug therapy alter the prognosis of childhood seizures and prevent the development of chronic epilepsy? *Seminars in Pediatric Neurology, 1,* 111–117.

Shinnar, S., Berg, A.T., Moshé, S.L., et al. (1990). Risk of seizure recurrence following a short unprovoked seizure in childhood: A prospective study. *Pediatrics, 85,* 1076–1085.

Shorvon, S. (2000). *Handbook of epilepsy treatment.* Malden, MA: Blackwell Science.

Sillanpää, M. (2000). Long-term prognosis of epilepsy. *Epileptic Disorders, 2,* 79–88.

Singh, R., Scheffer, I.E., Crossland, K., et al. (1999). Generalized epilepsy with febrile seizures plus: A common childhood-onset genetic epilepsy syndrome. *Annals of Neurology, 45,* 75–81.

Stein, A.G., Eder, H.G., Blum, D.E., et al. (2000). An automated drug delivery system for focal epilepsy. *Epilepsy Research, 39,* 103–114.

Steinhoff, B.J., Neususs, K., Thegeder, H., et al. (1996). Leisure time activity and physical fitness in patients with epilepsy. *Epilepsia, 37,* 1221–1227.

Szabó, C.A.,& Lüders, H.O. (2000). Todd's paralysis and postictal aphasia. In H.O. Lüders & S. Noachtar (Eds.), *Epileptic seizures: Pathophysiology and clinical semiology* (pp. 652–657). New York: Churchill Livingstone.

Tal, Y., Even, L., Kugelman, A., et al. (1997). The clinical significance of rigors in febrile children. *European Journal of Pediatrics, 156,* 457–459.

Tramonte, J.V., & Barron, T.F. (1998). Infantile spasms: A proposal for a staged evaluation. *Pediatric Neurology, 19,* 368–371.

Tuchman, R.F. (1997). Acquired epileptiform aphasia. *Seminars in Pediatric Neurology, 4,* 93–101.

Velasco, A.L., Velasco, M., Velasco, F., et al. (2000). Subacute and chronic electrical stimulation of the hippocampus on intractable temporal lobe seizures: Preliminary report. *Archives of Medical Research, 31,* 316–328.

Verrotti, A., Moresi, S., Cutarella, R., et al. (2000). Predictive value of EEG monitoring during drug withdrawal in children with cryptogenic partial epilepsy. *Neurophysiologie Clinique, 30,* 240–245.

Wallace, S.J. (1998). Myoclonus and epilepsy in childhood: A review of treatment with valproate, ethosuximide, lamotrigine, and zonisamide. *Epilepsy Research, 29,* 147–154.

Wasterlain, C.G. (1997). Recurrent seizures in the developing brain are harmful. *Epilepsia, 38,* 728–734.

Werlin, S.L., D'Souza, B.J., Hogan, W.J., et al. (1980). Sandifer syndrome: An unappreciated clinical entity. *Developmental Medicine and Child Neurology, 22,* 374–378.

Wiebe, S., Blume, W.T., Girvin, J.P., et al. (2001). A randomized, controlled trial of surgery for temporal-lobe epilepsy. *New England Journal of Medicine, 345,* 311–318.

Willmore, L.J. (2000). Clinical pharmacology of new antiepileptic drugs. *Neurology, 55*(11, Suppl. 3), S17–S24.

Wolf, P. (1992). Epilepsy with grand mal on awakening. In J. Roger, M. Bureau, C. Dravet, et al. (Eds.), *Epileptic syndromes in infancy, childhood and adolescence* (2nd ed., pp. 329–342). London: John Libbey & Co. Ltd.

Wolf, P. (1994). *Epileptic seizures and syndromes.* London: John Libbey & Co. Ltd.

Wyllie, E., Glazer, J.P., Benbadis, S., et al. (1999). Psychiatric features of children and adolescents with pseudoseizures. *Archives of Pediatric and Adolescent Medicine, 153,* 244–248.

Ziemann, U., Steinhoff, B.J., Tergau, F., et al. (1998). Transcranial magnetic stimulation: Its current role in epilepsy research. *Epilepsy Research, 30,* 11–30.

Zucconi, M., Oldani, A., Ferini-Stambi, L., et al. (1997). Nocturnal paroxysmal arousals with motor behaviors during sleep: Frontal lobe epilepsy or parasomnia? *Journal of Clinical Neurophysiology, 14,* 513–522.

26 Traumatic Brain Injury

Linda J. Michaud, Jennifer Semel-Concepción,
Ann-Christine Duhaime, and Mary F. Lazar

Upon completion of this chapter, the reader will:

- know the major causes of traumatic brain injury in children
- be able to distinguish among mild, moderate, and severe traumatic brain injury
- be able to identify prognostic factors for traumatic brain injury in children
- understand the long-term effects of the injury on the child and family
- be able to identify preventive means to reduce the incidence of traumatic brain injury

Most head trauma in children is minor and not associated with persisting impairments (Homer & Kleinman, 1999). However, severe head injury (with associated brain injury) occurs with sufficient frequency to make it the most common cause of acquired disability in childhood (Adelson & Kochanek, 1998; Mansfield, 1997; Zuckerman & Conway, 1997). Even when obvious physical complications are minimal, neuropsychological impairments may lead to chronic academic, behavior, and interpersonal difficulties that pose an enormous challenge to the child, family, and society. Effective acute management and long-term rehabilitation are vital after traumatic brain injury (TBI) in order to optimize the child's outcome (National Institutes of Health [NIH] Consensus Development Panel, 1999; Rosenthal et al., 1999). The best approach to TBI, however, is prevention.

CARMEN

When Carmen was 9 years old, she fell from the top of a 6-foot ladder during her summer vacation. She hit her head on the concrete pavement and immediately lost consciousness. Emergency medical services (EMS) rushed her to the hospital, where she opened her eyes on command, withdrew her feet to pain, and spoke some garbled words. Physicians then administered the Glasgow Coma Scale (GCS; discussed later in this chapter); Carmen scored a 10 out of a possible 15. Her neurological examination and cranial computed tomography (CT) scan were normal, with no evidence of hemorrhage or edema. Carmen improved so rapidly that in 1 week she seemed back to normal and was discharged.

Yet, after Carmen returned home, her parents noticed that she was very irritable, which was unusual for her. They initially attributed this to her stay in the hospital. They became concerned, however, when the irritability persisted for the next 2 months. They also noticed that Carmen was becoming quite aggressive toward her brother, her friends, and her dog.

When Carmen returned to school in the fall, her teachers also noticed these changes in her behavior. In addition, they were concerned by deterioration in her school performance. She had previously been a straight A student but was now receiving Cs and Ds in most subjects. Carmen's teachers requested a conference with her parents to discuss these changes.

Carmen's parents, wondering whether the changes in her personality, behavior, and school performance could be attributed to her brain injury, consulted a neurologist, who was unable to detect any neurological abnormalities. The physician then referred Carmen for a neuropsychological assessment. Her score on the Wechsler Intelligence Scale for Children–Third Edition (WISC-III; Wechsler, 1991) indicated average intellectual functioning with no significant verbal–performance discrepancy. Her scores were also average in arithmetic, spelling, and reading achievement tests. The tests, however, did indicate impairments in auditory memory, abstract problem-solving abilities, and attention span.

As a result of this evaluation, Carmen was provided with special education support (see Chapter 30) in math and social studies, the subjects that were most difficult for her. Her behavior and school performance gradually improved over the next few months, and it was anticipated that she would not require resource help during the next school year. Also, Carmen's parents thought that her personality was gradually returning to normal.

ETHAN

Ethan was 7 years old when he was hit by a car while riding his bicycle without a helmet. Minutes after the collision, EMS arrived and found him unresponsive and with an abnormal flexion motor response. A cranial CT scan performed on admission to the hospital showed a large **subdural hematoma** over the left frontal, temporal, and parietal lobes. There were no other injuries. Ethan was taken to the operating room within an hour, and the neurosurgeon removed the hematoma and placed an intracranial pressure monitor in him. He was found to have elevated intracranial pressure that was eventually reduced with mannitol and controlled hyperventilation.

Ethan remained unresponsive for 10 weeks but then began to follow the command, "Move your hand," by opening his left hand. He also followed objects placed in his field of vision but did not speak. He was transferred to the neurorehabilitation service, where he received physical, occupational, and speech-language therapy twice daily. Gradually, over the next 12 weeks, his motor control improved, although he had spasticity on the right side of his body. He began to walk with an ankle-foot orthosis (brace) and was able to complete self-care activities independently, primarily using his left arm, with some assistance from the right. Communication remained a major problem, as both expressive and receptive language impairments were evident. Cognitive testing (WISC-III) revealed persisting impairments, with scores on both verbal and performance subtests more than 2 standard deviations below the norms.

Ethan was eventually discharged and enrolled in an outpatient rehabilitation program, in which he received physical and occupational therapy weekly and speech-language therapy three times weekly. Three months later he returned to school in a self-contained class for children with communication disorders; he also received physical and occupational therapy.

At 1-year follow-up, Ethan's right hand functioning had gradually improved, but he continued to prefer using his left hand. Both expressive and receptive language skills had significantly increased. His individualized education program (IEP; see Chapter 30) for the next school year included continued placement in a class for children with communication disorders, with participation in a general education third-grade class for 20% of the day. He continued to receive physical and occupational therapies. Ethan was not able to keep up with his old friends but was making new ones. It is likely that he will continue to have disabilities, but he will also continue to gain new skills and knowledge that should help him cope with his disabilities.

INCIDENCE OF HEAD INJURIES

Each year, approximately 1 in 25 children receive medical attention because of a head injury (Brookes et al., 1990; Lam & MacKersie, 1999). These injuries range from confined areas of scalp or skull trauma to more diffuse and severe brain damage. TBI, defined as trauma sufficient to result in a change in level of consciousness and/or an anatomical abnormality of the brain, occurs in approximately 1 in 500 children per year (Adesunkanmi et al., 1998; Baker, O'Neill, & Karpf, 1984; Guerrero, Thurman, & Sniezek, 2000). Head injuries most commonly occur in the spring and summer, on weekends, and in the afternoons, when children are most likely to be outside playing or riding in cars. Although TBI can occur at any age, there are two stages in a child's life when the risk is notably higher. The first is from birth until 5 years, when cognitive and motor functions are most actively developing, and the second is in adolescence, when peer approval, impulsivity, and a sense of immortality increase risk-taking behaviors (Luerssen, Klauber, & Marshall, 1988).

CAUSES OF TRAUMATIC BRAIN INJURY

Common causes of TBI include falls from heights; sports- and recreation-related injuries; motor vehicle crashes; and assaults, including child abuse. The frequency of these types of brain injuries varies with age. Young children are more likely to sustain brain injuries as a result of falls, whereas teenagers are more often involved in motor vehicle crashes (Sosin, Sacks, & Webb, 1996). The frequency of gunshot wounds to the head has increased dramatically in children living in urban areas (Sheehan et al., 1997).

Certain psychosocial factors may increase the risk of childhood head trauma. Children with a conduct disorder or hyperactive-impulsive behavior (as seen in children with attention-deficit/hyperactivity disorder [ADHD]) may act in a dangerous manner, although hyperactive behavior itself does not necessarily increase the risk of injury (Gerring et al., 1998; Light et al., 1998). Adolescents who are severely depressed may attempt suicide. In addition, head injury from child abuse occurs more commonly in children who were born prematurely, who have a preexisting developmental disability, who were born to young parents, and who live with unstable family dynamics (Duhaime et al., 1998).

TYPES OF BRAIN INJURIES

The type of brain injury that a child sustains depends primarily on the nature of the force that caused the injury and the severity of the insult. Head trauma can be caused by both **impact** and **inertial** forces. Impact, or contact, forces occur when the head strikes a surface or is struck by a moving object. Impact forces can result in scalp injuries, skull fractures, focal brain bruises **(contusions),** or blood collections beneath the skull (i.e., **epidural hematomas**). Inertial forces occur when the brain undergoes violent motion inside the skull, which tears the nerve fibers and blood vessels. The severity of injuries caused by inertial forces depends on the magnitude and the direction of the motion. Angular acceleration/deceleration forces, such as those that might occur in a high-speed motor vehicle crash, cause much more serious damage than do straight-line (translational) forces, such as those that might occur in a fall. Injuries caused by inertial forces range from relatively mild **concussions** to more serious injuries, such as **diffuse axonal injuries (DAIs)** and **subdural hematomas.**

Most clinical brain injuries include both impact and inertial components, with several injury types occurring simultaneously. Thus, the injuries discussed in the following sections do not usually occur singly.

Scalp and Skull Injuries

Impact forces cause scalp and skull injuries. Although scalp injuries sometimes cause considerable blood loss, they have no neurological consequence. Skull fractures can be either ben̄ ̄ ̄or serious. A **linear fracture,** in which there is no visible injury but a crack in the skull is ̄ on an X ray, is sometimes seen in young children who have fallen from low heights. Th̄ tures do not cause significant neurological damage. A **depressed fracture,** in which the skull is broken and presses against the underlying brain tissue, however, may be associated with significant brain injury and associated disabilities. For example, a depressed fracture directly over the motor cortex (the part of the brain that controls movement) may result in weakness on the opposite side of the body.

Brain Contusions

Brain contusions, or bruises of the brain, most often result from direct impact to the head. As is true of bruises in other areas of the body, brain contusions often evolve during the first few days after the injury, such that clinical symptoms (e.g., blurred vision, changes in speech, uncharacteristic behavior) may worsen. Associated hemorrhages occasionally require surgical evacuation. Impairments depend on the extent of the bruise and resultant damage to the brain.

Epidural Hematomas

Although epidural hematomas can lead to serious impairments or even death, if detected promptly they can be treated effectively, increasing the chance for a favorable outcome. A hematoma, or blood clot, forms between the skull and the outer covering of the brain (i.e., dura) and may originate in either an artery or a vein. An arterial hematoma occurs when the brain's covering, usually containing the middle meningeal artery, is torn due to impact. This is usually associated with a skull fracture and is the only life-threatening brain injury to result from a low-height fall in young children. In older children, epidural hematomas may occur from falls and other contact injuries, such as sports injuries. Venous epidural hematomas occur when there is bleeding from a fractured bone or from a tear in a large vein in the dura. Because veins generally bleed more slowly than arteries, venous epidural hematomas are usually self-limited and less serious than arterial hematomas are.

The classic clinical hallmark of an arterial epidural hematoma is delayed onset of symptoms (Maggi et al., 1998). Thus, when a child sustains the injury, neurological symptoms may be minimal or absent. As the hematoma enlarges, however, secondary injury, caused by increased pressure on the brain, may occur. This can lead to headaches, confusion, vomiting, **focal neurological impairment** (e.g., one-sided weakness), and agitation. This may progress to lethargy, coma, and even death if left untreated. Specific symptoms associated with arterial epidural hematoma vary, depending on other concomitant injuries and/or the age of the individual. Venous epidural hematomas, which typically occur from bleeding at a fracture in the skull, may be asymptomatic or present with more delayed symptomatology. These do not always require surgical intervention. If surgery is performed before secondary injury becomes irreversible, outcome is remarkably favorable (Ben Abraham et al., 2000; Lee et al., 1998), and these children quickly return to normal functioning. If surgery is delayed, various physical and cognitive impairments are likely to persist.

Concussions

Concussions are brain injuries sufficient to cause a brief loss of consciousness or amnesia for the event. Physiologically, a concussion indicates a relatively mild injury to the nerve fibers in the brain. In children, concussions occur most commonly from falls and contact sports and represent one of the most frequent reasons for trauma admissions to the hospital (Poirier & Wadsworth, 2000). Usually, a brief loss of consciousness (typically a few minutes) is followed by a complete return to normal mental status and behavior. In some children, however, a period of headache, drowsiness, confusion, or irritability may occur, often several hours after the injury; these symptoms may last for a few days to weeks (Mittenberg, Wittner, & Miller, 1997). The CT scan of a child with a concussion will be normal, differentiating this child from one whose deterioration is caused by a blood clot requiring surgery.

Diffuse Axonal Injuries

Although concussion is at the mild end of the spectrum of diffuse injuries, children with more severe symptoms are classified as having sustained a DAI, in which nerve fibers (i.e., axons) throughout the brain have been damaged or torn, usually by violent motion (e.g., during motor vehicle crashes). The individual may have been a passenger, a pedestrian, or a bicycle rider (Senturia et al., 1997; Wills et al., 1997). Children are more prone to develop DAI because their heads are proportionally larger compared with their bodies, their neck muscles are relatively weaker, and their brain development (myelination) is not mature (Adelson & Kochanek, 1998).

Children who have sustained DAI lapse into immediate unconsciousness. For practical purposes, a diagnosis of DAI is given if unconsciousness lasts at least 6 hours without other causes, such as seizures or increased intracranial pressure from a hematoma. Depending on the severity of the injury, the child also may exhibit abnormal movements (i.e., posturing), abnormal reactions of the pupils, and difficulty regulating breathing and blood pressure. CT and magnetic resonance imaging (MRI) scans often reveal small, scattered brain tissue tears and hemorrhages. In more mild cases, the CT scan may show no abnormalities (Bigler, 1999; Ewing-Cobbs, Kramer, et al., 1998; Grasso & Keller, 1998). Because of the large mechanical forces involved in this type of injury, trauma to other organ systems or to the spine is not uncommon, and lack of oxygen or blood loss may exacerbate the primary insult to the central nervous system.

Recovery from DAI occurs over weeks to years, depending on the severity of injury. Long-lasting impairments may include motor, communicative, cognitive, and behavior problems and range from mild to severe (Paterakis et al., 2000). A few individuals with severe injuries may remain in a chronic unresponsive state, but the majority regain consciousness.

Acute Subdural Hematomas

Acute subdural hematomas are blood clots that form beneath the dura, over the surface of the brain itself. Unlike an epidural hematoma, hemorrhages in the subdural compartment occur not from impact but from shearing forces applied to the veins that course between the brain surface and the large, draining dural veins. Tremendous angular acceleration/deceleration forces are required to displace the brain from the dura sufficiently to rupture these bridging veins. As a result, a large acute subdural hematoma usually accompanies a major generalized injury to the brain itself. The damage done by direct pressure from the overlying blood clot thus adds to the damage from the primary injury, explaining why morbidity and mortality rates are so high among children with subdural hematomas and why surgical evacuation of the clot often appears to make only a small difference in the clinical status of the individual (Koc et al., 1997). This contrasts with the epidural hematoma, for which prompt surgical evacuation markedly improves outcome.

Recovery from a subdural hematoma is quite similar to that from a DAI; in fact, the two injuries often occur together. A subdural hematoma may cause major brain swelling and stroke and is almost always unilateral (i.e., on one side of the brain). Individuals with subdural hematomas often have a large area of brain damage on the affected side in addition to having DAI throughout the brain.

INFLICTED HEAD INJURY

Though most brain injuries are unintentional, inflicted injuries (i.e., due to physical abuse) do occur and pose special problems for the practitioner. Inflicted injuries are most commonly seen in children younger than 3 years of age (Reece & Sege, 2000) and are the leading cause of traumatic death in infancy (Duhaime et al., 1998; McCabe & Donahue, 2000). Reece and Sege (2000) found that confirmed abuse accounted for 19% of hospital admissions for head injury in children younger than 6½ years old and for 33% of those younger than 3 years old. The term *shaken baby syndrome* is frequently used to describe this type of injury. Some suggest that the use of the term *shaken-impact syndrome* better reflects the fact that when the child is shaken, the head usually hits a surface such as a bed, floor, or wall (David, 1999).

Clues that the injury might have been inflicted rather than accidental include a history that is inconsistent with the injuries or a delay in reporting the injury and seeking medical attention. For example, a fall from a low height (less than 4 feet) or from an infant swing or trivial forces encountered in childhood play are rarely sufficient to cause a significant head injury (Duhaime et al., 1998).

Certain injuries can alert the practitioner that the trauma may have been inflicted. These include complex skull fractures, subdural hematomas, and subarachnoid hemorrhage. Retinal hemorrhages, although not diagnostic, are strongly suggestive of abuse (Reece & Sege, 2000). The abused child may also show signs of previous injuries, including bone fractures and bruises that are in different stages of the healing process. Ewing-Cobbs, Kramer, et al. (1998) reported that 45% of children with inflicted head injuries showed signs of prior head injuries, even when the children were as young as 6 weeks old.

Children with inflicted head injuries are more likely to die than those with unintentional injuries (Duhaime et al., 1998). Seizures are also more common in this group, being seen in up to 70% (Duhaime et al., 1998). Those children who survive have poorer recovery, greater disability, and are more likely to have mental retardation (Ewing-Cobbs, Kramer, et al., 1998).

DETECTING SIGNIFICANT BRAIN INJURY

As noted previously, most head trauma is minor and does not require treatment or result in significant consequences. But how does a caregiver know whether head trauma warrants treatment? Generally speaking, if a child hits his or her head and does not lose consciousness, no treatment is necessary unless the child develops symptoms. Medical evaluation (a visit to a physician or the emergency room) is needed, however, if the child becomes lethargic, confused, or irritable; has a severe headache; demonstrates acute impairments in speech, vision, or movements of the arms or legs; has significant bleeding from the wound; or vomits repeatedly.

If the child is momentarily unconscious and then resumes activities, he or she may have a mild concussion. If there has been more than a momentary loss of consciousness or confusion, the child should be taken to the emergency room, where a neurological examination will be performed. A brain imaging study may be performed to determine whether there is significant brain injury (Bruce, 2000). If there are no abnormal neurological or radiological findings, the child may then be sent home. Parents will be given instructions to make sure the child can be roused from sleep, is not confused, and develops no new neurological symptoms.

If the child remains unconscious for more than a few minutes, EMS should be called. If, upon arrival at the hospital, the child is still unconscious, he or she will be stabilized in the emergency room and then usually transferred to the intensive care unit. Immediate coma after head trauma is the result of primary injury to neural pathways. There may be worsening in the subsequent 24 hours as a consequence of secondary hemorrhaging or brain swelling.

SEVERITY OF BRAIN INJURY

The duration and severity of coma indicate the seriousness of a brain injury. The most frequently used scale for coma severity is the GCS (Table 26.1; Jennett et al., 1977; Brain Trauma Foundation, the American Association of Neurological Surgeons, & the Joint Section on Neurotrauma and Critical Care, 2000). Although this scale was devised for use in adults and can be difficult to apply to very young children, it remains the most useful method available for classifying severe brain injuries in the early period after trauma. Using this scale within the first 6 hours after injury, the trauma team assigns the child a score based on the degree and quality of movement, vocalization, and eye opening. Individuals receive a score between 3 and 15. The best score is 15, representing the least severe brain injury. An individual with a score of 3 has no eye opening, movement, or verbal response and is in deep coma. An individual who looks about, moves limbs in response to requests, and is oriented to the environment receives a score of 15. Someone who opens his or her eyes when physically prodded, withdraws a limb that is touched, and makes only incomprehensible sounds receives a score of 8. Severe brain injury is defined as a score of 8 or less (Langfitt & Gennarelli, 1982). Scores of 9–12 reflect moderate brain injury, and scores of 13–15 reflect minor brain injury. Fatality rate after severe brain injury is between 20% and 40% (Feickert, Drommer, & Heyer, 1999).

Another tool to assess the severity of brain injury is the duration of posttraumatic amnesia (PTA), which includes the period of coma and the subsequent time during which the individual with TBI is unable to store and remember new events. The duration of PTA in mild head injuries is less than 1 hour, in moderate brain injuries is 1–24 hours, and in severe injuries is greater than 24 hours (Zafonte et al., 1997). Duration of PTA in children can be reliably and validly measured using the Children's Orientation and Amnesia Test (COAT; Ewing-Cobbs et al., 1990).

TREATMENT APPROACHES

Approaches to therapy depend on the stage of recovery from coma and associated medical and physical problems. Treatment can be divided into an acute medical phase and a later rehabilitative phase. Initial rehabilitation, which may last for weeks to months, is often provided in an inpatient setting after severe injury. Subsequent outpatient rehabilitation can be provided in a hospital, rehabilitation center, or school (Farmer et al., 1996).

The societal and financial costs of brain injury in children are monumental. Each year the cost of acute and rehabilitative care for new cases of TBI totals more than $9 billion (NIH Consensus Development Panel, 1999). Jaffe et al. (1993) found that the median cost of acute and rehabilitative care for a child with severe brain injury was more than $50,000. When the costs of rehospitalizations and/or long-term care, outpatient rehabilitation, medical equipment, provision of special education services, and loss of future earnings are added, the figure is vastly greater. Unfortunately, due to caps on insurance policies, rehabilitative services are often time-limited. Furthermore, schools may be ill-prepared to care for these children, who may have complex neuropsychological impairments. These problems can adversely affect recovery and outcome.

Table 26.1. Glasgow Coma Scale (GCS)

Response	Score
Eye opening	
Spontaneous	4
To speech	3
To pain	2
Nil	1
Best motor response	
Obeys	6
Localizes	5
Withdraws	4
Abnormal flexion	3
Extensor response	2
Nil	1
Verbal response	
Oriented	5
Confused conversation	4
Inappropriate words	3
Incomprehensible sounds	2
Nil	1

From Jennett, B., Teasdale, G., Galbraith, S., et al. (1977). Severe head injuries in three countries. *Journal of Neurology, Neurosurgery, and Psychiatry, 40,* 293; reprinted by permission of BMJ Publishing Group.

Acute Medical Management

The first priority in the emergency room is to address the ABCs of advanced life support: airway, breathing, and circulation. Immediate goals are to stop any hemorrhaging, aid respiration, and support blood pressure (Kokoska et al., 1998; Lavelle & Shaw, 1998). Once vital signs are stable, the attending physician identifies fractures and damage to various internal body organs. A neurological examination is also performed that includes an assessment of the child's level of consciousness. The physician directs a light into the child's eyes to see whether the pupils constrict equally in bright light and dilate equally in the dark. If these responses are absent, delayed, or asymmetrical, then brain swelling or injury is likely. Movement of limbs and reflexes are also tested to see whether there are tone changes or asymmetry that would indicate brain injury. For example, left-side weakness usually indicates damage to the right side of the brain.

Certain physical findings suggest damage to a specific region of the skull or brain. Blood behind the eardrum, cerebrospinal fluid drainage from the nose or ear, and bruising around the orbits of the eye all suggest the presence of a fracture at the base of the skull. Hemorrhages in the retina of the eye may be associated with subdural hematoma and are nearly always associated with child abuse.

Each year more than 500,000 children are seen in emergency rooms nationwide following head trauma (Schutzman et al., 2001). The majority of these visits are for minor head trauma. Until the late 1990s, there had been no consensus on the best management for these children (Murgio et al., 1999; Savitsky & Votey, 2000). Less than 0.02% (1 in 5,000) of children older than 2 years of age with minor closed head injury and no loss of consciousness develop intracranial bleeding that requires medical or surgical intervention (Quayle, 1999; Schutzman & Greenes, 2001). When the injury is associated with a brief loss of consciousness, this figure increases to 2%–5% (American Academy of Pediatrics [AAP], Committee on Quality Improvement, & American Academy of Family Physicians [AAFP], Commission on Clinical Policies and Research, 1999). In infants this figure is even higher at 3%–6% (Schutzman et al., 2001). Beginning in 1999, guidelines for both infants and older children were developed by experts in the field to aid in the evaluation and management of children with minor head trauma (AAP & AAFP, 1999; Schutzman et al., 2001).

Neurosurgical consultation is recommended for all children who have sustained more than a mild head trauma (Varney & Roberts, 1999). A child with an open-skull fracture may require surgery to prevent infection of the brain. Children with epidural or subdural hematomas also may require surgery to prevent or treat potentially life-threatening increased intracranial pressure (Meyer, Legros, & Orliaguet, 1999). Concern over increased intracranial pressure also may lead the neurosurgeon to insert a device to monitor intracranial pressure or a drainage tube (ventriculostomy) to both monitor and reduce intracranial pressure.

A CT scan is used routinely following significant head trauma to diagnose intracranial hemorrhage, swelling, DAI, and skull fractures. MRI scans are used during recovery to determine more clearly the extent of residual brain damage. Single photon emission computed tomography (SPECT) measures blood flow in the brain and may be particularly sensitive in cases of mild head injury when a CT scan is normal or inconclusive (Emanuelson et al., 1997; Novotny, Ashwal, & Shevell, 1998).

The medical management of coma primarily aims to prevent or limit secondary brain damage, which can result from a buildup of intracranial pressure, a lack of oxygen, a lack of sufficient metabolic energy supply, or an accumulation of neurotoxins (Tasker, 1999). Intracranial pressure often builds as a result of brain swelling. If this is found, drainage of spinal fluid, control of breathing rate, or administration of intravenous fluids (hypertonic saline) or medications (e.g., mannitol, barbiturates, pressors) may be used to decrease the pressure within the head and increase blood perfusion to the brain, thus improving blood flow to the brain (Khanna et al., 2000). Blood flow to the brain affects both pressure within the brain and the supply of nutrients and oxygen. Thus, blood supply must be carefully controlled. Research suggests that brain damage following TBI is, at least in part, intensified by excitatory neurotransmitters that are released in toxic amounts at the time of injury (Felderhoff-Mueser & Ikonomidou, 2000). These neurotoxins lead to swelling and death of nerve cells. Experimental trials with drugs that block receptors for these chemicals have shown some promise in protecting the brain. Therapeutic hypothermia and other strategies to protect the brain against delayed cellular processes are actively being investigated (Biagas & Gaeta, 1998; Meyer et al., 1999; Natale et al., 2000).

The occurrence of seizures immediately after the injury or within the first few days after a brain injury is rather common, even in children with only mild concussions. Young children are particularly susceptible to early seizures, whereas older children and adults are prone to late posttraumatic seizures (Asikainen, Kaste, & Sarna, 1999a; Gruskin & Schutzman, 1999). Less than 2% of children with early seizures will subsequently develop a seizure disorder (Asikainen et al., 1999a; Ylvisaker, 1985). Factors that increase this risk include bleeding into the brain and penetrating injury that may cause the formation of scar tissue (Annegers, 1998). Antiepileptic medication may be given preventively for a week after the injury, but prolonged treatment is generally used only if the child develops recurrent seizure activity (see Chapter 25).

Recovery from Coma

Although type and severity of injuries differ, certain patterns of behavior are observed in children recovering from TBI-induced coma. Initially, the child may not respond at all to external stimuli or may respond in stereotypical ways. For example, the child's response to a painful stimulus administered to one extremity may be generalized, with movement of all the extremities and an elevation in blood pressure and intracranial pressure. The child may not respond to a voiced command, such as "Open your eyes," or the child may open his or her eyes spontaneously, a sign that does not by itself signify wakefulness.

Fortunately, most children with TBI-induced coma regain consciousness, and only a very small number remain in a permanent unresponsive state (Zeman, 1997). Even in these individuals there is evidence that innovative drug treatments, such as the use of bromocriptine (Parlodel), may be of benefit (Passler & Riggs, 2001). Emergence from coma does not occur suddenly or smoothly but typically follows a saw-toothed pattern of waxing and waning levels of consciousness. The first signs are often heightened responses to external stimuli, especially to the voices of family members. Eye opening that occurs as a response to external stimuli reflects improving neurological status.

At about this time in recovery, the child may become intermittently agitated and combative, for instance, pulling at tubes, moaning, and trying to sit up. Although the child's eyes may be open, there appears to be little meaningful perception of the environment. This stage can be extremely difficult emotionally for family members, who should be reassured that this is expected during recovery and that the child will not remember these events. Occasionally, medications can be helpful in reducing agitation, including anticonvulsants, antidepressants, narcotics (especially if other injuries make it likely that the child is in pain), sedatives, and sympathetic blocking agents such as propranolol (Inderal).

As agitation subsides, the child will show increasing awareness of the environment. He or she will usually begin to visually fixate, with clear recognition and memory of familiar objects and people. Speech begins with short words or phrases, with delayed responses. These responses are usually inconsistent in the early stages of recovery.

Return of consciousness can be defined functionally as the ability to follow commands reliably. In preverbal or aphasic children, more general responsiveness must be used to ascertain the end of coma. Once consciousness has returned, therapeutic strategies increasingly utilize active participation by the individual with TBI. At variable rates, children with TBI become oriented to the environment, and behavior becomes progressively more age appropriate, purposeful, and complex. Motor, communicative, cognitive, sensory, and behavior impairments can be assessed and long-range goals set at this stage.

Rehabilitation

Rehabilitation aims to 1) avert complications that arise from immobilization, disuse, and neurological dysfunction; 2) augment the use of abilities regained as a result of recovery from coma; 3) teach adaptive compensation for impaired or lost function; and 4) alleviate the effect of chronic disability on the process of growth and development (NIH Consensus Development Panel, 1999; Rose, Johnson, & Attree, 1997; see Chapter 33). Rehabilitation begins almost immediately after vital signs have been stabilized, often while the child is still in coma.

Acute rehabilitative care following TBI aims to limit secondary musculoskeletal damage by passive range-of-motion exercises, positioning, and splinting of limbs. These efforts can help to prevent the later development of contractures, which could interfere with seating, ambulation, and participation in daily activities. Other important acute rehabilitative measures include changing body position and caring for the skin to prevent the development of pressure sores. In addition, adequate nutrition promotes wound healing. These measures, taken together, appear to shorten hospitalization and improve outcome.

Evaluating and Treating Functional Impairments

As the child begins to recover from coma, physical, cognitive, and emotional problems may become evident (Vieth, Johnstone, & Dawson, 1996). The nature and severity of functional impairments will determine the rehabilitative strategies. Severe DAI is likely to result in impairment in all areas of functioning, whereas focal damage may result in more localized abnormalities. Interdisciplinary services typically include medical, nutritional, physical, occupational, speech-language, and recreational therapies, as well as rehabilitation nursing, psychological, special education, and social services. Services are discussed in relation to the specific impairments that they are intended to remediate.

Addressing Motor Impairments   The site(s) of brain injury determines the type of motor dysfunction that follows. Spasticity, rigidity, and ataxia/tremor are the most common motor abnormalities, indicating damage to the corticospinal (pyramidal) tract, basal ganglia, and cerebellum (see Chapter 13; Mysiw, Corrigan, & Gribble, 1990).

Medication and surgery have had varying success in treating motor impairments. As of 2002, there is no effective medical or surgical approach to treating ataxia. Tremor, however, may respond to propranolol. Useful medications to treat spasticity and rigidity include those that are used to treat spastic cerebral palsy: diazepam (Valium), baclofen (Lioresal), and dantrolene (Dantrium) (Armstrong et al., 1997; "The Management of Spasticity," 2000; Meythaler et al., 1999; see also Chapter 23). Baclofen can be administered intrathecally (into the spinal fluid) as well as orally.

Management of spasticity may also include nerve blocks (injecting anesthetic agents at a variety of sites in the peripheral nervous system), and selective dorsal rhizotomy (see Chapter 23). The effects of nerve blocks last for a number of weeks or months, but repeated injections are required if spasticity persists. Intramuscular injections of botulinum toxin A appear safe and effective in reducing localized spasticity in children (Bakheit et al., 2001).

Orthopedic surgery may be required in some cases. Long-term contractures or dislocations may need to be treated by performing tendon releases, femoral osteotomies, or scoliosis surgery (see Chapter 23). Serial casting may be used to correct a limb deformity in some cases of spasticity.

Medical and surgical approaches may be helpful, but they offer no cure. The child may continue to have motor impairments that interfere with the ability to ambulate and to participate in self-care skills. Furthermore, cognitive and visual-perceptual impairments may exacerbate motor impairments. Active physical and occupational therapy is needed to assist the child in regaining motor function. Exercises and activities are designed to increase strength, balance, and coordination; to reduce spasticity; and to prevent contractures and dislocations. The child may need to relearn how to walk and may require crutches, walkers, or a wheelchair (see Chapter 33). The importance of addressing these issues cannot be overstated because long-term outcome (including long-term survival) following TBI in the school-age years is highly correlated with the degree of mobility and ability to self-feed (Strauss, Shavelle, & Anderson, 1998).

Managing Feeding Disorders   Feeding disorders often accompany motor impairments (Klodell et al., 2000). Food intake may decrease if the child is unable to communicate hunger; if the ability to obtain food or to eat is compromised because of impaired motor skills; or if there are problems with swallowing or gastroesophageal reflux.

Nutritional treatment during coma may involve intravenous hyperalimentation (see Chapter 9). Even after coma has resolved, children who are unable to take in sufficient sustenance by mouth will require temporary or long-term nasogastric or gastrostomy tube-feedings (see Chapter 27) with high-calorie formulas.

A number of rehabilitation therapies also are involved in treating feeding disorders. An occupational therapist may work on proper positioning for feeding. A speech-language pathologist may use desensitization techniques; may stimulate the swallowing reflex; and may facilitate tongue, lip, and jaw control to improve swallowing. Nutritionists provide advice concerning the textures, taste, temperature, and caloric density of the food (see Chapter 9). Finally, medication to control reflux may improve the child's ability to eat and gain weight (see Chapter 27).

Managing Sensory Impairments   Vision and hearing can both be affected by TBI. The most common vision complication is diplopia (i.e., double vision), caused by eye muscle palsy (Poggi et al., 2000). Nystagmus, caused by injury to the cerebellum, is also quite common among children with severe TBI. Less commonly, a crush injury (e.g., blunt object) may damage an eye or a missile injury (e.g., gunshot) may sever a portion of the visual pathway; both types of injury cause irreversible damage. Finally, a TBI accompanied by severe brain swelling can result in a stroke or cortical blindness. Cortical blindness involves an abnormality in the visual cortex, but not the eye itself, and partial or complete recovery can occur (see Chapter 10). As a result of these problems, vision testing should be included in the evaluation after recovery from coma.

Sensorineural hearing loss after TBI most commonly results from a fracture of the temporal bone and is usually unilateral (Lubinski, Moscato, & Willer, 1997; Roizen, 1999). Longitudinal fractures involving the middle-ear structures are associated with a conductive hearing loss. Transverse fractures can affect the cochlea and result in sensorineural hearing loss. Formal hearing assessment should be conducted following severe TBI because of the frequency with which hearing loss occurs. Because involvement is usually unilateral, deafness does not generally result. Even a mild hearing loss, however, should be identified and corrected with amplification so that the child can benefit maximally from all of his or her senses when working toward recovery (see Chapter 11).

Managing Communication Impairments   If the left hemisphere of the brain is damaged, speech and language impairments are likely. Language disorders may be expressive, receptive, or mixed. Dysarthria and **dysphasia** are the most common expressive language problems seen in children with TBI (see Chapter 12). Receptive language impairments most commonly involve auditory-perceptual problems. Recovery of speech motor function often is more complete than recovery of receptive language abilities (Yorkston et al., 1997). Usually when language is disordered, cognition also is affected (Chapman, 1995; Chapman et al., 1995). Intervention by a speech-language pathologist is directed at improving both the speech disorder and the language and cognitive impairments. Initially, this involves using simple commands and discussing uncomplicated topics related to the surroundings. The speech-language pathologist will also help to train the nursing staff and parents to use simple commands and, if needed, alternate means of communication.

Addressing Cognitive Impairments   Recovery of cognitive functioning is typically not as complete as recovery of motor functioning following severe TBI (Gagnon et al., 1998; Massagli, Michaud, & Rivara, 1996; Max et al., 2000). Furthermore, children who are preschoolers at the time of injury may have delayed manifestation of cognitive impairments, showing difficulty handling more complex tasks as they get older (Lazar & Menaldino, 1995).

Investigations of mild TBI in children have demonstrated no significant long-term adverse consequences on cognitive functioning (Fay et al., 1993). Studies of children who have sustained moderate to severe TBI, however, document significant cognitive impairments (Jaffe et al., 1995). Intellectual and neuropsychological impairment is increased with greater severity of injury (Jaffe et al., 1995). The cognitive sequelae most often associated with pediatric TBI are lowered performance on visuospatial and visual-motor tasks as compared with performance on verbal tasks; problems with attention, learning, and memory (Anderson, Catroppa, Rosenfeld, et al., 2000; Mateer, Kearns, & Eso, 1996); and diminished speed of information processing (Massagli, Jaffe, et al., 1996). Impairments in judgment, problem solving, reasoning, and organizational skills have also been demonstrated (Hanson & Clippard, 1992).

To identify impairments, neuropsychologists evaluate children using measures of intelligence as well as assessments of more discrete and/or subtle impairments in cognition that typically result from significant brain injury (Lord-Maes & Obrzut, 1996). This assessment involves a series of standardized tests that measure concept formation, reasoning, adaptive problem-solving skills, language, memory, concentration, visuospatial skills, sensory-perceptual and sensorimotor abilities, and academic performance. Results of such evaluations are used in planning appropriate rehabilitation programs and educational curricula (Clark, 1996; Kinsella et al., 1997; Tyler & Mira, 1999; Ylvisaker et al., 2001).

Performance on cognitive tasks varies in different settings. In a typical neuropsychological evaluation, the examiner meets individually with the child in a quiet room under very structured conditions. Because this situation is unlike the typical classroom with its many distractions, these tests alone may not accurately represent the child's ability to function in a general classroom setting. For this reason, it is recommended that such evaluations be augmented by contextual assessments (Telzrow, 1991) as well as by functional assessment measures (Milton et al., 1991).

Impairments in intellectual and neuropsychological functioning are generally proportional to the severity of the injury (Jaffe et al., 1995). Although significant recovery occurs during the first 6 months to 1 year after severe injury in children, the recovery rate slows subsequently (Ewing-Cobbs et al., 1997; Taylor et al., 1999). Much remains to be learned about the role of rehabilitative and educational interventions in influencing the rate and extent of recovery of specific cognitive functions.

Interventions to address cognitive impairments may be useful even during the inpatient phase of management. Multidisciplinary cognitive remediation may use a combination of memory training exercises (psychology), language therapy (speech-language pathology), and educational programming (special education). The strategy is to improve areas of impairment and encourage the development of compensatory techniques, such as the use of assistive technology (including computer-assisted learning) (Ried et al., 1995). Impairments in communication and cognition often are the main deterrents to successful reintegration into home, school, and community. Social inclusion (i.e., full, meaningful inclusion in the social fabric of the culture) should be a major goal of provision of assistive technology for children with impairments after TBI.

Modifying the Academic Environment   Research has consistently documented that children who have sustained a moderate to severe TBI tend to experience academic problems. Although these difficulties may be demonstrated in a particular area, such as reading or math (Goldstein & Levin, 1985), impairments in attention, problem solving, and speed of information processing more typically compromise all academic performance (Fenwick & Anderson, 1999). Standardized school achievement tests are not able to detect subtle learning disabilities and should not be used in place of the more comprehensive individual neuropsychological evaluation (Ewing-Cobbs, Fletcher, et al., 1998). It is important to recognize that a child with a mild to moderate head injury may appear to be unaffected initially. It is possible for a child to score typically when tested at a young age and subsequently develop learning difficulties as she or he reaches adolescence. Thus, repeat testing may be required as the young child grows, to determine whether the child has subtle impairments in domains that could not be tested at the age of injury.

Following a moderate or severe TBI, the child often requires modifications to the general education curriculum, ranging from self-contained, special education classes to assistance in a resource room or in the classroom. Focused instruction based on each child's specific skill or memory impairments is most useful, especially when the instruction is both highly structured and motivating with feedback and correction. In addition, physical, occupational, and/or speech-language therapy may be provided as part of the child's IEP (see Chapter 30).

TBI is recognized as a specific category of disability within special education, as mandated by the Individuals with Disabilities Education Act (IDEA) of 1990 (PL 101-476) and its amendments and reauthorization in 1997 (PL 105-17). There has been, however, a lag between the passage of this legislation and its actual implementation, and the definition of brain injury has not been interpreted consistently on a state-by-state basis. Because there are so few children with TBI in any given school and so many school systems lack adequate resources (e.g., funding, school personnel with training in TBI), these children often receive inadequate educational programming (Carney & Schoenbrodt, 1994). Although children with TBI may be identified as having behavior disorders (Michaud et al., 1993) or learning problems, their patterns of cognitive impairment are actually quite different from those seen in ADHD or in a specific learning disability. Unlike these disorders, two hallmarks of TBI are highly variable performance within and across academic subjects and continued change over time. Depending on the time since the injury, recovery may still be proceeding rapidly, with abilities changing from month to month. As a result, an appropriate educational approach in September may be outdated by November. Thus, flexibility and innovative approaches are needed to teach the child who is recovering from TBI. Above all, careful management of school reentry and long-term monitoring are essential in facilitating a successful academic outcome.

Mitigating Psychobehavioral Impairments Changes in personality and behavior also often follow severe TBI (Guthrie et al., 1999; Kehle, Clark, & Jenson, 1996; Max et al., 2000). Behavioral outcomes after mild to moderate injuries seem to be more varied (Max et al., 1997; Stoler & Hill, 1998). Injuries to certain areas of the brain, specifically the thalamus and basal ganglia, are particularly associated with the development of secondary attentional and memory difficulties (Anderson et al., 1999; Gerring et al., 2000).

Even with adequate cognitive functioning, significant behavior challenges can be expected (Bloom et al., 2001). Changes may include inattention, increased or decreased activity, impulsivity, irritability, lowered frustration tolerance, emotional lability, apathy, aggression, and/or social withdrawal (Andrews, Rose, & Johnson, 1998; Bloom et al., 2001). As a result of these behavioral problems, children with TBI often develop problems with peer relationships. Treatment for behavior problems may include counseling, behavior management, medication, or a combination of these approaches (Green, Stevens, & Wolfe, 1997; Schoenbrodt, 2001). These behavioral problems also have a profound impact on other family members that must be considered by the rehabilitation team (Gronwall, Wrightson, & Waddell, 1998; Junque, Bruna, & Mataro, 1997; Marsh et al., 1998; Stanton, 1999).

Addressing Social and Family Difficulties The effects of severe TBI on the family can be enormous (Rivara et al., 1996). In many ways, they are similar to the challenges faced by all families of children newly diagnosed with a developmental disability (see Chapter 36). Parents of children with TBI, in addition, may face overwhelming feelings of guilt and remorse, particularly if the child was in the parents' care when the injury occurred or if the parents feel otherwise responsible. Siblings also may feel guilty that they were left unharmed or did not protect their brother or sister. In addition, prolonged hospitalization and rehabilitation can place a heavy financial burden on the family. One parent may be forced to take a leave of absence from work to be with the child. This loss of income combined with the additional costs of modifying a home or providing outpatient rehabilitation can have a devastating effect on family finances.

Even after less severe TBI, psychosocial problems may develop (Watts & Perlesz, 1999). The family may rush to put the experience behind them and thus deny or ignore mild but persistent impairments, especially if the child appears to have recovered well. This can lead parents (and teachers) to expect normal achievement from the child, even if subtle cognitive impairments persist. If these impairments go undetected, they can lead to frustration, behavior problems, and poor learning (Wade, Taylor, & Drotar, 1998; Warschausky, Kewman, & Kay, 1999).

Studies have shown that the family's preinjury level of functioning is predictive of family functioning 1 and 3 years after the child's TBI (Rivara et al., 1996). Family functioning, in combination with injury severity and the child's preinjury functioning, is also predictive of the child's functioning 1 year after injury (Rivara et al., 1993). These investigations strongly support the need to identify families at risk very early in the rehabilitation process. Families can be assisted by individual and family counseling, by participation in support groups, and by information and support from teachers and health professionals. In addition, families may need ongoing service coordination, especially if they are having difficulty gaining access to resources (Hellawell, Taylor, & Pentland, 1999).

Fostering Vocational Endeavors   TBI also may have a major effect on the child's vocational development and outcome. In one follow-up study of Finnish adults who had sustained severe TBI during their preschool years, only one fourth were able to work full time, although half had achieved average school performance (Koskiniemi et al., 1995; Nybo & Koskiniemi, 1999). In these adults, vocational success was associated with better scores on tests involving speed, memory, and executive function (Nybo & Koskiniemi, 1999). The Finnish investigators also found that the individual's sense of identity was a major predictor of the capability to care for oneself in adulthood. Asikainen, Kaste, and Sarna (1999b) also found that adults who suffered a severe TBI before 8 years of age were less often independently employed than their counterparts who were older at the time of the severe TBI. This age association was not seen with mild or moderate head injuries (Verger et al., 2000). Vocational services for children and adolescents with TBI have generally not been provided through either the medical rehabilitation or educational systems. IDEA '97, however, mandates provision of transition services that include vocational evaluation and training for students with disabilities, beginning no later than age 14. This legislation is too recent for its impact to be known but is certainly a step in the right direction in aiding children with disabilities, including those with TBI, to achieve the ability to work and live independently in adulthood (see Chapter 37).

OUTCOME

Almost 95% of children admitted to a hospital following a TBI survive. For these children, a number of factors have been identified as predictors of outcome: GCS scores, duration of coma, duration of PTA, type of brain injury, age at injury, and preinjury functional level (Celli, Fruin, & Cervoni, 1997; Taylor & Alden, 1997).

Lower GCS scores generally indicate greater severity of TBI and a poorer outcome (Feickert et al., 1999; Michaud et al., 1992). As in the cases of Carmen and Ethan, the duration of unresponsiveness (i.e., not following commands) is a major index of the severity of the TBI (Massagli, Michaud, et al., 1996). Children who become responsive within 6 weeks have a good prognosis for recovery. When duration of unresponsiveness is between 6 weeks and 3 months, outcome is variable; and when the duration is longer than 3 months, prognosis for recovery of functioning is generally poor (Brink & Hoffer, 1978). Those children who do recover motor functioning after a prolonged period of unresponsiveness have impairments in cognitive functioning and changes in personality.

The duration of PTA is also a prognostic indicator (Ewing-Cobbs et al., 1990; Haviland & Russell, 1997). Longer duration of PTA indicates more severe TBI and is associated with worse outcome.

The type of brain injury also is important in determining outcome (Asikainen, Kaste, & Sarna, 1998). Children with focal lesions in addition to DAI have been observed to have poorer outcomes than those with only DAI (Paterakis et al., 2000). Outcomes are usually good for children who have epidural hematomas but poor for those with subdural hematomas (Levi et al., 1998). Injuries resulting in multiple organ damage also carry a poor prognosis, as the associated oxygen deprivation and low blood pressure cause secondary hypoxic-ischemic injury to the brain (Walker et al., 1985). As previously noted, younger children with brain injuries due to physical abuse (e.g., shaken impact syndrome) have significantly worse cognitive and motor outcomes than age-matched children with brain injury from other causes (e.g., motor vehicle accidents) (Kriel, Krach, & Panser, 1989).

The impact of age is complex, and the results of different studies have been inconsistent (Ewing-Cobbs, Duhaime, & Fletcher, 1995). In some studies, poorer outcomes have been observed in children who are quite young at the time of injury (Koskiniemi et al., 1995; Verger et al., 2000). In other studies, however, outcome has been found to be unrelated to age at the time of injury (Berger et al., 1985; Zuccarello et al., 1985). Researchers have distinguished among TBI severity: Young children with severe TBI do worse than their adult counterparts, whereas adults and young children with moderate and mild TBI fare equally well (Anderson, Catroppa, Morse, et al., 2000). Contrasting findings may reflect the fact that different areas of functional outcome were being assessed. The brain of the young child may have a greater degree of plasticity (see Chapter 13) than that of the older child or adult. Yet, this advantage may be offset by the fact that brain injury impairs new learning more than the retention of prior information. The young child has had less time to develop learning strategies and to store knowledge before the injury and therefore may experience a greater impairment in cognitive functioning.

Finally, one must consider any preexisting developmental disability in predicting outcome. If ADHD or mental retardation is evident in a child after recovery from TBI, it is important to know whether this predated the injury. Cognitive impairments following an injury should be compared with any preexisting cognitive test scores. In one study, children with ongoing problems following mild TBI were found to be more likely to have premorbid neurological or psychiatric problems, family stressors, or learning difficulty or to have had a previous head injury (Ponsford et al., 1999). Another large study conducted in England suggests that these cognitive impairments seen in some children with multiple mild head injuries are related more to social and personal factors than to the head injury itself (Bijur, Haslum, & Golding, 1996).

PREVENTION

Most childhood head trauma is preventable (Dowd, 1999; MacKenzie, 2000; Rivara, 1999). Because a number of factors contribute to the risk of injury, however, no single intervention will be completely effective. Rather, specific preventive strategies must be employed for each major category of TBI (i.e., motor vehicle crashes, including those associated with pedestrian and bicycle injuries; assaults and abuse; household incidents, including falls and near drownings; sports- and recreation-related injuries; and suicide attempts) (Chorley, 1998; Murray et al., 2000). Prevention also is important in children who have already sustained TBI, as the effect of subsequent injury is cumulative. Persistent neurological impairments that result in impulsivity or hyperactivity place these children at high risk for additional injury.

Laws in all states requiring restraint of children who are passengers in motor vehicles have been highly (but not completely) effective in lowering the frequency and severity of TBI (Bull & Sheese, 2000; Schieber, Gilchrist, & Sleet, 2000; Tyroch et al., 2000). Passive restraints such as airbags have also been found to be effective. When small children are seated in the front seat, however, airbag deployment can lead to injury and even death (Huff, Bagwell, & Bachman, 1998), emphasizing the importance of placing children in approved properly placed car seats or restraints in the back seat (Kohn, Chausmer, & Flood, 2000). The number of motor vehicle crashes in which teenagers sustain brain injuries continues to be too high. Education about the risks of drinking and driving has had some impact. Many experts believe, however, that further effective prevention efforts must include nighttime curfews and other graduated licensing measures, delaying licensure to 17 years of age, eliminating driver education courses that allow teenagers to obtain their licenses at younger ages, and random breath testing for alcohol (Agran, Castillo, & Winn, 1990; Durbin, 1999).

Efforts also should be supported to improve pedestrian safety. Although children can improve street-crossing skills somewhat with training, children younger than 11–12 years of age have developmental limitations in their ability to assess distances and speeds and negotiate traffic safely (Christoffel et al., 1996). Reducing the speed of traffic, separating pedestrians from traffic, and enforcing laws that govern motor vehicle–pedestrian interactions have been recommended as community strategies to reduce childhood pedestrian injuries (Rivara, 1994).

Bicycle helmets have been found to reduce the risk of TBI due to bicycle-related trauma by 88%, and their use should be strongly promoted (Miller, Binns, & Christoffel, 1996). Researchers at the National Center for Injury Prevention and Control reported that if all children were to wear bicycle helmets when riding, as many as 184 deaths and 116,000 head injuries might be prevented each year (Sosin et al., 1996). Individuals riding on motorcycles, as well as those who participate in contact sports (e.g., football, hockey) and certain recreational activities (e.g., horseback riding, rollerblading, skateboarding) should also wear adequate head protection (Rivara, 1994).

Falls could be reduced through measures including maximizing safety of playground surfaces and reducing the height of playground equipment and increasing house safety by placing bars on windows. Use of infant walkers increases exposure to household hazards such as stairs and should be discouraged (Rivara, 1994).

Although assaults and physical abuse theoretically represent entirely preventable causes of childhood TBI, society is making little progress in preventing them. Programs that provide in-home support and teaching of parenting skills to young mothers have been used in an attempt to decrease the risk of child abuse (Olds et al., 1986).

Most suicides in children also are preventable. A suicide attempt in a child is usually an impulsive act, a cry for help. If caregivers are attuned to recognize signs of depression, drug abuse, or other problems leading to this gesture, many suicide attempts could be prevented. Parent and teacher awareness needs to improve in this area. Reduced availability of firearms to children and adolescents could also reduce pediatric suicide (and homicide) rates (Powell, Sheehan, & Christoffel, 1996; Senturia, Christoffel, & Donovan, 1996). Gun control legislation represents one important attempt to limit access to lethal weapons, but enactment has proven a political minefield (Christoffel, 1995).

Finally, parents, teachers, and community groups need to be educated regarding the appropriate restraint of children in motor vehicles; safe pedestrian behavior; use of helmets for appropriate activities; and the prevention of falls from heights, playground injuries, pool drownings, and sports injuries.

SUMMARY

Head trauma is a common childhood event, and the spectrum of consequences is broad. Depending on the severity, type, and location of the injury, outcome may range from complete recovery to severe functional disability. Persistent motor, communication, cognitive, behavior, and sensory impairments may result from TBI. Restoration of function in affected areas is the goal of rehabilitation and requires the participation of multiple medical specialists, allied health professionals, and educators. Although treatment is important, most head injuries in children are preventable. Injury prevention programs must be supported if there is to be a significant decrease in TBI in the future.

REFERENCES

Adelson, P.D., & Kochanek, P.M. (1998). Head injury in children. *Journal of Child Neurology, 13*, 2–15.

Adesunkanmi, A.R., Oginni, L.M., Oyelami, A.O., et al. (1998). Epidemiology of childhood injury. *The Journal of Trauma, 44*, 506–512.

Agran, P., Castillo, D., & Winn, D. (1990). Childhood motor vehicle occupant injuries. *American Journal of Diseases of Children, 144*, 653–662.

American Academy of Pediatrics (AAP), Committee on Quality Improvement, & American Academy of Family Physicians (AAFP), Commission on Clinical Policies and Research. (1999). The management of minor closed head injury in children. *Pediatrics, 104*, 1407–1415.

Anderson, V.A., Catroppa, C., Morse, S.A., et al. (1999). Functional memory skills following traumatic brain injury in young children. *Pediatric Rehabilitation, 3*(4), 159–166.

Anderson, V., Catroppa, C., Morse, S., et al. (2000). Recovery of intellectual ability following traumatic brain injury in childhood: Impact of injury severity and age at injury. *Pediatric Neurosurgery, 32*, 282–290.

Anderson, V.A., Catroppa, C., Rosenfeld, J., et al. (2000). Recovery of memory function following traumatic brain injury in pre-school children. *Brain Injury, 14*, 679–692.

Andrews, T.K., Rose, F.D., & Johnson, D.A. (1998). Social and behavioral effects of traumatic brain injury in children. *Brain Injury, 12*, 133–138.

Annegers, J.F. (1998). A population based study of seizures after traumatic brain injuries. *New England Journal of Medicine, 338*, 20–24.

Armstrong, R.W., Steinbok, P., Cochrane, D.D., et al. (1997). Intrathecally administered baclofen for treatment of children with spasticity of cerebral origin. *Journal of Neurosurgery, 87*, 409–414.

Asikainen, I., Kaste, M., & Sarna, S. (1998). Predicting late outcome for patients with traumatic brain injury referred to a rehabilitation programme: A study of 508 Finnish patients 5 years or more after injury. *Brain Injury, 12*, 95–107.

Asikainen, I., Kaste, M., & Sarna, S. (1999a). Early and late posttraumatic seizures in traumatic brain injury rehabilitation patients: Brain injury factors causing late seizures and influence of seizures on long-term outcome. *Epilepsia, 40*(5), 584–589.

Asikainen, I., Kaste, M., & Sarna, S. (1999b). Patients with traumatic brain injury referred to a rehabilitation and re-employment programme: Social and professional outcome for 508 Finnish patients 5 or more years after injury. *Brain Injury, 10*, 883–899.

Baker, S.P., O'Neill, B., & Karpf, R.S. (1984). *The injury fact book*. Lanham, MD: Lexington Books.

Bakheit, A.M., Severa, S., Cosgrove, A., et al. (2001). Safety profile and efficacy of botulinum toxin A (Dysport) in children with muscle spasticity. *Developmental Medicine and Child Neurology, 43*, 234–238.

Ben Abraham, R., Lahat, E., Sheinman, G., et al. (2000). Metabolic and clinical markers of prognosis in the era of CT imaging in children with acute epidural hematomas. *Pediatric Neurosurgery, 33*, 70–75.

Berger, M.S., Pitts, L.H., Lovely, M., et al. (1985). Outcome from severe head injury in children and adolescents. *Journal of Neurosurgery, 62*, 194–199.

Biagas, K.V., & Gaeta, M.L. (1998). Treatment of traumatic brain injury with hypothermia. *Current Opinion in Pediatrics, 10*, 271–277.

Bigler, E.D. (1999). Neuroimaging in pediatric traumatic head injury: Diagnostic considerations and relationships to neurobehavioral outcome. *The Journal of Head Trauma Rehabilitation, 14*, 406–423.

Bijur, P.E., Haslum, M., & Golding, J. (1996). Cognitive outcomes of multiple mild head injuries in children. *Journal of Developmental and Behavioral Pediatrics, 17*, 143–148.

Bloom, D.R., Levin, H.S., Ewing-Cobbs, L., et al. (2001). Lifetime and novel psychiatric disorders after pediatric traumatic brain injury. *Journal of American Academy of Child and Adolescent Psychiatry, 40*, 572–579.

Brain Trauma Foundation, the American Association of Neurological Surgeons, & the Joint Section on Neurotrauma and Critical Care. (2000). Glasgow coma scale score. *Journal of Neurotrauma, 17*(6–7), 573–581.

Brink, J.D., & Hoffer, M.M. (1978). Rehabilitation of brain injured children. *Orthopedic Clinics of North America, 9*, 451–454.

Brookes, M., MacMillan, R., Cully, S., et al. (1990). Head injuries in accident and emergency departments: How different are children from adults? *Journal of Epidemiology and Community Life, 44*, 147–151.

Bruce, D.A. (2000). Imaging after head trauma: Why, when and which. *Child's Nervous System, 16*, 755–759.

Bull, M.J., & Sheese, J. (2000). Update for the pediatrician on child passenger safety: Five principles for safer travel. *Pediatrics, 106*, 1113–1116.

Carney, J., & Schoenbrodt, L. (1994). Educational implications of traumatic brain injury. *Pediatric Annals, 23*, 47–52.

Celli, P., Fruin, A., & Cervoni, L. (1997). Severe head trauma. Review of the factors influencing the prognosis. *Minerva Chirurgica, 52*, 1467–1480.

Chapman, S.B. (1995). Discourse as an outcome measure in pediatric head-injured populations. In S.H. Broman & M.E. Michel (Eds.), *Traumatic head injury in children* (pp. 95–116). New York: Oxford University Press.

Chapman, S.B., Levin, H.S., Matejka, J., et al. (1995). Discourse ability in children with brain injury: Correlations with psychosocial, linguistic, and cognitive factors. *The Journal of Head Trauma Rehabilitation, 10*(5), 36–54.

Chorley, J.N. (1998). Sports-related head injuries. *Current Opinion in Pediatrics, 10*, 350–355.

Christoffel, K.K. (1995). The "guns" debate. *Pediatrics, 95*, 619.

Christoffel, K.K., Donovan, M., Schofer, J., et al. (1996). Psychosocial factors in childhood pedestrian injury: A matched case-control study. Kids'n'Cars Team. *Pediatrics, 97*, 33–42.

Clark, E. (1996). Children and adolescents with traumatic brain injury: Reintegration challenges in educational settings. *Journal of Learning Disabilities, 29*, 549–560.

David, T.J. (1999). Shaken baby (shaken impact) syndrome: Non-accidental head injury in infancy. *Journal of the Royal Society of Medicine, 92*, 556–561.

Dowd, M.D. (1999). Childhood injury prevention at home and play. *Current Opinion in Pediatrics, 11*, 578–582.

Duhaime, A.-C., Christian, C.W., Rorke, L.B., et al. (1998). Non-accidental head injury in infants: The "shaken-baby syndrome." *New England Journal of Medicine, 18*, 1822–1829.

Durbin, D.R. (1999). Preventing motor vehicle injuries. *Current Opinion in Pediatrics, 11*, 583–587.

Emanuelson, I., von Wendt, L., Bjure, J., et al. (1997). Computed tomography and single-photon emission computed tomography as diagnostic tools in acquired brain injury among children and adolescents. *Developmental Medicine and Child Neurology, 39*, 502–507.

Ewing-Cobbs, L., Duhaime, A.-C., & Fletcher, J.M. (1995).

Inflicted and noninflicted traumatic brain injury in infants and preschoolers. *The Journal of Head Trauma Rehabilitation, 10*(5), 13–24.

Ewing-Cobbs, L., Fletcher, J.M., Levin, H.S., et al. (1997). Longitudinal neuropsychological outcome in infants and preschoolers with traumatic brain injury. *Journal of the International Neuropsychological Society, 3,* 581–591.

Ewing-Cobbs, L., Fletcher, J.M., Levin, H.S., et al. (1998). Academic achievement and academic placement following traumatic brain injury in children and adolescents: A two year longitudinal study. *Journal of Clinical and Experimental Neuropsychology, 20,* 769–781.

Ewing-Cobbs, L., Kramer, L., Prasad, M., et al. (1998). Neuroimaging, physical, and developmental findings after inflicted and noninflicted traumatic brain injury in young children. *Pediatrics, 102,* 300–307.

Ewing-Cobbs, L., Levin, H.S., Fletcher, J.M., et al. (1990). The Children's Orientation and Amnesia Test: Relationship to severity of acute head injury and to recovery of memory. *Neurosurgery, 27,* 683–691.

Farmer, J.E., Clippard, D.S., Luehr-Wiemann, Y., et al. (1996). Assessing children with traumatic brain injury during rehabilitation: Promoting school and community reentry. *Journal of Learning Disabilities, 29,* 532–548.

Fay, G.C., Jaffe, K.M., Polissar, N.L., et al. (1993). Mild pediatric traumatic brain injury: A cohort study. *Archives of Physical Medicine and Rehabilitation, 74,* 895–901.

Feickert, H.J., Drommer, S., & Heyer, R. (1999). Severe head injury in children: Impact of risk factors on outcome. *The Journal of Trauma, 47,* 33–38.

Felderhoff-Mueser, U., & Ikonomidou, C. (2000). Mechanisms of neurodegeneration after paediatric brain injury. *Current Opinion in Neurology, 13,* 1–5.

Fenwick, T., & Anderson, V. (1999). Impairments of attention following childhood traumatic brain injury. *Neuropsychology, Development, and Cognition: Section C, Child Neuropsychology, 5*(4), 213–223.

Gagnon, I., Forget, R., Sullivan, S.J., et al. (1998). Motor performance following a mild traumatic brain injury in children: An exploratory study. *Brain Injury, 12,* 843–853.

Gerring J.P., Brady K.D., Chen A., et al. (1998). Premorbid prevalence of ADHD and development of secondary ADHD after closed head injury. *Journal of the American Academy of Child and Adolescent Psychiatry, 37,* 647–654.

Gerring, J., Brady, K., Chen, A., et al. (2000). Neuroimaging variables related to development of secondary attention deficit hyperactivity disorder after closed head injury in children and adolescents. *Brain Injury, 14,* 205–218.

Goldstein, F.C., & Levin, H.S. (1985). Intellectual and academic outcome following closed head injury in children and adolescents: Research strategies and empirical findings. *Developmental Neuropsychology, 1,* 195–214.

Grasso, S.N., & Keller, M.S. (1998). Diagnostic imaging in pediatric trauma. *Current Opinion in Pediatrics, 10,* 299–302.

Green, B.S., Stevens, K.M., & Wolfe, T.D.W. (1997). *Mild traumatic brain injury: A therapy and resource manual.* San Diego: Singular Publishing Group.

Gronwall, D.M.A., Wrightson, P., & Waddell, P. (1998). *Head injury: The facts* (2nd ed.). Oxford, England: Oxford University Press.

Gruskin, K.D., & Schutzman, S.A. (1999). Head trauma in children younger than 2 years: Are there predictors for complications? *Archives of Pediatric and Adolescent Medicine, 153,* 15–20.

Guerrero, J.L., Thurman, D.J., & Sniezek, J.E. (2000). Emergency department visits associated with traumatic brain injury: United States, 1995–1996. *Brain Injury, 14,* 181–186.

Guthrie, E., Mast, J., Richards, P., et al. (1999). Traumatic brain injury in children and adolescents. *Child and Adolescent Psychiatric Clinics of North America, 8,* 807–826, ix.

Hanson, S.L., & Clippard, D. (1992). Assessment of children with traumatic brain injury: Planning for school reentry. *Physical Medicine and Rehabilitation: State of the Art Reviews, 6,* 483–494.

Haviland, J., & Russell, R.I. (1997). Outcome after severe non-accidental head injury. *Archives of Disease in Childhood, 77,* 504–507.

Hellawell, D.J., Taylor, R.T., & Pentland, B. (1999). Cognitive and psychosocial outcome following moderate or severe traumatic brain injury. *Brain Injury, 13,* 489–504.

Homer, C.J., & Kleinman, L. (1999). Technical report: Minor head injury in children. *Pediatrics, 104,* e78.

Huff, G.F., Bagwell, S.P., & Bachman, D. (1998). Airbag injuries in infants and children: A case report and review of the literature. *Pediatrics, 102,* e2.

Individuals with Disabilities Education Act Amendments of 1997, PL 105-17, 20 U.S.C. §§ 1400 *et seq.*

Individuals with Disabilities Education Act (IDEA) of 1990, PL 101-476, 20 U.S.C. §§ 1400 *et seq.*

Jaffe, K.M., Massagli, T.L., Martin, K.M,. et al. (1993). Pediatric traumatic brain injury: Acute and rehabilitation costs. *Archives of Physical Medicine and Rehabilitation, 74,* 681–686.

Jaffe, K.M., Polissar, N.L., Fay, G.C., et al. (1995). Recovery trends over three years following pediatric traumatic brain injury. *Archives of Physical Medicine and Rehabilitation, 76,* 17–26.

Jennett, B., Teasdale, G., Galbraith, S., et al. (1977). Severe head injuries in three countries. *Journal of Neurology, Neurosurgery, and Psychiatry, 40,* 291–298.

Junque, C., Bruna, O., & Mataro, M. (1997). Information needs of the traumatic brain injury patient's family members regarding the consequences of the injury and associated perception of physical, cognitive, emotional and quality of life changes. *Brain Injury, 11,* 251–258.

Kehle, T.J., Clark, E., & Jenson, W.R. (1996). Interventions for students with traumatic brain injury: Managing behavioral disturbances. *Journal of Learning Disabilities, 29,* 633–642.

Khanna, S., Davis, D., Peterson, B., et al. (2000). Use of hypertonic saline in the treatment of severe refractory posttraumatic intracranial hypertension in pediatric traumatic brain injury. *Critical Care Medicine, 28,* 1144–1151.

Kinsella, G.J., Prior, M., Sawyer, M., et al. (1997). Predictors and indicators of academic outcome in children 2 years following traumatic brain injury. *Journal of the International Neuropsychological Society, 3,* 608–616.

Klodell, C.T., Carroll, M., Carrillo, E.H., et al. (2000). Routine intragastric feeding following traumatic brain injury is safe and well tolerated. *American Journal of Surgery, 179,* 168–171.

Koc, R.K., Akdemir, H., Oktem, I.S., et al. (1997). Acute subdural hematoma: Outcome and outcome prediction. *Neurosurgical Review, 20*(4), 239–244.

Kohn, M., Chausmer, K., & Flood, M.H. (2000). Anticipatory guidance about child safety seat misuse: Lessons from safety seat "checkups." *Archives of Pediatrics and Adolescent Medicine, 154,* 606–609.

Kokoska, E.R., Smith, G.S., Pittman, T., et al. (1998). Early hypotension worsens neurological outcome in pediatric patients with moderately severe head trauma. *Journal of Pediatric Surgery, 33*(2), 333–338.

Koskiniemi, M., Kyykka, T., Nybo, T., et al. (1995). Long-term outcome after severe brain injury in preschoolers is worse than expected. *Archives of Pediatrics and Adolescent Medicine, 149,* 249–254.

Kriel, R.L., Krach, L.E., & Panser, L.A. (1989). Closed head injury: Comparison of children younger and older than 6 years of age. *Pediatric Neurology, 5*, 296–300.

Lam, W.H., & MacKersie, A. (1999). Paediatric head injury: Incidence, aetiology and management. *Paediatric Anaesthesia, 9*(5), 377–385.

Langfitt, T.W., & Gennarelli, T.A. (1982). Can the outcome from head injury be improved? *Journal of Neurosurgery, 56*, 19–25.

Lavelle, J.M., & Shaw, K.N. (1998). Evaluation of head injury in a pediatric emergency department: Pretrauma and posttrauma system. *Archives of Pediatrics and Adolescent Medicine, 152*, 1220–1224.

Lazar, M.F., & Menaldino, S. (1995). Cognitive outcome and behavioral adjustment in children following traumatic brain injury: A developmental perspective. *The Journal of Head Trauma Rehabilitation, 10*(5), 55–63.

Lee, E.J., Hung, Y.C., Wang, L.C., et al. (1998). Factors influencing the functional outcome of patients with acute epidural hematomas: Analysis of 200 patients undergoing surgery. *The Journal of Trauma, 45*, 946–952.

Levi, L., Guilburd, J.N., Bar-Yosef, G., et al. (1998). Severe head injury in children: Analyzing the better outcome over a decade and the role of major improvements in intensive care. *Child's Nervous System, 14*, 195–202.

Light, R., Asarnow, R., Satz, P., et al. (1998). Mild closed-head injury in children and adolescents: Behavior problems and academic outcomes. *Journal of Consulting and Clinical Psychology, 66*, 1023–1029.

Lord-Maes, J., & Obrzut, J.E. (1996). Neuropsychological consequences of traumatic brain injury in children and adolescents. *Journal of Learning Disabilities, 29*, 609–617.

Lubinski, R., Moscato, B.S., & Willer, B.S. (1997). Prevalence of speaking and hearing disabilities among adults with traumatic brain injury from a national household survey. *Brain Injury, 11*, 103–114.

Luerssen, T.G., Klauber, M.R., & Marshall, L.F. (1988). Outcome from head injury related to patient's age: A longitudinal prospective study of adult and pediatric head injury. *Journal of Neurosurgery, 68*, 409–416.

MacKenzie, E.J. (2000). Epidemiology of injuries: Current trends and future challenges. *Epidemiologic Reviews, 22*(1), 112–119.

Maggi, G., Aliberti, F., Petrone, G., et al. (1998). Extradural hematomas in children. *Journal of Neurosurgical Sciences, 42*(2), 95–99.

The management of spasticity. (2000). *Drug and Therapeutics Bulletin, 38*(6), 44–46.

Mansfield, R.T. (1997). Head injuries in children and adults. *Critical Care Clinics, 13*, 611–628.

Marsh, N.V., Kersel, D.A., Havill, J.H., et al. (1998). Caregiver burden at 6 months following severe traumatic brain injury. *Brain Injury, 12*, 225–238.

Massagli, T.L., Jaffe, K.M., Fay, G.C., et al. (1996). Neurobehavioral sequelae of severe pediatric traumatic brain injury: A cohort study. *Archives of Physical Medicine and Rehabilitation, 77*, 223–231.

Massagli, T.L., Michaud, L.J., & Rivara, F.P. (1996). Association between injury indices and outcome after severe traumatic brain injury in children. *Archives of Physical Medicine and Rehabilitation, 77*, 125–132.

Mateer, C.A., Kerns, K.A., & Eso, K.L. (1996). Management of attention and memory disorders following traumatic brain injury. *Journal of Learning Disabilities, 29*, 618–632.

Max, J.E., Koele, S.L., Castillo, C.C., et al. (2000). Personality change disorder in children and adolescents following traumatic brain injury. *Journal of the International Neuropsychological Society, 6*, 279–289.

Max, J.E., Lindgren, S.D., Knutson, C., et al. (1997). Child and adolescent traumatic brain injury: Psychiatric findings from a paediatric outpatient specialty clinic. *Brain Injury, 11*, 699–711.

McCabe, C.F., & Donahue, S.P. (2000). Prognostic indicators for vision and mortality in shaken baby syndrome. *Archives of Ophthalmology, 118*, 373–377.

Meyer, P., Legros, C., & Orliaguet, G. (1999). Critical care management of neurotrauma in children: New trends and perspectives. *Child's Nervous System, 15*, 732–739.

Meythaler, J.M., Guin-Renfroe, S., Grabb, P., et al. (1999). Long-term continuously infused intrathecal baclofen for spastic-dystonic hypertonia in traumatic brain injury: 1-year experience. *Archives of Physical Medicine and Rehabilitation, 80*, 13–19.

Michaud, L.J., Rivara, F.P., Grady, M.S., et al. (1992). Predictors of survival and severity of disability after severe brain injury in children. *Neurosurgery, 31*, 254–264.

Michaud, L.J., Rivara, F.P., Jaffe, K.M., et al. (1993). Traumatic brain injury as a risk factor for behavioral disorders in children. *Archives of Physical Medicine and Rehabilitation, 74*, 368–375.

Miller, P.A., Binns, H.J., & Christoffel, K.K. (1996). Children's bicycle helmet attitudes and use: Association with parental rules. The Pediatric Practice Research Group. *Archives of Pediatric and Adolescent Medicine, 150*, 1259–1264.

Milton, S.B., Scaglione, C., Flanagan, T., et al. (1991). Functional evaluation of adolescent students with traumatic brain injury. *The Journal of Head Trauma Rehabilitation, 6*, 35–46.

Mittenberg, W., Wittner, M.S., & Miller, L.J. (1997). Postconcussion syndrome occurs in children. *Neuropsychology, 11*(3), 447–452.

Murgio, A., Andrade, F.A., Sanchez Munoz, M.A., et al. (1999). International multicenter study of head injury in children: ISHIP Group. *Child's Nervous System, 15*, 318–321.

Murray, J.A., Chen, D., Velmahos, G.C., et al. (2000). Pediatric falls: Is height a predictor of injury and outcome? *American Surgeon, 66*(9), 863–865.

Mysiw, W.J., Corrigan, J.D., & Gribble, M.W. (1990). The ataxic subgroup: A discrete outcome after traumatic brain injury. *Brain Injury, 4*, 247–255.

Natale, J.E., Joseph, J.G., Helfaer, M.A., et al. (2000). Early hyperthermia after traumatic brain injury in children: Risk factors, influence on length of stay, and effect on short term neurologic status. *Critical Care Medicine, 28*, 2608–2615.

National Institutes of Health (NIH) Consensus Development Panel on Rehabilitation of Persons with Traumatic Brain Injury. (1999). Consensus conference: Rehabilitation of persons with traumatic brain injury. *Journal of the American Medical Association, 282*, 974–983.

Novotny, E., Ashwal, S., & Shevell, M. (1998). Proton magnetic resonance spectroscopy: An emerging technology in pediatric neurology research. *Pediatric Research, 44*, 1–10.

Nybo, T., & Koskiniemi, M. (1999). Cognitive indicators of vocational outcome after severe traumatic brain injury in childhood. *Brain Injury, 13*, 759–766.

Olds, D.L., Henderson, C.R., Jr., Chamberlin, R., et al. (1986). Preventing child abuse and neglect: A randomized trial of nurse home visitation. *Pediatrics, 78*, 65–78.

Passler, M.A., & Riggs, R.V. (2001). Positive outcomes in traumatic brain injury-vegetative state: Patients treated with bromocriptine. *Archives of Physical Medicine and Rehabilitation, 82*, 311–315.

Paterakis, K., Karantanas, A.H., Komnos, A., et al. (2000). Outcome of patients with diffuse axonal injury: The significance and prognostic value of MRI in the acute phase. *The Journal of Trauma, 49,* 1071–1075.

Poggi, G., Calori, G., Mancarella, G., et al. (2000). Visual disorders after traumatic brain injury in developmental age. *Brain Injury, 14,* 833–845.

Poirier, M.P., & Wadsworth, M.R. (2000). Sports-related concussions. *Pediatric Emergency Care, 16*(4), 278–283; quiz 284–286.

Ponsford, J., Willmott, C., Rothwell, A., et al. (1999). Cognitive and behavioral outcome following mild traumatic head injury in children. *The Journal of Head Trauma Rehabilitation, 14,* 360–372.

Powell, E.C., Sheehan, K.M., & Christoffel, K.K. (1996). Firearm violence among youth: Public health strategies for prevention. *Annals of Emergency Medicine, 28,* 204–212.

Quayle, K.S. (1999). Minor head injury in the pediatric patient. *Pediatric Clinics of North America, 46,* 1189–1199, vii.

Reece, R.M., & Sege, R. (2000). Childhood head injuries: Accidental or inflicted? *Archives of Pediatric and Adolescent Medicine, 154,* 11–15.

Ried, S., Strong, G., Wright, L., et al. (1995). Computers, assistive devices, and augmentative communication aids: Technology for social inclusion. *The Journal of Head Trauma Rehabilitation, 10,* 80–90.

Rivara, F.P. (1994). Epidemiology and prevention of pediatric traumatic brain injury. *Pediatric Annals, 23,* 12–17.

Rivara, F.P. (1999). Pediatric injury control in 1999: Where do we go from here? *Pediatrics, 103,* 883–888.

Rivara, J.B., Jaffe, K.M., Fay, G.C., et al. (1993). Family functioning and injury severity as predictors of child functioning one year following traumatic brain injury. *Archives of Physical Medicine and Rehabilitation, 74,* 1047–1055.

Rivara, J.B., Jaffe, K.M., Polissar, N.L., et al. (1996). Predictors of family functioning and change 3 years after traumatic brain injury in children. *Archives of Physical Medicine and Rehabilitation, 78,* 754–764.

Roizen, N.J. (1999). Etiology of hearing loss in children. Nongenetic causes. *Pediatric Clinics of North America, 46*(1), 49–64, x.

Rose, F.D., Johnson, D.A., & Attree, E.A. (1997). Rehabilitation of the head-injured child: Basic research and new technology. *Pediatric Rehabilitation, 1*(1), 3–7.

Rosenthal, M., Griffith, E.R., Kreutzer, J.S., et al. (Eds.). (1999). *Rehabilitation of the adult and child with traumatic brain injury* (3rd ed.). Philadelphia: F.A. Davis.

Savitsky, E.A., & Votey, S.R. (2000). Current controversies in the management of minor pediatric head injuries. *American Journal of Emergency Medicine, 18,* 96–101.

Schieber, R.A., Gilchrist, J., & Sleet, D.A. (2000). Legislative and regulatory strategies to reduce childhood unintentional injuries. *Future Child, 10*(1), 111–136.

Schoenbrodt, L. (Ed.). (2001). *Children with traumatic brain injury: A parent's guide.* Bethesda, MD: Woodbine House.

Schutzman, S.A., Barnes, P., Duhaime, A.-C., et al. (2001). Evaluation and management of children younger than 2 years old with apparently minor head trauma: Proposed guidelines. *Pediatrics, 107,* 983–993.

Schutzman, S.A., & Greenes, D.S. (2001). Pediatric minor head trauma. *Annals of Emergency Medicine, 37,* 65–74.

Senturia, Y.D., Christoffel, K.K., & Donovan, M. (1996). Gun storage patterns in US homes with children: A pediatric practice-based survey. Pediatric Practice Research Group. *Archives of Pediatric and Adolescent Medicine, 150,* 265–269.

Senturia, Y.D., Morehead, T., LeBailly, S., et al. (1997). Bicycle-riding circumstances and injuries in school-aged

children. A case-control study. *Archives of Pediatric and Adolescent Medicine, 151,* 485–489.

Sheehan, K., DiCara, J.A., LeBailly, S., et al. (1997). Children's exposure to violence in an urban setting. *Archives of Pediatric and Adolescent Medicine, 151,* 502–504.

Sosin, D.M., Sacks, J.J., & Webb, K.W. (1996). Pediatric head injuries and deaths from bicycling in the United States. *Pediatrics, 98,* 868–870.

Stanton, B.R. (1999). Does family functioning affect outcome in children with neurological disorders? *Pediatric Rehabilitation, 3*(4), 193–199.

Stoler, D.R., & Hill, B.A. (1998). *Coping with mild traumatic brain injury.* New York: Avery Penguin Putnam.

Strauss, D.J., Shavelle, R.M., & Anderson, T.W. (1998). Long-term survival of children and adolescents after traumatic brain injury. *Archives of Physical Medicine and Rehabilitation, 79,* 1095–1100.

Tasker, R.C. (1999). Pharmacological advance in the treatment of acute brain injury. *Archives of Diseases in Childhood, 81,* 90–95.

Taylor, H.G., & Alden, J. (1997). Age-related differences in outcomes following childhood brain insults: An introduction and overview. *Journal of the International Neuropsychological Society, 3,* 555–567.

Taylor, H.G., Yeates, K.O., Wade, S.L., et al. (1999). Influences on first-year recovery from traumatic brain injury in children. *Neuropsychology, 13*(1), 76–89.

Telzrow, C.F. (1991). The school psychologist's perspective on testing students with traumatic brain injury. *The Journal of Head Trauma Rehabilitation, 6*(1), 23–34.

Tyler, J.S., & Mira, M.P. (1999). *Traumatic brain injury in children and adolescents: A sourcebook for teachers and other school personnel* (2nd ed.). Austin, TX: PRO-ED.

Tyroch, A.H., Kaups, K.L., Sue, L.P., et al. (2000). Pediatric restraint use in motor vehicle collisions: Reduction of deaths without contribution to injury. *Archives of Surgery, 135,* 1173–1176.

Varney, N.R., & Roberts, R.J. (Eds.). (1999). *The evaluation and treatment of mild traumatic brain injury.* Mahwah, NJ: Lawrence Erlbaum Associates.

Verger, K., Junque, C., Jurado, M.A., et al. (2000). Age effects on long-term neuropsychological outcome in paediatric traumatic brain injury. *Brain Injury, 14,* 495–503.

Vieth, A.Z., Johnstone, B., & Dawson, B. (1996). Extent of intellectual, cognitive, and academic decline in adolescent traumatic brain injury. *Brain Injury, 10,* 465–470.

Wade, S.L., Taylor, H.G., & Drotar, D. (1998). Family burden and adaptation during the initial year after traumatic brain injury in children. *Pediatrics, 102,* 110–116.

Walker, M.L., Mayer, T.A., Storrs, B.B., et al. (1985). Pediatric head injury: Factors which influence outcome. *Concepts in Pediatric Neurosurgery, 6,* 84–97.

Warschausky, S., Kewman, D., & Kay, J. (1999). Empirically supported psychological and behavioral therapies in pediatric rehabilitation of TBI. *The Journal of Head Trauma Rehabilitation, 14,* 373–383.

Watts, R., & Perlesz, A. (1999). Psychosocial outcome risk indicator: Predicting psychosocial outcome following traumatic brain injury. *Brain Injury, 13,* 113–124.

Wechsler, D. (1991). *Wechsler Intelligence Scale for Children– Third Edition (WISC-III).* San Antonio, TX: The Psychological Corporation.

Wills, K.E., Christoffel, K.K., Lavigne, J.V., et al. (1997). Patterns and correlates of supervision in child pedestrian injury: The Kids 'N' Cars Research Team. *Journal of Pediatric Psychology, 22*(1), 89–104.

Ylvisaker, M. (Ed.). (1985). *Head injury rehabilitation: Children and adolescents.* San Diego: College-Hill.

Ylvisaker, M., Todis, B., Glang, A., et al. (2001). Educating students with TBI: Themes and recommendations. *The Journal of Head Trauma Rehabilitation, 16,* 76–93.

Yorkston, K.M., Jaffe, K.M., Polissar, N.L., et al. (1997). Written language production and neuropsychological function in children with traumatic brain injury. *Archives of Physical Medicine and Rehabilitation, 78,* 1096–1102.

Zafonte, R.D., Mann, N.R., Millis, S.R., et al. (1997). Post-traumatic amnesia: Its relation to functional outcome. *Archives of Physical Medicine and Rehabilitation, 78,* 1103–1106.

Zeman, A. (1997). Persistent vegetative state. *Lancet, 350,* 795–799.

Zuccarello, M., Facco, E., Zampieri, P., et al. (1985). Severe head injury in children: Early prognosis and outcome. *Child's Nervous System, 1,* 158–162.

Zuckerman, G.B., & Conway, E.E., Jr. (1997). Accidental head injury. *Pediatric Annals, 26,* 621–632.

IV

Interventions, Families, and Outcomes

27 Feeding

Peggy S. Eicher

Upon completion of this chapter, the reader will be able to:

- describe the typical swallowing process and how it changes from infancy to adulthood
- understand the influence of medical, motor, and motivational dysfunction on the process of feeding in children
- recognize some of the feeding problems that commonly occur in children with developmental disabilities
- identify the basic components of a treatment approach to feeding problems

Feeding problems frequently arise in children with developmental disabilities, interfering with the ability to obtain adequate nutrition (Stevenson, 1995; Sullivan & Rosenbloom, 1996). The manifestations vary from difficulty advancing the texture of food, to incompetent swallowing with aspiration, to total food refusal. Likewise, the factors contributing to the development of these feeding problems may result from an anatomical abnormality, a motor or sensory dysfunction, or a medical or psychological condition. Most commonly, a feeding problem results from a combination of several factors. In this chapter, the typical swallowing process is described so that the influences of various medical and developmental conditions on it can be understood. Specific feeding and digestive disorders are discussed, along with approaches to therapy.

HECTOR

Hector is a 15-month-old referred for evaluation because of his difficulty in initiating spoon-feeding, resulting in total bottle dependence. Found to have glaucoma at 1 month of age, Hector was diagnosed with Sturge-Weber syndrome (see Appendix B), a genetic disorder associated with a facial hemangioma (birthmark involving blood vessels), mental retardation, and seizures. Hector was fed by bottle from birth, initially taking good volumes and gaining weight well. Spoon feeding was introduced at 8 months of age, with repeated attempts being made over several weeks until he finally accepted baby foods. After 2–3 months, table foods were introduced and Hector stopped accepting all purees. For the past 3 months, he has eaten only Cheerios, cheese curls, French fries, chicken nuggets, and fish sticks. Hector eats in a highchair with an insert to help him maintain a balanced, upright sitting position. Oral-motor problems include difficulty with tongue control and chewing, use of the bottle to help transport food into the pharynx, and oral defensiveness. Hector drinks 3 ounces of his formula at breakfast and 4–5 ounces every 3 hours for a total of 25–27 ounces per day. He eats two cheese curls and half of a fish stick or chicken nugget for lunch and dinner. Breakfast is his worst meal, with Hector accepting only three Cheerios. Meals end when he becomes irritable and pushes the food away. Hector's mother also reports that her son extends his neck during meals and frequently pulls away from the nipple while drinking. Stooling is effortful with one hard, difficult-to-pass stool every 2–3 days.

On physical examination, Hector is hypotonic with a lax jaw and open mouth posture. He can breathe through his nose if his mouth is closed and his tonsils are not enlarged. He demonstrates difficulty moving his tongue separately from his jaw and tends to move his tongue and head to the side as a unit. As a result, the food becomes pocketed in his cheek, and he drinks from the bottle to help clear the food. As the meal progresses, Hector becomes increasingly irritable, turning his head away from the spoon, and pushing the food away, ending the meal.

THE FEEDING PROCESS

Swallowing

Swallowing can be divided into four phases (Figure 27.1). During the initial **oral preparatory phase** food is readied for swallowing and collected; then it is transported backward during the second phase, the **oral transport phase.** As the tongue propels the **bolus** past the faucial arches (near the tonsils), it starts the third phase, the **pharyngeal transfer phase,** and triggers the swallowing cascade, an involuntary sequence of highly coordinated movements of the **pharyngeal** (throat) and esophageal (tube to the stomach) muscles. With each swallow, respiration ceases as the trachea (entrance to the lungs) is covered by the **epiglottis** (a projecting piece of cartilage) so that food does not slip into the airway. A wave-like motion originating in the back wall of the throat propels the bolus past the airway and into the esophagus, marking the start of the fourth and final phase, the **esophageal transport phase.**

Development of the Swallowing Process

The process of swallowing evolves as the nervous system matures. Reflexive oral-motor patterns in the infant are integrated into learned oral-motor patterns through practice. Cortical maturation enables more independent and finely graded tongue and jaw movements to develop under increasing volitional control (Arvedson & Lefton-Greif, 1996; Bosma, 1986; Miller, 1993). This stepwise progression in oral-motor skills is similar to the sequential development of gross motor skills.

Suckling

Suckling is the most primitive oral pattern. The tongue rides up and down with the jaw but also moves in and out, creating a wave-like motion. Suckling motions and swallowing activity have been reported in fetuses as early as 12–17 weeks' gestation. They are gradually coupled over the course of gestation so that the fetus can swallow half an ounce at 20 weeks' gestation and up to 15 ounces at 38–40 weeks' gestation. Only following delivery and with some practice, however, does the suck/swallow pattern become coordinated with breathing to allow functional feeding. This stepwise coupling of suck/swallow and then suck/swallow/breath is one of the reasons that even healthy premature infants usually require tube feedings during the first weeks of life (Comrie & Helm, 1997). Initially, suckling is a reflexive activity that occurs involuntarily whenever something enters the child's mouth. With brain maturation, the reflex is integrated and the pattern is refined through practice to the voluntary act of sucking.

Sucking

During sucking, the lips purse, the jaw opening is narrower and more controlled than in suckling, and the tongue is raised and lowered independently of the jaw. When sucking replaces the anterior–posterior pattern of suckling, usually around 5 months of age, the child can more easily progress to spoon feeding. Food can be moved posteriorly without first riding out of the

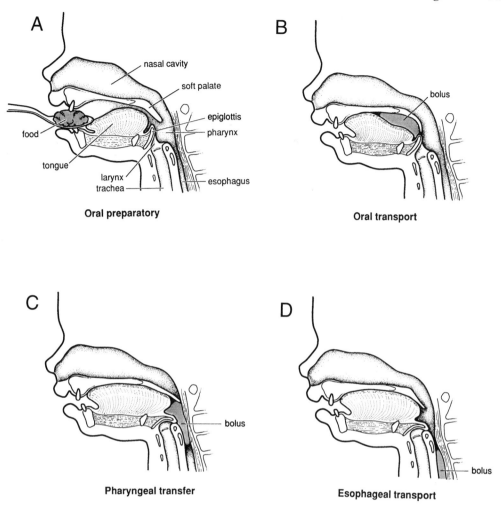

Figure 27.1. The four phases of swallowing. A) Oral preparatory: Food is taken into the mouth, processed to a manageable consistency, and then collected into a small parcel, or bolus. B) Oral transport: The bolus is then pushed backward by the tongue toward the pharynx. C) Pharyngeal transfer: As swallowing begins, the epiglottis normally folds over the opening of the trachea to direct food down the esophagus and not into the lungs. D) Esophageal transport: The peristaltic wave moves the bolus down the esophagus toward the stomach.

mouth with the tongue. Hector's feeding history suggests that he has had difficulty advancing to spoon feeding as a result of a persistent suckle pattern. It is possible he has continued to prefer his stronger but more immature suckle pattern because of his oral muscular hypotonia, which would hinder stability and development of independent tongue and jaw movements.

Munching

With munching, small pieces of food are broken off, flattened, and then collected for swallowing. Munching consists of a rhythmical bite-and-release pattern with a series of well-graded jaw openings and closings. The emergence of tongue lateralization at this stage enables the child to move food from side to side and return it to midline. *Chewing* food and breaking it into smaller pieces does not occur until the child acquires a rotary component to jaw movement. This emerges around 9 months and is gradually modified with practice to the adult pattern by around 3 years of age (Gisel, 1994). Munching is the level at which Hector demonstrates obvious problems. He has decreased and asymmetric bite strength and difficulty lateralizing the tongue to recollect the spoonful of food into the midline, resulting in pocketing. Despite his interest in his favorite finger foods, it is very hard for Hector to successfully prepare them for swallowing, contributing to his refusal to continue eating after only a few bites.

Oral-Motor Structures and Growth

Typically, the attainment of new oral-motor skills is timed to integrate with the change in oral-motor structures occurring with growth. The infant, for example, is perfectly equipped for nipple feeding. The cheek fat pads confine the oral cavity. The soft tissue structures, tongue, soft palate, and epiglottis fill much of the mouth cavity, making it easier to generate the vacuum necessary to draw fluids out of the nipple. The larynx is almost tucked under the tongue, necessitating less throat control to guide the liquid past the airway and into the esophagus (Bosma, 1986).

With growth, the jaw and palate enlarge in relation to the soft tissue structures, allowing room for teeth (Figure 27.2). The larger oral cavity (even without teeth) is not as efficient for nipple feeding but facilitates spoon entry and lateralization (pushing the food to the side). The larynx (voice box at the entry way to the lungs) descends and moves backward as the neck elongates. This elongation requires increased control of the position of the head and neck to enable safe swallowing. Control of head and neck positioning is achieved as the child develops control of head and neck movement and the ability to sit independently. Meanwhile, the changes occurring in the child's oral-motor pattern afford the tongue increasing control of collection and propulsion of the food in the mouth, enhancing the child's ability to guide the food safely past the airway. A delay in gross motor or oral-motor development can interfere with the integration of oral-motor skills with growth, resulting in decreased feeding efficiency (Stevenson, 1995).

Any anatomical defect involving the oral or nasal cavities, pharynx, or esophagus can adversely affect swallowing. Clefts such as those in the lip and especially the palate interfere with sealing off the oral cavity, decreasing the child's efficiency at generating negative pressure and

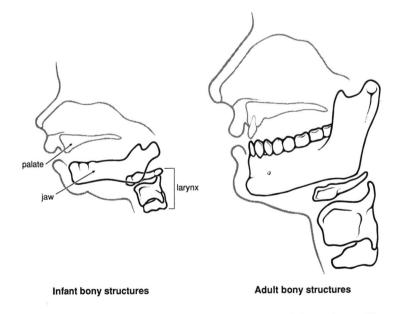

Infant bony structures   **Adult bony structures**

Figure 27.2. The influence of growth on the bony structures of the oropharynx. The mandible (jaw) enlarges, enabling room for teeth and a larger oral cavity. The larynx descends and moves posteriorly, necessitating increased control of bolus propulsion to guide it past the airway.

collecting the food in preparation for swallowing. A structural change that affects coordination can also be a significant problem; for example, enlarged adenoids may render the child dependent on his or her mouth as an airway, influencing suck/swallow/breath coordination.

FEEDING AND THE INFLUENCE OF MEDICAL CONDITIONS

Successful feeding is dependent not only on the anatomy and function of the oral and pharyngeal structures involved in swallowing but also on the child's medical status, especially with regard to respiration and digestion (Gisel & Alphonce, 1995). Sensory information from the lungs and heart input directly into the swallowing center in the brain. Thus, a child with breathing difficulty (e.g., when wheezing from asthma) may start to drool because swallowing frequency has decreased (Timms et al., 1993).

Input from the gastrointestinal (GI) tract also has a significant impact on the feeding process. Typically as the bolus of food travels to the stomach, the lower esophageal sphincter works as a one-way valve to prevent the backward flow, or reflux, of food after it has entered the stomach. Meanwhile, the stomach secretes acids to further break down the food. Contractions of the stomach wall mix the food, acids, and added fluids and push this mass gradually into the **duodenum,** the upper part of the small intestine (Figure 27.3). Enzymes and other substances from the pancreas and bile ducts are released into the duodenum and aid in the breakdown of food particles into their major components: proteins, fats, and carbohydrates. These compounds are further simplified into sugars (e.g., lactose), fatty acids, amino acids, vitamins, and minerals. The **jejunum** and **ileum,** the middle and lower portions of the small intestine, absorb these digested nutrients.

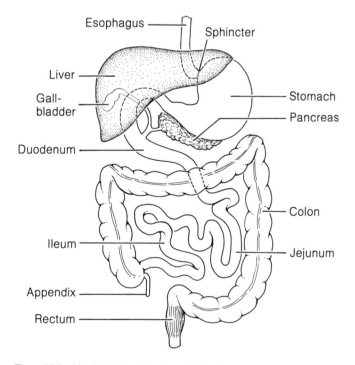

Figure 27.3. After food enters the stomach, it is mixed with acid and is partially digested. Then it passes through the three segments of the small intestine (duodenum, jejunum, and ileum). There, digestive juices are added, and nutrients are removed. The remaining water and electrolytes pass through the colon, where water is removed. Voluntary stooling is controlled by the rectal sphincter muscles.

The nonabsorbable nutrients, called **bulk** or *fiber*, pass to the large intestine or colon. Movement through the colon is much slower than through the rest of the digestive tract and is influenced by the volume of the nonabsorbable nutrients contained in food. Although movement from the stomach to the end of the ileum may take only 30–90 minutes, passage through the colon may require 1–7 days. Rapid movement, which happens, for example, during a bout of gastroenteritis, leads to diarrhea. Conversely, slower movement causes more water to be absorbed and results in hard stools and constipation. Constipation can lead to slower transit through the entire system and even vomiting. For proper bowel evacuation to take place, an individual needs fluid, fiber, and coordinated propulsive muscle activity (Williams, Bollella, & Wynder, 1995). This includes control of the rectal muscles that facilitate voluntary defecation.

Any medical condition that impairs the function of the respiratory or GI tract can influence the feeding and swallowing process. Asthma, gastroesophageal reflux (GER), constipation, kidney disease, and inborn errors of metabolism (see Chapter 18) can each contribute to the development of a feeding problem (Eicher et al., 2000; Stark, 1999). Moreover, these disorders can interact with one another. A respiratory condition that increases the work of breathing may influence the function of the GI tract by changing pressure relationships between the chest and abdomen. For example, when a child has to generate increased negative lung pressure to breathe, as during an asthma attack, abdominal pressure increases relative to chest pressure, increasing the probability of GER. Likewise, GER can contribute to reactive airway narrowing, wheezing, and increased work of breathing. Thus, a vicious cycle can start fairly easily. Unfortunately, if oral feeding is stopped for prolonged periods of time for any reason, the child may lose oral-motor skills and require gradual retraining (Monahan, Shapiro, & Fox, 1988). If the medical issue interfering with feeding becomes chronic, it can result in aversion to feeding and food refusal.

In Hector's case, constipation slows his gastrointestinal motility and increases abdominal pressure and the possibility of GER, which could contribute to his food selectivity and refusal. His neck extension with meals and frequent interruptions in nipple feeding are consistent with 1) fatigue, 2) the need for increased respiratory support, or 3) GER and resultant discomfort.

FEEDING AND THE INFLUENCE OF TONE, POSTURE, AND DEVELOPMENT

A child's developmental function influences the feeding process in several ways. Abnormal muscle tone and/or persistent primitive reflex activity (as seen in cerebral palsy; see Chapter 23) interfere with trunk support and body alignment. Lack of adequate trunk support greatly hinders rib cage expansion, which interferes with respiration and increases pressure on the stomach and abdominal cavity. With inadequate support and restricted respiration, the shoulders typically elevate, reducing the stability of the base of support for the head and neck. Improper head and neck alignment makes guiding a bolus past the airway harder, increasing the risk of aspiration of food into the lungs (Larnert & Ekberg, 1995). Malalignment also limits tongue movement, thereby interfering with oral-motor patterns. For all these reasons, a child should be seated during feedings, with a firm base of support and adequate trunk support to allow proper alignment of the head and neck. This may require a slight recline if the child has not yet accomplished independent sitting.

The child's fine motor and adaptive skills influence the choice of utensils and level of independence at mealtime, and cognitive abilities help to shape how the child interacts with the mealtime environment. Because children are dependent on their caregivers for nutrition, effective caregiver–child communication during mealtime is crucial. An understanding of the child's cognitive level and sensitivity to nonverbal cues prepare the caregiver to effectively communicate with the child. The absence of effective communication increases the likelihood of maladaptive behaviors at mealtime, such as expelling, refusal, or tantrums. Approaching the child at his or her cognitive level also engages the child's interest and makes meals more enjoyable.

Many feeding transitions occur in the first 3 years of life, and a child with a developmental disability may have more difficulty adjusting to the changes in textures, utensils, and settings that happen during this period. This heightens the importance of a stable mealtime environment and consistent interactions between the caregiver and child (Babbitt et al., 1994). Consistency imparts a sense of familiarity that enables children to be comfortable and more tolerant of mealtimes.

In light of his hypotonia, Hector uses an adapted insert for feeding in order to maintain good head, neck, and trunk alignment in sitting. Because pulling away from the nipple, neck extension, and pocketing were not recognized by parents as subtle signs of discomfort or fatigue, Hector has escalated his behavior to include head turning, pushing food away, and refusal in order to force his mother to end the meal.

FEEDING PROBLEMS IN CHILDREN WITH DISABILITIES

One third of all children with a developmental disability will develop a feeding problem significant enough to interfere with their nutrition, medical well-being, or social integration (Rogers et al., 1994; Waterman et al., 1992). Manifestations of a feeding disorder can be as subtle as increased congestion or gagging with meals or as dramatic as total food refusal, choking, or failure to thrive. The symptoms depend on the severity of the medical problem, the time of its occurrence, and the child's motor and sensory function. A feeding interruption may result from structural or neurological abnormalities affecting the mouth, nose, or respiratory or GI tract that interfere with safe feeding. Or, a feeding problem may develop if a medical or developmental condition chronically prevents the child from having a positive feeding experience. The child then starts to associate discomfort and pain with feeding and learns to avoid feeding situations. This food avoidance or aversion can continue even after the medical condition has resolved, especially in children who have difficulty interpreting or integrating sensory input from elsewhere in the body. An explanation of some of the more common feeding problems follows.

Increased Oral Losses

Loss of food from the mouth signals oral-motor dysfunction (Chigira et al., 1994). The child may have poor lip closure or jaw instability related to abnormal tone in the facial muscles. Once in the mouth, food may be carried out on the tongue as a result of a persistent suckle pattern. Sometimes food may be exhaled from the mouth if the oral cavity also serves as the primary airway. It must be remembered that a dietary history will not accurately reflect a child's caloric intake in the presence of significant oral losses (Stallings, Zemel, & Davies, 1996). A speech-language pathologist or an occupational therapist skilled in feeding can give helpful information and suggestions for improving a child's oral-motor patterns and tone.

Prolonged Feeding Time

Prolonged feeding time (greater than 30 minutes) usually results from a combination of factors. Oral transport may be slowed by difficulty in collecting food in the mouth or by weakened tongue movements. If pharyngeal transfer is weak or uncoordinated, the child may need more swallows between bites to clear the food bolus from the pharynx. The child may also slow the meal to allow more time for breathing between bites or to complete transport through the esophagus. Prolonged feeding time is a difficult problem for both the child and caregiver and signals the need for an evaluation (Kedesdy & Budd, 1998). Again, consultation with a speech-language pathologist or an occupational therapist skilled in feeding is a good place to start to get helpful information on the factors that could be playing a role in prolonging mealtime.

Pocketing

Food pocketing (holding food in the cheeks or the front of the mouth for prolonged periods) suggests either problematic oral transport or food refusal. Children who have difficulty moving their tongue from side to side often have trouble bringing food back to the midline before a swallow; as a result, mashed food or chunks migrate toward the cheeks. Alternatively, if a child does not want to swallow the food because of its texture or taste, he or she may trap it in the cheeks. If a child appears to have trouble moving his or her tongue to the sides, a speech-language pathologist can provide exercises that will help the child practice and strengthen tongue movements.

Coughing, Gagging, and Choking

Coughing and gagging indicate difficulty with swallowing. Both are normal defense mechanisms that prevent aspiration. The times when coughing and gagging occur during the meal may indicate which textures are troublesome (Casas, Kenny, & McPherson, 1994). For example, if a child gags on lumpy foods but not on purees, he or she may have difficulty adequately chewing or transporting the more highly textured food. The child who coughs while drinking may have a problem controlling flow through the pharynx and past the airway. If the child coughs or gags at the end of or after a meal but not during the meal, GER should be considered. Coughing or gagging during meals persisting for several weeks is a serious warning sign and requires evaluation as soon as possible (Kosko et al., 1998).

Choking occurs when a piece of food becomes stuck in the pharynx or airway and the child has difficulty dislodging it. This happens most commonly when large pieces of soft solids are given to a child who has an inadequate munching pattern or suckle transport. It also occurs if the child tends to stuff his or her mouth before swallowing. In this case, cutting foods up into smaller pieces or offering only a couple of pieces at a time may decrease choking. After some practice and with positive reinforcement, the child may be able to gradually advance the size and/or number of chunks accepted.

Aspiration

Aspiration refers to the entry of food or a foreign substance into the airway (Figure 27.4). It may occur before, during, or after a swallow or as a result of reflux. Everyone aspirates small amounts of food occasionally, but our protective responses—gagging and coughing—help to clear them from the airway. Children with developmental disabilities that affect sensory or motor coordination of the oropharynx, larynx, or trachea, however, are at increased risk for recurrent aspiration. Furthermore, these children often have impaired protective responses that limit their ability to clear their airway once aspiration has occurred. Signs of aspiration are influenced by the age of the child. In infants, it may present as apnea and bradycardia during meals, whereas in older infants and children, it may appear as coughing, congestion, or wheezing. Some children aspirate without evoking any protective response; this is called *silent aspiration* and is particularly dangerous because it often goes undetected. Recurrent aspiration and resultant accumulation of foodstuffs in the airway causes irritation and inflammation that can lead to pneumonia, bronchitis, or tracheitis (Loughlin & Lefton-Greif, 1994; Rogers et al., 1994). If you are concerned that a child may be aspirating, have him or her seen by a medical provider, who is likely to order testing such as a chest X ray and a modified barium swallow.

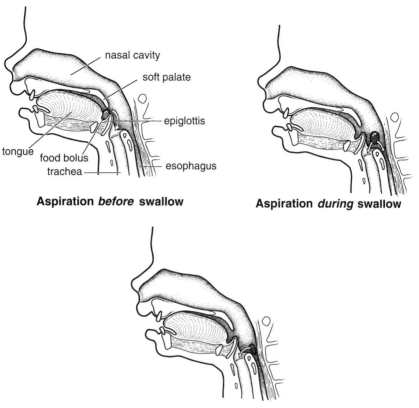

Figure 27.4.   Aspiration. a) If a part of the bolus leaks past the soft palate before a swallow is triggered, it can flow past the open epiglottis and into the trachea. b) If the epiglottis is not completely closed as the bolus passes, aspiration can also occur. c) Food residua in the pharynx after a swallow can be carried into the airway with the next breath, resulting in aspiration after the swallow.

Food Refusal

Food refusal can be total, in which the child does not accept and swallow any food, or partial, in which the child eats some food but not enough to sustain adequate growth and nutritional health. Food refusal is most often associated with an ongoing medical problem such as asthma or GER. Because of the resulting lack of practice eating, these children also commonly show immaturity or dysfunction in their oral-motor skills that further complicates matters. Food refusal requires a coordinated approach between the child's medical provider and a feeding specialist.

Food Selectivity

Food selectivity implies that the child will accept only a small number of foods, although he or she may eat large quantities of these items. There are four types of food selectivity: selectivity by number of foods (the child's total diet consists of fewer than 10 food items), selectivity by type of food (the child avoids all foods from one or more of the main food groups, e.g., starch, fruits, vegetables, meats), selectivity by type and number, and selectivity by texture (the child only accepts foods of a certain texture, e.g., purees, crunchy foods). Selectivity by number is often seen in children with pervasive developmental disorders (see Chapter 20). Selectivity by texture is most commonly seen in children with cerebral palsy who have oral-motor problems.

Selectivity by both number and type may be associated with an underlying medical condition initially but then becomes a learned response perpetuated by environmental or interactional factors even after the instigating factor has resolved (Babbitt et al., 1994). Food selectivity is a difficult problem that requires the coordinated efforts of a medical care provider, oral-motor specialist, and behavioral therapist.

Gastroesophageal Reflux and Delayed Gastric Emptying

GER involves the backward flow of stomach contents into the esophagus (Figure 27.5). Reflux can result in vomiting, and if the stomach contents enter the airway, the reflux can cause coughing, wheezing, and even pneumonia (Bagwell, 1995). In addition, the escape of stomach acid into the esophagus can cause irritation (esophagitis) that makes eating painful. The child may respond by vomiting, refusing to eat, or taking frequent breaks in the meal. GER can result from a number of abnormalities, and some forms can be inherited (Hu et al., 2000). The most common problem is inappropriate opening of the muscle at the base of the esophagus, which allows reflux of gastric contents. Reflux also can result from increased abdominal pressure caused by spasticity, posture problems, or constipation. Delayed stomach emptying may also lead to stomach distension that increases the risk for reflux. It can be caused by abnormal stomach contractions, poor intestinal motility, or a meal containing a large amount of fat or protein.

Not all vomiting is a consequence of GER. Increased intracranial pressure, obstruction of the stomach's outflow tract, kidney disease, and food allergies are other medical conditions that produce vomiting and gastric intolerance that mimic reflux (American Academy of Pediatrics, Committee on Nutrition, 2000). Therefore, an appropriate medical evaluation is important. Sometimes the pattern or content of emesis can suggest a cause (e.g., bilious vomiting suggests obstruction; repeated emesis immediately after a certain food suggests an allergy).

Vomiting is not the only impact that GER can have on the feeding process. A child with GER who feels uncomfortable all the time may not be interested in eating (food refusal) or may only accept a few favorite foods (food selectivity). GER can also influence the movement of the tongue, throat, and esophagus, causing the child to choose foods that are easier to swallow. Because of the resulting lack of practice with higher textured food, a child's oral-motor development may be delayed.

Abnormal Digestion: The Small Intestine

Although children with disabilities often have problems with sucking and swallowing, they usually are able to absorb nutrients once the food reaches the small intestine. Occasionally, however, there may be malabsorption that interferes with adequate nutrition (Brady et al., 1986). The most common malabsorptive disorder is lactose intolerance. Approximately 10%–20% of African American, Asian, and Jewish children are lactose intolerant (Rings, Grand, & Buller, 1994). Symptoms include vomiting and diarrhea after ingesting milk products. The cause of the intolerance is an inherited deficiency of the enzyme lactase, which normally breaks down

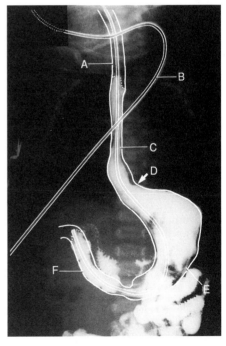

Figure 27.5. Gastroesophageal reflux (GER). Food passes down the esophagus (A), through the lower esophageal sphincter (D), and into the stomach (E) and duodenum (F). If the sphincter does not remain closed after the passage of food, reflux (C) occurs, as shown in this barium study in a child with a nasogastric tube (B) in place.

milk sugar (lactose) and allows its absorption. Unabsorbed lactose irritates the gastrointestinal wall and causes vomiting and diarrhea. An individual with this disorder can prevent or at least decrease the symptoms by taking lactase in a capsule form before ingesting a milk product or by using lactase-containing dairy products.

The function of the small intestine also can be compromised by a "dumping syndrome," in which the stomach is emptied too rapidly. When this happens, the duodenal receptors are presented with an excess of gastric contents. Symptoms of dumping include nausea, vomiting, diarrhea, heart palpitations, and weakness. Children receiving carbohydrate-based high-calorie supplements or formulas are particularly at risk. Avoiding dumping requires slowing the rate of stomach emptying or decreasing the concentration of food delivered to the duodenum. This can be accomplished by 1) slowing the feeding rate by using continuous feeding, 2) using fat-based instead of carbohydrate-based calorie supplements, or 3) changing to a formula with a lower caloric concentration.

Inconsistent Stooling: The Large Intestine

Constipation is a major problem for many children with developmental disabilities. This is caused by an inadequate intake of fluid and fiber combined with uncoordinated muscle contractions and poor rectal sphincter control (Williams et al., 1995). The result is the retention of stool for prolonged periods of time. The longer the stool remains in the colon, the more water is absorbed and the harder and more immobile the stool becomes; the result is constipation. Besides increasing abdominal pressure and thereby the risk of reflux, constipation can be associated with cramping and discomfort that interferes with appetite, positioning, and sleep.

Overly loose stools also can be a problem. This may be caused by a lack of dietary fiber, dumping, overaggressive use of laxatives or enemas, or passage of loose stool around an impaction. If diarrhea or constipation is a problem, the child's diet and bowel regimen should be evaluated and adjusted.

Failure to Thrive

Failure to thrive is the term used to describe growth that is falling away from the normal growth curve or from the child's previously established growth curve. It can result from an inadequate caloric intake, excessive caloric expenditures, or an inability to use the calories that have been ingested (Stevenson, 1995). Children with developmental disabilities are at increased risk of failure to thrive for both nutritional and nonnutritional reasons (see Chapter 9).

EVALUATION

Because of the complexity of the process and the multiple influences on it, evaluation of a feeding problem should have a multidisciplinary perspective. Information is needed regarding how and when the feeding problem started, how it has changed over time, and what interventions have been used. Background information regarding the child's medical, motor, and behavioral history is also important. A thorough evaluation includes the child's medical history and physical examination, neurodevelopmental assessment, oral-pharyngeal evaluation, feeding history, and mealtime observation (Kosko et al., 1998; Lefton-Greif & Arvedson, 1997). The information gleaned will identify the feeding problem and the medical, motor, and motivational factors contributing to it. For Hector, hypotonia has affected his oral facial musculature, contributing to an inefficient munching pattern. Hypotonia, however, did not explain his volume limitation with liquids or refusal of purees. The constipation and arching reported suggested that he had some GI dysmotility contributing to volume limitation, food selectivity, and food refusal. Hector has stumbled upon an effective communication strategy; when he cries and pushes food away, his mother offers him only his favorite foods.

Diagnostic procedures may be needed to provide further information to support or clarify the clinical impression. If GER is suspected, an upper GI series may be done to rule out anatomical problems. Barium, a milk-like substance visible on an X ray, is either ingested by the child or infused into the stomach by a nasogastric (NG) tube. As the fluid courses through the esophagus, stomach, and small intestine, the radiologist can identify structural abnormalities and reflux (Figure 27.5; Kramer & Eicher, 1993).

A second procedure, a milk scan, provides information about the frequency of GER episodes and assesses the rate of gastric emptying (Figure 27.6; Heyman, Eicher, & Alavi, 1995). Delayed gastric emptying can lead to vomiting and aspiration, whereas an increased rate of gastric emptying can lead to diarrhea. During the milk scan, the child swallows a formula to which a small amount of a radioactive tracer has been added, enabling the radiologist to track the milk as it moves through the GI tract. In addition to measuring gastric emptying and reflux, if the radioactive tracer is found in the lung after several hours, it suggests that aspiration has occurred during a reflux episode.

The final two studies, the pH probe and gastroesophageal duodenoscopy (endoscopy), are considered the gold standards in the evaluation of GER and esophagitis, respectively (Willging, 1995). For the pH probe study, an NG-like tube is inserted through the nose and passed down the esophagus to just above the junction of the stomach and esophagus. At the tip of the tube is a small sensor, which detects the pH, or acidity, above the gastroesophageal junction. If acid in the stomach refluxes through an incompetent sphincter muscle, the sensor records a sudden drop in the pH level, signaling GER (Figure 27.7). Reflux is most likely to occur in the hour following a meal or during sleep, when the child is reclining. For this reason, the pH

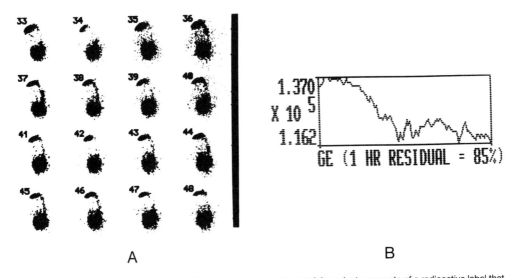

A   B

Figure 27.6. Milk scan. In this study, the child is fed a milk formula containing minute amounts of a radioactive label that can be seen on scanning. A) Shown here is a sequence of images taken after the child drinks the milk. The images are generated by a computer from information obtained by the scanner every 120 seconds. The area of radioactivity at the top of each image represents residual formula in the mouth, whereas the lower area of radioactivity is the stomach. Images 34–39 show increased activity in the mouth and esophagus reflecting a reflux episode to the mouth and descending back to the stomach. In frames 44–48, radioactivity can be seen flowing up from the stomach into the mid-esophagus, indicating another episode of reflux. A repeat scan after the child was placed on antireflux medication would show an absence of stomach reflux. B) In addition to diagnosing reflux, the milk scan can also evaluate whether the stomach is emptying food into the small intestine at a normal rate. Delayed gastric emptying increases stomach pressure and the possibility of reflux or vomiting. In the study shown, residual gastric radioactivity decreased by 15% 1 hour after the labeled milk was ingested (decreasing from 1.370×10^5 counters per minute to 1.162×10^5). This 85% 1-hour residual is high, the normal being 67% or less. Prokinetic agents such as metoclopramide (Reglan) not only decrease gastroesophageal reflux directly but also indirectly by increasing gastric emptying. Following effective medication, the gastric emptying would be expected to increase, potentially to normal levels.

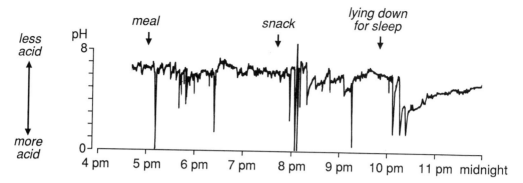

Figure 27.7. A pH probe study is done by passing a tube containing a pH electrode down the esophagus and positioning it just above the stomach. If there is reflux, the pH should drop as the acid contents of the stomach reach the lower esophagus, where the probe is placed. Shown here is an abnormal study with multiple episodes of low pH, occurring about half an hour after feeding and when the child is laid down to sleep. (From Batshaw, M.L. [1991]. *Your child has a disability: A complete sourcebook of daily and medical care* [p. 224]. Baltimore: Paul H. Brookes Publishing Co.; reprinted by permission. Copyright © 1991 Mark L. Batshaw. Illustration copyright © 1991 by Lynn Reynolds. All rights reserved.)

probe is left in place for 24 hours to record the presence of reflux and the circumstances of its occurrence. This may have important therapeutic implications in terms of positioning after feeding. The other method, endoscopy, entails passing a fiber-optic tube through the mouth down the esophagus and into the stomach (Leder, 1998). The child is sedated during this procedure. The gastroenterologist can then visualize the esophagus and stomach and take small biopsy specimens to look for inflammation.

If aspiration of oral feedings is suspected, a modified barium swallow with video fluoroscopy is the best test to use. In this study, the child is positioned in the usual feeding position and offered foods to which barium has been added. The radiologist uses a video fluoroscope to visualize the pharynx and watch how the pharyngeal muscles guide the food bolus past the airway. The texture of the food and liquids can be changed to evaluate whether the child has more difficulty with one texture than another (Logemann, 1997).

MANAGING FEEDING PROBLEMS

Because feeding difficulties in children with developmental disabilities usually result from the interaction of multiple factors, managing them can be difficult, time consuming, and frustrating. Effective treatment usually requires intervention from more than one therapeutic discipline and a plan of intervention that can be effectively applied across the child's environment whether it is the home, school, or therapist's office. The treatment team, which should include the child's caregiver, teacher, nurse, and therapists, should prioritize the goals of treatment and outline an integrated plan within the context of the child's medical, nutritional, and developmental needs (Schwartz, Corredor, & Fisher-Medina, 2001). The primary caregiver, with input from the team, oversees the plan and monitors progress toward the goals. Clear lines of communication among all members of the team are essential for success. Components of a successful treatment strategy include 1) minimizing negative medical influences; 2) ensuring positioning for feeding; 3) facilitating oral-motor function; 4) improving the mealtime environment; 5) promoting appetite; and 6) if needed, using alternative methods of feeding. All of these components should involve constant monitoring of the child's progress. Recognizing the interaction among the medical, motor, and motivational components enables the team to anticipate changes and work on several components at the same time (Arvedson, 1998). Obviously, for a feeding program to be successful, the therapists working with the child need to be consistent in and mindful of how the skills they are working on will impact the child's feeding function.

Minimize Negative Medical Influences

Because feeding is a complex skill, a child's feeding function may be very sensitive to even minor medical issues. Thus, parents' and therapists' observations of subtle changes in the child's behaviors, especially during and after feedings, are important and should be shared with medical care providers. Because problems with GI dysmotility such as constipation and GER can adversely affect respiratory and GI function as well as the child's level of comfort, they should be treated aggressively. For instance, Hector began to have daily soft stools that are easily passed, and he has stopped extending his neck and pulling away from the nipple during nipple feedings. This has increased his volume of intake and interest in purees and a wider variety of soft solid foods. Although no cure for constipation is known, the following suggestions may be helpful. Have the toddler or older child sit briefly on the toilet 30–60 minutes after meals to establish a regular pattern of bowel movements and to take advantage of the gastrocolic reflex that occurs after meals to expel stool. As much fluid as possible should be added to the diet. Bulky and high-fiber foods, such as whole-grain cereals, bran, and raw fruits and vegetables, should also be included in the diet to increase movement through the GI tract (Hillemeier, 1995; Williams et al., 1995). Fiber products such as those containing psyllium (e.g., Metamucil) may also be helpful. Prune, apricot, or papaya juice can serve as a mild laxative and are especially helpful if the child needs additional calories. Stool softeners, such as docusate (Colace) or mineral oil (Kondremul), may be used regularly to help coat the stool and facilitate its movement through the intestines. Active or passive physical exercise will also aid movement of the stool.

When constipation is persistent, additional measures may be needed. Laxatives and suppositories can be used, including milk of magnesia, malt soup **extract** (Malt-Supex), senna concentrate (Senokot), bisacodyl (Dulcolax), or glycerin suppositories. Enemas, such as Fleet Enema for Children, also may help, but constant use of enemas can interfere with normal rectal sphincter control and should be avoided. A combination of these approaches may be needed to establish regular bowel movements.

Constipation can increase the potential for GER. If GER is present, a number of therapeutic modalities, including proper positioning, meal modification, medications, and surgery, are available (Lewis et. al., 1994). The goal is to protect the esophagus from reflux of stomach acid, either by reducing the amount of food in the stomach at any one time or by decreasing stomach acid production.

Small, frequent meals and/or medications that promote stomach emptying help to decrease the volume of food in the stomach. In addition, studies have found that whey-based formulas improve stomach emptying and decrease vomiting in children with certain forms of spastic cerebral palsy (Fried et al., 1992). Upright positioning and thickened feedings use gravity to help keep stomach contents from refluxing into the esophagus. Medications such as urecholine (Bethanechol) and metoclopramide (Reglan) increase the tone in the esophageal sphincter, making it harder for reflux to occur (McCallum, 1990). Cimetidine (Tagamet), ranitidine (Zantac), or famotidine (Pepcid) often are used to decrease stomach acidity and thereby lower the risk of inflammation of the esophagus from reflux. (See Appendix C for more information on these medications.)

When GER cannot be controlled by positioning and medication alone, surgery may be needed to prevent problems associated with prolonged reflux that include failure to thrive, recurrent aspiration pneumonia, and gastroesophageal bleeding. The most common surgical procedure is **fundoplication** (Fonkalsrud et al., 1995), in

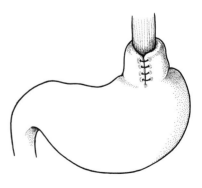

Figure 27.8. In the surgical procedure of fundoplication, the upper stomach is wrapped around the lower esophagus to create a muscular valve that prevents reflux.

which the top of the stomach is wrapped around the opening of the esophagus (Figure 27.8). This decreases reflux while permitting continued oral feeding. An alternative to fundoplication is the surgical placement of a gastrojejunal (G-J) tube that allows access to the stomach as well as the jejunum, permitting some portion of the feeds to bypass the stomach, thereby decreasing the risk of reflux (Figure 27.9; Albanese et al., 1993).

Ensure Proper Positioning

Feeding is a **flexor** activity that requires good breath support. Appropriate positioning maximizes the child's ability to both flex and breathe (Larnert & Ekberg, 1995). The child should be firmly supported though the hips and trunk to provide a stable base. The head and neck should be aligned in a neutral (upright) position, which decreases extension through the oral musculature while maintaining an open airway. Such positioning allows improved coordination and more control of the steps in oral-motor preparation and transport. This, in turn, results in more positive feedback to the child and caregiver as a result of good feeding experiences (Kerwin, Osborne, & Eicher, 1994). If the child does not appear comfortable or appropriately supported for feeding in the currently constructed chair, the child's occupational or physical therapist can make changes to improve the support and alignment.

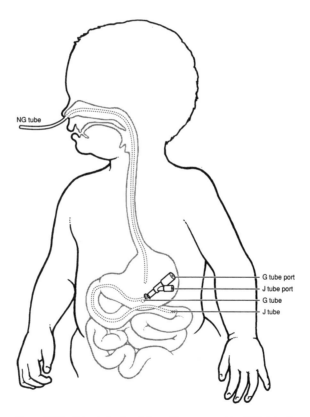

Figure 27.9. Enteral feeding tubes. The nasogastric (NG) tube is placed through the nostril and into the stomach. An NG tube is helpful when problems with the child's oral function are the primary obstacle to adequate nutrition and are temporary. A gastrojejunal (G-J) tube allows access to the stomach as well as directly into the intestine. The G-J tube has 2 openings, or ports, and two parts of tubing. The G port connects with the G tube, which empties the stomach. The J port connects with the J tube, which empties into the intestine. A G-J tube can be helpful when the stomach is unable to tolerate the quantity of nutrients needed for adequate growth.

Facilitate Oral-Motor Function

Chewing can be enhanced by placing food between the upper and lower back teeth. This encourages the child to move the jaw and use the tongue in an effort to dislodge the food. Other techniques include manipulating food textures to facilitate safe, controlled swallowing (Gisel, 1994; Takada, Miyawaki, & Tatsuta, 1994). Thickening of liquids slows their rate of flow, allowing more time for the child to organize and initiate a swallow. Thickening agents (e.g., Thick-It, instant pudding powders) can transform any thin liquid into a nectar-, honey-, or milkshake-like consistency. Almost any food can be chopped fine or pureed to a texture that the child can more competently manage.

It is important to remember that the primary goal of eating is to achieve adequate nutrition. Thus, when a child is first learning to accept a higher texture of foods, these foods should be presented during snacktime, when volumes are smaller. At mealtimes, easier textures should be used to ensure consumption of adequate calories for continued growth during this transition period. A speech-language pathologist or an occupational therapist can provide information about the child's oral-motor patterns and the appropriate food textures to facilitate improvement in feeding efforts.

Improve the Mealtime Environment

Eating requires more coordination among muscle groups than any other motor activity, including speech. Failure to perform the work competently can result in aspiration, which is unpleasant, frightening, and dangerous. Therefore, it is important to make eating as easy as possible (Babbitt et al., 1994; Kerwin et al., 1995). This can be accomplished by increasing the child's focus on the meal and including foods in each meal that are desirable and easier for the child to control (Luiselli, 1994). Let the child know that mealtime is coming so that he or she can prepare for the work to be done. This may entail a premeal routine of going to a special corner of the room and putting on a bib or napkin or relaxation therapy followed by oral stimulation to get the needed muscles ready for eating. Children with feeding difficulties usually eat better in one-to-one situations or in small groups because there is less distraction and they are better able to focus on the eating process (Kerwin, 1999). Undivided attention also makes mealtimes more reinforcing.

When a child is eating well and interested in self-feeding, a number of adaptive devices can promote independence in feeding. These include bowls with high sides, spoons with built-up or curved handles, and cups with rocker bottoms. The satisfaction children get from eating can be increased by social attention during the meal or earning time for a favorite activity after the meal is completed.

Social interaction is an important part of mealtime as well, although it can be distracting. When peer interaction is the focus, it may be helpful to make the meal small (e.g., a snack) and provide less challenging foods that do not require as much concentration for the child to be successful.

Promote Appetite

Some children have little or no appetite, whether or not they are receiving enough calories to progress along their growth curve. Poor appetite may be caused by an underlying medical condition such as a kidney or metabolic disorder or zinc deficiency, or it may be a sign that a chronic medical condition (e.g., diabetes) is inadequately controlled. Alternately, some children's appetite may be poor as a consequence of their schedule of tube or supplemental feedings. In Hector's case, bottle feedings of a formula have been offered on awakening and then every 3 hours, leaving little time for him to become interested in spoon feedings. In consultation with his nutritionist, the spacing of bottle feedings has been increased to 4-hour intervals, resulting in Hector's having an increased interest in spoon feeding and an increased overall nutritional intake. There are differing opinions about whether day versus night or bolus versus continuous tube feedings are better for promoting appetite. Actually, the important thing is to look at how the child is tolerating the tube feedings. If the child retches, gags, vomits, or needs time to recover after tube feedings, he or she is not tolerating them adequately. Sometimes it takes hours for the child to feel comfortable enough to eat orally again. With this in mind, the best tube-feeding schedule to promote a child's appetite is the one that is tolerated without GI discomfort, even if this involves continuous feedings.

Use Alternative Methods of Feeding

In some cases, oral feeding may not be safe or sufficient to permit adequate nutrition (Inder & Volpe, 1998; Kovar, 1997; Tilton, Miller, & Khoshoo, 1998). For these children, NG tube feedings or the placement of a gastrostomy (G) feeding tube is required (Figure 27.9). A commercially prepared enteral formula (e.g., Nutren Jr., Pediasure) can be used with any of these tubes. Although blenderized feedings can be given through an NG or a G tube, they are not appropriate for a jejunostomy (J) tube because they will obstruct it. With an NG or a G tube, feedings can be given as single large volumes (boluses) of 3–8 ounces every 3–6 hours or as a continuous drip throughout the day or overnight. J tube feedings must be given continuously, not as a bolus. The advantage of large-volume feedings is that they do not interfere with typical daily activities. The feeding itself takes about 30 minutes. As mentioned previously, however, the large volume may be difficult for the child to tolerate and may lead to vomiting or abdominal discomfort (Strauss et al., 1997). If this happens, continuous drip feedings can be instituted. A Kangaroo or similar type of automated pump is then used to deliver the formula at a set rate. Sometimes tube feedings are used to supplement oral feedings. In this case, the tube feedings generally are used at night so that the child remains hungry for oral feedings during the day.

SUMMARY

Feeding a child with a developmental disability often requires a number of creative approaches and the involvement of a variety of health care professionals (Eicher, 2001). When well integrated, these methods not only allow the child to have optimal oral feeding experiences with their positive social and developmental ramifications but also allow him or her to receive the necessary combination of nutrients and fluids needed to grow and remain healthy.

REFERENCES

Albanese, C.L., Towbin, R.B., Ulman, T., et al. (1993). Percutaneous gastrojejunostomy versus Nissen fundoplication for enteral feeding of the neurologically impaired child with gastroesophageal reflux. *Journal of Pediatrics, 123,* 371–375.

American Academy of Pediatrics, Committee on Nutrition. (2000). Hypoallergenic infant formulas. *Pediatrics, 106,* 346–349.

Arvedson, J.C. (1998). Management of pediatric dysphagia. *Otolaryngology Clinics of North America, 3,* 453–476.

Arvedson, J.C., & Lefton-Greif, M.A. (1996). Anatomy, physiology and development of feeding. *Seminars in Speech and Language, 17,* 261–268.

Babbitt, R.L., Hoch, T.A., Coe, D.A., et al. (1994). Behavioral assessment and treatment of pediatric feeding disorders. *Journal of Developmental and Behavioral Pediatrics, 15,* 278–291.

Bagwell, C.E. (1995). Gastroesophageal reflux in children. *Surgery Annual, 27,* 133–163.

Batshaw, M.L. (1991). *Your child has a disability: A complete sourcebook of daily and medical care.* Baltimore: Paul H. Brookes Publishing Co.

Bosma, J.F. (1986). Development of feeding. *Clinical Nutrition, 5,* 210–218.

Brady, M.S., Richard, K.A., Fitzgerald, J.F., et al. (1996). Specialized formulas and feedings for infants with malabsorption or formula intolerance. *Journal of the American Dietetic Association, 86,* 191–200.

Casas, M.J., Kenny, D.J., & McPherson, K.A. (1994). Swallowing/ventilation interactions during oral swallow in normal children and children with cerebral palsy. *Dysphagia, 9,* 40–46.

Chigira, A., Omoto, K., Mukai, Y., et al. (1994). Lip closing pressure in disabled children: A comparison with normal children. *Dysphagia, 9,* 193–198.

Comrie, J.D., & Helm, J.M. (1997). Common feeding problems in the intensive care nursery: Maturation, organization, evaluation, and management strategies. *Seminars in Speech and Language, 18,* 239–260.

Eicher, P.S. (2001). Nutrition and feeding. In M.L. Batshaw

(Ed.), *When your child has a disability: The complete sourcebook of daily and medical care* (Rev. ed., pp. 85–97). Baltimore: Paul H. Brookes Publishing Co.

Eicher, P.S., McDonald-McGinn, D.M., Fox, C.A., et al. (2000). Dysphagia in children with a 22q11.2 deletion: Unusual pattern found on modified barium swallow. *Journal of Pediatrics, 137*, 158–164.

Fonkalsrud, E.W., Ellis, D.G., Shaw, A., et al. (1995). A combined hospital experience with fundoplication and gastric emptying procedure for gastroesophageal reflux in children. *Journal of the American College of Surgeons, 180*, 449–455.

Fried, M.D., Khoshoo, V., Secker, D.J., et al. (1992). Decrease in gastric emptying time and episodes of regurgitation in children with spastic quadriplegia fed a whey-based formula. *Journal of Pediatrics, 120*, 569–572.

Gisel, E.G. (1994). Oral motor skills following sensorimotor intervention in the moderately eating-impaired child with cerebral palsy. *Dysphagia, 9*, 180–192.

Gisel, E.G., & Alphonce, E. (1995). Classification of eating impairments based on eating efficiency in children with cerebral palsy. *Dysphagia, 10*, 268–274.

Heyman, S., Eicher, P.S., & Alavi, A. (1995). Radionuclide studies of the upper gastrointestinal tract in children with feeding disorders. *Journal of Nuclear Medicine, 36*, 351–354.

Hillemeier, C. (1995). An overview of the effects of dietary fiber on gastrointestinal transit. *Pediatrics, 96*, 997–999.

Hu, F.Z., Preston, R.A., Post, J.C., et al. (2000). Mapping of a gene for severe pediatric gastroesophageal reflux to chromosome 13q14. *Journal of the American Medical Association, 284*, 325–334.

Inder, T.E., & Volpe, J.J. (1998). Recovery of congenital isolated pharyngeal dysfunction: Implications for early management. *Pediatric Neurology, 9*, 222–224.

Kedesdy, J.H., & Budd, K.S. (1998). *Childhood feeding disorders: Behavioral assessment and intervention.* Baltimore: Paul H. Brookes Publishing Co.

Kerwin, M.E. (1999). Empirically supported treatments in pediatric psychology: Severe feeding problems. *Journal Pediatric Psychology, 24*, 193–214.

Kerwin, M.E., Ahearn, W.H., Eicher, P.S., et al. (1995). The costs of eating: A behavioral economic analysis of food refusal. *Journal of Applied Behavior Analysis, 28*, 245–260.

Kerwin, M.E., Osborne, M., & Eicher, P.S. (1994). Effect of position and support on oral-motor skills of a child with bronchopulmonary dysplasia. *Clinical Pediatrics, 33*, 8–13.

Kosko, J.R., Moser, J.D., Erhart, N., et al. (1998). Differential diagnosis of dysphagia in children. *Otolaryngology Clinics of North America, 31*, 435–451.

Kovar, A.J. (1997). Nutrition assessment and management in pediatric dysphagia. *Seminars in Speech and Language, 18*, 5–11.

Kramer, S.S., & Eicher, P.M. (1993). The evaluation of pediatric feeding abnormalities. *Dysphagia, 8*, 215–224.

Larnert, G., & Ekberg, O. (1995). Positioning improves the oral and pharyngeal swallowing function in children with cerebral palsy. *Acta Paediatrica, 84*, 689–692.

Leder, S.B. (1998). Serial fiberoptic endoscopic swallowing evaluations in the management of patients with dysphagia. *Archives of Physical Medicine and Rehabilitation, 79*, 1264–1269.

Lefton-Greif, M.A., & Arvedson, J.C. (1997). Pediatric feeding/swallowing teams. *Seminars in Speech and Language, 18*, 5–11.

Lewis, D., Khoshoo, V., Pencharz, P.B., et al. (1994). Impact of nutritional rehabilitation on gastroesophageal reflux in neurologically impaired children. *Journal of Pediatric Surgery, 29*, 167–169.

Logemann, J.A. (1997). Role of the modified barium swallow in management of patients with dysphagia. *Otolaryngology—Head and Neck Surgery, 116*, 335–338.

Loughlin, G.M., & Lefton-Greif, M.A. (1994). Dysfunctional swallowing and respiratory disease in children. *Advances in Pediatrics, 41*, 135–162.

Luiselli, J.K. (1994). Oral feeding treatment of children with chronic food refusal and multiple developmental disabilities. *American Journal of Mental Retardation, 98*, 646–655.

McCallum, R.W. (1990). Gastric emptying in gastroesophageal reflux and the therapeutic role of prokinetic agents. *Gastroenterology Clinics of North America, 19*, 551–564.

Miller, A.J. (1993). The search for the central swallowing pathway: The quest for clarity. *Dysphagia, 8*, 185–194.

Monahan, P., Shapiro, B., & Fox, C. (1988). Effect of tube feeding on oral function. *Developmental Medicine and Child Neurology, 30*, 7.

Rings, E.H., Grand, R.J., & Buller, H.A. (1994). Lactose intolerance and lactase deficiency in children. *Current Opinion in Pediatrics, 6*, 562–567.

Rogers, B., Arvedson, J., Buck, G., et al. (1994). Characteristics of dysphagia in children with cerebral palsy. *Dysphagia, 9*, 69–73.

Schwartz, S.M., Corredor, J., & Fisher-Medina, J. (2001). Diagnosis and treatment of feeding disorders in children with developmental disabilities. *Pediatrics, 108*, 671–676.

Stallings, V.A., Zemel, B.S., & Davies, J.C. (1996). Energy expenditure of children and adolescents with severe disabilities: A cerebral palsy model. *American Journal of Clinical Nutrition, 64*, 627–634.

Stark, L.J. (1999). Commentary: Beyond feeding problems. The challenge of meeting dietary recommendations in the treatment of chronic diseases in pediatrics. *Journal of Pediatric Psychology, 24*, 221–222.

Stevenson, R.D. (1995). Feeding and nutrition in children with developmental disabilities. *Pediatric Annals, 24*, 255–260.

Strauss, D., Kastner, T., Ashwal, S., et al. (1997). Tubefeeding and mortality in children with severe disabilities and mental retardation. *Pediatrics, 99*, 358–362.

Sullivan, P.B., & Rosenbloom, L. (Eds.). (1996). *Clinics in Developmental Medicine: No. 140. Feeding the disabled child.* Cambridge, England: Cambridge University Press.

Takada, N., Miyawaki, S., & Tatsuta, M. (1994). The effects of food consistency on jaw movement and posterior temporalis and inferior orbicularis oris muscle activities during chewing in children. *Archives of Oral Biology, 39*, 793–805.

Tilton, A.H., Miller, M.D., & Khoshoo, V. (1998). Nutrition and swallowing in pediatric neuromuscular patients. *Seminars in Pediatric Neurology, 5*, 106–115.

Timms, B.J.M., Defiore, J.M., Martin, R.J., et al. (1993). Increased respiratory drive as an inhibitor of oral feeding of preterm infants. *Journal of Pediatrics, 123*, 127–131.

Waterman, E.T., Koltai, P.J., Downey, J.C., et al. (1992). Swallowing disorders in a population of children with cerebral palsy. *International Journal of Pediatric Otorhinolaryngology, 24*, 63–71.

Williams, C.L., Bollella, M., & Wynder, E.L. (1995). A new recommendation for dietary fiber in childhood. *Pediatrics, 96*, 985–988.

Willging, J.P. (1995). Endoscopic evaluation of swallowing in children. *International Journal of Pediatric Otorhinolaryngology, 32*(Suppl.), S107–S108.

28 Dental Care

Promoting Health and Preventing Disease

George Acs, Man Wai Ng,
Mark L. Helpin, and Howard M. Rosenberg

Upon completion of this chapter, the reader will:

- be familiar with the patterns of dental development and tooth emergence, as well as potential factors affecting them

- understand the causes of dental decay and periodontal disease and be familiar with preventive strategies and treatment

- be aware of the special oral considerations for children with disabilities

Increasingly, the important association between dental disease and nutrition, growth, and development has been recognized (Acs et al., 1992; Acs et al., 1999; Beck et al., 1996; Offenbacher et al., 1996). Children with developmental disabilities are at a particularly high risk for dental disease that may affect their overall health and development. Yet, for many of these children, oral health is given a low priority in the presence of other major health concerns. Many families of children with disabilities also face barriers to receiving adequate dental care, including transportation difficulties, architectural and physical barriers, unwilling or unprepared dental providers, lack of awareness of available services, and inadequate financing of dental care (Mouradian, Wehr, & Crall, 2000; Newacheck et al., 2000; Schultz, Shenkin, & Horowitz, 2001). This chapter introduces basic concepts of dentistry for children, with a focus on children with special needs. It describes the causes, prevention, and treatment of common dental diseases and the relationship between developmental disabilities and dental problems.

CRYSTAL, ALAN, AND DOMINIQUE

Crystal is a 10-year-old with cerebral palsy. Because of feeding difficulties, all of her food must be pureed. Feeding times are prolonged because she uses her tongue to first push food against her teeth and then propel it backward for swallowing. Although Crystal has had dental checkups, it is difficult for both her parents and the dental hygienist to visualize or brush her front teeth due to her tongue thrusting. Crystal's caregivers will need to devote considerable attention to maintaining her oral hygiene in order to prevent dental decay and periodontal disease. They may require special appliances, such as a nonlatex mouth prop, to help keep Crystal's mouth open during toothbrushing.

Alan is an 8-year-old with Down syndrome. The first of his permanent teeth is only now erupting, even though his younger brother had his first permanent teeth at age 5 years. Alan's baby teeth are very crowded. His first permanent tooth, in the lower jaw, is erupting behind the baby teeth. As Alan gets older, he may require extraction of a number of **primary**

(baby) teeth because they may not fall out as the permanent teeth erupt. Interestingly, even though Alan loves to eat sweets, he has never had a cavity. He does, however, accumulate significant amounts of plaque on his crowded teeth. He will require frequent dental cleanings to prevent gingival inflammation that may contribute to periodontal disease as he gets older.

Dominique is an 8-year-old who has a seizure disorder. Phenytoin (Dilantin) was prescribed to control her seizures, following unsuccessful attempts with a number of other antiepileptic drugs. Although Dominique's parents attempted toothbrushing, her clenching, tight lip musculature, and head movements made it very difficult. Because of poor oral hygiene and phenytoin therapy, Dominique's gums have overgrown most of her teeth. Despite previous surgery to remove the gingival overgrowth, it has recurred.

FORMATION AND EMERGENCE OF TEETH

Human tooth formation begins when the embryo is only 4–6 weeks old. The oral ectodermal (outer) layer of tissue forms the **dental lamina,** a thickened band of cells along the future dental arches. At specific points along the dental lamina, rapid growth of cells occurs. This forms small knobs that press downward into the underlying mesodermal (middle) layer of tissue (Fig-

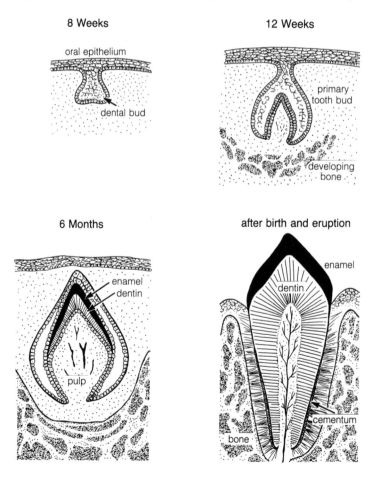

Figure 28.1. Development of teeth. By the time the fetus is 8 weeks old, the dental bud has formed, and by 12 weeks it begins to assume a tooth-like shape. At 6 months' gestation, the layers of the tooth (enamel, dentin, and pulp) are evident. About 16 months after birth, the primary cuspid, completely formed, erupts.

ure 28.1). There is one such knob (**dental organ, or tooth bud**) for each of the 20 primary teeth, 10 in the **maxilla** (upper jaw) and 10 in the **mandible** (lower jaw; Sicher, 1991) as shown in Figure 28.2. With time, permanent incisors, canines, and premolars develop from the corresponding primary tooth bud predecessors. In contrast, permanent molars develop from the dental lamina itself. Calcification of primary teeth begins at approximately 14 weeks in utero; permanent teeth begin to develop around the time of birth, and the vast majority of calcification occurs during early childhood (McDonald & Avery, 1994).

The calcified layer of the tooth is made up of **enamel,** which arises from the ectoderm (Figure 28.1). The layer under the enamel, called **dentin,** arises from the mesodermal cells. The soft tissue under the dentin, called the **pulp,** also arises from the mesoderm. The pulp contains the vital parts of the tooth: its blood vessels, lymph vessels, connective tissue, and nerve fibers (Sicher, 1991).

Although it is commonly said that the first baby tooth should erupt by 6 months of age, there is actually a wide variation in the age of eruption; the first baby teeth can erupt anywhere between 4 and 17 months of age. The full complement of primary teeth takes 2–3 years to appear. The first permanent tooth typically emerges around 6 years of age, and most permanent teeth have erupted by 12–13 years of age. Although frequently congenitally absent, the third molars ("wisdom teeth") may erupt between 17 and 21 years of age, making a total of 32 permanent teeth.

When a permanent tooth emerges, a primary tooth is shed, except in the case of the first, second, and third molars, which do not have primary teeth counterparts (McDonald & Avery, 1994). As noted previously, caution should be taken when evaluating tooth eruption in relation to tables and time schedules, especially in children with developmental disabilities, as each

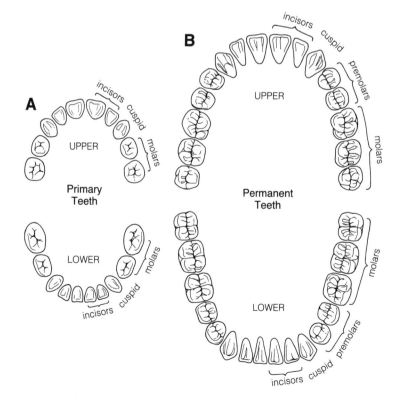

Figure 28.2. Primary and permanent teeth. A) There are 20 primary teeth: 4 incisors, 2 cuspids, and 4 molars on the top and on the bottom of the mouth. B) There are 32 permanent teeth: 4 incisors, 2 cuspids, 4 premolars, and 6 molars on the top and bottom.

child has his or her own timetable. Symmetry in eruption is more important than adherence to a strict time schedule. What occurs on the right side should occur, within a few months, on the left; and what occurs in the mandible should occur in the maxilla, again within a few months.

PROBLEMS AFFECTING THE DEVELOPMENT OF TEETH

Many genetic syndromes associated with developmental disabilities have characteristic developmental dental alterations. These include the presence of extra teeth, congenital absence of multiple teeth, unusually shaped teeth, and abnormalities in their mineralization. These abnormalities may contribute to orthodontic **malocclusion** (e.g., an overbite) and/or to an increased risk for dental caries (decay; Poole & Redford-Badwal, 1991). Anodontia (the absence of all teeth) is rare, but oligodontia (the absence of one or several teeth) can be seen in children with a number of genetic syndromes (see Appendix B), including Hallermann-Streiff syndrome, chondroectodermal dysplasia, Williams syndrome, Crouzon syndrome, achondroplasia, incontinentia pigmenti, ectodermal dysplasia, and cleft lip and palate (see Chapter 14 and Appendix B). Disorders affecting development of teeth may also lead to thinly enameled and abnormally shaped teeth. This can be seen in children with chromosomal disorders such as Down syndrome, inborn errors of metabolism such as mucopolysaccharidoses and Lesch-Nyhan syndrome, and inherited disorders of bone formation such as osteogenesis imperfecta. Environmental influences can also affect intrauterine tooth development. For example, nutritional deficiencies, especially of calcium; phosphorus; and vitamins A, C, and D, may result in generalized enamel hypoplasia (underdevelopment), reflecting a disruption in the mineralization of the teeth during their development. Although many syndromes are characterized by specific dental alterations, each child must be individually assessed to determine the treatment that is most appropriate. Malocclusions may be treated with a range of orthodontic approaches, whereas missing, hypoplastic, and abnormally shaped teeth may be treated with cosmetic bonding procedures. As with many elective procedures, however, the individual desires and abilities of the patient and primary caregivers to participate in treatment and to maintain treatment outcomes must be considered.

Because **secondary** (permanent) teeth are formed after birth, malformations of these teeth may occur as a result of childhood illness or its treatment. For example, if a child takes the antibiotic tetracycline between 4 months and 8 years of age, the permanent teeth may be discolored yellow, brown, or gray when they erupt. Traumatic injury to a tooth can cause a small white or brown spot on a single tooth, whereas infectious diseases (e.g., measles, chickenpox) and chronic diseases (e.g., liver failure, congenital heart disease) can cause hypoplasia of multiple teeth (Pinkham, 1994).

ORAL DISEASES

There are two basic types of oral diseases: dental caries and periodontal diseases. Both are usually initiated by specific bacteria and, therefore, can be considered infectious in nature.

Dental Caries

Dental caries, commonly called *dental decay* or *cavities*, occurs mainly in children and adolescents and is related to the presence of the bacteria *Streptococcus mutans* and *Lactobacillus acidophilus*. Decay is a multifactorial process that involves the teeth themselves, bacteria, diet, saliva, the immune system, biochemistry, and physiology. The "chain of decay" is as follows (Figure 28.3): Bacteria adhering to the teeth break down food, creating acid as a by-product. The acid damages the integrity of the enamel, and cavity formation begins. Tooth breakdown and ultimately abscess formation can occur when caries is left untreated.

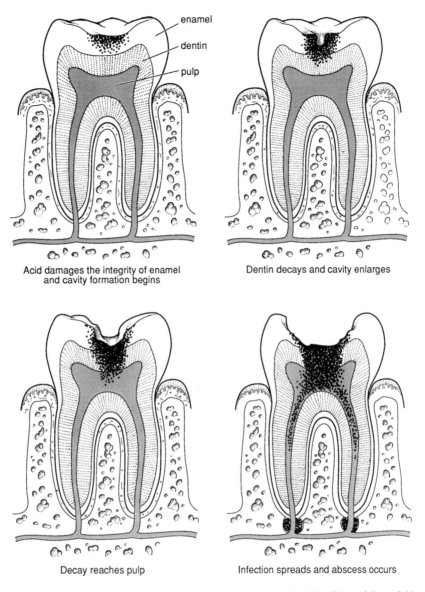

Acid damages the integrity of enamel
and cavity formation begins

Dentin decays and cavity enlarges

Decay reaches pulp

Infection spreads and abscess occurs

Figure 28.3. The chain of decay. In the presence of adverse factors, the chain of decay follows: Acid formed from the action of bacteria on carbohydrates damage the enamel, leading to cavity formation. If untreated, the decay eventually affects the dentin and pulp layer of the tooth and may lead to abscess formation.

Bacteria adhere to the teeth in an organized mass called **dental plaque.** Plaque consists of bacteria, bacterial by-products, **epithelial** cells (from the linings of the lips and mouth), and food particles (Pinkham, 1994). When plaque becomes calcified, it is called **calculus,** or *tartar.* Plaque as well as unremoved tartar can cause inflammation, tenderness, and swelling of the gums. This is an early phase of periodontal, or gum, disease and can lead to loss of stability of the teeth. The process of decay is one of demineralization of enamel and dentin. The prevalence of dental caries has been cited as more than 40% in 5-year-olds and 85% in 17-year-olds (Edelstein & Douglas, 1995).

One form of caries that merits special attention is nursing or early childhood caries, caused by falling asleep while sucking on a juice-filled bottle. The causative factor is prolonged contact of the juice's acids and acid breakdown products with the tooth surface, leading to demineralization. Because this starts on the tongue side of the top teeth, it is often detected late; by this time the same process may have begun on the upper and lower back teeth. In patients with developmental abnormalities of the teeth, particularly those affecting mineralization, the ravages of nursing caries may be even more pronounced.

For young children who are receiving carbohydrate-enriched diets to treat growth failure or who require chronic liquid medications that contain sugar, rampant cavities may also occur, even in the absence of a juice-filled nighttime bottle. Evidence suggests that the impact of infant formula on the development of early childhood caries depends on the specific properties of the formula. Until more definitive information is available, children should not be allowed to fall asleep with a nursing bottle containing any liquid other than water. The same principle applies to children who are breast-fed. Prolonged breast feeding and falling asleep with the nipple in the mouth can also promote decay by acid demineralization. In addition, dipping pacifiers in sweetened solutions increases the risk of cavities.

In considering the role of bacteria in the cycle of tooth decay, it is important to note that children acquire cavity-causing bacteria during the early phases of eruption of their first few teeth. They usually contract the bacteria from their primary caregiver. If that person has a high bacterial count or possesses bacteria that are more efficient in causing cavities, the child is at increased risk for future cavities. Parents can help reduce the risk of bacterial spread by undergoing frequent dental cleanings and repairing all of their own cavities.

Periodontal Diseases

Periodontal diseases involve the gingiva (gums) and bony sockets of the teeth. Like caries, gingivitis (the most common form of periodontal disease) is associated with plaque and specific bacterial organisms (Matthewson & Primosch, 1995). The early signs of periodontal disease involve swelling and bleeding of the gums. It is often an insidious process that can go unrecognized for years. Later phases lead to loss of the alveolar bone that supports the tooth. Periodontal disease involves both local and systemic factors. Local factors include dental crowding, poor oral hygiene, overly aggressive oral hygiene, and destructive dental habits. Systemic factors include certain chronic medications, hormonal alterations, and immune deficiency states. For example, patients requiring long-term use of the drugs phenytoin (an antiepileptic), cyclosporine (Sandimmune; an immune suppressant agent), and nifedipine (Procardia; a blood pressure medication) are at particular risk for overgrowth of the gums. Although the exact cause of this condition is unknown, the overgrowth is generally regarded as an exaggerated response to a local irritant. Overall, gingivitis can be found in up to half of children 6–12 years of age (Pinkham, 1994).

MALOCCLUSION

Malocclusion is the improper interdigitation or relationship of the teeth or jaws. It can interfere with oral functions such as speech and chewing and increase the risk of dental caries and periodontal diseases. In addition, it can create problems with facial appearance and self-image. Although many malocclusions are minor and require attention only for cosmetic reasons, others are more severe and debilitating. The prevalence of severe malocclusion has been reported to be as high as 14%; children with certain developmental disabilities, such as cerebral palsy, have an even higher prevalence (McDonald & Avery, 1994). In these children, the correction of this improper alignment of the teeth by orthodontic treatment to position the teeth properly also decreases the risk of dental disease by making routine oral hygiene easier.

Certain habits, including tooth grinding (**bruxism**) and pacifier/thumb sucking, may predispose to malocclusion. Bruxism is often an adaptive mechanism that allows the child to develop a comfortable occlusion or bite, but typically, the tooth grinding stops by school age when the permanent teeth erupt. In some children, however, especially those with mental retardation, cerebral palsy, and autism, bruxism becomes abnormal in intensity and persistence. Both behavior management techniques and dental appliances have been used to arrest the habit before it causes permanent dental changes. These techniques, however, only work when the child is motivated to stop the habit and is compliant in using the device.

DENTAL TRAUMA

It is estimated that half of all children experience traumatic injury to the primary or permanent teeth prior to graduation from high school. Injuries to the primary teeth are more frequent than injuries to permanent teeth. Although the incidence of primary tooth injury is approximately equal in boys and girls, males have twice as many injuries to permanent teeth (Andreasen & Andreasen, 1994). The risk of dental trauma in children with cerebral palsy and seizure disorders is increased because of their more frequent falls. The maxillary incisors, both primary and permanent, are the teeth most frequently traumatized. The presence of prominent maxillary anterior "buck" teeth, a consequence of malocclusion, is an important predisposing factor to injury of the teeth. Trauma to primary teeth generally causes tooth displacement. This is a result of the softer, spongier quality of the young bone that supports the teeth. Trauma to permanent teeth most often results in fracture of tooth structure (chipped teeth; Andreasen & Andreasen, 1994).

The management of trauma to the primary dentition is relatively straightforward. Either no treatment is necessary, or the damaged tooth requires extraction. Treatment considerations of traumatized permanent teeth, however, are more complex and merit dental evaluation the same day. Although primary teeth are not reimplanted, a permanent tooth that has been knocked out should be replaced into the tooth socket by a caregiver as soon as possible after the accident. Reimplantation within 30 minutes maximizes the likelihood of successful tooth retention. If immediate reimplantation is not possible, the tooth should be kept in cold milk or in the child's saliva, as this appears to extend the time a tooth may be out of the mouth before successful reimplantation.

Because many dental injuries can be avoided, prevention is extremely important. Athletic mouth guards, when they can be tolerated, significantly decrease the risk of dental injuries in children participating in contact sports and in children with developmental disabilities, who are at high risk for falls or self-injury (Andreasen & Andreasen, 1994).

PREVENTION OF DENTAL CARIES AND PERIODONTAL DISEASE

The three most important factors in protecting the teeth from dental decay are maintaining good oral hygiene, limiting ingestion of carbohydrates, and eliminating or reducing cavity-causing bacteria. Tools for preventive dentistry include brushing, flossing, and the use of fluoride and **dental sealants.**

Brushing

Children younger than 6 years generally have not developed the manual dexterity to effectively remove plaque from teeth. They should be encouraged to participate in their own oral hygiene; however, adults must take an active role and be responsible for adequately cleaning the teeth and gum regions. A soft, nylon bristle brush with polished, rounded ends works best. A scrubbing motion of the brush is a quick and easy method with which to begin. An electric toothbrush can be helpful and may be advantageous for gingival health (Barnes, Weatherford, & Menaker, 1993). When brushing, a small, pea-sized amount of toothpaste with fluoride may be used. If bubbles and foam from the paste cause a problem for the child, however, use water alone. Positioning the child in a supine (reclining) position facilitates good vision, access, and head control and will be helpful for the adult doing the brushing (McDonald & Avery, 1994; Pinkham, 1994).

Flossing

Adults should floss for a child until he or she has demonstrated facility with this procedure. Improper flossing can harm gingival tissues. Flossing should be performed wherever teeth are in contact with each other and the toothbrush cannot clean between the teeth. Unwaxed floss is preferred; however, any floss may be used. Floss-holding devices are available and can be employed by parents and/or caregivers when dexterity is a problem or when the child closes or bites (McDonald & Avery, 1994).

Fluorides

Whether present in the municipal water supply, taken as a daily supplement found in toothpaste, contained in a mouth rinse, or professionally applied, fluoride treatment has been shown to significantly reduce the incidence of dental decay and is an integral part of a preventive program. Studies have demonstrated that fluoride in water can decrease the prevalence of tooth decay by up to 60% (Pinkham, 1994). Fluoride makes enamel more resistant to decay and remineralizes new carious lesions, making them hard again. Fluoride supplementation should be considered if fluoride is not available in the community drinking water or in the water where child care is provided. Although reverse osmosis home filtration does remove fluoride from water, other systems do not. Bottled water must disclose its fluoride content if fluoride has been added but not if it is naturally occurring. On the basis of the child's needs and abilities, specific fluoride supplements may be recommended. It should be noted that excessive systemic fluoride, however, can cause fluorosis, a condition in which permanent teeth are discolored or malformed.

Many different fluoride formulations are available, each with specifically indicated uses. For children who are capable of rinsing, low potency over-the-counter fluoride rinses may be helpful in preventing cavities. In addition, there may be indications for the use of prescribed fluoride rinses or gels that contain higher concentrations of fluoride. Very often, these higher concentrations are provided to attempt reversal of the early stages of cavity formation. For some patients at high risk for developing cavities, and for those for whom it may be difficult to apply daily fluoride supplements, professionally applied fluoride varnishes may be of benefit. These varnish applications may provide benefits for up to 3 months.

Dental Sealants

Sealants consist of a plastic coating that is bonded to the chewing surface of molars to prevent decay. Most children have deep grooves on their permanent molars that are difficult to keep clean, but the molars can be protected by the application of sealants. Sealants are most indicated within the first 3–4 years of eruption of the permanent molars (commonly around 6–10 years of age). Studies have shown that in the absence of sealants, two thirds of children will have a cavity on at least one of their first permanent molars (Pinkham, 1994).

For sealants to be successfully applied, the tooth must be kept dry and free of moisture or salivary contamination for at least 1 minute. Otherwise, the sealant will fail or may place the child at increased risk for developing a cavity underneath the faulty sealant. If the only mechanism for ensuring a dry environment is sedation or general anesthesia, the benefit gained from applying the sealant may be outweighed by the risk of anesthesia. Thus, children with cerebral palsy may not be good candidates, and children with Down syndrome (who have few grooves) may not need it.

Diet

Frequent feedings or snacking, as needs to occur in children with failure to thrive, increase the total amount of time that teeth are exposed to foods or liquids that facilitate the development of dental caries. For prevention of caries, these children require more frequent and intensive oral hygiene measures. Similarly, children with neuromuscular disorders that result in decreased oral-motor abilities need an extended period of time to clear food from their mouths. The increased contact time between food, especially pureed carbohydrates, and teeth places these children at greater risk for cavity development. Children with food "squirreling/pocketing" habits are also more likely to develop caries. In addition, children with gastroesophageal reflux (see Chapter 27) are at increased risk because of the contact of stomach acid with the enamel of teeth. Even for typically developing children, the consistency, frequency, and timing of snacks contribute to their potential for decay. Snacks that are sticky (not just caramels but also foods such as sweet rolls, pretzels, and potato chips), eaten frequently, and eaten between meals have a high potential for causing dental decay. (See Table 28.1 for a list of snacks that do not compromise dental health.)

PROVIDING DENTAL AND ORTHODONTIC TREATMENT

The American Academy of Pediatric Dentistry recommends that all children have their first dental visit by 12 months of age. At this time, parents or primary caregivers are educated about likely events during development that affect the teeth and are taught strategies to effectively prevent dental disease. Greatest benefit is derived when a combination of preventive dentistry techniques is used. Usually, very little if any treatment is necessary at this time (American Academy of Pediatric Dentistry, 2000–2001; Edelstein, 1994; Griffen & Goepferd, 1991; Newbrun, 1992).

This first visit should be followed by checkups at regular intervals, depending on the child's risk for oral disease. During these checkups, cleaning and topical fluoride application will be performed to help minimize the risk of caries and periodontal disease. If, despite all preventive efforts, caries do appear, the dentist will treat this by removing the decay and placing a filling material or a crown. The newest dental materials offer the advantages of good strength, aesthetics, and anticaries activity.

Table 28.1. Foods that are good to use as snacks to maintain dental health

Raw vegetables

Carrot sticks	Green pepper rings
Celery sticks	Lettuce wedges
Cauliflower bits	Radishes
Cucumber sticks	Tomatoes

Drinks

Milk	Unsweetened vegetable juices
Sugar-free carbonated beverages	

Other snacks

Nuts	Unsweetened peanut butter
Popcorn	Cheese
Unsweetened plain yogurt	Sugarless gum or candy

Source: American Dental Association, 1983.

To minimize anxiety and help the child cope with the stress of treatment, the dentist may employ behavior management techniques or use sedation agents (e.g., nitrous oxide [laughing gas], sedative medications). Behavior management techniques focus on increasing the occurrence of desired behaviors and decreasing inappropriate behaviors (see Chapter 31). These approaches may be very effective in both improving compliance with dental health at home and in the dentist's office. For children requiring dental procedures, nitrous oxide and oxygen inhalation sedation may be used. Onset of sedation is fast; the depth of the sedation can be controlled; and recovery is rapid and complete. Nitrous oxide sedation may also be very effective in delivering dental treatment to young children and to those with attention-deficit/hyperactivity disorder (see Chapter 21) or with cognitive impairments that limit attention and cooperation. Inhalation sedation, however, requires a patient to voluntarily breathe the agent. If the child is combative, the use of medical sedation or general anesthesia may be considered. Here, the risks and benefits must be weighed to determine if the dental needs warrant this approach. There is usually consultation with the child's primary care provider or other specialists, such as neurologist or cardiologist, to review any unique considerations or precautions required in using sedation (Pinkham, 1994).

In terms of orthodontic care, the objectives are to move the teeth into new positions using retainers and other techniques. Although malocclusion is the most common reason to recommend orthodontic care, there may be other esthetic, functional, or periodontal considerations. Orthodontic care may be particularly helpful in certain genetic syndromes associated with developmental dental abnormalities. For patients with Down syndrome, cleft palate, or ectodermal dysplasia, for example, orthodontic therapy may be used to create more room for teeth, to create a more appropriate shape for the dental arches, or to align teeth to fabricate a well-fitting and functional partial denture, bridge, or implant. In patients with poor oral hygiene or who have a history of high caries activity, however, orthodontic braces should be deferred until there is an improved level of oral hygiene. This is necessary to protect against the development of new cavities or periodontal disease, both of which are more likely to occur if braces are worn for extended periods.

DENTAL CARE FOR CHILDREN WITH DEVELOPMENTAL DISABILITIES

The basic principles of pediatric dental care and oral health apply to all children. There are, however, specific issues related to several common developmental disabilities, including Down syndrome, cerebral palsy, meningomyelocele, and seizure disorders, that deserve further discussion.

Down Syndrome

In addition to having mental retardation, children with Down syndrome have congenital anomalies and crowded dentition that place them at increased risk for oral disease. Their midface hypoplasia and extra, missing, or small teeth contribute to the development of malocclusion and periodontal disease by adolescence (Cooley & Sanders, 1991). Their open-mouth posture with mouth breathing can lead to dry gum tissue that bleeds easily. Excellent oral hygiene methods may delay the onset, but tight musculature and oral hypersensitivity may lead to brushing difficulties and inadequate plaque removal. An additional consideration is congenital heart disease, which places these children at increased risk for bacterial **endocarditis** (a severe infection of the inner lining of the heart chambers) and may require antibiotic prophylaxis prior to dental procedures. Interestingly, children with Down syndrome seem to be at less risk than usual for dental caries, because their biting surfaces are smooth rather than having the typical grooving that shelters plaque formation.

Cerebral Palsy

Poor motor control and altered muscle tone may interfere with routine dental care in children with cerebral palsy (see Chapter 23). Although no specific oral problems are unique to children with cerebral palsy, several findings are more common or more severe in this population. Malocclusion is more likely to occur as a consequence of the uncoordinated movements of the muscles of the jaws, lips, and tongue. Persistent tongue thrusting or a forward positioned tongue is a particular concern. As the tongue is a powerful muscle, it can reposition the teeth, leading to an open bite and flared, widely spaced teeth.

The predilection for falling and the frequent prominence of the maxillary incisors also place these children at increased risk for dental trauma. In addition, mouth breathing and bruxism are often present (Cooley & Sanders, 1991; McDonald & Avery, 1994; Nowak, 1976). Furthermore, the incidence of caries and periodontal disease is higher because of problems in the oral clearing of food; difficulty in brushing and flossing; and the soft, sticky, high-carbohydrate diet that may be needed to maintain adequate nutrition. Despite receiving limited or no nutrition by mouth, children with cerebral palsy who are fed through gastrostomy tubes (see Chapter 27) are still susceptible to reflux of stomach acid as well as plaque and calculus buildup, placing them at increased risk for dental caries.

A number of treatment approaches can help. Providing dental care in the child's wheelchair or using positioning supports such as pillows in the dental chair adds to the comfort of the child. If toothbrushing after eating is not possible, wiping soft food debris from the mouth using a moistened face cloth or gauze pad is of benefit. In older children, an adapted toothbrush with handle modifications, an electric toothbrush, and floss holders can be of assistance in maintaining good oral hygiene.

Meningomyelocele

Individuals with meningomyelocele have a caries rate similar to that found in the general population. As a result of compromised oral hygiene, however, they have a high level of periodontal disease. Because of the spinal curvatures so often seen in these individuals and considering that many of these individuals ambulate using a wheelchair, positioning and comfort are important in dental care. The presence of hydrocephalus with a shunt may also have a bearing on the child's dental treatment; individuals with ventricular shunts may require antibiotic prophylaxis prior to dental procedures. Also, individuals with meningomyelocele have an increased risk of developing an allergic reaction to latex (Engibous, Kittle, & Jones, 1993); thus, latex gloves and other latex products should not be used.

Seizure Disorders

In children with seizure disorders, the major issues are side effects from certain antiepileptic drugs (see Chapter 25), as discussed previously, and from dental trauma. Approximately half of the children receiving the antiepileptic drug phenytoin (Dilantin), and occasionally those receiving phenobarbital (Luminal), develop overgrowth of the gingiva. Stopping the medication may begin to reverse the condition, but often the child will require surgical removal of the overgrown tissue. In children with poorly controlled generalized tonic-clonic seizures, the use of a helmet throughout the day to reduce risk of dental trauma from falls may be appropriate until seizure control is gained (Cooley & Sanders, 1991; McDonald & Avery, 1994; Nowak, 1976).

Other Conditions

The range of special dental considerations in patients with chronic medical illnesses or developmental disabilities is very large. For example, although patients with sickle cell disease tend to have a very low decay rate, they may experience jaw pain that is a sign of an infarction, or sickle crisis. Children with cystic fibrosis also tend to have a low decay rate, but when dental care is needed, nitrous oxide should not be used because of its potential for adversely affecting respiration. Due to the large number of conditions that have special and ongoing dental considerations, parents should seek consultation with the pediatric dentist and create a "dental home" for their child that will attend to near- and long-term oral health needs and coordinate care among the child's medical specialists.

SUMMARY

Oral health is an important component of overall health (U.S. Department of Health and Human Services, National Institutes of Health, National Institute of Dental and Craniofacial Research, 2000). It contributes to wellness of the child, eliminates pain and discomfort, and enhances quality of life. Furthermore, good oral health maximizes the chances for adequate nutrition, speech, and appearance. The emphasis in oral care for the child with a developmental disability should be the same as it is for a typically developing child: prevention through home dental care and regular office checkups.

REFERENCES

Acs, G., Lodolini, G., Kaminsky, S., et al. (1992). Effect of nursing caries on body weight in a pediatric population. *Pediatric Dentistry, 14,* 302–305.

Acs, G., Shulman, R., Ng, M.W., et al. (1999). The effect of dental rehabilitation on the body weight of children with early childhood caries. *Pediatric Dentistry, 21,* 109–113.

American Academy of Pediatric Dentistry. (2000–2001). American Academy of Pediatric Dentistry reference manual. *Pediatric Dentistry, 22,* 43–116.

American Dental Association. (1983). *Diet and dental health.* Chicago: American Dental Association, Bureau of Health Education and Audiovisual Services.

Andreasen, J.O., & Andreasen, F.M. (1994). *Textbook and color atlas of traumatic injuries to the teeth* (3rd ed.). St. Louis: Mosby.

Barnes, C.M., Weatherford, T.W., & Menaker, L. (1993). A comparison of the Braun Oral-B plaque remover electric and a manual toothbrush in affecting gingivitis. *Journal of Dentistry for Children, 4,* 48–51.

Beck, J., Garcia, R., Heiss, G., et al. (1996). Periodontal disease and cardiovascular disease. *Journal of Periodontology, 67*(10, Suppl,), 1123–1137.

Cooley, R.O., & Sanders, V.J. (1991). The pediatrician's involvement in prevention and treatment of oral disease in medically compromised children. *Pediatric Clinics of North America, 38,* 1265–1288.

Edelstein, B.L. (1994). Medical management of dental caries. *The Journal of the American Dental Association, 125*(Suppl.), 31S–39S.

Edelstein, B.L., & Douglas, C.W. (1995). Dispelling the myth that 50% of U.S. school children have never had a cavity. *Public Health Report, 110,* 6–13.

Engibous, P.J., Kittle, P.E., & Jones, H.L. (1993). Latex allergy in patients with spina bifida. *Pediatric Dentistry, 15,* 364–366.

Griffen, A.L., & Goepferd, S.J. (1991). Preventive oral health for the infant, child, and adolescent. *Pediatric Clinics of North America, 38,* 1209–1226.

Matthewson, R.J., & Primosch, R.E. (1995). *Fundamentals of pediatric dentistry* (3rd ed.). Chicago: Quintessence Publishing.

McDonald, R.E., & Avery, D.R. (1994). *Dentistry for the child and the adolescent* (6th ed.). St. Louis: Mosby.

Mouradian, W.E., Wehr, E., & Crall, J.J. (2000). Disparities in children's oral health and access to dental care. *Journal of the American Medical Association, 284,* 2625–2631.

Newacheck, P.W., McManus, M., Fox, H.B., et al. (2000). Access to health care for children with special health care needs. *Pediatrics, 105,* 760–766.

Newbrun, E. (1992). Preventing dental caries: Current and prospective strategies. *The Journal of the American Dental Association, 123,* 68–73.

Nowak, A.J. (1976). *Dentistry for the handicapped patient.* St. Louis: Mosby.

Offenbacher, S., Katz, V., Fertik, G., et al. (1996). Periodontal infection as a possible risk factor for preterm low birth weight. *Journal of Periodontology, 67*(10, Suppl.), 1103–1113.

Pinkham, J.R. (1994). *Pediatric dentistry: Infancy through adolescence* (2nd ed.). Philadelphia: W.B. Saunders.

Poole, A.E., & Redford-Badwal, D.A. (1991). Structural abnormalities of the craniofacial complex and congenital malformations. *Pediatric Clinics of North America, 38,* 1089–1125.

Schultz, S.T., Shenkin, J.D., & Horowitz, A.M. (2001). Parental perceptions of unmet dental need and cost barriers to care for developmentally disabled children. *Pediatric Dentistry, 20,* 321–325.

Sicher, H. (1991). *Orban's histology and embryology* (11th ed.). St. Louis: Mosby.

U.S. Department of Health and Human Services, National Institutes of Health, National Institute of Dental and Craniofacial Research. (2000). *Oral health in America: A report of the Surgeon General.* Rockville, MD: U.S. Department of Health and Human Services.

29

Early Intervention

Charles J. Conlon

Upon completion of this chapter, the reader will:

- know the definition of the term *early intervention services*
- understand the history of the development of early intervention
- recognize issues of referral and assessment
- be aware of the services provided
- understand the results of outcome studies

Early childhood is both the most critical and the most vulnerable period in a child's development. Research has confirmed that during the first few years of life, neurons form most of the connections that will be maintained throughout a child's lifetime (Diamond & Hopson, 1999; see Chapter 13). The neurons sprout dendrites, form synapses, and modify the strength of some connections while eliminating others (Schrader & Friedlander, 1999). During this period there is a degree of developmental plasticity that allows neurons to adapt in very specific ways to changing demands and for experiences to help shape the connections (Hohnke & Sur, 1999). As a result, each child's unique biology can be sculpted by the nurturing, support, and stimulation provided by his or her environment (e.g., family, community; Shonkoff & Phillips, 2000).

If a child presents with a delay in a developmental domain, a disability, or a condition that places him or her at high risk for a delay or disability, then early identification and intervention can be crucial in fostering this nature–nurture duet that will determine the developmental outcome of the child. In the context of federal mandates, the term *early intervention* (EI) refers to services and supports provided to children younger than 3 years of age and their families. These services and supports include a wide range of developmental, educational, and therapeutic activities that enhance a child's development and his or her relationships with family members. To be effective, EI services must take into account cultural diversity and family strengths, challenges, and priorities. Because of the multidisciplinary nature of EI, the EI professional must also take into account the boundaries between disciplines, the potential for conflict, and the need for new service delivery models. This chapter provides an overview of these EI services for children with disabilities.

CARL

Carl is a 6-month-old who was born at a gestational age of 26 weeks. After a difficult 4-month hospitalization in the neonatal intensive care unit, he was discharged home. Neurodevelopmental assessment just prior to discharge showed that he had cognitive function at a newborn level and markedly increased tone in his legs. Carl was considered to have significant developmental delays and was referred to the local EI program. After a comprehensive, multidisciplinary assessment, he was found to be eligible for services, and a treatment plan (individualized family service plan, or IFSP) was developed. Because both of Carl's parents worked outside the home, a physical therapist and early childhood educator came to Carl's child care center once a week to provide EI services. Carl's parents arranged their work schedules so that at least one of them could meet with the EI professional every other week at the child care center. Together, Carl's parents, educators, and child care workers have come up with creative activities that encourage Carl to develop his motor skills. As a result of these interactions, both parents are feeling increasingly comfortable in caring for Carl and in playing with him at home.

LEGISLATION AND PHILOSOPHY OF EARLY INTERVENTION

The first EI (previously referred to as *infant stimulation*) programs focused on improving the function of children with mental retardation, cerebral palsy, and genetic conditions/syndromes such as Down syndrome (Denhoff, 1981; Skeels & Dye, 1939). Subsequently, these programs have evolved into including not only children with established disabilities but also those at high risk for developmental disabilities because of other biological conditions (e.g., prematurity, perinatal asphyxia, certain congenital malformations, atypical neuromuscular findings). Certain environmental risk factors, such as parental mental retardation and psychiatric disorders (including substance abuse), have also been used to define infants who are at risk.

The landmark legislation, the Education for All Handicapped Children Act of 1975 (PL 94-142; see Chapter 30) paved the way for the development of EI programs. Part of this legislation (which later became Part B of the Individuals with Disabilities Education Act) encouraged states to identify and serve children ages 3–5 years. Subsequently, PL 94-142 was reauthorized and renamed the Individuals with Disabilities Education Act (IDEA) of 1990 (PL 101-476). The Education of the Handicapped Act Amendments of 1986 (PL 99-457) had required states to provide services to preschoolers, and amendments to IDEA in 1991 (PL 102-119) gave incentives to states to serve infants and toddlers (birth until age 3) under Part H, known as the Handicapped Infants and Toddlers Program. These laws also sought to decrease the need for special education and related services when the child reached school age and to provide family support (Blackman, Healy, & Ruppert, 1992).

Reauthorization of IDEA in 1997 (PL 105-17) changed and renamed Part H as Part C, Program for Infants and Toddlers with Disabilities. Under this legislation, families with infants or toddlers who meet the criteria for eligibility receive a comprehensive and multidisciplinary assessment, the development of an IFSP, service coordination, and procedural safeguards (Grzywacz, 1998). These services are provided at no cost to the family, but private medical insurance and Medicaid can be billed for certain services.

Part C of IDEA '97 provides a legislative foundation for ensuring that the system of EI is family directed, community based, comprehensive, and well coordinated. Federal legislation requires that each state governor establish a lead agency for the Part C system. This agency is responsible for the administration and supervision of all required components of the EI system. In addition, the legislation mandates that a state interagency coordinating council be appointed by the governor to help establish state policies and procedures for EI services. In keeping with the family-directed philosophy, strong representation from parents of children with disabilities (at least 20% of council members) is a requirement.

Allowing the family to direct decisions, based on a partnership with professionals, is the basic philosophy underlying EI legislation (Bailey et al., 1999; Edelman, 1991). Family-directed care recognizes that the family is the one constant in the child's life and must be involved in all decision-making about the child's care. It further implies that the family's physician and other professionals will provide information, evaluations, and recommendations that will help the family make informed decisions. Because the needs of the child and family are often many and complex, EI should involve a coordinated system of care that is community based, minimizes family disruption, and helps prevent gaps in services or duplication of effort.

To meet this goal, a service coordinator is named to assist the family in accomplishing coordination of care. The Division for Early Childhood of the Council for Exceptional Children (see Appendix D) has established specific recommended practices in EI and early childhood special education to address these goals (Sandall, McLean, & Smith, 2000).

IDENTIFICATION AND REFERRAL

A well-coordinated Child Find program is essential to identify infants at risk for developmental delay or disability who could benefit from an EI program. This involves a process of identifying and evaluating infants and toddlers who have developmental delays so that they and their families can receive appropriate services at the earliest point possible in the child's development. Child Find efforts are most effective when coordinated with other early identification programs such as Medicaid's Early and Periodic Screening, Diagnosis, and Treatment (EPSDT) program. Primary care providers (e.g., physicians, nurses, social workers) are in a key position to identify young children who are at risk for or who have developmental delays or disabilities (American Academy of Pediatrics, Committee on Children with Disabilities, 2001a; Palfrey, 1987).

Often the first step in the identification and referral of infants and toddlers who could benefit from EI services is developmental screening. When this occurs in the context of a well-child visit, it reinforces the concept that health and development are interrelated. An equally valid approach is to recognize parental concerns about a child's development as an effective method for early identification. Parental concern has, in fact, been shown to be as effective in identifying developmental delay as professional opinion and/or standardized testing is (Diamond, 1993; Glascoe, 1997). Thus, an infant or toddler can be referred to the local EI program directly by anyone (including a relative or friend) who suspects that the child has a developmental delay or disability.

Developmental screening is mandated in Part C of IDEA. It should involve the family and other sources of information, using a process that is culturally sensitive. It should be reliable, valid, cost-effective, and time-efficient. It should be seen not only as a means of early identification but also as a service that helps the family understand the child's developmental progress. Several developmental screening tests are commercially available (Table 29.1). The two most commonly used are 1) the Denver II (Frankenburg et al., 1992) and 2) the Ages & Stages Questionnaires (ASQ): A Parent-Completed Child-Monitoring System, Second Edition (Bricker & Squires, 1999).

The Denver II, a revision of the Denver Developmental Screening Test (Frankenburg & Dodds, 1969) is widely used in primary care clinics and EI programs for children from birth to 6 years of age. It is designed to compare a child's performance on various age-appropriate tasks with the performance of other children who are the same age. It is not, however, an evaluation tool and does not lead to standard scores, developmental quotients, or diagnostic labels (e.g., mental retardation). The Denver II, which can be completed in 10–20 minutes by a trained administrator, consists of tasks that are arranged in four sections to screen these developmental areas: personal-social, fine motor, language, and gross motor. In addition, the Denver II includes five test behavior items that are based on observation and confirmed by parental report.

The ASQ is used for identifying children at risk for developmental delays from 4 months to 5 years of age. The questionnaire is designed to be completed by families in the home environment but can also be used in waiting rooms, clinics, and child care settings. Parents take 10–15 minutes to complete the questionnaire, usually with the assistance of EI service providers or other professionals, who can then score it. The 30 items per age group are divided into five developmental domains: communication, gross motor, fine motor, problem solving, and personal-social. An "overall" section allows family members to address any of their concerns. Individual questionnaires are available for the following ages: 4, 6, 8, 10, 12, 14, 16, 18, 20, 22,

Table 29.1.   Developmental screening instruments for infants and toddlers

Measure	Age range	Areas assessed
Developmental Profile II (DP-II; Alpern, Boll, & Shearer, 1986)	Birth to 9 years	Physical, self-help, social, academic, and communication
Bayley Infant Neurodevelopmental Screener (BINS; Aylward, 1995)	3–24 months	Basic neurological, auditory and visual receptive, verbal and mother expressive, and cognitive
Ages & Stages Questionnaires (ASQ): A Parent-Completed, Child-Monitoring System, Second Edition (Bricker & Squires; 1999)	4–60 months	Communication, gross and fine motor, personal-social, problem solving
Early Language Milestone Scale–Second Edition (ELM Scale–2; Coplan 1993)	Birth to 36 months	Auditory expressive, auditory receptive, and visual skills
Infant/Toddler Symptom Checklist (DeGangi, Poisson, Sickel, et al.; 1995)	7–30 months	Self-regulation, attention, modulation of sleep/wake states, responses to sensory stimuli, and attachment and emotional functioning
Developmental Activities Screening Inventory (DASI-II; Fewell & Langley, 1984)	Birth to 60 months	Sensory intactness, means-ends relationships, causality to memory, seriation, and reasoning
Denver Prescreening Questionnaire–II (PDQ-II; Frankenburg,1988)	Birth to 6 years	Items across developmental areas
Denver II (Frankenburg, Dodds, Archer, et al.,1992)	Birth to 6 years	Gross motor, language, fine motor-adaptive, personal-social, and test behavior
Child Development Inventory (CDI; Ireton, 1992)	15 months to 6 years	Social, self-help, gross motor, fine motor, expressive language, and preacademic
Infant Development Inventory (IDI; Ireton; 1994)	Birth to 18 months	Social, self-help, gross motor, fine motor, and language

24, 27, 30, 33, 36, 42, 48, 54, and 60 months. These ages match the usual times for well-child visits to the pediatrician.

ASSESSMENT FOR EARLY INTERVENTION SERVICES

Assessment is the process used to identify a child's strengths and needs. It often begins when the family first calls the infant and toddler (EI) program for assistance and is the link to develop an effective treatment plan. Once a referral is made to the local agency that coordinates EI services, assessment, eligibility determination, and the IFSP meeting must be completed within 45 calendar days. After a family is referred, a service coordinator is assigned to help plan and coordinate all of the steps leading to the development of a service plan (provided that the child is found to be eligible for EI).

Each assessment must be timely, comprehensive, and multidisciplinary. Pertinent records relating to the child's current health status as well as medical history must be reviewed. The assessment should be comprehensive and include the child's level of functioning in five development domains: physical (including vision/hearing and gross and fine motor development), cognition, communication, social-emotional, and adaptive. The multidisciplinary assessment team must include a family member and two professionals representing different disciplinary expertise (Bagnato & Neisworth, 1999). For example, the professionals might include an early childhood special educator and a speech-language pathologist or perhaps a motor therapist such as an occupational or physical therapist. The qualified personnel are usually chosen on the basis of the strengths and needs of the child and family (Berman & Shaw, 1995). They cannot, however, both be from the same discipline, such as two special educators. The assessment must reflect the unique strengths and needs of the child. In addition, family members provide information about their circumstances, priorities, and resources that may have an impact on their child. It appears that the more active the family's involvement in designing and participating in their child's program, the greater the child's developmental progress (Ramey & Ramey, 1998).

It is now well accepted that the procedures and instruments used for assessment of infants and toddlers cannot simply be professionally directed and test-driven. This is based on the fact that the standardized tests for children from birth to age 3 years are not as predictive as psychological testing instruments used in older children are. In addition, young children are changing rapidly in the first 3 years of life. Thus, their assessment must be seen as an evolving process rather than one determined by a single test or test battery. Present-day assessment practices emphasize a play-based approach using developmental and behavioral checklists, direct observations, and criterion-referenced instruments. In addition, for the assessment process to be most productive, it should take place in an environment that is familiar to the child and family, ideally at home or in a child care center with active parental participation. This assessment approach yields a more realistic understanding of the child's strengths and delays and can aid in the development of intervention priorities (Bagnato, Neisworth, & Munson, 1997; Linder, 1993; Neisworth & Bagnato, 2000). A list of such instruments is provided in Table 29.2.

Play-based assessments involve a child's being observed in structured and unstructured play opportunities with family members and EI personnel. This model allows for flexibility in content, and the sequence of events can follow the lead of the child or family. This is often less stressful for both parent and child. EI professionals demonstrate a flexible approach when they choose toys that are motivating for the child, often using the child's preferred playthings. Play-based assessment can provide information on the five mandated domains; it also may address the child's learning style, temperament, motivation, and social interaction. Observations can include information about the child's alertness, attention, problem-solving skills, muscle tone, and overall emotional stability. Although standardized instruments may be needed to help determine eligibility for EI services, the information gathered through a flexible developmental and play-based approach may be more useful in planning the intervention program (Bagnato & Neisworth, 2000; Linder, 1993; Sandall et al., 2000).

In addition to assessing the child's level of development, every assessment should identify the family's concerns, priorities, and resources. Concerns are what family members identify as needs, issues, or problems that they want addressed. Priorities allow for a family to set its own agenda and make choices about how EI will be involved in their life. Resources include finances, strengths, abilities, and formal and informal supports that can be mobilized to meet the family's concerns, needs, and desired outcomes (Kaufmann & McGonigel, 1991). Identifying these issues leads to the development of EI outcomes, strategies, and activities that will help families achieve their goals.

Table 29.2.   Evaluation and assessment instruments for infants and toddlers

Measure	Age range	Areas assessed
Bayley Scales of Infant Development–Second Edition (Bayley, 1993)	1 week to 30+ months	Mental and motor
Early Intervention Developmental Profile (Schafer & Moersch, 1981)	Birth to 7 months	Motor, language, and adaptive skills
Receptive-Expressive Emergent Language Scale–Second Edition: A Method for Assessing the Language Skills of Infants (REEL-2; Bzoch & League, 1991)	Birth to 36 months	Receptive/expressive language
The Rossetti Infant-Toddler Language Scale (Rossetti, 1990)	Birth to 36 months	Interaction, attachment, pragmatics, gesture, play/language, comprehension, and expression

DEVELOPING AN INDIVIDUALIZED FAMILY SERVICE PLAN

The development of the IFSP is based on the information gathered through the assessment of the child and family and is directed by the family's concerns, priorities, and resources. It can be reviewed and updated at any time but it must be reviewed every 6 months and rewritten at least yearly. Its elements (Content of an IFSP, 1998) include the following:

- A statement of the child's present levels of development in all five domains, based on objective criteria
- With the concurrence of the family, a statement of the family's resources, concerns, and priorities as they relate to facilitating the development of the infant or toddler
- Major outcomes to be achieved with the criteria, procedures, and time lines used to determine the degree of progress toward achieving the outcomes
- A listing of specific EI services to be provided and the frequency (how many times per week or month), intensity (how long the sessions will last per visit), and methods of delivering services (e.g., direct, consultative, in a playgroup)
- Identification of where services will be provided. Ideally this should be in the natural environment (i.e., where the infant or toddler usually spends his or her day). This could be at home, in a child care center, or in a family home care setting. Often services are provided in a number of environments; one visit might be at home and another at the child care center.
- An outline of linkage or support services not required under Part C (e.g., medical services)
- Projected dates for services to start and the anticipated duration of these services
- The name of the service coordinator who will assist the family through the assessments and link them to needed resources
- Outline of the transition of the toddler to preschool or other appropriate services

A strong link between the parents, the EI team, and the primary care provider fosters an open sharing of concerns and allows for true collaboration (American Academy of Pediatrics, Committee on Children with Disabilities, 2001b). If a physician is not able to attend the IFSP meeting, then he or she can share health information and recommendations with the rest of the team by providing written reports, by giving telephone or e-mail consultation, or by sending a representative to the IFSP meeting. When the pediatrician or other primary care provider is not a part of the assessment team, he or she should review the IFSP, discuss it with the family and be prepared to comment as needed. This primary care provider should determine if the proposed health-related services are appropriate and sufficiently comprehensive. These services could include clean intermittent catheterization, tracheostomy care, the changing of dressings, and the administration of medication. Health services should also include consultation by physicians with EI service providers concerning the special health care needs to be addressed in the course of providing intervention services. When health services are included in the IFSP, they should be carried out by the primary care provider or by an appropriate pediatric subspecialist (e.g., cardiologist, neurologist, surgeon; American Academy of Pediatrics, Committee on Children with Disabilities, 1999).

SERVICE COORDINATION

Service coordination (sometimes referred to as *case management*) is the process by which EI services are monitored and linked to ensure that the needs of young children and their families are addressed in a coordinated and systematic fashion. The service coordinator must be capable of performing multiple roles that support and strengthen family functioning. This individual acts as a link between the child and family and all aspects of the EI program, from assessment through development of the IFSP, ensuring provision of services, advocacy, and ultimately transition from the program. Although service coordination is usually provided by a professional, it can be done by other parents who are hired specifically for this purpose. Many families prefer this approach as it builds on parent-to-parent support, but it is not accepted by all states.

PROVIDED SERVICES

Based on the family's priorities, concerns, and resources and in collaboration with the EI team's ongoing assessment, desired outcomes are listed in the IFSP. The strategies and activities needed to achieve the outcomes often require a broad range of EI services. The most common strategy is for special instruction to be provided by an early childhood special educator or developmental specialist who guides caregivers in promoting developmentally appropriate activities and play (Shonkoff & Meisels, 2000). In addition, parents often find family training and/or counseling to be a key service that helps them understand their child's developmental strengths and weaknesses. This in turn results in improved advocacy and intervention planning.

A broad range of services and supports are mandated by the federal regulations regarding Part C of IDEA '97 (Early Intervention Services, 1999), including but not limited to the following:

- Assistive technology devices and services
- Audiology
- Family training, counseling, and home visits
- Health services
- Medical services for diagnosis or evaluation
- Nursing services
- Nutrition services
- Occupational therapy
- Physical therapy
- Psychological services
- Service coordination
- Social work services
- Special instruction
- Speech-language pathology
- Transportation and related costs
- Vision services

Infants and toddlers with more complex problems and those who have multiple disabilities may require and benefit from several services. This need for multidisciplinary therapy has spawned a number of new service delivery models. These include consultation, coaching, collaboration, and so forth. It is a quite common and accepted practice for an EI provider to expand his or her role and work. For example, children with motor disabilities often require the services of an occupational or physical therapist. Although the focus of these professionals is on motor skills, they may facilitate language during the movement activities. Periodic consultation with rather than direct service by the speech-language pathologist may be an effective way to accomplish the desired outcomes.

The frequency and intensity of EI services continue to be controversial topics. Frequent hands-on intervention, similar to a medical rehabilitation model, is often expected by families as well as by some EI providers. Yet, choosing services to assist young children and families to achieve specific outcomes is a complex process. It requires that meaningful outcomes be identified and that EI professionals provide an array of consultative and direct services. This approach often departs from the traditional frequency and intensity model of "so many times per week." Meaningful outcomes should go beyond specific disciplinary goals (e.g., increasing the mean length of utterance, reducing limb spasticity) to effectively address the child's and family's functioning within the home and/or in a child care setting and during play or while the child is learning in any environment.

Different services as well as service levels may be needed, depending on the number of caregivers and the number of locations of care. A biweekly visit with a parent and child who spend the day together at home may be sufficient to accomplish the desired outcome. On the other hand, a multiple caregiver situation often requires more frequent contacts to demonstrate strategies and allow for more collaboration with key adults. It should be noted that not all goals can be worked on at the same time. A flexible model might emphasize sequential rather than simultaneous services; for example, once one goal is accomplished, a new one can be introduced. Each goal should have distinct services, frequency, intensity, and location identified prior to its implementation. Frequency and intensity of services are not as important as what providers do with their time in guiding the child and family. Shifting to a flexible, outcomes-guided model that is family directed increases the likelihood that the recommendations for services will emerge from a thorough analysis of child and family priorities. This contrasts with the traditional medical model of providing a predetermined group of services by specific disciplines that are driven by a particular disability rather than by the specific goals of the family (Hanft & Feinberg, 1997).

TRANSITION FROM EARLY INTERVENTION TO PRESCHOOL SERVICES

Transition is a process that children and families go through as they move from one program or setting to another. Families of young children with developmental delays and disabilities may need to move between home and hospital or from one community-based program to another. At about 3 years of age, the child will need to make the transition from EI to early childhood special education services, such as an inclusive preschool or child care program. Careful planning and preparation for each transition can ensure that change occurs in a timely and effective manner. Transition planning may also help to alleviate parental stress and may be an opportunity for family growth as new skills are developed that can be applied to new settings. To ensure a seamless move from EI to preschool services, the IFSP must include a transition plan.

EFFICACY OF EARLY INTERVENTION

There is growing evidence that EI can have a substantial impact on children with developmental delays/disabilities and on their families (Ramey & Ramey, 1999). EI services have been shown to improve performance on developmental outcome measures (psychological testing), strengthen parent–child interactions, and provide a supportive environment for families. One of the most important studies, the Infant Health and Development Program (IHDP) provided a comprehensive, well-structured curriculum for 985 low birth weight (LBW) premature infants (IHDP, 1990; Ramey et al., 1992). This controlled clinical trial evaluated the efficacy of developmental and support services (with pediatric follow-up) in reducing cognitive, behavioral, and health problems in the LBW infant. The experimental group received a home-based EI program with parental support and information on health and development. After 1 year of age, children in this group attended a structured center-based EI program with concurrent parent group meetings. The control group of LBW infants received developmental surveillance and referrals as needed, but no EI services were provided. The program ended at 3 years of age. At 3 years of age, the experimental group was found to have significantly higher IQ scores (about 10 points higher), an increased receptive vocabulary, and fewer behavioral problems (IHDP, 1990; Ramey et al., 1992). At 5 years of age, however, only the children from the experimental group who had been heavier (but still LBW) at birth continued to show higher cognitive measures (Brooks-Gunn et al., 1994). At 8 years this heavier LBW group continued to show modest intervention-related differences in cognitive and academic skills, although these differences were less than at 3 years of age (McCarton et al., 1997). This emphasizes the challenge in sustaining the benefits of EI into the elementary school years. Finally, although this study showed significant benefits to infants in lower socioeconomic groups, there were less clear benefits in higher socioeconomic groups. In sum, EI was found to have a modest benefit for infants at high risk for developmental delays as a result of prematurity, especially if they came from lower socioeconomic settings.

The efficacy of EI in treating children with established biologic disorders such as Down syndrome, cerebral palsy, or autism has been more difficult to document (Guralnick, 1997a, 1997b). The diversity and severity of childhood impairments (e.g., in the pervasive developmental disorders), the broad range of EI service models, and different outcomes measured make interpretation of studies difficult. It does appear, however, that the short-term impact of EI services on cognitive and social development of children with disabilities is greater when the intervention is more structured and focused on the relationship between child and caregiver (Bailey et al., 1999; Farran, 2000; Guralnick, 1998; Guralnick, 1999). In these settings, EI programs may improve play behavior and provide some short-term gains in developmental achievement, particularly in children with less severe disabilities. There seems, however, to be an even greater beneficial effect on family acceptance and caregiving activities, such as feeding and handling, than on developmental progress (Majnemer, 1998).

SUMMARY

As EI programs have developed into well-organized systems, they have become better able to respond to the many stresses that are faced by children with disabilities and their families. These families need information and guidance about health matters, identification and referral to community professionals, and advice on behavior management. They may also need resources such as financial assistance and respite care. Interpersonal and family distress may also need to be addressed. This may include reassessment of long-term expectations, redefining parental roles, and identifying threats to parental competency. The connections between stressors, family interaction patterns, and developmental outcomes of children are now being understood within a developmental framework (Guralnick, 1997a, 1999). It is becoming clear that EI can produce beneficial effects for children and their families. Sophisticated professional services that are primarily child focused and family directed are very important, but these services should constitute only one component of a larger system of EI services. Success depends on the comprehensiveness of an EI program and its ability to identify and address episodic and chronic stresses in the everyday lives of families.

REFERENCES

Alpern, G., Boll, T., & Shearer, M. (1986). *Developmental Profile II (DP-II)*. Los Angeles: Western Psychological Services.

American Academy of Pediatrics, Committee on Children with Disabilities. (1999). Pediatrician's role in development and implementation of an individual education plan (IEP) and/or an individual family service plan (IFSP). *Pediatrics, 104*, 124–127.

American Academy of Pediatrics, Committee on Children with Disabilities. (2001a). Developmental surveillance and screening of infants and young children. *Pediatrics, 108*, 192–196.

American Academy of Pediatrics, Committe on Children with Disabilities. (2001b). Role of the pediatrician in family-centered early intervention services. *Pediatrics, 107*, 1155–1157.

Aylward, G.P. (1995). *Bayley Infant Neurodevelopmental Screener (BINS)*. San Antonio, TX: The Psychological Corporation.

Bagnato, S., & Neisworth, J. (1999). Collaboration and teamwork in assessment for early intervention. *Child and Adolescent Psychiatric Clinics of North America, 8*, 347–363.

Bagnato, S., Neisworth, J., & Munson, S.M. (1997). *LINKing assessment and early intervention: An authentic curriculum-based approach*. Baltimore: Paul H. Brookes Publishing Co.

Bailey, D.B., Jr., Aytch, L.S., Odom, S.L., et al. (1999). Early intervention as we know it. *Mental Retardation and Developmental Disabilities Research Reviews, 5*, 11–20.

Bayley, N. (1993). *Bayley Scales of Infant Development—Second Edition Manual*. San Antonio, TX: The Psychological Corporation.

Berman, C., & Shaw, E. (1995). *Family-directed child evaluation and assessment under IDEA: Lessons from families and programs*. Chapel Hill, NC: National Early Childhood Technical Assistance System.

Blackman, J., Healy, A., & Ruppert, E. (1992). Participation by pediatricians in early intervention: Impetus from Public Law 99-457. *Pediatrics, 89*, 98–102.

Bricker, D., & Squires, J. (with assistance from Mounts, L., Potter, L., Nickel, R., Twombly, E., & Farrell, J.). (1999). *Ages & Stages Questionnaires (ASQ): A parent-completed, child-monitoring system* (2nd ed.). Baltimore: Paul H. Brookes Publishing Co.

Brooks-Gunn, J., McCarton, C.M., Casey, P.H., et al. (1994). Early intervention in low-birth-weight premature infants: Results through age 5 years from the Infant Health and Development Program. *Journal of the American Medical Association, 272*, 1257–1262.

Bzoch, K.R., & League, R. (1991). *Receptive-Expressive Emergent Language Scale–Second Edition: A Method for Assessing the Language Skills of Infants (REEL-2).* Austin, TX: PRO-ED.

Content of an IFSP, 34 C.F.R. § 303.344 (1998).

Coplan, J. (1993). *Early Language Milestone Scale, Second Edition (ELM Scale–2).* Austin, TX: PRO-ED.

DeGangi, G., Poisson, S., Sickel, R., et al. (1995). *Infant/Toddler Symptom Checklist.* San Antonio, TX: The Psychological Corporation.

Denhoff, E. (1981). Current status of infant stimulation or enrichment programs for children with developmental disabilities. *Pediatrics, 67,* 32–37.

Diamond, K. (1993). The role of parents' observations and concerns in screening for developmental delays in young children. *Topics in Early Childhood Special Education, 13,* 68–81.

Diamond, M., & Hopson, J. (1999). *Magic trees of the mind: How to nurture your child's intelligence, creativity and healthy emotions from birth through adolescence.* New York: Plume.

Early Intervention Services, 34 C.F.R. § 303.12 (1999).

Edelman, L. (1991). Recognizing family-centered care. In L. Edelman (Ed.), *Getting on board: Training activities to promote the practice of family-centered care.* Bethesda, MD: Association for the Care of Children's Health.

Education for All Handicapped Children Act of 1975, PL 94-142, 20 U.S.C. §§ 1400 *et seq.*

Farran, D. (2000). Another decade of intervention for children who are low income or disabled: What do we do now? In J.P. Shonkoff & S.J. Meisels (Eds.), *Handbook of early childhood intervention* (2nd ed., pp. 510–548). Cambridge, England: Cambridge University Press.

Fewell, R., & Langley, M.B. (1984). *Developmental Activities Screening Inventory (DASI-II).* Austin, TX: PRO-ED.

Frankenburg, W.K. (1998). *Prescreening Developmental Questionnaire–II (PDQ-II).* Denver, CO: Denver Developmental Materials.

Frankenburg, W.K., & Dodds, J.B. (1969). *The Denver Developmental Screening Test.* Denver: University of Colorado Medical Center.

Frankenburg, W.K., Dodds, J.B., Archer, P., et al. (1992). *Denver II.* Denver, CO: Denver Developmental Materials. (Available from the publisher, Post Office Box 371075, Denver, CO 80237-5075; 800-419-4729)

Glascoe, F.P. (1997). Parents' concerns about children's development: Prescreening technique or screening test? *Pediatrics, 99,* 522–528.

Grzywacz, P. (1998). Year in review, part 2: Part C changes focus on early intervention, natural environments, and transitions. *Early Childhood Report, 9*(3), 1–11.

Guralnick, M.J. (Ed.). (1997a). *The effectiveness of early intervention.* Baltimore: Paul H. Brookes Publishing Co.

Guralnick, M. (1997b). Organizing themes in early intervention. *Infants and Young Children, 10*(2), v–vii.

Guralnick, M. (1998). The effectiveness of early intervention for vulnerable children: A developmental perspective. *American Journal on Mental Retardation, 102,* 319–345.

Guralnick, M. (1999). Family and child influences on the peer-related social competence of young children with developmental delays. *Mental Retardation and Developmental Disabilities Research Reviews, 5,* 21–29.

Hanft, B., & Feinberg, E. (1997). Toward the development of a framework for determining the frequency and intensity of early intervention services. *Infants and Young Children, 10*(1), 27–37.

Hohnke, C.D., & Sur, M. (1999). Development of the visual pathways: Effects of neural activity. *Mental Retardation and Developmental Disabilities Research Reviews, 5,* 51–59.

Individuals with Disabilities Education Act Amendments of 1997, PL 105-17, 20 U.S.C. §§ 1400 *et seq.*

Individuals with Disabilities Education Act (IDEA) of 1990, PL 101-476, 20 U.S.C. §§ 1400 *et seq.*

Infant Health and Development Program. (1990). Enhancing the outcomes of low-birth-weight premature infants: A multisite, randomized trial. *Journal of the American Medical Association, 263,* 3035–3042.

Ireton, H. (1992). *Child Development Inventory (CDI).* Minneapolis, MN: Behavior Science Systems. (Available from the publisher, Box 580274, Minneapolis, MN 55458)

Ireton, H. (1994). *Infant Development Inventory (IDI).* Minneapolis, MN: Behavior Science Systems. (Available from the publisher, Box 580274, Minneapolis, MN 55458)

Kaufmann, R., & McGonigel, M. (1991). Identifying family concerns, priorities, and resources. In M. McGonigel, R. Kaufmann, & B. Johnson (Eds.), *Guidelines and recommended practices for the individualized family service plan* (2nd ed., pp. 47–56). Bethesda, MD: Association for the Care of Children's Health.

Linder, T.W. (Ed.). (1993). *Transdisciplinary play-based assessment: A functional approach to working with young children* (Rev. ed.). Baltimore: Paul H. Brookes Publishing Co.

Majnemer, A. (1998). Benefits of early intervention for children with developmental disabilities. *Seminars in Pediatric Neurology, 5,* 62–69.

McCarton, C.M., Brooks-Gunn, J., Wallace, I.F., et al. (1997). Results at age 8 years of early intervention for low-birth-weight premature infants. *Journal of the American Medical Association, 277,* 126–132.

Neisworth, J., & Bagnato, S. (2000). Recommended practices in assessment. In S. Sandall, M. McLean, & B. Smith (Eds.), *DEC recommended practices in early intervention/early childhood special education.* Longmont, CO: Sopris West.

Palfrey, J. (1987). Early identification of children's special needs: A study in five metropolitan communities. *Journal of Pediatrics, 111,* 561.

Ramey, C.T., Bryant, D.M., Wasik, B.H., et al. (1992). Infant health and development program for low birth weight, premature infants: Program elements, family participation, and child intelligence. *Pediatrics, 93,* 454–465.

Ramey, C., & Ramey, S. (1998). Early intervention and early experience. *American Psychologist, 53*(2), 109–120.

Ramey, S.L., & Ramey, C.T. (1999). Early experience and early intervention for children "at risk" for developmental delay and mental retardation. *Mental Retardation and Developmental Disabilities Research Reviews, 5,* 1–10.

Rossetti, L.M. (1990). *The Rossetti Infant-Toddler Language Scale: A measure of communication and interaction.* East Moline, IL: LinguiSystems.

Sandall, S., McLean, M., & Smith, B. (Eds.). (2000). *DEC recommended practices in early intervention/early childhood special education.* Longmont, CO: Sopris West.

Schafer, D.S., & Moersch, M.S. (Eds.). (1981). *Developmental programming for infants and young children* (Vol. 2). Ann Arbor: University of Michigan Press.

Schrader, L., & Friedlander, M.J. (1999). Developmental regulation of synaptic mechanisms that may contribute to learning and memory. *Mental Retardation and Developmental Disabilities Research Reviews, 5,* 60–71.

Shonkoff, J., & Meisels, S.J. (Eds.). (2000). *Handbook of early childhood intervention* (2nd ed.). New York: Cambridge University Press.

Shonkoff, J., & Phillips, D. (Eds.). (2000). *From neurons to neighborhoods: The science of early childhood development.* Washington, DC: National Academy Press.

Skeels, H., & Dye, H. (1939). A study of the effects of differential stimulation on mentally retarded children. *Proceedings of the American Association of Mental Deficiency, 44,* 114–136.

30 Special Education Services

Elissa Batshaw Clair, Robin P. Church, and Mark L. Batshaw

Upon completion of this chapter, the reader will:

- be aware of the history of special education services
- understand the components of an individualized education program
- be familiar with the Individuals with Disabilities Education Act Amendments of 1997 and other legislation pertaining to education for children with disabilities
- be knowledgeable about services and supports available for children with disabilities

As defined by the Education for All Handicapped Children Act of 1975 (PL 94-142), *special education* involves a set of individualized supports provided to a student with a disability based on his or her needs and delivered in the least restrictive environment, or LRE. The Individuals with Disabilities Education Act (IDEA) Amendments of 1997 (PL 105-17) mandates two types of services to be provided as part of a free appropriate public education, or FAPE: special education and related services. IDEA '97 defines *special education* as "specially designed instruction . . . to meet the unique needs of a child with a disability, including instruction conducted in the classroom, in the home, in hospitals and institutions, and in other settings; and instruction in physical education" (§ 602[25]). *Related services* are defined as "transportation and . . . developmental, corrective, and other supportive services" (§ 602[22]) and include occupational and physical therapy. The cornerstone of providing special education services is the individualized education program, or IEP. This chapter discusses the history of special education legislation in the United States, IDEA '97, the components of an IEP, and the education-related supports and services available to children with disabilities.

JOHN

John was considerably slower than his siblings were in gaining early developmental milestones. He didn't walk or speak his first word until 18 months. As a toddler John received speech therapy in his home once per week in accordance with an individualized family service plan (IFSP) provided under Part C (Infants and Toddlers with Disabilities) of IDEA '97. These services were designed to help John's parents facilitate their son's communication skills. When John entered kindergarten, he was soon identified as having significant delays as compared with his classmates and in need of assessment for special education services. His parents gave permission for testing, which showed him to be functioning in the range of mild mental retardation and thus eligible for special education services. An IEP was developed with input from a team consisting of a psychologist, general and special education teacher, speech-language pathologist, and John's parents. The IEP identified the goals John would work toward, the amount of time he would spend receiving special education services, and the related services that would be provided to support his educational progress. The IEP team decided to place John in an inclusive environment, a class that was co-taught by a general education teacher and a special education teacher. The class contained children with and without disabilities. The two teachers worked together so that all children could have access to the same core curriculum, with differentiated instruction and modifications to the schoolwork. The team also decided that John would require related services from a speech-language pathologist. Sometimes this therapist would teach all or part of the class a lesson; at other times she would work with John individually. John made good progress in this program and was reassessed on an ongoing basis so that adjustments to his IEP could be made. When John was 14 years old, he began the transition planning process mandated by IDEA '97. With his input during a transition planning inventory, an individualized transition plan (ITP) was developed as part of his IEP. John was very interested in cooking, often preparing creative meals at home. He chose to attend prevocational food service classes in addition to his academic courses. The high school offered career cluster experiences in culinary arts, and John continued taking vocational classes, honing his skills as a chef. With the help of a job coach provided by the Bureau of Vocational Rehabilitation, John secured a summer job at a local restaurant. He continued in his school program through age 21 because special education legislation mandates services through this age for students with disabilities 1) who have not earned all of their credits toward graduation, 2) who need additional transition services, or 3) who are earning an alternative certificate rather than a general education diploma. Beginning in eleventh grade, when John was 19, he began to work half days at the restaurant while continuing to go to school part time. At 20 years old, he enrolled in culinary classes at a community college as part of his ITP. At 21, he completed his public education, receiving a diploma, and has subsequently been hired full time as an assistant chef at the restaurant.

HISTORY OF SPECIAL EDUCATION SERVICES

Federal mandates for special education services in the United States began in the 1960s as an outgrowth of the civil rights movement. Congress sought to ensure that economically disadvantaged children received the same quality of education as their privileged peers. In 1965, the Elementary and Secondary Education Act (PL 89-10) was signed into law. This law attempted to correct unequal educational opportunities that resulted from a child's economic condition. Congress eventually determined that another group of children, children with disabilities, was not receiving the same quality of education as their peers (U.S. Department of Education, Office of Special Education and Rehabilitative Services [OSERS], 2000). As the first step in correcting this disparity, the Education of the Handicapped Act of 1970 (EHA; Part B of PL 91-230) was enacted. This amendment to earlier legislation established a core grant program for local education agencies (LEAs) to provide services for children with disabilities.

Although the EHA was helpful in improving conditions for some children with disabilities, many other children were still being excluded from school entry. In 1971 the Pennsylvania Association for Retarded Children (PARC) sued the Commonwealth of Pennsylvania for not providing an education for all children with mental retardation. They argued that Pennsylvania was violating both state statutes and the equal protection clause of the Fourteenth Amendment to the Constitution in not providing an education for these students. During this case PARC was able to prove four points about the education of children with mental retardation: 1) that all children with mental retardation are capable of benefiting from a program of education and training; 2) that education cannot be defined as only the provision of academic experiences for children; 3) that having undertaken to provide all children with a free public education, the state could not deny students with mental retardation access to free public education and training; and 4) that the earlier students with mental retardation were provided education, the better the predictable learning outcomes (Yell, 1998). The judge ruled for PARC, and Pennsylvania was forced to provide a public education for all students with disabilities. Subsequent to this ruling, Congress passed the Education for All Handicapped Children Act of 1975 (PL 94-142), which created special education in the form we know it today. This was the first law requiring that a free appropriate education be provided to all children, regardless of their disability. No child could legally be excluded from school. Unlike the EHA, which lacked funding, PL 94-142 was a funded program, resulting in states' being more motivated to follow the statutes. This law defined the disabilities that would be covered and established guidelines for fair evaluation and assessment. PL 94-142 also established the IEP and guaranteed parents the right to due process in settling disputes with schools about appropriate program development (Mercer, 1997).

In PL 94-142, however, special education programs were mandated only for school-age children. Some private organizations offered early intervention programs, but the majority of young children with disabilities were not provided services until they reached kindergarten age. This deficiency was corrected in the Education of the Handicapped Act Amendments of 1986 (PL 99-457), which extended the mandate for special education services to infants and preschoolers. PL 99-457 also required the development of an IFSP for infants and toddlers in early intervention programs (Mercer, 1997; see Chapter 29).

The next step in the history of special education services in the United States was the Individuals with Disabilities Education Act of 1990 (PL 101-476), also known as IDEA, which superseded the EHA and its amendments. A major philosophic decision in IDEA was to use person-first language and to replace the word *handicap* with *disability* throughout the text of the law. In doing this Congress acknowledged that "disability is a natural part of the human experience and in no way diminishes the right of individuals to participate in or contribute to society" (PL 101-476, § 601[c]). The new law also required that transition planning occur to help students progress from high school into postsecondary education, vocational training, integrated employment, adult services, and community participation (Mercer, 1997). The law added assistive technology to the list of services that must be considered when creating an IEP (Horne, 1996). In addition, it included a mandate for a greater emphasis on meeting the needs of ethnically and culturally diverse children with disabilities. Finally, it mandated the development of early intervention programs to address the needs of children who were exposed prenatally to maternal substance abuse (Mercer, 1997).

In IDEA '97 (PL 105-17), a major change is the focus on maximizing student participation in the general education curriculum. In addition, Congress viewed the reauthorization process as an opportunity to improve IDEA by doing the following (S. Rep. No. 105-17, 1997):

- Strengthening the role of parents
- Giving increased attention to racial, ethnic, and linguistic diversity to prevent inappropriate identification and mislabeling
- Ensuring that schools are safe and conducive to learning
- Encouraging parents and educators to work out their differences using nonadversarial means

IDEA '97 guarantees a free appropriate public education for all children with disabilities ages 3–21. Children older than 18 who have received a regular high school diploma as opposed to a certificate of completion, however, are no longer eligible for these free services. A zero-reject provision mandates that even students who have severe and multiple impairments have the right to a free appropriate education in the least restrictive environment. Money is also available through Part C of this law for states that wish to provide an IFSP for children under the age of 3, but these services are not mandatory.

DEFINING DISABILITY FROM AN EDUCATIONAL PERSPECTIVE

For a child to receive special education services, he or she must have a physical, cognitive, or behavioral impairment that interferes with the ability to benefit from instruction in the general classroom curriculum. Among these impairments, emotional disturbance is the fastest growing segment of the special education population. The specific disabilities that are recognized by IDEA '97 legislation are:

- Mental retardation
- Hearing impairments (including deafness)
- Speech or language impairments
- Visual impairments (including blindness)
- Emotional disturbance
- Orthopedic impairments
- Autism
- Traumatic brain injury
- Other health impairments [added to IDEA '97, this may be interpreted to include attention-deficit/hyperactivity disorder]
- Specific learning disabilities
- Developmental delays [expanded from ages 3–5 years in the 1990 law to 3–9 years in IDEA '97] (PL 105-17, § 602[3])

SECTION 504 OF THE REHABILITATION ACT AND THE AMERICANS WITH DISABILITIES ACT

If a child does not satisfy the IDEA '97 criteria for disabilities, he or she may still receive special education services through Section 504 of the Rehabilitation Act of 1973 (PL 93-112) or through the Americans with Disabilities Act of 1990 (PL 101-336), whose objectives and language are very similar. These two acts are intended to establish a "level playing field" by eliminating barriers that exclude people with disabilities from participation in the community and workplace. The acts try to eliminate hurdles and discrimination from participation, be they physical (e.g., steps instead of ramps) or programmatic (e.g., exclusion of a child with HIV from the classroom).

In addition, the definition of disability is broader under Section 504 than under IDEA '97; although all students covered by IDEA '97 would also be covered by Section 504, the reverse is not the case. Specifically, Section 504 protects all people who 1) have a physical or mental impairment that substantially limits one or more major life activities, 2) have a record of such an impairment, or 3) are regarded as having such an impairment. The following are examples of students who may be covered by Section 504 to receive special education services but are not covered by IDEA '97:

- Students with communicable diseases (e.g., HIV)
- Students who are addicted to drugs, including alcohol
- Students with temporary disabilities resulting from accidents who may need short-term hospitalizations or homebound recovery
- Students with attention disorders without significant academic deficiencies
- Students with Tourette syndrome

ASSESSMENT AND EVALUATION

Public schools are obliged to evaluate any child suspected of having a disability. This includes children enrolled in private schools and children ages 3–5 years who are not yet registered for school. The implementation of this requirement varies from state to state, but in addition to having access to official preschool Child Find programs, generally parents can bring their child to the local school district and request an evaluation. The stated purpose of the initial evaluation is to determine whether a child has a disability and, if present, to establish the educational needs of the child (PL 105-17, § 614 [a][1][B]).

Parental consent is required prior to an evaluation. This consent, however, does not serve as consent for placement of the child in a special education program, which must be obtained separately. A child usually is evaluated by a multidisciplinary team consisting of a psychologist and one or more of the following education professionals: speech-language pathologist, occupational therapist, physical therapist, and social worker. The evaluation team should use a comprehensive assessment process to address strengths, interests, goals, and needs of the child in order to determine whether and what special education services are required. The typical evaluation may include tests of intelligence, memory, visual-motor integration, adaptive behavior, reading, math, social-emotional skills, and language. For children whose cognitive functioning is at a preschool level, testing of communication, social, and adaptive skills is performed.

The multidisciplinary team must follow specific guidelines during the evaluation of the child. These guidelines were created in response to faulty evaluation practices in the past, which had led to many children (especially minority children) being incorrectly placed in special education. Many of these children were labeled "mentally retarded" on the basis of one test, typically an IQ test. With these children in mind, a number of mandates for appropriate evaluation procedures were put in place as part of IDEA '97. The key mandates are that a number of tests must be used to determine if the child has a disability and that parental input must be included. Specific guidelines include (§§ 614[b][2][A–C] and 614[b][3][A]):

- Use of a variety of assessment tools and strategies
- Consideration of information provided by the parent
- Use of multiple procedures to determine whether a child has a disability
- Use of multiple procedures to determine an appropriate educational program for the child
- Use of technically sound instruments that may assess the relative contribution of cognitive and behavioral factors, in addition to physical or developmental factors
- Use of the child's native language in all evaluation procedures

With increasing concerns about the rising number of students classified as having a learning disability, IDEA '97 prohibits eligibility decisions from being made based on a lack of instruction or as a result of limited English proficiency.

In sum, the formal assessment and evaluation procedures of IDEA '97 are intended to ensure that 1) special education services are provided to all children and youth who demonstrate the need for such services, 2) decisions for service provision are fair and defensible, and 3) all requirements for evaluation are implemented consistently in all districts and states and monitored for appropriateness and compliance (Shriner & Spicuzza, 1995).

REEVALUATION

In addition to the initial evaluation, there must be a reevaluation of the need for and progress in special education. The reevaluation process, however, has been streamlined in IDEA '97. The previous reevaluation often involved extensive assessments of the student, even if these were not warranted. Under IDEA '97, the reevaluation may rely on existing information and assessment, and retesting is only to be done for valid reasons. In addition, parental consent is now required for reevaluation. Furthermore, all reevaluations must now include information about the student's involvement and progress in the general curriculum to ensure that the parents have a more complete picture of what is happening with their child.

THE INDIVIDUALIZED EDUCATION PROGRAM

The IEP is a written plan that maps out the goals that the child is expected to achieve over the course of the school year. According to IDEA '97, these goals must be developed based on the strengths of the child, the concerns of the parents, and the results of the most recent evaluation of the child (§ 614[d][3][A]). A new IEP must be written at least once per year and should be modified as often as needed based on an assessment of the child's progress. The IEP is created by a team that consists of professionals and the child's parents. The child is also encouraged to participate in the process, when appropriate. To ensure that parents are active participants, parents who are not well versed in education law can bring a surrogate to the IEP planning meeting; parents whose native language is not English and who have difficulty understanding or speaking English must be provided a translator for the meeting; and parents who are unable to comprehend for any reason aspects of the disability or IEP must be given explanations they can understand. The following sections describe the process of developing an IEP, the provisions that must be covered, and examples of IEPs for children with varying disabilities.

Participants in Developing an IEP

The individuals who may be involved as team participants in the IEP process include the parent(s), the child (when appropriate), the special education teacher, and representatives of related services. In addition, IDEA '97 requires that a general education teacher be involved if a student is likely to participate in the general education environment. This reflects the finding that most children with disabilities are in inclusive environments for at least part of the day. Another requirement of IDEA '97 is participation by a representative of the local school who has the authority to provide or supervise the provision of specially designed instruction to meet the needs of children with disabilities, who has knowledge of the general curriculum, and who has knowledge of the resources of the LEA. A psychologist is no longer specified as a required participant but instead can be replaced by a person who can interpret the instructional implications of evaluation results. School nurses are mentioned as likely IEP team members as schools are assuming increased responsibility for educationally related health-care needs (S. Rep. No. 105-17, 1997).

Development of Annual Goals and Benchmarks

IDEA '97 requires the development of measurable annual goals to enable parents and educators to determine a student's progress. These goals should address both academic and nonacademic concerns and be based on the student's current level of educational and behavioral function. The child's parents are to be informed of the progress toward achievement of annual goals as often as parents of children without disabilities are. So, if report cards are given out quarterly, so too must reports be given to parents of children receiving special education services. Progress toward reaching these benchmarks does not necessarily require a letter grade but can be performance based or criterion referenced and can be rated on a spectrum, for example, from "no progress" to "completed."

The Contents of an IEP

The law is very specific about what must be included in an IEP. According to IDEA '97, an IEP must contain the following items:

- A statement of the child's present level of educational performance, including how the child's disability affects his or her involvement and progress in the general education curriculum.

- A statement of measurable annual goals, including benchmarks or short-term objectives, related to meeting the child's special needs...to enable the child to be involved in and progress in the general curriculum.
- A statement of how the child's progress toward the annual goals...will be measured and how the child's parents will be regularly informed of [this] progress.
- A statement of the special education and related services and supplementary aids and services to be provided to the child, or on behalf of the child and ... the frequency, location, and duration of those services and modifications.
- An explanation of the extent, if any, to which the child will not participate with nondisabled children in the regular class.
- A statement of any individual modifications [that are needed for the child to participate in state- or districtwide assessments of student achievement or a statement of how and why the child will be alternately assessed if he or she is not to participate in state- or districtwide assessments]. (§ 614[d][1][A])

Individualized Transition Plan

An adolescent with a disability needs to start preparing for life in the community. According to IDEA '97, these transition plans may include preparing for "post-secondary education, vocational training, integrated employment (including supported employment), competitive employment, continuing and adult education, adult services, independent living, or community participation" (§ 602[30][A]). Beginning when the child is age 14, a formal ITP must be part of the IEP and should be based on the individual student's needs, interests, and choices. A transition planning inventory such as the one in Figure 30.1 can be helpful in beginning this process. The inventory identifies comprehensive aspects for planning, such as the likely postschool environment, vocational interests, further training needs, daily living skills, future living arrangements, recreation and leisure interests, transportation or mobility needs, legal planning, health and medical concerns, interpersonal relationships, financial resources, existing supports and those needed for the future, and links to outside agencies. A transition plan will map out "instruction, related services, community experiences, the development of employment and other post-school adult living objectives, and, when appropriate, acquisition of daily living skills and functional vocational evaluation" (§ 602[30][C]).

The specific items to be included within the IEP relating to transition are as follows:

- Beginning at age 14, and updated annually, a statement of the transition service needs of the child (such as participation in advanced-placement courses or a vocational education program)...that focuses on the child's course of study.
- Beginning at age 16 (or younger, if determined appropriate by the IEP Team), a statement of needed transition services for the child, including, when appropriate, a statement of the interagency responsibilities or any needed linkages.
- Beginning at least one year before the child reaches the age of majority under State law, a statement that the child has been informed of his or her rights ... that will transfer to the child on reaching the age of majority. (PL 105-17, § 614[d][1][A][vii])

Establishment of the Least Restrictive Environment

IDEA '97 emphasizes that the general education curriculum is presumed to be the appropriate beginning point for planning an IEP (§ 614[d][1][A][iv]). Only when participation in the general education curriculum with supplementary support and services can be demonstrated as not benefiting the student should an alternative curriculum be considered (Table 30.1). It should be emphasized that many variables go into making a decision about placement (e.g., what the parents want for their child, what the child wants, what cultural and ethnic issues affect the decision).

Transition Planning Inventory

Student information

Name: _____ Date: _____ Social Security number: _____

Date of birth: _____ Age: _____ Grade/program: _____

Name(s) of person(s) completing this form: _____

Relationship to student: _____

Likely postschool settings *Check based on what you expect will happen for the student after high school.*

Employment/further education or training	Living arrangements

___ Competitive employment
   ___ full time   ___ part time
___ Supported employment
   ___ full time   ___ part time
___ Other employment (*specify*): _____
___ College/university
___ Other education or training (*specify*): _____
	___ Will live by him- or herself
	___ Will live with parents or other relatives
	___ Will live with others who are not relatives
	   (without adult supervision)
	___ Will live with others who are not relatives
	   (with adult supervision)
	___ Other (*specify*): _____
	___ Contingency plan (*specify*): _____

Present level of life domains

Vocational	Y/N	Comments
1. Knows requirements and demands of his or her preferred occupations		
2. Makes informed choices among occupational alternatives, based on his or her interests, preferences, and abilities		
3. Knows how to get a job		
4. Demonstrates general job skills and work attitudes preferred by employers for keeping a job and advancing; may include supported employment		
5. Has the specific knowledge and skills needed to perform a particular skilled, semiskilled, or entry-level job; may include supported employment		
6. Supports that are needed to help student maintain employment	→	
7. Factors keeping student from being independent on the job	→	
8. Natural supports existing at the jobsite	→	
9. Student's vocational interests, skills, and needs	→	
10. Student's work experience	→	
11. Has a Plan for Achieving Self Support (PASS)		
12. Has a portfolio		
Further education/training	**Y/N**	**Comments**
1. Knows how to gain entry into an appropriate post-school community employment training program		
2. Knows how to gain entry into an appropriate vocational/technical school		
3. Knows how to gain entry into an appropriate college or university		

Figure 30.1. Transition planning inventory. (Adapted by Marlena Clementson of the Kennedy Krieger Institute from Clark, G. & Patton, J. [1997]. *Transition Planning Inventory: Profile and Further Assessment Recommendations Form.* Austin, TX: PRO-ED; adapted by permission.)

4.	Can succeed in an appropriate postsecondary program		
5.	Knows how his or her disability affects learning/work		
6.	Support services that are needed to help student succeed	→	
Daily living/living arrangements		**Y/N**	**Comments**
1.	Maintains personal grooming and hygiene		
2.	Knows how to locate a place to live in the community; may include using agencies that provide supported living options		
3.	Knows how to set up an apartment, house, or other living quarters		
4.	Performs everyday household tasks		
5.	Length of time student is able to stay by him- or herself	→	
6.	Times of the day support is needed	→	
7.	What student would do in an emergency situation	→	
8.	In-home or out-of-home respite needed. How often?		
Recreation/leisure		**Y/N**	**Comments**
1.	Partakes in various indoor leisure activities		
2.	Partakes in various outdoor activities		
3.	Uses settings that provide various types of entertainment		
4.	Anything student would like to do, but isn't doing. Why?		
5.	Student's leisure/hobby interests	→	
Transportation/mobility		**Y/N**	**Comments**
1.	Uses local transportation systems when needed		
2.	How student currently travels	→	
3.	Reads a map		
4.	Can follow directions		
5.	Can identify common community signs		
6.	Exercises pedestrian safety		
7.	Is able to use public transportation		
8.	Is able to get to work. How?		
9.	Types of public transportation available in student's area	→	
Community participation/advocacy		**Y/N**	**Comments**
1.	Knows his or her basic legal rights		
2.	Participates as an active citizen		
3.	Makes legal decisions affecting his or her life		
4.	Locates appropriate community services and resources		
5.	Knows how to use a variety of services and resources successfully		

(continued)

Figure 30.1.   (*continued*)

Legal	Y/N	Comments
1. Has life insurance		
2. Guardianship arranged for		
3. Durable power of attorney in place		
4. Has a living will		
5. Has burial plans		
Health/medical	**Y/N**	**Comments**
1. Maintains good physical health		
2. Addresses physical problems that arise		
3. Maintains good mental health		
4. Addresses mental health problems that arise		
5. Exercises good judgment		
6. Knows how body systems work		
7. Makes informed choices regarding sexual behavior		
8. Makes medical appointments		
9. Knows basic first aid		
10. Knows 911 protocol		
11. Has medical insurance now. Any restrictions now? Any restrictions in the future?		
12. Takes medication? By self? Monitored?		
13. Knows about proper nutrition		
14. Specialty services received (*specify which*)		
Interpersonal relationships/personal management	**Y/N**	**Comments**
1. Recognizes and accepts own strengths and limitations		
2. Expresses feelings and ideas to others appropriately		
3. Expresses feelings and ideas to others confidently		
4. Sets personal goals		
5. Makes personal decisions		
6. Gets along well with family members		
7. Demonstrates knowledge and skills of parenting		
8. Establishes and maintains close and/or casual friendships in a variety of settings		
9. Displays appropriate social behavior in a variety of settings		
10. Demonstrates skills for getting along well with co-workers		
11. Demonstrates skills for getting along well with supervisors		
12. Receives counseling now		
13. Will need counseling services after exiting school		
14. Shows respect for property of others		
15. Who are the student's friends?	→	
16. Student's personal values?	→	
17. Is able to problem-solve. How?		

Financial/income	Y/N	Comments
1. Receives Supplemental Security Income (SSI)		
2. Student's current or future representative/payee	→	
3. Parent has adequate estate planning		
4. Gets an allowance		
5. Can maintain a budget		
6. Can count change		
7. Can balance a checkbook		
8. Can make purchases		
9. Has a credit card		
10. Uses an ATM		
11. Has a savings account		
12. Uses tax forms		
13. Can read a paystub		
Supports	**Y/N**	**Comments**
1. Supports that already exist for student	→	
2. Receives services from Developmental Disabilities Administration, Division of Rehabilitation Services, or Mental Health Administration (*specify which organizations*)		
Communication	**Y/N**	**Comments**
1. How student communicates his or her needs, wants, and frustrations	→	
Occupational	**Y/N**	**Comments**
1. Student's motor capabilities? Challenges?	→	

Participation in State- and Districtwide Assessments

IDEA '97 states that students with disabilities shall be included in state- and districtwide assessments when possible (§ 612[a][17][A]). The reasoning is that exclusion from such evaluations may severely limit the student's opportunities for postsecondary education and employment (S. Rep. No. 105-17, 1997). The degree of participation in assessment relates to the issue of individuals with disabilities receiving separate certificates of completion that are not equivalent to a high school diploma. To carry out the intention of the law, the IEP team must document which portions of the general education curriculum, and therefore which goals and standards, are relevant. If the student's instruction addresses only some of the general education curricular goals, partial participation in statewide testing is indicated.

The IEP must include a statement of whatever modifications may be needed in state- or districtwide testing. The basic intention is that all students should have the opportunity to demonstrate what they have learned. Alternate assessments are intended for only a small percentage of students: 1) those with the most severe disabilities who cannot complete a standardized test, even with assistance (e.g., scribe or some other type of facilitator), and 2) those who will earn a differentiated diploma or certificate of completion. In these cases, a portfolio of work is often used as an alternate assessment tool. For example, Maryland developed the Independent Mastery Assessment Program, which measures a student's progress in four domains: 1) personal management, 2) community functioning, 3) career vocational skills, and 4) leisure/recreation skills.

The overall goal of these alternative assessments is to ensure that the child is achieving his or her personal best and that the child continues to achieve at progressively higher levels. To ac-

Table 30.1. Levels of educational placement, from least to most restrictive

Environment	% of all students with disabilities	Means of service provision
General education classroom	46	*General education class:* The child with a disability receives no special help or materials from the teacher or any other service provider.
		General education class with consulting teacher services and special materials: A special education teacher assists the general education teacher in adapting the general education curriculum to best meet the needs of the child with a disability. The special education teacher may also come into the classroom a few times a week to work directly with the child.
		General education class with related services: One or more times a week (less than 21% of the school day) a related services provider (e.g., physical therapist, occupational therapist, speech-language pathologist) works with the child in the classroom or in a separate location.
General education classroom and resource room	26	*General education class with resource room services:* The child joins a small group of students in a separate classroom (21%–60% of the school day) to work on areas of need with a special education teacher.
		Part-time special education class and part-time general education class: The child spends part (less than 61%) of the academic day in a special education class and part of the academic day in the general education class.
Resource room or other segregated environment	23	*Full-time special education class:* The child is in a separate special education class for all academic classes (61%–100% of the school day) but typically has lunch and nonacademic classes with peers without disabilities.
	3.3	*Special day school:* The child attends a school that serves only children with disabilities, and he or she spends no time during the school day with children without disabilities.
	0.63	*Residential school:* The child attends an overnight special education program.
	0.75	*Hospital or home instruction:* The child is unable to attend school and is educated in the hospital during a hospital stay or is educated at home.

Sources: Mercer, 1997; U.S. Department of Education, Office of Special Education and Rehabilitative Services, 1998; Ysseldyke & Algozzine, 1995.

complish this, the student's curriculum should fit his or her needs, rather than having the student fit into a particular existing curriculum. The intention of IDEA '97 is that the child's special education and related services are in addition to and affected by the general curriculum, not separate from it (PL 105-17, § [d][1][A][iii][III]; S. Rep. No. 105-17, 1997).

IDEA '97 addresses the issue of accountability by making data public about the results of educating children with disabilities. This includes a requirement for states to report the number of children with disabilities who are participating in general assessments or in alternate assessments and their overall performance on these evaluations. States are also required to publish dropout, graduation, and postsecondary education and employment rates. These rates are to be compared with and reported in the same amount of detail as those of students without disabilities (§§ 653[b][2][iii] and 612[a][17][b], respectively). The purpose of gathering and reporting this information is to increase efforts toward attaining improved student results and has implications for funding streams at the school, district, and/or state level.

The National Center on Educational Outcomes was established in 1990, with funding from the Office of Special Education Programs, to increase participation of students with disabilities in large-scale assessments. Two state assessment programs, in Maryland and Kentucky, currently have fully inclusive participation policies and have been used as national models. Reporting information on students with disabilities is important because it ensures that these students are represented in the accountability system. There is great variability in reporting practices, however, from district to district and from state to state, making comparisons difficult. Complicating this issue is the concern that when students with disabilities are included in large-scale assessments, the results may not be comparable to those of other students because of the special testing circumstances (The Council for Exceptional Children [CEC], 1998).

Mediation of IEP Disputes

As part of IDEA '97, all states must offer mediation as an initial avenue for conflict resolution between parents and the school in developing an IEP (§ 615[e]). The goal is to increase the speed and quality of decision making regarding programming for students and to decrease the burden on the due process system and litigation. States are required to maintain a listing of trained mediators. Agreements reached during mediation are to be set forth in writing. Discussions during mediation, however, are confidential and cannot be used as evidence in any subsequent due process hearing or civil proceeding.

DISCIPLINING STUDENTS RECEIVING SPECIAL EDUCATION SERVICES

There have been ongoing concerns that school officials face a lack of parity in making decisions about disciplining students with and without disabilities who have violated the same school rules (S. Rep. No. 105-17, 1997). IDEA '97 attempts to balance the obligation for ensuring that schools are safe and orderly environments that are conducive to learning with the need to ensure that students with disabilities receive a free appropriate public education. The basic tenet of IDEA '97 is that school officials may discipline a student with a disability in the same manner as a student without disabilities, with a few notable exceptions. A major exception is that suspensions may not exceed 10 school days (§ 615[k][1][A][i]). If the student brings a weapon to school, however, removal can be for as long as 45 days. In addition, a hearing officer can order a 45-day change in placement if a student with disabilities presents a substantial risk to the safety of others (§ 615[k][2][A]).

In these instances, the school must develop an appropriate IEP and alternative placement that meets the requirements of a free appropriate public education. Under normal circumstances, however, a review of the relationship between the student's disability and misconduct (termed a *manifestation determination*) must be conducted within 10 days of the action. If a determination is made that no relationship exists between the misconduct and the disability, the same disciplinary procedures should be used as for a student who does not have a disability. Education services, however, must be continued at home during the suspension. If the team finds a relationship between the disability and the disciplinary problem, school officials may seek a change in placement but cannot mandate a long-term suspension or expulsion. Furthermore, there is a "stay-put" provision if parents request a due process hearing. In this case, the school placement is not changed until the hearing process is completed (unless there is a weapons charge).

In terms of avoidance of suspensions, IDEA '97 requires that if a student with a disability has behavior problems, the IEP team should consider strategies such as positive behavior interventions and supports to address these problems. It is mandated that the behavior intervention program should use the principles of functional behavioral analysis (see Chapter 31) and delineate expected behaviors, inappropriate behaviors, and positive and negative consequences.

PROVISION OF SPECIAL EDUCATION SERVICES TO PRIVATE SCHOOLS

IDEA '97 extends some benefits to students in private schools. It requires that local public school districts provide special education and related services to children whom they have referred to a private school. In addition, if a school district fails to provide a free appropriate public education to a student with a disability and the parents unilaterally place their child in a private school, the public school must reimburse the parents for the private school placement (*School Comm. of Burlington v. Department of Ed. of Mass.*, 1985). If the parents, however, choose to place their child in a private school rather than in a public school without first showing that the public school is not providing a free appropriate public education, the public school is not liable for paying expenses. For parents to recover reimbursement for private school placements, four conditions must be met: 1) the student must have been first enrolled in the LEA, 2) the parents must have notified the LEA of their intention to enroll their child in a private school, 3) the LEA must not have consented to or referred the child to the private school; and 4) the LEA must have failed to provide a free appropriate public education in a timely manner.

FEDERAL FUNDING

Federal funding for IDEA '97 services is received by the state education agency and then distributed to the LEA. It should be noted, however, that federal funds cover only about 10% of the total cost of special education services; the remainder is funded by the state and local school districts. Furthermore, the federal government caps the number of students in special education in each state to 12% of the total number of school-age students. Thus, although IDEA '97 is the law of the land, the federal government supports but a fraction of the total costs of special education and related services. This level of funding accounts to some extent for the variability of its application across states and districts. At the federal level, there are ongoing discussions and proposed plans for fully funding IDEA.

APPROACHES FOR PROVIDING SERVICES

If the IEP evaluation determines that a child has a disability that interferes with his or her ability to benefit from the general education curriculum, the multidisciplinary team must determine the level and approach to providing special educational services. The team uses the principle of the least restrictive environment, in which children are educated as much as possible with their peers without disabilities in an inclusive environment. This means that a child with disabilities usually will be educated within the general education classroom, with special supports from the teacher and appropriate modification of schoolwork and assignments. In accordance with the principles of the least restrictive environment, this approach is superior to any placement in which the child with a disability is educated in a segregated environment. Table 30.1 summarizes the different approaches/environments for providing special education services and the distribution of students within these environments in the late 1990s.

Although the inclusivity of the environment is a factor in a student's academic or social success, the classroom environment and quality of instruction are of great importance. The most effective interventions for a student with disabilities have the following components: 1) a case-by-case approach to decision making about the student's instruction and placement, 2) intensive and reasonably individualized instruction combined with close cooperation between the general and special education teachers, and 3) careful and frequent monitoring of the student's progress (Hocutt, 1996; Kauffman, 1995).

INCLUSION PRACTICES

For inclusion to be effective, it cannot simply mean placing a child with a disability in a general education classroom; it must incorporate all of the supports necessary for the child to have access to the core curriculum or to a modification of it. A number of practices have been developed to accomplish this goal. One is *cooperative learning*, a term used to describe a range of team-based learning strategies. Students are divided into small teams with varying abilities and are assigned a task they complete together. Team members monitor, assist, and provide feedback to each other. Methods such as direct instruction, small-group instruction, and independent practice can be combined with cooperative learning to teach skills and information. This strategy may be helpful in teaching both academic and social skills.

A second strategy is peer tutoring, in which one student acts as a teacher, providing instruction to a peer. A third strategy involves the use of instructional tools. These may include mnemonic devices, flow charts, study guides, and role-playing activities. Content enhancement routines that combine an interactive instructional sequence with instructional tools can be particularly helpful when combined with strategies of instruction that assist students in becoming self-regulated learners (Fisher, Schumaker, & Deshler, 1995). Finally, curriculum revisions (accommodations) can be used when teaching more complex subjects, such as math.

ACCOMMODATIONS AND MODIFICATIONS TO THE GENERAL CURRICULUM

Students with disabilities can be supported within the general education curriculum in many ways. An inclusion placement alone is not sufficient to help a student with a disability succeed. Accommodations are defined as changes made in *how* a student has access to the curriculum or demonstrates learning. Accommodations provide equal access to learning, do not substantially change the instructional level or content, are based on individual strengths and needs, and may vary in intensity or degree. Modifications and/or accommodations can also be provided during assessment. Within the classroom, accommodations can be made for organizational problems, for attention difficulties and motivation, for difficulty in content areas such as reading or writing, for auditory processing concerns, or for assessment (CEC & IDEA Partnerships, 2000). In testing situations, *accommodations* usually refer to changes in format, response, environment, timing, or scheduling that do not alter in a significant way what the test measures or the comparability of the scores. In contrast, when changes in the assessment alter what the test is supposed to measure or the comparability of scores, the term *modification* is used.

In addition to supporting students through accommodations and/or modifications, instruction can be differentiated to meet the needs of high-, low-, and average-achieving students with disabilities in the classroom. As each student with a disability has individual interests and learning styles, differentiating instruction is also a way to meet the needs of a diverse class and engage everyone in the learning process (Smith et al., 2000; Tomlinson, 2000). Instructional elements that can be differentiated include content, process, product, and learning environment. Successful differentiation involves ongoing assessment that is closely tied to the curriculum, creating quality work that is interesting and appealing, and using flexible groupings that give students the opportunity to work in a variety of environments and with a mix of their peers (CEC, 1993).

ROLE OF THE SPECIAL EDUCATION TEACHER IN THE GENERAL CURRICULUM

It is the responsibility of the special education teacher to support students who qualify for special education services during instruction in the general education classroom. The amount of support needed depends on the individual needs of the child. The special education teacher may take on one of two roles, that of a collaborator or of a co-teacher. As a collaborator, the special education teacher must familiarize the general education teacher with the adaptations and modifications that will be necessary to enable the child to benefit from instruction in the general education classroom. The two teachers then discuss who will be responsible for which aspects of the student's instructional needs. For a student who needs only limited support, the special education teacher might create modified tests and check on the student at the end of the day to make sure that all of the homework assignments have been written down. On the advice of the special education teacher, the general education teacher might assign only even-numbered test problems or give the student extended time. For a student who needs more extensive supports, the special education teacher may supply adapted assignments that cover the same content as the general education lesson but are at the student's functional level.

As a co-teacher, the special education teacher shares the classroom with a general education teacher. The two teachers share responsibility for all of the students in the class, regardless of ability. The teachers take turns teaching lessons. While one teaches the entire class, the other one helps any students in need. The two teachers may divide the class into small groups for instruction, but grouping is not made according to disability.

RELATED SERVICES

In addition to the academic services provided by the teacher, children with disabilities are eligible to receive related services that enable the child to benefit from general or special education (Table 30.2). According to IDEA '97, these services include

- Speech-language pathology and audiology services
- Psychological services
- Physical and occupational therapy
- Recreation, including therapeutic recreation
- Social work services
- Counseling services, including rehabilitation counseling
- Orientation and mobility services
- Medical services (§ 602[22])

These services can be provided in or outside of the classroom. Services provided in the classroom have the advantage of allowing teachers to know what is going on with their students by integrating the special education services into the general academic curriculum and preventing the children from missing material during a period outside the classroom. In recognition of these benefits, the principle of the least restrictive environment requires that related services be provided in the classroom whenever appropriate.

One type of related services that is changing significantly is medical services. As a result of the 1999 U.S. Supreme Court ruling in the case of *Cedar Rapids Community School District v. Garret F.*, cost cannot be a consideration in providing needed medical related services for a child to receive a free appropriate public education. Thus, children who use technology assistance (see Chapter 32) must be provided the medical supervision necessary for their attendance in the public school.

SUMMARY

Special education and related services are mandated by federal law to be provided to all students with defined disabilities. They are to receive a free appropriate public education in the least restrictive environment. IDEA '97 emphasizes student participation in the general education curriculum. The focus is on how to address the student's needs that result from his or her disability in a way that permits the student to participate, to the greatest possible extent, in the general curriculum offered to all students. A more collaborative relationship between general education and special education teachers is also implied by this law. The most popular approach to providing this service is by inclusion. Whether this is the best approach for all children with disabilities is still unclear, and there remains a spectrum of approaches and strategies to provide special education services. Outcome is best when support services are provided early and in the quantity and quality required for progress to be made. The IEP guides this process, and assessment of progress at regular intervals is critical for success.

Table 30.2. Examples of disabilities and typical related services provided

Disability	Services									
	Speech-language pathology	Audiology	Behavior support and counseling	Physical therapy	Occupational therapy	Vision (orientation and mobility)	Social work	Assistive technology	Transportation	Medical services
Vision impairment	X		X	X	X	X	X	X		
Hearing impairment	X	X	X				X	X		
Mental retardation	X		X				X			
Autism	X		X				X			
Attention-deficit/ hyperactivity disorder			X				X			
Learning disabilities			X				X			
Cerebral palsy	X		X	X	X	X	X	X	X	X
Traumatic brain injury	X		X	X	X	X	X	X	X	X

REFERENCES

Americans with Disabilities Act (ADA) of 1990, PL 101-336, 42 U.S.C. §§ 12101 *et seq.*

Cedar Rapids Community School Dist. v. Garret F., 526 U.S. 66 (1999).

Clark, G., & Patton, J., (1997). *Transition Planning Inventory: Profile and Further Assessment Recommendations Form.* Austin, TX: PRO-ED.

The Council for Exceptional Children (CEC). (1993). *Including students with disabilities in general education classrooms.* Reston, VA: Author. (ERIC Document Reproduction Service No. ED 434435)

The Council for Exceptional Children (CEC). (1998). State-wide assessment programs: Including students with disabilities. *Research Connections in Special Education, 2,* 1–8.

The Council for Exceptional Children (CEC) & IDEA Partnerships. (2000). *Making assessment accommodations: A toolkit for educators.* Reston, VA: Author.

Education for All Handicapped Children Act of 1975, PL 94-142, 20 U.S.C. §§ 1400 *et seq.*

Education of the Handicapped Act Amendments of 1986, PL 99-457, 20 U.S.C. §§ 1400 *et seq.*

Education of the Handicapped Act of 1970 (EHA), PL 91-230, 84 Stat. 121-154, 20 U.S.C. §§ 1400 *et seq.*

Elementary and Secondary Education Act of 1965, PL 89-10, 20 U.S.C. §§ 241 *et seq.*

Fisher, J.B., Schumaker, J.B., & Deshler, D.D. (1995). Searching for validated inclusive practices: A review of the literature. *Focus on Exceptional Children, 28*(4), 1–20.

Hocutt, A.M. (1996). Effectiveness of special education: Is placement the critical factor? *The Future of Children, 6,* 77–102.

Horne, R.L. (1996). The education of children and youth with special needs: What do the laws say? *NICHCY News Digest, 15,* 1–16.

Individuals with Disabilities Education Act Amendments of 1997, PL 105-17, 20 U.S.C. §§ 1400 *et seq.*

Individuals with Disabilities Education Act (IDEA) of 1990, PL 101-476, 20 U.S.C. §§ 1400 *et seq.*

Kauffman, J.M. (1995). Why we must celebrate a diversity of restrictive environments. *Learning Disabilities: Research & Practice, 10,* 225–232.

Mercer, C.D. (1997). *Students with learning disabilities.* Upper Saddle River, NJ: Prentice-Hall.

Pennsylvania Association for Retarded Citizens v. Commonwealth of Pennsylvania, 334 F. Supp. 1257 (E.D. Pa. 1971).

Rehabilitation Act of 1973, PL 93-112, 29 U.S.C. §§ 701 *et seq.*

S. Rpt. No. 105-17 at 2 (1997) (Document No. 941; Filename sr017.105). Retrieved January 22, 2002, from United States Congress Online via GPO Access: http://frwebgate .access.gpo.gov/cgi-bin/useftp.cgi? IPaddress=162.140.64 .21 & filename = sr017.pdf & directory = / diskc/ wais / data / 105_cong_reports

School Comm. of Burlington v. Department of Ed. of Mass., 471 U. S. 359 (1985).

Shriner, J.G., & Spicuzza, R.J. (1995). Procedural considerations in the assessment of students at risk for school failure. *Preventing School Failure, 38,* 33–39.

Smith, T.E.C., Polloway, E.A., Patton, J.R. et al. (2001). *Teaching students with special needs in inclusive settings* (3rd ed.). Needham Heights, MA: Allyn & Bacon.

Tomlinson, C.A. (2000, August). Differentiation of instruction in the elementary grades. *ERIC Digest.* (ERIC Document Reproduction Service No. ED 443572)

U.S. Department of Education, Office of Special Education and Rehabilitative Services (OSERS). (1998). *Twentieth annual report to Congress on the implementation of the Individuals with Disabilities Education Act.* Retrieved January 21, 2002, from http://www.ed.gov/offices/OSERS/OSEP/Research/ OSEP98AnlRpt/

U.S. Department of Education, Office of Special Education and Rehabilitative Services (OSERS). (2000). *Twenty-second annual report to Congress on the implementation of the Individuals with Disabilities Education Act.* Retrieved January 21, 2001, from http://www.ed.gov/offices/OSERS/OSEP/ Products/OSEP2000AnlRpt/ExecSumm.html

Yell, M.L. (1998). *The law and special education.* Upper Saddle River, NJ: Merrill.

Ysseldyke, J.E., & Algozzine, B. (1995). *Special education: A practical approach for teachers.* Boston: Houghton Mifflin.

31 Promoting Adaptive Behavior While Addressing Challenging Behavior

John M. Parrish

Upon completion of this chapter, the reader will:

- be acquainted with selected principles and methods of improving child behavior
- be familiar with clinical and/or medical contexts in which specific behavior strategies and tactics are applicable

The definition of *challenging behavior* depends on who is doing what, who is observing it, under what circumstances it is occurring, and how frequently it occurs. Thus, the "terrible twos" are less acceptable in a 5-year-old; grandparents may be less tolerant of rambunctious behavior than young parents; acceptable behavior at a friend's house differs from acceptable behavior at home; and infrequent mild tantrums are of less concern than tantrums that occur daily. Although children with disabilities often display adaptive behavior, about half of them also exhibit challenging behaviors with enough frequency or severity to interfere with their interpersonal relationships, educational progress, life at home, and/or medical management (Table 31.1). Parents, teachers, and other professionals often adopt informal approaches to address these troubling behaviors or, more important, to support the child in developing adaptive behaviors. With the benefit of professional consultation, however, such efforts can become more creative and systematic and thereby enhance the child's motivation and learning. This chapter provides an overview of selected principles and procedures to support children with disabilities to develop adaptive behavior while addressing their challenging behavior.

ORIGIN OF BEHAVIOR

Our behavior arises from an interaction of genetic and environmental factors. Given our burgeoning knowledge about the human genome and molecular biology, we may soon understand much more about the genetic and biological basis for our behavior. In some cases, we already know that specific genetic defects contribute to maladaptive behavior. Examples include self-injury in Lesch-Nyhan syndrome, tics in Tourette syndrome, hyperphagia in Prader-Willi syndrome, and hand wringing in Rett syndrome. As of 2002, however, environmental events that trigger and serve to maintain either adaptive or challenging behavior have received the most study. They form the basis of applied behavior analysis.

A fundamental assumption underlying child behavior analysis is that both adaptive and aberrant behavior are typically learned (i.e., the child's behavior is largely a result of its immediate **antecedents** and **consequences**). Antecedents are events that trigger a behavior (e.g., teasing that provokes aggression). Consequences are events that follow the behavior (e.g., aggression results in loss of a privilege). Other concurrent events (e.g., the child's level of arousal or fatigue) and historical events (e.g., a recent argument) may influence the child's behavior.

Table 31.1. Common behavioral excesses and impairments in children with disabilities

Aerophagia (excessive swallowing of air)
Aggression
Attentional impairments
Disruptive behavior
Elopement
Excessive activity
Feeding problems (e.g., food selectivity by type or texture)
Hair pulling
Impulsivity
Inappropriate sexual behavior
Lack of community survival skills (e.g., crossing streets safely)
Lack of self-help skills (e.g., dressing, feeding, toileting)
Medical noncompliance (refusal to complete prescribed regimens)
Noncompliance with parental or teacher instructions
Obesity
Pica
Property destruction
Rumination
Self-injury
Sleep disturbances (e.g., spontaneous awakenings)
Social skills impairments
Somatic complaints (e.g., recurrent abdominal pain)
Stereotypies (e.g., hand flapping, arm waving, body rocking)
Tantrums
Thumb sucking
Truancy

Adaptive and challenging behaviors typically serve multiple purposes, even for the same child. Being polite may result in making new friends or in garnering additional praise from a parent. Tantrums may help the child gain access to what he or she wants (e.g., an extra turn in a game), to escape from work or unpleasant situations (e.g., an assigned chore, bedtime), or to attain desired objects or attention.

The goal of a behavior analytic approach to a child's behavior is to enable the child to live as independently as possible while being fully included socially in the least restrictive environments that offer ample opportunity for physical, cognitive, emotional, and social growth and enrichment (Koegel, Koegel, & Dunlap, 1996). Priority is assigned to supporting the child's overall development and quality of life, not merely to ameliorating the child's challenging behavior (Bijou, 1995; Novak, 1996). Accordingly, behavior analysts emphasize opportunities not only for instructional supports regarding adaptive behavior but also for exploration and fun.

Effective intervention also requires accurate identification of events that instigate and maintain challenging behaviors. These events are subsequently altered to decrease challenging behaviors while at the same time teaching **prosocial** (i.e., alternative adaptive) behavior. The behavior selected for assessment and intervention is termed the **target behavior.**

FUNDAMENTAL PRINCIPLES AND PROCEDURES OF APPLIED BEHAVIOR ANALYSIS

There are four principal approaches to applied behavior analysis: positive reinforcement, **planned ignoring (extinction), negative reinforcement,** and **punishment** (Catania, 1984). Figure 31.1 presents a graphic model of each.

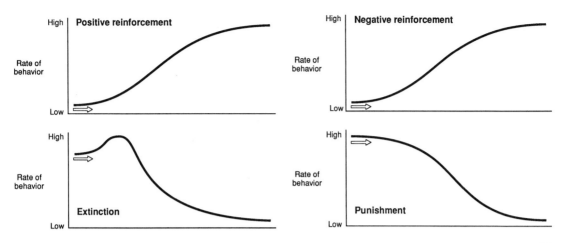

Figure 31.1. The four principal approaches to behavior management are illustrated. Positive and negative reinforcement both result in an increase in the rate of occurrence of a behavior over time, while extinction and punishment procedures reduce the behavior. The arrows indicate baseline observation periods and the arrowhead, the start of the behavior management procedure.

Positive Reinforcement

Positive reinforcement occurs when consequences following a behavior result in an increase in that behavior in the future (Martin & Pear, 1996). For example, when Paul, a 9-year-old boy with mental retardation, receives a compliment for using his utensils correctly during mealtimes, subsequent use of utensils is likely to increase. Such consequences are referred to as **positive reinforcers.** Events that function as positive reinforcers may center on social activities, toys, or food (O'Donahue, 1998). Table 31.2 presents examples of common positive reinforcers.

Positive Side Effects of Positive Reinforcement

Effective use of positive reinforcement not only increases appropriate behavior but also reduces challenging behavior (Parrish et al., 1986). For instance, as Paul's parents acknowledge his display of manners during mealtimes and involve him in casual conversation about his preferred topics, Paul is less likely to be disruptive (e.g., by interrupting adult-to-adult conversations) to attract attention.

Variation in Positive Reinforcers

Reinforcers vary widely in type (i.e., what events the child prefers) and value (i.e., how much the child prefers them) among different children and within each child over time. Reinforcers are defined solely on the basis of their effect on a given child's behavior, not on their form, content, appearance, or assumed value. Every child, without exception, has preferences that can be identified by asking or observing the child, asking others familiar with him or her, and/or by structuring systematic reinforcer assessments (e.g., Fisher et al., 1992). Specific events and items become positive reinforcers for the given child because they have been paired previously with biological essentials (e.g., food, water, warmth) and/or with other events that are already positive reinforcers for the child (e.g., the presence of a friend).

Importance of Selecting Age-Appropriate Reinforcers

Selecting positive reinforcers that are appropriate both for the child's chronological and developmental age is important. For example, given Paul's age and cognitive disability, it would be appropriate to provide him with opportunities to listen to music, look at picture books, or

Table 31.2.   Examples of positive reinforcers

Social reinforcers	Manipulative reinforcers
Affection	Bicycles
Allowing child to be left alone on child's request	Books, magazines
Arranging for child to demonstrate a mastered skill	Computers
Casual conversation	Games
Descriptive praise	Gifts
Gesture of approval	Money
Offering assistance on child's request	Musical instruments
Physical proximity	Pencils, pens, crayons
Talking about topics of interest to child	Small toys (e.g., dolls, ball)
	Tickets to preferred events
Edible reinforcers	**Activity reinforcers**
Celery, carrots	Assembling a puzzle
Chips	Dining at a restaurant
Cookies	Going to an arcade
Crackers	Painting with watercolors
Dry cereals	Playing outside
Fruit	Singing
Ice cream	Talking on the telephone
Juice or soft drinks	Visiting friends
Popcorn	Watching a videotape
Raisins	

enjoy time with friends. Selection of everyday positive reinforcers also is important. For instance, when teaching Paul to say, "Please make me a peanut butter and jelly sandwich," it is better to provide such a sandwich as a reinforcer as opposed to some other arbitrary reinforcer. Use of natural reinforcers increases the likelihood that the newly learned behavior will continue to occur in appropriate, everyday situations.

Factors Influencing the Effectiveness of Positive Reinforcement

Several factors influence the effectiveness of an item or event as a positive reinforcer (Miller, 1980). Effectiveness is enhanced if the event or item is delivered contingently, that is, only when the targeted appropriate behavior occurs. Another key factor is the child's degree of **deprivation** in relation to the specific reinforcing item or event. For instance, if Paul is hungry, a snack may be an effective reinforcer. Offering Paul a snack just after he has had a meal is less likely to be effective, however. Varying the positive reinforcers offered to the child is also important.

Another critical dimension is the timing of reinforcer delivery. Reinforcers may be delivered immediately after a target behavior or on a delayed basis. In general, immediate reinforcement is more effective than delayed reinforcement. With a prolonged time interval, the child may have difficulty understanding the relationship between his or her behavior and the delivery of positive reinforcement. Also, delayed reinforcement for appropriate behavior is likely to reinforce challenging behavior that may have occurred during the interim.

The amount of reinforcement provided is also important. If the child receives a lot of a reinforcer, **satiation** can occur and the reinforcing effect of an item or event will be diminished or temporarily lost. In general, the amount of positive reinforcement provided should be proportional to the effort required of the child to behave appropriately. At the beginning of a program, larger amounts of reinforcement may be needed to establish a desired behavior because more initial effort by the child is required.

A fourth factor influencing effectiveness pertains to the schedule of reinforcement. Positive reinforcement can be provided after a set number of responses have occurred (i.e., **ratio schedules**) or after the passage of a certain amount of time relative to the child's performance (i.e., **interval schedules**). Ratio schedules are typically used when the behavior being reinforced has a definite beginning and end. For instance, Paul receives praise after he puts each toy away or solves two spelling problems. Interval schedules are more suitable when behaviors are continuous or of extended duration. For example, Paul receives praise for playing appropriately with a peer for 3 minutes or doing homework for 10 minutes. Positive reinforcement can also be administered on a continuous or intermittent basis. Continuous reinforcement involves provision of positive reinforcement following every occurrence of a targeted appropriate behavior. All other schedules are intermittent. Continuous reinforcement is often necessary to establish new behaviors. Satiation, however, needs to be avoided. Once a behavior is established, intermittent reinforcement may effectively maintain it.

The quality or value of the positive reinforcer is also important. The more the child values a reinforcer, the more effective it is likely to be. The value of a reinforcer is always relative to other available reinforcers. Positive reinforcers are typically more effective if they are novel and varied. Introducing new reinforcers periodically, and otherwise varying reinforcers previously administered, better ensures that the child does not get too much of any one reinforcer.

Although positive reinforcement procedures can be designed to promote the child's prosocial behavior, in everyday life the process of positive reinforcement also may increase inappropriate behavior unintentionally. For instance, if Paul's father complies with Paul's persistent demands for attention, Paul's attention-seeking behavior may increase in the future.

Planned Ignoring (Extinction)

When a child has received positive reinforcement for misbehavior, that behavior is likely to continue or intensify. In such situations, a procedure termed *planned ignoring* can be effective in decreasing the rate of the challenging behavior (Lerman & Iwata, 1996; Martin & Pear, 1996). Planned ignoring is based on the process of extinction, in which positive reinforcement (e.g., adult attention) is withheld when the child's challenging behavior occurs. For example, if his mother regularly interrupts her telephone conversations to console Paul, he may seek her undivided attention by whining whenever she gets on the telephone. If she, however, continues her telephone conversation, withholding her attention from Paul as long as he continues to whine, his mother is using planned ignoring to minimize the frequency and amount of positive reinforcement he receives for the misbehavior.

Behavior May Worsen Before It Improves

Consistent ignoring of nondangerous, nondestructive behavior (e.g., nagging, whining, crying, complaining, noise-making, talking back) will usually result in an eventual decline in the behavior. The desired effects of planned ignoring, however, are seldom immediate. Often there is a temporary increase, or **extinction burst,** in the frequency and intensity of the challenging behavior before a subsequent reduction (Lerman & Iwata, 1996). For instance, when a parent or teacher first ignores Paul, Paul is likely to whine persistently or have a tantrum. Although this burst of inappropriate behavior may appear to be a setback, it actually indicates that previously dispensed positive reinforcement is the culprit and that planned ignoring is likely to be an effective intervention over time.

Challenging Behavior May Reappear

Even after an undesirable behavior has been extinguished, it may recur. This phenomenon, known as **spontaneous recovery,** occurs when the child tests to see whether his or her old behavior (e.g., whining) results in positive reinforcement, as it once did. If the parent or teacher continues to ignore the behavior, a rapid and sustained decrease in the challenging behavior typically occurs. This illustrates the importance of being consistent when responding to a child's behavior.

Ignoring Challenging Behavior Is Difficult

Routine application of planned ignoring may be difficult because many parents and teachers confuse planned ignoring with "doing nothing," especially when they hold to the notion that they must not allow a child's misbehavior to go unpunished. Furthermore, because planned ignoring sometimes results in the challenging behavior becoming "worse" before it gets "better," it should not be used when the child's challenging behavior places someone's safety (including the child's) at risk or may cause property damage or loss.

Negative Reinforcement

As with positive reinforcement, negative reinforcement leads to an increased frequency of a target behavior (Iwata, 1987). Negative reinforcement occurs when, as a result of an individual's behavior, an unpleasant event is avoided or escaped, causing an increase in this behavior in the future. Examples of negative reinforcement abound in everyday life, such as when someone chooses to use an umbrella to avoid getting wet or duck his or her head when walking under a low tree branch.

Negative Reinforcement Is Not Punishment

Negative reinforcement is often confused with punishment because both processes include an aversive event or outcome. Nonetheless, negative reinforcement and punishment can be distinguished readily, and their effects could not be more dissimilar. The key difference is whether the process increases or decreases the behavior that it follows. If the behavior increases in frequency, reinforcement, whether positive or negative, has occurred. If the behavior decreases in frequency, punishment has occurred.

Negative Reinforcement Can Contribute to Challenging Behavior

As is true with positive reinforcement, negative reinforcement may function to increase unacceptable as well as acceptable behaviors. For example, when Paul's father "gives in" to Paul's tantrums in a public place, Paul receives positive reinforcement for oppositional behavior, and his father's giving in is reinforced negatively via the cessation of Paul's difficult behavior. As a result, Paul is more likely to have a tantrum in a public place when his father denies his request; and his father is more likely to give in if and when Paul's escalating behavior causes a sufficient public disturbance.

Similarly, negative reinforcement processes are at work when a parent chooses to respond to the child's demanding behavior with threats, yelling, or spanking, and the child concedes. As a result of this negative reinforcement, the parent is more likely to rely on coercive interventions in the future when the child's behavior becomes annoying. Hence, the process of negative reinforcement must be used judiciously or it can worsen challenging behaviors on the part of the child, the caregiver, or both.

Punishment

In contrast to positive and negative reinforcement, punishment procedures seek to decrease the occurrence of a behavior (Matson & Taras, 1989). Punishment is frequently thought of as doing something mean or hurtful to someone because that person made a mistake. Yet, the same event that is a positive reinforcer for one person may be another person's punisher. For instance, some people love horror movies; others find it punishing to watch them. Generalizations regarding what is a punisher are unwise. Defining an event or action on the basis of its impact on the behavior that it follows is wiser.

Formats of Punishment

Punishment typically occurs in two formats. A punisher may be applied (**contingent stimulation**) or access to a reinforcer may be withdrawn (**contingent withdrawal**) following the occurrence of a misbehavior (Miller, 1980). For example, when Paul grabs his mother's eyeglasses, she may shout at him, thereby providing punishment via contingent stimulation. When a teacher withdraws recess privileges from Paul after he has broken a classroom rule, she is effecting punishment by contingent withdrawal.

Use of Punishment Is Controversial

The process of punishment is an element of the natural order, just as is gravity. The purposeful use of punishment to effect behavior change, however, is controversial. Skillful behavior analysts altogether avoid or significantly minimize the use of punishment procedures for at least three reasons. First, positive reinforcement strategies are typically as or more effective than punishment. Before a punishment strategy is even considered for implementation in a classroom, the teacher should strive to select a curriculum that is appropriate for the student, define specific learning objectives that are meaningful and functional for the student, and enrich the variety and quality of instruction to augment the student's ability and motivation to learn.

Second, punishment may damage relationships. For instance, before intervening, the teacher should consider the possible adverse impact of each alternative disciplinary tactic on the feelings and behavior of the student. Segregating a student from group instruction for disciplinary reasons may be counterproductive. In fact, suspensions and expulsions often fail to correct challenging behavior and may inadvertently positively reinforce the very behavior they are intended to punish.

Third, punishment procedures can be misapplied and cause harm (Harris & Handleman, 1990; Matson & DiLorenzo, 1983; Repp & Singh, 1990). Excessive use of punishment can spawn a vicious cycle of coercive and potentially abusive behavior (Patterson, 1982). Less restrictive and less intrusive strategies that emphasize positive reinforcement for desired behavior should be attempted first and are typically found to be sufficient.

Purposes of Punishment

Punishment procedures should be considered only to reduce challenging behaviors that may cause some injury to the child or others. When used, they should be monitored and evaluated throughout the entire period of their application by an expert to ensure that they are warranted; implemented safely and correctly; and are not overused, misused, or abused. They are also best implemented in conjunction with positive reinforcement strategies, thereby providing differential consequences for appropriate versus inappropriate behavior.

SELECTED INSTRUCTIONAL PROCEDURES

Differential Reinforcement

In many cases, several inappropriate behaviors, as well as a number of adaptive behaviors, are targeted for change. Correspondingly, positive reinforcement and planned ignoring are often used in combination through a process termed **differential reinforcement**. The purpose of differential reinforcement is to reinforce acceptable behavior while simultaneously withholding reinforcement for challenging behavior. This is the essence of promoting adaptive behavior while addressing challenging behavior. For example, the teacher ignores Paul when he speaks out of turn but calls on him when he raises his hand. Table 31.3 presents selected types of differential reinforcement.

Table 31.3. Selected types of differential reinforcement

Type	Goal	Example
DRO (differential reinforcement of other behavior)	Absence of targeted problem behavior during observation interval	Child may continue to play team sport during recess so long as aggression does not occur.
DRA (differential reinforcement of appropriate behavior)	Increased occurrence of targeted appropriate behavior in absence of targeted inappropriate behavior	Child is acknowledged for sharing; child's dawdling is ignored.
DRC (differential reinforcement of communicative skill)	Increased occurrence of functional communication skill	Child uses functional speech to request help (e.g., "Help me...") rather than aggression against teacher to escape from academic demand.
DRI (differential reinforcement of incompatible behavior)	Increased occurrence of a targeted appropriate behavior that is incompatible with a targeted problem behavior	Child's "on task" behavior is reinforced; child's "off task" behavior is not reinforced.
DRL (differential reinforcement of low-rate behavior)	Occurrence of challenging behavior at acceptably low rates	Child receives privilege contingent on low rates of complaining.

Differential reinforcement often is preferred over planned ignoring because it is more effective for teaching the child with disabilities that specific behaviors are appropriate and others are not. The effectiveness of differential reinforcement depends not only on the consistency of its administration, but also on the unavailability of positive reinforcement for challenging behavior. For example, if Paul receives positive reinforcement (e.g., laughter) from his fellow students for speaking out of turn, the teacher's efforts to ignore this behavior will probably be ineffective. Consistent application of differential reinforcement by numerous caregivers across diverse environments and situations is required for behavior change to occur and endure.

Instructional and Imitation Training

With many children with disabilities, it is sufficient to simply "show and tell" when teaching new behaviors while using differential reinforcement procedures. During **instructional training,** the teacher 1) describes the behavior he or she wants, 2) asks the child to perform the described action, 3) gives the child a supervised opportunity to initiate and complete the directed activity, and 4) and provides positive reinforcement upon satisfactory completion of the task. In **imitation training,** the teacher 1) demonstrates what the child is to do, 2) asks the child to repeat the action, 3) gives the child an opportunity to initiate and complete the targeted activity, and 4) provides the child with positive reinforcement when the task is completed. Imitation training requires less verbal skill and is often used when the child's receptive vocabulary is limited. When the child learns how to follow directions and to imitate what is observed, then the child is better able to learn important daily living and social skills that prevent or replace challenging behaviors (Martin & Pear, 1996).

Compliance Training

Some children first need to learn how to follow instructions through highly systematic teaching. **Compliance training** is often a pivotal intervention for children with disabilities. Teaching a child to follow directions and to complete requested actions independently facilitates cooperative learning and has been found to prevent or significantly reduce the occurrence of challenging behaviors (Parrish et al., 1986). During compliance training, the instructor orients the child to attend to the instructor and then issues a developmentally appropriate "do" request. A "do" request is a statement that specifies an action (e.g., "give me 10 pennies"). The instructor issues the "do" request using a firm, but matter-of-fact tone. The instructor then waits quietly for about 10–20 seconds (the duration of the wait is dependent on the complexity of the requested action), giving the child an opportunity to follow through. The instructor avoids nagging, lecturing, or apologizing for the request. If the child complies with the developmentally appropriate request, the instructor provides praise and perhaps a **tangible** item (e.g., a raisin) as well.

If the child does not comply, the instructor reissues the request using the same words and tone. The only change in the procedure is that the instructor pairs the repetition of the verbal request with a gesture, such as pointing to the pennies and then to the instructor's outstretched hand. The instructor waits quietly. If the child complies with the first repetition of the request, the instructor provides praise but not a tangible reinforcer. If the child again does not comply, the caregiver immediately provides gentle physical guidance (e.g., a light touch) to assist the child in completing the requested action. Verbal requests and gestural hints, and contingent reinforcement are faded gradually as the child increasingly demonstrates independent task completion (see Forehand & Long, 1996; Forehand & McMahon, 1981; and Foxx, 1982b).

Building Momentum

Sometimes standard methods of teaching the child to follow instructions are unsuccessful. In such cases, it is helpful to identify requests to which the child has complied routinely. These requests are termed "high-p," which is an abbreviation for high probability. Once high-p requests are identified, the instructor issues a few of them one at a time, in sequence, prior to issuing a "low-p" request to which the child has seldom complied. For example, Paul frequently refuses to get ready for bed. Upon request, however, he often agrees to sing his favorite song, go to his bedroom to get a preferred book, and exchange "high fives." Knowing these "high-p" requests, his mother works to build behavioral momentum with Paul when redirecting him to begin his bedtime routine. She first issues the three "high-p" requests and excitedly acknowledges his compliance with each. Then, she firmly but matter-of-factly asks him to get dressed for bed. (For more information about building behavioral momentum as a means of promoting compliance, see Mace et al., 1990).

Shaping Through Graduated Guidance and Guided Compliance

Among children with more severe disabilities, the desired behavior may not yet be in the child's repertoire at all or may occur infrequently. More is needed than simply issuing an instruction, demonstrating an appropriate behavior, or building momentum. Often the child exhibits challenging behaviors because he or she has not learned how to respond appropriately. Through a systematic procedure known as **shaping**, new prosocial behaviors can be built and added to the child's skill base. Gradual development of a new behavior is encouraged by reinforcing small advances or improvements in the child's repertoire. Training and reinforcement occur in a step-by-step manner in which each step toward skillful demonstration of the target behavior is reinforced. As steps are performed more and more consistently, they are no longer reinforced. Reinforcement, however, continues to be provided for performing new or more advanced steps. As the skill is shaped, the amount of structure and degree of direct involvement by the instructor is gradually faded away, so the child eventually demonstrates skill mastery independently (Martin & Pear, 1996).

For instance, Paul is taught to self-feed. Initially, he receives praise paired with a preferred treat for merely touching his spoon. Once Paul consistently touches the spoon, positive reinforcement is discontinued for spoon touching, and he receives positive reinforcement only if he grasps the spoon. When Paul grasps the spoon independently on a consistent basis, he is then required to grasp the spoon and move it toward his mouth to receive reinforcement. This procedure continues until the target behavior, self-feeding, is learned.

Prompting

A desired behavior can be developed through the use of **graduated guidance** and **guided compliance.** Here, *graduated* refers to providing only that level of assistance (i.e., guidance) necessary for the child to complete a task satisfactorily. Graduated guidance involves using **prompts** (e.g., verbal, gestural, manual, visual, or auditory cues) that direct the child to participate in a targeted activity (e.g., sharing, waiting, putting on a shirt). Table 31.4 presents examples of prompts. Guided compliance involves the use of graduated guidance in the context of compliance training, which attempts to teach the child to accomplish tasks independently.

Teaching in a Functional Context

For graduated guidance and guided compliance to be effective, instructors must select developmentally appropriate activities that fit the situation in which instruction is to take place (Horner, Sprague, & Flannery, 1993). For example, graduated guidance could be used to teach Paul to select a coat appropriate to the weather. With graduated guidance, less is better than more. The minimum number of cues necessary to accomplish the targeted activity should be provided.

Forward Chaining

Graduated guidance and guided compliance are often used to teach a sequence of skills (Foxx, 1982a), such as toothbrushing, using the toilet, and getting dressed. During **forward chaining,** the initial step (i.e., skill) in the sequence is taught first; the last skill is taught last. For instance, if Paul were learning to brush his teeth independently, he would first receive the minimal assistance necessary for him to grasp and hold a toothbrush, at which point he would receive a reinforcer. Next, he would be guided to wet the toothbrush, receive a reinforcer, apply toothpaste, receive a reinforcer, and so forth.

Backward Chaining

Sometimes it is more effective to teach the child skills in the reverse order, using a technique called **backward chaining** (Foxx, 1982a). This makes sense when the child's repertoire is very limited and the last step in the sequence is associated with a potent positive reinforcer. In this event, Paul would first learn the last step in the sequence. For example, if Paul were to learn to use a spoon for feeding, he would first be assisted minimally to place a spoon loaded with his preferred food in his mouth. Then he would learn how to balance a loaded spoon when carrying it from a dish toward his mouth. Then he would learn how to load the spoon and place it in his mouth, and so on.

Adjusting Amount of Guidance

Usually, when graduated guidance is implemented, the entire skill sequence is completed. Graduated guidance is especially helpful to the child who does not understand verbal or gestural prompts or the child whose motivation to respond to such prompts is insufficient. During the graduated guidance procedure, the amount of the instructor's gentle guidance is adjusted frequently, depending on the child's behavior. The degree of graduated guidance provided can range from full to partial, from guidance to **shadowing.** The instructor provides only that amount of gentle guidance required for the child to initiate the requested action and decreases the guidance gradually as the child develops the needed skills.

Moving from Full to Partial Guidance

The degree of required guidance varies from one individual to the next and within each individual over time. During **full graduated guidance,** the instructor keeps his or her hands in full contact with the child's hands throughout the planned activity and provides descriptive

Table 31.4.   Selected types of prompts

Prompt	Example
Verbal	Teacher says "Paul, please turn to page 20 of your math book and complete the word problems."
Gestural	Parent points to pepper shaker while saying "Paul, please pass the pepper."
Manual	Occupational therapist provides hand-over-hand guidance while saying "Paul, pick up your pencil and write your name."
Visual	Teacher scores Paul's completed seatwork with a red pencil. Teacher says "Paul, please rework the problems circled in red."
Auditory	When bell rings, Paul proceeds to his next class.

praise whenever the child completes the targeted task. For example, Paul receives guidance to load his spoon with mashed potatoes. As the spoon is being loaded, the instructor says "Paul, good scooping! You have a spoonful of mashed potatoes to enjoy now!" With **partial graduated guidance,** the instructor does less and less as the child's learning proceeds. The instructor uses minimal physical contact and verbal encouragement as long as the activity is continued independently. In this way, the instructor adjusts his or her effort according to the child's skill and motivational level to complete the task.

Shadowing

Once the child reliably completes the activity while requiring less and less guidance, the instructor begins to shadow. This involves the instructor keeping his or her hands within an inch or so of the child's hands, as the child proceeds to complete the task. If and when the child ceases to complete the activity or makes a mistake, the caregiver provides only that degree of partial guided compliance necessary for the child to complete the task. During shadowing, the instructor issues verbal prompts, as needed, and provides praise. In this way, the instructor gradually reduces the child's reliance on physical prompts while increasing the extent to which the child is guided and motivated solely by verbal prompts. Thus, the child simultaneously acquires a skill, learns to demonstrate it more and more independently, and learns to follow verbal instructions. The use of shadowing is then faded out by gradually increasing the distance between the child's hands and the instructor's hands. (For more information about graduated guidance, see Foxx, 1982a.)

Fading Prompts and Positive Reinforcement

The long-term use of prompts and positive reinforcement can be time and labor intensive. It may foster dependency in the child. **Fading** is a process by which prompts and/or positive reinforcers are withdrawn gradually, such that the child participates in a target activity competently while being less and less reliant on systematic cues and consequences (Martin & Pear, 1996). For example, initially Paul's mother verbally prompts Paul to put his lunch money in his pocket prior to leaving home. When Paul complies, she provides him with an extra quarter. Later, he receives praise only for doing this without prompts. Eventually prompts and reinforcers are no longer needed, although his mother occasionally comments on how pleased she is when Paul leaves home with lunch money on his own.

Use of fading increases the likelihood that desired behaviors will occur spontaneously and in situations other than the one(s) in which training occurred. Fading can be accomplished by decreasing the frequency of prompts preceding a target behavior or by delaying use of prompts. Similarly, fading can be achieved by decreasing the frequency and amount of reinforcement provided following a target behavior or by requiring more occurrences of a target behavior before providing a reinforcer.

BEHAVIORAL DIAGNOSIS AND TREATMENT

Table 31.5 outlines the steps required for the design and implementation of an effective behavior management program. These steps are differential diagnosis, examining setting events, treatment planning and intervention, prioritizing target behaviors, considering the importance of functional equivalence, providing parent education and case-centered consultation, fading the intervention and programming for generalization, and follow-up assessment and care.

Differential Diagnosis

Assessment techniques include semistructured interviews with key informants (e.g., parents, teachers), administration and scoring of questionnaires and rating scales, viewing of available videotapes, and direct observation of the child's target behavior(s) during interactions with specific individuals and environmental conditions. During interviews, the behavior analyst first obtains an overall evaluation of the child's challenging behaviors. Measures such as the Parent Rating Scales of the Behavior Assessment System for Children (BASC; Reynolds & Kamphaus, 1992) and the Child Behavior Checklist (CBCL; Achenbach, 1991a, 1991b, 1991c; Achenbach & Rescorla, 2000) are often incorporated into the interview.

The behavior analyst then either 1) selects measures focused on a particular problem (e.g., aggression) or on a specific diagnosis (e.g., attention-deficit/hyperactivity disorder) or 2) develops individually tailored assessment tools (see Kamphaus & Frick, 1996; Mash & Terdal, 1997). Detailed assessments of the behaviors of greatest concern are then completed. The analyst helps informants describe target behaviors through greater reliance on verbs than adjectives. For instance, the informant may initially describe the child as being "hyperactive," "stubborn," and "lazy." More useful definitions of these concerns may become "leaves seat without permission more than once per minute," "satisfactorily responds to fewer than three of every five requested actions," and "does not initiate accurate and timely completion of assigned seatwork or homework."

Table 31.5. Typical steps during construction of behavior management program

1. Differential diagnosis	Review available records; conduct clinical interview; complete rating scales and questionnaires; view videotapes; make direct observations; do descriptive analyses; conduct functional assessments; and do functional analyses to 1) define target behaviors operationally, 2) pinpoint conditions under which they occur, 3) collect baseline data, and 4) determine environmental variables that maintain and/or exacerbate problem behavior.
2. Treatment planning	Design protocols based on differential diagnosis; protocols specify what is to be done, how, by whom, and when; protocols articulate "do's and don'ts" in everyday language, how to assess progress, expected effects, common pitfalls, and clinical/ethical safeguards.
3. Intervention	Parents, teachers, other direct services providers undergo training in effective and safe implementation of recommended protocol(s) prior to intervention; obtain data; direct management decisions on whether to continue, revise, or discontinue protocol(s) in effect.
4. Fading intervention	Upon stabilization of occurrence of newly acquired skills, contingencies are gradually withdrawn.
5. Programming generalization	Effort is made to demonstrate behavioral progress across people, behaviors, settings, other environmental conditions, and time.
6. Follow-up assessment/care	Individual's performance is monitored regularly, with remedial therapy provided as indicated.

The informants are then guided to describe the frequency, duration, and/or intensity of each behavior of concern. The analyst is likely to ask where and under what conditions each behavior does or does not occur. Upon identifying the setting(s) of the target behaviors, the analyst then seeks to ascertain the specific environmental conditions (i.e., variables or factors) that precipitate or maintain the challenging behavior. Those events that typically precede or trigger the behavior (i.e., antecedents) are carefully identified. For example, Paul's tantrums may often be preceded by an adult's instruction for him to complete a difficult task or by denial of Paul's request for a toy. See Luiselli and Cameron (1998) for an in-depth account of how to assess antecedent causes and how to rearrange the day-to-day environment to provide improved antecedent supports for the individual.

Behavior is also a function of its consequences. The behavior analyst defines the events or conditions that typically follow the occurrence of the target behavior(s). Many challenging behaviors are followed, and thereby maintained, by positive or negative reinforcement. For instance, Paul's tantrums may be reinforced positively if his parents console him. Alternatively, withdrawal of a request for Paul to complete a task or completing the task for him allows him to avoid or escape from performing the task, thereby providing negative reinforcement. The behavior analyst assesses the consequences that occur in response to the target behavior(s).

The behavior analyst works to determine the specific functions (i.e., motivational factors) served by the challenging behavior and the environmental variables that support the continuance of this behavior (Iwata et al., 1993; Mace et al., 1993). In fact, more and more professionals in the field of applied behavior analysis are moving away from adopting teaching and behavior reduction strategies merely based on their understanding of the "laws" of behavior and are increasingly determining their interventions through the generation and testing of motivational hypotheses in individual circumstances. Application of tactics derived from data-based hypothesis testing reflects a heightened sensitivity on the part of behavior analysts to individual differences that arise in motivation and learning among all people, including those with developmental disabilities. (For more information about the importance of hypothesis-testing in behavioral diagnosis and interventions based upon hypothesis testing, see Carr, 1994; Carr et al., 1994; Horner & Carr, 1997; Jackson & Panyan, 2002; Lohrmann-O'Rourke, Knoster, & Llewellyn, 1999; Repp, 1999; and Vittimberga, Scotti, & Weigle, 1999.)

Examining Setting Events (Establishing Operations)

Increasingly, behavior analysts recognize that influences other than those that occur immediately before or after the target behavior are important determinants of that behavior (Carr, Reeve, & Magito-McLaughlin, 1996). Events that are more complex or temporally distant also influence current behavior. For example, complex concurrent factors, such as physiological variables including fatigue, deprivation, satiation, infections, discomfort, and pain, influence how the child with disabilities responds. Other complex concurrent factors include the presence or absence of other people, amount of space available, access to alternative or preferred activities, and level of task difficulty or preference.

In addition to concurrent factors, prior events influence a child's behavior. For example, Paul's aggression against a classroom peer on a Monday morning may be related to an argument he had with his father during the previous weekend, a history of being teased by the peer, or having been corrected for mistakes by his teacher earlier that morning. Such historical events are no longer available as immediate stimuli, but they may nonetheless contribute to current arousal states that continue over time and may compound the influence of current triggering events, such as the peer's refusing to share a snack with Paul. Identification of previous or concurrent influences (also referred to as *setting events* or *establishing operations*) is important to the selection and use of effective behavior management strategies. (For more information about setting events and establishing operations, see Horner et al., 1996; Kennedy, 1994; Kennedy & Itkonen, 1993; and Vollmer & Iwata, 1991.)

Additional relevant information is often obtained, including accounts of previous efforts to teach or address target behavior(s), prior professional contacts to resolve reported concerns, pertinent medical history, current medications and dosages, present school placement and academic status, daily routines, and potential obstacles to delivery of indicated services. Particular attention is dedicated to an understanding of the child's strengths. A focus on the child's endearing qualities and what the child enjoys and does well (i.e., the child's preferences and skills) serves to orient adult caregivers to relate (i.e., "listen") to children with disabilities warmly, compassionately, and with respect (Lovett, 1996). The behavior analyst aims to design interventions based on the child's competencies and choices. The behavior analyst also identifies the child's preferred objects, activities, events, and treats, in preparation for development of a program centered on positive reinforcement.

Whenever practicable, the behavior analyst observes videotapes of the child's behavior at home and at school and observes the target behavior(s) directly. Table 31.6 presents definitions and examples of the methods/measures of direct observation typically used.

Behavior analysts increasingly conduct systematic observations of the target behavior(s) using **descriptive and functional analysis** (Iwata et al., 1982; Iwata et al., 1993; Mace et al., 1993; Sasso et al., 1992). Descriptive analysis involves observation of the child's behavior during routine activities that are often associated with either a very high or a very low frequency of the target behavior(s). The aim is to conduct each activity in a routine manner while providing typical antecedents and consequences.

On the basis of interviews and completion of rating scales and questionnaires (e.g., the Motivation Assessment Scale, Durand, 1988), as well as direct observations, the behavior analyst develops hypotheses regarding the roles played by different antecedents and consequences in eliciting (i.e., precipitating) or maintaining the target behavior(s). For example, specific hypotheses may implicate the role of adult or peer attention, access to reinforcers contingent on the challenging behavior, or avoidance of or escape from demands. These hypotheses are then tested under conditions of varying levels of control in which the hypothesized environmental variables are manipulated more or less systematically to determine their effects on the frequency, duration, and intensity of the target behavior(s).

For instance, to test whether Paul's disruptive behavior is precipitated by attention given to him, a series of observational trials may be conducted during which an adult, on a rotating basis, does the following: 1) withholds attention until Paul becomes disruptive, 2) enables Paul

Table 31.6. Definitions and examples of typical methods and measures of direct observation

Method	Description	Example
Yes/no determination	Record of whether a target behavior occurred during one preset interval	"Yes" indicates Paul took a multivitamin as prescribed.
Frequency count	Tally of each occurrence of target behavior	Series of check marks indicates how many times Paul had tantrums during one targeted afternoon.
Outcome recording	Record of whether desired outcome occurred	Paul is asked to clean his room by 7 P.M.; at this time, his room is checked.
Event recording	Record of specific occurrence of a target behavior and its antecedents and consequences	The following events are recorded in a log: Paul is criticized by a classmate; Paul hits classmate; classmate cries.
Time sampling	Periodic observation of high-rate target behavior	Paul is observed as being "in seat" or "out of seat" at each half-hour.
Interval recording	Record of occurrence of target behavior during a series of timed intervals	Frequency of sharing within 60 15-second intervals during 15 minutes of direct observation is recorded.

to avoid or escape from a chore contingent on disruptive behavior, or 3) offers Paul access to a preferred activity or toy contingent on disruptive behavior (Cooper et al., 1990; Derby et al., 1992; Northup et al., 1991). If the rate of disruptive behavior is highest during the first or third phases, then the role of positive reinforcement by way of contingent adult attention or access to preferred events, respectively, is provisionally implicated as a causative factor. If the rate of disruptive behavior is highest during the second phase, then the role of negative reinforcement is suggested. (To obtain more information about the methods of descriptive and functional analysis, see O'Neill et al., 1990; Reichle & Wacker 1993; and Van Houten & Axelrod, 1993.)

Treatment Planning and Intervention

At the conclusion of the initial assessment sequence, the behavior analyst consults with the family to discuss whether intervention is warranted and, if so, what form it should take. Every effort is made to incorporate the individual child's and family's perspectives and preferences in the planning of the child's instructional or behavior reduction program. This effort is often termed *person-* or *family-centered planning*. Furthermore, care is taken to design an acceptable context in which treatment can be effective (Favell & McGimsey, 1993; Horner et al., 1993; Van Houten et al., 1998). Family members receive the necessary training and consultation to make informed decisions as advocates for the child. The behavior analyst then works with the child and family to develop individually tailored interventions based on the systematic assessments just completed. (For more information about designing appropriate and effective interventions, see Albin et al., 1996; Axelrod et al., 1993; Carr et al., 1994; Jackson & Leon, 1998; Jackson & Panyan, 2002; Jones & Jones, 1998; Knoster & Bambara, 1998; Ruef et al., 1998; and Scotti & Meyer, 1999). Once the indicated interventions are defined and begun, the behavior analyst provides instruction to empower family members so that they can implement the interventions that meet with the child and family's approval. Interventions typically involve direct learning trials with the child, parent education and training, and teacher/staff consultation. Interventions are typically aimed at strengthening the child's repertoire of skills more than at the child's diagnosis per se. During parent education and teacher consultation sessions, the behavior analyst recommends problem-specific protocols designed to enable these key care providers to implement interventions in the home, school, and community.

Prioritizing Target Behaviors

Factors frequently considered when prioritizing among target behaviors are 1) the availability of effective interventions, 2) the relative severity of each presenting challenging behavior, 3) the degree of effort and skill required of the child and primary care providers to implement the recommended problem-specific protocols, and 4) the preferences of the child and care providers. Behaviors that can be addressed solely through positive reinforcement strategies and other **positive practices** or dangerous/destructive behaviors that require immediate attention are often selected for intervention first. Interventions for behaviors that are not dangerous or destructive yet are relatively difficult to address may be delayed until some success has been achieved in implementing basic interventions that work with less difficult behaviors.

Considering the Importance of Functional Equivalence

If, as a result of competently delivered interventions, the child acquires an adaptive behavior that serves a function equivalent to that of a problematic behavior, then the child will increasingly display acceptable behavior accompanied by a concomitant decrease in challenging behavior (Carr, 1988). For example, higher rates of self-injurious behavior are often associated with impairments in communication skills (Carr et al., 1994; Durand, 1990). The acquisition and use of appropriate communication responses that are functionally equivalent to the challenging behavior have been demonstrated to be an effective intervention for many difficult behaviors (Carr & Durand, 1985a, 1985b; Carr et al., 1994). Through functional communication training, the child learns to exhibit communicative responses (e.g., using words, gesturing, signing, pressing **microswitches**) that provide the same positive or negative reinforcement as the challenging behavior to be replaced. Typically, speech is the modality of choice because of its universality. If, through differential reinforcement, the child's communicative response results in more positive reinforcement than the challenging behavior, then a reduction in the challenging behavior should occur. For example, rather than disrupt a peer to acquire the teacher's attention, the student learns to ask, "Am I doing good work?" Rather than have a tantrum to avoid work, the student learns to say, "Help me, please." Similarly, rather than take something without asking for permission, the child learns to ask, "May I have that?" Independent communication is a pivotal skill that facilitates learning and social relationships. (For more information about functional communication training as a means of teaching communication skills while managing challenging behavior, see Carr et al., 1994; Durand, 1990; and Reichle & Wacker, 1993.)

Providing Parent Education

Parent education and training procedures range from informal tips extended to parents on the telephone to intensive, highly structured curricula presented over a series of sessions (Sanders, 1998b). These procedures are often supplemented by "how to" books on child behavior management and articles, lectures, and workshops on effective parenting. Numerous books regarding child behavior management are available for parents (e.g., Baker & Brightman, 1997; Blechman, 1985; Christophersen, 1988; Garber, Garber, & Spizman, 1987; Koegel, Koegel, Kellegrew, et al., 1996; Sanders, 1998a).

Intensive programs usually begin with the behavior analyst describing the procedures to be implemented in the home and community, along with a rationale for their use. Predicted effects and possible side effects are reviewed. Common challenges and pitfalls are anticipated. Once the plan of action is determined, a major aspect of many intervention packages is competency-based training of the child care providers. Such training consists of the following steps: 1) identification of target skills; 2) breakdown of these skills into specific steps to be taught; 3) identification of each learner's skills prior to training; and 4) provision of systematic training through verbal description, modeling, and practice. Assessment of the learner's skill acquisition is ongoing, with remedial instruction provided when indicated.

Often, the behavior analyst gives the parents a brief written protocol that is procedure- or problem-specific. These protocols serve as easy-to-use summaries of do's and don'ts. Parents are frequently given homework assignments to implement newly learned intervention strategies while collecting data to determine the impact of their efforts on the child's target behavior. Homework assignments and obtained data are reviewed during subsequent sessions. When necessary, previously recommended intervention protocols are revised. Ideally, parent education and training sessions continue until the following three criteria are met: 1) the parents demonstrate mastery of requisite intervention strategies; 2) the parents show evidence that such strategies are in routine use; and 3) the child's behavior displays stable improvement.

Providing Case-Centered Consultation

Approaches to consultation with teachers and care providers are similar to those used with parents. Consultation usually begins with a telephone contact and brief interview, followed by a field visit at the site where care is provided to the child. During a school visit, for example, the behavior expert usually conducts a semistructured interview and may ask the teacher to respond to selected rating scales and questionnaires. Together, the consultant and teacher examine the key parameters of the child's target behaviors, often observing and recording the target behaviors to obtain objective **baseline** measures. The consultant recommends observational procedures and periodically returns to the classroom to assist the teacher in obtaining valid data regarding the child's behavior.

Once relevant baselines have been established, the consultant collaborates with the teacher to design an intervention program and, if necessary, to demonstrate selected intervention procedures. The teacher is often given an opportunity to practice intervention tactics while the consultant observes and offers feedback. Consultants usually choose positive reinforcement interventions designed to increase appropriate behavior. In many cases, the consultant simultaneously collaborates with the child's parents to initiate a home-based program designed to supplement the school-based interventions. The teacher and parents are guided to collaborate effectively with one another via daily school–home communication systems. (See Kelly, 1990, for details regarding design and implementation of school–home communication systems.)

Several works written for professional behavior analysts who provide parent education and training, and/or consultation to professional and paraprofessional care providers are available (e.g., Aaron & Joshi, 1992; Bagnato & Neisworth, 1991; Barkley, 1990; Bradley-Johnson & Lesiak, 1989; Carr et al., 1994; Christophersen, 1994; Christophersen & Mortweet, 2001; Dangel & Polster, 1988; Durand, 1990; Forehand & McMahon, 1981; Foxx, 1982a, 1982b; Horne & Sayger, 1990; Marks, 1995; Reichle & Wacker, 1993; Rosenfeld & Gravois, 1995; Schaefer & Briesmeister, 1989; Shapiro, 1989; Shapiro & Cole, 1994).

Fading Intervention and Programming for Generalization

A child's behavior differs from one situation to the next. If a behavior is reinforced repeatedly (either positively or negatively) in a particular situation, it is likely to recur in that situation. It also may occur in similar situations. Examples of such transfer of behavior across environments (i.e., *stimulus generalization*) are common in everyday life.

Generalization occurs across behaviors as well as across situations. Changing one behavior often may cause changes in other behaviors. This is termed *response generalization.* For instance, positive reinforcement of a child's compliance with adult requests also may result in reductions in aggression, disruption, and property destruction. Reinforcement of a behavior may increase the frequency of behaviors that are similar in form or function.

Behavior analysts usually evaluate and address specific target behaviors in specific environments. For example, the behavior analyst may target for change Paul's aggression against a particular peer. The procedures described previously often result in substantive improvements. Such outcomes are of little benefit, however, if intervention effects do not endure or do not generalize to new situations and behaviors. Unfortunately, the impact of treatment is sometimes highly specific and temporary.

Behavior analysts use various strategies to ensure that positive outcomes maintain (i.e., extend over time) and generalize (i.e., transfer, spread) across situations and behaviors (Dunlap, 1996; Stokes & Baer, 1977). One of the most common strategies is referred to as **sequential modification.** If desired changes in behavior are not observed to occur across environments and behaviors, concrete steps are taken to introduce the effective intervention (e.g., positive reinforcement) to each of the behaviors or environments to which transfer of effects is inadequate. For instance, Paul is learning to follow instructions issued by each of his five teachers. The initial intervention has been demonstrated to be effective in two of the five classrooms. In this instance, the intervention is refined further and introduced sequentially into each of the other three classrooms. This altered intervention is continued until Paul follows instructions issued by every teacher.

A second strategy is to bring the target behavior under the control of consequences that occur every day. The behavior analyst sets "behavior traps." For example, when teaching Paul to share, the instructor may offer praise and tokens each time Paul shares. As Paul increasingly initiates sharing, peers become more cooperative and increasingly reciprocate. Such cooperation and reciprocal reinforcement may be sufficient to sustain (i.e., "trap") Paul's sharing without continuation of the instructor's contingent praise and tokens.

Offering multiple examples of the desired behavior during training is a third method of increasing maintenance and generalization. This involves providing the child with opportunities to observe and practice newly acquired skills across slightly altered situations. For example, if the target skill is learning how to engage in conversation, Paul is given opportunities to initiate conversation with many different people in different contexts. The instructor prompts Paul to select one of several available topics for conversation and then introduces Paul to several people with whom he is to discuss the chosen topic. This continues until Paul demonstrates a generalized ability to converse.

Maintenance and generalization also may be promoted through training loosely, that is, by teaching a behavior imprecisely in poorly controlled environments. For instance, if Paul learns to speak only when spoken to, he will be at a loss when encountering someone who is reticent to speak. If Paul, however, learns to initiate conversation as well as to continue it, his skills may become proficient across diverse, nonstructured environments with different people.

When the instructional focus is to facilitate the child's acquisition of new skills, it is important that the contingencies in effect be clear and be consistently applied. When the goal is to enhance the maintenance and generalization of an already acquired skill, however, use of unclear and inconsistent contingencies may be indicated. Here, contingencies are arranged so that the child cannot easily distinguish whether or not they are in effect. As a result, the child behaves acceptably across many situations and people in hopes of receiving positive reinforcement while avoiding punishment. For example, Paul's father aims to manage four of Paul's inappropriate behaviors (i.e., tantrums, object-throwing, talking back, cursing) by occasionally putting contingencies in effect for only one or two of these behaviors. Paul is not informed which behaviors do or do not "count." By bedtime, if the rate of occurrence of the target behavior is below a preset criterion frequency, Paul earns a privilege.

Another method to support maintenance and transfer of appropriate behavior is to use the same materials under the same conditions during training as the child will use in everyday situations. This is termed *programming for common stimuli*. For instance, when teaching a child with physical disabilities how to use a wheelchair, it is optimal to introduce the child to the wheelchair to be used everyday and to teach the child how to maneuver it in the context of daily routines in his or her home, school, and community.

If the child can learn to direct his or her own behavior, lessons learned are more likely to maintain and transfer across relevant environments. This may require teaching children general-case problem-solving and choice-making skills. Teaching children with disabilities to exercise choice and to make sound decisions independently is another major focus of behavior analysts (see Bannerman et al., 1990; Guess, Benson, & Siegel-Causey, 1985; and Houghton, Bronicki, & Guess, 1987). Research has demonstrated that many children with disabilities can learn to monitor their own behavior, establish performance criteria for reinforcement, and ascertain the amount of positive reinforcement earned. For example, it may be feasible to teach Paul to accomplish assigned seatwork using self-instruction and self-reinforcement across academic tasks.

Near the completion of training, gradual removal (i.e., fading) of positive reinforcement contingencies increases the probability that the child's progress will be maintained. Sudden withdrawal of differential consequences may result in a setback. Gradual withdrawal of reinforcers can be accomplished by altering the amount and timing of reinforcement. For example, Paul may receive fewer points contingent on satisfactory completion of home chores, or he may be allowed to earn points every other day only, rather than every day. On alternate days, Paul's performance merely results in praise by his parents.

Gradual withdrawal prepares the child for the real world, in which consequences for behavior often are not systematic, may be delayed, or may not be provided at all. During the initial phase of skill acquisition or behavior change, it is important that consequences be provided immediately and consistently. Maintenance of acquired skills or altered behavior, however, is enhanced if consequences are progressively delayed and provided intermittently. Behaviors taught using an intermittent schedule of reinforcement are typically more resistant to extinction than those with continual high levels of reinforcement. Hence, once a new skill is in the child's repertoire or a desired behavior occurs routinely, it is preferable to acknowledge the acceptable behavior every so often rather than each time the behavior occurs. Finally, children can be instructed to exhibit new skills or behaviors at different times in different forms and environments. Parents and teachers often do this by asking the child to change clothes, complete another math problem, or speak with grandmother on the telephone. These methods of generalization and fading are not mutually exclusive. Each can be employed in isolation or combination.

Follow-Up Assessment and Care

Individually tailored interventions that are applied over time frequently result in substantial improvements that are both clinically significant and socially important. Nonetheless, in many cases, sustained follow-up assessment and care is required because the child's behavioral repertoire and the environments influencing it are everchanging. Learned behavior seldom remains static. Revisions to the management protocols are often indicated in adapting to changing behaviors and environments. In some instances, the impact of previously effective interventions diminishes or new behaviors of concern emerge.

Perhaps one of the most common misconceptions about applied behavior analysis is that a permanent "cure" or "fix" can be achieved. In fact, although intervention goals are frequently attained, once a behavior is in a child's repertoire, seldom can it be eliminated altogether. Rather, at best it can be addressed under the specific conditions in which it recurs. Thus, the behavior analyst develops and implements a plan for ongoing care in anticipation of the continuance or occasional reemergence of the target behavior(s) of concern. Periodic assessments and "booster" training sessions are typically provided. Between such planned events, the behavior analyst frequently troubleshoots on an as-needed basis.

POSITIVE BEHAVIORAL SUPPORT

In the 1990s a theory emerged that has perhaps far-reaching implications for the future of applied behavior analysis. It is often referred to as *positive behavioral support*. Some of its defining characteristics are 1) interventions that are responsive to the context in which the target behavior occurs, 2) interventions that are designed in light of the motivational bases of this behavior, 3) interventions that are justified by the outcomes that they achieve, and 4) outcomes that are acceptable to key participants (the individual, his or her family, and the community members, both professional and nonprofessional, who participate in or are responsible for the support provided) (Haring & DeVault, 1996).

Furthermore, positive behavioral support increasingly represents a set of attitudes toward what constitutes appropriate and effective care and an expanding array of interdisciplinary practices in clinical, educational, work, home, and community environments. Such practices include, but are by no means limited to, hypothesis-based interventions, person- and family-centered planning, and vision setting. Individual differences in growth and development, motivation and learning, and preferences and choices, not only are taken into account but also are actively supported in a manner that expands the resources and opportunities available to the individual with disabilities and his or her community. (For more information about positive behavioral support, see Artesi & Mallar, 1998; Carr et al., 1999; Carr et al., 1994; Horner & Carr, 1997; Horner et al., 1990; Jackson & Leon, 1998; Jones & Jones, 1998; Koegel, Koegel, & Dunlap, 1996; Lohrmann-O'Rourke et al., 1999; Lucyshyn, Dunlap, & Albin, 2002; Ruef et al., 1998; and Weigle, 1997.)

SUMMARY

Children with developmental disabilities possess many strengths, competencies, and preferences. Nonetheless, more often than their typically developing peers, they also exhibit skill impairments and challenging behaviors. It is exceedingly important to a child's optimal development that these behavioral concerns be addressed. The principles and procedures of applied behavior analysis are based on fundamental processes that define our everyday experiences, including positive reinforcement, extinction, negative reinforcement, and punishment. Specific interventions often emphasize acquisition and maintenance of adaptive alternate behaviors that enable the child to function independently in least restrictive environments that present opportunities for choice-making and learning. Priority is assigned to building skills in a framework that promotes the child's self-determination.

REFERENCES

Aaron, P.G., & Joshi, R.M. (1992). *Reading problems: Consultation and remediation.* New York: Guilford Press.

Achenbach, T.M. (1991a). *Integrative guide for the 1991 CBCL/4–18, YSR, and TRF profiles.* Burlington: University of Vermont, Department of Psychiatry.

Achenbach, T.M. (1991b). *Manual for the Child Behavior Checklist/4–18 and 1991 profile.* Burlington: University of Vermont, Department of Psychiatry.

Achenbach, T.M. (1991c). *Manual for the Teacher's Report Form and 1991 profile.* Burlington: University of Vermont, Department of Psychiatry.

Achenbach, T.M., & Rescorla, L.A. (2000). *Manual for the ASEBA preschool forms and profiles.* Burlington: University of Vermont, Department of Psychiatry.

Albin, R.W., Lucyshyn, J.M., Horner, R.H., et al. (1996). Contextual fit for behavioral support plans: A model for "goodness of fit." In L.K. Koegel, R.L. Koegel, & G. Dunlap (Eds.), *Positive behavioral support: Including people with difficult behavior in the community* (pp. 81–98). Baltimore: Paul H. Brookes Publishing Co.

Artesi, A.J., & Mallar, L. (1998). Positive behavior supports in general education settings: Combining person-centered planning and functional analysis. *Intervention in School and Clinic, 34*(1), 33–38.

Axelrod, S., Spreat, S., Berry, B., et al. (1996). A decision-making model for selecting the optimal treatment procedure. In R. Van Houten & S. Axelrod (Eds.), *Behavior analysis and treatment* (pp. 183–202). New York: Kluwer Academic/Plenum Publishers.

Bagnato, S.J., & Neisworth, J.T. (1991). *Assessment for early intervention: Best practices for professionals.* New York: Guilford Press.

Baker, B.L., & Brightman, A.J. (with Blacher, J.B., Heifetz, L.J., Hinshaw, S.P., & Murphy, D.M.). (1997). *Steps to independence: Teaching everyday skills to children with special needs* (3rd ed.). Baltimore: Paul H. Brookes Publishing Co.

Bannerman, D.J., Sheldon, J.B., Sherman, J.A., et al. (1990). Balancing the right to habilitation with the right to personal liberties: The rights of people with developmental

disabilities to eat too many doughnuts and take a nap. *Journal of Applied Behavior Analysis, 23,* 79–89.

Barkley, R.A. (1990). *Hyperactive children: A handbook for diagnosis and treatment.* New York: Guilford Press.

Bijou, S.W. (1995). *Behavior analysis of child development* (2nd rev. ed.). Reno, NV: Context Press.

Blechman, E.A. (1985). *Solving child behavior problems at home and school.* Champaign, IL: Research Press.

Bradley-Johnson, S., & Lesiak, J.L. (1989). *Problems in written expression: Assessment and remediation.* New York: Guilford Press.

Carr, E.G. (1988). Functional equivalence as a mechanism of response generalization. In R.H. Horner, G. Dunlap, & R.L. Koegel (Eds.), *Generalization and maintenance: Lifestyle changes in applied settings* (pp. 221–241). Baltimore: Paul H. Brookes Publishing Co.

Carr, E.G. (1994). Emerging themes in the functional analysis of problem behavior. *Journal of Applied Behavior Analysis, 27,* 393–399.

Carr, E.G., & Durand, V.M. (1985a). Reducing behavior problems through functional communication training. *Journal of Applied Behavior Analysis, 18,* 111–126.

Carr, E.G., & Durand, V.M. (1985b). The social-communicative basis of severe behavior problems in children. In J. Reiss & R.R. Bootzin (Eds.), *Theoretical issues in behavior therapy* (pp. 219–254). San Diego: Academic Press.

Carr, E.G., Horner, R.H., Turnbull, A., et al. (1999). *Positive behavior support for people with developmental disabilities.* Washington, DC: American Association on Mental Retardation.

Carr, E.G., Levin, L., McConnachie, G., et al. (1994). *Communication-based intervention for problem behavior: A user's guide for producing positive change.* Baltimore: Paul H. Brookes Publishing Co.

Carr, E.G., Reeve, C.E., & Magito-McLaughlin, D. (1996). Contextual influences on problem behavior in people with developmental disabilities. In L.K. Koegel, R.L. Koegel, & G. Dunlap (Eds.), *Positive behavioral support: Including people with difficult behavior in the community* (pp. 403–424). Baltimore: Paul H. Brookes Publishing Co.

Catania, A.C. (1984). *Learning* (2nd ed.). Upper Saddle River, NJ: Prentice-Hall.

Christophersen, E.R. (1988). *Little people: Guidelines for common sense child rearing* (3rd ed.). Kansas City, MO: Westport Publishers.

Christophersen, E.R. (1994). *Pediatric compliance: A guide for the primary care physician*. New York: Kluwer Academic/Plenum Publishers.

Christophersen, E.R., & Mortweet, S.L. (2001). *Treatments that work with children: Empirically supported strategies for managing childhood problems*. Washington, DC: American Psychological Association.

Cooper, L.J., Wacker, D.P., Sasso, G.M., et al. (1990). Using parents as therapists to evaluate the appropriate behavior of their children: Application to a tertiary diagnostic clinic. *Journal of Applied Behavior Analysis, 23*, 285–296.

Dangel, R.F., & Polster, R.A. (1988). *Teaching child management skills*. Elmsford, NY: Pergamon.

Derby, K.M., Wacker, D.P., Sasso, G., et al. (1992). Brief functional assessment techniques to evaluate maladaptive behavior in an outpatient setting: A summary of 79 cases. *Journal of Applied Behavior Analysis, 18*, 713–721.

Dunlap, G. (1996). Promoting generalization: Current status and functional considerations. In R. Van Houten & S. Axelrod (Eds.), *Behavior analysis and treatment* (pp. 269–296). New York: Kluwer Academic/Plenum Publishers.

Durand, V.M. (1988). Motivation Assessment Scale. In M. Hersen & A. Bellack (Eds.), *Dictionary of behavior assessment techniques* (pp. 309–310). Elmsford, NY: Pergamon.

Durand, V.M. (1990). *Severe behavior problems: A functional communication training approach*. New York: Guilford Press.

Favell, J.E., & McGimsey, J.F. (1993). Defining an acceptable treatment environment. In R. Van Houten & S. Axelrod (Eds.), *Behavior analysis and treatment* (pp. 25–45). New York: Kluwer Academic/Plenum Publishers.

Fisher, W., Piazza, C.C., Bowman, L.G., et al. (1992). A comparison of two approaches for identifying reinforcers for persons with severe and profound disabilities. *Journal of Applied Behavior Analysis, 25*, 491–498.

Forehand, R.L., & Long, N. (1996). *Parenting the strong-willed child*. Chicago: Contemporary Books.

Forehand, R.L., & McMahon, R.J. (1981). *Helping the noncompliant child: A clinician's guide to parent training*. New York: Guilford Press.

Foxx, R.M. (1982a). *Decreasing behaviors of severely retarded and autistic persons*. Champaign, IL: Research Press.

Foxx, R.M. (1982b). *Increasing behaviors of severely retarded and autistic persons*. Champaign, IL: Research Press.

Garber, S.W., Garber, M.D., & Spizman, R.F. (1987). *Good behavior*. New York: Villard Books.

Guess, D., Benson, H.A., & Siegel-Causey, E. (1985). Concepts and issues related to choice-making and autonomy among persons with severe disabilities. *Journal of The Association for Persons with Severe Handicaps, 10*, 79–86.

Haring, N.G., & De Vault, G. (1996). Discussion: Family issues and family support. In L.K. Koegel, R.L. Koegel, & G. Dunlap (Eds.), *Positive behavior support: Including people with difficult behavior in the community* (pp. 115–120). Baltimore: Paul H. Brookes Publishing Co.

Harris, S.L., & Handleman, J.S. (Eds.). (1990). *Springer series on behavioral therapy: Vol. 25. Aversive and nonaversive interventions: Controlling life-threatening behavior by the developmentally disabled*. New York: Springer Publications.

Horne, A.M., & Sayger, T.V. (1990). *Treating conduct and oppositional defiant disorders in children*. Elmsford, NY: Pergamon.

Horner, R.H., & Carr, E.G. (1997). Behavioral support for students with severe disabilities: Functional assessment and comprehensive intervention. *Journal of Special Education, 31*(1), 84–104.

Horner, R.H., Dunlap, G., Koegel, R.L., et al. (1990). Toward a technology of "nonaversive" behavioral support. *Journal of The Association for Persons with Severe Handicaps, 15*, 125–132.

Horner, R.H., Sprague, J.R., & Flannery, K.B. (1993). Building functional curricula for students with severe intellectual disabilities and severe problem behaviors. In R. Van Houten & S. Axelrod (Eds.), *Behavior analysis and treatment* (pp. 47–71). New York: Kluwer Academic/Plenum Publishers.

Horner, R.H., Vaughn, B.J., Day, H.M., et al. (1996). The relationship between setting events and problem behavior: Expanding our understanding of behavioral support. In L.K. Koegel, R.L. Koegel, & G. Dunlap (Eds.), *Positive behavioral support: Including people with difficult behavior in the community* (pp. 381–402). Baltimore: Paul H. Brookes Publishing Co.

Houghton, J., Bronicki, G.J.B., & Guess, D. (1987). Opportunities to express preferences and make choices among students with severe disabilities in classroom settings. *Journal of The Association for Persons with Severe Handicaps, 12*, 18–27.

Iwata, B.A. (1987). Negative reinforcement in applied behavior analysis: An emerging technology. *Journal of Applied Behavior Analysis, 20*, 361–378.

Iwata, B.A., Dorsey, M.F., Slifer, K.J., et al. (1982). Toward a functional analysis of self-injury. *Analysis and Intervention in Developmental Disabilities, 2*, 3–20.

Iwata, B.A., Vollmer, T.R., Zarcone, J.R., et al. (1993). Treatment classification and selection based on behavioral function. In R. Van Houten & S. Axelrod (Eds.), *Behavior analysis and treatment* (pp. 101–125). New York: Kluwer Academic/Plenum Publishers.

Jackson, L.B., & Leon, M.Z. (1998). *Developing a behavior support plan: A manual for teachers and behavioral specialists* (2nd ed.). Colorado Springs, CO: PEAK.

Jackson, L.B., & Panyan, M.V. (2002). *Positive behavioral support in the classroom: Principles and practices*. Baltimore: Paul H. Brookes Publishing Co.

Jones, V.F., & Jones, L.S. (1998). *Comprehensive classroom management: Creating communities of support and solving problems*. Needham Heights, MA: Allyn & Bacon.

Kamphaus, R.W., & Frick, P.J. (1996). *Clinical assessment of child and adolescent personality and behavior*. Needham Heights, MA: Allyn & Bacon.

Kelly, M.L. (1990). *School-home notes: Promoting children's classroom success*. New York: Guilford Press.

Kennedy, C.H. (1994). Manipulating antecedent conditions to alter the stimulus control of problem behavior. *Journal of Applied Behavior Analysis, 27*, 161–170.

Kennedy, C.H., & Itkonen, T. (1993). Effects of setting events on the problem behavior of students with severe disabilities. *Journal of Applied Behavior Analysis, 26*, 321–327.

Koegel, L.K., Koegel, R.L., & Dunlap, G. (Eds.). (1996). *Positive behavioral support: Including people with difficult behavior in the community*. Baltimore: Paul H. Brookes Publishing Co.

Koegel, L.K., Koegel, R.L., Kellegrew, D., et al. (1996). Parent education for prevention and reduction of severe problem behaviors. In L.K. Koegel, R.L. Koegel, & G. Dunlap (Eds.), *Positive behavioral support: Including people with difficult behavior in the community* (pp. 3–30). Baltimore: Paul H. Brookes Publishing Co.

Lerman, D.C., & Iwata, B.A. (1996). Developing a technology for the use of operant extinction in clinical settings:

An examination of basic and applied research. *Journal of Applied Behavior Analysis, 29,* 345–382.

Lohrmann-O'Rourke, S., Knoster, T., & Llewellyn, G. (1999). Screening for understanding: An initial line of inquiry for school-based settings. *Journal of Positive Behavioral Interventions, 1*(1), 35–52.

Lovett, H. (1996). *Learning to listen: Positive approaches and people with difficult behavior.* Baltimore: Paul H. Brookes Publishing Co.

Lucyshyn, J.M., Dunlap, G., & Albin, R.W. (Eds.). (2002). *Families and positive behavior support: Addressing problem behaviors in family contexts.* Baltimore: Paul H. Brookes Publishing Co.

Luiselli, J.K., & Cameron, M.J. (Eds.). (1998). *Antecedent control: Innovative approaches to behavioral support.* Baltimore: Paul H. Brookes Publishing Co.

Mace, F.C., Lalli, J.S., Pinter-Lalli, E., et al. (1993). Functional analysis and treatment of aberrant behavior. In R. Van Houten & S. Axelrod (Eds.), *Behavior analysis and treatment* (pp. 75–99). New York: Kluwer Academic/Plenum Publishers.

Mace, F.C., Lalli, J.S., Shea, M.C., et al. (1990). The momentum of human behavior in a natural setting. *Journal of the Experimental Analysis of Behavior, 54,* 163–172.

Marks, E.S. (1995). *Entry strategies for school consultation: Self-management interventions.* New York: Guilford Press.

Martin, G., & Pear, J. (1996). *Behavior modification: What it is and how to do it.* (5th ed.). Upper Saddle River, NJ: Prentice-Hall.

Mash, E.J., & Terdal, L.G. (1997). *Assessment of childhood disorders* (3rd ed.). New York: Guilford Press.

Matson, J.L., & DiLorenzo, T. (1983). *Punishment and its alternatives: A new perspective for behavior modification.* New York: Springer-Verlag.

Matson, J.L., & Taras, M.E. (1989). A 20 year review of punishment and alternative methods to treat problem behaviors in developmentally delayed persons. *Research in Developmental Disabilities, 10,* 85–104.

Miller, L.K. (1980). *Principles of everyday behavior analysis* (2nd ed.). Pacific Grove, CA: Brooks/Cole Thomson Learning.

Northup, J., Wacker, D., Sasso, G., et al. (1991). A brief functional analysis of aggressive and alternative behavior in an outclinic setting. *Journal of Applied Behavior Analysis, 24,* 509–522.

Novak, G. (1996). *Developmental psychology: Dynamical systems and behavior analysis.* Reno, NV: Context Press.

O'Donahue, W. (Ed.). (1998). *Learning and behavior therapy.* Needham Heights, MA: Allyn & Bacon.

O'Neill, R.E., Horner, R.H., Albin, R.W., et al. (1990). *Functional analysis of problem behavior: A practical assessment guide.* Sycamore, IL: Sycamore.

Parrish, J.M., Cataldo, M.F., Kolko, D.J., et al. (1986). Experimental analysis of response covariation among compliant and inappropriate behaviors. *Journal of Applied Behavior Analysis, 19,* 241–254.

Patterson, G.R. (1982). *Coercive family process.* Eugene, OR: Castalia.

Reichle, J., & Wacker, D.P. (Vol. Eds.) & Warren, S.F. & Reichle, J. (Series Eds.). (1993). *Communication and language intervention series: Vol. 3. Communicative alternatives to challenging behavior: Integrating functional assessment and in-tervention strategies.* Baltimore: Paul H. Brookes Publishing Co.

Repp, A.C. (1999). Naturalistic functional assessment with regular and special education students in classroom settings. In A.C. Repp & R.H. Horner (Eds.), *Functional analysis of problem behavior: From effective assessment to effective support* (pp. 238–258). Belmont, CA: Wadsworth.

Repp, A.C., & Singh, N.N. (Eds.). (1990). *Perspectives on the use of nonaversive and aversive interventions for persons with developmental disabilities.* Sycamore, IL: Sycamore.

Reynolds, C.R., & Kamphaus, R.W. (1992). *Behavior assessment system for children (BASC).* Circle Pines, MN: American Guidance Service.

Rosenfeld, S.A., & Gravois, T. (1995). *Instructional consultation teams: Collaborating for change.* New York: Guilford Press.

Ruef, M.B., Higgins, C., Glaeser, B.J., et al. (1998). Positive behavior support: Strategies for teachers. *Intervention in School and Clinic, 34*(1), 21–32.

Sanders, M.R. (1998a). *Every parent: A positive approach to children's behavior.* Milton, Australia: Families International Publishing.

Sanders, M.R. (1998b). *Practitioner's manual for enhanced Triple P (Positive Parenting Program).* Milton, Australia: Families International Publishing.

Sasso, G.M., Reimers, T.M., Cooper, L.J., et al. (1992). Use of descriptive and experimental analyses to identify the functional properties of aberrant behavior in school settings. *Journal of Applied Behavior Analysis, 25,* 809–821.

Schaefer, C.E., & Briesmeister, J.M. (1989). *Handbook of parent training: Parents as co-therapists for children's behavior problems.* New York: John Wiley & Sons.

Scotti, J.R., & Meyer, L.H. (Eds.). (1999). *Behavioral intervention: Principles, models, and practices.* Baltimore: Paul H. Brookes Publishing Co.

Shapiro, E.S. (1989). *Academic skills problems: Direct assessment and intervention.* New York: Guilford Press.

Shapiro, E.S., & Cole, C.L. (1994). *Behavior change in the classroom: Self-management interventions.* New York: Guilford Press.

Stokes, T.F., & Baer, D.M. (1977). An implicit technology of generalization. *Journal of Applied Behavior Analysis, 10,* 349–367.

Van Houten, R., & Axelrod, S. (Eds.). (1993). *Behavior analysis and treatment.* New York: Kluwer Academic/Plenum Publishers.

Van Houten, R., Axelrod, S., Bailey, J.S., et al. (1988). Report by the Association for Behavior Analysis task force on the right to effective treatment. *Journal of Applied Behavior Analysis, 21,* 381–384.

Vittimberga, G.L., Scotti, J.R., & Weigle, K.L. (1999). Standards of practice and critical elements in an educative approach to behavioral intervention. In J.R. Scotti & L.H. Meyer (Eds.), *Behavioral intervention: Principles, models, and practices* (pp. 47–69). Baltimore: Paul H. Brookes Publishing Co.

Vollmer, T.R., & Iwata, B.A. (1991). Establishing operations and reinforcement effects. *Journal of Applied Behavior Analysis, 24,* 279–291.

Weigle, K.L. (1997). Positive behavior support as a model for promoting educational inclusion. *Journal of The Association for Persons with Severe Handicaps, 22,* 36–48.

32 Technological Assistance
Innovations for Independence

Susan E. Levy and Maureen O'Rourke

Upon completion of this chapter, the reader will:

- know the definition of medical technology assistance in children
- be aware of the incidence and types of medical technology assistance
- understand conditions leading to a need for medical technology assistance, especially those relating to chronic respiratory failure
- acknowledge the psychosocial stresses on children assisted by medical technology and on their families

Advances in medical and surgical care have resulted in improved survival of children with complex medical disorders, including complications associated with premature birth; neuromuscular diseases; spinal cord injury; cancer; human immunodeficiency virus (HIV); and chronic diseases of the kidney, respiratory system, gastrointestinal tract, and liver. Some children with these disorders, however, require temporary or permanent support by medical assistive devices, such as mechanical ventilators or feeding tubes. This chapter focuses on the uses of medical assistive technology and the resulting psychological, educational, and socioeconomic impact on the child and family.

DEFINITION AND INCIDENCE OF MEDICAL TECHNOLOGY ASSISTANCE

The Office of Technology Assessment (OTA) defines a child who receives medical technology assistance as one who requires a mechanical device and substantial daily skilled nursing care to avert death or further disability. These medical devices replace or augment a vital body function and include respiratory technology assistance (e.g., **nasal cannulae** for oxygen supplementation, mechanical ventilators, positive airway pressure devices, artificial airways such as tracheostomy tubes), surveillance devices (e.g., cardiorespiratory monitors, pulse oximeters), nutritive assistive devices (e.g., nasogastric or gastrostomy feeding tubes), equipment for intravenous therapy (e.g., parenteral nutrition, medication infusion), devices to augment or protect kidney function (e.g., dialysis, urethral catheterization), and ostomies (e.g., colostomy; Office of Technology Assessment, 1987). Only about 1 in 1,000 children requires medical technology assistance (Palfrey et al., 1991; Storgion, 1996). The incidence does appear to be increasing in children younger than 1 year of age, however, primarily as a consequence of improved survival of very low birth weight infants (Palfrey et al., 1994).

RAY

Ray is a 3-year-old who was hospitalized for the first 2 years of his life for management of chronic respiratory failure. He was born prematurely at 27 weeks' gestation and required oxygen administration and mechanical ventilation at the outset due to hyaline membrane disease (HMD; see Chapter 6). He had a stormy early course in the neonatal intensive care unit (NICU), with a number of the complications commonly associated with very premature infants. At 3 months of age, a tracheostomy (insertion of an artificial airway) was performed because Ray's doctors determined that Ray would require long-term mechanical ventilator support. Other medical complications included intracerebral hemorrhage, retinopathy of prematurity (see Chapter 6), and gastroesophageal reflux (GER; see Chapter 27).

At 10 months of age, Ray still had lung disease, or bronchopulmonary dysplasia (BPD; see Chapter 6) and was transferred from the NICU to a subacute nursing facility with a specialized unit for children who require mechanical ventilatory support. The medical, nursing, and therapy staff collaborated with Ray's family in developing a plan and time line to accomplish the goals of enhancing Ray's growth and development and of teaching his parents to care for him at home. Because Ray had been so sick, he had to rely on a feeding tube (gastrostomy tube, or G tube) for nutrition and lacked experience and skills in oral feeding. The tube feedings were effective in helping him grow but made his GER worse, and the doctors and nurses worked closely with his parents to adjust his medications and the rate of tube feeding to minimize reflux and provide Ray with the best opportunity to grow and develop his oral skills. By the time Ray was discharged at 2 years of age, he could be placed on a portable ventilator, which was mounted on an adapted stroller. He could tolerate being off the ventilator for 6 hours during the day, allowing him to attend a preschool program to address his delays in development, particularly those involving speech, language, and gross motor skills.

Ray's parents were active members of the interdisciplinary team. By the time Ray was ready for discharge, they were able to care for him independently. Ray went home with his family with extensive home nursing and therapy support. The team social worker worked closely with Ray's family to ensure funding for nursing care through the family's insurance and the state Medicaid waiver system.

One year later, Ray is doing well at home and has not required readmission to the hospital. Important factors in his family's success have been the extensive medical, nursing, and therapy supports in the home. Ray now attends a preschool program three mornings per week, where he receives services from speech-language, occupational, and physical therapists. His parents are working closely with the school district and nursing agency to ensure continued provision of services including nursing supervision of his medical problems. His lungs have improved to the point that he only requires oxygen at night, and his doctors believe that within the next few months this may also be discontinued. The family is optimistic that he may be able to be decannulated (have his tracheostomy removed) by the summer. Despite Ray's complex medical and developmental challenges, he is an integral member of his family and enjoys his life.

MEDICAL TECHNOLOGY ASSISTANCE AND DISORDERS THAT REQUIRE ITS USE

Ironically, dependence on medical technology is a consequence of improvements in medical care. Many children are now able to survive what were once fatal diseases. In a 1987–1990 survey of children in Massachusetts who are dependent on technology, more than half of the children (57%) had neurological involvement; 13% had multisystem involvement (more than one organ involved); 9%, cancer or hematological disorders; 7%, cardiac or respiratory disorders; 7%, gastrointestinal disorders; 4%, kidney disorders; and 3%, musculoskeletal disorders (Palfrey et al., 1994). Table 32.1 lists the types of medical assistive devices that are required in a number of these conditions. The types of medical technology assistance have been divided into four categories for the purposes of federally mandated programs (Table 32.2). Of these types, the most frequently used technology is Type IV, which includes respiratory assistance and cardio-respiratory monitoring (Table 32.3).

Respiratory Technology Assistance

Health care professionals must provide children who have chronic respiratory failure with medical technology support that is sufficient to maintain normal oxygen levels in the blood, prevent ongoing lung injury from recurrent infection, and promote growth and development (Table 32.4). These goals usually can be accomplished using a combination of oxygen supplementation, continuous positive airway pressure (CPAP), chest physiotherapy, medications, and adequate nutrition. When these measures are insufficient, however, mechanical ventilation and tracheostomy tube placement are considered. Surveillance of the child's cardiorespiratory status may also be required.

Oxygen Supplementation

Oxygen is the single most effective agent in treating the infant with chronic lung disease. In these infants, hypoxia can be precipitated by even simple caregiving activities such as handling or feeding. Recurrent hypoxic episodes result in an increased risk of **pulmonary hypertension,** which may lead to further lung damage. Continuous oxygen therapy prevents hypoxia and improves growth and development (Goodman et al., 1988). Many infants with chronic respiratory failure require supplemental oxygen for months or even years. Too much oxygen, however, can adversely affect the lungs. To avoid this, oxygen saturation (the oxygen carrying capacity of red blood cells) may be monitored using a device called a pulse oximeter (Figure 32.1). Oxygen saturation in the blood greater than 90% is optimal for typical growth and well-being. Oxygen can be administered by nasal cannulae (plastic prongs placed in the nose and connected to a tube which delivers an oxygen/air mixture), face mask, oxygen tent or hood, or an artificial airway (e.g., tracheostomy). Portable oxygen sources and delivery systems are available (such as the one that Ray used) so that the child is not tethered to the home or hospital room.

Continuous Positive Airway Pressure

For the child with a moderate disturbance of pulmonary function, such as mild respiratory failure and obstructive sleep apnea, CPAP may be employed (Downey, Perkin, & MacQuarrie, 2000). CPAP is created by a device (Figure 32.1) that imposes resistance to exhalation, thereby preventing recurrent collapse of the small air passages. It also improves oxygenation by maintaining the alveoli in an open position so that they can engage in gas exchange. CPAP can be applied to the child's natural airway (via a tight-fitting mask or **nasal pillows**), as is done in the hospital; more commonly, it is given through a tracheostomy tube (Kurz, 1999).

Table 32.1. Types of medical technology assistance required in certain conditions

Condition	Types of technical assistance
Spinal cord injury	Mechanical ventilation
	Tube feeding
	Bladder catheterization
Neuromuscular disorder	Mechanical ventilation
	Tube feeding
Cerebral palsy	Tube feeding
Prematurity	Mechanical ventilation
	Oxygen supplementation
	Tube feeding
	Intravenous nutrition
	Ostomy
	Cardiorespiratory monitor
Kidney failure	Dialysis
Cancer and HIV infection	Intravenous medication
	Intravenous nutrition
	Central venous line

Table 32.2. Categories of technology assistance

Type	Description
I	Mechanical ventilation for at least part of each day
II	Prolonged intravenous nutrition or drug therapy
III	Support for tracheostomy tube care, suctioning, oxygen supplementation, or tube feeding
IV	Cardiorespiratory monitoring, kidney dialysis, or ostomy care

Source: Office of Technology Assessment (1987).

When necessary, positive pressure can be administered between mechanical breaths, in which case the technique is referred to as *positive end expiratory pressure* (PEEP).

Chest Physiotherapy and Suctioning

Children with respiratory illness or failure also may produce excessive secretions (e.g., saliva) and/or be unable to cough effectively. Chest physiotherapy and suctioning, which can be taught to all caregivers, help clear pulmonary secretions (Krause & Hoehn, 2000). Chest physiotherapy involves the repetitive manual percussion of the chest wall (for infants, often using a vibrator). Secretions are loosened and can then be cleared by coughing or, in children with tracheostomies, by suctioning (Oberwaldner, 2000). This procedure requires the insertion of a catheter through the tracheostomy tube and into the trachea. Suction then is applied in order to remove secretions. Typically, supplemental oxygen is administered before and after suctioning to prevent hypoxia during the procedure (Flenady & Gray, 2000). Chest physiotherapy and suctioning are done as often as necessary, usually several times a day.

Table 32.3.   Usage of technology assistance

Assistance	%
Suction, oxygen, tracheostomy care	31
Cardiorespiratory monitoring	25
Mechanical ventilator support	17
Intravenous medications or nutrition	12
Tube feedings	10
Kidney dialysis	1
Other	4

Source: Millner (1991).

Mechanical Ventilation and Tracheostomy

Mechanical ventilation is the process by which a device augments or replaces the child's own breaths (Carlo & Ambalavanan, 1999). Mechanical breaths can be generated either by applying negative pressure to the outside of the chest wall or by delivering positive pressure through the airway. Negative pressure ventilators are used primarily in children with respiratory muscle pump failure (Heulitt, 2000). Positive pressure ventilation can be effective for pump failure or for lung disease. Positive pressure ventilation can be noninvasive (i.e., applied to the natural airway by a mask) or invasive (i.e., delivered via a surgically inserted tracheostomy tube; MacDonald & Johnson, 1996; Roberts, 1999). This chapter focuses on invasive positive pres-

Table 32.4.   Components in the care of the child requiring ventilator assistance

Medical	Ventilation should support physical growth and minimize shortness of breath and fatigue that can interfere with development.
	Intercurrent illnesses should be treated aggressively.
Developmental	Children must be evaluated on a regular basis by an interdisciplinary team of developmental pediatricians, child psychologists, and therapists. Problems are identified, and individualized programs should be designed to enhance developmental functioning.
	Early intervention programs with groups of children should be utilized when appropriate.
	Physical, occupational, and speech-language therapists should work with children individually as needed.
Environmental	A physical environment that is less restrictive than the typical intensive care unit should be provided.
	A regular routine of care, bathing, dressing, mealtimes, play periods, and naps must be provided.
Social	Families may require group and individual psychosocial support.
	Families should be encouraged to visit and participate in the child's care.
	Families must become an integral part of the caregiving team and should assume an advocacy and decision-making role.
	Foster families should be sought when biological families are unable to participate in the child's care.
	Primary nursing programs should be used to ensure continuity of care.

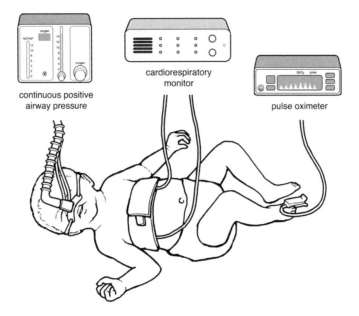

continuous positive
airway pressure

cardiorespiratory
monitor

pulse oximeter

Figure 32.1. This illustration shows an infant receiving nasal continuous positive airway pressure (CPAP) for mild chronic respiratory failure and being monitored for oxygen saturation by a pulse oximeter and for respiratory arrests by a cardiorespiratory monitor.

sure ventilation because it is currently the most commonly used method of mechanical ventilation in children.

A tracheostomy usually involves the insertion of a plastic tube through a surgically created incision in the cartilage of the trachea just below the Adam's apple. It is secured around the neck with foam-padded strings. This open airway is then attached to a mechanical ventilator or to a CPAP device with tubing that provides humidified air or an air/oxygen mixture. The tracheostomy tube also allows the caregiver to have direct access to the airway, permitting suctioning of secretions or removal of other blockages.

Numerous positive pressure ventilators are available and appropriate for children with chronic respiratory failure. Ventilator selection is affected by a number of factors: the child's size, the underlying disorder, where the ventilator will be used (home versus hospital or school), whether portability is necessary (battery-powered ventilators exist), and other special features that may be helpful to the child.

Surveillance Devices

Children with disorders that affect the heart or lungs are likely to require the use of surveillance devices. Although these instruments provide no direct therapeutic benefit, they give early warning of problems and thereby improve care indirectly. The two most common types of electronic surveillance devices are pulse oximeters and cardiorespiratory monitors (Figure 32.1). They can be used individually or in combination in the hospital and at home (Poets & Southall, 1994).

The oximeter measures oxygen saturation in the arterial blood using a probe that is attached with a special tape or a bandage to one of the child's fingers or toes (Hunt, 1996; Nadkarni, Shah, & Deshmukh, 2000). The probe measures the amount of oxygen bound to hemoglobin, the oxygen-carrying protein in blood cells that gives blood its red color. An alarm can be set to sound below a certain oxygen saturation level. This can occur as a consequence of delivery failure (e.g., depletion of oxygen in the oxygen tank) or a change in the child's condition (e.g., an increased need for supplemental oxygen because of a respiratory infection). In the latter situation, the current activity may need to be curtailed and the oxygen concentration increased. Because this device reflects how well oxygen is being delivered to vital organs, it is an important monitor; unfortunately, it is quite susceptible to false alarms resulting from probe displacement, movement of the extremity, or electrical interference.

The cardiorespiratory monitor has electrodes that are pasted to the child's chest to record heart and respiratory rate (Figure 32.1; Cote et al., 1998). An alarm is part of the system and is set off by rates that are either too high or too low. If the alarm sounds, the caregiver should examine the child's respiratory, cardiovascular, and neurological status. Like the oximeter, the cardiorespiratory monitor can produce false alarms, most commonly resulting from the inadvertent detachment of the chest leads. In the very rare event, however, that the alarm sounds because of a cardiorespiratory arrest (i.e., cessation of breathing and heart rate), cardiopulmonary resuscitation (CPR) must be instituted immediately.

Conditions that May Require Respiratory Technology Assistance and Surveillance

Children like Ray, who have chronic respiratory failure (i.e., the inability of the respiratory system to maintain adequate gas exchange in the lungs), require respiratory technology assistance. Gas exchange in the lung normally involves the uptake of oxygen (O_2) and the elimination of carbon dioxide (CO_2). Oxygen is essential for energy-generating chemical reactions in the body, whereas carbon dioxide is a waste product of the chemical reactions and must be eliminated by the lungs and kidneys (Figure 32.2).

Respiratory failure can originate from problems with the respiratory muscle pump or problems with the lungs themselves (Figure 32.3). For gas exchange to occur, oxygen and car-

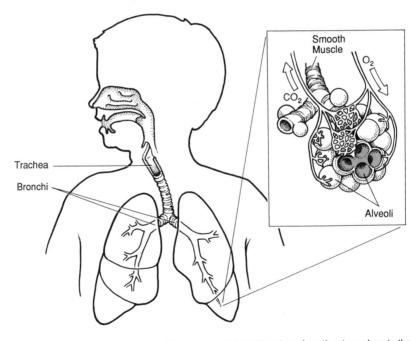

Figure 32.2.   The airways and lungs. The airways conduct inhaled gas from the atmosphere to the alveoli. Air enters the nose (and/or mouth) and then the voice box. It then descends into the chest via the windpipe, or trachea. The trachea divides into two bronchi, one serving each lung. The main bronchus to each lung divides repeatedly into a series of progressively smaller tubes that ultimately deliver gas to the alveoli, where gas exchange occurs. The carbon dioxide is eliminated by exhalation from the lungs. It also goes into the bloodstream and then is delivered to the kidney, where it is eliminated.

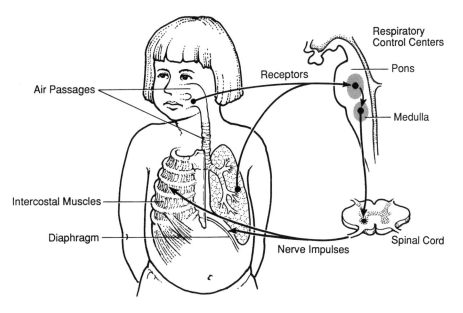

Figure 32.3. Respiratory failure can originate from problems with the respiratory muscle pump, problems with the lungs themselves, or defects in the respiratory control centers in the central nervous system (pons) or spinal cord.

bon dioxide must be moved in and out of the lungs, respectively, by the action of the respiratory pump. This consists of the rib cage and the breathing apparatus (i.e., diaphragm and muscles of the chest wall) and is driven by the respiratory center in the brainstem (Figure 32.3). Signals from this center are transmitted via the spinal cord and peripheral nerves to the respiratory muscles, which raise and lower the diaphragm and relax and contract the muscles of the chest wall. During inhalation, contraction of the respiratory muscles expands the chest cavity and moves gas into the lungs. With normal breathing, the respiratory muscles then relax and exhalation occurs (gas moves out of the lungs). Dysfunction of any component of the respiratory pump or its neurological control can cause respiratory failure.

In children, respiratory pump failure can be caused by neuromuscular disorders such as spinal cord injury; spinal muscular atrophy; Duchenne muscular dystrophy; and, in rare cases, cerebral palsy. Respiratory pump failure contrasts with HMD, which involves damage to the lung itself.

Hyaline Membrane Disease Prematurity is associated with immaturity of many organ systems (see Chapter 6). Immaturity of and subsequent damage to the lungs can lead to HMD or respiratory distress syndrome (RDS), a disorder that accounts for a significant proportion of mortality and morbidity in low birth weight infants (Majnemer et al., 2000). A child with HMD or RDS frequently depends on some form of respiratory technology assistance, including oxygen supplementation, tracheostomy tube with CPAP, and/or mechanical ventilation.

Premature infants may also have immaturity of the respiratory control centers in the brainstem. This may lead to apneic episodes (periodic, brief respiratory arrests). If respiration is not restored quickly, the cardiovascular system may collapse due to lack of oxygen, and the child may have a cardiorespiratory arrest. To prevent this from occurring, premature infants who have episodes of apnea and bradycardia (low heart rate) are placed on electronic surveillance using a cardiorespiratory monitor and alarm (Bhatia, 2000). This alerts caregivers so that they can respond quickly to apneic episodes to avert hypoxic-ischemic brain damage.

Neuromuscular Disorders Neuromuscular disorders, a group of diseases associated with acquired or congenital dysfunction of the central nervous system, spinal cord, peripheral nerves, or muscles, lead to severe weakness. Examples include polio, Duchenne muscular dystrophy, spinal muscular atrophy, and Guillain-Barré syndrome (see Chapter 14). Any of these disorders can severely affect the respiratory muscles, making mechanical ventilation necessary to avert respiratory failure (Bach, Niranjan, & Weaver, 2000; Bach & Zhitnikov, 1998; Gozal, 2000). In addition, if the swallowing musculature is affected, tube feedings may be required.

Spinal Cord Injury   Children who have sustained a severe spinal cord injury require diverse types of technology assistance. In addition to paralysis below the injury, children with spinal cord injury may have respiratory insufficiency resulting from impaired neurological control of the muscles of respiration, as well as impaired swallowing and bowel and bladder control (McKinley et al., 1999). Medical technology assistance may include mechanical ventilation, tube feeding, and bladder catheterization.

Cerebral Palsy   Children with spastic cerebral palsy may develop curvature of the spine (scoliosis) leading to rib cage distortion and stiffness. This chest wall abnormality can cause a decrease in respiratory muscle power and impede typical lung development and function.

Issues for the Caregiver

The caregiver must be aware of a number of issues in the child who is receiving some form of respiratory technology assistance or surveillance. If the child is receiving oxygen supplementation, it is important that the child gets the oxygen mixture. This requires that the tank not be empty, that the tube connecting the tank to the child be attached correctly, and that the mask or nasal cannulae be correctly positioned (and not dislodged by the child). Aside from being monitored by simple observation to make sure all equipment is in place, the child usually will have a surveillance device attached that will sound an alarm if something is amiss. A child with critical airway needs should always have a professional or a parent who is well trained in the emergency care of the child and emergency back-up equipment (e.g., portable suction, extra tracheostomy tubes). Children in school may need to have a nurse present or rapid availability of a nurse in the classroom.

Accidental displacement of the tracheostomy tube is the most common complication in mechanical ventilation (Posner, 1999). This is often a relatively minor problem; the tube can be repositioned, and a child who is not completely dependent on the ventilator can breathe spontaneously around the tube during this process. Displacement, however, can be life threatening to a child who has a narrow trachea above the tracheostomy and, as a result, is totally dependent on the device. In this case, a dislodged or blocked tube can be life threatening and must be replaced immediately. A child with narrow trachea should be closely observed and electronically monitored with a cardiorespiratory monitor and/or pulse oximeter.

The ventilator contains an alarm that sounds under conditions of low or high mechanical pressure and can be set to the individual child's needs. The most common reason for a low-pressure alarm is accidental disconnection of the tracheostomy tube from the ventilator tubing. This may occur when the child moves from one position to another. It is usually not a serious problem; the tube is simply reattached. A high-pressure alarm most commonly sounds because something is obstructing the flow of gas into the child. This may be external to the child (e.g., kinked or obstructed tubing) or within the child (e.g., a mucous plug inside the tracheostomy tube, a **bronchospasm**, a cough). Humidifying the gas mixture that passes through the tubing usually prevents mucous plugging, and if plugging occurs, it can be removed by suctioning. Thus, in addition to being trained for emergency care, the caregiver often has ongoing responsibilities, which may include providing chest physiotherapy or tube suctioning.

All personnel working with children who have respiratory needs should be trained in the performance of CPR. As respiratory arrest almost always precedes cardiac arrest in children, proper technique for artificial ventilation is essential. In the child with a tracheostomy, breaths of 100% oxygen should be delivered through a resuscitation bag that is attached to the tracheostomy tube. For a child without a tracheostomy or for a child whose tube has come out and cannot be reinserted, a tight-fitting mask should be applied to the child's face and oxygen given by resuscitation bag. For further details, the reader is encouraged to review guidelines for the performance of CPR (Nadkarni et al., 1997; "Part 9: Pediatric Basic Life Support," 2000).

Nutritional Assistive Devices and Ostomy Care

Good nutrition is a vital component in the medical management of children with chronic illnesses including cancer, cystic fibrosis, congenital heart disease, inflammatory bowel disease, immunodeficiency, and HIV infection (Akobeng, Miller, & Thomas, 1999; Hofner et al., 2000; Pedersen et al., 1999; Thomas et al., 2000). Children with chronic respiratory failure or certain forms of cerebral palsy (e.g., dyskinetic type) may need up to twice the normal caloric intake because of the considerable energy expended in rapid breathing or in involuntary movements (de Meer et al., 1997). Because lung growth parallels height growth, recovery from HMD is linked to the child's nutritional status. Similarly, development in children with cerebral palsy is often limited by undernutrition (see Chapter 23). Despite needing an increased food intake, these children may be unable to ingest even a typical intake because of oral-motor impairments, GER, or behavior problems (see Chapter 27). In these instances, nutritional assistance devices may prove helpful.

Children with oral intake that is insufficient to maintain normal growth may require tube feedings temporarily through a cannula inserted into one nostril and passed into the stomach (nasogastric tube) or into the second part of the intestine (nasojejunal tube). When long-term feedings are required, as in Ray's case, a permanent tube can be placed directly into the stomach (G tube; Figure 32.4) or intestine (jejunostomy tube or J tube). A G-J tube combines a G tube and a J tube (Figure 27.9). The J tube portion travels through the stomach, the duode-

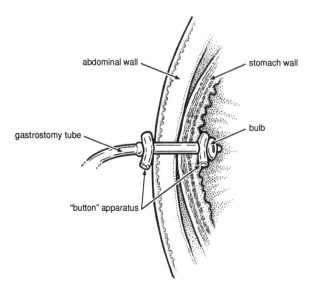

Figure 32.4. When long-term feedings are required, as in Ray's case, a permanent gastrostomy tube (G tube) can be placed directly into the stomach and is secured by a button apparatus to the skin so that the feeding tube does not dislodge.

num, and into the jejunum (second portion of the small intestine) to prevent reflux of the nutrients. New techniques allow insertion of G and/or J tubes **percutaneously** (through the skin) or laparoscopically (by "closed" surgery using a laparoscope, an instrument that uses fiber optics, to place the tube), thus avoiding a prolonged surgical procedure performed under general anesthesia (Campos & Marchesini, 1999). The percutaneous procedure is called a *percutaneous endoscopic gastrostomy* (PEG; Hofner et al., 2000; Khattak et al., 1998; Nicholson, Korman, & Richardson, 2000). If the child has GER, the intervention of choice may be a combination of a surgical antireflux procedure (e.g., fundoplication; see Chapter 27 and Figure 27.8) by open or laparoscopic route and insertion of a G or G-J tube. Once the feeding tube is inserted, nutrition can be provided using a specially prepared commercially available formula, such as Jevity and Ensure, or using foods from the family's meals that have been blenderized (see Chapter 9).

An **ostomy** is the connection of an internal organ through the abdominal wall to the outside of the skin. The most common ostomy in older children and adults is a colostomy, an opening that permits the evacuation of bowel contents. A colostomy or ileostomy (an ostomy permitting evacuation from the ileum) is sometimes necessary in a premature infant who has undergone bowel surgery as a result of necrotizing enterocolitis. In most cases, the bowel can be reattached in a few months after healing has occurred. In older children, a colostomy or ileostomy is often performed for inflammatory bowel disease (e.g., ulcerative colitis, Crohn disease). Less common ostomies include a vesicostomy (opening from the bladder through the abdominal wall) and **ureterostomy** (opening of the tubes leading from the kidney to the bladder), which are used to treat urinary tract obstructions.

Conditions that May Require Nutritional Assistive Devices

Cerebral Palsy   Children with cerebral palsy are at increased risk for developing feeding problems as a consequence of swallowing dysfunction and/or GER (see Chapter 23; Del Giudice et al., 1999). Treatment may include the use of tube feedings and special formulas.

Prematurity   Tube feedings may be required in very low birth weight infants because of an immature pattern of suck and swallow, which prevents adequate oral intake of formula. In addition, in a child with necrotizing enterocolitis (see Chapter 6), damage to the gastrointestinal tract may necessitate the surgical removal of a substantial percentage of the small or large bowel, thereby interfering with normal digestion of food. This surgery involves the placement of an ostomy to permit the evacuation of gastrointestinal secretions from the small intestine or feces from the colon.

Issues for Caregivers

Parents, school nursing staff, teachers, and other caregivers of children with feeding tubes need to learn certain skills. If the tube falls out, it must be replaced or fed back into the opening. To prevent this from occurring, the tube may be anchored to the abdominal wall and skin by a button apparatus or internally by a bulb that is inflated by water or that widens in a mushroom shape (Figure 32.4). Sometimes the tube comes out simply because the bulb has deflated. Depending on state regulations, a trained teacher, therapist, nurse, or parent may be able to reinsert the tube and then reinflate the bulb. The gastrostomy tube site must be washed daily with soap and water and the tube changed every few months.

Irritation around the gastrostomy site signals that it may be infected or that stomach acid is leaking. If an infection has been ruled out, the use of Duoderm or another occlusive ointment such as Vaseline may be applied to protect the area. If the skin around the tube bleeds, it may need to be cauterized using silver nitrate sticks.

The care of other ostomy sites (called *stomas*, or openings), such as a colostomy site, is similar to the care of the gastrostomy site (Garvin, 1994). In addition, special bags are used to collect feces, urine, and other secretions and must be emptied and replaced at routine intervals.

Long-Term Intravenous Therapy

Long-term intravenous therapy, generally provided through a **central venous line,** is most often required to provide nutrition and/or to administer medication (Chung & Ziegler, 1998). Total parenteral nutrition involves the provision of a high-calorie, high-protein solution directly into the bloodstream by intravenous administration. Prolonged intravenous access may also be needed to provide antibiotics (e.g., when a child has osteomyelitis, a deep bone infection) or chemotherapy. In these situations, a catheter (often called a *Broviac line*) may be placed into a vein under radiological guidance and advanced to a more central position (Chung & Ziegler, 1998). This type of catheter prevents the need for repeated placement of **peripheral venous lines.** In addition, a central venous catheter allows the child to receive chemotherapy, antibiotics, and/or parenteral nutrition at home rather than having to remain in the hospital. Central lines are more stable than peripheral lines and can be maintained for months or years, provided that there is strict adherence to sterile techniques and proper care.

Conditions that May Require Long-Term Intravenous Therapy

Cancer and HIV Infection   The provision of intravenous medication, nutrition, or blood products may be required for weeks or months in children with certain chronic illnesses such as cancer, immunodeficiency, and HIV infection (Jayabose et al., 1992; Shulman, 2000; Thureen & Hay, 2000).

Prematurity   Premature infants may require prolonged total parenteral hyperalimentation (i.e., intravenous nutrition) after an episode of necrotizing enterocolitis that leads to a short gut syndrome (see Chapter 6; Thureen & Hay, 2000). In this case, intravenous nutrition provides a bypass around the gastrointestinal tract.

Chronic Illnesses   Total parenteral nutrition may also be required by older children with a range of disorders, including chronic malabsorption (e.g., due to cystic fibrosis), intestinal inflammation (e.g., Crohn disease), and end-stage renal disease (Kuizon & Saluski, 1999; Ramage et al., 1999).

Issues for Caregivers

The parent or nurse is responsible for administering the parenteral nutrition solution or medication at the proper intervals and for the correct duration. The caregiver must be trained in the maintenance of sterility of the central venous catheter and be able to recognize catheter detachment and infection. Signs of an infection include redness of the surrounding skin and discharge of pus. Most children with a central venous catheter have a **hemostat,** or clamp, that can be placed over the plastic tubing to prevent significant blood loss if the catheter becomes detached.

Kidney Dialysis

The two principal forms of kidney dialysis are hemodialysis and **peritoneal** dialysis. Although hemodialysis has been used in adults for years, it has been less commonly employed in children (Hingorani & Watkins, 2000). Home peritoneal dialysis, however, has been used since the mid-1980s in children with kidney failure (Miller, Ruley, & Bock, 1995). To prepare for the child's peritoneal dialysis, a catheter is surgically inserted through the abdominal wall and into the underlying peritoneal space. This catheter permits dialysis solution to flow into the peritoneal space, equilibrate, and then drain. This procedure eliminates toxins that would normally be metabolized by the kidney. It takes several hours and may be necessary 3–5 days per week. Families can be trained to perform peritoneal dialysis independently at home.

Renal or kidney failure can occur in children as a result of a congenital malformation, chronic infection, or inherited disease. Chronic kidney failure or end-stage renal disease leads to the accumulation of fluid in the body and metabolic imbalances that can result in poor weight gain and muscle weakness (Warady & Watkins, 1998). If severe, the accumulation of metabolic toxins can cause coma, brain damage, and death. In many cases, a "cure" is possible with kidney transplantation. Many children who will eventually become eligible for a renal transplant, however, may initially be too young or too small or a suitable donor organ may be unavailable. These children require medical technology assistance through kidney dialysis (Conger, 1998; Hingorani & Watkins, 2000).

EFFECTS OF MEDICAL TECHNOLOGY ASSISTANCE ON THE CHILD AND FAMILY

Children with illnesses that require medical technology assistance may be hospitalized for prolonged periods of time among noisy and frightening pieces of machinery. Much of the child's social contact may be relegated to nursing care that involves unpleasant procedures (Baumgardner & Burtea, 1998; Kirk, 1998). Prolonged hospitalization places emotional and financial stresses on the family and may isolate the child from his or her family (Murphy, 1997). Even very involved families may find it difficult to spend extended periods in the hospital with their child because of distance or work commitments. Professionals may need to assist families to bond with their infant or provide support for their older child who may feel abandoned when the parents are unable to visit frequently.

Once home, social isolation may not disappear. In school, the child is likely to be treated as different because of the accompanying equipment and medical/nursing needs. This can be partially offset by educating classmates and providing psychological counseling for the child. Teams of nurses and care managers working on discharge planning from the hospital or subacute nursing facility can ease this transition.

The child and family must also learn to deal with the underlying medical problem that led to the technology dependence. It is generally easier for a child and family to cope with technology dependence on a short-term basis, such as when intravenous antibiotics are necessary to treat a severe infection or when a temporary ostomy is required following abdominal surgery. If the child has a severe chronic disease, however, adaptation to technology assistance is only one issue that the child and family must deal with (see Chapter 36; Watson, 1995).

Social issues may also adversely affect the child's emotional well-being. For example, the same factors that led to prematurity (e.g., young maternal age, low socioeconomic status, maternal substance abuse) may also limit the family's ability to cope with the stress of caring for a child who has an ongoing medical condition (Corbett, 1998; Petr, Murdock, & Chapin, 1995). Under these circumstances, parental visitation may be infrequent and home care impossible. Nursing and therapy staff may become the primary emotional caregivers in addition to fulfilling their roles as medical caregivers. In these instances, a pediatric subacute nursing facility or a special medical foster home (individual or group) may be an appropriate alternative to prolonged hospitalization.

In most families, however, the parents remain very involved with their child and are willing and able to learn to care for their child at home once he or she becomes medically stable. Home care enables the entire family to be together with less disruption but also causes stress for family members who often experience chronic fatigue, financial concerns, and the demands of meeting their child's needs during a prolonged period of time (Bond, Phillips, & Rollins, 1994). Parents may be concerned about making a mistake that could injure or even cause the death of their child. If ongoing home nursing care is required, the lack of privacy caused by the presence of nurses may be an additional stressor. Studies have suggested that families can do well if the technology assistance lasts less than 2 years. More prolonged periods, however, are associated with an increased risk of parental stress and depression (Ahmann & Bond, 1992; Murphy, 1997). The provision of in-home respite care and family-to-family support systems can be extremely helpful in these situations.

FUNDING MEDICAL TECHNOLOGY ASSISTANCE

Medical technology assistance can be very expensive, depending on the type of equipment required, the extent of the disability (Miller et al., 1998; Smith, 1998), and the staffing needs of the child. Therefore, before the child who requires medical technologic support can be discharged, a number of financial issues must be addressed. The two major issues are nursing care and equipment/supplies. The requirement for nursing care depends on the severity of illness. In individuals who require mechanical ventilation, nursing care is often required for more than 12 hours per day (Fields et al., 1991). Yet, many insurance policies do not provide reimbursement for this much nursing care (Mele & Flowers, 2000). Even insurance polices that do reimburse for these needs may have ceilings beyond which they will not pay. Although these ceilings may be many hundreds of thousands of dollars, the benefits can be exhausted in less than a year of intensive nursing care. Yet, the child may require many years of home nursing care and technology assistance.

In addition, certain out-of-pocket expenses are not compensated for by federal programs or private insurance policies. These include remodeling of the home, increased utility costs, loss of income from work absences, transportation costs, and child care expenses. Approaches to funding are discussed in Chapter 38.

PREPARING FOR HOME CARE

Despite financial and psychosocial difficulties, more children who require medical technology assistance are being reintegrated into the community each year (Capen & Dedlow, 1998; Cross et al., 1998; Petit de Mange, 1998). Home care, especially when ventilator assistance is required, becomes a viable option only after a number of requirements have been met. The family must master the child's medical and nursing care (Bosworth & Nielson, 1997; Shipley, 1997; Toder & McBride, 1997). They need to select a nursing agency if home nursing services are required and a durable medical equipment supplier for equipment, disposable supplies, and in-home support (e.g., equipment maintenance and monitoring). The funds to pay for all these services also must be arranged. In addition, modifications to the family's home may be needed. These may include changing existing electrical systems and adding ramps for wheelchair or stroller accessibility. If mechanical ventilation is required, local electric, ambulance, and telephone companies must be notified that a person dependent on life-support technology will be living in the family's home so that the household can be placed on a priority list in the event of a power failure or a medical emergency.

Medical, educational, and rehabilitative services also need to be arranged before discharge. A pediatrician or family physician in the community should be identified to provide general medical care. The discharging team should contact this individual prior to the child's hospital discharge to introduce the child and encourage the community physician's active participation in the child's care. If the child requires special rehabilitation therapies after discharge, either center- or home-based providers should be arranged. Educational services also need to be identified, and the child's health care and rehabilitative plans should be written into an individualized family service plan for early intervention services (see Chapter 29) if the child is younger than age 3 or into an individualized education program (see Chapter 30) if the child is preschool or school age (Palfrey et al., 1994). In addition, the school nurse needs to develop an individualized health care plan as well as emergency plans for the child (Porter et al., 1997). A center- or school-based educational program offers the child the opportunity to interact with other children in a stimulating environment. This should be encouraged if the child's physical condition permits and appropriate medical or nursing supports are available.

OUTCOME

The neurodevelopmental outcome of the child who requires medical technology assistance depends more on the underlying condition than on the type of technology assistance provided (Stutts, 1994). Therefore, outcome is best discussed for the individual disorders. As the outcomes for HIV, neuromuscular disorders, and cerebral palsy are discussed in other chapters (see Chapters 8, 14, and 23, respectively), the following sections focus on the child who requires ventilator assistance.

Liberation from Mechanical Ventilation

A child's prognosis for liberation from mechanical ventilation depends on the disease causing the respiratory failure. Complete liberation from mechanical ventilation is usually a realistic goal for children with HMD. Satisfactory growth, normal gas exchange on the current level of support, sufficient stamina for activities of daily living, and absence of intercurrent illness usually indicate that the child can tolerate a gradual reduction in the level of mechanical support. The speed of weaning from the ventilator is dictated by the child's clinical status and contributing psychosocial factors (Frader, 2000; Lemanek, Zanoli, & Levy, 1997).

Several techniques are used to wean a child from mechanical ventilation (Zeggwagh et al., 1999). The number of mechanical breaths delivered per minute can be reduced gradually, or the child may spend increasingly longer periods off the ventilator. The "time off" approach has the advantage of allowing the child greater mobility. Nighttime mechanical ventilation is usually the last support to be withdrawn. After the child has functioned without mechanical ventilation and supplemental oxygen for several months, removal of the tracheostomy tube may be considered.

If the disorder is not expected to improve over time, such as in cases of muscular dystrophy or spinal cord injury, complete liberation from the ventilator may not be a realistic goal, yet partial liberation may still be possible. To promote mobility and independence, the child's schedule can be arranged so that ventilation is provided while the child is resting. For the child who completely depends on mechanical ventilation, mobility is still possible using a portable ventilator. These devices, with external batteries capable of powering the ventilator for up to 12 hours, can be mounted on specially designed trays attached to wheelchairs or carts. Though somewhat bulky, the portable mechanical ventilator and battery enable the child to attend school and travel with the family.

Developmental and Behavioral Complications Associated with Long-Term Mechanical Ventilator Support

Developmental complications associated with long-term mechanical ventilation are most commonly a function of the underlying medical condition that caused the respiratory failure and include language, behavior, and feeding problems (Gregoire, Lefebvre, & Glorieux, 1998). A number of studies, however, have suggested that some of the impairments in language production, syntax, and articulation are exacerbated by the presence of a tracheostomy during the critical period of early language development (Fraser, Pengilly, & Mok, 1998; Kertoy et al., 1999). Thus, speech-language therapy is very important for these children. Treatment focuses on oral exercises to encourage the sounds the child can produce as well as various augmentative and alternative communication systems (see Chapter 12). For the school-age child, the educator and speech-language pathologist collaborate to build a system of communication that incorporates the child's existing means of expression with communication aids. For example, a Passy-Muir **speaking valve** can be used to enhance vocalizations and speech at the same time that the therapist encourages the child to use sounds, gestures, and facial expressions (Fraser et al., 1998). This approach is combined with augmentative and alternative communication systems that use object, graphic, or picture modes of expression displayed in a variety of ways, such as a communication board or wallet, a conversation photograph notebook, a loop audiotape and a cassette recorder, or a computer system with voice or written output. These systems can greatly expand a child's ability to communicate.

Few studies have been published concerning the developmental outcome of children who require long-term mechanical ventilation. One of the most extensive studies describes moderate to severe developmental delay in almost half of premature infants with HMD who required long-term ventilation (Gray et al., 1995). This is about three times the rate of delay in premature infants who do not require ventilator assistance. The question remains whether prolonged mechanical ventilation itself is causally related to the poorer outcome or is a marker for other preexisting neurological impairments that adversely affect development. For example, the premature infant with severe HMD may have had sustained prolonged hypoxia or a significant intracerebral hemorrhage. One study provides evidence that neurodevelopmental outcome is a function of previous neurological complications and not the duration of mechanical ventilation (Luchi, Bennett, & Jackson, 1991).

Children who depend on a ventilator may also have behavior problems (Fridy & Lemanek, 1993). The absence of audible speech may lead to frustration in attempts at communication and may result in aggressive or acting-out behavior. Noncompliant behavior may also occur because of inconsistencies in caregiving during prolonged hospitalizations. Some children have developmental disabilities that resemble autism and are associated with perseverative, self-stimulatory, and self-injurious behaviors. Treatment often utilizes behavior management therapy, medication, and supportive counseling for the family and other caregivers (Levy, 1996). In addition, providing assistive communication strategies, which may enhance the ability of caregivers to understand the child, is likely to decrease the challenging behaviors (Carr et al., 1994).

Children who use ventilators also are at increased risk for GER and resultant vomiting. Over time, a child with GER may associate eating with the subsequent negative experience of vomiting and, as a result, may refuse to eat. In addition, the child may experience oral-motor dysfunction or frequent interruptions in periods of oral feeding due to acute illnesses (Starrett, 1991). The young child may lose the skills needed for effective feeding during these periods. Effective treatment includes medical management of any underlying disorder (e.g., GER) as well as teaching behavior management skills to the child's parents and caregivers.

SUMMARY

A medical technology device replaces or augments a vital bodily function. These devices include respiratory technology assistance, surveillance devices, nutritive assistive devices, ostomies, and dialysis. Approximately 1 in 1,000 children will require the long-term use of a medical assistive device, but the incidence among children with developmental disabilities is significantly higher. The requirement for prolonged technology assistance places both financial and emotional stresses on the entire family. It also provides considerable challenges to health care professionals and other caregivers. Knowledge about the correct use of medical devices and confidence in dealing with potential emergencies is important for both parents and caregivers. Training in medical technology assistance should occur while the child is hospitalized. Arrangement for financial, nursing, and equipment support is essential before the child goes home. Ultimately, outcome for the child who depends on medical technology appears to be more a function of the underlying disorder than the type of technology. The role of parents, however, cannot be overemphasized.

REFERENCES

Ahmann, E., & Bond, N.J. (1992). Promoting normal development in school-age children and adolescents who are technology dependent: A family centered model. *Pediatric Nursing, 18*, 399–405.

Akobeng, A.K., Miller, V., & Thomas, A. (1999). Percutaneous endoscopic gastrostomy feeding improves nutritional status and stabilizes pulmonary function in patients with cystic fibrosis. *Journal of Pediatric Gastroenterology and Nutrition, 29*, 485–486.

Bach, J.R., Niranjam, V., & Weaver, B. (2000). Spinal muscular atrophy type 1: A noninvasive respiratory management approach. *Chest, 117*, 1100–1105.

Bach, J.R., & Zhitnikov, S. (1998). The management of neuromuscular ventilatory failure. *Seminars in Pediatric Neurology, 5*, 92–105.

Baumgardner, D.J., & Burtea, E.D. (1998). Quality-of-life in technology-dependent children receiving home care and their families—a qualitative study. *WMJ, 97*, 51–55.

Bhatia, J. (2000). Current options in the management of apnea of prematurity. *Clinical Pediatrics, 39*, 327–336.

Bond, N., Phillips, P., & Rollins, J.A. (1994). Family-centered care at home for families with children who are technology dependent. *Pediatric Nursing, 20*, 123–130.

Bosworth, D.G., & Nielson, D.W. (1997). Effectiveness of home versus hospital care in the routine treatment of cystic fibrosis. *Pediatric Pulmonology, 24*, 42–47.

Campos, A.C., & Marchesini, J.B. (1999). Recent advances in the placement of tubes for enteral nutrition. *Current Opinion in Clinical Nutrition and Metabolic Care, 2*, 265–269.

Capen, C.L., & Dedlow, E.R. (1998). Discharging ventilator-dependent children: A continuing challenge. *Journal of Pediatric Nursing, 13*, 175–184.

Carlo, W.A., & Ambalavanan, N. (1999). Conventional mechanical ventilation: Traditional and new strategies. *Pediatric Reviews, 20*, 117–126.

Carr, E.G., Levin, L., McConnachie, et al. (1994). *Communication-based intervention for problem behavior: A user's guide for producing positive change.* Baltimore: Paul H. Brookes Publishing Co.

Chung, D.H., & Ziegler, M.M. (1998). Central venous catheter access. *Nutrition, 14*, 119–123.

Conger, J. (1998). Dialysis and related therapies. *Seminars in Nephrology, 18*, 533–540.

Corbett, N.A. (1998). Homecare, technology, and the management of respiratory disease. *Critical Care Nursing Clinics of North America, 10*, 305–313.

Cote, A., Hum, C., Brouillette, R.T., et al. (1998). Frequency and timing of recurrent events in infants using home cardiorespiratory monitors. *Journal of Pediatrics, 132*, 783–789.

Cross, D., Leonard, B.J., Skay, C.L., et al. (1998). Extended hospitalization of medically stable children dependent on technology: A focus on mutable family factors. *Issues in Comprehensive Pediatric Nursing, 21*, 63–84.

de Meer, K., Westerterp, K.R., Houwen, R.H., et al. (1997). Total energy expenditure in infants with bronchopulmonary dysplasia is associated with respiratory status. *European Journal of Pediatrics, 156*, 299–304.

Del Giudice, E., Staiano, A., Capano, G., et al. (1999). Gastrointestinal manifestations in children with cerebral palsy. *Brain Development, 21*, 307–311.

Downey, R., III, Perkin, R.M., & MacQuarrie, J. (2000). Nasal continuous positive airway pressure use in children with obstructive sleep apnea younger than 2 years of age. *Chest, 117*, 1608–1612.

Fields, A.I., Rosenblatt, A., Pollock, M.M., et al. (1991). Home care cost-effectiveness for respiratory technology-dependent children. *American Journal of Diseases of Children, 145*, 729–733.

Flenady, V.J., & Gray, P.H. (2000). Chest physiotherapy for preventing morbidity in babies being extubated from mechanical ventilation. *Cochrane Database of Systemic Reviews, 2*, CD000283.

Frader, J.E. (2000). Withdrawing mechanical ventilation in children. *Critical Care Medicine, 28*, 3119–3120.

Fraser, J., Pengilly, A., & Mok, Q. (1998). Long-term ventilator dependent children: A vocal profile analysis. *Pediatric Rehabilitation, 2*, 71–75.

Fridy, J., & Lemanek, K. (1993). Developmental and behavioral issues. In K. Bleile (Ed.), *The care of children with long-term tracheotomies* (pp. 141–167). San Diego: Singular Publishing Group.

Garvin, G. (1994). Caring for children with ostomies. *Nursing Clinics of North America, 29*, 645–654.

Goodman, G., Perkin, R.M., Anas, N.G., et al. (1988). Pulmonary hypertension in infants with bronchopulmonary dysplasia. *Journal of Pediatrics, 112*, 72–80.

Gozal, D. (2000). Pulmonary manifestations of neuromuscular disease with specific reference to Duchenne muscular dystrophy and spinal muscular atrophy. *Pediatric Pulmonology, 29*, 141–150.

Gray, P.H., Burns, Y.R., Mohay, H.A., et al. (1995). Neurodevelopmental outcome of preterm infants with bronchopulmonary dysplasia. *Archives of Disease in Childhood, 73*, F128–F134.

Gregoire, M.C., Lefebvre, F., & Glorieux, J. (1998). Health and developmental outcomes at 18 months in very preterm infants with bronchopulmonary dysplasia. *Pediatrics, 101*, 856–860.

Heulitt, M.J. (2000). The use of negative pressure ventilation in infants with acute respiratory failure: Old technology, new idea. *Respiratory Care, 45*, 479.

Hingorani, S., & Watkins, S.L. (2000). Dialysis for end-stage renal disease. *Current Opinion in Pediatrics, 12*, 140–145.

Hofner, G., Behrens, R., Koch, A., et al. (2000). Enteral nutritional support by percutaneous endoscopic gastrostomy in children with congenital heart disease. *Pediatric Cardiology, 21*, 241–246.

Hunt, C.E., Hufford, D.R., Bourguignon, C., et al. (1996). Home documented monitoring of cardiorespiratory pattern and saturation in healthy infants. *Pediatric Research, 39*, 216–222.

Jayabose, S., Escobedo, V., Tugal, O., et al. (1992). Home chemotherapy for children with cancer. *Cancer, 69*, 574–579.

Kertoy, M.K., Guest, C.M., Quart, C.M., et al. (1999). Speech and phonological characteristics of individual children with a history of tracheostomy. *Journal of Speech, Language, and Hearing Research, 42*, 621–635.

Khattak, I.U., Kimber, C., Kiely, E.M., et al. (1998). Percutaneous endoscopic gastrostomy in paediatric practice: Complications and outcome. *Journal of Pediatric Surgery, 33*, 67–72.

Kirk, S. (1998). Families' experiences of caring at home for a technology-dependent child: A review of the literature. *Child: Care, Health and Development, 24*, 101–114.

Krause, M.F., & Hoehn, T. (2000). Chest physiotherapy in mechanically ventilated children: A review. *Critical Care Medicine, 28*, 1648–1651.

Kuizon, B.D., & Salusky, I.B. (1999). Growth retardation in

children with chronic renal failure. *Journal of Bone and Mineral Research, 14,* 1680–1690.

Kurz, H. (1999). Influence of nasopharyngeal CPAP on breathing pattern an incidence of apnoeas in preterm infants. *Biology of the Neonate, 76,* 129–133.

Lemanek, K., Zanolli, K., & Levy, S.E. (1997). Environmental factors influencing weaning of a young child from mechanical ventilation. *Journal of Developmental and Behavioral Pediatrics, 18,* 166–170.

Levy, S.E. (1996). Nonpharmacologic management of disorders of behavior and attention. In A.J. Capute & P.J. Accardo (Eds.), *Developmental disabilities in infancy and childhood: Vol. II. The spectrum of developmental disabilities.* (2nd ed., pp. 451–457). Baltimore: Paul H. Brookes Publishing Co.

Luchi, J.M., Bennett, F.C., & Jackson, J.C. (1991). Predictors of neurodevelopmental outcome following bronchopulmonary dysplasia. *American Journal of Diseases of Children, 145,* 813–817.

MacDonald, K.D., & Johnson, S.R. (1996). Volume and pressure modes of mechanical ventilation in pediatric patients. *Respiratory Care Clinics of North America, 2,* 607–618.

Majnemer, A., Riley. P., Shevell, M., et al. (2000). Severe bronchopulmonary dysplasia increases risk for later neurological and motor sequelae in preterm survivors. *Developmental Medicine and Child Neurology, 42,* 53–60.

McKinley, W.O., Jackson, A.B., Cardenas, D.D., et al. (1999). Long-term medical complications after traumatic spinal cord injury: Regional model systems analysis. *Archives of Physical Medicine and Rehabilitation, 80,* 1402–1410.

Mele, N.C., & Flowers, J.S. (2000). Medicaid managed care and children with special health care needs: Case study analysis of demonstration waivers in three states. *Journal of Pediatric Nursing, 15,* 63–72.

Miller, V.L., Rice, J.C., DeVoe, M., et al. (1998). An analysis of program and family costs of case managed care in technology-dependent infants with bronchopulmonary dysplasia. *Journal of Pediatric Nursing, 13,* 244–251.

Miller, D.H., Ruley, J., & Bock, G.H. (1995). Current status of pediatric home peritoneal dialysis training in the United States. *Advances in Peritoneal Dialysis, 11,* 274–276.

Millner, B.N. (1991). Technology-dependent children in New York state. *Bulletin of the New York Academy of Medicine, 67,* 131–142.

Murphy, K.E. (1997). Parenting a technology-assisted infant: Coping with occupational stress. *Social Work in Health Care, 24,* 113–126.

Nadkarni, V., Hazinski, M.F., & Zideman, D., et al. (1997). Pediatric resuscitations: An advisory statement from the Pediatric Working Group of the International Liaison Committee on Resuscitation. *Circulation, 95,* 2185–2195.

Nadkarni, U.B., Shah, A.M., & Deshmukh, C.T. (2000). Non-invasive respiratory monitoring in paediatric intensive care. *Journal of Postgraduate Medicine, 46,* 149–152.

Nicholson, F.B., Korman, M.G., & Richardson, M.A. (2000). Percutaneous endoscopic gastrostomy: A review of indications, complications and outcome. *Journal of Gastroenterology and Hepatology, 15,* 21–25.

Oberwaldner, B. (2000). Physiotherapy for airway clearance in paediatrics. *European Respiratory Journal, 15,* 196–204.

Office of Technology Assessment. (1987). *Technology-dependent children: Hospital versus home care: A technical memorandum* (DHHS Publication No. TM-H-38). Washington, DC: U.S. Government Printing Office.

Palfrey, J.S., Haynie, M., Porter, S., et al. (1994). Prevalence of medical technology assistance among children in Mass-

achusetts in 1987 and 1990. *Public Health Reports, 109,* 226–233.

Palfrey, J.S., Walker, D.K., Haynie, M., et al. (1991). Technology's children: Report of a statewide census of children dependent on medical supports. *Pediatrics, 87,* 611–618.

Part 9: Pediatric basic life support. European Resuscitation Council. (2000). *Resuscitation, 46,* 401–441.

Pedersen, A.M., Kok, K., Petersen, G., et al. (1999). Percutaneous endoscopic gastrostomy in children with cancer. *Acta Paediatrica, 88,* 849–852.

Petit de Mange, E.A. (1998). Pediatric considerations in homecare. *Critical Care Nursing Clinics of North America, 10,* 339–346.

Petr, C.G., Murdock, B., & Chapin, R. (1995). Home care for children dependent on medical technology: The family perspective. *Social Work in Health Care, 21,* 5–22.

Poets, C.F., & Southall, D.P. (1994). Noninvasive monitoring of oxygenation in infants and children: Practical considerations and areas of concern. *Pediatrics, 93,* 737–746.

Porter, S., Haynie, M., Bierle, T., et al. (Eds.). (1997). *Children and youth assisted by medical technology in educational settings: Guidelines for care* (2nd ed.). Baltimore: Paul H. Brookes Publishing Co.

Posner, J.C. (1999). Acute care of the child with a tracheostomy. *Pediatric Emergency Care, 15,* 49–54.

Ramage, I.J., Geary, D.F., Harvey, E., et al. (1999). Efficacy of gastrostomy feeding in infants and older children receiving continuous ambulatory peritoneal dialysis. *Peritoneal Dialysis International, 19,* 231–236.

Roberts, K.E. (1999). Ventilatory strategies for the critically ill infant and child. *Critical Care Nursing Clinics of North America, 11,* 501–509.

Shipley, L. (1997). Technology-dependent children at home. *Nursing in Critical Care, 2,* 235–238.

Shulman, R.J. (2000). New developments in total parenteral nutrition for children. *Current Gastroenterology Reports, 2,* 253–258.

Smith, D.C. (1998). Assistive technology: Funding options and strategies. *Mental and Physical Disability Law Reports, 22,* 115–123.

Starrett, A.L. (1991). Growth in developmental disabilities. In A.J. Capute & P.J. Accardo (Eds.), *Developmental disabilities in infancy and childhood* (pp. 181–187). Baltimore: Paul H. Brookes Publishing Co.

Storgion, S.A. (1996). Care of the technology-dependent child. *Pediatric Annals, 25,* 677–684.

Stutts, A.L. (1994). Selected outcomes of technology dependent children receiving home care and prescribed child care services. *Pediatric Nursing, 20,* 501–505, 507.

Thomas, T.S., Berto, E., Scribano, M.L., et al. (2000). Treatment of esophageal Crohn's disease by enteral feeding via percutaneous endoscopic gastrostomy. *Journal of Parenteral and Enteral Nutrition, 24,* 176–169.

Thureen, P.J., & Hay, W.W., Jr. (2000). Intravenous nutrition and postnatal growth of the micropremie. *Clinical Perinatology, 27,* 197–219.

Toder, D.S., & McBride, J.T. (1997). Home care of children dependent on respiratory technology. *Pediatric Reviews, 18,* 273–281.

Warady, B., & Watkins, S.L. (1998). Current advances in the therapy of chronic and renal failure and end stage renal disease. *Seminars in Nephrology, 18,* 341–354.

Watson, A.R. (1995). Strategies to support families of children with end-stage renal failure. *Pediatric Nephrology, 9,* 628–631.

Zeggwagh, A.A., Abouqal, R., Madani, N., et al. (1999). Weaning from mechanical ventilation: A model for extubation. *Intensive Care Medicine, 25,* 1077–1083.

33 Rehabilitation

Physical Therapy and Occupational Therapy

Lisa A. Kurtz

Upon completion of this chapter, the reader will:

- understand the theoretical principles guiding physical therapy and occupational therapy

- be familiar with some common approaches to rehabilitation intervention, including neurodevelopmental therapy, sensory integration, orthotics, and nonmedical assistive technology

KIA: A CHILD WITH CEREBRAL PALSY AND ASSISTIVE TECHNOLOGY NEEDS

Kia was born at 30 weeks' gestation and was diagnosed with periventricular leukomalacia (see Chapter 6) shortly after birth. Physical therapy intervention began in the neonatal intensive care unit in the form of consultation with the parents and unit staff regarding positioning and handling techniques that would facilitate optimal postural control and help Kia to maintain a quiet, alert state during her waking hours. By 6 months of age, Kia was actively engaged with her environment, playing with toys and interacting with people. The muscle tone in her legs, however, was noted to be increased relative to the tone in her arms, and she was unable to sit alone. A diagnosis of spastic diplegic cerebral palsy was made. Outpatient physical therapy focused on a home management program, bilateral foot orthoses, adaptive seating, and helping her learn to sit and crawl. By 3 years of age, Kia could walk independently with canes and was enrolled in preschool, where she started occupational therapy with an emphasis on learning dressing and other self-care skills. Although she had typical intellectual development and was not a candidate for special education, Kia was eligible for consultative therapy in school once she entered kindergarten under the provisions of Section 504 of the Rehabilitation Act of 1973 (PL 93-112).

At age 6, Kia underwent orthopedic surgery to lengthen her lower extremity muscles, followed by a period of intensive physical therapy to improve her hip and knee control. Shortly thereafter, she became a community ambulator with the use of canes, although she continued to use a manual wheelchair for extended trips. By third grade, Kia was falling behind in schoolwork due to handwriting difficulties, and the occupational therapist recommended several simple modifications to a standard computer that allowed her to complete school assignments more efficiently.

Kia has continued her schooling, attending general education classes, receiving good grades, and participating fully in extracurricular programs. She is now ready to enter high school and is considering a power scooter to improve speed and freedom of mobility in her expanded school environment and in the community with her peers. She continues to be monitored in a tertiary care center by occupational and physical therapists to address current and/or potential problems.

GEORGE: A CHILD WITH PERVASIVE DEVELOPMENTAL DISORDER AND BEHAVIORAL DIFFICULTIES

Although George was a healthy baby whose early development seemed typical, he had some unusual habits, including a fascination for letters and numbers, extreme tantrums, and unusual food preferences. At age 3, George was diagnosed as having a pervasive developmental disorder (PDD), and was enrolled in an early intervention program. With intellectual functioning measuring in the low-average range, George progressed fairly well, although he continued to display limited play interests, delayed self-care skills, and frequent tantrums. At the age of 4½ years, he was referred for occupational therapy, at which time an evaluation revealed evidence of severe sensory defensiveness and poor motor planning skills. Therapy combining sensory integration and behavioral interventions was initiated. A typical session would proceed as follows:

1. With assistance, George removes his outer clothes, goes to the toilet, and washes his hands, with behavioral intervention strategies used to ensure his compliance.
2. Next, George is given a choice of two play activities that incorporate firm touch or other input to enhance body awareness. Firm touch usually produces a calming effect and helps to reduce tactile defensiveness and distractibility. For example, George may pretend to be a "hot dog" by wrapping himself in a foam mat (the "roll"), then invite his mother to apply make-believe mustard, relish, and onions, giving him a squeeze between each "condiment." He more willingly allows hand-over-hand instruction for subsequent tasks after this game.
3. George is next engaged in gross motor play selected to promote body awareness and motor planning, such as following a "map" that helps him to visualize the sequence of movements needed to maneuver an obstacle course.
4. Again using behavioral strategies, George is assisted in putting away his toys, washing his hands, and donning his coat, thus ending the session.

After 6 months of therapy, George was independent in most areas of self-care and showed a greater range of play interests. Although he continued to be overly sensitive, his parents could better anticipate potentially distressing situations and modify both the environment and their expectations accordingly to help him to maintain calmer behavior. When George entered kindergarten as a special education student, occupational therapy was included in his individualized education program (IEP; see Chapter 30). His therapist regularly visited his class. She offered many suggestions to his teachers to help them modify his school environment and to help him stay calm. For example, she suggested using a classroom chair with arms and a nonslip seat to prevent squirming and substituting a glue stick for the typical classroom paste that George found irritating to touch.

Children with disabilities or significant developmental delays often benefit from physical and occupational therapy interventions designed to promote inclusion in society. A variety of intervention options are available. Therapy may be provided on an individual, group, or consultative basis. It may be delivered in hospital, school, home, or community environments. It may be required daily or as needed. For example, an early intervention program with frequent physical and occupational therapy is often beneficial for the infant with cerebral palsy; during this period, the child undergoes rapid developmental changes; meanwhile, the parents are first learning to cope with their child's impairments. Once the child enters school, therapy may decrease in frequency and assume a more consultative role around the child's specific educational needs. The child may, however, periodically benefit from additional short-term therapy to address specific functional concerns, such as the need to improve ambulation following orthopedic surgery or the desire to learn adapted techniques for engaging in a new recreational setting.

PHYSICAL AND OCCUPATIONAL THERAPY APPROACHES TO INTERVENTION

Although physical and occupational therapists receive similar basic educational preparation, tend to hold congruent philosophies regarding approaches to intervention, and may acquire similar levels of skill in the use of selected therapeutic procedures, there are important differences in their primary roles (Conner-Kerr, Wittman, & Muzzarelli, 1998; Kurtz & Scull, 1993). Table 33.1 reviews some of the ways in which occupational and physical therapists might approach similar goals from different perspectives. Often, however, the roles of therapists overlap based on the interests and talents of the individual therapist as well as the philosophy of the workplace.

Pediatric physical therapy focuses on evaluating and treating sensorimotor development, musculoskeletal alignment, cardiopulmonary status, and neurobehavioral organization in children with physical disabilities or developmental delays that place them at risk for decreased functional mobility or for qualitative problems with mobility or postural control (Heriza & Sweeney, 1994). Pediatric occupational therapy also addresses sensorimotor development and neurobehavioral organization, as well as functional mobility, perceptual maturation, and psychosocial adjustment of children who have or are at risk for disabilities. Occupational therapists particularly focus on disabilities that limit the child's ability to develop the necessary skills and attitudes for independence in self-care, play, and school performance, which are the primary "occupations" of childhood (O'Brien, 1993). Although play is the therapy medium of choice for most young children, both occupational and physical therapy incorporate a wide variety of other modalities, including exercise, sensory stimulation, physical agents, splinting or casting, adaptive aids and equipment, and behavioral training (American Occupational Therapy Association, 1999; American Physical Therapy Association, 2001).

The nature of rehabilitation services has changed dramatically since the early 1900s, the formative years of occupational and physical therapy. Early models for rehabilitation were based in hospital settings and focused on the diagnosis and corrective treatment of pathological conditions resulting from disease or impairment (McNary, 1947; Weiss & Betts, 1967). Since then, interventions have focused on helping the child and family achieve confidence and independence with personally meaningful daily activities (Haley, Coster, & Binda-Sundberg, 1994; Law et al., 1998). This requires therapy to be family centered, culturally relevant, and community based. In addition, there is increasing emphasis on interventions for health promotion and prevention of the secondary complications, such as obesity, social isolation, and

Table 33.1. Comparison of occupational therapy (OT) and physical therapy (PT)

Rehabilitation goal	Typical OT emphasis	Typical PT emphasis
Promote developmental progression of skills	Fine motor, adaptive, and personal-social domains	Gross motor domain
Teach functional skills needed for daily living	Dressing, eating, toileting, personal hygiene, and household chores	Ambulation, transfers, and other mobility demands
Maintain or increase range of motion and muscle strength	Upper body	Lower body
Promote environmental accessibility	Organizing work and play areas for efficiency	Reducing architectural barriers to mobility
	Modifying the environment to promote attention and information processing	Providing adapted car seats or other transportation devices
Provide assistive technology	Adapted toys, school materials, computers, self-care aids, and environmental controls	Wheelchairs, ambulation aids, and transfer equipment

depression, that may arise from the presence of a disability (Canadian Association of Occupational Therapists, 1997; Kniepmann, 1997; Rimmer, 1999).

GUIDELINES FOR REFERRAL

Referral to physical therapy is indicated whenever there is a known physical impairment, a reason to suspect a delay in gross motor development, or a qualitative impairment in postural or movement skills. Referral to occupational therapy is indicated whenever there is reason to suspect delay or qualitative impairment in the performance of daily tasks and routines, including self-care, play, social interaction, or the performance of school-related tasks (American Academy of Pediatrics, Committee on Children with Disabilities, 1996). Referral is recommended as soon as a problem is identified to help the family learn about the diagnosis, identify additional supportive services, and master child care practices that will promote development and prevent further complications.

ASSESSMENT AND PLANNING FOR INTERVENTION

Initial assessment usually includes 1) an interview with the parents or other caregivers to determine their needs and concerns and 2) observation of the child at play or performing functional tasks. Therapists then clinically assess the child for muscle tone and strength, joint range of motion, sensory responses and perception, neurological maturation and organization, and social and behavior responses. Standardized tests of motor, perceptual, and adaptive development are also commonly administered.

The treatment plan will take into account results of these assessments as well as recommendations from all other people involved in the care of the child. The plan should address the model of intervention that will be used (e.g., individual, group, consultation), the optimal frequency of intervention, recommendations for special equipment or environmental adaptations, and the plan for parent or caregiver instruction. Goals should be developed for a specific time period with objective and measurable outcomes delineated. Periodically, the plan should be reevaluated and revised as necessary.

It is extremely important that the referring physician, the family, and all other team members are in agreement with the plan. Also, because learning is enhanced by practice and repetition, parents, teachers, and all other caregivers need to understand how to reinforce the skills learned in therapy throughout the child's day.

THERAPY IN EARLY INTERVENTION PROGRAMS

Therapy services in early intervention programs (see Chapter 29) may include screening for motor or perceptual difficulties, monitoring the development of children over time, consulting with families and other members of the interdisciplinary team, and providing direct therapy. Generally, early intervention programs focus more on helping families adjust to their child's developmental delay or disability than on correcting the problems. Attention is given to encouraging parents to develop a satisfying and nurturing relationship with their child and to learn practical methods for supporting their child's development in the natural environments of the home and community. Through the process of developing an individualized family service plan (IFSP), therapy goals are organized around the family's needs and priorities, taking into account the infant's unique abilities. Table 33.2 presents examples of how family goals for therapy might be expressed in an IFSP.

Table 33.2. Examples of therapy goals for early intervention

	Karen	Rasheed
Parent statement	"I want Karen to be able to get around on her own."	"We would like Rasheed to have more fun playing with his toys."
Individualized family service plan (IFSP) goal(s)	Karen will crawl using a reciprocal hand/knee pattern.	Rasheed will improve his ability to visually guide and control his hands to reach for toys.
		Rasheed will use his hands to activate a busy box or a simple cause-and-effect toy.
Intervention(s)	Provide neurodevelopmental facilitation to promote proximal stability and weight shift while in a quadruped position.	Provide corner seat with trunk harness to promote stability and scapular protraction during sitting.
	Use strategically placed toys directly in Karen's line of vision to encourage forward movement.	Provide resting hand splints to maintain range of motion.
		Provide several cause-and-effect toys that can be activated by a simple switch strategically within Rasheed's available reach.
Criterion	Karen will crawl for a distance of 3 feet using reciprocal hand/knee pattern at least once during each scheduled physical therapy session.	When positioned in his corner seat, Rasheed will actively reach towards a jellybean switch and apply sufficient force to activate a battery-operated toy in three of five trials.

THERAPY IN THE SCHOOL

Under the Individuals with Disabilities Act (IDEA) Amendments of 1997 (PL 105-17), students may be eligible for occupational or physical therapy services if the services allow the child to benefit from special education or to gain access to a general education program. Therapists may fulfill multiple roles in support of the educational objectives for the student (Table 33.3). Because provisions for therapy under IDEA '97 were designed to support the student's performance only in the school environment, some children with disabilities may require additional therapy in a clinical setting for their functional needs to be fully addressed.

A variety of service models may be used for implementing school-based therapy (American Occupational Therapy Association, 1997; Hanft & Place, 1997; Lowes & Effgen, 1996; Rainforth, York, & Macdonald, 1992). Direct service means that the therapist has frequent contact with the student, either individually or in a group; this service model is often recommended for students with severe or newly acquired disabilities that limit school performance or for those who require consistent, hands-on therapy to meet educational objectives. Monitoring involves the development of an intervention plan that can be effectively carried out by the classroom teacher or other personnel. Infrequent direct contact by the therapist is required to establish the effectiveness of the intervention and to update and revise the plan based on the student's progress. Consultation refers to the sharing of specialized knowledge with other education team members to support the overall goals and objectives of the educational program.

Table 33.3. Functions of occupational and physical therapy in school environments

Promoting safe and efficient mobility

Recommending classroom positioning to promote optimal postural control and function

Modifying classroom materials and routines to improve attention and organization

Treating specific perceptual and motor difficulties that interfere with academic achievement

Promoting independence in self-care (e.g., toileting, using the cafeteria)

Contributing to prevocational training

Consultation may be oriented toward the student (e.g., recommending an adaptation to sports equipment that allows a student to participate with peers in physical education; see Chapter 34); colleagues (e.g., providing in-service training to teachers regarding techniques for supporting the development of good handwriting habits); or the educational system (e.g., recommending environmental adaptations that allow all students with mobility limitations to have access to extracurricular activities). Current practice supports the provision of therapy in inclusive environments such that interventions are carried out in the student's natural environment, in the presence of peers, and using the typical tasks and materials that are expected of other students (Case-Smith & Cable, 1996).

Even children with disabilities who do not require special education (e.g., those with juvenile rheumatoid arthritis or spinal cord injury) may be eligible for special services and accommodations under other entitlements, including the Americans with Disabilities Act (ADA) of 1990 (PL 101-336), Section 504 of the Rehabilitation Act of 1973, or state regulations governing education.

SELECTED INTERVENTIONS

Neurodevelopmental Therapy

Neurodevelopmental therapy (NDT), based on the work of Drs. Karel and Berta Bobath, has been widely accepted and used by occupational and physical therapists since the 1960s (Bobath & Bobath, 1984). This treatment approach, based on a developmental model, emphasizes sensorimotor experience to facilitate the development of normal movement and postural responses and is most commonly used with young children diagnosed with cerebral palsy (see Chapter 23) or other neurodevelopmental disorders (Bly, 1991).

NDT focuses on the use of individualized handling techniques that are selected according to the child's specific problems with muscle tone and control, cognitive abilities, and motivation to engage in tasks. Through handling, therapists attempt to control abnormal patterns of movement while facilitating more normal motor patterns, thus promoting motor learning through the sensory feedback associated with active movement. Caregivers are taught to incorporate these handling techniques into the child's daily routine, hopefully increasing the caregivers' level of comfort with routine child care as well as promoting frequent practice of newly acquired skills (Breslin, 1996; Darrah & Bartlett, 1995).

Although a number of research studies suggest that therapy incorporating a neurodevelopmental approach increases the rate of improvement in motor development and the quality of motor control, some of these studies have been criticized for having design flaws (Ottenbacher et al., 1986; Palisano, 1991; Stern & Gorga, 1988). In addition, newer theories of motor learning suggest that a systems approach to motor development may be more efficacious than a purely developmental approach. Therapists are beginning to question whether the NDT approach results in adequate carryover of facilitated normal movement patterns to daily functional activities (Law et al., 1998). Multiple factors involving the musculoskeletal system, cognition, the environment, motivation, task requirements, and practice effects appear to be variables that should be manipulated in various combinations to effect lasting changes in motor behavior (Campbell, 2000; Heriza, 1991).

Sensory Integration Therapy

Children with developmental disabilities including specific learning disabilities, attention-deficit/hyperactivity disorder, and PDDs are commonly referred to therapists for evaluation and remediation of problems with motor coordination, self-care, handwriting, or the social isolation that may result from clumsiness and avoidance of playground activities or recreational sports.

Treatment approaches for these children are varied but commonly incorporate principles of sensory integration (SI) theory (Fisher, Murray, & Bundy, 1991; Parham & Mailloux, 1996), based on the work of A. Jean Ayres (1979). Ayres defined *sensory integration* as a normal developmental process involving the ability of the child's central nervous system to organize sensory feedback from the body and the environment in order to make successful adaptive responses. Problems with normal SI are suggested when 1) the child exhibits difficulty with planning and execution of motor or behavior responses; 2) there is evidence of perceptual impairment, especially involving the auditory, tactile, proprioceptive, vestibular, or visual systems; and 3) these problems are not attributable to overt brain damage or to a specific visual or hearing impairment. SI therapy advocates the use of controlled sensory input to create a milieu that promotes the child's success in making adaptive responses to environmental challenges. Proponents of SI contend that therapy enhances neural organization, leading to more mature learning and behavior patterns. Thus, rather than teach specific functional skills, the goal of intervention is to enhance the brain's ability to learn. As with many other developmental interventions, however, there is limited scientific evidence to support the efficacy of SI (Cermak & Henderson, 1989, 1990; Fallon, Mauer, & Neukirch, 1994; Ottenbacher, 1991; Wilson & Kaplan, 1994). Direct SI therapy requires frequent sessions (usually one to two times per week) and the use of a specially designed therapy area, making it difficult to provide within some school environments.

Many therapists recommend a holistic approach that combines SI therapy principles with more traditional approaches to promoting skill development. For example, modification of classroom materials and routines to reduce motor challenges during school or homework assignments can help students with mild motor difficulties to focus their attention more effectively on the cognitive aspects of learning. Examples of such modifications include providing a chair with armrests and a nonslip seat for the child who fidgets in his or her seat, a pencil grip for the child who has an immature grasp and fatigues during writing, or page separators for the child who is slow to locate a particular assignment in a workbook. Perceptual-motor interventions, usually involving the teaching and practice of specific motor skills, may help to improve the child's coordination for selected tasks, enhance self-esteem, and increase motivation for participation in physical education or recreational sports, although the effect on academic achievement has yet to be demonstrated (Schaffer et al., 1989). Group therapy organized around a common recreational interest may focus on preventing or minimizing the negative social consequences frequently associated with learning disabilities, including problems with self-esteem and social and behavioral interactions with peers (Tupper & Miesner, 1992; Williamson, 1993).

Splinting and Bracing

Orthotic management refers to the use of splints or braces to improve motor function. It may be used as an isolated intervention or as an adjunct to occupational and/or physical therapy. Splints may be either **static** (rigid) or **dynamic** (with movable parts). They may serve a variety of purposes, including 1) to support weak muscles, 2) to increase or maintain muscle length needed for mobility, 3) to control involuntary movement, 4) to immobilize a body part, or 5) to serve as a base of support for the attachment of toys or self-care devices (Blanchet & McGee, 1996).

Lower extremity orthotics, such as molded plastic ankle-foot orthoses (MAFOs), are worn inside the shoes. For example, they are commonly used to enhance ambulatory function in children who have spastic diplegia, like Kia. Children with significant lower extremity weakness may require more extensive orthoses that support the knees and/or hips to achieve ambulatory skills.

Static resting hand splints are often used to maintain muscle length and prevent the development of secondary musculoskeletal deformity in children with increased muscle tone. Their use during periods of inactivity, such as sleep, may promote increased flexibility and improved hand function when they are removed. Other static splints provide support to the hand in positions that improve function during purposeful activity. For example, a splint that supports the wrist in slight extension may make it easier for the child to oppose the thumb to the fingers, allowing a more functional grasp of objects. Dynamic hand splints may be designed to selectively increase muscle strength and/or control patterns of movement. Figure 33.1 presents two examples of splints commonly used by physical and occupational therapists.

Assistive Technology

The broad term *assistive technology* (AT) is used to describe a variety of devices and services that help children with disabilities to be included in a full range of social experiences and to function more independently, thus improving their quality of life. AT may be as simple as an enlarged spoon handle to compensate for a weak grasp, as commonplace as a wheelchair to promote mobility within the environment, or as futuristic as sophisticated computerized systems for augmentative and alternative communication (see Chapter 12) and environmental control. AT devices include products that are purchased commercially, modified, or custom made according to the specific needs of the user.

Even very young children may benefit from early training in the use of technology. For example, infants as young as 6 months may be capable of understanding the cause-and-effect relationships necessary to operate a single-switch computer program (Swinth, Anson, & Dietz, 1993). Early intervention programs teach young children how to use devices that promote their independence because children who are able to enter school with these technologies in place may be able to achieve greater success in general education classrooms (Butler, 1988).

A number of laws, including the Technology-Related Assistance for Individuals with Disabilities Act of 1988 (PL 100-407), ADA, and IDEA, have improved access to AT devices and services for children and have provided funding to support not only the purchase or lease of equipment but also services to ensure success with their use. These services include 1) evaluation of the child's technological needs, 2) maintenance and repair of equipment, 3) training in use of the devices, and 4) coordination of technology with other therapy services. Schools are required to specifically address the special education student's AT needs. If an evaluation indicates that a student requires AT to benefit from special education, it must be provided as an integral part of the IEP. This means that schools hold the legal responsibility for evaluation, device selection and acquisition, and training in the use of educationally relevant assistive devices. It should be noted, however, that when assistive devices are recommended for purposes that are not related to educational objectives, creative strategies for funding equipment often must be used. Some examples of potential funding sources include Medicaid (also referred to as *Medical Assistance*), Supplemental Security Income (SSI), private foundations or donors, and durable medical equipment riders on private insurance policies.

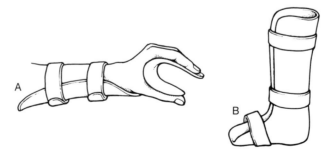

Figure 33.1.   a) Resting hand splint prevents deformity by maintaining a flaccid or spastic hand in a functional position; b) molded ankle-foot orthosis (MAFO) maintains the ankle in a desired position and prevents unwanted motion during gait.

OUTCOMES MEASUREMENT

The importance of identifying valid, sensitive, and practical tools that can be used to measure and document the outcome of rehabilitative care cannot be overemphasized (Campbell, 1996; Ketelaar, Vermeer, & Helders, 1998; Law et al., 1999). In the current health care climate, rehabilitation professionals are under increasing pressure to identify creative alternatives for delivering high-quality care at lower cost. Outcomes measurement can be extremely useful in demonstrating the validity of various therapeutic regimens. Use of consultative rather than direct service models, group rather than individual therapy, cross-training of providers from different disciplines in selected aspects of intervention, and nonlicensed aides as therapy extenders are emerging practices that are under debate by the health care industry.

Accurate and appropriate measures of functional outcome are needed to compare the relative benefits of these various approaches to rehabilitation. The most commonly used tools for measurement of outcome focus on functional changes that may occur during the course of rehabilitation. Examples of pediatric functional assessment tools in common use include the Pediatric Evaluation of Disability Inventory (PEDI; Coster & Haley, 1992) and the Uniform Data Set for Medical Rehabilitation for Children (WeeFIM; Msall, DiGaudio, & Duffy, 1993).

Although progress has been made in the area of outcomes measurement, there remain many unresolved problems. Quality rehabilitation strives for more than the reduction of functional impairment. Ultimately, the goal of rehabilitative intervention is to prevent or ameliorate social disadvantages that may develop as consequences of the underlying impairment (Christiansen, 1993). (See Chapter 15 for a discussion of the *terminology in disability classification*, a conceptual model of disablement that focuses on overcoming such functional limitations of impairment.) Therefore, outcome measures need to demonstrate not only that gains made during therapy can be sustained over time and in the child's natural environment but also that they result in an improved quality of life for the child and family (Mayhan, 1994; Smith & Illig, 1995). For example, children with cerebral palsy frequently receive physical and occupational therapy to improve mobility skills. One typical outcomes measure, easy to obtain during therapy, is increased joint range of motion as measured by goniometry. The real value of this therapy must be questioned, however, unless mobility gains can be easily maintained by parents or other caregivers at home; prevent the need for more invasive orthopedic or other medical intervention; reduce the costs for special education and related services; or promote access to social, educational, or recreational experiences that are desired by the child and family. Therapists must be increasingly prepared to demonstrate that recommended interventions are appropriate (i.e., address the needs as stated by the consumer), effective (i.e., achieve targeted outcomes), and efficient (i.e., at the lowest cost possible).

SUMMARY

Pediatric occupational and physical therapy strive to minimize the effects of impairment, to promote full inclusion in society, and to enhance the overall quality of life for children with disabilities and their families. Although the two disciplines may overlap in certain knowledge and skills, there are important differences in their primary roles and methods of care. A holistic approach to rehabilitation incorporates many different options for intervention selected according to therapeutic significance, as well as the family's unique needs and priorities. Examples of intervention methodology include exercise, sensory stimulation, environmental adaptation, positioning, NDT, SI, behavior therapy, orthotics, and AT. Some of these (splinting, exercise) are widely accepted, whereas others (NDT, SI) are in need of further research to support clinical efficacy.

REFERENCES

American Academy of Pediatrics, Committee on Children with Disabilities. (1996). The role of the pediatrician in prescribing therapy services for children with motor disabilities. *Pediatrics, 98,* 308–310.

American Occupational Therapy Association. (1997). *Occupational therapy services for children and youth under the Individuals with Disabilities Education Act.* Bethesda, MD: Author.

American Occupational Therapy Association. (1999). The guide to occupational therapy practice. *The American Journal of Occupational Therapy, 53,* 247–322.

American Physical Therapy Association. (2001). Guide to physical therapist practice (2nd ed.). *Physical Therapy, 81,* 9–746.

Americans with Disabilities Act (ADA) of 1990, PL 101-336, 42 U.S.C. §§12101 et seq.

Ayres, A.J. (1979). *Sensory integration and the child.* Los Angeles: Western Psychological Services.

Blanchet, D., & McGee, S.M. (1996). Principles of splint design and use. In L.A. Kurtz, P.W. Dowrick, S.E. Levy, et al. (Eds.), *Handbook on developmental disabilities: Resources for interdisciplinary care* (pp. 465–480). Gaithersburg, MD: Aspen Publishers.

Bly, L. (1991). A historical and current view of the basis of NDT. *Pediatric Physical Therapy, 3,* 131–135.

Bobath, K., & Bobath, B. (1984). Neuro-developmental treatment. In D. Scrutton (Ed.), *Clinics in developmental medicine: No. 90. Management of the motor disorders of children with cerebral palsy* (pp. 6–18). Cambridge, England: Cambridge University Press.

Breslin, D.M. (1996). Motor-learning theory and the neurodevelopmental treatment approach: A comparative analysis. *Occupational Therapy in Health Care, 10*(1), 25–40.

Butler, C. (1988). High tech tots: Technology for mobility, manipulation, communication, and learning in early childhood. *Infants and Young Children, 1*(2), 66–73.

Campbell, S.K. (1994). The child's development of functional movement. In S. Campbell (Ed.), *Physical therapy for children* (pp. 3–37). Philadelphia: W.B. Saunders.

Campbell, S.K. (1996). Quantifying the effects of interventions for movement disorders resulting from cerebral palsy. *Journal of Child Neurology, 11*(Suppl. 1), S61–S70.

Canadian Association of Occupational Therapists. (1997). *Enabling occupation: An occupational therapy perspective.* Ottawa, Ontario: CAOT Publications.

Case-Smith, J., & Cable, J. (1996). Perceptions of occupational therapists regarding service delivery models in school-based practice. *The Occupational Therapy Journal of Research, 16*(1), 23–44.

Cermak, S., & Henderson, A. (1989). The efficacy of sensory integration procedures: Part I. *Sensory Integration Quarterly, 17*(3), 1–5.

Cermak, S., & Henderson, A. (1990). The efficacy of sensory integration procedures: Part II. *Sensory Integration Quarterly, 18*(1), 1–5.

Christiansen, C. (1993). Continued challenges of functional assessment in rehabilitation: Recommended changes. *American Journal of Occupational Therapy, 47,* 258–259.

Conner-Kerr, T.A., Wittman, P., & Muzzarelli, R. (1998). Analysis of practice-role perceptions of physical therapy, occupational therapy, and speech-language therapy students. *Journal of Allied Health, 27,* 128–131.

Coster, W.J., & Haley, S.M. (1992). Conceptualization and measurement of disablement in infants and young children. *Infants and Young Children, 4*(4), 11–22.

Darrah, J., & Bartlett, D. (1995). Dynamic systems theory and management of children with cerebral palsy: Unresolved issues. *Infants and Young Children, 8*(1), 52–59.

Fallon, M.A., Mauer, D.M., & Neukirch, M. (1994). The effectiveness of sensory integration activities on language processing in preschoolers who are sensory and language impaired. *Infant and Toddler Intervention, 4*(3), 235–243.

Fisher, A.G., Murray, E.A., & Bundy, A.C. (1991). *Sensory integration: Theory and practice.* Philadelphia: F.A. Davis.

Haley, S.M., Coster, W.J., & Binda-Sundberg, K. (1994). Measuring physical disablement: The contextual challenge. *Physical Therapy, 74*(5), 443–451.

Hanft, B., & Place, P. (1997). *The consulting therapist: A guide for physical and occupational therapists in the schools.* San Antonio, TX: Therapy Skill Builders.

Heriza, C.B. (1991). Motor development: Traditional and contemporary theories. In M.J. Lister (Ed.), *Contemporary control of motor problems: Proceedings of the Step II Conference* (pp. 99–126). Alexandria, VA: Foundations for Physical Therapy.

Heriza, C.B., & Sweeney, J.K. (1994). Pediatric physical therapy, Part I: Practice, scope, scientific basis, and theoretical foundation. *Infants and Young Children, 7*(2), 20–32.

Individuals with Disabilities Education Act (IDEA) Amendments of 1997, PL 105–17, 20 U.S.C. §§ 1400 *et seq.*

Ketelaar, M., Vermeer, A., & Helders, P.J. (1998). Functional motor abilities of children with cerebral palsy: A systematic literature review of assessment measures. *Clinical Rehabilitation, 12,* 369–380.

Kniepmann, K. (1997). Prevention of disability and maintenance of health. In C. Christiansen & C. Baum (Eds.), *Occupational therapy: Enabling function and well-being* (pp. 530–555). Thorofare, NJ: Slack.

Kurtz, L.A., & Scull, S.A. (1993). Rehabilitation for developmental disabilities. *Pediatric Clinics of North America, 40,* 629–643.

Law, M., Darrah, J., Pollack, N., et al. (1998). Family-centered functional therapy for children with cerebral palsy: An emerging practice model. *Physical and Occupational Therapy in Pediatrics, 18*(1), 83–102.

Law, M., King, G., Russell, D., et al. (1999). Measuring outcomes in children's rehabilitation: A decision protocol. *Archives of Physical Medicine and Rehabilitation, 80,* 629–636.

Lowes, L.P., & Effgen, S. (1996). The Americans with Disabilities Act of 1990: Implications for pediatric physical therapists. *Pediatric Physical Therapy, 8,* 111–116.

Mayhan, Y.D. (1994). The importance of outcomes measurement in managed care. *American Occupational Therapy Association, Administration and Management Special Interest Section Newsletter, 10*(4), 2–4.

McNary, H. (1947). The scope of occupational therapy. In H. Willard & C.S. Spackman (Eds.), *Occupational therapy.* Philadelphia: Lippincott Williams & Wilkins.

Msall, M.E., DiGaudio, K.M., & Duffy, L.C. (1993). Use of functional assessment on children with developmental disabilities. *Physical Medicine and Rehabilitation Clinics of North America, 4,* 517–527.

O'Brien, S.P. (1993). Human occupation frame of reference. In P. Kramer & J. Hinojosa (Eds.), *Frames of reference for pediatric occupational therapy* (pp. 307–350). Philadelphia: Lippincott Williams & Wilkins.

Ottenbacher, K. (1991). Research in sensory integration: Empirical perceptions and progress. In A.G. Fisher, E.A.

Murray, & A.C. Bundy (Eds.), *Sensory integration: Theory and practice* (pp. 387–399). Philadelphia: F.A. Davis.

Ottenbacher, K.J., Biocca, Z., DeCremer, G., et al. (1986). Quantitative analysis of the effectiveness of pediatric therapy: Emphasis on the neurodevelopmental approach. *Physical Therapy, 66,* 1095–1101.

Palisano, R.J. (1991). Research on the effectiveness of neurodevelopmental treatment. *Pediatric Physical Therapy, 3*(3), 143–148.

Parham, L.D., & Mailloux, Z. (1996). Sensory integration. In J. Case-Smith & P.N. Pratt (Eds.), *Occupational therapy for children* (3rd ed., pp. 307–355). St. Louis: Mosby.

Rainforth, B., York, J., & Macdonald, C. (1992). *Collaborative teams for students with severe disabilities: Integrating therapy and educational services.* Baltimore: Paul H. Brookes Publishing Co.

Rehabilitation Act of 1973, PL 93-112, 29 U.S.C. §§ 701 et seq.

Rimmer, J.M. (1999). Health promotion for people with disabilities: The emerging paradigm shift from disability prevention to prevention of secondary conditions. *Physical Therapy, 79,* 495–502.

Schaffer, R., Law, M., Polatajko, H., et al. (1989). A study of children with learning disabilities and sensorimotor problems, or let's not throw the baby out with the bathwater.

Physical and Occupational Therapy in Pediatrics, 9(3), 101–117.

Smith, P.M., & Illig, S.B. (1995). Measuring post-discharge functional outcomes. *Far Horizons, 2*(1), 1–2.

Stern, F.M., & Gorga, D. (1988). Neurodevelopmental treatment (NDT): Therapeutic intervention and its efficacy. *Infants and Young Children, 1,* 22–32.

Swinth, Y., Anson, D., & Dietz, J. (1993). Single-switch computer access for infants and toddlers. *American Journal of Occupational Therapy, 47,* 1031–1038.

Technology-Related Assistance for Individuals with Disabilities Act of 1988, PL 100-407, 29 U.S.C. §§ 2201 *et seq.*

Tupper, L.C., & Miesner, K.E.K. (1992, March). The role of occupational therapy with the learning disabled child. *Sensory Integration Quarterly, 20*(1), 8–9.

Weiss, H., & Betts, H.B. (1967). Methods of rehabilitation in children with neuromuscular disorders. *Pediatric Clinics of North America, 14,* 1009–1016.

Williamson, G.G. (1993). Enhancing the social competence of children with learning disabilities. *Sensory Integration Special Interest Section Newsletter, 16*(1), 1–2.

Wilson, B.N., & Kaplan, B.J. (1994). Follow-up assessment of children receiving sensory integration treatment. *Occupational Therapy Journal of Research, 14,* 244–266.

34 Exercise, Sports, and Recreation

Terry Adirim and Kenneth M. Fine

Upon completion of this chapter, the reader will:

- Understand the importance of helping all children participate in sports and recreation

- Be familiar with the specific benefits of exercise for the child with special needs

- Be familiar with the laws regarding the inclusion of children with physical and cognitive disabilities in physical education and community programs

- Understand how to incorporate physical education adaptations into a child's individualized education program based on his or her abilities

- Be aware of community sports and recreation programs available to children with special needs

- Know about the pre-participation evaluation for children and adolescents with disabilities

- Have knowledge of the types of injuries encountered in athletes with disabilities

One of the goals of the U.S. government's Healthy People 2010 initiative (a statement of national health objectives identifying the most significant preventable threats to health and establishing national goals to reduce these threats) is to have 85% of adolescents participate in vigorous physical activity for more than 20 minutes, three times per week (U.S. Public Health Service, 2000). Yet, it has been noted that people with disabilities tend to engage in very low rates of physical activity. As a result of this finding, there has been increased interest in incorporating exercise, sports, and recreation into their lives. In addition to the improved health that results from increased fitness, the impetus for this increased interest is a commitment to full inclusion of children with disabilities in all aspects of life.

Ideally, all children should have the opportunity to participate in recreational activities and sports that capitalize on their abilities. For any child, free play and sporting activities promote fitness, endurance, coordination, and self-esteem. Physical activity has also been credited with maximizing muscle and bone growth and strength, increasing lean muscle mass, reducing body fat, and preventing or reducing symptoms of depression and anxiety (Chang, 2000). In addition, sports provide children with achievable goals that promote a sense of accomplishment and increase self-esteem. Recreational activities also provide the opportunity for children with developmental disabilities to be included in their broader community. This is beneficial to children with and without disabilities; children with disabilities develop important social skills, and typically developing children learn sensitivity to others who are different. Very few conditions preclude an individual from participating in exercise and sport. Thus, professionals working with children with disabilities should actively promote participation in sport and recreation activities.

JAMIE

Jamie is a 14-year-old with Down syndrome who is interested in playing on a Special Olympics basketball team. He became interested in the Special Olympics because one of his classmates plays in a local league. In preparation for his participation Jamie visited his pediatrician for an evaluation. She noted that Jamie has not had many of the medical complications associated with his condition. In considering Jamie's request, his doctor was aware that individuals with Down syndrome have physical differences that may affect their ability to participate in contact sports or those requiring vigorous effort. Approximately 15% of people with Down syndrome have atlantoaxial subluxation (see Chapter 16), a condition caused by laxity of the ligament that holds the first neck vertebra (C1) in place. Excessive motion at this level has the potential to cause permanent damage to the spinal cord (Sullivan & Anderson, 2000). As a result, screening for this problem is mandated by the Special Olympics prior to an individual's participating in certain sports: "butterfly stroke and diving starts in swimming [as well as individual medley events], pentathlon, high jump, squat lifts, equestrian sports, artistic gymnastics, football (soccer), alpine skiing, snowboarding, and any warm-up exercises placing undue stress on the head and neck" (Special Olympics, n.d.-b, p. 14). Children with significant atlantoaxial subluxation are encouraged to take part in lower impact sports.

Jamie's pediatrician first asked about symptoms suggestive of atlantoaxial subluxation, including neck pain, stiff neck, torticollis (wry neck), progressive loss of bowel or bladder control, or change in gait pattern. Jamie's mother indicated that her son had not had any of these symptoms. The pediatrician then examined Jamie and concluded that he was mildly overweight and had mild to moderate ligamentous laxity (hyperflexible, flat feet) but had no neurologic signs or symptoms suggestive of atlantoaxial subluxation. After discussing the findings with Jamie's family, the pediatrician decided to obtain special cervical spine (neck) X rays to screen for atlantoaxial subluxation; these were found to be normal. As a result of the examination, the pediatrician signed the form permitting Jamie's participation in sports activities without specific limitations. She also told the family that this physical activity could be helpful to Jamie in a number of ways. It could aid in weight control, which is often an issue for people with Down syndrome. It could also support his emerging social skills and self-esteem. The pediatrician, however, counseled the family about certain injuries that Jamie was at higher risk to sustain as a result of his generalized ligamentous laxity. To avoid these she suggested that he perform certain warm-up exercises and avoid certain sustained activities that would predispose him to injury.

PHYSICAL ACTIVITY IN CHILDREN WITH DISABILITIES

Developmental disabilities carry varied challenges for participation in physical activities. For example, cerebral palsy is associated with significantly impaired movements (see Chapter 23), and musculoskeletal disorders (e.g., muscular dystrophy) may be associated with decreased levels of cardiorespiratory fitness and muscular endurance. Yet, the lack of participation in physical activity by these individuals predisposes them to more health problems than involvement poses, including osteoporosis and obesity (Dykens, Rosner, & Butterbaugh, 1998; Fernhall, 1992; Takeuchi, 1994). Rates of obesity are especially high in people with Down syndrome, muscular dystrophy, and meningomyelocele (see Chapter 24) (Fernhall et al., 1996; Prasher, 1995).

Exercise, particularly aerobic activity, has been shown to aid in weight control and to be feasible in most children (Rimmer, 1992). In addition, it can improve self-confidence and offer opportunities for social interactions. Studies have shown that low self-esteem is a particular concern in children with mental retardation (Bybee, Ennis, & Zigler, 1990; Johnson, 1981;

MacMahon & Gross, 1987; Rogers & Saklofske, 1985; Widaman et al., 1992) and that participants in Special Olympics have greater self-esteem and confidence as compared with nonparticipating individuals (Edmiston, 1990; Klein, Gilman, & Zigler, 1993).

People with mental retardation are also at increased risk for maladaptive behaviors and behavioral disorders, including aggression, impulsivity, stereotypies, and self-injurious behaviors (Dykens et al., 1998; see Chapter 19). Studies have shown that exercise may be beneficial in reducing some of these behaviors, especially in individuals with pervasive developmental disorders (Kern et al., 1982; see Chapter 20). For example, one study of children with autism demonstrated that jogging was associated with a reduction in self-stimulatory behaviors for 40 minutes after the activity (Celiberti et al., 1997).

Another area that is being actively investigated is the effect of sports on improving social competence in individuals with mental retardation. In one study, participants in Special Olympics programs were shown to be more involved in extracurricular activities, hobbies, and friendships than nonparticipants were (Dykens & Cohen, 1996). Other studies have demonstrated that sports activities improve social adjustment in children with learning disabilities (Bachman & Sluyter, 1988; Kern et al., 1982; Rosenthal-Malek & Mitchell, 1997). A few studies have explored the effects of exercise on learning, but no significant improvement has been noted. One study in boys, however, did show that aerobic exercise improved self-concept and physical fitness (MacMahon & Gross, 1987). There is also a controversial study suggesting that physical exercise prior to classroom activities may improve performance on tests of concentration (Caterino & Polak, 1999). Despite the paucity of data, taken as a whole, these studies suggest that children with developmental disabilities should be encouraged to participate in some form of exercise or sport activity on an ongoing basis. In support of such a conclusion, the American Academy of Orthopaedic Surgeons (1985/1992) issued a report strongly endorsing the participation of people with physical disabilities in sports and recreational activities. These activities could include both regular sports (e.g., track and field, martial arts, swimming) and adapted sports (e.g., horseback riding to improve balance in the child with cerebral palsy, wheelchair races for individuals with meningomyelocele).

Individual sports may be a better choice for children with disabilities than team sports. In contrast to team sports that tend to be organized for the youth population (e.g., Little League Baseball, soccer), individual sports (e.g., swimming) allow participation throughout a person's life span. Individual sports also allow the individual with a disability to improve at his or her own pace, without being compared with other children. As a result, even small improvement can lead to a sense of accomplishment. It should be emphasized that although individual activities are not conducted with a team of other athletes, they can be performed in the company of other children. In this inclusive setting, the child with a disability can benefit from learning to cooperate with other children and to engage in socially appropriate behavior. The participation of a child with a disability in community recreation programs should be presented in a positive manner to the other participating children. Children without disabilities may benefit from inclusion policies by becoming more accepting of individuals with disabilities not only in sporting activities but in other aspects of life as well.

INCLUSION OF THE CHILD WITH DISABILITIES
IN EXERCISE AND SPORTS PROGRAMS IN SCHOOL

According to the National Association for Sport and Physical Education (n.d.), a physically educated person

> Has learned the skills necessary to perform a variety of physical activities, is physically fit, does participate regularly in physical activity, knows the implication of and the benefits from involvement in physical activities, and values physical activity and its contributions to a healthful lifestyle

In fact, the Individuals with Disabilities Education Act (IDEA) Amendments of 1997 (PL 105-17) includes a provision that exercise and recreation is part of a free appropriate public education and should be incorporated into educational curriculum for a student with disabilities as part of his or her individualized education program (IEP). These planned exercise and recreation programs should support the goals and objectives of the IEP (see Chapter 30).

Yet, despite these goals and IDEA '97 legislation, children with disabilities continue to be excluded from many physical education programs. To prevent this exclusion, specific goals and objectives for physical education should be included in each IEP. These should be developmentally appropriate for the child and include the provision of adaptive techniques and technology when needed. Adapted physical education programs are those that have the same objectives as general physical education but involve adjustments in the regular program to meet the needs and abilities of students with special needs. Some examples of adaptations include modifying equipment, changing the rules of the game, having a student in alternate activities, and providing peer assistance. The purpose of these adaptations is to allow the child to be included in the general physical education class with peers without disabilities to the greatest extent possible. A specific example of adaptation in a physical education class is that while the children without disabilities are warming up (e.g., doing jumping jacks), a child in a wheelchair can do exercises or stretches specifically adapted for his or her upper-arm abilities. Or, an ambulatory child with mild cerebral palsy could be given extra opportunities to hit a ball (e.g., allowed 5 strikes) during a game of softball.

Accommodations to team and individual sports can be made for children with physical and sensory disabilities. For example, ball sports can be adapted to a child's disability by using larger or smaller balls, by varying the distance required to travel while dribbling in basketball or soccer, by using textured balls that facilitate catching, by using brightly colored balls for a child with visual impairments, or by using softer balls for safety. A student who uses a wheelchair can play these sports by holding the ball on his or her lap while moving the chair to the basket or goal or by being permitted to push the wheelchair a few times, bounce the ball, and then move the wheelchair again. Also, a student who uses a wheelchair should be encouraged to pass the ball by throwing overhead instead of from the chest. In softball, an athlete can hit the ball off a tee or use larger balls. In addition, an athlete with visual impairments can receive verbal cues when the ball is pitched. During a game, the bases can be placed closer together so that there is less distance to run, the pitcher could stand closer to the player and pitch slowly, or different rules for scoring could be used. During a game, a peer without a disability could be paired with the athlete with a disability to provide assistance (Block, 2000).

COMMUNITY SPORTS PROGRAMS

In the United States, federal legislation has been instrumental in both the creation of special/adapted community recreation programs for children with disabilities and in the inclusion of these children in general community recreation programs. This movement started with the Rehabilitation Act of 1973 (PL 93-112), which prohibited discrimination in recreation programs on the basis of disability. In 1990, the Americans with Disabilities Act (PL 101-336) opened doors for the nondiscriminatory participation of individuals with disabilities in all aspects of public life, including recreational activities.

Still, there remain barriers to participation in both special/adapted and inclusive recreational programs. For example, in any one school or community there may not be sufficient children with a particular disability to form a special team, or the special program that is available may be too far for a family to travel to. Barriers to inclusion also include reluctance on the part of athletes without disabilities and their families, coaches, and teachers to allow children with disabilities to participate.

Yet, there are clearly effective ways for these individuals to be included in existing recreation/sports programs or to develop special programs (Schleien et al., 1997). Many of the more innovative programs are taking place in community centers and in parks and recreation programs that are supported by federal funds and, therefore, must be responsive to federal mandates. These include swimming, adapted sports, and camp programs geared for the child with physical or cognitive impairments. Many sports can be adapted for the athlete with a disability by modifying the rules or by the athlete's using adaptive equipment (Chang, 1994).

A number of national organizations (with local affiliates) provide an infrastructure for programs involving athletes with disabilities. Perhaps the most widely known of these is Special Olympics; others include the International Paralympic Committee for athletes with physical disabilities and Disabled Sports USA. Certain organizations address specific disabilities (see Appendix D), such as the United States Association of Blind Athletes, the International Committee of Sport for the Deaf, and the National Disability Sports Alliance (formerly known as the United States Cerebral Palsy Athletic Association. There are also sports-specific organizations (see Appendix D) such as the Challenger Division of Little League Baseball, TOPSoccer (Total Outreach Program for Soccer), and Yoga for the Special Child. TOPSoccer, affiliated with the US Youth Soccer organization, is an example of a community-based program that enables young athletes with physical or intellectual disabilities to practice and play soccer. The Little League Challenger Division, affiliated with the Little League Baseball organization, does the same for youth baseball. These organizations not only provide the opportunity for children with disabilities to play specific sports but also allow these children to partner with peers without disabilities.

As communities are becoming aware of the barriers to participation in recreational activities for children with disabilities, new opportunities and ideas for inclusion are being created. An example is the construction of adapted playgrounds that have ramps and wheelchair-accessible equipment. Model recreation programs include Project TRAIL, Jewish community centers, and Trail Partners: A Creative Step Toward Access in Park Districts.

Each of these organizations has criteria for determining how athletes are grouped according to similar abilities. For example, the International Paralympic Committee (2000) criteria state that a person is eligible to participate in the Paralympic Games if he or she "cannot participate on reasonably equal terms in a sport for 'able-bodied' because of a functional disadvantage due to a permanent disability." Impairment classifications within Paralympics include athletes with 1) cerebral palsy; 2) spinal cord lesions, meningomyelocele, or polio; 3) blindness; and 4) neuromuscular disorders or amputations. Each category and sport is further broken down into specific functional categories. A wide range of sports are available including archery, track and field, cycling, equestrian, fencing, judo, powerlifting, sailing, soccer, swimming, table tennis, wheelchair basketball, wheelchair rugby, wheelchair tennis, volleyball, alpine and cross-country skiing, ice-sledge hockey, and wheelchair dance sport.

The Special Olympics, which Jamie wanted to participate in, is probably the best known of the private agencies promoting sports programs for individuals with cognitive impairments such as mental retardation. Its mission is stated as providing

> Year-round sports training and athletic competition in a variety of Olympic-type sports for all children and adults with mental retardation, giving them continuing opportunities to develop physical fitness, demonstrate courage, experience joy, participate in the sharing of gifts, skills and friendship with their families, other Special Olympic athletes and the community (Special Olympics, n.d.-a)

Goals of the Special Olympics include enhancing physical fitness, social development, and acceptance in the community. Athletes are grouped for competition by sex, age, and ability. More than 1 million Special Olympic athletes participate in more than 150 programs worldwide (Special Olympics, n.d.-a). There are six international regions; the region for North

America is subdivided into state/territory organizations. Each of these subdivisions is organized into local affiliate groups that provide year-round activities for their athletes, including both training and competition. Individuals of all ability levels are accommodated, including individuals with severe mental retardation. For example, a local organization may hold a basketball tournament that along with typical basketball games has dribbling races and shooting contests for individuals who do not have the skills to participate in the team sport activity. On a national and international level, the Special Olympics offers winter and summer events similar to those offered in the Paralympic Games.

THE PRE-PARTICIPATION EXAMINATION

Every athlete with a disability should have a pre-participation examination performed at least once a year by a physician knowledgeable about sports medicine issues (American Academy of Pediatrics, Committee on Sports Medicine and Committee on Children with Disabilities, 1987). The purpose of this examination is not to determine whether a child should be excluded from participation but rather to provide an opportunity for the physician to recommend prevention measures and/or adapted activities based on development skills and physical challenges. As was the case with Jamie, this evaluation may include special tests to uncover conditions problematic or hazardous to the athlete. In addition, it can provide advice in choosing an appropriate sport and/or the adaptive equipment needed for that sport.

The annual pre-participation examination should ideally be performed by a physician who is familiar with the child's needs. Each year, the physician should identify new physical/developmental accomplishments and challenges as well as address ongoing issues. Topics to review should include use of adaptive equipment (e.g., wheelchair); presence of allergies; special dietary needs; risk of exercise-induced wheezing; emotional, psychiatric, or behavioral problems that could interfere with participation in sports; bone or joint disorders; hearing impairment and hearing aid use; contact lens or eyeglasses use; use of dentures; immunization record (especially tetanus); and long-term medications that could enhance (e.g., steroids) or interfere with (e.g., sedating medication) performance. The physician should also ask about past medical problems that may place the child at increased risk for sports injury. These include exercise-induced fainting or seizures; past heat or cold injury; prior fractures or dislocations; history of menstrual problems; prior medical disqualification; and level of previous sports participation.

The physical examination should include all organ systems, with a special focus on those areas affected by the child's disability. For example, children with Down syndrome should have careful attention paid to their cardiovascular and musculoskeletal systems (see Chapter 16). Finally, athletes who use wheelchairs, prosthetics, or other medical assistive devices such as ostomies (see Chapter 32) should have this equipment checked periodically for fit and wear.

Some sports are clearly inappropriate for children with certain disabilities. For example, contact sports are contraindicated in a child with brittle bones due to osteogenesis imperfecta (see Chapter 14) or for the child with Down syndrome who has atlantoaxial subluxation. In the past, however, children with disabilities were often excluded from sports unnecessarily. Take the example of swimming and diving for children with seizure disorders (see Chapter 25). Previously, neither swimming nor diving was permitted; now it is clear that provided that there is adequate supervision and the child's seizures are under adequate control, these activities carry little risk of injury.

The Committee on Sports Medicine and Fitness of the American Academy of Pediatrics (2001) has devised a classification system for sports. They are classified as either contact or noncontact and then further subclassified into strenuous, moderately strenuous, and nonstrenuous activities. The committee also set forth recommendations for participation by children with various medical conditions on the basis of this classification system. In this system, very few conditions exclude a child from playing all sport activities. Even children with Down syndrome who have complex congenital cardiac malformations may be able to participate in some sporting activity, depending on the severity of the condition and following consultation with the child's cardiologist. Some children, such as those with osteogenesis imperfecta, are excluded from contact sports but are cleared for participation in nonstrenuous, noncontact activities. These individuals should consult with their physician before deciding on a sport.

SPORT INJURIES IN THE ATHLETE WITH DISABILITIES

The types of sport injuries sustained by children with disabilities are usually the same as those in typically developing children, and injury should be assessed in a similar manner. If the child is unable to describe what happened, obtaining a history of the injury from witnesses or parents is helpful. In an injured child with no history of acute trauma, overuse injuries ranging from muscle strains to stress fractures should be considered. After the history is taken, a thorough physical examination is performed, including a careful evaluation of the affected extremity and related body regions. For example, the hips should be examined in a child with knee pain because hip pain often is referred to (perceived to be coming from) the knee. In some children a more comprehensive examination is indicated to uncover unappreciated injuries. Finally, tests may be taken, including blood work, bone density measurements, X rays of the injured extremity, or more advanced imaging techniques (e.g., computed tomography, magnetic resonance imaging).

Certain developmental disabilities are more likely to be associated with specific risks from injury from exercise or sports. One example is that the child with meningomyelocele or spinal cord injury may not be able to perceive pain in an injured area. As a result, he or she is at risk for undetected soft-tissue damage from contusions, abrasions, lacerations, or crush injuries. Furthermore, many of these individuals will be participating in sports using their wheelchairs. This shifts the site of the most common injuries from the lower extremities to the upper extremities; wrist and shoulder sprains and pain are common. These athletes may also have poor thermoregulation, so careful attention to appropriate dress and hydration is essential.

In cerebral palsy there is an increased risk for ligament sprains and muscle strains because of tone abnormalities and inadequate muscle control. In addition, the presence of contractures is more likely to place stress on affected joints, leading to a higher risk of injury with exercise. Attention to using appropriately sized adaptive equipment (e.g., braces, wheelchairs) and padding of the equipment is essential in preventing these problems.

As mentioned previously, individuals with Down syndrome have other specific physical concerns with regard to sports and recreation, especially involving the cervical spine. Thus, these children should be screened for an abnormality prior to participating in exercises or sports that place the neck at risk for injury (e.g., gymnastics, contact sports, diving). If a child is found to have a cervical spine abnormality, alternative sports activities should be chosen. Another medical concern for some children with Down syndrome is congenital heart disease that may decrease endurance or predispose the individual to arrhythmias during intense exercise. In this case, consultation with a pediatric cardiologist should be sought. Children with Down syndrome also have a higher incidence of orthopedic issues resulting from hypotonia and ligamentous laxity. This can lead to flat feet, scoliosis, a slipped capital femoral epiphysis, and patellar instability (see Chapter 16). These conditions can be caused or exacerbated by physical activity. Awareness that the child with Down syndrome is at risk for these problems can help anticipate and prevent these complications. For example, orthotic shoe inserts can be used to treat flat feet, and orthoses may help patellar instability.

Wheelchair athletes are particularly susceptible to injuries related to the extensive use of their upper extremities. These sports include road racing, basketball, track, and tennis. Injuries most commonly involve sprains and strains of the wrists and shoulders. To avoid these problems it is important that athletes use appropriate equipment and stretch, train, and rest properly. Healing also may be an issue in these athletes, especially among those who have meninogmyelocele (see Chapter 24), so careful attention to skin care of blisters and lacerations is important. Proper attire is also important in wheelchair athletes because they may have poor temperature control or decreased sensation and may suffer from heat- or cold-related illnesses.

SUMMARY

Sports and recreational activities are important to promote both the physical and emotional health of children with disabilities. Virtually all children can participate in these activities, although some modification or use of adaptive equipment may be required. An effective exercise/ sports program can improve weight control, socialization, self-esteem, and acceptance into the community. There are many organizations whose mission is to assist the family of a child with disabilities identify appropriate sport and recreational opportunities. Medical assessment prior to participation in sports, however, is important, especially for individuals with disorders that carry enhanced risks of injury.

REFERENCES

American Academy of Orthopaedic Surgeons. (1992). *Support of sports and recreational programs for physically disabled people* (Document No. 1123). Rosemont, IL: Author. (Original work published 1985)

American Academy of Pediatrics, Committee on Sports Medicine and Committee on Children with Disabilities. (1987). Exercise for children who are mentally retarded. *Pediatrics, 80*, 447–448.

American Academy of Pediatrics, Committee on Sports Medicine and Fitness. (2001). Medical conditions affecting sports participation. *Pediatrics, 107*, 1205–1209.

Americans with Disabilities Act (ADA) of 1990, PL 101-336, 42 U.S.C. §§ 12101 *et seq.*

Bachman, J.E., & Sluyter, D. (1988). Reducing inappropriate behaviors of developmentally disabled adults using antecedent aerobic dance exercises. *Research in Developmental Disabilities, 9*, 73–83.

Block, M.E. (2000). *A teacher's guide to including students with disabilities in general physical education* (2nd ed.). Baltimore: Paul H. Brookes Publishing Co.

Bybee, J., Ennis, P., & Zigler, E. (1990). Effects of institutionalization on the self-concept and outerdirectedness of adolescents with mental retardation. *Exceptionality, 1*, 215–216.

Caterino, M.C., & Polak, E.D. (1999). Effects of two types of activity on the performance of second-, third-, and fourth-grade students on a test of concentration. *Perceptual and Motor Skills, 89*, 245–248.

Celiberti, D.A., Bobo, H.E., Kelly, K.S., et al. (1997). The differential and temporal effects of antecedent exercise on the self-stimulatory behavior of a child with autism. *Research in Developmental Disabilities, 18*, 139–150.

Chang, F.M. (1994). The child athlete with chronic disease. In C.L. Stanitski, J.C. De Lee, and D. Drez, Jr. (Eds.), *Pediatric and adolescent sports medicine* (Vol. 3, pp. 34–43). W.B. Saunders.

Chang, F.M. (2000). Physically challenged athletes. In J.A. Sullivan & S.J. Anderson (Eds.), *Care of the young athlete.* Rosemont, IL: American Academy of Orthopaedic Surgeons.

Dykens, E.M., & Cohen, D.J. (1996). Effects of Special Olympics International on social competence in persons with mental retardation. *Journal of American Academy of Child and Adolescent Psychiatry, 35*, 223–229.

Dykens, E.M., Rosner, B.A., & Butterbaugh, G. (1998). Exercise and sports in children and adolescents with developmental disabilities: Positive physical and psychosocial effects. *Child and Adolescent Psychiatric Clinics of North America, 7*, 757–771.

Edmiston, P.A. (1990). *The influence of participation in a sports training program on the self concepts of the educable mentally retarded attending a one-week Special Olympics sports camp* (Special Olympics International, Inc., research monograph). Washington, DC, Joseph P. Kennedy Jr. Foundation.

Fernhall, B. (1992). Physical fitness and exercise training of individuals with mental retardation. *Medicine and Science in Sports and Exercise, 25*, 442–450.

Fernhall, B., Pitetti, K.H., Rimmer, J.H., et al. (1996). Cardiorespiratory capacity of individuals with mental retardation including Down syndrome. *Medicine and Science in Sports and Exercise, 28*, 366–371.

Individuals with Disabilities Education Act Amendments of 1997, PL 105-17, 20 U.S.C. §§ 1400 *et seq.*

International Paralympic Committee. (2000, January). *Sports: Classifications. Section II: Eligibility of competitors.* Retrieved January 14, 2002, from http://www.paralympic.org.

Johnson, D.S. (1981). Naturally acquired learned helplessness: The relationship of school failure to achievement, behavior, attribution, and self-concept. *Journal of Educational Psychology, 73*, 174–180.

Kern, L., Koegel, R.L., Dyer, K., et al. (1982). The effects of physical exercise on self-stimulation and appropriate responding in autistic children. *Journal of Autism and Developmental Disorders, 12*, 399–419.

Klein, T., Gilman, E., & Zigler, E. (1993). Special Olympics: An evaluation by parents and professionals. *Mental Retardation, 31*, 15–23.

MacMahon, J.R., & Gross, R.T. (1987). Physical and psychological effects of aerobic exercise in boys with learning disabilities. *Developmental and Behavioral Pediatrics, 8*, 274–277.

National Association for Sport and Physical Education. (n.d.). *National standards for physical education.* Retrieved January 14, 2002, from http://www.aahperd.org/naspe/template.cfm?template=publicationsnationalstandards.html

Prasher, V.P. (1995). Overweight and obesity amongst Down syndrome adults. *Journal of Intellectual Disability Research, 39,* 437–441.

Rehabilitation Act of 1973, PL 93-112, 29 U.S.C. §§ 701 *et seq.*

Rimmer, J.H. (1992). Cardiovascular fitness programming for adults with mental retardation: Translating research into practice. *Adapted Physical Activity Quarterly, 9,* 237–248.

Rogers, H., & Saklofske, D.H. (1985). Self-concepts, locus of control, and performance expectations of learning-disabled children. *Journal of Learning Disabilities, 18,* 273–278.

Rosenthal-Malek, A., & Mitchell, S. (1997). Brief report: The effects of exercise on the self-stimulatory behaviors and positive responding of adolescents with autism. *Journal of Autism and Developmental Disorders, 27,* 193–202.

Schleien S.J., Ray, M.T., & Green, F.P. (1997). *Community recreation and people with disabilities: Strategies for inclusion* (2nd ed.). Baltimore: Paul H. Brookes Publishing Co.

Special Olympics. (n.d.-a) *About Special Olympics.* Retrieved January 14, 2002, from http://www.specialolympics.org/about_special_olympics/index.html

Special Olympics. (n.d.-b). *Official Special Olympics summer sports rules, 2000–2003* (Rev. ed.) [PDF file]. Washington, DC: Author. Available from Special Olympics web site, http://www.specialolympics.org/sports/index.html

Sullivan, J.A., & Anderson, S.J. (Eds.). (2000). *Care of the young athlete.* Rosemont, IL: American Academy of Orthopaedic Surgeons.

Takeuchi, E. (1994). Incidence of obesity among school children with mental retardation in Japan. *American Journal of Mental Retardation, 99,* 283–288.

U.S. Public Health Service. (2000). *Healthy People 2010: National health promotion and disease prevention objectives.* Washington, DC: U.S. Department of Health and Human Services.

Widaman, K.F., MacMillan, D.L., Hemsley, R.E., et al. (1992). Differences in adolescents' self-concept as a function of academic level, ethnicity, and gender. *American Journal on Mental Retardation, 96,* 387–404.

35 Ethical Dilemmas

Evaluation and Decision Making

Tomas Jose Silber and Mark L. Batshaw

Upon completion of this chapter, the reader will:

- understand parental rights, best interests of the child, informed consent, surrogate decision making, and the mature minor doctrine

- become familiar with moral reasoning as an activity that may include application of competing ethical theories, principles, and casuistry to resolve ethical dilemmas

- understand the difference between ethical decision making and legal requirements

- be aware of current ethical dilemmas concerning people with disabilities, including withholding of treatment, advance directives, genetic screening, prenatal diagnosis, selective abortion, sexual and reproductive rights, and human subject research

Moral issues are interwoven into professional practice, and it is the task of each educator and health care professional to reflect about and process issues in an ethical manner. This obligation is no different, and the responsibility no less, than that of making a clinical decision. The purpose of this chapter is to empower those taking care of children with disabilities for the daily practice of clinical ethics. We need to recognize that we do not come to ethical deliberations in a naïve state. Our membership in a culture, religion, gender, and so forth, has immersed us in the world of ethics since childhood. People come to their professions with certain core beliefs and biases and must be careful to suppress or at least acknowledge these in their clinical ethical considerations. This is especially important because there is a power differential between professionals and the families they serve. Parents come as suppliants to have professionals care for their child; clinicians are the ones with the power. Recognition needs to be given to parents, who, over time, working with their child, have become "experts" in the disease, the care issues, and the availability or lack of availability of appropriate services, and more. Parents have also been thinking about ethical dilemmas involving the care of their child. Clinicians and educators therefore need to look at the parents' expertise and acknowledge the parents' values and abilities in ethical decision making. The vicissitudes of a newborn with severe developmental disabilities can serve as introduction to this topic.

ALICE

Alice was noted to have marked hypotonia and great difficulty sucking in the newborn period. She was found to have severe brain atrophy on a magnetic resonance imaging scan. Her abnormal swallowing function led to a progressive worsening of her nutritional status accompanied by occasional bouts of respiratory distress. Alice's mother, who is a physician, was very concerned that her baby faced a diminished life and one filled with pain, similar to that of many of her own patients. When Alice's pediatrician proposed that Alice have a tracheostomy placed to protect her airway and a gastrostomy feeding tube inserted to improve her nutrition, Alice's mother refused to give consent. A number of the nursing staff were very upset with her decision and requested a consultation from the medical ethics team.

During the consultation it became clear that the family was very caring and loving of Alice, their first child. They considered quality of life, however, to be a paramount issue. They wanted to protect their child from suffering during a series of potentially painful future medical and/or surgical interventions. They noted that they had thought through their decision with the help of their extended family and that they felt comfortable with it. A case conference was conducted with the medical and nursing staff. After considering the issues, the medical ethics consultation team recommended that because of the serious nature and uncertain outcome of the condition and because the parents' decision was congruent with their value system, they should be allowed to exercise their parental right of surrogate decision making. Following this ethics consult, the parents formally refused any further intervention and took Alice home, where she died 2 weeks later.

This painful story raises many issues: Was this decision right? Who has the right to make the decision? What are the legitimate considerations on which to base a decision? What should be done regarding dissent? The sheer number of ethical dilemmas that relate to children with disabilities and the importance of the possible outcomes call for careful and deliberate reflection. For instance, in the preceding case there is a clear tension between the precepts of disability rights and options of care (including palliative care only) for children with disabilities. Respect for the rights of the individual with disabilities and willingness to advocate for them should not prevent or inhibit discussions about limiting aggressive life-sustaining therapy. This style of thoughtful balancing of competing values is traditionally referred to as moral reasoning and is the function of clinical ethics.

THE VOCABULARY OF ETHICS

Many concepts have been considered necessary ingredients in the activity of moral reasoning. These include understanding concepts such as *ethical principles, ethical theory,* and *casuistry,* as well as grasping the difference between *ethical decision making* and *legal requirements.* Understanding these issues may help in communication with ethicists, and may serve as a stimulus to enrich the assessment of ethical dilemmas.

Ethical Principles

Ethical principles are general statements about what types of actions are right and wrong. These principles include autonomy (the right of self-determination), beneficence (an obligation to act to benefit the individual), nonmaleficence (invoking the Hippocratic Oath); and justice (fairness in the distribution of resources; Beauchamp & Childress, 1994; Jecker, Jonsen, & Pearlman, 1997).

Ethical Theories

Ethical theories are attempts at constructing an approach to evaluate moral issues (Mappes & Degrazia, 2000). They involve developing systematic connections among moral principles. The main difference among ethical theories is the criterion utilized to decide what is "good" and "right." Some theories focus on what will be the consequence of a behavior (consequentialist ethics). Others see pleasure (or the avoidance of suffering) as the deciding criterion (hedonism). Others still look at the consequences and embrace the greatest happiness for the greatest number (utilitarianism).

A different viewpoint has been taken in so-called self-development ethics, in which the right behavior is the one that promotes self-realization. This is reminiscent of the Aristotelian view that the moral person will make moral decisions. The formalists, in contrast, appeal to the concept of deontological ethics (from the Greek word *deon*, meaning duty). They postulate that the rightness of an act does not flow from the goodness of the outcome but rather from the *kind* of act it is. Usually the kind of act is specified in terms of the conformity of structural features of the act to general principles of moral duty.

Ethical theories do not give a concrete answer to specific problems but may serve as guides to how to look for an answer and how to determine which factors are relevant. A theory of morality aspires to explain decisions, illuminate conclusions, and test for consistency (Englehardt, 1986).

Casuistry

A frequent criticism of both principled ethics and ethical theory is the potential in bioethics of separating theory from practice. *Casuistry*, the fine tuning of ethical choices based on previous resolutions of similar dilemmas, emphasizes the point that theory finds its meaning mostly in the context of practice. In the last decades of the 20th century, new thoughts enriched the field of bioethics from a feminist perspective that focuses on the ethics of care, from an urban ethics view, and from an international perspective that addresses issues of discrimination and disparity in health care (Cecire, Blustein, & Fleischman, 2000).

Examples of Ethics in Practice

To illustrate how these concepts are put into practice, one can return to the case of Alice. When the dilemma of treatment versus nontreatment was brought to the ethics committee, the ensuing discussion was built spontaneously around principles and theories. Some examples follow.

One committee member expressed concern that there was a duty to protect those who were most vulnerable and that therefore a newborn with a severe disability was entitled to all available treatment (deontological theory, principle of beneficence). Another member objected to this idea because it did not take into account the suffering and limitations that this infant would be facing. This team member was also concerned about the distress this would cause the family, as they would be responsible for the infant continuing in such a state of existence (consequentialist theory, situational ethics). Yet another person voiced the need to give preeminence to "the best interests of the child." This turned out to be difficult to discern as it involved comparing a state of frequent suffering and discomfort with a state of nonbeing.

Many other themes emerged in an attempt to resolve the ethical dilemma, including the *doctrine of double effect, ordinary versus extraordinary means,* and *surrogate decision making* (discussed later). For example, the doctrine of double effect makes it ethically permissible to have a bad outcome if the *intention* is to pursue a benefit and not to inflict harm (casuistry). In this case it was clear that Alice's parents wanted to protect her from a life burdened by incomprehensible pain and with scant possibility for social interaction. This was the reason they were refusing treatment rather than simply wanting to take steps to end her life. The concept of ordinary versus extraordinary treatment is understood to apply not to the treatment technology itself—after all, gastrostomy and tracheostomy are "ordinary" procedures—but to how a procedure relates to a patient's situation (e.g., Alice's parents considered these to be extraordinary interventions for their neurologically devastated child).

ETHICS AND THE LAW

Some familiarity with the law is also needed in dealing with moral dilemmas. This may involve specific issues in the legal code related to advance directives (described later in this chapter), child abuse/neglect, sterilization of adolescents with mental retardation, and so forth, as well as to such issues as the use of courts to intervene in health care decisions, appointment of guardians, and interpretation of statutes. In most instances the law is informed by ethical principles. Legal dispositions, however, do not necessarily subsume ethical obligations; on some occasions it may be necessary to challenge the law on moral grounds.

PEDIATRIC CLINICAL ETHICS

A number of clinical ethical issues are specific to children. These include informed parental consent, surrogate decision making, child assent, parental rights, and the rights of minors (Cassidy & Fleischman, 1996). These are discussed next.

Informed Consent and Assent

Informed consent means that a person who will be affected by a proposed treatment has the right to learn about the condition, the alternative treatments (or nontreatment), and the possible outcomes (American Academy of Pediatrics [AAP], Committee on Bioethics, 1995; Bartholome, 1995). Although studies have shown that older children have the capacity to understand and make medical decisions, from a legal perspective it is the parents who make binding decisions for their child. Parents therefore exercise a right of surrogate decision making; they give clinicians permission to treat. These parental rights are seldom questioned unless unusual circumstances arise (e.g., cases of parental abuse or neglect).

Despite their inability to give consent, children should receive explanations about any evaluation proposed or treatment to be received (AAP Committee on Bioethics, 1995). This concept has been extended to the requirement of obtaining a minor's assent to participate in nontherapeutic research (Broome, 1999).

Medical Rights of Minors

Special ethical issues arise during adolescence, when the budding autonomy of the adolescent challenges the need for parental consent for treatment. In colonial America, under the concept of parental sovereignty, parents assumed a claim of ownership of their children. This doctrine continues to be reflected in court rulings on custody, foster care, and adoption. In the late 19th century, however, legal limits were imposed on parental ownership in circumstances in which the children were considered to be in danger. This doctrine became known as the child welfare position and is reflected by laws regarding child abuse and compulsory education (Goldstein, Freud, & Solnit, 1980).

A serious flaw in the parental sovereignty and child welfare doctrines is that neither distinguishes the stages of complete dependency that characterize early childhood from the emerging autonomy that develops in adolescence. Since the 1970s a new philosophy dealing with the civil rights of adolescents has emerged, taking into account differences in age and maturity (Zinner, 1995). This approach allows parents or the state to represent the minors' interest only as long as the minor is not able to represent him- or herself. Often referred to as the *mature minor doctrine*, this concept is exemplified in legislation on freedom of speech in schools and the minor's right to obtain contraceptives.

The medical rights of minors are an outgrowth of this notion, allowing adolescents to give consent without parental notification for some determined circumstances (e.g., reproductive health care, mental health care). The mature minor doctrine acknowledges the changes that come with the increasing cognitive competence of teenagers and affirms that they can make rational decisions and therefore are capable of giving informed consent. It is congruent with current knowledge about child development and has long been accepted by the AAP Committee on Bioethics (1973). This pivotal idea has been expressed in the legal literature as follows: "A 'mature minor' makes his or her decisions on daily affairs; is mobile, independent, and can manage financial affairs; can initiate ... appointments; [and] understands risks, benefits, and informed consent" (Brown & Truitt, 1979).

The medical rights of minors need to be taken into consideration in determining the degree of participation in decisions by older children and teenagers with disabilities. Doesn't the adolescent who has lived with a disability for 15 years have some insight into the situation and a right to participate in decisions? Although consent legally belongs to the parents (with exceptions allowed by statutes and state laws), mature minors should participate in decision making to varying degrees. This concept may also have relevance to adults with mental retardation who function intellectually at the level of a young adolescent. Such individuals may be considered to have incomplete competence from a legal perspective but may be able to give informed consent. Reluctance of parents to allow this participation or conflicts among parents, adolescents, and professionals are common dilemmas.

ISSUES OF CLINICAL ETHICS RELATING TO CHILDREN WITH DISABILITIES

Advances in reproductive, genetic, and life-support technology have raised a number of unique ethical questions in the care of children with severe disabilities (O'Neill, 1998; Roleff, 1998; Shevell, 1998). For example, are there instances in which medical care can ethically be withheld from a newborn infant with a disability; if so, who decides? Should all technologically feasible genetic screening be done? Should screening and prenatal diagnosis be offered to women who are genetically at risk of having children with severe disabilities? These and other ethical questions are examined next from various perspectives.

Withholding and Refusal of Treatment

Some children with developmental disabilities are born with medical conditions that are life threatening in the newborn period. Decisions about whether and how to treat these conditions require weighing the risks and benefits of treatment options (AAP Committee on Bioethics, 1996; Street et al., 2000). For example, children with Down syndrome are at increased risk for having a narrowing of the small intestine called duodenal atresia (see Chapter 16). This condition leads to vomiting and dehydration and, if not surgically repaired, results in death by starvation during the first weeks after life. Another example is open meningomyelocele (see Chapter 24). The exposed spinal cord places affected infants at risk for developing meningitis, an infection of the spinal cord that carries a high mortality rate. For both of these disorders, the surgical correction of these problems could be considered routine. The damaged portion of the small intestine can be removed, and the child can then eat and drink. Likewise, the spinal opening can be closed, thereby preventing meningitis. But these children have persisting disabilities that last a lifetime. Should parents, like Alice's, have the right to withhold treatment from these infants because of quality-of-life issues? (AAP Committee on Bioethics, 1994; Anspach, 1993).

As mentioned previously, it is accepted that because the infant is not able to make medical decisions, the parents of the child may act as surrogate decision makers. To give informed consent, however, the parents must receive information from the physician about the risks of the procedure, the possible benefits, and the long-term outcome. Yet, in giving information, physicians and other health care professionals may be influenced by their own personal or professional experiences and biases concerning a particular infant's disability (Silverman, 1987). Studies have shown that physicians and nurses are often disinclined to treat infants with severe disabilities based on issues of quality of life, effect on the family, and cost of care. They are also less optimistic about achieving a satisfactory outcome than are occupational and physical therapists, social workers, teachers, and parents (Lee, Penner, & Cox, 1991a, 1991b). This is a strong argument in favor of bringing these other individuals into the ethics consultation process. As a result of biases, physicians and nurses may consciously or unconsciously accentuate certain risks, underestimate the quality of life of people with disabilities, and as a result unduly influence the parents' treatment decisions (Bach & Campagnolo, 1992; Gerhart et al., 1994). From the perspective of medical ethics, professionals need to be aware of their own biases and attempt to suppress or acknowledge them in providing information about the risks and benefits of a procedure or treatment.

Even if parents have received and processed the information, some clinicians maintain that parents are still not in a position to give informed consent. These clinicians argue that parents faced with the birth of a child with severe disabilities are in such a state of shock and are so overwhelmed by fear, guilt, and horror that they are not capable of making an informed decision. Others argue that even though parents have these feelings, they still retain their right to decide and their wishes should not be overridden. Generally, studies have found that parents' decisions in these situations are thoughtful and responsible, especially if the parents are given sufficient time to consider their choices (Strong, 1984). In most instances, a delay of a few days will not adversely affect the infant's outcome, will lead to more informed decision making, and will help preserve the parents' right to make decisions about their child's care (Charney et al., 1985). Most important, parents need to be reassured that they are good parents no matter what decision they make.

Although parents' rights are usually paramount, in some instances society has permitted health care providers to override the parents' autonomy in making treatment decisions about their children. It is now generally accepted by the medical community that the benefits of life as a person with Down syndrome or meningomyelocele exceeds the risk of surgery and the burden of having these disorders. Current guidelines propose that when treatment of an ill infant has a reasonable chance of being successful and the infant is likely to survive and be able to interact with his or her environment, even with a serious disability, the best interests of that infant are served by treatment. When treatment is likely to be futile, however, it need not be instituted (Loewy, 1994). These guidelines intend to establish the boundaries of parental decision making and the health care provider's moral obligation to treat illness and preserve life. Ambiguity remains, however, because the guidelines require a determination of futility.

Probably in response to concerns relating to intrusion by the state, a presidentially appointed commission has clearly acknowledged the importance of parental involvement in decision making for their child: "In nearly all cases, parents are best suited to collaborate with practitioners in making decisions about an infant's care, and the range of choices practitioners offer should typically reflect the parents' preferences regarding treatment" (President's Commission for the Study of Ethical Problems in Medicine and Biomedical and Behavioral Research, 1983, p. 214).

Advance Directives (Do Not Resuscitate Orders)

The term *advance directive* originates from the world of adult medicine and refers to instructions a patient leaves about the medical care he or she desires in advance of a time when loss of consciousness or incompetence prevents the individual from giving directives. More loosely, advance directives refer to a physician's order in a patient's medical chart to prospectively limit the amount of intervention that should occur in the event of a medical emergency (Walsh-Kelly et al., 1999). Such an order might indicate that in the event of a cardiopulmonary arrest, no resuscitative actions should be taken. Alternatively, it might limit rather than exclude intervention. For example, in the event of a cardiopulmonary arrest, resuscitation should be undertaken but the individual should not be placed on a ventilator.

These advance directives have also been used for children with disabilities who are neurologically devastated and have no hope of improvement. In this case, parents stipulate that normal care is to be provided but that extraordinary measures are not to be taken simply to prolong life. A do not resuscitate (DNR) order is written by the attending physician after discussion with and consent of the parents. This order can be rescinded at any time during the hospitalization at the parents' request. The DNR terminology is imbedded in the medical culture and can at times be misinterpreted as abandonment of the patient, with a sense that "nothing can be done." This should never be the case, as palliative and comfort care are important treatment modalities that are continued. Many clinicians have concluded that a DNR decision would benefit families more if it could be understood as an accepting natural death (AND) decision (Morrow, 2000).

Genetic Testing and Screening Programs

Tests for genetic conditions such as fragile X syndrome (see Chapter 17) can provide information not only about the child who is being tested but also about that family (Davis, Krasnewich, & Puck, 2000; Juengst, 1997–1998; Ross & Moon, 2000). This is a potential ethical problem; people who do not want to know this information about themselves may have their autonomy violated as a consequence of another individual's test. Furthermore, genetic tests may be used to predict the development of a currently asymptomatic disease in the future (e.g., Huntington disease, Alzheimer's disease, breast cancer) rather than to diagnose a current illness (McConnell et al., 1999; Terrenoire, 1992). If the test results become part of a medical record, insurance companies can easily gain access to them and could use them as a basis for denying health care or disability or life insurance coverage for the tested individual or other family members (Miller, 1998; Roth & Painter, 2000).

As new genetic tests become available, society will need to consider whether the benefit to the individual being tested outweighs the possible harm to the person and others in the family (American Society of Human Genetics, Board of Directors, & American College of Medical Genetics, Board of Directors, 1995). Some of these issues include whether a treatment exists for the condition, how accurate the test is, what the consequences of false positive and false negative test results are, and whether any family members will be at risk of losing insurance because of a test result (Andrews et al., 1994).

Screening programs differ from genetic testing because they are performed on large populations that consist mostly of individuals who are at low risk of having the condition. The purpose of screening is usually to identify individuals at high risk for a condition before it becomes clinically apparent (Seashore, 2000). This is beneficial if it permits early institution of therapy to prevent or lessen the impact of the disease. Common examples are blood pressure and cholesterol screening programs. If an individual is identified as having an abnormal screen, after further testing to confirm the risk, he or she may receive medications or be placed on a special diet to control the blood pressure or to reduce the cholesterol level. This, in turn, may decrease the risk of stroke or heart attack. Most people agree that these screening programs are in the best interest of the individual and do not represent ethical dilemmas. But if the benefits are not substantial, screening programs can be at odds with the principles of voluntary participation, privacy, confidentiality, and informed consent. For example, if these tests were required prior to a person's being hired for a job, problems could arise if abnormal test results were used to prevent that individual from obtaining the job or health insurance (Ad Hoc Committee on Genetic Testing/Insurance Issues, 1995; Ostrer et al., 1993).

Newborn screening programs represent another ethical dilemma (Fryer, 1995). In the early 1960s, a newborn blood screening test was developed for phenylketonuria (see Chapter 18). Subsequent studies showed that affected children identified and treated in infancy with a special diet developed typically, whereas late identification was universally associated with mental retardation. States were so enthusiastic about the potential of preventing a source of mental retardation that most mandated screening of every newborn prior to discharge from the hospital. Yet, even considering the test's worthwhile nature, was it ethical to require this test? Some parents may object to the requirement on the grounds that it violates their right to give informed consent. In the mid-1970s, Maryland became the first state to repeal the law requiring this test, instead offering it on a voluntary basis. More than 95% of parents agreed to have the screening test performed (Culliton, 1976). The end result, therefore, was close to what had been previously legislated, and the rights of both the state and the individual were protected. Other states subsequently followed Maryland's lead.

Advances in genetic research promise great improvements in the diagnosis and treatment of many childhood diseases. Yet, although emerging genetic technology may facilitate testing and screening, this often occurs before prevention or treatment can be established. It is therefore crucial to consider each genetic discovery from the perspective of what is in the best interest of the child. The AAP Committee on Bioethics (2001a), tackled this issue and made a series of recommendations, including 1) that periodic review and evaluation of established newborn screening is needed; 2) that informed consent of parents and older adolescents prior to genetic testing should be required; 3) that genetic testing for adult onset conditions should be deferred until adulthood, whenever this does not affect morbidity or mortality; and 4) that counseling about the limits of genetic knowledge should be offered.

Prenatal Diagnosis, Therapeutic Abortion, and Fetal Therapy

Closely linked to the question of genetic screening are the issues surrounding prenatal diagnosis and abortion (Silber, 1981). The ethics of abortion is one of the most difficult questions to resolve, as discussion is often complicated by religious, legal, and political arguments. The main ethical questions revolve around the issues of the "personhood" of the fetus versus the autonomy of the woman (Crosby, 1993).

The possibility of fetal therapy has added a new dimension to the prenatal diagnosis and termination of pregnancy debate (Yang, Flake, & Adzick, 1999). As treatment of the fetus for certain congenital disorders becomes more common (see Chapters 2 and 24), important questions will be raised about the rights of the mother and the rights of the fetus. Some view prenatal diagnosis as nothing more than an attempt to "eliminate" individuals with disabilities (Glover & Glover, 1996). Their view is that if the human variances that are reflected in disabilities are devalued, then the person with a disability also is devalued. On this basis, they oppose prenatal screening tests as well as prenatal diagnosis. Others argue that if a family is given information about an identified genetic disorder, they have a wider range of choices about the intervention they wish to undertake (Kenner & Dreyer, 2000). They argue that if this knowledge is available, families should not be deprived of it but rather taught how to use it in an effective and ethical manner. Obviously, if there were effective prenatal treatment so that the disorder could be prevented and the person's quality of life preserved, this would speak to both sides of the issue.

A prominent thinker about the intersection of the disability rights movement and the feminist movement asked,

> How is it possible to contest the eugenic and stigmatizing definition of disabilities, which seems to underlie prenatal diagnosis, while still upholding the rights of the individual women to determine what kind of medical care and what sort of pregnancy decisions are in their own best interest? (Rapp, 1999)

A plausible answer is to support reproductive rights *and* optimal services for children with disabilities. Finally, a strong argument can be made that prevention of the conception or gestation of an infant with a severe disability does not equate with unwillingness to provide comprehensive care and support after the birth of a child with the same disability.

A related issue is preimplantation diagnosis using in vitro fertilization (IVF; Fost, 1999; Nagy et al., 1998; Tasca & McClure, 1998). This offers the possibility of choosing the genetic makeup of children in ways that were not previously possible, of creating designer babies. By removing a single cell from an early embryo prior to implanting it, one can now test for sex and certain genetic diseases and chromosomal abnormalities. With the advent of gene chip technology, thousands of potential mutations could be screened (Persidis, 1999). This development raises obvious ethical dilemmas. Could this technology be used to choose gender? Should all embryos carrying genetic disorders be discarded? Should IVF be used to create babies who have a genetic makeup that will help another family member? The last of these questions has already become a reality with the birth of a baby chosen by preimplantation diagnosis to be a donor of umbilical cord blood to treat his sister, who had a potentially fatal blood disorder (Associated Press, 2000).

Sexual and Reproductive Rights

Progress in medicine has allowed most people with disabilities to reach reproductive age, leading to new concerns related to the rights of people with mental retardation to have sexual relationships, marry, and bear children. Sexual drive is presumed to be as strong in individuals with mental retardation as it is in the general population, although it may be somewhat delayed or less evident in individuals with severe mental retardation (Monat-Haller, 1992). Nevertheless, the attitude that previously ignored sexual drive and the right to sexual activity in individuals with mental retardation is now considered invalid and unacceptable (Melberg Schwier & Hingsburger, 2000).

In the past, this paternalistic attitude toward sexuality and individuals with mental retardation resulted in institutional policies of separating individuals by gender and punishing sexual "acting out" behavior. This policy is now considered ethically suspect because it denies individual autonomy to engage in activities that are pleasurable and not necessarily harmful to anyone (Crichton, 1998). Obviously, guidelines for appropriate and inappropriate times and places to engage in sexual behavior can be learned. For example, people with mental retardation can learn that masturbation is an acceptable but private expression of sexuality. Similarly, most individuals with mental retardation can learn to use contraception, take precautions against sexually transmitted diseases (STDs), and decline sexual opportunities.

Although in some states laws remain that forbid marriage and sexual relationships among individuals with mental retardation, these laws have not been enforced; furthermore, they may be unconstitutional. The rights to marry and bear children are protected under the Fourteenth Amendment to the U.S. Constitution. The right to bear children, however, is not absolute; it is accompanied by responsibility for the new human being that is created (Robertson, 1995). Therefore, decisions about marriage and childbearing in individuals with disabilities may involve not only the couple but also the broader family unit, which may benefit from professional guidance.

Sterilization of Adolescents with Mental Retardation

From an ethical perspective it is problematic to consider sterilization for a person with mental retardation simply because of concerns about his or her capacity to care for children. After all, typical intellectual function does not ensure responsible parenting, nor does mental retardation provide a sufficient reason to require sterilization. Some traditions (e.g., Catholic doctrine) consider this procedure an inadmissible practice, a mutilation. Moreover, they consider that the reproductive organs exist to benefit the species and cannot be subordinated to benefit an individual (Lebacqz, 1978). Other traditions (e.g., libertarian philosophy) fear the potential abuse of technology by the power of the state and proponents of eugenics (Robitsher, 1973). Some clinicians invoke the right of people with mental retardation not to be invaded by a surgical procedure they cannot understand. These clinicians maintain that rather than sterilization these individuals require more parental and societal support, protection, and supervision. These clinicians further observe that on occasion parents do not act in the best interests of their children and might make decisions for their own benefit (Goldstein et al., 1980). Circumstances can be envisioned, however, in which sterilization would be permissible. The principle of beneficence calls for the protection of the vulnerable. If sterilization is determined to be the most effective form of contraception with the fewest side effects, it can be a legitimate consideration. Such "justified paternalism," though, requires that the decision be made publicly and following a multidisciplinary assessment (American College of Obstetricians and Gynecologists, 1988; Rauh et al., 1989).

Organ Donation and Rationing of Care

There is a significant need for hearts, livers, and kidneys to be transplanted in infants who have been born with life-threatening malformations of these organs. Yet, few infant organ donors are available. One potential source of organs is infants with anencephaly, a uniformly fatal birth defect (see Chapter 24). Paradoxically, although these infants have a severe brain malformation, their other body organs are usually unaffected. These infants would seem to be ideal candidates as organ donors, and they have been donors in the past. Since 1988, however, a moratorium has precluded the use of organs from infants with anencephaly for the purpose of transplantation. In 1995 the Council on Ethical and Judicial Affairs of the American Medical Association reversed its position and indicated that it was "ethically permissible to consider the anencephalic neonate as a potential organ donor" (p. 1617). Such a furor ensued, however, that the council suspended the new position. As a consequence of this decision, very few organ donors are available for infants. Research is now focusing on the use of partial transplants of organs from adults, organs from nonhuman primates, and artificial organs.

Another ethical issue regarding transplantation is whether individuals with disabilities should have equal access to organ transplants (Bowling, 1996). Traditionally, organ transplantation was reserved for typically developing individuals. In the 1990s, however, access has increased for people with disabilities, although these individuals still remain at a disadvantage and prone to discrimination in organ transplantation. Quality of life and ability to comply with posttransplant drug regimens are among the many reasons given for assigning a low priority to individuals with disabilities. National attention has been drawn, however, to the rights of such individuals to receive organs through the successful heart-lung transplant of Sandra Jensen, who has Down syndrome (Goldberg, 1996).

The basic issue of rationing of care is likely to become more rather than less pervasive in this era of managed care and concern about health care costs. It will be important to be vigilant that individuals with disabilities are not discriminated against when these decisions are being made (Mori & Basauri, 1999; Woodstock Theological Center, 1999).

Research Involving Individuals with Disabilities

Many of the guidelines for medical research were developed in response to research studies that took what would now be considered unethical advantage of the vulnerable nature of children, individuals with disabilities, and individuals in institutions (Dresser, 1996). One of the most egregious examples occurred in the mid-1950s, when research was conducted on healthy children with mental retardation in Willowbrook State School in New York. Uproar resulted when the public learned that some parents were not able to admit their child to the institution unless they permitted researchers to enroll the child in a study (Levine, 1988) that infected children with hepatitis to study a new vaccine (Krugman, 1986). Subsequently, the National Commission for the Protection of Human Subjects formulated guidelines for research on children and other vulnerable individuals, which were codified as federal regulations (Additional DHHS Protections for Children Involved as Subjects in Research, 1983; Protection of Human Subjects, 1981).

These regulations stipulate that to be ethical, research must be scientifically sound, have a favorable ratio of risks to benefits, be performed with the informed consent of the participating individuals, and select individuals fairly so that no one group bears the brunt of the risks nor preferentially reaps the benefits of research (Glantz, 1998; McNeill, 1993). Furthermore, because individuals with severe disabilities may be unable to give consent, researchers must maximize the chances of benefit from the research if risks are more than minimal (Gaylin, 1982). When there is no direct benefit to the participant, the research is acceptable only if the risk is no more than a minor increase over minimal (e.g., drawing blood; Additional DHHS Protections for Children Involved as Subjects in Research, 1983) and if the research is likely to yield knowledge that is vital to the understanding and treatment of the individual's disability (Jonsen, 1978). Finally, if at all possible, research should be done first on animals, followed by typically developing adults and older children, before using young children or individuals with disabilities. When children or individuals with severe disabilities are used as research subjects, their participation should be voluntary (i.e., with their assent if mental age is at least 7 years and consent if 18 years or older). If the intervention holds the promise of direct benefit to the individual and is available only in the context of the research study, then an exception can be made (National Commission for the Protection of Human Subjects of Biomedical and Behavioral Research, 1977). Other exceptions may be brought to the forefront in the near future with the testing of novel treatment approaches such as gene therapy (Fletcher, 1995; Vanderpool, 1996).

ETHICS CONSULTATION AND ETHICS COMMITTEES

Most clinical and ethical decisions are resolved between professionals and families following the process of moral reasoning, the give-and-take as outlined so far. On occasion, however, this does not work and questions are raised. For example, when is an ethics consultation needed? Who should have access? Who should be notified? How does the ethics consultant/committee get called? What are the role and function of ethics consultant or committee? Ethics consultation for a patient with disabilities usually occurs when there is concern about the ethical appropriateness of a decision or when there is disagreement among members of the health care team or between the professionals and the family. The variety of issues involved may cover a wide range, from informed consent to withdrawal of treatment (American Society for Bioethics and Humanities, 1998).

Access to ethics consultation should be made available to patients, families, surrogates, health care providers, and any other involved party. This open access ensures that the rights and values of all involved parties are respected (AAP Committee on Bioethics, 2001b). Notification of an ethics consultation request should be given to patients or family whenever their participation is required. This may not be needed if the consultation is for a professional's benefit (value clarification) or for resolving a dispute among professionals (mediation). Notification includes giving the reason for the consultation, describing the process of ethics consultation, and inviting participation. The attending physician should always be notified because he or she is ultimately responsible for the patient's medical care.

SOCIAL JUSTICE

Children with disabilities face life issues that go beyond health care (Savage, 1998). Those children affected by socioeconomic circumstances such as lack of or late prenatal care are overrepresented in this group.

Another disturbing fact is that as "the life expectancy and the overall health of Americans have improved greatly over the last century . . . not all Americans are benefiting equally from advances in health prevention and technology" (Satcher, 2001, p. 1). Indeed, there is compelling evidence that race and ethnicity correlate with persistent health disparities in the burden of chronic illness and death. The development of a formal racial and ethnic initiative by the U.S. Department of Health and Human Services is a step in the right direction.

Finally, a gender perspective needs to be included. For instance, insufficient attention has been paid to the unfairness in our society toward those who provide most of the care: mothers and low-paid women. How will dependency workers, the vast majority of whom are female, have the time, energy, and resources to represent their personal interests in a public sphere designed for autonomous individuals? It has been proposed that equality cannot be obtained without altering the way our society meets the needs of dependent individuals (MacIntyre, 1999).

SUMMARY

Ethical problems often arise in the medical treatment of children with severe disabilities because these individuals may not be able to make autonomous choices, participate voluntarily in medical care, or give informed consent. Parents or guardians become the substitute decision makers who ideally make choices in the best interests of the child. When treatment decisions are made by proxy, professionals must try to ensure a higher benefit-to-risk ratio than what people who are making decisions on their own behalf would select. It is generally assumed that parents can make the best decisions about their child's care; parental authority, however, is not absolute in the United States. Here, the state has affirmed society's strong interest in the well-being of its children, and the principle of beneficence is sometimes allowed to override parental wishes if the two appear to be in conflict.

Issues such as withholding treatment, organ donation, genetic screening, prenatal diagnosis, and research on children with developmental disabilities all present ethical dilemmas. These issues can be analyzed to determine which ethical considerations apply. After identifying the relevant principles, one can then decide which takes precedence and what is ethically permissible. Therefore, ethical concerns ought to be discussed in an open and frank manner. All educators and health care professionals can enhance their capacity for ethical reflection and should participate in these important decision-making processes.

REFERENCES

Ad Hoc Committee on Genetic Testing/Insurance Issues. (1995). Genetic testing and insurance. *American Journal of Human Genetics, 56*, 327–331.

Additional DHHS Protections for Children Involved as Subjects in Research, 45 C.F.R. §§ 46.401–46.409 (1983, March 8).

American Academy of Pediatrics (AAP), Committee on Bioethics. (1973). A model act providing for consent of minors for health services. *Pediatrics, 51*, 293–294.

American Academy of Pediatrics (AAP), Committee on Bioethics. (1994). Guidelines on forgoing life-sustaining medical treatment. *Pediatrics, 93*, 532–536.

American Academy of Pediatrics (AAP), Committee on Bioethics. (1995). Informed consent, parental permission, and assent in pediatric practice. *Pediatrics, 95*, 314–317.

American Academy of Pediatrics (AAP), Committee on Bioethics. (1996). Ethics and the care of critically ill infants and children. *Pediatrics, 98*, 149–152.

American Academy of Pediatrics (AAP), Committee on Bioethics (2001a). Ethical issues with genetic testing in pediatrics. *Pediatrics. 107*, 1451–1455.

American Academy of Pediatrics (AAP), Committee on Bioethics (2001b). Institutional Ethic Committees. *Pediatrics. 107*, 205–209.

American College of Obstetricians and Gynecologists, Committee on Ethics. (1988). *Sterilization of women who are mentally handicapped* (Committee Opinion No. 63). Washington, DC: Author.

American Medical Association, Council on Ethical and Judicial Affairs. (1995). The use of anencephalic neonates as organ donors. *Council Report, 273*, 1614–1618.

American Society for Bioethics and Humanities. (1998). *Core competencies for health care ethics consultations.* Glenview, IL: Author.

American Society of Human Genetics, Board of Directors, & American College of Medical Genetics, Board of Directors. (1995). Points to consider: Ethical, legal, and psychological implications of genetic testing in children and adolescents. *American Journal of Human Genetics, 57*, 1233–1241.

Andrews, L.B., Fullarton, J.E., Holtzman, N.A., et al. (Eds.). (1994). *Assessing genetic risks: Implications for health and social policy.* Washington, DC: National Academy Press.

Anspach, R.R. (1993). *Deciding who lives: Fateful choices in the intensive-care nursery*. Berkeley: University of California Press.

Associated Press. (2000, October 19). Umbilical cord blood transplant a success. *The Washington Post*, p. A13.

Bach, J.R., & Campagnolo, D.I. (1992). Psychosocial adjustment of post-poliomyelitis ventilator assisted individuals. *Archives of Physical Medicine and Rehabilitation, 73*, 934–939.

Bartholome, W.G. (1995). Informed consent, parental permission, and assent in pediatric practice. *Pediatrics, 96*(5, Pt. 1), 981–982.

Beauchamp, T.L., & Childress, J.F. (1994). *Principles of biomedical ethics* (4th ed.). New York: Oxford University Press.

Bowling, A. (1996). Health care rationing. *British Medical Journal, 312*, 670–674.

Broome, M.E. (1999). Consent (assent) for research with pediatric patients. *Seminars in Oncology Nursing, 15*, 96–103.

Brown, R.H., & Truitt, R.B. (1979). Rights of minors to Medicaid treatment. *De Paul Law Review, 28*, 290–295.

Cassidy, R.C., & Fleischman, A.R. (1996). *Pediatric ethics: From principles to practice*. Amsterdam: Harwood Academic Publishers

Cecire, V.R., Blustein, J., & Fleischman, A.R. (2000). Urban bioethics. *Kennedy Institute of Ethics Journal, 10*, 1–21.

Charney, E.B., Weller, S.C., Sutton, L.N., et al. (1985). Management of the newborn with myelomeningocele: Time for a decision-making process. *Pediatrics, 75*, 58–64.

Crichton, J. (1998). Balancing restriction and freedom in the care of people with intellectual disability. *Journal of Intellectual Disability Research, 42*(Pt. 2), 189–195.

Crosby, J.F. (1993). The personhood of the human embryo. *Journal of Medicine and Philosophy, 18*, 399–411.

Culliton, B.J. (1976). Genetic screening: States may be writing the wrong kinds of laws. *Science, 191*, 926–929.

Davis, J., Krasnewich, D., & Puck, J.M. (2000). Genetic testing and screening in pediatric populations. *Nursing Clinics of North America, 35*, 43–51.

Dresser, R. (1996). Mentally disabled research subjects: The enduring policy issues. *Journal of the American Medical Association, 276*, 67–72.

Englehardt, H.T., Jr. (1986). *The foundations of bioethics*. New York: Oxford University Press.

Fletcher, J.C. (1995). Gene therapy in mental retardation: Ethical considerations. *Mental Retardation and Developmental Disabilities Research Reviews, 1*, 7–13.

Fost, N. (1999). Access to IVF. *Pediatrics in Review, 20*(8), e36–e37; discussion e38–e39.

Fryer, A. (1995). Genetic testing of children. *Archives of Disease in Childhood, 73*, 97–99.

Gaylin, W. (1982). The competence of children: No longer all or none. *Hastings Center Report, 12*, 33–38.

Gerhart, K.A., Koziol-Mclain, J., Lowenstein, S.R., et al. (1994). Quality of life following spinal cord injury: Knowledge and attitude of emergency care providers. *Annals of Emergency Medicine, 23*, 807–812.

Glantz, L.H. (1998). Research with children. *American Journal of Law and Medicine, 24*, 213–244.

Glover, N.M., & Glover, S.J. (1996). Ethical and legal issues regarding selective abortion of fetuses with Down syndrome. *Mental Retardation, 34*, 207–214.

Goldberg, C. (1996, March 3). Her survival proves doubters wrong. *The New York Times*, p. A12.

Goldstein, J., Freud, A., & Solnit, A. (1980). *Beyond the best interest of the child*. New York: The Free Press.

Jecker, N.S., Jonsen, A.R., & Pearlman, R.A. (1997). *Bioethics: An introduction to the history, methods, and practice*. Sudbury, MA: Jones & Bartlett.

Jonsen, A.R. (1978). Research involving children: Recommendations of the National Commission for the Protection of Human Subjects of Biomedical and Behavioral Research. *Pediatrics, 62*, 131–136.

Juengst, E.T. (1997–1998). Caught in the middle again: Professional ethical considerations in genetic testing for health risks. *Genetic Testing, 1*, 189–200.

Kenner, C., & Dreyer, L.A. (2000). Prenatal and neonatal testing and screening: A double-edged sword. *Nursing Clinics of North America, 35*, 627–642.

Krugman, S. (1986). The Willowbrook hepatitis studies revisited: Ethical aspects. *Reviews of Infectious Diseases, 8*, 157–162.

Lebacqz, K. (1978). Sterilization: Ethical aspects. In W.T. Reich (Ed.), *Encyclopedia of bioethics* (Vol. 4, pp. 1609–1613). New York: The Free Press.

Lee, S.K., Penner, P.L., & Cox, M. (1991a). Comparison of the attitudes of health care professionals and parents toward active treatment of very low birth weight infants. *Pediatrics, 88*, 110–114.

Lee, S.K., Penner, P.L., & Cox, M. (1991b). Impact of very low birth weight infants on the family and its relationship to parental attitudes. *Pediatrics, 88*, 105–109.

Levine, R.J. (1988). *Ethics and regulation of clinical research* (2nd ed.). New Haven, CT: Yale University Press.

Loewy, E.H. (1994). Limiting but not abandoning treatment in severely mentally impaired patients: A troubling issue for ethics consultants and ethics committees. *Cambridge Quarterly of Healthcare Ethics, 3*, 216–225.

MacIntyre, A. (1999). *Dependent rational animals: Why human beings need the virtues*. New York: Open Court.

Mappes, T., & Degrazia, D. (Eds.). (2000). *Biomedical ethics* (5th ed.). New York: McGraw Hill Higher Education.

McConnell, L.M., Koenig, B.A., Greely, H.T., et al. (1999). Genetic testing and Alzheimer disease: Recommendations of the Stanford Program in Genomics, Ethics, and Society. *Genetic Testing, 3*, 3–12.

McNeill, P.M. (1993). *The ethics and politics of human experimentation*. New York: Cambridge University Press.

Melberg Schwier, K., & Hingsburger, D. (2000). *Sexuality: Your sons and daughters with intellectual disabilities*. Baltimore: Paul H. Brookes Publishing Co.

Miller, P.S. (1998). Genetic discrimination in the workplace. *The Journal of Law, Medicine and Ethics, 26*, 189–97, 178.

Monat-Haller, R.K. (1992). *Understanding and expressing sexuality: Responsible choices for individuals with developmental disabilities*. Baltimore: Paul H. Brookes Publishing Co.

Mori, K., & Basauri, L. (1999). Ethical issues in managed and rationed care for children with severe neurological disabilities: A questionnaire survey. *Child's Nervous System, 15*, 342–346.

Morrow, J. (2000). Making mortal decisions at the beginning of life: The case of impaired and imperiled infants. *Journal of the American Medical Association, 284*, 1146–1147.

Nagy, A.M., De Man, X., Ruibal, N., et al. (1998). Scientific and ethical issues of preimplantation diagnosis. *Annals of Medicine, 30*, 1–6.

National Commission for the Protection of Human Subjects of Biomedical and Behavioral Research. (1977). *Reports and recommendations: Research involving children* [DHEW Publication No. OS 77-0004] (Vol. 1, pp. 112–113). Washington, DC: U.S. Government Printing Office.

O'Neill, P. (1998). Communities, collectivities, and the ethics of research. *Canadian Journal of Community Mental Health, 17*, 67–78.

Ostrer, H., Allen, W., Crandall, L.A., et al. (1993). Insurance and genetic testing: Where are we now? *American Journal of Human Genetics, 52*, 565–577.

Persidis, A. (1999). Biochips: An evolving clinical technology. *Hospital Practice (Office Edition), 34*(12), 67–68, 73–76, 83–85.

President's Commission for the Study of Ethical Problems in Medicine and Biomedical and Behavioral Research. (1983). *Deciding to forgo life-sustaining treatment.* Washington, DC: U.S. Government Printing Office.

Protection of Human Subjects. 21 C.F.R. § 50 (1981, January 27).

Rapp, R. (1999). *Testing women, testing the fetus: The social impact of amniocentesis in America.* New York: Routledge.

Rauh, J.S., Dine, M.S., Biro, F.M., et al. (1989). Sterilization for the mentally retarded adolescent. *Journal of Adolescent Health Care, 10,* 467–472.

Robertson, J.A. (1995). Norplant and irresponsible reproduction. *Hastings Center Report, 25,* S23–S26.

Robitsher, J. (1973). *Eugenic sterilization.* Springfield, IL: Charles C Thomas.

Roleff, T.L. (Ed.). (1998). *Biomedical ethics: Opposing viewpoints.* San Diego: Greenhaven Press.

Ross, L.F., & Moon, M.R. (2000). Ethical issues in genetic testing of children. *Archives in Pediatric and Adolescent Medicine, 154,* 873–879.

Roth, M.T., & Painter, R.B. (2000). Genetic discrimination in health insurance: An overview and analysis of the issues. *Nursing Clinics of North America, 35,* 731–756.

Satcher, D. (2001). Our commitment to eliminate racial and ethnic health disparities. *Yale Journal of Health Policy, Law and Ethics, 1*(1), 1–14.

Savage, T.A. (1998). Children with severe and profound disabilities and the issue of social justice. *Advanced Practice Nursing Quarterly, 4*(2), 53–58.

Seashore, M.R. (2000). Genetic screening and the pediatrician. *Pediatric Annals, 29,* 272–276.

Shevell, M.I. (1998). Clinical ethics and developmental delay. *Seminars in Pediatric Neurology, 5,* 70–75.

Silber, T.J. (1981). Amniocentesis and selective abortion. *Pediatric Annals, 10,* 31–34.

Silverman, D. (1987). *Communication and medical practice: Social relations in the clinic.* Thousand Oaks, CA: Sage Publications.

Street, K., Ashcroft, R., Henderson, J., et al. (2000). The decision making process regarding the withdrawal or withholding of potential life-saving treatments in a children's hospital. *Journal of Medical Ethics, 26,* 346–352.

Strong, C. (1984). The neonatologist's duty to patient and parents. *Hastings Center Report, 14,* 10–16.

Tasca, R.J., & McClure, M.E. (1998). The emerging technology and application of preimplantation genetic diagnosis. *The Journal of Law, Medicine and Ethics, 26,* 7–16.

Terrenoire, G. (1992). Huntington's disease and the ethics of genetic prediction. *Journal of Medical Ethics, 18,* 79–85.

Vanderpool, H.Y. (Ed.). (1996). *Research ethics with human subjects: Facing the 21st century.* Frederick, MD: University Publishing Group.

Walsh-Kelly, C.M., Lang, K.R., Chevako, J., et al. (1999). Advance directives in a pediatric emergency department. *Pediatrics, 103*(4, Pt. 1), 826–830.

Woodstock Theological Center. (1999). *Ethical issues in managed health care organizations.* Washington, DC: Georgetown University Press.

Yang, E.Y., Flake, A.W., & Adzick, N.S. (1999). Prospects for fetal gene therapy. *Seminars in Perinatology, 23,* 524–534.

Zinner, S.E. (1995). The elusive goal of informed consent by adolescents. *Theoretical Medicine, 16,* 323–331.

36

Providing Family-Centered Services

Paula J. Beckman

Upon completion of this chapter, the reader will:

- understand ecological influences on families
- be aware of the family life cycle
- appreciate approaches to providing family-centered services
- understand the influence that cultural issues may have on service delivery

With the evolution of services for children with disabilities, professionals have increasingly recognized the importance of working effectively with families (Beckman, 1996b; Dunst, 1996). With this recognition has come a growing awareness of the complex array of influences that affect families and the way in which families adapt to the birth of a child with a severe disability. Increasingly, service providers understand that the family is the constant in the child's life and expert in knowing the needs of the child. Rather than assuming that professionals are always the "experts," providers now acknowledge the important expert contribution of parents. This has led to an emphasis on providing services in a way that is family centered. For services to be family centered, professionals work collaboratively with families to address the child's needs in a way that is consistent with the priorities of the entire family (Shelton & Stepanek, 1994). The ability of service providers to deliver family-centered services, however, effectively depends on how well they understand the multiple influences that affect families and their ability to adapt professional practice accordingly.

TANYA

When Tanya was born 8 weeks prematurely, her parents, John and Carla, were bombarded with highly technical information from several medical professionals and were asked to make a number of important decisions that they felt ill-equipped to address. At first, they felt a sense of disbelief and were overwhelmed by the need to make numerous decisions for Carla and, at the same time, attend to the needs of other family members. It helped, however, that Carla's parents lived nearby and were able to care for Tanya's 4-year-old brother, Tyler, while Carla and John spent long hours at the hospital.

As Tanya's health stabilized and the time for Tanya to go home from the hospital approached, Carla decided to take a leave of absence from her job as a teacher so that she could be at home to care for Tanya. John and Carla learned to care for Tanya at home and respond to her medical needs. But as Tanya grew older, they began worrying that she wasn't doing many things that they thought she should be able to do, such as rolling over and sitting up. They talked to many doctors and medical professionals about her development, and after several anxious months, it was determined that Tanya had a mild to moderate form of cerebral palsy and a seizure disorder. At 9 months of age, Tanya began participating in a home-based early intervention program. Carla worked closely with Tanya's early childhood educator and physical therapist so that she could learn special strategies for feeding, dressing, and positioning Tanya as well as ways to promote her cognitive and language development. Carla also joined a support group for parents of children with disabilities.

At age 3, Tanya began to attend a preschool program for children with disabilities in an early childhood center. When Carla and John visited the classroom, however, they noticed that none of the other children were talking and were disappointed. Tanya's parents had hoped that their daughter would have an opportunity to be around children without disabilities because they believed it would help promote her language development. When Carla asked about changing classrooms to achieve this goal, she was told that no other placements were available. John, who was an attorney, then initiated discussions with school system administrators. John and Carla spent many hours and a considerable amount of money seeking outside evaluations to support their concern about Tanya's placement.

After a series of meetings, Tanya was placed in an inclusive preschool program that was co-taught by a special education teacher and a regular preschool teacher. Physical therapy and speech-language therapy were provided in the classroom. Tanya flourished in the new program, and Carla and John were delighted. Carla volunteered in the classroom and developed a strong working relationship with Tanya's teachers and therapists. She began helping the teachers identify activities that would motivate Tanya. When she told the special education teacher about the problems she was having maneuvering Tanya's equipment at home, the teacher and physical therapist made a home visit to see how they could help.

ECOLOGICAL INFLUENCES ON FAMILIES

One of the most useful conceptual models to understand the multiple factors that influence children and their families is the ecological framework proposed by Bronfenbrenner (1979, 1986). Bronfenbrenner originally proposed this model as a way of understanding influences on child development. Subsequently, other investigators have found an ecological perspective useful as a way of understanding the issues facing families of children with disabilities as well (Beckman, 1996a, 1996b; Dunst, Trivette, & Deal, 1988). From this perspective, an understanding of factors influencing families requires professionals to understand the larger social context in which each family operates. In this conceptualization, children and families are part of a series of nested systems, each of which exerts an impact on the other.

The first level of the system is known as the *microsystem* and consists of the immediate settings in which children participate for significant periods of time. Although children participate in several different settings, the immediate family setting is paramount. Important intrafamily influences include family structure, the resources available to the family (e.g., time, financial resources), patterns of interaction between family members, and the characteristics, experiences, and beliefs of individual family members.

A relatively large body of literature has focused on the effect of a disability on the family at the level of the microsystem. The results, however, have been far from clear. One example is the effect of the child's disability on the marital relationship. Although an increased rate of divorce was found in families of children with disabilities in some studies, others noted that it strengthened the marriage, and still other studies found no differences (Turnbull & Turnbull, 1997).

A child with a disability may also affect his or her siblings in different ways (Powell & Gallagher, 1993). Among the reported positive effects are increased maturity, independence, responsibility, and tolerance of differences in others (Lobato, 1993; Powell & Gallagher, 1993). Negative effects include a sense of loneliness and isolation, as well as feelings of jealousy, resentment, and embarrassment (Frank, 1996; Powell & Gallagher, 1993). To some extent, effects on siblings are mediated by age, gender, family characteristics, the sibling's sense of competence, and the type of disability (Frank, 1996; Powell & Gallagher, 1993). For example, older siblings, especially older sisters, are sometimes expected to assume increased child-care responsibilities (Powell & Gallagher, 1993). Younger siblings are more likely than older children to believe that something that they did caused the disability (Lobato, 1993). Frank (1996) suggested several ways to help siblings with these issues. She stated that it is important to 1) provide clear information about the disability at an appropriate developmental level, 2) support the siblings' feelings, 3) balance responsibilities within the family, and 4) enhance the siblings' sense of competence and self-esteem.

In the example of Tanya's family, both Carla and John had professional skills that worked to their advantage when they had to negotiate with school professionals about Tanya's placement. They also had sufficient financial resources that allowed Carla to leave her job to stay home with Tanya, volunteer in Tanya's preschool program, and seek outside evaluations during a dispute with the school system. These circumstances contributed to the way in which the family adapted effectively to Tanya's special needs. Families who do not have the same professional skills, knowledge about the educational system, and access to the financial resources are likely to have a very different experience. Particularly vulnerable are families from diverse cultures in which authority figures are not questioned.

The *mesosystem* is the relationship that exists between the different settings in which the child participates. Bronfenbrenner (1986) emphasized that the processes operating in different settings are not independent but rather exert important, mutual influences on one another. For example, the parent–professional relationship is an important influence at the level of the mesosystem. Parental satisfaction with an intervention program is often related to whether the parents have had a good relationship with the professionals in the program (Hanson et al., 2000). In the vignette about Tanya and her family, the relationship between Carla and Tanya's preschool teacher was an important part of Tanya's success in the classroom. This relationship promoted the exchange of relevant information between the family and service provider. Moreover, when John and Carla found themselves in a disagreement with the school about Tanya's kindergarten placement, the preschool teacher remained a long-term source of support. In addition, John and Carla received ideas and encouragement from the support group that Carla attended.

The *exosystem* refers to the social structures and organizations in which the child and family are not direct participants but which exert an indirect influence on family adaptation. For example, the service system consists of a variety of agencies and organizations such as hospitals, schools, social service agencies, health maintenance organizations (HMOs), and other systems. Each of these organizations operates programs and offers services that are needed by children with disabilities and their families. As a result, the policies and practices of these organizations can exert a profound influence on families. Families may be empowered or disempowered and may be supported or may face increased stress depending on the nature of these organizations' policies and practices. For example, the policies and practices of HMOs and insurance companies affect the nature and quality of services children receive, thereby exerting an important influence on the child's development and the family's well-being. Similarly, school policies concerning the way an individualized education program (IEP; see Chapter 30) is developed and the IEP meetings are conducted determine whether families feel that they are valued partners on the team. In the case of Tanya, the lack of an appropriate program in the neighborhood forced Tanya to ride a bus for lengthy periods and even compromised her health during the winter months. This uncertainty forced Carla to abandon her plans to return to work. In addition, school policies regarding Tanya's placement decisions forced John and Carla to challenge the system and required them to expend time and financial resources to advocate effectively for their daughter.

Finally, the larger social, cultural, economic, and political context constitutes the *macrosystem*. This includes such broad-based influences as political trends, economic conditions, and culturally based views of disability. For example, culture may influence interactions with families in many ways (Barnwell & Day, 1996). Language differences may make communication between families and caregivers more difficult and result in families' having limited information on which to base decisions (Barnwell, 2001; Lynch & Hanson, 1998). Families may also hold different beliefs about such factors as the meaning of disability, the importance of independence, the role of extended family members, medical practices, and behavioral discipline (Harry, 1992). For example, if families do not subscribe to Western views of medicine and medical practice, conflicts may arise with professionals who view a particular medical intervention as critical to a child's future development. From a family-centered perspective, it is important for service providers to recognize how their own cultural backgrounds affect the way in which they interact with families, and they need to learn to respect cultural differences in the individuals to whom they provide services.

Other factors at the level of the macrosystem can exert important influences on families. For John and Carla, federal policies concerning the rights of children with disabilities (see Chapters 29 and 30) provided them with an important tool with which they could influence Tanya's educational placement.

An ecological conceptualization of factors influencing children with disabilities has also made an important contribution to the understanding of family adaptation. It recognizes that influences on families exist at all levels of the system and that these can have a profound effect on the family's well-being. From this perspective, it is important to understand that factors at any one level of the system exert an influence on factors at other levels and that these factors change over time (Bronfenbrenner, 1986). There are many practical examples of such effects. The particular policies and practices of agencies with which parents come in contact (e.g., HMOs, school programs) are associated with the levels of stress experienced by family members (Beckman, 1996b). A family with limited financial resources may need both parents to work and/or to work multiple jobs. This may make it difficult for the family to attend meetings and clinic appointments. If the child's mother or father is young or has a limited educational background, she or he may find it more difficult to find a place as an equal partner in the intervention planning team.

THE FAMILY LIFE CYCLE

Another way to understand the complexity of issues facing families is to use a life-cycle approach (Carter & McGoldrick, 1980; Turnbull & Turnbull, 1997). This perspective describes the changes that occur in families throughout the life span. Although the designation of specific stages in the life span is somewhat arbitrary, each represents a period during which the family's life style is relatively stable. Stages are typically determined by the age of the oldest child, changes in family size, and the work status of the parent(s). Although stress can occur at any point within the life cycle, points of transition between stages have particular potential for stress, because families must readjust based on changing circumstances. While this approach provides a useful general overview of the life-span process, it must be recognized that there is considerable heterogeneity among families. For example, in families from diverse cultural traditions, blended families, households headed by single parents, and nontraditional families, the life cycle may be considerably different from that of a family with Anglo American roots.

Turnbull and Turnbull (1997) have noted that a child with a disability can exert a considerable impact on the family's life cycle. In addition to the common adaptations that families of typically developing children must make, there may be additional or different transitions for families of children with disabilities. Although various authors describe the number of life-span stages slightly differently, Turnbull and Turnbull (1997) noted key periods that are particularly relevant for families of children with disabilities. One of these stages is the birth of a first child, when parents must make a variety of adaptations, such as changes in sleep patterns and changes in financial responsibilities.

For a family whose child has a disability however, there are additional changes. They will have to deal with the process of obtaining a diagnosis, finding appropriate services, and caring for the child's special needs at home. In the vignette about Tanya, John and Carla spent several anxious months worrying about Tanya's failure to achieve key developmental milestones prior to obtaining an accurate diagnosis and establishing a "medical home" for Tanya's care (see Chapter 38). Moreover, Carla gave up her job to stay home and address Tanya's special needs. As this family moves through the life stages, they will need to make other adjustments, for example, as they consider school placements and ultimately when John and Carla help Tanya make the transition to adulthood.

Carla's decision highlights the fact that there are often increased caregiving demands associated with parenting a child with a disability (Beckman, 1991). Although these demands may persist throughout the life cycle, they are often most acute during infancy and early childhood. In this period, families may need to spend extra time or use special techniques to complete relatively routine child care tasks, such as feeding, dressing, and bathing. They also may need to spend more time attending appointments to address the medical, educational, and therapy needs of their child.

Another key life-cycle stage occurs when the child enters school. Some families may just be learning that their child has a disability. If they have not participated in a preschool intervention program, parents must learn to navigate the IEP process, develop an understanding of their child's legal rights, and learn to negotiate the educational system. School entry is also a time when families may begin to experience the social stigma that sometimes occurs with a disability. Parents must also deal with the judgments of school professionals, both about themselves and about their child. Sometimes these judgments can be negative, with professionals labeling parents as "in denial," "hostile," or "overprotective." For parents, the difficulty is that almost any behavior can be interpreted in a negative light. At other times, judgments may focus on a child's "deficits" rather than strengths.

Adolescence is the next major stage in the life cycle. For most families, this period presents numerous difficulties, including their child's increased self-determination, sexual maturation, and identity and body image development. During this period, parents may find that their son or daughter is increasingly isolated or that addressing emerging sexuality and fostering healthy sexuality and self-image in their son or daughter present special challenges (Melberg Schwier & Hingsburger, 2000).

The launching of children into adulthood is another important period. Although there are some cultural variations, during this period, most people entering adulthood are expected to find ways of supporting themselves economically and move away from home. Individuals with disabilities and their families, however, may need to search for appropriate postschool programs, employment, and living arrangements.

Although Tanya and her family have experienced only the first two stages described here, they have already gone through several key transitions. For this family, changes took place with Tanya's birth, her transition from the hospital to home, her transition to preschool, and her transition to elementary school. Each of these changes required adjustment and adaptation on the part of her family.

IMPLICATIONS FOR SERVICE PROVIDERS: FAMILY-CENTERED SERVICES

The conceptual approaches just described have important implications for the way in which service providers work with families. One of the most far reaching of these recommendations has been the emphasis on family-centered services. This concept first received attention in the 1980s and has been increasingly accepted, particularly in programs for young children (Bailey et al., 1992; Beckman, 1996a, 1996b; Beckman et al., 1994; Dunst et al., 1990; Shelton & Stepanek, 1994).

A number of specific principles have been identified as key elements of family-centered care (Shelton & Stepanek, 1994). These include recognizing the following:

1. Although service systems and personnel fluctuate, the family is the constant in the child's life.
2. Facilitating collaboration between families and professionals is important.
3. There should be a complete and unbiased exchange of information between families and professionals.
4. Policies and practices should recognize and honor cultural diversity as well as the strengths and individuality of all families.
5. It should be understood that families have different methods of coping and that the policies and programs that are implemented should address these diverse needs.
6. Family-to-family support and networking should be encouraged.
7. Service systems for children with special needs should be flexible, accessible, and comprehensive.
8. Families and children possess a range of strengths, concerns, emotions, and aspirations beyond their need for specialized services.

Therefore, central to the family-centered approach are the principles of empowering families, providing social supports, building relationships with families, building communication skills, and maintaining effective communication. Each of these is described next.

Empowering Families

An emphasis on empowerment has been implicit within a family-centered approach to patient care (Dunst, 2000; Dunst et al., 1988; Kirkham, 1993; Singer, Powers, & Olson, 1996). This focus recognizes the strengths and assets of individual families and views the locus of decision making as being within the family. It encourages providers to build upon the strengths that already exist in families and to help families develop new capacities (Dunst, 2000). Such an approach emphasizes the importance of self-determination, discourages interventions that diminish the families' capacity or that create dependency, and encourages families' active involvement in decision making (Epps & Jackson, 2000).

As families become empowered, they may disagree with the advice of professionals. It is important to recognize that families have the right to ask questions and, when they feel it is appropriate, the right to challenge professionals. Service providers have a responsibility to try to understand the basis for the disagreement and to make an effort to resolve it effectively. Such a resolution will be more successful if service providers approach families with an attitude of respect and make an effort to be nonjudgmental (Beckman, Frank, & Stepanek, 1996). This is particularly important when families come from cultural, religious, or ethnic backgrounds that differ from those of their service providers. Service providers also need to learn strategies for effective communication and conflict resolution so that they can work more effectively with families with whom they disagree. Strategies for dealing effectively with conflict can be found in Beckman, Frank, et al. (1996).

Providing Social Supports

Equally important is social support as a factor that mediates stressful life experiences and promotes family adaptation and well-being (Beckman, 1991; Crnic et al., 1983; Dunst et al., 1988). There appears to be a positive relationship between social support and child outcome (Dunst, Lowe, & Bartholomew, 1990). Moreover, the stress of having a child with a disability can often be lessened by such factors as strong social support, a strong marital relationship, good financial resources, and good problem-solving skills. The informal support provided by the family's social network (e.g., extended family, friends, neighbors) is likely to be an additional important factor (Beckman, 1991, 1996b). For this reason, advocates of family-centered intervention emphasize the importance of building upon existing informal networks of support when addressing the needs of children and their families. In addition, families frequently report that access to information and availability of empathic, trustworthy professionals are critical to helping them meet their child's needs (Beckman, 1996b).

As a result, interventions that promote the use of natural, informal support systems are viewed as a critical component of effective intervention (Dunst, 2000). This means that whenever possible, service providers need to build upon existing strengths in the family.

Building Relationships with Families as the Basis for Intervention

Providing services in a way that is family centered, empowers families, and gives support depends on the ability of the service provider to establish and maintain good working relationships with families. Indeed, many have argued that the basis for providing good services, regardless of discipline, lies in the relationship that is formed between the family and the service provider (Beckman, Newcomb, et al., 1996; Kalmanson & Seligman, 1992; Shulman, 1978, 1992, 1993). Good working relationships need nurturing and usually take time to develop (Beckman, Newcomb, et al., 1996). During this process, it is important to recognize that initial contacts with professionals and with the systems they represent can often set the tone for the subsequent relationship. A core goal during this evolution is to build trust, and professionals can best do this by being trustworthy. At a minimum, this means that service providers need to follow through on commitments (even those that may seem relatively small or unimportant); provide complete information; maintain confidences; and remain nonjudgmental, respectful, and empathic. For example, service providers must be sure to call when they say they will, take time to talk to parents, keep appointments on time, answer questions honestly, offer choices and options, and provide enough information so that parents can make informed decisions. Service providers can also learn and practice good communication skills such as active listening and sensitively asking questions. If conflicts arise between the service provider and families, it is important for the professional to remain calm and actively listen to the family's concerns. The service provider should address issues that are important to the family by offering potential solutions and options. It is particularly important during conflicts for the professional to assume that the parents are simply concerned about their child and trying to obtain services that they feel are most appropriate.

Building Communication Skills

For any participant to engage effectively in the decision-making process, he or she needs access to relevant information. This includes information about the child, the family, and the service system. In relationships between families and service providers, each participant has access to some information, but in most cases, no one has access to all of the relevant information. It is for this reason that the concepts of collaboration and partnership are so critical. Typically, service providers have a wealth of knowledge about their particular discipline, about the service system in which the child is involved, and about the services that are available within that system. In contrast, families have a wealth of information about their child and the needs of their family. In addition, as individuals with disabilities mature, they will have their own opinions and preferences about available options. Only when this information is shared openly can all participants make the best decisions. In addition, parents need adequate time to review the information they have been given so that they can come to a decision that is appropriate for their family. This is very much an individual process, and different families will need differing amounts of time to come to a decision. Finally, service providers need to remain available to answer questions and provide additional information. Such support can be critical for the family to make a decision that will work effectively for both their child and the family over time.

Parents often do not have access to important information that might affect decisions about their child. For example, families may have limited knowledge of the programs in which their children are enrolled, may be unaware of options that they have within a particular system, or be unaware that they have the right to challenge recommendations of professionals (Green & Shinn, 1994). There may be many reasons for this lack of information, but it often lies in a failure of service providers to communicate basic details to families. Service providers need to understand the link between information, communication, and decision making. No one can participate in decisions without adequate information that is communicated in an effective way. Providers need to be particularly sensitive to these issues when working with families who speak other languages or who have limited access to knowledge of the health care and educational systems.

Maintaining Effective Communication

Both the central nature of the relationship between families and service providers and the link between communication, information, and decision making for families suggest that the ability to communicate effectively is essential to high-quality intervention. As mentioned previously, three important qualities that providers need in order to establish good working relationships and communication with families are respect for the family, empathy, and a nonjudgmental attitude. When service providers ask families about their priorities and preferences, they are reflecting respect for families. There are several key skills that all providers can learn that will help them reflect these qualities. These include effective questioning; active listening; and providing clear, accurate information. Providers must also avoid verbal barriers to good communication such as criticizing, prematurely offering advice, moralizing (e.g., "you should," "you ought"), blaming, labeling the parent (e.g., "he is in denial," "she is hostile," "she is overprotective"), and interrupting. Other nonverbal behaviors, such as staring, yawning, or looking at a watch also create barriers to good communication. In addition, it is important to recognize how language, cultural, and educational differences can influence communication. For example, in some cultures it is considered rude to look at a person directly while he or she is speaking. Also, in some cultures the professional is viewed as an authority figure, and parents may feel reluctant to verbalize disagreements. Professionals may need to deliberately create opportunities for parents to express concerns in such situations. Professionals need to make special efforts to communicate with families for whom such barriers may influence access to information. To work effectively with children and families, good communication skills are often as important as discipline-specific skills.

SUMMARY

Ecological and life-span approaches to understanding families of children with disabilities have helped professionals understand the complexity of the issues facing families. By viewing children and families in the context of a larger system, it becomes easier to identify the multiple influences that may be operating for a particular child and family at any given time. Thus, a family's adaptation is likely to be influenced not only by the nature of a particular disability but also by factors at every level of the ecological system. Moreover, these systems are dynamic and change over time. As a result, family priorities and needs are likely to change as well. This points to the importance of building relationships with families over time rather than basing recommendations that may affect families on brief, short-term contacts. Finally, there is considerable evidence that the service delivery system can exert a powerful influence on families (Beckman, 1996a, 1996b). Whether that influence is ultimately positive or negative will depend on the sensitivity and responsiveness of individual professionals and the ability of the agencies and organizations that are in the business of serving families to be responsive to their needs.

REFERENCES

Bailey, D.B., Buysse, V., Edmondson, R., et al. (1992). Creating family-centered services in early intervention: Perceptions of professionals in four states. *Exceptional Children, 58,* 298–309.

Barnwell, D.A. (2001). *An ethnographic study of Latino families' perceptions of transition from early intervention to preschool.* Doctoral dissertation submitted to the University of Maryland, College Park.

Barnwell, D.A., & Day, M. (1996). Providing support to diverse families. In P.J. Beckman (Ed.), *Strategies for working with families of young children with disabilities* (pp. 47–68). Baltimore: Paul H. Brookes Publishing Co.

Beckman, P.J. (1991). Comparison of mothers and fathers perceptions of the effect of young children with and without disabilities. *American Journal of Mental Retardation, 95,* 585–595.

Beckman, P.J. (1996a). The service system and its effects on families: An ecological perspective. In M. Brambring & A. Beelmann (Eds.), *Early intervention: Theory, evaluation, and practice.* Bielefeld, Germany: Universitat Bielefeld.

Beckman, P.J. (Ed.). (1996b). *Strategies for working with families of young children with disabilities.* Baltimore: Paul H. Brookes Publishing Co.

Beckman, P.J., Frank, N., & Stepanek, J.S. (1996). Resolving conflicts with families. In P.J. Beckman (Ed.), *Strategies for working with families of young children with disabilities,* (pp. 127–150). Baltimore: Paul H. Brookes Publishing Co.

Beckman, P.J., Newcomb, S., Frank, N., et al. (1996). Evolution of working relationships with families. In P.J. Beckman (Ed.), *Strategies for working with families of young children with disabilities* (pp. 17–30). Baltimore: Paul H. Brookes Publishing Co.

Beckman, P.J., Robinson., C.C., Rosenberg, S., et al. (1994). Family involvement in early intervention: The evolution of family-centered services. In L.J. Johnson, R.J. Gallagher, M.J. LaMontagne, et al. (Eds.), *Meeting early intervention challenges: Issues from birth to three* (2nd ed., pp. 13–31). Baltimore: Paul H. Brookes Publishing Co.

Bronfenbrenner, U. (1979). *The ecology of human development: Experiments by nature and design.* Cambridge, MA: Harvard University Press.

Bronfenbrenner, U. (1986). Ecology of the family as a context for human development: Research perspectives. *Developmental Psychology, 22,* 723–742.

Carter, E.A., & McGoldrick, M. (Eds.). (1980). *The family life cycle: A framework for family therapy.* New York: Gardner Press.

Crnic, K.A., Greenberg, M.T., Ragozin, A.S., et al. (1983). Effects of stress and social support on mothers and premature and full-term infants. *Child Development, 54,* 209–217.

Dunst, C.J. (1996). Early intervention in the USA: Programs, models, and practices. In M. Brambring, H. Rauh, & A. Beelmann (Eds.), *Early childhood intervention: Theory, evaluation, and practice* (pp. 11–52). Hawthorne, New York: Walter de Gruyter.

Dunst, C.J. (2000). Revisiting "Rethinking Early Intervention." *Topics in Early Childhood Special Education, 20,* 95–104.

Dunst, C.J., Lowe, L., & Bartholomew, P. (1990). Contingent social responsiveness, family ecology, infant communicative competence. *National Student Speech, Language, Hearing Association Journal, 17,* 39–49.

Dunst, C.J., Trivette, C.M., & Deal, A.G. (1988). *Enabling and empowering families: Principles and guidelines for practice.* Cambridge MA: Brookline Books.

Dunst, C.J., Trivette, C.M., Hamby, D., et al. (1990). Family systems correlates of the behavior of young children with handicaps. *Journal of Early Intervention, 14,* 204–218.

Epps, S., & Jackson, B.J. (2000). *Empowered families, successful children: Early intervention programs that work.* Washington, DC: American Psychological Association.

Frank, N. (1996). Helping families support siblings. In P.J. Beckman (Ed.), *Strategies for working with families of young children with disabilities* (pp. 169–189). Baltimore: Paul H. Brookes Publishing Co.

Green, S.K., & Shinn, M.R. (1994). Parent attitudes about special education and reintegration. What is the role of student outcomes? *Exceptional Children, 61,* 269–281.

Hanson, M.J., Beckman, P.J., Horn, E., et al. (2000). Entering preschool: Family and professional experiences in the transition process. *Journal of Early Intervention, 23,* 279–293.

Harry, B. (1992). Developing cultural self-awareness: The first step in values clarification for early interventionists. *Topics in Early Childhood Special Education, 12,* 333–350.

Kalmanson, B., & Seligman, S. (1992). Family-provider relationships: The basis of all interventions. *Infants and Young Children, 4*(4), 46–52.

Kirkham, M.A. (1993). Two-year follow-up of skills training with mothers of children with disabilities. *American Journal on Mental Retardation, 97,* 509–520.

Lobato, D.J. (1993). Issues and interventions for young siblings of children with medical and developmental problems. In Z. Stoneman & P.W. Berman (Eds.), *The effects of mental retardation, disability, and illness on sibling relationships: Research issues and challenges* (pp. 85–98). Baltimore: Paul H. Brookes Publishing Co.

Lynch, E.W., & Hanson, M.J. (1998). *Developing cross-cultural competence: A guide for working with children and their families* (2nd ed.). Baltimore: Paul H. Brookes Publishing Co.

Melberg Schwier, K., & Hingsburger, D. (2000). *Sexuality: Your sons and daughters with intellectual disabilities.* Baltimore: Paul H. Brookes Publishing Co.

Powell, T.H., & Gallagher, P.A. (1993). *Brothers and sisters: A special part of exceptional families* (2nd ed.). Baltimore: Paul H. Brookes Publishing Co.

Shelton, T.L., & Stepanek, J.S. (1994). Family-centered care for children needing specialized health and development services. *Journal of Special Education, 27*(1), 82–106.

Shulman, L. (1978). A study of practice skill. *Social Work, 23,* 274–281.

Shulman, L. (1992). *The skills of helping: Individuals, families, and groups.* Itasca, IL: F.E. Peacock Publishers.

Shulman, L. (1993). Developing and testing a practice theory: An interactional perspective. *Social Work, 38,* 91–97.

Singer, G.H.S., Powers, L.E., & Olson, A.L. (Eds.). (1996). *Redefining family support: Innovations in public–private partnerships.* Baltimore: Paul H. Brookes Publishing Co.

Turnbull, A.P., & Turnbull, H.R. (1997). *Families, professionals, and exceptionality: A special partnership.* Columbus, OH: Charles E. Merrill.

37 Future Expectations

Transition from Adolescence to Adulthood

Patience H. White, Vincent Schuyler,
Andrea Edelman, Adadot Hayes, and Mark L. Batshaw

Upon completion of this chapter, the reader will:

- be aware of the importance of planning for the transition to adulthood for youth with disabilities.

- know the general principles and major components of a transition plan

- understand the resources and mandated laws available to assist youth with disabilities

- know the role of employment and postsecondary education in the transition process

- recognize the importance of addressing community involvement and sexuality for youth with disabilities

- be aware of the value of future planning for individuals with disabilities

Individuals with mental retardation and/or developmental disability (MR/DD) encounter the same life transitions as typically developing people do. Perhaps the most difficult of these is the transition to adulthood, a period of complex biological, social, and emotional change. This transition involves learning to move 1) from dependence to independence, 2) from school to postsecondary education, 3) from school to work, 4) from pediatric to adult health care, 5) to independent participation in leisure activities, and 6) toward the formation and maintenance of adult social and sexual relationships.

As the individual with MR/DD makes the transition to adulthood, parents and professionals need to acknowledge the importance of self-determination in maximizing quality of life. This involves allowing the individual to make choices and to learn from them. It also means that the individual has rights and must learn the skills to advocate for them and to use them wisely. This approach allows the person with MR/DD to communicate his or her interests, beliefs, and values to others (Menchetti & Piland, 1998). This chapter focuses on the steps involved in the successful transition of an individual with MR/DD from youth to adulthood.

BRYAN

Bryan is a 23-year-old former premature infant who has cerebral palsy and mental retardation. Since he completed his public school education 2 years ago, Bryan has worked in a supported employment position at a local supermarket. He receives support and guidance from co-workers who were trained by a local job placement program to provide natural supports in the workplace. After work he participates in many recreational and leisure activities with friends. With his increasing job satisfaction and financial independence, this past year Bryan expressed a desire to live on his own. He and his parents contacted the local United Cerebral Palsy Association and with assistance from the staff found an apartment and a personal care attendant to live with him. Bryan still comes to his parent's house for family dinners and events at least once a week and spends additional time with his two younger siblings, ages 16 and 18, who come to visit him frequently in his apartment. Bryan has recently started dating a young woman he met at his job.

GENERAL PRINCIPLES OF TRANSITION

In the context of youth with MR/DD, *transition* can be defined as the planned movement from childhood to adulthood. By this point, the adolescent should have been prepared through a planned process to assume these responsibilities. The goal of this transition planning is to identify what the individual with MR/DD wants in his or her future and how to achieve it, that is, choice and self-determination. Any services needed to accomplish this goal should be uninterrupted, coordinated, developmentally and age appropriate, psychologically sound, and comprehensive (Blum et al., 1993).

Transition planning should involve a partnership between the individual, his or her family, school personnel, local community and adult service organization representatives, and interested others. The focus of this team should be to assist the individual in identifying opportunities and experiences during the school years that will help prepare him or her for adult life that is as independent as possible. Certain general principles apply to all transition planning (Blum, 1995):

- Transition is a process, not an event. It must take into account the young person's developmental stage and the functional impact of the disability.
- Inadequate planning for transition is second only to financial problems as the most common reason for failure of an individual to move successfully into adulthood (National Center for Youth with Disabilities, 1993).
- The transition process should begin as early as possible. It should include goals for independence and self-determination that are centered on a flexible schedule that recognizes the young person's increasing capacity for making choices and growing independence.
- Different options for moving toward adulthood should be discussed with the adolescent, who should be an integral part of the decision-making process. Self-advocacy skills are a key component to growing up and should be fostered throughout this process.
- Family members need to understand their changing roles as the focus shifts toward a confidential relationship between the adolescent and his or her teachers, physicians, and other individuals providing assistance.
- Transition to adult services should occur **prospectively** rather than during a crisis. Professionals (including those from the health and education fields) and parents must prepare to "let go" of the developing young adult.
- Coordination between health care, educational, vocational, and social service systems is essential.
- The maturational process during adolescence should focus on basic tasks that are both sequential and overlapping. Attempting to address a later task before the individual has mastered an earlier one increases the risk of failure (McKenzie, 1990).

MOVING TOWARD INDEPENDENCE

Teachers and other individuals providing assistance to families can and should begin preparing children with MR/DD for independence as early as possible. Developing age-appropriate independent tasks and goals increases a person's chances of making a successful transition to adulthood. For example, young children between 3 and 5 years of age can begin to incorporate chores into their daily routine that are appropriate for their developmental level. By the developmental age of 6–11 years, children can begin making decisions on how to spend their allowance. Between 12 and 18 years, the individual should be actively engaged in a career development process (University of Washington, Center on Human Development and Disability, Adolescent Health and Transition Project, n.d.). All of these tasks work to build self-determination and to set the expectation that the young person will become as independent as possible as an adult (Quinn, 1997).

DEVELOPING SOCIAL COMPETENCE

Research has shown that it is not just the disability that has an effect on outcome, but also that the social and family environment does (Kennedy, 2001). Werner and Smith (1992) demonstrated that positive relationships and connectedness with adults are central to an individual's success as an adult because they give the young person clear messages of support and capability. Similarly, societal expectations are a key component of social functioning. Social competence may be a challenge for the teenager whose disability affects physical, emotional, or cognitive maturation (Blum & Gehn, 1992; Groce, 1985). For example, an adolescent with meningomyelocele may have growth delay, resulting in his or her being treated like a younger child. In general, teenagers with MR/DD tend to worry more about their physical appearance than their typically developing peers do, although this only rarely translates into psychopathology.

Another issue for youth with MR/DD is that they can be socially isolated, even when included in a general education classroom. They tend to have fewer friends than their typically developing peers, and this can make them lonely and occasionally depressed (David et al., 1994). A consequence of social isolation may be an individual's excessive physical and psychological dependence on and overprotection by his or her parents. Overprotection impedes the attainment of competencies in life skills. Studies have shown that teenagers with MR/DD who reported being overprotected were less happy and had lower self-esteem, higher anxiety, and more self-conscious behavior (Blum et al., 1991). In contrast, opportunities for accepting responsibility and expectations of success were markers for a good outcome.

MOVING TOWARD POSTSECONDARY EDUCATION

Postsecondary education can take many forms. Although traditionally thought of as college, it may be any form of education or training that takes place after a young adult leaves high school. Postsecondary education can take place at a trade or professional school (e.g., computer training, instruction in auto repair), through an on-the-job training program, through an apprenticeship, in specialized coursework, at a 2-year community college or a university, or even through postgraduate study. Because postsecondary education or training positively affects employment outcomes and quality of life in adulthood, it should be considered for all individuals with MR/DD.

Role of Professionals, Parents, and Youth

After exiting the school system, most young adults with MR/DD have the potential to live independently, acquire additional education or training in preparation for employment, and become employed. By setting appropriate expectations for the future, teachers and health care professionals can play an important role in facilitating a young adult's successful transition from school to postsecondary education or training (American Academy of Pediatrics, Committee on Children with Disabilities, 2000). Expectations can be set early and revisited as the child grows into young adulthood.

Professionals play a central role in this process by providing information about the nature of the student's disability, offering insights about abilities and limitations, and assisting the student in identifying compensatory strategies and accommodations (see Table 37.1). Taking the time to have an interactive dialogue with the student about future goals is essential in promoting transition to adulthood.

Parents are an equally important partner in their child's education and can be excellent collaborators in the development of short- and long-range goals and transition plans. They are the primary individuals providing assistance and serving as advocates for their child. They possess special knowledge and insights about their son's or daughter's abilities and disabilities and how these affect functioning at home and at school. Parents should collaborate with the school to ensure that disability-related needs are accommodated as the young person matures.

The adolescent with a MR/DD also plays a crucial role. He or she should be encouraged to develop self-determination skills over time and take on an increasingly active role in the management of his or her disability. It is important that parents hear, share, and incorporate their child's expectations and choices in the many activities they do together in transition planning.

The Individualized Transition Plan

As part of the Individuals with Disabilities Act (IDEA) of 1997 (PL 105-17), transition planning must be addressed by 14 years of age with the development of an individualized transition

Table 37.1.   Postsecondary education for people with disabilities: elements of effective transition planning

Transition planning should assess the impact of disability on the student.

Education
Has the disability necessitated any special accommodations at school?
Was class missed at certain times of day to perform a health-care routine?
Did the disability affect attendance?
Did medication affect the student's ability to concentrate or participate in school? (Was the student more alert at certain times of the day? Were frequent breaks from class required to take medications or to rest?)
Was extra time necessary for the student to complete classwork, tests, or homework?
Was technology (e.g., computers) used in the classroom or at home to fulfill academic requirements?
Was in-class assistance required, such as a person to take notes?

Medical Care
Are any activities restricted?
Does the student require specialized medical care (e.g., gastrostomy tube feedings)?
Does the student require the coordinated care of many health care providers?
Does the student have a care routine that must be performed at a specific time of day?
Does the student have a care routine that can only be done by a specially trained individual (e.g., physical therapist, respiratory therapist, nurse)?
Is there a medication schedule that must be strictly adhered to?
Are required drugs difficult to find?
Is the care of a medical specialist required? If so, how frequently?

Environment
Do certain environmental factors (e.g., heat, cold, molds, dust, odors, humidity) affect the student's health and well-being?
Does the student need to limit exposure to noise and distractions?
Does the student require a special living environment?
Are certain activities (e.g., walking long distances, climbing stairs) difficult?

Activities of Daily Living
Is assistance with getting out of bed required?
Is assistance with food preparation/eating needed?
Does the student require a special diet?
Does the student need assistance with bathing or with using the bathroom?
Is assistance with dressing necessary?
Is assistance with mobility required?

From Edelman, A., Schuyler, V., & White, P. (1998). *Maximizing success for young adults with chronic health related illnesses.* Washington, DC: HEATH Resource Center, American Council on Education; adapted by permission.

plan (ITP) as part of the child's individualized education program (IEP). As mentioned in Chapter 30, transition services must include "instruction, related services, community experiences, the development of employment and other post-school adult living objectives and, when appropriate, acquisition of daily living skills" (§ 602[30]). The planning team should include the parents, the student (if developmentally able), the student's general education and special education teachers, a vocational rehabilitation (VR) specialist, a developmental disabilities services coordinator (or case manager), and other professionals who can help in designing the ITP. The planning process involves gathering information about the individual's interests, skills, and abilities and applying that information to the formation of future goals. This includes ensuring that the course of future study is appropriate to the individual's abilities and aligned with the type of employment and education chosen. Planning also involves identifying the type of postsecondary education or training to be pursued and assessing any impact the disability may have in the postsecondary environment and the accommodations required to adapt to the environment.

The ITP is meant to prepare the student to make the transition from the world of school to the world of adult life by engaging in transition-related activities while at school. Community-based resources and support services should be identified and linkages made. For students who plan to pursue additional education or training after high school, their ITP should identify coursework needed to achieve those goals and list specific activities that will assist them in moving into the postsecondary school environment. This topic is discussed further in Chapter 30.

Vocational Rehabilitation Services

Until 1997, schools provided all disability-related services to their students; VR agencies would only become involved after the student had exited the school program. Today, with transition planning mandated under IDEA '97, VR counselors must participate in transition planning before the student exits the school system, usually starting at age 16. Parents and students can request their participation, and this is highly desirable as it provides a seamless transition from school to adult service provision.

Frequently, it is through linkages made as part of the ITP process that a student and his or her family become aware of community-based providers of disability-related services. The VR agency can provide or arrange for a host of training, educational, medical, and other services individualized to the needs of the person. VR services are intended to help individuals acquire and maintain gainful employment. A VR counselor will work with the young adult to assess the disability and help him or her develop an individualized plan for employment (IPE). This plan will identify an employment goal and the means for achieving it, often including some form of postsecondary education or training. The IPE takes into account any disability-related needs and accommodations necessary to achieve success in the workplace.

Although VR counselors can provide direct services to the young adult, they more often refer the individual to appropriate community-based agencies that can assist in achieving postsecondary education goals. Services provided may include self-advocacy training, the development of employment readiness skills, identification and procurement of and instruction in the use of assistive technology, and so forth. Many programs prepare the individual for employment in specific occupations; some provide a job coach to assist with job training at a community-based employment site.

Disability Support Services in College

For individuals continuing their education in college, VR counselors can also assist in identifying resources. Most colleges and universities have either a disability support services (DSS) office or some other office or individual designated to assist students with disabilities. To receive assistance or request accommodations for disability-related needs, a student must take the lead in disclosing his or her disability, providing documentation of the disability, and identifying needed accommodations. The documentation of the disability must support the requested accommodations (e.g., extra time in test taking for an individual with attention-deficit/hyperactivity disorder or learning disabilities, a sign language interpreter for an individual with deafness).

The DSS office should be able to assist a student with disclosing the disability to instructors; requesting accommodations; identifying supports, services, and assistive technology; and addressing other disability-related needs presented by the student. There is a great deal of variability across schools as to the steps undertaken on behalf of the student with the disability as well as to the types of accommodations provided. Universities that receive federal funding, however, are mandated to provide reasonable accommodations to qualified individuals with disabilities under Section 504 of the Rehabilitation Act of 1973 (PL 93-112) and under Title II of the Americans with Disabilities Act (ADA) of 1990 (PL 101-336). Private institutions and vocational schools must also provide reasonable accommodations as mandated by the amendments to the Rehabilitation Act of 1973 and Title III (public accommodations) of the ADA. The student's physician will need to provide documentation of the disability and justification for the requested accommodations. A number of organizations can give students and parents information about laws that have an impact on the education of individuals with disabilities (see Appendix D).

ENTERING THE WORK FORCE

When adolescents with disabilities are asked what they want for their future, they are clear that they seek an interesting and remunerative job. This was demonstrated by one of the largest surveys of young people with disabilities, conducted in 1995 by the PACER Center in Minneapolis, Minnesota (Wright, 1996). More than 11,000 households with young adults with disabilities were mailed a survey that asked questions about what these young people wanted in transition services. A total of 1,314 teenagers with a variety of disabilities (e.g., learning disabilities, chronic illnesses, mental health problems, physical disabilities, sensory impairments) responded. All groups identified job training as the most important issue, with independent living skills and college or vocational guidance close behind.

Even with these individuals' interest in obtaining a job, as of 2002 the long-term outcome of workforce participation by young adults with disabilities is not encouraging. Three to five years after leaving school, fewer than 8% of young adults with disabilities in the United States are reported to be fully employed or enrolled in postsecondary education, active socially, and living independently in the community (Hughes, 2001). A 1999 NOD/Harris poll found that only 32% of people with disabilities between the ages of 18 and 65 worked full or part time, compared with 81% in the population as a whole. Perhaps as a consequence of this, people with disabilities are three times more likely to live in a household with an income of less than $15,000 per year (Lou Harris Assoc., Inc., 1999).

Essentials for Obtaining a Job

Education is essential in today's knowledge-based economy. Studies show that the level of education attained is directly correlated with employment status and lifetime earnings (Mortenson, 2001). Thus, making postsecondary education available for young people with disabilities is central to their future success in the marketplace. This is exemplified by the fact that 32% of individuals with disabilities have indicated that it is their lack of skills, education, and training that accounts for their lack of employment (Lou Harris Assoc., Inc., 1999).

Early work experience is equally important. A 1996 survey of 300 employers by *The New York Times* revealed the top three qualities they valued in employees were attitude, communication skills, and previous work experience. In several American studies, between 30% and 50% of typically developing 13-year-olds were found to be involved in a work experience at least once a week, such as babysitting or delivering newspapers. Youth with disabilities need to be exposed to the world of work at a similar developmental age as those without disabilities and to be introduced to role models of adults with disabilities who are successful in the workplace.

Finally, social isolation and late incorporation into a peer group predisposes individuals with disabilities to have delayed exposure to appropriate social skills and to future job networks (Chadsey & Beyer, 2001). Even today, family/friend networks are the most common way people obtain jobs. Social skills impairments may also interfere with their job performance and need to be addressed (Smith, Belcher, & Juhrs, 1995).

Federal Laws Related to Work and Disability

Several federal laws related to work and disability can be helpful in obtaining a position for a young adult with disabilities:

- Provisions of *Section 504 of the Rehabilitation Act of 1973* include 1) the prohibition of discrimination by employers receiving federal funds, 2) a mandate for equal opportunities and programs for individuals with disabilities, and 3) provision of federal funds to agencies that develop programs for people with disabilities.
- The *Rehabilitation Act Amendments of 1978* (PL 95-602) improved the 1973 initiative by guaranteeing access to programs for all individuals, even if gainful employment is not the expected outcome.
- The *Rehabilitation Act Amendment of 1992* (PL 102-569) emphasized the role of VR counselors in working with adolescents with disabilities.
- The *Americans with Disabilities Act (ADA) of 1990* (PL 101-336) prohibits discrimination in the workplace against individuals with disabilities and mandates reasonable accommodations so that the individual can fulfill his or her job responsibilities.
- *Supplemental Security Income (SSI)* can be applied for through the Social Security Administration. This program provides financial resources to a qualifying individual that can be used to purchase adaptive equipment (e.g., a van equipped with a lift, a ramp, an adapted computer) that increases accessibility to the workplace. It also makes the individual eligible for Medicaid coverage.

Work Options

Work options for individuals with disabilities include the same as for those without disabilities (i.e., competitive employment) but also include a range of alternatives:

- An individual engaged in *competitive employment* is working in a job in which he or she is expected to perform at the same level as other employees without disabilities and to not require assistance in performing the job. The employee can, however, expect appropriate accommodations in line with the mandates of the ADA. This could include adaptive seating, computer input devices, large-print text, and so forth. To succeed in a competitive employment setting, the employee needs good social and communication skills, motivation, reading, writing, computing skills, independent living skills with or without an attendant, transportation (if not telecommuting), and mobility independence. Because of these requirements it remains unusual for an individual with mental retardation requiring extensive support to find competitive employment.
- *Supported employment* is defined by the Rehabilitation Act Amendments of 1986 (PL 99-506) and 1992 as competitive employment in an integrated setting with ongoing support services for an individual with a disability. This program is administered through the state-level Bureaus of Vocational Rehabilitation and state MR/DD agencies. These agencies have

aided people with disabilities in obtaining employment with needed supports through supervisor or co-worker assistance (natural supports) or job coaches (Rogan, Hagner, & Murphy, 1993). A job coach or employment consultant is a person who is hired by the individual or the placement agency to provide specialized on-site training to assist the employee with a disability in learning and performing his or her job and adjusting to the work environment (Chadsey et al., 1997). It should be recognized, however, that a job coach sometimes interferes with worksite inclusion (Chadsey et al., 1997).

- *Sheltered workshops* focus on developing specific work skills in a segregated environment. They are being replaced by supported employment options that integrate the individual into the community.
- Adults with mental retardation requiring extensive to pervasive support may be served in *day treatment programs* that focus on the development of daily living skills rather than job skills.

COMMUNITY LIVING

The home has many functions, including providing shelter, being a social space, and enhancing the quality of life. Since the move away from institutionalization in the 1970s, the quality and quantity of homes for individuals with disabilities has greatly expanded. As of 2001, approximately 35% of individuals with MR/DD were living in their own homes, 15% were in publicly funded residential settings, and 60% continued to live with their families (Braddock et al., 2001; Seltzer & Krauss, 2001). According to the Bureau of the Census, between 1990 and 2000 the number of group home residents in Maryland increased from 793 to 4,132, exemplifying the growth in community-based homes. In many communities, however, the need for community living programs for young adults with MR/DD still exceeds the supply, and waiting lists are the norm. It is important to keep in mind that an individual's options may be limited not only by the resources available in the community but also by his or her own abilities to develop strategies to fill the gaps in services. Fortunately, the range of community living options and support services is expanding thanks to federal laws such as the ADA. In addition, each state has a developmental disabilities administration and a bureau of vocational rehabilitation that can provide a vital link to appropriate community-based services. A range of living options involving various levels of support is discussed next.

Independent/Supported Living

As more services and programs have become available in the community to assist individuals with MR/DD in activities of daily living, more people are choosing supported/independent living. As recently as 1990, it was virtually unheard of for an individual with quadriplegia to live independently. In 2000, many of these individuals do so with the assistance of an aide in the home, accessible transportation, VR, and assistive technology. The appropriate combination of resources permits these individuals to live independently or with support and to own their homes (Cummins, 2001; Klein, 2000).

Family Home

Many families whose grown children have MR/DD will choose for the individual to continue to live at home. This setting promotes close family relationships. There is strong emotional support, and the individual can participate in all family activities and events. The individual, however, is also less likely to participate in formal external activities (e.g., day programs, supported employment), have fewer friends, and show greater dependence on his or her parents (Seltzer & Krauss, 2001). If the individual has a job, outside friends, and activities, however, living in the family home can be an excellent life choice.

Assisted Living Programs (Group Homes)

As of 2002, group homes are perhaps the most common form of assisted living program (outside of the family home) available for individuals with mental retardation requiring extensive support. Most group homes have living space for five to seven individuals. Assistance varies depending on the individual's disability. Most group homes, however, have on-site counselors who provide supervision and support in daily living skills, employment, and recreation.

Intermediate Care Facilities

Intermediate care facilities are community-based residential facilities that provide for the needs of individuals with MR/DD who require complex care but not in an in-patient care facility. Most intermediate care facilities are small, providing care for fewer than 25 individuals at a time. These facilities provide a complex level of care in an integrated setting with opportunities for socialization and activities.

Residential Care Facilities

The majority of residential care facilities were opened in the beginning of the 20th century and are state owned and operated. These institutions traditionally had hundreds of beds for individuals with mental retardation. Since the move toward deinstitutionalization, many such facilities have closed and placement in these facilities is now rare.

ADULT HEALTH CARE SERVICES

Adults with MR/DD have increased risk factors associated with poor health outcomes (e.g., obesity), more chronic diseases that go unrecognized or inadequately treated, and an increased prevalence of mental health disorders (Seltzer & Krauss, 2001). Yet, identifying a regular source of medical and mental health care for these individuals can prove difficult. The best way of ensuring adult health care is for individuals with MR/DD to make the transition from the pediatric system prospectively as they reach the age of majority.

The process of transition in health care should be a collaborative one between health care professionals, the adolescent, and the parents. The components of health care needed by the person with MR/DD should be identified, such as which professionals (e.g., occupational therapist, physical therapist, speech-language therapist) are needed to provide the necessary care and who the care manager will be. In addition, health-related skills (e.g., clean intermittent catheterization in meningomyelocele; see Chapter 24) need to be identified so that the individual can manage his or her disability. Similarly, financing options to pay for health care need to be identified.

The transition plan should involve not only the transfer of medical information from pediatric to adult providers but also the transition of responsibility for health-related issues from the parent to the individual with MR/DD. To be ready to move to the adult system, the adolescent needs to develop the ability to understand and discuss his or her disability, to be responsible for taking medications (with supervision when necessary), and to use required adaptive equipment or appliances. During this process, health care professionals should consider when to start seeing the individual alone and when to develop a confidential relationship with him or her.

Often the teenager or family asks, "Why the need to change from a pediatric health care provider to an adult provider?" One answer is that an adult should obtain health care services from an adult health care system. If this process is expected, then the message to the teenager is that he or she, like all other teenagers, should be treated as an adult from a medical perspective.

This promotes progress toward self-determination. In contrast, staying in a parent-oriented pediatric system can send a message to the adolescent with MR/DD that he or she is not expected to make or capable of making independent decisions about and taking responsibility for health care. The only exception is when the young adult is declared incompetent, a condition usually associated with mental retardation requiring extensive to pervasive support.

It must be recognized, however, that there are barriers to this transition to the adult health care system. Unlike pediatric providers, adult health care providers rarely work in multidisciplinary teams and may not have the time to assist the family with all aspects of care. Also, adult health providers may not be as knowledgeable about the care of childhood-onset disabilities. As a result, parents may worry that their child will receive less quality and quantity of care in the adult system and may have difficulty "letting go" of the pediatric health system. Finally, pediatric health care providers may become very attached to their patients and may be conflicted about having the individual leave their practice. Perhaps the best option is to have a collaborative arrangement in which pediatric and adult health care providers work together, at least during the transition period.

In terms of funding of health care services, youth with MR/DD can often qualify for the federal Medicaid or state Children's Health Insurance Program (CHIP; see Chapter 38). Until recently, however, when an individual reached majority (18 years in most states), he or she was no longer eligible for this coverage. Congress, however, passed the Ticket to Work and Work Incentives Improvement Act of 1999 (PL 106-170), which expanded Medicaid coverage for workers with disabilities. This law permits states to disregard income, assets, and resource limitations for workers with disabilities and allows these individuals to buy into Medicaid. Thus, a person with a disability can continue to receive Medicaid coverage even though they have begun to earn an income that previously would have made them ineligible.

PARTICIPATION IN SPORTS, LEISURE, AND COMMUNITY ACTIVITIES

Our lives are segmented into time spent in education, work, and leisure. Because a young adult with MR/DD may have only partial employment, leisure time expands. If leisure time means idle time, the hours will drag, the individual may become socially isolated, and the quality of life will be less. Leisure time, however, can be a source of enjoyment and may contribute to skill development, participation in family activities, and meeting people in the community. It should be recognized that participation in these activities is correlated with adaptive skills; people with MR/DD requiring extensive to pervasive support are less likely to participate (Felce & Emerson, 2001).

Leisure activities are as varied as personalities and interests. They can be passive, such as watching television or reading a book, or active, such as participating in sports, playing computer games, or attending community or religious events. Individuals with MR/DD should have the training, experience, and opportunity to participate in a range of activities. Persistence, flexibility, planning, and choice are the keys to success in developing an effective leisure and recreation program. If special recreational settings are needed, many types of programs are available such as the Special Olympics, therapeutic horseback riding, and wheelchair sports (see Chapter 34).

Leisure activities are also a time for socialization. This is particularly important for young adults with developmental disabilities, who tend to become socially isolated. Preparation for participation in these activities should be one of the goals in an ITP. Social skills training, using role-playing activities, can be very helpful in improving these skills and can assist these individuals in becoming more attuned to others' reactions to their behavior. This training can also help a person develop conversation skills, maintain eye contact, use appropriate body language, or recover from rejection.

ISSUES OF SEXUALITY

The onset of puberty, including the beginning of menstruation, is a time of emerging sexuality in children with MR/DD, much as in typically developing adolescents (Suris et al., 1996). This is sometimes a sensitive subject for parents, who may have a difficult time accepting that adolescents and young adults with MR/DD have sexual feelings. Parents also may worry that their child (especially if they have a daughter) will be taken advantage of sexually, become pregnant, or be the victim of sexual abuse or sexually transmitted diseases. Because of these concerns parents may try to shield their child from social contacts and knowledge about sex. It is important for professionals to counsel parents that, contrary to their beliefs, educating their child about sexuality is the most effective way of protecting him or her from abuse and the consequences of unprotected sexual activity (Melberg Schwier & Hingsburger, 2000). Sexual education can foster responsible decision-making skills and offer young people support and guidance in exploring and affirming their own value and rights as individuals. This education also should encourage adolescents to delay sexual behaviors until they are ready physically, cognitively, and emotionally for mature sexual relationships and their consequences. The American Academy of Pediatrics, Committee on Psychosocial Aspects of Child and Family Health and Committee on Adolescence (2001), has suggested that the goals of sexual education should include

* Developing an appreciation of one's own body
* Learning to interact with both genders in respectful and appropriate ways
* Learning appropriate ways to express affection and love
* Encouraging the development of meaningful interpersonal relationships
* Learning to be assertive in protecting the privacy of one's own body
* Learning about contraception, conception, and protection from sexually transmitted diseases

DEVELOPING A LIFE PLAN

In most states an individual with MR/DD becomes emancipated at the age of 18 unless a surrogate court declares the individual incompetent. Although most individuals with MR/DD will assume independence, some will require lifetime assistance, whether from a professional or family member. For these individuals, families should develop a life plan. The concept of crafting a life plan emerged in response to the desire of parents to ensure that their child will be cared for in a loving, clean, and comfortable environment by competent people when the parents are no longer able to provide such care themselves.

Yet, in one study, less than half of families had made future plans for their adult child with mental retardation requiring extensive to pervasive support (Smith, Tobin, & Fullmer, 1995). Parents were more likely to have made plans if their child was receiving a greater number of services, when parents had serious health problems, when siblings were already actively involved in care, and when the family was not using avoidant coping mechanisms. Parents who had designated a successor caregiver (e.g., another family member) tended to feel less stress and more satisfaction with life. In contrast, those relying on a waiting list for residential placement felt more of a burden. Siblings were more willing to become the caregiver when 1) their brother or sister had more mild impairments, 2) the sibling was already involved with his or her care, 3) there were close family relationships, and 4) they did not feel pessimistic about their sibling's future (Griffiths & Unger, 1994).

Appropriate life planning coordinates all aspects of the person's life, including legal and financial issues, residential care, medical care, employment, and socialization. Because plans should be based on the particular needs of the person and family, issues such as religious and/or spiritual needs and special family considerations can be included. Table 37.2 provides recommended steps to take in comprehensive life planning for an individual with MR/DD.

Table 37.2. Comprehensive life and estate planning for people with disabilities

Prepare a comprehensive life plan that includes all pertinent areas, including residential, employment, social, medical, religion, legal, and financial issues.

Write a Letter of Intent as a guide for individuals providing assistance in the future.

Recommend future guardians/advocates.

Determine a realistic cost for the life care plan.

Select a combination of resources to provide for the plan, (e.g., government benefits, family assets, inheritance, savings, life insurance).

Prepare a Last Will and Testament.

Decide on the establishment of a Special Needs Trust that can coordinate resources and protect the finances of a person with a disability into the future.

Combine all the materials into a "life planning binder" so that all of the information is readily accessible. Ensure that there are several copies of the binder and that all pertinent parties know where these are located.

Meet with all of the parties involved to discuss the plan and build consensus.

Review the plan at least once a year, and make revisions as needed.

Source: Prudential Life Insurance Company, Estate Planning for Persons with Disabilities (n.d.).

SUMMARY

Youth with MR/DD should expect to become happy and effective participants in the adult world. They should have opportunities to learn about their strengths, abilities, skills, needs, and interests. They should also be allowed to take certain risks and to learn from failure. They need to assume responsibility for themselves and need to understand the difference between the protected world of school and home and the world of work and adult life. Most of all, they must believe they are capable of success. These goals can be accomplished through comprehensive transition planning for the child's movement into adulthood.

REFERENCES

American Academy of Pediatrics, Committee on Children with Disabilities. (2000). The role of the pediatrician in transitioning children and adolescents with developmental disabilities from school to work or college. *Pediatrics, 106,* 854–856.

American Academy of Pediatrics, Committee on Psychosocial Aspects of Child and Family Health & Committee on Adolescence. (2001). Sexuality education for children and adolescents. *Pediatrics, 108,* 498–502.

Americans with Disabilities Act (ADA) of 1990, PL 101-336, 42 U.S.C. §§ 12101 *et seq.*

Blum, R.W. (1995). Transition to adult health care: Setting the stage. *Journal of Adolescent Health, 17,* 3–5.

Blum, R.W., Garrell, D., Hodgeman, C.H., et al. (1993). Transition from child-centered to adult health care systems for adolescents with chronic conditions: A position paper of the Society for Adolescent Medicine. *Journal of Adolescent Health, 14,* 570–576.

Blum, R.W., & Gehn, O. (1992). Chronically ill youth. In E.R. McAnarney, R.E. Kreipe, & D.P. Orr (Eds.), *Textbook of adolescent medicine* (pp. 222–228). London: W.B. Saunders.

Blum, R.W., Resnick, M.D., Nelson, R., et al. (1991). Family and peer issues among adolescents with spina bifida and cerebral palsy. *Pediatrics, 88,* 280–285.

Braddock, D., Emerson, E., Felce, D., et al. (2001). Living circumstances of children and adults with mental retardation or developmental disabilities in the United States, Canada, England and Wales, and Australia. *Mental Retardation and Developmental Disabilities Research Reviews, 7,* 115–121.

Chadsey, J., & Beyer, S. (2001). Social relationships in the workplace. *Mental Retardation and Developmental Disabilities Research Reviews, 7,* 128–144.

Chadsey, J., Linneman, D., Rusch, R., et al. (1997). The impact of social integration interventions and job coaches in work settings. *Education and Training in Mental Retardation and Developmental Disabilities, 32,* 281–292.

Cummins, R.A. (2001). Living with support in the community: Predictors of satisfaction with life. *Mental Retardation and Developmental Disabilities Research Reviews, 7,* 99–104.

David, J., Cooper, C., Hickey, D., et al. (1994). The functional and psychological outcomes of juvenile chronic arthritis in young adulthood. *British Journal of Rheumatology, 33,* 876–881.

Edelman, A., Schuyler, V., & White, P. (1998). *Maximizing success for young adults with chronic health related illnesses.* Washington, DC: HEATH Resource Center, American Council on Education.

Felce, D., & Emerson, E. (2001). Living with support in a home in the community: Predictors of behavioral development and household and community activity. *Mental Retardation and Developmental Disabilities Research Reviews, 7,* 75–83.

Griffiths, D.L., & Unger, D.G. (1994). Views about planning for the future among parents and siblings of adults with mental retardation. *Family Relations, 43,* 221–227.

Groce, N. (1985). *Everyone here spoke sign language.* Cambridge, MA: Harvard University Press.

Hughes, C. (2001). Transition to adulthood: Supporting young adults to access social, employment, and civic pursuits. *Mental Retardation and Developmental Disabilities Research Reviews, 7,* 84–90.

Individuals with Disabilities Education Act (IDEA) Amendments of 1997, PL 105-17, 20 U.S.C. §§ 1400 *et seq.*

Kennedy, C.H. (2001). Social interaction interventions for youth with severe disabilities should emphasize interdependence. *Mental Retardation and Developmental Disabilities Research Reviews, 7,* 122–127.

Klein, J. (2000). Postcards on the refrigerator: Changing the power dynamic in housing and assistance. In J. Nisbet & D. Hagner (Eds.), *Part of the community: Strategies for including everyone* (pp. 177–201). Baltimore: Paul H. Brookes Publishing Co.

Lou Harris Assoc., Inc. (1999). *NOD/Harris Survey of People with Disabilities Study.* Washington, DC: Author.

McKenzie, N.G. (1990). Approach to the adolescent in the clinical setting. *Medical Clinics of North America, 74,* 1085–1095.

Melberg Schwier, K., & Hingsburger, D. (2000). *Sexuality: Your sons and daughters with intellectual disabilities.* Baltimore: Paul H. Brookes Publishing Co.

Menchetti, B., & Piland, V. (1998). The personal career plan: A person-centered approach to vocational evaluation and career planning. In F. Rusch & J. Chadsey (Eds.), *Beyond high school: Transition from school to work* (pp. 319–339). Belmont, CA: Wadsworth.

Mortenson, T. (2001, October 15). *Student employment and higher education opportunity: Good, bad and ugly.* Paper presented at National Student Employment Association National Conference, San Antonio, TX. Retrieved February 5, 2002, from http://www.postsecondary.org/archives/Reports/SanAntonioTX101501.pdf

National Center for Youth with Disabilities. (1993). *Teenagers at risk: A national perspective of state level services for adolescents with chronic illnesses or disability.* Minneapolis, MN: Author.

Prudential Life Insurance Company, Estate Planning for Persons with Disabilities. (n.d.). *Planning for the future* [Brochure]. Birmingham, AL: Author.

Quinn, P. (1997). *Understanding disability: A lifespan approach.* Thousand Oaks, CA: Sage Publications.

Rehabilitation Act Amendments of 1978, PL 95-602, 29 U.S.C. §§ 701 *et seq.*

Rehabilitation Act Amendments of 1986, PL 99-506, 29 U.S.C. §§ 701 *et seq.*

Rehabilitation Act Amendments of 1992, PL 102-569, 29 U.S.C. §§ 701 *et seq.*

Rehabilitation Act of 1973, PL 93-112, 29 U.S.C. §§ 701 *et seq.*

Rogan, P., Hagner, D., & Murphy, S. (1993). Natural supports: Reconceptualizing job coach roles. *Journal of the Association for Persons with Severe Handicaps, 18,* 275–281.

Seltzer, M.M., & Kraus, M.W. (2001). Quality of life of adults with mental retardation/developmental disabilities who live with family. *Mental Retardation and Developmental Disabilities Research Reviews, 7,* 105–114.

Smith, G.C., Tobin, S.S., & Fullmer, E.M. (1995) Elderly mothers caring at home for offspring with mental retardation: A model of permanency planning. *American Journal of Mental Retardation, 99,* 487–489.

Smith, M., Belcher, R., & Juhrs, P. (1995). *Guide to successful employment for individuals with autism.* Baltimore: Paul H. Brookes Publishing Co.

Suris, J., Resnick, M.D., Cassuto, N., et al. (1996). Sexual behavior of adolescents with chronic disease and disabilities. *Journal of Adolescent Health, 19,* 124–131.

Ticket to Work and Work Incentives Improvement Act of 1999, PL 106-170, 42 U.S.C. §§ 1305 *et seq.*

University of Washington, Center on Human Development and Disability, Adolescent Health Transition Project. (n.d.). *Transition timeline for children and adolescents with special health care needs.* Retrieved November 16, 2001, from http://depts.washington.edu/healthtr/timeline.htm

Werner, E., & Smith, R. (1992). *Overcoming the odds: High risk children.* Ithaca, NY: Cornell University Press.

Wright, B. (1996, Fall). Teens say job training their top need. *Point of Departure, 2*(2), 8.

38 Health Care Delivery Systems and Financing Issues

Angelo P. Giardino, Alan E. Kohrt, Lowell Arye, and Nora Wells

Upon completion of this chapter, the reader will:

- understand the definition of the term *children with special health care needs* and see how such a definition affects health care delivery and financing issues
- appreciate the complexity involved in developing a system that adequately coordinates various services and supports
- be aware of insurance coverage issues that affect the provision of health care to these children
- recognize the various public health care programs and benefits that may be of value to these children and their families

CHILDREN WITH SPECIAL HEALTH CARE NEEDS

Not all children with developmental disabilities have special health care needs, and not all children with special health care needs have developmental disabilities. For example, children with learning disabilities do not generally have special medical needs, and children with asthma, who do have special medical needs, do not generally have developmental disabilities. Therefore, the term *children with special health care needs* includes both a subgroup of children with developmental disabilities (e.g., children with cerebral palsy or meningomyelocele) and a group of typically developing children with complex medical problems. Children with special health care needs are defined by the federal Maternal and Child Health Bureau as "those who have or are at increased risk for a chronic physical, developmental, behavioral or emotional condition and who also require health and related services of a type or amount beyond that required by children generally" (McPherson et al., 1998, p. 138). Approximately 18% of children in the United States who are younger than 18 years (12.5 million children) satisfy these criteria (Newacheck, McManus, et al., 2000). These include children with ongoing medical conditions such as hemophilia, diabetes, and asthma, as well as children with developmental disabilities such as autism, mental retardation, sensory impairments, and cerebral palsy (Newacheck et al., 1998). Many of these children are also considered to have a disability according to definitions from the World Health Organization (1980) and various federal agencies; a side-by-side comparison of these definitions is provided in Table 38.1.

Developing an effective health care system for children with special health care needs is the focus of this chapter. Several of the core features of this system, however, are important for all children. Children with special health care needs may require an array of services beyond the primary care doctor, including those provided by specialists, therapists, pharmacists, mental health providers, and home health providers (Wells et al., 2000). The most important principles are that children should be provided comprehensive health care, that care should be coordinated, and that children should have a "medical home" (more fully defined later but essentially means that health care delivery is sensitive to the unique situation of the child and his or her family).

707

Table 38.1. Definitions of children with special health care needs, based on various approaches

List of diagnoses (not all-inclusive)	World Health Organization (1980; 2001) disablement model	Social Security Administration (2001)	Census Bureau: Survey of Income and Program Participation (McNeil, 1993)	Maternal and Child Health Bureau (McPherson et al., 1998)
Children with special health care needs are defined as (but not limited to) those having the following conditions: Asthma Autism Central nervous system injury Cerebral palsy Cleft lip/palate Congenital heart disease Cystic fibrosis Diabetes Down syndrome Hearing impairment Hemophilia Inborn errors of metabolism Learning disabilities Leukemia Mental retardation Muscular dystrophy Sickle cell disease Seizure disorder Spina bifida Visual impairment	*Impairment* is an abnormality of an anatomical, physiological, or psychological structure and/or function. *Disability* is a person's limitation in performance in an activity or ability within the range functioning from an impairment. *Handicap* is the social consequence or disadvantage resulting from the impairment and disability when the person interacts with the environment.	A child younger than 18 years is defined as having a disability "if he or she has a medically determinable physical or mental impairment or combination of impairments that causes marked and severe functional limitations, and that can be expected to cause death or that has lasted or can be expected to last for a continuous period of not less than 12 months" (p. 3). A medically determinable impairment is "an impairment that results from anatomical, physiological, or psychological abnormalities which can be shown by medically acceptable clinical and laboratory diagnostic techniques. A physical or mental impairment must be established by medical evidence consisting of signs, symptoms, and laboratory findings—not only by the individual's statement of symptoms" (p. 3).	From birth to 5 years old, a child is defined as having a disability if he or she 1) has limitation in the usual activities done by most children the same age or 2) is receiving therapy or diagnostic service for developmental needs. For children older than 6 years, disability is defined as any limitation in the ability to do regular schoolwork. Additional indicators of disability for children 3–14 years old include a long-lasting condition that limits ability to walk, run, or use stairs. Additional indicators of disability for children 15–17 years old include problems with personal care, activities of daily living, and basic mobility and the use of assistive devices such as wheelchairs.	Children with special health care needs are defined as "those who have or are at increased risk for a chronic physical, developmental, behavioral or emotional condition and who also require health and related services of a type or amount beyond that required by children generally" (p. 138).

PROBLEMS IN ARRANGING COORDINATION OF CARE

Given the many services needed and the number of providers and professionals involved in co-ordinating the various health care services required by a child with special health care needs, there are many challenges for the child's family and health care providers. The complexity of the child's needs requires a great deal of time, energy, and skill to ensure that efforts of different agencies, institutions, and professionals work effectively together to develop a comprehensive care plan (American Academy of Pediatrics [AAP], 1998, 1999; Perrin, 1990). This coordination is difficult as a consequence of a lack of comprehensive case management services and because of the child's needs, which may span a range of services. These services may include some that are not traditionally seen as health related, such as education and housing. Many children and families do not have comprehensive case management services. As a result families, health care professionals, and various child advocates expend an enormous amount of time and energy attempting to align the available programs and services with the child's needs (Liptak & Revell, 1989). Even when obtained, many services are not available in convenient, community-based settings, thus further depleting the families' energy and resources.

In an attempt to deal with these issues, insurers, hospitals, and public and private agencies have developed case management programs as a form of care coordination (Silva, Sofis, & Palfrey, 2000). The purpose and scope of these programs vary with the type of agency. Hospitals use case management to provide information to payers and assist with discharge planning. Case management done for insurers and managed care organizations (MCOs) focuses more on benefits management and resource utilization and less on care coordination, although some Medicaid MCOs do organize and coordinate a broader package of benefits (Abt Associates, 2000). Many social agencies and public programs provide case management services because these are often mandated by public policy. Title V programs, which are state programs for children with special health care needs that are funded via block grants from the federal Maternal and Child Health Bureau, have a special mandate to monitor and provide care coordination, but programs vary from state to state. Although Medicaid payment for case management may be allocated for a child, families often find that their case manager lacks the necessary medical information or adequate communication with clinicians. Many specialty programs in children's hospitals have nurse specialists who help coordinate the medical care. These specialty-based care coordinators may have the most information about the particular specialty (e.g., diabetes) but may lack knowledge of resources and other aspects of comprehensive medical care at the community or primary care level. This rather disjointed system often results in the community-based primary care physicians saying that they want to be the care coordinators; the specialty clinicians and their team providing some coordination; the insurers, including Medicaid MCOs, providing benefits management; early intervention, mental health, and Title V programs paying for and delivering different aspects of case management; and families valuing whatever help with coordination they receive but often doing most of the coordination themselves and asking for more organized and consistent help (Wells et al., 2000).

THE CONCEPT OF A MEDICAL HOME

To help families with care coordination and to improve care, the AAP has called for all children to have "a *medical home* that provides accessible, continuous, comprehensive, family centered, coordinated, and compassionate health care in an atmosphere of mutual responsibility and trust among clinician, child, and caregiver(s)" (1992, p. 774). The federal Maternal and Child Health Bureau strongly supports these concepts and has also emphasized the importance of culturally competent and community-based care. Table 38.2 describes the ideal medical home.

Prior to the emergence of managed care as a dominant force in health care delivery, primary care was beginning to be recognized as a valuable component in the highly specialized, technology dependent, tertiary care–based health care delivery system in the United States. Starfield (1992) defined *primary care* as health care that is first contact (involving an initial physician to whom the family goes to for routine and nonroutine care), community based (accessible), longitudinal (continuous), coordinated, and comprehensive. In addition, primary care clinicians for children (e.g., community pediatricians, family physicians, nurse practitioners) provide preventive care such as well-child examinations; immunizations; and vision, hearing,

Table 38.2. Attributes of the ideal medical home

Attributes	Description
A medical home provides care that is *accessible.*	The family can obtain care in the community, and there are no barriers to receiving care based on race, ethnic, or cultural background; based on type of health insurance, including Medicaid and the Children's Health Insurance Program (CHIP); or based on lack of insurance coverage. When families are forced to change insurance because of employer decisions, the health care practice makes an effort to accommodate the change and maintain continuity of care.
The medical home is *family centered.*	Family members are recognized by the clinicians and staff as the principal caregivers, and information is shared with them in an unbiased, ongoing, and complete manner. All care plans reinforce the family as the center of support for the child.
Care from a medical home is *continuous.*	Families and children value the ongoing relationship with primary care providers, subspecialty clinicians, and staff. The medical home provides continuity of care as the child and family make the transition from the hospital to the community and to child care, to school, or to home-based care. The continuity of care from infancy through young adulthood is the foundation of the medical home; it allows the clinician to know the family and patient and permits the family to trust the physician and his or her staff. This continuity shapes clinical judgment so that unnecessary tests are avoided and psychosocial factors can be weighed in decision making. The long-term relationship finally allows the young adult and family to make the transition to adult-based care with a new provider with support and information from the pediatrician or pediatric nurse practitioner.
Primary care medical homes provide care that is *comprehensive.*	Families can receive health care 24 hours per day, 7 days per week. The child can receive preventive, acute, or chronic care within the scope and knowledge of the clinician. Because of the complexity of medical conditions today, many children require appropriate referral to subspecialists for management of acute and chronic conditions.
Medical homes *coordinate care.*	Not only are families assisted in contacting and utilizing appropriate support, educational and community based services, but also the care provided in hospital, ambulatory, and community settings is planned and coordinated to the benefit of the family and child. Medical records and other information are shared between providers to avoid duplication and fragmentation.
Medical homes are characterized by *compassion.*	The clinic- and office-based teams in the medical home demonstrate concern for the well-being of the child and family. This compassion is communicated by every member of the staff.
Care in the medical home also must be *culturally competent.*	The medical home must be able to deliver care in cross-cultural situations; therefore, the staff must value diversity, be aware of how their own culture affects their thoughts and actions, understand the dynamics when cultures interact, and have a practice-wide cultural education program that helps ensure culturally competent clinical care and service delivery.
Care delivered by the medical home is *community based.*	Primary care is community based. Although children and families with special health care needs often require care by subspecialists who may not be available in their own community, the medical home whenever possible should be in the community where the family lives. The staff and clinicians of the medical home coordinate and communicate with the subspecialists. In addition, other providers, including pediatric physical, occupational, speech, and feeding therapists; home nursing staff; and providers of other important services should be available in the community or as close to home as possible.

Source: American Academy of Pediatrics, 1992.

developmental, and medical screening. Primary care also includes personalized care that demonstrates the clinician's knowledge of the patient and family environment, including work; personal; emotional; and, often, financial concerns. For the child and family, often the primary care team's medical home coordinates care with the pediatric subspecialist(s), staff, and community providers to ensure comprehensive care. In a few instances, the subspecialist assumes the majority of the responsibilities for the medical home; in some albeit unusual cases, the specialist may even provide well-child care.

THE HEALTH CARE ENVIRONMENT AND FINANCING

For most of its history, the health care system in the United States utilized a fee-for-service model in which the health care provider received a payment for each unit of service rendered (MacLeod, 2001). The typical fee has been based on a "usual and customary" charge for the service. This system is a **retrospective** payment system; payment is made after the service is rendered. This approach has been criticized because of its potential to encourage health care professionals to provide too many services. In response to skyrocketing costs, the U.S. health care system experienced a revolution in the later years of the 20th century, and it continues to evolve toward a **prospective,** or prepayment, approach (Deal, Shiono, & Behrman, 1998; Wagner, 2001).

Managed Care

The notion of prepayment is a defining feature of what has become known as *managed care.* In its purest form, the provider is paid a set fee based solely on the number of individuals to be served, in an arrangement referred to as *capitation.* No additional payment is made when services are provided. This approach is expected to result in the provision of only appropriate services because providers are not compensated for "doing more." A criticism of managed care is that such a system may encourage providers to "do less" than is optimal. This point is of particular concern to children with ongoing and disabling conditions because their care, in general, is significantly more expensive than that of typically developing children (Neff & Anderson, 1995; U.S. General Accounting Office, 1996, 2000). In looking at how financial aspects of the health care environment relate to children with special health care needs, it is important to consider managed care as an approach; to review types of insurance coverage, including private and public programs; and to weigh the overall importance of Medicaid (also referred to as *Medical Assistance* or *MA*) to these children and their families.

Managed care in its purest form includes five key elements: 1) prospective payment, 2) networks of selected providers, 3) credentialing of providers using explicit standards, 4) quality assurance and utilization review programs, and 5) incentives for use of network providers (Freund & Lewit, 1993). Using these components, MCOs in theory develop a more comprehensive range of health care services with incentives and oversight devices intended to maximize health benefits while limiting unnecessary utilization and expenditures. MCOs usually reimburse providers on a capitated basis, providing a set payment each month for each individual covered regardless of the amount of services that the individual uses (typically referred to as the *per-member-per-month rate* or the *PMPM;* Fox & Fama, 1996; Nash, 1994). If the individuals, on average, use fewer services than expected that month, the providers may realize a financial gain; if the individuals use more services than expected, the providers may face a financial loss (Kongstvedt, 2001). Thus, the MCOs seek to keep health care expenditures at or below monthly or annual expectations to maximize potential financial gain. Because the financial incentive structure discourages overuse of services, this prepaid approach to providing health care should lead to a system in which only appropriate services are delivered.

Insurance Coverage: Public and Private

Access and use of health care services is affected by insurance coverage, family income, and sociodemographics (Newacheck, McManus, et al., 2000). The principal form of health insurance for all Americans younger than age 65 is private or commercial insurance that is provided by employers. The number of workers who receive employer-provided insurance, however, has declined since the mid- to late 1990s with a subsequent reduction in the number of children covered under such plans (Children's Defense Fund, 1998). As employer-based insurance coverage for children declines, coverage from public forms of insurance needs to increase. If this increase occurs at a slower rate than the decrease in private insurance, it could result in an expanding number of uninsured children.

To avoid the problem of uninsured children, the federal government has developed several publicly funded insurance programs that provide avenues for children to receive health care coverage. Table 38.3 lists comprehensive details about each program. In 1965, Medicaid (Title XIX of the Social Security Act Amendments of 1965, PL 89-97) was launched. Medicaid is a jointly funded federal/state program that serves as a societal safety net for children who are inadequately covered by private insurance, who do not have private insurance, or who meet other eligibility criteria. It should be noted that coverage under Medicare, the other kind of public insurance, is uncommon in children except for children with end-stage kidney disease. In addition, Congress created the Children's Health Insurance Program (CHIP; Title XXI) in 1997 (modified in 1999), which provides states with an incentive to extend health care coverage to uninsured children who do not qualify for traditional Medicaid (Deal & Shiono, 1998). Some states have expanded Medicaid for CHIP-eligible children, whereas others use commercial benefit plans ("CHIP & Seamless Health Care," 1999; "State Legislative Agendas," 1999). Despite the availability of public coverage via Medicaid and CHIP, there remain children (including some with special health care needs) who do not have adequate health insurance coverage (Brodsky & Somers, 1997; Newacheck, Halfon, & Inkelas, 2000). A few states have developed specific benefits plans for children with special health care needs, but these remain the exception.

The federal and state governments provide several other avenues for children with disabilities and their families to gain access to a range of health care services and funding for these services. These include the Social Security Administration's Supplemental Security Income (SSI) program, which provides income support and/or access to Medicaid; the Maternal and Child Health Bureau's Title V programs, which provide enhanced services (e.g., case management) above the covered Medicaid services; and the Individual's with Disability Education Act (IDEA) Amendments of 1997's Parts B and C benefits, which link educational and health care needs with Medicaid funding. In practical terms, these programs may demonstrate considerable state-to-state variability in eligibility criteria, types of services covered or offered, and amount of care provided.

Private–public insurance coverage issues and programmatic variability further complicate the task of fashioning care plans for children with special health care needs. Children and families experience this variability most acutely when they must navigate through a number of agencies, institutions, and providers, each with its own set of eligibility requirements, regulations, and service provisions that may or may not meet the child's needs. In addition, publicly funded programs are coming under increased scrutiny as legislative and budgetary debates focus on cost and quality. One may only assume that over time public resources for providing health care services for these children will be closely scrutinized (National Research Council & Institute of Medicine, 1996). Therefore, strong advocacy efforts and partnering with families and concerned professionals will be essential to work on appropriate access to highly efficient and cost-effective care for children with special health care needs.

Children and Managed Care

Looking in general at managed care approaches to caring for children, one sees both possible advantages and disadvantages. Owing to its preventive focus, managed care approaches to pediatric care could conceivably encourage payers and providers to work toward keeping children healthy and thus avoid the higher costs of taking care of children when their clinical situations becomes more serious. In the ideal situation, more efficiently coordinated care could generate cost savings. These savings, in turn, could be invested in increasing access, providing the highest quality of services, and promoting new venues of care that are less costly. These could include outpatient sites and community-based initiatives as opposed to inpatient settings or hospital-based programs (Deal et al., 1998). In the ideal world, managed care approaches that include both physical and behavioral health coverage hold a particular advantage for children with chronic or disabling conditions (Stroul et al., 1998). This theoretical benefit has yet to be demonstrated on a nationwide basis, and it relies on MCOs' adopting a long-term perspective rather than a more traditional, short-term budgetary cycle perspective.

Because of its inherent cost consciousness, managed care also has potential disadvantages for children. Managed care approaches initially were developed to cover working adults in an effort to minimize costs. Children, because of their dynamic growth and developmental trajectory, are different from adults and may be vulnerable in a typical managed care environment that seeks to limit expenditures for services that do not have immediate or easily defined impacts (Hughes & Luft, 1998). Concerns have been raised about the financial disincentives inherent in capitation that may exist in caring for medically fragile children that may create financial pressure on MCOs to select low-risk pediatric enrollees. This could also result in limitation of the number of pediatric specialist providers and implementation of policies and procedures that reduce ancillary services whose benefits may not be immediately obvious (Bodenheimer, Lo, & Casalino, 1999; Hughes & Luft, 1998). Another concern is that MCOs may not be interested in tailoring programs to meet the unique needs of children because expenditures for children, in general, only account for 14% of all expenditures in a given health plan (Deal et al., 1998). At the extreme, some contend that managed care is a market-based tool that will lead to the rationing of health care services; this would be especially damaging to high-cost populations such as children with special health care needs (Pear, 2000).

Managed Care and Children with Special Health Care Needs

Children with special health care needs could potentially experience benefits from managed care, especially as compared with the parameters of the traditional fee for service plans. In the best-case scenario MCOs provide the following: 1) increased flexibility to design programs that will meet the children's special needs; 2) coverage of well-child care, routine immunizations, and other preventive care that are often excluded in traditional plans; 3) protection of families from excessive medical costs; and 4) point-of-service (POS) plans that provide families with the benefits of managed care while retaining the choice of physicians even if they are not in the standard network of providers (Smith & Ashbaugh, 1995). With respect to children with special health care needs, a national survey examining the benefits structure of 59 MCOs identified a number of potential advantages, including the availability of ancillary therapies, home care, outpatient mental health services, case management, and the absence of lifetime benefit maximums (Fox, Wicks, & Newacheck, 1993).

Managed care systems, however, can also work to the disadvantage of these children, especially because more than 90% of child health care expenditures are consumed by approximately 15% of children who have disabilities or chronic illnesses (Deal et al., 1998; Fox et al., 1993; Kuhithau et al., 1998; Smith & Ashbaugh, 1995). Children with special health care needs, therefore, represent a group of high service utilizers, which makes them ready cost-

Table 38.3. Overview of assistance programs for children with special health care needs

Program history	Description	Comments	Family perspectives
The *Supplemental Security Income (SSI)* program for children was started in 1974 to "reduce the additional deleterious environmental effects that a low family income can have on the growth and development of the disabled child" (Academy of American Pediatrics [AAP], 1995). In the Personal Responsibility and Work Opportunity Reconciliation Act of 1996 (PL 104-193), Congress redefined SSI's definition of disability for children and removed individual functional assessment from the determination process. An eligible child must have a medically determinable impairment (defined in Table 38.1). Many previously eligible children were declared ineligible under the new law.	SSI provides benefits to low-income people who meet financial and other eligibility requirements. SSI qualifies children and adults (including those with disabilities) for Medicaid health care services in many states. In some states, a child on SSI automatically qualifies for Medicaid. SSI recipients represent slightly more than one quarter of the Medicaid population but more than two thirds of all Medicaid expenditures (Hillman & Arye, 1995). A child with SSI is ensured referral to Title V programs for children with special health care needs. Families can call 1-800-772-1213 to make an appointment for a telephone interview. An application should be filed even if the family may not be eligible financially.	A team consisting of a disability examiner and a medical or psychological professional determines if the child is eligible from written information, which can come from schools, physicians, psychologists, teachers, therapists, parents, friends, relatives, the child, and others. The team will use only the written information to determine degree of disability for the previous 12 months, so accurate, timely data is critical. Reports should include a 12-month medical history; use specific terms; have complete, detailed clinical and laboratory results; should contain a clear diagnosis (when possible), type, response to treatments, prognosis, and duration of treatment; should indicate ability to function in an age-appropriate manner and perform activities of daily living with description of any limitations; and should include school reports. If a decision cannot be made, a consultation examination can be requested (SSA, 2001).	SSI is a critical safety net for low-income children with disabilities. Family income must be very low for the child to qualify. The level of disability required is also severe enough that many children with special health care needs do not meet the requirements. For an eligible child, the cash benefit from the SSI program allows families to decide which additional services the child needs that may not be covered by Medicaid or another third-party payer.

Program history	Description	Comments	Family perspectives
Medicaid, the primary public health program for low-income individuals, was passed into law in 1965 (Title XIX of the Social Security Act Amendments of 1965, PL 89-97). For fiscal year 1998, 22 million children were enrolled in Medicaid during the year. Approximately 50% were enrolled in Medicaid managed care programs (AAP, 2000). Medicaid pays for approximately 35% of all births in the United States in a given year. During 1996 close to 1 million children with disabilities who received Medicaid also received SSI benefits. In most states, Medicaid is the single largest and fastest-growing budget item, accounting for more than 18% of states' total expenditures and 77% of states' health-related expenditures.	Medicaid provides access to a comprehensive benefit package of health coverage (e.g., ancillary therapies, home care, mental health care, transportation to medical services, ongoing maintenance services, preventive services, nursing home care, hospitalization, physician services). All states are mandated to cover a core set of benefits (e.g., hospital; outpatient physician services; laboratory and X ray; basic home health services; and early and periodic screening, diagnosis, and treatment [EPSDT]). Under EPSDT, states must cover all medically necessary services for children, even those considered optional for adults (e.g., services by other health professionals, optometrist services and eyeglasses, intermediate care facility services, nursing facility services for children younger than 21 years, prescribed drugs, dental services, prosthetic devices, services provided in clinics). States may provide home- and community-based waiver services to qualifying individuals. States are not limited in the scope of services provided under such waivers for people who would otherwise be institutionalized as long as the services are cost-effective (but room and board other than for respite care is not covered).	Under EPSDT, children must receive screening and diagnostic services and medically necessary treatments, even those not available under a state's Medicaid program but that are allowable under federal Medicaid law. This requirement makes EPSDT an important vehicle for children with disabilities. Case management services can be covered under Medicaid.	Medicaid provides the most appropriate benefit package for children with special health care needs and thus is a safety net for these children. Many children with less severe disabilities who need this coverage, however, do not qualify for it.

(continued)

Table 38.3. *(continued)*

Program history	Description	Comments	Family perspectives
Title V was created in 1935 as part of the Social Security Act (PL 74-271). The Omnibus Budget Reconciliation Act (OBRA) of 1981 (PL 97-35) created the Maternal and Child Health Bureau block grants, adding benefits for children with disabilities receiving SSI, lead poisoning, sudden infant death syndrome, genetic testing and counseling, and adolescent pregnancy to existing Title V programs. States must spend 30% of the federal funds on services for children with special health care needs. In 2000, 970,044 children received medical services via children with special health care needs programs (U.S. Department of Health and Human Services, 2002).	Title V block grants provide health and related services to women of child-bearing age, infants, children, and adolescents. For children with special health care needs and their families, Title V helps to ensure that services (e.g., case management or care coordination, transportation, home visiting, health education) are family centered, coordinated, and community based. Title V helps to provide wraparound services (individualized direct services designed to support a child in his or her home, school, and community) and provides rehabilitation services for individuals younger than 16 who are blind or who have disabilities and who receive SSI if the services are not covered under Medicaid. In many states, Title V provides partial funding for categorical programs (e.g., for children with spina bifida, cerebral palsy, sickle cell disease, hemophilia, and others).	States determine eligibility requirements for defining children with special health care needs and determine what services are provided. Tremendous variability in eligibility and services exists among states. Most states provide screening and treatment of disabling conditions as well as ongoing support services (e.g., case management, counseling).	Family involvement in the planning and program aspects of Title V has been mandated since 1989. In some states, family involvement has become the hallmark of the program.

Program history	Description	Comments	Family perspectives
Before the Education for All Handicapped Children Act of 1975 (PL 94-142) was implemented, almost 1 million children with disabilities could not attend school and hundreds of thousands were not provided with appropriate services. The current version of the law, the *Individuals with Disabilities Education Act (IDEA) Amendments of 1997 (PL 105-17)* guarantees all students with disabilities ages 3–21 the right to a free appropriate public education in the least restrictive environment; provides federal funds to states and local school districts to help pay the costs of special education, including related services such as speech-language and physical therapy; and includes early intervention provisions for infants/toddlers. (See Chapter 30 for discussion of services mandated by IDEA '97.) From 1997 to 1998, the law provided for school-based services for more than 5.5 million children ages 6–21 and 570,000 preschoolers ages 3–5. From 1998 to 1999, 190,000 children up to 3 years of age received services (U.S. Department of Education, Office of Special Education and Rehabilitative Services [OSERS], 2000). Approximately 7.7% of all students received special education services during the 1993–1994 academic year (Lewit & Baker, 1996).	States and localities fund the majority of special education services, but the federal government provides some funds. Part B of IDEA '97 deals with related services for children age 3 and older who need special education services. Part C (formerly known as Part H) deals with early intervention services for infants/toddlers with disabilities. Part B services include classroom instruction, physical education, home instruction, and instruction in hospitals and institutions. Other related services are transportation and corrective or supportive services (e.g., speech-language pathology, audiology, psychological services, physical and occupational therapy, early identification and assessment of disabilities, counseling, school health services, social work in schools, medical evaluation and diagnosis). Part C funds state planning for early intervention services to promote children's development from birth to age 3 years. States determine eligibility guidelines, develop needs assessments, and create a process for an individualized family service plan (U.S. Department of Education, Office of Special Education and Rehabilitative Services [OSERS], 2000; U.S. Department of Health and Human Services, Assistant Secretary for Planning and Evaluation, 1991).	State Medicaid programs can pay for related services provided through IDEA '97 that are specified in the federal Medicaid law and determined to be medically necessary by the state Medicaid agency.	Many children with special health care needs also need special services in schools, and IDEA '97 is the vehicle for these needed services. A major problem for families is the lack of coordination between the school-based services and the child's health-related services.

(continued)

Table 38.3. *(continued)*

Program history	Description	Comments	Family perspectives
Created in 1997, the **Children's Health Insurance Program** (CHIP; Title XXI) will provide more than $40 billion over 10 years, entitling participating states to annual federal allotments to purchase "child health assistance" for "targeted low-income children" not eligible for other forms of insurance, including Medicaid ("Implementing Title XII," 1997). As of January 2001, 3.3 million children were enrolled in and 1.36 million children were eligible for CHIP.	CHIP may 1) expand Medicaid coverage; 2) establish new, subsidized state insurance programs; or 3) subsidize enrollment in employer health plans or in comprehensive community-based programs with federal waivers. Low-income children are eligible, meaning children younger than 19 years with family incomes below 200% of poverty level or 50 percentage points higher than a state's Medicaid eligibility levels. Children may not be excluded for having preexisting conditions or for having certain conditions (Ullman, Bruen, & Holahan, 1998).	CHIP funds states to insure children from working families with incomes too high to qualify for Medicaid but too low to afford private health insurance.	CHIP programs that mandate Medicaid-level health benefits will help to meet the needs of children with special health care needs. CHIP programs that have less adequate benefit packages, however, will result in significant problems for these children and their families.

718

reduction targets in a system that is essentially designed to manage routine populations and that usually limits access to specialists and reduces utilization of high-cost services. Taking this into account, potential downsides identified for children with special health care needs include 1) a lack of choice, 2) decreased access to specialty providers, 3) availability of specialized services only when significant improvement is expected over a short period, 4) high copayments especially for out-of-network providers, and 5) lack of information about the needs of these children. Decreased access is a particular concern in the care of such children, who often require the services of pediatric specialists. In addition, limiting therapy services to those resulting in immediate improvement would exclude treatment for children who require ongoing treatment to improve age-appropriate function (e.g., children with cerebral palsy or meningomyelocele).

The findings in the literature on the impact of managed care on children in general and those with special health care needs in particular have been equivocal (Szilagyi, 1998). What is clear is that some plans can successfully implement strategies that reduce 1) inpatient hospital bed days (which account for between 40% and 50% of total health care expenditures) and 2) emergency department usage by enrollees. Impact on primary care in the outpatient setting and access to specialists is less clear. A trend is emerging, however, showing that MCOs may reduce the use of specialty services, especially of high-cost procedures (Szilagyi, 1998). Thus, although more research is needed to define the impact of managed care on children with special health care needs, the unique vulnerability of these children to inadequate access to health care services causes concern about the already identified trends.

Recognizing the potential disadvantages of a managed care approach for these children and realizing that a significant number of these children receive some or all of their overall health care coverage under state-run Medicaid programs, the Centers for Medicare & Medicaid Services (CMS; formerly called the Health Care Financing Administration), which has federal oversight responsibility for Medicaid, has established a set of safeguards to promote attention to the unique aspects of caring for these children in a managed care environment (Table 38.4). These safeguards provide protection for children and families involved in Medicaid programs and serve as an outline for some of the potentially problematic areas that children with special health care needs may face in managed care. To deal with this issue, some states have conceived "carve-outs" for these children in which the children are handled separately from the general population. Components from several perspectives on what constitutes an optimal care system for these children include the following (AAP, 1998; McManus & Fox, 1996a, 1996b; Sandy & Gibson, 1996):

- Integration of primary and specialty care in a way that combines the expertise of the specialists with the breadth of perspective provided by a generalist
- Integration of medical care with home- and community-based services that effectively link the person with visiting nurses, Meals on Wheels, transportation, respite care, housekeeping, and housing services
- Integration of patient and family perspectives into the care process and planning, using patient-centered communication and a consumer-oriented focus to service delivery
- Emphasis on functional status and quality of life so that the systems are tracked to be accountable for their effectiveness
- Improved screening and risk assessment to identify children early, when specialized services developmentally have the most effect
- Individual and group health education targeted to improve self-care skills and appropriate use of health care services
- Flexible gatekeeping that allows children and families access to a variety of services on a limited basis without prior authorization
- Comprehensive case management that moves beyond benefit management and achieves real case coordination

Table 38.4. Centers for Medicare & Medicaid Services (formerly Health Care Financing Administration) safeguards for children with special health care needs

Types of safeguards	Requirements for state managed care programs
Public process	Stakeholders such as advocates, providers, and consumer groups are included during waiver development.
Definition of children with special needs	Definition includes at least the Balanced Budget Act (BBA) of 1997 (PL 105-33) categories of children with special health care needs based on eligibility for five federal and state programs: 1. Supplemental Security Income (SSI) 2. A discretionary Medicaid eligibility category known as the Katie Beckett state plan option that covers children living at home who would be eligible for Medicaid had they been placed in an institution 3. Maternal and Child Health Bureau block grants for children with special health care needs under Title V of the Social Security Act (PL 74-271) 4. Federal foster care or adoption assistance under Title IV-E of the Social Security Act 5. Foster care or out-of-home placements funded from other sources
Identification	Children with special health care needs are identified, and specific data are collected on these children.
Enrollment/ disenrollment	Enrollment includes outreach activities and assistance from specially trained personnel, and children with special health care needs can disenroll or reenroll in another plan for good cause. The auto-assignment process assigns these children to an existing or otherwise capable provider.
Provider capacity	Health plans should have sufficient experienced providers to serve children with special health care needs, and the state will monitor their capacity.
Specialists	Capacity standards (regarding credentialing and accessibility) are set for specialists to whom children with special health care needs have direct access or can use as primary care physicians. Specific types of specialist are included in health plan networks, or children are allowed to see specialists outside of the networks.
Coordination	Children with special health care needs must receive a needs assessment and subsequent treatment plan, along with case management services. Coordination is required among agencies, advocates, and other systems of care or funding sources serving children with special health care needs.
Quality of care	Specific performance measures and performance improvement projects addressing children with special health care needs are developed.
Payment methodology	A payment methodology accounts for children with special health care needs enrolled in capitated managed care.
Plan monitoring	Access to specialists and services, quality of care, coordination of care, and enrollee satisfaction are monitored. Americans with Disabilities Act of 1990 (PL 101-336) access standards are monitored. Medical necessity is defined for health plans, and its application is monitored.
BBA guidance	The state adequately addresses CMS guidance regarding relevant BBA provisions.

From U.S. General Accounting Office. (2000, March). *Medicaid managed care: Challenges in implementing safeguards for children with special needs.* (Report No. GAO/HEHS-00-37). Washington, DC: Author.

- Coordination with public health, education, and social services, including collaborative arrangements, to organize and provide services
- An understanding of the differences between adult and childhood disability and the need for managed care models to be flexible in meeting pediatric needs
- Access to a medical home
- Fair reimbursement that compensates physicians for the increased time and complexity associated with care coordination (sometimes refereed to as *risk-adjusted rates* in capitated systems)
- Viable systems of monitoring the care delivered

LOOKING TOWARD THE FUTURE

Measuring outcomes and demonstrating high quality will become increasingly necessary in order to justify the enhanced service delivery and higher costs for children with special health care needs in what is increasingly a market-based system. This will require rigorous collection of data on the health care services delivered and analysis of the data using increasingly sophisticated health services techniques. The success that various HIV/AIDS programs have had in achieving adequately funded comprehensive sets of service for patients with this specific special need serves as a model for what can be done with rigorously collected data that supports the care delivered (Havens et al., 1997).

Classically, the measurable dimensions of health care quality are the structure, the process, and the actual outcomes (Donabedian, 1980). Structure, from a quality and health services perspective, describes aspects of the health care system such as facilities, staffing patterns, and qualifications. Process in this context deals with the policies and procedures that govern aspects of care such as technical and professional skills, documentation of care, safety practices, and the use of assessment tools. Finally, outcomes deal with the health status of the people served, their health-related knowledge and behavior, and their satisfaction with care (Monahan & Sykora, 1999). Table 38.5 lists the types of quality questions that can be answered when looking at structure, process, and outcomes. When considering children with special health care needs, potential problems with assessing outcomes include the following (Monahan & Sykora, 1999):

- Self-limited conditions may improve or resolve on their own even without therapy over time, so attributing the improvement to the treatment may be difficult.
- Treatment of some chronic conditions is only partially effective and is not expected to be curative, so the presence of the condition can not be used as a measure because the diagnosis does not change even though the treatment makes an improvement.
- Lack of understanding of the natural history of some chronic conditions leads some authorities to disagree on what is expected and what the result of therapy should be.

Table 38.5.   Quality indicators in health care and the questions they address

Dimension	Indicators examined	Examples of questions
Structure	Facilities Equipment Conformance to standards Staffing patterns Personnel qualifications and experience Organizational structure descriptions Financing patterns	Are primary care and specialty care clinics and hospitals accessible? How is the service delivery system structured? Do clinicians providing care communicate with each other? Are the health care professionals well educated, well trained, and board certified? Are medical records well maintained?
Process	Technical and professional skill Documentation of care Safety practices Monitoring assessment tools	Was the blood test for lead done for a child at risk for lead poisoning? Was the child with asthma treated in the most up-to-date manner?
Outcome	Health status Health-related knowledge Health-related behavior Satisfaction with care	Did the patient get better? Was disability reduced? Does a child with special health care needs have the highest level of functioning possible given what is known to be possible? If not, why not?

Source: Monahan & Sykora, 1999.

Note: Not all outcomes are the result of purely clinical decision making. Clinicians need to acknowledge that parents of children with special health care needs and other consumers of health care also consider personal preferences and experience when making health care plan choices.

- External factors that may be involved in improvement, such as supportive family involvement and the responsiveness of community supports, are not easily measured but surely can have an impact on outcome.

Despite the difficulties of monitoring quality and working to improve outcomes, this outcomes measurement has an immense potential to improve the care delivered to children who have special health care needs. In addition, the data collection, analysis, and subsequent actions illuminate why various services are indicated based on the patient outcome and allow for monitoring of improvement (Ireys, Grason, & Guyer, 1996). The amount of data available on these children is beginning to increase. Despite the limitations just listed, health care providers need to increase their efforts in this regard to continue to make a strong case for the increased spending on health care and for the appropriate amount of care coordination for these children and their families.

SUMMARY

Given the many services needed and the number of providers and professionals involved, coordinating health care services for children with special health care needs presents a challenge to the child's family and to health care providers. The complexity of the child's needs mean that a great deal of time, energy, and skill are required to coordinate the efforts of different agencies, institutions, and professionals so that they work effectively together in a comprehensive care plan. This coordination is particularly complex both because of the relative lack of comprehensive case management and care coordination services and because the child's needs may span a range of services, including some that are not traditionally seen as health related. Further complicating matters are the many federal and state agencies and programs involved in providing and funding services and the revolutionary changes in the heath care marketplace. Managed care may prove to be a combination of a blessing and a curse for children with special health care needs. All of this points to the importance of each child having a medical home and effective case management to navigate this system.

REFERENCES

Abt Associates, Inc. (2000, June). *Evaluation of the District of Columbia's demonstration program, "Managed Care System for Disabled and Special Needs Children": Final report summary.* Retrieved November 20, 2001, from http://aspe.hhs.gov/daltcp/reports/dc-frs.htm.

American Academy of Pediatrics. (AAP). (1992). American Academy of Pediatrics Ad Hoc Task Force on Definition of the Medical Home: The medical home (RE9262). *Pediatrics, 90,* 774.

American Academy of Pediatrics. (AAP). (1995). Why Supplemental Security Income is important for children and adolescents. *Pediatrics, 95,* 603–608.

American Academy of Pediatrics. (AAP). (1998). Managed care and children with special health care needs: A subject review (RE9814). *Pediatrics, 102,* 657–660.

American Academy of Pediatrics. (AAP). (1999). Care coordination: Integrating health and related systems of care for children with special health care needs (RE9902). *Pediatrics, 104,* 978–981.

American Academy of Pediatrics. (AAP). (2000). *Medicaid state report.* Elk Grove Village, IL: American Academy of Pediatrics, Division of Health Policy Research.

Americans with Disabilities Act (ADA) of 1990, PL 101-336, 42 U.S.C. §§ 12101 *et seq.*

Balanced Budget Act of 1997, PL 105-33, 111 Stat. 251.

Bodenheimer, T., Lo, B., & Casalino, L. (1999). Primary care physicians should be coordinators, not gatekeepers. *Journal of the American Medical Association, 282,* 2045–2049.

Brodsky, K.L., & Somers, S.A. (1997). Medicaid managed care for special needs population: Making it work. *Health Strategies Quarterly, 1*(2), 1–2.

Chen, A., Brown, R., Archibald, N., et al. (2000). *Best practices in coordinated care* (Contract No. HCFA 500-95-0048 [04]; MPR Reference No. 8534-004). Baltimore, MD: Health Care Financing Administration.

Children's Defense Fund. (1998). *The state of America's children: Yearbook 1998.* Washington, DC: Children's Defense Fund.

CHIP & seamless health care: New programs expand both coverage and confusion. (1999, March). *State Initiatives in Health Care Reform*(30), 7–10.

Deal, L.W., & Shiono, P.H. (1998). Medicaid managed care and children: An overview. *The Future of Children, 8*(2), 93–104.

Deal, L.W., Shiono, P.H., & Behrman, R.E. (1998). Children and Managed Health care: Analysis and recommendations. *The Future of Children, 8*(2), 4–24.

Donabedian, A. (1980). *The definition of quality and approaches to its assessment.* Ann Arbor, MI: Health Administration Press.

Education for All Handicapped Children Act of 1975, PL 94-142, 20 U.S.C. §§ 1400 *et seq.*

Fox, H.B., Wicks, L.B., & Newacheck, P.W. (1993). Health maintenance organization and children with special needs. *American Journal of Diseases of Children, 147,* 546–552.

Fox, P.D., & Fama, T. (Eds.). (1996). *Managed care and chronic illness: Challenges and opportunities.* Gaithersburg, MD: Aspen Publishers.

Freund, D.A., & Lewit, E.M. (1993). Managed care for children and pregnant women: Promises and pitfalls. *The Future of Children, 3*(2), 92–122.

Havens, P.L., Cuene, B.E., Waters, D., et al. (1997). Structure of a primary care support system to coordinate comprehensive care for children and families infected/affected by human immunodeficiency virus in a managed care environment. *The Pediatric Infectious Disease Journal, 16,* 211–216.

Health Care Financing Administration. (2001). *State Children's Health Insurance Program (SCHIP): Aggregate enrollment statistics for the 50 states and the District of Columbia for federal fiscal years (FFY) 2000 and 1999.* Retrieved from http://www.hcfa.gov/init/fy99-00.pdf

Hillman, A., & Arye, L. (1995). *States as payers: Managed care for Medicaid populations* [Policy syntheses]. Philadelphia: University of Pennsylvania, Leonard Davis Institute of Health Economics.

Hughes, D.C., & Luft, H.S. (1998). Managed care and children: An overview. *The Future of Children, 8*(2), 25–38.

Implementing Title XXI: States face choices. (1997). *Health Policy and Child Health, 4*(4), 1–4.

Individuals with Disabilities Education Act Amendments of 1997, PL 105-17, 20 U.S.C. §§ 1400 *et seq.*

Individuals with Disabilities Education Act (IDEA) of 1990, PL 101-476, 20 U.S.C. §§ 1400 *et seq.*

Ireys, H.T., Grason, H.A., & Guyer, B. (1996). Assuring quality care for children with special needs in managed care organizations: Roles for pediatricians. *Pediatrics, 98,* 178–185.

Kongstvedt, P.R. (Ed.). (2001). *The managed health care handbook* (4th ed.). Gaithersburg, MD: Aspen Publishers.

Kuhlthau, K., Perrin, J.M., Ettner, S.L., et al. (1998). High-expenditure children with Supplemental Security Income. *Pediatrics, 102,* 610–615.

Lewit, E.M., & Baker, L.S. (1996). Children in special education: The future of children. *Special Education for Students with Disabilities, 6*(1), 139–151.

Liptak, G.S., & Revell, G.M. (1989). Community physician's role in case management of children with chronic illnesses. *Pediatrics, 84,* 465–471.

MacLeod, G.K. (2001). An overview of managed health care. In P.R. Kongstvedt (Ed.), *The managed health care handbook* (4th ed., pp. 3–16). Gaithersburg, MD: Aspen Publishers.

McManus, M.A., & Fox, H.B. (1996a). Enhancing preventive and primary care. *Managed Care Quarterly, 4*(3), 19–29.

McManus, M.A., & Fox, H.B. (1996b). Enhancing preventive and primary care for children with chronic or disabling conditions served in health maintenance organizations. In P.D. Fox & T. Fama (Eds.), *Managed care and chronic illness: Challenges and opportunities* (pp. 197–112). Gaithersburg, MD: Aspen Publishers.

McNeil, J.M. (1993). Americans with disabilities, 1991–1992. *Current Population Reports, P70-33.* Washington, DC: U.S. Department of Commerce, Bureau of Census.

McPherson, M., Arango, P., Fox, H., et al. (1998). A new def-inition of children with special needs. *Pediatrics, 102,* 137–140.

Monahan, C.A., & Sykora, J. (1999). *Developing and analyzing performance measures: A guide for assessing quality care for children with special health care needs.* Vienna, VA: National Maternal and Child Health Clearinghouse.

Nash, D.B. (Ed.). (1994). *The physician's guide to managed care.* Gaithersburg, MD: Aspen Publishers.

National Research Council & Institute of Medicine. (1996). *Paying attention to children in a changing health care system: Summaries of workshops.* Washington, DC: National Academy Press.

Neff, J.M., & Anderson, G. (1995). Protecting children with chronic illness in a competitive marketplace. *Journal of the American Medical Association, 274,* 1866–1869.

Newacheck, P.W., Halfon, N., & Inkelas, M. (2000). Commentary: Monitoring expanded health insurance for children. Challenges and opportunities. *Pediatrics, 105,* 1004–1005.

Newacheck, P.W., McManus, M., Fox, H.B., et al. (2000). Access to health care for children with special health care needs. *Pediatrics, 105,* 760–766.

Newacheck, P.W., Strickland, B., Shonkoff, J.P., et al. (1998). An epidemiologic profile of children with special health care needs. *Pediatrics, 102,* 117–122.

Omnibus Budget Reconciliation Act (OBRA) of 1981, PL 97-35, 95 Stat. 357.

Pear, R. (2000, June 18). The "R" word; Justice Souter takes on a health care taboo. *The New York Times,* p. 3.

Perrin, J.M. (1990). Children with special health needs: A United States perspective. *Pediatrics, 6,* 1120–1123.

Personal Responsibility and Work Opportunity Reconciliation Act of 1996, PL 104-193, 42 U.S.C. §§ 211 *et seq.*

Sandy, L.G., & Gibson, R. (1996). Managed care and chronic care: Challenges and opportunities. In P.D. Fox & T. Fama (Eds.), *Managed care and chronic illness: Challenges and opportunities* (pp. 8–17). Gaithersburg, MD: Aspen Publishers.

Silva, T.J., Sofis, L.A., & Palfrey, J.S. (2000). *Practicing comprehensive care: A physician's operations manual for implementing a medical home for children with special health care needs.* Boston: Institute for Community Inclusion/UAP.

Smith, G., & Ashbaugh, J. (1995). *Managed care and people with developmental disabilities: A guidebook.* Alexandria, VA: National Association of State Directors of Developmental Disabilities Services.

Social Security Act, PL 74-271, 42 U.S.C. §§ 301 *et seq.*

Social Security Act Amendments of 1965, PL 89-97, 42 U.S.C. §§ 101 *et seq.*

Social Security Administration, Office of Disability. (2001, January). *Disability evaluation under Social Security* (SSA Pub. No. 64-039). Washington, DC: Government Printing Office.

Starfield, B. (1992). *Primary care: Concept, evaluation and policy.* New York: Oxford University Press.

State legislative agendas focus on managed care and CHIP: Potential and value of further state reform debated. (1999, March). *State Initiatives in Health Care Reform*(No. 30), 1–3, 10.

Stroul, B.A., Pires, S.A., Armstrong, M.I., et al. (1998). The impact of managed care on mental health services for children and their families. *The Future of Children, 8*(2), 119–133.

Szilagyi, P.G. (1998). Managed care for children: Effect on access to care and utilization of health services. *The Future of Children, 8*(2), 39–59.

Ullman, F., Bruen, B., & Holahan, J. (1998). *The State Chil-

dren's Health Insurance Program: A look at the numbers. Retrieved November 20, 2001, from http://newfederalism .urban.org/html/occ4.html

U.S. Department of Education, Office of Special Education and Rehabilitative Services (OSERS). (2000). *Twenty-second annual report to Congress on the implementation of the Individuals with Disabilities Education Act.* Retrieved November 20, 2001, from http://www.ed.gov/offices/OSERS/OSEP/ Products/OSEP2000AnlRpt/ExecSumm.html

U.S. Department of Health and Human Services. (2002). *Program data: Number of individuals served by Title V, by class of individuals* [As reported by states in their Title V Block Grant FY 2000 annual reports and FY 2002 applications]. Retrieved February 6, 2002, from http://tvispast.mchdata .net/Reports_Graphs_2001/prgsch04.htm

U.S. Department of Health and Human Services, Assistant Secretary for Planning and Evaluation. (1991). *Medicaid coverage of health-related services for children receiving special education* [Brochure]. Washington, DC: Lewin/ICF and Fox Health Policy Consultants.

U.S. General Accounting Office. (1996, July). *Medicaid managed care: Serving the disabled challenges state programs. Report to the Chairman and Ranking Minority Member, Subcommittee on Medicaid and Health Care for Low-Income Families, Committee on Finance, U.S. Senate* (Report No. GAO/ HEHS-96-136). Washington, DC: Author.

U.S. General Accounting Office. (2000, March). *Medicaid managed care: Challenges in implementing safeguards for children with special needs.* (Report No. GAO/HEHS-00-37). Washington, DC: Author.

Wagner, E.R. (2001). Types of managed care organizations. In P.R. Kongstvedt (Ed.), *The managed health care handbook* (4th ed., pp. 28–41). Gaithersburg, MD: Aspen Publishers.

Wells, N., Knauss, M.W., Anderson, B., et al. (2000). *What do families say about health care for children with special health care needs?: Your voice counts!! The Family Partners Project report to families.* Unpublished manuscript. Boston: Family at the Federation for Children with Special Needs.

World Health Organization. (1980). *International classification of impairments, disabilities, and handicaps: A manual of classification relating to the consequences of disease.* Geneva: Author.

World Health Organization. (2001). *International classification of functioning, disability, and health (ICF).* Geneva: Author.

A Glossary

Mark L. Batshaw

abduction   Moving part of the body away from one's midline.

ABR   *See* auditory brainstem response.

abruptio placenta   Premature detachment of a normally situated placenta; *also called* placental abruption.

abscesses   Localized collections of pus in cavities caused by the disintegration of tissue, usually the consequence of bacterial infections.

accommodation   1) In special education, a change in *how* a student gains access to the curriculum or demonstrates his or her learning that does not substantially alter the content or level of instruction (e.g., allowing a student to record test answers in the test booklet instead of on a separate bubble sheet); 2) the change in the shape of the lens of the eye that allows it to focus on objects at varying distances.

acetabulum   The cup-shaped cavity of the hip bone that holds the head of the femur in place, creating a joint.

acid–base balance   In metabolism, the ratio of acidic to basic compounds (about 7.42).

acidosis   Too much acid in the bloodstream. The normal pH is 7.42; acidosis is generally less than 7.30.

acquired immunodeficiency syndrome (AIDS)   Severe immune deficiency disease caused by human immunodeficiency virus (HIV; *see Chapter 8*).

actin   Protein involved in muscle contraction.

acute inflammatory peripheral neuropathy   Ascending paralysis following a viral infection; *also called* Guillain-Barré syndrome *(see Chapter 14)*.

adduction   Moving a body part, usually a limb, toward the midline.

adenoids   Lymphatic tissue located behind the nasal passages.

adenoma sebaceum   Benign cutaneous growths, usually seen around the nose, that resemble acne; these occur in individuals with tuberous sclerosis *(see Appendix B)*.

adjustment disorders   A group of psychiatric disorders, usually of childhood, associated with difficulty adjusting to life changes.

adrenaline   A potent stimulant of the autonomic nervous system. It increases blood pressure and heart rate and stimulates other physiological changes needed for a "fight or flight" response.

advance directives   Orders in a patient's medical chart limiting the level of resuscitation or other interventions that should be undertaken in the event of incapacitating illness when the patient cannot give direct consent. They are often part of a living will. In children with severe disabilities, the term is used to define the level of intervention a parent wants provided in the event of life-threatening emergency or illness in the child.

afferent   Pertaining to the neural signals sent from the peripheral nervous system to the central nervous system (CNS).

AFP   *See* alpha-fetoprotein.

afterbirth   *See* placenta.

agenesis of the corpus callosum   Absence of the band of white matter that normally connects the two hemispheres of the brain.

agonist   1) A medication that enhances certain neural activity; 2) a muscle that works in concert with another muscle to produce movement.

agyria   Absence of normal convolutions on the surface of the brain.

AIDS   *See* acquired immunodeficiency syndrome.

alcohol-related neurodevelopmental disorder (ARND)   *Previously called* fetal alcohol effects (FAE); *see Chapter 7.*

alleles   Alternate forms of a gene that may exist at the same site on the chromosome.

alopecia   Hair loss.

alpha-fetoprotein (AFP)   Fetal protein found in amniotic fluid and serum of pregnant women. Its measurement is used to test for meningomyelocele and Down syndrome in the fetus.

alveoli   Small air sacs in the lungs. Carbon dioxide and oxygen are exchanged through their walls.

amaurosis   Blindness.

amblyopia   Partial loss of sight resulting from disuse atrophy of neural circuitry during a critical period of development, most often associated with untreated strabismus in children.

amino acids   The building blocks of protein needed for normal growth.

amniocentesis   A prenatal diagnostic procedure performed in the second trimester in which amniotic fluid is removed by a needle inserted through the abdominal wall and into the uterine cavity.

amniotic fluid   Fluid that surrounds and protects the developing fetus. This fluid is sampled through amniocentesis.

anaphase   The stage in cell division (mitosis and meiosis) when the chromosomes move from the center of the nucleus toward the poles of the cell.

anaphylaxis   A life-threatening hypersensitivity response to a medication or food, marked by breathing difficulty, hives, and shock.

anemia   Disorder in which the blood has either too few red blood cells or too little hemoglobin.

anencephaly   Neural tube defect (NTD) in which either the entire brain or all but the most primitive regions of the brain are missing.

anophthalmia   Congenital absence of the eyes.

anorexia   A severe loss of appetite.

antagonists   Working at cross-purposes (e.g., the adductor and abductor muscles of the hip oppose each others' actions and are called antagonists).

antecedents   Events or contextual factors that precede or coincide with a behavior.

anterior   In front of or the front part of a structure.

anterior fontanelle   The membrane-covered area on the top of the head; *also called* the soft spot. It generally closes by 18 months of age.

anterior horn cells   Cells in the spinal column that transmit impulses from the pyramidal tract to the peripheral nervous system.

anthropometrics   Measurements of the body and its parts.

antibody   A protein formed in the bloodstream to fight infection.

anticipation   In genetics, process in which certain abnormalities (e.g., triplet repeat expansion) become more severe from one generation to the next.

antidepressants   Medications used to control major depression.

antihistamine   A drug that counteracts the effects of histamines, substances involved in allergic reactions.

antipsychotic medications   Medications used to treat psychosis, most commonly phenothiazines such as thioridazine (Mellaril).

anxiety disorders   Psychiatric disorders characterized by feelings of anxiety. These include panic attacks, separation anxiety, obsessive-compulsive disorder (OCD), and posttraumatic stress disorder (PTSD).

aorta   The major artery of the body. It originates in the left ventricle of the heart and carries oxygenated blood to the rest of the body.

Apgar scoring system   Scoring system developed by Virginia Apgar to assess neurological status in the newborn infant. Scores range from 0 to 10.

apical   At the tip of a structure.

apneic   Pertaining to an episodic arrest of breathing.

aqueous humor   The fluid in the eyeball that fills the space between the lens and the cornea.

architectonic dysplasias   Developmental malformations affecting the neuronal architecture of the brain.

ARND   Alcohol-related neurodevelopmental disorder *(see Chapter 7)*.

arthritis   An inflammatory disease of joints.

articular   Referring to the surface of a bone at a joint space.

articulation   1) The formulation of individual speech sounds; 2) the connection at a joint.

asphyxia   Interference with oxygenation of the blood that leads to loss of consciousness and possible brain damage.

aspiration   Inhalation of a foreign body, usually a food particle, into the lungs.

aspiration pneumonia   Inflammation of the lung(s) caused by inhaling a foreign body, such as food, into the lungs.

astigmatism   A condition of unequal curvature of the cornea that leads to blurred vision.

asymmetrical tonic neck reflex (ATNR)   A primitive reflex, *also called* fencer's response, found in infants; usually is no longer evident by 3 months of age. When the neck is turned in one direction, the arm shoots out on the same side and flexes on the opposite side; similar changes occur in the legs.

ataxia   An unbalanced gait caused by a disturbance of cerebellar control.

ataxic cerebral palsy   A form of cerebral palsy in which the prominent feature is ataxia.

athetoid cerebral palsy   A form of dyskinetic cerebral palsy associated with athetosis.

athetosis   Constant random, writhing involuntary movements of the limbs.

ATNR   *See* asymmetric tonic neck reflex.

atonic   Pertaining to the absence of normal muscle tone.

atresia   Congenital absence of a normal body opening; *adjective:* atretic.

atria   The upper chambers of the heart.

atrophy   A wasting away of a cell, tissue, or organ.

audiometry   A hearing test, using a device called an *audiometer,* that yields results in the form of a graph showing hearing levels in sound intensity at various wavelengths of sound presented through earphones.

auditory brainstem response (ABR)   A test of central nervous system (CNS) hearing pathways.

aura   A sensation, usually visual and/or olfactory, marking the onset of a seizure.

auricle   The outer ear.

autoimmune   Pertaining to a reaction in which one's immune system attacks other parts of the body.

automatic movement reactions   *See* postural reactions.

automatisms   Automatic fine motor movements (e.g., unbuttoning one's clothing) that are part of a seizure.

autonomic   Describing the part of the nervous system that regulates certain automatic functions of the body—for example, heart rate, sweating, and bowel movement.

autosomal dominant   Mendelian inheritance pattern in which a single copy of a gene leads to expression of the trait.

autosomal recessive   Mendelian inheritance pattern in which two carrier parents have a 25% chance of passing the trait to each child.

autosomes   The first 22 pairs of chromosomes. All chromosomes are autosomes except for the two sex chromosomes.

aversive   Pertaining to a stimulus, often unpleasant, which decreases the likelihood that a particular response will subsequently occur.

backward chaining   Method of teaching a task in which the instructor begins by teaching the last step in a sequence because this step is most likely to be associated with a potent positive reinforcer.

bacteremia   Spread of a bacterial organism throughout the bloodstream.

banding   In genetics, pertaining to a series of dark and light bars that appear on chromosomes after they are stained. Each chromosome has a distinct banding pattern.

barotrauma   Injury related to excess pressure, especially to the lungs or ears.

basal   1) Near the base; 2) relating to a standard or reference point (e.g., basal metabolic rate).

baseline   In behavior management, the frequency, duration, and intensity of a behavior prior to intervention.

beriberi   Disease caused by a deficiency of the vitamin B_1 (thiamin) and manifested as edema, heart problems, and peripheral neuropathy.

beta-adrenergic blockers   Medications, including propranolol (Inderal), that were initially used to control high blood pressure and have subsequently been found to be useful in treating aggressive behavior, tremor, and migraine headache.

binocular vision   The focusing of both eyes on an object to provide a stereoscopic image.

biotin   One of the B-complex vitamins needed to activate a number of important enzymatic reactions in the body.

bipolar disorder   A psychiatric disorder manifested by cycles of mania and depression; *previously called* manic depression.

blastocyst   The embryonic group of cells that exists at the time of implantation.

blood poisoning   *See* sepsis.

bolus   1) A small rounded mass of food made ready by tongue and jaw movement for swallowing; 2) a single dose of a large amount of medication given to rapidly attain a therapeutic drug level.

botulism   Poisoning by botulin toxin and manifested as muscle weakness or paralysis.

BPD   *See* bronchopulmonary dysplasia.

brachialis   A muscle in the upper arm.

brachycephaly   Tall head shape with flat back part of the skull.

bradycardia   Abnormal slowing of the heart rate, usually to fewer than 60 beats per minute.

brainstem   The primitive portion of the brain that lies between the cerebrum and the spinal cord.

branchial arches   A series of archlike thickenings of the body wall in the pharyngeal region of the embryo.

bronchopulmonary dysplasia (BPD)   A chronic lung disorder that occurs in a minority of premature infants who previously had respiratory distress syndrome. It is associated with "stiff" lungs that do not permit adequate exchange of oxygen and carbon dioxide and frequently leads to dependence on ventilator assistance for extended periods.

bronchospasm   Acute constriction of the bronchial tube, most commonly associated with asthma.

bruxism   Repetitive grinding of the teeth.

bulk   Foodstuffs that increase the quantity of intestinal contents and stimulate regular bowel movements. Fruits, vegetables, and other foods containing fiber provide bulk in the diet.

caffeine   A central nervous system (CNS) stimulant found in coffee, tea, and cola.

calcify   To become hardened through the laying down of calcium salts.

calculus   An abnormal collection of mineral salts on the tooth, predisposing it to decay; *also called* tartar.

callus   A disorganized network of bone tissue that forms around the edges of a fracture during the healing process.

camptodactyly   Deformity of fingers or toes in which they are permanently flexed.

cancellous   Referring to the lattice-like structure in long bones (e.g., the femur).

catalyze   To stimulate a chemical reaction via a compound that is not used up.

cataracts   Clouding of the lenses of the eyes.

catheterization   Use of a tube to infuse or remove fluids.

celiac disease   Congenital malabsorption syndrome that leads to failure to gain weight and passage of loose, foul-smelling stools. It is caused by intolerance of cereal products that contain gluten (e.g., wheat).

central nervous system (CNS)   The portion of the nervous system that consists of the brain and spinal cord. It is primarily involved in voluntary movement and thought processes.

central venous line   A catheter that is advanced through a peripheral vein to a position directly above the opening to the right atrium of the heart. It is used to infuse long-term medication and/or nutrition.

centrioles   Tiny organelles that migrate to the opposite poles of a cell during cell division and align the spindles.

centromere   The constricted area of the chromosome that usually marks the point of attachment of the sister chromatids to the spindle during cell division.

cephalocaudal   From head to tail; refers to neurological development that proceeds from the head downward.

cephalohematoma   A swelling of the head resulting from bleeding of scalp veins. Often found in newborn infants, it is usually not harmful.

cerebral hemisphere   Either of the two halves of brain substance.

cerebral palsy   A disorder of movement and posture due to a nonprogressive defect of the immature brain *(see Chapter 23)*.

cerumen   Ear wax.

cervical   Pertaining 1) to the cervix or 2) to the neck.

choanal atresia   Congenital closure of the nasal passage; part of the CHARGE association *(see Appendix B)*.

cholesteatoma   A complication of otitis media, in which skin cells from the ear canal migrate through the perforated eardrum into the middle ear, or mastoid region, forming a mass that must be removed surgically.

choreoathetosis   Movement disorder, characteristic of dyskinetic cerebral palsy, involving frequent involuntary spasms of the limbs.

chorioamnionitis   Infection of the amniotic sac, which surrounds and contains the fetus and amniotic fluid.

chorion   The outermost covering of the membrane surrounding the fetus.

chorionic villus sampling (CVS)   A prenatal diagnostic procedure done in the first trimester of pregnancy to obtain fetal cells for genetic analysis.

chorioretinitis   An inflammation of the retina and choroid that produces severe visual loss.

choroid   The middle layer of the eyeball between the sclera and the retina.

choroid plexus   Cells that line the walls of the ventricles of the brain and produce cerebrospinal fluid.

chromatids   Term given to chromosomes during cell division.

ciliary muscles   Small muscles that affect the shape of the lens of the eye, permitting accommodation.

CK   *See* creatine kinase.

clonus   Alternate muscle contraction and relaxation in rapid succession.

clubfoot   A congenital foot deformity; *also called* talipes equinovarus.

CMV   *See* cytomegalovirus.

CNS   *See* central nervous system.

coarctation   A congenital narrowing, such as of a blood vessel, most commonly of the aorta.

cochlea   The snail-shaped structure in the inner ear containing the organ of hearing.

codons   Triplets of nucleotides that form the DNA code for specific amino acids.

coloboma   Congenital cleft in the retina, iris, or other ocular structure.

compliance training   An important prerequisite to instructional training, the instructor orients the child to attend to the instructor and then issues a developmentally appropriate "do" request.

computed tomography (CT)   An imaging technique in which X-ray "slices" of a structure are viewed and synthesized by a computer, forming an image. It is most commonly used to visualize the brain. CT scans are less clear than magnetic resonance imaging (MRI) scans but are better at localizing certain tumors and areas of calcification.

concave   Having a curved, indented surface.

concussion   A clinical syndrome caused by a blow to the head, characterized by transient loss of consciousness.

cones   Photoreceptor cells of the eye associated with color vision.

congenital   Originating prior to birth.

congenital myopathies   A group of inherited muscle disorders often associated with mitochondrial dysfunction.

consanguinity   Relationship by blood.

consequences   Events or contextual factors that occur subsequent to a behavior and may or may not be causally related to it.

contiguous gene syndrome   A genetic syndrome resulting from defects in a number of adjacent genes.

contingent stimulation   Applying punishment following the occurrence of a misbehavior.

contingent withdrawal   The removal of access to positive reinforcement following a misbehavior.

contracture   A shortening of muscle fibers that causes decreased joint mobility and is almost always irreversible.

contusion (of brain)   Structural damage limited to the surface layer of the brain, caused by a blow to the head.

convex   Having a curved, elevated/protruding surface, such as a dome.

cordocentesis   *See* percutaneous umbilical blood sampling (PUBS).

cornea   The transparent, dome-like covering of the iris.

corpus callosotomy   Surgical procedure in which the corpus callosum is cut to prevent the generalized spread of seizures from one hemisphere to another.

corpus callosum   The bridge of white matter connecting the two cerebral hemispheres.

cortical   Pertaining to the cortex or gray matter of the brain.

corticospinal tract   *See* pyramidal tract.

craniofacial   Relating to the skull and bones of the face.

craniosynostosis   Premature closure of cranial bones.

creatine kinase (CK)   An enzyme released by damaged muscle cells. Its level is elevated in muscular dystrophy.

crib death   *See* sudden infant death syndrome (SIDS).

crossover   The exchange of genetic material between two closely aligned chromosomes during the first meiotic division.

cryotherapy   The use of freezing temperatures to destroy tissue. A cryotherapy probe has been used to treat retinoblastoma and retinopathy of prematurity.

cryptorchidism   Undescended testicles.

CT   *See* computed tomography.

CVS   *See* chorionic villus sampling.

cystic fibrosis   An autosomal recessively inherited disorder of the secretory glands leading to malabsorption and lung disease.

cytomegalovirus (CMV)   A virus that may be asymptomatic or cause symptoms in adults that may resemble mononucleosis. In the fetus, however, it can lead to severe malformations similar to congenital rubella.

cytoplasm   The contents of the cell outside the nucleus.

DAIs   *See* diffuse axonal injuries.

DDH   *See* developmental dislocation of the hip.

debridement   The removal of dead tissue (e.g., after a burn or infection).

deletion   Loss of genetic material from a chromosome.

delirium   An organically based psychosis characterized by impaired attention, disorganized thinking, altered and fluctuating levels of consciousness, and memory impairment. It may be caused by encephalitis, diabetes, or intoxication and is usually reversed by treating the underlying medical problem.

delusions   False beliefs, often quite bizarre, that are symptoms of psychosis or drug intoxication.

dementia   A progressive neurological disorder marked by loss of memory, decreased speech, impairment in abstract thinking and judgment, other disturbances of higher cortical function, and personality change. One example is Alzheimer's disease.

dental caries   Tooth decay.

dental lamina   A thickened band of tissue along the future dental arches in the human embryo.

dental organ   The embryonic tissue that is the precursor of the tooth; *also called* tooth bud.

dental plaque   Patches of bacteria, bacterial by-products, and food particles on teeth that predispose them to decay.

dental sealant   Plastic substance administered to teeth, most commonly the molars, to increase their resistance to decay.

dentin   The principal substance of the tooth surrounding the tooth pulp and covered by the enamel.

deoxyribonucleic acid (DNA)   The fundamental component of living tissue. It contains an organism's genetic code.

depolarization   The eliminating of the electrical charge of a cell.

depressed fracture   Fracture of bone, usually the skull, that results in inward displacement of the bone at the point of impact. It requires surgical intervention to prevent damage to underlying tissue.

deprivation   In behavior management, denial of access to a reinforcing item or event.

descriptive and functional analysis   Observation period in behavior management that precedes treatment.

detoxification   The conversion of a toxic compound to a nontoxic product.

developmental dislocation of the hip (DDH)   A congenital hip dislocation, usually evident at birth, occurring more commonly in girls.

dialysis A detoxification procedure of the blood (hemodialysis) or across the peritoneum (peritoneal dialysis), used to treat kidney failure.

diaphysis The shaft of a long bone lying under the epiphysis.

differential reinforcement A behavior management technique in which a preferred alternate behavior is positively reinforced while a less preferred behavior is ignored.

diffuse axonal injuries (DAIs) Diffuse injuries to nerve cell components, usually resulting from shearing forces. This type of traumatic brain injury is commonly associated with motor vehicle accidents.

diopters Units of refractive power of a lens.

diploid Having paired chromosomes in nondividing cells (i.e., 46 chromosomes in 23 pairs).

dislocation The displacement of a bone out of a joint space.

distal Pertaining to the part farthest from the midline or trunk.

diuretics Medications used to reduce intercellular fluid buildup in the body (edema), especially in the lungs.

DMD Duchenne muscular dystrophy; *see Chapter 14 and Appendix B.*

DNA *See* deoxyribonucleic acid.

dominant In genetics, referring to a trait that only requires one copy of a gene to be expressed phenotypically. For example, brown eyes is a dominant trait, so a child receiving a gene for brown eyes from his or her mother or father (or from both parents) will have brown eyes.

double helix The coiled structure of DNA.

dual diagnosis Mental retardation and psychiatric disorder.

Duchenne muscular dystrophy (DMD) *See Chapter 14 and Appendix B.*

ductus arteriosus An arterial connection, open during fetal life, that diverts the blood flow from the pulmonary artery into the aorta, thereby bypassing the not yet functional lungs.

duodenal atresia Congenital absence of a portion of the first section of the small intestine; often seen in individuals with Down syndrome.

duodenum First part of the small intestine.

dynamic In the context of orthotics, capable of active movement.

dysarthria Difficulty with speech due to impairment of oral motor structures or musculature.

dyscalculia Learning disability affecting skills in mathematics.

dysgraphia Learning disability in areas of processing and reporting information in written form.

dyskinetic cerebral palsy Type of "extrapyramidal" cerebral palsy often involving abnormalities of the basal ganglia and manifesting as rigidity, dystonia, or choreoathetosis.

dyslexia Learning disability affecting reading skills.

dysostosis An abnormal bony formation.

dysphagia Difficulty in swallowing function.

dysphasia Impairment of speech consisting of a lack of coordination and failure to arrange words in proper order; due to a central brain lesion.

dysplasia Abnormal tissue development.

dyspraxia Inability to perform coordinated movements despite normal function of the central and peripheral nervous systems and muscles.

dysthymia A mild form of depression characterized by a mood disturbance that is present most of the time and is associated with feelings of low self-esteem, hopelessness, poor concentration, low energy, and changes in sleep and appetite. Often seen in depressed adolescents.

dystocia Structural abnormalities of the uterus that cause a difficult labor or childbirth.

dystonia A disorder of the basal ganglia associated with altered muscle tone, leading to contorted body positioning.

dystonic cerebral palsy A form of dyskinetic cerebral palsy whose prominent feature is dystonia.

E. coli *See* Escherichia coli.

ECG *See* electrocardiogram.

echocardiography An ultrasonic method of imaging the heart. It can be used to detect congenital heart defects.

echolalic Pertaining to immediate or delayed repetition of a word or phrase said by others; often evident in children with certain pervasive developmental disorders (PDDs).

ectodermal dysplasia Abnormal skin development.

ectopias Congenital displacement of a body organ or tissue.

ectrodactyly   Congenital absence of all or parts of digits.

EDC   *See* estimated date of confinement.

EDD   Estimated due date; *See* estimated date of confinement.

edema   An abnormal accumulation of fluid in the tissues of the body.

EEG   *See* electroencephalogram.

efferent   Pertaining to the impulses that go to a nerve or muscle from the central nervous system (CNS).

effusion   Fluid escaping from blood vessels or lymphatics that collects in body cavities (e.g., a pleural, or lung, effusion).

ELBW   *See* extremely low birth weight.

electrocardiogram (EKG, ECG)   The graphic record of an electronic recording of heart rate and rhythm.

electroencephalogram (EEG)   A recording of the electrical activity in the brain that is often used in the evaluation of seizures.

electrolytes   Minerals contained in solution (e.g., in the blood).

enamel   The calcified outer layer of the tooth.

encephalitis   Inflammation of the brain, generally from a viral infection.

encephalocele   Congenital cystic malformation of the brain associated with severe disabilities.

encephalopathy   Disorder or disease of the brain.

endocarditis   Inflammation of the inner lining of the heart.

endochondral ossification   Formation of bone from cartilage.

epicanthal folds   Crescent-shaped fold of skin on either side of the nose, commonly associated with Down syndrome.

epidemiology   The study of factors determining the frequency and distribution of diseases (e.g., an outbreak of food poisoning).

epidural anesthesia   Pain relief by infusing an anesthetic agent into the epidural space of the spine.

epidural hematoma   Localized collection of clotted blood lying between the skull and the outer (dural) membrane of the brain, resulting from the hemorrhage of a blood vessel resting in the dura. This most commonly results from traumatic head injury.

epiglottis   A lid-like structure that hangs over the entrance to the windpipe and prevents aspiration of food or liquid into the lungs during swallowing.

epiphyses   The end plates of long bones; linear growth occurs here.

epithelial   Pertaining to cells that are found on exposed surfaces of the body, (e.g., skin, mucous membranes, intestinal walls).

equinus   Involuntary extension (plantarflexion) of the foot (like a horse). This position is often found in spastic cerebral palsy.

Escherichia coli (E. coli)   Bacteria that can cause infections ranging from diarrhea, to urinary tract infection, to sepsis.

esophageal transport phase   Phase of swallowing in which the rhythmic contraction of esophageal muscles to transport food from pharynx to stomach.

esophagus   Tube through which food passes from the pharynx to the stomach.

esotropia   A form of strabismus in which one or both turn in; "cross eyed."

estimated date of confinement (EDC)   Expected date of delivery; *also called* estimated due date (EDD).

estrogen   Female sex hormone.

eustachian tube   Connection between oral cavity and middle ear, allowing equilibration of pressure and drainage of fluid.

everted   Turned outward.

excitotoxic   Pertaining to excitotoxins, chemicals that can cause neuronal cell death and have been implicated in hypoxic brain damage and acquired immunodeficiency syndrome (AIDS) encephalopathy.

executive function   Brain processing involved in planning; it is thought to be deficient in individuals with learning disabilities.

exotropia   A form of strabismus in which one or both eyes turn out; "wall-eyed."

expressive language   Communication by spoken language, gesture, signing, or body language.

extension   Movement of a limb at a joint to bring the joint into a more straightened position.

extinction   *See* planned ignoring.

extinction burst   A transient increase in the frequency and intensity of a challenging behavior before a subsequent reduction occurs.

extract   In the context of medication, a concentrated preparation.

extremely low birth weight (ELBW)   Term often used to describe an infant with a birth weight less than 1,000 grams (2 ¼ pounds).

fading   Behavioral instruction process by which prompts are withdrawn gradually.

failure to thrive (FTT)   Inadequate growth of both weight and height in infancy or early childhood caused by malnutrition, chronic disease, or a congenital anomaly.

FAS   Fetal alcohol syndrome; *see Chapter 8.*

febrile   Having an elevated body temperature. A child is considered febrile when the fever is above 100.4 degrees Fahrenheit (38 degrees Celsius).

femur   Long bone in the thigh connecting the hip to the knee.

fencer's response   *See* asymmetrical tonic neck reflex (ATNR).

fetal alcohol effects (FAE)   *Former term for* alcohol-related neurodevelopmental disorder (ARND; *see Chapter* 7).

fetal alcohol syndrome (FAS)   *See Chapter* 7.

flexion   Movement of a limb to bend at a joint.

flexor   A muscle with the primary function of flexion or bending at a joint.

flora   In medicine, bacteria normally residing within a body organ and not causing disease, such as *E. coli* in the intestine.

fluency   Aspect of speech production; producing speech in a fluid manner.

focal   Localized.

focal neurological changes   Findings on neurological exams that are abnormal and indicative of a lesion in a particular part of the brain; *also called* focal neurological impairments.

forebrain   The front portion of the brain during fetal development; *also called* the prosencephalon.

forward chaining   A behavior management technique in which the first skill in a sequence is taught first and the last skill is taught last.

fovea centralis   The small pit in the center of the macula; the area of clearest vision, containing only cones.

frame shift   A type of gene mutation in which the insertion or deletion of a single nucleotide leads to the misreading of all subsequent codons.

free level   In pharmacotherapy, the amount of active drug that is able to produce an effect on the body.

free radicals   Chemical compounds, the abnormal accumulation of which has been linked to cancer and neurotoxicity.

frequency   Cycles per second, or hertz (Hz), a measure of sound.

FTT   *See* failure to thrive.

full graduated guidance   Behavior management technique in which the instructor keeps his or her hands in contact with child's hands while teaching a task.

fundoplication   An operation in which the top of the stomach is wrapped around the opening of the esophagus to prevent gastroesophageal reflux (GER).

gastroenteritis   An acute illness marked by vomiting and diarrhea usually associated with a viral infection (e.g., rotavirus in infants) that generally lasts a few days; *also called* stomach flu.

gastroesophageal reflux (GER)   The backward flow of food into the esophagus after it has entered the stomach.

gastroschisis   Congenital malformation of the abdominal wall resulting in the protrusion of abdominal contents.

gastrostomy   An operation in which an artificial opening is made into the stomach through the wall of the abdomen. This is usually done in order to place a feeding tube into the stomach.

gene   A unit of genetic material (DNA) that encodes a single protein.

genome   The complete set of hereditary factors (genes) in an organism.

genomic imprinting   A condition manifested differently depending on whether the trait is inherited from the mother or father; *also called* uniparental disomy. An example is a deletion in chromosome

15q11–q13, which when inherited from the mother results in Angelman syndrome and when inherited from the father results in Prader-Willi syndrome *(see Appendix B)*.

genotype   The genetic composition of an individual.

GER   *See* gastroesophageal reflux.

germ cells   The cells involved in reproduction (i.e., sperm, eggs).

German measles   *See* rubella.

glaucoma   Increased pressure within the anterior chamber of the eye, which can cause blindness.

glial cells   Cells that compose the white matter and provide a support function for neurons.

glossoptosis   Protruding tongue.

glucose   A sugar, *also called* sucrose, contained in fruits and other carbohydrates.

glycogen   The chief carbohydrate stored in the body, primarily in the liver and muscles.

goiter   Enlargement of the thyroid gland.

graduated guidance   A behavior management technique in which only the level of assistance (guidance) necessary for the child to complete the task is provided.

graft versus host disease   A mechanism of the body's immune system that destroys foreign proteins. When it occurs in an immunosuppressed child who has received a bone marrow or organ transplant, it can be life threatening. Symptoms include diarrhea, skin breakdown, and shock.

grammar   The system of and rules for using units of meaning (morphemes) and syntax in language.

grapheme   A unit, such as a letter, of a writing system.

guided compliance   A behavior management technique involving the use of graduated guidance to teach functional tasks.

Guillain-Barré syndrome   An acute neuropathy *(see Chapter 14)*.

gynecomastia   Excessive breast growth in males.

gyri   Convolutions of the surface of the brain; singular: gyrus.

habilitation   The teaching of new skills to children with developmental disabilities. It is called *habilitation* rather than *rehabilitation* because these children did not possess these skills previously.

hallucinations   Sensory perceptions without a source in the external world. These most commonly occur as symptoms of psychosis, drug intoxication, or seizure.

haploid   Having a single set of human chromosomes, 23, as in the sperm or egg.

hCG   *See* human chorionic gonadotropin.

hemangiomas   Congenital masses of blood vessels.

hematocrit   Percentage of red blood cells in whole blood, normally about 35%–40%.

hematopoietic   Relating to the formation of red blood cells.

hemihypertrophy   Asymmetric hypertrophy of face or limbs.

hemiplegia   Paralysis of one side of the body.

hemodialysis   A detoxification procedure in which an individual's blood is gradually removed through an artery, passed through an artificial kidney machine, and then returned cleansed. It is used most commonly to treat chronic renal (kidney) failure.

hemoglobin   Blood protein capable of carrying oxygen to body tissues.

hemostat   A small surgical clamp used to constrict a tube or blood vessel.

herpes simplex virus (HSV)   A virus leading to symptoms that range from cold sores, to genital lesions, to encephalitis; also a cause of fetal malformations and sepsis in early infancy.

heterotopia   Migration and development of normal neural tissue in an abnormal location in the brain.

heterozygous   Carrying genes dissimilar for one trait.

HIV   Human immunodeficiency virus; *see Chapter 8*.

homeostasis   Equilibrium of fluid, chemical, and temperature regulation in the body.

homozygous   Carrying identical genes for any given trait.

human chorionic gonadotropin (hCG)   The hormone secreted by the embryo that prevents its expulsion from the uterus. A pregnancy test measures the presence of this hormone in the blood or urine.

human immunodeficiency virus (HIV)   *See Chapter 8*.

hybrid   Offspring of parents of dissimilar species.

hydrocephalus   A condition characterized by the abnormal accumulation of cerebrospinal fluid within the ventricles of the brain. In infants, this leads to enlargement of the head.

hyperalimentation   *See* parenteral nutrition.

hyperbilirubinemia   Excess accumulation of bilirubin in the blood, which can result in jaundice, a yellowing of the complexion and the whites of the eyes, or kernicterus, the yellow staining of certain central parts of the brain.

hyperglycemia   High blood sugar level, as seen in diabetes.

hyperimmune globulin   Blood that is especially rich in antibodies against a virus.

hyperopia   Farsightedness.

hyperparathyroidism   High level of blood parathyroid hormone, which causes abnormalities in calcium and phosphorous metabolism.

hypersynchronous   In the context of the central nervous system (CNS), pertaining to the discharge of many neurons at the same time that leads to a seizure.

hypertelorism   Widely spaced eyes.

hypertension   High blood pressure.

hyperthyroidism   Condition resulting from excessive production of thyroid hormone.

hypertrichosis   Excessive hair growth.

hypertrophy   Overgrowth of a body part or organ.

hypocalcemia   Low blood calcium level.

hypogenitalism   Having small genitalia.

hypoglycemia   Low blood sugar level.

hypogonadism   Decreased function of sex glands with resultant retarded growth and sexual development.

hypoplasia   Defective formation of a tissue or body organ.

hypospadias   Abnormal urethral opening in penis.

hypothermia   Excessively low body temperature.

hypothyroidism   Condition resulting from deficient production of thyroid hormone.

hypotonia   Decreased muscle tone.

hypoxic   Having reduced oxygen content in body tissues.

hypsarrhythmia   Electroencephalographic (EEG) abnormality seen in infants with infantile spasms. It is marked by chaotic spike–wave activity.

ictal   Pertaining to a seizure event.

IEP   *See* individualized education program.

IFSP   *See* individualized family service plan.

ileostomy   A surgically placed opening from the small intestine through the abdominal wall to divert bowel or bladder contents after an operation.

ileum   Lower portion of the small intestine.

immunoglobulin   An antibody produced by the body after exposure to a foreign agent, such as a virus.

impact   In reference to traumatic head injury, the forcible striking of the head against an object.

imperforate   Lacking a normal opening in a body organ. The most common example in childhood is an absent or closed anus.

imitation training   A behavior management technique in which the teacher demonstrates the desired behavior, asks the child to complete the action, and provides positive reinforcement when the task is completed.

implantation   The attachment and imbedding of the fertilized egg into the mucous lining of the uterus.

in utero   Occurring during fetal development.

inborn error of metabolism   An inherited enzyme deficiency leading to the disruption of normal bodily metabolism, an example being phenylketonuria (PKU).

incidence   The rate of occurrence of new cases of a disorder in a population.

individualized education program (IEP)   A written plan, mandated by federal law, that maps out the objectives and goals that a child receiving special education services is expected to achieve over the course of the school year.

individualized family service plan (IFSP)   A written plan detailing early intervention and related services to be provided to an infant or toddler with disabilities in accordance with federal law.

individualized transition plan (ITP)   A written plan for an adolescent receiving special education services that maps out his or her postschool education, services, and employment and adult living goals; required by federal law to be part of the student's individualized education program (IEP) starting at age 14.

inertial   Pertaining to inertia, which is the tendency to keep moving in the same direction as the force that produced a movement.

inferior   In anatomy, below.

influenza   An acute illness caused by a virus; attacks respiratory and gastrointestinal tracts.

informed consent   The written consent of a child or guardian to undergo a procedure or treatment after its risks and benefits have been explained in easily understood language.

instructional training   A behavior management technique in which the teacher describes the desired behavior, asks the child to perform it, and provides positive reinforcement upon completion of the task.

insult   An attack on a body organ that causes damage to it. This may be physical, metabolic, immunological, or infectious.

intensity   Strength.

interictal   In an individual with a seizure disorder, pertaining to the periods when seizures are not occurring.

interphase   The period in the cell life cycle when the cell is not dividing.

interval schedules   Provision of reinforcement based on the passage of a certain amount of time relative to the child's performance of a behavior or task.

intubation   Insertion of a tube through the nose or mouth into the trachea to permit mechanical ventilation.

inversion   The result of two breaks on a chromosome followed by the reinsertion of the missing fragment at its original site but in the inverted order.

inverted   1) Reversed; 2) in anatomy, turned inward.

ionic   Pertaining to mineral ions, a group of atoms carrying a charge of electricity.

iris   The circular, colored membrane behind the cornea, surrounding the pupil.

ischemia   Having decreased blood flow to an area of the body; leads to tissue death.

isochromosome   A chromosome with two copies of one arm and no copy of the other.

ITP   *See* individualized transition plan.

jaundice   A yellowing of the complexion and the whites of the eyes resulting from hyperbilirubinemia.

jejunum   Second portion of the small intestine.

karyotyping   Photographing the chromosomal makeup of a cell. In a human, there are 23 pairs of chromosomes in a normal karyotype.

ketosis   The buildup of acid in the body, most often associated with starvation, inborn errors of metabolism, or diabetes.

kyphoscoliosis   A combination of humping and curvature of the spine.

kyphosis   Humping deformity of the spine; "hunchback."

lactase   Enzyme necessary to digest the milk sugar lactose.

lactose   Milk sugar composed of glucose and galactose.

lag of mineralization of bone   *See* spondyloepiphyseal dysplasia.

lanugo   Fine body hair.

lateral   To the side; away from the midline.

lateral ventricles   Cavities in the interior of the cerebral hemisphere containing cerebrospinal fluid. They are enlarged with hydrocephalus or with brain atrophy.

LBW   *See* low birth weight.

lens   The biconvex, translucent body that rests in front of the vitreous humor of the eye and refracts light.

lesions   Injuries or loss of function.

ligaments   Fibrous tissue connecting bones.

linear fracture   Break of a bone in a straight line; refers to a type of skull fracture or fracture of a long bone (arm or leg).

lipoma   A benign, fatty tissue tumor.

low birth weight (LBW)   Term often used to describe an infant with a birth weight less than 2,500 grams (5½ pounds).

lumbar   Pertaining to the lower back.

lumbar puncture   The tapping of the subarachnoid space to obtain cerebrospinal fluid from the lower back region. This procedure is used to diagnose meningitis and to measure chemicals in the spinal fluid; *also called* a spinal tap.

lymphocyte   A type of white blood cell.

lymphoma   A cancerous growth of lymphoid tissue.

lyonization   The genetic principle discovered by Mary Lyon that there is X-chromosome inactivation in females.

lysosomes   Minute organelles in a cell that contain enzymes used to digest potentially toxic material.

macrocephaly   Large head size.

macroorchidism   Having abnormally large testicles; found in fragile X syndrome.

macrosomia   Large body size.

macrostomia   Large mouth.

macula   The area of the retina that contains the greatest concentration of cones and the fovea centralis.

magnetic resonance imaging (MRI)   Imaging procedure that uses the magnetic resonance of atoms to provide clear images of interior parts of the body. It is particularly useful in diagnosing structural abnormalities of the brain.

magnetic resonance spectroscopy (MRS)   A study that can be done as part of a regular MRI scan. Instead of giving a picture of the brain, it analyzes the presence and amount of certain metabolic components in various brain regions. It has been particularly helpful in diagnosing certain inborn errors of metabolism, such as mitochondrial disorders *(see Appendix B)*.

major depression   A prolonged period of depressed mood.

malnutrition   Inadequate nutrition for normal growth and development to occur.

malocclusion   The improper fitting together of the upper and lower teeth.

mandible   Lower jaw bone.

mania   A distinct period of abnormally and persistently elevated, expansive, or irritable mood. The mood disturbance is sufficiently severe to cause impairment in function.

manic depression   *See* bipolar disorder.

mastoiditis   Infection of the mastoid air cells that rest in the temporal bone behind the ear. This is an infrequent complication of chronic middle-ear infection.

maxilla   The bony region of the upper jaw.

maxillary hypoplasia   Incomplete development of the upper jaw.

medial   Toward the center or midline.

median plane   The midline plane of the body; it runs vertically and separates the left and right halves of the body.

medium chain fatty acids   Fatty acids that can bypass normal uptake process and go directly to the liver.

megavitamin therapy   The use of at least 10 times the required amount of vitamins; *also called* orthomolecular therapy.

meiosis   Reductive cell division occurring only in eggs and sperm in which the daughter cells receive half (23) the number of chromosomes of the parent cells (46).

Mendelian traits   Dominant and recessive traits inherited according to the genetic principles put forward by Gregor Mendel.

meningeal   Related to the meninges, the three membranes enveloping the brain and spinal cord.

meningitis   Infection of the meninges.

meningocele   Protrusion of the meninges through a defect in the skull or vertebral column.

meningomyelocele   Protrusion of meninges and malformed spinal cord through a defect in the vertebral column; *also called* myelomeningocele.

menses   Menstrual flow.

messenger ribonucleic acid (mRNA)   RNA involved in the translation of genetic information.

metaphase   The stage in cell division in which each chromosome doubles.

metaphyses   The ends of the shaft of long bones; connected to the epiphyses.

microcephaly   Small head size.

microdeletion   A microscopic deletion in a chromosome associated with a contiguous gene syndrome.

micrognathia   Receding chin.

microphthalmia   Small eye.

micropreemie   Term often used to describe an infant weighing less than 800 grams (1 ¼ pounds).

microswitches   Switches, usually used to control computers, environmental control systems, or power wheelchairs, that have been adapted so that less pressure than normal is required for activation.

microtia   Small ear.

milligram   One thousandth of a gram.

milliliter   One thousandth of a liter; equal to about 15 drops.

missense mutation   Gene error resulting from the replacement of a single nucleic acid for another, resulting in a misreading of the DNA code.

mitochondrial myopathies   Congenital muscle disorders caused by a mutation in the mitochondrial DNA.

mitosis   Cell division in which two daughter cells of identical chromosomal composition to the parent cell are formed; each contains 46 chromosomes.

mixed cerebral palsy   A form of cerebral palsy with spastic and dyskinetic components.

modification   In special education, a substantial change in the method or scoring scale used to assess a student's academic performance or knowledge (e.g., using a portfolio of work to demonstrate a student's learning).

monosomy   Chromosome disorder in which one chromosome is absent; the most common example is Turner syndrome, XO *(see Appendix B)*.

monosomy X   Turner syndrome *(see Appendix B)*.

morbidity   Medical complication of an illness, procedure, or operation.

Moro reflex   Primitive reflex present in the newborn in which the infant throws the arms out as if to give an embrace.

morphemes   The smallest linguistic units of meaning.

morula   The group of cells formed by the first divisions of a fertilized egg.

mosaicism   The presence of two genetically distinct types of cells in one individual (e.g., in a child with Down syndrome who has some cells containing 46 chromosomes and some cells containing 47 chromosomes).

motor point block   The injection of a denaturing agent into the nerve supply of a spastic muscle.

MRI   *See* magnetic resonance imaging.

mRNA   *See* messenger ribonucleic acid.

MRS   *See* magnetic resonance spectroscopy.

mucopolysaccharides   Product of metabolism that may accumulate in cells and cause a progressive neurological disorder (e.g., Hurler disease, *see Appendix B*).

multifactorial   Describing an inheritance pattern in which environment and heredity interact.

muscle spindles   Muscle fibers that are part of the reflex arc that controls muscle contraction.

muscular dystrophy   *See Chapter 14 and Appendix B.*

mutation   A change in a gene that occurs by chance.

myasthenia gravis   *See Chapter 14.*

myelination   The production of a coating called *myelin* around an axon. This quickens neurotransmission.

myelomeningocele   *See* meningomyelocele.

myoclonus   Irregular, involuntary contraction of a muscle.

myopia   Nearsightedness.

myosin   Protein necessary for muscle contraction.

myotonia   Abnormal rigidity of muscles when voluntary movement is attempted.

myringotomy   The surgical incision of the eardrum. It is usually accompanied by the placement of pressure-equalization tubes to drain fluid from the middle ear.

nasal cannulae   Plastic prongs placed in the nostrils to deliver oxygen.

nasal pillows   A prop attached to an oxygen line to permit the flow of oxygen directly into the nose.

nasogastric (NG) tube   A plastic feeding tube placed in the nose and extended into the stomach.

nasopharynx   Posterior portion of the oral cavity above the palate.

NDT   *See* neurodevelopmental therapy.

necrosis   Death of tissue.

necrotizing enterocolitis (NEC) Severe inflammation of the small intestine and colon, more common among premature infants.

negative reinforcement Behavioral phenomenon in which an individual's behavior permits an unpleasant event to be avoided or escaped, with a resultant increase in this behavior in the future.

nerve blocks Direct injection of denaturing agents into motor nerves.

neural fold During embryonic life, the fold created when the neural plate expands and rises; later it becomes the spinal column.

neural network A network involving many brain regions working in concert to store and use information obtained from the environment.

neural plate During embryonic life, the elongated, shoe-shaped body that forms from part of the ectoderm; it is a precursor to the spinal column.

neural tube The precursor of the spinal column.

neural tube defects (NTDs) *See Chapter 24.*

neurodevelopmental therapy (NDT) Therapy that includes an understanding and utilization of normal developmental stages in working with children; commonly used theory underlying physical and occupational therapy.

neuroleptic malignant syndrome A rare toxic reaction to a phenothiazine medication (e.g., thioridazine [Mellaril]) in which there is a potentially life-threatening high fever.

neurotoxin A chemical compound that can damage neurons.

neurotransmitter A chemical released at the synapse that permits transmission of an impulse from one nerve to another.

neutropenia Low white blood cell count.

NG tube *See* nasogastric tube.

nondisjunction Failure of a pair of chromosomes to separate during mitosis or meiosis, resulting in an unequal number of chromosomes in the daughter cells.

nonsense mutation Gene defect in which a single base pair substitution results in the premature termination of a message and the resultant production of an incomplete and inactive protein.

NTDs Neural tube defects; *see Chapter 24.*

nucleotide bases The four nucleic acids that form DNA and RNA—adenine, guanine, cytosine, and thymine—and a fifth, uracil, which is found in RNA.

nystagmus Involuntary rapid movements of the eyes.

obsessive-compulsive disorder (OCD) A psychiatric disorder in which recurrent and persistent thoughts and ideas that cannot be suppressed (obsessions) are associated with repetitive behaviors (compulsions), such as excessive handwashing.

ocular Pertaining to the eye.

oligohydramnios The presence of too little amniotic fluid. It may result in fetal deformities, including clubfoot and atretic lungs.

omphalocele Congenital herniation of abdominal organs through the navel.

operant control Control established and maintained by operant contingencies (i.e., the relationships in effect between the behavior and its consequences).

ophthalmologist Physician specializing in treatment of diseases of the eye.

opiate antagonists A category of medications that block endorphin receptors of the brain. These drugs, such as naltrexone (REVIA), have been used to treat self-injurious behavior.

opisthotonos Positioning of the body in which the back is arched, while head and feet touch the bed.

ophthalmoscope An instrument containing a mirror and a series of magnifying lenses used to examine the interior of the eye.

optokinetic Pertaining to movement of the eyes.

oral preparatory phase The step preceding swallowing in which food is formed into a bolus in the mouth.

oral transport phase The transport of a bolus of food to the back of the mouth so that it can then be swallowed.

organ of Corti A series of hair cells in the cochlea that form the beginning of the auditory nerve.

organic acidemias Inborn errors of organic acid metabolism (e.g., methylmalonic aciduria; *see Appendix B*).

orthomolecular therapy   *See* megavitamin therapy.

orthopedic   Relating to bones or joints.

orthoses   Orthopedic devices, most commonly splints or braces, used to support, align, or correct deformities or to improve the function of limbs; *also called* orthotics.

orthotist   Professional trained in the fitting and construction of splints, braces, and artificial limbs.

ossicles   The three small bones in the middle ear: the stapes, incus, and malleus.

osteoarthritis   Degenerative joint disease.

osteoblasts   Cells that produce bony tissue.

osteoclast   Cell that absorbs and removes bone.

osteoid   The substrate of bone.

osteopenia   The loss of bony tissue.

osteopetrosis   A genetic disorder marked by deficient osteoclastic activity. A buildup of bone encroaches on the eye, brain, and other body organs, leading to early death. Treatment with bone marrow transplantation has been successful in some cases.

ostomy   An artificial opening in the abdominal region, for example, for discharge of stool or urine.

otoacoustic emissions   Low-intensity sound energy emitted by the cochlea subsequent to sound stimulation as measured by a microphone coupled to the external ear canal.

oxidative phosphorylation   A chemical reaction occurring in the mitochondrion resulting in energy production.

oxygenation   The provision of sufficient oxygen for bodily needs.

pachygyria   Abnormal convolutions on the surface of brain.

palatal   Relating to the palate, the back portion of the roof of the mouth.

panic disorder   A psychiatric disorder in which the patient has episodes of sudden and irrational fears associated with hyperventilation and palpitations.

parenteral nutrition   Intravenous provision of high-quality nutrition (i.e., carbohydrates, protein, fat), used in children with malabsorption, malnutrition, and short bowel syndrome; *also called* hyperalimentation.

Parkinson's disease   A progressive neurological disease usually occurring in older people; associated with tremor, slowed movements, and muscular rigidity.

parvovirus   A group of extremely small DNA viruses. Intrauterine infection with one type of parvovirus increases the risk of miscarriage but has not been shown to result in fetal malformations.

partial graduated guidance   Instructor uses minimal physical contact but much praise in helping the child learn a desired task.

patent ductus arteriosus (PDA)   The persistence of a fetal passage permitting blood to bypass the lungs.

patterning   Controversial therapy program that involves repetition of movements in order to facilitate developmental progress.

PDA   *See* patent ductus arteriosus.

PDDs   Pervasive developmental disorders; *see Chapter 20.*

penetrance   The percentage of people with a particular genetic mutation who express symptoms of the disorder. A disorder shows reduced penetrance when some people with the genetic defect are completely without symptoms.

percutaneous umbilical blood sampling (PUBS)   A prenatal diagnostic procedure for obtaining fetal blood for genetic testing; *also called* cordocentesis.

percutaneously   Through the skin.

perfusion   The passage of blood through the arteries to an organ or tissue.

periodontal disease   Disease of the gums and bony structures that surround the teeth.

periosteum   Fibrous tissue covering and protecting all bones.

peripheral nervous system   The parts of the nervous system other than the brain and spinal cord.

peripheral venous lines   Catheters that are placed in a superficial vein of the arm or leg to provide medication.

peritoneal   Referring to the membrane surrounding the abdominal organs. In kidney failure, dialysis can be performed by perforating the peritoneum and "washing out" the abdominal cavity.

periventricular leukomalacia (PVL)   Injury to part of the brain near the ventricles; caused by lack of oxygen; occurs principally in premature infants.

peroxisome   A cellular organelle involved in processing fatty acids.

pervasive developmental disorders (PDDs)   *See Chapter 20.*

pes cavus   High-arched foot.

PET   *See* positron emission tomography.

phalanges   Bones of the fingers and toes.

pharyngeal   Pertaining to the pharynx.

pharyngeal transfer phase   The transfer of a food bolus from the mouth to the pharynx on its way to being swallowed.

pharynx   The back of the throat.

phenothiazines   Drugs that affect neurochemicals in the brain and are used to control behavior.

phenotype   The physical appearance of a genetic trait.

phenylketonuria (PKU)   *See Chapter 18.*

philtrum   Groove between nose and mouth.

phobias   Irrational fears.

phocomelia   Congenitally foreshortened limbs.

phoneme   The smallest unit of sound in speech.

phonetic   Pertaining to the sounding out of words.

phonology   The set of sounds in a language and the rules for using them.

photoreceptors   Receptors for light stimuli; the rods and cones in the retina.

physes   Growth plates of a developing long bone.

pica   The hunger for or ingestion of nonfood items.

pitch   The frequency of sounds, measured in cycles per second, or hertz (Hz). Low-pitched sounds have a frequency less than 500 Hz and a bass quality. High-pitched sounds have a frequency greater than 2,000 Hz and a tenor quality.

PKU   Phenylketonuria; *see Chapter 18 and Appendix B.*

placenta   The organ of nutritional exchange between the mother and the embryo. It has both maternal and embryonic portions and is disc shaped and about 7 inches in diameter. The umbilical cord attaches in the center of the placenta. *Also called* the afterbirth; *adjective:* placental.

placenta previa   Condition in which the placenta is implanted in the lower segment of the uterus, extending over the cervical opening. This often leads to bleeding during labor.

placental abruption   *See* abruptio placenta.

planned ignoring   A behavior management technique based on withholding positive reinforcement following an occurrence of a nondangerous, nondestructive challenging behavior; *also called* extinction.

plasma   The noncellular content of blood; *also called* serum.

plasmapheresis   The removal of blood followed by filtering the plasma and reinfusing the blood products. This procedure is done to remove toxins and antibodies as in Guillain-Barré syndrome.

plasticity   The ability of an organ or part of an organ to take over the function of another damaged organ.

***Pneumocystis carinii* pneumonia**   Lung infection often seen in immunocompromised individuals, such as those with acquired immunodeficiency syndrome (AIDS).

polar bodies   The nonviable eggs formed during meiosis.

polio   Viral infection of the spinal cord causing an asymmetrical ascending paralysis, now prevented by vaccination.

polydactyly   Extra fingers or toes.

polyhydramnios   The presence of excessive amniotic fluid; often associated with certain fetal anomalies such as esophageal atresia.

polysomnogram   Procedure performed during sleep that involves monitoring electroencephalogram (EEG), electrocardiogram (EKG), and respiratory efforts. It is used to investigate individuals with sleep disorders, including sleep apnea.

positive practices   Behavior management techniques requiring the child to demonstrate repeatedly a relevant prosocial alternative to a challenging behavior.

positive reinforcement   A method of increasing desired behaviors by rewarding them.

positive reinforcers   Any tangible (e.g., food, toy) or action (e.g., hug) that is reinforcing to an individual and will lead to a subsequent increase in the behavior that preceded it.

positive support reflex (PSR)   Primitive reflex present in an infant, in which the child reflexively accepts weight on the feet when bounced, appearing to stand briefly.

positron emission tomography (PET)   Imaging study utilizing radioactive labeled chemical compounds to study the metabolism of an organ, most commonly the brain.

posterior   In back of or the back part of a structure.

postictal   Immediately following a seizure episode.

postterm birth   Birth after the 42nd week of gestation.

posttraumatic stress disorder (PTSD)   Psychiatric disorder in which a previously experienced stressful event is reexperienced psychologically many times, associated with anxiety and fear.

postural reactions   Normal reflex-like protective responses of an infant to changes in position; *also called* automatic movement reactions.

pragmatics   System describing how language should be adapted to specific social situations, to convey emotion, and to emphasize meanings.

preeclampsia   Illness of late pregnancy characterized by high blood pressure with swelling and/or protein in the mother's urine, seen especially in teenagers and women older than 35 years; *also called* toxemia.

presbyopia   A decrease in the accommodation of the lens of the eye that occurs with aging.

preterm birth   Birth prior to the 37th week of gestation; prematurity.

prevalence   The percentage of a population that is affected by a disorder at any given time.

primary teeth   Baby teeth.

prompts   Cues (e.g., verbal, visual) that direct the child to participate in a targeted activity.

prone   Face down.

prophase   The initial stage in cell division when the chromosomes thicken and shorten to look like separate strands.

prophylaxis   Use of a preventive agent.

proptosis   Appearance of protruding eyes.

prosencephalon   *See* forebrain.

PSR   *See* positive support reflex.

ptosis   Drooping of eyelid.

PTSD   *See* posttraumatic stress disorder.

prosocial   Socially acceptable.

prospective   Pertaining to 1) treatment in anticipation of the development of a disorder or 2) a managed health care model based on payment (e.g., of insurance premiums) before services are rendered.

proximal   Describing the part nearest the midline or trunk.

pseudohypertrophy   Enlarged but weak muscle, as found in muscular dystrophy.

psychoeducational   Pertaining to the testing of intelligence, academic achievement, and other types of psychological and educational processes.

psychosis   A psychiatric disorder characterized by hallucinations, delusions, loss of contact with reality, and unclear thinking; *adjective:* psychotic.

psychotherapy   Nonpharmacological treatment for an individual with an emotional disorder. There are varying types of psychotherapy ranging from supportive counseling to psychoanalysis. These services are usually provided by a psychologist, psychiatrist, or social worker.

PUBS   *See* percutaneous umbilical blood sampling.

pulmonary   Pertaining to the lungs.

pulmonary hypertension   Increased back pressure in the pulmonary artery leading to decreased oxygenation and right heart failure.

pulp   The soft tissue under the dentin layer in teeth, containing blood vessels, lymphatics (lymph vessels), connective tissue, and nerve fibers.

punishment   In behavior management, a procedure or consequence that decreases the frequency of a behavior through the use of a negative stimulus or withdrawal of a preferred activity/object.

pupil   The aperture in the center of the iris.

purine   A type of organic molecule found in RNA and DNA.

PVL   *See* periventricular leukomalacia.

pyramidal tract   A nerve tract, *also called* the corticospinal tract, leading from the cortex into the spinal column, which is involved in the control of voluntary motor movement. Damage to this tract leads to spasticity, commonly seen in cerebral palsy.

quickening   The first signs of life felt by the mother as a result of fetal movements in the fourth or fifth month of pregnancy.

rad   A measure of radioactivity.

radiograph   A medical X ray.

ratio schedules   Provision of reinforcement following a set number of correct responses.

real-time ultrasonography   The use of sound waves to provide a moving (real-time) image, used in fetal monitoring.

rebound   A phenomenon in which as a medication dose wears off, a person's behavior or symptoms become worse than when completely off medication.

receptive aphasia   Impairment of receptive language due to a disorder of the central nervous system (CNS).

receptive language   The understanding of language.

recessive   Pertaining to a trait that is expressed only if the child inherits two copies of the gene.

refracted   Deflected through a substance, such as through a lens.

reinforcer   A response to a behavior that increases the likelihood that the behavior will occur again.

related services   Services (e.g., transportation, occupational and physical therapy) that supplement the special education services provided to a child with a disability under the Individuals with Disabilities Education Act (IDEA) Amendments of 1997 (PL 105-17).

resonance   In linguistics and speech-language pathology, the balance of air flow between the nose and the mouth.

retina   The photosensitive nerve layer of the eye.

retinoscope   An instrument used to detect errors of refraction in the eye.

retrospective   1) Looking backward; 2) pertaining to a fee-for-service health care model in which payment occurs after services are rendered.

retrovirus   A type of DNA virus that is involved in gene therapy; also the class of viruses in which human immunodeficiency virus (HIV), the causative agent of acquired immunodeficiency syndrome (AIDS), belongs.

Rh incompatibility   Condition occurring when an Rh$^+$ baby is born to an Rh$^-$ mother. This leads to breakdown of red blood cells in the baby and the excessive release of bilirubin predisposing the Rh$^+$ baby to kernicterus (*see Chapter 5*). This condition is prevented by the use of the drug RhoGAM in the Rh$^-$ mother who is carrying an Rh$^+$ fetus.

ribonucleic acid (RNA)   A molecule essential for protein synthesis within the cell.

ribosome   Intracellular structure concerned with protein synthesis.

rickets   Bone disease resulting from nutritional deficiency of vitamin D.

rigid   Pertaining to increased tone marked by stiffness; seen in dyskinetic cerebral palsy.

ring chromosome   A ring-shaped chromosome formed when deletions occur at both tips of a normal chromosome, with subsequent fusion of the tips forming a ring.

RNA   *See* ribonucleic acid.

rods   Photoreceptor cells of the eye associated with low-light vision.

rootlets   Small branches of nerve roots.

rubella   A viral infection, *also called* German measles, that generally causes a mild elevation of temperature and skin rash and resolves in a few days. However, when it occurs in a pregnant woman during the first trimester, it can lead to intrauterine infection and severe birth defects. Congenital rubella syndrome has largely disappeared in developed countries as a result of the universal use of a rubella vaccine in childhood.

salicylates   Chemicals found in many food substances and in aspirin.

sarcomeres   The contractile units of the muscle fiber.

satiation   Having had enough or too much of something.

saturated fatty acid   A type of fatty acid in the diet that has been linked to heart disease more frequently than unsaturated fatty acids have been.

schizophrenia   A psychiatric disorder with characteristic psychotic symptoms, including prominent delusions, hallucinations, catatonic behavior, and/or flat affect.

sclera   The white, outer covering of the eyeball.

scoliosis   Lateral curvature of the spine.

secondary   1) Occurring as a consequence of a primary disorder; 2) pertaining to the permanent teeth.

seizure threshold   Tolerance level of the brain for electrical activity. If level of tolerance is exceeded, a seizure occurs.

semantics   The study of and conventions governing meanings of words.

separation anxiety   Excessive concern about separation, usually of mother from child (e.g., school phobia).

sepsis   Life-threatening infection that has spread throughout the bloodstream; *also called* blood poisoning.

sequential modification   If desired changes in behavior are not observed to occur across settings and behaviors, concrete steps are taken to introduce the effective intervention (e.g., positive reinforcement) to each of the behaviors or settings to which transfer of effects is inadequate.

serotonin reuptake inhibitors   A group of psychoactive drugs, an example being fluoxetine (Prozac), used to treat depression.

serum   *See* plasma.

sex chromosomes   Chromosomes that determine gender, the X and Y chromosomes.

sex-linked trait   *See* X-linked trait.

shadowing   Technique in which the instructor keeps his or her hands within an inch of the child's hands as the child proceeds to complete the task.

shaping   Reinforcing successive approximations to the goal behavior.

SIDS   *See* sudden infant death syndrome.

single photon emission computed tomography (SPECT)   An imaging technique that permits the study of the metabolism of a body organ, most commonly the brain.

sleep apnea   Brief periods of arrested breathing during sleep, most commonly found in premature infants and in older children and adults with morbid obesity.

sleep myoclonus   Sudden jerking movements of the body associated with various sleep stages that may be confused with a seizure.

soft neurological signs   A group of neurological findings that are normal in young children but when found in older children suggest immaturities in central nervous system (CNS) development. Example includes difficulty performing sequential finger–thumb opposition or rapid, alternating movements.

soft spot   *See* anterior fontanelle.

somatic   Relating to the body.

spastic   Pertaining to increased muscle tone sin which muscles are stiff and movements are difficult. Caused by damage to the pyramidal tract in the brain.

spastic diplegia   A form of cerebral palsy, primarily seen in former premature infants, that is manifested as spasticity of both lower extremities with only mild involvement of upper extremities.

spastic hemiplegia   A form of cerebral palsy in which one side of the body demonstrates spasticity and the other side is unaffected.

spastic quadriplegia   A form of cerebral palsy in which all four limbs are affected. Increased muscle tone (i.e., spasticity) is caused by damage to the pyramidal tract in the brain.

spasticity   Abnormally increased muscle tone.

speaking valve   A valve that can be used by children who have tracheostomy tubes to permit vocalizations.

SPECT   *See* single photon emission computed tomography.

spina bifida   A developmental defect of the spine *(see Chapter 24)*.

spina bifida occulta   Generally benign congenital defect of the spinal column not associated with protrusion of the spinal cord or meninges.

spinal muscular atrophy   Congenital neuromuscular disorder of childhood associated with progressive muscle weakness.

spinal tap   *See* lumbar puncture.

spindle   In mitosis and meiosis, a web-like figure along which the chromosomes are distributed. *Not to be confused with* muscle spindle.

spondyloepipheseal dysplasia   Congenital structural abnormality of vertebral column caused by a lack of mineralization of bone; *also called* lag of mineralization of bone.

spontaneous recovery   In behavior management, the recurrence of an undesirable behavior after it has been extinguished.

sporadic In genetics, describing a disease that occurs by chance and carries little risk of recurrence.

standardized rating scales Questionnaires concerning specific behaviors that have been completed for large samples of children so that norms and normal degrees of variation are known.

static Unchanging.

stereotypic movement disorder Disorder characterized by recurring purposeless but voluntary movements (e.g., hand flapping in children with autism); *also called* stereotypies.

stereotypies *See* stereotypic movement disorder.

steroids 1) Medications used to treat severe inflammatory diseases and infantile spasms; 2) certain natural hormones in the body.

stimulant Medication used to treat attention-deficit/hyperactivity disorder (e.g., methylphenidate [Ritalin]).

stomach flu *See* gastroenteritis.

strabismus Deviation of one or both eyes during forward gaze.

subarachnoid Beneath the arachnoid membrane, or middle layer, of the meninges.

subdural Resting between the outer (dural) and middle (arachnoid) layers of the meninges.

subdural hematoma Localized collection of clotted blood lying in the space between the dural and arachnoid membranes that surround the brain. This results from bleeding of the cerebral blood vessels that rest between these two membranes.

subluxation Partial dislocation.

substrate A compound acted upon by an enzyme in a chemical reaction.

sucrose *See* glucose.

suction Removal of secretions by suction, for example by the advancing of a catheter through the nose or throat and into the trachea.

sudden infant death syndrome (SIDS) Diagnosis given to a previously well infant (often a former premature baby) who is found lifeless in bed without apparent cause; *also called* crib death *(see Chapter 6)*.

sulci Furrows of the brain; *singular:* sulcus.

superior In anatomy, above.

supine Lying on the back, face upward.

surfactant Substance that coats the alveoli in the lungs, keeping them open. A deficiency of it leads to respiratory distress syndrome in premature infants.

sutures In anatomy, the fibrous joints between certain bones (e.g., skull bones).

synapses The minute spaces separating one neuron from another. Neurochemicals breach this gap.

syndactyly Webbed hands or feet.

synophrys Confluent eyebrow.

syphilis A sexually transmitted disease that can cause an intrauterine infection in pregnant women and result in severe birth defects.

systemic Involving the whole body.

tachycardia Rapid heart rate.

talipes equinovarus *See* clubfoot.

tangibles Rewards given in positive reinforcement procedures (e.g., food, toys).

tardive dyskinesia A potentially severe movement disorder resulting from the long-term use of phenothiazines or other antipsychotic medication.

target behavior Behavior selected for assessment and management.

tartar *See* calculus.

telangiectasia Abnormal cluster of small blood vessels.

telophase The final phase in cell division, in which the daughter chromosomes are at the opposite poles of the cell and new nuclear membranes form.

tendons Fibrous cords by which muscles are attached to bone or to one another.

teratogens Agents that can cause malformations in a developing embryo.

testosterone Male sex hormone.

tetraploid Having four copies of each chromosome (i.e., 92 chromosomes). This is incompatible with life.

thrombocytopenia Low platelet count.

thrush Monilial (fungal) yeast infection of the oral cavity sometimes seen in infants.

tics   Brief repetitive movements or vocalizations that occur in a stereotyped manner and do not appear to be under voluntary control.

time-out   A procedure whereby the possibility of positive reinforcement is withdrawn for a predetermined brief amount of time following the occurrence of a targeted challenging behavior.

tocolysis   Use of medications to stop premature labor.

tonic labyrinthine reflex (TLR)   Primitive reflex in which the infant retracts the arms and extends the legs when the neck is tilted backwards, stimulating the labyrinth.

tonic-clonic   Spasmodic alteration of muscle contraction and relaxation.

tonotopically   Arranged spatially by tone as found in the cochlea or inner ear.

tooth bud   *See* dental organ.

torticollis   Wry neck, in which the neck is painfully tilted to one side; a form of dystonia.

toxemia   *See* preeclampsia.

toxoplasmosis   An infectious disease caused by a microorganism. It may be asymptomatic in adults but can lead to severe fetal malformations.

trachea   Windpipe.

tracheoesophageal fistula   A congenital connection between the trachea and esophagus leading to aspiration of food and requiring surgical correction.

tracheomalacia   Softening of the cartilage of the trachea.

tracheostomy   1) The surgical creation of an opening into the trachea to permit insertion of a tube to facilitate mechanical ventilation; 2) also the tube itself.

trachoma   A bacterial infection causing blindness in developing countries.

transcription   The process in which mRNA is formed from a DNA template.

translation   The process in which an amino acid sequence is assembled according to the pattern specified by mRNA.

translocation   The transfer of a fragment of one chromosome to another chromosome.

triplet repeat expansion   Abnormal number of copies of identical triplet nucleotides (as occurs in fragile X syndrome; *see Chapter 17*).

triploid   Having three copies of each chromosome (i.e., 69 chromosomes). This is generally incompatible with life.

trisomy   A condition is which there are three copies of one chromosome rather than two (e.g., trisomy 21, Down syndrome).

tubers   Benign congenital tumors found in the brain of an individual with tuberous sclerosis *(see Appendix B)*.

twinning   The production of twins.

tympanometry   The measurement of flexibility of the tympanic membrane as an indicator of a middle-ear infection or fluid in the middle ear.

undernutrition   Inadequate nutrition to sustain normal growth.

uniparental disomy   *See* genomic imprinting.

unsaturated fatty acid   A type of dietary fat, certain kinds of which have been linked to heart disease.

urea   End product of protein metabolism.

ureterostomy   Surgical procedure creating an outlet for the ureters through the abdominal wall.

valgus   Condition in which the distal body part is angled away from the midline.

varicella   The virus that causes chickenpox and shingles.

varus   Condition in which the distal body part is angled toward the midline.

vasoconstriction   The decrease in diameter of blood vessels.

ventilator   A machine that provides a mixture of air and oxygen to an individual in respiratory failure. The oxygen content, pressure, volume, and frequency of respirators can be adjusted.

ventricles   Small cavities, especially in the heart or brain.

ventriculoperitoneal shunt   Tube connecting a cerebral ventricle with the abdominal cavity; used to treat hydrocephalus.

vertebral arches   The bony arches projecting from the body of the vertebra.

vertex presentation   Downward position of infant's head during vaginal delivery.

very low birth weight (VLBW)   Term often used to describe an infant with a birth weight less than 1,500 grams ($3\frac{1}{3}$ pounds).

vesicles   Small, fluid-containing elevations in the upper layer of skin, as seen in chickenpox.

vesicostomy   The surgical creation of an opening for the bladder to empty its contents through the abdominal wall.

vestibular system   Three ring-shaped bodies located in the labyrinth of the ear that are involved in maintenance of balance and sensation of the body's movement through space.

villi   Tiny vascular projections, such as those coming from the embryo that become part of the placenta; *singular:* villus.

vitreous humor   The gelatinous content of the eye located between the lens and retina.

VLBW   *See* very low birth weight.

watershed area   Area of tissue lying between two major arteries and thus poorly supplied by blood.

watershed infarct   Injury to brain due to lack of blood flow in the brain tissues between interfacing blood vessels.

X-linked trait   A trait transmitted by a gene located on the X chromosome; *previously called* sex-linked.

B Syndromes and Inborn Errors of Metabolism

Cheryl Scacheri

The underlying cause of a developmental disability can be explained in some children by a single genetic or teratogenic mechanism. An understanding of the etiology can shed light on the reason for clinical features such as physical malformations, cognitive impairments, and behavior problems. Making a diagnosis in such cases may be important for physicians to implement appropriate medical management or to provide genetic or prenatal counseling. Other professionals may also find that a diagnosis assists them in the development of more global aspects of the child's care, including educational, physical, occupational, and speech-language therapy. Families, too, benefit from having a diagnosis that enables them to gather information specific to their child's condition and often provides them with the opportunity to belong to support groups, to attend conferences on the disorder, and to communicate with other families. The advent of the Internet has brought together families with rare disorders who may not otherwise have met. Some of the larger disease-oriented organizations may even provide financial and other assistance to families and may help educate health care professionals about the condition. For all these reasons, the search for an etiology of a child's developmental disability may focus on syndrome identification.

By definition, a *syndrome* is a collection of two or more features that have a single origin. Syndromes may have a genetic basis or can be caused by teratogens (see Chapter 7). Genetic syndromes affect multiple organ systems because the genetic defect is usually contained in every cell of the body. This abnormality may interfere with typical development or cause abnormal differentiation of more than one tissue of the body. Most genetic and teratologic syndromes are of prenatal onset and are evident at birth, usually because of an unusual appearance (i.e., dysmorphic features) or multiple congenital abnormalities. Syndromes are usually stable conditions, and neurological regression is uncommon. An association, or a sequence, is a single localized anomaly and its secondary defects.

Unlike most syndromes, *inborn errors of metabolism* are usually not evident at birth. During gestation the mother's normal metabolism protects the fetus. After delivery, however, there may be accumulation of toxic metabolites as a result of an enzyme deficiency. The presentation of inborn errors varies from metabolic crisis and death within days of birth to occasional episodes in response to external factors later in childhood. Some metabolic disorders are treatable, and many in this category of genetic conditions are detectable with newborn screening through biochemical or molecular testing (see Chapter 2).

Although the clinical features associated with certain syndromes and inborn errors of metabolism have been known for centuries (e.g., Down syndrome, congenital hypothyroidism), the chromosomal and molecular bases of the disorders have been characterized only since the 1960s or so. An increasing number of genetic and biochemical tests can now be utilized to confirm a clinically suspected diagnosis. This is of particular importance because different therapeutic options (or the opportunity to participate in clinical research trials) may be available to individuals on the basis of a genetic diagnosis, particularly in the cases of gene therapy and other molecularly based therapies. In addition, a genetic diagnosis allows for accurate recurrence risk estimates and appropriate genetic counseling for other family members.

Research on the cognitive abilities of individuals with genetic syndromes is uncovering specific patterns of learning and behavior for many syndromes; these patterns are called *behavioral phenotypes*. These patterns of behavior can be used to establish rational and attainable educational goals to promote the child's attainment of his or her full cognitive and functional potential (see Finegan, J.A. [1998]. Study of behavioral phenotypes: Goals and methodological considerations. *American Journal of Medical Genetics, 81,* 148–155). In addition, researchers believe that understanding altered behavior in specific genetic syndromes will further the understanding of the genes that may underlie specific behaviors in the typically developing population. References addressing the cognitive and behavioral abilities of individuals with specific genetic conditions are included in this appendix.

On-line and other helpful resources for children with disabilities that are available to professionals and families alike are listed in Appendix D. Excellent resources also exist for genetic disorders. These include the Genetic Alliance, which has a directory of support groups, foundations, research organizations, patient advocacy groups, and tissue registries. Based in Washington, D.C., the Genetic Alliance (202-966-5557; http://www.geneticalliance.org; e-mail: info@geneticalliance.org) also has an annual conference, a listserv, and information on public policies. Two other excellent resources are GeneTests and GeneReviews (206-527-5742; http://www.genetests.org; e-mail: genetests@genetests.org), both administered by the University of Washington and funded by the National Institutes of Health, the Health Resources and Services Administration, and the U.S. Department of Energy. GeneTests has a directory of clinics and laboratories and provides some educational tools for professionals, whereas GeneReviews provides a medical knowledge base relating genetic testing to the diagnosis, management, and genetic counseling of individuals and families with specific inherited disorders. The National Organization for Rare Disorders (NORD; 203-746-6518; http://www.rarediseases.org) is a patient advocacy organization dedicated to so-called orphan diseases. This organization's rare disease database, newsletter, and directory of participating organizations (including support groups and foundations) are useful to families and clinicians alike. NORD also offers research grants and fellowships to physician-scientists. The Online Mendelian Inheritance in Man (OMIM; http://www.ncbi.nlm.nih.gov/omim) catalog describes all known Mendelian disorders, providing clinical, biochemical, genetic, and therapeutic information.

This appendix lists a number of syndromes and inborn errors of metabolism that are often associated with developmental disabilities. Included in each listing are the principal characteristics, pattern of inheritance, frequency of occurrence (**prevalence** or **incidence**), and recent references that further define the syndrome. Cognitive and behavioral changes are noted for disorders in which common developmental abnormalities are widely accepted as part of the syndrome or inborn error. When known, the causative gene or chromosome location is listed. In describing the chromosomal location, the first number or letter indicates the chromosome on which there is a genetic change (mutation), and the subsequent letter (p or q) indicates the short or long arm of the chromosome, respectively. The term *ter* is used when the site is at the terminal end of one arm of the chromosome; *cen* is used when the site is near the **centromere**. The numbers following the p or q specify the location on the chromosome. For example, Aarskog-Scott syndrome is located on the short arm of the X chromosome at position 11.21, designated as Xp11.21. The inheritance patterns of genetic traits are listed as *autosomal recessive (AR), autosomal dominant (AD), X-linked recessive (XLR), X-linked dominant (XLD), mitochondrial (M),* or *sporadic (SP)* (i.e., noninherited or a new genetic mutation). In the rare syndromes for which a treatment is available, it is included in the description. Treatment is more often available for inborn errors of metabolism. This appendix lists a number of the more commonly recognized syndromes associated with developmental disabilities but is not intended to be all-inclusive. Specific medical terminology is defined in the glossary (see Appendix A); glossary terms that appear here for the first time are presented in boldface type.

Aarskog-Scott syndrome (faciodigitogenital dysplasia [FGDY]) *Clinical features:* short stature, brachydactyly (short fingers and toes), widow's peak, broad nasal bridge with small nose, hypertelorism, shawl scrotum, **cryptorchidism** (undescended testes). *Associated complications:* Ptosis, eye movement problems, strabismus, orthodontic problems, occasional cleft lip/palate. *Cause:* mutations in the *FGD1* gene at Xp11.21. *Inheritance:* XLR with partial expression in some females; rare AD cases reported. *Prevalence:* Unknown, considered to be very rare.
   References: Logie, L.J., & Porteous, M.E.M. (1998). Intelligence and development in Aarskog syndrome. *Archives of Disease in Childhood, 79,* 359–360.
   Teebi, A.S., Rucquoi, J.K., & Meyn, M.S. (1993). Aarskog syndrome: Report of a family with review and discussion of nosology. *American Journal of Medical Genetics, 46,* 501–509.

achondroplasia *Clinical features:* Disproportionate short stature, relatively large head with prominent forehead, depressed nasal bridge, short limbs, trident-shaped hand; intelligence is usually unaffected. *Associated complications:* Risk for spinal cord compression, apnea, hypotonia, delays in motor milestones, occasional hearing loss, and occasional hydrocephalus. *Cause:* Mutations in fibroblast growth factor receptor 3 (*FGFR3*) gene on chromosome 4p16.3. *Inheritance:* AD; most cases are caused by new mutations, and there may be no family history. Offspring of two affected individuals are at 25% risk to inherit a homozygous mutation, which is lethal. *Prevalence:* 1/10,000. *Treatment:* growth hormone has been used to increase height potential. *See also* Chapter 14.
   References: American Academy of Pediatrics, Committee on Genetics. (1995). Health supervision for children with achondroplasia. *Pediatrics, 95,* 443–451.

Thompson, N.M., Hecht, J.T., Bohan, T.P., et al. (1999). Neuroanatomic and neuropsychological outcome in school-age children with achondroplasia. *American Journal of Medical Genetics, 88,* 145–153.

acrocephalosyndactyly, type I *See* Apert syndrome.

acrocephalosyndactyly, type II *See* Carpenter syndrome.

acrocephalosyndactyly, type V *See* Pfeiffer syndrome.

acrofacial dysostosis (Nager syndrome) *Clinical features:* **Micrognathia** (small jaw), malar hypoplasia (underdeveloped cheeks), downward slant of eyelids, high nasal bridge, external ear defects, occasional cleft lip/palate, asymmetric limb anomalies (hypoplastic thumb or radius [a bone in the lower arm]). *Associated complications:* Scoliosis, severe conductive hearing loss, occasional heart or kidney defects, mental retardation present in 16%. *Cause:* Gene linked to chromosome 9q32. *Inheritance:* AR in most cases. *Prevalence:* Rare.
References: Fryns, J.P. (1999). On the nosology of severe acrofacial dysostosis with limb deficiency. *American Journal of Medical Genetics, 82,* 282–283.

McDonald, J.T., & Gorski, J.L. (1993). Nager acrofacial dysostosis. *Journal of Medical Genetics, 30,* 779–782.

adrenoleukodystrophy (X-linked ALD) (*For neonatal form, see* adrenoleukodystrophy, neonatal form.) *Clinical features:* Progressive neurological disorder of white matter resulting from accumulation of very long chain fatty acids and characterized by spasticity, ataxia, peripheral neuropathy (functional disturbance of the peripheral nerves), and speech disturbance. Primary adrenal insufficiency is a hallmark. The disease process commonly begins in late childhood. *Associated complications:* Progressive intellectual deterioration, seizures, endocrine abnormalities, conductive hearing loss. *Cause:* Mutations in *ALD* gene at Xq28. The ALD protein product is localized to the peroxisomal membrane. *Inheritance:* XLR, with intrafamilial variability ranging from classical ALD to Addison disease in adulthood. Incidence: 1/100,000 males in the United States. *Treatment:* Dietary modifications, "Lorenzo's oil" (oleic acid and erucic acid), and bone marrow transplant have each been attempted with minimal success. The potential benefit of Lorenzo's oil or bone marrow transplant when used in presymptomatic individuals with the *ALD* gene is yet to be determined.
References: Moser, H.W. (1995). Adrenoleukodystrophy. *Current Opinion in Neurology, 8,* 221–226.

van Geel, B.M., Assies, J., Haverkort, E.B., et al. (1999). Progression of abnormalities in adrenomyeloneuropathy and neurologically asymptomatic X-linked adrenoleukodystrophy despite treatment with "Lorenzo's oil." *Journal of Neurology, Neurosurgery, and Psychiatry, 67,* 290–299.

adrenoleukodystrophy, neonatal form (*For childhood form, see* adrenoleukodystrophy [X-linked ALD].)
Clinical features: A disorder of peroxisomes (minute organelles in certain cells that are involved in the processing of long chain fatty acids) characterized by onset in early infancy of seizures, hypotonia, and adrenal insufficiency; mild dysmorphic facial features include high forehead, epicanthal folds (vertical fold of skin on either side of the nose), broad nasal bridge, and anteverted (forward-tipping) nostrils. Death in early childhood is usual, but there are known cases of affected individuals surviving until the second or third decade. *Associated complications:* Mental retardation, cataracts, visual impairment. *Cause:* Absence of peroxisomes, which results from mutations in a number of autosomal peroxin (*PEX*) genes. *Inheritance:* AR. *Prevalence:* Rare.
Reference: Moser, A.B., Rasmussen, M., Naidu, S., et al. (1995). Phenotype of patients with peroxisomal disorders subdivided into sixteen complementation groups. *Journal of Pediatrics, 127,* 13–22.

Aicardi syndrome *Clinical features:* Infantile spasms, absence or hypoplasia of the corpus callosum, abnormalities of eyes (including the retina), vertebral or rib anomalies, severe mental retardation. *Associated complications:* Poorly controlled seizures, visual impairment. *Cause:* Gene linked to Xp22. *Inheritance:* XLD; it is presumed that mutations in this gene are lethal in males. *Prevalence:* Rare.
Reference: Manezes, A.V., MacGregor, D.L., & Buncic, J.R. (1994). Aicardi syndrome: Natural history and possible predictors of severity. *Pediatric Neurology, 11,* 313–318.

alcohol-related neurodevelopmental defects (ARND) *Previously called* fetal alcohol effects (FAE); *see* Chapter 7.

Alexander disease *Clinical features:* Progressive neurological disorder characterized by **macrocephaly,** exaggerated startle response, optic atrophy, intellectual decline, seizures, early death. *Associated complications:* Hydrocephalus, demyelination, progressive spasticity, visual impairment. *Cause:* One case demonstrates mutations in NADH dehydrogenase (ubiquinone) flavoprotein 1 (*NDUFV1*) gene on chromosome 11q13; other evidence supports the involvement of the *GFAP* gene, which codes for glial fibrillary acidic protein at 17q21. *Inheritance:* AD, usually SP. *Prevalence:* Rare.
References: Johnson, A.B. (1996). Alexander disease. *Handbook of Clinical Neurology, 22,* 701–710.

Pridmore, C.L., Baraitser, M., Harding, B., et al. (1993). Alexander's disease: Clues to diagnosis. *Journal of Child Neurology, 8,* 134–144.

Angelman syndrome　*Clinical features:* "Puppet-like" gait, large mouth, small head with **brachycephaly** (short head), prominent jaw, ataxia, sudden bursts of inappropriate laughter, generalized depigmentation of hair. *Associated complications:* Seizures, severe mental retardation, paucity of speech. *Cause:* Deletion of 15q11–q13 on the maternally inherited chromosome or paternal inheritance of both copies of chromosome 15 (uniparental disomy). *Inheritance:* AD, most cases are new mutations; uniparental disomy is SP. *Prevalence:* 1/10,000–1/20,000.

> *References:* Clarke, D.J., & Marston, G. (2000). Problem behaviors associated with 15q– Angelman syndrome. *American Journal of Mental Retardation, 105,* 25–31.
>
> Laan, L.A., van Haeringen A., & Brouwer O.F. (1999). Angelman syndrome: A review of clinical and genetic aspects. *Clinical Neurology and Neurosurgery, 101,* 161–170.

Apert syndrome (acrocephalosyndactyly, type I)　*Clinical features:* Premature fusion of the cranial sutures **(craniosynostosis)** with misshapen head, high forehead, and flat occiput (back part of head); hypertelorism with downward slant; flat midface and nasal bridge; severe **syndactyly** (webbing of fingers or toes); limb anomalies; cleft palate. *Associated complications:* Hydrocephalus, varying degrees of mental retardation, hearing loss, teeth abnormalities, occasional heart and kidney anomalies. *Cause:* Mutations in the fibroblast growth factor receptor-2 (*FGFR2*) gene on chromosome 10q26. *Inheritance:* Most are sporadic; occasional AD; recurrence risk for individual's offspring is 50%. *Prevalence:* 1.5/100,000. *Treatment:* Neurosurgical correction of sutures improves appearance and may reduce risk of mental retardation; plastic/orthopedic surgery for limb anomalies.

> *References:* Cohen, M.M., Kreiborg, S., & Odont, D. (1993). An updated pediatric perspective on Apert syndrome. *American Journal of Diseases of Children, 147,* 989–993.
>
> Lajeunie, E., Cameron, R., El Ghouzzi, V., et al. (1999). Clinical variability in patients with Apert's syndrome. *Journal of Neurosurgery, 90,* 443–447.

ARND　alcohol-related neurodevelopmental defects; *see Chapter* 7.

arthrogryposis multiplex congenita　*Clinical features:* Nonprogressive joint contractures that begin prenatally; flexion contractures at the fingers, knees, and elbows, with muscle weakness around involved joints. *Associated complications:* Occasional kidney and eye anomalies, cleft palate, defects of abdominal wall, scoliosis. *Cause:* Multiple; most frequently related to an underlying neuropathy, myopathy (muscle weakness), or in utero crowding; may be associated with maternal myasthenia gravis. *Inheritance:* usually SP or may be caused by teratogenic exposure; occasionally AD or AR. *Prevalence:* Unknown. *Treatment:* Casting of affected joints or surgery, if indicated.

> *References:* Gordon, N. (1998). Arthrogryposis multiplex congenita. *Brain Development, 20,* 507–511.
>
> Sodergard, J., Hakamies-Blomqvist, L., Sainio, K., et al. (1997). Arthrogryposis multiplex congenita: Perinatal and electromyographic findings, disability, and psychosocial outcome. *Journal of Pediatric Orthopaedics, Part B, 6,* 167–171.

ataxia telangiectasia　*Clinical features:* Slowly progressive ataxia, telangiectasias (dilation of capillaries, especially in the sclera and behind the earlobe), immune defects, elevated alpha-fetoprotein in blood. *Associated complications:* Dystonia or choreoathetosis, increased risk of malignancy (often **lymphoma**), eye movement abnormalities, finger contractures, increased risk of sinus and pulmonary infections; intelligence is typically unaffected but may decline with disease progression. *Cause:* Mutation in the *ATM* gene on chromosome 11q22.3. *Inheritance:* AR. *Prevalence:* 1/100,000–1/300,000.

> *References:* Crawford, T.O., Mandir, A.S., Lefton-Greif, M.A., et al. (2000). Quantitative neurologic assessment of ataxia-telangiectasia. *Neurology, 54,* 1505–1509.
>
> Kastan, K. (1995). Clinical implications of basic research: Ataxia-telangiectasia. Broad implications for a rare disorder. *New England Journal of Medicine, 333,* 662–663.

Bardet-Biedl syndrome　*Clinical features:* Obesity, genital anomalies, **polydactyly** (extra fingers or toes), retinal anomalies. *Associated complications:* Mental retardation, abnormal liver functioning, cataracts, occasional cardiac and renal (kidney) anomalies, delayed puberty, ataxia, spasticity, night blindness. (Bardet-Biedl syndrome and Laurence-Moon syndrome were previously called Laurence-Moon-Bardet-Biedl syndrome but are now known to be separate disorders.) *Cause:* Linked to five distinct chromosomal loci: 2q31, 3p11–p13, 11q13, 15q22.3–q23, 16q21. *Inheritance:* AR. *Prevalence:* Rare in most populations; increased frequency in Arab population in Kuwait and in Bedouin population.

> *References:* Beales, P.L., Elcioglu, N., Woolf, A.S., et al. (1999). New criteria for improved diagnosis of Bardet-Biedl syndrome: Results of a population survey. *Journal of Medical Genetics, 36,* 437–446.
>
> Carmi, R., Elbedow, K., Stone, E.M., et al. (1995). Phenotypic differences among patients with Bardet-Biedl syndrome linked to three different chromosome loci. *American Journal of Medical Genetics, 59,* 199–203.

Batten disease (neuronal ceroid lipofuscinosis, juvenile)   *Clinical features:* Typical development for first 2–4 years of life; rapid vision loss; gradual onset of ataxia, myoclonic or major motor seizures, and retinal degeneration; typically no survival beyond adolescence. *Associated complications:* Gradual intellectual decline, spasticity, psychosis, kyphoscoliosis. *Cause:* At least eight genes (*CLN1–CLN8*) have been implicated, all of which are necessary to prevent accumulation of lysosomal proteins. *Inheritance:* AR. *Incidence:* 7/100,000 live births in Iceland; 0.71/100,000 live births in Germany; rarer elsewhere.

> *References:* Goebel, H.H. (1995). The neuronal ceroid-lipofuscinoses. *Journal of Child Neurology, 10,* 424–437.
>
> Rider, J.A., & Rider, D.L. (1999). Thirty years of Batten disease research: Present status and future goals. *Molecular Genetics and Metabolism, 66,* 231–233.

Becker muscular dystrophy (BMD)   *See* muscular dystrophy.

Beckwith-Wiedemann syndrome   *Clinical features:* Omphalocele (congenital defect in abdominal wall containing intestine); macrosomia (large body size); large organs, especially the tongue; neonatal hypoglycemia. *Associated complications:* Advanced growth for the first 6 years, with advanced bone age, occasional **hemihypertrophy** (enlargement of one side of the body), kidney or adrenal anomalies, increased risk of malignancy (liver, kidney, muscle), occasional mental retardation (may be due to hypoglycemia). *Cause:* Presumed failure to suppress gene for insulin-like growth factor, type 2 (*IGF2*), caused by a duplication (including uniparental disomy) of paternal chromosome 11p15.5, maternal chromosomal rearrangements involving chromosome 11p15.5, or mutations in one or more critical genes in this region. *Inheritance:* most often SP; possible AD with variable **penetrance.** *Prevalence:* 0.07/1,000. *Treatment:* Early treatment of hypoglycemia is critical; surgical repair of omphalocele.

> *References:* Elliot, M., & Maher, E.R. (1994). Beckwith-Wiedemann syndrome. *Journal of Medical Genetics, 31,* 560–564.
>
> Nicholls, R.D. (2000). The impact of genomic imprinting for neurobehavioral and developmental disorders. *Journal of Clinical Investigation, 105,* 413–418.

biotinidase deficiency   *See* multiple carboxylase deficiency, late onset, juvenile form.

BMD   muscular dystrophy, Becker type; *see* muscular dystrophy.

Börjeson-Forssman-Lehmann syndrome   *Clinical features:* Obesity; short stature; postpubertal **gynecomastia** (breast enlargement in males); long, thick ears; coarse facial appearance; protruding tongue; hypogonadism (small testes), cataracts or other eye anomalies, tapering fingers, varying degrees of mental retardation. *Associated complications:* Seizures, microcephaly, hypotonia. *Cause:* Potential gene linked to chromosome Xq26.3. *Inheritance:* XLD, with females less severely affected than males. *Prevalence:* Rare.

> *References:* Gunay-Aygun, M., Cassidy, S.B., & Nicholls, R.D. (1997). Prader-Willi and other syndromes associated with obesity and mental retardation. *Behavior Genetics, 27,* 307–324.
>
> Turner, G., Gedeon, A., Mulley, J., et al. (1989). Borjeson-Forssman-Lehmann: Clinical manifestations and gene localization to Xq26–q27. *American Journal of Medical Genetics, 34,* 463–469.

Brachmann de Lange syndrome   *See* de Lange syndrome.

Canavan disease (spongy degeneration of central nervous system)   *Clinical features:* Progressive neurological disease consisting of macrocephaly, hypotonia, visual impairment, and early death; symptoms begin at 3–6 months of age. *Associated complications:* Feeding difficulties with progressive swallowing problems, gastroesophageal reflux, severe mental retardation. *Cause:* Deficiency in the enzyme aspartoacylase, caused by a mutation in the *ASPA* gene on chromosome 17pter–p13. *Inheritance:* AR. *Prevalence:* Rare in most populations; about 1/5,500 in Ashkenazi Jewish population.

> *Reference:* Matalon, R.M., & Michals-Matalon, K. (2000). Spongy degeneration of the brain, Canavan disease: Biochemical and molecular findings. *Frontiers in Bioscience, 5,* D307–D311.

Carpenter syndrome (acrocephalosyndactyly, type II)   *Clinical features:* Craniosynostosis, flat nasal bridge, malformed and low-set ears, short digits, syndactyly and/or polydactyly, obesity, **hypogenitalism** and/or cryptorchidism. *Associated complications:* congenital heart defects, hearing loss; 75% have mild mental retardation. *Cause:* Unknown. *Inheritance:* Presumed AR. *Prevalence:* Rare.

> *References:* Robinson, L.K., James, H.E., Mubarak, S.J., et al. (1985). Carpenter syndrome: Natural history and clinical spectrum. *American Journal of Medical Genetics, 20,* 461–469.
>
> Katzen, J.T., & McCarthy, J.G. (2000). Syndromes involving craniosynostosis and midface hypoplasia. *Otolaryngology Clinics of North America, 33,* 1257–1284.

cerebrohepatorenal syndrome   *See* Zellweger syndrome.

CHARGE association   *Clinical features: c*oloboma (defect in iris or retina), *h*eart defect, choanal *a*tresia (congenital blockage of the nasal passages), *r*etarded growth and development, *g*enital anomalies, and *e*ar anomalies with or without hearing loss. *Associated complications:* Hypogenitalism, cryptorchidism, occasional cleft lip/palate, varying degrees of mental retardation, potentially severe visual and hearing impairments. *Cause:* Unknown. *Inheritance:* Usually SP; approximately 8% of cases are familial. *Prevalence:* 1/10,000; more common in females than males.

References: Blake, K.D., Davenport, S.L., Hall, B.D., et al. (1998). CHARGE association: An update and review for the primary pediatrician. *Clinical Pediatrics, 37,* 159–173.

Keller, J.L., & Kacker, A. (2000). Choanal atresia, CHARGE association, and congenital nasal stenosis. *Otolaryngology Clinics of North America, 33,* 1343–1351.

chondroectodermal dysplasia   *See* Ellis-van Creveld syndrome.

chromosome 22q11 microdeletion syndromes (e.g., DiGeorge syndrome, velocardiofacial syndrome [VCFS])   *Clinical features:* Microdeletions within the long arm of chromosome 22 have varying presentations, including DiGeorge syndrome, VCFS, and isolated outflow tract defects of the heart. Characteristic facial appearance that includes a small, open mouth; short palpebral fissures (eyelid openings); flat nasal bridge; bulbous nasal tip; protuberant, low-set ears; varying degrees of **palatal** abnormalities ranging from cleft to velopharyngeal insufficiency. Classic DiGeorge syndrome is associated with hypoplastic thymus, hypoparathyroidism, and congenital heart defect. *Associated complications:* Feeding problems in infancy, rare seizures, hypernasal speech, characteristic pattern of nonverbal learning disability. *Cause:* Deletion on chromosome 22q11.2. *Inheritance:* Usually SP; occasionally one parent has a chromosomal rearrangement involving 22q, which increases the risk for recurrence; risk to offspring of affected individuals is 50%. *Prevalence:* Unknown.

References: Driscoll, D.A., & Emanuel, B.S. (1996). DiGeorge and velocardiofacial syndromes: The 22q11 deletion syndrome. *Mental Retardation and Developmental Disabilities Research Reviews, 2,* 130–138.

Moss, E.M., Batshaw, M.L., Solot, C.B., et al. (1999). Psychoeducational profile of the 22q11.2 microdeletion: A complex pattern. *Journal of Pediatrics, 134,* 193–198.

Wang, P.P., Solot, C., Moss, E.M., et al. (1998). Developmental presentation of 22q11.2 deletion (DiGeorge/velocardiofacial syndrome). *Journal of Developmental and Behavioral Pediatrics, 19,* 342–345.

Cohen syndrome   *Clinical features:* Obesity; microcephaly; short stature; long hands with tapering fingers; characteristic facial features, including micrognathia, short philtrum, prominent incisors; varying degrees of mental retardation. *Associated complications:* Hypotonia, joint laxity, ocular abnormalities, occasional heart defect. *Cause:* Gene linked to chromosome 8q21–q22. *Inheritance:* AR. *Prevalence:* Unknown.

References: Kivitie-Kallio, S., Larsen, A., Kajasto, K., et al. (1999). Neurological and psychological findings in patients with Cohen syndrome: A study of 18 patients aged 11 months to 57 years. *Neuropediatrics, 30,* 181–189.

Kivitie-Kallio, S., & Norio, R. (2001) Cohen syndrome: Essential features, natural history, and heterogeneity. *American Journal of Medical Genetics, 102,* 125–135.

congenital facial diplegia   *See* Moebius sequence.

Cornelia de Lange syndrome   *See* de Lange syndrome.

craniofacial dysostosis   *See* Crouzon syndrome.

cri-du-chat syndrome (5p– syndrome)   *Clinical features:* Pre- and postnatal growth retardation, cat-like cry in infancy, hypertelorism with downward slant, microcephaly, low-set ears, micrognathia, single palmar crease, severe mental retardation. *Associated complications:* Severe respiratory and feeding difficulties in infancy, hypotonia, inguinal (groin) hernias, occasional congenital heart defects. *Cause:* Partial deletion of chromosome 5p15.2. *Inheritance:* Usually SP new mutation; in 12% of cases, a parent carries a balanced translocation. *Prevalence:* 1/20,000–1/50,000.

References: Cornish, K.M., Bramble, D., Munir, F., et al. (1999). Cognitive functioning in children with typical cri du chat (5p–) syndrome. *Developmental Medicine and Child Neurology, 41,* 263–266.

Dykens, E.M., & Clarke, D.J. (1997). Correlates of maladaptive behavior in individuals with 5p– (cri du chat) syndrome. *Developmental Medicine and Child Neurology, 39,* 752–756.

Crouzon syndrome (craniofacial dysostosis)   *Clinical features:* Craniosynostosis, shallow orbits with **proptosis** (protuberant eyeballs), hypertelorism, strabismus, parrot-beaked nose, short upper lip, **maxillary hypoplasia** (small upper jaw), conductive hearing loss. *Associated complications:* Mental retardation, seizures, visual impairment, agenesis of corpus callosum, occasional cleft lip or palate, obstructive airway problems. *Cause:* Mutations in fibroblast growth factor receptor-2 (*FGFR2*) gene on chromosome 10q25.3–q26. *Inheritance:* AD with variable expression; up to 25% may represent new mutations. *Prevalence:* Unknown.

Reference: Proudman, T.W., Moore, M.H., Abbott, A.H., et al. (1994). Noncraniofacial manifestations of Crouzon's disease. *The Journal of Craniofacial Surgery, 5,* 218–222.

de Lange syndrome (Brachmann de Lange syndrome, Cornelia de Lange syndrome)   *Clinical features:* Prenatal growth retardation, postnatal short stature, **hypertrichosis** (excessive body hair), **synophrys** (confluent eyebrow), anteverted nostrils, depressed nasal bridge, long philtrum, thin upper lip, microcephaly, low-set ears, limb and digital anomalies, eye problems (myopia, ptosis, or nystagmus). *Associated complications:* Severe mental retardation, occasional heart defect, gastrointestinal problems, features of pervasive developmental disorders, self-injurious behavior, occasional hearing loss. *Cause:* Gene linked to chromosome 3q26.3. *Inheritance:* Usually SP; possibly AD in some families. *Prevalence:* 1/50,000.

References: Berney, T.P., Ireland, M., & Burn, J. (1999). Behavioural phenotype of Cornelia de Lange syndrome. *Archives of Disease in Childhood, 81,* 333–336.

Goodban, M.T. (1993). Survey of speech and language skills with prognostic indicators in 116 patients with Cornelia de Lange syndrome. *American Journal of Medical Genetics, 47,* 1059–1063.

DiGeorge syndrome   *See* chromosome 22q11 microdeletion syndromes.

DMD   muscular dystrophy, Duchenne type; *see* muscular dystrophy.

Down syndrome   *Clinical features:* Hypotonia, flat facial profile, upward-slanting palpebral fissures, small ears, small nose with low nasal bridge, single palmar crease, short stature, mental retardation, congenital heart disease. *Associated complications:* Atlantoaxial (upper cervical spine) instability; hyperextensible large joints; strabismus; thyroid dysfunction; predisposition toward immune disorders and leukemia; eye abnormalities, including strabismus, nystagmus, cataracts, or glaucoma; narrow ear canals and high incidence of middle-ear infections with potential hearing loss. Neurological abnormalities include risk of seizures and early-onset Alzheimer's disease. *Cause:* Extra chromosome 21 caused by trisomy, mosaicism, or translocation. *Inheritance:* SP; usually nondisjunction chromosome abnormality. Recurrence risk in the absence of translocation is 1%–2% in women younger than 35 years and the same as the typical maternal age-related risk in women over 35 years old at delivery. If translocation is present in parent, recurrence risk is higher and is dependent on sex of carrier parent. *Prevalence:* 1/100,000–1.5/100,000. *(Incidence:* 1/800 births.) *See also Chapter 16.*

References: Chapman, R.S., & Hesketh, L.J. (2000). Behavioral phenotype of individuals with Down syndrome. *Mental Retardation and Developmental Disabilities Research Reviews, 6,* 84–95.

Hauser-Cram, P., Warfield, M.E., Shonkoff, J.P., et al. (1999). Family influences on adaptive development in young children with Down syndrome. *Child Development, 70,* 979–989.

Dubowitz syndrome   *Clinical features:* Prenatal onset of growth deficiency; postnatal short stature; eczema; sparse hair; mild microcephaly; cleft palate; dysmorphic facial features, including high forehead, broad nasal bridge, ptosis, epicanthal folds. *Associated complications:* Mental retardation, behavioral disturbances, recurrent infections, increased frequency of malignancy, occasional **hypospadias** (abnormality in the location of the male urethra) or cryptorchidism, hypoparathyroidism. *Cause:* Unknown. *Inheritance:* AR. *Prevalence:* Rare.

References: Hansen, K.E., Kirkpatrick, S.J., & Laxova, R. (1995). Dubowitz syndrome: Long term follow-up of an original patient. *American Journal of Medical Genetics, 55,* 161–164.

Tsukahara, M., & Opitz, J.M. (1996). Dubowitz syndrome: Review of 141 cases including 36 previously unreported patients. *American Journal of Medical Genetics, 63,* 277–289.

Duchenne muscular dystrophy (DMD)   *See* muscular dystrophy.

ectrodactyly–ectodermal dysplasia–clefting (EEC) syndrome   *Clinical features:* **Ectrodactyly** (split hands or feet), **ectodermal dysplasia** (abnormal skin development), sparse hair, cleft lip and palate, lacrimal (tear) duct abnormalities; intelligence is not usually affected. *Associated complications:* Occasional renal (kidney) or genital anomalies, hearing impairment, hypodontia (underdeveloped teeth). *Cause:* Mutations in *p63* gene at 3q27; some cases linked to chromosome 7q21–q22. *Inheritance:* AD with variable penetrance and expressivity. *Prevalence:* Unknown.

References: Buss, P.W., Hughes, H.E., & Clarke, A. (1995). Twenty-four cases of the EEC syndrome: Clinical presentation and management. *Journal of Medical Genetics, 32,* 716–723.

Celli, J., Duijf, P., Hamel, B.C., et al. (1999). Heterozygous germline mutations in the p53 homolog p63 are the cause of EEC syndrome. *Cell, 99,* 143–153.

Roelfsema, N.M., & Cobben, J.M. (1996). The EEC syndrome: A literature study. *Clinical Dysmorphology, 5,* 115–127.

Edwards syndrome   *See* trisomy 18 syndrome.

EEC syndrome   *See* ectrodactyly–ectodermal dysplasia–clefting syndrome.

Ehlers-Danlos syndrome   *Clinical features:* At least 10 distinct forms have been described. All include aspects of skin fragility, easy bruisability, joint hyperextensibility, and hyperelastic skin. Types I and III are most commonly described and have similar clinical presentations with the previously mentioned features; type IV is characterized by severe blood vessel involvement with risk of spontaneous arterial rupture; type VI is characterized by eye involvement, including corneal fragility; type VIII includes periodontal disease; type IX has bladder diverticula (pouches or sacs in the bladder wall), and chronic diarrhea. *Associated complications:* Occasional mental retardation, premature loss of teeth, mitral valve prolapse, intestinal hernias, premature delivery from premature rupture of membranes, scoliosis, abnormalities of thymus. *Cause:* Each form is associated with an abnormality in the formation of collagen. *Inheritance:* Types I, II, III, IV, VII, and VIII are AD with variable expression; types VI and X are AR; types V and IX are XLR. *Prevalence:* Unknown.

References: Burrows, N.P. (1999). The molecular genetics of the Ehlers-Danlos syndrome. *Clinical and Experimental Dermatology, 24,* 99–106.

Byers, P.H. (1994). Ehlers-Danlos syndrome: Recent advances and current understanding of the clinical and genetic heterogeneity. *Journal of Investigative Dermatology, 103*(Suppl. 5), 47S–52S.

Ellis-van Creveld syndrome (chondroectodermal dysplasia)   *Clinical features:* Short-limbed dwarfism (final height 43–60 inches), polydactyly, nail abnormalities, neonatal teeth, underdeveloped and premature loss of teeth, congenital heart defect in 50%; intelligence is usually not affected. *Associated complications:* Severe cardiorespiratory problems in infancy, hydrocephalus, severe leg deformities. *Cause:* Caused by mutations in the *EVC* gene on chromosome 4p16. *Inheritance:* AR. *Prevalence:* Rare, increased in Amish.

Reference: Avolio, A., Jr., Berman, A.T., & Israelite, C.L. (1994). Ellis-van Creveld syndrome (chondroectodermal dysplasia). *Orthopedics, 17,* 735–737.

facio-auriculo-vertebral spectrum   *See* oculoauriculovertebral spectrum.

faciodigitogenital dysplasia (FGDY)   *See* Aarskog-Scott syndrome.

FAE   Fetal alcohol effects; *former term for* alcohol-related neurodevelopmental defects (ARND; *see Chapter* 7).

familial dysautonomia (Riley-Day syndrome)   *Clinical features:* Absent or sparse tears, absence of fungiform papillae (knoblike projections) on tongue, postural hypotension, abnormal sweating, episodic vomiting, swallowing disorder, ataxia. *Associated complications:* Feeding difficulties, scoliosis, joint abnormalities, hypertension, aseptic **necrosis** of bones (damage to bony tissue unassociated with infection or injury). *Cause:* Mutation of the gene coding for beta-nerve growth factor localized to chromosome 9q31–q33. *Inheritance:* AR. *Prevalence:* Rare; 3% carrier frequency in Ashkenazi Jewish population.

References: Axelrod, F.B. (1998). Familial dysautonomia: A 47-year perspective. How technology confirms clinical acumen. *Journal of Pediatrics, 132,* S2–S5.

Blumenfeld, A., Slaugenhaupt, S.A., Axelrod, F.B., et al. (1993). Localization of the gene for familial dysautonomia on chromosome 9 and definition of DNA markers for genetic diagnosis. *Nature Genetics, 4,* 160–164.

FAS   *See* fetal alcohol syndrome; *see also Chapter* 7.

fetal alcohol effects (FAE)   *Former term for* alcohol-related neurodevelopmental effects (ARND); *see Chapter* 7.

fetal alcohol syndrome (FAS)   *See Chapter* 7.

References: American Academy of Pediatrics, Committee on Substance Abuse & Committee on Children with Disabilities. (2000). Fetal alcohol syndrome and alcohol-related neurodevelopmental disorders. *Pediatrics, 106,* 358–361.

Weinberg, N.Z. (1997). Cognitive and behavioral deficits associated with parental alcohol use. *Journal of the American Academy of Child and Adolescent Psychiatry, 36,* 1177–1186.

fetal face syndrome   *See* Robinow syndrome.

fetal hydantoin syndrome   phenytoin syndrome; *see Chapter* 3.

FGDY   faciogenital dysplasia; *see* Aarskog-Scott syndrome.

5p– syndrome   *See* cri-du-chat syndrome.

45,X   *See* Turner syndrome.

47,X   *See* XXX, XXXX, and XXXXX syndromes.

fragile X syndrome   *Clinical features:* Prominent jaw, macroorchidism (large testes), large ears, attention-deficit/hyperactivity disorder, or autism-like behavior. Affected males (full mutation) often have moderate to severe mental retardation. Of females with a full mutation, 33% have average intelligence; 33% have average intelligence with significant learning disabilities; and 33% have mental retardation, occasional pervasive developmental disorder, or psychiatric disorders. *Associated complications:* Abnormalities of connective tissue with finger joint hypermobility or joint instability, mitral valve prolapse. *Cause:* Mutation in *FMR1* gene on Xq27–q28; molecular analysis reveals an increase in cytosine-guanine-guanine (CGG) trinucleotide repeats in the coding sequence of the FMR1 gene. Normal allele sizes vary from 6 to 50 CGG repeats. Phenotypically unaffected individuals have premutations, with allele size ranging from 50 to 200. Allele sizes of greater than 230 CGG repeats generally indicate a full mutation with phenotypic expression of the syndrome. *Inher-*

itance: X-linked with genetic imprinting (full mutations are not inherited from the father) and anticipation (number of repeats may increase in subsequent generations). *Prevalence:* 1/2,000 males; 1/4,000 females. *See also Chapter 17.*

References: Fisch, G.S., Carpenter, N.J., Holden, J.J., et al. (1999). Longitudinal assessment of adaptive and maladaptive behaviors in fragile X males: Growth, development, and profiles. *American Journal of Medical Genetics, 83,* 257–263.

Maes, B., Fryns, J.P., Ghesquiere, P., et al. (2000). Phenotypic checklist to screen for fragile X syndrome in people with mental retardation. *Mental Retardation, 38,* 207–215.

Friedreich ataxia   *Clinical features:* Slowly progressive neurological disorder characterized by limb and gait ataxia, dysarthria, nystagmus, **pes cavus** (high-arched feet), kyphoscoliosis. In rare cases, progression is rapid. Onset is before adolescence. *Associated complications:* Delayed motor milestones, cardiomyopathy (heart muscle weakness), and/or congestive heart failure; increased risk of insulin-dependent diabetes mellitus; impaired color vision. *Cause:* Usually homozygous guanine-adenosine-adenosine (GAA) expansions in the *frataxin* gene on chromosome 9q13. *Inheritance:* AR. *Prevalence:* Approximately 1/100,000. *Treatment:* Supportive care includes physical therapy, orthopedic surgery to correct progressive scoliosis, close cardiology follow-up. Some groups have had minimal success with a diet restrictive in carbohydrates.

References: Shapiro, F., & Specht, L. (1993). The diagnosis and orthopaedic treatment of childhood spinal muscular atrophy, peripheral neuropathy, Friedreich ataxia, and arthrogryposis. *Journal of Bone and Joint Surgery, 75,* 1699–1714.

Wood, N.W. (1998). Diagnosing Friedreich's ataxia. *Archives of Disease in Childhood, 78,* 204–207.

G syndrome   *See* Opitz syndrome.

galactosemia   *Clinical features:* Jaundice, lethargy, hypotonia in the newborn period; failure to thrive with vomiting and diarrhea; cataracts; liver dysfunction. Varying degrees of intellectual impairment (severe if untreated). In 70% of treated children, IQ score is less than 90; 50% have significant visual-perceptual impairments. Verbal dyspraxia is also seen in 62% of treated infants. *Associated complications:* Ovarian failure, hemolytic anemia, increased risk of sepsis (particularly *E. coli* in neonate), cerebellar ataxia, tremors, choreoathetosis. *Cause:* A deficiency of the enzyme galactose-1-phosphate uridyltransferase or, less commonly, galactokinase (both are enzymes required for digestion of galactose, a natural sugar found in milk). The *GALT* gene is on chromosome 9p13. *Inheritance:* AR. *Prevalence:* 1/50,000–1/70,000 in the United States. *Treatment:* Galactose-free diet.

References: Hansen, T.W., Henrichsen, B., Rasmussen, R.K., et al. (1996). Neuropsychological and linguistic follow-up studies of children with galactosaemia from an unscreened population. *Acta Paediatrica, 85,* 1197–1201.

Schweitzer, S., Shin, Y., Jakobs, C., et al. (1993). Long-term outcome in 134 patients with galactosemia. *European Journal of Pediatrics, 152,* 36–43.

Gaucher disease   *Clinical features:* Three clinically distinct forms, the most common of which (type I) has onset in adulthood and no central nervous system involvement. Types II and III have enlarged spleen, hematological abnormalities, bony lesions, abnormalities of skin pigmentation, and varying degrees of mental retardation. *Associated complications:* Seizures, oculomotor abnormalities. *Cause:* Accumulation of glucosylceramide due to deficiency of the enzyme beta-glucosidase on chromosome 1q21. *Inheritance:* AR. *Prevalence:* Rare; type I increased in Ashkenazi Jewish population. *Treatment:* Enzyme replacement therapy, bone marrow transplantation.

References: Elstein, D., Abrahamov, A., Hadas-Halpern, I., et al. (1999). Recommendations for diagnosis, evaluation, and monitoring of patients with Gaucher disease. *Archives of Internal Medicine, 159,* 1254–1255.

Frenkel, E.P. (1993). Gaucher disease: A heterogeneous clinical complex for which effective enzyme replacement has come of age. *American Journal of the Medical Sciences, 305,* 331–344.

globoid cell leukodystrophy   *See* Krabbe disease.

glutaric acidemia, type I   *Clinical features:* A disorder of organic acid metabolism, hypotonia, movement disorder and seizures present during the first year of life; macrocephaly is common. This disorder may mimic extrapyramidal cerebral palsy. *Associated complications:* Episodic acidosis, vomiting, lethargy, and coma. Mental retardation is usual, although intellectual functioning may remain intact. *Cause:* Mutations in the glutaryl-CoA dehydrogenase gene on chromosome 19p13.2 result in accumulation of glutaric acid and to a lesser degree of 3-hydroxyglutaric and glutaconic acids. *Inheritance:* AR. *Prevalence:* Rare; 1/30,000 in Sweden and more common in the Amish population. *Treatment:* Diet low in lysine and supplemental oral carnitine.

References: Baric, I., Zschocke, J., Christensen, E., et al. (1998). Diagnosis and management of glutaric aciduria type I. *Journal of Inherited Metabolic Disease, 21,* 326–340.

Hoffmann, G.F., & Zschocke, J. (1999). Glutaric aciduria type I: From clinical, biochemical and molecular diversity to successful therapy. *Journal of Inherited Metabolic Disease, 22,* 381–391.

glutaric acidemia, type II (multiple acyl-CoA dehydrogenase deficiency)   *Clinical features:* An inborn error of metabolism that may present in infancy with severe metabolic acidosis, hypoglycemia, and cardiomyopathy. The urine has a characteristic odor of sweaty feet similar to that present in isovaleric acidemia. Dysmorphic facial features (macrocephaly, large anterior fontanelle [soft spot], high forehead, flat nasal bridge, and malformed ears) are seen in one half of cases. This condition also can present later in life with episodic vomiting, acidosis, and hypoglycemia. *Associated complications:* Muscle weakness, liver disease, cataracts, respiratory distress, renal (kidney) cysts. *Cause:* Defective dehydrogenation of isovaleryl-CoA and butyryl-CoA; gene linked to chromosome 15q23–q25. *Inheritance:* AR. *Prevalence:* Rare. *Treatment:* Diet with supplemental riboflavin and carnitine.

> *References:* al-Essa, M.A., Rashed, M.S., Bakheet, S.M., et al. (2000). Glutaric aciduria type II: Observations in seven patients with neonatal- and late-onset disease. *Journal of Perinatology, 20,* 120–128.
>
> Frerman, F.E., & Goodman, S.I. (1995). Glutaric acidemia type II. In C.R. Scriver, A.L. Beaudet, W.S. Sly, et al. (Eds.), *The metabolic and molecular bases of inherited disease* (pp. 1619–1623). New York: McGraw-Hill.

glycogen storage diseases (glycogenoses)   *Clinical features:* More than 12 forms of glycogen storage diseases are currently known, and there is a wide spectrum of clinical features among them. They share varying degrees of liver and muscle abnormalities, and patient organs have excessive glycogen accumulation. Types I (glucose-6-phosphate deficiency), II (Pompe disease, acid alpha-glucosidase deficiency), III (amylo-1,6-glycosidase deficiency), and VI (hepatic phosphorylase deficiency) are the most common and represent almost 90% of cases. Common clinical features include hypoglycemia, short stature, enlarged spleen, and muscle weakness. *Associated complications:* Hypotonia, renal (kidney) abnormalities, gouty arthritis, bleeding abnormalities, hypertension, respiratory distress. Type II disease characteristically has severe cardiac, muscle, and neurological involvement. *Cause:* Deficiencies in the various enzymes involved in the synthesis or degradation of glycogen. There are many genes and chromosome locations associated with glycogenoses. *Inheritance:* All except type VIII are inherited as AR; type VIII is XLR. *Prevalence:* Combined prevalence of 1/20,000–1/25,000. *Treatment:* Dietary treatment has been shown to reduce hypoglycemia, prevent growth and developmental problems, and can mollify the biochemical abnormalities. (No specific treatment is yet available for any of the glycogenoses. Increased protein intake and overnight tube feeding of starch to maintain normoglycemia have been shown to be useful for supportive care.) Liver transplantation has been attempted in types I, III, and IV, with correction of the biochemical abnormalities but not all sequelae.

> *References:* Chen, Y.T., & Burchell, A. (1995). Glycogen storage diseases. In C.R. Scriver, A.L. Beaudet, W.S. Sly, et al. (Eds.), *The metabolic and molecular bases of inherited disease* (pp. 935–965). New York: McGraw-Hill.
>
> Wolfsdorf, J.I., Holm, I.A., & Weinstein, D.A. (1999). Glycogen storage diseases: Phenotypic, genetic, and biochemical characteristics, and therapy. *Endocrinology and Metabolism Clinics of North America, 28,* 801–823.

GM2 gangliosidosis, type I   *See* Tay-Sachs disease.

Goldenhar syndrome   *See* oculoauriculovertebral spectrum.

Hallermann-Streiff syndrome (oculomandibulodyscephaly with hypotrichosis)   *Clinical features:* Proportionate short stature; characteristic facial appearance, including small eyes, small, pinched nose, and small mouth; sparse, thin hair; frontal bossing (prominent central forehead). *Associated complications:* Various eye abnormalities, including nystagmus, strabismus, cataracts, and/or decreased visual acuity; neonatal teeth and other dental abnormalities; narrow upper airway or **tracheomalacia** (softening of the tracheal cartilages), with related respiratory difficulty; frequent respiratory infections, snoring, and feeding difficulties. *Cause:* Unknown, believed to be genetic. *Inheritance:* Most reported cases SP. *Prevalence:* 150 cases known to exist.

> *References:* Cohen, M.M., Jr. (1991). Hallermann-Streiff syndrome: A review. *American Journal of Medical Genetics, 41,* 488–499.
>
> David, L.R., Finlon, M., Genecov, D., et al. (1999). Hallermann-Streiff syndrome: Experience with 15 patients and review of the literature. *The Journal of Craniofacial Surgery, 10,* 160–168.

hemifacial microsomia   *See* oculoauriculovertebral spectrum.

hereditary progressive arthroophthalmopathy   *See* Stickler syndrome.

holocarboxylase synthetase deficiency   *See* multiple carboxylase deficiency, infantile or early form.

holoprosencephaly   *Clinical features:* This classification encompasses a spectrum of midline defects of the brain and face. The most severe are incompatible with life. Individuals who survive have varying degrees of disability ranging from typical development with hypotelorism (widely spaced eyes) to alobar holoprosencephaly (brain without segmentation into hemispheres) and cyclopia (single central eye). *Associated complications:* Seizures, endocrine abnormalities, micropenis, cleft of retinae. *Cause:* Genetically heterogeneous; sonic hedgehog (*SHH*) gene on chromosome 7q36 implicated in some cases; many cases have involved mutations in different genes, such as those located at 2p21 (*SIX3* gene), 13q32 (*ZIC2* gene), or 18p11.3 (*TGIF* gene). *Inheritance:* May be part of a syndrome or caused by teratogenic exposure; as an isolated birth defect may be AD or AR. *Prevalence:* 1/16,000.

> *References:* Barr, M., Jr., & Cohen, M.M., Jr. (1999). Holoprosencephaly survival and performance. *American Journal of Medical Genetics, 89,* 116–120.
>
> Elias, D.L., Kawamoto, H.K., & Wilson, L.F. (1992). Holoprosencephaly and midline facial anomalies: Redefining classification and management. *Plastic and Reconstructive Surgery, 90,* 951–958.

Holt-Oram syndrome *Clinical features:* Upper-limb defect ranging from hypoplastic (incompletely formed), abnormally placed or absent thumbs; to hypoplasia of radius, ulna, or humerus (arm bones); to complete **phocomelia** (foreshortened limbs); affected individuals also have congenital heart defect (atrial septal defect, ventricular septal defect most common). *Associated complications:* Occasional abnormalities of chest muscles and vertebral anomalies. *Cause:* Mutations in the *TBX5* gene on chromosome 12q2. *Inheritance:* AD with variable expression; may increase in severity with each generation. *Prevalence:* Unknown.

> *References:* Basson, C.T., Cowley, G.S., Solomon, S.D., et al. (1994). The clinical and genetic spectrum of Holt-Oram syndrome (heart-hand syndrome). *New England Journal of Medicine, 330,* 885–891.
>
> Newbury-Ecob, R.A., Leanage, R., Raeburn, J.A., et al. (1996). Holt-Oram syndrome: A clinical genetic study. *Journal of Medical Genetics, 33,* 300–307.

homocystinuria *Clinical features:* Downward dislocation of lens of the eye (with myopia); tall, slim physique; hypopigmentation (fair skin); and sparse, thin hair. Two forms have been described, differing in their responsiveness to pyridoxine (vitamin B_6). *Associated complications:* Mild to moderate mental retardation in one half to three fourths of untreated individuals; increased risk of myocardial infarction and stroke because of thrombosis (blood clot); behavioral disorders, cataracts, or glaucoma; scoliosis; osteoporosis. *Cause:* Inherited defect in the enzyme cystathionine beta-synthetase caused by mutations in a gene on chromosome 21q22. *Inheritance:* AR. *Prevalence:* 1/200,000. *Treatment:* Folic acid supplementation, use of betaine hydrochloride, and dietary restriction of methionine have shown promise; pyridoxine is used in the rare individuals who have the pyridoxine-responsive form of the disease. Early treatment with pyridoxine in responsive cases may allow typical intelligence.

> *References:* Kraus, J.P. (1994). Molecular basis of phenotype expression in homocystinuria. *Journal of Inherited Metabolic Disease, 17,* 383–390.
>
> Yap, S., & Naughten, E. (1998). Homocystinuria due to cystathionine beta-synthase deficiency in Ireland: 25 years' experience of a newborn screened and treated population with reference to clinical outcome and biochemical control. *Journal of Inherited Metabolic Disease, 21,* 738–747.

Hunter syndrome (MPS II) *See* mucopolysaccharidoses (MPS).

Huntington disease (*previously called* Huntington chorea), juvenile *Clinical features:* Progressive neurological disorder that can present in childhood, although the mean age of onset is 40 years. Children present with dysarthria, clumsiness, hyperreflexia, rigidity, and oculomotor disturbances. *Associated complications:* Joint contractures, swallowing dysfunction, seizures. *Cause:* Expansion of CAG (cytosine-adenine-guanine) trinucleotide repeat in *huntingtin* gene on chromosome 4p16.3; normal number of CAG repeats is 11–34; affected individuals have 37–86 CAG repeats. *Inheritance:* AD; affected children have a greater number of repeats, and the disease allele is always paternally inherited. Progression in children with paternally inherited disease is more rapid than in children with maternally inherited disease. *Prevalence:* 4/100,000–7/100,000.

> *References:* Gomez-Tortosa, E., del Barrio, A., Garcia Ruiz, P.J., et al. (1998). Severity of cognitive impairment in juvenile and late-onset Huntington disease. *Archives of Neurology, 55,* 835–843.
>
> Prudon, S.E., Mohr, E., Ilivitsky, V., et al. (1994). Huntington's disease: Pathogenesis, diagnosis and treatment. *Journal of Psychiatry and Neuroscience, 19,* 359–367.

Hurler syndrome (MPS IH) *See* mucopolysaccharidoses (MPS).

hypophosphatasia *Clinical features:* A disorder of calcium and phosphate metabolism with a severe infantile form (which can be rapidly fatal) and a relatively mild childhood form. The neonatal form presents as short limbs and poor ossification of the skeleton. Features of both include short stature, bowed long bones, craniosynostosis, hypocalcemia. *Associated complications:* Seizures, multiple fractures, premature loss of teeth. *Cause:* Mutations in the bone/liver/kidney alkaline phosphatase gene on chromosome 1p36. *Inheritance:* AR. *Prevalence:* 1/100,000.

References: Whyte, M.P. (1995). Hypophosphatasia. In C.R. Scriver, A.L. Beaudet, W.S. Sly, et al. (Eds.), *The metabolic and molecular bases of inherited disease* (pp. 4095–4111). New York: McGraw-Hill.

Zurutuza, L., Muller, F., Gibrat, J.F., et al. (1999). Correlations of genotype and phenotype in hypophosphatasia. *Human Molecular Genetics, 8,* 1039–1046.

incontinentia pigmenti   *Clinical features:* Swirling patterns of hyperpigmented skin lesions; tooth abnormalities; microcephaly; ocular abnormalities; thin, wiry hair; mental retardation in approximately one third of cases. *Associated complications:* Spasticity, seizures, vertebral or rib abnormalities; hydrocephalus. *Cause:* Mutations in *NEMO* gene on chromosome Xq28. *Inheritance:* XLD with lethality in males. *Prevalence:* Rare.

References: Landy, S.J., & Donnai, D. (1993). Incontinentia pigmenti (Bloch-Sulzberger syndrome). *Journal of Medical Genetics, 30,* 53–59.

Smahi, A., Courtois, G., Vabres, P., et al. (2000). Genomic rearrangement in NEMO impairs NF-kappa-B activation and is a cause of incontinentia pigmenti. *Nature, 405,* 466–472.

infantile Refsum disease   *See* Refsum disease, infantile.

isovaleric acidemia   *Clinical features:* A disorder of organic acid metabolism. An acute, often fatal neonatal form is characterized by acidosis and coma; a chronic form presents with recurrent attacks of ataxia, vomiting, lethargy, and ketoacidosis. Attacks are generally triggered by infection or increased protein load. Urine smell of sweaty feet is characteristic. *Associated complications:* Seizures, mental retardation if untreated, enlarged liver, vomiting, hematologic abnormalities. *Cause:* Deficiency of the enzyme isovaleryl-CoA dehydrogenase; gene linked to chromosome 15q14–q15. *Inheritance:* AR. *Prevalence:* Rare. *Treatment:* Treatment consisting of a low-protein diet with supplemental oral glycine and carnitine has resulted in a relatively good cognitive outcome.

References: Berry, G.T., Yudkoff, M., & Segal, S. (1988). Isovaleric acidemia: Medical and neurodevelopmental effects of long-term therapy. *Journal of Pediatrics, 113,* 58–64.

Mehta, K.C., Zsolway, K., Osterhoudt, K.C., et al. (1996). Lessons from the late diagnosis of isovaleric acidemia in a five-year-old boy. *Journal of Pediatrics, 129,* 309–310.

Joubert syndrome   *Clinical features:* Structural cerebellar abnormalities, abnormal eye movements, retinal dysplasia or coloboma, episodic hyperventilation. *Associated complications:* Hypoplasia of corpus callosum, encephalocele (hernia of part of the brain and meninges through a skull defect), kidney cysts, microcephaly, abnormalities of the tongue, hypotonia, mental retardation. *Cause:* Gene linked to 9q34.3 in some families. *Inheritance:* AR. *Prevalence:* Rare.

References: Fennell, E.B., Gitten, J.C., Dede, D.E., et al. (1999). Cognition, behavior, and development in Joubert syndrome. *Journal of Child Neurology, 14,* 592–596.

Gitten, J., Dede, D., Fennell, E., et al. (1998). Neurobehavioral development in Joubert syndrome. *Journal of Child Neurology, 13,* 391–397.

juvenile neuronal ceroid lipofuscinosis   *See* Batten disease.

Kearns-Sayre syndrome   *See* mitochondrial disorders.

kinky hair syndrome   *See* Menkes syndrome.

Klinefelter syndrome (XXY syndrome)   *Clinical features:* Occurring only in males; tall, slim stature; long limbs; relatively small penis and testes; gynecomastia in 40%. *Associated complications:* Intention tremor (involuntary trembling arising when attempting a voluntary, coordinated movement) in 20%–50%, low to average intelligence, infertility, behavioral disorders, scoliosis, 8% have diabetes mellitus as adults. *Cause:* Chromosomal nondisjunction resulting in 47,XXY karyotype. *Inheritance:* SP. *Prevalence:* 1/500 males. *Treatment:* Hormone treatment is needed in adolescence for the development of secondary sex characteristics.

References: Geschwind, D.H., Boone, K.B., Miller, B.L., et al. (2000). Neurobehavioral phenotype of Klinefelter syndrome. *Mental Retardation and Developmental Disabilities Research Reviews, 6,* 107–116.

Smyth, C.M., & Bremner, W.J. (1998). Klinefelter syndrome. *Archives of Internal Medicine 158,* 1309–1314.

Klippel-Feil syndrome   *Clinical features:* Cervical vertebral fusion, hemivertebrae (incomplete development of one side of one or more vertebrae). *Associated complications:* Torticollis; low hairline; sacral agenesis; hearing loss; occasional congenital heart defect; extra, fused, or missing ribs; middle ear abnormalities. *Cause:* Subgroup has been linked to chromosome 8q22.2. *Inheritance:* AD with variable expressivity and reduced penetrance most common; AR and nongenetic causes have been reported. *Prevalence:* Unknown.

References: Clarke, R.A., Catalan, G., Diwan, A.D., et al. (1998). Heterogeneity in Klippel-Feil syndrome: A new classification. *Pediatric Radiology, 28,* 967–974.

McGaughran, J.M., Kuna, P., & Das, V. (1998). Audiological abnormalities in the Klippel-Feil syndrome. *Archives of Disease in Childhood, 79,* 352–355.

Klippel-Trenauny-Weber syndrome   *Clinical features:* Asymmetric hypertrophy of limb, hemangiomas (benign congenital tumors made up of newly formed blood vessels). *Associated complications:* Platelet deficiency. *Cause:* Unknown. *Inheritance:* Believed to be SP. *Prevalence:* Unknown.

References: Berry, S.A., Peterson, C., Mize, W., et al. (1998). Klippel-Trenauny syndrome. *American Journal of Medical Genetics, 79,* 319–326.

Samuel, M., & Spitz, L. (1995). Klippel-Trenauny-Weber syndrome: Clinical features, complications, and management in children. *British Journal of Surgery, 82,* 757–761.

Krabbe disease (globoid cell leukodystrophy)   *Clinical features:* In the classic form of this progressive neurological disorder, symptoms begin at 4–6 months of age with irritability, progressive stiffness, optic atrophy, mental deterioration, and early death. Approximately 10%–15% of cases have onset of symptoms between 15 months and 17 years and have slower disease progression. *Associated complications:* Hypertonicity, opisthotonos (back arching), visual and hearing impairment, episodic unexplained fevers, seizures. *Cause:* Accumulation of psychosine galactosylceramide caused by a galactocerebrosidase enzyme deficiency resulting from a mutation in the *GALC* gene on chromosome 14q24.3–q32.1. *Inheritance:* AR. *Prevalence:* 0.5/100,000–1/100,000; may be increased in Jewish, Sicilian, and Scandinavian populations. *Treatment:* Hematopoietic stem cell transplantation has been performed in a small number of patients, but success is unclear.

References: Krivit, W., Shapiro, E.G., Peters, C., et al. (1998). Hematopoietic stem-cell transplantation in globoid-cell leukodystrophy. *New England Journal of Medicine, 338,* 1119–1126.

Wenger, D.A., Rafi, M.A., Luzi, P., et al. (2000). Krabbe disease: Genetic aspects and progress toward therapy. *Molecular Genetics and Metabolism, 70,* 1–9.

Landau-Kleffner syndrome   *Clinical features:* Selective aphasia (loss of speech), regression in receptive and/or expressive language ability, with some recovery in older children; seizures; paroxysmal electroencephalogram; electrical status epilepticus in slow wave sleep with or without clinical seizures. *Associated complications:* Behavioral disturbances similar to those in pervasive developmental disorders (see Chapter 20). *Cause:* Unknown. *Inheritance:* Possibly AR. *Prevalence:* Unknown; at least 170 children have been reported in the medical literature. *Treatment:* Treatment of seizures with antiepileptic medications. *See also Chapter 25.*

References: Appleton, R.E. (1995). The Landau-Kleffner syndrome. *Archives of Disease in Childhood, 72,* 386–387.

Gordon, N. (1997). The Landau-Kleffner syndrome: Increased understanding. *Brain Development, 19,* 311–316.

Laurence-Moon-Bardet-Biedl syndrome   *See* Bardet-Biedl syndrome.

Leber hereditary optic neuropathy   *See* mitochondrial disorders.

Leber's congenital amaurosis   *See* mitochondrial disorders.

Leigh syndrome   *See* mitochondrial disorders.

Lennox-Gastaut syndrome   *See Chapter 25.*

Lesch-Nyhan syndrome   *Clinical features:* An inborn error of purine metabolism associated with elevated levels of uric acid in blood and urine. Affected males appear normal at birth but dyskinetic movements and spasticity develop, accompanied by severe self-injurious behavior, including biting of fingers, arms, and lips. *Associated complications:* Seizures in 50%, hematuria (blood in urine), kidney stones, and ultimate kidney failure. *Cause:* Defect in enzyme hypoxanthine-guanine phosphoribosyltransferase caused by a mutation in the *HPRT* gene on Xq26–q27.2. *Inheritance:* XLR. *Prevalence:* Rare. *Treatment:* Allopurinol is useful in preventing kidney and joint deposition of uric acid. Numerous medications have been used in management of self-injurious behavior without much success.

References: Matthews, W.S., Solan, A., Barabas, G., et al. (1999). Cognitive functioning in Lesch-Nyhan syndrome: A 4-year follow-up study. *Developmental Medicine and Child Neurology, 41,* 260–262.

Olson, L., & Houlihan, D. (2000). A review of behavioral treatments used for Lesch-Nyhan syndrome. *Behavior Modification, 24,* 202–222.

lissencephaly syndromes (e.g., Miller-Dieker syndrome)   *Clinical features:* A group of disorders in which Miller-Dieker syndrome is the prototype. Features include agyria or **pachygyria** (absent or decreased cerebral convolutions, respectively); progressive spasticity; microcephaly; characteristic facial appearance with short nose, broad nasal bridge, upturned nose, hypertelorism, prominent upper lip, malformed or malpositioned ears. *Associated complications:* Mental retardation, infantile spasms, late tooth eruption, failure to thrive, **dysphagia** (swallowing difficulty), congenital heart defect, intestinal atresia (congenital closure), agenesis of corpus callosum (90%). *Cause:* Incomplete development of the brain, with resulting smooth surface; 90% of affected individuals have submicroscopic deletions on chromosome 17p13.3. *Inheritance:* SP; possibly increased recurrence risk if one parent has a balanced chromosomal translocation of chromosome 17p. *Prevalence:* Rare.

References: Dobyns, W.B., & Truwit, C.L. (1995). Lissencephaly and other malformations of cortical development: 1995 update. *Neuropediatrics, 26,* 132–147.

Leventer, R.J., Pilz, D.T., Matsumoto, N., et al. (2000). Lissencephaly and subcortical band heterotopia: Molecular basis and diagnosis. *Molecular Medicine Today, 6,* 277–284.

Lowe syndrome (oculocerebrorenal syndrome)   *Clinical features:* Bilateral cataracts at birth, hypotonia, absent deep tendon reflexes, kidney dysfunction. *Associated complications:* Failure to thrive, vitamin D–resistant rickets, visual impairment, glaucoma, mental retardation in 75%, behavioral problems, intention tremor, craniosynostosis, peripheral neuropathy (damage to nerves). *Cause:* Abnormal inositol phosphate metabolism, caused by mutations in the *OCRL1* gene on chromosome Xq26.1. *Inheritance:* XLR. *Prevalence:* Rare.

References: Charnas, L.R., Bernardini, I., Rader, D., et al. (1991). Clinical and laboratory findings in the oculocerebrorenal syndrome of Lowe, with special reference to growth and renal function. *New England Journal of Medicine, 324,* 1318–1325.

Kenworthy, L., & Charnas, L. (1995). Evidence for a discrete behavioral phenotype in the oculocerebrorenal syndrome of Lowe. *American Journal of Medical Genetics, 59,* 283–290.

mandibulofacial dysostosis   *See* Treacher Collins syndrome.

maple syrup urine disease (MSUD)   *Clinical features:* A disorder of branched chain amino acid metabolism with four identified clinical variants (classic, intermittent, intermediate, and thiamine-responsive). The classic form comprises 75% of cases and is characterized by severe opisthotonos, hypertonia, hypoglycemia, lethargy, and respiratory difficulties. It is most often fatal within 1 month. Untreated survivors have severe mental retardation and spasticity. The intermittent form presents with periods of ataxia, behavior disturbances, drowsiness, and seizures. Attacks are triggered by infections, excessive protein intake, or other physiological stresses. Individuals with the intermediate form usually demonstrate mild to moderate mental retardation. *Associated complications:* Acidosis, hypoglycemia, growth retardation, feeding problems. *Cause:* Deficiency in branched chain alpha-ketoacid dehydrogenase caused by mutations in the genes (at chromosomal locations 1p31, 6p22–p21, and 19q13.1–q13.2) making up this enzyme complex. *Prevalence:* 1/220,000; increased prevalence in Mennonite population. *Inheritance:* AR. *Treatment:* High-calorie diet with restriction of branched chain amino acids. If instituted early (within 2 weeks of birth), the prognosis is good for typical intelligence. Thiamine is used in the thiamine-responsive form.

References: Chuang, D.T. (1998). Maple syrup urine disease: It has come a long way. *Journal of Pediatrics, 132*(3, Pt. 2), S17–S23.

Chuang, D.T., & Shih, V.E. (1995). Disorders of branched-chain amino acid and ketoacid metabolism. In C.R. Scriver, A.L. Beaudet, W.S. Sly, et al. (Eds.), *Metabolic and molecular bases of inherited disease* (pp. 1239–1277). New York: McGraw-Hill.

Marfan syndrome   *Clinical features:* Tall, thin body; upward dislocation of ocular lens; myopia; spider-like limbs; hypermobile joints. Average intelligence expected. *Associated complications:* Aortic dilatation, congestive heart failure, mitral valve prolapse, emphysema, sleep apnea, and scoliosis. *Cause:* Mutation in the *fibrillin* gene located on chromosome 15q15–q21.3. *Inheritance:* AD with wide clinical variability. *Prevalence:* 1/10,000.

References: Gray, J.R., & Davies, S.J. (1996). Marfan syndrome. *Journal of Medical Genetics, 33,* 403–408.

Pyeritz, R.E. (2000). The Marfan syndrome. *Annual Review of Medicine, 51,* 481–510.

Maroteaux-Lamy syndrome (MPS VI)   *See* mucopolysaccharidoses (MPS).

McCune-Albright syndrome (polyostotic fibrous dysplasia)   *Clinical features:* Large café-au-lait spots with irregular borders, fibrous dysplasia of bones (thinning of the bone with replacement of bone marrow with fibrous tissue, producing pain and increasing deformity), bowing of long bones, premature onset of puberty, advanced bone age. *Associated complications:* Hearing or visual impairment, hyperthyroidism, **hyperparathyroidism** (increased activity of the parathyroid gland, which controls calcium metabolism), abnormal adrenal function, increased risk of malignancy, occasional spinal cord anomalies. *Cause:* Mutation in the *GNAS1* gene (causing a defect in the enzyme adenyl cyclase) localized to 20q13. *Inheritance:* AD; theoretically lethal unless present in the mosaic form. *Prevalence:* Unknown.

Reference: de Sanctis, C., Lala, R., Matarazzo, P., et al. (1999). McCune-Albright syndrome: A longitudinal clinical study of 32 patients. *Journal of Pediatric Endocrinology and Metabolism, 12,* 817–826.

MELAS   *m*itochondrial myopathy, *e*ncephalopathy, *l*actic *a*cidosis, and *s*troke-like episodes; *see* mitochondrial disorders.

Menkes syndrome (kinky hair syndrome)   *Clinical features:* An inborn error of copper metabolism presenting at age 1–2 months with "steely" texture of hair and characteristic face with pudgy cheeks. *Associated com-*

plications: Seizures, feeding difficulties; severe mental retardation; recurrent infections; visual loss; bony abnormalities, with tendency toward easy fracture; early death. *Cause:* Copper deficiency from decreased absorption and/or missing enzymes, caused by mutations in the adenosine triphosphatase *ATP7A* gene at Xq13. *Inheritance:* XLR. *Prevalence:* 1/200,000.

References: Bankier, A. (1995). Menkes disease. *Journal of Medical Genetics, 32,* 213–215.

Menkes, J.H. (1999). Menkes disease and Wilson disease: Two sides of the same copper coin. Part I: Menkes disease. *European Journal of Paediatric Neurology, 3,* 147–158.

MERRF   *m*yoclonic *e*pilepsy with *r*agged *r*ed *f*ibers; *see* mitochondrial disorders.

metachromatic leukodystrophy (sulfatide lipidosis)   *Clinical features:* One of a group of lysosomal storage disorders in which *lysosomes,* the cell structures that digest toxic materials, are missing a necessary enzyme. The resulting accumulation of toxins leads to varying degrees of progressive neurological impairment ranging from unsteady gait to severe rigidity and choreoathetosis. Muscle weakness and ataxia are common. Onset of the infantile form is by age 2 years and usually results in death by age 5. The juvenile form generally begins between 4 and 10 years of age, is more rare, and progresses more slowly. *Associated complications:* Seizures, abdominal distension, mental deterioration. *Cause:* Mutations in the arylsulfatase A (*ASA*) gene on chromosome 22q cause ASA enzyme deficiency. *Inheritance:* AR. *Prevalence:* 1/40,000 in Sweden; rarer elsewhere. *Treatment:* Bone marrow transplantation may slow the progression of the illness in juvenile-onset cases.

Reference: Gieselmann, V., Zlotogora, J., Harris, A., et al. (1994). Molecular genetics of metachromatic leukodystrophy. *Human Mutation, 4,* 233–242.

methylmalonic aciduria   *Clinical features:* In symptomatic cases, this disorder of organic acid metabolism is characterized by repeated episodes of vomiting, lethargy, and coma resulting from acidosis. On newborn screening analyses, some individuals with this metabolic abnormality may remain asymptomatic. *Associated complications:* Seizures, neutropenia (decreased white blood count), osteoporosis, infections, feeding abnormalities, mental retardation. *Cause:* Deficiency of enzyme methylmalonyl-CoA mutase (caused by mutation in the *MUT* gene at 6p21). *Inheritance:* AR. *Prevalence:* 1/20,000. *Treatment:* Treatment consists of a low-protein diet and supplemental vitamin B_{12} in those who have a B_{12}-responsive form; supplementation with carnitine is also used.

Reference: van der Meer, S.B., Poggi, F., Spada, M., et al. (1994). Clinical outcome of long-term management of patients with vitamin B_{12}-unresponsive methylmalonic acidemia. *Journal of Pediatrics, 125,* 903–908.

Miller-Dieker syndrome   *See* lissencephaly syndromes.

mitochondrial disorders (mitochondrial encephalopathies and myopathies)   *Clinical features:* This diverse group of disorders is linked by a common etiology: abnormal function of the mitochondria (energy-producing cell structures) or mitochondrial metabolism. Common features seen in patients with mitochondrial disorders include ptosis, external ophthalmoplegia (paralysis of the external eye muscles), myopathy, cardiomyopathy. *Associated complications:* Seizures, sensorineural deafness, optic atrophy, retinitis pigmentosa (changes in retina causing loss of peripheral vision and clumping of pigment), diabetes, migraine, exercise intolerance. *Cause:* Genes encoding nuclear DNA and mitochondrial DNA (mtDNA) are known to cause mitochondrial disorders. Mutations in different genes may cause the same symptoms. *Inheritance:* AR, AD, SP, or may be inherited from the mother through mtDNA. *Prevalence:* 1/8,500 for all mitochondrial disorders combined. *Treatment:* Early diagnosis and treatment of diabetes, eye abnormalities, and cardiac disease. Coenzyme Q10 and riboflavin have been used with some reported benefit. Five mitochondrial disorders are discussed next.

References: Chinnery, P.F., & Turnbull, D.M. (1999). Mitochondrial DNA and disease. *Lancet, 354*(Suppl. 1), S117–S121.

Read, C.Y., & Calnan, R.J. (2000). Mitochondrial disease: Beyond etiology unknown. *Journal of Pediatric Nursing, 15,* 232–241.

Kearns-Sayre syndrome   *Clinical features:* Short stature, progressive ophthalmoplegia, cardiomyopathy, retinitis pigmentosa. *Associated complications:* visual impairment, hearing loss, myopathy, ataxia, endocrine abnormalities, diabetes mellitus. *Cause:* Rearrangements in mtDNA. *Inheritance:* Maternal, through mtDNA.

Leber hereditary optic neuropathy (Leber's congenital amaurosis)   *Clinical features:* Bilateral central vision loss. *Associated complications:* Occasionally seen with multiple sclerosis, dystonia, or movement disorder. *Cause:* Primarily associated with point mutations in mtDNA. *Inheritance:* Maternal, through mtDNA.

Leigh syndrome (subacute necrotizing encephalomyopathy)   *Clinical features:* Encephalopathy, ophthalmoplegia, optic atrophy, myopathy. *Associated complications:* Developmental delay and regression, ataxia, spasticity, early death. *Cause:* Deficiency of cytochrome *c* oxidase (COX) or another enzyme involved in energy metabolism. *Inheritance:* Maternal, AR, XLR.

MELAS (*m*itochondrial myopathy, *e*ncephalopathy, *l*actic *a*cidosis, and *s*troke-like episodes)   *Clinical features:* Migraine headaches, seizures, stroke-like episodes, encephalopathy (degenerative disease of the brain), myopathy. *Associated complications:* Progressive hearing loss, cortical blindness, ataxia, dementia, and lactic acidosis. *Cause:* A mutation in mtDNA encoding transfer RNA causes reduced mitochondrial protein synthesis. *Inheritance:* Maternal, through mtDNA.

MERRF (*m*yoclonic *e*pilepsy with *r*agged *r*ed *f*ibers)   *Clinical features:* Myoclonic epilepsy, ataxia, spasticity, myopathy. *Associated complications:* Optic atrophy, sensorineural hearing loss, peripheral neuropathy, diabetes, cardiomyopathy. Characteristic ragged red muscle fibers are seen on muscle biopsy examination. *Cause:* Mutations in mtDNA encoding transfer RNA. *Inheritance:* Usually maternal, through mtDNA.

Moebius sequence (congenital facial diplegia)   *Clinical features:* Expressionless face and facial weakness due to palsies of the 6th, 7th, and occasionally 12th cranial nerves; occasional abnormalities of fingers; micrognathia. *Associated complications:* Feeding difficulties, oral motor dysfunction, articulation disorder, occasional tracheal or laryngeal anomalies. Mental retardation in 10%–50%. *Cause:* Linked to chromosomes 13q12–q13 and 1p34. *Inheritance:* Mostly SP; rare reports of AD with variable expressivity. *Prevalence:* Rare. *References:* Johansson, M., Wentz, E., Fernell, E., et al. (2001). Autistic spectrum disorders in Mobius sequence: A comprehensive study of 25 individuals. *Developmental Medicine and Child Neurology, 43*, 338–345. Kumar, D. (1990). Moebius syndrome. *Journal of Medical Genetics, 27*, 122–126.

monosomy X   *See* Turner syndrome.

Morquio syndrome (MPS IV)   *See* mucopolysaccharidoses (MPS).

MSUD   *See* maple syrup urine disease.

mucopolysaccharidoses (MPS)   *Clinical features:* A group of lysosomal storage disorders (defined in the entry about metachromatic leukodystrophy) in which glycosaminoglycans accumulate within the lysosomes. There are seven distinguishable forms, each with two or more subgroups. Features shared by most include coarse facial features, thick skin, corneal clouding, and organomegaly (enlargement of spleen and liver). Growth deficiency, mental retardation, and skeletal dysplasia are also seen. Most are AR. The various MPS disorders are differentiated by their clinical features, enzymatic defects, genetic transmission, and urinary **mucopolysaccharide** pattern. Hunter (MPS II), Hurler (MPS IH), and Sanfilippo (MPS III) syndromes are discussed next. Others include Morquio (MPS IV), Scheie (MPS V), Maroteaux-Lamy (MPS VI), and Sly (MPS VII) syndromes. *References:* Bax, M.C., & Colville, G.A. (1995). Behaviour in mucopolysaccharide disorders. *Archives of Disease in Childhood, 73*, 77–81. Neufeld, E.F., & Muenzer, J. (1995). The mucopolysaccharidoses. In C.R. Scriver, A.L. Beaudet, W.S. Sly, et al. (Eds.), *The metabolic and molecular bases of inherited disease* (pp. 2465–2494). New York: McGraw-Hill.

Hurler syndrome (MPS IH)   *Clinical features:* Short stature; gradual coarsening of facial features in early childhood, including hypertrichosis; large skull; organomegaly; prominent lips; corneal clouding; **dysostosis** (soft bones); stiffening of joints. There is progressive mental deterioration and spasticity. *Associated complications:* Chronic ear infections, hearing loss, occasional hernia and cardiac valve changes, visual impairment, brain cysts, airway obstruction. *Cause:* Deficiency of enzyme alpha-L-iduronidase caused by mutations in the iduronidase gene on 4p16.3. *Inheritance:* AR. *Prevalence:* 1/144,000. *Treatment:* Bone marrow transplantation has shown some success in early treated cases.

Hunter syndrome (MPS II)   *Clinical features:* Type IIA is severe; type IIB is mild. Features include short stature; enlarged liver and spleen; coarsening of facial features, with hypertrichosis beginning in early childhood. Mental retardation is mild or absent in type IIB; this subtype is compatible with survival to adulthood. Type IIA is highlighted by progressive mental deterioration first noted between 2 and 3 years of age; death occurs before age 15 in most cases and is similar to MPS IH, but with clear corneas. *Associated complications:* Sensorineural deafness; retinitis pigmentosa with visual loss; macrocephaly; stiffening of joints, particularly those in the hands; cardiac valve disease in 90%, hernia; respiratory insufficiency; chronic diarrhea in 65%; seizures in 66%. *Cause:* Deficiency of enzyme iduronate 2-sulfatase caused by mutations in this gene on Xq28. *Inheritance:* XLR. *Prevalence:* 1/110,000–1/132,000. *Treatment:* Minimal success has been reported with bone marrow transplantation.

Sanfilippo syndrome (MPS III)   *Clinical features:* Four distinct types representing four different enzyme defects with similar clinical features. There is mild coarsening of facial features, absence of corneal clouding, mild enlargement of liver, joint stiffness, and progressive mental deterioration. Deterioration is most rapid in type IIIA; death occurs by 10–20 years in most cases. *Associated complications:* Severe behavioral disturbances by age 4–6 years, dysostosis, diarrhea in 50%, progressive spasticity and ataxia, central breathing problems with advancing disease. *Cause:* Type IIIA: deficiency of enzyme heparan sulfatase caused by mutations in sulfamidase gene on 17q25.3. Type IIIB: deficiency of enzyme alpha-*N*-acetylglucosaminidase caused by mutations in the *NAGLU* gene on 17q21. Type IIIC: deficiency of enzyme acetyl-CoA:alpha-glucosaminide *N*-acetyltransferase caused by mutations in a gene linked to chromosome 14. Type IIID: deficiency of enzyme *N*-acetyl-alpha-glucosaminine-6-sulfatase caused by mutations in the *G6S* gene linked to chromosome 12q14. *Inheritance:* AR. *Prevalence:* 1/24,000. *Treatment:* Treatment is supportive only. Bone marrow transplantation has not been successful.

multiple acyl-CoA dehydrogenase deficiency   *See* glutaric acidemia, type II.

multiple carboxylase deficiency, infantile or early form (holocarboxylase synthetase deficiency)   *Clinical features:* Disorder of organic acid metabolism characterized by seizures, lethargy, coma, skin rash, alopecia (loss of hair from skin areas where it is normally present), and acidosis. Often, the presenting feature is respiratory distress. *Associated complications:* Mental retardation, hearing impairment, optic atrophy with visual impairment, recurrent infections, vomiting. *Cause:* Mutations causing enzyme deficiencies of holocarboxylase synthetase, biotinidase, or 3-methylcrotonyl-CoA carboxylase. *Inheritance:* AR. *Prevalence:* Rare. *Treatment:* Oral biotin supplementation. Prenatal treatment with oral biotin corrects lethargy, hypotonia, and vomiting. *Reference:* Wolf, B. (1995). Disorders of biotin metabolism. In C.R. Scriver, A.L. Beaudet, W.S. Sly, et al. (Eds.), *The metabolic and molecular bases of inherited disease* (pp. 3151–3177). New York: McGraw-Hill.

multiple carboxylase deficiency, late onset, juvenile form (biotinidase deficiency)   *Clinical features:* A disorder characterized by varying degrees of mental retardation, hypotonia, seizures (often infantile spasms), alopecia, skin rash, and lactic acidosis. The onset of symptoms usually occurs between 2 weeks and 2 years of age. *Associated complications:* Hearing and visual impairment, respiratory difficulties and apnea, recurrent infections. *Cause:* Defects in various enzymes for biotin transport or metabolism. Genetic mutations have been identified in the biotinidase gene on chromosome 3p25 and the holocarboxylase synthetase gene on chromosome 21q22.1. *Inheritance:* AR. *Prevalence:* 1/166,000. *Treatment:* Supplementation with oral biotin; response is better if used early in the course of the disease.

References: Baumgartner, E.R., & Suormala, T. (1997). Multiple carboxylase deficiency: Inherited and acquired disorders of biotin metabolism. *International Journal for Vitamin and Nutrition Research, 67,* 377–384.

Wolf, B. (1995). Disorders of biotin metabolism. In C.R. Scriver, A.L. Beaudet, W.S. Sly, et al. (Eds.), *The metabolic and molecular bases of inherited disease* (pp. 3151–3177). New York: McGraw-Hill.

muscular dystrophy, Duchenne (DMD) and Becker (BMD) types   *Clinical features:* Progressive proximal muscular degeneration, muscle wasting, hypertrophy (enlargement) of calves, cardiomyopathy. Onset of symptoms in DMD occurs before 3 years. Loss of ability to walk independently by adolescence. The onset in BMD is later, and the progression is slower. *Associated complications:* Congestive heart failure, scoliosis, flexion contractures, respiratory compromise, and intestinal motility dysfunction (causing constipation). Approximately one third of boys with DMD have learning disabilities. *Cause:* Mutations in the gene that encodes dystrophin localized to Xp21.1. *Inheritance:* XLR. *Incidence:* DMD 1/3,500 male births; BMD 1/20,000 males. *Treatment:* Glucocorticosteroids have been shown to prolong ambulation. *See also Chapter 14.*

References: Billard, C., Gillet, P., Barthez, M., et al. (1999). Reading ability and processing in Duchenne muscular dystrophy and spinal muscular atrophy. *Developmental Medicine and Child Neurology, 40,* 12–20.

Escolar, D.M., & Scacheri, C.G. (2001). Pharmacologic and genetic therapy for childhood muscular dystrophies. *Current Neurology and Neuroscience Reports, 1,* 168–174.

myotonic dystrophy   *Clinical features:* The most prominent feature is **myotonia,** a form of dystonia involving increased muscular contractility combined with decreased power to release (e.g., a strong handshake with the inability to release it). Other features include myopathy, ptosis, and frontal balding. The age of onset varies from childhood to adulthood. The congenital form is severe, with neonatal hypotonia, motor delay, mental retardation, and facial muscle palsy. In the congenital form, feeding difficulties and severe respiratory problems are common. Classic myotonia does not begin until around 10 years of age. *Associated complications:* Cataracts, cardiac conduction abnormalities, diabetes, and hypogonadism. *Cause:* Cytosine-thymine-guanine (CTG) expansion mutations in muscle protein kinase gene on chromosome 19q13. Severity varies with the number of CTG repeats: Unaffected people have 5–30 repeat copies. Those with the classical adult form have more than 80 copies, and individuals with the childhood onset form usually have more than 500 copies. The correlation between the number of repeats and severity and age of onset, however, is not always consistent. *Inheritance:* AD with genetic anticipation. With rare exception, it is the mother who transmits mutations causing the congenital form. *Prevalence:* 1/10,000–1/25,000; increased prevalence in certain areas of Quebec.

References: Perini, G.I., Menegazzo, E., Ermani, M., et al. (1999). Cognitive impairment and (CTG)n expansion in myotonic dystrophy patients. *Biological Psychiatry, 46,* 425–431.

Steyaert, J., Umans, S., Willekens, D., et al. (1997). A study of the cognitive and psychological profile in 16 children with congenital or juvenile myotonic dystrophy. *Clinical Genetics, 52,* 135–141.

Nager syndrome   *See* acrofacial dysostosis.

neonatal adrenoleukodystrophy   *See* adrenoleukodystrophy, neonatal form.

neurofibromatosis, type I (von Recklinghausen disease)   *Clinical features:* Multiple café-au-lait spots, axillary (armpit) and inguinal (groin) freckling, nerve tumors (fibromas) in body and on skin, Lisch nodules (brown bumps on the iris of the eye). *Associated complications:* Glaucoma, scoliosis, hypertension, attention-deficit/hyperactivity disorder, macrocephaly or hydrocephalus, visual and hearing impairments, increased risk of numerous malignant and benign tumors, increased risk of learning disabilities. *Cause:* Mutation in *NF1* gene, which codes for neurofibromin protein, on chromosome 17q11.2. *Inheritance:* AD with variable expression. Approximately 50% represent new mutations. *Prevalence:* 1/3,500.

References: Johnson, N.S., Saal, H.M., Lovell, A.M., et al. (1999). Social and emotional problems in children with neurofibromatosis type 1: Evidence and proposed interventions. *Journal of Pediatrics, 134,* 767–772.

North, K.N., Riccardi, V., Samango-Sprouse, C., et al. (1997). Cognitive function and academic performance in neurofibromatosis 1: Consensus statement from the NF1 Cognitive Disorders Task Force. *Neurology, 48,* 1121–1127.

neurofibromatosis, type II   *Clinical features:* Bilateral vestibular schwannomas (benign tumors of auditory nerve), cranial and spinal tumors, neuropathy. Café-au-lait spots (usually fewer than six). In contrast to type I, no Lisch nodules or axillary freckling are seen. *Associated complications:* Deafness (average age of onset is 20 years), cataracts or other ocular abnormalities. *Cause:* Mutation in tumor-suppressor (*NF2*) gene encoding merlin protein on chromosome 22q12.2. *Inheritance:* AD; up to 50% may represent new mutations. *Prevalence:* 1/200,000 Incidence: 1/40,000.

References: MacCollin, M., & Mautner, V.F. (1998). The diagnosis and management of neurofibromatosis 2 in childhood. *Seminars in Pediatric Neurology, 5,* 243–252.

Martuza, R.L., & Eldridge, R. (1988). Neurofibromatosis 2 (bilateral acoustic neurofibromatosis). *New England Journal of Medicine, 318,* 684–688.

neuronal ceroid lipofuscinosis, juvenile   *See* Batten disease.

Niemann-Pick disease, types A and B   *Clinical features:* Lysosomal storage disorder. Type A presents in infancy with failure to thrive, enlarged liver and spleen, rapidly progressive neurological decline. Death occurs by age 2–3 years. Type B is variable but is compatible with survival to adulthood and may cause few or no neurological abnormalities. *Associated complications:* Mental retardation, ataxia, myoclonus, eye abnormalities, coronary artery disease, lung disease. *Cause:* Sphingomyelinase enzyme deficiency caused by mutations in the sphingomyelinase (*SMPD*) gene on chromosome 11p15.4. *Inheritance:* AR. *Prevalence:* Rare; increased in Ashkenazi Jewish population.

References: Kolodny, E.H. (2000). Niemann-Pick disease. *Current Opinion in Hematology, 7,* 48–52.

Schuchman, E.H., & Desnick, R.J. (1995). Niemann-Pick disease types A and B: Acid sphingomyelinase deficiencies. In C.R. Scriver, A.L. Beaudet, W.S. Sly, et al. (Eds.), *The metabolic and molecular bases of inherited disease* (pp. 2601–2624). New York: McGraw-Hill.

Noonan syndrome   *Clinical features:* Short stature; characteristic facial features, including triangular shape, deep philtrum, downslanting palpebral fissures, ptosis; low-set ears; low posterior hair line; short or webbed neck; congenital heart defects (usually pulmonary valve stenosis); shield-shaped chest. *Associated complications:* Sensorineural deafness, malocclusion of teeth, articulation difficulties, bleeding abnormalities. *Cause:* Unknown. *Inheritance:* Half of reported cases are SP; may be AD with variable expression. *Prevalence:* 1/1,000–1/2,500.

References: van der Burgt, I., Thoonen, G., Roosenboom, N., et al. (1999). Patterns of cognitive functioning in school-aged children with Noonan syndrome associated with variability in phenotypic expression. *Journal of Pediatrics, 135,* 707–713.

Wood, A., Massaran, A., Super, M., et al. (1995). Behavioral aspects and psychiatric findings in Noonan syndrome. *Archives of Disease in Childhood, 72,* 153–155.

oculoauriculovertebral spectrum (facio-auriculo-vertebral spectrum; Goldenhar syndrome; hemifacial microsomia)   *Clinical features:* Unilateral external ear deformity ranging from absence of ear to microtia (tiny ear), preauricular (earlobe) tags or pits, middle-ear anomaly with variable hearing loss, facial asymmetry with small size unilaterally, **macrostomia** (large mouth), occasional cleft palate, microphthalmia or eyelid coloboma. *Associated complications:* Vertebral anomalies, occasional heart and renal (kidney) defects, mental retardation in 10%. *Cause:* Unknown. *Inheritance:* Usually SP, occasionally AD; genetically heterogeneous. *Prevalence:* 1/45,000 in Northern Ireland, presumably less common in other populations.

References: Cohen, M.S., Samango-Sprouse, C.A., & Stern, H.J., et al. (1995). Neurodevelopmental profile of infants and toddlers with oculo-auriculo-vertebral spectrum and the correlation of prognosis with physical findings. *American Journal of Medical Genetics, 60,* 535–540.

Schaefer, G.B., Olney, A.H., & Kolodziej, P. (1998). Oculo-auriculo-vertebral spectrum. *Ear, Nose, and Throat Journal, 77,* 17–18.

oculocerebrorenal syndrome   *See* Lowe syndrome.

oculomandibulodyscephaly with hypotrichosis   *See* Hallermann-Streiff syndrome.

Optiz syndrome (Opitz-Frias syndrome; Opitz oculogenitolaryngeal syndrome; *previously called* G syndrome)   (G refers to surname of original patient described.) *Clinical features:* Hypertelorism, hypospadias, dysphagia, bifurcated (divided) nasal tip, widow's peak, occasional cleft lip/palate, mild to moderate mental retardation in two thirds of affected individuals. *Associated complications:* Gastroesophageal reflux; esophageal dysmotility (poor movement of food through the esophagus); hoarse cry; occasional congenital heart defect or agenesis of corpus callosum; platelet abnormalities; structural cerebellar anomalies, including Dandy-Walker malformation. *Cause:* Genes believed to cause Opitz syndrome are linked to 22q11.2 and Xp22. *Inheritance:* AD and XLR. *Prevalence:* Unknown.

References: Bershof, J.F., Guyuron, B., & Olsen, M.M. (1992). G syndrome: A review of the literature and a case report. *Journal of Cranio-Maxillo-Facial Surgery, 20,* 24–27.

Conlon, B.J., & O'Dwyer, X. (1995). The G syndrome/Opitz oculo-genital-laryngeal syndrome/Opitz BBB/G syndrome/Opitz-Frias syndrome. *Journal of Laryngology and Otology, 109,* 244–246.

osteogenesis imperfecta   *Clinical features:* Four clinically distinct forms of this metabolic disease of bone have been described. Type I is characterized by bone fragility and blue sclera. Type II usually presents with severe bone deformity and death in the newborn period. Type III is characterized by progressive bone deformity. Type IV is clinically similar to type I but presents with normal sclerae, milder bone deformity, variable short stature, and dental abnormalities. *Associated complications:* Increased prevalence of fractures (may be confused with physical abuse) that decreases after puberty; scoliosis; mitral valve prolapse; occasionally progressive adolescent-onset hearing loss. *Cause:* Mutations in one of the genes regulating collagen formation. All types map to 17q21–q22 (*COLA1*) and 7q21–q22 (*COLA2*). *Inheritance:* Type I and IV: AD; type II: AD (all type II cases are new mutations; recurrence risk is 6% due to gonadal mosaicism); type III is occasionally AR. *Prevalence:* 1/30,000. *Treatment:* Cyclic intravenous pamidronate therapy to increase bone mineral density. *(See Chapter 14.)*

References: Binder, H., Conway, A., Hason, S., et al. (1993). Comprehensive rehabilitation of the child with osteogenesis imperfecta. *American Journal of Medical Genetics, 45,* 265–269.

Cinman, N. (2001). Osteogenesis imperfecta: A life not so fragile. *Lancet, 358*(Suppl.), S46.

pentasomy X   *See* XXX, XXXX, and XXXXX syndromes.

Pfeiffer syndrome (acrocephalosyndactyly, type V)   *Clinical features:* Mild craniosynostosis with brachycephaly, flat midface, broad thumbs and toes, hypertelorism, and partial syndactyly. *Associated complications:* Hydrocephalus, hearing impairment, seizures, occasional mental retardation. *Cause:* Mutations in the genes that code for fibroblast growth factor receptors 1 and 2 (*FGFR1* and *FGFR2*) on chromosomes 8p11.2–p11.1 and 10q26, respectively. *Inheritance:* AD with many cases due to new mutations. *Prevalence:* Unknown.

References: Plomp, A.S., Hamel, B.C., Cobben, J.M., et al. (1998). Pfeiffer syndrome type 2: Further delineation and review of the literature. *American Journal of Medical Genetics, 75,* 245–251.

Robin, N.H., Scott, J.A., Arnold, J.E., et al. (1998). Favorable prognosis for children with Pfeiffer syndrome types 2 and 3: Implications for classification. *American Journal of Medical Genetics, 75,* 240–244.

phenylketonuria (PKU)   *Clinical features:* Inborn error of amino acid metabolism without acute clinical symptoms. Mental retardation, microcephaly, abnormal gait, and seizures may develop in untreated individuals. Pale skin and blond hair are common features. *Associated complications:* Behavioral disturbances, cataracts, skin disorders, movement disorders. *Cause:* Classically caused by a deficiency of the enzyme phenylalanine hydroxylase, which is caused by a mutation in the *PAH* gene at 12q24.1. *Inheritance:* AR. *Prevalence:* 1/10,000 among Caucasians in the United States. *Treatment:* Early identification is available through newborn screening. A phenylalanine-restricted, low-protein diet should be continued at least throughout childhood and, in females, during childbearing years. Specialized formulas are available for individuals who need to be on the restricted diet. *See also Chapter 18.*

References: Berenbaum, S.A. (1999). Neuropsychological follow-up in neonatal screening: Issues, methods and findings. *Acta Paediatrica Supplement, 88*(432), 83–87.

Sullivan, J.E., & Chang, P. (1999). Review: Emotional and behavioral functioning in phenylketonuria. *Journal of Pediatric Psychology, 24,* 281–299.

phenytoin syndrome (fetal hydantoin syndrome)   *See Chapter 3.*

Reference: Buehler, B.A., Rao, V., & Finnell, R.H. (1994). Biochemical and molecular teratology of fetal hydantoin syndrome. *Neurologic Clinics, 12,* 741–748.

Pierre-Robin sequence   *Clinical features:* Micrognathia, cleft palate, **glossoptosis** (downward displacement of tongue). *Associated complications:* Neonatal feeding problems, apnea or respiratory distress, upper airway obstruction. *Cause:* Impaired closure of the posterior palatal shelves early in development. This defect can be an isolated finding or can be associated with trisomy 18 or other syndromes. *Inheritance:* AR; a rare X-linked form also exists. *Prevalence:* Unknown.

References: Caouette-Laberge, L., Bayet, B., & Larocque, Y. (1994). The Pierre Robin sequence: Review of 125 cases and evolution of treatment modalities. *Plastic and Reconstructive Surgery, 93,* 934–942.

Kapp-Simon, K.A., & Krueckeberg, S. (2000). Mental development in infants with cleft lip and/or palate. *The Cleft Palate-Craniofacial Journal, 37,* 65–70.

PKU   *See* phenylketonuria.

polyostotic fibrous dysplasia   *See* McCune-Albright syndrome.

Prader-Willi syndrome   *Clinical features:* Short stature; failure to thrive in infancy, hyperphagia (increased appetite); almond-shaped eyes; viscous (thick) saliva; hypotonia, particularly in neck region; hypogonadism with cryptorchidism; small hands and feet. *Associated complications:* Mental retardation, behavior problems, obstructive sleep apnea, neonatal temperature instability. *Cause:* Approximately 75% have a microdeletion on the long arm of the paternally inherited chromosome 15 (15q11–q13); 25% have maternal uniparental disomy. *Inheritance:* AD, usually SP. *Prevalence:* 1/25,000.

References: Einfeld, S.L., Smith, A., Durvasula, S., et al. (1999). Behavior and emotional disturbance in Prader-Willi syndrome. *American Journal of Medical Genetics, 82,* 123–127.

Holland, A.J., Treasure, J., Coskeran, P., et al. (1995). Characteristics of the eating disorder in Prader-Willi syndrome: Implications for treatment. *Journal Intellectual Disability Research, 39*(Pt. 5), 373–381.

propionic acidemia   *Clinical features:* A disorder of organic acid metabolism characterized by episodes of vomiting, lethargy, and coma; hypotonia; bone marrow suppression; characteristic facies with puffy cheeks and exaggerated Cupid's bow upper lip. *Associated complications:* Impaired antibody production, mental retardation, seizures in half, abnormalities of muscle tone. *Cause:* Deficiency of enzyme propionyl-CoA carboxylase caused by mutations in the *PCCA* gene on chromosome 13q32 and the *PCCB* gene on chromosome 3q21–q22. *Inheritance:* AR. *Prevalence:* 1/2,000–1/5,000 in Saudi Arabia; rare elsewhere. *Treatment:* Treatment consists of a diet low in valine, isoleucine, threonine, and methionine, with supplement of carnitine. A commercial formula is available.

Reference: North, K.N., Korson, M.S., Gopal, Y.R., et al. (1995). Neonatal-onset propionic acidemia: Neurologic and developmental profiles, and implications for management. *Journal of Pediatrics, 126,* 916–922.

Refsum disease, infantile   *Clinical features:* Failure to thrive, absent or tiny ear lobes, high forehead, single palmar crease, flat facial profile and nasal bridge, retinal degeneration, hypotonia, liver enlargement and dysfunction. *Associated complications:* Sensorineural hearing impairment, mental retardation, peripheral neuropathy, hypercholesterolemia (elevated blood cholesterol level). There is also a late-onset form of this disease. *Cause:* Accumulation of phytanic acid, very long chain fatty acids, di- and trihydroxycholestanoic acids, and pipecolic acid, due to defect in peroxisomal function. *Inheritance:* AR. *Prevalence:* Rare.

References: Moser, A.B., Rasmussen, M., Naidu, S., et al. (1995). Phenotype of patients with peroxisomal disorders subdivided into sixteen complementation groups. *Journal of Pediatrics, 127,* 13–22.

Weinstein, R. (1999). Phytanic acid storage disease (Refsum's disease): Clinical characteristics, pathophysiology and the role of the therapeutic apheresis in its management. *Journal of Clinical Apheresis, 14,* 181–184.

retinitis pigmentosa   *Clinical features:* A group of diseases associated with retinal degeneration, constricted visual fields, and progressive blindness. Initial symptom is night blindness occurring in adolescence or adult life. *Associated complications:* May occur as an isolated condition or as part of a genetic syndrome (e.g., Usher syndrome, mitochondrial disorders). *Cause:* Believed to have many different genetic causes. *Inheritance:* AR in 70% of cases; AD and XLR less commonly seen. Recurrence risk depends on cause and family history. *Prevalence:* 1/2,000–1/7,000.

References: Pagon, R.A. (1988). Retinitis pigmentosa. *Survey of Ophthalmology, 33,* 137–177.

Sharma, R.K., & Ehinger, B. (1999). Management of hereditary retinal degenerations: Present status and future directions. *Survey of Ophthalmology, 43,* 427–444.

Rett syndrome (Rett disorder)   *Clinical features:* Normal development for 6–9 months, followed by progressive encephalopathy. Features of autism, loss of purposeful hand use with characteristic ringing of hands, hyperventilation, ataxia, spasticity. *Associated complications:* Postnatal onset of microcephaly, seizures. *Cause:* Mutations in the methyl-CpG binding protein 2 (*MeCP2*) gene at Xq28. *Inheritance:* XLD with severe, neonatal encephalopathy or lethality in males. *Prevalence:* 1/10,000–1/15,000 among females. *See also Chapter 20.*
References: Budden, S.S. (1997). Rett syndrome: Habilitation and management reviewed. *European Child and Adolescent Psychiatry, 6*(Suppl. 1), 103–107.
Hoffbuhr, K., Devaney, J., LaFleur, B., et al. (2001). MeCP2 mutations in children with and without the phenotype of Rett syndrome. *Neurology, 56,* 1486–1495.

Riley-Day syndrome   *See* familial dysautonomia.

Robinow syndrome (fetal face syndrome)   *Clinical features:* Slight to moderate short stature; short forearms; macrocephaly with frontal bossing (prominent central forehead); flat facial profile with apparent hypertelorism; small, upturned nose; hypogenitalism; micrognathia. *Associated complications:* Vertebral or rib anomalies, dental malocclusion, genital hypoplasia, inguinal (groin) hernia, enlarged liver and spleen. *Cause:* Mutations in the *ROR2* gene on 9q22. *Inheritance:* Rarely AD; AR form is most common, is clinically more severe, and is often accompanied by rib anomalies. *Prevalence:* Rare.
References: Robinow, M. (1993). The Robinow (fetal face) syndrome: A continuing puzzle. *Clinical Dysmorphology, 2,* 189–198.
Van Steensel, M. (1998). Robinow syndrome. *Journal of Medical Genetics, 35,* 349–350.

Rubinstein-Taybi syndrome   *Clinical features:* Growth retardation, broad thumbs and toes, maxillary hypoplasia (small upper jaw), slanted palpebral fissures, pouting lower lip, short upper lip, occasional agenesis of corpus callosum. *Associated complications:* Apnea, constipation, cardiac defects, keloid scar formation, glaucoma, mental retardation. *Cause:* Mutations of the CREB binding protein (*CBP*) gene on chromosome 16p13.3, most often an interstitial microdeletion of this chromosome locus. *Inheritance:* SP. *Prevalence:* 1/125,000.
References: Hennekam, R.C. (1993). Rubinstein-Taybi syndrome: A history in pictures. *Clinical Dysmorphology, 2,* 87–92.
Hennekam, R.C., Baselier, A.C., Beyaert, E., et al. (1992). Psychological and speech studies in Rubinstein-Taybi syndrome. *American Journal of Mental Retardation, 96,* 645–660.

Russell-Silver syndrome (Silver-Russell syndrome)   *Clinical features:* Short stature of prenatal onset; skeletal asymmetry with hemihypertrophy (enlargement of one side of the body) in 60%; triangular facies; beaked nose; thin upper lip; narrow, high-arched palate; blue sclerae; occasional café-au-lait spots; fifth finger clinodactyly; genital anomalies in males. *Associated complications:* Delayed fontanelle (soft spot) closure, hypocalcemia in neonatal period with sweating and rapid breathing, increased risk of fasting hypoglycemia as toddler, feeding difficulties, precocious sexual development, vertebral anomalies. *Cause:* Duplications or maternal uniparental disomy at 7p12–p11.2; some evidence that chromosome 17q25 may be a cause in subset of cases. *Inheritance:* AD (usually new mutation); maternal uniparental disomy in 10%; AR in rare cases. *Prevalence:* Unknown.
References: Hitchins, M.P., Stanier, P., Preece, M.A., et al. (2001). Silver-Russell syndrome: A dissection of the genetic aetiology and candidate chromosomal regions. *Journal of Medical Genetics, 38,* 810–819.
Price, S.M., Stanhope, R., Garrett, C., et al. (1999). The spectrum of Silver-Russell syndrome: A clinical and molecular genetic study and new diagnostic criteria. *Journal of Medical Genetics, 36,* 837–842.

Sanfilippo syndrome (MPS III)   *See* mucopolysaccharidoses (MPS).

Scheie syndrome (MPS V)   *See* mucopolysaccharidoses (MPS).

Silver-Russell syndrome   *See* Russell-Silver syndrome.

Sly syndrome (MPS VII)   *See* mucopolysaccharidoses (MPS).

Smith-Lemli-Opitz syndrome   *Clinical features:* Microcephaly, short nose with upturned nostrils, low serum cholesterol, syndactyly of second and third toes, genitourinary abnormalities. *Associated complications:* Hypotonia, moderate to severe mental retardation, seizures, feeding difficulties and vomiting, photosensitivity, occasional heart defect. *Cause:* Defect in cholesterol metabolism caused by mutations in the sterol delta-7-reductase gene on chromosome 11q12–q13. *Inheritance:* AR. *Prevalence:* 1/20,000–1/40,000. *Treatment:* Dietary modifications, including increased cholesterol ingestion.
References: Elias, E.R., Irons, M.B., Hurley, A.D., et al. (1997). Clinical effects of cholesterol supplementation

in six patients with the Smith-Lemli-Opitz syndrome (SLOS). *American Journal of Medical Genetics, 68,* 305–310.

Opitz, J.M. (1994). RSH/SLO ("Smith-Lemli-Opitz") syndrome: Historical, genetic, and developmental considerations. *American Journal of Medical Genetics, 50,* 344–346.

Smith-Magenis syndrome   *Clinical features:* Short stature, brachycephaly, cleft palate, congenital heart defect, myopia, midface hypoplasia, prominent chin, varying degrees of mental retardation. *Associated complications:* Genital or vertebral anomalies, scoliosis, hearing impairment, self-injurious behavior, other behavior problems. *Cause:* Microdeletion of 17p11.2. *Inheritance:* AD (most represent new mutations). *Prevalence:* 1/25,000.

References: Dykens, E.M., & Smith, A.C. (1998). Distinctiveness and correlates of maladaptive behaviour in children and adolescents with Smith-Magenis syndrome. *Journal of Intellectual Disability Research, 42*(Pt. 6), 481–489.

Greenberg, F., Lewis, R.A., Potocki, L., et al. (1996). Multi-disciplinary clinical study of Smith-Magenis syndrome (deletion 17p11.2). *American Journal of Medical Genetics, 62,* 247–254.

Sotos syndrome   *Clinical features:* An overgrowth syndrome characterized by a distinctive head shape, macrocephaly, downslanting eyes, flat nasal bridge, accelerated growth with advanced bone age, high forehead, hypertelorism, prominent jaw. *Associated complications:* Increased risk of abdominal tumors, hypotonia, marked speech delay, congenital heart defects, varying degrees of cognitive impairment. *Cause:* Gene that may be linked to chromosome 3p21. *Inheritance:* AD. *Prevalence:* At least 105 cases have been reported in the medical literature.

References: Cole, T.R.P., & Hughes, H.E. (1994). Sotos syndrome: A study of the diagnostic criteria and natural history. *Journal of Medical Genetics, 31,* 20–32.

Opitz, J.M., Weaver, D.W., & Reynolds, J.F., Jr. (1998). The syndromes of Sotos and Weaver: Reports and review. *American Journal of Medical Genetics, 79,* 294–304.

spongy degeneration of central nervous system   *See* Canavan disease.

Stickler syndrome (hereditary progressive arthroophthalmopathy)   *Clinical features:* Flat facies, myopia, cleft of hard or soft palate, **spondyloepiphyseal dysplasia** (lag of mineralization of bone). *Associated complications:* Hypotonia, hyperextensible joints, occasional scoliosis, risk of retinal detachment, cataracts, arthropathy in late childhood or adulthood, occasional hearing loss or cognitive impairment. *Cause:* Mutations in type 2 and type 11 procollagen genes (*COL2A1, COL11A1, COL11A2*), which have been linked to 12q13.11–q13.2, 1p21, and 6p21.3, respectively. *Inheritance:* AD with variable expression. *Prevalence:* 1/20,000.

References: Lewkonia, R.M. (1992). The arthropathy of hereditary arthroophthalmopathy (Stickler syndrome). *Journal of Rheumatology, 19,* 1271–1275.

Snead, M.P., & Yates, J.R. (1999). Clinical and molecular genetics of Stickler syndrome. *Journal of Medical Genetics, 36,* 353–359.

Sturge-Weber syndrome   *Clinical features:* Flat facial "port wine stains," seizures. *Associated complications:* Glaucoma, hemangiomas (benign congenital tumors made up of newly formed blood vessels) of meninges. May be progressive in some cases, with gradual visual or cognitive impairment. *Cause:* Unknown. *Inheritance:* Usually SP, AD in a few reported cases. *Prevalence:* 0.15/1,000.

References: Powell, J. (1999). Update on hemangiomas and vascular malformations. *Current Opinion in Pediatrics, 11,* 457–463.

Sujansky, E., & Conradi, S. (1995). Outcome of Sturge-Weber syndrome in 52 adults. *American Journal of Medical Genetics, 57,* 35–45.

subacute necrotizing encephalomyopathy   Leigh syndrome; *see* mitochondrial disorders.

sulfatide lipidosis   *See* metachromatic leukodystrophy.

TAR syndrome   *See* thrombocytopenia-absent radius syndrome.

Tay-Sachs disease (GM2 gangliosidosis, type I)   *Clinical features:* A lysosomal storage disorder leading to a progressive neurological condition characterized by deafness, blindness, and seizures. Development is typical for the first several months of life. Subsequently, there is an increased startle response, hypotonia followed by hypertonia, cherry-red spot in maculae, optic nerve atrophy. Rapid decline and fatality by age 5 years. An adult form of this enzyme deficiency presents with ataxia. *Associated complications:* Feeding abnormalities, aspiration. *Cause:* Deficiency of the enzyme hexosaminidase A caused by mutation in the gene at 15q23–q24. *Inheritance:* AR. *Prevalence:* 1/112,000; 1/3,800 in Ashkenazi Jewish population.

Reference: Gravel, R.A., Clarke, J.T.R., Kaback, M.M., et al. (1995). The GM2 gangliosidoses. In C.R. Scriver, A.L. Beaudet, W.S. Sly, et al. (Eds.), *The metabolic and molecular bases of inherited disease* (pp. 2839–2879). New York: McGraw-Hill.

tetrasomy X   *See* XXX, XXXX, and XXXXX syndromes.

thrombocytopenia-absent radius syndrome (TAR syndrome)   *Clinical features:* Radial aplasia (absence of one of the lower arm bones) with normal thumbs, thrombocytopenia (platelet deficiency). *Associated complications:* Knee joint abnormalities, neonatal foot swelling, occasional congenital heart or renal (kidney) defect. *Cause:* Unknown. *Inheritance:* AR. *Prevalence:* Unknown.

References: MacDonald, M.R., Schaefer, G.B., Olney, A.H., et al. (1994). Hypoplasia of the cerebellar vermis and corpus callosum in thrombocytopenia with absent radius syndrome on MRI studies. *American Journal of Medical Genetics, 50,* 46–50.

McLaurin, T.M., Bukrey, C.D., Lovett, R.J., et al. (1999). Management of thrombocytopenia-absent radius (TAR) syndrome. *Journal of Pediatric Orthopedics, 19,* 289–296.

Treacher Collins syndrome (mandibulofacial dysostosis)   *Clinical features:* Characteristic facial appearance with malformation of external ears, small chin, flattened midface, cleft palate. *Associated complications:* Conductive or mixed (conductive and sensorineural) hearing loss, defects of middle and inner ear, respiratory and feeding problems, apnea. Intelligence is average in 95% of cases. *Cause:* Mutations in *TCOF1* gene on chromosome 5q32–q33. *Inheritance:* AD. *Prevalence:* Unknown. *Treatment:* Surgical repair of most malformations.

References: Posnick, J.C. (1997). Treacher Collins syndrome: Perspectives in evaluation and treatment. *Journal of Oral and Maxillofacial Surgery, 55,* 1120–1133.

Winter, R.M. (1996). What's in a face? *Nature Genetics, 12,* 124–129.

trisomy 13 syndrome   *Clinical features:* Microphthalmia, coloboma, corneal opacity, cleft lip and palate, polydactyly, scalp defects, dysmorphic features, low-set ears, flexion deformity of fingers. *Associated complications:* Cardiac defects, kidney and gastrointestinal tract anomalies, eye abnormalities, visual impairment, sensorineural hearing loss, profound mental retardation, cerebral palsy. *Cause:* Nondisjunction resulting in extra chromosome 13; rarely parental translocation. *Inheritance:* SP; may recur in families in presence of parental translocation. *Incidence:* 1/8,000 births.

References: Baty, B.J., Blackburn, B.L., & Carey, J.C. (1994). Natural history of trisomy 18 and trisomy 13: I. Growth, physical assessment, medical histories, survival, and recurrence risk. *American Journal of Medical Genetics, 49,* 175–188.

Matthews, A.L. (1999). Chromosomal abnormalities: Trisomy 18, trisomy 13, deletions, and microdeletions. *Journal of Perinatal and Neonatal Nursing, 13,* 59–75.

trisomy 18 syndrome (Edwards syndrome)   *Clinical features:* prenatal onset of growth retardation, low-set ears, clenched fists, congenital heart defects, microphthalmia, coloboma, corneal opacity; 30% die within first month of life, 50% by second month, and only 10% survive their first year. *Associated complications:* Feeding problems, aspiration, conductive hearing loss, profound mental retardation. *Cause:* Nondisjunction resulting in extra chromosome 18. *Inheritance:* SP. *Incidence:* 1/6,600 births.

References: Baty, B.J., Blackburn, B.L., & Carey, J.C. (1994). Natural history of trisomy 18 and trisomy 13: I. Growth, physical assessment, medical histories, survival, and recurrence risk. *American Journal of Medical Genetics, 49,* 175–188.

Matthews, A.L. (1999). Chromosomal abnormalities: Trisomy 18, trisomy 13, deletions, and microdeletions. *Journal of Perinatal and Neonatal Nursing, 13,* 59–75.

trisomy 21   *See* Down syndrome; *see also Chapter 16.*

trisomy X   *See* XXX, XXXX, and XXXXX syndromes.

tuberous sclerosis   *Clinical features:* Hypopigmented areas on skin, adenoma sebaceum (acne-like facial lesions), infantile spasms, iris depigmentation, retinal defects, calcium deposits in brain. *Associated complications:* Seizures, mild to moderate mental retardation, tumors of the heart, increased risk of malignancy, hypoplastic tooth enamel and dental pits, renal (kidney) cysts, hypertension. *Cause:* Mutations in the *TSC1* and *TSC2* genes on chromosomes 16p13 and 9q34, respectively. *Inheritance:* AD with variable expressivity. *Prevalence:* 1/10,000–1/50,000.

References: Curatolo, P. (1996). Neurological manifestations of tuberous sclerosis complex. *Child's Nervous System, 12,* 515–521.

Kwiatkowski, D.J., & Short, M.P. (1994). Tuberous sclerosis. *Archives of Dermatology, 130,* 348–354.

Turner syndrome (45,X; monosomy X)   *Clinical features:* Affecting females only, the physical features include short stature, broad chest with widely spaced nipples, short neck with low hairline and extra skin at nape ("webbed" appearance). *Associated complications:* "Streak" ovaries causing infertility and delayed puberty, congenital heart defect (often coarctation of aorta), small ear canals, chronic otitis media in 90% with frequent hearing loss, occasional thyroid or renal (kidney) disease. Intelligence is usually average, but prevalence of learning disabilities is high. *Cause:* Nondisjunction chromosome abnormality resulting in one copy of sex chromosome. *Inheritance:* SP. *Prevalence:* 1/5,000. *Treatment:* Growth hormone has been used successfully to increase eventual adult height. *(See also Chapter 1.)*

References: Saenger, P. (1996). Turner's syndrome. *New England Journal of Medicine, 335,* 1749–1754.

Siegel, P.T., Clopper, R., & Stabler, B. (1998). The psychological consequences of Turner syndrome and review of the National Cooperative Growth Study psychological substudy. *Pediatrics, 102*(2, Pt. 3), 488–491.

Usher syndromes   *Clinical features:* Approximately 10 subtypes exist; all have progressive sensorineural deafness, nystagmus, retinitis pigmentosa, central nervous system defects (e.g., loss of sense of smell, vertigo, epilepsy). *Associated complications:* Ataxia, psychosis, cataracts, occasional cognitive impairment. *Cause:* Genes linked to chromosomes 1q32.3, 1q41, 3p23–p24.2, 3q21–q25, 5q, 10q, 11p15.1, 11q13, and 14q32. *Inheritance:* AR. *Prevalence:* 3/100,000–5/100,000.

References: Keats, B.J., & Corey, D.P. (1999). The Usher syndromes. *American Journal of Medical Genetics, 89,* 158–166.

Smith, R.J., Berlin, C.I., Hejtmancik, J.R., et al. (1994). Clinical diagnosis of the Usher syndromes: Usher Syndrome Consortium. *American Journal of Medical Genetics, 50,* 32–38.

VATER/VACTERL association   *Clinical features:* *v*ertebral defects, *a*nal atresia (imperforate anus), *t*racheo-esophageal fistula (problem with connection between trachea and esophagus), *e*sophageal anomalies, *r*adial (lower arm) defects, *r*enal (kidney) anomalies, and other *l*imb defects. *Associated complications:* Respiratory, cardiac, and renal (kidney) abnormalities can be severe. Intelligence is usually not affected. *Cause:* Unknown. *Inheritance:* Usually SP; rare families with AR pattern. *Prevalence:* Unknown.

References: Botto, L.D., Khoury, M.J., Mastroiacovo, P., et al. (1997). The spectrum of congenital anomalies of the VATER association: An international study. *American Journal of Medical Genetics, 71,* 8–15.

Lubinsky, M. (1986). VATER and other associations: Historical perspectives and modern interpretations. *American Journal of Medical Genetics, 45,* 313–319.

velocardiofacial syndrome (VCFS)   *See* chromosome 22q11 microdeletion syndromes.

von Recklinghausen disease   *See* neurofibromatosis, type I.

Waardenburg syndrome, types I, II, and III   *Clinical features:* Widely spaced eyes (type I), heterochromia (irises of different colors), white forelock, nonprogressive sensorineural hearing loss, musculoskeletal abnormalities (type III). *Associated complications:* Impaired vestibular function leading to ataxia, premature graying, vitiligo (patches of skin depigmentation), occasional glaucoma. *Cause:* Types I and III: mutations in *PAX3* gene on chromosome 2q35; type II: mutations in various genes, including the microphthalmia-associated transcription factor (*MITF*) gene on chromosome 3p14.1–p12.3. *Inheritance:* AD. *Prevalence:* 1/20,000–1/40,000.

References: Lee, D., Lanza, J., & Har-El, G. (1996). Waardenburg syndrome. *Otolaryngology—Head and Neck Surgery, 114,* 166–167.

Read, A.P., & Newton, V.E. (1997). Waardenburg syndrome. *Journal of Medical Genetics, 34,* 656–665.

Weaver syndrome   *Clinical features:* Micrognathia; distinctive chin with dimple; hypertelorism; macrocephaly; downslanting palpebral fissures; long philtrum; depressed nasal bridge; hoarse, low-pitched cry. *Associated complications:* Accelerated growth with advanced bone age, hypertonia, **camptodactyly** (permanently flexed fingers), mental retardation. *Cause:* Unknown. *Inheritance:* All reported cases have been sporadic; question of possible AR. *Prevalence:* Unknown.

References: Cole, T.R.P., Dennis, N.R., & Hughes, H.E. (1992). Weaver syndrome. *Journal of Medical Genetics, 29,* 332–337.

Opitz, J.M., Weaver, D.W., & Reynolds J.F., Jr. (1998). The syndromes of Sotos and Weaver: Reports and review. *American Journal of Medical Genetics, 79,* 294–304.

Williams syndrome   *Clinical features:* Characteristic "elfin" facies (full lips and cheeks, fullness of area around the eyes); short stature; star-like pattern to iris; hoarse voice; friendly, talkative, extroverted personality; congenital heart defect (often supravalvular aortic stenosis). *Associated complications:* Hypercalcemia (increased blood calcium level), stenosis (stricture) of blood vessels, kidney anomalies, hypertension, joint contractures, mild to moderate mental retardation (characteristic strength in verbal abilities). *Cause:* Deletion of the *elastin* gene locus at chromosome 7q11. *Inheritance:* AD. *Prevalence:* 1/10,000.

References: Brewer, C.M., Morrison, N., & Tolmie, J.L. (1996). Clinical and molecular cytogenetic (FISH) diagnosis of Williams syndrome. *Archives of Disease in Childhood, 74,* 59–61.

Greer, M.K., Brown, F.R., III, Pai, G.S., et al. (1997). Cognitive, adaptive, and behavioral characteristics of Williams syndrome. *American Journal of Medical Genetics, 74,* 521–525.

Wilson disease   *Clinical features:* Liver dysfunction, Kayser-Fleischer ring in cornea, low serum ceruloplasmin (enzyme important in regulation of copper in body). *Associated complications:* Movement disorders, dysphagia (difficulty swallowing) or other oral-motor dysfunction, behavioral disturbances. If left untreated, death from liver failure within 1–3 years of onset. *Cause:* Mutations in the copper metabolism gene, *ATP7B,* on chromosome 13q14.3–q21.1 lead to intracellular accumulation of copper in liver. *Inheritance:* AR. *Prevalence:* 1/50,000. *Treatment:* Administration of copper-chelating agents in conjunction with a low copper diet.

References: Akil, M., & Brewer, G.J. (1995). Psychiatric and behavioral abnormalities in Wilson's disease. *Advances in Neurology, 65,* 171–178.

Shimizu, N., Yamaguchi, Y., Aoki, T. (1999). Treatment and management of Wilson's disease. *Pediatrics International, 41,* 419–422.

Wolf-Hirschhorn syndrome *Clinical features:* Hypertelorism; characteristic broad, beaked nose; microcephaly; marked intrauterine growth retardation; ear anomalies; severe mental retardation. *Associated complications:* Hypotonia, seizures, occasional heart defect or cleft palate. *Cause:* Partial deletion of short arm of chromosome 4; some research shows that the *HOX7* gene may be responsible. *Inheritance:* SP; inherited if parent has a balanced translocation. *Prevalence:* 1/50,000.

References: Battaglia, A., Carey, J.C., Cederholm, P., et al. (1999). Natural history of Wolf-Hirschhorn syndrome: Experience with 15 cases. *Pediatrics, 103,* 830–836.

Estabrooks, L.L., Lamb, A.N., Aylsworth, A.S., et al. (1994). Molecular characteristics of chromosome 4p deletions resulting in Wolf-Hirschhorn syndrome. *Journal of Medical Genetics, 31,* 103–107.

X-linked ALD *See* adrenoleukodystrophy.

XXX (trisomy X; 47,XXX); XXXX (tetrasomy X); and XXXXX (pentasomy X) syndromes *Clinical features:* Females with XXX syndrome generally have above-average stature but otherwise normal physical appearance; 70% have significant learning disabilities. XXXX syndrome is associated with a mildly unusual facial appearance, behavioral problems, moderate mental retardation. XXXXX syndrome presents with severe mental retardation and multiple physical defects. *Associated complications:* Infertility, delayed pubertal development. *Cause:* Nondisjunction during meiosis. *Inheritance:* SP. *Incidence:* 1/800 live-born females.

References: Harmon, R.J., Bender, B.G., Linden, M.G., et al. (1998). Transition from adolescence to early adulthood: Adaptation and psychiatric status of women with 47,XXX. *Journal of the American Academy of Child and Adolescent Psychiatry, 37,* 286–291.

Linden, M.G., Bender, M.G., & Robinson, A. (1995). Sex chromosome tetrasomy and pentasomy. *Pediatrics, 96*(4, Pt. 1), 672–682.

XXY syndrome *See* Klinefelter syndrome.

XYY syndrome *Clinical features:* Subtle findings, including tall stature, severe acne, large teeth. *Associated complications:* Poor fine motor coordination; learning disabilities (characteristically language based); varying degrees of behavioral disturbances, including tantrums and aggression. *Cause:* Extra Y chromosome resulting from nondisjunction. *Inheritance:* SP. *Prevalence:* 1/1,000.

References: Fryns, J.P. (1998). Mental status and psychosocial functioning in XYY males. *Prenatal Diagnosis, 18,* 303–304.

Fryns, J.P., Kleczkowska, A., Kubien, E., et al. (1995). XYY syndrome and other Y chromosome polysomies: Mental status and psychosocial functioning. *Genetic Counseling, 6,* 197–206.

Zellweger syndrome (cerebrohepatorenal syndrome) *Clinical features:* The most severe of the known peroxisomal disorders. Affected infants have intrauterine growth retardation, characteristic facies (high forehead, upslanting palpebral fissures, hypoplastic supraorbital ridges, and epicanthal folds), hypotonia, eye abnormalities (cataracts, glaucoma, corneal clouding, retinitis pigmentosa), early onset of seizures. Death occurs by 1 year of age in most cases. *Associated complications:* Severe feeding difficulties with failure to thrive, liver disease, occasional cardiac disease, extremity contractures, kidney cysts. *Cause:* Impaired peroxisome synthesis caused by mutations in a number of genes, including peroxin-1 (*PEX1*) at chromosome 7q21–q22, peroxin-5 (*PEX5*) at chromosome 12, peroxin-2 (*PEX2*) at chromosome 8, peroxin-6 (*PEX6*) at chromosome 6, and peroxin-12 (*PEX12*). (The peroxisome is a cellular organelle involved in processing fatty acids.) *Inheritance:* AR. *Prevalence:* 1/100,000. *Treatment:* Docosahexaenoic acid (DHA) ethyl ester was shown to be helpful in a small group of patients.

References: Martinez, M. (2001). Restoring the DHA levels in the brains of Zellweger patients. *Journal of Molecular Neuroscience, 16,* 309–316.

Raymond, G.V. (1999). Peroxisomal disorders. *Current Opinion in Pediatrics, 11,* 572–576.

C Commonly Used Medications

Karl F. Gumpper, B.S. Pharm, BCNSP

This appendix contains information about commonly used medications but is not meant to be used to prescribe medication. The generic name of each drug is in CAPITAL LETTERS; the trade name is in parentheses. Table C.1 lists the drug categories, uses, standard applications, and side effects; Table C.2 lists medications by trade name. Specific medical terminology is defined in the glossary (see Appendix A).

It should be noted that uses and standard applications may change during the life of this edition and that additional side effects may be discovered. Furthermore, this appendix does not provide detailed info on drug interactions and contraindications for use; these should be discussed with a health care provider.

REFERENCES

Children's National Medical Center. (2002). *CNMC Hospital Formulary (Intranet version)*. Washington, DC: Author.

Lacy, C.F., Armstrong, L.L., Goldman, M.P., et al. (Eds.). (2001–2002). *Drug information handbook* (9th ed.). Cleveland, OH: Lexicomp.

Taketomo, C.K., Hodding, J.H., & Kraus, D.M. (Eds.). (2001–2002). *Pediatric dosage handbook* (6th ed). Cleveland: Lexicomp.

Thomson Healthcare/MICROMEDEX. (1974–2002). *MICROMEDEX Healthcare Series: Vol. 112*. Greenwood Village, CO: Author.

Table C.1. Information about commonly used medications

Medication	Category	Use(s)	Standard application[a]	Side effects
ACYCLOVIR (Zovirax)	Antiviral agent	Used primarily in children who are immunocompromised to treat or protect against herpes simplex and varicella (chickenpox) infections	**C, L, O, and injection:** Depending on clinical situation	Kidney impairment
ALPRAZOLAM (Xanax)	Psychopharmacological agent	Anxiety, aggression, panic attacks	**T:** Titrate starting at minimal doses of 0.125 mg three times daily; safety and efficacy in children younger than 18 years has not been established.	Drowsiness, insomnia, decreased salivation
AMITRIPTYLINE (Elavil)	Psychopharmacological agent	Attention-deficit/hyperactivity disorder, depression	**T:** 1–1.5 mg/kg/day, given in three doses; not recommended for children younger than 12 years	Sedation; dry mouth; blurred vision; very rarely, sudden death from cardiac arrhythmia
AMOXICILLIN (Amoxil)	Antibiotic	First-line drug for otitis media	**C, T, L, chewables:** 20–80 mg/kg/day, given in two to three doses	Diarrhea, rash
AMOXICILLIN AND CLAVULANIC ACID (Augmentin)	Antibiotic	Otitis media	**T, L, chewables:** 45–80 mg/kg/day, given in two doses	Diarrhea (worse than with amoxicillin alone), rash
AMPHETAMINE AND DEXTROAMPHETAMINE (Adderall)	Psychopharmacological agent	Attention-deficit/hyperactivity disorder, obesity	**T:** One to three doses daily; not recommended for children younger than 3 years; 3- to 5-year-olds: 2.5 mg/day initially, with an increase of 2.5 mg/week until optimal response; children older than 6 years: 5 mg once or twice daily initially, with an increase of 5 mg/week until optimal response	Insomnia, loss of appetite, emotional lability (moodiness), addictive potential, arrhythmia

Drug	Classification	Indications	Dosage	Side effects
BACLOFEN	Antispasticity agent	Spasticity of cerebral or spinal origin	**T:** 5 mg/dose, two or three times daily initially; increase by 5 mg every 4–7 days to a maximum of 30–80 mg/day. **Intrathecal:** 50–600 mcg/day delivered by implantable pump	Drowsiness, muscle weakness; rarely, nausea, dizziness, or paresthesia (numbness and tingling); abrupt withdrawal can cause hallucinations and seizures
BENZTROPINE (Cogentin)	Anticholinergic	Movement disorders associated with antipsychotics such as haloperidol	**T:** Initiate therapy with low dosage; gradually increase in increments of 0.5 mg twice daily; maximum dosage: 6 mg/day	Gastrointestinal upset, drowsiness, dizziness or blurred vision, dry mouth, difficult urination, constipation
BOTULINUM TOXIN A (Botox)	Antispasticity agent	Spasticity in cerebral palsy and spinal cord injury	**Injection:** Administered by a qualified practitioner. Based on review of clinical trials, dosage use in management of cerebral palsy should not exceed 4 units/kg per 2 months.	Diffuse skin rash, paralysis with overdose
BUPROPRION (Wellbutrin)	Psychopharmacological agent	Antidepressant, attention-deficit/hyperactivity disorder	**T:** Safety and efficacy in children younger than 18 years has not been established.	Decreased seizure threshold
BUSPIRONE (BuSpar)	Psychopharmacological agent	Attention-deficit/hyperactivity disorder, anxiety, aggression	**T:** Safety and efficacy in children younger than 18 years has not been established.	Chest pain, ringing in the ears, sore throat, nasal congestion
CALCIUM UNDECYLENATE (10%) (Caldesene powder)[b]	Skin agent	Diaper rash	**O, P:** Apply three or four times daily after bathing or changing.	Irritation, allergic reaction
CARBAMAZEPINE (Carbatrol; Tegretol, Tegretol XR)	Antiepileptic	Generalized tonic-clonic, complex partial, and simple partial seizures; also used to treat aggression	**T, L:** 5–20 mg/kg/day; blood level should be maintained at 4–14 mcg/ml	Unsteady gait, double vision, drowsiness, slurred speech, dizziness, tremor, headache, nausea, abnormalities in liver function, low white blood cell count

[a]Key: **C,** capsules; **T,** tablets; **L,** liquid suspension, elixir, or syrup; **O,** ointment; **P,** powder; **S,** suppositories.

[b]Available without a prescription.

[c]Available with or without a prescription. The nonprescription and prescription formulations may vary in strength.

Medication	Category	Use(s)	Standard application[a]	Side effects
CARNITINE (*also called* L-CARNITINE) (Carnitor)	Nutritional supplement	Primary and secondary carnitine deficiency, especially in inborn errors of metabolism; valproic acid–induced deficiency	**T, L, injection:** 50–100 mg/kg/day divided into doses given every 6 hours. Give higher dosages with caution. Start dosage at 50 mg/kg/day, and increase slowly to a maximum of 3 g/day while assessing tolerance and therapeutic response.	Nausea, vomiting, abdominal cramps, diarrhea
CEPHALEXIN (e.g., Keflex)	Antibiotic	Used to treat susceptible infections of the respiratory tract, skin, and urinary tract	**C, T, L:** 25–100 mg/kg/day divided into doses given every 6–8 hours. Maximum dosage: 4,000 mg/day.	Headache, rash, nausea, vomiting, diarrhea
CHLORAL HYDRATE (Aquachloral [supplement], Noctec)	Psychopharmacological agent	Sedation	**C, L, S:** 5–15 mg/kg every 8 hours to a maximum dosage of 2 g/day	Mucous membrane and gastrointestinal irritation, paradoxical excitement, hypotension
CHLORPROMAZINE (Thorazine)	Psychopharmacological agent	Psychosis, anxiety, aggression, severe hyperactivity in mental retardation (rarely used now because of newer drugs with fewer side effects)	**T, L, S:** 2.5–6 mg/kg/day to a maximum of 40 mg in children younger than 5 years or 75 mg in children 5–12 years old	Drowsiness, tardive dyskinesia, electrocardiogram changes, agranulocytosis (i.e., low white blood cell count leading to infection), rash, hyperpigmentation of skin
CIMETIDINE (Tagamet)[c]	Gastrointestinal agent	Gastroesophageal reflux, gastric/duodenal ulcers; inhibits gastric acid secretion	**T, L:** 10–40 mg/kg/day, given four times daily	Rarely, diarrhea, headache, decreased white blood cell count, or liver toxicity
CISAPRIDE (Propulsid)	Gastrointestinal agent	Gastroesophageal reflux; increases gastric emptying	**T, L:** 0.7–1 mg/kg/day, given three or four times daily. (**Note:** Cisapride was removed from U.S. market in July 2000 because of serious adverse events; limited-access program is available through Janssen Pharmaceutica.)	Abdominal pain, diarrhea

Drug	Classification	Indications	Dosage	Side Effects
CLARITHROMYCIN (Biaxin)	Antibiotic	Wide-spectrum drug used against staph, strep, and mycoplasma ("walking pneumonia") infections	**T, L:** 15 mg/kg/day, given twice daily for 10 days	Stomach upset, but tolerated better than erythromycin
CLOMIPRAMINE (Anafranil)	Psychopharmacological agent	Obsessive-compulsive disorder	**C:** Initiate at 25 mg/day; gradually increase during the first 2 weeks, as tolerated, to a daily maximum of 3 mg/kg or 100–200 mg, whichever is smaller.	Drowsiness, dry mouth, blurred vision
CLONAZEPAM (Klonopin)	Antiepileptic	Lennox-Gastaut syndrome; absence, atonic, myoclonic, and partial seizures; infantile spasms	**T:** 0.01–0.2 mg/kg/day (usual maintenance dosage is 0.5–2 mg/day, given twice daily)	Sedation, hyperactivity, confusion, depression, especially if withdrawn quickly; tolerance to the drug can develop
CLONIDINE (Catapres)	Psychopharmacological agent	Hypertension, attention-deficit/hyperactivity disorder, Tourette syndrome	**T:** 0.005–0.025 mg/kg/day, four times daily; increase every 5–7 days as needed; ***sustained-release patch*** also available	Dry mouth, sedation, hypotension, headache, nausea
CLORAZEPATE (Tranxene)	Antiepileptic	Adjunctive therapy for partial seizures	**T:** 3.75–7.5 mg/dose twice daily; increase dosage by 3.75 mg at weekly intervals; maximum dosage: 60 mg/day in two to three divided doses	Hypotension, drowsiness, dizziness (see also side effects of DIAZEPAM)
CLOTRIMAZOLE (Lotrimin, Mycelex)[b]	Antifungal	Candida albicans (yeast) infections	***Cream:*** Apply twice daily for 2–4 weeks.	Skin irritation, peeling

[a]Key: **C,** capsules; **T,** tablets; **L,** liquid suspension, elixir, or syrup; **O,** ointment; **P,** powder; **S,** suppositories.

[b]Available without a prescription.

[c]Available with or without a prescription. The nonprescription and prescription formulations may vary in strength.

779

Medication	Category	Use(s)	Standard application[a]	Side effects
CLOZAPINE (Clozaril)	Psychopharmacological agent	Schizophrenia in which standard antipsychotic drug treatment has not worked	**T:** 25 mg once or twice daily, then continued with daily dosage increments of 25–50 mg/day, if well tolerated, to a target dosage of 300 to 450 mg/day by the end of 2 weeks. (**Note:** All patients must be registered in Novartis's distribution system prior to starting the medication.)	Hypotension, seizure, sedation, agranulocytosis (i.e., low white blood cell count leading to infection), myocarditis (i.e., inflammation of the heart)
COLLOIDAL OATMEAL (e.g., Aveeno)[b]	Skin treatment	Dry skin, itching	**Oil, cleansing bar, cream, lotion:** Add to bath or apply as needed.	Allergic reaction
CORTICOTROPIN (Acthar, ACTH)	Antiepileptic	Infantile spasms and Lennox-Gastaut syndrome	**Intramuscular injection:** 20–40 units/day; many regimens exist, but corticotropin is generally used for weeks to months and then tapered off slowly	Glucose in urine, hypertension, cataracts, brittle bones
DANTROLENE SODIUM (Dantrium)	Antispasticity agent	Spasticity in cerebral palsy or spinal cord injury	**C:** 0.5 mg/kg twice daily initially; increase by 0.5 mg/kg every 4–7 days to a maximum of 3 mg/kg/dose, given two to four times daily	Weakness; drowsiness; lethargy; dizziness; tingling sensation; nausea; diarrhea; rarely, liver toxicity (liver function should be monitored); long-term side effects in children are not known
DESIPRAMINE (Norpramin)	Psychopharmacological agent	Depression, anxiety, attention-deficit/hyperactivity disorder	**T:** Not recommended in children younger than 12 years; 1–4.5 mg/kg/day; maximum dosage: 100 mg/day	Hypotension, ringing in the ears, gastrointestinal discomfort, dry mouth, blurred vision; sudden death from cardiac arrhythmia has been reported in a few cases

DEXTROAMPHETAMINE (Dexedrine, Dexedrine Spansules, DextroStat)	Psychopharmacological agent	Attention-deficit/hyperactivity disorder	**T:** 0.1 mg/kg, twice daily initially; increase to 0.5–1 mg/kg/dose, two to three times daily; **sustained-release capsules** (Dexedrine Spansules) are available (5, 10, and 15 mg)	Insomnia, restlessness, headache, abdominal cramps
DIAZEPAM (Valium, Diastat)	Antispasticity agent, anti-epileptic, psychopharmacological agent	Sedation, aggression, anxiety, spasticity, seizures	**C, T, L:** 0.12–0.8 mg/kg/day, given three to four times daily. **Rectal gel** (Diastat): not recommended for infants younger than 6 months; safety and efficacy in children younger than 2 years has not been established; 2–5 years, 0.5 mg/kg; 6–11 years, 0.3 mg/kg; older than 11 years, 0.2 mg/kg; not to exceed 20 mg/dose	Sedation, weakness, depression, ataxia, memory disturbance, difficulty handling secretions and chewing/swallowing foods, anxiety, hallucinations, agitation, insomnia, respiratory and cardiac depression, urinary retention or incontinence, rash, low white blood cell count; drug dependence can occur
DIPHENHYDRAMINE (Benadryl)[b]	Antihistamine	Sedation, nasal congestion, hives	**C, T, L:** 5 mg/kg/day given at 6–8 hour intervals to a maximum of 300 mg/day	Sedation, insomnia, dizziness, euphoria
DUODERM	Skin treatment	Skin ulcers/sores, second-degree burns, and minor abrasions	**Sterile occlusive dressing with hydroactive or gel formula:** Apply as directed; caregiver may apply to patient's wound but should do so under direction of a physician or a wound care specialist.	Allergic reaction to tape or gel formula
ERYTHROMYCIN (various brands)	Antibiotic	Used against staph, strep, and mycoplasma ("walking pneumonia") infections; used in combination with sulfisoxazole (Pediazole) for otitis media	**C, T, L:** 30–50 mg/kg/day, given four times daily	Nausea, vomiting, interactions with other drugs

[a]*Key:* **C,** capsules; **T,** tablets; **L,** liquid suspension, elixir, or syrup; **O,** ointment; **P,** powder; **S,** suppositories.
[b]Available without a prescription.
[c]Available with or without a prescription. The nonprescription and prescription formulations may vary in strength.

Medication	Category	Use(s)	Standard application[a]	Side effects
ERYTHROMYCIN (2%) (T-STAT)	Skin treatment	Acne	**Solution on pads:** Apply to clean area twice daily.	Skin dryness, peeling, skin irritation
ETHOSUXIMIDE (Zarontin)	Antiepileptic	Absence seizures	**C, L:** 15–40 mg/kg/day, given twice daily to a maximum of 1.5 g/day; blood level: 40–80 mcg/liter	Sedation, unsteady gait, rash, stomach distress, low white blood cell count
FAMOTIDINE (Pepcid)[c]	Gastrointestinal agent	Gastresophageal reflux; decreases stomach acidity	**T, L:** 1 mg/kg/day, given twice daily with meals; maximum dosage: 80 mg/day	Headache, dizziness
FELBAMATE (Felbatol)	Antiepileptic	Lennox-Gastaut syndrome; also effective in generalized tonic-clonic, complex partial, and secondary generalized seizures	**T, L:** 15–45 mg/kg/day	Anorexia, vomiting, insomnia, headache, rash, risk of life-threatening hepatitis and aplastic anemia (Food and Drug Administration recommends complete blood count and liver function tests every 1–2 weeks)
FLUCONAZOLE (Diflucan)	Antifungal	Treatment of susceptible fungal infections including oral and vaginal *Candida albicans* (yeast) infections	**L, T:** 6 mg/kg once on first day of therapy, then 3 mg/kg/dose daily for 14–21 days. For vaginal candidiasis a single 150-mg dose may be given.	Dizziness, headache, rash, nausea; inhibits the metabolism of many drugs, so patients must be screened for possible drug interactions
FLUOXETINE (Prozac)	Psychopharmacological agent	Depression, self-injurious behavior, Tourette syndrome, obsessive compulsive disorder	**C, L:** Safety and efficacy in children younger than 12 years has not been established; adults should initially receive 20 mg/day in morning to a maximum of 80 mg/day.	Anxiety, agitation, sleep disruption, decreased appetite, seizures
FOSPHENYTOIN (Cerebyx) Closely related to phenytoin.	See PHENYTOIN	See PHENYTOIN	See PHENYTOIN	See PHENYTOIN

Drug	Type	Use	Dosage	Side effects
FUROSEMIDE (Lasix)	Diuretic	Diuresis	**T, L, injection:** 1 mg/kg/dose one to four times daily	Electrolyte abnormalities
GABAPENTIN (Neurontin)	Antiepileptic	Adjunctive therapy in partial and secondarily generalized seizures	**C, L:** 20–30 mg/kg/day; safety and efficacy in children younger than 12 years has not been established	Sedation, dizziness, unsteady gait, fatigue
GLYCOPYROLATE (Robinul)	Anticholinergic	Decrease drooling in cerebral palsy	**T:** 0.05 mg/kg/dose every 3–4 hours as needed for secretions	Rapid heart rate, orthostatic hypotension, drowsiness, blurred vision, dry mouth
GUANFACINE (Tenex)	Psychopharmacological agent	Hypertension, attention-deficit/hyperactivity disorder, Tourette syndrome	**T:** Dosages of 2–4 mg/day have been described in case reports.	Dry mouth, sedation, hypotension, headache, nausea
HALOPERIDOL (Haldol)	Psychopharmacological agent	Self-injurious behavior (SIB), severe agitation, psychosis, Tourette syndrome	**T, L:** 0.01–0.03 mg/kg/day for agitation; 0.05–0.15 mg/kg/day, in two or three daily doses for psychosis; and 0.05–0.075 mg/kg/day, in two or three daily doses for Tourette syndrome	Movement disorder, neuroleptic malignant syndrome, lower seizure threshold in epilepsy
HYDROCORTISONE (e.g., Caldecort, Cort-Dome, Hytone)[c]	Skin treatment	Eczema, dermatitis	**O, cream:** Apply thin film two to four times daily.	Skin irritation, dryness, rash
HYDROCORTISONE, POLYMYXIN-B, AND NEOMYCIN (Cortisporin)	Skin treatment	Steroid-responsive skin conditions with secondary infection	**O, cream:** Apply sparingly and massage into skin two or three times daily.	Local irritation, kidney/ear toxicity (if neomycin is absorbed in large amounts)
IMIPRAMINE (Tofranil, Janimine)	Psychopharmacological agent	Depression, enuresis	**C, T:** 1.5 mg/kg/day, given in in three daily doses to a maximum of 5 mg/kg/day; therapeutic blood level for depression is 150–225 nanograms/ml	Dry mouth, drowsiness, constipation, electrocardiogram abnormalities, increased blood pressure

[a]*Key:* **C,** capsules; **T,** tablets; **L,** liquid suspension, elixir, or syrup; **O,** ointment; **P,** powder; **S,** suppositories.
[b]Available without a prescription.
[c]Available with or without a prescription. The nonprescription and prescription formulations may vary in strength.

Medication	Category	Use(s)	Standard application[a]	Side effects
ISOTRETINOIN (Accutane)	Skin treatment	Severe acne in adolescents (or adults)	**C:** 0.5–2 mg/kg/day, given twice daily for 15–20 weeks	Drying of mucous membranes, photosensitivity, teratogenicity (do not use during pregnancy), depression
LAMOTRIGINE (Lamictal)	Antiepileptic	Adjunctive therapy in partial and secondarily generalized seizures; may be effective in primary generalized seizures	**T:** 5–15 mg/kg/day (1–5 mg/kg/day if co-administered with valproic acid); safety and efficacy in children younger than 12 years has not been established	Sedation, dizziness, potentially life-threatening Stevens-Johnson syndrome (allergic skin condition)
LANOLIN, PETROLATUM, VITAMINS A AND D, AND MINERAL OILS (A & D Ointment)[b]	Skin treatment	Diaper rash	**O:** Apply thin film at each diaper change.	Allergic reaction
L-CARNITINE, see CARNITINE				
LEVETIRACETAM (Keppra)	Antiepileptic	Adjunctive therapy in partial seizures	**T:** Initially, 20 mg/kg/day divided in two doses; increase to 40–60 mg/kg/day as tolerated; maximum dosage: 3,000 mg/day.	Somnolence, coordination difficulties, dizziness
LEVOTHYROXINE (Levothroid, Synthroid)	Hormone	Hypothyroidism	**T:** 1–5 years, 5–6 mcg/kg/day; 6–12 years, 4–5 mcg/kg/day; older than 12 years, 2–3 mcg/kg/day	Heart palpitations, nervousness, tremor, excessive sweating
LINDANE (Kwell)	Skin treatment	Scabies and lice	***Cream, lotion:*** Apply thin layer and massage into body from neck down; wash off after 8–12 hours. ***Shampoo:*** Apply to dry hair, massage thoroughly into hair and leave on for 4 minutes, then form lather and rinse well.	None with prescribed use; risk of seizures with overuse in small children. Should be reserved for patients who do not respond to other treatments (e.g., permethrin).

LITHIUM CARBONATE (Eskalith)	Psychopharmacological agent	Mood stabilizer, bipolar disorders, and depression	**C, T, L:** 15–60 mg/kg/day divided in three to four doses. Maximum dosage: 1,800 mg/day; therapeutic range: mania, 0.6–1.5 mEq/liter; bipolar disorder, 0.8–1 mEq/liter	Sedation, confusion, seizures, rash, hypothyroidism, diarrhea, muscle weakness
LORAZEPAM (Ativan)	Psychopharmacological agent	Anxiety, status epilepticus	**T, L, injection:** 0.05 mg/kg/dose every 6 hours as needed; do not exceed 4 mg/dose	Sedation, weakness, depression, unstable gait, memory disturbance, difficulty handling secretions and chewing/swallowing foods, anxiety, hallucinations, agitation, insomnia, respiratory and cardiac depression, urinary retention or incontinence, rash, low white blood cell count; drug dependence can develop
MAGNESIUM HYDROXIDE AND ALUMINUM HYDROXIDE (Maalox)[b]	Gastrointestinal agent	Antacid for reflux, also helps treat constipation	**L:** 1–2 teaspoons with meals and at bedtime	Minimal
METHYLPHENIDATE (e.g., Concerta, Metadate, Metadate CD, Metadate ER, Methylin, Methylin ER, Ritalin)	Psychopharmacological agent	Attention-deficit/hyperactivity disorder	**T:** 0.6 mg/kg/day, given twice daily initially; increase to 1–2 mg/kg/day given two or three times daily when pain using regular Ritalin. **Sustained-release tablets** (Ritalin SR; 20 mg) last 5–6 hours; **long-acting capsules** (Concerta; 18 and 36 mg) last 12 hours.	Appetite suppression, insomnia, arrhythmia, hypo- or hypertension, abdominal pain
METHYLPREDNISOLONE (Medrol, Solu-Medrol)	Respiratory agent	Reduction of airway inflammation during acute asthma attacks	**Injection:** 1 mg/kg/dose; orally: 1 mg/kg/dose, twice daily for 3–5 days	Side effects usually mild with short-term use
METOCLOPRAMIDE (Reglan)	Gastrointestinal agent	Antireflux, increases gastric emptying	**T, L:** 0.1–0.5 mg/kg/day, given four times daily	Acute movement disorder (dystonia), drowsiness

[a]Key: **C**, capsules; **T**, tablets; **L**, liquid suspension, elixir, or syrup; **O**, ointment; **P**, powder; **S**, suppositories.

[b]Available without a prescription.

[c]Available with or without a prescription. The nonprescription and prescription formulations may vary in strength.

Medication	Category	Use(s)	Standard application[a]	Side effects
MICONAZOLE (2%) (e.g., Monistat)[b]	Antifungal	*Candida albicans* (yeast) infections	*Cream:* Apply twice daily for 2–4 weeks.	Skin irritation, peeling
MINERAL OIL (e.g., Alpha Keri)[b]	Skin treatment	Emollient for dry skin	*Soap, oil, spray:* Add to bath or rub into wet skin as needed; rinse.	Allergic reaction
MINERAL OIL, PETROLATUM, AND LANOLIN (Nivea, Lubriderm)[b]	Skin treatment	Emollient for dry skin	*Cream, lotion, bath oil:* Apply as needed.	Allergic reaction
MUPIROCIN (2%) (Bactroban)	Skin treatment	Antibiotic for impetigo, skin ulcers, burns	*O:* Apply sparingly three times daily, may cover with gauze.	Burning, itching, pain at site of application
NALTREXONE (ReVia)	Psychopharmacological agent	Opiate antagonist for treatment of self-injurious behavior	*T:* 50 mg/day in adults; safety and efficacy in children younger than 18 years has not been established	None in opioid-free individuals
NORTRIPTYLINE (Aventyl, Pamelor)	Psychopharmacological agent	Depression	*C, L:* 10 mg three times daily and 20 mg at bedtime; not recommended for children younger than 12 years	Dry mouth, drowsiness, constipation, electrocardiogram abnormalities, increased blood pressure, mania, sudden death from cardiac arrhythmia has been reported in a few cases with overdose
NYSTATIN (Mycostatin)	Antifungal	Treatment of yeast and thrush infections such as in the mouth and gastrointestinal tract	*O, P, cream:* Apply twice daily. *L:* 0.5–1 ml to each side of mouth four times daily; up to 5 cubic centimeters, swish, and swallow	Diarrhea (reported with oral form), redness, skin irritation, gastrointestinal upset
OXCARBAZEPINE (Trileptal)	Antiepileptic	Generalized tonic-clonic, complex partial, and simple partial seizures as both adjunctive and monotherapy	*T, L:* 8–10 mg/kg in two divided doses, usually not to exceed 600 mg/day	Headache; drowsiness; dizziness; blurred or double vision; trouble walking, speaking, or controlling body movement; abnormalities in liver function; low white blood cell count

Drug	Category	Use	Dosage	Side Effects
PAROXETINE (Paxil)	Psychopharmacological agent	Depression, obsessive compulsive disorder, anxiety disorder	**T, L:** 10–20 mg/day to start; increase dosage as needed by 10 mg/day weekly until a maximum of 50–60 mg/day is achieved	Heart palpitations, headache, anxiety, constipation, weakness
PEMOLINE (Cylert)	Psychopharmacological agent	Attention-deficit/hyperactivity disorder	**T:** 37.5 mg/day in morning initially; increase weekly to desired dosage; maximum dosage: 112.5 mg/day; not recommended for children younger than 6 years	Insomnia, anorexia, abdominal discomfort; potentially life-threatening liver toxicity has been reported
PENICILLIN (e.g., Pen V K)	Antibiotic	Drug of choice for strep throat, which alternatively can be treated by a single intramuscular injection of penicillin (Bicillin)	**T, L:** 25–50 mg/kg/day, given four times daily for 7 days	Allergic reactions, diarrhea
PERMETHRIN (Nix,[b] Elimite)	Skin treatment	Scabies and lice	**Cream, lotion:** Apply thin layer and massage into body from neck down; wash off after 8–14 hours. **Shampoo:** Apply to dry hair, massage thoroughly into hair, and leave on for 10 minutes, then form lather and rinse well. May repeat in 1 week if live mites reappear.	None with prescribed use
PETROLATUM, MINERAL OIL AND WAX, AND ALCOHOL (Eucerin)[b]	Skin treatment	Emollient for dry skin, itching	**Cream, lotion, facial lotion with sunscreen, cleansing bar:** Apply as needed.	Allergic reactions
PHENOBARBITAL (Luminal)	Antiepileptic	Generalized tonic-clonic, simple partial, and secondarily generalized seizures	**C, T, L:** 2–5 mg/kg/day for children; 1–2 mg/kg/day for adolescents; therapeutic blood level: 15–40 mcg/ml	Paradoxical hyperactivity, sedation, learning difficulties in older children, behavioral difficulties in 50% of children younger than 10 years, rash, irritability, unsteady gait

[a]Key: **C,** capsules; **T,** tablets; **L,** liquid suspension, elixir, or syrup; **O,** ointment; **P,** powder; **S,** suppositories.
[b]Available without a prescription.
[c]Available with or without a prescription. The nonprescription and prescription formulations may vary in strength.

787

Medication	Category	Use(s)	Standard application[a]	Side effects
PHENYTOIN (Dilantin)	Antiepileptic	Generalized tonic-clonic and complex partial seizures	*C, T, injection, L:* Maintenance dosage: 4–8 mg/kg/day; blood level: 10–20 mcg/ml; free level: 1–2 mcg/ml	Swelling of gums, excessive hairiness, rash, coarsening of facial features, possible adverse effects on learning and behavior, risk of birth defects if taken during pregnancy, nystagmus and unsteady gait with toxic levels
PREDNISOLONE (Prelone)	Respiratory agent	Reduction of airway inflammation during acute asthma attacks	*L:* 1 mg/kg/dose, twice daily for 3–5 days	Side effects usually mild with short-term use
PREDNISONE (Deltasone)	Respiratory agent	Reduction of airway inflammation during acute asthma attacks	*T, L:* 1 mg/kg/dose, twice daily for 3–5 days	Side effects usually mild with short-term use
PRIMIDONE (Mysoline)	Antiepileptic	Generalized tonic-clonic and complex partial seizures	*T, L:* 10–25 mg/kg/day for children; 125–250 mg three times daily for adolescents; therapeutic blood level: 5–12 mcg/ml; also metabolized to phenobarbital (of which therapeutic blood level is 15–40 mcg/ml)	Drowsiness, dizziness, nausea, vomiting, personality change (see also side effects of PHENOBARBITAL)
RANITIDINE (Zantac)[c]	Gastrointestinal agent	Gastroesophageal reflux (decreases stomach acidity)	*T, L:* 2–4 mg/kg/day, given twice daily	Headache, gastrointestinal upset, rarely liver toxicity
RISPERIDONE (Risperdal)	Psychopharmacological agent	Self-injurious behavior, psychosis, Tourette syndrome	*T, L:* Pediatric patients may start with 0.25–0.5 mg twice daily; slowly increase to the optimal range of 4–8 mg/day; dosages greater than 10 mg/day should be avoided.	Hypotension, sedation, dizziness, movement disorder, cessation of menses, constipation, weight gain, urinary retention, agranulocytosis (i.e., low white blood cell count leading to infection)
SELENIUM SULFIDE (2.5%) (e.g., Selsun Blue)[b]	Skin treatment	Scalp conditions (dandruff or seborrhea)	*Lotion, shampoo:* Apply to wet scalp, wait 3 minutes, rinse, repeat; use twice a week for 2 weeks, then as needed.	Skin irritation, dry or oily scalp

Drug	Classification	Uses	Dosage	Side Effects
SERTRALINE (Zoloft)	Psychopharmacological agent	Depression	*T, L:* 50 mg/day initially to a maximum of 200 mg/day in adults; safety and efficacy in children has not been established	Anxiety, agitation, sleep disruption, decreased appetite, seizures
SULFISOXAZOLE (Gantrisin; Pediazole)	Antibiotic	Prevention of otitis media	*T, L:* 50–75 mg/kg/day, given four to six times daily (see erythromycin dosage information when using Pediazole)	Bone marrow suppression, allergic reactions
THEOPHYLLINE (Aerolate, Slo-Bid, Theo-Dur, Uniphyl)	Respiratory agent	Bronchodilator; may be used in conjunction with other treatments for asthma	*T, C, L:* Ages 6 weeks to 6 months: 10 mg/kg/day; children ages 6 months to 1 year: 12–18 mg/kg/day; children ages 1–9 years: 20–24 mg/kg/day; children ages 9–12 years: 20 mg/kg/day; children ages 12–16 years: 18 mg/kg/day; maximum adult dosage: 900 mg/day	Nausea, vomiting, and stomach pain (especially common at high blood levels)
THIORIDAZINE (Mellaril)	Psychopharmacological agent	Self-injurious behavior, psychosis	*T, L:* Not recommended for children younger than 2 years; children ages 2–12 years: 0.5–3 mg/kg/day; children older than 12 years with mild disorders: 10 mg, two or three times daily; children older than 12 years with severe disorders: 25 mg, two or three times daily	Drowsiness, movement disorder, electrocardiogram abnormalities, retinal abnormalities
THIOTHIXENE (Navane)	Psychopharmacological agent	Self-injurious behavior, psychosis	*T, L:* 2 mg, three times daily, increase to 15 mg/day if needed; not recommended for children younger than 12 years	Movement disorder (tardive dyskinesia), neuroleptic malignant syndrome, rapid heart rate, hypotension, drowsiness, bone marrow suppression

*a*Key: *C*, capsules; *T*, tablets; *L*, liquid suspension, elixir, or syrup; *O*, ointment; *P*, powder; *S*, suppositories.
*b*Available without a prescription.
*c*Available with or without a prescription. The nonprescription and prescription formulations may vary in strength.

Medication	Category	Use(s)	Standard application[a]	Side effects
TIAGABINE (Gabitril)	Antiepileptic	Partial seizures that are unresponsive to other antiepileptic drugs	*T:* 12–18 years: initially 4 mg once daily for 1 week; then 8 mg/day in two divided doses for 1 week; then increase weekly by 4–8 mg/day in two to four divided doses daily; titrate dosage to response; maximum dosage: 32 mg/day (dosages greater than 32 mg/day have been used in select adolescent patients for short periods)	Dizziness, headache, sleepiness, central nervous system depression, memory disturbance, unsteady gait, emotionality, tremors, weakness
TOLNAFTATE (Tinactin)[b]	Skin treatment	Antifungal, ringworm	*P, cream:* Apply small amount to affected area two to three times a day for 2–4 weeks.	Nontoxic
TOPIRAMATE (Topamax)	Antiepileptic	Refractory partial seizures, Lennox-Gastaut syndrome	*T, sprinkles:* Initially give 0.5–1 mg/kg/day in two divided doses for 1 week, then increase by 0.5–1 mg/kg/day each week; titrate dosage to response. Usual minimally effective dosage: 6 mg/kg/day in two divided doses; some children may require more than 15 mg/kg/day; dosages as high as 50 mg/kg/day have been used in select patients receiving concomitant enzyme-inducing agents (e.g., carbamazepine)	Edema (swelling), language problems, abnormal coordination, depression, difficulty concentrating, fatigue, dizziness, unsteady gait, sleepiness, constipation, weight loss, muscle pain, weakness, nystagmus
TRIAMCINOLONE (e.g., Aristocort [skin], Azmacort [respiratory], Kenalog)	Skin treatment; respiratory agent	Eczema, dermatitis; inhibition of airway inflammation in patients with chronic asthma symptoms	*O, P, cream, lotion:* Apply thin film two to four times daily. *Inhaler:* 100 mcg per spray; children ages 6–12 years: 1–2 puffs three or four times daily; adults: 2 puffs three or four times daily	Skin irritation, rash, dryness, cough, hoarseness, dry mouth, increased wheezing; rinse mouth after use to prevent thrush

790

Drug	Type	Use	Dosage	Side Effects
TRIMETHOPRIM AND SULFAMETHOXAZOLE (TMP/SM) (Bactrim, Septra)	Antibiotic	Convenient dosing for otitis media and for urinary tract infections	***T, L:*** 8–10 mg/kg/day, given twice daily	Bone marrow suppression, allergic reactions, photosensitivity
VALPROIC ACID (Depacon, Depakene, Depakote)	Antiepileptic	Myoclonic, simple absence, and generalized tonic-clonic seizures; Lennox-Gastaut syndrome; infantile spasms; also used to treat aggression and mood disorders	***C, L, sprinkle, injection:*** 15–60 mg/kg/day; therapeutic blood level: 50–100 mcg/ml. Depakote ER may be dosed less frequently than other preparations of valproic acid.	Hair loss, weight loss or gain, abdominal distress, tremor, low platelet count; risk of birth defects if taken during pregnancy; potentially fatal liver damage (risk is 1/800 in children with developmental disabilities younger than 2 years on more than one antiepileptic drug)
ZINC OXIDE, COD LIVER OIL, LANOLIN, AND PETROLATUM (Caldesene ointment)[b]	Skin treatment	Diaper rash	***O:*** Apply three or four times daily after diaper change or bath.	Allergic reaction
ZONISAMIDE (Zonegran)	Antiepileptic	Adjunctive therapy in partial seizures, infantile spasms, Lennox-Gastaut syndrome	***C:*** 2–4 mg/kg, gradually increased at 1- to 2-week intervals to 4–8 mg/kg. Maximum dosage: 12 mg/kg/day (not to exceed 400 mg/day); may be administered as a single dose or in two or three divided doses	Somnolence, dizziness, loss of appetite, headache, agitation/irritability, confusion, rash, visual disturbances

[a]*Key:* ***C,*** capsules; ***T,*** tablets; ***L,*** liquid suspension, elixir, or syrup; ***O,*** ointment; ***P,*** powder; ***S,*** suppositories.
[b]Available without a prescription.
[c]Available with or without a prescription. The nonprescription and prescription formulations may vary in strength.

Table C.2. Medications according to trade name

Trade name	Generic name
A & D Ointment	LANOLIN, PETROLATUM, VITAMINS A AND D, AND MINERAL OILS
Accutane	ISOTRETINOIN
ACTH	CORTICOTROPIN
Acthar	CORTICOTROPIN
Adderall	AMPHETAMINE AND DEXTROAMPHETAMINE
Aerolate	THEOPHYLLINE
Alpha Keri	MINERAL OIL
Amoxil	AMOXICILLIN
Anafranil	CLOMIPRAMINE
Aquachloral	CHLORAL HYDRATE
Aristocort	TRIAMCINOLONE
Ativan	LORAZEPAM
Augmentin	AMOXICILLIN AND CLAVULANIC ACID
Aveeno	COLLOIDAL OATMEAL
Aventyl	NORTRIPTYLINE
Azmacort	TRIAMCINOLONE
Bactrim	TRIMETHOPRIM AND SULFAMETHOXAZOLE (TMP/SM)
Bactroban	MUPIROCIN (2%)
Benadryl	DIPHENHYDRAMINE
Biaxin	CLARITHROMYCIN
Botox	BOTULINUM TOXIN A
BuSpar	BUSPIRONE
Caldecort	HYDROCORTISONE
Caldesene ointment	ZINC OXIDE, COD LIVER OIL, LANOLIN, AND PETROLATUM
Caldesene powder	CALCIUM UNDECYLENATE (10%)
Carbatrol	CARBAMAZEPINE
Carnitor	CARNITINE (*also called* L-CARNITINE)
Catapres	CLONIDINE
Cerebyx	FOSPHENYTOIN (*see* PHENYTOIN in Table C.1)

Trade name	Generic name
Clozaril	CLOZAPINE
Cogentin	BENZTROPINE
Concerta	METHYLPHENIDATE
Cort-Dome	HYDROCORTISONE
Cortisporin	HYDROCORTISONE, POLYMYXIN-B, AND NEOMYCIN
Cylert	PEMOLINE
Dantrium	DANTROLENE SODIUM
Deltasone	PREDNISONE
Depacon	VALPROIC ACID
Depakene	VALPROIC ACID
Depakote	VALPROIC ACID
Dexedrine	DEXTROAMPHETAMINE
Dexedrine Spansules	DEXTROAMPHETAMINE
DextroStat	DEXTROAMPHETAMINE
Diastat	DIAZEPAM
Diflucan	FLUCONAZOLE
Dilantin	PHENYTOIN
Elavil	AMITRIPTYLINE
Elimite	PERMETHRIN
Eskalith	LITHIUM CARBONATE
Eucerin	PETROLATUM, MINERAL OIL AND WAX, AND ALCOHOL
Felbatol	FELBAMATE
Gabitril	TIAGABINE
Gantrisin	SULFISOXAZOLE
Haldol	HALOPERIDOL
Hytone	HYDROCORTISONE
Janimine	IMIPRAMINE
Keflex	CEPHALEXIN
Kenalog	TRIAMCINOLONE
Keppra	LEVETIRACETAM
Klonopin	CLONAZEPAM
Kwell	LINDANE
Lamictal	LAMOTRIGINE
Lasix	FUROSEMIDE
Levothroid	LEVOTHYROXINE

Trade name	Generic name
Lotrimin	CLOTRIMAZOLE
Lubriderm	MINERAL OIL, PETROLATUM, AND LANOLIN
Luminal	PHENOBARBITAL
Maalox	MAGNESIUM HYDROXIDE AND ALUMINUM HYDROXIDE
Medrol	METHYLPREDNISOLONE
Mellaril	THIORIDAZINE
Metadate	METHYLPHENIDATE
Metadate CD	METHYLPHENIDATE
Metadate ER	METHYLPHENIDATE
Methylin	METHYLPHENIDATE
Methylin ER	METHYLPHENIDATE
Monistat	MICONAZOLE (2%)
Mycelex	CLOTRIMAZOLE
Mycostatin	NYSTATIN
Mysoline	PRIMIDONE
Navane	THIOTHIXENE
Neurontin	GABAPENTIN
Nivea	MINERAL OIL, PETROLATUM, AND LANOLIN
Nix	PERMETHRIN
Noctec	CHLORAL HYDRATE
Norpramin	DESIPRAMINE
Pamelor	NORTRIPTYLINE
Paxil	PAROXETINE
Pediazole	ERYTHROMYCIN AND SULFISOXAZOLE
Pen V K	PENICILLIN
Pepcid	FAMOTIDINE
Prelone	PREDNISOLONE
Propulsid	CISAPRIDE
Prozac	FLUOXETINE

Trade name	Generic name
Reglan	METOCLOPRAMIDE
ReVia	NALTREXONE
Risperdal	RISPERIDONE
Ritalin	METHYLPHENIDATE
Robinul	GLYCOPYROLATE
Selsun Blue	SELENIUM SULFIDE (2.5%)
Septra	TRIMETHOPRIM AND SULFAMETHOXAZOLE (TMP/SM)
Slo-Bid	THEOPHYLLINE
Solu-Medrol	METHYLPREDNISOLONE
Synthroid	LEVOTHYROXINE
Tagamet	CIMETIDINE
Tegretol	CARBAMAZEPINE
Tegretol XR	CARBAMAZEPINE
Tenex	GUANFACINE
Theo-Dur	THEOPHYLLINE
Thorazine	CHLORPROMAZINE
Tinactin	TOLNAFTATE
Tofranil	IMIPRAMINE
Topamax	TOPIRAMATE
Tranxene	CLORAZEPATE
Trileptal	OXCARBAZEPINE
T-STAT	ERYTHROMYCIN (2%)
Uniphyl	THEOPHYLLINE
Valium	DIAZEPAM
Wellbutrin	BUPROPION
Xanax	ALPRAZOLAM
Zantac	RANITIDINE
Zarontin	ETHOSUXIMIDE
Zoloft	SERTRALINE
Zonegran	ZONISAMIDE
Zovirax	ACYCLOVIR

D Resources for Children with Disabilities

Margaret Rose

Listed in this appendix are a number of organizations that provide services in the area of developmental disabilities. A brief description of the purpose of the organization follows each listing. Some recommended web sites and journals are also listed. This appendix is a representative sample and is not intended to be all-inclusive. We have tried to ensure that the information, addresses, and telephone numbers are as current as possible. We apologize if readers find that any of these have changed.

GENERAL

American College of Obstetricians and Gynecologists (ACOG)

409 12th Street SW, Post Office Box 96920, Washington, DC 20090-6920 (http://www.acog.org/; e-mail: resources@acog.org). Professional organization of obstetrician-gynecologists dedicated to the advancement of women's health through education, advocacy, practice, and research. Provides on-line physician directory. Bookstore offers patient information pamphlets, professional resources, and multimedia resources.

American Medical Association (AMA)

515 North State Street, Chicago, IL 60610 (312-464-5000; http://www.ama-assn.org). Develops and promotes standards in medical practice, research, and education; advocates for patients and physicians.

Barnes & Noble/B. Dalton Booksellers

(http://www.bn.com; see local yellow pages under "bookstores, retail"). Provides a Children with Special Needs collection of useful books for families with children with disabilities in the Family and Child Care section of their stores.

Canadian Health Network

(http://www.canadian-health-network.ca/). Canadian health information service web site that features 26 topic areas focused on major health issues and population groups.

Center for the Advancement of Health

2000 Florida Avenue NW, Suite 210, Washington, DC 20009-1231 (202-387-2829; fax: 202-387-2857; http://www.cfah.org; e-mail: cfah@cfah.org). Organization dedicated to translating research on health and behavior into effective policy and practice.

Cochrane Library

Update Software Inc., 1070 South Santa Fe Avenue, Suite 21, Vista, CA 92084 (760-631-5844; fax: 760-631-5848 (http://www.update-software.com/; e-mail: info@updateusa.com). On-line, searchable database of systematic reviews of the effects of health care interventions related to pregnancy and neonatal outcomes. Also available on CD-ROM.

Disability Resources

NSNET Nova Scotia Community Organization Network, Technical Resource Centre, c/o Kings Regional Rehabilitation Centre, Post Office Box 128, Waterville, Nova Scotia, Canada B0P 1V0 (902-538-3103 x112; fax: 902-538-7022; http://www.nsnet.org/resource.html; e-mail: trc@nsnet.org). Internet-based network of community organizations, information, and resources in Nova Scotia to help assist parents and families, professionals and other agencies. Any organization or agency that supports individuals with disabilities can become an associated member at no cost.

Easter Seals

230 West Monroe Street, Suite 1800, Chicago, IL 60606 (800-221-6827; TTY: 312-726-4258; fax: 312-726-4258; http://www.easter-seals.org; e-mail: info@easter-seals.org). Nonprofit, community-based health agency dedicated to increasing the independence of people with disabilities. Offers a range of quality services, research, and programs. Serves more than a million people in the United States and Puerto Rico each year through a nationwide network of more than 400 service centers.

March of Dimes

1275 Mamaroneck Avenue, White Plains, NY 10605 (888-663-4637; http://www.modimes.org). Awards grants to institutions and organizations for development of genetic services, perinatal care in high-risk pregnancies, prevention of premature delivery, parent support groups, and other community programs. Campaign for Healthier Babies distributes information about birth defects and related newborn health problems. Spanish-language materials are available.

National Center for Education in Maternal and Child Health

2000 15th Street North, Suite 701, Arlington, VA 22201-2617 (703-524-7802; fax: 703-524-9335; http://www.ncemch.org; e-mail: info@ncemch.org). Disseminates publications and fact sheets to the public and professionals in the field and develops and maintains database of topics, agencies, and organizations related to maternal and child health.

National Library of Medicine (NLM)

8600 Rockville Pike, Bethesda, MD 20894 (888-346-3656; http://www.nlm.nih.gov/; e-mail: publicinfo@nlm.nih.gov). Part of the National Institutes of Health, NLM is the world's largest medical library and is a national resource for all U.S. health sciences libraries. It collects materials in areas of biomedicine; health care; biomedical aspects of technology; humanities; and the physical, life, and social sciences. The Medline Plus Health Information web site (http://www.medlineplus.gov/) presents health information from NLM and contains extensive information for professionals and the public on diseases/conditions and medicines, lists of hospitals, a medical encyclopedia/dictionary, information in Spanish, and links to current clinical trials.

DEVELOPMENTAL DISABILITIES AND RELATED ILLNESSES

ACQUIRED IMMUNODEFICIENCY SYNDROME (AIDS)

Centers for Disease Control and Prevention (CDC)
National Sexually Transmitted Diseases (STD) and AIDS Hotline

(English: 800-342-2437; Spanish: 800-344-7432; TTY: 800-243-7889). A weekday hotline that provides confidential information on transmission and prevention of human immunodeficiency virus (HIV)/AIDS and other STDs, testing, local referrals, and educational materials to the public.

Office of National AIDS Policy

The White House, Washington, DC 20500 (202-456-5594; http://www.whitehouse.gov/onap/aids.html). Provides broad direction for federal AIDS policy and fosters interdepartmental communication on HIV and AIDS. Works closely with the AIDS community in the United States and around the world.

ATTENTION-DEFICIT/HYPERACTIVITY DISORDER (ADHD)

A.D.D. WareHouse

300 Northwest 70th Avenue, Suite 102, Plantation, FL 33317 (800-233-9273; fax: 954-792-8545; http://www.addwarehouse.com; e-mail: sales@addwarehouse.com). A mail-order resource for ADHD-related books, games, videotapes, and so forth for clinicians, parents, teachers, adults, and students.

CHADD (Children and Adults with Attention-Deficit/Hyperactivity Disorder)

8181 Professional Place, Landover, MD 20785 (800-233-4050; fax: 301-306-7090; http://www.chadd.org; e-mail: national@chadd.org). Support group for parents of children with attention disorders. Provides continuing education for both parents and professionals, serves as a community resource for information, and advocates for appropriate educational programs.

Attention Deficit Disorder Association

1788 Second Street, Suite 200, Highland Park, IL 60035 (847-432-2332 [to leave a message]; fax: 847-432-5874; http://www.add.org; e-mail: mail@add.org). National organization that provides education, research, and public advocacy. Especially focused on the needs of adults and young adults with ADHD.

AUTISM AND OTHER PERVASIVE DEVELOPMENTAL DISORDERS (PDDs)

Autism Research Institute

4182 Adams Avenue, San Diego, CA 92116 (619-281-7165; fax: 619-563-6840; http://www.autism.com/ari). Information and referral for parents, teachers, physicians, and students working with children with autism and similar developmental disabilities. Publishes quarterly newsletter, *Autism Research Review International.*

Autism Society of America

7910 Woodmont Avenue, Suite 300, Bethesda, MD 20814-3067 (800-328-8476; fax: 301-657-0869; http://www.autism-society.org/; e-mail: info@autism-society.org). Provides information about autism, including options, approaches, methods, and systems available to parents and family members of children with autism and the professionals who work with them. Advocates for the rights and needs of individuals with autism and their families.

Center for the Study of Autism

Post Office Box 4538, Salem, OR 97302 (http://www.autism.org). Provides information about autism to parents and professionals. Performs research on the efficacy of various therapeutic interventions.

International Rett Syndrome Association

9121 Piscataway Road, Clinton, MD 20735 (800-818-7388; fax: 301-856-3336; http://www.rettsyndrome.org; e-mail: irsa@rettsyndrome.org). Provides information, referral, and support to families and acts as a liaison with professionals. Also facilitates research on Rett syndrome.

CEREBRAL PALSY

American Academy for Cerebral Palsy and Developmental Medicine (AACPDM)

6300 North River Road, Suite 727, Rosemont, IL 60018-4226 (847-698-1635; fax: 847-823-0536; http://www.aacpdm.org; e-mail: woppenhe@ucla.edu). Multidisciplinary scientific society that fosters professional education, research, and interest in the problems associated with cerebral palsy.

United Cerebral Palsy Associations

1660 L Street NW, Suite 700, Washington, DC 20036 (800-872-5827; TTY: 202-973-7197; fax: 202-776-0414; http://www.ucpa.org; e-mail: national@ucp.org). Direct services to children and adults with cerebral palsy that include medical diagnosis, evaluation and treatment, special education, career development, counseling, social and recreational programs, and adapted housing.

CHRONIC ILLNESS

Candlelighters Childhood Cancer Foundation

Post Office Box 498, Kensington, MD 20895 (800-366-2223; fax: 301-962-3521; http://www.candlelighters.org; e-mail: info@candlelighters.org). Provides support, information, and advocacy to families of children with cancer, adults who had childhood cancer, and the professionals who work with these individuals. Publishes newsletters, reports, and other publications. Provides network of support groups.

Families of Children Under Stress (FOCUS)

3050 Presidential Drive, Suite 114, Atlanta, GA 30340 (770-234-9111; fax: 770-234-9131; http://www.focus-ga.org; e-mail: focus-ga@mindspring.com). Publishes bimonthly newsletter for families of chronically or terminally ill children.

Guillain-Barré Syndrome Foundation International

Post Office Box 262, Wynnewood, PA 19096 (610-667-0131; fax: 610-667-7036; http://www.guillain-barre.com; e-mail: gbint@ix.netcom.com). Provides emotional support to individuals with Guillain-Barré syndrome and their families; fosters research; educates the public about the disorder; develops nationwide support groups; and directs people with this syndrome to resources, meetings, newsletters, and symposia.

CLEFT LIP AND PALATE

AboutFace USA

Post Office Box 969, Batavia, IL 60510 (888-486-1209; fax: 815-444-1943; http://www.aboutfaceUSA.org; e-mail: AboutFace2000@aol.com). Provides information, emotional support, public education programs, and community awareness to individuals with facial differences and their families.

CYSTIC FIBROSIS

Cystic Fibrosis Foundation

6931 Arlington Road, Bethesda, MD 20814 (800-344-4823; fax: 301-951-6378; http://www.cff.org; e-mail: info@cff.org). Provides referral for diagnostic services and medical care; offers professional and public information and supports research and professional training.

DOWN SYNDROME

The Association for Children with Down Syndrome

4 Fern Place, Plainview, NY 11803 (516-933-4700; fax: 516-933-9524; http://www.acds.org). Offers information and referral services, including a free list of publications.

National Down Syndrome Congress (NDSC)

1370 Center Drive, Suite 102, Atlanta, GA 30338 (800-232-6372; http://ndsccenter.org; e-mail: info@ndsccenter .org). Provides information and referral materials and publishes a newsletter.

National Down Syndrome Society (NDSS)

666 Broadway, New York, NY 10012 (800-221-4602; fax: 212-979-2873; http://www.ndss.org). Provides information and publishes a newsletter and clinical care booklets.

EPILEPSY

American Epilepsy Society

342 North Main Street, West Hartford, CT 06117-2507 (860-586-7505; fax: 860-586-7550; http://www.aesnet .org; e-mail: Info@aesnet.org). Promotes research and education for professionals dedicated to the prevention, treatment, and cure of epilepsy.

Epilepsy Foundation (formerly Epilepsy Foundation of America)

4351 Garden City Drive, Landover, MD 20785-7223 (800-332-1000; http://www.efa.org; e-mail: webmaster @efa.org). Provides programs of information and education, advocacy, support of research, and the delivery of needed services to people with epilepsy and their families.

International League Against Epilepsy

avenue Marcel Thiry 204, B-1200, Brussels, Belgium (http://www.ilae-epilepsy.org/; e-mail: ndevolder @ilae-epilepsy.org). Global nonprofit organization that disseminates knowledge about epilepsy and fosters research, education and training, and improved services and care. Has official working relationship with the World Health Organization.

FETAL ALCOHOL SYNDROME

Family Empowerment Network (FEN)

610 Langdon Street, Room 517, Madison, WI 53703-1195 (800-462-5254; fax: 608-265-3352; http://www .dcs.wisc.edu/pda/hhi/fen/; e-mail: fen@dcs.wisc.edu). National, nonprofit organization that exists to empower families affected by fetal alcohol syndrome and other drug-related birth defects through education and support; also publishes a newsletter, *The FEN Pen.*

National Organization on Fetal Alcohol Syndrome (NOFAS)

216 G Street NE, Washington, DC 20002 (202-785-4585; fax: 202-466-6456; http://www.nofas.org; e-mail: information@nofas.org). Nonprofit organization founded in 1990 dedicated to eliminating birth defects caused by alcohol consumption during pregnancy and improving the quality of life for those individuals and families affected. NOFAS, which applies a multicultural approach in its prevention and healing strategies, is the only national organization focusing solely on fetal alcohol syndrome.

PREVLINE: Prevention Online
(National Clearinghouse for Alcohol and Drug Information)

11426–11428 Rockville Pike, Suite 200, Rockville, MD 20852 (800-729-6686; http://www.health.org; e-mail: info@health.org). The world's largest resource for current information and materials concerning substance abuse. Distributes brochures, offers resources for parents and teachers on prevention, and has English- and Spanish-speaking information service staff available to answer questions.

FRAGILE X SYNDROME

FRAXA Research Foundation

45 Pleasant Street, Newburyport, MA 01950 (978-462-1866; http://www.fraxa.org; e-mail: info@fraxa.org). Supports scientific research aimed at finding a treatment and a cure for fragile X syndrome. Funds grants and fellowships at universities worldwide. Runs a listserv on which individuals may post strategies and questions. Publishes *FRAXA Newsletter, Medication Guide for Fragile X Syndrome* (by Michael Tranfaglia), and *Fragile X— A to Z: A Guide for Families* (edited by Wendy Dillworth; downloadable from the web site free of charge).

National Fragile X Foundation

Post Office Box 190488, San Francisco, CA 94119 (800-688-8765; fax: 925-938-9315; http://www.fragilex.org; e-mail: natlfx@fragilex.org). Promotes education concerning diagnosis of, treatment for, and research on fragile X syndrome and provides referral to local resource centers. Sponsors a biannual conference. Offers extensive audiovisual and teaching aids.

GENETIC SYNDROMES AND INBORN ERRORS OF METABOLISM

There are many support organizations and networks for children with various syndromes and inborn errors of metabolism and their families. A representative sample is listed here. For a more complete listing, contact the National Organization for Rare Disorders (NORD [see later listing]).

The American Society of Human Genetics

9650 Rockville Pike, Bethesda, MD 20814-3998 (866-486-4363; fax: 301-530-7079; http://www.ashg.org). Organization for professionals specializing in human genetics. Publishes *The American Journal of Human Genetics* and other resources.

Arnold-Chiari Family Network

c/o Kevin and Maureen Walsh, 67 Spring Street, Weymouth, MA 02188 (617-337-2368). Informal family support network for individuals with Chiari I and Chiari II malformations and their families. Literature and occasional newsletter provided on request.

Avenues

Post Office Box 5192, Sonora, CA 95370 (209-928-3688; http://www.sonnet.com/avenues; e-mail: avenues @sonnet.com). Publishes a semiannual newsletter that provides lists of parents, physicians, and experienced medical centers that are concerned with people with arthrogryposis multiplex congenita.

Cornelia de Lange Syndrome Foundation, Inc.

302 West Main Street, #100, Avon, CT 06001 (800-223-8355; fax: 860-676-8337; http://cdlsoutreach.org; e-mail: info@cdlsusa.org). Supports parents and children affected by de Lange syndrome, encourages research, and disseminates information to increase public awareness through a newsletter and informational pamphlet.

5p– Society

Post Office Box 268, Lakewood, CA 90714 (888-970-0777; fax: 714-890-9112; http://www.fivepminus.org; e-mail: fivepminus@aol.com). Family support and information group for parents, grandparents, and guardians of individuals with 5p– (cri-du-chat) syndrome. Publishes a newsletter and sponsors an annual meeting.

GeneTests•GeneClinics

(206-527-5742; 206-221-4674; http://www.geneclinics.org; http://www.genetests.org; e-mail: geneclinics @geneclinics.org; genetests@genetests.org). Free medical genetics information resource developed for physicians, other health care providers, researchers, and the public. Provides *GeneReviews*, peer-reviewed articles describing the application of genetic testing to the diagnosis, management, and genetic counseling of patients; international directories for genetic testing laboratories and genetic and prenatal diagnosis clinics; and various educational materials.

Genetic Alliance, Inc.

4301 Connecticut Avenue NW, Suite 404, Washington, DC 20008-2304 (800-336-4363; fax: 202-966-8553; http://www.geneticalliance.org; e-mail: info@geneticalliance.org). International organization of families, health professionals, and genetic organizations dedicated to enhancing the lives of individuals living with genetic conditions through the provision of education, policy, and information services. Helpline staff are available to address questions about genetics and to connect callers with support groups and informational resources.

Genetics Society of America

9650 Rockville Pike, Bethesda, MD 20814-3998 (866-486-4363; fax: 301-530-7079; http://www.faseb.org /genetics/gsa/gsamenu.htm). Professional organization that aims to bring together genetic investigators and provide a forum for sharing research findings. Cooperates in the organization of an international congress held every five years under the auspices of the International Genetics Federation. Publishes the journal *GENETICS* and other resources.

Howard University Center for Sickle Cell Disease

2121 Georgia Avenue NW, Washington, DC 20059 (202-806-7930; fax: 202-806-4517; http://www.huhosp .org/sicklecell). Screening and counseling for sickle cell disease; provides services to both adults and children, including medical treatment and psychosocial intervention.

Little People of America, Inc.

Post Office Box 745, Lubbock, TX 79408 (English and Spanish helpline: 888-572-2001; http://www.lpaonline .org; e-mail: LPADataBase@juno.com). Nationwide organization dedicated to helping people of short stature. Provides fellowship, moral support, and information to "little people," or individuals with dwarfism. The toll-free helpline provides information on organizations, products and services, and doctors in the caller's area.

National Gaucher Foundation

5410 Edson Lane, Suite 260, Rockville, MD 20852 (800-428-2437; fax: 301-816-1516; http://www.gaucherdisease .org; e-mail: ngf@gaucherdisease.org). Publishes quarterly newsletter, operates support groups and chapters, provides referrals to organizations for appropriate services, and funds research on Gaucher disease.

The National Neurofibromatosis Foundation, Inc.

95 Pine Street, 16th Floor, New York, NY 10005 (800-323-7938; fax: 212-747-0004; http://www.nf.org; e-mail: NNFF@nf.org). Supplies information to lay people and professionals and offers genetic counseling and support groups throughout the United States.

National Organization for Rare Disorders (NORD)

Post Office Box 8923, New Fairfield, CT 06812-8923 (203-746-6518; fax: 203-746-6481; http://www.rarediseases .org; e-mail: orphan@rarediseases.org). Nonprofit group of voluntary health organizations serving people with rare disorders and disabilities. Dedicated to the identification, treatment, and cure of rare disorders through education, advocacy, research, and service.

National Tay-Sachs and Allied Diseases Association

2001 Beacon Street, Suite 204, Brighton, MA, 02135 (800-906-8723; fax: 617-277-0134; http://www.NTSAD .org; e-mail: NTSAD-boston@worldnet.att.net). Promotes genetic screening programs nationally; has updated listing of Tay-Sachs disease prevention centers in a number of countries; provides educational literature to general public and professionals; and coordinates a peer group support for parents.

National Urea Cycle Disorders Foundation

4841 Hill Street, La Cañada, CA 91011 (http://www. nucdf.org/; e-mail: info@nucdf.org). Provides information and support for families. Supports and stimulates medical research and increased awareness by the public and the legislators of issues related to urea cycle disorders.

Online Mendelian Inheritance in Man (OMIM)

(http://www.ncbi.nlm.nih.gov/Omim/). Web site database of human genes and genetic disorders with textual information, pictures, and reference information.

Osteogenesis Imperfecta Foundation, Inc.

804 West Diamond Avenue, Suite 210, Gaithersburg, MD 20878 (800-981-2663; fax: 301-947-0456; http://www.oif.org; e-mail: bonelink@oif.org). Supports research on osteogenesis imperfecta and provides information to those with this disorder, their families, and other interested people.

Prader-Willi Syndrome Association

5700 Midnight Pass Road, Sarasota, FL 34242 (800-926-4797; fax: 941-312-0142; http://www. pwsausa.org; e-mail: national@pwsausa.org). National organization that serves as a clearinghouse for information on Prader-Willi syndrome; shares information with parents, professionals, and other interested people.

Sickle Cell Disease Association of America, Inc.

200 Corporate Pointe, Suite 495, Culver City, CA 90230-8727 (800-421-8453; fax: 310-215-3722; http://www.sicklecelldisease.org; e-mail: scdaa@sicklecelldisease.org). Provides education, screening, genetic counseling, technical assistance, tutorial services, vocational rehabilitation, and research support in the United States and Canada.

Support Organization for Trisomy 18, 13, and Related Disorders (SOFT)

2982 South Union Street, Rochester, NY 14624 (800-716-7638; Spanish: 631-226-3986; http://www.trisomy .org; e-mail: barbsoft@aol.com). Chapters in most states provide support and family packages with a newsletter and appropriate literature underscoring the common problems for children with trisomy 13 or trisomy 18. Holds yearly conference for families and professionals.

Tourette Syndrome Association

42-40 Bell Boulevard, Bayside, NY 11361 (718-224-2999; fax: 718-279-9596; http://www.tsa-usa.org; e-mail: ts@tsa-usa.org). Offers information, referral, advocacy, education, research, and self-help groups to those affected by Tourette syndrome.

Treacher Collins Foundation

Post Office Box 683, Norwich, VT 05055 (http://www.treachercollinsfnd.org; e-mail: geomrf@hotmail.com). Resource and referral for families, individuals, and professionals who are interested in developing and sharing knowledge and experience about Treacher Collins syndrome and related disorders. Publishes newsletter and makes print and videotape resources available by loan.

Tuberous Sclerosis Alliance

801 Roeder Road, Suite 750, Silver Spring, MD 20910 (800-225-6872; fax: 301-562-9870; http://www.tsalliance. org; e-mail: info@tsalliance.org). Offers public information about manifestations of the disease to newly diagnosed individuals, their families, and interested professionals. Referrals are made to support groups located in most states. Funds research through membership fees and donations.

HEARING, SPEECH, AND LANGUAGE IMPAIRMENTS

ADARA (formerly Professional Workers with the Adult Deaf [PRWAD] and the American Deafness and Rehabilitation Association)

Post Office Box 727, Lusby, MD 20657 (http://www.adara.org; e-mail: ADARAorgn@aol.com). Serves professionals who work with deaf individuals and people interested in learning about deafness. Publishes a journal and newsletter by subscription; offers memberships.

Alexander Graham Bell Association for the Deaf

3417 Volta Place NW, Washington, DC 20007 (202-337-5220; TTY: 202-337-5221; fax: 202-337-8314; http://www.agbell.org; e-mail: info@agbell.org). Umbrella organization for International Organization for the Education of the Hearing Impaired (IOEHI), Parents' Section (PS), and Oral Hearing Impaired Section. Provides general information and information on resources. Encourages improved communication, better public understanding, and detection of early hearing loss. Works for better educational opportunities; provides scholarships and training for teachers.

American Hyperlexia Association

195 West Spangler, Suite B, Elmhurst, IL 60126 (630-415-2212; fax: 630-530-5909; http://www.hyperlexia.org; e-mail: info@hyperlexia.org). Nonprofit organization composed of families of children, speech-language professionals, and educators dedicated to identifying hyperlexia, promoting effective teaching techniques, and educating the general public about hyperlexia.

American Society for Deaf Children

Post Office Box 3355, Gettysburg, PA 17325 (voice/TTY: 717-334-7922; parent hotline: 800-942-2732; fax: 717-334-8808; http://www.deafchildren.org; e-mail: asdc1@aol.com). Provides information and support to parents and families with children who are deaf or who have hearing impairment.

American Speech-Language-Hearing Association (ASHA)

10801 Rockville Pike, Rockville, MD 20852 (voice/TTY: 800-638-8255; http://www.asha.org; e-mail: actioncenter @asha.org). This professional and scientific organization and certifying body for professionals providing speech-language and hearing therapy conducts research in communication disorders; publishes several journals; provides consumer information and professional referral.

Boys Town National Research Hospital

555 North 30th Street, Omaha, NE 68131 (http://www.boystownhospital.org/home.asp). Professionals can access a variety of resources relating to children with hearing, language, and learning disabilities and the research currently underway at Boys Town National Research Hospital.

Captioned Media Program (formerly Captioned Films/Videos)

1447 East Main Street, Spartanburg, SC 29307 (800-237-6213; TTY: 800-237-6819; fax: 800-538-5636; http://www.cfv.org; e-mail: info@cfv.org). Government-sponsored distribution of open-captioned materials to eligible institutions, individuals, and families. Application sent on request.

Deafness Research Foundation

1050 17th Street NW, Suite 701, Washington, DC 20036 (http://www.drf.org; e-mail: webmaster@drf.org). Solicits funds for the support of research into the causes, treatment, and prevention of deafness and other hearing disorders.

International Hearing Society

16880 Middlebelt Road, Livonia, MI 48154 (http://www.insinfo.org). Provides information on how to proceed when hearing loss is suspected; free consumer kit, facts about hearing aids, and a variety of literature on hearing-related subjects are available.

National Center for Stuttering

200 East 33rd Street, New York, NY 10016 (800-221-2483; http://www.stuttering.com). Provides free information for parents of young children just starting to show symptoms of stuttering; runs training programs in current therapeutic approaches for speech-language professionals; provides treatment for people older than 7 years of age who stutter.

National Deaf Education Network and Clearinghouse

Laurent Clerc National Deaf Education Center; Gallaudet University, 800 Florida Avenue NE, Washington, DC 20002-3695 (voice/TTY: 202-651-5031; http://clerccenter.gallaudet.edu/Clearinghouse/index.html; e-mail: clearinghouse.Infotogo@gallaudet.edu). Provides information related to deafness; has a multitude of resources and experts available for individuals with hearing impairment, their families, and professionals. Collects information about resources around the country.

Self Help for Hard of Hearing People (SHHH)

7910 Woodmont Avenue, Suite 1200, Bethesda, MD 20814 (301-657-2248; TTY: 301-657-2249; fax: 301-913-9413; http://www.shhh.org; e-mail: National@shhh.org). Educational organization that provides assistance to individuals with hearing impairments to participate fully in society. Publishes journal, newsletter, and other materials; provides advocacy and outreach programs and extensive network of local chapters and self-help groups; and hosts an annual convention.

Signing Exact English (SEE) Center for the Advancement of Deaf Children

Post Office Box 1181, Los Alamitos, CA 90720 (562-430-1467; fax: 562-795-6614; http://www.seecenter.org; e-mail: seectr@aol.com). Offers information and referral services for parents of children newly diagnosed with hearing impairments.

Speech Therapy Activities

(http://www.speechtx.com/). Web site provides free, printable speech-language activities for speech-language pathologists and parents.

LEARNING DISABILITIES

Dyslexia Research Institute

5746 Centerville Road, Tallahassee, FL 32308 (850-893-2216; fax: 850-893-2440; http://www.dyslexia-add .org; e-mail: dri@dyslexia-add.org). Provides training, workshops, and seminars for professionals. Literature sent on request.

International Dyslexia Association (IDA; formerly the Orton Dyslexia Society)

8600 LaSalle Road, Chester Building Suite 382, Baltimore, MD 21286-2044 (410-296-0232; fax: 410-321-5069; http://www.interdys.org; e-mail: info@interdys.org). Devoted to the study and treatment of dyslexia; provides information and referrals; sponsors conferences, seminars, and support groups; and has two regular publications and more than 40 branches in the United States and abroad.

LD Online

(http://www.ldonline.org/; e-mail: info@ldonline.org). Web site resource on learning disabilities for parents, students, teachers, and other professionals. This interactive web site provides basic information on learning disabilities, as well as the latest research and news; also offers e-mail consultation by experts on learning disabilities, resource lists, personal stories, bulletin boards, and materials/resources for purchase.

Learning Disabilities Association of America (LDA)

4156 Library Road, Pittsburgh, PA 15234 (412-341-1515; fax: 412-344-0224; http://www.ldanatl/.org; e-mail: info@ldaamerica.org). Encourages research and the development of early detection programs, disseminates information, serves as an advocate, and works to improve education for individuals with learning disabilities.

National Center for Learning Disabilities (NCLD)

381 Park Avenue, South, Suite 1401, New York, NY 10016 (888-575-7373; fax: 212-545-9665; http://www .ld.org). Promotes public awareness of learning disabilities; provides computerized information and referral services to consumers and professionals on learning disabilities. Publishes *Their World*, an annual magazine for parents and professionals.

MENTAL RETARDATION

American Association on Mental Retardation (AAMR)

444 North Capitol Street NW, Suite 846, Washington, DC 20001 (800-424-3688; fax: 202-387-2193; http:// www.aamr.org). Professional organization that promotes cooperation among those involved in services, training, and research in mental retardation. Encourages research, dissemination of information, development of appropriate community-based services, and the promotion of preventive measures designed to further reduce the incidence of mental retardation.

The Arc of the United States

1010 Wayne Avenue, Suite 650, Silver Spring, MD 20910 (301-565-3842; fax: 301-565-5342; http://thearc.org; e-mail: info@thearc.org). National advocacy organization working on behalf of individuals with mental retardation and their families; has more than 1,000 state and local chapters.

President's Committee on Mental Retardation (PCMR)

370 L'Enfant Promenade SW, Suite 701, Washington, DC 20447-0001 (202-619-0634; fax: 202-205-9519; http://www.acf.dhhs.gov/programs/pcmr; e-mail: pcmr@acf.dhhs.gov). Advises the President and the Secretary of Health and Human Services on all matters pertaining to mental retardation; publishes annual reports and information on the rights of people with mental retardation.

MUSCULAR DYSTROPHY

Muscular Dystrophy Association

3300 East Sunrise Drive, Tucson, AZ 85718 (800-572-1717; http://www.mdausa.org; e-mail: mda@mdausa.org). Health care agency that fosters research and provides direct services to individuals with muscular dystrophy; is concerned with conquering muscular dystrophy and other neuromuscular diseases.

SCOLIOSIS

National Scoliosis Foundation

5 Cabot Place, Stoughton, MA 02072 (800-673-6922; fax: 781-341-8333; http://www.scoliosis.org; e-mail: NSF @scoliosis.org). Nonprofit organization with state chapters dedicated to informing the public about scoliosis and promoting early detection and treatment of scoliosis. Publishes *Spinal Connection* newsletter.

Scoliosis Research Society

611 East Wells Street, Milwaukee, WI 53202 (414-289-9107; fax: 414-276-3349; http://www.srs.org). Sponsors and promotes research on the etiology and treatment of scoliosis and spinal disorders.

SEVERE/MULTIPLE DISABILITIES

Helen Keller National Center for Deaf-Blind Youths and Adults

111 Middle Neck Road, Sands Point, NY 11050 (516-944-8900; TTY: 516-944-8637; fax: 516-944-7302; http://www.helenkeller.org/national). Has specialists at its New York training center as well as representatives in 10 regional offices who can assist with locating assistive/adaptive devices. Also offers technical assistance to local agencies that are serving deafblind individuals.

TASH

29 West Susquehanna Avenue, Suite 210, Baltimore, MD 21204 (410-828-8274; fax: 410-828-6706; http://www.tash.org; e-mail: info@tash.org). Advocates inclusive education and community opportunities for people with disabilities, disseminates research findings and practical applications for education and community living, encourages sharing of experience and expertise. Publishes a newsletter and a journal.

SPINA BIFIDA AND OTHER NEURAL TUBE DEFECTS (NTDs)

Spina Bifida Association of America

4590 MacArthur Boulevard NW, Suite 250, Washington, DC 20007-4226 (800-621-3141; fax: 202-944-3295; http://www.sbaa.org; e-mail: sbaa@sbaa.org). Provides information and referral for new parents and literature on spina bifida; supports a public awareness program; advocates for individuals with spina bifida and their families; supports research; and conducts conferences for parents and professionals.

TRAUMATIC BRAIN INJURY (TBI)

Brain Injury Association of America (formerly National Head Injury Foundation)

105 North Alfred Street, Alexandria, VA 22314 (helpline: 800-444-6443; 703-236-6000; fax: 703-236-6001; http://www.biausa.org; e-mail: FamilyHelpLine@biausa.org). Provides information to educate the public, politicians, businesses, and educators about brain injury, including effects, causes, and prevention.

Traumatic Brain Injury Resource Guide

(http://www.neuroskills.com). Web site includes educational information, books, local support groups, and research.

VISUAL IMPAIRMENTS

American Foundation for the Blind (AFB)

11 Penn Plaza, Suite 300, New York, NY 10011 (800-232-5463; fax: 212-502-7777; e-mail: afbinfo@afb.net; http://www.afb.org). Works in cooperation with other agencies, organizations, and schools to offer services to individuals who are blind or who have visual impairments; provides consultation, public education, referrals,

and information; produces and distributes talking books; publishes and sells materials for professionals in the blindness field.

American Printing House for the Blind (APH)

Post Office Box 6085, Louisville, KY 40206-0085 (800-223-1839; fax: 502-899-2274; http://www.aph.org; e-mail: info@aph.org). Nonprofit publishing house for people with visual impairments; books in braille and large type and on audiotape and computer disk are available. A range of aids, tools, and supplies for education and daily living are also available. Free catalog.

National Association for Visually Handicapped

22 West 21st Street, 6th Floor, New York, NY 10010 (212-889-3141; fax: 212-727-2931; http://www.navh.org; e-mail: staff@navh.org) (in AK, AZ, CA, CO, HI, ID, MT, NV, NM, OR, UT, WA, and WY: 3201 Balboa Street, San Francisco, CA 94121; 415-221-3201; fax: 415-221-8754; http://www.navh.org; e-mail: staffca@navh .org). Provides informational literature, guidance and counseling in the use of visual aids, emotional support, and referral services for parents of partially sighted children and those who work with these children. Publishes free large-print newsletter.

National Braille Association

3 Townline Circle, Rochester, NY 14623-2513 (585-427-8260; fax: 585-427-0263; http://www.nationalbraille .org; e-mail: nbaoffice@compuserve.com). Produces and distributes braille reading materials for people with visual impairment. Collection consists of college-level textbooks, materials of general interest, standard technical tables, and music.

National Federation of the Blind

1800 Johnson Street, Baltimore, MD 21230 (410-659-9314; fax: 410-685-5653; http://www.nfb.org; e-mail: nfb@nfb.org). Strives for complete integration of blind people into society on a basis of equality. Offers advocacy services for the blind in such areas as discrimination in housing and insurance. Operates a job referral and listing system to help blind individuals find competitive employment. Runs an aids and appliances department to assist blind people in independent living. Has a scholarship program for blind college students and a loan program for blind people who are going into business for themselves. Publishes monthly and quarterly publications.

National Library Service for the Blind and Physically Handicapped

1291 Taylor Street NW, Washington, DC 20011 (202-707-5100; TTY: 202-707-0744; fax: 202-707-0712; http://www.loc.gov/nls; e-mail: nls@loc.gov). Administers a national library service through a network of participating public libraries that provides braille and recorded books and magazines on free loan to anyone who cannot read standard print because of visual or physical disabilities.

Prevent Blindness America

500 East Remington Road, Schaumburg, IL 60173 (800-331-2020; http://www.preventblindness.org; e-mail: info@preventblindness.org). Committed to the reduction of preventable blindness. Provides information to people who are blind, professionals working with these individuals, and the public.

Recording for the Blind & Dyslexic (RFB&D)

20 Roszel Road, Princeton, NJ 08540 (609-452-0606; http://www.rfbd.org). Produces and distributes textbooks on audiotape, computer disk, and CD-ROM; individuals or institutions who have memberships may borrow these materials. Also provides reference librarian services for individual members.

INTERVENTIONS, SUPPORTS, AND SERVICES

ACCESSIBILITY AND COMMUNITY INCLUSION

Association of University Centers on Disabilities (formerly American Association of University Affiliated Programs for Persons with Developmental Disabilities)

8630 Fenton Street, Suite 410, Silver Spring, MD 20910 (301-588-8252; fax: 301-588-2842; http://www.aucd .org; e-mail: kmusheno@aucd.org). Represents the professional interests of the national network of 61 university centers for excellence in developmental disabilities education, research, and service (UCEs; formerly called university affiliated programs, or UAPs) that serve people with developmental disabilities.

The Center for Universal Design

North Carolina State University College of Design, Campus Box 8613, Brooks Hall, Room 220, Pullen Road, Raleigh, NC 27695-8613 (800-647-6777; fax: 919-515-3023; http://www.design.ncsu.edu:8120/cud/; e-mail: cud@ncsu.edu). Provides publications and information to parents and professionals concerning accessible housing design and financing issues; makes referrals to local organizations.

Center on Human Policy

Syracuse University, 805 South Crouse Avenue, Syracuse, NY 13244-2280 (800-894-0826; TTY: 315-443-4355; fax: 315-443-4338; http://soeweb.syr.edu/thechp/; e-mail: thechp@sued.syr.edu). Involved in a range of local, state, national, and international activities, including policy studies, research, information, and referral.

Job Accommodation Network (JAN)

West Virginia University, Post Office Box 6080, Morgantown, WV 26506-6080 (in the U.S.: voice/TTY: 800-526-7234; worldwide: voice/TTY: 304-293-7186; fax: 304-293-5407; http://janweb.icdi.wvu.edu; e-mail: jan @jan.icdi.wvu.edu). Information and resources to make workplaces accessible to those with disabilities.

National Association of Developmental Disabilities Councils

1234 Massachusetts Avenue NW, Suite 103, Washington, DC 20005 (202-347-1234; fax: 202-347-4023; http://www.naddc.org; e-mail: mgray@naddc.org). Organization of Developmental Disability Councils that exist in each state to provide information on and advocate for resources and services for people with developmental disabilities and their families.

National Center on Accessibility

Indiana University, 2805 East 10th Street, Suite 190, Bloomington, IN 47408-2698 (812-856-4422; TTY: 812-856-4421; fax: 812-856-4480; http://www.ncaonline.org; e-mail: nca@indiana.edu). Works with departments of parks, recreation, and tourism throughout the United States to improve accessibility. Sponsors several training sessions each year throughout the United States to educate employers on making their workplaces accessible.

National Council on Independent Living

1916 Wilson Boulevard, Suite 209, Arlington, VA 22201 (703-525-3406; TTY: 703-525-4153; fax: 703-525-3409; http://www.ncil.org; e-mail: ncil@ncil.org). A national membership association of nonprofit corporations that advances the full integration and participation of people with disabilities in society and the development of centers for independent living. Provides members with technical assistance and training, a quarterly newsletter, and sponsors a national conference.

National Home of Your Own Alliance

University of New Hampshire, Institute on Disability, Center for Housing and New Community Economics (CHANCE), 7 Leavitt Lane, Suite 101, Durham, NH 03824-3522 (http://alliance.unh.edu/nhoyo.html; e-mail: drv@cisunix.unh.edu). This program is dedicated to helping people with disabilities in becoming homeowners and in controlling their homes.

National Organization on Disability

910 16th Street NW, Suite 600, Washington, DC 20006 (202-293-5960; fax: 202-293-7999; TTY: 202-293-5968; www.nod.org; e-mail: ability@nod.org). Promotes the acceptance and understanding of the needs of citizens with disabilities through a national network of communities and organizations and facilitates exchange of information regarding resources available to people with disabilities.

U.S. Architectural and Transportation Barriers Compliance Board

1331 F Street NW, Suite 1000, Washington, DC 20004-1111 (800-872-2253; TTY: 800-993-2822; fax: 202-272-5447; http://www.access-board.gov; e-mail: info@access-board.gov). An organization created by Section 504 of the Rehabilitation Act of 1973 (PL 93-112) to enforce the Architectural Barriers Act of 1968 (PL 90-480). Offers free publications and answers to technical questions about accessibility.

ADAPTIVE TECHNOLOGY AND EQUIPMENT

ABLEDATA

8630 Fenton Street, Suite 950, Silver Spring, MD 20910 (800-227-0216; TTY: 301-608-8912; fax: 301-608-8958; http://www.abledata.com; e-mail: abledata@macroint.com). National database of information on assistive technology and rehabilitation equipment.

Alliance for Technology Access

2175 East Francisco Boulevard, Suite L, San Rafael, CA 94901 (415-455-4575; TTY: 415-455-0491; fax: 415-455-0654; http://www.ataccess.org; e-mail: ATAinfo@ATAccess.org). A resource and demonstration center open to people with disabilities and their families as well as professionals and others interested in adaptive technology.

Independent Living Aids, Inc.

200 Robbins Lane, Jericho, NY 11753 (800-537-2118; fax: 516-937-3906; http://www.independentliving.com; e-mail: can-do@independentliving.com). Sells aids that make daily tasks easier for those with physical disabilities; also carries clocks, calculators, magnifying lamps, and easy-to-see low vision and talking watches for individuals with visual impairments. Will send free catalog.

Michigan's Assistive Technology Resource

1023 South U.S. Route 27, St. Johns, MI 48879 (800-274-7426; TTY: 989-224-0246; fax: 989-224-0330; http://www.matr.org; e-mail: matr@match.org). Provides free information on low-tech devices and equipment available for individuals with disabilities.

Rehabilitation Engineering and Assistive Technology Society of North America (RESNA)

1700 North Moore Street, Suite 1540, Arlington, VA 22209-1903 (703-524-6686; TTY: 703-524-6639; fax: 703-524-6630; http://www.resna.org). Multidisciplinary organization of professionals interested in the identification, development, and delivery of technology to people with disabilities. Offers numerous publications.

BEHAVIOR AND MENTAL HEALTH

American Academy of Child and Adolescent Psychiatry (AACAP)

3615 Wisconsin Avenue NW, Washington, DC 20016-3007 (202-966-7300; fax: 202-966-2891; http://www.aacap.org). National, nonprofit organization composed of child and adolescent psychiatrists. Provides information for professionals and families to aid in the understanding and treatment of childhood and adolescent developmental, behavioral, and mental disorders. Parent and caregiver fact sheets and information on research, practice, and membership are available on the web site.

American Psychiatric Association (APA)

1400 K Street NW, Washington, DC 20005 (888-357-7924; fax: 202-682-6850; http://www.psych.org/; e-mail: apa@psych.org). International organization for physicians dedicated to the diagnosis and treatment of mental and emotional illnesses and substance use disorders.

American Psychological Association (APA)

750 First Street, NE, Washington, DC 20002-4242 (800-374-2721; TTY: 202-336-6123; http://www.apa.org/). National scientific and professional organization that develops and promotes standards in psychological practice, research, and education. Dedicated to the dissemination of psychological knowledge to professionals, students, and the general public through meetings, reports, and publications.

Association for Behavior Analysis (ABA)

213 West Hall, Western Michigan University, 1903 West Michigan Avenue, Kalamazoo, MI 49008-5301 (616-387-8341; fax: 616-387-8354; http://www.wmich.edu/aba/; e-mail: 76236.1312@compuserve.com). International organization that promotes the experimental, theoretical, and applied analysis of behavior. Disseminates professional and public information. Also publishes two scholarly journals: *The Behavior Analyst* and *The Analysis of Verbal Behavior.*

Behaviour Change Consultancy

24 Rochdale, Harold Road, London SE19 3TF, England (http://www.advice4parents.free-online.co.uk/; e-mail: bcc@behaviourchange.com). Provides advice, support, project management, policy development, and training to schools, local educational authorities, and parents on the subjects of disaffection; social, emotional, and behavioral difficulties; and behavior management.

Internet Mental Health

(http://www.mentalhealth.com/; e-mail: editor@mentalhealth.com). Free web site encyclopedia of mental health information for mental health professionals, patients, friends and families of patients, mental health support groups, students, and the general public.

Journal of Applied Behavior Analysis

(http://www.envmed.rochester.edu/wwwrap/behavior/jaba/jabahome.htm). Psychology journal that publishes research about applications of the experimental analysis of behavior to social problems. Published by The Society for the Experimental Analysis of Behavior.

CAREERS

ENTRY POINT! and ACCESS (Achieving Competence in Computing, Engineering, and Space Science) Internship Programs

American Association for the Advancement of Science (AAAS), 1200 New York Avenue NW, Washington, DC 20005 (voice/TTY: 202-326-6649; fax: 202-371-9849; http://www.entrypoint.org; e-mail: lsummers@aaas.org). The ENTRY POINT! internship program seeks to increase the number of college and graduate students with disabilities who enter and advance in science, mathematics, and engineering fields. The similar ACCESS program, which has the same application process as ENTRY POINT!, is coordinated by AAAS and NASA.

Fedcap Rehabilitation Services, Inc.

119 West 19th Street, New York, NY 10011 (212-727-4200; TTY: 212-727-4384; fax: 212-727-4374; http://www.fedcap.org; e-mail: info@fedcap.org). Services include vocational training and job placement for adults with severe disabilities and/or other disadvantages.

CHILD DEVELOPMENT AND PEDIATRICS

American Academy of Pediatrics (AAP)

141 Northwest Point Boulevard, Elk Grove Village, IL 60007-1098 (847-434-4000; fax: 847-434-8000; http://www.aap.org; e-mail: kidsdocs@aap.org). Professional membership association for board-certified pediatricians that offers professional continuing education, health education materials, and other programs.

Child Development Institute

17853 Santiago Boulevard, Suite 107-328, Villa Park, CA 92861 (714-998-8617; fax: 714-637-6957; http://www.childdevelopmentinfo.com/; e-mail: webmaster@childdevelopmentinfo.com). Web site for parents on child development, parenting, child psychology, teenagers, health, safety, and learning disabilities.

Pediatric Development and Behavior: Developmental-Behavioral Pediatrics Online Community

880 6th Street South, Suite 340, St. Petersburg, FL 33701 (727-502-8035; fax: 727-892-8244; http://www.dbpeds.org/). Web site resource for clinical information and educational material on developmental, learning, and behavioral problems. Main audience is physicians, but the web site may also be of interest to psychologists, nurses, social workers, therapists, educators, and parents.

Society for Developmental and Behavioral Pediatrics

19 Station Lane, Philadelphia, PA 19118 (215-248-9168; http://www.sdbp.org; e-mail: nmspota@aol.com). Interdisciplinary organization that promotes research and teaching in developmental and behavioral pediatrics. Sponsors the *Journal of Developmental and Behavioral Pediatrics* and conducts annual scientific meetings.

Society for Developmental Pediatrics

Post Office Box 23836, Baltimore, MD 21203 (410-550-9446). Provides list of pediatricians who specialize in evaluation and treatment of children with disabilities. Sponsors the scientific journal *Mental Retardation and Developmental Disabilities Research Reviews*.

DENTAL CARE

American Academy of P ediatric Dentistry

211 East Chicago Avenue, #700, Chicago, IL 60611-2663 (312-337-2169; fax 312-337-6329; http://www.aapd.org). National organization representing the specialty of pediatric dentistry. Dedicated to improving and maintaining the oral health of children, adolescents, and people with special health care needs. Publishes the journal *Pediatric Dentistry*.

American Society of Dentistry for Children

211 East Chicago Avenue, #710, Chicago, IL, 60611-2663 (312-943-1244; fax: 312-943-5341; http://www .asdckids.org; e-mail: asdckids@aol.com). Professional organization for specialists in pediatric dentistry. Dedicated to improving the dental health of children through the dissemination of knowledge to professionals and the general public through educational programs, public service efforts, and research. Publishes the *Journal of Dentistry for Children.*

National Institute of Dental and Craniofacial Research

National Institutes of Health, Bethesda, MD 20892-2190 (301-496-4261; http://www.nidr.nih.gov; e-mail: nidcrinfo@mail.nih.gov). Institute dedicated to the promotion of oral, dental, and craniofacial health through study of ways to promote health, prevent diseases and conditions, and develop new diagnostics and therapeutics.

Oral Health in America: A Report of the Surgeon General

(http://www.nidr.nih.gov/sgr/oralhealth.asp). First-ever Surgeon General's report (2000) on oral health. Identifies a silent epidemic of dental and oral diseases in some populations and calls for a national effort to improve oral health among all Americans. Available in English and Spanish.

Special Care Dentistry

211 East Chicago Avenue, 5th Floor, Chicago, IL 60611 (312-440-2660; fax: 312-440-2824; http://www.SCDonline .org; e-mail: SCD@SCDonline.org). National organization of dentists, dental hygienists, dental assistants, non-dental health care providers, health program administrators, hospitals, agencies that serve people with special needs, and other advocacy and health care organizations. Publishes the journal *Special Care in Dentistry.*

EDUCATION

American Educational Research Association (AERA)

1230 17th Street NW, Washington, DC 20036-3078 (202-223-9485; fax: 202-775-1824; http://www.aera.net). International professional organization with the goal of advancing educational research and its practical education. Members are educators, counselors, evaluators, graduate students, behavioral scientists, and directors or administrators of research, testing, or evaluation.

Association for Supervision and Curriculum Development (ASCD)

1703 North Beauregard Street, Alexandria, VA 22311 (800-933-2723; fax: 703-575-5400; http://www.ascd.org). Professional membership organization for educators with interest in instruction, curriculum, and supervision. Publishes the journal *Educational Leadership.*

Association on Higher Education and Disability (AHEAD)

University of Massachusetts, 100 Morrissey Boulevard, Boston, MA 02125 (617-287-3880; TTY: 617-287-3882; fax: 617-287-3881; http://www.ahead.org). Professional organization committed to full participation in higher education for people with disabilities.

Council for Exceptional Children (CEC)

1110 North Glebe Road, Suite 300, Arlington, VA 22201 (888-232-7733; TTY: 703-264-9446; fax: 703-264-9494; http://www.cec.sped.org; e-mail: service@sped.org). Provides information to teachers, administrators, and others concerned with the education of gifted children and children with disabilities. Maintains a library and database (ERIC Clearinghouse on Disabilities and Gifted Education; http://www.ericec.org) on research in special and gifted education; provides information and assistance on legislation.

National Association of Private Special Education Centers (NAPSEC; formerly National Association of Private Schools for Exceptional Children)

1522 K Street NW, Suite 1032, Washington, DC 20005 (202-408-3338; fax: 202-408-3340; http://www .napsec.com; e-mail: napsec@aol.com). A nonprofit association that represents more than 200 schools nationally and more than 600 at the state level through its Council of Affiliated State Associations, which provides special education and therapeutic services for children in public or private educational placements. NAPSEC provides a free referral service to parents and professionals seeking an appropriate placement for a child with a disability and publishes a directory of member schools.

National Information Center for Educational Media (NICEM)

Post Office Box 8640, Albuquerque, NM 87198-8640 (800-926-8328; fax: 505-998-3372; http://www.nicem .com; e-mail: nicem@nicem.com). Provides database of educational audiovisual materials, including videotapes, motion pictures, filmstrips, audiotapes, and slides.

FAMILY AND SIBLING SUPPORTS

Beach Center on Families and Disability

University of Kansas, 3111 Haworth Hall, Lawrence, KS 66045 (785-864-7600; fax: 785-864-7605; http://www .beachcenter.org; e-mail: beach@dole.lsi.ukans.edu). Research and training center that disseminates information about families with members who have developmental disabilities. Publishes newsletter and offers many other publications.

Caring for the Special Child

(http://www.baby-place.com/disabilities.htm). Web site provides information and links on topics related to education and disabilities such as school placements, community programs, and camps.

The Compassionate Friends

Post Office Box 3696, Oak Brook, IL 60522-3696 (877-969-0010; fax: 630-990-0246; http://www .compassionatefriends.org; e-mail: nationaloffice@compassionatefriends.org). National and worldwide organization that supports and aids parents in the positive resolution of the grief experienced upon the death of their child; fosters the physical and emotional health of bereaved parents and siblings.

Exceptional Parent

65 East Route 4, River Edge, NJ 07661 (201-489-4111; fax: 201-489-0074 http://www.eparent.com; subscriptions: Post Office Box 2078, Marion, OH 43306-2178; 877-372-7368). This magazine, published since 1971, provides straightforward, practical information for families and professionals involved in the care of children and young adults with disabilities; many articles are written by parents.

Family Village: A Global Community of Disability-Related Resources

Waisman Center, University of Wisconsin–Madison, 1500 Highland Avenue, Madison, WI 53705-2280 (http:// www.familyvillage.wisc.edu; e-mail: familyvillage@waisman.wisc.edu). This web site serves as a global community that integrates information, resources, and communication opportunities on the Internet for people with cognitive and other disabilities, for their families, and for people that provide services and support to these individuals.

Federation for Children with Special Needs

1135 Tremont Street, Suite 240, Boston, MA 02120 (800-331-0688 [in MA only]; 617-236-7210; fax: 617-572-2094; http://www.fcsn.org; e-mail: fcsninfo@fcsn.org). Offers parent-to-parent training and information; projects include Technical Assistance for Parent Programs (TAPP), Collaboration Among Parents and Health Professionals (CAPP), and Parents Engaged in Educational Reform (PEER). The federation is part of the National Early Childhood Technical Assistance System (NEC*TAS) consortium.

National Information Center for Children and Youth with Disabilities (NICHCY)

Post Office Box 1492, Washington, DC 20013-1492 (voice/TTY: 800-695-0285; fax: 202-884-8441; http:// www.nichcy.org/; e-mail: nichcy@aed.org). National information and referral center. Provides information on disabilities and disability-related issues for families, educators, and other professionals.

PACER Center (Parent Advocacy Coalition for Educational Rights)

8161 Normandale Boulevard, Minneapolis, MN 55437 (800-537-2237 [in MN only]; 952-838-9000; TTY: 952-838-0190; fax: 952-838-0199; http://www.pacer.org; e-mail: pacer@pacer.org). Provides education and training to help parents understand special education laws and to obtain appropriate school programs for their children. Workshops and program topics include early intervention, emotional disabilities, and health/medical services. Also provides disability awareness puppet program for schools, child abuse prevention program services, newsletters, booklets, extensive written materials, and videotapes.

Parent Educational Advocacy Training Center (PEATC)

6320 Augusta Drive, Suite 1200, Springfield, VA 22150 (800-869-6782 [in VA only]; voice/TTY: 703-923-0010; Spanish: 703-569-6200; fax: 703-923-0030; http://www.peatc.org; e-mail: partners@peatc.org). Professionally staffed organization that helps parents to become effective advocates for their children with school personnel and the educational system.

Parent to Parent

c/o Beach Center on Families and Disability, University of Kansas, 3111 Haworth Hall, Lawrence, KS 66045 (785-864-7600; http://www.beachcenter.org/frames.php3?id=48&category=Family [click on Parent Support, then click on Parent to Parent]). State and local chapters provide one-to-one, parent-to-parent support by matching trained parents to newly referred parents on the basis of their children's disabilities and/or family issues they are encountering or have encountered.

Sibling Information Network

The A.J. Pappanikou Center, 249 Glenbrook Road, U-64, Storrs, CT 06269-2064 (860-486-4985; fax: 860-486-5037). Assists individuals and professionals interested in serving the needs of families of individuals with disabilities; disseminates bibliographic material and directories; places people in touch with each other; publishes a newsletter written for and by siblings and parents.

The Sibling Support Project

c/o Donald Meyer, Director, the Sibling Support Project, The Arc of the United States, 6512 23rd Avenue, NW, Suite 213, Seattle, WA (206-297-6368; http://www.thearc.org/siblingsupport; e-mail: donmeyer@siblingsupport. org). National program dedicated to the interests of brothers and sisters of people with special health and developmental needs. The project's primary goal is to increase the availability of peer support and education programs for such siblings.

Team Advocates for Special Kids (TASK)

100 Cerritos Avenue, Anaheim CA 92805 (714-533-8275; fax: 714-533-2533; www.taskca.org; e-mail: taskca @yahoo.com). Provides services to enable children with disabilities to reach their highest potential. Offers training, education, support, information, resources, and community awareness programs to families of children with disabilities and the professionals who serve them. TASK's Tech Center, a member of the Alliance for Technology Access, conducts one-to-one guided exploration of technology to determine appropriate adapted hardware and software for people with disabilities. Conducts an advocacy training course and other workshops; publishes a bimonthly newsletter.

FEDERAL AGENCIES

National Information Center for Children and Youth with Disabilities (NICHCY)

Post Office Box 1492, Washington, DC 20013 (voice/TTY: 800-695-0285; fax: 202-884-8441; http://nichcy .org; e-mail: nichcy@aed.org). Provides information to assist parents, educators, caregivers, advocates, and others in helping children and youth with disabilities become participating members of the community. Services include personal responses to specific questions, referrals to other organizations or sources of help, prepared information packets, and publications on current issues.

Office of Disability Employment Policy

1331 F Street NW, Suite 300, Washington, DC 20004-1107 (202-376-6200; TTY: 202-376-6205; fax: 202-376-6859; http://www.dol.gov/dol/odep/welcome.html; e-mail: infoodep@dol.gov). One of the oldest presidential committees in the United States. Promotes acceptance of people with physical and mental disabilities in the world of work, both the public and the private sectors. Promotes the elimination of barriers, both physical and attitudinal, to the employment of people with disabilities.

Office of Special Education and Rehabilitative Services (OSERS)

U.S. Department of Eduction, 400 Maryland Avenue SW, Washington, DC 20202 (202-205-5465; http://www.ed .gov/offices/OSERS). Part of the U.S. Department of Education. Responds to inquiries and researches and documents information operations serving the field of disabilities. Specializes in providing information on federal funding for programs serving people with disabilities, federal legislation affecting individuals with disabilities, and federal programs benefiting people with disabilities.

FEEDING, GROWTH, AND NUTRITION

American Academy of Allergy, Asthma, and Immunology

611 East Wells Street, Milwaukee, WI 53202 (414-272-6071; patient information and physician referral: 800-822-2762; http://www.aaaai.org; e-mail: info@aaaai.org). Professional association offering an online disease management center and annual meetings for practitioners; provides educational resources, referral services, and activities for children.

American Dietetic Association

216 West Jackson Boulevard, Chicago, IL 60606-6995 (800-877-1600; http://www.eatright.org). World's largest association of food and nutrition professionals. Its web site offers healthy lifestyle and nutrition tips and referrals to registered dieticians. Publishes *Journal of the American Dietetic Association*.

Comeunity's Resources for Feeding and Growth of Children

(http://www.comeunity.com/premature/child/growth/resources.html). This web site contains links to recommended parent discussion lists, articles, and hospitals/institutions that offer feeding therapy.

Dysphagia Resource Center

(http://www.dysphagia.com). This web site contains links to resources on swallowing and swallowing disorders.

Food Allergy and Anaphylaxis Network

(http://www.foodallergy.org). This web site promotes education, advocacy, research, and awareness about food allergies and provides information to schools on managing students with food allergies, as well as information geared toward children and adolescents.

Food and Drug Administration (FDA)

5600 Fishers Lane, Rockville, MD 20857-0001 (888-463-6332; http://www.fda.gov). Part of the U.S. Department of Health and Human Services. Provides the latest federal warnings and updates about foods, drugs, medical devices, vaccines, animal feed, cosmetics, and radiation-emitting products. Has links for children, consumers, patients, and health care professionals.

Formula Manufacturers

The following web sites contain information about special formulas required by some infants with developmental disabilities:

  http://www.meadjohnson.com (Enfamil, ProSobee, metabolic formulas)
  http://www.ross.com (Similac, Isomil, metabolic formulas)
  http://www.shsna.com (metabolic formulas)
  http://www.verybestbaby.com (Nestlé's Carnation)

New Visions

1124 Roberts Mountain Road, Faber, VA 22938 (434-361-2285; fax: 434-361-1807; http://www.new-vis.com; e-mail: sem@new-vis.com). Provides education and therapy services to professionals and parents working with children with feeding, swallowing, oral-motor, and prespeech problems. Therapy materials, tapes, and books may be ordered from the *Mealtimes* catalog.

The Vegetarian Resource Group

Post Office Box 1463, Baltimore, MD 21203 (410-366-8343; http://www.vrg.org; e-mail: vrg@vrg.org). Nonprofit organization that disseminates information on vegetarianism/veganism and the interrelated issues of health, nutrition, ecology, ethics, and world hunger. Its web site offers vegetarian and vegan recipes, nutrition information, cookbooks, and travel hints.

LEGAL ISSUES

American Bar Association Center on Children and the Law

740 15th Street NW, Washington, DC 20005-1019 (http://www.abanet.org/child/; e-mail: ctrchildlaw@abanet .org). Offers information and advocacy to professionals and parents of children and adolescents with disabilities.

American Civil Liberties Union (ACLU)

125 Broad Street, New York, NY 10004-2400 (212-549-2500; to order publications: 800-775-2258; http://www .aclu.org; e-mail: aclu@aclu.org). This nonprofit organization, the largest public-interest law firm in the United States, offers links to disability rights topics.

Children's Defense Fund (CFD)

25 E Street NW, Washington, DC, 20001 (202-628-8787; http://www.childrensdefense.org/; e-mail: cdfinfo @childrensdefense.org). Private nonprofit organization dedicated to educating about, advocating for, and studying the needs of children, especially low-income and minority children and children with disabilities. Their mission focuses on giving children a head start (child care), a healthy start (child health), a fair start (family income), a safe start (violence prevention, child welfare, and mental health), and a moral start (ethics, morality, and self-discipline).

Disabilities Rights Education and Defense Fund (DREDF)

2212 Sixth Street, Berkeley, CA 94710 (voice/TTY: 510-644-2555; fax: 510-841-8645; http://www.dredf.org; e-mail: dredf@dredf.org). Law and policy center to protect the rights of people with disabilities. Referral and information regarding rights of people with disabilities is offered. This organization educates legislators and policymakers about issues affecting the rights of people with disabilities and also educates the public about the Americans with Disabilities Act of 1990 (PL 101-336).

Judge David L. Bazelon Center for Mental Health Law

1101 15th Street NW, Suite 1212, Washington, DC 20005-5002 (202-467-5730; TTY: 202-467-4342; fax: 202-223-0409; http://www.bazelon.org; e-mail: webmaster@bazelon.org). Nonprofit legal advocacy program that works to define, establish, and protect the rights of children and adults with mental disabilities, using test-case litigation, federal policy advocacy, and training and technical assistance for lawyers and other advocates nationwide.

National Association of Protection and Advocacy Systems (NAPAS)

900 Second Street NE, Suite 211, Washington, DC 20002 (202-408-9514; TTY: 202-408-9521; fax: 202-408-9520; http://www.protectionandadvocacy.com; e-mail: napas@earthlink.net). The NAPAS web site provides links to protection and advocacy agencies located across the United States. These agencies are mandated by federal law to serve and protect the rights of people with disabilities.

MEDICATIONS

AmericasDoctor

1325 TriState Parkway, Suite 300, Gurnee, IL 60031 (847-855-7500; fax: 847-855-8787; http://www.americas doctor.com/). Private pharmaceutical services company that integrates information, marketing and research resources for professionals and the general public. Provides clinical research services, offers patient recruitment services for clinical trials, and displays articles that discuss current medical science information.

Drug InfoNet

(http://www.druginfonet.com). This web site provides information about drugs, diseases, and pharmaceutical manufacturing, as well as links to related sites.

OCCUPATIONAL THERAPY

American Occupational Therapy Association (AOTA)

4720 Montgomery Lane, Post Office Box 31220, Bethesda, MD 20824 (301-652-2682; TTY: 800-377-8555; fax: 301-652-7711; http://www.aota.org). Professional organization of occupational therapists; provides such services as accreditation of educational programs, professional publications, public education, and continuing education for practitioners.

PHYSICAL THERAPY

American Physical Therapy Association (APTA)

1111 North Fairfax Street, Alexandria, VA 22314 (800-999-2782; TTY: 703-683-6748; fax: 703-684-7343; www.apta.org). Professional membership association of physical therapists, physical therapist assistants, and physical therapy students. Operates clearinghouse for questions on physical therapy and disabilities. Publishes bibliographies on a range of topics.

RECREATION AND SPORTS

American Alliance for Health, Physical Education, Recreation and Dance (AAHPERD)

1900 Association Drive, Reston, VA 20191 (800-213-7193; http://www.aahperd.org). National organization supporting and assisting individuals involved in physical education, recreation, dance, and health, leisure, fitness, and education. An alliance of six national associations, AAHPERD offers numerous publications.

American Amputee Soccer Association

(http://www.ampsoccer.org; e-mail: rgh@ampsoccer.org). Promotes social interactivity, self-esteem and self-confidence among adult, and especially among new and youthful amputees, through recreational and competitive amputee soccer programs. The association's web site provides links to other sporting programs for individuals with disabilities.

American Association of Adapted Sports Programs

Post Office Box 538, Pine Lake, GA 30072 (404-294-0070; fax 404-294-5758; http://www.aaasp.org; e-mail: aaasp@bellsouth.net). This organization's mission is to enhance the health, independence and future economic self-sufficiency of youths with physical disabilities by facilitating a national disabled sports movement, assisting communities in creating the best member programs possible for youth with disabilities who wish to compete.

Disabled Sports USA (DS/USA)

451 Hungerford Drive, Suite 100, Rockville, MD 20850 (301-217-0960; TTY: 301-217-0963; fax: 301-217-0968; http://www.dsusa.org; e-mail: dsusa@dsusa.org). DS/USA offers summer programs and competitions, fitness programs, "fitness is for everyone" videotapes, and winter ski programs. Local chapters offer such activities as camping, hiking, biking, horseback riding, 10K runs, water skiing, white water rafting, rope courses, mountain climbing, sailing, yachting, canoeing, kayaking, aerobic fitness, and snow skiing. Provides year-round sports and recreational opportunities to people with orthopedic, spinal cord, neuromuscular, and visual impairments through a national network of local chapters.

Girl Scouts of the USA

420 5th Avenue, New York, NY 10018 (800-478-7248; http://www.girlscouts.org; e-mail: misc@girlscouts.org). Open to all girls ages 5–17 (or kindergarten through grade 12). Runs camping programs, sports and recreational activities, and service programs. Incorporates children with disabilities into general Girl Scout troop activities. Published book *Focus on Ability: Serving Girls with Special Needs.*

International Committee of Sports for the Deaf

814 Thayer Avenue, Suite #350, Silver Spring, MD 20910 (http://www.ciss.org; e-mail: info@ciss.org). Gives history of accomplishments of deaf athletes. Links to regional confederations and technical delegates throughout the world.

International Paralympic Committee

(http://www.paralympic.org). Organizes international multidisability competitions, such as the winter and summer Paralympic Games, which take place after the Olympic Games in the same host city. Posts competition results. Publishes online newsletter.

Little League Baseball, Challenger Division

(http://www.littleleague.org/programs/challenger.htm). Provides boys and girls with disabilities the opportunity to experience the emotional development and the fun of playing Little League Baseball.

National Center on Physical Activity and Disability

1640 West Roosevelt Road, Chicago, IL 60608-6904 (voice/TTY: 800-900-8086; http://ncpad.cc.uic.edu). Encourages and supports people with disabilities who wish to increase their overall level of activity and participate in some form of regular physical activity. Offers searchable directories of organizations; programs and facilities that provide opportunities for accessible physical activity; adaptive equipment vendors; conferences and meetings; and references to journal articles, books, videotapes, and more. Provides fact sheets on a variety of physical activities for people with disabilities.

The National Sports Center for the Disabled

P.O. Box 1290, Winter Park, CO 80482 (970-726-1540; fax: 970-726-4112; http://www.nscd.org; e-mail: info @nscd.org). Provides therapeutic recreation programs that are designed for individuals with disabilities who require adaptive equipment and/or special instruction. Offers summer and winter programs and has some scholarships.

Special Olympics International

1325 G Street NW, Suite 500, Washington, DC 20005 (202-628-3630; fax: 202-824-0200; http://www.special olympics.org; e-mail: info@specialolympics.org). Largest organization to provide year-round sports training and athletic competition for children and adults with mental retardation and certain other significant cognitive impairments. Local, state, and national games are held throughout the United States and in more than 150 countries; world games are held every four years.

United States Association of Blind Athletes (USABA)

33 North Institute Street, Colorado Springs, CO 80903 (719-630-0422; fax: 719-630-0616; http://www.usaba .org). Aims to ensure that legally blind individuals have the same opportunities as their sighted peers in recreation and sports programs at all levels from developmental to elite. Works to change negative stereotypes relating to the abilities of blind individuals and other people with disabilities. Publishes newsletter (also available on cassette). Web site has links to related sites and event calendars with sport descriptions.

Very Special Arts

1300 Connecticut Avenue NW, Suite 700, Washington, DC 20036 (800-938-8721; TTY: 202-737-0645; fax: 202-737-0725; http://www.vsarts.org; e-mail: info@vsarts.org). Nonprofit gallery that represents artists with disabilities.

Wheelchair Sports, USA

3595 East Fountain Boulevard, Suite L-1, Colorado Springs, CO 80910 (719-574-1150; fax: 719-574-9840; http://www.wsusa.org; e-mail: wsusa@aol.com). Governing body of various sports of wheelchair athletics, including swimming, archery, weightlifting, track and field, table tennis, and air weapons. Publishes a newsletter.

Yoga for the Special Child

1521 Chicago Avenue, Evanston, IL 60201 (888-900-9642; fax: 847-869-8329; http://www.specialyoga.com). A comprehensive program of yoga techniques designed to enhance the natural development of children with special needs.

REHABILITATION

National Institute on Disability and Rehabilitation Research (NIDRR)

400 Maryland Avenue SW, Washington, DC 20202-2572 (202-205-8134; TTY: 202-205-4475; http://www.ed .gov/offices/OSERS/NIDRR/). NIDRR provides leadership and support for a comprehensive program of research related to the rehabilitation of individuals with disabilities.

National Rehabilitation Information Center (NARIC)

4200 Forbes Boulevard, Suite 202, Lanham, MD 20706 (800-346-2742; fax: 301-562-2401; http://www.naric .com; e-mail: naric@heitechservices.com). Rehabilitation information service and research library; provides quick-reference and referral information, bibliographic searches, and photocopies of documents. Publishes several directories and resource guides.

REFERENCE

2002 resource guide [Special issue]. (2002, January). *Exceptional Parent, 32*.

Index

Page numbers followed by *f* indicate figures; those followed by *t* indicate tables.